SIMILES DICTIONARY

SIMILES DICTIONARY

Second Edition

ELYSE SOMMER

VISIBLE
INK
PRESS

Detroit

SIMILES DICTIONARY

Visible Ink Press®
43311 Joy Rd., #414
Canton, MI 48187-2075

Visible Ink Press is a registered trademark of Visible Ink Press LLC.

Most Visible Ink Press books are available at special quantity discounts when purchased in bulk by corporations, organizations, or groups. Customized printings, special imprints, messages, and excerpts can be produced to meet your needs. For more information, contact Special Markets Director, Visible Ink Press, www.visibleinkpress.com, or 734-667-3211.

Managing Editor: Kevin S. Hile
Art Director: Mary Claire Krzewinski
Typesetting: Marco Di Vita
Proofreaders: Sharon R. Gunton

Library of Congress Cataloging-in-Publication Data
Sommer, Elyse.
Similes dictionary / by Elyse Sommer. — Second Edition.
     pages cm.
   Includes index.
   ISBN 978-1-57859-433-7 (pbk.)
   1. Quotations, English. 2. Simile—Dictionaries. I. Sommer, Elyse, editor of compilation. II. Title.
   PN6084.S5S55 2013
   082—dc23

                                                                        2013000154

Printed in the United States of America

10 9 8 7 6 5 4 3 2 1

CONTENTS

How to Use This Book vii

Introduction ix

Table of Thematic Categories

1

The Similes

45

Author Index 565

How to Use This Book

Similes Dictionary is designed for the browser's enjoyment and inspiration and as a thesaurus for writers and speakers. Because many similes are complete little quotes, the book also serves as a quotation finder.

To best fulfill all these functions, the more than 16,000 entries have been grouped into nearly 1,300 thematic categories to ease and expedite access to them. The Table of Thematic Categories at the front of the book contains an alphabetical list that includes the subject categories, synonyms, and See and See Also cross references. All categories and synonyms with their cross references are also included in the text.

Cross references pertaining to the category in general appear after the thematic heading.

How to Locate Similes through the Subject Headings

Since this is a phrase book, most readers will be best served by searching through the thematic categories to find the phrases that interest them. Taking the thesaurus approach, turn first to the Table of Thematic Categories and go to a heading most likely to lead you to the similes that interest you. If you looked up ABILITY, you will find that it is a main heading and also a cross reference to a thematically related heading, ACCOMPLISHMENT. If you looked under ACCURACY, you would find it listed as a synonym, with a cross reference to the main heading, CORRECTNESS.

How to Locate Similes by Browsing

Taking the browser's approach, go right to the entries and let the thematic headings and cross references in the text guide you through your ramble.

How to Locate Similes by a Specific Author

If you're curious who said what, turn to the Author's Index and look up the categories for the author whose similes you want to see. If an author's listing includes many entries, you can limit your search to just a few thematic categories.

How to Locate Familiar Similes

The search for a specific familiar phrase can often be narrowed down to similes from Shakespeare, early writers and poets like Chaucer, Shelley, Swinburne, Tennyson and Longfellow. All can be tracked through the Authors Index.

Things to Bear in Mind When Reading the Entries

Spelling and punctuation in entries from printed sources is as it appeared there. The exception to this are words with spelling common only in England, e.g.: colour, favour, grey, honour, moustaches, odour, which appear as color, favor, gray, honor, mustaches, odour.

Some similes contain modernized words and phrases, but such changes are always called to the reader's attention, with the original form in a comment paragraph after the entry. The same holds true for dialect words and phrases.

When the descriptive reference frame for a simile is not crucial to its meaning but would enhance reading or shed light on its use, a word or phrase preceding the simile is included in the entry. Such additional text is enclosed in parenthethes. This keeps the focus on the simile and maintains the alphabetizing by simile system. Unless the parenthesized text is a complete sentence, the first word of the actual entry is not capitalized, e.g.:

(Gaze as) innocent as a teddy bear —Babs H. Deal

When additional text is in square brackets, the words are not the author's but inserted for clarity by the editors. If this bracketed text precedes the simile, the entry is capitalized since it does not continue the author's words, e.g.:

[School boys] Frail, like thin-boned fledgling birds clamoring for food —Sylvia Berkman

Words in parenthethes or brackets may also appear in the middle or at the end of an entry, e.g.:

My efforts [to stir husband out of a sense of doom] have been like so many waves, dashing against the Rock of Ages —Robert E. Sherwood

To enhance the browser's enjoyment and increase the book's utility, many similes include brief comments. These can include any or all of the following: information about the simile, its source, examples of variations, cross references specific to that simile.

INTRODUCTION

I'm as corny as Kansas in August,
I'm as normal as blueberry pie.
Oscar Hammerstein "A Wonderful Guy" South Pacific

The simile that describes the resemblance between two dissimlar things, usually flagging up the comparison with "as" or "like," has been a literary device to lend color to the English language since time immemorial. Musical theater legend Oscar Hammerstein was a master "similist," often piling on his vivid comparisons for added effect. "A Wonderful Guy," from the classic *South Pacific,* expanded on the famous "I'm corny as Kansas in August / I'm as normal as blueberry pie" with "I'm as trite and as gay as a daisy in May" and "I'm bromidic and bright / As a moon-happy night / Pourin' light on the dew!"

Its effectiveness for expressing thoughts more clearly and vividly makes the simile one of most widely used figures of speech in written and spoken English. Similes crop up in newspaper and magazine articles, fiction and nonfiction, dramas as well as daily conversations. The ones with the most zip tend to metamorphose into common expressions that are are used unchanged or refreshed. In the age of sound bites and tweets they are more than ever timely and, to borrow an ever-popular simile, useful as a Swiss army knife for drawing pithy word sketches that are more robust than a single word and more spontaneous than a formal quote.

Since many similes are "as old as old as the hills" and also as fresh as today's newspaper headline—whether printed or online—a collection of examples can never really be complete. The seemingly overflowing well of similes from biblical times to the present keeps filling up. Thus, a book like *Similes Dictionary* is never really finished. I'm therefore delighted to have a chance to amend and update the first edition.

Besides expanding on the entries of writers with a special propensity for the simile, this new edition has afforded me a chance to include comparison phrases from works published in the last few years, some of which proved especially fertile. That meant adding similes from

Cynthia Ozick's latest books, as well as newly published authors like Helen Simonson (*Major Pettigrew's Last Stand*).

My main activity since compiling the first edition post has been as editor and publisher of *Curtainup,* an online theater magazine. Naturally, this has led me to many apt examples in dramatic dialogue and songs with which to enrich this new edition. Few song writers can match Oscar Hammerstein's gift for poetic figures of speech that sing gloriously. However, there are plenty of pithy examples from old-timers like Irving Berlin (When I'm with a pistol / I sparkle like a crystal, / Yes, I shine like the morning sun. / But I lose all my luster / When with a Bronco Buster. "You Can't Get a Man with a Gun" from *Annie Get Your Gun*).

Living song writers also incorporate similes into their oeuvre, like this one from singer / songwriter Sting: Like a circle in a spiral / Like a wheel within a wheel / Never ending or beginning, / On an ever spinning wheel / As the images unwind / Like the circles that you find / In the windmills of your mind. Sting's title, "The Windmills Of Your Mind," introduces a metaphor to the song's panoply of similes.

The similes included in this sort of collection tend to be more fragmentary than quotes in a book of quotations. The first edition cited the author but in most instances omitted the title of the source. Since a number of readers wrote asking for the plays in which to find the many Shakespeare citations, I've added them for this edition and decided to also include book, play, or song titles as well as the author's name for all new entries.

Still on the subject of source attribution, we decided to give the author-plus-title treatment to one other writer, Raymond Chandler. The prolific detective novelist is noted for his terse, witty tropes, so much so that they've come to be known as Chandlerisms and are often given new life; for example, *New York Times* columnist Maureen Dowd (in her April 10, 2012 Op-Ed piece "State of Cool") incorporated one of Chandler's sharp similes to describe photo images of Secretary of State Hillary Clinton as follows: "The pictures, as Raymond Chandler would say, make Hillary look 'as inconspicuous as a tarantula on a slice of angel food.'"

Sources tapped for new entries once again include books; print, broadcast, and electronic media; stage and screen. With the large mass of contemporary material to choose from, you might wonder why similes that have been used again and again were not eliminated. Granted, overuse has caused what was once fresh and original to metamorphose into cliché. However, sometimes a familiar phrase is something a writer or puzzle solver will find useful.

A simile's pungency can also be retained by using it in a fresh context or giving it a life-extending twist. Since *The Similes Dictionary* is also intended as an inspirational guide for fine tuning your own colorful phrase making skills, expressions that have entered the lexicon of common usage can become stepping stones towards nurturing one's own comparative wit and wisdom. With this in mind, I've added some specific tips for readers to use this book to sharpen their writing with similes at the end of this introduction.

The basic organizational principle remains the same as in the original edition and the companion dictionary, Visible Ink's *Metaphors Dictionary:* A thematic category arrangement with extensive See and See Also cross references. Because the simile is so frequently used to draw a graphic physical and character description, headings pertaining to these are significantly represented, often sub-divided into more specific headings. In addition to FACE(S), for example, readers will find categories for FACIAL COLOR; FACIAL DETAILS; FACIAL EXPRESSIONS, BLANK; FACIAL EXPRESSIONS, MISCELLANEOUS; FACIAL EXPRESSIONS, SERIOUS; and FACIAL SHAPE.

The simile maker's penchant for irony and disparaging remarks is also reflected in the headings. Besides a whole category of INSULTS, numerous thematic synonyms lead the way to more. Many other headings encompass both positive and negative expressions, with the negative entries often outnumbering the positive ones.

To sum up aims for this collection, No matter what your primary use for *The Similes Dictionary,* here's hoping you'll enjoy the casual pleasure of browsing, which will in turn heighten your appreciation for the simile as a simple and useful linguistic device. Most have focused on proverbs and quotations. This applies to books published before this century, as well as more contemporary references. Two notable exceptions are John Ray, whose simile-rich collection of proverbs was published in the seventeenth century, and Frank J. Wilstach, whose *Dictionary of Similes* was published in 1916. The Wilstach book represents a worthy effort to give the simile its just due. However, besides lacking the many fresh similes coined during the last seventy years, its keyword organization makes it difficult to find anything unless you know exactly what you're looking for.

10 Tips for Creating and Using Similes

1. For a heightened appreciation of similes, jot down similes that catch your eye in a notebook. To move from inspiration to originality, expand that notebook by rewriting some of your jottings and adding some that rise from your own creative wellsprings, but don't expect to really use even the best ones. These jottings are simply a warm-up for getting into the colorful comparison habit.

2. Keep your similes appropriate to the subject. You'll make stronger connections between your topic and what you are comparing if there's a subtle link between the two. In reviewing the 2012 revival of Gore Vidal's *The Best Man, Village Voice* critic Michael Feingold remarked that "seeing [James Earl] Jones and [Angela] Lansbury 'take stage,' in the blatant way they do here, is something like watching a monarch annex a neighboring province, except that the consequences are delightful rather than dire." Feingold's comparing the actors to a monarch was perfectly suited to a play about a presidential election.

3. Keep your similes appropriate in style. A successful simile must fit its stylistic landscape as a hollow fits the circle. Robert Burns's beautiful "my luv is like a red, red rose" would be misplaced in a business article or a spy novel.

4. Surprise reader or listeners. Really stimulating similes are rarely the obvious and therefore ordinary ones. The eighteenth-century wit Sydney Smith counseled us to choose phrases "remote from all the common tracks and sheep-walks made in the mind." While most people would never think of a stale cake in relation to a decaying house, it's this element of surprise that enhances novelist Jonathan Valin's description of a crumbling white house in *Life's Work* as "crumbling at the corners like stale cake left out on a plate. It's a most unusual image, but it makes perfect sense.

5. Appeal to all the senses by drawing comparisons that a reader will hear or taste or feel in their minds, as well as see. The anthem song of the musical *Billy Elliott* is a good example: "And then I feel a change, like a fire deep inside / Something bursting me wide open, impossible to hide / And suddenly I'm flying, flying like a bird / Like electricity, electricity / Sparks inside of me, and I'm free, I'm free.

6. Combine similes with other figures of speech. British playwright Mike Bartlett used the metaphor of a cock fight for his 2012 play about a fraught sexual relationship. A description of an attractive young men starts with a simile—"Some people might think you were scrawny but I think you're like a picture drawn with a pencil"—and concludes with a metaphor: "I like it. You haven't been coloured in, you're all Wire."

7. Emphasize your point by extending or expanding the comparison. My favorite example of unrestrained comparative excess comes from Donald E. Westlake's *The Fugitive Pigeon,* which works not only because it's genuinely funny but because it successfully links all the extensions to the play on the character's name: "(Up till then I'd assumed that Gross was the man's name, but it was his description.) He looked like something that had finally come up out of its cave because it has eaten the last phosphorescent little fish in the cold pool at the bottom of the cavern. He looked like something that better keep moving because if it stood still someone would drag it out back and bury it. He looked like a big white sponge with various diseases at work on the inside. He looked like something that couldn't get you if you held a crucifix up in front of you. He looked like the big fat soft white something you might find under a tomato plant leaf on a rainy day with a chill in the air"

8. Moderation works, too. Just as some people like more seasoning than others, so you must follow your own creative taste buds. Bear in mind Roman philosopher Seneca's belief that "excellence resides in quality, not quantity" and be aware that a single simile is often all you need for impact. If the image is strong, neither does it need to be elaborate. In fact, our most memorable—the ones that pass from literature into quotation books and everyday language—are usually short and direct.

9. Don't fuss too much about adding similes to your writing. Similes should be an enhancement not the sole objective of any writers. But do fuss over the ones you create. Revise, and judge your similes mercilessly. A good story without a good simile can still be a good story. But add a bunch of great similes to a bad story and it will be like a jeweled handle on a dull, broken knife.

10. Make sure it works. This is the most important tip of all, for a simile's whole purpose is to cause a reader to say "Yes, that's what it's like." To have that effect, the image you're creating must be correct. To say that something grew like a brick wall does not create much of a picture since a wall does not grow but is built. To say that rush hour traffic flowed like blood from a wound is also faulty.

TABLE OF
THEMATIC CATEGORIES

In the following table, categories used throughout the text and synonyms that are cross-referenced to categories are combined in one list in alphabetic order.

❧ **ABANDONMENT**
See Also: ALONENESS, BEARING, FRIENDSHIP, REJECTION

❧ **ABILITY**
See Also: ACCOMPLISHMENT

❧ **ABSORBABILITY**

❧ **ABSURDITY**
See Also: DIFFICULTY, FUTILITY

❧ **ABUNDANCE**
See Also: CLOSENESS, GROWTH, SPREADING

❧ **ACCEPTIBILITY**
See: BELONGING

❧ **ACCESSIBILITY**
See: AVAILABILITY, COURTESY

❧ **ACCIDENT**
See: FATE

❧ **ACCOMPLISHMENT**
See Also: ABILITY, CLEVERNESS, SUCCESS/ FAILURE

❧ **ACCUMULATION**
See: GROWTH

❧ **ACCURACY**
See: CORRECTNESS

❧ **ACCUSATION**
See: CRITICISM

❧ **ACTING**
See Also: STAGE AND SCREEN

❧ **ACTIONS**
See Also: BEHAVIOR, CAUTION, LEAPING, JUMPING, MOVEMENTS, VIOLENCE

❧ **ACTIVENESS**
See Also: ALERTNESS, BEHAVIOR, BUSINESS, ENERGY, ENTHUSIASM, EXCITEMENT, MOVEMENTS, PERSONALITY PROFILES

❧ **ACTORS**
See: STAGE AND SCREEN

❧ **ADAPTABILITY**
See: BELONGING, FLEXIBILITY/INFLEXIBILITY

❧ **ADJUSTMENT**
See: FLEXIBILITY/INFLEXIBILITY, HABIT

❧ **ADMIRATAION**
See: FLATTERY, WORDS OF PRAISE

❧ **ADULTERY**
See: MARRIAGE

❧ **ADVANCING**
See Also: ENTRANCES AND EXITS,
    MOVEMENTS

❧ **ADVANTAGEOUSNESS**
See Also: COST

❧ **ADVERSARY**

❧ **ADVERSITY**
See: FORTUNE/MISFORTUNE

❧ **ADVERTISING**
See Also: BUSINESS

❧ **ADVICE**
See Also: FRIENDSHIP, FUTILITY

❧ **AFFABILITY**
See: AVAILABILITY, COURTESY, FRIENDSHIP

❧ **AFFECTION**
See Also: FRIENDSHIP, LOVE

❧ **AFFLICTIONS**
See: HEALTH, PAIN

❧ **AFFLUENCE**
See: RICHES

❧ **AGE**
See Also: LIFE, MANKIND, YOUTH

❧ **AGGRESSION**
See: PERSONAL TRAITS, VIOLENCE

❧ **AGILITY**
See Also: MOVEMENTS, SPEED, TURNING
    AND TWISTING, WALKING

❧ **AGITATION**
See Also: EXCITEMENT, HEARTBEAT,
    NERVOUSNESS, TREMBLING

❧ **AGREEMENT/DISAGREEMENT**
See Also: COMPATIBILITY, FIGHTING

❧ **AILMENTS**
See: ILLNESS

❧ **AIM**
See: PURPOSEFULNESS

❧ **AIMLESSNESS**
See Also: BELONGING, EMPTINESS

❧ **AIR**
See Also: ATMOSPHERE, HEAT

❧ **AIRPLANES**
See: VEHICLES

❧ **ALCOHOL**
See: DRINKING

❧ **ALERTNESS**
See Also: ATTENTION/ATTENTIVENESS,
    EYES, SCRUTINY, WATCHFULNESS

❧ **ALIENATION**
See Also: ALONENESS, REMOTENESS

❧ **ALIKENESS**
See: SIMILARITY

❧ **ALIMONY**
See: MARRIAGE

❧ **ALLURE**
See: ATTRACTIVNESS

♣ ALONENESS
See Also: ABANDONMENT

♣ ALOOFNESS
See: PERSONAL TRAITS, RESERVE

♣ AMAZEMENT
See: SURPRISE

♣ AMBITION
See Also: PURPOSEFULNESS

♣ ANCESTORS
See: PAST, THE

♣ ANGER
See Also: EMOTIONS, IRRITABLENESS

♣ ANIMALS
See Also: BIRDS

♣ ANIMATION
See: ACTIVENESS, ENERGY, ENTHUSIASM

♣ ANNOYANCE
See Also: IRRITABLENESS

♣ ANTICIPATION
See Also: HOPE

♣ ANXIETY
See Also: EMOTIONS, NERVOUSNESS, TENSION

♣ APARTNESS
See: ALONENESS

♣ APATHY
See: REMOTENESS

♣ APPAREL
See: CLOTHING

♣ APPEARENCE
See: PHYSICAL APPEARANCE

♣ APPETITE
See: HUNGER

♣ APPLAUSE
See: NOISE

♣ APPRECIATION

♣ ARGUMENTS
See Also: FIGHTING

♣ ARITHMITIC
See: MATHEMATICS AND SCIENCE

♣ ARM(S)
See Also: ARM MOVEMENTS, FINGER(S), HAND(S)

♣ ARM MOVEMENTS
See Also: HAND MOVEMENTS

♣ ARMY

♣ ART AND LITERATURE
See Also: BOOKS, MUSIC, POETS/POETRY, WRITERS/WRITING

♣ ASTONISHMENT
See Also: SURPRISE

♣ ATMOSPHERE
See Also: AIR

♣ ATTENTION
See Also: ALERTNESS, SCRUTINY, WATCHFULNESS

♣ ATTIRE
See: CLOTHING

♣ ATTRACTION

❧ ATTRACTIVENESS
See Also: BEAUTY, DESIRABILITY, PHYSICAL
 APPEARANCE

❧ AUTHENTICITY
See: TRUENESS/FALSENESS

❧ AUTHORITY
See: POWER

❧ AUTHORSHIP
See: POETS/POETRY, WRITERS/WRITING

❧ AUTOMOBILES
See: VEHICLES

❧ AVAILABILITY

❧ AVARICE
See: GREED

❧ AWARENESS
See: REALIZATION

❧ AWKWARDNESS
See Also: MOVEMENT(S)

❧ BACHELOR
See: MEN AND WOMEN

❧ BAD LUCK
See: FORTUNE/MISFORTUNE

❧ BADNESS
See: CRUELTY, EVIL

❧ BALANCE
See: REGULARITY/IRREGULARITY

❧ BALDNESS
See Also: HAIR

❧ BARENESS

❧ BARGAINS
See: ADVANTAGEOUSNESS

❧ BARRENNESS
See: EMPTINESS

❧ BASEBALL
See Also: SPORTS

❧ BASKETBALL
See: SPORTS

❧ BEACHES
See: OCEAN/OCEANFRONT

❧ BEARD(S)
See Also: HAIR, PHYSICAL APPEARANCE

❧ BEARING
See Also: FACIAL EXPRESSIONS,
 MISCELLANEOUS, LYING, PERSONALITY
 PROFILES, PHYSICAL APPEARANCE,
 POSTURE, SITTING, STANDING,
 WALKING

❧ BEAUTY
See Also: BEAUTY DEFINED, FACE,
 PHYSICAL APPEARANCE

❧ BEAUTY DEFINED

❧ BEGINNINGS AND ENDINGS
See Also: BIRTH, ENTRANCES AND EXITS

❧ BEHAVIOR
See Also: ACTION, LIFE, MANKIND,
 PROPRIETY/IMPROPRIETY

❧ BELIEFS
See Also: GOVERNMENT, POLITICS,
 RELIGION

❧ BELIEVABILITY

♣ **BELONGING**

♣ **BENDING/BENT**

♣ **BENEFITS**
See: ADVANTAGEOUSNESS

♣ **BEREAVEMENT**
See: GRIEF, SADNESS

♣ **BEWILDERMENT**
See Also: EMOTIONS, STRANGENESS

♣ **BIBLE**
See: BOOKS

♣ **BICYCLING**
See: SPORTS

♣ **BIGNESS**
See Also: FATNESS, PHYSICAL APPEARANCE,
    TALLNESS

♣ **BIGOTRY**
See: INTOLERANCE

♣ **BIOGRAPHY**
See: BOOKS, WRITERS/WRITING

♣ **BIRDS**
See Also: ANIMALS, INSECTS, SINGING

♣ **BIRTH**
See Also: BEGINNINGS AND ENDINGS,
    DEATH, ENTRANCES AND EXITS, LIFE

♣ **BITTERNESS**
See Also: ANGER, FRIENDSHIP, LOVE

♣ **BLACK**
See Also: COLORS; FACIAL EXPRESSIONS,
    SERIOUS; GLOOM

♣ **BLESSEDNESS**
See: FORTUNE/MISFORTUNE

♣ **BLINDNESS**
See Also: EYE(S); EYE EXPRESSIONS, BLANK

♣ **BLOOD**
See Also: VIOLENCE

♣ **BLOOMING**
See: GROWTH

♣ **BLUE**
See Also: COLORS

♣ **BLUSHES**
See Also: FACIAL COLOR, RED, SHAME,
    SHYNESS

♣ **BOATS**
See: SEASCAPES

♣ **BODY**
See Also: AGILITY, AWKWARDNESS, BODY
    ORGANS, FATNESS, MUSCLES, PHYSICAL
    APPEARANCE, SHOULDERS, STOMACH,
    STRENGTH, THINNESS

♣ **BODY ORGANS**
See Also: SEX, TONGUE

♣ **BOISTEROUSNESS**
See: NOISE

♣ **BOLDNESS**
See: COURAGE

♣ **BONDS**
See: CONNECTIONS

♣ **BOOKS**
See Also: READERS/READING

❧ BOREDOM/BORING
See Also: DULLNESS, LIFE

❧ BOUNCING
See: ROCKING AND ROLLING

❧ BOUNDLESSNESS
See: CONTINUITY

❧ BOXING AND WRESTLING
See Also: SPORTS

❧ BRAIN
See: INTELLIGENCE, MIND

❧ BRAVERY
See: COURAGE

❧ BREASTS
See Also: BODY, BODY ORGANS

❧ BREATHING

❧ BREVITY
See Also: TIME

❧ BRIGHTNESS
See Also: GLIMMER, GLITTER, AND GLOSS,
*   LIGHTING, SHINING*

❧ BRITTLENESS
See: FRAGILITY

❧ BROWN
See Also: COLORS

❧ BRUTALITY
See: CRUELTY, VIOLENCE

❧ BUILDINGS
See: HOUSES

❧ BURST
See Also: DISINTEGRATION, SUDDENNESS

❧ BUSINESS
See Also: ADVERTISING, SUCCESS/FAILURE

❧ BUSYNESS
See Also: ACTIVENESS, WORK

❧ CALMNESS
See Also: PEACEFULNESS

❧ CANDOR
See Also: HONESTY

❧ CAPABILITY
See: ABILITY

❧ CAREFULNESS
See: ATTENTION, CAUTION, CORRECTNESS

❧ CARELESSNESS

❧ CARES
See: PROBLEMS AND SOLUTIONS

❧ CAUSE AND EFFECT

❧ CAUTION
See Also: BEHAVIOR

❧ CELEBRITY
See: FAME

❧ CENSORSHIP
See: CONTROL, CRITICISM

❧ CERTAINTY

❧ CESSATION
See: PAUSE

❧ CHANGE
See Also: ENTRANCES AND EXITS,
*   PERMANENCE*

♣ **CHAOS**
See: ORDER/DISORDER

♣ **CHARACTER**
See Also: PERSONAL TRAITS, REPUTATION

♣ **CHARACTERISTICS, NATIONAL**

♣ **CHARITY**
See: KINDNESS

♣ **CHARM**
See: ATTRACTIVENESS

♣ **CHASTITY**
See: VIRTUE

♣ **CHEAPNESS**
See: COST, THRIFT

♣ **CHEEKS**
See Also: BLUSHES, FACIAL COLOR, SKIN

♣ **CHEERFULNESS**
See Also: BRIGHTNESS, GAIETY, HAPPINESS, SMILES

♣ **CHILDISHNESS**
See: YOUTHFULNESS

♣ **CHILDREN**
See Also: PARENTHOOD

♣ **CHIN**
See Also: CHEEKS, FACE(S), MOUTH

♣ **CHOICES**

♣ **CHURCHES**
See: HOUSES

♣ **CITIES/STREETSCAPES**
See: PLACES

♣ **CIVILIZATION**
See: SOCIETY

♣ **CLARITY**

♣ **CLEANLINESS**
See Also: ORDER/DISORDER

♣ **CLEVERNESS**
See Also: ALERTNESS

♣ **CLICHÉ**
See: ORIGINALITY, MAXIMS, PROVERBS, AND SAYINGS

♣ **CLINGING**
See Also: PERSISTANCE; PEOPLE, INTERACTION; RELATIONSHIPS

♣ **CLOSENESS**
See Also: COMPATIBILITY, FRIENDSHIP

♣ **CLOTHING**
See Also: CLOTHING ACCESSORIES; CLOTHING, ITS FIT

♣ **CLOTHING ACCESSORIES**
See Also: JEWELRY

♣ **CLOTHING, ITS FIT**
See Also: CLOTHING

♣ **CLOUD MOVEMENTS**
See Also: RAIN

♣ **CLOUD(S)**
See Also: CLOUD MOVEMENTS, SKY

♣ **CLUMSINESS**
See: AWKWARDNESS

♣ **COLDNESS**
See Also: REMOTENESS, RESERVE

☙ **COLLAPSE**
See Also: DISINTEGRATION

☙ **COLORS**
See Also: BLACK, BLUE, BRIGHTNESS,
*   BROWN, GREEN, PALLOR, PINK, RED,*
*   WHITE*

☙ **COMEDY**

☙ **COMFORT**

☙ **COMMONPLACE**
See Also: FAMILIARITY

☙ **COMPASSION**
See: KINDNESS, PITY

☙ **COMPATIBILITY**
See Also: BELONGING

☙ **COMPETENCE**
See: ABILITY, ACCOMPLISHMENT

☙ **COMPETITION**
See Also: BUSINESS, SPORTS

☙ **COMPLACENCY**
See: CONTENTMENT

☙ **COMPLAINTS**
See: ANGER, CRITICISM

☙ **COMPLETENESS**

☙ **COMPLEXION**
See Also: SKIN, WRINKLES

☙ **COMPLEXITY**
See Also: DIFFICULTY

☙ **COMPLIMENTS**
See: FLATTERY, WORDS OF PRAISE

☙ **COMPOSITION**
See: MUSIC

☙ **COMPREHENSIBLENESS**
See: UNDERSTANDABILITY

☙ **CONCEIT**
See: VANITY

☙ **CONCNENTRATION**
See: ATTENTION, SCRUTINY

☙ **CONCISENESS**
See: BREVITY

☙ **CONDEMNATION**
See: CRITICISM

☙ **CONFIDENCE**
See: SELF-CONFIDENCE, TRUST

☙ **CONFIDENTIALITY**
See: SECRECY

☙ **CONFUSION**
See: BEWILDERMENT

☙ **CONNECTIONS**
See Also: CLINGING

☙ **CONSCIENCE**
See Also: REGRET

☙ **CONSIDERATION**
See: THOUGHT

☙ **CONSPICUOUSNESS**

☙ **CONTAGION**
See: SPREADING

☙ **CONTEMPT**

♣ **CONTENTMENT**
See Also: HAPPINESS, JOY

♣ **CONTINUITY**
See Also: PERMANENCE

♣ **CONTROL**

♣ **CONVERSATION**

♣ **CONVICTION**
See: BELIEFS

♣ **COOKERY**
See: FOOD, DRINK

♣ **COOLNESS**
See: CALMNESS

♣ **COOPERATION**
See: AGREEMENT

♣ **CORPORATIONS**
See: BUSINESS

♣ **CORPULENCE**
See: FATNESS

♣ **CORRECTNESS**
See Also: TRUENESS/FALSENESS, MANNERS, REPUTATION

♣ **CORRESPONDENCE**
See Also: WRITERS/WRITING

♣ **COST**
See Also: ADVANTAGEOUSNESS, THRIFT

♣ **COUNSEL**
See: ADVICE

♣ **COURAGE**

♣ **COURTESY**
See: BEHAVIOR, MANNERS

♣ **COURTSHIP**
See: MEN AND WOMEN

♣ **COVERTNESS**
See: SECRECY

♣ **COWARDICE**
See: FEAR

♣ **COZINESS**
See: COMFORT

♣ **CRAFTINESS**
See: CLEVERNESS

♣ **CRAVING**
See: DESIRE

♣ **CRAZINESS**
See: MADNESS

♣ **CREDIT**

♣ **CRIME**
See Also: DISHONESTY, EVIL

♣ **CRISPNESS**
See: SHARPNESS

♣ **CRITICISM**
See Also: CRITICISM, DRAMATIC AND LITERARY

♣ **CRITICISM, DRAMATIC AND LITERARY**
See Also: POETS/POETRY, WRITERS/ WRITING,

♣ **CROOKEDNESS**
See: BENDING/BENT

❖ CROWDS
See Also: CLOSENESS

❖ CRUELTY
See Also: COLDNESS, EVIL

❖ CRYING
See Also: GROANS AND WHISPERS,
SCREAMS

❖ CUNNING
See: CLEVERNESS

❖ CURIOSITY

❖ CURSES
See Also: WORDS

❖ CUSTOM
See: HABIT

❖ DAMPNESS
See: DISCOMFORT

❖ DANCING
See Also: AGILITY, INSULTS, WORDS OF
PRAISE

❖ DANGER
See Also: RISK

❖ DARING
See: COURAGE

❖ DARKNESS

❖ DAY
See Also: NIGHT, SLOWNESS, TIME

❖ DEATH
See Also: ADVANCING; BEGINNINGS AND
ENDINGS; DEATH DEFINED; DEATH,
FINALITY OF; ENTRANCES AND EXITS;
SUDDENNESS; TIMELINESS

❖ DEATH DEFINED

❖ DEATH, FINALITY OF

❖ DEBT
See: CREDIT

❖ DECEPTION
See: TRUENESS/FALSENESS

❖ DECISIONS
See: CHOICES

❖ DECORATIVENESS
See: ATTRACTIVENESS

❖ DECREASE

❖ DEDICATION
See: ATTENTION

❖ DEEDS
See: ACTIONS

❖ DEJECTION
See Also: EMOTIONS, GLOOM

❖ DELAY
See: LINGERING

❖ DELIBERATENESS
See: PURPOSEFULNESS

❖ DELIGHT
See: JOY

❖ DEMOCRACY
See: FREEDOM, GOVERNMENT

❖ DENIAL
See: BEHAVIOR

❖ DENSITY
See: ABUNDANCE, THICKNESS

♣ **DEPARTURE**
See: EXITS

♣ **DEPENDABILITY**
See: RELIABILITY/UNRELIABILITY

♣ **DEPLETION**
See: DECREASE

♣ **DEPRESSION**
See: DEJECTION, GLOOM

♣ **DESERTION**
See: ABANDONMENT

♣ **DESIRABILITY**
See Also: PLEASURE

♣ **DESIRE**
See Also: SEX

♣ **DESOLATION**
See: ABANDONMENT

♣ **DESPERATION**

♣ **DESTITUTION**
See: POVERTY

♣ **DESTRUCTION/
DESTRUCTIVENESS**
See Also: DISINTEGRATION

♣ **DETACHMENT**
See: REMOTENESS

♣ **DETERIORATION**
See: DISINTEGRATION

♣ **DETERMINATION**
See: PURPOSEFULNESS

♣ **DEVOTION**
See: LOYALTY/DISLOYALTY

♣ **DEW**
See: NATURE

♣ **DICTION**
See: SPEECH PATTERNS

♣ **DICTIONARIES**
See: BOOKS

♣ **DIETS**
See: EATING AND DRINKING

♣ **DIFFERENCES**

♣ **DIFFICULTY**
See Also: FUTILITY, IMPOSSIBILITY

♣ **DIGNITY**
See: PRIDE

♣ **DILEMMAS**
See: PROBLEMS AND SOLUTIONS

♣ **DIPLOMACY**
See: TACT

♣ **DIRECTNESS**
See: CANDOR, STRAIGHTNESS

♣ **DISAGREEMENT**
*See: AGREEMENT/DISAGREEMENT,
ARGUMENT*

♣ **DISAPPEARANCE**

♣ **DISAPPOINTMENT**
See Also: DESPAIR, FACIAL EXPRESSION

♣ **DISAPPROVAL**
See: CONTEMPT

♣ **DISASTER**
See: FORTUNE/MISFORTUNE

♣ **DISCOMFORT**
See Also: PAIN

♣ **DISCONTENT**
See Also: DEJECTION, GLOOM

♣ **DISCORD**
See: AGREEMENT/DISAGREEMENT

♣ **DISCOURAGEMENT**
See: DEJECTION

♣ **DISCRETION**
See: CAUTION, TACT

♣ **DISCRIMINATION**
See: STYLE

♣ **DISHONESTY**
See Also: BELIEVABILITY, CRIME, LIES AND LIARS

♣ **DISILLUSIONMENT**
See: DISAPPOINTMENT

♣ **DISINTEGRATION**
See Also: DESTRUCTION

♣ **DISLOYALTY**
See: LOYALTY/DISLOYALTY

♣ **DISORDER**
See: ORDER/DISORDER

♣ **DISPERSAL**

♣ **DISPOSABILITY**
See: TRANSIENCE

♣ **DISSATISFACTION**
See: DISCONTENT

♣ **DISSENSION**
See: AGREEMENT/DISAGREEMENT, ARGUMENTS, FIGHTING

♣ **DISSIMILARITY**
See: DIFFERENCES

♣ **DISTANCE**
See: REMOTENESS

♣ **DISTINCTIVENESS**
See: ORIGINALITY

♣ **DIVERSENESS**
See Also: DIFFERENCES, PERSONAL TRAITS

♣ **DIVORCE**
See: MARRIAGE

♣ **DOCILITY**
See: MEEKNESS

♣ **DOCTORS**
See Also: PROFESSIONS

♣ **DOGS**
See: ANIMALS

♣ **DOMINATION**
See: POWER

♣ **DOUBT**
See: TRUST/MISTRUST

♣ **DREAM(S)**
See Also: AMBITION, HOPE, SLEEP

♣ **DRINKING**
See Also: EATING AND DRINKING, FOOD AND DRINK

♣ **DRIVERS/DRIVING**
See: VEHICLES

♣ DRYNESS

♣ DULLNESS
See Also: BOREDOM/BORING

♣ DUMBNESS
See: STUPIDITY

♣ DUTY
See: RELIABILITY/UNRELIABILITY

♣ EAGERNESS
See: ENTHUSIASM

♣ EARS
See: FACIAL DETAILS

♣ EARTH
See: NATURE

♣ EASE

♣ EASE, OPPOSITE MEANING
See: DIFFICULTY

♣ EATING AND DRINKING
See Also: FOOD AND DRINK, MANNERS

♣ ECONOMICS

♣ EDUCATION
See Also: KNOWLEDGE

♣ EERINESS
See: STRANGENESS

♣ EFFECT
See: CAUSE AND EFFECT

♣ EFFECTIVENESS
*See: ABILITY, CAUSE AND EFFECT,
    SUCCESS/FAILURE,
    USEFULNESS/USELESSNESS*

♣ EFFORTLESSNESS
See: EASE

♣ EGO
See Also: VANITY

♣ ELASTICITY
See: FLEXIBILITY/INFLEXIBILITY

♣ ELATION
See: JOY

♣ ELEGANCE
See: CLOTHING, STYLE

♣ ELOQUENCE
See: PERSUASIVENESS, SPEECHMAKING

♣ ELUSIVENESS
See Also: DIFFICULTY

♣ EMBARRASSMENT
See: SHAME, SHYNESS

♣ EMBRACE
*See Also: KISSES, MEN AND WOMEN,
    PEOPLE, INTERACTION, SEXUAL
    INTERACTION*

♣ EMINENCE
See: FAME

♣ EMOTIONS
*See Also: ANXIETY, CHEERFULNESS,
    DEJECTION, ENVY, GLOOM, GRIEF,
    HAPPINESS, HATE, LONELINESS, LOVE,
    SADNESS, TENSION, WEARINESS*

♣ EMPTINESS
See Also: ABANDONMENT, ALONENESS

♣ ENDURANCE
See: CONTINUITY, PERMANENCE

♣ **ENEMY**
See: ADVERSARY

♣ **ENERGY**
See Also: ACTIVENESS, BUSYNESS,
    ENTHUSIASM

♣ **ENJOYMENT**
See: PLEASURE

♣ **ENTHUSIASM**
See Also: ENERGY, EXCITEMENT

♣ **ENTRANCES AND EXITS**
See Also: BEGINNINGS AND ENDINGS,
    DEATH, EXITS

♣ **ENTRAPMENT**
See Also: ADVANCING

♣ **ENVY**

♣ **EPITAPHS**
See: DEATH, PRIDE

♣ **ERECTNESS**
See: POSTURE

♣ **ERRORS**

♣ **ETERNITY**
See: CONTINUITY

♣ **EVASIVENESS**
See: ELUSIVENESS

♣ **EVENNESS**
See: STRAIGHTNESS

♣ **EVIL**
See Also: ACTION, CRUELTY

♣ **EXACTNESS**
See: CORRECTNESS

♣ **EXAMINATION**
See: SCRUTINY

♣ **EXCITEMENT**
See Also: AGITATION, ENERGY,
    ENTHUSIASM

♣ **EXERCISE**
See: MOVEMENT(S), SPORTS

♣ **EXHAUSTION**
See: WEARINESS

♣ **EXITS**
See Also: BEGINNINGS AND ENDINGS,
    DISAPPEARANCE, ENTRANCES AND
    EXITS

♣ **EXPANSION**
See: GROWTH

♣ **EXPECTATION**
See: ANTICIPATION, HOPE

♣ **EXPENSIVENESS**
See: COST

♣ **EXPERIENCE**
See Also: KNOWLEDGE

♣ **EXPLOSION**
See: BURST, SUDDENNESS

♣ **EYE(S)**
See Also: EYES, BRIGHT; EYEBROWS; EYE
    COLOR; EYE EXPRESSIONS,
    MISCELLANEOUS; EYELASHES; EYE
    MOVEMENTS

♣ **EYEBROWS**

♣ **EYE COLOR**
See Also: BLACK, BLUE, BROWN, EYES,
    GRAY, GREEN

♣ EYE EXPRESSIONS, MICELLA-
  NEOUS

♣ EYELASHES

♣ EYELIDS

♣ EYE MOVEMENTS

♣ EYES BRIGHT

♣ FACE(S)
*See Also: BLUSHES; CHEEKS; EYES;
  EYEBROWS; EYELASHES; EYELIDS;
  FACIAL EXPRESSION, MICELLANEOUS;
  FACIAL DETAILS; HAIR; LIPS; MOUTH;
  MUSTACHES; PHYSICAL APPEARANCE;
  SKIN; WRINKLES*

♣ FACIAL COLOR
*See Also: BLUSHES, COLOR, PALLOR, RED,
  WHITE*

♣ FACIAL DETAILS

♣ FACIAL EXPRESSIONS, BLANK
*See Also: EYE EXPRESSIONS,
  MISCELLANEOUS*

♣ FACIAL EXPRESSIONS,
  MISCELLANEOUS
*See Also: EYE EXPRESSIONS,
  MISCELLANEOUS*

♣ FACIAL EXPRESSIONS, SERIOUS
*See Also: EYE EXPRESSIONS,
  MISCELLANEOUS*

♣ FACIAL SHAPE

♣ FACTS
See Also: TRUTH

♣ FAILURE
*See: COLLAPSE, DISINTEGRATION,
  SUCCESS/FAILURE*

♣ FAITH
See: BELIEF, RELIGION

♣ FAITHFULNESS/FAITHLESSNESS
See: LOYALTY/DISLOYALTY

♣ FALL
See: SEASONS

♣ FALLING
See: COLLAPSE

♣ FALSENESS
See: TRUENESS/FALSENESS

♣ FAME
See Also: GREATNESS

♣ FAMILIARITY
See Also: COMMONPLACE

♣ FAMILY
*See: PEOPLE, INTERACTION;
  RELATIONSHIPS*

♣ FASCINATION
See: ATTRACTIVENESS

♣ FASHION
See: CLOTHING, STYLE

♣ FATE
See Also: HELPLESSNESS, LIFE

♣ FATIGUE
See: WEARINESS

♣ FATNESS
*See Also: BODY, INSULTS, PHYSICAL
  APPEARANCE*

❧ **FEAR**
See Also: ANXIETY, EMOTIONS,
*   NERVOUSNESS*

❧ **FEELINGS**
See: EMOTIONS, PHYSICAL FEELINGS

❧ **FEET**
See: LEG(S)

❧ **FEROCITY**
See Also: SCREAMS

❧ **FERTILITY**
See: GROWTH

❧ **FERVOR**
See: ENTHUSIASM

❧ **FICKLENESS**
See: LOYALTY/DISLOYALTY

❧ **FICTION**
See: STORIES

❧ **FIGHT**
See Also: FIGHTING

❧ **FIGHTING**
See Also: ARGUMENTS

❧ **FIGURE**
See: BODY

❧ **FINANCE**
See: ECONOMICS

❧ **FINGER(S)**
See Also: HAND(S)

❧ **FIRE AND SMOKE**
See Also: TOBACCO

❧ **FIRMNESS**
See Also: FLEXIBILITY/INFLEXIBILITY

❧ **FISHING**
See: SPORTS

❧ **FITNESS**
See: HEALTH

❧ **FLATNESS**
See: SHAPE

❧ **FLATTERY**
See Also: FRIENDSHIP, WORDS OF PRAISE

❧ **FLAVOR**
See: FOOD AND DRINK

❧ **FLAWS**
See: ERRORS

❧ **FLEXIBILITY/INFLEXIBILITY**
See Also: HABIT

❧ **FLOWERS**
See Also: NATURE

❧ **FOG**
See Also: MIST

❧ **FOOD AND DRINK**
See Also: EATING AND DRINKING

❧ **FOOLISHNESS**
See Also: ABSURDITY, FUTILITY, STUPIDITY

❧ **FOOTBALL**
See Also: SPORTS

❧ **FORCEFULNESS**
See: POWER

❧ **FOREBODING**
See: ANXIETY, FEAR

❧ FOREHEAD
See Also: FACE(S)

❧ FORGETFULNESS
See: MEMORY, MIND

❧ FORGIVENESS

❧ FORLORNNESS
See: ABANDONMENT, ALONENESS

❧ FORMALITY
See Also: ORDER/DISORDER

❧ FORTUNE/MISFORTUNE

❧ FRAGILITY
See Also: WEAKNESS

❧ FRANKNESS
See Also: CANDOR

❧ FRAUD
See Also: CRIME, DISHONESTY

❧ FRECKLES
See Also: FACIAL DETAILS

❧ FREEDOM

❧ FRESHNESS

❧ FRIENDLINESS
See: SOCIABILITY

❧ FRIENDSHIP
See Also: LOVE, SOCIABILITY

❧ FRIENDSHIP DEFINED

❧ FROWNS
*See Also: FACIAL EXPRESSIONS,
MISCELLANEOUS; LOOKS; STARES*

❧ FRUSTRATION
See Also: DEJECTION, EMOTIONS

❧ FUN
See: PLEASURE

❧ FURNITURE AND FURNISHINGS
See Also: HOUSES, ROOMS

❧ FURTIVENESS
See: SECRECY

❧ FURY
See: ANGER

❧ FUTILITY
*See Also: ABSURDITY, DIFFICULTY,
IMPOSSIBILITY,
USEFULNESS/USELESSNESS*

❧ FUTURE

❧ GAIETY
See Also: CHEERFULNESS

❧ GAIT
See: WALKING

❧ GARDEN SCENES
See: FLOWERS, LANDSCAPES, NATURE

❧ GENEROSITY
See: KINDNESS

❧ GENIUS
See: GREATNESS

❧ GENTLENESS
See Also: KINDNESS

❧ GESTURES
See: HAND MOVEMENTS

❧ GIDDINESS
See: LIGHTNESS

❧ GIFTS
See: KINDNESS

❧ GLANCE
See: LOOKS

❧ GLIMMER, GLITTER, AND GLOSS
See Also: BRIGHTNESS, LIGHTING, SHINING

❧ GLOOM
See Also: BEHAVIOR; DEJECTION; FACIAL EXPRESSIONS, SERIOUS; SADNESS

❧ GLORY
See: FAME, SUCCESS/FAILURE

❧ GLUTTONY
See: GREED, EATING AND DRINKING

❧ GOD
See: FORGIVENESS, RELIGION

❧ GOLD
See: COLORS, MONEY

❧ GOLF
See Also: SPORTS

❧ GOOD HEALTH
See: HEALTH

❧ GOODNESS
See: HEART, KINDNESS

❧ GOSSIP

❧ GOVERNMENT
See Also: LAW, POLITICS

❧ GRACEFULNESS
See: AGILITY, BEAUTY

❧ GRACIOUSNESS
See: BEHAVIOR, MANNERS

❧ GRAVENESS
See: SERIOUSNESS

❧ GRAY
See Also: COLORS, GLOOM, HAIR COLOR, SKY, WEATHER

❧ GREATNESS
See Also: FAME, INTELLIGENCE, MIND

❧ GREED
See Also: EATING AND DRINKING, ENVY

❧ GREEN
See: COLORS, ENVY

❧ GRIEF
See Also: SADNESS

❧ GRIN(S)
See Also: LAUGHTER, SMILES

❧ GROANS AND WHISPERS
See Also: SIGHS

❧ GROWTH
See Also: SPREADING

❧ GRUMBLING
See: COMPLAINTS

❧ GUILT
See Also: CONSCIENCE

❧ HABIT
See Also: BEHAVIOR, FLEXIBILITY/INFLEXIBILITY

❧ HAIR
See Also: HAIR COLOR; HAIR, CURLY; HAIR STYLES; HAIR TEXTURE

♣ HAIR COLOR
See Also: BLACK, BROWN, GRAY, RED, WHITE

♣ HAIR, CURLY
See Also: HAIR STYLES

♣ HAIR STYLES

♣ HAIR TEXTURE

♣ HAND MOVEMENTS
See Also: HANDSHAKE

♣ HAND(S)
See Also: ARM(S), FINGER(S), HAND MOVEMENTS, HANDSHAKE

♣ HANDSHAKE

♣ HANDWRITING

♣ HAPPINESS
See Also: CONTENTMENT, JOY, PLEASURE

♣ HARD-HEARTEDNESS
See: CRUELTY

♣ HARDNESS
See: FIRMNESS, TOUGHNESS

♣ HARDSHIP
See: FORTUNE/MISFORTUNE

♣ HARD WORK
See: AMBITION, WORK

♣ HARMLESSNESS
See Also: INNOCENCE, KINDNESS

♣ HARMONY
See: AGREEMENT, COMPATIBILITY, PEACEFULNESS

♣ HARSHNESS
See Also: FIRMNESS, VOICE(S)

♣ HASTE
See: SPEED

♣ HASTINESS
See: CARELESSNESS

♣ HATRED

♣ HEAD MOVEMENTS

♣ HEAD(S)
See Also: HEAD MOVEMENTS

♣ HEALTH
See Also: PAIN

♣ HEART(S)
See Also: AGITATION, HEARTBEAT

♣ HEARTBEAT
See Also: AGITATION

♣ HEARTINESS
See: EMOTIONS

♣ HEAT
See Also: WEATHER

♣ HEAVINESS

♣ HELPFULNESS
See: KINDNESS

♣ HELPLESSNESS

♣ HESITANCY
See: UNCERTAINTY

♣ HILLS
See: MOUNTAINS

♣ HISTORY
See Also: MEMORY; PAST, THE

♣ HOCKEY
See: SPORTS

♣ HOLLOWNESS
See: EMPTINESS

♣ HOME
*See: FURNITURE AND FURNISHINGS,
    HOUSES,ROOMS*

♣ HOMELESSNESS

♣ HONESTY
See Also: RELIABILITY/UNRELIABILITY

♣ HONOR
See: REPUTATION

♣ HOPE
See Also: DREAM(S)

♣ HORROR
See: FEAR

♣ HOSPITALITY

♣ HOSTILITY
See: ANGER

♣ HOUSES
*See Also: FURNITURE AND FURNISHINGS,
    ROOMS*

♣ HOVERING
See: LINGERING

♣ HOWLS
See: SCREAMS

♣ HUMANITY
See: MANKIND

♣ HUMILITY
See: MEEKNESS, MODESTY

♣ HUMOR
See Also: CLEVERNESS, LAUGHTER

♣ HUNGER
See Also: EATING AND DRINKING

♣ HURRYING
See: SPEED

♣ ICICLES
See: SNOW

♣ IDEALS
See: BELIEFS

♣ IDEAS

♣ IDLENESS
See Also: SITTING

♣ IGNORANCE
See Also: STUPIDITY

♣ ILLNESS
See Also: HEALTH

♣ ILL TEMPER
See: ANGER

♣ ILLUSTRIOUSNESS
See: FAME

♣ IMAGINATION
See: IDEAS

♣ IMITATION
See: SIMILARITY

♣ IMMEDIACY
See: SPEED

♣ **IMMOBILITY**
See Also: DEATH, LYING, POSTURE, SITTING
    STANDING

♣ **IMPARTIALITY**

♣ **IMPASSIVENESS**
See: COLDNESS, REMOTENESS, RESERVE

♣ **IMPATIENCE**
See: RESTLESSNESS

♣ **IMPERMANENCE**
See: FRAGILITY, LIFE

♣ **IMPOLITENESS**
See: MANNERS

♣ **IMPORTANCE/UNIMPORTANCE**
See Also: MEMORY, NECESSITY

♣ **IMPOSSIBILITY**
See Also: ABSURDITY, DIFFICULTY,
    FUTILITY, OPPORTUNITY

♣ **IMPROBABILITY**
See: IMPOSSIBILITY

♣ **IMPROPRIETY**
See: PROPRIETY/IMPROPRIETY

♣ **INACCURACY**
See: ERRORS

♣ **INACTIVITY**
See: IDLENESS, IMMOBILITY

♣ **INAPPROPRIATENESS**
See Also: BELONGING

♣ **INCISIVENESS**
See: SHARPNESS

♣ **INCOMPLETENESS**

♣ **INCONGRUITY**
See: ABSURDITY

♣ **INCORRECTNESS**
See: ERRORS

♣ **INCREASE**
See: GROWTH

♣ **INDECISION**
See: CHOICES

♣ **INDEPENDENCE**
See: FREEDOM

♣ **INDIFFERENCE**
See: REMOTENESS, RESERVE

♣ **INDIGNATION**
See: ANGER

♣ **INDISTINCTION**
See: VAGUENESS

♣ **INDIVIDUALITY**
See: ORIGINALITY

♣ **INDOLENCE**
See: IDLENESS

♣ **INDUSTRIOUSNESS**
See: AMBITION, WORK

♣ **INEFFECTIVENESS**
See: FUTILITY, USEFULNESS/USELESSNESS

♣ **INEVITABILITY**
See: CERTAINTY

♣ **INEXORABILITY**
See: CERTAINTY

♣ **INFATUATION**
See: LOVE

❧ **INFLATION**
See: ECONOMICS

❧ **INFLUENCE**
See: POWER

❧ **INFORMATION**

❧ **INGRATITUDE**
See: PARENTHOOD, SHARPNESS

❧ **INHERITANCE**
See: PAST, THE

❧ **INJUSTICE**
See: JUSTICE

❧ **INNOCENCE**
See Also: HARMLESSNESS

❧ **INQUISITIVENESS**
*See: CURIOSITY, QUESTIONS AND
    ANSWERS*

❧ **INSECTS**
See Also: ANIMALS

❧ **INSEPARABILITY**
*See: CLOSENESS, FRIENDSHIP,
    RELATIONSHIPS*

❧ **INSIGHT**
See: WISDOM

❧ **INSIGNIFICANCE**
See: MEMORY, IMPORTANCE

❧ **INSTINCTIVENESS**
See: NATURALNESS

❧ **INSULT**

❧ **INTELLIGENCE**
See Also: MIND

❧ **INTENSITY**
See Also: SHARPNESS, STARES

❧ **INTIMACY**
See: CLOSENESS, RELATIONSHIPS

❧ **INTOLERANCE**

❧ **IRONY**
See: HUMOR

❧ **IRREGULARITY**
See: REGULARITY/IRREGULARITY

❧ **IRRITABLENESS/IRRITATING**
See Also: ANGER, NERVOUSNESS, TENSION

❧ **ISOLATION**
See: ALONENESS

❧ **JEALOSY**
See: ENVY

❧ **JEWELRY**
See Also: CLOTHING

❧ **JOBS**
See: WORK

❧ **JOKES**
See: HUMOR

❧ **JOURNALISM**
See: PROFESSIONS, WRITERS/WRITING

❧ **JOY**
*See Also: CONTENTMENT, HAPPINESS,
    PLEASURE*

❧ **JUDGMENTS**
See: OPINIONS

❧ **JUMPING**
See Also: LEAPING; ROCKING AND ROLLING

♣ **JUSTICE**

♣ **KINDNESS**
See Also: GENTLENESS, SWEETNESS

♣ **KISSES**
See Also: INSULTS

♣ **KNOWLEDGE**
See Also: EDUCATION, INTELLIGENCE,
*   MIND*

♣ **LANDSCAPES**
See Also: MOUNTAINS; NATURE; PONDS,
*   RIVERS AND STREAMS; ROAD SCENES;*
*   TREES*

♣ **LANGUAGE**
See Also: SPEAKING, WORD(S)

♣ **LAUGHTER**
See Also: GAIETY, GRINS, HUMOR, SMILES

♣ **LAWS**
See Also: LAWYERS

♣ **LAWYERS**
See Also: LAW, PROFESSIONS

♣ **LAZINESS**
See: IDLENESS

♣ **LEAPING**
See Also: JUMPING, ROCKING AND
*   ROLLING*

♣ **LEARNING**
See: EDUCATION

♣ **LEAVES**
See Also: FLOWERS, NATURE, TREES

♣ **LEG(S)**
See Also: PAIN, PHYSICAL FEELING

♣ **LETTER-WRITING**
See: CORRESPONDENCE

♣ **LIBERTY**
See: FREEDOM

♣ **LIES AND LIARS**
See Also: DISHONESTY

♣ **LIFE**
See Also: AGE, LIFE DEFINED, MANKIND

♣ **LIFE DEFINED**

♣ **LIGHTING**
See Also: BRIGHTNESS, SHINING

♣ **LIGHTNESS**
See Also: SOFTNESS

♣ **LIGHTNING**
See: THUNDER AND LIGHTNING

♣ **LIKELIHOOD**
See: IMPOSSIBILITY

♣ **LIKENESS**
See: SIMILARITY

♣ **LIMBS**
See: ARM(S), LEG(S)

♣ **LIMPNESS**
See: GAIETY, SOFTNESS

♣ **LINGERING**

♣ **LIPS**
See Also: MOUTH

♣ **LITERATURE**
See: ART AND LITERATURE, BOOKS,
*   WRITERS/WRITING*

♣ **LIVELINESS**
See: ACTIVENESS, ENTHUSIASM, ENERGY

♣ **LOCALITIES**
See: PLACES

♣ **LOGIC**
See: SENSE

♣ **LONELINESS**
See: ABANDONMENT, ALONENESS

♣ **LONGING**
See: DESIRE

♣ **LONG-WINDEDNESS**
See: TALKATIVENESS

♣ **LOOKS**
*See Also: FROWNS AND SCOWLS,
    SCRUTINY, STARES*

♣ **LOOSENESS**

♣ **LOUDNESS**
See: NOISE

♣ **LOVE**
*See Also: FRIENDSHIP, LOVE DEFINED, MEN
    AND WOMEN*

♣ **LOVE DEFINED**

♣ **LOYALTY/DISLOYALTY**
See: FRIENDSHIP, LOVE

♣ **LUCIDITY**
See: CLARITY

♣ **LUCK**
See: FORTUNE/MISFORTUNE

♣ **LUNACY**
See: MADNESS

♣ **LUSHNESS**
See: ABUNDANCE

♣ **LUST**
See: DESIRE, SEX

♣ **LYING**
*See Also: BEARING, BENDING/BENT,
    IMMOBILITY, POSTURE, SITTING, SLEEP,
    STANDING*

♣ **MADNESS**

♣ **MANIPULATION**
See: POWER

♣ **MANKIND**
See Also: HELPLESSNESS, LIFE

♣ **MANNERS**
*See Also: BEHAVIOR,
    PROPRIETY/IMPROPRIETY*

♣ **MARRIAGE**
*See Also: MEN AND WOMEN,
    RELATIONSHIPS*

♣ **MATHEMATICS AND SCIENCE**

♣ **MATRIMONY**
See: MARRIAGE

♣ **MAXIMS, PROVERBS, AND SAYINGS**

♣ **MEANINGFULNESS/
    MEANINGLESSNESS**
*See Also: MEMORY, IMPORTANCE/
    UNIMPORTANCE, NECESSITY*

♣ **MEANNESS**
See: CRUELTY

♣ **MEEKNESS**
See Also: MODESTY

♣ **MEETINGS**

♣ **MELANCHOLY**
See: DESPAIR

♣ **MEMORY**
See Also: PAST, THE

♣ **MEN AND WOMEN**
See Also: LOVE, MARRIAGE, SEXUAL
INTERACTION

♣ **MERCY**
See: KINDNESS

♣ **MERIT**
See: VIRTUE

♣ **MERRIMENT**
See: GAIETY, JOY

♣ **METHOD**
See: PURPOSEFULNESS

♣ **MIDDLE AGE**
See: AGE

♣ **MIND**
See Also: ATTENTION, INSULTS, MIND
DEFINED, THOUGHT

♣ **MIND DEFINED**

♣ **MIRTH**
See: GAIETY

♣ **MISERLINESS**
See: THRIFT

♣ **MISERY**
See: DEJECTION, GLOOM

♣ **MISFORTUNE**
See: FORTUNE/MISFORTUNE

♣ **MIST**
See Also: FOG

♣ **MISTAKES**
See: ERRORS

♣ **MISTRESS**
See: MEN AND WOMEN

♣ **MIXTURES**
See: CONNECTIONS

♣ **MOANS**
See: GROANS AND WHISPERS

♣ **MODESTY**
See Also: MEEKNESS, PERSONAL TRAITS

♣ **MONARCHY**
See: GOVERNMENT

♣ **MONEY**
See Also: COST, GREED, RICHES

♣ **MONOTONY**
See: DULLNESS, REPETITION

♣ **MONTHS**
See: SEASONS

♣ **MOOD CHANGES**
See: CHANGE

♣ **MOODINESS**
See: GLOOM

♣ **MOON**

♣ **MORALITY**
See Also: BELIEFS, VIRTUE

♣ **MORTALITY**
See: DEATH

♣ **MOTHERHOOD**
See: CHILDREN, PARENTHOOD

♣ **MOTHERS-IN-LAW**
See: PARENTHOOD

♣ **MOTIONLESSNESS**
See: IMMOBILITY

♣ **MOTIVATION**
See Also: AMBITION, PURPOSEFULNESS

♣ **MOUNTAINS**
See Also: LANDSCAPES, NATURE

♣ **MOURNING**
See: GRIEF

♣ **MOUTH**
*See Also: CHEEK; CHIN; MOUTH,
    OPEN/SHUT*

♣ **MOUTH, OPEN/SHUT**

♣ **MOVEMENT(S)**
*See Also: ADVANCING, JUMPING, LEAPING,
    ROCKING AND ROLLING, RUNNING,
    TURNING AND TWISTING, WALKING*

♣ **MOVIES**
See: STAGE AND SCREEN

♣ **MURDER**
See: CRIME

♣ **MUSCLES**
See Also: STRENGTH

♣ **MUSIC**
See Also: SINGING

♣ **MUSTACHES**
See Also: BEARD(S), HAIR

♣ **MYSTERIOUSNESS**
See: STRANGENESS

♣ **NAKEDNESS**
See: BARENESS

♣ **NAMES**
See Also: MEMORY

♣ **NARROWNESS**
See: THINNESS

♣ **NATIONS**
*See: CHARACTERISTICS, NATIONAL;
    GOVERNMENTS*

♣ **NATURALNESS**

♣ **NATURE**
*See Also: FLOWERS, LEAVES, MOON,
    OCEAN/OCEANFRONT; PONDS, RIVERS
    AND STREAMS; RAIN; SEASCAPES,
    SKYSCAPES; SNOW; STARS; SUN;
    THUNDER AND LIGHTNING; TREES;
    WEATHER*

♣ **NEARNESS**
See: CLOSENESS

♣ **NEATNESS**
See: CLEANLINESS, ORDER/DISORDER

♣ **NECESSITY**
See Also: IMPORTANCE/UNIMPORTANCE

♣ **NECK**
*See Also: CHIN, CHEEKS, PHYSICAL
    APPEARANCE*

♣ **NEED**
See: DESIRE

♣ **NEGLECT**
See: ABANDONMENT, REJECTION

♣ **NEGLIGENCE**
See: CARELESSNESS

♣ **NERVE**
See: COURAGE

♣ **NERVOUSNESS**
See Also: ANXIETY, TENSION, TREMBLING

♣ **NEUTRALITY**
See: IMPARTIALITY

♣ **NEWNESS**
See: FRESHNESS, TIMELINESS/
    UNTIMELINESS

♣ **NEWS**
See Also: GOSSIP, KNOWLEDGE

♣ **NIGHT**
See Also: DARKNESS

♣ **NIGHTMARES**
See: DREAM(S)

♣ **NOISES**
See Also: IRRITABLENESS

♣ **NOSE(S)**
See Also: FACIAL DETAILS

♣ **NONSTALGIA**
See: MEMORY, SENTIMENT

♣ **NOURISHMENT**
See: FOOD AND DRINK

♣ **NOVELS**
See: BOOKS

♣ **NUMBNESS**
See: RESERVE

♣ **OATH**
See: PROMISE

♣ **OBEDIANCE**
See: MEEKNESS

♣ **OBESITY**
See: FATNESS

♣ **OBJECTS, MISCELLANEOUS**

♣ **OBLIVION**
See: BLINDNESS, MEMORY

♣ **OBSCURITY**
See: VAGUENESS

♣ **OBSERVATION**
See: SCRUTINY

♣ **OBSOLESCENCE**
See: TIMELINESS/UNTIMELINESS

♣ **OBSTINANCY**
See: PERSISTENCE

♣ **OBVIOUSNESS**
See Also: CLARITY, VISIBILITY

♣ **OCEAN/OCEANFRONT**
See Also: SEASCAPES

♣ **OCCUPATIONS**
See: DOCTORS, LAWYERS, PROFESSIONS

♣ **ODOR**
See: SMELL

♣ **OLD**
See: AGE

♣ **OPAQUENESS**
See: VAGUENESS

♣ OPEN AND SHUT

♣ OPENNESS
See: CANDOR

♣ OPERA
See: MUSIC

♣ OPINION
See Also: IDEAS

♣ OPPORTUNENESS
See: TIMELINESS/UNTIMELINESS

♣ OPPORTUNITY
See Also: FORTUNE/MISFORTUNE,
  IMPOSSIBILITY

♣ OPTIMISM
See: CHEERFULNESS

♣ ORANGE
See: COLORS

♣ ORATORY
See: SPEECHMAKING

♣ ORDER/DISORDER
See: CLEANLINESS

♣ ORDINARINESS
See: COMMONPLACE

♣ ORIGINALITY

♣ OUTBURST
See: BURST

♣ OUT OF PLACE
See: BELONGING

♣ PAIN
See Also: HEALTH

♣ PAINTINGS
See: ART AND LITERATURE

♣ PALLOR
See Also: FACIAL COLOR, GRAY, RED, WHITE

♣ PARENTAL LOVE
See Also: PARENTHOOD

♣ PARENTHOOD

♣ PARTING
See: BEGINNINGS AND ENDINGS

♣ PASSION
See Also: DESIRE, LOVE, SEX

♣ PAST, THE
See Also: HISTORY, MEMORY

♣ PATIENCE

♣ PATRIOTISM
See: BELIEFS

♣ PAUNCHINESS
See: BODY, FATNESS, STOMACH

♣ PAUSE
See Also: CAUTION

♣ PEACEFULNESS
See Also: CALMNESS

♣ PECULIARITY
See: STRANGENESS

♣ PENETRATION
See: PERVASIVENESS

♣ PENNANTS
See: OBJECTS, MISCELLANEOUS

♣ PENSIVENESS
See: THOUGHT

♣ PEOPLE, INTERACTION
*See Also: CROWDS, FRIENDSHIP, MEN AND
    WOMEN, RELATIONSHIPS*

♣ PERCEPTIVENESS
See Also: ALERTNESS, SENSITIVENESS

♣ PERMANENCE/IMPERMANENCE
See Also: CONTINUITY

♣ PERPLEXITY
See: BEWILDERMENT

♣ PERSISTENCE
See Also: CLINGING, PURPOSEFULNESS

♣ PERSONAL TRAITS
See Also: DULLNESS

♣ PERSONALITY PROFILES
See Also: PERSONAL TRAITS

♣ PERVASIVENESS
See Also: CLINGING

♣ PHYSICAL APPEARANCE
*See Also: ARM(S), ATTRACTIVENESS,
    BEAUTY, BODY, EYE(S), FACE(S),
    FATNESS, HAIR, HAND(S), THINNESS,
    UNATTRACTIVENESS*

♣ PHYSICAL FEELINGS
See Also: HEALTH, PAIN

♣ PHYSICIANS
See: DOCTORS

♣ PICTURES
See: ART AND LITERATURE

♣ PINK
See Also: CHEEKS, COLORS, FACIAL COLOR

♣ PITY
See Also: KINDNESS

♣ PLACES
See Also: CITY/STREETSCAPES, INSULTS

♣ PLAINNESS
See: SIMPLICITY

♣ PLANNING
See: PURPOSEFULNESS

♣ PLAYS
See: STAGE AND SCREEN

♣ PLEASURE
See Also: GAIETY, HAPPINESS, JOY

♣ PLENTY
See: ABUNDANCE

♣ POETS/POETRY
See Also: WRITERS/WRITING

♣ POISE
See: BEARING

♣ POLITENESS
See: MANNERS

♣ POLITICS/POLITICIANS

♣ PONDS, RIVERS, AND STREAMS
See Also: NATURE, SEASCAPES

♣ POPULARITY

♣ POSSIBILITY
See: OPPORTUNITY

♣ **POSTURE**
See Also: BEARING, BENT, STRAIGHTNESS

♣ **POVERTY**
See Also: ECONOMICS

♣ **POWER**

♣ **POWERLESSNESS**
See: HELPLESSNESS

♣ **PRAISE**
See: FLATTERY, WORDS OF PRAISE

♣ **PRAISEWORTHINESS**
See: VIRTUE

♣ **PRAYER**
See: RELIGION

♣ **PRECARIOUSNESS**
See: DANGER

♣ **PRECISION**
See: CORRECTNESS

♣ **PREDICTABILITY**
See: CERTAINTY

♣ **PREJUDICE**
See: INTOLERANCE

♣ **PREPAREDNESS**

♣ **PRESENT, THE**

♣ **PRESERVATION**
See: PROTECTIVENESS

♣ **PRETTINESS**
See: BEAUTY

♣ **PREVENTION**
See: PROBLEMS AND SOLUTIONS

♣ **PRICE**
See: COST

♣ **PRIDE**

♣ **PROBABILITY**
See: CERTAINTY

♣ **PROBLEMS AND SOLUTIONS**

♣ **PROCRASTINATION**
See: LINGERING

♣ **PROFANITY**
See: CURSES

♣ **PROFESSIONS**
See Also: DOCTORS, LAWYERS

♣ **PROFICIENCY**
See: ABILITY

♣ **PROFUSION**
See: ABUNDANCE

♣ **PROGRESS**
See: GROWTH

♣ **PROLIFERATION**
See: SPREADING

♣ **PROMISE**
See Also: RELIABILITY/UNRELIABILITY

♣ **PROMPTNESS**

♣ **PRONUNCIATION**
See: SPEECH PATTERNS

♣ **PROPRIETY/IMPROPRIETY**
See Also: MANNERS

♣ **PROSE**
See: POETS/POETRY, WRITERS/WRITING

♣ **PROSPERITY**
See: RICHES, SUCCESS/FAILURE

♣ **PROTECTIVENESS**
See Also: WATCHFULNESS

♣ **PROTRUSION**
See Also: BELONGING, OBVIOUSNESS,
   VISIBILITY

♣ **PROVERBS**
See: MAXIMS, PROVERBS, AND SAYINGS

♣ **PROXIMITY**
See: CLOSENESS

♣ **PRUDENCE**
See: CAUTION

♣ **PSYCHOLOGY**
See: PROFESSIONS

♣ **PUBLIC OPINION**
See: OPINION

♣ **PUBLIC, THE**
See: POLITICS

♣ **PURITY**
See Also: VIRTUE

♣ **PURPLE**
See: COLORS

♣ **PURPOSEFULNESS**

♣ **PURSUIT**

♣ **PUZZLEMENT**
See: BEWILDERMENT

♣ **QUESTIONS AND ANSWERS**
See Also: PROBLEMS AND SOLUTIONS

♣ **RAIN**
See Also: WEATHER

♣ **RANTING**
See: ROARS

♣ **RAPIDITY**
See: SPEED

♣ **RARITY**
See Also: ORIGINALITY

♣ **RASHNESS**
See: SPEED

♣ **READERS/READING**
See Also: BOOKS

♣ **READINESS**
See: PREPAREDNESS

♣ **REALIZATION**
See Also: TRUTH

♣ **REALNESS/UNREALNESS**

♣ **REAPPEARANCE**

♣ **REASON**
See: SENSE

♣ **RECOLLECTION**
See: MEMORY

♣ **RED**
See Also: BLUSHES, CHEEKS, COLORS, HAIR,
   LIPS, MOUTH

♣ **REDUCTION**
See: DECREASE, DISAPPEARANCE

♣ **REFLECTION**
See: THOUGHT

❧ **REFORM**
See: CHANGE

❧ **REGRET**
See Also: CONSCIENCE

❧ **REGULARITY/IRREGULARITY**

❧ **REJECTION**
See Also: ABANDONMENT

❧ **RELATIONSHIPS**
See Also: MARRIAGE; MEN AND WOMEN;
PARENTHOOD; PEOPLE, INTERACTION

❧ **RELENTLESSNESS**
See: PERSISTENCE

❧ **RELIABILITY/UNRELIABILITY**
See Also: FIRMNESS, STEADINESS

❧ **RELIEF**
See: EMOTIONS

❧ **RELIGION**
See Also: BELIEFS

❧ **REMEDY**
See: PROBLEMS AND SOLUTIONS

❧ **REMORSE**
See: REGRET

❧ **REMOTENESS**
See Also: RESERVE

❧ **RENOWN**
See: FAME

❧ **REPETITION**
See Also: CONTINUITY, DULLNESS

❧ **REPUTATION**

❧ **RESENTMENT**
See: ANGER

❧ **RESERVE**
See Also: EMOTIONS, PERSONALITY TRAITS,
REMOTENESS

❧ **RESIGNATION**
See: MEEKNESS

❧ **RESPONSE**
See: QUESTIONS AND ANSWERS, WORD(S)

❧ **RESPONSIBILITY**
See: RELIABILITY/UNRELIABILITY

❧ **RESTLESSNESS**

❧ **RESTRAINT**
See: CONFINEMENT, EMOTIONS

❧ **RESULTS**
See: CAUSE AND EFFECT

❧ **RETREAT**
See: DISAPPEARANCE, EXITS

❧ **RETURN**
See: PAST, THE; REAPPEARANCE

❧ **REVELRY**
See: GAIETY

❧ **REVENGE**
See Also: BITTERNESS

❧ **REVOLUTIONS**
See: POLITICS

❧ **RHETORIC**
See: SPEECHMAKING, WORD(S)

♣ **RICHES**
See Also: *ABUNDANCE, FORTUNE/MISFORTUNE, MONEY, SUCCESS/FAILURE*

♣ **RICHNESS**

♣ **RIDICULE**
See: *INSULTS*

♣ **RIGHTEOUSNESS**
See: *JUSTICE, VIRTUE*

♣ **RIGHTNESS**
See: *CORRECTNESS, TRUENESS/FALSENESS*

♣ **RISING**
See Also: *BEARING, STANDING*

♣ **RISK**
See Also: *DANGER*

♣ **RIVERS**
See: *PONDS, RIVERS, AND STREAMS*

♣ **ROAD SCENES**
See Also: *NOISE, VEHICLES*

♣ **ROARS**
See Also: *SCREAMS*

♣ **ROBBERY**
See: *DISHONESTY*

♣ **ROCKING AND ROLLING**
See Also: *MOVEMENT(S), UNSTEADINESS, VIBRATION*

♣ **ROMANCE**
See: *LOVE, MEN AND WOMEN*

♣ **ROOMS**
See Also: *FURNITURE AND FURNISHINGS, HOUSES*

♣ **ROUNDNESS**
See: *SHAPE*

♣ **ROWDINESS**
See: *NOISE*

♣ **RUDENESS**
See: *MANNERS*

♣ **RUMOR**
See: *GOSSIP*

♣ **RUNNING**
See Also: *MOVEMENT(S), SPEED*

♣ **RUTHLESSNESS**
See: *CRUELTY*

♣ **SADNESS**
See Also: *DEJECTION, EMOTIONS, GLOOM*

♣ **SAFETY**
See Also: *DANGER, RISK*

♣ **SALES**
See: *SUCCESS/FAILURE*

♣ **SARCASM**
See: *HUMOR*

♣ **SATISFACTION**
See: *CONTENTMENT*

♣ **SAYINGS**
See: *MAXIMS, PROVERBS, AND SAYINGS*

♣ **SCANDAL**
See: *REPUTATION, SHAME*

♣ **SCARCITY**
See: *RARITY*

♣ **SCARS**
See: *FACIAL DETAILS*

❧ **SCATTERING**
See: DISPERSAL

❧ **SCIENCE**
See: MATHEMATICS AND SCIENCE

❧ **SCREAMS**
See Also: NOISE, ROARS

❧ **SCRUPULOUSNESS**
See: CORRECTNESS

❧ **SCRUTINY**
See Also: INTENSITY

❧ **SEASCAPES**
See Also: NATURE; OCEAN/OCEANFRONT; PONDS, RIVERS, AND STREAMS

❧ **SEASONS**

❧ **SECRECY**

❧ **SEDATENESS**
See: SERIOUSNESS

❧ **SELF-CONFIDENCE**
See Also: PRIDE, VANITY

❧ **SELF-CONCIOUSNESS**
See: DISCOMFORT, NATURALNESS

❧ **SELFISHNESS**

❧ **SENSATIONS**
See: EMOTIONS

❧ **SENSE**
See Also: INTELLIGENCE

❧ **SENSELESSNESS**
See: ABSURDITY

❧ **SENSITIVENESS**
See Also: KINDNESS

❧ **SENTIMENT**

❧ **SEPARATION**
See: BEGINNINGS AND ENDINGS

❧ **SERENITY**
See: PEACEFULNESS

❧ **SERIOUSNESS**

❧ **SERMONS**
See: SPEECHMAKING

❧ **SERVILITY**
See: MEEKNESS

❧ **SEX**
See Also: ATTRACTIVENESS, BODY ORGANS, BREASTS, MEN AND WOMEN, SEXUAL INTERACTION, RELATIONSHIPS

❧ **SEXUAL INTERACTION**
See Also: INSULTS

❧ **SEXUALITY**
See: SEX

❧ **SHADOW**

❧ **SHALLOWNESS**
See: IMPORTANCE/UNIMPORTANCE

❧ **SHAME**
See Also: BLUSHES

❧ **SHAPE**

❧ **SHARPNESS**
See Also: PAIN, PARENTHOOD

❧ **SHINING**
See Also: BRIGHTNESS; GLIMMER, GLITTER, AND GLOSS

❧ **SHOCK**
See Also: CAUSE AND EFFECT, SURPRISE

❧ **SHOULDERS**
See Also: BODY

❧ **SHOUTS**
See: SCREAMS

❧ **SHREWDNESS**
See: CLEVERNESS

❧ **SHRIEKS**
See: SCREAMS

❧ **SHUT**
See: OPEN/SHUT

❧ **SHYNESS**
See Also: MEEKNESS, PERSONAL TRAITS

❧ **SICKNESS**
See: ILLNESS

❧ **SIDEBURNS**
See: BEARD(S)

❧ **SIGHS**
See Also: GROANS AND WHISPERS

❧ **SIGNIFICANCE**
See: IMPORTANCE/UNIMPORTANCE

❧ **SILENCE**
See Also: SECRECY

❧ **SILLINESS**
See: ABSURDITY, FOOLISHNESS, IMPOSSIBILITY, STUPIDITY

❧ **SIMILARITY**
See Also: DISSIMILARITY

❧ **SIMILES**
See: MAXIMS, PROVERBS, AND SAYINGS

❧ **SIMPLICITY**
See Also: EASE

❧ **SIN**
See: EVIL

❧ **SINCERETY**
See: CANDOR

❧ **SINGING**
See Also: MUSIC

❧ **SITTING**
See Also: BEARING, IMMOBILITY

❧ **SKEPTICISM**
See: TRUST/MISTRUST

❧ **SKILLS**
See: ABILITY, ACCOMPLISHMENT

❧ **SKIN**
See Also: BALDNESS, COMPLEXION, FACIAL COLOR, FACIAL DETAILS, PALLOR, WRINKLES

❧ **SKY**
See Also: CLOUDS, MOON, SKY COLOR

❧ **SKY COLOR**

❧ **SLANDER**

❧ **SLEEP**
See Also: DREAM(S), SNORE(S)

❧ **SLIGHTNESS**
See: WEAKNESS

❧ **SLIMNESS**
See: THINNESS

❧ **SLOPPINESS**
See: CARELESSNESS, ORDER/DISORDER

❧ **SLOWNESS**
See Also: MOVEMENT(S)

❧ **SMALLNESS**

❧ **SMELL**
See Also: AIR, SWEAT

❧ **SMILE**
See Also: BRIGHTNESS; FACIAL EXPRESSIONS, MISCELLANEOUS; GRINS; LAUGHTER

❧ **SMOKE**
See: FIRE AND SMOKE

❧ **SMOKING**
See: TOBACCO

❧ **SMOOTHNESS**

❧ **SNORE(S)**
See Also: SLEEP

❧ **SNOW**
See Also: NATURE, WEATHER

❧ **SOAP OPERA**
See Also: STAGE AND SCREEN

❧ **SOCIABILITY/UNSOCIABILITY**
See Also: BEHAVIOR

❧ **SOCIETY**

❧ **SOFTNESS**

❧ **SOLIDITY**
See: FIRMNESS, STEADINESS, STRENGTH

❧ **SOLITUDE**
See: ALONENESS

❧ **SORROW**
See: GRIEF

❧ **SOUL**

❧ **SOUNDNESS**
See Also: HEALTH

❧ **SOUNDS**
See: NOISE

❧ **SPEAKING**
See Also: CONVERSATION, SPEECH PATTERNS, TALKATIVENESS

❧ **SPEECHLESSNESS**
See: SILENCE

❧ **SPEECHMAKING**

❧ **SPEECH PATTERNS**

❧ **SPEED**
See Also: RUNNING

❧ **SPIRIT**
See: COURAGE

❧ **SPOILAGE**
See: DISINTEGRATION

❧ **SPONTANEITY**
See: NATURALNESS

❧ **SPORTS**
See Also: BASEBALL, BOXING AND WRESTLING, FOOTBALL, GOLF

❧ **SPREADING**
See Also: GROWTH, PERVASIVENESS

♣ **SPRIGHTLINESS**
See: ACTIVENESS

♣ **SPRING**
See: SEASONS

♣ **STAGE AND SCREEN**
See Also: ACTING

♣ **STALENESS**
See: TIMELINESS/UNTIMELINESS

♣ **STANDING**
See Also: BEARING, IMMOBILITY,
    PERSONALITY PROFILES, POSTURE

♣ **STARES**
See Also: FROWNS, LOOKS

♣ **STARS**

♣ **STARTING AND STOPPING**
See: BEGINNINGS AND ENDINGS, PAUSE

♣ **STATELINESS**
See: BEARING

♣ **STATISTICS**
See: FACTS

♣ **STEADINESS**
See Also: FIRMNESS

♣ **STEALTH**
See: SECRECY

♣ **STERILITY**
See: BARRENNESS, EMPTINESS

♣ **STICKINESS**
See: CLINGING

♣ **STILLNESS**
See: IMMOBILITY, PEACEFULNESS, SILENCE

♣ **STINGINESS**
See: THRIFT

♣ **STOMACH**
See Also: BODY, FATNESS, SHAPE, THINNESS

♣ **STOP**
See: PAUSE

♣ **STORIES**
See Also: BOOKS, WRITERS/WRITING

♣ **STRAIGHTNESS**
See Also: POSTURE

♣ **STRANGENESS**

♣ **STREETSCAPES**
See: CITY/STREETSCAPES

♣ **STRENGTH**
See Also: BODY, COURAGE, MUSCLES,
    TOUGHNESS

♣ **STRUGGLE**
See Also: BEHAVIOR, FUTILITY, LIFE

♣ **STUBBORNNESS**
See: PERSISTENCE

♣ **STUDENTS**
See: EDUCATION

♣ **STUPIDITY**
See Also: ABSURDITY, DULLNESS,
    FOOLISHNESS, INSULTS, MIND

♣ **STURDINESS**
See: FIRMNESS, STRENGTH

♣ **STYLE**
See Also: CLOTHING

♣ SUBSERVIENCE
See: MEEKNESS

♣ SUBTLTY
See: TACT

♣ SUCCESS/FAILURE
See Also: BUSINESS; GROWTH; PAST, THE

♣ SUDDENNESS
See Also: ENTRANCES AND EXITS, SHOCK,
*   SURPRISE*

♣ SUMMER
See: SEASONS

♣ SUN
See Also: MOON, SKY, SUNSET

♣ SUNSET

♣ SURPRISE
See Also: SHOCK, SUDDENNESS

♣ SURVIVAL
See: IMPOSSIBILITY, SUCCESS/FAILURE

♣ SUSPENSE
See: EXCITEMENT

♣ SUSPICION
See: TRUST/MISTRUST

♣ SWEARING
See: CURSES, WORD(S)

♣ SWEAT
See Also: SMELLS

♣ SWEETNESS
See Also: PLEASURE, TASTE

♣ SWIMMING
See: SPORTS

♣ SYMMETRY
See: REGULARITY/IRREGULARITY

♣ SYMPATHY
See: KINDNESS, PITY

♣ TACT
See Also: INSULTS

♣ TALENT
See: ABILITY, ACCOMPLISHMENT

♣ TALKATIVENESS
See Also: CONVERSATION

♣ TALLNESS

♣ TASTE

♣ TEACHERS/TEACHING
See: EDUCATION

♣ TEARS
See Also: CRYING

♣ TEDIUM
See: BOREDOM, DULLNESS, REPETITION

♣ TEETH
See Also: WHITE

♣ TEMPER
See: ANGER

♣ TEMPERAMENT
See: PERSONAL TRAITS

♣ TEMPTATION
See: ATTRACTION

♣ TENACITY
See: PERSISTENCE

❧ **TENDERNESS**
*See: AFFECTION, GENTLENESS, KINDNESS,
   LOVE*

❧ **TENNIS**
See: SPORTS

❧ **TENSION**
See Also: ANXIETY, NERVOUSNESS

❧ **TENTATIVENESS**
See: UNCERTAINTY

❧ **TERROR**
See: FEAR

❧ **THEATER**
See: STAGE AND SCREEN

❧ **THEORIES**
See: IDEAS

❧ **THICKNESS**
See Also: ABUNDANCE

❧ **THIGHS**
See: LEG(S)

❧ **THINNESS**
See Also: BODY

❧ **THOUGHTS**
See Also: IDEAS, INTELLIGENCE

❧ **THREATS**
See: VIOLENCE

❧ **THRIFT**

❧ **THROAT**
See: NECK

❧ **THUNDER AND LIGHTNING**
See Also: NATURE, WEATHER

❧ **TIDINESS**
See: ORDER/DISORDER

❧ **TIGHTNESS**
See: FIRMNESS, TENSION, THRIFT

❧ **TIME**
See Also: DAY, DEATH, LIFE

❧ **TIMELINESS/UNTIMELINESS**
See Also: STALENESS

❧ **TIREDNESS**
See: WEARINESS

❧ **TOBACCO**
See Also: SMELLS

❧ **TONGUE**
See Also: MOUTH, SHARPNESS

❧ **TOUGHNESS**

❧ **TRADING**
*See: ADVANTAGEOUSNESS,
   SUCCESS/FAILURE*

❧ **TRAFFIC**
See: ROAD SCENES, VEHICLES

❧ **TRAIL**
See: PURSUIT

❧ **TRANQUILITY**
See: PEACEFULNESS

❧ **TRANSIENCE**
See Also: BREVITY, DEATH, LIFE

❧ **TRANSPORTATION**
See: VEHICLES

❧ **TRAVEL**

❦ TREES
See Also: LEAVES,NATURE

❦ TREMBLING
See Also: ROCKING AND ROLLING,
VIBRATION

❦ TRITENESS
See: STALENESS

❦ TRIUMPH
See: SUCCESS/FAILURE

❦ TROUBLES
See: PROBLEMS AND SOLUTIONS

❦ TROUBLESOMENESS
See: DIFFICULTY

❦ TRUENESS/FALSENESS

❦ TRUST/MISTRUST
See Also: UNCERTAINTY

❦ TRUTH
See Also: CANDOR, HONESTY

❦ TURNING AND TWISTING

❦ TYRANNY
See: POWER

❦ UMBRELLAS
See: OBJECTS, MISCELLANEOUS

❦ UNATTRACTIVENESS
See Also: UNDESIRABILITY

❦ UNAWARENESS
See: BLINDNESS

❦ UNCERTAINTY
See Also: FATE

❦ UNCOMFORTABLENESS
See: DISCOMFORT

❦ UNCONCIOUSNESS
See: NATURALNESS

❦ UNDEMONSTRATIVENESS
See: COLDNESS

❦ UNDERSTANDABILITY
See: CLARITY

❦ UNDERSTANDING
See: KNOWLEDGE

❦ UNDESIRABILITY

❦ UNEMPLOYMENT
See: WORK

❦ UNEXPECTEDNESS
See: SUDDENNESS, SURPRISE

❦ UNFAIRNESS
See: INTOLERANCE

❦ UNFRIENDLINESS
See: SOCIABILITY

❦ UNGRACIOUSNESS
See: MANNERS

❦ UNHAPPINESS
See: DEJECTION, DISCONTENT, GLOOM

❦ UNHELPFULNESS
See: USEFULNESS/USELESSNESS

❦ UNIQUENESS
See: ORIGINALITY

❦ UNKINDNESS
See: CRUELTY

♣ **UNLIKELIHOOD**
See: IMPOSSIBILITY

♣ **UNNATURALNESS**
See: NATURALNESS

♣ **UNPLEASANTNESS**
See: UNDESIRABILITY

♣ **UNPREDICTABILITY**
See: SURPRISES, UNCERTAINTY

♣ **UNPROFITABILITY**
See: ADVANTAGEOUSNESS

♣ **UNREALITY**
See: REALNESS/UNREALNESS

♣ **UNRELIABILITY**
See: RELIABILITY/UNRELIABILITY

♣ **UNRESPONSIVENESS**
See: COLDNESS, REMOTENESS, RESERVE

♣ **UNSTEADINESS**
See Also: MOVEMENT(S)

♣ **UNTIDINESS**
See: ORDER/DISORDER

♣ **UNTIMELINESS**
See: TIMELINESS/UNTIMELINESS

♣ **UNTRUSTWORTHINESS**
See: TRUST/MISTRUST

♣ **UNTRUTH**
See: LIES AND LIARS

♣ **UNWELCOMENESS**
See: UNDESIRABILITY

♣ **UPRIGHTNESS**
See: POSTURE, STRAIGHTNESS

♣ **UP-TO-DATENESS**
See: TIMELINESS/UNTIMELINESS

♣ **URGENCY**
See: IMPORTANCE/UNIMPORTANCE

♣ **USEFULNESS/USELESSNESS**
See Also: FUTILITY, NECESSITY

♣ **VAGUENESS**

♣ **VALOR**
See: COURAGE

♣ **VALUE**
See: IMPORTANCE/UNIMPORTANCE

♣ **VANITY**
See Also: PRIDE

♣ **VARIETY**
See: DIVERSENESS

♣ **VEHICLES**
See Also: ROAD SCENES

♣ **VEHICLES, OPERATION OF**

♣ **VERBOSENESS**
See: TALKATIVENESS

♣ **VEXATION**
See: ANGER, IRRITABLENESS/IRRITATING

♣ **VIBRATION**
See Also: TREMBLING

♣ **VICE**
See: EVIL

♣ **VICTORY**
See: SUCCESS/FAILURE

❧ VIGILANCE
See: ALERTNESS, WATCHFULNESS

❧ VIGOR
See: ENTHUSIASM, STRENGTH

❧ VIOLENCE
See Also: ADVANCING, BEHAVIOR

❧ VIRTUE
See Also: ACCOMPLISHMENT, MORALITY,
*   PURITY*

❧ VISIBILITY
See Also: CLARITY, OBVIOUSNESS,
*   PROTRUSION*

❧ VIVIDNESS
See: BRIGHTNESS

❧ VOCATION
See: PROFESSIONS

❧ VOICE(S)
See Also: CRYING; GROANS AND WHISPERS;
*   SINGING; VOICE, EFFECT OF; VOICE,*
*   HARSH; VOICE, MONOTONOUS; VOICE,*
*   MUSIC-RELATED; VOICE, SOFT; VOICE,*
*   WEAK*

❧ VOICE, EFFECT OF

❧ VOICE, HARSH
See Also: HARSHNESS

❧ VOICE, MONOTONOUS

❧ VOICE, MUSIC-RELATED

❧ VOICE, SOFT

❧ VOICE, WEAK

❧ VOTERS
See: POLITICS

❧ VULGARITY
See: TASTE

❧ VULNERABILITY
See: SENSITIVENESS

❧ WALKING
See Also: AWKWARDNESS, CAUTION,
*   MOVEMENT(S), RUNNING*

❧ WAR
See Also: ARMY

❧ WARMTH
See: COMFORT, HEAT

❧ WASTE

❧ WATCHFULNESS
See Also: ATTENTION, PROTECTIVENESS,
*   SCRUTINY*

❧ WATER
See: OCEAN/OCEANFRONT; PONDS, RIVERS,
*   AND STREAMS; SEASCAPES*

❧ WEAKNESS

❧ WEALTH
See: RICHES

❧ WEARINESS

❧ WEATHER
See Also: CLOUDS, COLDNESS, FOG, HEAT,
*   MIST, RAIN, SUN, THUNDER AND*
*   LIGHTNING, WIND*

❧ WEDDINGS
See: MARRIAGE

♣ **WEIGHT**
See: HEAVINESS, LIGHTNESS

♣ **WELCOMENESS**
See: DESIRABILITY

♣ **WELL-BEING**
See: HEALTH

♣ **WHISPERS**
See: GROANS AND WHISPERS

♣ **WHITE**
See Also: COLORS, COMPLEXION, PALLOR

♣ **WICKEDNESS**
See: EVIL

♣ **WILDNESS**
See: FEROCITY

♣ **WIND**
See Also: WEATHER

♣ **WINNING**
See: SPORTS, SUCCESS/FAILURE

♣ **WINTER**
See: SEASONS

♣ **WISDOM**
See Also: EDUCATION, KNOWLEDGE

♣ **WISH**
See: DESIRE

♣ **WIT**
See Also: CLEVERNESS, HUMOR, WISDOM

♣ **WIVES**
See: MARRIAGE

♣ **WOMEN**
See: HEART(S), MEN AND WOMEN

♣ **WORD(S)**
See Also: SPEAKING; WORDS, DEFINED; WORDS, EFFECT OF; WORDS OF PRAISE; WRITERS/WRITING

♣ **WORDS, DEFINED**

♣ **WORDS, EFFECT OF**

♣ **WORDS OF PRAISE**

♣ **WORK**
See Also: ATTENTION, BOREDOM, DOCTORS, LAWYERS, PROFESSIONS

♣ **WORLD**
See Also: LIFE

♣ **WORRY**
See: AGITATION, ANXIETY

♣ **WOUND**
See: PAIN

♣ **WRINKLES**
See Also: COMPLEXION, FOREHEAD, SKIN

♣ **WRITERS/WRITING**
See Also: POETS/POETRY

♣ **YEARNING**
See: DESIRE

♣ **YELLOW**
See Also: COLORS, HAIR

♣ **YELLS**
See: SCREAMS

♣ **YOUTH**
See Also: AGE

♣ **ZEAL**
See: AMBITION, ENTHUSIASM

THE SIMILES

❧ ABANDONMENT

See Also: ALONENESS, BEARING, FRIEND-SHIP, REJECTION

Abandoned as a used Kleenex —Anon

Abandoned, like the waves we leave behind us —Donald G. Mitchell

Cast off friends, as a stripper her clothes —Anon

Cast off his friends, as a huntsman his pack —Oliver Goldsmith

(My youth has been) cast aside like a useless cigar stump —Anton Chekov

Chuck me in the gutter like an empty purse —Edith Wharton

Deserted as a playwright after the first night of an unsuccessful play —Somerset Maugham

Deserted as a cemetery —Anon

Desolate ... as the dark side of the moon —Pat Conroy

Discard like a withered leaf, since it has served its day —John Gould Fletcher

(What have we come to when people ... could be) discarded ... like an old beer cans —May Carton

Discarded ... like used bandages —Louis MacNeice

Discard like a bad dream —Anon

Divest himself of his profoundest convictions and his beliefs as though they were a pair of old shoes whose soles had come loose and were flapping in the rain —Irving Stone

Feeling quite lost ... like a fly that has had its head taken off —Luigi Pirandello

Felt stranded, as if some solid security has left him, as if he had, recklessly and ruthlessly, tossed away the compass which for years had kept him straight and true —Carolyn Slaughter

Leaving me alone like a shag on a rock —John Malcolm

Left like balloons with the air let out —Gloria Norris

Left high and dry like a shipwreck in a drained reservoir —Thomas McGuire

Like a little lost lamb I roamed about —Leo Robin lyric "A Little Girl from Little Rock" from the musical *Gentlemen Prefer Blondes*

Neglected as the moon by day —Jonathan Swift

People had fallen away like veils —Susan Richards Shreve

Put off [as religious faith] quite simply, like a cloak that he no longer needed —Somerset Maugham

Shed [adult reality for past] like a snake sheds an old and worn skin —Guy Vanderhaeghe

Vanderhaeghe used the snake comparison to describe someone shedding the reality of the present for the past

Stood like a forgotten broom in the corner —Eudora Welty

❧ ABILITY

See Also: ACCOMPLISHMENT

Able to absorb punishment as open buds absorb the dew —Grantland Rice

The abilities of man must fall short on one side or the other, like too scanty a blanket —Sir William Temple

The ability to make a great individual fortune … is a sort of sublimated instinct in a way like the instinct of a rat-terrier for smelling out hidden rats —Irvin S. Cobb

Being creative without talent is a bit like being a perfectionist and not being able to do anything right —Jane Wagner

Chose [people] with swift skill, like fruit tested for ripeness with a pinch —Paul Theroux

(My wife …) cooks like Escoffier on wheels —Moss Hart

Cuts like a saw through soft pine through the chatter of freeloaders, time-wasting delegations —Stephen Longstreet

In Longstreet's novel, Ambassador, *from which this is extracted, the efficiency tactics are diplomatic.*

Efficient as a good deer rifle —Bruce DeSilva

Functioned as smoothly as a hospital kitchen —Laurie Colwin

Resourceful and energetic as a street dog —James Mills

Having communists draft the law for the most capitalist society on earth is like having a blind man guide you through the Louvre museum —Mark Faber, *Wall Street Journal,* June

19, 1986 Faber's simile pertained to the basic law that will govern Hong Kong in the future.

His [Brendan Sullivan's] management (of Oliver North) is like one of those pictures that museum directors settle for labeling "Workshop of Veronese" because the hand of the master is not there for certain but his touch and teaching inarguably are —Murray Kempton, New York Post, December 12, 1986

Kempton's simile describes the legal abilities of a member in the Edward Bennett Williams law firm, representing Colonel North during the Iran weapons scandal.

I can walk like an ox, run like a fox, swim like an eel … make love like a mad bull —David Crockett, speech to Congress

Instinct as sure as sight —Edgar Lee Masters

Native ability without education is like a tree without fruit —Aristippus

Natural abilities are like natural plants, that need pruning by study —Francis Bacon

Played bridge like an inspired card sharp —Marjory Stoneman Douglas

To see him [Chief Justice Hughes] preside was like witnessing Toscanini lead an orchestra —Justice Felix Frankfurter

Skilled … like a mischievous and thieving animal —Émile Zola

Skillful as jugglers —Daphne du Maurrier

Talent is like a faucet. While it is open, one must write (paint, etc.) —Jean Anouilh, *New York Times,* October 2, 1960

Talent, like beauty, to be pardoned, must be obscure and unostentatious —Marguerite Countess Blessington

You must work at the talent as a sculptor works at stone, chiseling, plotting, rounding, edging and making perfect —Dylan Thomas

❧ ABSORBABILITY

Absorbed them [the influences of women around whom I grew up] as I would chloroform on a cloth laid against my face —Vivian Gornick

Absorbent as a sponge —Anon

Absorbent as blotting paper —Anon

Absorbent as cereal soaking up cream —Anon

It [a huge Christmas tree] soaked up baubles and tinsel like melting snow —Truman Capote

❧ ABSURDITY

See Also: DIFFICULTY, FUTILITY

Absurd as a monkey in a dinner jacket —Anon

Absurd as an excuse —Anon

Absurd ... as expecting a drowning man to laugh —German proverb

Time and use often transform proverbs into similes. In this case, the original proverb was "A fool will laugh when he is drowning."

Absurd as hiring a street vendor to run major corporation —Anon

Absurd as looking for hot water under the ice —Latin proverb

Absurd as mathematics without numbers —Anon

Absurd as to expect a harvest in the dead of winter —Robert South

Absurd as to instruct a rooster in the laying of eggs —H. L. Mencken

Absurd as ... to put bread in a cold oven —Latin proverb

Absurd as ... to put water in a basket —Danish proverb

Absurd as trying to drink from a colander —Latin proverb

Absurd ... like baking snow in the oven —German proverb

The simile has evolved from "he baked snow in the oven."

Absurd ... like jumping into the water for fear of the rain —French proverb

Absurd, like using a guillotine to cure dandruff —Clare Booth Luce

Absurd ... like vowing never to be sick again —Lynne Sharon Schwartz

As logical as trying to put out a fire with applications of kerosene —Tallulah Bankhead

Attending the Gerald R. Ford Symposium on Humor and the Presidency is sort of like attending the Ayatollah Khomeini Symposium on the sexual revolution —Pat Paulsen, at September 19, 1986 symposium in Grand Rapids, Mich.

Bizarre and a little disconcerting, like finding out that the Mona Lisa was a WAC —Jonathan Valin

(His ...) body so sleek with health, that his talk of death seemed ludicrous, like the description of a funeral by a painted clown —Christopher Isherwood

Comparing [Ronald] Reagan with [Franklin D.] Roosevelt is like comparing [*Peanuts* cartoonist] Charles Schultz to Rembrandt —Mike Sommer

Incongruous as a mouse dancing with an elephant —Anon

Incongruous as a priest going out with a prostitute —Anon

Looks as well as a diamond necklace about a sow's neck —H. G. Bohn's *Hand-Book of Proverbs*

Makes about as much sense ... as it would to put army shoes on a ... French poodle —William Diehl

Ridiculous as monkeys reading books —Delmore Schwartz

Stupid and awkward, like chimpanzees dressed up in formal gowns —Scott Spencer

That's like Castro calling Tito a dictator —John Wainwright

You just can't go around thinking that McDonald's food is going to be steaming hot. It's like expecting the hamburger to be served on a French roll —Ann Beattie

♣ ABUNDANCE

See Also: CLOSENESS, GROWTH, SPREADNG

Abound like street vendors on a Spring day —Anon

Abound like blades of grass —George Sandys

Abundant as the light of the sun —Thomas Carlyle

Abundant as the salt in the sea —Anon

Abundant as air —Anon

> *Modern day life has added "Abundant as polluted air and water."*

Abundant as June graduates in search of jobs —Anon

Abundant as poverty —Anon

Ample as the wants of man —William Wadsworth Longfellow

As full as fruit tree in spring blossom —Janet Flanner

> *The simile refers to a letter filled with good news.*

As stuffed (with idle hopes and false illusions) as any Whitsun goose crammed with bread and spices —George Garrett

As stuffed with ideas as a quilt is with batting —Anon

Bountiful as April rains —William Cowper

Bountiful as the showers that fall into the Spring's green bosom —James Shirley

Bulging like a coin purse fallen on the ground —D. Snodgrass

[Dreams] came like locusts —Isaac Bashevis Singer

(The big racket money) comes in like water from a pipe in your bathroom, a steady stream that never stops flowing —Raymond Chandler, *The Long Goodbye*

Ladled out fines like soup to breadline beggars —Bernard Malamud

> *In Malamud's novel* The Natural *the simile refers to fines issued by a baseball coach to rule-breaking players.*

Lush as a Flemish oil painting —Anon

Numerous as a bank or trust company's vice-presidents —New York Tribune, January 6, 1921

> *With the lean-and-mean management style coming into vogue since the mid-eighties this long enduring simile may well be headed for obsolescence.*

(Children appearing here and there …) numerous as fireflies —Alice McDermott

Overdo … like a host who stuffs his guests with too many hors' d'oeuvres —Tom Shales, Public Radio, January 10, 1986

> *The simile referred to the directorial touches used in the movie* The Color Purple

Plentiful as blackberries —William Shakespeare. *Henry IV, Part II*

Plentiful as New Year's Eve predictions and resolutions —Elyse Sommer

Plentiful as oak leaves, as plentiful as the fireflies that covered the lawn at evening —Ellen Gilchrist

Plentiful as tabby cats —W. S. Gilbert

Pour … over everything like ketchup —Gore Vidal

> *President Art Hochstater reminiscing about political campaigning in the days when what made a speech was the frequent references to God.*

Stuffed like a Strasbourg goose

> *Strasbourg geese are over-fed and under-exercised in order to obtain the largest possible liver for making pate. Being stuffed like a Strasbourg goose is linked to any kind of excess.*

They're like plums on a tree —H.E. Bates

> *Bates compared the abundance of plums on a tress to an abundance of admirers.*

Thick as autumnal leaves —John Milton

Thick as fleas —American colloquialism, attributed to New England

> Some variations from the American South: "Thick as fleas on a fat pup" "thick as flies on flypaper."

[The Reports came in] thick as hail —William Shakespeare, *Macbeth*

(You have fallen into ripeness) thick as honey —Marge Piercy

Thick as Japanese beetles —Herman Wouk

> Wouk's simile from Inside, Outside *refers to the behavior of people working for the president of the United States.*

(Eyelashes) thick as June grass —Elizabeth Spencer

Thick as summer stars —William Blake

Thick as buttercups in June —Henry James

Thick as … freckles —George Garrett

> *In his novel* Death of the Fox, *Garrett refers specifically to the freckles of Sir Francis Drake.*

Thick as the green leaves of a garden —Henry James

♣ ACCEPTABILITY
See: BELONGING

♣ ACCESSIBILITY
See: AVAILABILITY, COURTESY

♣ ACCIDENT
See: FATE

♣ ACCOMPLISHMENT
See Also: ABILITY, CLEVERNESS, SUCCESS/ FAILURE

Accomplishment and authority hang on him like a custom-tailored suit —Alvin Boretz

Encased in talent like a uniform —W. H. Auden

He uses irony as a surgeon uses a scalpel … with the same skill and to the same effect —Anon

Like a hog he does no good till he dies? —Thomas Fuller

Rise to the occasion like a trout to the hook —Anon

Skilled and coordinated as an NFL backfield —James Mills

Something positive had been accomplished, like wrapping up a package in smooth paper, firm, taut, with a tight knot —Belva Plain

(Slowly he crept upon the heart of Manhattan, his) talent poised like a knife —Scott Spencer

To watch him is like watching a graceful basketball player sink shot after shot —Anon

♣ ACCUMULATION
See: GROWTH

♣ ACCURACY
See: CORRECTNESS

♣ ACCUSATION
See: CRITICISM

♣ ACTING

Acting is like letting your pants down; you're exposed —Paul Newman

Acting is like prize fighting. The downtown gyms are smelly, but that's where the champions are —Kirk Douglas

Acting is like making love. It's better if your partner is good —Jeremy Irons

Acting is like roller skating. Once you know how to do it, it is neither stimulating nor exciting —George Sanders

Being given good material is like being assigned to bake a cake and having the batter made for you —Rosalind Russell

The body of an actor is like a well in which experiences are stored, then tapped when needed —Simone Signoret

❧ ACTIONS

See Also: BEHAVIOR, CAUTION, LEAPING, JUMPING, MOVEMENT(S), VIOLENCE

Acting without thinking is like shooting without aiming —B.C. Forbes

The actions of men are like the index of a book; they point out what is most remarkable in them —Heinrich Heine

Actions of the last age are like almanacs of the last year —Sir John Denham

[Meaningless] Actions that seemed like a charade played behind thick glass —Franz Werfel

All action is involved in imperfection, like fire and smoke —*Bhagavad Gita*

Best understood not as a sharply defined operation, like beheading, but as a whole range of activities, more like cooking —James R. Kincaid, "Plagiarist's Tale," *New Yorker*, August 11, 2011

Driven to make a move, like a dilatory chess player prodded on by an impatient opponent —Harvey Swados

Evil deeds are like perfume, difficult to hide —George Herzog

A good deed will stick out with an inclination to spread like the tail of a peacock —Bartlett's *Dictionary of Americanisms*

Most of us shell our days like peanuts —Amor Towles, *Rules of Civility*

Our deeds are like children born to us; they live and act apart from our own will —George Eliot

Our least deed, like the young of the land crab, wends its way to the sea of cause and effect as soon as born, and makes a drop there to eternity —Henry David

Reprehensible actions are like over-strong brandies; you cannot swallow them at a draught —Victor Hugo

The acts of my life swarm down the street like Puerto Rican kids —William Meredith

Trying to shake off the sun as a dog would shake off the sea —James Dickey

The vilest deeds like poison weeds bloom well in prison air —Oscar Wilde

❧ ACTIVENESS

See Also: ALERTNESS, BEHAVIOR, BUSINESS, ENERGY, ENTHUSIASM, EXCITEMENT, MOVEMENT(S), PERSONALITY PRO-FILES

About as active as a left-over fly in January —Anon

About as animated as a suit on a hanger —Elyse Sommer

(This region was as) active as a compost heap —Julia O'Faolain

Active as the sun —Isaac Watts

Alive as a vision of life to be —Algernon Charles Swinburne

(He looks) dead as a stump —Pat Conroy

> *In Conroy's Novel,* The Prince of Tides, *a character hearing someone described as above disagrees with another simile: "On the contrary, I think he looks as though he could rise up and whistle a John Philip Sousa march."*

Frisky as a Frisbee —Helen

Frisky as a colt —Geoffrey Chaucer

He was behaving as though the party were his: like an energetic octopus, he was shaking martinis, making introductions, manipulating the phonograph —Truman Capote

He is like a moving light, never still. He has the temperature and metabolism of a bird —Joy Williams

He [James Cagney] was like fireworks going off —Television obituary, 1986

Lively as a boy, kind like a fairy godfather —Robert Louis Stevenson

Lively as a weasel —Wallace Stegner

Lusty as June —Wallace Stevens

Mechanically animated, like the masterwork of some fiendishly inventive undertaker —Sharon Sheehe Stark

Pert as a sparrow —Walker Percy

(She had) rolled up her sleeves with all the vigor of a first-class cook confronting a brand-new kitchen —Mary McCarthy

She is active and strong as little lionesses —William James

> *From a letter to James' family, describing the energy of a Dresden women, July 24, 1867.*

She was like a strong head wind —Marguerite Young

Simmering … like a coal fire in the Welsh mines —Marvin Kittman about British actor Roy Marsden whose popularity thus simmers "in the collective unconscious of the American public" and bursts into flame whenever he makes an appearance in a new British import, *Newsday,* March 27, 1987

Sprightly as a Walt Disney cricket —Jean Thompson

Tireless as a spider —Eudora Welty

Vibrant as an E string —Carl Van Vechten

We were blazing through our lives like comets through the sky —William Finn, from the song "When the Earth Stopped," *Elegies: A Song Cycle*

❧ ACTORS
See: STAGE AND SCREEN

❧ ADAPTABILITY
See: BELONGING, FLEXIBILITY/INFLEXIBILITY

She'd taken to the suburbs like an actress getting into character. —Jonathan Tropper, *This Is Where I Leave You*

❧ ADJUSTMENT
See: FLEXIBILTY/INFLEXIBILITY, HABIT

❧ ADMIRATION
See: FLATTERY, WORDS OF PRAISE

❧ ADULTERY
See: MARRIAGE

❧ ADVANCING
See Also: ENTRANCES AND EXITS, MOVEMENT(S)

Advanced like armies —Anon

> *This simile is used to describe forward sweeps in a figurative as well as literal sense. For example, book critic Anatole Broyard used the simile about William Faulkner's sentences in a* New York Times Book Review *on May 17, 1987.*

(The terrible old miser) advanced, like the hour of death to a criminal —Honoré de Balzac

Advance like the shadow death —John Ruskin

Approached … as stealthily as a poacher stalking a hind —Donald Seaman

Bearing down like a squad of tactical police —Marge Piercy

Bearing down like a tugboat busily dragging a fleet of barges —Frank Swinnerton

Came on like a last reel of a John Wayne movie —Line from *L.A. Law,* television drama segment, 1987

Came [toward another person] … like a tidal wave running toward the coast —Isak Dinesen

Came with slow steps like a dog who exhibits his fidelity —Honoré de Balzac

Come down, like a flock of hungry corbies, upon them —George Garrett

> *Garrett is comparing the corbies to a group of beggars.*

Come like a rolling storm —Beryl Markham

Coming after me … like a wave —Calder Willingham

Coming at him like a fullback —Wallace Stegner

(She'd seen it) coming like a red caboose at the end of a train —Denis Johnson

(Cancer) coming like a train —William H. Gass

Coming like a truck —James Crumley

Here the strong advance describes an aggressive woman

(People) converged upon them, like a stream of ants —Hortense Calisher

(Faith's father) descended … like a storm —Charles Johnson

Descend on me like age —Margaret Atwood

Forges ahead, lashing over the wet earth like a whipcrack —T. Coraghessan Boyle

Glide toward them, as softly and slyly as a fly on a windowpane —Donald Seaman

was upon them like a sun-flushed avalanche —Frank Swinnerton

Invade like weeds, everywhere but slowly —Margaret Atwood

Leaned forward like a magnificent bird of prey about to swallow its victim whole —Mike Fredman

Like a figurehead on the prow of a foundering ship his head and torso pressed forward —John Updike

Like fowls in a farm-yard when barley is scattering, out came the children running —Robert Browning

Moved forward [towards an attractive woman] like so many iron filings to a magnet —J. B. Priestley

(He was) moving toward me like a carnivorous dinosaur advancing on a vegetarian sibling —Joan Hess

Pressing forward like the wind —Sir Walter Scott

Pushed forward like the nervous antennae of a large insect —Rita Mae Brown

[An odor] Roll up … like fog in a valley —C.D.B. Bryan

Slid forward slowly as an alligator —Rudyard Kipling

(He could hear the roar of darkness) sweeping toward him like a fist —Jay McInerney

Swooped like chickens scrambling for a grain of corn —Aharon Megged

Went firmly on as if propelled —Stephen Crane

⟡ ADVANTAGEOUSNESS

See Also: COST

Beneficial … like water to a garden —Anon

Benefits, like bread, soon become stale —Caroline Forne

Benefits, like flowers, please most when they are fresh —George Herbert

Free [things] … free as a well to get into, but like a rat trap, not exactly free to get out of —Josh Billings

Billings wrote in a phonetic dialect. Here's the dialect version of the above: "I hav found a grate menny things in this wurld that was free —free az a well tew git into, but like a rat trap, not edzackly free tu git out ov."

A good deal … like trading an apple for an orchard —Anon

The opposite of this is a German proverb: "Like trading the hen for the egg."

Like parenthood, you bid [at an auction], then see what you've got —John Ciardi

Privileges she could list as a prisoner might count out the days of his sentence —Margaret Sutherland

⟡ ADVERSARY

An adversary as easily wiped out as writing on a chalkboard —Elyse Sommer

Being in the same room with the two men was like dropping in on a reunion of Capulets and Montagues —P. G. Wodehouse

A dead enemy is as good as a cold friend —German proverb

Fill me with strength against those who ... like water held in the hands would spill me —Louis MacNeice

✤ ADVERSITY

See: FORTUNE/MISFORTUNE

✤ ADVERTISING

See Also: BUSINESS

Commercials on television are similar to sex and taxes; the more talk there is about them the less likely they are to be curbed —Jack Gould, *New York Times,* October 20, 1963

Doing business without advertising is like winking at a girl in the dark. You know what you are doing, but nobody else does —Stewart Henderson Britt, *New York Herald-Tribune,* October 30, 1956

A good ad should be like a good sermon: It must not only comfort the afflicted, it also must afflict the comfortable —Bernice Fitz-Gibbon

✤ ADVICE

See Also: FRIENDSHIP, FUTILITY

Advice after an evil is done is like medicine after death —Danish proverb

It's quite common to substitute the word "mischief" for "evil."

Advice is like kissing: it costs nothing and is a pleasant thing to do —Josh Billings

Advice is like snow; the softer it falls ... the deeper it sinks into the mind —Samuel Taylor Coleridge

Advice, like water, takes the form of the vessel it is poured into —*Punch,* August 1, 1857

The advice of old age gives light without heat, like winter sun —Marquis de Luc de Clapiers Vauvenargues

Advice is like castor oil, easy enough to give but dreadful uneasy to take —Josh Billings

Good advice is like a tight glove; it fits the circumstances, and it does not fit other circumstances —Charles Reade

His (Ariel Sharon's) advice on that subject (Lebanon 1984-1985) ... was akin to a man with seven traffic accidents opening a driving school —Abba Eban, *New York Times,* February, 1986

It [excellent advice] is a good deal like giving a child a dictionary to learn a language with —Henry James

A proposal is like a flashlight. It's completely useless in the spotlight, but in the shadows it can do lots of good —Professor Steven Carvell, *Wall Street Journal*, December 11,1986

Professor Carvell's simile was specific to a proposal for investment research.

Telling a runner he can't run ... is a bit like being advised not to breathe —Thomas Rogers on runner Fred Lebow's being so advised for medical reasons, *New York Times,* 1986

To heed bad advice is like eating poisoned candy —Anon

To listen to the advice of a treacherous friend, is like drinking poison from a golden cup —Demophilus

✤ AFFABILITY

See: AVAILABILITY, COURTESY, FRIENDSHIP

✤ AFFECTION

See Also: FRIENDSHIP, LOVE

Affectionate as a miser toward his money —Anon

(She had an) affection for her children almost like a cool governess —D.H. Lawrence

Affection is the youth of the heart, and thought is the heart's maturity —Kahil Gibran

Gibran completed the simile with "but oratory is its senility."

Affection, like melancholy, magnifies trifles —Leigh Hunt

Affection, like spring flowers, breaks through the most frozen ground at last —Jeremy Bentham

Affection, like the nut within the shell, wants freedom —Dion Boucicault

Affection or love that ... intended for someone else and spilled accidentally like a bottle of ink under a dragging sleeve —Diane Wakoski

Affections are like slippers; they will wear out —Edgar Saltus

The affections, like conscience, are rather to be led than driven —Thomas Fuller

Her cowlike, awkward affection surrounding him like a moist fog —Hank Searls

The human affections, like the solar heat, lose their intensity as they depart from the center —Alexander Hamilton

My affection has no bottom, like the Bay of Portugal —William Shakespeare

The shorter, more commonly used "Affection is like a bottomless well" was more than likely inspired by this comparison from "As You Like It."

She was like a cat in her fondness for nearness, for stroking, touching, nestling —Katherine Anne Porter

♣ AFFLICTIONS

See: HEALTH, PAIN

♣ AFFLUENCE

See: RICHES

♣ AGE

See Also: LIFE, MANKIND, YOUTH

Age covered her like a shawl to keep her warm —Rose Tremain

Age ... indeterminate as a nun —Sharon Sheehe Stark

Age is a sickness, and youth is an ambush —John Donne

Age is like love, it cannot be hid —Thomas Dekker

Age, like a cage, will enclose him —Alastair Reid

Age, like distance, lends a double charm —Oliver Wendell Holmes

Age like winter weather ... age like winter bare —William Shakespeare, "Sonnet 73," *The Passionate Pilgrim*

These comparisons of age to the weather are alternated with you and the weather similes.

Age, like woman, requires fit surroundings —Ralph Waldo Emerson

Ageless as the sun —Algernon Charles Swinburne

The age of man resembles a book: infancy and old age are the blank leaves; youth, the preface, and man the body or most important portion of life's volume —Edward Parsons Day

(Each year in me) ages as quickly as lilac in May —F. D. Reeve

The simile marks the opening of a poem entitled "Curriculum Vitae."

Antique as the statues of the Greeks —Edward Bulwer-Lytton

As a white candle in a holy place, so is the beauty of an aged face —Joseph Campbell

At middle age the soul should be opening up like a rose, not closing up like a cabbage —John Andrew Holmes

At thirty-nine, the days grow shorter, and night kneels like a rapist on the edge of your bed —Richard Selzer

At twenty man is like a peacock, at thirty a lion, at forty a camel, at fifty a serpent, at sixty a dog, at seventy an ape, at eighty nothing at all —Valtasar Gracian

Awareness [of one's own age] comes ... like a slap in the eye —Ingrid Bergman, on seeing a friend no longer young

Being seventy-five means you sometimes get up in the morning and feel like a bent hairpin —Hume Cronyn, "Sixty Minutes" interview with Mike Wallace, April 12, 1987

He could account for his age as a man might account for an extraordinary amount of money he finds has slipped through his fingers —John Yount

In his novel, Hardcastle, *Yount expands on the Simile as follows: "Sure, he could think back and satisfy himself that nothing was lost, but merely spent. Yet the odd notion persists that, if he knew just how to do it, he might shake himself awake and discover that he is young after all."*

Grow old before my eyes … as if time beat down on her like rain in a thunderstorm, every second a year —Erich Maria Remarque

He had reached the time of life when Alps and cathedrals become as transient as flowers —Edith Wharton

He who lives to see two or three generations is like a man who sits some time in the conjurer's booth —Arthur Schopenhauer

How earthy old people become … moldy as the gravel —Henry David Thoreau

Old as Methuselah —Seventeenth century proverb

This has inspired many variations including another cliché "As old as the hills," generally attributed to Sir Walter Scott's The Monastery *and Dickens'* David Copperfield.

I feel age like an icicle down my back —Dyson Carter

A man of fifty looks old as Santa Claus to a girl of 20 —William Feather

A man's as old as his arteries —Dr. Pierre J. G. Cabanis

Most old men are like old trees, past bearing themselves, will suffer no young plants to flourish beneath them —Alexander Pope

My age is as a lusty winter, frosty but kind —William Shakespeare, *As You Like It*

My body … continues to be a good sport. Provided my marvelous doctor pumps steroids into my hip or spine when needed, it runs along on the leash like a nondescript mutt and wags its tail —Louis Begley, "Age and Its

Awful Discontents," *New York Times*, March 17, 2012

Old age is a tyrant which forbids the pleasures of youth on pain of death —François, Duc de La Rochefoucauld

Old age is false as Egypt is, and, like the wilderness, surprises —Babette Deutsch

Old age is like an opium-dream. Nothing seems real except what is unreal —Oliver Wendell Holmes, Sr.

Old age is like a plane flying through a storm. Once you're board there's nothing you can do —Golda Meir, quoted on being over 70 by Oriana Fallaci, *L'Europe*, 1973

Old age is like being engaged in a war. All our friends are going or gone and we survive amongst the dead and dying as on a battlefield —Muriel Spark

Old Age is like everything else. To make a success of it, you've got to start young —Fred Astaire

Old age is rather like fatigue, except that you cannot correct it by relaxing or taking a vacation —B.F. Skinner and M.E. Vaughan

Old age is rather like another country. You will enjoy it more if you have prepared yourself before you go —B.F. Skinner & M.E. Vaughan

Old age took her [Queen Elizabeth] by surprise, like a frost —Anon

Old as a garment the moths shall eat up —The Holy Bible/Isaiah

Old as a hieroglyph —John Berryman

Old as civilization —Morley Safer, "60 Minutes" segment on torture, November 9, 1986

Old as death —Elizabeth Barrett Browning

Old as God —Delmore Schwartz

Old as the sun —Slogan, Sun Insurance Co.

Old as history —Slogan, Anheuser-Busch beer

(I'm as) old as my tongue and a little older than my teeth —Jonathan Swift

(Made her feel) older than coal —Joseph Wambaugh

The old man is like a candle before the wind —Hilda Doolittle

An old man, like a spider, can never make love without beating his own death watch —Charles Caleb Colton

The old man who is loved is winter with flowers —German proverb

(The Jewish women were as …) old as nature, as round as the earth —Thomas Wolfe

(The problem now is as) old as realism —Max Apple

Old as stone —Marge Piercy

Old as the most ancient of cities and older —Saul Bellow

Old women and old men … huddle like misers over their bag of life —Randall Jarrell

Some men mellow with age, like wine; but others get still more stringent, like vinegar —Henry C. Rowland

The span of his seventy-five years had acted as a magic bellows —the first quarter century had blown him full with life, and the last had sucked it all back —F. Scott Fitzgerald

To be seventy years old is like climbing the Alps —William Wadsworth Longfellow

Wrinkled and weathered like old leather, emphysemic and broken down, like hard times —Jamie M. Saul, *Light of Day*

Years steal fire from the mind as vigor from the limb —Lord Byron

You know you're getting older when every day seems like Monday —Kitty Carlisle, quoting her mother, 1985 television interview

Youth is like a dream, middle age a forlorn hope, and old age a nostalgia with a pervasive flavor of newly turned earth —Gerald Kersh

♣ AGGRESSION
See: PERSONAL TRAITS, VIOLENCE

♣ AGILITY
See Also: MOVEMENT(S), SPEED, TURNING AND TWISTING, WALKING

Agile as a fish —William Humphrey

Agile as a monkey —Alexandre Dumas, Pere

Agile as squirrels —Luigi Pirandello

As graceful as an elk, as nimble as a fawn —Leo Robin, "I'm A 'Tingle, I'm A 'Glow," from *Gentlemen Prefer Blondes*

(Moved) as lightly as a bubble —Hans Christian Andersen

As nimble as a cow in a cage —Thomas Fuller

Feet as fleet as Mercury's —Richard Adler and Jerry Ross, "Shoeless Joe from Hannibal MO," from the musical *Damn Yankees*

Deft as spiders' catenation —C. S. Lewis

Frisky and graceful as young lambs at play —George Garrett

Graceful as joy —Babette Deutsch

Graceful as a panther —Raymond Chandler, *The Long Goodby*

Graceful as a premiere danseuse —Natascha Wodin

Graceful as a Stillson wrench —Diane Wakoski

Graceful as the swallow's flight —Julian Grenfell

Graceful figure … which was as tough as hickory and as flexible as a whip —Thomas Wolfe

He could leap like a grasshopper and melt into the tree-tops like a monkey —G. K. Chesterton

Light-footed as a dancer waiting in the wings —Vita Sackville-West

(Her tiny body as) limber as a grass —Jean Stafford

Lithe as a swan —Richard Ford

Lithe as a whip —Raymond Chandler, *The Long Goodbye*

Nimble as a cat —Anon

Herman Melville used this to begin chapter 78 of Moby Dick, *but it probably dates back well before that.*

Nimble as a deer —Geoffrey Chaucer

Quick as a wrestler —Edward Hoagland

Spring [out of his bed] like a mastiff —T. Coraghessan Boyle

Springy as a trampoline —Marge Piercy

Spry as a yearling —Eugene O'Neill

Step as elastic as a cat's —Jo Bannister

Supple as a cat —Irwin Shaw

> *This is a variation of the often used "Agile as a cat" and "Agile as a cat, and just as sly"*

Supple as a red fox —Maxine Kumin

Swift and light as a wild cat —D. H. Lawrence

There was something breath-taking in the face of his big body which made his very entrance into a room like an abrupt physical impact —Margaret Mitchell

> *Mitchell is describing Rhett Buttler, the hero of her epic* Gone with the Wind.

♣ AGITATION

See Also: EXCITEMENT, HEARTBEAT, NERVOUSNESS, TREMBLING

Agitated with delight as a waving sea —*Arabian Nights*

Agitation ... like insects coming alive in the spring —William Goyen

Calm as a tornado —Anon

Composed as an egg gatherer in a rattlesnake pit —Harry Prince

Disturbing as decay in a carcass —Julia O'Faolain

Feel like he had a mouse water skiing in his stomach —Joseph Wambaugh

Feel my insides slipping away as if they are on a greased slide —W. P. Kinsella

Felt as if his heart was beating itself to death in some empty hollow —Oscar Wilde

Felt her heart make little leaps, as though it might creep onto her tongue and expose something —Leigh Allison Wilson

Felt his heart quicken, as a horse quickens at the faint warning touch of the spur —Ben Ames Williams

(Arrived in the library with every nerve twittering) felt like a tree full of starlings —M. J. Farrell

Froze my heart like a block of ice —T. Coraghessan Boyle

Hearts drumming like wings —Paul Horgan

Her heart leaped like a fish —Katherine Mansfield

Her heart ... plucking inside her chest like a bird in a bag —Brian Moore

His heart pumping like a boiler about to blow —Ira Wood

Her heart ... thundering like ten hearts —Sharon Sheehe Stark

Her stomach leaped up inside her like a balloon —William Styron

His heart beat so hard he sometimes fondled it with his hands as though trying to calm a wild bird that wanted to fly away —Bernard Malamud

His heart chilled like a stone in a creek —John Farris

His heart ... like a madly bouncing ball, beating the breath out of his body —Helen Hudson

Heart moving so fast it was like one of those motorcycles at fairs that the fellow drives around the walls of a pit —Flannery O'Connor

His heart racing like a quick little animal in a cage —T. Coraghessan Boyle

His heart sinks like a soap in a bucket —Robert Coover

His heart thundered like horses galloping over a wooden bridge —Gerald Kersh

His heart whammed like a wheezing steam engine —Bernard Malamud

His soul seething within him like a Welsh rabbit at the height of its fever —P. G. Wodehouse

I could hear my heart, like somebody hammering on a tree —John D. MacDonald

It seemed like something snapped inside of me, something like a suspender strap —John Steinbeck

(Scandal and chaos …) kicked up like chicken feathers —Pat Ellis Taylor

My heart behaved like a fresh-caught trout —Lael Wertenbaker

My heart felt like a rabbit running wildly around inside my rib cage —James Crumley

My heart jumped like a fox —Scott Spencer

My heart leaped like a big bass after a willow fly —Borden Deal

My heart pounded like a drowning swimmer's —Frank Conroy

My heart pounded … like the hoofbeats of a horse —Charles Johnson

My heart stopped as if a knife had been driven through it —Rudyard Kipling

My heart turned over like a dirt bike in the wrong gear —T. Coraghessan Boyle

My heart would flutter like a duck in a puddle, and if I tried to outdo it and speak, it would get right smack up in my throat and choke me like a cold potato —Irving Stone

My stomach plunged like an elevator out of control —T. Coraghessan Boyle

Nerves melt like jellyfish —Derek Walcott

Placid as a riptide —Joseph Wambaugh

The pressure was building in me like beer on a full bladder —T. Coraghessan Boyle

Seemed to smolder like a tar-barrel on the point of explosion —Lawrence Durrell

The sense of horror and failure had clutched his spine like the wet, wrinkled hand of a drowned woman —William Styron

Set my heart to rocking like a boat in a swell —Edna St. Vincent Millay

She explodes like a chestnut thrown on the fire —Colette

❧ AGREEMENT/DISAGREEMENT

See Also: COMPATABILITY, FIGHTING

About as far apart as an atheist and a born-again Christian —Anon

Acquiesced like an old man acquiescing in death —Wilfrid Sheed

(Nobody can be as) agreeable as an uninvited guest —Frank McKinney

Humorists like McKinney are notable phrase converters. This simile may be a case in point, evolving from William Wordsworth's sonnet To a Snowdrop which describes a flower bending its forehead "As if fearful to offend, like an unbidden guest."

Agree like a finger and a thumb —Anon

Agree like two cats in a gutter —John Heywood's *Proverbs*

Agree like cats and dogs —John Ray's *Proverbs*

This sarcastic twist to the more commonly used "Fight like cats and dogs" dates back to the nineteenth century.

Agree like pickpockets in a fair —John Ray's *Proverbs*

Agree like the clocks of London —Richard Brinsley Sheridan

As coals are to burning coals, and wood to fire, so is a contentious man to kindle strive —The Holy Bible

As far apart as the atheists who claim there is no soul, and the Christian Scientists who declare there is no body —Anon

Co-operate about as much as two tomcats on a fence —Raymond Chadler

Far apart as the poles —Anon

Flock together in consent, like so many wild geese —William Shakespeare, *Henry IV, Part II*

Like the course of the heavenly bodies, harmony in national life is a resultant of the struggle between contending forces —Judge Louis D. Brandeis

Sentiments as equal as if weighed on a golden scale —Janet Flanner

We are made for cooperation, like feet, like hands, like eyelids, like the row of the upper and lower teeth. To act against one another is contrary to nature —Marcus Aurelius

❧ AILMENTS

See: ILLNESS

❧ AIM

See: PURPOSEFULNESS

❧ AIMLESSNESS

See Also: BELONGING, EMPTINESS

Aimless as a cloud in the sky —Oscar Hammerstein, "The Man I Used to Be," *Pipe Dream*

Aimless as a leaf in a gale. Oscar Hammerstein. "The Man I Used to Be," *Pipe Dream*

Aimless as an autumn leaf borne on November's idle winds —Paul Hamilton Hayne

Chuckled aimlessly, like an old man searching for his spectacles —James Crumley

The crowd scurried aimlessly away like ants from a disturbed crumb —O. Henry

Drift about … aimlessly as a ghost —Lawrence Durrell

Drifted like winter moons —Richard Wilbur

Drifting like breath —Robert Penn Warren

Drifts like a cloud —Dante Gabriel Rossetti

He was without subject matter, like a tennis player in the Arctic or a skier in Sahara's sand —Delmore Schwartz

How does it feel / To be on your own / With no direction home / Like a complete unknown / Like a rolling stone? —Bob Dylan, from the song "Like a Rolling Stone"

Kept going … like a car without a driver —Cornell Woolrich

Woolrich's description of aimlessness is a variant of "Aimless as a ship without a rudder;" in fact, in his story Dawn to Dusk *Woolrich used the two similes together.*

Lived from day to day as if the years were circular —Alice McDermott

Never really taking hold of anything, he slides in and out of jobs like a wind-up toy sledding about until the inevitable slowdown —Alvin Boretz, film treatment

Ran out of motives, as a car runs out of gas —John Barth

Walking in aimless circles like children during a school fire drill —James Crumley

Wandered about at random, like dogs that have lost the scent —Voltaire

❧ AIR

See Also: ATMOSPHERE, HEAT

Air as clear as water —Maya Angelou

Air … as cool as water —Ethan Canin

The air, as in a lion's den, is close and hot —William Wordsworth

The air brightens as though ashes of lightning bolts had been scattered through it —Galway Kinnell

The air flowed like a liquid —Dan Jacobson

The air had a sweet, keen taste like the first bite of an apple —Phyllis Bottome

Air … hot like the air of a greenhouse —Rose Tremain

The air hovered over the city like a fine golden fog —Isak Dinesen

Air had lain about us like a scarf —Irving Feldman

The air … lay stifling upon the city, like a cat indifferently sprawled upon a dying mouse —Brian W. Aldiss

The air in the room was jumpy and stiff like it is before a big storm outside —Lee Smith

The air is calm as a pencil —Frank O'Hara

The air is pure and fresh like the kiss of a child —Mikhail Lermontov

Air light and pleasant as children's laughter —James Crumley

Air like a furnace —Benjamin Disraeli, about Spain

Air like bad breath —T. Coraghessan Boyle

Air like honey —John Updike

The [hazy] air muffles your head and shoulders like a sweater you've got caught in —William H. Gass

Air pure as a theorem —Lawrence Durrell

The air smelled like wet clothes —Andrew Kaplan

The air softly began a low sibilance that covered everything, like the night expiring —Richard Ford

Air so thick and slow its like swimming —Jayne Anne Phillips

Air streams into me like cold water —Erich Maria Remarque

Air sweet and fresh like milk —George Garrett

Air thicker than chowder —Peter Meinke

The air was like soup —Derek Lambert

The air was like the silk dress Sharai wore, clean and complex and sensual —A. E. Maxwell

Sharai is the name of a character in a novel entitled The Frog and the Scorpion

The air was mild and fresh, and shone with a faint unsteadiness that was exactly like the unsteadiness of colors inside a seashell —Maeve Brennan

The air was smoky and mellow as if the whole earth were being burned for its fragrance like a cigar —John Braine

The air was so heavy that we could feel it pressing down on us like mattresses —Jean Stafford

The air was so rich and balmy it seemed that it could be scooped up with the hand —Rosine Weisbrod

The air was still as if it were knotted to the zenith —Saul Bellow

The cold air was like a quick shower —Paul M. Fitzsimmons

The crystal air cut her like glass —Sharon Sheehe Stark

(The air was moist, odorous and black; one) felt it [the air] like a soft weight —Saul Bellow

The gray air in summer burned your eyes and throat like tractor exhaust trapped in a machine shed —Will Weaver

There was a slow pulsation, like the quiver of invisible wings in the air —Ellen Glasgow

In Glasgow's novel, Barren Ground, *this simile sets the scene for an approaching storm.*

The warm air and moisture … close in around her like a pot —Susan Neville

❧ AIRPLANES
See: VEHICLES

❧ ALCOHOL
See: DRINKING

❧ ALERTNESS
See Also: ATTENTION/ATTENTIVENESS, EYES, SCRUTINY, WATCHFULNESS

Alert as a bird in the springtime —George Moore

Alert as a bloodhound at dinnertime —T. Coraghessan Boyle

Bright as a bee —Julia O'Faolain

Bright as a cigar band —Rita Mae Brown

Bright as a salesman in a car showroom —Donald Seaman

Bright-eyed as hawks —Walt Whitman, on the pioneer cowboys of the West

(It helps to have a friend at City Hall with) ear like a redskin, always to the ground —Arthur A. Cohen

Ears … as sensitive as two microphones —Robert Culff

Ears quick as a cat's —Frank Swinnerton

Head cocked to one side like a lizard waiting for its prey to wander into range —Michael Korda, *Another Life*

His brain [when free of restrain] skips like a lambkin —Calder Willingham

His mind … was crackling like a high-tension wire —Cornell Woolrich

Keen as a hawk's eye —Barbara Howes

Keen as robins —Frank Swinnerton

(His alertness is nearly palpable,) keenness trembling within him like his pilot light —Philip Roth about Primo Levi, *New York Times Book Review,* October 12, 1986

On the watch [for recurring problem], like a captain at sea, riding the unknown forces which may produce the known disaster all over again —Paul Horgan

Quest about like a gun-dog —Lawrence Durrell

Saw like Indian scouts and heard like blind people … and smelt like retrievers —Wilfrid Sheed

Sharp-eyed as a lynx —Sir Walter Scott

Wait like a set trap for a mouse —Anon

Wide awake as a lie detector —Wallace Stegner

Wide awake, brain cells flashing like free-game in a pinball machine —T. Coraghessan Boyle

❧ ALIENATION
See: ALONENESS, REMOTENESS

❧ ALIKENESS
See: SIMILARITY

❧ ALIMONY
See: MARRIAGE

❧ ALLURE
See: ATTRACTIVENESS

❧ ALONENESS
See Also: ABANDONMENT

Alone as a nomad —Richard Ford

Alone as a scarecrow —Truman Capote

Alone as a wanderer in the desert —Anon

Alone … like a lost bit of driftwood —Harvey Swados

Alone, like a planet —Richard Lourie

Alone … like bobbing corks —Jean Anouilh
> *Playwright Anouilh's simile from* Thieves' Carnival *describes two characters who thus bob about because their adventures are over.*

Alone like some deserted world —Bayard Taylor

Like the moon am I, that cannot shine alone —Michelangelo

[Building] As isolated as an offshore lighthouse —Nicholas Proffitt

By himself he felt cold and lifeless, like a match unlighted in a box —Stefan Zweig
> *The simile, from a short story entitled* The Burning Secret, *describes a man content only in the company of others.*

Feel lonely as a comet —Anton Chekhov, letter to his wife

Felt like an island —Derek Lambert

In your absence it is like rising every day to a sunless sky —Benjamin Disraeli

Isolated as if it were a fort in the sea or a log-hut in the forest —Israel Zangwill

Isolated like a tomb —Ian Kennedy Martin

Left him standing like a stump —Willa Cather

Like the deserted bride on her wedding night / All alone and shaking with fright —Fred Ebb, "I Can't Do It Alone," from the musical *Chicago*

Loneliness became as visible as breath that turned to vapor —Tennessee Williams

Loneliness fell over me and covered my face like a sheet —Susan Fromberg Schaeffer

Loneliness overcame him like a suffocating guilt —Irving Stone

Loneliness … rises like an exhalation from the American landscape —Van Wyck Brooks

Loneliness surrounded Katherine like a high black fence —Tess Slesinger

(I wandered) lonely as a cloud —William Wordsworth

One of the poet's most famous lines.

Lonely as a Hopper landscape —Brian Moore

Lonely as a lighthouse —Raymond Chandler, *Farewell, My Lovely*

Lonely as a wave of the sea —Katherine Anne Porter

Lonely as priests —Anon

Lonely as Sunday —Mark Twain

The lonely, like the lame, are often drawn to one another —Harvey Swados

Lonesome as a walnut rolling in a barrel —Edna Ferber

Lonesome … like the a sharp way down at the left-hand end of the keyboard —O. Henry

Lone women, like empty houses, perish —Christopher Marlowe

(And I) Sit by myself like a cobweb on a shelf —Oscar Hammerstein II, from lyric for *Oklahoma*

Solitary as a lonely eel —Richard Ford

Solitary as a tomb —Victor Hugo

Solitary as an explorer —Donald Hall

Solitary as an oyster —Charles Dickens

A solitary figure, like the king on a playing card —Marcel Proust

Solitary … like a swallow left behind at the migrating season of his tribe —Joseph Conrad

Solitude affects some people like wine; they must not take too much of it, for it flies to the head —Mary Coleridge

Solitude is as needful to the imagination as society is wholesome for the character —James Russell Lowell

Solitude … is like Spanish moss which finally suffocates the tree it hangs on —Anais Nin

Solitude swells the inner space like a balloon —May Sarton

Solitude wrapped him like a cloak —Francine du Plessix Gray

Stand … alone, like a small figure in a barren landscape in an old book —John D. MacDonald

Stand alone on an empty page like a period put down in a snowfall —William Gass

Survive like a lonely dinosaur —Mary McCarthy

(Celibate and) unattached, like a pathetic old aunt —Alice McDermott

Undisturbed as some old tomb —Edgar Allen Poe

Walk alone like one that had the pestilence —William Shakespeare, *The Two Gentlemen of Verona*

In common usage, most generally, "Like one who has the plague," or whatever contagious disease might be afoot.

We whirl along like leaves, and nobody knows, nobody cares where we fall —Katherine Mansfield

When I am alone, I feel like a day-old glass of water —Diane Wakoski

♣ ALOOFNESS
See: PERSONAL TRAITS, RESERVE

♣ AMAZEMENT
See: SURPRISE

❧ AMBITION

See Also: PURPOSEFULNESS

Ambition ... coursed like blood through her —Vita Sackville-West

(One woman's) ambition expanded like yeast —Rita Mae Brown

Ambition is as hollow as the soul of an echo —Anon

Ambition is a sort of work —Kahil Gibran

Ambition is like a treadmill ... you no sooner get to the end of it then you begin again —Josh Billings

Ambition is like hunger; it obeys no law but its appetite —Josh Billings

Ambition is like love, impatient both of delays and rivals —Sir John Denham

Ambition is like the sea wave, which the more you drink the more you thirst —Alfred, Lord Tennyson

Ambition, like a torrent, never looks back —Ben Jonson

Ambitions thin with age —James Goldman

Ambitious as the devil —Francis Beaumont

As ambitious as Lady Macbeth —James Huneker

Aspirations prancing like an elephant in a skirmish —Frank O'Hara

Good intentions ... like very mellow and choice fruit, they are difficult to keep —G. Simmons

How like a mounting devil in the heart rules the unrestrained ambition! —N.P. Willis
The word "unrestrained" has been substituted for "unrein'd."

A man without ambition is like a woman without beauty —Frank Harris

Overambitious ... like a musician trying to play every instrument in the band —Anon

People aim for the stars, and they end up like goldfish in a bowl —Muriel Barbery, *The Elegance of the Hedgehog*

(I think of) that ambition of his like some sort of little engine tick, tick, ticking away, and never stopping ... —Gore Vidal about Abraham Lincoln

To reach the height of ambition is like trying to reach the rainbow; as we advance it recedes —William Talbot Burke

Zeal without knowledge is like an expedition to a man in the dark —John Newton

❧ ANCESTORS

See: PAST, THE

❧ ANGER

See Also: EMOTIONS, IRRITABLENESS

Anger ... flowing out of me like lava —Diane Wakoski

Anger.... hard, like varnished wood —Lynne Sharon Schwartz

Anger ... hot as sparks —Wallace Stegner

Anger is a short madness —Horace

Anger is as useless as the waves of the ocean without wind —Chinese proverb

Anger is like wind is like a stone cast into a wasp's nest —Malabar proverb

Anger like a scar disfiguring his face —William Gass

Anger like grief, is a mark of weakness; both mean being wounded and wincing —Marcus Aurelius

Anger ... like Mississippi thunderstorms, full of noise and lightning, but once it passed, the air was cleared —Gloria Norris

The anger of a meek man is like fire struck out of steel, hard to be got out, and when got out, soon gone —Matthew Henry

Anger spreading through me like a malignant tumor —Isabel Allende

Angers ... crippling, like a fit —May Sarton

The anger [of a crowd of people] shot up like an explosion —H.E. Bates

Anger … smoldered within her like an unwholesome fire —Charles Dickens

Anger … spreading like a fever along my shoulders and back —Philip Levine

Anger standing there gleaming like a four-hundred-horsepower car you have lost your license to drive —Marge Piercy

Anger surged suddenly through his body like a quick pain —Beryl Markham

(His) anger was quick as a flame —Phyllis Bottome

Anger welled up in him like lava —Frank Ross

Angry as a hornet —George Garrett

A variation by movie critic Rex Reed: "angry as a ruptured hornet."

Angry as a wasp —John Heywood's *Proverbs*

Angry as a bear with a sore head —Stanley Weyman

Some variations of this popular simile are "Angry as a grizzly bear with a bad tooth" and "Cross as a bear with a sore head."

Angry words fan the fire like wind —Epigram

Bounced with indignation, as if she had robbed him of his reputation, of the esteem of honest people, of his humor, of something rare that was dearer to him than life —Guy de Maupassant

(He was) burning like a boiler —Saul Bellow

Carried on as though he had uremic poisoning —Rita Mae Brown

Cold, vicious rage that covered every inch of me like a rank sweat —Jonathan Valin

Come boiling out like bloodhounds —Richard Ford

Could feel her fury buzzing and burrowing into the meat under my skull like a drill bit —Stephen King

Die in a rage, like a poisoned rat in a hole —Jonathan Swift

A draft of anger and deep hurt trailing her like a cheap perfume —Paul Kuttner

Feel as though I had swallowed a hand grenade —Erich Maria Remarque

Feeling mean … like a bull gator —Robert Campbell

A feeling of rage cut him as with a sharp knife and took possession of him —Mikhail P. Arzybashev

Felt furious and helpless as if she had been insulted by a child —Flannery O'Connor

Few of the authors mention e-books. Those who do tend to regard with dread and disgust, like a farmhand studying a handful of fallen locusts —Robert Moor, "Bones of the Book"

A fit of anger is as fatal to dignity as a dose of arsenic to life —Josiah Gilbert Holland

Fumed like champagne that is fizzy —Bliss Carman

Fumes like Vesuvius —Cole Porter, lyrics from "*I've Come to Wive It* Wealthy In Padua," one of the songs from *Kiss Me Kate,* the musical adaptation of Shakespeare's *Taming of the Shrew.*

Since Porter rarely used similes, it's natural to wonder if working on a play by as prolific a simile creator as Shakespeare inspired not just this but the several other similes in this one song.

Fuming anger like a toaster with crust jammed against its heating coil —Ira Wood

Furious … like a wounded bull in an arena —Alexandre Dumas, Pere

Fury pervading her like a bloat —Lynne Sharon Schwartz

Fury was running all through his blood and bones like an electric flood —Robert Campbell

Gall … like a crown of flowering thorn —W. D. Snodgrass

The poem from which this simile is extracted is about a dead marriage and the narrator's regret

that his love has become a galling thing. He follows up the flowering thorn comparison with: "My love hung like a gown of lead that pulled you down."

Getting angry is like worshipping idols —L'Olam Midrash

Growling like a fox in a trap —William Diehl

Heaven has no rage like love to hatred turned, nor hell a fury like a woman scorned —William Congreve

Her rage ... damned up regularly as water —Louise Erdrich

Her resentment was like a coagulant ... she felt sullen, dull, thick —Nancy Huddleston Packer

He's like a scalded cat —William Alfred

He was like the mule in the story that kept running into the trees; he wasn't blind, he was just so mad he didn't give a damn —Rex Stout

His cheeks quiver with rage —Walker Percy

Hissed like an angry kettle —Herbert Lieberman

(Barcaloo's rage took about five seconds to boil up) It was like dropping cold water into a pot of hot iron. —Robert Campbell

Let it [anger at wife] all come out of him, like air from a tire —Bruce Jay Friedman

Like ice, anger passes away in time —Anon

Mad as a bobcat —James Kirkwood

Mad as a buck —William Shakespeare, *The Comedy of Errors*

Mad as a bull among bumble bees —Anon

Mad as a cat that's lost a mouse —O'Henry

Mad as all wrath —Anon

Mad the sea and wind —William Shakespeare, *Hamlet*

Mad as a wet hen —American colloquialism

    A variation from George Garrett's novel The Finished Man: *Mad as a doused rooster.*

Mad as hops —American colloquialism

In *Picturesque Expressions*," Lawrence Urdang speculates that this is a twist on being 'hopping' mad.

On the warpath [against world's injustices], like a materialistic Don Quixote —Clarence Day

Outrage which was like sediment in his stomach —Paule Marshall

Outrage ... worked like acid in his temper —Frank Swinnerton

Puffed up with rage like a squid (my psyche let out angry ink) —Saul Bellow

Rage ... as infectious as fear —Christopher Isherwood

Rage, as painful as a deep cut —Jean Stafford

Rage ... burst in the center of my mind like a black bubble of fury —Lawrence Durrell

Rage sang like a coloratura doing trills —Marge Piercy

Rages like a chafed bull —William Shakespeare, *Henry VI, Part II*

Rage swells in me like gas —Marge Piercy

Rage whistling through him like night wind on the desert —Paige Mitchell

Raging back at her [an angry woman] like a typhoon —T. Coraghessan Boyle

Raging like some crazed Othello —Suzi Gablik describing Marc Chagall's behavior in review of *My Life with Chagall* by Virginia Haggard, *New York Times Book Review,* August 17, 1986

(Enemy chase me) sore as a bird —The Holy Bible/Lamentations

Sore as a boil —American colloquialism

Sore as a crab —John Dos Passos

Stammering with anger like the clucking of a hen —Émile Zola

Stewing hostility and mordant self-pity ... pooled like poison almost daily in his soul —Joseph Heller

surges of anger, like the rush of an incoming tide —P. D. James, *Death Comes to Pemberly*

Tempers boil over like unwatched spaghetti —Tonita S. Gardner

Turned crimson with fury —Lewis Carroll

When he (Woody Hayes) is angry he is like those creatures that lurk in hollow trees. His glare … causes brave men to run like scalded cats —George F. Will

The angry man described by Will is football coach Woody Hayes.

Words heat up room like an oven with door open —Anon

(The young man's) wrath is like straw of fire, but like red hot steel is the old man's ire —Lord Byron

♣ ANIMALS

See Also: BIRDS

The cat … carried his tail like a raised sword —Helen Hudson

The cat was sleeping on the floor like a tipped-over roller skate —Paul Theroux

Crows … circle in the sky like a flight of blackened leaves —Stephen Vincent Benét

Dogs … all snarls and teeth like knives —George Garrett

Dog … with a marking down his breast like a flowing polka-dot tie. He was like a tiny shepherd —Eudora Welty

Dour as a wet cat —Warren Beck

Fins [on fish] like scimitars —Richard Maynard

Frogs sparkling like wet suns —Margaret Atwood

He [a dog] dragged her around the block like a horse pulling a wheelless carriage —Margaret Millar

A herd of black and white cows moved slowly across a distant field, like pieces of torn paper adrift on a dark pond —Hilary Masters

His tail [a cat's] waved like a pine tree —Sheila Kaye-Smith

The Llama is a wooly sort of fleecy hairy goat with an indolent expression and an undulating throat. Like an unsuccessful literary man —Hilaire Belloc

[A cow] lying on her back like a fat old party in a bathtub —Edward Hoagland

[A cat] purring like a Packard engine. It worked like a lullaby —Harold Adams

Sheep huddled likes fallen clouds —George Garrett

Silver whiskers … like rice-threads —D. H. Lawrence

The silver whiskers described by Lawrence belong to a fox, from which his story takes its title.

Squirrels … fat as housecats —Doris Lessing

Swarms of bees like a buzzing cloud flew from flower to flower —Erich Maria Remarque

A white poodle … like an animated powder puff —Penelope Gilliatt

Wings of the swans are folded now like the sheets of a long letter —Donald Justice

♣ ANIMATION

See: ACTIVENESS, ENERGY, ENTHUSIASM

♣ ANNOYANCE

See: IRRITABLENESS

♣ ANTICIPATION

See Also: HOPE

Anticipation went through me like a ripple of discordant notes —A. E. Maxwell

Lay in waiting like a giant crab —August Strindberg

In Strindberg's play,, The Stranger, a character named Mrs. X thus compares the woman who wants her husband.

Like chill dawn waiting for sunrise, I am waiting for you —Rainer Maria Rilke

Wait, breathless as a bride —George Garrett

Waited … keenly as fisherman waiting for a bite —Lawrence Durrell

Waiting for her like a king awaiting the arrival of a courtier —Harvey Swados

Waiting [without thought or action], like a radio set equipped with a receiver only, for a signal from a distance which he wasn't even certain would be transmitted —Kenzaburo Oe

Wait … like a dog expecting to be taken for a walk —Rosamund Pilcher

Wait … like a pair of sea captains' wives in their widow's walks —Thomas McGuane

❧ ANXIETY

See Also: EMOTIONS, NERVOUSNESS, TENSION

Anxiety flowed through the core of his bones like lava —Calder Willingham

(It is in those marriages and love affairs which are neither good or bad … that) anxiety flows like a muddy river —Norman Mailer

An anxiety had settled like a fine dust on everything she did —Howard Jacobson, *The Finkler Question*

An anxiety hung like a dark impenetrable cloud —Anon

Anxiety … is somewhat like a blow on the head —Delmore Schwartz

Anxiety moved like a current through his belly —Bernard Malamud

Anxiety receives them like a grand hotel —W. H. Auden

Anxious as a law associate during his sixth year with a major law firm —Elyse Sommer

Anxious as a mid-level manager in a corporate takeover —Mike Sommer

Anxious as an aspiring Miss Universe contestant sequestered in a soundproof booth and brought out moments later to tell what she loves most about America —Susan Barron, *New York Times*

Anxious as a mid-level manager in a corporate takeover —Mike Sommer

Anxious as an investor watching his stock go down —Anon

Anxious as a tax payer with an audit notice from the IRA —Anon

As worried as she would have been over a lover she had cared for passionately —Sumner Locke Elliot

A case of the dreads so thick they seemed to whistle out the heating ducts and swarm the room like a dark mistral —Richard Ford

Desperation rising from him like a musk —Paule Marshall

A feeling of foreboding … like a wind stirring the tapestry, an ominous chill —Evelyn Waugh

A feeling of vague anxiety … snuffling about me like cold-nosed rodents, like reading of a favorite baseball player whose star has descended to the point where he parks cars at a restaurant or sits in a room above a delicatessen in Indianapolis, drinking vodka and waiting for his pension —W. P. Kinsella

Felt as if a serpent had begun to coil round his limbs —George Eliot

Felt as if her nerves were being stretched more tightly, like strings on violin pegs —Leo Tolstoy

Felt chilled as by the breath of death's head —Victor Hugo

Felt like a switchboard with all my nerves on Emergency Alert —Dorothy B. Francis

Frantic as a mouse in a trap —Anon

Had a chill and heavy feeling in his stomach like a lump of lead —Vicki Baum

Her mild, constant worries had engraved no lines in her bisque china face but had gradually cracked it like a very old plate —Lael Wertenbaker

His heart seemed to slide like the hook on a released pulley —Frank Swinnerton

I'm 'bout as worried as a pregnant fox in a forest fire —Peter Benchley

Over it [a face that had looked hopeful] now lay like a foreign substance a film of anxiety —Thomas Hardy

Second-hand cares, like second-hand clothes, come easily off and on —Charles Dickens

Stress is like an iceberg. We can see one-eighth of it above, but what about what's below —Patrice O'Connor

Suspended in his own anxiety as if in a cloudy solution of some acid —Lawrence Durrell

That news went through me like a cold wind. —Susan Vreeland, *Clara and Mr. Tiffany*

There is the same pain and panic when your computer locks up as when you have an attack of appendicitis —Brendan Gill, quoted *New York Times,* August 2, 1986, in article by William E. Geist about a man (computer tutor Bruce Stark) who helps people with their computer problems.

This is typical of similes that are borrowed and modified to fit a personal sphere of interest.

Unease … it slipped out without his being able to control it, like sweat from his pores —Clive Barker

Worry is like a rocking chair. It gives you something to do, but it doesn't get you anywhere —Anon

❧ APARTNESS
See: ALONESS

❧ APATHY
See: REMOTENESS

❧ APPAREL
See: CLOTHING

❧ APPEAREANCE
See: PHYSICAL APPEARANCE

❧ APPETITE
See Hunger

❧ APPLAUSE
See: NOISE

Applause … like pebbles being rattled in a tin —Francis King

❧ APPRECIATION
Cherish like a secret —D.H. Lawrence

Poorly appreciated … like a fine landscape in dull weather —Arthur Schopenhauer

She looked on him as a kind of gigantic treat, a prize won in a lottery —Anita Brookner

Ungrateful as children, who can never pay their debt of gratitude because they owe so much —Honoré de Balzac

An ungrateful man is like a hog under a tree eating acorns, but never looking up to see where they come from —Timothy Dexter

❧ ARGUMENTS
See Also: FIGHTING

Argue like geese —Ben Hecht

Argued like a lawyer —Edith Wharton

Arguing like sparring fish in a tank —Graham Swift

Arguing with Owen was like fencing with a bag of wool —Julia O'Faolain

The argument broke open, porous as cheese —Julia O'Faolain

Arguments are like the grinding of rusty blades —Elizabeth Hardwick

Can't help arguing like I can't help the man in the moon —Louise Erdrich

Clash like the coming and retiring wave —Alfred, Lord Tennyson

Clash, like waves of the sea —John Hall Wheelock

Contention is like fire, both burn so long as there is any exhaustible matter to contend with —Thomas Adams

Grabbed the argument as if it were a beach ball we were tossing between us —Dorothy B. Francis

Her argument clung to its point like a frightened sharp-clawed animal —Edith Wharton

Her arguments are like elephants. They squash you flat —Rumer Godden

His argument is as thin as the homeopathic soup that was made by boiling the shadow of a pigeon that had been starved to death —Abraham Lincoln

Protesting like children at nap time —George Garrett

Split [in disagreement] like an egg —Paige Mitchell

Talking to Oscar [Levant] is like fighting a man who has three fists instead of the regulation two —Alexander Woolcott

True disputants are like true sportsmen, their whole delight is in the pursuit —Alexander Pope

Words ... flew between them like sparks between steel striking steel —Edna Ferber

The words [during an argument] whipped away like weightless leaves —Lael Tucker Wertenbaker

❧ ARITHMETIC

See: MATHEMATICS AND SCIENCE

❧ ARM(S)

See Also: ARM MOVEMENTS, FINGER(S), HAND(S)

Arm ... like a fat bread roll —James Lee Burke

Arms and legs like tendrils —Jonathan Kellerman

(Her bare) arms and legs were like white vines —James Robison

Arms delicate as daisy stems —Sharon Sheehe Stark

Arms folded across his chest as primly as two blades in a Swiss Army knife —Pat Conroy

(An old man with) arms like driftwood scoured by salt and wind —Marge Piercy

Arms like gateposts —Leslie Thomas

Arms like logs —James Crumley

Arms like pythons —Nicholas Proffitt

Arms loose ... like ropes dangling toward the floor —Cornell Woolrich

Arms ... pink and thick as country hams —Robert B. Parker

Arms ... rounded and graceful and covered with soft down, like a breath of gold —Wilbur Daniel Steele

Arms, soft and smooth; they must be like peeled peaches to the touch —Stefan Zweig

Arms spread like a crucifix —Carolyn Chute

Arms swinging wildly, like a great gull flapping toward the sea —Kay Boyle

Arms thick as firs —Paige Mitchell

Arms ... thick as hickory logs —Elinor Wylie

Arms thick like a butcher's —Richard Maynard

Arms ... very thin and pale, as though they'd been tucked away in some dark place, unused —Margaret Millar

Bent arms like pothooks —Erich Maria Remarque

Delicate wrists that moved bonelessly as snakes —Margaret Millar

Elbows ... pointy, like a hard lemon —Ann Beattie

Forearms so hard and well-defined that the skin looked as if it had been flayed away, like drawings in an anatomy book —Jonathan Valin

Held their arms like bundles to their chest —William H. Gass

It [arm] was so thin ... its covering didn't look like flesh but like paper wrapped around a bone to take home to a dog —Margaret Millar

Let her arms drop like folded wings —Julie Hayden

My arms fit you like a sleeve —Anne Sexton

The descriptive frame of reference in Sexton's poem "Unknown Girl" is a baby.

My arms lie upon the desk like logs sogged with rain —David Ignatow

One of her arms hung down to the floor like an overfed white snake —Ross Macdonald

Skinny, muscular arms ... like the twisted branches of an old apple tree —Arthur Miller

Swarthy arms like rolls of copper —Aharon Megged

Thin arms ... ridged like braided leather —R. Wright Campbell

Upper arms big as legs —Will Weaver

Wrists like twigs —Eleanor Clark

Wrists ... like two by fours —Charles Bukowski

Wrists ... looked thin as a dog's foreleg —John Updike

Wrist ... small like the throat of a young hen —Philip Levine

Wrist that looked like a lean ham —William Faulkner

♣ ARM MOVEMENTS

See Also: HAND MOVEMENTS

Arms extended over his head, fists clenched, like a soccer player running mad with triumph —Daniel Curley

Arms spread out like wasps —James Patterson

Arms upraised like two giant branches —Harvey Swados

(His) arms waggled like duck wings —Martin Cruz Smith

Arms working like a windmill —Mike Fredman

Crook his arm like an usher at a wedding —Susan Neville

Crooking her arms like broken branches —Bernard Malamud

Folded her arms like hemp cord —Leigh Alison Wilson

Opened your arms like cupboard doors —Marge Piercy

Raised his arms like a fight announcer —Harvey Swados

Spreading their arms wide like galleons in full sail —Lawrence Durrell

Waving his arms like a deranged pelican —George Garrett

Waved ... like a queen in a passing coach —William McIlvanney

♣ ARMY

An army, like a snake, goes on its belly —Frederick the Great

Military intelligence has about as much to do with intelligence as military music has to do with music —John le Carré

Soldiers in peace are like chimneys in summer —John Ray's *Proverbs*

The word 'chimneys' has been modernized from 'chimnies.'

♣ ART AND LITERATURE

See Also: BOOKS, MUSIC, POETS/POETRY, WRITERS/WRITING

Aesthetics is for the artist like ornithology is for the birds —Barnett Newman, *New York Times Book Review*, February 18, 1968

Art is a jealous mistress —Ralph Waldo Emerson

Art is an absolute mistress —Charlotte Cushman

Art is like a border of flowers along the course of civilization —Lincoln Steffens Forbes S

Art is like baby shoes. When you coat them with gold they can no longer be worn —John Updike

Art is like religion. As long as you do your best to stamp it out of existence, it flourishes in spite of you, like weeds in a garden. But if you try and cultivate it, and it becomes a popular success, it goes to the dogs at once —Jane Wardle

Art is science in the flesh —Jean Cocteau

Art is wild as a cat and quite separate from civilization —Stevie Smith

The artist, like the neurotic, has withdrawn from an unsatisfying reality into this world of imagination; but, unlike the neurotic, he knew how to find a way back from it and once more to get a firm foothold in reality —Sigmund Freud

Artists ... like bees, they must put their lives into the sting they give —Ralph Waldo Emerson

Art, like Eros, stirs senses to full life, demands devotion —Steven Millhauser

Art like life is an open secret —Lawrence Durrell

Art, like life, should be free, since both are experimental —George Santayana

Art, like morality, consists of drawing the line somewhere —Gilbert Keith Chesterton

Art, like the microscope, reveals many things that the naked eye does not see —George Moore

As the sun colors flowers, so does art color life —Sir John Lubbock

Great art is as irrational as great music. It is mad with its own loveliness —George Jean Nathan

I have seen the beauty evaporate from poems and pictures, exquisite not so long ago, like hoar frost before the morning sun —W. Somerset Maugham

In art, as in diet, as in spiritual life, the same rules of elimination apply: the more one can do without the better —Anne Freemantle

In art, as in love, instinct is enough —Anatole France

In art, as in politics, there is no such thing as gratitude —George Bernard Shaw

In literature, as in love, we are astonished at what is chosen by others —André Maurois, *New York Times,* April 14, 1963

(Nine times out of ten,) in the arts as in life, there is actually no truth to be discovered; there is only error to be exposed —H. L. Mencken

Literature, like a gypsy, to be picturesque, should be a little ragged —Douglas Jerold

Literature, like virtue, is its own reward —Lord Chesterfield

Literature's like a big railway station ... there's a train starting every minute —Edith Wharton
In her short story, The Angel at the Grave, *Wharton continues the simile as follows: "People are not going to hang around the waiting room. If they can't get to a place when they want to, they go somewhere else."*

It [empty white canvas] looks like an anemic nun in a snow storm —James Rosenquist, quoted in television documentary about his work, 1987

Modern paintings are like women. You'll never enjoy them if you try to understand them —Harold Coffin

Most works of art, like most wines, ought to be consumed in the district of their fabrication —Rebecca West

Naiveté in art is like zero in a number; its importance depends on the figure it is united with —Henry James

One must act in painting as in life, directly —Pablo Picasso, *Time* interview

Two modern paintings ... like Rorschach inkblots gone to seed —Pat Conroy

A painting requires as much cunning as the perpetration of a crime —Edgar Degas

A picture is a poem without words —Latin proverb

(Some of the canvases had no pictures at all, just colors,) swirls and patches and planes of color, thickened and lumped, like hunks of emotion —Dan Wakefield

Without favor art is like a windmill without wind —John Ray's *Proverbs*

The youth of an art is, like the youth of anything else, its most interesting period —Samuel Butler

♣ ASTONISHMENT

See Also: SURPRISE

♣ ATMOSPHERE

See Also: AIR

Air … full of unspoken words, unformulated guilts, a vicious silence, like the moments before a bridge collapses —John Fowles

The atmosphere (of the room) was as vapid as a zephyr wandering over a Vesuvian lava-bed —O. Henry

Evil which hung in … air like an odorless gas —Ross Macdonald

(The circle in which I moved was a self-contained world …) it was like being in the treacly, supersaturated air of a hothouse filled with luxuriant vegetation, or in an aquarium with its own special heating unit and food supply, its own species of plankton —Natascha Wodin

(The whole place seemed restless and troubled and) people were crowding and flitting to and fro, like shadows in an uneasy dream —Charles Dickens

Sensed a wrongness around me, like an alarm clock that had gone off without being set —Maya Angelou

They [women who run shops in a town] have given the Square a fussy, homespun air that reminds you of life pictured in catalogs —Richard Ford

Thick and sultry the atmosphere steams like an island in the Pacific —T. Coraghessan Boyle

♣ ATTENTION

See Also: ALERTNESS, SCRUTINY, WATCH-FULLNESS

(When listening he is) as focused and as still as a chipmunk spying something unknown from atop a stone wall —Philip Roth about Primo Levi, *New York Times Book Review*, October 12, 1986

The attention [of listeners] is like a narrow mouthed vessel; pour into it what you have to say cautiously, and, as it were drop by drop —Joseph Joubert

Attention rolled down like a window shade —Sharon Sheehe Stark

Attention [of students] sinking … like sluggish iron from the cooling crust —John Updike

Attentive and indifferent as a croupier —George Garrett

Attracted about as much attention as a flea in a dog pound —Ross Thomas

Attracted about as much attention (in the artistic world) as the advent of another fly in a slaughter house —James L. Ford

Attracted as little attention as a dirty finger nail in the third grade —Ring Lardner

Attracted attention like the principal heads in a picture —Honoré de Balzac

Collected attention like twists of silver paper or small white pebbles —Elizabeth Bowen

Concentrates … like a cancer victim scanning a medical dictionary in hopes that the standard definitions have been repealed overnight in favor of good news —James Morrow

Curiosity, keen and cold as a steel knife —Maxim Gorky

Deaf as a door nail —Thomas Wilson

This is the best known of many "Deaf as" similes. It's used in its literal sense as well as to describe inattentiveness. Popular variants include "Deaf as a post," "Deaf as a door," and"Deaf as a stone."

Deaf as a piecrust —Lawrence Durrell

(Had honed her ability to turn) deaf as a snail —Joseph Wambaugh

Drinking it [information] like a bomber pilot getting ready for a mission —Harvey Swados

(The hoot of laughter that always made Mary) flick him off like television —Sumner Locke Elliott

Had taken in her every anecdote as completely as a recording machine —Louis Auchincloss

Heads are turning like windmills —Arthur Miller

Heedless as the dead —Lord Byron {

His eyes wandered, like a mind —Penelope Gilliatt

His mind keeps slipping away like a fly —John Rechy

Inattentive, like the ear of a confessor —Mary McCarthy

Intent as a surgeon —Jean Stafford

Interest spread like a net —Nadine Gordimer

(She could not keep her mind on anything;) it [her mind] kept darting around like a darning needle —Jean Stafford

Leaned forward ... like hounds just before they get the fox —Steven Vincent

Leapt from theme to theme like a water-bug —Eleanor Clark

Listened as intently as a blind woman —Rita Mae Brown

Listened, very still, like a child who is being told a fascinating and gruesome fairy tale —Isak Dinesen

Listen like an uncle —Herbert Gold

Listen ... like snakes to a charmer's flute —Jan de Hartog

Mind jumps from one thing to another like drops of water bouncing off a larded pan when you test whether the griddle is hot enough to pour the pancake batter in —John Hagge

My mind wanders like smoke —Clifford Odets

Pricked up his ears like two railroad signals —Lewis Carroll

[Poets] Receive the same care as xylophones and equestrian statues —Delmore Schwartz

Seems not to listen to her words, but rather watches her forming them ... like some fervent anthropologist —William Boyd

Snaps to attention like a thumb —Irving Feldman

(He tried to apply his mind to the work he was doing but his) thoughts fluttered desperately, like moths in a trap —W. Somerset Maugham

The words bounced off Harry, like pebbles skipped on water —Paul Kuttner

(So scatter-brained that) words went by him like the wind —Louisa May Alcott

❧ ATTIRE
See CLOTHING

❧ ATTRACTION

Absorbing as a love affair —Elyse Sommer

(A charismatic man) attracting young men to himself like filings to a magnet —Linda West Eckhardt

Come at him [girls to a boy] like ducks to popcorn —Max Apple

Drawn to as bathers to sea shore —Anon

Drawn to as children to amusement parks —Anon

Drawn to as readers to a library —Anon

Drawn to us warily but helplessly, like a starved deer —Louise Erdrich

Drew ... like pipers charming rats —Lynne Sharon Schwartz

In her novel, Disturbances in the Field, *Schwartz alludes to ideas that are attractive to the heroine and her college friends.*

Drew (many confidences ...) as unintentionally as a magnet draws steel filings —Vita Sackville-West

Enchanted ... like a meadow full of four-leaf clovers —Mary McCarthy

Fascinated like sick people are fascinated by anything ... scrap of news about their own case —James Thurber

Fascinating and fantastic as toys in a shop window to a little poor boy in the street —Isak Dinesen

Fascinating as a burning fuse —William McGivern, about fellow writer Michael Gilbert's espionage novel *Overdrive*.

Whenever a simile is used to praise a book, it is invariably highlighted on the book jacket or in ads, as this one was.

(The salesgirls) fell on me like pigeons on breadcrumbs —Judith Rascoe

Had drawn her to him like a flower to the sun —John le Carré

(The warm sweet center of her) had taken hold of him like a hand —John Yount

Held her mesmerized like a snake —Julia O'Faolain

He moves to you like a stable hand to a new horse —Allan Miller

This comes from Miller's dramatization of D. H. Lawrence's short novel, The Fox. *It did not appear in the Lawrence text.*

Irresistible [thoughts] as intruders who force their way into your house —Dan Wakefield

Like children taking peeps at pantry shelves, we think we're tempted when we tempt ourselves —Arthur Guiterman

Men just love to buzz around me like there was a sweet smell coming from me —Pat Conroy

Mesmerizing as a flickering neon sign —Anon

(Kept watching because) something about her stayed with me. Like a cold matzo ball —Nat Hentoff

Take to the way a hypochondriac takes to a bed —Lorrie Moore

Temptation leapt on him like the stab of a knife —Edith Wharton

Temptations, like misfortunes, are sent to test our moral strength —Marguerite de Valois

Took to as an ant to a picnic —Harry Prince

Took to it ... like a retriever to water-ducks —Ouida

Was drawn to ... as if by strong cords —Aharon Appelfeld

You pull me like the moon pulls on the tide —Richard Thompson, "The Dimming of the Day"

❧ ATTRACTIVENESS

See Also: BEAUTY, DESIRABILITY, PHYSICAL APPEARANCE

Adorable as a baby —Anon

Babies have long been linked with adjectives that equate appealing (or peaceful) qualities. This commonly used form may have its origins in Swinburne's "Adorable as is nothing save a child."

Alluring as a ripe peach —Guy de Maupassant

Appealing as power to a politician —Anon

Appealing as something for nothing —Anon

Appealing as sunlight after a storm —Anon

An appeal shone from her as light from a twisted filament —John Updike

As handsome as a movie legend —Julie Orringer, *The Invisible Bridge*

As likable as a jaguar —William Beechcroft

Charm is almost as poor a butter for parsnips as good intentions —Heywood Broun

Charm rolled off him like a halo off an angel —James Kirkwood

In the television movie adaptation of Kirkwood's There Must Be a Pony *the character played by Elizabeth Taylor's uses this simile to characterize the man played by Robert Wagner.*

Cute as a bug's ear —Bobbie Ann Mason

Dazzle like an Impressionistic painting in which every brush stroke tells and contains something germane to the whole —V.S. Pritchett on George Meredith

Decorative as the scalps of an Indian brave —Frank Swinnerton

(The novel is often as) disarming as a work of folk art —Bethami Probst, *New York Times Book Review,* April 12, 1987

Have all the charm of a black widow —Pia Lindstrom, television movie review, 1986

Interesting, like a plot in the mystery books —Louise Erdrich

Inviting as a down comforter —Anon

The last time he was on Broadway, critics called him the hottest leading man since Hugh Jackman. This time many thought he was as sexy (and as wooden) as a tree stump —Michael Riedel, *New York Post,* January 6, 2012, about Jackman in *On a Clear Day You Can See Forever*

Look like something that ought to be eaten for dessert —Irwin Shaw

More alluring than an invitation to visit rich and charming friends on the Cote d'Or —Ogden Nash

Seductive as Cleopatra —Louis Bromfield

She's like a mound of nectarines —Saul Bellow

Unappealing as a meringue with hardly any crust —Anon

❧ AUTHENTICITY
See: TRUENESS/FALSENESS

❧ AUTHORITY
See: POWER

❧ AUTHORSHIP
See: POETS/POETRY, WRITERS/WRITING

❧ AUTOMOBILES
See: VEHICLES

❧ AVAILABILITY

About as hard to get as lion shit in Africa —Stephen Longstreet

Accessible a candidate looking for another hand to shake —Mike Sommer

Accessible as a hooker plying her trade —Anon

As unapproachable as a star —Anon

As unattainable, as desirable, as beauty —Margaret Sutherland

(Drinks here) flow like cement —John Mortimer, Public Television series, *Paradise Postponed,* 1986

Has been handed round like snuff at a wake —Ellen Currie
The descriptive frame of reference is a promiscuous girl.

Inaccessible as time —Alice McDermott
In her novel That Night, *the author talks about old neighborhoods of which parents who have moved away say "You can't go there anymore" as if change made a place inaccessible as time.*

Laying around like pop-corn —Clifford Odets
Odets follows this up with "You think good boys are laying around like pop-corn?"

Like an apple hanging on a tree, waiting for somebody to come along and pick it —Lee Smith

Like Meissen china in a glass case, the admiration [for an appealing but inaccessible woman] had to be kept at a distance —Jilly Cooper

Lived high up [in an apartment complex] ... as accessible as a bald Rapunzel —William McIlvanney

Unobtainable as a taxi when it rains —Anon

Untouchable as God —Erich Maria Remarque

❧ AVARICE
See: GREED

❧ AWARENESS
See: REALIZATION

♣ AWKWARDNESS

See Also: MOVEMENT(S)

Awkward as a bull in a china shop —Anon

> *This still-popular simile endures with many substitutions for the bull such as "a blind dog," "a gorilla," "a monkey." Often, instead of a substitute comparison, a different context can lift a simile like this beyond the cliché for example, "Like wild bulls in a china shop … are my awkward hands of love" from poet Delmore Schwartz's journals and notes*

Awkward as learning newly learned —Adrienne Rich

Awkward in her movements, as if she had been in solitary for years —Ross Macdonald

Awkward … like a guest at a party to whose members he carried bad news he had no right to know, no right to tell —Hortense Calisher

Awkward like a leaden ballet dancer lifting a fat partner —Ed McBain

Awoke as stiff as if I'd been spray-starched —Jonathan Kellerman

Blunder and fumble like a moth … a rabbit caught in the glare of a torch —William Faulkner

Bumbled up to him like a mole —Wilfrid Sheed

Clumsy as two kids on their first date —Anon

Clumsy … like a leaky old engine with the driving belt slipping and steam escaping from every joint —Christopher Isherwood

Feel awkward like a boy on a date with an older girl —Bobbie Ann Mason

Graceless as a pelican on the ground —George Garrett

Had about as much grace as a hippopotamus in a bubble bath —Harry Prince

Has the grace of an arthritic elephant on roller skates —Corey Sandler

Moved thickly, like a clumsy, good-tempered horse —William Faulkner

Moving stiffly like a man in a body cast —Martin Cruz Smith

She ran on like a clumsy goat, trampling and trespassing on land and that was preserved —Daphne du Maurier

Stiff as a gaffer —Richard Wilbur

Stiff as a line in Euclid —Saul Bellow

Stiff as a poker grew —Wallace Irwin

Stumbling about like a drunken bear —James Crumley

Uncoordinated as a rag doll —Dorothea Straus

Unwieldy as a pregnant elephant —Anon

♣ BACHELOR

See: MEN AND WOMEN

♣ BAD LUCK

See: FORTUNE/MISFORTUNE

♣ BADNESS

See: CRUELTY, EVIL

♣ BALANCE

See: REGULARITY/IRREGULARITY

♣ BALDNESS

See Also: HAIR

Bald as a ballpeen hammer —Thomas Lux

Bald as a brass knob —Beverly Farmer

Bald as a nun —Patrick White

Bald and wrinkled as a lizard —Sarah Bird

Bald as a balloon —Percival Wilde

Bald as a barefaced lie —Anon

Bald as a bearing —Loren D. Estleman

Bald as a billiard ball —Anon

> *Of the many objects used as comparisons comparatively liked with baldness, the billiard or cue ball probably ranks at the very top.*

Bald as a brick —Raymond Chandler, *The Long Goodbye*

Bald as an egg —Raymond Chandler, *The Long Goodbye*

Bald as a football —William Boyd

Bald as an orange —Thomas Bailey Aldrich

Bald as a winter tree —William Morris

Bald as convicts —George Garrett

Bald as peeled onion —Margaret Laurence

Bald as the beach —William Diehl

Bald as the palm of your hand —Richard Harris Barham

Bald as time —Richard Prome

Bald head shining like a polished stone —George Garrett

The gleaming skull [of bald-headed man] shone like a supernatural sun —Sholom Ash

Had gone completely bald very young as though to get that over with as soon as possible —Helen Hudson

Hair beginning to recede like the polar ice cap in warm weather —Jean Thompson

Head as smooth as a knob —Russell Baker, *New York Times*, May 17, 1986

He had a bald patch on the top of his head which made him look rather like a monk —Guy de Maupassant

He was bald, his back hair was thick and projected like one of those large tree mushrooms that grow on the mossy side of a trunk —Saul Bellow

His bald head coming to a point, like an egg —Richard Llwellyn

His bald head shone ... like an agitated moon —Erich Maria Remarque

His head [bald, with ring of grey-brown hair] was like the brown edges of a leaf in fall, a sign that the tree, however tall and green from a distance, was being eaten away at the edges, dying from the outside in —Jay Parini

His strong, bald head had a dull glow, like old ivory —Ivan Bunin

No more hair than a stone —John MacDonald

A semi-circular fringe of white hair surrounding his bald pate like a broken halo —Margaret Millar

✤ BARENESS

Bare as the back of my hand —John Ray's *Proverbs*

As naked as the last leftover clap in a theatre —Joe Coomer

Bare as a birch at Christmas —Sir Walter Scott
> *Scott used this in both* The Fortunes of Nigel *and* Quentin Durward.

Bare as a bird's tail —Edward Ward

Bare as a newly shorn sheep —John Lydgate
> *The simile has been modernized from "Bare as a sheep that is but newe shorn."*

(There she was, on the bed beside me, as) bare-assed as Eve in Eden —George Garrett

Bare as shame —Algernon Charles Swinburne

Bare as winter trees —William Wordsworth

Bare like a carcass picked by crows —Jonathan Swift

More desolate than the wilderness —The Holy Bible/Ezekiel

Naked as an egg —F. van Wyck Mason

Naked as a peach pit —Helen Dudar, *Wall Street Journal*, November 26, 1986
> *Even writers not given to using similes often use them as attention-grabbers at the beginning of an article, as Helen Dudar did to introduce her subject, novelist Paget Powell.*

Naked as a stone —Angela Carter

Naked as a table cloth —Frank O'Hara

Naked as a weather report —Robert Traver

Naked as rain —Wallace Stevens

Nude as fruit on limb —George Garrett

(Voice wearing) raw as a rubbed heel —Sharon Sheehe Stark

(I'm simply against) showing girls as if they were pork chops —Germaine Greer on Playmate features in *Playboy Magazine*, January, 1972

Standing naked as a dead man's shadow —A. D. Winans

❧ BARGAINS
See: ADVANTAGEOUSNESS

❧ BARRENNESS
See: EMPTINESS

❧ BASEBALL
See Also: SPORTS

The ball … came floating up to the plate like a generous scoop of vanilla ice cream bobbing to the top of a drugstore soda —Howard Frank Mosher

A ballpark at night is more like a church than a church —W. P. Kinsella

The ball … sailed through the light and up into the dark, like a white star seeking an old constellation —Bernard Malamud

The ball was coming in like a Lear jet —T. Glen Coughlin

Baseball games are like snowflakes and fingerprints, no two are ever alike —W. P. Kinsella

Baseball is like writing. You can never tell with either how it will go —Marianne Moore

Baseball, like writing, was a passion for Marianne Moore

Boston hit Dwight Gooden like they were his wicked stepparents —Vin Scully, commenting on the second game of the 1986 World Series

(He) bats like a lightning rod —W.P. Kinsella

The catcher is padded like an armchair —*London Times*, 1918

Defeat stains a pitcher's record as cabernet stains a white carpet —Marty Noble, *Newsday*, August 25, 1986

The dirt flew as if some great storm had descended and would have ripped up the entire [baseball] field —Craig Wolff, *New York Times* August 3, 1986

Dwight Gooden [of New York Mets] pitching without his fastball was like Nureyev dancing on a broken leg or Pavarotti singing with a sore throat —Anon, *Newsday*, October 25, 1986

The earth around the base is … soft as piecrust. Ground balls will die on the second bounce, as if they've been hit into an anthill —W. P. Kinsella

[Baseball] field … cool as a mine, soft as moss, lying there like a cashmere blanket —W. P. Kinsella

(He) bats like a lightning rod —W. P. Kinsella

He gets power from his bat speed … it's like he has cork in his arms —Pete Rose about Eric Davis, David Anderson, *New York Times*, May 7, 1987

He ran the bases as if he was hauling William H. Taft in a rickshaw —Heywood Broun

His fastball crackling, his curveball dropping as suddenly as a duck shot in the air, [Dwight Gooden] has begun his charge for a third straight award-winning season —Ira Berkow, *New York Times*/Sports of the Times, August 3, 1986

Homers are like orgasms. You run out of them after a time —Norman Keifetz

It [the patched-up Shea Stadium field] was dangerous underfoot as the Mets and the cubs tiptoed their way through a 5-0 Met victory the way soldiers would patrol a mine field —George Vecsey, *New York Times*/Sports of the Times, September 19, 1986

The ball players has to navigate their way through the field like soldiers because their fans had behaves so destructively the day before.

Knowing all about baseball is just about as profitable as being a good whittler —Frank McKinney

Outfielders ran together as if directed by poltergeists —George Vecsey, *New York Times/ Sports of The Times* column on dreadful things that happen to the Mets when they play against the Houston Outfielders, October 8, 1986

Someone once described the pitching of a no-hit game as like catching lightning in a bottle (How about catching lightning in a bottle on two consecutive starts?) —W. P. Kinsella

Sometimes I hit him like I used to hit Koufax, and that's like drinking coffee with a fork. Did you ever try that? —Willie Stargell on Steve Carlton, *Baseball Illustrated*, 1975

Stepping up to the plate now like the Iron Man himself. The wind-up, the delivery, the ball hanging there like a pinata like a birthday gift, and then the stick flashes in your hands like an archangel's sword —T. Coraghessan Boyle

To be an American and unable to play baseball is comparable to being a Polynesian and unable to swim —John Cheever

Trying to sneak a pitch past him is like trying to sneak the sunrise past a rooster —Amos Otis, baseball outfielder, about Rod Carew, former first baseman

Twenty years ago rooting for the Yankees was like rooting for IBM —George F. Will, on the Chicago Cubs, *Washington Post*, March 20, 1974

❧ BASKETBALL
See: SPORTS

❧ BEACHES
See: OCEAN/OCEANFRONT

❧ BEARD(S)
See Also: HAIR, PHYSICAL APPEARANCE

Bearded as Abraham —George Garrett

Bearded like a black sky before a storm —George Garrett

Beard not clipped, but flowing like a bridal veil —Sinclair Lewis

Beards like Spanish moss —T. Coraghessan Boyle

Beard stiff and jutting like a Michelangelo prophet —Harvey Swados

Bristly gray beard … as rusted as old iron —Paige Mitchell

Flecks of premature gray in his beard, like the first seeds of age beginning to sprout in him —Ross Macdonald

Gray beard like a goat's chin tuft —Ernest Hemingway

A heavy black beard that grew high on his cheeks like a mask —James Crumley

His beard is like a bird's nest, woven with dark silks —Bobbie Ann Mason

His red beard looked like a toy doctor's beard stuck on a child's face —Gloria Norris

His sideburn, shaped like the outline of Italy, juts out onto his jaw —Bobbie Ann Mason

Long beard was spread out like a little blanket on his chest —Willis Johnson

Massive sideburns hung like stirrups on either side of his face —Ross Macdonald

A neat little beard, like a bird's nest, cupped his chin —Bobbie Ann Mason

A shadow of beard lay over his bony cheeks like soot on a chimney sweep —W. T. Tyler

Sideburns like brackets —Max Shulman

Sideburns stood like powerful bushy pillars to the beard —Saul Bellow

A small goatee stuck to his chin like a swab of surgical cotton —Dorothea Straus

A two-day growth of beard that made him look like a cactus —Sue Grafton

Whiskers grew like small creeper upon a scorched face —Frank Swinnerton

❧ BEARING

See Also: FACIAL EXPRESSIONS, MISCELLA-
NEOUS; LYING; PERSONALITY PRO-
FILES; PHYSICAL APPEARANCE; POS-
TURE; SITTING; STANDING; WALKING

Carried it [a bright, haggard look] ... like a mask
or a flag —William Faulkner

Exuded an air, almost an aroma, of justification,
like a mother who has lived to see her ma-
ligned boy vindicated at last —Harvey Swados

Sitting up against the pillow, head back like a
boxer between rounds —John le Carré

Head lifted as though she carried life as lightly
there as if it were a hat made of tulle —Paule
Marshall

Held her body with a kind of awkward pride
mixed with shame, like a young girl suddenly
conscious of her flesh —Ross Macdonald

Held herself like a daughter of the Caesars —W.
Somerset Maugham

Held his shoulders like a man conscious of responsibility —Willa Cather

He leaned back and crossed his legs, as if we were
settling in front of the television set to watch
"Masterpiece Theater" —Joan Hess

Her head ... carried well back on a short neck,
like a general or a statesman sitting for his
portrait —Willa Cather

He seemed enduringly fixed on the sofa, the one
firm object in a turbulent world ... like a
lighthouse ... the firm, majestic lighthouse
that sends out its kindly light —Isak Dinesen

He seemed to have collapsed into himself, like a
scarecrow in the rain —Christopher Isherwood

His chin hung on his hand like dead weight on
delicate scales —Reynolds Price

His erect figure carrying his white hair like a flag
—John Updike

His shoulders slumped like a man ready to take a
beating —James Crumley

His straight black hair and craggy face gave off a
presence as formidable as an Indian in a gray
flannel suit —Norman Mailer,

Holding herself forward [as she walks] like a
present —Alice Adams

I felt that if he [man with threatening presence]
were to rise violently to his feet, the whole
room would collapse like paper —Margaret
Drabble

Lay piled in her armchair like a heap of small rubber tires —Patricia Ferguson

Leaned forward eagerly ... looking like a bird that
hears a worm in the ground —Robert Lowry

A lofty bearing ... like a man who had never
cringed and never had a creditor —Herman
Melville

Looked like a prisoner in the dock, hangdog and
tentative —T. Coraghessan Boyle

Looking regal as a king —Gloria Norris

Perched on her armchair like a granite image on
the edge of a cliff —Edith Wharton

(Sat) prim and watchful as a school girl on her
first field trip —Robert Traver

Relaxed and regal as a Siamese cat —Harold
Adams

(They were mute, immobile, pale —as) resigned
as prisoners of war —Ignazio Silone

Sat like a bronze statue of despair —Louisa May
Alcott

Sat like a Greek in a tragedy, waiting for the gods
to punish her for her way of life —Jonathan
Valin

Sat helpless and miserable, like a man lashed by
some elemental force of nature —Flannery
O'Connor

Sat like a man dulled by morphine —Albert Maltz

(The leading members of the Ministry) sat like a range of exhausted volcanoes —Benjamin Disraeli

Sat on the arm of the sofa with a kind of awkward arrogance, like a workman in a large strange house —Paul Theroux

(Professor Tomlinson) sat up in the witness chair like a battleship raising its most powerful gun turret into position to fire —Henry Denker

She drew herself up with a jerk like a soldier standing easy called to stand-at-ease position —Kingsley Amis

She holds up her head like a hen drinking —Scottish proverb

She walked like a woman at her lover's funeral —Derek Lambert

She was still and soft in her corner [of the room] like a passive creature in its cave —D. H. Lawrence

She wore defeat like a piece of cheap jewelry —Pat Conroy

Slumped into her seat like a Pentecostal exhausted from speaking in tongues —Sarah Bird

Spread his arms and went springy like a tennis player —Graham Swift

Slumps in his chair like a badly hurt man, half life-size —Ted Hughes

Standing like a lost child in a nightmare country in which there was no familiar landmark to guide her —Margaret Mitchell

Standing … poised and taut as a diver —George Garrett

Standing still alone, she seemed almost somber, like a statue to some important but unpopular virtue in a formal garden —Douglas Adams

Stands there like a big shepherd dog —Clifford Odets

Stands there like a prizefighter, like somebody who knows the score —Raymond Carver

Stands there vacantly, like a scared cat —Bobbie Ann Mason

Stately [movement] like a sailing ship —William H. Gass

Stood around casual as tourists —James Crumley

Stood before them, like a prisoner at the bar, or rather like a sick man before the physicians who were to heal him —Edith Wharton

Stood in one place, staring back into space and grinding fist into palm, like a bomb looking for someplace to go off —William Diehl

Stood looking at us like a figure of doom —Edith Wharton

Stood morosely apart, like a man absorbed in adding millions of pennies together, one by one —Frank Swinnerton

Stood stiffly as a hanged man —Leigh Allison Wilson

Stood … stiffly, like a page in some ancient court, or like a young prince expecting attention —Mary Hedin

Stood there like an angry bull that can't decide who to drive his horns in next —Danny Santiago

Walked like a man through ashes, silent and miserable —Robert Culff

Went about looking as though she had had a major operation that had not proved a success —Josephine Tey

Wore abuse like widow's weeds —Lael Wertenbaker

Wore their beauty and affability like expensive clothes put on for the occasion —Edith Wharton

❧ BEAUTY

See Also: BEAUTY, DEFINED; FACE; PHYSICAL APPEARANCE

(He was) all beauty, as the sun is all light —Phyllis Bottome

Beautiful and faded like an old opera tune played upon a harpsichord —Amy Lowell

Beautiful and freckled as a tiger lily —O. Henry, "The Voice of the City" (*The Complete Works of O. Henry*), 1926

Beautiful as a feather in one's cap —Thomas Carlyle

(He is) beautiful as a law of chemistry —Robert Penn Warren

Beautiful as a motherless fawn —Bruce de Silva

Beautiful as an angel —William Paterson

Beautiful as an icon —Rachel Ingalls

Beautiful as an illusion —Angela Carter

Beautiful as a prince in a fairy story —Mary Lee Settle

Beautiful as a rainbow —John Dryden

Beautiful as a well-handled tool —Stephen Vincent Benét

Beautiful as a woman's blush and as evanescent too —Letitia Landon

(For he was) beautiful as day —Lord Byron

Beautiful as fire —Ambrose Bierce

Beautiful as honey poured from a jar —*People* book review

(There was a woman) beautiful as morning —Percy Bysshe Shelley

Beautiful as nature in the spring —O. S. Wondersford

Beautiful as sky and earth —John Greenleaf Whittier

(She was) as beautiful as the devil, and twice as dangerous —Dashiell Hammett

Beautiful as youth —Dollie Radford

Beautiful … like a dream of youth —Oliver Wendell Holmes

Beauty … extraordinary, as if it were painted —Anita Brookner

Beauty in a woman's face, like sweetness in a woman's lips, is a matter of taste —M. W. Little

Beauty is as good as ready money —German proverb

Beauty is striking as deformity is striking —Edmund Burke

Beauty, like a lantern's light, will shine outward from within him —George Garrett

Beauty … like fine cutlery —John Gardner

Donned beauty like a robe —Iris Murdoch

Exquisite as the jam of the gods —Tennessee Williams

Fair as the lily —Henry Constable, "Damelus Song to His Diaphenia," 1859

One of the most popular and enduring flower/ beauty comparisons.

Fair as any rose —Christina Rossetti

Fair as a star —William Wordsworth

Fair as heaven or freedom won —Algernon Charles Swinburne

Fair as is the rose in May —Geoffrey Chaucer

Fair as marble —Percy Bysshe Shelley

Fairer than the morning star —Oscar Wilde

A fair face without a fair soul is like a glass eye that shines and sees nothing —John Stuart Blackie

Gorgeous as Aladdin's cave —Eleanor Mercein Kelly

(In the dingy park) her beauty fled as swiftly as the marmalade kitten had leapt from her grasp —William Trevor

Her beauty was as cool as this damp breeze, as the moist softness of her own lips —F. Scott Fitzgerald

He's as pretty as those long-defunct lover-gods —Charles Simic

(A novel that would be as) lovely as a Persian carpet, and as unreal —Oscar Wilde

Lovely as Spring's first rose —William Wordsworth

Lovely as the evening moon —Amy Lowell

Outstanding beauty, like outstanding gifts of any
kind, tends to get in the way of normal emotional development, and thus of that particular success in life which we call happiness
—Milton R. Sapirstein

Pretty as a diamond flush —Alfred Henry Lewis

(Face …) pretty as a greeting card —Donald E.
Westlake

Pretty as a new-laid egg —American colloquialism, attributed to Midwest

(There sat Mary) pretty as a rose —Jump Rope
Rhyme

Pretty as a spotted pony —American colloquialism, attributed to Southeast

Pretty as a spotted pup —Mary Hood

Pretty as a wax doll —Katherine Mansfield

Pretty as the carved face on a … cameo —Davis
Grubb

Pretty like children on their birthdays —Truman
Capote

Shed beauty like winter trees —George Garrett

She walks in beauty like the night —Lord Byron

*A timeless and much-quoted Byron line. It con-
tinues with "of cloudless nights and starry skies."*

She was as cute as a washtub —Raymond Chandler, *Farewell, My Lovely*

She was lovely as a flower, and, like a flower, she
passed away —Richard Le Gallienne

There is in true beauty, as in courage, something
which narrow souls cannot dare to admire
—William Congreve

In the original manuscript of The Old Bachelor
the word "something" was "somewhat."

A thing of beauty is a joy forever —John Keats

*A Keats classic that proves discretion is best when
it comes to including or implying "like" or "as."*

You boys are as cute as a couple of lost golf balls
—Raymond Chandler, *The High Window*

❧ BEAUTY DEFINED

Beauty as definite as that of a symphony by
Beethoven or a picture by Titan —W. Somerset Maugham

Beauty can pierce one like a pain —Thomas
Mann

Beauty in a modest woman is like a distant fire or
a sharp-edged sword: the one does not burn,
the other does not cut, those who do not
come near it —Miguel de Cervantes

Beauty is a fading flower —The Holy Bible/Isaiah

Beauty is like an almanac; if it lasts a year, it is
well —Thomas Adam

Beauty is like summer fruits which are easy to
corrupt and cannot last —Francis Bacon

*Transposed for modern style from "beauty is as
summer fruits."*

Beauty … is like the morning dew —Samuel
Daniel

Beauty is like the surf that never ceases
—Struthers Burt

Beauty is the virtue of the body, as virtue is the
beauty of the soul —Ralph Waldo Emerson

Beauty, like supreme dominion is best supported
by opinion —Jonathan Swift

Beauty, like truth and justice, lives within us
—George Bancroft

Beauty, like wit, to judges should be shown
—Lord Lyttleton

The beauty of a lovely woman is like music
—George Eliot

Beauty passes like a breath —Alfred, Lord Tennyson

Beauty vanishes like vapor —Harriet Prescott
Spofford

Beauty without grace is the hook without the bait
—Ralph Waldo Emerson

Beauty without modesty is like a flower broken from its stem —Anon

Beauty without virtue is a rose without fragrance —German and Danish proverbs

Glorious beauty is like a fading flower —The Holy Bible/Isaiah

Women's beauty, like men's wit, is generally fatal to the owners —Lord Chesterfield

Had Chesterfield lived to become attuned to non-sexist language he might have eliminated the gender references as follows: "Beauty, like wit, is generally fatal to the owners."

❧ BEGINNINGS AND ENDINGS

See Also: BIRTH, ENTRANCES AND EXITS

Breaking off with a hard dry finality, like a human relationship —Lawrence Durrell

[A distressing event] Came like a door banging on to a silent room —Hugh Walpole

Comes and goes like a cyclone —Marianne Hauser

Comes and goes like a fever —George Garrett

(My urge to gamble) comes and goes like hot flashes —Tallulah Bankhead

Come to a final end like a step climbed or a text memorized —John Cheever

[The ecstasies and tears of youth] Die like the winds that blew the clouds from overhead —Noel Coward, lyrics for "Light Is the Heart"

Ebbing then flowing in again, like mud tides around a mollusk —Julia O'Faolain

Finished, like the flipped page of a book (this day was finished …) —Isaac Bashevis Singer

The first springs of great events, like those of great rivers, are often mean and little —Jonathan Swift

It was over, gone like a furious gust of black wind —William Faulkner

Leaving [a place to which one has become accustomed] is like tearing off skin —Larry McMurtry

Like a horse breaking from the gate, my life had begun —Scott Spencer

Like some low and mournful spell, we whisper that sad word, "farewell" —Park Benjamin

Parted [husband and wife] as an arrow from the bowstring —Amy Lowell

Parting is inevitably painful … like an amputation —Anne Morrow Lindbergh

(You and that money are going to be) separated like yolks and whites —Saul Bellow

Spent is my passion like a river dried up by the sun's fierce rays —W. Somerset Maugham

Things [like, popularity] come and go, like the business cycle —William Brammer

❧ BEHAVIOR

See Also: ACTION, LIFE, MANKIND, PROPRIETY/IMPROPRIETY

Accepted the crisp bills with a certain famished delicacy, like an aristocrat determined not to slaver at the sight of food —John Farris

Accumulated [information] like a nest-building bird —Louis Auchincloss

Act badly … like a man hitting a woman in the breast —G.B. Shaw

Acted bored but patient, as though an enthusiastic acquaintance had just shown him the picture of a new grandchild —Joel Swerdlow

Allowed himself to be absorbed (into the softly palpitating life about him,) like a tired traveler sinking, at his journey's end, into a warm bath —Edith Wharton

As touchy as cabaret performers and as stubborn as factory machinists —Justin Cartwright, *To Heaven by Water*

Ate like Satan, and worked like a gnat —A. E. Coppard

Attention-getting behavior … like I was screaming at the universe [to fulfill my ambitions] —Mel Brook, *Playboy*, April, 1973

Battled failure like the seven plagues —Anon

Behave ... like a sort of love-crazed sparrow —Roald Dahl

Behavior is a mirror in which every one shows his image —Johann Wolfgang von Goethe

Bluster like the north wind —Mrs. Centlivre

Butters it [the truth] over like a slice of bread —Erich Maria Remarque

In his novel, All Quiet on the Western Front, *Remarque uses the simile to explain that man is "Essentially a beast" but covers up this truth "With a little decorum."*

(All he was doing was) calling attention to himself, rather like those movie stars who go around wearing dark glasses on cloudy days —Loren D. Estleman

Carrying on like a revivalist facing a full tent —Robert Traver

Charm was put forward like a piece of acting in a theatre —Hugh Walpole

Clutched at her throat like one stifled for want of air —Anzia Yezierska

Crawl into (his secret life) and nestled there, like the worm in the rose —Mary McCarthy

Dangled herself [before men] ... like a drum majorette —Margaret Millar

Deny like a piano player in a bordello who claimed he didn't know what went on upstairs —Ed McBain

Flinched as if someone had thrown a baseball directly at his face —Graham Masterton

Flinched back like a box turtle into its shell —F. van Wyck Mason

Flirtatious as a Southern belle —Alice McDermott

For the promise of favor he will kneel down and lick boots like a spaniel —George Garrett

Glancing around him like a hunting dog nosing for a spoor —Kenzaburo Oe

Go forward like a stoic Roman —Edwin Arlington Robinson

Gripped life like a wrestler with a bull, impetuously —Stephen Vincent Benét

He had a way of ... suddenly pouncing on something [someone says] that interested him, like a heron spearing a fish —Antonia White

Her not doing it was like the Baskerville hound that didn't bark —William Dieter

In public, they act like flat-chested old maids preaching temperance —Charles Simic

Intruded upon my vision like a truck on an empty road —Mary Gordon

I talk half the time to find out my own thoughts, as a schoolboy turns his pockets inside out to see what is in them —Oliver Wendell Holmes

Jerked at the [fishing] net like a penitent —T. Coraghessan Boyle

Like a nun withdrawing, or a child exploring a tower, she went upstairs —Virginia Woolf

Lived and behaved like that sandpiper [in my poem] ... just running along the edges of different countries, looking for something —Elizabeth Bishop, acceptance speech at University of Oklahoma, 1976 on receiving an Books Abroad/Neustadt International Prize for Literature

Looked round ... desperately like someone trying to find a way of crossing a muddy path without getting her shoes soiled —Franz Werfel

Lurking like a funeral director at a christening —W. P. Kinsella

Many talk like philosophers, and live like fools —H. G. Bohn's *Hand-Book of Proverbs*

Men's behavior should be like their apparel, not too straight ... but free for exercise or motion —Francis Bacon

Nodded judiciously like someone making a mental note —Lynne Sharon Schwartz

Pedestrians in the East behave like lemmings rushing dispassionately to their deaths —W. P. Kinsella

People loll upon the beaches ripening like gaudy peaches —Ogden Nash

Play with ... like a clever cat with a rubber mouse —Maureen Howard

(She) poured out feelings and thoughts that most people keep to themselves like a prodigal flinging gold pieces to a scrambling crowd —W. Somerset Maugham

Pushed me across [stage] like a broom —Edith Pearlman

Pull rank like a little red wagon (if it'd get her a place in the shade) —Tom Robbins

(Mary) pulled nerves like string in a blanket —Louise Erdrich

Pushing and jostling like a stormy sea —Stephen Vincent Benét

Raving, but soundlessly ... so that she looked like a film of herself without a sound-track —Lawrence Durrell

Recoiled ... like a man walking in his sleep, awakened from a frightful dream —Charles Dickens

Rose like a trout to the fly or a pickerel to the spoon —Mary McCarthy

The simile as used in the short story, "Yellowstone Park," describes a character who's an easy prey for any appeal for money to be spent for educational purposes.

(A day after helping the Giants to their victory over the Raiders in Los Angeles, Lionel Manuel, the third-year wide receiver) sauntered through the locker room like an explorer just back from a glorious expedition —William R. Rhoden, *New York Times*, September 23, 1986

(She sat in bed,) sharpening her charms and her riddles like colored pencils —Yehuda Amichai

She went toward the sitting room seeking him like a cold animal seeking the fire —Margaret Mitchell

Shook himself like an angry little dog coming out of the water —Barbara Pym

Shrugged their shoulders as if to shake off whatever chips of responsibility might have lodged there —Helen Hudson

Spoke like a fool, and acted like a fiddler —Saul Bellow

Stuffed his own emptiness with good work like a glutton —Flannery O'Connor

Swallowed his temper but it left a sour taste in his stomach like heartburn —Donald McCaig

Swallowing hard like a stiff-necked goose —Paige Mitchell

Talk like a saint and behave like a fool —Jerome K. Jerome

Talks like a prophet and acts like a comedian —Amos Oz

Thought and action ... were simultaneous in her, rather like thunder and lightning —Leigh Allison Wilson

Took them [spectacles] off, polished the lenses, and held them to the light like a spinster checking her crystal —Donald MacKenzie

Were MacKenzie writing the novel from which this is culled, Postscript to a Dead Letter, *he might well use a new bride or a proud homeowner instead of spinster, which has fallen into disfavor.*

Toys with ... as with a yo-yo —Benjamin Netanyahu, Israeli representative to the United Nations, *New York Times*, November 23, 1986

This simile was used in connection with an article on Syrian terrorism. Typically, the simile was highlighted as a blurb!

Treat us like mushroom ... keep us in the dark and throw shit at us —Loren D. Estleman

Used tranquilizing drugs ... like the inhabitants of besieged medieval cities who, surprised by death, went back to bed, trying to fall asleep by telling themselves that the threatening flames were only a nightmare —Marguerite Yourcenar

Using a ... flippant tone, as if he were talking about people in a play, or watching the ceiling at the dentist's —Ross Macdonald

Wore abuse like widow's weeds —Lael Wertenbaker (*Unbidden Guests*, 1970)

BELIEFS

See Also: GOVERNMENT, POLITICS, RELIGION

Belief is as necessary to the soul as pleasures are necessary to the body —Elsa Schiaparelli

Belief, light as a drum rattle, touches us —A. R. Ammons

Communism is like Prohibition, it's a good idea but it won't work —Will Rogers

Conservatives, like embalmers, would keep intact the forms from which the vital principle has fled —John Lancaster Spalding

Convictions ... the deeper you went the filmier the convictions got, until they were like an underwater picture, shifting, dreamy, out of focus —Wilfrid Sheed

Fascism would sprout to life like a flower through a coffin's cracks, watered by the excreta of the dead —Dylan Thomas

Faith is like a lily lifted high and white —Christina Georgina Rossetti

Faith, like a jackal, feeds among the tombs, and even from these dead doubts she gathers her most vital hope —Herman Melville

Faith ... stronger than a bank vault —Jimmy Breslin

His religious ethics fell like drowned fences —Graham Masterson

Ideals are like comets, revisit the earth periodically after long cycles of years —always excepting the enormous ideas that so many sublime donkeys envision of themselves —*Punch*, 1850

Ideals are like the stars: we never reach them, but like the mariners of the sea, we chart our course by them —Carl Schurz speech, Faneuil Hall, Boston, April 18, 1859

(He was fast in the clutches of his theory.) It seemed to guide him like some superior being seated at the helm of his intelligence —Edith Wharton

(Fanatics are a pain.) It's like talking to a rock trying to talk to a fanatic —Robert Campbell

Living up to ideals is like doing every day work with your Sunday clothes on —Ed Howe

Love of country is like love of woman ... he loves her best who seeks to bestow on her the highest good —Felix Adler

A man's ideal, like his horizon, is constantly receding from him as he advances toward it —W. G. T. Shedd

(Like many another big boss,) nationalism is largely bogus ... like a bunch of flowers made out of plastics —J. B. Priestly

One by one, like leaves from a tree all my faiths have forsaken me —Sara Teasdale

Our dogmas have been greatly enlarged to make them fit in with all sorts of necessities, so that they are like a patched coat, well-worn, and comfortable to wear. Our religion is as variegated as a Harlequin's dress —Anatole France

Patriotism is a kind of religion: it is the egg from which wars are hatched —Guy de Maupassant

Patriotism is as fierce as a fever, pitiless as the grave, blind as a stone and irrational as a headless man —Ambrose Bierce

(I think) patriotism is like charity —it begins at home —Henry James

Principles are like mountains; they rise very near heaven, but when they stand in our way, we drive a tunnel through them —Cardinal Rampolla

Skepticism [in preference to superstition] ... it seems to be like a choice between lunacy and idiocy, death by fire or by water —Henry

James, letter to Thomas Sergeant Perry, November 1, 1863

The theory towered up ... like some high landmark by which travelers shape their course —Edith Wharton

We naturally lose illusions as we get older, like teeth —Sydney Smith

When a man takes an oath, Meg, he's holding his own self in his own hands. Like water. And if he opens his fingers then, he needn't hope to find himself again. —Sir Thomas More in *A Man for All Seasons,* in response to his daughter's pleas to compromise his ideals and save his life.

A wise conviction is like light —Sir Arthur Helps

❧ BELIEVABILITY

As full of shit as a Christmas goose —American colloquialism

Believable as a declaration of eternal love from a call girl —Elyse Sommer

Believable as a forced confession —Anon

Believable as the testimony of a proven perjurer —Anon

Giving up credibility in a free society is like giving up force in a totalitarian society —Mario M. Cuomo, commenting on President's Special Review Board findings on the Reagan Administration's involvement in Iran-Contra affair, *New York Times,* March 1, 1987

It's [my growing cold towards him] unbelievable ... as if I had suddenly waked and found this lake dried up and sunk in the ground —Anton Chekhov

The comparison from Chekhov's play The Sea Gull *refers the relationship between two of the characters, Nina and Trepleff.*

Like a man who dreams he sees a friend run on him sword in hand, felt not pain so much as a wild incredulity —Dorothy Canfield

Shadowy and plausible as a ghost —W. D. Snodgrass

Some circumstantial evidence is very strong, as when you find a trout in milk —Henry David Thoreau

That this feeble, unintelligent old man was possessed of such power ... seemed as impossible to believe as that he had once been a pink-and white baby —F. Scott Fitzgerald

To tell a soldier defending his country that this is The War That Will End War is exactly like telling a workman, naturally rather reluctant to do his day's work, that this is The Work That Will End Work —G. K. Chesterton

Unimaginable as hate in heaven —John Milton

The word 'heaven' has been modernized from 'heav'n' as it appeared in Paradise Lost.

Unthinkable as an honest burglar —H. L. Mencken

The whole idea was fantastic, like a polar bear in the Sahara desert —Ken Follett

❧ BELONGING

As much at home ... as a fish in water —Honoré de Balzac

An enduring comparison, as illustrated by a 1986 quote from the New York Times: *"We belong ... like fish in water. We're in our environment."*

As much out of his element as an eel in a sandbag —H. G. Bohn's *Hand-Book of Proverbs*

As well adapted to the purpose as a one-pronged fork for pitching hay —Herman Melville

(She had) clicked into place [as teacher in school] like a well-hung door closing evenly —Barry Targan

Felt as well placed in the world as a fresh loaf of bread —Laurie Colwin

Fit [poor fit] like a breeching on a pig —Anon

Fit like a duck's foot in the mud —Anon

Fit ... like a tongue into a groove —Jonathan Valin in the novel *Life's Work,* the simile refers to the way a man's body fits into a chair.

Fits as a hollow fits a circle —Anon

Fits him as easily as his skin —Thomas Hughes

Fits like the skin on a sausage —Anon

Fitted (into their scheme of life) as a well-made reel fits the butt of a good rod —Henry Van Dyke

Fitted in like a Marine in a parade —William Beechcroft

Fitted (its new home) like a coin in a slot —George Garrett

Fitting comfortable and heavy like a gun in a holster —George Garrett

I belonged in Idle Valley like a pearl onion on a banana split —Raymond Chandler, *The Long Goodbye*

Like a barber's chair, fit for everyone —Thomas Fuller

Like Miniver Cheevy, he had been born too late —Joseph Heller

Looking as lost as a shipwrecked mariner —Yisrael Zarchi

[Feel] misplaced … as if she had been expelled from a dream which she would have dearly loved to remain —Milan Hundera

Part of the landscape, like a tree —John Updike

Salander fitted into this picture about as well as a buffalo at a boat show —Stieg Larsson, *The Girl with the Dragon Tattoo*

Swam as happily in society as a fish swam in schools —Susan Fromberg Schaeffer

❧ BENDING/BENT

As crooked as a corkscrew —George Kaufman and Moss Heart

As crooked as a dog's elbow —F.T. Elworthy

As crooked as a ram's horn —Charles Caleb Colton

Bending from the waist as if he was going to close up like a jackknife —John Dos Passos

Bend like a finger joint —Charles Wright

Bend like sheets of tin —Palmer Cox

Bends with her laugh … like a rubber stick being shaken —Alice McDermott

Bent as a country lane —John Wainwright

Bent double like a tree in a high wind —Caryl Phillips

Bent down like violets after rain —Thomas Bailey Aldrich

Bent like a birch ice-laden —James Agee

Bent like a bow —Aharon Megged

> *A variation on the bent bow image from William McIlvanney's novel,* Laidlow: *"Arching his body like a bow."*

Bent like a broken flower —Algernon Charles Swinburne

Bent like a rainbow —Robert Southey

> *Another way to express this image is to be "Bent like a rainbow arch."*

Bent … like a soldier at the approach of an assault —Victor Hugo

Bent like a wishbone —William Kennedy

Bent slightly like a man who has been shot but continues to stand —Flannery O'Connor

(The headwaiter) bowed like a poppy in the breeze —Ogden Nash

Bows down like a willow tree in a storm —Erich Maria Remarque

Coiled like a fetus —William H. Gass

> *A variation by Derek Lambert: "Curled up like a bulky fetus."*

Coiled up like the letter "s" —Damon Runyon

Crooked like a comma —Sharon Sheehe Stark

Curled himself like a comma into the waiting cab —William H. Hallhan

Curled like a ball —Sterling Hayden

Curled up in a ball like a wet puppy —Amos Oz

Curled up [in sleeping position] like a fist around an egg —Leonard Michaels

Curled up like a gun-dog —Colette

(Bent over your books) curled up like a porcupine with a bellyache —Marge Piercy

Curled up like fried bacon —Anon

Curling up like a small animal —Nina Bawden

Curling up like burning cardboard —Lawrence Durrell

[A cat] Curls up like a dormer mouse —Jayne Anne Phillips

Drooped like a flower in the frost —John Greenleaf Whittier

Folded over like a ruler from the waist —William Gass

Folded up, like a marionette with cheap wooden hinges, and sat down —Graham Masterton

(Never will I be) gibbous like the moon —Diane Ackerman

Lean forward like firemen pulling a hose —Miller Williams

Tilting like a paper cutout —Susan Minot

Twisted as an old paint tube —Fannie Hurst

A very old lady, her back curved over like a snail's —Daphne Merkin

❧ BENEFITS
See: ADVANTAGEOUSNESS

❧ BEREAVEMENT
See: GREIF, SADNESS

❧ BEWILDERMENT
See Also: EMOTIONS, STRANGENESS

As confounding as the groom who drives into a stop sign on the way to his wedding —Amy Hempel

As puzzling as a page in an unknown language —Henry James
  In James' story, The Pupil, *the personality of one of the characters serves as a frame of reference for the comparison.*

Bewildering like a fruitless spring —Jean Garrigue

Confounded utterly, like an orphan in solitary confinement —Jean Stafford

Confused, like a mourner who has wandered into the wrong funeral parlor —James Crumley

He's as mixed up as the twentieth century —Clifford Odets

Inexplicable as the birth of a star —Stephen Vincent Benét

It [Speaking candidly] muddled her like wine, or like a first breath of freedom —Kate Chopin

Mysterious as the sea —Robert Traver

So confused he's like a hypnotized rabbit —Derek Lambert

Wrinkled his long nose uncertainly, like a hound robbed of the scent by heavy rain —Donald Seaman

❧ BIBLE
See: BOOKS

❧ BICYCLING
See: SPORTS

❧ BIGNESS
See Also: FATNESS, PHYSICAL APPEARANCE, TALLNESS

Ample as a fat man's waistline —Anon

As large as life —Maria Edgeworth

As large as life and twice as natural —Anon
  While this is most commonly attributed to Lewis Carroll, who used it in Through the Looking Glass *in 1873,* Stevenson's Proverbs, Maxims and Famous Phrases *includes an earlier (though likely not the earliest) source, Cuthbert Bede's 1853 work,* Verdant Green.

Big as a braggart's mouth —Anon

Big as a den bear —Richard Ford

Big as a draft animal —William Brammer

Big as all out of doors —Anon

[A man] big as an express train —T. Coraghessan Boyle

(Bombers) big as bowling alleys —Marge Piercy

A big man, filling the chair like a great mound of wheat —H.R.F. Keating

Great as man's ambition —Dame Edith Sitwell

Huge as a planet —Lord Byron

Huge as mountains —Walter Savage Landor

Immense as whales —Sir William Davenant

Large as a log of maple —Refrain from "Yankee Doodle," early American folk song

(My disappointment) large as capsized tugs —Richard Eberhart

A large business organization is like a damn big dragon. You kick it in the tail, and two years later, it feels it in the head —Frederick Kappell, *Look*, August 28, 1962

Kappell, chairman of American Telephone and Telegraph, began his comparison with "the Bell System is ... " instead of the more general phrase used here.

A list big as a comedian's gag file —Anon

Over-sized like a clown's shoes —Anon

She's big as a damned barn and tough as knife metal —Ken Kesey

She was big as three women —Ernest Hemingway

Vast a water —Madeleine L'Engle

Vast like the inside of a Pharaoh's tomb —Arthur A. Cohen. Taken from Cohen's novel *In the Days of Simon Stern*, the comparison describes New York's Madison Square Garden.

♣ BIGOTRY
See: INTOLERANCE

♣ BIOGRAPHY
See: BOOKS, WRITERS/WRITING

♣ BIRDS
See Also: ANIMALS, INSECTS, SINGING

Bird, its little black feet tucked under its belly like miniature bombs —Peter Meinke

Birds afloat, like a scarf —Babette Deutsch

Birds ... bobbed like clothespins on the telephone line —Elizabeth Savage

Birds ... circling like black leaves —Hugh Walpole

Birds flew up like black gloves jerked from a line —Paul Theroux

Birds ... gliding like pieces of dark paper abandoned suddenly by an erratic wind —John Rechy

Bird, shaped like the insides of a yawning mouth —Charles Simic

Birds in flight, fluid as music on a page —Anne Morrow Lindberg

Birds ... like planes stacked up over the airport, circling until they get a permission-to-land signal —Italo Calvino

Bird songs rang in the air like dropped coins —George Garrett

Birds rose into the air like blown leaves (at his approach) —Margaret Millar

The birds sang as if every sparkling drop were a fountain of inspiration to them —Charles Dickens

Birds ... they roll like a drunken fingerprint across the sky —Richard Wilbur

(Birds) twitter louder than a flute —Phyllis McGinley

Birds ... white as scraps of paper —Willa Cather

Crows whirled lazily in the sky like flakes of black ash rising from a fire —Guy Vanderhaeghe

A dove ... glistening like a pearl —Hans Christian Andersen

The eagles were reveling in the air like bank robbers who had broken into the vault —Edward Hoagland

A flight of egrets … flying low, and scattered … like a ripple of white notes, sweet and pure and springlike, which an unseen hand drew forth, like a divine arpeggio, from an unseen harp —W. Somerset Maugham

A flock of white swans flew like a long white veil over the water —Hans Christian Andersen

The fluttering, honking formation of birds was like a ship borne by the wind into the high invisible distance —Bernard Malamud

Geese … blackening the sky like a shake of pepper —Diane Ackerman

Gulls cry like hurt children —George Garrett

Gulls … settling and stirring like blown paper —Sylvia Plath

A handful of thrushes set down in an oak tree, like a flurry of leaves —Linda Bierds

This simile marks the closing of Bierds' poem "Mid-Plains Tornado."

(The great) hawk circling like a black planet —Ellen Gilchrist

Hens … like dowager women, plump and impeccably arrayed in brown and grey —Rolf Yngve

His wings [Jonathan Livingston Seagull's] were smooth and perfect as sheets of polished silver —Richard Bach

Hummingbird … with a beak that looked as long as a darning needle and about as sharp —A. E. Maxwell

A jaybird … flying in a feathered flash of blue and white like a swift piece of the sky —George Garrett

The parrots shriek as if they were on fire —Ted Hughes

In a poem entitled "The Jaguar," the parrots not only shriek but "strut like cheap tarts to attract the stroller with the nut."

The pigeons lolloped from illusory pediment to window-ledge like volatile, feathered madmen, chattering vile rhymes and laughing in hoarse, throaty voices —Angela Carter

Pigeons … settled into trees that shone with them like soft blue and gray fruit —Marge Piercy

Pigeons … with spreading wings like falling snow —Émile Zola

Soared high above the other birds, climbing like a dart —R.Wright Campbell

A solid line of pelicans flew … in graceful unison like a crew of oarsman in a racing shell —George Garrett

Sparrows scatter like handfuls of gravel —William H. Gass

Storks and pelicans flew in a line like waving ribbons —Hans Christian Andersen

Swans floated about like white lanterns —Lawrence Durrell

Swans go by like a snowy procession of Popes —George Garrett

Terns rise like seafoam from the breaking surf —Robert Hass

White gulls … in such close formation they were like a cloud —Phyllis Roberts

❧ BIRTH

See Also: BEGINNINGS AND ENDINGS, DEATH, ENTRANCES AND EXITS, LIFE

Birth and death are like two ships in a harbor. There is no reason to rejoice at the ship setting out on a journey [birth], not knowing what she may encounter on the high seas, but we should rejoice at the ship returning to port [death] safely —Amora Levi

Into the world we come like ships launch'd from the docks, and stocks, and slips, for fortune fair or fatal! —Edward Fitzgerald

Once upon a time we were all born, popped out like jelly rolls —Anne Sexton

Passed like an envelope through a letter box [about an easy birth] –Anais Nin

The solemnity of birth, like that of death, is lost in repulsive or merely commonplace details for those who are in attendance —Marguerite Yourcenar

♣ BITTERNESS

See Also: ANGER, FRIENDSHIP, LOVE

Bitter and sharp as a pulled leek with earth still clinging to it —George Garrett

Bitter as a broken friendship –Anon

Bitter as acorns —Ann Tyler

Bitter as a day of mourning —Joseph Conrad

(My youth was) bitter as a hard green fruit —Marilyn Hacker

Bitter as alum —Reynolds Price

(The air was) bitter as a stiffed hooker —Loren D. Estleman

Bitter as a tear —Algernon Charles Swinburne

Bitter as blood —Algernon Charles Swinburne

Bitter as coffee that's set too long —Rebecca Rule
   A variation: "bitter as warmed up coffee."

(His voice was) bitter as dregs —Stephen Crane

Bitter as gall —John Webster

Bitter as self-sacrifice —Elizabeth Barrett Browning

Bitter as soot —Laurence Sterne

Bitter as the breaking down of love —Algernon Charles Swinburne

Bitter to me as death —William Shakespeare
   Cymbeline

Bitter as wormwood —The Holy Bible/Proverbs

Bitterness … kept coming back like a taste in the mouth after eating something bad —Rachel Ingalls

Embittered in mind, as a bear robbed of her whelps —The Holy Bible/Samuel

A flood of bitterness that washes over me every seven minutes like plagues visited upon a speeded-up pharaoh —William H. Gass

♣ BLACK

See Also: COLORS; FACIAL EXPRESSIONS, SERIOUS; GLOOM

(Hair) black and gleaming as a new galosh —Loren D. Estleman

(The newel post) black and shiny as a skull —W. P. Kinsella

Black as a black poodle's nose —Babette Deutsch

Black as a baker's shovel —Isaac Bashevis Singer

[A hall] Black as a billy goat's belly —Ruth Chatterton

Black as a bull-moose in December —Henry Van Dyke

Black as a child's midnight waking —Marge Piercy

Black as a crow —Petronius
   An ancient simile that's still going strong, with "Black as a raven" from The Holy Bible the most frequently used variant

Black as a funeral procession —Diane Ackerman

[Darkening sky] Black as a giant tortoise —Stefan Zweig

Black as a heavy smoker's lungs —Elyse Sommer

Black as a manic depressive's thoughts —Elyse Sommer

(The room was) black as an honest politician's prospects —Dashiell Hammett

Black as an undertaker's hat —Donald Seaman

Black as a pine at night —Stephen Vincent Benét

(Locks) black as a raven —The Holy Bible/Song of Solomon

Black as a stack of black cats in the dark —H.W. Thompson

Black as a tar-barrel —Lewis Carroll

Black as black —W.B. Yeats

(Eyes ...) black as bottomless water —Ellen du Pois Taylor

(Eyes) black as caverns —T. Coraghessan Boyle

(Black coats were) black as coffins —Rebecca West

Black as despair —John Phillips

Black as dusk —William Styron

Black as ebony —Oscar Wilde

Black like an oven (our kin was ...) —The Holy Bible/Lamentations

Black as fate —Dame Edith Sitwell

Black as hell —William Shakespeare

> *Shakespeare, the master of so many similes, can be credited for a fair share of the best-known "black as" comparisons. Besides this one from* Hamlet, *and Sonnet/147, they include "Black as ink," "Black as ebony," and "Black as jet."*

Black as midnight without a moon —Anon

Black as murder —Thomas Dekker

Black as perjury —Anon

(Our hands were) black as potatoes dug from the ground —T. Coraghessan Boyle

As black as some charred rafter —W. D. Snodgrass

Black as sorrow —Sir Philip Sidney

Black as the ace of spades —Anon

Black as the devil's hind foot —T.C. Haliburton

Black as the devil's heart —Ariel Dorfman

Black as the head of a hanged man —F. D. Reeve

(Black holes) black as the moments before birth and after death —T. Coraghessan Boyle

Black as thunder —William Makepeace Thackeray

(Their visages) blacker than coal —The Holy Bible/Lamentation

(Deep and) black like an abyss —Aharon Megged

Black ... like a subway tunnel —William Faulkner

It [a room] was black as the inside of a cat —Davis Grubb

The sky was as black as a monsoon —Dominique Lapierre

❧ BLESSEDNESS
See: FORTUNE/MISFORTUNE

❧ BLINDNESS
See Also: EYE(S), EYE EXPRESSIONS, BLANK

Blind as a bat —Anon

> *Attribution for this enduringly popular cliché dates back to the seventeenth century and a somewhat longer old English version from John Clarke' Paromiologia: "Blind as a bat at noone." Less used variants are "Blind as a beetle" and "blind as a buzzard."*

Blind as a flame of fire —Algernon Charles Swinburne

Blind as a fool's heart —Robert Browning

Blind [about understanding love and hate] as a newborn child —Marguerite Duras

Blind as a newt —Leigh Allison Wilson

Blind as a night fog —Daniel Berrigan

Blind as a stone —Anon

> *This still commonly used expression dates back to the fourteenth century, even before Chaucer used it in* Canterbury Tales: *"Blind as is a stoon."*

(Eyes staring) blind as glass —Rose Tremain

Blind as Hell —William Habbington

Blind as ignorance —Francis Beaumont and John Fletcher

Blind as inexperience —Victor Hugo

Blind as love —Percy Bysshe Shelley

Blind as maggots —Mark Helprin

Blind as night —Beryl Markham

(Bright and) blind as the moon in the blank midmorning sky —F. D. Reeve

Blind as the waves of the sea —Eva Gore-Booth

Oblivious of … as an ant or flea might be to the sound of the avalanche on which it rides —William Faulkner

♣ BLOOD

See Also: : VIOLENCE

Bleeding like a stuck pig —Anon

Bleed, like a can of cherries —D. H. Lawrence

Blood … hot and sticky like spilled wine —Harvey Swados

Blood is like a parachute. If it's not there when you need it, you'll probably never need it again —slogan for blood donor drive, June, 1987

Blood spouting … as generously as water from a fountain —Jack London

Blood like turpentine —George Garrett

Blood spurting out of his nose holes like tomato puree —Jay Parini

Bloodthirsty as a tick —Diane Ackerman

Blood … which flows like a scream through the woods —Charles Simic

Bubbled blood like a little red spring —William Goyen

Face bloody as raw pork —Nelson Algren

[Man in hopes of improving world] scatters blood like a fish leaping from a lake —Janet Flanner

Stale, coppery smell [of blood], like the taste of pennies on the tongue —Jonathan Valin

♣ BLOOMING

See: GROWTH

♣ BLUE

See Also: COLORS

Blue and delicate as spring sky reflected in an old window —Elizabeth Spencer

(Eyes) blue as chicory in bloom —Ed McBain

(Sky …) blue as a robin's egg —Lee Smith

Blue as a brochure sea —William McIlvanney

Blue as a jay bird's wing —Ellen Glasgow

(Eyes as) Blue as a peacock's neck —Flannery O'Connor

(Sky …) blue as a staring Northern eye —Elizabeth Enright

Blue as autumn mist —Thomas Hardy

(Eyes as) blue as corn-flowers —Lawrence Durrell

(Sea and sky are a matched set) blue as delftware —T. Coraghessan Boyle

(Eyes) blue as heaven —Lord Byron Other famous poets to link heaven and the color blue include Christina Rosetti with "Sapphires shining blue as heaven" and Percy Bysshe Shelley with "Blue as the overhanging heaven." For every day usage there's "Blue as the sky."

Blue as hyacinths —Richard Ford

Blue as melancholy —Anon

(Sky) blue as the core of a match flame —George Garrett

Blue as the decks of the sea —Dame Edith Sitwell

Blue as the glimpses of sea beyond —John Greenleaf Whittier

Blue as the nose that graduate drunkards wear —Don Marquis

Blue as the sky —American colloquialism, attributed to New England

Blue as with the cold —Israel Zangwill

Blue like a corpse —Nikolai V. Gogol

Blue [of a repelling place] … like the color of the lips of an asthmatic plumber dying of lead poisoning who has put himself out of his misery with cyanide —Gerald Kersh

Blue like the last thundercloud of a tempest dispersed —Alexander Pushkin

Pale blues like old people's eyes —Edna O'Brien

Your eyes were bluer than robin's eggs —Joan Baez, "Diamonds and Rust"

❧ BLUSHES

See Also: FACIAL COLOR, RED, SHAME, SHY-NESS

Blood gushed crimson to her cheek ... as though red wine had been poured into a crystal glass —Stefan Zweig

The blood showed clearly [on his face], like wine stains a pearly glass —Elinor Wylie

Blushed like a beetroot —Anatoly Rybakof

Blushed like a brick —Samuel Hopkins Adams

Blushed like a rose —Isak Dinesen

Blushed, like a wave of illness —Nadine Gordimer

Blushes rising like the tide —Lael Wertenbaker

Blushing like a strawberry —Marcel Proust

Blushing like a tomato —E. V. Lucas

Blushing pink as dawn —George Garrett

Blush like a black dog —John Ray's *Proverbs*

Blush like a geranium —Harry Graham

A blush that felt like a gasoline fire —R. V. Cassill

Color came to his face like blood on a galled fish —Loren D. Estleman

The color flew in her face like a flag —D. H. Lawrence

A deep flush enveloped him like darkness —Heinrich Böll

A delicate flush of pink ... like the flush in the face of the bridegroom when he kissed the lips of the bride —Oscar Wilde,

(I could feel my) face flaming as red as all the tomatoes in the world —H. C. Witwer

A faint blush, like the shadow of a rose in a mirror of silver came to her cheeks —Oscar Wilde

Felt shame flooding his cheeks like a hot geyser —Mark Helprin

His face went red as a peony —Julia O'Faolain

Red as a barn —Susan Fromberg Schaeffer

Red crawling across her face like a stain —Harvey Swados

Ruddiness spreading across her cheeks like a wound —Joseph Koenig

Turned all colors —as a peacock's tail, or sunset streaming through a Gothic skylight —Lord Byron

Turned as red as a winter apple —American colloquialism

The comparison of blushing cheeks to apples is common in every day language as well as literature. An example of the latter: "Color like an apple" from Truman Capote's short story "Children on Their Birthdays."

Turned red as ... a nectarine, as a dahlia, as the most divinely red thing in the world —Colette

❧ BOATS

See: SEASCAPES

❧ BODY

See Also: AGILITY, AWKWARDNESS, BODY ORGANS, FATNESS, MUSCLES, PHYSICAL APPEARANCE, SHOULDERS, STRENGTH, STOMACH, THINNESS

(A big soft) ass as wide as an axhandle —George Garrett

Body and mind, like man and wife, do not always agree to die together —Charles Caleb Colton

Body grown light as a shell, empty as a shell —Joyce Carol Oates

The body is like a piano. It is needful to have the instrument in good order —Henry Ward Beecher

The body, lady, is like a house: it don't go anywhere; but the spirit, lady, is like a automobile: always on the move —Flannery O'Connor

Body ... light as milk —Philip Levine

Body like a block of granite —Brian Glanville

Body like a spring —Marguerite Duras

(Had a) body like a stack of lumpy pillows —Robert Campbell

Body like dry bone —Robert Silverberg

Body … long like a weasel's —Anton Chekov

Body … shaped like a sack half full of cement —Sterling Hayden

Body … silvery like a white rose —Isak Dinesen

The body turns empty as the shell of an insect, or like something inflatable but flattened —Jayne Anne Phillips

Body warm and flat as beer that's been standing —Marge Piercy

Buddha-like body still as an onyx boulder —Ralph Ellison

Build like a sack of angle irons —Loren D. Estleman

Built like a bowling pin —Clive Cussler

(She's hard to fit, being) built like a cement root cellar —Louise Erdrich

Built like a Coke machine —Joseph Wambaugh

Built like a crate —William Diehl

Built like a fire plug —Pat Conroy

Built like a greyhound —Miles Gibson

Built like a hammer —Lee K. Abbott

Built like a Russian weightlifter —William Diehl

Built like a skyscraper —Slogan, Shaw-Walker steel filing cabinets

Built like a snowman. A small round head atop a large round body with no neck in between —Rick Borsten

Built like a vault —Anon

Built like refrigerators —Jonathan Valin

Built solid, firm and square, like an unencumbered pine —Sylvia Berkman

Built square, like a van —William Beechcroft

Built with curves like the hull of a racing yacht —Ernest Hemingway

A quick simile is about as much space as a master of conciseness like Hemingway devotes to physically describing a character. The woman with the racing yacht curves is Lady Brett from The Sun Also Rises

Chest like a nail keg —Peter Matthiessen

Chest like an oak wine cask —Ira Wood

Chest like an oyster barrel —Ogden Nash

Chests and bellies like a pair of avalanches —T. Coraghessan Boyle

Chunky, heavy, like a Samoan swimmer —Herbert Gold

Corded and tough as a short piece of tallowed cable —George Foy

The simile in Foy's novel Coaster *applies to a sailor.*

Delicate and softly rounded as a painting by Boucher —F. van Wyck Mason

(Against the light of the lamp) the delicate erotic lines of her slender body came up like a photographic print in a developing tray —Brian Moore

Even her hipbones [like rest of angular body] jutted out as if her skirt was draped on a coathanger —Richard Maynard

A figure like a beer barrel —Oscar Wilde

A variation by Charles Johnson: "Broad as a beer barrel."

Figure like a sack of flour —Josephine Tey

A figure like a two-armed Venus de Milo who had been on a sensible diet —David Niven

Being an actor as well as a writer Niven probably had a special appreciation for any device which would capture audience attention the minute the curtain rises; and so this simile in the first sentence of his autobiography, The Moon's a Balloon.

Figure … so delicate that she moved like a shadow —Inez Haynes Irwin

(She had) a figure that was like a swift unexpected blow to the diaphragm —that to linger on makes the beholder feel obscene —Frederick Exley

A fine small body, like a miniature dog bred for show —Maureen Howard

(He was) flat and wide as a gingerbread man —Charles Portis

Flat-chested and straight as a board —MacDonald Harris

Graceful figure —which was as tough as hickory and as flexible as a whip —Thomas Wolfe

He placed his hands on her hips, over the stretch marks that were like inlaid streaks of mother-of-pearl that would never fade, whose brilliance spoke only for the body's decay —Jhumpa Lahiri, *Unaccustomed Earth*

Her body seemed somehow to hang on her, like somebody else's clothing —William McIlvanney

Her broad sexless body made her resemble a dilapidated Buddha —Ross Macdonald

Her firm protruding ass looked like a split peach —Steve Shagan

Hips like hills of sand —*Arabian Nights*

Hips like jugs —Eugene McNamara

His ancient, emaciated body looked as though it were already attacked by the corruption of the grave —W. Somerset Maugham

His body was covered with a dense mat of black hair. He looked like an overfed chimpanzee —Andrew Kaplan

His body waved like a flame in the breeze —television obituary describing James Cagney's physical grace, 1986

His pectorals hung flabbily, like the breasts of an old woman —Gerald Kersh

It [worn body] was as if it were charred by a thunderbolt —Honoré de Balzac

Long body, devoid of developed muscles, was like a long, limp sash —Yukio Mishima

Look like a hot-air balloon with insufficient ballast —Anna Quindlen, *New York Times*, March 27, 1986

The cause for the hot-air balloon appearance is pregnancy.

(A man with) a middle like a flour bag —Sharon Sheehe Stark

(Kaplan was examining the) midriff bulge that ballooned out over his belt like an inflated inner tube —William P. Kennedy

The simile marks the opening of Kennedy's espionage novel The Masakado Lesson.

(Was halfway through the process of turning from muscular to fat, so that at present he was) of uncertain consistency, like a cheap mattress —Richard Francis

Round and curved as a marble statue —George Garrett

A small boned body as easy to fragment as a young grouse's —Penelope Gilliatt

A small, plump woman, with her waist cinctured in sternly, like a cushion with a noose around it —John Cheever

Spine … like an iron rod —Angela Carter

Square as a wooden block —T. Coraghessan Boyle

Square like a block of stone —Willis Johnson

(She no longer had her slim waist or rounded bosom but was) square like a stack of firewood —Isak Dinesen

(A massive woman …) square, rather like a great piece of oak furniture —Willa Cather

Still had an athlete's frame … but the flesh had sagged on the hanger, like an old suit with change left in the pockets —Jonathan Valin

Straight as a mast, muscled like a gorilla —Maxwell Anderson and Laurence Stallings

A strong, supple body, like a tigress —Anthony Powell

Torso … thick and circular, like the bole of a tree —Madison Smartt Bell

(His body looked soft, his) waist puffing out like rising bread dough —Sue Grafton

We are bound to our bodies like an oyster to its shell —Plato

Weight was … beginning to hang like slightly inferior clothing —William McIlvanney

(Jill Martin was what they call a healthy lady.) Well rounded, like something out of Rubens —Mike Fredman

(He was) wide as a door —Andre Dubus

♣ BODY ORGANS

See Also: SEX, TONGUE

A liver [from excessive drinking] like an old boot —J. B. Priestly

Penises as flaccid as ruined breasts —James Crumley

Penis … like a hard, live bedpost —Alice Walker

Penis like an upraised club —John Farris

Prostate like an Idaho potato —dialogue spoken by Marlon Brando in *The Last Tango in Paris*, 1972

Prostate … as round and elastic as a handball —Walker Percy The prostate comparison is made by the doctor-narrator of Percy's *Love In the Ruins* about an old male patient.

♣ BOISTEROUSNESS

See: NOISE

♣ BOLDNESS

See: COURAGE

♣ BONDS

See: CONNECTIONS

♣ BOOKS

See Also: READERS/READING

All the juice of a book is in an unpublished manuscript, and the published book is like a dead tree —just good for cutting up and building your house with —Christina Stead

Bad books are like intoxicating drinks; they furnish neither nourishment, nor medicine —Tryon Edwards

The *Bible* among books is as a diamond among precious stones —John Stoughton

A book is a friend whose face is constantly changing —Andrew Lang

A book is a mirror: if an ass peers into it, you can't expect an apostle to look out —Georg Christoph Lichtenberg

A book is like a garden carried in the pocket —Arab proverb

A book, like a child, needs time to be born —Heinrich Heine

A book, like a grape-vine, should have good fruit among its leaves —Edward Parsons Day

A book, like a landscape, is a state of consciousness varying with readers —Ernest Dimnet

A book may be as great a thing as a battle —Benjamin Disraeli

Books are like individuals; you know at once if they are going to create a sense within the sense … or if they will merely leave you indifferent —George Moore

Books … arranged carefully according to size, like schoolchildren lined up for recess —Helen Hudson

Books, like friends, should be few and well chosen —Thomas Fuller

Books, like men their authors, have no more than one way of coming into the world, but there are ten thousand to go out of it and return no more —Jonathan Swift

Books like proverbs receive their value from the stamp and esteem of ages through which they have passed —Sir William Temple

Books … as little read as tombstones —Frank Swinnerton

The [thick] book was just like a warm, thick eiderdown that she could pull over herself, snuggle into —Alice Munro

A book without an index is as incomplete as an eunuch —Theodore Stanton

A classic … is a successful book that has survived the reaction of the next period or generation. Then it's safe, like a style in architecture or furniture —F. Scott Fitzgerald

Dictionaries are like watches: the worst is better than none, and the best cannot be expected to go quite true —Samuel Johnson

Disliking a classic like disliking a nation one visits, it's the result of a blind spot, which goes away and leaves one embarrassed —Edward Hoagland

Each new book is as a ship that bears us away from the fixity of our limitations into the movement and splendor of life's infinite ocean —Helen Keller

Every book is like a purge, at the end of it one is empty … like a dry shell on the beach, waiting for the tide to come in again —Daphne Du Maurier, *Ladies Home Journal*, November, 1956

The harmonies of bound books are like the flowers of the field —Hilaire Belloc

It is with books as with new acquaintances. At first we are highly delighted, if we find a general agreement … with closer acquaintances differences come to light; and then reasonable conduct mainly consists in not shrinking back at once —Johann Wolfgang von Goethe

It is with books as with men: a very small number play a great part —Voltaire

Like the fortune teller who sees a long journey in the cards or death by water, they [books] influence the future —Graham Greene

Most books, like their authors are born to die —Joshua Swartz

A new book, like a young man, has a reputation to acquire —Clarence Walworth

A new book … not one of a number of similar objects, but like an individual man, unmatched —Marcel Proust

Novels are useful as bibles, if they teach you the secret that the best of life is conversation and the greatest success is confidence —Ralph Waldo Emerson

An old book, like an old man, is bound to have a good character already established, and must expect to be looked upon with suspicion if it has not —Clarence Walworth

The reading of good books is like a conversation with the finest men of past centuries —René Descartes

A room without books is like a body without a soul —Cicero

A twist to this, variously attributed to Hanna More and Henry Ward Beecher, is "A house without books is like a room without windows."

Such books are like frowzy old broads who have been handled by a thousand men —Peter De Vries

The books being compared to frowzy old broads are telephone directories in phone booths.

There is no frigate like a book —Emily Dickinson

Dickinson's simile serves as both title and first line for one of her best-known poems

Volumes [of books produced in America] by the dozens like doughnuts, big and soft and empty at the core —Helen Hudson

♣ BOREDOM/BORING

See Also: DULLNESS, LIFE

Bored as Greta Garbo —Alice McDermott

Boredom enveloped her like heavy bedding —Yukio Mishima

Boredom … like a cancer in the breast —Evelyn Waugh

Boredom, like hookworm, is endemic —Beryl Markham

Boredom wafted from her like the scent of stale sweat —Anon

Boredom was increasing ... like a silent animal sadly rubbing itself against the sultry grass —Yukio Mishima

Bore me the same as watching an industrial training film, or hearing a lecture on the physics of the three-point stance —Richard Ford

Boring as airline food —Anon

Boring as going to the toilet —Sylvia Plath

Boring, like reading the *Life Cycle of the Hummingbird* —Dan Wakefield

Could feel his boredom like an actual presence, like a big German shepherd that must be fed and restrained —Marge Piercy

Life is as tedious as a twice-told tale —William Shakespeare, *King John*

> *This famous simile also appeared in Homer's* Odyssey *the format of a question, "What's so tedious as a twice-told tale?"*

She felt her brain begin to soften like something forgotten at the back of the fridge. —David Nicholls, *One Day*

Yawns [caused by a dull discussion] inflated in his throat like balloons —Derek Lambert

❧ BOUNCING
See: ROCKING AND ROLLING

❧ BOUNDLESSNESS
See: CONTININUITY

❧ BOXING AND WRESTLING
See Also: SPORTS

A boxing match is like a cowboy movie. There's got to be good guys and there's got to be bad guys. What people pay for is to see the bad guys get beat —Sonny Liston, quoted from his obituary, *New York Times*

Fell on his face, kicking and heaving like a wounded leopard —Gerald Kersh

Fired himself across the ring like a stone from a catapult —Gerald Kersh

Got up the third time with blood like a livid splash of ripe fruit all over his face —H. E. Bates

He (Joe Louis) punches like he had a baseball bat in his both hands —Irwin Shaw

Louis —his nostrils like the mouth of a double-barreled shotgun took a quiet lead and let him have both barrels —Bob Considine, International News Service report on Louis-Schmeling fight, June 22, 1938

(Sharkey) kept coming in like the surf —Anon comment about the 1899 Jeffries-Sharkey fight

Their long, stiff jabs made their gloves dip and seem heavy, like big red balloons —Richard Ford

They clung together, spinning round and round like two twigs in a whirlpool —Gerald Kersh

Went down like a letter in a mail chute —Anon

When he (Jake La Motta) was in the ring, it was like he was in a cage fighting for his life —Ray Arcel, boxing trainer, quoted in Ira Berkow's Sports of the Times column, *New York Times*

Wrestled together, interlaced like snakes —Honoré de Balzac

❧ BRAIN
See: INTELLIGENCE, MIND

❧ BRAVERY
See: COURAGE

❧ BREASTS
See Also: BODY, BODY ORGANS

Bosom like a Spanish balcony —Colette

Bosom like the prow of a ship —M. J. Farrell

Bosoms ... large, like mounds of earth on the banks of a dug-up canal —R. K. Narayan

Bosoms like cheese-wheels —David Huddle

Bosoms like vast, half-filled hot-water bottles —M. J. Farrell

Bosoms set like two great prows of battleships —Brian Donleavy

Breasts as large and round as a bald man's head —James Crumley

Breasts hard as stone, project like a bulwark —Erich Maria Remarque

A breast divided into segments like a peeled orange, or a pair of thighs that converge into a single swollen knee —Kingsley Amis

Breasts heaving like a flight deck —Rita Mae Brown

Breasts … hung like water-filled balloons from her chest —Bernard Malamud

Breasts lie flat on her ribs like soft purses —Rose Tremain

Breasts, like a nursing mother's —Katherine Anne Porter

Breasts like a pair of piggies —Vladimir Nabokov

Breasts like armaments —T. Coraghessan Boyle

Breasts … like bread loaves hot from the oven —Francine du Plessix Gray

Breasts like … clusters of the vine —The Holy Bible/Song of Solomon

Breasts … like dried apples —Annette Sanford

Breasts like dunes —John D. MacDonald

Breasts … like empty purses except when they filled briefly and fed another child —H. E. Bates

Breasts like giant cabbages —W. Somerset Maugham

Breasts like overripe squash —Patricia Henley

Breasts like pennants —Irwin Shaw

Breasts like small hard apples —Francine du Plessix Gray

Breasts like smooth and ivory-colored hills —Marguerite Young

Breasts … sag from her chest like two plump gourds —Susan Yankowitz

Breasts sagging like overripe fruit —George Garrett

Breasts … shaped like crescent moons —Ira Wood

Breasts swaying like party balloons —Jilly Cooper

Breasts swelling … like rising bread —Marge Piercy

Breasts that drop, big as barrels —Dylan Thomas

Breasts were like long white grapes in the hot sun —D. H. Lawrence

Breasts, which were like apples cut in half —Colette

Breasts … whose fruits are dark as plums —C. J. Koch

Bursts like creamy milk-fed veal —Susan Lois

The character who thus pronounces and describes a woman's breast in a novel entitled Personals, *is a kosher butcher.*

Chest like a promontory —Daphne Merkin

Cleavage deep as the jungle —T. Coraghessan Boyle

Enormous breasts that seemed to rise up and nearly out of her gown with every deep breath, defying physical laws, like a half-finished bridge —William Brammer

Full breasts soaring all over the place like billowing pennants in a strong wind —Joseph Heller

Her bosom heaved like an opera singer's —Ruth Prawer Jhabvala

Her breasts are tiny and hang from her chest like a pair of prunes —Milan Kundera

(An ample woman) her breasts hung like calabashes inside her grey dress —Thomas Keneally

Her breasts looked like two five-pound flour sacks from which some of the contents had spilled —Sue Grafton

Her large heavy breasts seemed to lift like wings —James Crumley

Her nipples preceded her like scouts —Yehuda Amichai

Her small girlish breasts already sagged like little pockets on her white chest —Jonathan Valin

His bared breast glistened soft and greasy as though he had sweated out his fat in his sleep —Joseph Conrad

Jutting breasts like hills —Robinson Jeffers

Little mounds had appeared like soft marshmallows through her sweater —Carol Ascher

Long pointed breasts rearing like the muzzles of two Afghans —James Crumley

The nipple [of mother nursing child] looked like the end of a Tootsie Roll —Bobbie Ann Mason

Nipples … flat and wide as poker chips —Sue Miller

Nipples large as cookies —Ira Wood

Nipples … like buds of peonies —Amy Lowell

Nipples like two dark eyes —David Michael Kaplan

Nipples shaped like discs of milk chocolate —Ira Wood Wood's novel "The Kitchen Man," is filled with food-related images.

Nipples … small as buttons —Miles Gibson

Nipples standing out like two overgrown M&Ms —T. Glen Coughlin

The profile of her body stood forth like the prow of a clipper ship —Calder Willingham

She had fenders like a GMC truck —Loren D. Estleman

They [breasts] were wide mounds growing like muscles across her chest —Will Weaver

A woman without breasts is like a bed without pillows —Anon

❧ BREATHING

Alimentary canal … working like a derrick without a soul —Tess Slesinger

(His) breath came heavily, like puffs of wind over a stormy sea —Walter De La Mar

Breath came like puffs from a steam locomotive —Gerald Tomlinson

Breath clear and sweet like a child's —Flannery O'Connor

Breathed as if she had a fever —Mark Helprin

Breathed deeply like a swimmer coming up for air —George Garrett

(He) breathed like a prisoner set free —Willa Cather

Breathe hard like a horse when you take the saddle off —O. Henry

Breathe like a chugging train —Tony Ardizzone

Breathe like a second-hand bicycle pump —O. Henry

Breath [from snoring] grating like bark stripped from a tree —T. Coraghessan Boyle

Breathing as rapidly as an exhausted dog —Derek Lambert

Breathing as softly as a butterfly —Ellen Glasgow

Breathing as though steam engines were working his lungs —Pat Conroy

Breathing like a hard-run horse —James Crumley

Breathing like almost any sort of man who has just been chased for a mile or so uphill by a bull in the pink of condition —Kingsley Amis

Breathing like an escape valve —Joseph C. Lincoln

Breathing like a tire pump —Dashiell Hammett

Breathing like the friction of rusted gears —T. Coraghessan Boyle

Breathing like two hippos with a chest cold —Jane Wagner

This line, spoken by the character Paul (interpreted by Lily Tomlin), describes his participation at his wife's labor.

Breathing, quick and hoarse like a dog's panting —Albert Camus

Breathing ... slow and rhythmical, like the bellows at a forge rising and falling —Henri-Pierre Roché

Breathing [an overweight man's] sounded like someone sitting down on a leather couch —Sue Grafton

Breathing with irregularity, like an overworked horse. Breathing deeply like a man asleep —George Garrett

Breath is like the gentle air of Spring —Henry Wadsworth Longfellow

Breath ... like the steam of apple-pies —Robert Greene

Breath popping like steam valves in old boilers —Denis Johnson

(Rankin's) breath rushed out like an undertow beneath the words —Richard Moran

Breath sweet as May —Christina Rossetti

The breath was pumped from their bodies as though from machines —Vicki Baum

Breath [of dying woman] whistled like the wind in a keyhole —Edith Wharton

Each breath was expelled in a puff, as if one were blowing a trumpet, Dizzy Gillespie fashion —Stephen King

Each breath was like a hill to climb —Barbara Reid

Gasped for breath like a wounded animal —Vicki Baum

Gasped the air deeply, like a diver escaping from a watery grave —Jan Kubicki

Gasping like a fish stranded on a sandbank —F. van Wyck Mason

An extension of "Gasped like a stranded fish."

Gulped in air through her mouth, straining like a nearly drowned man dragged out of the water —William Moseley

Gulping in air like a swimmer exhausted from fighting a heavy surf —Margaret Millar

Hack and wheeze like an overworked horse —T. Coraghessan Boyle

Her breath seems to flow like the water in a frozen stream —Rochelle Ratner

His breath [as he kissed her hand] was between her fingers like a web on summer grass —Ellen Gilchrist

His breath was staccato, like obstructed sobs —Nancy Huddleston Packer

Holds her breath like a seal —John Berryman

Huff like windy giants —W. D. Snodgrass

Let out a long, whistling breath like a deflating tire —Cornell Woolrich

Lungs ... blowing like leathern bellows —Frank Ross

(Stearn's) lungs fluttered like a sparrow's heartbeat —Z. Vance Wilson

(I was panting and) my breath came like fire —Louise Erdrich

Pant like a fat man running for a bus —Lawrence Durrell

Panting like a steamboat —Joyce Cary

Puffed like a leaky steam pipe —O. Henry

Puffing like a blown shire horse —Donald Seaman

A rasping gasp as though he were swallowing his false teeth —W. P. Kinsella

Sharp intake of breath, like a toy balloon suddenly deflated —Ralph Ellison

Snort [while asleep] like a timid locomotive —MacDonald Harris

Sound of breathing ... like the soft crackle of tissue paper —Frank Swinnerton

Sucked air like a drowning fish —Miles Gibson

Took as much breath as if I'd heaved a shot put —Larry McMurtry

Wheezing ... like a horse with a progressive lung disease —T. Coraghessan Boyle

❧ BREVITY

See Also: TIME

As compact as a drop of pure water —Richard E. Shepard, *New York Times*, November 3, 1986
The simile attempts to explain the mystery of the Flamenco Puro dance troop's creative wellsprings.

Brief as a classified ad —Anon

Brief as a drop of dew —Cale Young Rice

Brief as a grouch's smile —Anon

Brief as a sinner's prayer —Anon

Brief as a twinge —Margaret Atwood

Brief as the Z column in a pocket dictionary —Irvin S. Cobb Or, to be even more specific, "Brief as the Z column in this dictionary."

Brief as youth in retrospect —Elyse Sommer

(Smiled) briefly —on and off like a light switch —Gavin Lyall

Concise as a telegram —Elyse Sommer

Short as any dream —William Shakespeare, *Midsummer Night's Dream*

Short, clear as a bird-note, trailing away —E. B. White

❧ BRIGHTNESS

See Also: GLIMMER, GLITTER, AND GLOSS; LIGHTING; SHINING

Blazing like the windows of the city —James Dickey

(He possessed a brainful of information) bright and beautiful as diamonds swaddled in midnight-blue velvet —W. P. Kinsella

Bright and light as the crest of a peacock —Alfred, Lord Tennyson

Bright and pleasing as a child's rattle —Virginia Woolf

Bright as a beach in the moonlight —Alfred Austin

(An image came to me across the years) bright as a coin from the mint —Norman Mailer

Bright as a frog's eyes —Hart Crane

Bright as all between cloudless skies and windless streams —Percy Bysshe Shelley

Bright as a nettle rash —Diane Ackerman

(Laugh …) bright as a new ensign's buttons —Frederic Wakeman

Bright as a newly painted toy —Hugh Walpole

Bright as an icon —Margaret Atwood

Bright as any glass —Geoffrey Chaucer

Bright as any meteor ever bred by the North Pole —Lord Byron

Bright as a parakeet —Dame Edith Sitwell

(Every day) bright as a postcard —Karl Shapiro

Bright as a roomful of crystal chandeliers —Anon

Bright as a splinter from a glazier's table —Beryl Markham

(A face) bright as a waterdrop —Padraic Fallon

Bright as day —Geoffrey Chaucer

Bright as foil —Molly Giles

Bright as freedom —Marge Piercy

Bright as joy —Hartley Coleridge

Bright as light —Alfred, Lord Tennyson

Bright as moonlight over snow —Wallace Stegner

Bright as Spring —Walter Savage Landor

(Eyes as) bright as the Dipper —Stephen Vincent Benét

Bright as the fullest moon in blackest air —*Arabian Nights*

Bright as the promises of a new administration —Elyse Sommer

Bright as the promise of life on commencement day —Elyse Sommer

Bright as the promise of a cloudless day —C.P. Wilson

Bright as the raindrops and roses in June —Dame Edith Sitwell

Bright as the world was in its infant years —John Banks

Bright as truth —Barry Cornwall

Bright like a brimming bowl of jewels —Peter De Vries

Bright, like a flash of sunlight —Earle Bulwer-Lytton

Bright (eyes) like agate —D. H. Lawrence

Bright like blood —Algernon Charles Swinburne

Brightness ... bright as dipper —Stephen Vincent Benét

Brilliant as a postage stamp —Lawrence Durrell

(Eyes) brilliant as fire —Nadine Gordimer

[Oranges and grapefruits] Brilliant as planets —Cynthia Ozick

Brilliant as the stars —Ouida

Brilliant as the sun —Slogan, Lustberg-Nast, Lustray shirts

Brilliant like a Chinese porcelain —W. Somerset Maugham

Brilliantly, gaudily colored as a Gypsy camp —Kate Simon

Dazzled the eyes like a second noonday sun —Edna Ferber

Growing brighter and brighter like a forest after a rain —Denis Johnson

Lights up like a Star Wars pinball machine —

Looking brighter than a Christmas tree —Oscar Hammerstein, "Everybody's Got a Home but Me," *Pipe Dream*

Vivid as sun through a thin brown bottle —Reynolds Price

Vivid as the granules of paint in a Dubuffet —John Updike

Again: In Cymbeline, old Belarius says of the "two princely boys" that are with him, —"They are as gentle / As zephyrs, blowing below the violet, / Not wagging his sweet head; and yet as rough

❧ BRITTLENESS
See: FRAGILITY

❧ BROWN
See Also: COLORS

(Wine) as brown as November leaves —Wilbur Daniel Steele

[Pupils of eyes] Brown and shiny like melting chocolate —Margaret Millar

Brown as a berry —Geoffrey Chaucer
The old English original read "Broun as is a berye."

(His face was) brown as an old boot —Christopher Isherwood

Brown as an old daguerreotype fading —Robert Penn Warren

Brown as a nut —Henry Wadsworth Longfellow

(Cheeks) brown as oak-leaves —Henry Wadsworth Longfellow

(Hair) brown as a pecan shell —Reynolds Price

Brown as cinnamon —Truman Capote

Brown as onion soup —Saul Bellow

Brown as rust —George Garrett

(A tan) brown as seven-grain bread —Patricia Henley

(A girl as) brown as the ground —Cynthia Ozick

Brown as tobacco spit brew —Truman Capote

Brown ... like the color of the basket —H. E. Bates

A dreggy brown, like bad coffee —Irvin S. Cobb

Pale brown, like canvas —Mary McCarthy

❧ BRUTALITY
See: CRUELTY, VIOLENCE

❧ BUILDINGS
SEE: HOUSES

❧ BURST

See Also: DISINTEGRATION, SUDDENNESS

(Your unexpected letter has just) burst into my existence like a meteor into the sphere of a planet —William James letter from Dresden to Oliver Wendell Holmes, Jr., May 15, 1868

(My poor head would) burst like a dropped watermelon —Maya Angelou

Burst like a raw egg —William Diehl

Burst like a ripe seedpod —Beryl Markham

Burst like a thunderbolt —Alfred, Lord Tennyson

(Seeds) burst like bullets —Anne Sexton

[Details of an event would] burst open like garbage from a bag dropped from a height —Thomas Keneally

Burst out like a rash —Nadine Gordimer

Bursting like an overdone potato —Sir Arthur Conan Doyle

Comes apart like a slow-ripping seam —Sharon Sheehe Stark

The character coming apart in the author's story, In the Surprise of Life, is a girl who has been trying to contain her laughter.

Flashed [a remark] like a sheet of heat lightning —Rita Mae Brown

(The cursing and grumbling) flashed like a storm —Enid Bagnold

Like the buds let us burst —Ogden Nash

(He had a real gift for those flaring exclamations, those raucous) outbursts, like wounds suddenly opened —Romain Gary

Sputtering like a leaky valve —John Peter Touhey

(Our imaginations seem to have been) torn open ... as by a charge of dynamite —Dorothy Canfield

❧ BUSINESS

See Also: ADVERTISING, SUCCESS/FAILURE

As oxygen is the disintegrating principle of life, working night and day to dissolve, separate, pull apart and dissipate, so there is something in business that continually tends to scatter, destroy and shift possession from this man to that. A million mice nibble eternally at every business venture —Elbert Hubbard

Business is like a man rowing a boat upstream. He has no choice; he must go ahead or he will go back —Lewis E. Pierson

Business is like oil. It won't mix with anything but business —J. Grahame

Business ... is very much like religion: it is founded on faith —William McFee

Business policy flows downhill from the mountain, like water —Anon

A business without customers is like a computer without bytes —Anon

As the entries that follow show, this concept lends itself to many additional twists.

A business without customers is like a stage without light —Anon

A business without orders is like a room without windows —Anon

Buying and selling like a Rockefeller —Arthur A. Cohen

A corporation is just like any natural person, except that it has no pants to kick or soul to damn —Ernst and Lindley

Playwrights Ernst and Lindley wrote this wrote this simile to be spoken by a judge in their 1930's play Hold Your Tongue.

Corporate politics is like the days of Andrew Jackson, the spoils system —Rita Mae Brown

Customers drop away like tenpins —Anon

Inventory that just sits there like it's nailed to the floor —Anthony E. Stockanes

Like a boxer who has taken a series of heavy blows, and starts to lose his legs, the mighty American economy had finally begun to sag —Edward Rutherfurd, *New York*

Nowadays almost every business is like show business, including politics, which has become more like show business than show business is —Russell Baker

Orders fell like stones —Anon

(Being in the microcomputer business is) risky, like going 55 miles an hour three feet from a cliff. If you make the wrong turn you're bankrupt so fast you don't know what hit you —George Morrow, quoted in *New York Times*, March 11, 1986 when his company went bankrupt

Some businesses are like desert flowers. They bloom overnight, and they're gone —George Morrow, quoted in *New York Times*, March 11, 1986

The first two words transposed from "Computer companies" to generalize the comparison.

Sometimes, it seemed to him, the market was nothing more than an aggregate of individuals, like a great school of fish, feeding upon small hopes until some fright causes them all to swerve together —Edward Rutherfurd, *New York*

The tide of business, like the running stream, is sometimes high and sometimes low, a quiet ebb, or a tempestuous flow, and always in extreme —John Dryden

Tradespeople are just like gardeners. They take advantage of your not knowing —Agatha Christie

♣ BUSYNESS

See Also: ACTIVENESS, WORK

Busier than a cat covering shit on a marble slab —American colloquialism

Busier than a gulag gravedigger —Joseph Wambaugh

Bustled about like so many ants roused by the approach of a foe —J. Hampden Porter

Ants rank with bees as a means to describe busyness. In modern day usage and literature the above is usually shortened; for example, "Busy as an ant" used by Ogden Nash in his poem "Children."

(I've been) busy as a bartender on Saturday night —Irwin Shaw

Busy as a bee —Geoffrey Chaucer

Chaucer's old English version of what has become a commonly used expression read "Bisy as bees ben they."

Busy as a dog with fleas —Anon

Busy as a fiddler's elbow —Harry Prince

As busy as a hen with one chicken —John Ray's *Proverbs*

To strengthen the impact of the simile, there's "As busy as a hen with ten chickens" and "As a hen with fifteen chickens," attributed to James Howell, and "As busy as a hen with fifteen chickens in a barnyard," attributed to John Russell Bartlett.

Busy as an oven at Christmas —Michael Denham

Busy as ants in a breadbox —Anon

(I am) busy as a one-armed paperhanger with the itch —American colloquialism This is often attributed to Theodore Roosevelt, who used it in a letter to his daughter. Some extensions on the one-armed paperhanger image include: "Busy as a one-armed paper-hanger with the hives" (one of the many common expressions in Carl Sanburg's *The People, Yes*), "Busy as a one-armed paperhanger with the seven-year itch" (H. W. Thompson, *Body, Boots and Britches*) and "Busy as a one-armed paper-hanger with the nettle rash" (O. Henry, *The Ethics of a Pig*).

As busy as a one-legged man in an ass-kicking contest all week long —Pat Conroy

About as busy as a pair of lizards on a warm brick —James Cain

Busy as a ticking clock —Anon (Wilstak.1st)

(Birds shrill and musical) busy as bullets —John Farris

Busy as catbirds —Hilary Masters

Busy as jumper cables at a Mexican funeral —Thomas Zigal

Busy as maggots —Marge Piercy

Busy as the day is long —Vincent Stuckey Lean

Busy as the devil in a gale of wind —Sir Walter Scott

Get busy like a bomb —Erich Maria Remarque

Humming like a hive —John Gardner

Hurried … like one who had always a multiplicity of tasks on hand —Charlotte Brontë

[The demands job of being secretary of Defense] It's like getting a shave and having your appendix out at the same time —Robert Lovett, *Saturday Evening Post,* May 28,1960

Like a squirrel in a cage, always in action —Aphra Behn

Like the bee, we should make our industry our amusement —Oliver Goldsmith

❧ CALMNESS

See Also: PEACEFULNESS

Calm as a bathtub —George Garrett

Calm as a Buddhist —Elizabeth Taylor

Calm as a convent —Anon

Calm as a cud-chewing cow —Harold Adams

Calm as a frozen lake when ruthless winds blow fiercely —William Wordsworth

Calm as a gliding moon —Samuel Taylor Coleridge

Calm as a marble head —Eudora Welty

(I'm) calm as a Mediterranean sky —Frank Swinnerton

Calm as a mirror —Alexandre Dumas, Pere

(The sky was) calm as an aquarium —Antoine de Saint-Exupéry

Calm as an iceberg —Gelett Burgess

Calm as a sea horse —Susan Vreeland, *Clara and Mr. Tiffany*

Calm as a slumbering babe —Percy Bysshe Shelley

As part of our daily language this has evolved into "Calm as a sleeping baby."

[Said it as] calm as a virgin discussing flower arrangement —George MacDonald Fraser

Calm as beauty —Robert Browning

Calm as dewdrops —William Wordsworth

Calm as fate —John Greenleaf Whittier

Calm as glass —Charlotte Brontë

Calm as ice —Nathaniel Hawthorne

Calm as if she were sitting for her portrait —Henry James

Calm as in the days when all was right —Frederich Von Schiller

Calm as night —Victor Hugo

(Voice) calm as the deepest cold —Sharon Sheehe Stark

Calm as the sky after a day of storm —Voltaire

Calm as virtue —William Shakespeare, *Cymbeline*

Calm as water in a glass —standing water in clean cut glass —Reynolds Price

Calm descended (on the pool hall) as nerve shattering as if the (long barnlike) room were the ship from which Jonah had been cast into the sea —Flannery O'Connor

Calmed down, like a Corinthian column —John Ashbery

A calm … like the deep sleep which follows an orgy —Mark Twain

Cold as cucumbers —Francis Beaumont and John Fletcher

In its original meaning this referred to sexual coldness. As currently used it meansbeing calm, collected, or "Cool as a cucumber." Poet Stevie Smith used the simile as a title for a poem which begins with this and two other cliché to describe the subject of the poem, a girl named Mary: "Cool as a cucumber calm as a mill pond sound as a bell was Mary."

Cool and collected as a dean sitting in his deanery —Ogden Nash

Cool and ordinary as a gallon of buttermilk —Borden Deal

Cool as a Buddha —Jan Epton Seale

> The simile, from a short story about a new mother entitled "Reluctant Madonna," reads as follows in full context: "Christie intends to be cool as a Buddha about this baby. Unflappable."

Cool as a cop with a clipboard —Gary Gildner

Cool as a cube of cucumber on ice —Carl Sandburg

> This extension of the familiar "Cool as a cucumber" is particularly apt in Sanburg's epic The People, Yes, which beautifully and cleverly incorporates many familiar similes.

Cool as a frozen daiquiri —Linda Barnes

Cool as an Easter lily —Erich Maria Remarque

Cool as a quarterback —Dan Wakefield

(He was) cool as a refrigerator —R.A. J. Walling

Cool as a veteran horse race jockey —Carl Sandburg

Cool as lettuce —Jay Parini

(He's as) cool as the other side of your pillow —Merlin Olsen, NBC-TV broadcaster, about Ken O'Brien, quarterback for the Jets, January 1987

Expression … as calm and collected as that of a doctor by a patient's bedside —Stefan Zweig

Felt a certain calm fall over me like a cloak —R. Wright Campbell

Have kept composure, like captives who would not talk under torture —Richard Wilbur

He lay as calm as a boulder in the sun —Loren D. Estleman, *Sugartown: An Amos Walker Mystery*

His calmness was like the sureness of money in the bank —Anzia Yezierska

Looked as cool as a yellow diamond —Robert Campbell

Looking calm as an eggshell —Edith Wharton

(The April morning) mellow as milk —Sharon Sheehe Stark

Mellow as moonlight —Slogan, Vogan Candy Co.

Mellow as old brandy —Anon

Mild as cottage cheese —Stephen Vincent Benét

Mild as milk —Dame Edith Sitwell

Nonchalant as a shoplifter in the checkout line —Donald McCaig

The sea was calm like milk and water —Isak Dinesen

The sense of rest, of having arrived at the long-promised calm center, filled him like a species of sleep —John Updike

Serene as a man who has just got a promotion and raise —Geoffrey Wolff

Stayed calm, like a hero before the battle when all the cameras are on him —Clancy Sigal

Unshakable as a pyramid in the desert —Joe Williams, *The Draft*

(Your opinion at the moment) worries me exactly as much as dandruff would a chopped-off head —William McIlvanney

♣ CANDOR

See Also: HONESTY

About as sincere as the look upon the face of an undertaker conducting a nine-hundred dollar funeral —H. L. Mencken

As candid as the C.I.A. —Anon

As devoted to candor as a high school valedictorian —Jonathan Valin

As forthcoming as *Pravda* —Joseph Wambaugh

As frank as a candid camera shot —Anon

As open [about revealing self] as an unsteamed clam —Elyse Sommer

As revealing as a locked diary —Anon

Candid as mirrors —Robert G. Ingersoll

Direct as a bullet —Flannery O'Conner

Penny's honesty has always been like nudity in an action movie: gratuitous, but no less welcome for it. —Jonathan Tropper, *This Is Where I Leave You*

Phony as a laugh track —Vincent Canby, about the movie *Murphy's Romance*, *New York Times*, January 17, 1986

Sincerity is like traveling on a plain beaten road, which commonly brings a man sooner to his journey's end than by-ways in which men often loose themselves —John Tillotson

Took off the mask of tranquility she had worn … like an actress returning weary to her room after a trying fifth act and falling half-dead upon a couch, while the audience retains an image of her to which she bears not the slightest resemblance —Honoré de Balzac

(You get right) to the point … like a knife in the heart —Harvey Fierstein

Two-sided, like Janus —L. P. Hartley

❧ CAPABILITY
See: ABILITY

❧ CAREFULNESS
See: ATTENTION, CAUTION, CORRECTNESS

❧ CARELESSNESS

Act with the calm forethought of a beheaded chicken —Herman Wouk

> *In his novel,* Inside, Outside, *Wouk used the comparison to describe the behavior of political characters.*

Careless as a child at play —William Winter

Careless as saints who live by faith alone —George Garrett

[Charles de Gaulle] Has been abysmally careless, like a man running a bus over mountains, who forgot to equip it with good brakes —Janet Flanner

Ignore caution like a gambler with a hot tip —Anon

❧ CARES
See: PROBLEMS AND SOLUTIONS

❧ CAUSE AND EFFECT

Affect me [with revulsion] like the smell of a cheap cigar left smoldering in an ashtray —Jonathan Valin

> *In Valin's novel,* Final Notice, *the descriptive frame of reference for the simile is a tattoo.*

The certainty [of his desire] landed in the bottom of my stomach like a flatiron —Mary Gordon

The change [in living accommodations] would be like going from Purgatory to Paradise —Louisa May Alcott

The conviction that I am loved and loving affects me like a military bracing —John Cheever

The effort made him choke like a tiger at a bone —Robert Frost

Every gesture … aroused a beat chant like the beat of the heart of the desert —Anais Nin

(This city) exacerbates loneliness in may the same way that water makes Alka-Seltzer fizz —Pat Conroy

The general effect was exactly like a microscopic view of a small detachment of black beetles in search of a dead rat —John Ruskin

Has a disruptive effect … like a torpedo coming down Main Street —Anon politician on Gramm-Rudman Law, February, 1986

Has as little effect on me as water on a duck's back —American colloquialism, attributed to South

> *A variation: "As water rolling off a duck's back."*

Her absence felt like a presence, an electrical charge of silence in the house —John Updike

His death served to remind me, like a custard pie in the face, that life is sometimes like one big savage joke —Sue Grafton

(A blast of Prince [music] …) hit me like a feather boa with a length of lead pipe in it —Jonathan Valin

The image hit him like a train —Julie Orringer, *The Invisible Bridge*

Its [melancholy] effect upon you is somewhat similar to what would probably be produced by a combined attack of toothache, indigestion and a cold in the head —Jerome K. Jerome

It [forcing an old priest into retirement] was just like ripping an old tree out of the ground —W. P. Kinsella

The kind whisper went into my heart like a dagger —Charlotte Brontë

Offering a flight attendant a $20 bill for a $2 drink is like spitting on an Alabama state trooper —Louis D. Wilson, *Wall Street Journal,* June 30, 1986

Pain and poverty and thwarted ambition … can break the virtues like brittle bones —George Garrett

[A dying woman being interviewed by a journalist] People must grow terribly upset when you turn up with a notepad. No? Like the undertaker arriving to measure the dowager —Tom Rachman, *The Imperfectionists*

Seeing her again … was like rediscovering a half-forgotten landmark —Ann Petry

[When a tired-looking woman smiles] Some of the years of hard living fell away like happy tears —James Crumley

♣ CAUTION

See Also: BEHAVIOR

Cagey as a feral cat —John Yount

Careful as a cat walking on egg shells —American colloquialism, attributed to New England

Carries it [a plant] as if it's made of Steuben glass —Ann Beattie

Carry … like a hot tureen —Eudora Welty

Caution flowed over the [telephone] wire like a wave —Robert M. Coates

Caution, like that of a wild beast that is fierce but feeble or like that of an insect whose little fragment of earth has given way, and made it pause in a palsy of distrust —George Eliot

Cautious as a burglar walking over a tin roof in cowhide boots —Wallace Irwin

Cautious as a good housekeeper —Honoré de Balzac

Cautious as a tightrope walker with a severe itch —Anon

> *This is yet another perversion of the popular "Busy as a one-armed paperhanger" comparison*

Cautious as his gray suit —John Dancy, NBC-TV about Robert Gates at CIA confirmation hearings, April, 1987

Cautiously, like a man handling sixteenth-century lace —Roald Dahl

Choosy as a stud in a harem —Mike Sommer

Discreet … as if you're trying to tail yourself —William McIlvanney

Going as if he trod upon eggs —Robert Burton

Like a weight-watcher at the feast of San Gennaro, I just nibbled a bit —Leonard M. Heine Jr., commenting on his cautious stock purchases when others were investing freely, quoted *Wall Street Journal* column by Vartanig G. Vartan, January 19, 1987

Peeped out carefully like a mole from its hole —Derek Walcott

Picked up the pieces as carefully as if they were cuttings from the Koh-I-Noor —Israel Zangwill

Picking his word like a man making his way through a minefield —Donald Seaman

Progressed like a man tracing and following a chalk line —Frank Swinnerton

A prudent man is like a pin; his head prevents him from going too far —Anon

Should be used with discretion, like cayenne pepper —Anon

So wary that he sleeps like a hare, with his eyes open —Thomas Fuller

Timid as hares —Anton Chekov

To take all you want is never as good as to stop when you should —Lao Tzu

(We must) treat him like Dresden china —Nikolai V. Gogol

Wary as a blind horse —Thomas Fuller

Wary as a pickpocket's confidence that the policeman on the beat will stay bought —H. L. Mencken

> This is slightly changed from Mencken's original words which identified the pickpocket as an American.

Watch what he said as carefully as if he were in court —John Updike

❖ CELEBRITY

See: FAME

❖ CENSORSHIP

See: CONTROL, CRITICISM

❖ CERTAINTY

Absolute as a miser's greed —Anon

An absolute, like the firmness of the earth —Tom Wolfe

Almost as predictable as the arrival of solstice and equinox —Russell Baker, *New York Times*, September 17, 1986

> Baker's comparison referred to Chief-Justice-to-be William Rehnquist's judicial opinions.

As certain as a gun —Samuel Butler

As certain as beach traffic in July —Anon

As certain as bodies moved with greater impulse, progress more rapidly than those moved with less —Voltaire

As certain as death and taxes —Daniel Defoe

> Often attributed to Benjamin Franklin, the simile continues to be popular, with many humorous twists such as "Certain as death and hay-fever" used in Philip Barry's 1923 play "You and I."

As certain as dye penetrates cotton —Daniela Gioseffi

The simile, from a poem, continues with "The orange is a part of the living animal."

As certain as end-of-the season inventories —Anon

As certain as June graduates scanning the want ads —Anon

As certain as leaves falling in September —Anon

As certain as lines at return counters after Christmas —Anon

As certain as rise of taxi meter —Anon

As certain as that a crooked tree will have a crooked shadow —Anon

As certain as that bread crumbs will attract a flock of pigeons —Anon

As certain as that leaves will fall in autumn —Anon

As certain as that night succeeds the day —George Washington

As certain as your shadow will follow you —Anon

As certain as the morning —Thomas Wolfe

As certain as the sunrise —Anon

As certain as thunderclap following lightning —Anon

As certain as wrinkles —Anon

As certainly as day follows day —Anon

As certainly as Segovia had been born to finger a fretboard or Willy Mays to swing a bat —T. Coraghessan Boyle

As inevitable as a dog at a hydrant —Anon

As inevitable as the turning of the earth on which you stand —Harvey Swados

As sure as a club —Mary Hedin

As sure as a goose goes barefoot —American colloquialism, attributed to the Northeast

As sure as a tested hypothesis —Lorrie Moore

As sure as a wheel is round —American colloquialism

As sure as behave and misbehave —John Ciardi

As sure as day —William Shakespeare, *King Henry IV, Part III*

As sure as death —William Shakespeare *King Henry IV, Part I*

The same simile was used by Ben Jonson in Every Man in His Humor. If not the first, it is certainly one of the earliest example of this simile.

As sure as meat will fry —American colloquialism, attributed to Southeast

As sure as rain —Ben Ames Williams

A more specific variation of this is "Sure as rain in April."

As sure as shooting —Anon

This common expression probably stems from the no longer used "Sure as a gun," variously attributed to the poet John Dryden and the playwright William Congreve.

As sure as snakes crawl —American colloquialism, attributed to the Midwest

As surely as that two ends of a seesaw cannot both be elevated at the same time —Alexander Woolcott

As surely as the eye tends to be long-sighted in the sailor and short-sighted in the student —Herbert Spencer

As surely as the harvest comes after the seedtime —Dr. John Brown

As surely as the tree becomes bulky when it stands alone and slender if one of a group —Herbert Spencer

As surely as water will wet us, as surely as fire will burn —Rudyard Kipling

As unpreventable as blinking your eyes when a light flashes suddenly —Anon

Certain things will follow inevitably, just like a little trail of horseshit behind a fat old draught horse —George Garrett

Definite as a counter-signed contract —Anon

Inevitable as a comet's return —Marge Piercy

Inevitable as noon —Thomas Wolfe

Inevitable as the snick of a mouse-trap —Carl Sandburg

Inevitable … like a stone rolling down a mountain —Mary Gordon

Predictable as a physical law —Charles Johnson

(The man was as) predictable as rainwater seeking a low spot —William Beechcroft

Predictable as the prints left by a three-legged dog —Sharon Sheehe Stark

Predictable as the arrival of Monday morning —Harry Prince

Predictable as the menu at charity dinner —Anon

Predictable, like a diplomatic reception —A. Alvarez

Secure as an obituary in the *Times* —Marge Piercy

So predictable … just like tuning in the same radio station every night —Lee Smith

A character in Smith's novel, The Last Day the Dog bushes Bloomed, *uses this simile to describe a dull suitor.*

Sweet and sure annuity; it's like taking a bath at Fort Knox —Moss Hart

This line from Light Up the Sky *likens a national tour for an ice show to sure-fire success.*

❖ **CESSATION**
See: PAUSE

❖ **CHANGE**
See Also: ENTRANCES AND EXITS, PERMANENCE

Anticipate change as though you had left it behind you —Rainer Maria Rilke

Any essential reform must, like charity, begin at home —John Macy

Changeable as a baby's diaper —Anon

Changeable as the weather —American colloquialism attributed to New England

The variations this has sprouted typify the simple simile's extension through more particularization.

Some examples: "Changeable/unpredictable as April weather or as the sky in April" and "Changeable like Midwestern weather —violent and highly volatile."

(Her expression would) change as quickly as a sky with clouds racing across the moon —Madeleine L'Engle

The change came about slowly, arriving like a pale mist that slipped into every crevice —Erik Larson, *In the Belly of the Beast: Love, Terror, and an American Family in Hitler's Berlin*

(Hopes) changed daily like the stock market —Margaret Millar

In her novel The Murder of Miranda, *Millar expands the Simile as follows: "Gaining a few points here, losing a few there."*

Changed his mind regularly, like shirts —Anon

Changed ... like the shift of key in a musical score —Lawrence Durrell

Changed moods like a strobe of shifting lights —Alvin Boretz

Changeful as a creature of the tropical sea lying under a reef —Saul Bellow

A change, like a shift of wind, overcame the judge —Truman Capote

Change of attitude ... like a fish gliding with a flick of its tail, now here, now there —Jean Rhys

(Life) changed like fluffy clouds —Rita Mae Brown

Changes ... as breath-taking as a Celtics fast break —Larry McCoy, *Wall Street Journal* article about changes at CBS network, December 4, 1986

The configuration of my life (of our lives) altered again, like a kaleidoscope turned with the gentle twist of a divine hand —Claire Messud, *A Life*

Changes his mood like a wizard —Joan Chase

Ever changing, like a joyless eye that finds no objects worth its constancy —Percy Bysshe Shelley

Every politician knows how the public mood can change. Sometimes the change is gradual. Sometimes, like water held back by a barrier, it will suddenly break through and rush down like a flood, sweeping all before it —Edward Rutherfurd, *New York*

Everything changed ... like the rug, the one that gets pulled —Alberto Alvaor Rios

Fickle as the sunlight —William Alfred

Fickle as the wind —Horace

Get used to [changes] ... like listening to your own heart —Marguerite Duras

In our changes we should move like a caterpillar, part of which is stationary in every advance, not like the toad —James A. Pike

Reverend Pike's advice was aimed at preventing anxiety.

[Moving from slow to fast-paced life] it was like stepping from a gondola to an ocean steamer —Edith Wharton

[Personality of a character] metamorphoses ... like a butterfly bursting out of a cocoon —Frank Rich, *New York Times,* January 21, 1986

Mood ... swinging like an erratic pendulum from being hurt to hurting —Ross Macdonald

Most reformers, like a pair of trousers on a windy clothesline, go through a vast deal of vehement motion but stay in the same place —Austin O'Malley

Popped out and disappeared like a heat rash —George Garrett

Sailing through change as effortlessly as gulls —Gail Godwin

(And all the shapes of this grand scenery) shifted like restless clouds before the steadfast sun —Percy Bysshe Shelley

(Streets) shift like dunes —Lisa Ress

The switch is like going from Star Wars to stage-coaches —David "Doc" Livingston, commenting on enforced job switch (from controlling air traffic to controlling commuter trains), as quoted in *New York Times* article about fired air controllers by N.R. Kleinfield, September 28, 1986

Up and down like mercury —May Sarton

(Moods may) veer as erratically as the wind —Milton R. Sapirstein

♣ CHAOS

See: ORDER/DISORDER

♣ CHARACTER

See Also: PERSONAL TRAITS, REPUTATION

As the sun is best seen at its rising and setting, so men's native dispositions are clearest seen when they are children and when they are dying —Robert Boyle

A character is like an acrostic ... read it forward, backward, or across, it still spells the same thing —Ralph Waldo Emerson

Character is like a tree, and reputation like its shadow. The shadow is what we think of it; the tree is the real thing —Abraham Lincoln

Character is like white paper; if once blotted, it can hardly ever be made to appear white as before —Joel Hawes

A character, like a kettle, once mended always wants mending —Jean-Jacques Rousseau

Character, like porcelain ware, must be painted before it is glazed. There can be no change after it is burned in —Henry Ward Beecher

A man of words and not of deeds is like a garden full of weeds. And when the weeds begin to grow, it's like a garden full of snow —Nursery rhyme
This dates back to the eighteenth century.

The reputation of a man is like his shadow, gigantic when it precedes him, and pigmy in its proportions when it follows —Alexandre de Talleyrand

Some people, like modern shops, hang everything in their windows and when one goes inside nothing is to be found —Berthold Auerbach

The soundness of his nature was like the pure paste under a fine glaze —Edith Wharton

A vein of iron buried inside her moral frame, like a metal armature inside a clay statue —Carlos Baker

Your moral character must be not only pure, but, like Caesar's wife, unsuspected —Lord Chesterfield

♣ CHARACTERISTICS, NATIONAL

America is more a ratatouille than a melting pot —Ken Holm, *New York Times Magazine,* October 12, 1986
The food image is particularly appropriate to Holm's article about mixing Eastern and Western ingredients when cooking.

America is rather like life. You can usually find in it what you look for —E.M. Forster

As American as a catcher's mitt —George Jean Nathan

As American as a Norman Rockwell painting —Max Shulman

As American as a sawed-off shotgun —Dorothy Parker about Dashiell Hammett, *The New Yorker,* April 15, 1931

As American as cheesecake —Samuel Yellen

As American as corn on the cob —Anon

As American as jazz —Anon

As American as shopping malls —Anon

As American as the dream of being a millionaire —Anon

As American as the two car garage —Anon

As British as roast beef —Anon

As British as tea and scones —Elyse Sommer

The variations to this are virtually limitless; to cite just a few: "English as the changing of the guards at Buckingham Palace," "English as clotted cream," "As English as Piccadilly," "As English as Trafalgar Square."

As in sex, the Japanese do not care for extended encounters: "in and out" is their motto in love and war —James Kirkup

Bullied and ordered about, the Englishman obeys like a sheep, evades like a knave, or tries to murder his oppressor —George Bernard Shaw

Countries are like fruit; the worms are always inside —Jean Giradoux

Energy in a nation is like sap in a tree, it rises from the bottom up —Woodrow Wilson, October 28, 1912 speech

Frenchmen are like grains of gunpowder, each by itself smutty and contemptible, but mass them together and they are terrible indeed —Samuel Taylor Coleridge

French woman dips into love like a duck into water, 'tis but a shake of the feathers and wag of the tail and all is well again but an English woman is like a heedless swan venturing into a pool who gets drowned —Washington Irving

Friendship in France as impossible to be attained as orange-trees on the mountains of Scotland —Lady Mary Wortley Montague letter to Lady Pomfret, July 12, 1744

(In America … people claim and disown 'identities') as easily as they slap on bumper stickers —Philip Roth

Nations like individuals, have to limit their objectives, or take the consequences —James Reston

Nations, like men, die by imperceptible disorders —Jean Giraudoux

Nations, like men, have their infancy —Henry St. John, Viscount Bolingbroke

A quiet Irishman is about as harmless as a powder magazine built over a match factory —James Dunne

Soviet action is like a riddle wrapped inside an enigma —Winston Churchill

The wheels of American foreign relations turn like the wheels of an ox cart —Clive Cussler

❧ CHARITY
See: KINDNESS

❧ CHARM
See: ATTRACTIVENESS

❧ CHASTITY
See: VIRTUE

❧ CHEAPNESS
See: COST, THRIFT

❧ CHEEKS
See Also: BLUSHES, FACIAL COLOR, SKIN

Cheekbones glistening as if they'd been oiled —T. Coraghessan Boyle

Cheekbones like bunions —Steve Stern

Cheekbones, like little gossamer-covered drums —Eudora Welty

Cheeks … always a bright inflamed red, as if they'd been scoured —Jean Thompson

Cheeks … big as a balloon —Njabulo Ndebele

Cheeks bright as a wooden doll's —Derek Lambert

Cheeks bulging like a trumpeter's —George Garrett

Cheeks glowing like one of those apples in an expensive fruit shop —Patrick White

Cheeks had turned to blotches of dull red, like some pigment which has darkened in drying —Edith Wharton

Cheeks had risen like puffy omelettes [from weight gain] —Phyllis Bottome

Cheeks ... just tinged, like the snow apple —Helga Sandburg

Cheeks ... like a raspberry patch —Truman Capote

Cheeks ... like caves —John Rechy

Cheeks like poppies —John Galsworthy

Cheeks ... pale as a winter snow upon which a few drops of blood have fallen —Arthur A. Cohen

Cheeks ... round and ruddy as marzipan fruit —Sylvia Plath

Cheeks ... sweet as flowers —The Holy Bible/ Song of Solomon

Cheeks the luscious pink of ripening strawberries —W. P. Kinsella

Jowls ... hanging like wineskins —Z. Vance Wilson

Red cheeks glistened like polished apples —Anon

Spots of rouge on her cheekbones like a couple of roses pressed into the pages of a book —George Garrett

❧ CHEERFULNESS

See Also: BRIGHTNESS, GAIETY, HAPPINESS, SMILES

All smiles ... as if ready for a thousand little curtseys —André Malraux

(She was) as bubbly as a magnum of champagne —Harry Prince

[A movie] as heart-warming as an approaching headache —Vincent Canby, New York Times, March 21, 1986

[A young girl] Blithe and airy as a wind-swept leaf —Sylvia Berkman

Blithe as a boy —Pamela Hansford Johnson

[A sunlit room] bright and bouncing as a newly bathed baby —John Braine

Bright as a chirping bird —Stephen Longstreet

Buoyant as a bride —Thomas McGuane

Cheerful as a grove in Spring —William Wordsworth

Cheerful as the rising sun in May —William Wordsworth

(Smile.... as) as cheerful as the winter solstice —William McIlvanney

A cheerful face is nearly as good for an invalid as healthy weather —Benjamin Franklin

Cheerfulness is like money well expended in charity; the more we dispense of it, the greater our possessions —Victor Hugo

Cheerfulness opens, like spring, all the blossoms of the inward man —J.P. Richter

Encouraging as a round of applause —Anon

(I am) gay as morning, light as snow —Dorothy Parker

Instead of flittin', I'll be sittin' / Next to her I'm cheerful like a kitten —Irving Berlin, from the song "The Girl That I Marry," from the musical Annie Get Your Gun

Optimistic as a sweepstake ticket buyer —Anon

Optimistic as a company spokesperson —Anon

Positive as good news —G. K. Chesterton

Positive as the forecast in a Chinese fortune cookie —Elyse Sommer

Radiant like a work of art, full of strange rays —Iris Murdoch

(She's always happy. She) shies away from misery like a petrified horse —Carolyn Slaughter

Sunny and open as a May morning —Willa Cather

❧ CHILDISHNESS
See: YOUTHFULNESS

❧ CHILDREN
See Also: PARENTHOOD

A baby is like a beast, it does not think —Aeschylus

Childhood is like a mirror, which reflects in after life the images first presented to it —Samuel Smiles

Childhood ... like so many oatmeal cookies —Frank O'Hara

Childhood shows the man, as the morning shows the day —John Milton

Children are like beggars; often coming without being called —Proverb

Children are like leaves on a tree —Marcus Aurelius

Children are like puppies: you have to keep them near you and look after them if you want to have their affection —Anna Magnani

Children are like pancakes: You should always throw out the first one —Peter Benchley

Children [in families] are like rival pretenders to a throne and their main object in life is to eliminate their competitors —Milton R. Sapirstein

Children in a family are like flowers in a bouquet: there's always one determined to face in an opposite direction from the way the arranger desires —Marcelene Cox

Children like apples ... good enough to eat —Donald Culross

Children ... like robins, pink-cheeked and rosy —Lawrence Durrell

Children ... they string our joys, like jewels bright, upon the thread of years —Edward A. Guest

The faces of the kids ... suddenly deprived by fear of their childhood, looked like ancient agonized adults —Herbert Gold

A happy childhood can't be cured. Mine'll hang around my neck like a rainbow —Hortense Calisher

This is the opening for the novel Queenie, *in which the author is much sparer with her similes than she is in her short stories*

Ladies touch babies like bankers touch gold —James Ferry

One of two similes from a little rhyme within a short story entitled Dancing Ducks.

Life without children is like a tree without leaves —Milan Kundera

A little girl without a doll is almost as unfortunate and quite as impossible as a woman without children —Victor Hugo

Maternal testimony not withstanding, babies are like biscuits in a pan —Ellery Sedgewick

My childhood clings to me like wet paint —Daphne Merkin

In Enchantment, *a novel about a young woman's search for self-discovery, the simile concludes: "Blotching the picture of who I am in the present."*

With children as with plants ... future character is indicated by their early disposition —Demophilus

CHIN
See Also: CHEEKS, FACE(S), MOUTH

A chin like an infant's elbow —Penelope Gilliatt

Chin like the butt end of a ham —Ross Macdonald

(A small) chin like half a rubber ball —Robert Campbell

Chin line ... shaped like a persimmon —Susan Minot

Her chin rising and falling upon her heaving bosom like the figurehead of a vessel upon a heavy harbor swell —Arthur Train

Chin stood out like the knuckles in a clenched hand —Max Apple

Chin was blue as if it had been shot full of gunpowder —Joyce Cary

Jaw as rigid as a shovel —John Yount

A jaw like a park bench —Raymond Chandler, *The Little Sister*

Jaw like the head of an ax slipped through at the last second like a curl of smoke —R. Wright Campbell

A jaw like the share of a plow —Sterling Hayden

Jawline like granite —William Diehl

Jaw set like a rock —Donald Seaman

(He popped a mint into his mouth and) snapped his jaws shut like a shark —Harvey Swados

Their shaven jowls looked like the hide of a fresh-scalded, fresh-scraped hog —William Humphrey

❧ CHOICES

Alternatives faced one like knives —Hortense Calisher

Feel like a piece of flux caught between two magnets —William Diehl

In Diehl's novel Hooligans, *the two magnets represent the choice between two lifestyles.*

Indecisive as a young boy in an ice cream parlor —Ira Berkow discussing George Steinbrenner's choices of field leaders for the Yankees, *New York Times*/Sports of the Times, September 20, 1986

I would sooner smarm like a fart-licking spaniel than starve in a world of fat poems —Dylan Thomas

It [making a choice] seems like a choice between lunacy and idiocy, death by fire or by water —Henry James, letter to Thomas Sergeant Perry, November 1, 1863

Like a kid jumping off the barn ... once they decide to go, they go —John D. MacDonald

Sudden resolutions, like the sudden rise of the mercury in the barometer, indicate little else than the changeableness of the weather —Julius Charles Hare

Took all things of life for hers to choose from and apportion, as though she were continually picking presents for herself from an inexhaustible counter —F. Scott Fitzgerald

❧ CHURCHES
See: HOUSES

❧ CITIES/STREETSCAPES
See Also: PLACES

Alleys open and fall around me like footsteps of a newly shod horse —Frank O'Hara

The ancient oaks ... marched over the avenue like a canopy —John Kennedy Toole

The asphalt shines like a silk hat —Derek Walcott

Bars were strung along the street like bright beads —Margaret Millar

In her novel Experiment in Springtime, *Millar strings the names of the bars to this simile.*

A big limestone church hangs like a gray curtain under the street lamp —John Updike

The black night falls like a shroud over the whole town —Lu Hsun

A brutally ugly, utilitarian place, like a mill town without the mill —Jonathan Valin

The city seems to uncurl like some hibernating animal dug out of its winter earth —Lawrence Durrell

The city unwrinkles like an old tortoise —Lawrence Durrell

Far below and around lay the city like a ragged purple dream —O. Henry

In the distance, the city rose like a cluster of warts on the side of the mountain —Flannery O'Connor

Men and women, streaming forth from all directions like giant lines of ants moving fast and earnestly —Alaa Al Aswany, *Chicago*

The noon sun put a glaze on them [the sidewalks], so that the cement burned and glittered like glass —Carson McCullers

The passing scene spread outside the windows like a plentiful, prim English tea —Dorothea Straus

People [on a crowded sidewalk] ... jostling along like sheep in a pen that has no end —Maeve Brennan

The public streets, like built canals of air —David Denby

Raw grass sprouted from the cobbles like hair from a deafened ear —Philip Levine

The shadows of the palms lay like splash marks of dark liquid on the pavement —Ross Macdonald

The shop fronts stood along that thoroughfare with an air of invitation, like rows of smiling saleswomen —Robert Louis Stevenson

A steep lane, like a staircase —Émile Zola

The street as gray as newspapers —Marge Piercy

The street lay still as a photograph —Jack Finney

The street shone … like a fire in a forest —Robert Louis Stevenson

The streets looked as if they were made of silver they were so bright and glistening —Oscar Wilde

The streets (of Bethany, Massachusetts) sparkled like high-gloss picture postcards sold in drugstores of small New England villages —Susan Richards Shreve

Streets tangled like old string —W. H. Auden

Street … that neither stank or sparkled but merely had a look of having been turned, like the collar on an old shirt —Hortense Calisher

That's how quickly New York City comes about—like a weather vane—or the head of a cobra. Time tells —Cynthia Ozick, *Heir to the Glimmering World*

The town, like an upturned sky, swollen with human lights —Albert Camus

The town [seen from a distance] looked small and clean and perfect, as if it were one of those miniature plastic towns sitting beside a child's electric railroad —Ann Tyler

A view (of Brewer) spread out below like a carpet —John Updike

Village … jumbled and colorful like a postcard —George Garrett

Wide, smooth, empty sidewalks looked like long canals of grey eyes —Ayn Rand

♣ CIVILIZATION

See: SOCIETY

♣ CLARITY

(The scents of the garden descended upon him, their contours) as precise and clear as the colored bands of a rainbow —Patrick Suskind

As sharp as the last daybreak —Joy Williamson
From a book jacket blurb about Tess Gallagher's ability to portray aging people's vision of irremediable loss in the novel The Lovers of Horses.

As unreadable as a piece of modern sculpture —Frank Swinnerton

(The image) blurred … like something familiar seen beneath disturbed though clear water —William Faulkner

(The consonants) blur together like ink on a wet page —Sue Grafton

Clear and diminished like a scene cut in cameo —Edna St. Vincent Millay

Clear as a bell —John Ray's *Proverbs*
One could compile a small book of just "Clear as" similes. The bell comparison along with "Clear as a whistle" and "Clear as crystal" are probably most frequently used and familiar.

[A theory synthesized from suppositions] as clear as a case history written in a book —Jean Stafford

Clear as a cloudless hour —Algernon Charles Swinburne

Clear as a cube of solid sunshine —Anon

[Eyes] clear as a fountain —Walter Savage Landor

Clear as a graph —Anon

Clear as a lake —Samuel Taylor Coleridge

Clear as a legal confession of murder —John Cheever

Clear as an oboe solo —Diane Ackerman

Clear as A on the piano in the middle of all the tuning instruments of an orchestra —Sylvia Plath

Clear as a tear —Sylvia Plath

Clear as cold water —Mark Helprin

(The morning was) clear as glass —Mark Helprin

Clear as infant's eyes —John Keats

(The creek flashed) clear as quartz —Ella Leffland

Clear as righteousness —Algernon Charles Swinburne

Clear as the A, B, C —George Washington

Clear as the day —Miles Coverdale

"Clear as" comparisons linked with the day, time of day, and the sun at different times of the day include: "Clear as noon" (shortened from the once popular "Clear as noon-day") and "Clear as the sun" (both attributed to Roger North); "Clear as is the summer's sun" (from William Shakespeare's The Life of King Henry the Fifth); "Clear as the mid-day sunshine" (Nathaniel Hawthorne); "Clear as day-light" (Arnold Bennett).

Clear as the figures at the bottom of a profit and loss statement —Anon

Clear as the lines in a wet leaf —Charles Johnson

Clear as the note of doom —Lord De Tabley

(The men were naked and) clear as the point of a sword in the sun —George Garrett

(The sky is as) clear as the song of a boy —Beryl Markham

Clear as the twanging of a harp —Alfred, Lord Tennyson

Clear as wind —Alfred, Lord Tennyson

Clear, like accusation —Paul Horgan

[Voice in the "silent dead of night"] distinct as a passing footstep's fall —Henry Wadsworth Longfellow

Distinctly as white lace on velvet —Thomas Hardy

(Shouldn't the soul of a man be as) limpid and cutting as a diamond —John Cheever

(The air is) lucid and lonely as wind chimes —Sharon Sheehe Stark

(The poet's work was about as) lucid as a polygraph —Joseph Wambaugh

Lucidity is positively flowing over me like the sweet oils of Persia —Lorraine Hansberry

Precise as a portrait photo —Natascha Wodin

To read [Descartes] was like swimming in a lake so clear that you could see the bottom —W. Somerset Maugham

(Lake) transparent as liquid chrysolite —T. H. White

Transparent as a white cloud in the moonshine —Hans Christian Andersen

(Lake) transparent as liquid chrysolite —T. H. White

Transparent like some holy thing —Thomas Moore

❧ CLEANLINESS

See Also: ORDER/DISORDER

Clean and smooth as a peeled onion —O. Henry

Clean and well-kept as a cemetery —Karl Shapiro

(Her face) clean and white as a handkerchief —John Ashberry

[a kitchen] clean and white as heaven —Amor Towles, *Rules of Civility*

Clean as a Band-Aid —Max Apple

Clean as a bleached bone —Wallace Stegner

Clean as a convent cell —Vita Sackville-West

Clean as a hound's tooth —American colloquialism, attributed to New England

(His heart felt) clean as a new green leaf —Stephen Vincent Benét

Clean as a New England kitchen —Anon

Clean as a newly laundered sheet —Rosamund Pilcher

Pilcher uses the "Clean as a sheet" simile to describe the smoothness and cleanliness of sand

when the tide is out in a story entitled "The White Birds."

Clean as a new pin of every penny of debt —Sir Walter Scott

Clean as a penny —William Robertson

A much used simile for anyone that is neatly and cleanly dressed.

Clean as a pig's whistle —American colloquialism, attributed to New England Just plain "Clean as a whistle," is said to stem from the fact that it takes a clean dry whistle to produce a good sound.

Clean as a piglet bathed in milk —Mary Gordon

Clean as a rose is after rain —James Whitcom Riley

Clean as a toilet bowl —Lincoln Kirstein

(The woman was as) clean as a white rose in the morning gauze of dew —Carl Sandburg

Clean as driftwood —Robert Hass

(Legs) clean as marble —Beryl Markham

Clean as new grass when the old grass burns —Carl Sandburg

Clean as water pouring from a silver tap —Tennessee Williams

Dirty as a glass roof in a train station —Leonard Cohen

Dust balls sail like galleons [on a carpet] on the dry sea —Robert Irwin

Feathers of dust clung like frightened children to the table legs —Loren D. Estleman, *Sugartown: An Amos Walker Mystery*

Fingernails … like watch crystals —Walker Percy

Immaculate as a laboratory —Ben Ames Williams

Spotless as naked innocence —John Smith

The water's (of the swimming pool) like bouillabaisse. It's got more things in it than Macy's window —Noel Coward

❧ CLEVERNESS

See Also: Alertness

Adroit as a rhinoceros —Franklin P. Adams

Brain as nimble as an aircraft —David Nicholls, *One Day*

Brains like the frogs, dispersed all over his body —Charles Dickens

Clever as a bird-dog —American colloquialism, attributed to New England

Clever as sin —Rudyard Kipling

Crafty as a new religious convert pledged to win over a sinner —Gloria Norris

Crafty as an exorcist —Miles Gibson

Crafty as the sea —W. B. Yeats

Cunning as a dead pig, but not half so honest —Jonathan Swift

Cunning is a sort of short-sightedness —Joseph Addison

Has as many tricks as a bear —John Ray's *Proverbs*

Hinted with the delicacy of a lilac bud —Sinclair Lewis

Ingenious as magicians —Delmore Schwartz

Like rats, his wits were beginning to busy themselves again —Walter de la Mare

Little clevernesses are like half-ripened plums, only good eating on the side that has had a glimpse of the sun —Henry James

Played on his misfortune as on a cello —Marguerite Yourcenar

Sharp and bright as a blade of sunlight —Alice Walker

Sharp as a cut-throat razor —Donald Seaman

Sharp as a knife —American colloquialism, attributed to New England

An equally popular variation, also attributed to New England folklore: "Sharp as a razor."

Sharp as a needle —Anon

Common usage has made this interchangeable with "Sharp as a pin." A variation of more recent vintage, "Sharp as a tack," has become a cliché in its own right.

Sharp as mustard —Ogden Nash

> *In Nash's poem, "The Tale of the Custard Dragon," the descriptive frame of reference is a little dog.*

Shrewd as a barrel-load of monkeys —Robin Sheiner

Shrewd as a sparrow —Janet Flanner

Shrewdness is often annoying, like a lamp in the bedroom —Ludwig Boerne

Sly and slick as a varmint —Robert Penn Warren

(Every move had been as stealthy and as) sly as a hungry coyote —William Humphrey

Smart as a whip —Anon

> *Used to the point of abuse since the seventeenth century. A variation in keeping with the phrase's origin which refers to the smarting pain caused by a whip: "Sharp as a whiplash."*

Smart as new nails —Sharon Sheehe Stark

Tricky as palmistry —Karl Shapiro

Wily as a fox —John Clarke

> *The fox continues to be a favorite link to clever, crafty behavior. Often 'cunning' is substituted for 'wily,' and the fox is not just any fox but an old one.*

♣ CLICHÉ

See: ORIGINALITY; MAXIMS, PROVERBS, AND SAYINGS

♣ CLINGING

See Also: PERSISTANCE; PEOPLE, INTERACTION; RELATIONSHIPS

Adhere like lint —Anon

Adhere like ticks to a sheep's back —Maurice Hewlett

Adhering … like shipwrecked mariners on a rock —J.M. Barrie

Between flashbacks that trace her journey from modest beginnings the phrase "grocer's daughter from Grantham" is attached to her like a Homeric epithet —A. O. Scott, review of movie *The Iron Lady, New York Times*, December 29, 2011.

> *The film's title is, of course, a metaphor.*

Clinging … like lichen to a rock —Ross Macdonald

Clinging like a limpet in the heaviest sea —William H. Hallhan

Clinging … like a monkey-on-a-stick —Julia O'Faolain

Clinging … stupidly, like a mule —Joseph Conrad

Clinging to her like chewing gum to a boot sole —Julian Gloag

Cling … like a wart —Tony Ardizzone

> *The simile, as used in The Heart of the Order, describes the way a cowboy clings to the back of a bull.*

Cling like chewing gum to a shoe sole —Anon

Cling like ivy —Robert Burton

Clings fiercely to all his titles, like an old soldier to his medals —Robert Traver

Clings to as a baby clings to its pacifier —Anon

Clings to me like a bed-bug —Maxim Gorky

Cling to (another person) as an exhausted man does to a rock —Brooks Bakeland

Cling to … like a drowning person to a piece of timber —Isak Dinesen

Cling to like a leech —American colloquialism, attributed to New England

Cling to like a vine —American colloquialism, attributed to New England

> *A variation is to "Cling like ivy."*

Cling to … like tenacious barnacles upon rocks —Mary Ellen Chase

Clung like a basket enfolding a tithe offering —Arthur A. Cohen

Clung [to an idea] like a shipwrecked sailor hanging on to the only solid part of his sinking universe —Marguerite Yourcenar

(The baby) clung like a sloth —Louise Erdrich

Clung ... like a tarantula —Terry Southern

(Rancor) clung like curses on them —Percy Bysshe Shelley

Clung ... like magnet to steel —T. Buchanan Read

Clung the way a tree animal clings to a branch —Rachel Ingalls

Clung to each other like double sweet peas —*A Broken-Hearted Gardener,* anonymous nineteenth-century verse

Clung together hand in hand like men overboard —George Garrett

Clung to her like a man on a swaying subway car whose grip on the overhead rail keeps him from tumbling to the floor —Paul Reidinger

Clung to his consciousness like a membrane —John Updike

Clutched [at her blanket] as a faller clutches at the turf on the edge of a cliff —Virginia Woolf

Clutching hold of ... with the grasp of a drowning man —Charles Dickens

Clutching is the surest way to murder love, as if it were a kitten, not to be squeezed so hard, or a flower to fade in a tight hand —May Sarton

(There she sat) glued to the tube like a postage stamp —A. Alvarez

Gummed together like wet leaves —Lawrence Durrell

[A term to describe a problem] had stuck with him like day-old oatmeal —T. Glen Coughlin

Hang on like a summer cold —Anon

Hang on ... like a tick —Rita Mae Brown

Hang on to ... [some small, unimportant point] ... like a dog to a bone —Barbara Greene, on her cousin Graham Greene

Some people like to get more specific; for example, "Hang on to ... like a terrier" is found in Iris Murdoch's novel The Good Apprentice.

Hang over like a heavy curtain —Anon

Hang over like a layer of smog —Anon

Hang over like crepe —Anon

Hang over like murder on a guilty soul —Sciller

Hang together like burrs —John Ray's *Proverbs*

Hung like bees on mountain-flowers —Percy Bysshe Shelley

(The thought ...) hung like incense around Francis —Dorothy Canfield

It [something that had been said] stuck up in the girl's consciousness like a fallen meteor —John Cheever

(A scar of horror, if not of guilt) lay consciously on his breast, like the scarlet letter —George Santayana

Clinging ... like starving children to a teat —Margaret Millar (Beyond

Like swarming bees they clung —Lord Byron

Remained like a black cloud —Frank Swinnerton

She clings to me like a fly to honey —Anton Chekov

She clung to him like a shadow —Margaret Mitchell

She's coiled around her family and her house like a python —Jane Bowles

She was like a sea-anemone —had only to be touched to adhere to what touched her —John Fowles

Sticking to [another person's side] like a melting snowbank —Marge Piercy

Stick like a wet leaf —Anton Chekov

Sticks like a burr to a cow's tail —Edward Noyes Westcott

Sticks like crazy glue —Anon

(My touch) sticks like mud —Marge Piercy

Stick together like overcooked pasta —Elyse Sommer

Stick together like peanut butter and jelly —Ed McBain

Sticky as fire —Terry Bisson

Sticky as rubber cement —Anon

Stuck … like a barnacle to a ship's keel, or a snail to a door, or a little bunch of toadstools to the stem of a tree —Charles Dickens

Stuck to [him or her] like shit to a blanket —American colloquialism

Stuck to my side like a lung infected with pleurisy —Patrick White

Stuck with … like gas on water —Will Weaver

Tenacious as a Boston bull —Anon

They [people who cling to outmoded political concepts] are like degenerates who are color blind, except that they see something which is NOT there, instead of failing to see something which is —Janet Flanner

They [narrator's daughters] cling together like Hansel and Gretel —Ogden Nash

Tied to each other back to back [long-married people] … like dogs unable to disengage after coupling —Lawrence Durrell

❧ CLOSENESS

See Also: COMPATIBILITY, FRIENDSHIP

Always together … like Siamese twins —Nina Bawden

[Cid and his wife Juena] are like the nail [finger nail] and the flesh —*The Lay of the Cid,* epic poem

According to a grad student at SUNY, Stony Brook, NY, this is the only simile in this 3500 verse epic poem dating back to 1140 C.E.

As close to him as sticking plaster —Cornell Woolrich

Close as an uncracked nut —Anon

Close as a dead heat —Anon

Close as fingers inside a pair of mittens —Anon

Close as flies in a bottle —Shana Alexander

Close as the bark to a tree —Sir Charles Sedley

This simile is also used to describe stinginess.

Close as the cu in cucumbers —Anon

Close as the gum on a postage stamp —Anon

Close as two peas in a pod —H. I. Phillips

Common usage has created twists such as "Close as two peas on a plate."

Close like exiles from a remote and forgotten land —A.R. Guerney Jr.

Close together as the two shells of an oyster —Leonard McNally

Get as close as an Eskimo does to a fire in his igloo in the tundra —Anon, from a radio broadcast

His face was so close to hers that it was out of focus, like a cloud passing in front of the sun —Michael Korda

Inseparable as a baseball fan and a bag of peanuts —Anon

Inseparable as finger and thumb —George Farquhar

Inseparable as a shadow to a body —Robert Burton

Inseparable as Don Quixote and Sancho Panza —Anon

Inseparable like ivy, which grows beautifully so long as it twines around a tree, but is of no use when it is separated —J. P. Molière

The original wording has been transcribed from "A woman is like ivy" for a less gender-oriented interpretation.

Intimate as two sardines in a can —Anon

Near as the end of one's nose —Anon

Near as twilight is to darkness —Thomas Paine

Strayed as close to that woman as a pimple —Charles Johnson

They're as thick as three in a bed —Scottish saying

They were all standing around him thick as bees —Cornell Woolrich

(It is proper that families remain) thick like good soup —J. P. Donleavy

Though you think he's far away / He's near to you, so near to you / As near as April is to May! —Richard Adler and Jerry Ross, "Near to You," *Damn Yankees*

We were like two kernels in one almond —Sadi

Wrapped tight an as eggroll —Donald McCaig

♣ CLOTHING

See Also: CLOTHING ACCESSORIES; CLOTH-ING, ITS FIT

A little-girl-type sundress that was about as sexy as a paper bag —Dan Wakefield

All dressed up like Christmas trees —Rosamund Pilcher

A baggy blue flowered housedress that looked like old slipcovers —Louise Erdrich

A bikini is like a barbed-wire fence. It protects the property without obstructing the view —Joey Adams

Blouses thin as the film of tears in your eyes —Bin Ramke

Clothes, pressed stiff as cardboard —Jay Parini

Coat like a discarded doormat —T. Coraghessan Boyle

A dark blue suit so rigidly correct that it looked like a uniform —Harvey Swados

Draped in a muumuu that covered her like a Christo curtain shrouding a California mountain —Paul Kuttner

Dressed all in brown, like a rabbit —Anon

Dressed as if she were going to a coronation —Shelby Hearon

Dressed in black jersey, without ornament, like a widow —Ross Macdonald

Dressed like a bookie —Gavin Lyall

Dressed like a Hollywood bit player hoping to be discovered leaning on a bar —Robert Campbell

In his novel, In La-La Land We Trust, *Campbell expands upon this simile for several sentences, detailing the outfit.*

Dressed up like a dog's dinner —American colloquialism

This means to be overdressed, and badly dressed at that.

Dresses conservatively as a corpse —Harvey Swados

(The Queen) dresses like a whistle-stop town librarian —Stephen Longstreet

Dresses like he's got a charge at Woolworth's —Robert B. Parker

With names of stores and companies and products constantly changing, Woolworth's may not always be synonymous with cheap. However, the simile could live on with an appropriate substitution.

Dress … gone limp in the heat, like a wilted plant —Louise Erdrich

A dress like ice-water —F. Scott Fitzgerald

Dress that was as small as a scarf —Laurie Colwin

Fancy as a rooster up for the fair —Linda Hogan

Garments as weathered as an old sail —George Eliot

A girl who dressed like an Arabian bazaar —T. Coraghessan Boyle

Her white silk robe flowed over her like a milk shower —Harold Adams

He was dressed for this death-watch job [hotel desk clerk] as if for a lively party —Christopher Isherwood

In her orange fringed poncho she looked like a large teepee —Michael Malone

Ladies wrapped like mummies in shawls with bright flowers on them —Virginia Woolf

Like her husband she carried clothes, carried them as a train carries passengers —Henry James

Looks like she's wearing her entire wardrobe all at once—and all of it hand-me-downs from someone bigger than she is —Julie Salamon

A description of the appearance of a character played by Debra Winger in the movie Black Widow, Wall Street Journal, *February 6, 1987.*

A party frock sticking out all around her [a little girl's] legs like a lampshade —Joyce Cary

Peeled off his trousers like shucking corn —Rita Mae Brown

Ragged as a scarecrow —Thomas Heywood

Shirt [heavily patched] lays on his body like a ratty dishtowel —Carolyn Chute

Skirts swirling like a child's pennant caught in a stiff breeze —Tony Ardizzone

Slickers [worn by cops] that shone like gun barrels —Raymond Chandler

Raymond Chandler used this simile in his early days as a pulp magazine writer, (Killer In the Rain, Black Mask Magazine, *1935) and again in his novel* The Big Sleep.

Starched clothes sat in the grass like white enameled teapots —Isaac Babel

[Formal attire] Suited them the way an apron suits a grizzly bear —William McIlvanney

Sweater as sopped as wet sheep —Susan Minot

Tailored and bejeweled like a pampered gigolo —James Mills

Tightly wrapped in a red skirt like a Christmas present —Helen Hudson

Trousers pressed as sleek as a show dog's flank —R. V. Cassill

A wedding gown like a silver cloud —Mazo de la Roche

A white robe, flowing, like spilled milk —Paige Mitchell

Wide sleeves fluttering like wings —Marcel Proust

Wore his clothes as if they were an official uniform —Vernon Scannell

You wear your clothes as if you want to be helped out of them —W. P. Kinsella

Zipped and buttoned into a polyester pantsuit, she was like a Christmas stocking half-filled with fruit —Mary Ward Brown

❧ CLOTHING ACCESSORIES

See Also: JEWELRY

Boots that shone like a well-rubbed table —Stephen Vincent Benét

A collar that looked like a pancake flapping around my head and it made me look like a pregnant penguin —Elizabeth Taylor

Glasses as thick as the bottom of a pop bottle —George Garrett

Handkerchief hoisted like a brave little flag from his breast pocket —Vicki Baum

Hat big as an Easter cake —Joyce Cary

A hat … perched right on top of her head, like a mushroom —Roald Dahl

Impenetrably black sunglasses like Batman's mask —John Rechy

Shoes gleaming like beer bottles —Loren D. Estleman

Shoes … shined up like patent leather —George Garrett

Shoes sticking out like tongues beneath the long black robe —Helen Hudson

Silk, like wrinkled skins on scalded milk —Oliver Wendell

Socks which fell like a couple of woolen concertinas over his dusty shoes —John Mortimer

Straw hat with a bow on it like the sails of a windmill —L. P. Hartley

A ten-gallon hat like a walking mushroom —Truman Capote

Tie … loose and awry like a long lazy tongue wore a costume as distinctive as a ballet dancer's tutu —Van Wyck Mason

Ties pulled loose from their collars, like weary gamblers —Graham Swift

♣ CLOTHING, ITS FIT

See Also: CLOTHING

Bathing suit so tight that it seemed any moment she would burst out of it like a cooked frankfurter —George Garrett

A blanket wrapped around her body as tight as a cigar —Scott Spencer

(Clothes which) clung like refractory cobwebs —Patrick White

A coat which seems to fit her as her life fits, barely, inadvertently, not at all —Herbert Morris

Everything she wears fits like a saddle on a sow —Harold Adams

(Her bathing suit that) fit her like a sack —Flannery O'Connor

Fit like a saddle fits a sow —Anon

> *A alliterative putdown for the way a person is dressed. It dates back to sixteenth-century England and became an American colloquialism shortly after it crossed the ocean.*

[A dress] fits like the skin of a grape —Charles Raddock

> *Raddok's scathing review of the play* Between the Covers *describes Jacqueline Susann's outfit by referring to the lines of the dress as its only good lines.*

Fits you like flannel washed in hot suds —O. Henry

Fitted her like a duck's foot in the mud —American colloquialism, attributed to New England

Her coat fit her like a cheese box —Mary Gordon

Her garments seeming to flutter round her like draperies —Barbara Pym

Her halter top that cradled her breasts like a hammock —Phyllis Naylor

Her sleeves dropped like a sigh —Anais Nin

Her slip was stretched over her breast, as firmly and simply as linen over an embroidery frame —Boris Pasternak

Her stockings hung about her ankles like Hamlet's when he exposed himself to Ophelia and called her a whore —Leonard Michaels

His [shirt] collar was so tight it felt like a string cutting his neck —Dan Wakefield

His jacket hung on him like a scarecrow —Ross Macdonald

His pants hung as full as an Arab tent from his global stomach —William Diehl

His shirt fit him like a sail at the back —Philip Gerard

His short-sleeved shirt and short pants fit him like a dirty sack —James Crumley

(The uniform) hung slack like a castoff on a scarecrow —Paige Mitchell

Jeans fit like a rubber glove —W. P. Kinsella

The jeans fitted like hand-me-ups from a younger, thinner sister —Margaret Millar

(A healthy blonde with) jeans so tight her hipbones looked like towel hooks —Erma Bombeck

[Pants] tight … like elastic bandages —Ann Petry

Jeans that made his legs look like tree trunks. The bright green fishnet shirt he wore made him look even more like a tree —Ann Beattie

Legs … hung straight and rigid as if she had iron shinbones and ankles —William Faulkner

She wears her clothes as if they were thrown on her with a pitchfork —Jonathan Swift

Snugger than the bark to a dead maple —Anon

(A yellow) tee shirt that clings to her arms, breast and round belly like the skin of a sausage —Russell Banks

They [too-large trousers] make you look like an elephant that has lost weight —Penelope Gilliatt

Tight blue jeans that grip her behind like two hands —Charles Bukowski

Tight … like a lobster shell —W. S. Gilbert

Trousers and jacket droop like a tailor's nightmare —T. Coraghessan Boyle

Trousers … as wrinkled at the crotch as if he'd had them pressed that way —Harvey Swados

The trousers fitted her legs closely, but she could come out of them as though she were peeling a banana —MacDonald Harris

❦ CLOUD(S)

See Also: CLOUD MOVEMENTS, SKY

A cloud like a torn shirt —Katherine Mansfield

Clouds are like Holy Writ, in which theologians cause the faithful or the crazy to see anything they please —Voltaire

Clouds … as white as leghorn feathers —Saul Bellow

The cloud showed motion within, like an old transport truck piled high with crate on crate of sleepy white chickens —Eudora Welty

The clouds hung above the mountains like puffs of white smoke left in the wake of a giant old-fashioned choo-choo train —Sue Grafton

The clouds lie over the chiming sky … like the dustsheets over a piano —Dylan Thomas

Clouds like a marble frieze across the sky —Helen Hudson

Clouds like cruisers in the heaven —Edna O'Brien

Clouds like dark bruises were massing and swelling [on the horizon] —George Garrett

Clouds … like drowsy lambs around a tree —Romain Gary

(The sky turned sooty with) clouds like enormous thumbprints —Helen Hudson

Clouds like lights among great tombs —Wallace Stevens

Clouds like tattered fur —Jean Thompson

Clouds piling up like a bubble bath —Sue Grafton

Clouds, plump and heavy as dumplings —Anthony E. Stockanes

The clouds were asses' ears —Dylan Thomas

The clouds were huddled on the horizon like dirty sheep from the steppes —Joyce Renwick

The clouds were like an alabaster palace —Johnny Mercer, from his 1954 lyrics for "Midnight Sun."

The clouds were like old fiddles —Joyce Cary

A few clouds were drawn against the light like streaks of lead pencils —John Cheever

Fluffy white clouds, like flecks of lather, were floating across the sky —Alexander Solzhenitsyn

Clouds … wild and black and rolling like locomotives —W. P. Kinsella

Frail clouds like milkweed floss —John Dos Passos

Gleaming, white fluffy clouds peeped over the hills … like kittens —Stella Benson

High fat clouds like globs of whipped cream —William Faulkner

Like a grave face, lit by some last, sad thought, a cloud, tinged by the fading glow of sunset —John Hall Wheelock

Like blurred lenses, winter clouds cast a shade over the sun —Truman Capote

(Above the falling sun,) like visible winds the clouds are streaked and spun —Roy Fuller

Little white clouds … like a row of ballet-girls, dressed in white, waiting at the back of the stage, alert and merry, for the curtain to go up —W. Somerset Maugham

Little white clouds like flags were whipped out in the scented wind —Paul Horgan

Little white puffs of cloud … like a cat steeped in milk —W. P. Kinsella

A long thin cloud crossed it [the moon] slowly, drawing itself out like a name being called —Eudora Welty

Low clouds, drooping at the edges like felt, sailed over the woods —Boris Pasternak

Low on the horizon hung a fugitive wisp of cloud, spiraled and upthrust like a genie emerging from a bottle —Robert Traver

A massive cloud like dirty cotton —William Faulkner

One cloud intruded [into the blue of the sky], puffy, precise, as if piped from a pastry bag —Margaret Sutherland

Parcels of clouds lying against the mountainside like ghosts of dead mackerel —Paul Theroux

A single puff of cloud so still, it seems as if it had been painted there —Delmore Schwartz

Small thin clouds like puffs of frosty breath —Joyce Cary

Some small clouds, like rosy petals, seemed to his eyes to be dancing, gently and carefully, against the blue —Hugh Walpole

They [the clouds] peel the morning like a fruit —Lawrence Durrell

When clouds appear like rocks and towers, the earth's refreshed by frequent showers —English weather rhyme

White and fluffy clouds … one looked like a fish and one looked like a movie star, all curvy, and another looked like Santa Claus gone wrong —Lee Smith

❧ CLOUD MOVEMENTS

See Also: RAIN

Black clouds lumbered off westward like ghosts of buffalo —W. P. Kinsella

Clouds floating around [in the sky] … like suds in a pan —Helen Hudson

Clouds … gathered like great boneless birds —Hugh Walpole

Clouds hastening like messengers through heaven —John Hall Wheelock

Clouds rising like a tide of ink just beneath the moon —John Farris

Clouds rose up from the meadows like soft creamy wings seeking the bodies of gigantic birds —Rita Mae Brown

Clouds sailing … like a flock of birds taking flight to distant lands —Hans Christian Andersen

Clouds that hung, like banners —Edgar Allen Poe

Clouds that swam like lonely white fish in the sky —Robie Macauley

Clouds would part like windows, as though to air the sky —Boris Pasternak

Gray clouds ballooned down like the dirty underside of a great circus tent —Brian Moore

Inky clouds, like funeral shrouds sail over the midnight skies —W S. Gilbert

Gilbert contributed many a simile to the famous Gilbert and Sullivan operettas, like this one from Ruddigore.

Rain clouds scudded past like big ships sailing out of harbor —Brian Moore

Lonely clouds were floating above, like guests strolling above the sky —Yehuda Yaari

Over my head the clouds thicken, then crack and split like a roar of cannonballs tumbling down a marble staircase —Edward Abbey, *Desert Solitaire: A Season in the Wilderness*

A rolling cloud boiled onto the horizon like black liquid —Dorothy Francis

The sailing clouds went by, like ships upon the sea —Henry Wadsworth Longfellow

There's a feathery little cloud floatin' by like a lonely leaf on a big blue stream —Oscar Hammerstein II, lyrics for "Two Little People" from *Carousel*

Troops of small feathery white clouds ranged over the sky, like grazing herds of the gods —Thomas Mann

♣ CLUMSINESS
See: AWKWARDNESS

♣ COLDNESS
See Also: REMOTENESS, RESERVE

(There was) a certain coldness, like that of a spinster about her —Boris Pasternak

Behave exactly like a block of ice —Noel Coward, lyrics for "I'm So In Love"

The chill in the air was like a constant infinitely small shudder —M. J. Farrell

(Some laughs are as) cold and meaningless as yesterday's buckwheat pancake —Josh Billings
   Billings often used a phonetic dialect writing the "as" and "az."

Cold as a dead man's nose —William Shakespeare, *Winter's Tale*

Cold as a fish —American colloquialism, attributed to New England

Cold as a fish caught through the ice —F. van Wyck Mason

Cold as a hole in the ice —Bertolt Brecht

(It grew as) cold as a key —Thomas Heywood

Cold as a lizard —Walter Savage Landor
   In one of Landor's Conversation *pieces, he has Fra Filippo Lippi commenting to Pope Eugenius IV that while an ordinary person could use an expression like "Cold as ice," a true poet would reach for more originality. The above is one suggestion; "cold as a lobster" is another.*

Cold as a miser's heart —Donald Seaman

[A smile] cold as a moan —Marge Piercy

Cold as a murderer's heart —Richard Ford

Cold as an igloo —Reynolds Price

As cold as any stone —William Shakespeare, *Henry V*

Cold ... as a pane of glass —Reynolds Price

Cold as a snowman's dick —William H. Gass

(A kiss) cold as bacon —Joyce Cary

Cold as charity —Anon
   An English phrase in use since the seventeenth century.

Cold as coldest hell —Sylvia Berkman
   In a short story entitled "Who Killed Cock Robin," Beckman uses this simile to describe a character's personality and continues as follows: "cruel to every fingernail, and invariably polite."

Cold as dew to dropping leaves —Percy Bysshe Shelley

Cold as fears —Algernon Charles Swinburne

[I felt] as cold as Finnegan's feet (the day they buried him) —Raymond Chandler, *Farewell, My Lovely*

As cold as if I had swallowed snowballs —William Shakespeare, *The Merry Wives of Windsor*
   A variation of this snowball simile from The Merry Wives of Windsor *is found in another Shakespeare play,* Pericles: *"She sent him away as cold as a snowball."*

(Your heart would be as heavy and) cold as iron shackles —George Garrett

Cold as Monday morning's barrenness —F. D. Reeve

Cold as moonlight —Yvor Winters

(Face) cold as newsprint —Philip Levine

(Eyes) cold as river ice —Davis Grubb

As cold as snakes —American colloquialism, attributed to the Northeast

(Men) cold as spring water —Julia O'Faolain

(The wet air was as) cold as the ashes of love —Raymond Chandler, *Farewell, My Lovely*

Cold as the cold between the stars —Terry Bisson

Cold as the north side of a gravestone in Winter —Proverb

Cold as the snow —Lewis J. Bates

Cold as the tomb of Christ —Maxwell Anderson

Colder than a banker's heart —William Diehl

Colder than a dead lamb's tail —Anon

Colder than a lawyer's heart —George V. Higgins

Colder than a witch's tits —American colloquialism, attributed to the South

> *Like many regional expressions that gained national currency during World War II, this one is often referred to as an Army expression.*

(It was) colder than ice —Hans Christian Andersen

> *Whether used as a pure simile "Cold as ice" or as cited above, the linking of snow and ice to cold has become as "Common as snowflakes in winter." A story in the January 23, 1987 edition of the* New York Times *about a planned freedom march in Atlanta was highlighted with a blurb stating "We are going to march if it's cold as ice … " proving once again that even without a new twist, a simile usually wins the spotlight.*

Cold like a sea mist and as ungraspable —Sylvia Townsend

Cold [in manner] like Christmas morning —Grace Paley

The cold was like a sleep —Wallace Stevens

The cold was like a thick vast sleep —Davis Grubb

Cool and smooth, like the breath of an air conditioner —T. Coraghessan Boyle

Cool as a snowbank —Louisa May Alcott

(Her bare arms and shoulders felt as) cool as marble —Leo Tolstoy

(Skin) cool as steel —Elizabeth Hardwick

(Voice) cool as water on shaded rocks —Beryl Markham

Could feel the cold climbing up his ankles like ships' rats —Penelope Gilliatt

Hardened her heart, like God had hardened Pharaoh's heart against the Jews —Daphne Merkin

> *The simile was particularly appropriate in* Enchantment, *a novel about an orthodox Jewish family.*

A heart as cold as English toast —Harry Prince

It [TV show] was hard as fiberglass —Norman Mailer

My flesh was frozen for an inch below my skin, it was as if I were wearing icy armour —Rebecca West

Unresponding … like a wall —D. H. Lawrence

❧ COLLAPSE

See Also: DISINTEGRATION

Caved in like a sinkhole —Jonathan Valin

Caving in like a mud dam —Kurt Rheinheimer

(Periods in one's life that once seem important until you look back on them) collapsed as flat as packing cartons —Jonathan Penner

> *In a short story entitled "Emotion Recollected in Tranquility," the author tied the image of collapsed packing cartons to the collapse of part of one's life.*

Collapsed like an elephant pierced by a bullet in some vital spot —Kingsley Amis

Collapsed like a rotten tree —Erich Maria Remarque

Collapsed like a rump-shot dog —T. Coraghessan Boyle

(Half a dozen career daydreams) collapsed like a telescope —Thomas McGuane

Collapsed like a wounded soldier in the mud —Z. Vance Wilson

Collapsed to the floor like a tent that has had all the guy ropes and poles removed at the same time —Jimmy Sangster

Collapsed upon the sea as if his body had telescoped into itself, like a picnic beaker —Joyce Cary

(His body) collapsed vertically like a punctured concertina —Frank Ross

> *An older variation of this by Irving Cobb is "Fold up like a concertina."*

(One day would) collapse like a peony —Jilly Cooper

Collapse like a sack of meal —Anon

The sack of meal as a comparison linked to falling, collapsing or toppling has seeded so much use and extension that one can only list some of its in-print appearances: "Went over like a sack of meal" (Frank O'Connor); "Fall heavily, like a sack of meal" (S.J. Perelman); "Went down ... like an empty sack" (John M. Synge); "Dropped, like a flour sack falling from a loft" (Gerald Kersh). Most commonly overheard in everyday conversation is "Collapse like an empty paper bag."

Collapse like a snowman in the sun —Anon

Collapse like a tent when the pole is kicked out from under it —Loren D. Estleman

Collapse ... like empty garments —Joyce Cary

Collapse like sandcastles against the ocean tide —Anon

Collapse like a punctured blister —Mike Sommer

Collapse like the cheeks of a starved man —Charles Dickens

Collapsing like a cardboard carton thrown on a bonfire —Margaret Atwood

Comes apart [no longer able to control laughter] like a slow-ripping seam —Sharon Sheehe Stark

Crashed on the leather sofa, going down like a B-52 with a bellyful of shrapnel —Jonathan Kellerman

[Souvenirs of a romance] Crumble like flowers pressed in dictionaries —Judith Martin

Crumble like tinder —Anon

(A small white house that was) crumbling at the corners like stale cake left out on a plate —Jonathan Valin

Crumbling like one of those dry sponge cakes —Francis King

Crumpled like caterpillars on mulberry leaves —James Purdy

(She) crumpled like paper crushed in a fist and began to cry —Harold Adams

Crumpled up as if he were a paper flower —Ruth Prawer Jhabvala

Crumples like a used-up piece of paper —Daphne Merkin

[Gulls] Downed ... like a tumbled kite —John Hall Wheelcock

(The bird) dropped like an arrow —Leo Tolstoy

Dropped like an elephant's trunk —Eudora Welty

Dropped like one hit in the head by a stone from a sling —Eudora Welty

Drops like a piece of flotsam —T. Coraghessan Boyle

Falling as gently and slowly as a kite —Elizabeth Hardwick

Fall over like a frozen board —William H. Gass

Fall to the floor like misfired cannon balls —John Updike

(She's welcome to climb with man if she wishes ... and) fall with a crash like a trayful of dishes —Amy Lowell

Fell as low as a toad —American colloquialism, attributed to the Midwest

(Accents of peace and pity) fell like dew (upon my heart) —Percy Bysshe Shelley

Fell ... like insects knocked off by a gardener's spray —Derek Lambert

Fell like one who is seized with sleep —Dante Alighieri

Fell slowly forward like a toppling wall —Stephen Crane

Fell to her knees like a nun seeking sudden forgiveness —James Crumley

Flopped like the ears of a dog —Edgar Allan Poe

Folded up like a pocket camera —George Ade

Fold up like a cheap camera —Anon

[First baseman] Goes down slow as a toppling tree —W. P. Kinsella

Going under [dying] like shipwrecked sailors —Thomas Keneally

(Let life face him with a new demand on his understanding and then watch him) go soggy, like a wet meringue —D. H. Lawrence

He dropped like a bullock—he lay like a block —Rudyard Kipling

(When I tell him he must go, he suddenly) hits the floor like a toppled statue —Louise Erdrich

Hit the floor like an anvil —Joseph Wambaugh

(Slumped to the floor and) lay there like a punctured balloon —Myron Brinig

Some variations on the balloon comparison: "I was going down ... like a child's balloon as it gradually lets out air" (Eugene Ionesco's play, The Stroller in the Air); "Ripples to the pavement like a deflated balloon" from T. Coraghessan Boyle's novel Water Music, Little.

Like an emptying tube, after a couple of minutes he collapses —Erich Maria Remarque

Over she went ... like a little puff of milkweed —Eudora Welty

Pitched forward like a felled tree —Oakley Hall

(His heaving bulk suddenly) sagged, like a sail bereft of wind —Jan Kubicki

[Old man] Scrunched like an old gray fetus —Grace Paley

Thudded like a bird against the glass wall —Ross Macdonald

Topple over like a doll with a round base —Wilfrid Sheed

Tumble down like a house of cards —George Du Maurier

The many twists on tumbling, falling or collapsing cards as comparisons include Robert Browning's "Fell like piled-up cards" and Edith Wharton's "Collapsed like a playing card."

Tumbled down like the Tower of Babel —Bernard Malamud

Tumbling dumb as a ninepin —Sharon Sheehe Stark

We fell to the carpet like leaves circling in a light wind —James Crumley

Went down like a ninepin —Edith Wharton

This still popular simile to describe falling with a thud was probably in use before its appearance in Wharton's story, The Pelican.

Went down like a plumb line —Lawrence Durrell

Went down like a pole-axed steer —Donald Seaman

Went over [after being hit] like a paper cut-out and lay just as flat as one —Cornell Woolrich

❧ COLORS

See Also: BLACK, BLUE, BRIGHTNESS, BROWN, GREEN, PALLOR, PINK, RED, WHITE

An amber mixture like autumn leaves —François Maspero

[Go to the woods and bring me back / One: the cow] as white as milk Stephen Sondheim, "Epilogue," *Into the Woods*

The lyric continues with witch's additional items, all similes linked to colors, "Two: the cape as red as blood, Three: the hair as yellow as corn, Four: the slipper as pure as gold."

Bright gold like a diadem —Angela Carter

(Sky damp and) colorless as a cough —Sharon Sheehe Stark

Colorless as a desert —Alice McDermott

Colorless like the white paper streamer a Chinaman pulls out of his mouth —editor, *Dragonfly magazine,* 1880

The simile appeared in a rejection letter to Anton Chekhov when he was still a fledgling writer.

Colors are as soft as a Mediterranean dawn —Bryan Miller, *New York Times,* July 3, 1987

Miller's simile pertained to the colors of a restaurant.

Colors as clear as notes perfectly played —A. E. Maxwell

Colors [of Christmas candy] … as piercing as the joys and sufferings of the poor … red like the love that was celebrated in doorways … yellow like the flames in a drunk man's brain —Heinrich Böll

Colors clear as fresh-cut flowers —Joan Chase

Deep colored as old rugs —Eudora Welty

As full of color as blood —John Logan

Gold as the seeds of a melon —Dame Edith Sitwell

A good soldier, like a good horse, cannot be of a bad color —Oliver Wendell Holmes

Orange as the sunset —Dashiell Hammett

Orange bright like golden lamps in a green light —Andrew Marvell

[A taxi] Painted in an arabesque of colors, like a psychedelic dream gone wild —Andrew Kaplan

(His split lip is as) purple as a nightcrawler stuck on a hook —Robert Flanagan

This simile begins Flanagan's short story "Naked to Naked Goes."

[Cabbage] purply as cheap stained glass —Babette Deutsch

The reds and browns and golds of the trees seem ready to drip from their branches like wet dye —Alice McDermott

Silvery as sleighbells —Diane Ackerman

Two-toned like a layer cake —Donald McCaig

♣ COMEDY

Comedy is rather like a dessert; a bit like meringue —Woody Allen

♣ COMFORT

(Feel as) comfortable as a Cossack in Kiev —Richard Ford

(Eugene was) comfortable as a saggy armchair —Donald McCaig

Comfortable as matrimony —Nathan Bailey

Comfortable … like sleeping on a cloud —Slogan, Sealy Inc.

Comforting as a long soak in a hot tub after a short walk in a freezing rainstorm —Elyse Sommer

Comforting as the Surgeon General's statement on a pack of Lucky Strikes —Harry Prince

Comfort [memory of a lover] like a rosary —Sumner Locke Elliott

Cozy and dark as a dreary day —Sharon Sheehe Stark

Cozy as a cup of tea —Anon

Cozy as a nest —Émile Zola

Cozy as visiting your grandmother —Mary Lee Settle

Easy as an old shoe —English proverb

New Englanders brought this from the old country as "Comfortable as an old shoe," an expression still very much in use. There's also a Ukrainian proverb which incorporates a somewhat different form of this simile.

Feels comfortable like in a cloud —François Maspero

Reassured … like a sheltering wing over a motherless bird —Louisa May Alcott

Restful as one's favorite armchair —Frank Swinnerton

(Here Skugg lies) snug as a bug in a rug —Benjamin Franklin, letter to Georgiana Shipley, September, 1772

Snug as the yolk in an egg —Henrik Ibsen

Soothing as mother's milk —Anon

[Conversation] Soothing, like the quiet, washing sound of an ocean —Donald Justice

Supported [by attentive performance] as a bold swimmer by the waves —Ivan Turgenev

[Prospect of someone's being there] sustained him like a snug life jacket —Lynne Sharon Schwartz

Sustain like a stream does a trout —Andre Dubus

Warm and cozy and private as a nursery —John Braine

Warm and old-fashioned as a potbellied stove —Anon, capsule movie review, *Newsday*, January, 1986

(Walls look as) warm and sturdy as a fisherman's hand-knitted sweater —Sheila Radley

(The whole room was as equally and agreeably) warm as a bath full of water —Anon

Warm as piss —American colloquialism

Warm as sunshine, light as floating clouds —Slogan, Torefeaco bedding,

Warm like love —Sharon Sheehe Stark

❧ COMMONPLACE

See Also: FAMILIARITY

As corny as Kansas in August … as normal as blueberry pie —Oscar Hammerstein II, "A Wonderful Guy," *South Pacific*

This joyous declaration of love keeps piling on the similes: such as "I'm as trite and as gay as a daisy in May" and "I'm bromidic and bright/As a moon-happy night/Pourin' light on the dew!" Another famous simile from the same score: "High as a flag on the Fourth of July."

As daily as bread —Thomas Lux

Common as adultery, and hardly less reprehensible —Lord Altringham

Societal changes have seeded "Common as divorce" and "Common as sex before marriage."

Common as bag ladies on city streets —Anon

(Angels were as) common as birds or butterflies —Donald Justice

Common as dentists who molest female patients —Loren D. Estleman

Common as dirt —American colloquialism attributed to New England

A popular variation: "Common as mud."

Common as frozen dinners —Anon

Another up-and-coming one from our fast food age: "Common as microwave dinners."

Common as get out —William Hazlitt

This has become known and used as "Common as all get-out."

Common as graduation parties in June —Anon

Common as hot spells in July and snowflakes in winter —Elyse Sommer

Common as pig's tracks —H. W. Thompson

American folklore has simplified this to "Common as dirt."

Common … as potatoes —Hugh Walpole

Common as the highway —John Ray's *Proverbs*

Common as the New York cockroach —Erik Sandberg-Diment, writing about the increased use and availability of personal computer clones of the original IBM model, *New York Times*, December 12, 1986

New Yorkers might well argue that they have no exclusiveness when it comes to cockroaches.

(Charles's conversation was) commonplace as a street pavement —Gustave Flaubert

Commonplace as birth —Anon

Commonplace as slumber —Phyllis McGinley

Ordinary as walking a straight line —Lee K. Abbott

Taken for granted like a nose bob —Alistair Cooke, *New York Times* interview, referring to the television teleprompter, January 1, 1985

Traditional as a seven-layer wedding cake —Jonathan Valin

❧ COMPASSION

See Also: KINDNESS, PITY

❧ COMPATIBILITY

See Also: BELONGING

Companionable as a cat and a goldfish —Anon

Companionable [a mother and son] as a pair of collusive old whores —David Leitch

Compatible as the stars and stripes on the American flag —Elyse Sommer

Get on like a house on fire —Ngaio Marsh

Get on like salt and iron —Loren D. Estleman

Good taste and humor are a contradiction in terms, like a chaste whore —Malcom Muggeridge quoted in *Time*, September 14, 1953

Got along like Siamese twins —George Garrett

Go together like a computer and an abacus —Anon

Go together like apples and pie crust —Elyse Sommer

These "go-togethers" provide endless opportunity for additional twists.

Go together like bagels and cream cheese —Anon

Go together like blueberries and cream —Anon

Go together like coffee and danish —Anon

Go together like ice cream and salt —Anon

Go together like meatballs and spaghetti —Anon

Go together like paper and pencil —Anon

Go together like tea and lemon —Anon

Got on like twin souls —Edward Marsh

Irreconcilable as a jazz band and a symphony orchestra —Paul Mourand

No more affinity for each other than a robin for a goldfish —Eleanor Kirk

Struck [Flanner and Mike Wallace] it off together like a pair of lighted pinwheels —Janet Flanner

♣ COMPETENCE
See: ABILITY, ACCOMPLISHMENT

♣ COMPETITION
See Also: BUSINESS, SPORTS

As competitive as two dogs after a bitch in heat —Anon

Asking him to compete fairly is like asking a hungry lion to leave the lambs alone —Mike Sommer

Competition is like sugar sprinkled on cobbler pie —Elmer Kelton

A non-competitive businessman is like an honest crook —Elyse Sommer

Playing tennis without keeping score is like apple pie sans la mode —Anon

♣ COMPLACENCY
See: CONTENTMENT

♣ COMPLAINTS
See: ANGER, CRITICISM

♣ COMPLETENESS

Fragmentary, like the text of a corrupt manuscript whose words have been effaced in the wind and rain —Arthur A. Cohen

Completely as hydrogen mixes with oxygen to become water ... the orange is part of the living animal —Daniela Gioseffi

Incomplete as a circus without clowns —Elyse Sommer

Incomplete ... like cabbage with all the flavor boiled out —Richard Brookhiser, *Wall Street Journal* book review, April 1, 1987

The simile refers to an author's effort to serve up election information without politics.

Playing cards without money is like a meal without salt —Bertolt Brecht

A store without customers is like a library without books —Anon

(The antismoking zealots never tell you these things ... colds, weight gain can happen to you after kicking the habit.) They [people giving incomplete information] are like Karl Malden, who is always telling you how happy American Express will be to replace your stolen traveler's checks but never bothers to tell you that if their serial numbers are stolen too, you're out of luck —Russell Baker, *New York Times Magazine*, September 21, 1986

❧ COMPLEXION

See Also: SKIN, WRINKLES

A blotchy complexion like salami —Jilly Cooper

The cluster of red veins, like Rorschach patterns, sticking out on his cheeks —Henry Van Dyke

Complexion … as red as a boiled shrimp —Kenzaburo Oe

Complexion … as smooth as white mushrooms —Bobbie Ann Mason

Complexion dark as cholera —Cynthia Ozick

Complexion like a choir boy's —Robert Campbell

A complexion like the blossoms of apples —W. B. Yeats

A complexion like the moon at short range —Harry Prince

Complexion … like the skin on porridge —Frank Swinnerton

Complexion like twelve-year-old Scotch going down —Loren D. Estleman

Complexion the colour of porridge —Christopher Isherwood

Complexion, which had become pale in the dimness of the house, … shone as if it had been varnished —Guy de Maupassant

Face glistened as if it were covered with scar tissue from a newly healed burn —Kenzaburo Oe

Face … pock-marked like a wall against which men had stood to take the bullets of a firing squad —Penelope Gilliatt

Her complexion in its pallor showed clear as a lily petal —Ethel Cook Eliot

His face had an unnatural smoothness as though it were massaged and nourished with cold creams —W. Somerset Maugham

Suntan that looks like it was done on a rotisserie —Tom Wolfe describing actor Cary Grant

The thin veins on his massive cheeks were like the engraving on gilt-edged securities —Ludwig Bemelmans

A tracery of red veins, distinct as mapped rivers and tributaries, showed on his cheeks —Anne Tyler

❧ COMPLEXITY

See Also: DIFFICULTY

(He was) as complex as the double helix and sometimes as simple as a paramecium —Mike Sommer

As complicated and unavailing as a cut-out paper snowflake —Eudora Welty

As complicated as a full-bore, rollicking infidelity right in their own homes —Richard Ford

As complicated as the flush valve on a water closet —Anon

[A family's history] convoluted as a Greek Drama —Gail Godwin

(Character is) as detailed, as intricately woven as the intricate Oriental carpets and brocades in Freud's office —Vincent Canby, *New York Times*, September 24, 1986

The Oriental carpet and brocade comparison was particularly apt for Canby's review of Nineteen-Nineteen, *a movie about two Freud patients, with many scenes in Freud's heavily carpeted Vienna office.*

The detail was astonishing, like the circuits on a computer chip —James Morrow

(By marriage she had to assume a whole new family of blood kin) elaborate as a graph —George Garrett

(Their relationship seems as) intricate as a DNA blueprint —Joseph Wambaugh

To say Freud was complex is like saying Tolstoy could write —Anon

❧ COMPLIMENTS

See: FLATTERY, WORDS OF PRAISE

❧ COMPOSITION

See: MUSIC

❧ COMPREHENSIBLENESS
See: UNDERSTANDABILITY

❧ CONCEIT
See: VANITY

❧ CONCENTRATION
See: ATTENTION, SCRUTINY

❧ CONCISENESS
See: BREVITY

❧ CONDEMNATION
See: CRITICISM

❧ CONFIDENCE
See: SELF-CONFIDENCE, TRUST

❧ CONFIDENTIALITY
See: SECRECY

❧ CONFUSION
See: BEWILDERMENT

❧ CONNECTIONS
See Also: CLINGING

Attached [to an idea] like a slug to its shell —Paige Mitchell

Bonds (of family) as immutable as a tribal code —Anon

Bonds frail as spider webs —George Garrett

The bonds which I had thought bound me … turned out to be as flimsy and insubstantial as a kindergartner's paper chain —Harvey Swados

Bound as the sun to the world's wheel —Algernon Charles Swinburne

Bound together as two trees with interwoven roots —Edith Wharton

Bound together … like stepsisters with completely different backgrounds forced to live together under the same roof —Margaret Millar

The comparison as used in the mystery novel, Beyond This Point Are Monsters, *is applied to cities which are different in sight and sound but bound together by geography and economics.*

(Different professional groups in an organization) bundled together, as carrots or sticks of asparagus are bundled together —Frank Swinnerton

Closely connected … as a mother with her baby's belly button —Bertolt Brecht

Connect like a recurring musical leitmotif —Anon

Drawn together and held like snowflakes in a glass glove —Arthur A. Cohen

(Lives and limbs) entwined like the roots of trees —John Logan

Held together as backbone holds together the ribs and limbs and head to a body —H. G. Wells

Holds together like a quilt —James Dickey

Joined together as in a wedding of rivers —George Garrett

Linked [together] like mountain climbers —Frank Swinnerton

Linked together by bonds as deep and mysterious as those which tie the mother to her young —Harvey Swados

Lives crossing like swords —Paige Mitchell

Mixes like alphabet soup —Diane Ackerman

Roped together like climbers on a rockface —Lawrence Durrell

❧ CONSCIENCE
See Also: REGRET

A bad conscience is a kind of illness, in the sense that pregnancy is an illness —Freidrich Nietzsche

A clear conscience is like a wall of brass —Latin proverb

Conscience as big as the Alps —Walter Goodman, *New York Times,* May 27, 1987

Conscience … a terrifying little sprite, that bat-like winks by day and wakes by night —John Wolcott

Conscience is God's presence in man —Anon

Conscience is like a sun-dial; if you let truth shine upon it, it will put you right —Hamilton Bower

The author expanded upon the simile as follows: "But you may cover it over so that no truth can fall upon it, or you may let false light gleam upon it and then it will lead you astray."

(His) conscience rose like a shining light —Honoré de Balzac

Conscience wide as hell —William Shakespeare, *Henry V*

Gets little attacks of conscience, like hot flashes —Jonathan Valin

Going through life with a conscience is like driving your car with the brakes on —Budd Schulberg

A healthy conscience is like a wall of bronze —Erasmus

He that has a scrupulous conscience, is like a horse that is not well wayed [well-taught]; he starts at every bird that flies out of the hedge —John Selden

The word 'hath' from the original simile has been modernized to 'has.'

The sting of conscience, like the gnawing of a dog at a bone, is mere foolishness —Freidrich Nietzsche

Weather-beaten conscience … as elastic as his heart —Arthur Train

❧ CONSIDERATION
See: THOUGHT

❧ CONSPICUOUSNESS
Even on Central Avenue, not the quietest dressed street in the world, he looked about as inconspicuous as a tarantula on a slice of angel food —Raymond Chandler, *Farewell, My Lovely*

❧ CONTAGION
See: SPREADING

❧ CONTEMPT
As the air to a bird or the sea to a fish, so is contempt to the contemptible —William Blake

Contempt is kind of gangrene, which if it seizes one part of a character corrupts all the rest by degrees —Samuel Johnson

(His voice had turned idle) contemptuous, uncaring, like a king throwing a handful of coppers at the feet of children —Borden Deal

Disdain as a gourmet disdains TV dinners —Anon

Disdain as a lover of literature disdains a potboiler —Anon

(He started) handling my exam paper like it was a turd —J. D. Salinger

(A waiter who) looked as if he had been cornstarched in arrogance —Pat Conroy

More haughty than the devil —William Shakespeare, *Henry VI*

Scorn will curl suddenly round silent corners like bell-less bicycles —W. R. Rodgers

Sneered, like a waiter in a French restaurant who has just taken an order for a Chardonnay that he disdains —Ira Berkow, *New York Times* September 29, 1986

(They) treat me like a snakebit cowpoke just in from the range —Thomas Zigal

Watch … distastefully, as though she were a cigar being smoked in the presence of a lady without permission —Penelope Gilliatt

❧ CONTENTMENT
See Also: HAPPINESS, JOY

(There she lay) as complacently feminine as a turtle-dove —Christopher Isherwood

Content as a Parsee priestess who had duly paid her morning devotions to the deity —Israel Zangwill

Content as a tick sitting quietly on a tree and living off a tiny drop of blood plundered years before —Patrick Suskind

(She wanted us to be as) content as trees in a rain-forest —Max Apple

Contented as a baby on a schedule —Hollis Summers

Contented as a cobra full of warm milk —Rubert Hughes

Content ... like a little white kitty in a basket —Eudora Welty

Feel rewarded, like a gardener who's cutting roots —Margaret Sutherland

Hummed ... like a cook with things coming out right —William Beechcroft

Like jellyfish that lie beneath the warm ocean waters here [Hilton Head], there is discontent beneath the surface bonhomie (of the governors' annual conference) —David Shieman, *Wall Street Journal*, August 26, 1986

(She prospered, and could expect to prosper more ... but) like someone in exile, uncertain of deliverance, she was restless and dissatisfied —Robert Henson

Looked about as satisfied as a millionaire's mistress —William Beechcroft

Mood of complacency ... like a man who, having been under dire threat of burglary, suddenly increases his insurance and changes all the locks on his house and is convinced that these emergencies will make him for ever immune —H .E. Bates

Pleased as a cat with two tails —American colloquialism, attributed to New England

A common variation: "Proud as a dog with two tails."

Psyche ... topped up like the tanks of the automobiles —Frank Conroy

The simile from Conroy's novel, Stop-Time, refers to more than one automobile because the scene is in a gas station. Removed from this con- text, *"topped up like the tank of an automobile" would have the same meaning.*

Satisfying as getting a refund on your income tax —Anon

Sitting pretty, like a batter with three balls and no strikes against him —James Thurber

Take it (killing and bloodshed) in like the sun shines and the rain falls —Eileen O'Casey

Wears contentment like a wreath —Barbara Howes

❧ CONTINUITY

See Also: PERMANENCE

As never ending as a brook —Anon

Bottomless as Hell —Ben Jonson

Bottomless as the foundation of the Universe —Thomas Carlyle

[My bounty is as] Boundless as the sea —William Shakespeare, *Romeo and Juliet*

Boundless as the wind —Jonathan Swift

(Restaurants) come and go steadily as Bedouin tribesmen —Ed McBain

A constant figure in her life, like a white knight or a black mammy —Julia Whedon

Continued as on an endless escalator —Eleanor Clark

Continuous as an endless circle —Anon

Continuous as the beat of death —Amy Lowell

Continuous as the stars that shine and twinkle on the Milky Way —William Wordsworth

A variation: "infinite as the stars."

Endless as prairies —Margaret Atwood

Endless as the line around a circle —Anon

(She was, for him,) eternal like the seasons —Dorothea Straus

Eternal as mediocrity —James G. Huneker

Go on like an eternal flame —Lyn Lifshin

Had gone on like a bad sleep —Jean Stafford

Keeps rolling along like the Big River —John Gross

Lived on like names in a legend —John Hall Wheelcock

Numberless as the sands of the desert —American colloquialism

An equally popular variation is "numberless as the fish in the sea."

Steadily as a shell secretes its beating leagues of monotone —Hart Crane

Timeless as a churchyard —Sharon Sheehe Stark

❧ CONTROL

Abstinent as a reformed sinner —Anon

Censorship is like an appendix. When it is inert it is useless; when active it is extremely dangerous —Maurice Edelman

Censorship, like charity, should begin at home —Clare Booth Luce

The combinations for this comparison are virtually limitless.

Censure is like the lightning which strikes the highest mountains —Baltasar Gracian

Censorious ... as a superannuated sinner —William Wycherly

Circumscribed like a dog chained to a tree —Beth Nugent

(Always trying to) confine things into the shape of a phrase, like pouring water into a ewer —Vita Sackville-West

(Ordered lives) contained like climbers huddled to a rock ledge —W. D. Snodgrass

Feel like a dog on a short leash —Joanne Kates, *New York Times*, September 18, 1986

He kept it [emotional feeling] rigidly at the back of his mind, like a fruit not ripe enough to eat —H. E. Bates

He that has no rule over his own spirit is like a city without walls —The Holy Bible/Proverbs

"Hath" has been modernized to "has."

Imprison like a stone girdle —Anon

Irrepressible, like flame catching kindling —George Garrett

I wear my chains [of sexual and social roles] like ornaments, convinced they make a charming jingle —Phyllis McGinley

Manageable as chess pieces —George Meredith

[My wife's society] oppressed me like a spell —Edgar Allen Poe

In another version of the tale Morelia, *Poe kept the comparison but changed the frame of reference to the mystery of the wife's manner instead of her company.*

Suffocating as the interior of a sepulcher —Anon

The restriction is like saying to an avid reader he can't see a book for nine months —Kent Hannon on ruling restricting basketball practice for players who don't have C average, *New York Times*, July 21, 1986

To be with her was like living in a room with shuttered windows —Edith Wharton

Uncontrollable as a swift tide with a strong undertow —Anon

Uncontrollable as the wind —Robert Traver

❧ CONVERSATION

The American's conversation is much like his courtship ... he gives in and watches for a reaction; if the weather looks fair, he inkles a little —Donald Lloyd, *Harper's Magazine*, September 19, 1963

Chattering as foolishly as two slightly mad squirrels —James Crumley

Conversation ... as edifying as listening to a leak dropping in a tin dish-pan at the head of the bed when you want to go to sleep —O. Henry

A conversation between the two of you must be like listening to two pecans in a bowl —Geoffrey Wolff

The character who utters this simile in Wolff's novel Providence *follows it up as follows: "Why*

don't you let him shoot 500 cc of Thorazine right in your heart and get it over."

Conversation … crisp and varied as a freshly tossed salad —Anon

Conversation … it was like talk at a party, leap-frogging, sparring, showing-off —Nina Bawden

Conversation, like lettuce, requires a good deal of oil to avoid friction, and keep the company smooth —Charles Dudley Warner

Conversation … like dialogue from a play that had run too long and the acting had gone stale —John McGahern

Conversation … rapid and guttural as gunfire —Harvey Swados

The conversations … behaved like green logs, they fumed but would not fire —Truman Capote

Conversation should be like a salad, composed of various ingredients, and well stirred with salt, oil, and vinegar —Joaquin Setanti

Conversation … should flow, like waters after summer showers, not as if raised by mere mechanic powers —William Cowper

Conversation … sweet as clover —Ogden Nash

The conversation was just like clockwork. It recurred regularly, except that there was no need to wind anything up —Walter de la Mare

Conversation … was like trying to communicate with a ship sinking in mid-Atlantic when you're on shore —William McIlvanney

Conversationally, she'd been put into a grey zone, a lot like a bus station waiting room: cold air, silences, topics limited to states of health and the weather —Margaret Atwood, *Moral Disorder*

Conversed in whispers … like doctors consulting on a difficult case —Jean Stafford

Conversed like tennis players, back and forth, stroke for stroke —Jessamyn West

Converse with himself, like a prisoner alone in his cell or like a wayfarer lost in a wilderness —Joseph Conrad

Cutting off the small talk with an opening question like a serve —Elizabeth Spencer

Discourses on subjects above our comprehension … it's like listening to an unknown language —Henry Fielding

Even on Central Avenue, not the quietest dressed street in the world, he looked about as inconspicuous as a tarantula on a slice of angel food —Raymond Chandler, *Farewell, My Lovely*

A false and most unnatural kind of chatting, like fighters meeting at a weigh-in —Norman Mailer

Mailer was describing the beginning of an interview with Mike Wallace.

From time to time … talk becomes effective, conquering like war, widening the boundaries of knowledge like an exploration —Robert Louis Stevenson

Gabbing like college girls with the handsomest boys on campus waiting at the curb in big convertibles —Richard Ford

Good communication is as stimulating as black coffee, and just as hard to sleep after —Anne Morrow Lindberg

Good conversation, like any game, calls for equals in strength —Jacques Barzun

Good conversation unrolls itself like the spring or like the dawn —W. B. Yeats

A good talk is like a good dinner: one assimilates it —Jerome K. Jerome

Good talk is … like an impromptu piece of acting where each should represent himself to greatest advantage —Robert Louis Stevenson

Good talk is like good scenery—continuous, yet constantly varying, and full of the charm of novelty and surprise —Randolph S. Bourne

He [the inveterate punster] followed conversation as a shark follows a ship, or, to shift the metaphor, he was like Jack Horner and stuck in his thumb to pull out a pun —Stephen Leacock

(She) hit on the commonplace like a hammer driving a nail into the wall. She plunged into the obvious like a clown in a circus jumping through a hoop —W. Somerset Maugham

Maugham's biting similes describe a dull conversationalist in his story "Winter Cruise."

In conversation ... like playing on the harp; there is much in laying the hands on the strings to stop their vibration as in twanging them to bring out the music —Oliver Wendell Holmes, Sr.

In married conversation as in surgery, the knife must be used with care —André Maurois, February, 1955

The joke went on and on ... scaring away any other kind of conversation like a schoolyard bully —William Gass

Like the alternating patches of sun and shade that fell on the windshield as the clouds skidded overhead, the conversation inside the pickup went by fits and starts —Phyllis Naylor

(Their habit was to engage in this) mock banter, where they slipped truths into their jokes ... like filling cream puffs —David R. Slavitt

Natural talk, like plowing, should turn up a large surface of life, rather than dig mines —Robert Louis Stevenson

Stevenson elaborated on his simile as follows: "Masses of experience, anecdote, incident, crosslights, quotation, historical instances, the whole flotsam and jetsam of two minds forced in and in upon the matter in hand from every point of the compass, and from every degree of mental elevation and abasement, these are the materials with which talk is fortified, the food on which the talkers thrive."

(He had) practiced his portion of the conversation so many times ... that he felt like an actor in a stock company —Herbert Gold

Quips flew back and forth (between L and him) like balls between two long-experienced jugglers in a circus ring —Natascha Wodin

The room seethes with talk. Always a minimum of three conversations, like crosswinds —Rosellen Brown

Small talk is like the air that shatters the stalactites into dust again —Anais Nin

The talk came like the spilling of grain from a sack, in bursts of fullness that were shut off in mid-sentence as if someone had closed the sack abruptly and there was more talk inside —Shirley W. Schoonover

Talked ... like old friends in mourning —Nadine Gordimer

Talking to Bill is like opening a new bottle of ketchup; you gotta wait a while before anything comes out —Jonathan Valin

In his novel, Life's Work, *Valin expands on this as follows: "Sometimes you wait and nothing happens."*

Talking to him was like playing upon an exquisite violin. He answered to every touch and thrill of the bow —Oscar Wilde

Talking to them is like trying to get a zeppelin off the ground —Penelope Gilliatt

Talking to you is like addressing the Berlin Wall —Colin Forbes

Talking to you is like sending out your laundry. You never know what the hell is coming back —Neil Simon

Talking to you is like talking to my forearm —Geoffrey Wolff

Talking with him [George McGovern] is like eating a Chinese meal. An hour after its over, you wonder whether you really ate anything —Eugene McCarthy

Talking with you is more like boxing than talking —Larry McMurtry

The simile from Somebody's Darling *continues as follows: "You're always hitting me with a jab."*

Talk that warms like wine —Babette Deutsch

Their remarks and responses were like a Ping-Pong game with each volley clearing the net and flying back to the opposition —Maya Angelou

They bounced the conversation along like an India rubber ball —Claire Messud, *The Last Life*

Trading talk like blows —Anne Sexton

♣ CONVICTION
See: BELIEFS

♣ COOKERY
See: FOOD, DRINK

♣ COOLNESS
See: CALMNESS

♣ COOPERATION
See: AGREEMENT

♣ CORPORATIONS
See: BUSINESS

♣ CORPULANCE
See: FATNESS

♣ CORRECTNESS
See Also: TRUENESS/FALSENESS, MANNERS, REPUTATION

Accurate as a hole in one —Anon

Accurately as a geometrician —V.S. Pritchett

As scrupulous as a well-trained tailor —Robert Penn Warren

Exact as a blueprint —Anon

Exact as the technical jargon of a trade —Aldous Huxley

More exacting than a pasha with thirty wives —Guy de Maupassant

Proper as a butler —Charles Simmons

Respectable as Jane Austen —Marge Piercy

Right as a well-done sum —Sylvia Plath

♣ CORRESPONDENCE
See Also: WRITERS/WRITING

Correspondences are like small clothes before the invention of suspenders; it is impossible to keep them up —Sydney Smith

Letters are like bodies, and their meaning like souls —Abraham Ibn Mezra

A letter that was like a poem. It was … like listening to French it was so beautiful —Philip Roth

A lifelong sustained correspondence, like a lifelong unbroken friendship or happy marriage, requires explaining: all the cards are stacked against it —Max Lerner

Little letters cozy and innocent as a baby's layette —Truman Capote

A mess of a letter … it dribbles and mouths all over the place like Maurice Chevalier [the famous French performer] —Dylan Thomas

Printed [condolence] cards should be abolished; they're like canned music —Gwen Schwartz-Borden, director Bereavement Center, Family Service Association of Nassau County, quoted in *New York Times* article on bereavement notes November 24, 1986

The time is coming when letter writing with pen and ink and sent as a personal message from one person to another will be as much of a rarity as the gold pocket watch carried on a chain —Andy Rooney

A woman's love letters are like her child. They belong to her more than to anybody else —Edith Wharton

Writing to you is like corresponding with an aching void —Groucho Marx

Your letters … they're like telegrams —Dorothy Parker

♣ COST
See Also: ADVANTAGEOUSNESS, THRIFT

As cheap as pearls are costly —Robert Browning

Charge like a brain surgeon —Saul Bellow

Cheap as dirt —F.E. Smedley

Cheap as excuses —Anon

Cheap as lies —Anon

Cheap as old clothes —Horace Walpole

Cheap as old clothes used to be —Elyse Sommer

An update Horace Walpole's simile above, inspired by a change in both economic conditions and the status of old clothes.

Expensive as building an atomic reactor —Robert Traver

Expensive as Manhattan real estate —Anon

Expensive as sin —Anon

❧ COUNSEL

See: ADVICE

❧ COURAGE

Adventurous as a bee —William Wordsworth

As brave as hell —Petronius

As much backbone as an eel —American colloquialism

As much backbone as cooked spaghetti —Harry Prince

(There was) a tragic daring about her, like a moth dancing around a flame —Paige Mitchell

(He died) bold as brass —George Parker

Common usage has seeded modern-day modifications such as "bold as brass balls."

Bold as a dying saint —Elkanah Settle

Bold as a lion —The Holy Bible/Proverbs

Bold as an unhunted fawn —Percy Bysshe Shelley

(He died) bold as brass —George Parker

Common usage has seeded modern day modifications such as "bold as brass balls."

Bold as love —Edmond Gosse

Bold as Paul in the presence of Agrippa —William Cowper

Brave as a barrel full of bears —Ogden Nash

Brave as a tiger in a rage —Ogden Nash

Brave as winds that brave the sea —Algernon Charles Swinburne

Courage is like a disobedient dog, once it starts running away it flies all the faster for your attempts to recall it —Katherine Mansfield

Courage is like love; it must have hope to nourish it —Napoleon Bonaparte

Courage, like cowardice, is undoubtedly contagious, but some persons are not liable to catch it —Archibald Prentice

Courage, on nearly all occasions, inflicts as much of evil as it imparts of good —Walter Savage Landor

Courageous as a poker player with a royal flush —Mike Sommer

Courageous like firemen. The bell rings and they jump into their boots and go down the pole —Anon

Daring as tickling a tiger —Anon

Fend off pressure like a sharkhunter feeds off danger —Anon

Gallant as a warrior —Beryl Markham

Grew bold, like a general who is about to order an assault —Guy de Maupassant

Have the gall of a shoplifter returning an item for a refund —W.I.E. Gates

Indomitable as a lioness —Aharon Appelfeld

A man without courage is like a knife without edge —Anon

More guts than a gladiator —William Diehl

Nothing so bold as a blind horse —Greek proverb

Over-daring is as great a vice as over-fearing —Ben Jonson

Show nerve of a burglar —Anon

Stand my ground brave as a bear —American country ballad "If You Want to Go A-Courting"

Valiant as a lion —William Shakespeare

This simile from Henry the Fourth *has made lion comparisons part of our everyday language. Another lion simile by the bard is "walked like one of the lions" from* The Two Gentlemen of Verona.

With all the courage of an escaped convict —Honoré de Balzac

Valiant as Hercules —William Shakespeare, *Much Ado about Nothing*

(I've seen plenty of great big tough guys that was as) yellow and soft as a stick of butter —George Garrett

❧ COURTESY

See: BEHAVIOR, MANNERS

❧ COURTSHIP

See: MEN AND WOMEN

❧ COVERTNESS

See: SECRET

❧ COWARDICE

See: FEAR

❧ COZINESS

See: COMFORT

❧ CRAFTINESS

See: CLEVERNESS

❧ CRAVING

See: DESIRE

❧ CRAZINESS

See: MADNESS

❧ CREDIT

Credit buying is much like being drunk. The buzz happens immediately ... the hangover comes the day after —Dr. Joyce Brothers

Credit is like a looking glass.... once cracked [it] can never be repaired again —Sir Walter Scott

An anonymous rhymed version of this is: "Credit, like a lookin-glass, broken once, is gone, alas!" And, from John Ray's Proverbs *there is: "Credit lost is like Venice glass broken."*

Credit is like chastity, they can both stand temptation better than suspicion —Josh Billings

Creditors buzz like locusts —Anais Nin

Debts are like children: the smaller they are the more noise they make —Spanish proverb

The first step in debt is like the first step in falsehood, involving the necessity of going on in the same course, debt following debt, as lie follows lie —Samuel S. Smiles

It's [borrowing] like anticipating one's income, and making the future bear the expenses of the past —John Russell Bartlett

Lending to the feckless is like pelting a stray dog with dumplings —Arab proverb

No man's credit is as good as his money —Edward Watson Howe

❧ CRIME

See Also: DISHONESTY, EVIL

Crime, like virtue, has its degrees —Jean Racine

Crimes, like virtues, are their own rewards —George Farquhar

Murder, like a snowball rolling down a slope gathers momentum as it goes —Cornell Woolrich

Murder, like talent, seems occasionally to run in families —G. H. Lewes

Outlaws, like lovers, poets and tubercular composers who cough blood onto piano keys, do their finest work in the slippery rays of the moon —Tom Robbins

Passing statutes creating new crimes is like printing paper money without anything back of it; in the one case there isn't really any more money than there was before and in the other there isn't really any more crime either —Arthur Train

Trying to find out what ultimately drove a criminal to murder is as fruitful as trying to determine what drove fate to choose its victims —Lucinda Franks, reviewing two books about a murder case, *New York Times Book Review* March 1, 1987

❧ CRISPNESS

See: SHARPNESS

❧ CRITICISM

See Also: CRITICISM, DRAMATIC AND LITERARY

(They were) as critical as a fan-club —William McIlvanney

Blaming X [one group of an industry] for the decline of business is like blaming the iceberg for the demise of the *Titanic* —Bill Soutar, *Publishers Weekly*, 1985

Soutar was speaking specifically about poor business in his field of softcover book distribution.

Criticism is like champagne: nothing more execrable if bad, nothing more excellent if good —Charles Caleb Colton

Criticism, like rain, should be gentle enough to nourish a man's growth without destroying his roots —Frank A. Clark

Criticizing, like charity, should begin a home —B. C. Forbes

Impersonal criticism is like an impersonal fist fight, or an impersonal marriage, and as successful —George Jean Nathan

Like people rummaging in boxes for a knife, everyone searched deep in his memory for a grievance —Marguerite Yourcenar

Long harangue [of complaints] … was like a three-hour movie with no intermission —Elizabeth Spencer

Muttering thin complaints like little children called from play —James Crumley

Rattling off her woes like mea culpas —Rita Mae Brown

Safe from criticism as a stutter or a squint —Henry James

(Mothers) scolded in voices like amplified hens —Rumer Godden

Shot grievances like beads across an abacus —Cynthia Ozick

Sounded like a cranky old man who needs a stray Airedale to kick —*New York Times* editorial criticizing Mayor Edward Koch of NYC for a remark about his feeling for Soviet Government's arrest of American journalist, September 17, 1986

Squeaking like little pigs coming out of the barn door —Congressman Dale Lotta (Ohio), April 9, 1987

To criticize Glass for excessive reiteration is a little like complaining that the rain is too damp. —Justin Davidson, "Had I Never Listened Closely Enough?" *New York Magazine*, January 29, 2012

Philip Glass's 75th birthday prompted this article on trying to like his music.

❧ CRITICISM, DRAMATIC AND LITERARY

See Also: POETS/POETRY, WRITERS/WRITING

Aired their grievances like the wash —Daphne Merkin

[Reading about Frank Sinatra's wrong doings] as refreshing as inhaling carbon monoxide —Barbara Grizzuiti Harrison, reviewing Kitty Kelley's unauthorized biography of Frank Sinatra, *New York Times Book Review* November 2, 1986

[For author W. P. Kinsella] a baseball stadium is a window on the human heart, and his novel ... stirs it like the refreshing crack of a bat against the ball —*Miami Herald* review of *Shoeless Joe*, a baseball novel, by W. P. Kinsella

Like many comparisons, this one was pulled out of the review ad used as an attention-getting blurb on the back of the author's next novel.

The book is like a professor's joke. It's nothing if not erudite —Vincent Canby, review of movie of Umberto Echo's *The Name of the Rose*, *New York Times* September 24, 1986

Book reviews ... a kind of infant's disease to which newborn books are subject —Georg C. Lichtenberg

Critics are like brushers of other men's clothiers —Benjamin Disraeli

Critics are like eunuchs in a harem. They see how it should be done every night. But they can't do it themselves —Brendan Behan

Even when he's not at his best, his books still are appetizing, much like a box of popcorn —Tom Herman, book review (*The Panic of '89* by Paul Erdman), *Wall Street Journal*, January 16, 1987

His [author of pamphlet] words, like cavalry horses answering the bugle, group themselves automatically into the familiar dreary pattern —George Orwell

It [*The House of Seven Gables*] is like a great symphony, with no touch alterable without injury to the harmony —William James, letter to brother, Henry, January 19, 1869

It's [*Praying for Rain*, Jerome Weidman's autobiography] ... like a raisin-laced kugel, the noodles crammed with juicy morsels about some people, obscure and famous, who have been near and dear to him —Helen Dudar *New York Times Book Review*, September 21, 1986

Language is as precise as "Hello!" and as simple as "Give me a glass of tea" —Vladimir Mayakovsky about Anton Chekhov

Literary criticism is an art, like the writing of tragedies or the making of love, and similarly does not pay —Clifton Fadiman

Much of the text reads about as joyfully as a Volkswagen manual —George F. Will

The novel [*A Special Destiny* by Seymour Epstein] reads like the fictionalized autobiography of a young writer exorcising frustrations and resentments —Bethamy Probst, *New York Times Book Review*, September 21, 1986

Novels ... like literary knuckleballs —George F. Will, about Elmore Leonard's novels

One long evening of evasions, as if the playwright were taking the Fifth Amendment on advice of counsel —Frank Rich, *New York Times*, December 12, 1986

Drama critic Rich has the gift for perfectly suiting the comparison to what it describes ... in this case a play entitled "Dream of a Blacklisted Actor."

The prose lays there like a dead corpse on the page —Anon

Prose rushes out like a spring-fed torrent sweeping the reader away —Chuck Morris

Reviewing an autobiography is the literary equivalent of passing judgment on someone's life —Richard Lourie, prefacing his review of Eric Ambler's *Autobiography, New York Times Book Review* August 17, 1986

Style ... as strong and personal as Van Gogh's brushstrokes —George F. Will, about Elmore Leonard's novels

(The author's) style is as crisp as if it had been quick-frozen —Max Apple, about T. Coraghessan Boyle, *New York Times Book Review*, 1979

They [critics] bite like fish, at anything, especially at bookes [books] —Thomas Dekker

They [Gorky's stories] float through the air like songs —Isaac Babel, lecture, 1934

Thin stuff with no meat in it, like a woman, who has starved herself to get what she thinks is a good figure —Ben Ames Williams

This simile is used by the novelist-hero of Leave Her to Heaven, *to describe his current work.*

To criticize Glass for excessive reiteration is a little like complaining that the rain is too damp. —Justin Davidson, "Had I Never Listened Closely Enough?" *New York Magazine,* January 29, 2012

Philip Glass's 75th birthday prompted this article on trying to like Philip Glass.

To many people dramatic criticism must seem like an attempt to tattoo soap bubbles —John Mason Brown

The undisputed fame enjoyed by Shakespeare as a writer ... is, like every other lie, a great evil —Count Leo Tolstoy

Watching the movie is like being on a cruise to nowhere aboard a ship with decent service and above-par fast food. —Vincent Canby, *New York Times Book Review,* October 2, 1983

[Henry James] Writes fiction as if it were a painful duty —Oscar Wilde

(Tolstoy) writes like an ocean, in huge, rolling waves, and it doesn't look like it was processed through his thinking —Mel Brook, *Playboy,* 1975

Writes like an angel, a fallen, hard-driving angel —A. Alvarez about Robert Stone, *New York Review of Books,* 1986

♣ CROOKEDNESS

See: BENDING/BENT

♣ CROWDS

See Also: CLOSENESS

About as much privacy as a statue in the park —Anon

As lacking in privacy as a goldfish —Anon

Bunched and jammed together as solidly as the bristles in a brush —Mark Twain

Came crowding like the waves of ocean, one on the other —Lord Byron

Clustering like a swarm of bees —Amy Lowell

Crowded like a view of Venice —Frank O'Hara

Crowded [stores] like tightly woven multi-colored carpet of people —Richard J. Meislin, *New York Times*

The crowd in the lobby [of a hotel] was frozen in poses like the chorus at the curtain of a musical comedy —Vicki Baum

The crowd scattered in all directions, like a flock of chickens among which a stone had been thrown —Aharon Megged

Feel like a pressed flower —Edith Wharton

Flocking ... like geese —Sharon Sheehe Stark

(The public was) flowing in like a river —Enid Bagnold

Huddle together like birds in a storm —Robert Graves

Jostled like two steers in the stock yards —A.R. Guerney Jr.

Loaded up like a garbage truck —Paige Mitchell

Man ... still, like a hen, he likes his private run —W. H. Auden

Men milled everywhere, like cattle in a lightning storm —James Crumley

Mobs in their emotions are much like children, subject to the same tantrums and fits of fury —Euripides

No more privacy than a traffic cop —Anon

[People] Packed as closely as herring in a barrel —Sholom Aleichem

Packed like a cattle pen —Paige Mitchell

The people bunched like cattle in a storm —James Crumley

People [on a train] ... hanging from straps like sides of beef on a hook —Julio Cortázar

People [at a party] ... packed tight as a rugby scrum —Nadine Gordimer

If Gordimer's story, The Smell of Death and Flowers, *had been set in America, it might have had a football lineup for the rugby scrum.*

People streaming from the plane like busy insects on the march —Sylvia Berkman

Stood packed like matches in an upright box —William Faulkner

Swarm like bees —Anon

Swarm like summer flies —William Shakespeare, *Henry VI*

(Apartments) tenanted tight as hen-houses —Barbara Howes

When the bell rings and the school's 3,295 students spill out of classrooms into the maze of hallways, escalators and stairs like ants in a farm —Fernanda Santos, "To Be Black at Stuyvesant High," *New York Times*, February 26, 2012

❧ CRUELTY

See Also: COLDNESS, EVIL

(He's always been) a bigger shit than two tons of manure —William McIlvanney

Cruel and cold as the judgment of man —Lord Byron

Cruel as death —James Thomson

This is from a double simile, the second part being "Hungry as the grave."

Cruel as love or life —Algernon Charles Swinburne

Cruel as old gravestones knocked down and scarred faceless —James Wright

(Nothing so) cruel as panic —Robert Louis Stevenson

(She knew well the virtues of her singular attractiveness, as) cruel as shears —George Garrett

Cruel as winter —Lewis J. Bates

Crueler than hell —Algernon Charles Swinburne

Cruel, like the ostriches in the wilderness —The Holy Bible/Lamentations

The ostrich reference appears both in i>Lamentations and the Book of Job.

Cruelty on most occasions is like the wind, boisterous in itself, and exciting a murmur and bustle in all the things it moves among —Walter Savage Landor

Evil, like good, has its own heroes —François, Duc de La Rochefoucauld

Had a personality like a black hole —Jonathan Valin

In his novel Natural Causes, *from which this is taken, Valin expands upon the simile with "He sucked in everything around him and gave nothing back in return."*

A heart like a snake —Michael V. Gazzo

Her coarseness, her cruelty, was like bark rough with lichen —Virginia Woolf

He's like a cobra. No conscience —William Diehl

How could you be so cold as the winter wind when it breeze yo' —Kanye West, "Heartless."

Mean as a man who'd make knuckle-bones out of his aunt —Anon

Mean as a snake —John D. MacDonald

Mean as cat shit —James Kirkwood

Mean as cat's meat —Somerset Maugham, quoted in *New York Times Magazine* article by Thomas F. Brady, January 24, 1954

(That old scoundrel's) mean as ptomaine —Richard Ford

Mean as the man who tells his children that Santa Claus is dead —Anon

Merciless as ambition —Joseph Joubert

Merciless as bailiffs —Erich Maria Remarque

Ordered her about like a convict —Nicholas Monsarrat

Ruthless as any sea —Beryl Markham

So mean he would steal a dead fly from a blind spider —Anon

Spiteful as a monkey —Frank Swinnerton

Spiteful as the devil —Walter Savage Landor

Treat us like mud off the bottom of the Hudson River —Rebecca West

Use men ruthlessly like pawns —Honoré de Balzac

Walk all over [another person] like a carpet —Elyse Sommer

Whipping and abuse are like laudanum; you have to double the dose as the sensibilities decline —Harriet Beecher Stowe

Wickedness burns like fire —The Holy Bible/Isaiah The above has been modernized from "Wickedness burneth as the fire."

Would cut me down like a piece of grass —Jimmy Sangster

❧ CRYING

See Also: GROANS AND WHISPERS, SCREAMS

Bawling like sick monkeys —Henry Miller

Cried naggingly, half-heartedly, like the grinding of a non-starting engine that has drained its battery —John Updike

Cries out like an Arab, high wails like a dog or human in terrible pain. It rises and falls like sirens going by —Robert Campbell

Cry, hopelessly and passively, like a child in a dentist's waiting room —William Faulkner

Cry like a rain-water spout in a shower —Charles Dickens

Crying ... muffled, like faraway nighttime waves —Z. Vance Wilson

Crying out like an abandoned infant —T. Coraghessan Boyle

(Gave a) cry like a startled sea gull —Oscar Wilde

Her eyes [when she wept] were like syphon bottles under pressure —Erich Maria Remarque

Her sob broke like a bubble on a pink geranium —John Malcolm Brinnin

Kept on crying ... like persistent rain —Elizabeth Spencer

Like a waterpot I weep —*A Broken-Hearted Gardener,* anonymous nineteenth-century verse

A sad crying, like the birds going south for the steel winter to come —Ray Bradbury

The shrill cry of the new-born ... like the sound of the blade of a skate on ice —Angela Carter

Sobbed ... like an abandoned child —Maurice Hewlett

A sob broke the surface like a bubble of air from the bottom of a pond —Sue Grafton

Sobs ... died off softly, like the intermittent drops that end a day of rain —Edith Wharton

Sobs laboring like stones from her heaving breast —James Crumley

Sobs rippled like convulsions through her slim body —James Crumley

Thin cry [of a bluebird], like a needle piercing the ear —Theodore Roethke

Wailed like an uneasy animal in pain —Kenneth Grahame

Weeping like a calf —François Maspero

Weeping raw as an open sausage —A. D. Winans

Wept like a fountain —Erich Maria Remarque

Wept like a gutter on a rainy day —Guy de Maupassant

Wept like a woman deceived and forsaken by a lover —George Garrett

Whimpers like a hurt dog —Robin McCorquodale

Whine, as unctuous as old bacon grease —James Crumley

(The twangy voice was beginning to) whine like a loosening guitar string —François Camoin

❧ CUNNING

See: CLEVERNESS

❧ CURIOSITY

Aloof curiosity like that of sixth-formers watching a sword-swallower —Frank Swinnerton

Curious as a monkey —Anon

Curious as a two-year old —Anon

Curiosity … like thirst —Alice McDermott

Inquisitive as a goat —Erich Maria Remarque

Inquisitive as an X-ray —Anon

Inquisitive as a reporter smelling a scoop —Elyse Sommer

Pick and pry like a doctor or archeologist —Sylvia Plath

Poking his nose everywhere like a dog smelling out a trail —American colloquialism

Suppressed her curiosity as if squashing a cockroach —Marge Piercy

❧ CURSES

See Also: WORDS

The captain broke loose [with oaths] upon the dead man like a thunderclap —Jack London

Cried out a foreign legion of four-letter words like little prayers —George Garrett

Cursed like a sailor's parrot —Katherine Anne Porter

Cursed like highwaymen —Stephen Crane

Curse like a drunken tinker —George Garrett

Curses are like young chickens, they always come home to roost —Robert Southey

Curses, like processions; they return to the place from which they have come —Giovanni Ruffini

Probably taken from old Italian proverb.

Curses so dark they sounded like they were being fired all the way from a ghetto of hell —Ken Kesey

Cursing and crying like some sort of fitting had busted in her mind and this whole stream of words gushed out —Hilary Masters

Cursing like a jay —T. Coraghessan Boyle

Erupted like a volcano of profanity —Sholem Aleichem

Felt them [curse words] at the back of his tongue like dangerous little bombs —Thomas Williams

Made curses fly up like a covey of quail —George Garrett

Swear like men who were being branded —Stephen Crane

Swore like a trooper —D. M. Moir

To hear R curse was like hearing the Almighty tear through his own heavens and blow up the stars left and rightly —Marianne Hauser

❧ CUSTOM

See: HABIT

❧ DAMPNESS

See: DISCOMFORT

❧ DANCING

See Also: AGILITY, INSULTS, WORDS OF PRAISE

As light on your feet as a fairy —Rita Mae Brown

Danced like a faun —O. Henry

> *O. Henry was well known for perverting and extending existing sayings. This one can be traced Robert Lowell's "Dancing like naked fauns too glad for shame."*

Danced like a wave —Dame Edith Sitwell

Danced like a wet dream —Martin Amis

Danced like sandflies —Margaret Atwood

Danced like something dark and slithery from the Argentine —P. G. Wodehouse

(People) danced moving their bodies like thick rope —Susan Richards Shreve

Dancers swaying like wet washing in a high wind —Lawrence Durrell

Dances like a Mack truck —Cornell Woolrich

Dances like an angel —Joseph Addison

(Sometimes I think that) dancing, like youth, is wasted on the young —Max Lerner

Dancing with her must be a good deal like moving the piano or something —Ring Lardner

(Helga Danzing danced just the way she looked: big, clumsy, almost impossible to lead,) dancing with her was like pushing a weight uphill —Abraham Rothberg

(You've got) a foot movement like a baby hippopotamus trying to side-step a jab from a humming-bird … and your knees are about as limber as a couple of Yale pass-keys —O. Henry

Pirouetting like a Baryshnikov —T. Coraghessan Boyle

Sailed like a coquettish yacht convoyed by a stately cruiser —O. Henry

You dance like there's a stone in your shoe —John Updike

♣ DANGER

See Also: RISK

(His presence was) a foreboding, or dismal signal, like drawn blinds —Elizabeth Taylor

Dangerous as a gift from an enemy —Anon
   A twist on the Danish proverb "Gifts from enemies are dangerous."

Dangerous as cocaine —Pietro Mascagni
   The danger being described is modern music.

(I feel so many) dangers gathering round —like shadows —Davis Grubb

Feel as though I'm dancing on a volcano —Rita Mae Brown

Felt as if they were about to dive onto a postage stamp from the top of the Eiffel Tower —Fred Taylor

(One's life) hangs perilously in danger, like ripe fruit on a thin branch —Stephen Longstreet

Hazardous as sand traps for golfers —Anon

It [the need to risk] was like statistics or gambling; you had to compute probabilities —Mary McCarthy
   In her novel A Charmed Life, *McCarthy expands on her simile with this sentence: "And there was always the unforeseen, the little thing you overlooked that would catch you up in the end."*

The menace (of insanity) is like a warder, restricting my freedom of mind —Richard Maynard

(His) menaces … idle as the wind —W. S. Gilbert

Menacing as a fury —Natascha Wodin

Ominous and dark as the hour before a storm —Gerald Kersh

Ominous, like waves in a gathering mid-Atlantic storm —Anon

Rode precariously like high-wire artists —Ross Macdonald

The safe earth … grew narrow as a grave —Phyllis Bottome

There was a feeling like a concussion in the air —Eudora Welty

This faint shadow [of danger] lay upon his life … as discreetly as the shadow of cancer lies among cells —Thomas McGuane

Trying to maintain good relations with a Communist is like wooing a crocodile —Winston Churchill

We sit here talking and leave everything to Mangan {a businessman in the mold of many modern corporate executives} and to chance and to the devil …? It's madness: it's like giving a torpedo to a badly brought up child to play at earthquakes with —George Bernard Shaw, *Heartbreak House*

♣ DARING

See: COURAGE

♣ DARKNESS

Dark and cool as a cave —David Huddle

Dark and heavy like a surface stained with ink —John Ashberry

(It was) dark as a closet —Niven Busch

Dark as a dungeon —Anon
The simile is the title of a ballad from the American South.

(All was) dark as a stack of black cats —J.S. Rioss

Dark as anger —Sylvia Plath

Dark as a pocket —American colloquialism, attributed to Vermont

Dark as a thundercloud —Steven Vincent Benet

Dark as a troll —W. D. Snodgrass

Dark as a wolf's mouth —Miguel de Cervantes
"Dark as" and "Black as" have been used interchangeably, since the simile's appearance in Don Quixote.

Dark as a womb —T. Coraghessan Boyle

Dark as blackberries —Marge Piercy

(The room was) dark as dreamless sleep —Harry Prince

(Eyelashes …) dark as night —Lord Byron

Dark as sin —Mark Twain

Dark as the devil's mouth —Sir Walter Scott

Dark as the inside of a coffin —Gavin Lyall

Dark as the inside of a magician's hat —Robert Campbell

Dark as the inside of a cow —Mark Twain

Dark as the river bottom —Paige Mitchell

Dark like wet coffee grounds —Ella Leffland

The darkness ahead … looked like Alaska —Richard North Patterson

Darkness as deep and cold as Siberian midnight —Gerald Kersh

Darkness [in a rainstorm] came closer … like a sodden velvet curtain —Frank Swinnerton

Darkness falls like a wet sponge —John Ashberry
This is the opening line of an Ashberry poem entitled "The Picture of Little J.A. in a Prospect of Flowers."

Darkness fell like a swift blow —James Crumley

Darkness fills her like a carbohydrate —Daniela Gioseffi

The darkness flew in like an unwelcome bird —Norman Garbo

Darkness had begun to come in like water —Alice McDermott

Darkness hanging over them like a blotter —T. Coraghessan Boyle

Darkness like a black lake —Erich Maria Remarque

Darkness … like a warm liquid poured from the throat of an enormous bird —John Hawkes

Darkness settling down round them like a soft bird —Rose Tremain

Darkness should be a private matter, like thought, like emotion —William Dieter

Darkness so total it seemed and shifting, like deep water —William Boyd

The darkness was like a rising tide that covered the gardens and the houses, erasing everything as a still sea erased footprints on a beach —John P. Marquand

Darkness was sinking down over the region like a veil —Thomas Mann

The darkness was thin, like some sleazy dress that has been worn and worn for many winters and always lets the cold through to the bones —Eudora Welty

Dim as a cave of the sea —Richard Wilbur

Dim as a cellar in midafternoon —Joyce Cary

Dim as an ill-lit railroad coach —Natascha Wodin

(My sun has set, I) dwell in darkness as a dead man out of sight —Christina Rossetti

Light … drained out of the windows like a sink —William H. Gass

So dark and murky it [a movie, *The Fugitive Kind*] looked like everyone was drowning in chocolate syrup —Tennessee Williams, quoted in interview with Rex Reed

♣ DAY

See Also: NIGHT, SLOWNESS, TIME

The afternoon droops like a hot candle —Malcolm Cowley

The afternoon sways like an elephant —Babette Deutsch

This begins a poem entitled "July Day."

The beauty of the morning called to her like a signal bell —R. V. Cassill

Dawn came like a blanket of flowers —T. Coraghessan Boyle

The dawn came up like a Have-a-Nice-Day emblem —Tom Robbins

A day as fresh as spring itself —Wallace Stegner

(The next) day dawned like a yawning hole —Robert Barnard

The day drooped like a flag —Katherine Mansfield

The day goes by like a shadow over the heart (with sorrow where all was delight) —Stephen Foster

From Stephen Foster's famous "My Old Kentucky Home" with "over" instead of "o'er" as in the original.

The day is flat and intense, like a photograph of itself —Marge Piercy

The day [Sunday] is like wide water, without sound —Wallace Stevens

Day like a bated breath —Sharon Sheehe Stark

A day like an endless empty sea —Delmore Schwartz

Days and nights were shuffling like lame and overweight cattle —Don Robertson

Days are scrolls: write on them what you want to be remembered —Bahya

Days … arrive like crows in a field of stubble corn —Robert Hass

The days dripped away like honey off a spoon —Wallace Stegner

Days … followed one another in an undistinguished series, growing and then fading like the leaves on a tree —Stefan Zweig

The days go by, like caterpillars do —Johnny Mercer, opening stanza from 1947 song, "Lazy Mood"

The days go by like film, like a long written scroll —Maxwell Anderson

The days, like the leaves, seemed to fly from the trees, as if this year was intent on its own destruction —Susan Fromberg Schaeffer

The day smelled like clear water —Joan Chase

The days pass by like a wayward tune —H. B. Yeats

Days pass like papers from a press —Wallace Stevens

The days slipped by … like apple parings under a knife —Stephen Vincent Benét

The days walking along higher and higher, like the way teachers line you up to have pictures taken —Lee Smith

The days were truly endless and seemed like a single black night —Barbara Reid

The day was dry, rather misty; like a day pictured in a Japanese print —Frank Swinnerton

The day was still like a very glazed photograph —M. J. Farrell

Feel the pull of the long day, like a road he dragged behind him —Sharon Sheehe Stark

A fine morning makes you want to bust open like a pea pod —Joe Coomer

The gray winter morning descends like the huge lead-coated balloon —Jerry Bumpus

The middle of the day, like the middle of certain fruits, is good for nothing —Walter Savage Landor

Morning came like a stone breaking —Madison Smartt Bell

The morning crept out of a dark cloud like an unbidden guest uncertain of his welcome —W. Somerset Maugham

Morning … gray like a mouse —Jessamyn West

Morning hours of inactivity … like a beautiful sculpture-lined bridge across which I stroll from night into day, from dream into reality —Milan Kundera

(Night had died, and the) morning lay like a corpse. Like sadness, going from one end of the world to another, without a sound —Aharon Megged

My days are like a lengthening shadow —The Holy Bible/Psalms

One of those days that come as a surprise in the middle of winter, like a gift sent on no anniversary, so that the pleasure takes us unaware —Jean Stafford

Our days run as fast away as does the sun —Robert Herrick

Over the garden, day still hung like a pink flag —Elizabeth Bowen

Workday is finished, dead as the calendar page that bore its number —Beryl Markham

♣ DEATH

See Also: ADVANCING; BEGINNINGS AND ENDINGS; DEATH, DEFINED; DEATH, FINALITY OF; ENTRANCES AND EXITS; SUDDENNESS; TIMELINESS

As death comes on we are like trees growing in the sandy bank of a widening river —Bhartrihari

The body of Benjamin Franklin, Printer, like the cover of an old book, its contents torn out, and stripped of its lettering and gilding lies here food for worms —Benjamin Franklin

Franklin's epitaph for himself is a fine example of appropriately suiting the comparison to what's being compared.

(Kill him) dead as a beef —William Faulkner

[Sexual feelings] Dead as a burned-out cinder —Ellen Glasgow

Death arrives … sudden as a pasteboard box crushed by a foot —Marge Piercy

Death falling like snow on any head it chooses —Philip Levine

Death fell round me like a rain of steel —Herbert Read

A simile from one of Read's many war poems "Meditation of the Waking English Officer."

Death has many times invited me: it was like the salt invisible in the waves —Pablo Neruda

Death lies on her, like an untimely frost —William Shakespeare, *Romeo and Juliet*

Death, like roulette, turning our wish to its will —George Barker

Death lurking up the road like a feral dog abroad in the swirling snow —Marge Piercy

Death, you can never tell where else it will crop up —John Hale

Die alone like a dog in a ditch —Aldous Huxley

Died in beauty, like a rose blown from its parent stem —C.D. Sillery

Die like candles in a draft —Sharon Sheehe Stark

In the short story, The Johnstown Polka, *the simile has a literal frame of reference; specifically, a room in an old age home which is overheated because to open the windows would kill the people in it.*

Died like flies in a sugar bowls —Rita Mae Brown

(I won't) drown like a rat in a trap —G.B. Shaw

Like a swift-fleeting meteor, a fast flaying cloud, a flash of lightning, a break of the wave, man passes from life to his rest in the grave —William Knox

Dying is as natural as living —Thomas Fuller M. D.

Dying like flies —Anon

An even more frequently used variation is to "Drop like flies."

(I will) encounter darkness as a bride —William Shakespeare

(You couldn't) Expect death to come rushing in like a skivvy because you'd rung the bell —Paul Barker

Feel my death rushing towards me like an express train —John Updike

Felt death near, like a garment she had left hanging in her closet and could not see or find though she knew it was there —Abraham Rothberg

Go to their graves like flowers or creeping worms —Percy Bysshe Shelley

The intimations of mortality appear so gradually as to be imperceptible, like the first graying in of twilight —Richard Selzer

Like a clock worn out with eating time, the wheels of weary life at last stood still —John Dryden

Like a led victim, to my death I'll go —John Dryden

Like a swift-fleeting meteor, a fast flaying cloud, a flash of lightning, a break of the wave, man passes from life to his rest in the grave —William Knox

Like sheep they are laid in the grave —The Holy Bible/Psalms

(I now) look at death, the way we look at a house we plan to move into —William Bronk

Men fear death, as children fear to go in the dark; and as that natural fear in children is increased with tales, so is the other —Francis Bacon

Our fear of death is like our fear that summer will be short, but when we have had our swing of pleasure, our fill of fruit, and our swelter of heat, we say we have had our day —Ralph Waldo Emerson

Passed away, as a dry leaf passes into leaf mold —John Updike

[In old age] The shadow of Death ... like a sword of Damocles, may descend at any moment —Samuel Butler

She passed away like morning dew —Hartley Coleridge

(The passionate desire to be loved by a man, that had a thousand times before) swept like a storm over her body —Sherwood Anderson, *Winesburg, Ohio*

Talking over the fact of his approaching death as though it were a piece of property for agreeable disposition in the family —Elizabeth Spencer

There are no graves that grow so green as the graves of children —Oliver Wendell Holmes

From a letter of condolence to W. R. Sturtevant, September 17, 1878 in which the simile continues as follows: "Their memory comes back after a time more beautiful than that of those who leave us at any other age."

We are all kept and fed for death, like a herd of swine to be slain without reason —Palladas

We end our years like a sigh ... for it is speedily gone, and we fly away —The Holy Bible/Psalms

Wherever you go, death dogs you like a shadow —Anon

♣ DEATH DEFINED

Death is like a fisherman who catches fish in his net and leaves them for a while in the water; the fish is still swimming but the net is around him, and the fisherman will draw him up —?when he thinks fit —Ivan Turgenev

Death is like thunder in two particulars: we are alarmed at the sound of it and it is formidable only from that which preceded it —Charles Caleb Colton

Death is simply a shedding of the physical body, like the butterfly coming out of a cocoon —Elisabeth Kuebler-Ross

Death, like an overflowing stream, sweeps us away —Abraham Lincoln

Death, like birth, is a secret of nature —Marcus Aurelius

Death, like life, is an affair of being more frightened than hurt —Samuel Butler

Dying is an art, like everything else —Sylvia Plath

Dying is something ghastly, as being born is something ridiculous —George Santayana

If a person has reached the "age of strength" [eighty years old], a sudden death is like dying from a kiss —*Babylonian Talmud*

Like the dew on the mountain, like the foam on the river, like the bubble on the fountain, you are gone, and for ever —Sir Walter Scott

The above, taken from Scott's famous The Lady of the Lake, *substitutes "You are gone" for the old English "Thou art gone."*

The stroke of death is as a lover's pinch, which hurts, and is desir'd —William Shakespeare *Antony & Cleopatra*

(I) think of death as a sort of deleterious fermentation, like that which goes on in a bottle of Chateau Margaux when it becomes corked —H. L. Mencken

♣ DEATH, FINALITY OF

As the cloud is consumed and vanished away: so he that goes down to the grave comes up no more —The Holy Bible/Job

'Goes' is a modernization of the biblical 'goeth.'

Dead and as far away as yesterday —W. S. Gilbert

Dead as a dead mackerel —C. W. Grafton

Dead as a dodo bird —American colloquialism, attributed to New England

Dead as a doornail —English phrase

Many people attribute this much used simile to Shakespeare who used it in Henry VI *and* Henry IV. *In the first play the simile appears as follows: "If I do not leave you all as dead as a doornail, I pray God I may never eat grass more. In the sec-*

ond, in response to Falstaff asks "What, is the old king dead?" and Pistol answers, "As a nail in door."

Dead as a fried oyster —S. J. Perelman

This is one of four different twists on the familiar "Dead as a doornail" from Perelman's spoof on cliché Somewhere a Roscoe. *The others used are "Dead an iced catfish," "Dead as a stuffed mongoose," and "Dead as vaudeville."*

Dead as a hammer —Scotch Saying

Dead as a herring —Samuel Butler

Dead as a turd —Stephen King

Deader than a roast turkey on Thanksgiving —Joan Hess

Dead as the last year's leaves —W. S. Gilbert

♣ DEBT
See: CREDIT

♣ DECEPTION
See: TRUENESS/FALSENESS

♣ DECISIONS
See: CHOICES

♣ DECORATIVENESS
See: ATTRACTIVENESS

♣ DECREASE

Contract, like the pupil of an eye that confronts the sun —John Hall Wheelock

(My avarice) Cooled like lust in the chill of the grave —Ralph Waldo Emerson

Decrease like a cigar —the harder you puff on it, the shorter it gets —Anon

The cigar has also been likened to an actor, e.g., "An actor decreases like a cigar; the more you puff him, the smaller he gets."

Decrease like a lemon drop; the more you lick it the less it becomes —Anon

Decrease like hair after each decade —Mike Sommer

Devour [information] like baseball addicts devour box scores —David E. Sanger, *New York Times,* December 14, 1985

Diminished and flat, as after radical surgery —Sylvia Plath

(All my efforts) diminish like froth —Erich Maria Remarque

Drain (as a day's happenings) like water running out of a tub —Andre Dubus

Energy … draining out like sand —May Sarton

Gobble up cash the way electronic equipment gobbles up batteries —Anon

Goes down like an ebbing tide —Henry James

> *James let the hero of his play* Guy Domville, *use the ebbing tide comparison to explain the nature of his ignorance.*

Go through [as bottle of pills] like a bull breaks a fence —Anon

Pared like a carrot —John Russell

> *This is often used to mean cut down, humiliated.*

(The conversation was already) petering out like a smoldering cigarette-end —Stefan Zweig

Receding like a threatened headache which hasn't materialized —William McIlvanney

Shrinking as violets do in summer —Thomas Moore

> *The original ended with "As violets do in summer's rays."*

Shrinking like aches —Charles Wright

Shrivel up like the tendrils of a creeper when thrown on a bonfire —Francis King

Shrunken as a beggar's heart —Stephen Vincent Benét

Use up as fast as a ten dollar bill in the supermarket —Anon

Use up, like a cake of soap —Elyse Sommer

Wore off [feeling of self-confidence] quicker than champagne —Edith Wharton

♣ DEDICATION

See: ATTENTION

♣ DEEDS

See: ACTIONS

♣ DEJECTION

See Also: EMOTIONS, GLOOM

(There was about him) an air of defeat … as though all the rules he'd learned in life were, one by one, being reversed —Margaret Millar

Dampened my mood (as automatically) as would the news of an earthquake in Cincinnati or the outbreak of the Third World War —T. Coraghessan Boyle

Dejection seemed to transfix him, to reach down out of the sky and crash like a spike through his small rigid body —Niven Busch

Dejection settled over her like a cloud —Louis Bromfield

Depression crept like a fog into her mind —Ellen Glasgow

Depression … is like a light turned into a room—only a light of blackness —Rudyard Kipling

Depressions … like thick cloud covers: not a ray of light gets through —Larry McMurtry

Despair howled round his inside like a wind —Elizabeth Bowen

Despair is like forward children, who when you take away one of their playthings, throw the rest into the fire for madness —Pierre Charron

Despair, like that of a man carrying through choice a bomb which, at a certain hour each day, may or may not explode —William Faulkner

Despair passed over him like cold winds and hot winds coming from places he had never visited —Margaret Millar

Despondency … lurking like a ghoul —Richard Maynard

Emptied, like a collapsed balloon, all the life gone out of him —Ben Ames Williams

Feeling of desperation … as if caught by a chain that was slowly winding up —Victor Hugo

Feel like a picnicker who has forgotten his lunch —Frank O'Hara

(I'm not feeling very good right now. I) feel like I've been sucking on a lot of raw eggs —Dexter Manley, of the Washington Redskins after his team lost important game, quoted *New York Times* December 8, 1986

Feels his heart sink as if into a frozen lake —John Rechy

Felt depression settle on his head like a sick crow —Bernard Malamud

(He often) felt [suicidal] like a deep sea diver whose hose got cut on an unexpected rock —Diane Wakoski

Felt like Willie Loman at the end of the road —T. Coraghessan Boyle

Felt the future narrowing before me like a tunnel —Margaret Drabble

Forlorn … like Autumn waiting for the snow —John Greenleaf Whittier

(Her) heart dropped like a purse of coins falling through a ripped pocket —Joyce Reiser Kornblatt

His despair confronted me like a black beast —Natascha Wodin

His haughty self was like a robber baron fallen into the hands of rebellious slaves, stooped under a filthy load —Sinclair Lewis

His heart has withered in him and he has been left with the five senses, like pieces of broken wineglass —Lawrence Durrell

Hope and confidence … shattered like the pillars of Gaza —W. Somerset Maugham

Hope removed like a tree —The Holy Bible/Job

It was like having a part of me amputated —W. P. Kinsella

The character in the novel Shoeless Joe, *the comparison is a character's response to being suspended from his baseball team.*

(I was) like the old lion with a thorn in his paw, surrounded by wolves and jackals and facing his snaggle-toothed death in a political jungle —T. Coraghessan Boyle

Listless and wretched like a condemned man —Erich Maria Remarque

(They)live under dust covers like furniture —Michael Frayn

Frayn's simile vividly portrays the despair of the characters in his adaptation of an untitled Chekhov play, first produced under the title Wild Honey *in 1984.*

Looked suddenly disconsolate, like a scarecrow with no crows to scare —Graham Masterton

Looking forlorn, stricken, like a little brother who, tagging along, is being deserted by the big fellows —Edna Ferber

Crawl back [after unanticipated defeat at golf] looking like a toad under a harrow —P. G. Wodehouse

Look like a dog that has lost its tail —John Ray's *Proverbs*

Look like the picture of ill luck —John Ray's *Proverbs*

Miserable, like dead men in a dream —George MacDonald

Miserable, lonesome as a forgotten child —F. Scott Fitzgerald

Misery is manifold … as the rainbow, its hues are as various as the hues of that arch —Edgar Allen Poe

Misery rose from him like a stench —Marge Piercy

A mood as gypsy-dark as his eyes —Robert Culff

My life is just an empty road and people walk on me —Tony Ardizzone

Must live hideously and miserably the rest of his days, like a man doomed to live forever in a state of retching and abominable nausea of heart, brain, bowels, flesh and spirit —Thomas Wolfe

Put away his hopes as if they were old love letters —Anon

Relapsed into discouragement, like a votary who has watched too long for a sign from the altar —Edith Wharton

Saw himself like a sparrow on the Bank-top; sitting on the wherewithal for a thousand, thousand meals and dropping dead from hunger the first day of winter —Christina Stead

Seemed like a whipped dog on a leash —Ignazio Silone

The sense of desolation and of fear became bitterer than death —William Cullen Bryant

(I have been) so utterly and suicidally morbid that my letters would have read like an excerpt from the *Undertakers' Gazette* —Dylan Thomas

The simile is excerpted from a November, 1933 letter to Pamela Hansford Johnson apologizing for the delay in replying to her letter.

(Foster's) stomach felt like a load of wet clothes at the bottom of the dryer —Phyllis Naylor

There's a state of peace following despair … like the aftermath of an accident —C. J. Koch

Waves of black depression engulf one from time to time … like a rising tide —Gustave Flaubert

❧ DELAY
See: LINGERING

❧ DELIBERATENESS
See: PURPOSEFULNESS

❧ DELIGHT
See: JOY

❧ DEMOCRACY
See: FREEDOM, GOVERNMENT

❧ DENIAL
See: BEHAVIOR

❧ DENSITY
See: ABUNDANCE, THICKNESS

❧ DEPARTURE
See: EXITS

❧ DEPENDABILITY
See: RELIABILITY/UNRELIABILITY

❧ DEPLETION
See: DECRESAE

❧ DEPRESSION
See: DEJECTION, GLOOM

❧ DESERTION
See: ABANDONMENT

❧ DESIRABILITY
See Also: PLEASURE

Beckoning … like summer welcoming the swallows —Ariel Dorfman

Cherish like a secret —D.H. Lawrence

Dear as a pardon —Diane Ackerman

Hates (publicity) the way Polly hates crackers —Arthur Baer

Dear as remembered kisses after death —Alfred, Lord Tennyson

Dear as the mother to the son —Alfred, Lord Tennyson

(She was) desirable … like a dessert. Afterward you discarded the empty plate and forgot it —Derek Lambert

(Enigmatic remarks, as elusive and as) eagerly gobbled up as currants in a bun —Robert Culff

(Six years ago ... the idea of spending an afternoon at Shea Stadium) held about as much appeal as your basic monster traffic jam —Malcom Moran, *New York Times,* October 11, 1986

Like a box of chocolates ... seductive and satisfying —*Publishers Weekly* comment on a short novel

The simile expanded on the box of chocolates appeal with: "Readers will want to devour it in one sitting."

Welcome as a corpse is to a coroner —Mark Twain

Welcome as a dandelion in the bosom of winter —Josh Billings

Welcome as a free ticket to a hit show —Anon

Welcome as a letter from home —Anon

Welcome as a visit from an old friend —Anon

Welcome as happy tiding after fears —Thomas Otway

Welcome as sunshine after rain —Anon

A possible inspiration for this is: "Love comforteth like sunshine after rain" from Shakespeare's Venus and Adonis.

Welcome as the best dish in the kitchen —H. G. Bohn's *Hand-Book of Proverbs*

Welcome as the flowers in May —John Ray's *Proverbs*

Welcomed it as a Bedouin in the desert welcomes the flies that are the herald of an oasis —Richard Selzer

♣ DESIRE

See Also: SEX

A brief surge of sexual desire that crested and passed like a wave breaking —Paige Mitchell

Craves love like oxygen —Marge Piercy

Craving [for a man] ... like a cigarette smoker who knows his desire is unhealthy, knows that the next puff may set off a chain reaction of catastrophe, but nevertheless cannot by such logic tame the impulse —Paul Reidinger

Desire had run its course like a long and serious illness —Harvey Swados

Desire ... like the hunger for a definite but hard-to-come-by food —Mary Gordon

Desire overtook us like a hot, breaking wave —A. E. Maxwell

Desires ... hurried like the clouds —Elizabeth Bowen

Desire ... swept over her like a flame —Robin McCorquodale

Dying for ... like God for a repentant sinner —Bertolt Brecht

(She is) gaping after love like a carp after water on a kitchen table —Gustave Flaubert

Her needs stick out all over, like a porcupine's needles —Emily Listfield

His need for her was crippling ... like a cruel blow at the back of his knees —John Cheever

How passionate the mating instinct is, like a giant hippo chasing his mate through the underbrush and never stopping till he finally mounts her in the muddy waters of the mighty Amazon —Daniel Asa Rose

Longing ... afflicted her like a toothache —Harold Acton

(Miss) like sin —Lael Wertenbaker

The simile in full context from the novel Unbidden Guests: *reads as follows: "I woke up missing Alex like sin."*

Miss you like breath —Janet Flanner

More giddy in my desires than a monkey —William Shakespeare, *As You Like It*

My desire for her is so wild I feel as if I'm all liquid —W. P. Kinsella

My heart is yearning like the ocean that's running dry —Selena Gomez, "A Year without Rain"

A passion finer than lust, as if everything living is moist with her —Daniela Gioseffi

Worldly desires are like columns of sunshine radiating through a dusty window, nothing tangible, nothing there —Bratzlav Naham

Yearning radiating from his face like heat from an electric heater —Larry McMurtry

♣ DESOLATION

See: ABANDONMENT

♣ DESPERATION

Edgar [a journalist during a difficult interview] made one more approach, like a plane in bad weather that was running out of fuel. —Lionel Shriver in *The New Republic*

I felt my heart sinking, like a ship going under —Edward Rutherfurd, *New York*

♣ DESTITUTION

See: POVERTY

♣ DESTRUCTION/ DESTRUCTIVENESS

See Also: DISINTEGRATION

As killing as the canker to the rose —John Milton

(Bones) breaking like hearts —Bin Ramke

Break [a person's spirit] like a biscuit —Francis Beaumont and John Fletcher

Break like a bursting heart —Percy Bysshe Shelley

Break like dead leaves —Richard Howard

Cracked like parchment —Sin Ai

Cracked like the ice in a frozen daiquiri —Anon

(Her projects of happiness) crackled in the wind like dead boughs —Gustave Flaubert

Crack like walnuts —Rita Mae Brown

Crack like wishbones —Diane Ackerman

Cracks ... like a glass in which the contents turned to ice, and shiver it —Herman Melville

[Fender and hood of car] crumpled like tinfoil —T. Coraghessan Boyle

Crushed like an empty beer can —Anon

Crushed ... like rats in a slate fall —Davis Grubb

In Grubb's novel The Barefoot Man, *the simile refers to miners who lost their lives.*

Crushed like rotten apples —William Shakespeare, *Henry V*

Crushed me like a grape —Carla Lane, British television sitcom, *Solo*, May 19, 1987

(And I'll be)cut up like a pie —Irish ballad

Destructive as moths in a woolens closet —Anon

[Time's malevolent effect on body] Dragging him down like a bursting sack —Gerald Kersh

(The Communists are) eating us away like an old fruit —Janet Flanner

(Men) fade like leaves —Aristophanes

Flattened her pitiful attempt like a locomotive running on a single track full steam ahead —Cornell Woolrich

(Creditors ready to) gnaw him to bits ... like maggots at work on a carcass —George Garrett

The grass at Shea Stadium looked as if it had been attacked by animals that had not grazed for ages —Alex Yannis, *New York Times*, September 18, 1986

Yannis, in reporting on the Mets' winning the National League Eastern Division title, used the simile to describe the fans' destruction of the playing field.

If I do [give up] ... I'll be like a bullfighter gone horn-shy —Loren D. Estleman

Like a divorce ... goes ripping through our lives —jacket copy describing effect of Sharon Sheehe Stark's novel, *A Wrestling Season*

Marked for annihilation like an orange scored for peeling —Yehuda Amichai

My heroes [Chicago Cubs] had wilted like slugs —George F. Will

Pollutes ... like ratbite —William Alfred

Self-destructing like a third-rate situation comedy
—Warren T. Brookes, on Republican Party,
Wall Street Journal, July 15, 1986

Shattered like a walnut-shell —Charles Dickens
*In Dickens' A Tale of Two Cities, the comparison
refers to a broken wine cask.*

Shatter them like so much glass —Robert Louis
Stevenson

Shrivel up like some old straw broom —Joyce
Carol Oates

Snap like dry chicken bones —David Michael Kaplan

[Taut nerves] Snap like guy wires in a tornado
—Nardi Reeder Campion, *New York Times*

(Then the illusion) snapped like a nest of threads
—F. Scott Fitzgerald

Snapped off [due to frailness] like celery
—Lawrence Durrell

(Who can accept that spirit can be) snuffed as finally as a flame —Barbara Lazear Ascher, *New
York Times,* October 30, 1986

They [free-spending wife and daughter] ate holes
in me like Swiss cheese —Clifford Odets

Wear out their lives, like old clothes —John
Cheever

Your destruction comes as a whirlwind —The
Holy Bible/Proverbs

♣ DETACHMENT
See: REMOTENESS

♣ DETERIORATION
See: DISINTEGRATION

♣ DETERMINATION
See: PURPOSEFULNESS

♣ DEVOTION
See: LOYALTY/DISLOYALTY

♣ DEW
See: NATURE

♣ DICTION
See: SPEECH PATTERNS

♣ DICTIONARIES
See: BOOKS

♣ DIETS
See: EATING AND DRINKING

♣ DIFFERENCES

Alike as the gap between Little League and Major
League —Anon

Alike as an oil portrait and polaroid snapshot
—Anon

Alike as a cliché and a sonnet —Rod MacLeish,
National Public Radio, December 29, 1986
*In his obituary on mystery writer John MacDonald, MacLeish used the simile to point out the difference between MacDonald's Travis McGee
character and Raymond Chandler's Philip Marlowe.*

Alike as a mom and pop grocery store and a
multi-national corporation —Anon

Alike as an abacus and computer —Anon

Alike as an elephant and a giraffe —Anon

Alike as grains of sand —Anon

Alike as human faces —Anon

Alike as six pebbles on the beach —Eudora Welty

Alike as the gap between doing a gig at a neighborhood wedding and being on prime-time
TV —Anon

And I see the same skies through brown eyes /
That you see through blue / But we're worlds
apart, worlds apart / Just like the earth, just
like the sun —Roger Miller, "Worlds Apart,"
Big River

As like as an apple is to a lobster —John Ray's
Proverbs

A variation on the same theme, also from John Ray's Proverbs *is: "as alike as an apple is to an oyster." Other entries in this section merely hint at the endless twists possible.*

As like this as a crab's like an apple —William Shakespeare, *King Lear*

Here we have the above simile turned around, with the apple the comparison.

(In this world it is rarely possible to settle matters with an"either, or," since there are) as many gradations of emotion and conduct as there are stages between a hooked nose and one that turns up —Johann Wolfgang Von Goethe

Different as a moonbeam from lightning, as frost from fire —Emily Brontë

(You and I are as) different as chalk and cheese —John Ray's *Proverbs*

Opposite as yea and nay —Francis Quarles

(Two faces) different as hot and cold —Dannie Abse

Different as three men singing the same chorus from three men playing three tunes on the same piano —G. K. Chesterton

Different as ying from yang —Harry Prince

Everything has in fact another side to it, like the moon —G. K. Chesterton

Sharply defined as salt and pepper —Anon

The difference between vivacity and wit is the same as the difference between the lightning-but and lightning —Josh Billings

Various as the fancies of men in pursuit of a wife —James Ralph

♣ DIFFICULTY

See Also: FUTILITY, IMPOSSIBILITY

About as easy to ignore as a Salvation Army drum —William McIlvanney

As easy as buying a pair of solid leather shoes for $10 —Anon

As easy as combing your hair with a broom —Anon

Easy as doing one thing at a time and never putting off anything till tomorrow that could be done today —Baron Samuel von Puffendorf

As easy as drawing a picture in water —Anon

As easy as eating soup with a fork —Anon

As easy as finding a two-bedroom apartment on Manhattan's east side for $400 month —Anon

This is the sort of topical and location-specific comparison that is adapted to the user's own locale and economic conditions.

As easy as getting rid of cockroaches in a New York apartment —Anon

As easy as making an omelette without eggs —Anon

A simile probably inspired by the proverb "one can't expect to make an omelet without breaking eggs."

As easy as passing a bull in a close —William McIlvanney

As easy as roller skating on a collapsing sidewalk —Anon

As easy as running with a stitch in your side —Anon

As easy as trying to paint the wind —Anon

As easy as shaving with an axe —Anon

As easy as struggling through a waist-high layer of glue —Anon

As easy as taking a hair out of milk —Babylonian Talmud

As easy to scare Jack Cady [character in novel] as to scare an oak tree —Speer Morgan

As easy as trying to load a thermometer with beads of quicksilver —Bill Pronzini

Easy as trying to nail a glob of mercury —Anon

Easy as trying to open an oyster without a knife —Anon

Easy as trying to participate in your own funeral —Anon

Easy as trying to read a book on the deck of a sinking ship —Anon

Easy as trying to unscramble an egg —Anon

Another proverb that has become familiar is attributed to J. P. Morgan on the dissolution of trusts in 1905: "You can't unscramble eggs."

Easy as wading in tar —Anon

Easy as walking on one leg —Anon

Chasing a dream, a dream no one else can see or understand, like running after a butterfly across an endless meadow, is extremely difficult —W. P. Kinsella

Controlling the bureaucracy is like nailing Jell-O to the wall —John F. Kennedy

Dealing with him is like dealing with a porcupine in heat —Anon

The porcupine simile made by an anonymous White House reporter in 1986 referred to deputy chief Richard G. Darmon.

Demanding as a Dickens novel with a cast of hundreds —Ira Wood

Difficult as an elephant trying to pick up a pea —H. G Wells

Difficult as climbing pinnacles of ice —Elinor Wylie

Difficult as driving a Daimler at top speed on a slick road —Barry Tuckwell, quoted in an article by Barbara Jepson, *Wall Street Journal*, July 1, 1986

(Getting the truth in the *New York Post* has been as) difficult as finding a good hamburger in Albania —Paul Newman, *New York Post*, October 14, 1986

The actor's simile referred to the paper's efforts to prove that he is only 5 foot 8 inches tall

Difficult as getting a concession to put a merry-go-round on the front lawn of the White House —Kenneth L. Roberts

As true and timely a simile today as when it originated in the early part of the twentieth century.

Difficult as making a silk purse out of a sow's ear —Anon

This can be traced to the German proverb "you cannot make a silk purse of a sow's ear." A less well-known French version substitutes velvet for silk.

Difficult as making dreams come true —Anon

Difficult as putting a bandage on an eel —Anon

Difficult as to sell a ham to a kosher caterer —Elyse Sommer

Difficult as sighting a rifle in the dark with rain falling —Peter Greer

Difficult as trying to draw blood from a turnip —French proverb

Difficult as trying to be old and young at the same time —German proverb

Another proverb that has evolved into simile form, in this instance from "you cannot be old and young at the same time."

Difficult as trying to run and sit still at the same time —Scotch proverb

Difficult ... like trying to play the piano with boxing gloves —William H. Hallhan

Difficult ... like swimming upstream in Jell-O —Loren D. Estleman

Difficult ... like trying to grab a hold of Jell-O in quicksand —Philip K. Meyer, Eberstadt Fleming executive quoted in *New York Times*, July 25, 1986 on estimating an oilfield company's earnings

Difficult ... like walking a frisky, 220-pound dog —Henry D. Jacoby, on trying to manage crude oil prices in face of changing market conditions, *New York Times*, January 26, 1986

Difficult to absorb ... like trying to take a sip of water from a fire hose —Anon

The comment was a response to Uranus probe, January 22, 1987.

Difficult to get as trying to get a pearl out of a lock-jawed oyster —Robert Vinez quoted in

Wall Street Journal article on consumer campaign to get Ford to put air bags into all cars. *The difficulty in this instance involved getting the air bag out of Ford.*

(Satiety is as) difficult to stomach as hunger —Stefan Zweig

Finding a decent, affordable apartment in New York is … like trying to recover a contact lens from a subway platform at rush hour —Michael de Courcy Hinds, *New York Times*, January 16, 1986

Getting information from him was like squeezing a third cup from a tea bag —Christopher Buckley

[Getting stubborn George ready for the hospital was] like ushering a mule into a cage. —Susan Vreeland, *Clara and Mr. Tiffany*

Hard as building a wall of sand —Marge Piercy

(It was) hard to do, but quick, like a painful inoculation —Judith Rascoe

Hard to lift as a dead elephant —Raymond Chandler, *The Little Sister*

It [to get a woman character to admit feelings for her lover] would be rather like breaking rocks —Laurie Colwin

Keeping up with her is like trying to run after a departing train —Jhumpa Lahiri, *Unaccustomed Earth*

Laborious as idleness —Louis IV

Life is not an easy thing to embrace, like trying to hug an elephant —Diane Wakoski

(Waiting on a $175 check from the Amoco Traveler was) like trying to bail out a rowboat with an eyedropper while the cold, briny deep gushed through a hole the size of a rubber boot —Lionel Shriver, *The New Republic*

Lurching up those steep stairs was like climbing through a submarine —Scott Spencer

Not like making instant coffee —David Brierley

In his novel, Skorpion's Death, Brierley uses the comparison to describe the difficulty of learning how to fly.

A process that could be likened to trying to drain a swimming pool with a soda straw —Thomas J. Knudson, on project to reduce flooding of lake in Utah, *New York Times*, April 11, 1987

To get a cent out of this woman is like crossing the Red Sea dry-shod —Sholem Aleichem

Trying to define yourself is like trying to bite your own teeth —Alan Watts

Trying to get information out of Joe was like trying to drag a cat by its tail over a rug —F. van Wyck Mason

Trying to jump-start a business venture over breakfast is like working hard at going to sleep or devoting a year to falling in love —Anon participant at a business networking breakfast, *New York Times*, Michael Winerif, February 17, 1987

Walking [while feeling dizzy] was like a journey up the down escalator —Madison Smart Bell

With effort like rising out of deep water —Elizabeth Spencer

❧ DIGNITY

See: PRIDE

❧ DILEMMAS

See: PROBLEMS AND SOLUTIONS

❧ DIPLOMACY

See: TACT

❧ DIRECTNESS

See: CANDOR, STRAIGHTNESS

❧ DISAGREEMENT

See: AGREEMENT/DISAGREEMENT, ARGUMENT

❧ DISAPPEARENCE

Blown away like clouds —Henry Wadsworth Longfellow

Blows away like a deck of cards in a hurricane —George Garrett

Bobbed away like a soap-bubble —Sylvia Plath

(The premonition had) boiled off like a puff of bad air —Herbert Lieberman

Borne away like a cork on a stream —Lawrence Durrell

(The old worlds) died away like dew —Dame Edith Sitwell

Disappeared as if into fairyland —Peter Najarian

Disappeared ... effortlessly, like a star into a cloud —F. van Wyck Mason

Disappeared like a sigh —Tom Wolfe

[Food being served, vegetables] disappeared like leaves before locusts —Charlotte Brontë

Disappeared like raindrops which fall in the ocean —John T. Morse, about the loss of many of Oliver Wendell Holmes similes and other witticisms

Disappeared [huntsmen and hounds into a bewitched forest] like soap bubbles —Anne Sexton

Disappeared ... like sparks dropped into wet grass —James Crumley

Disappearing like the fastest fairy who ever lived —Brian Donleavy

Disappearing, like water poured out of a wide-necked bottle —Diane Wakoski

Disappear like a moon entering a cloud bank —Bernard Malamud

Disappear like quicksilver in the cracks —Booth Tarkington

Disappear like socks in the laundry —Elyse Sommer

Disappear like the dew on the mountain —Anon

Drift away into infinity, like a child's balloon at a circus —Robert Penn Warren

Everybody peeled away like an onion —official of a New York company on reason for his firm's bankruptcy, *New York Times*, December 12, 1986

(The vision of her early loveliness) faded from reality like dew licked up by the sun —Elinor Wylie

Faded like a cloud which has outswept its rain —Percy Bysshe Shelley

Faded ... like dew upon the sea —Oliver Wendell Holmes

(The restlessness in him) faded like fog before sunshine —Pearl S. Buck

(Light would) fade like a slow gray curtain dropping —Nelson Algren

Fades like the lustre of an evening cloud —William Wordsworth

[Awareness of children] Fading like old ink —Margaret Atwood

(The season) fading like woodwind music —George Garrett

Fading like young joy —Dame Edith Sitwell

Fall away like forgiven sins —Miller Williams

(All your joys start) falling like sand through a sieve —Lorenz Hart
   Hart's lyric for"A Lady Must Live" from America's Sweetheart omitted the letter 'g' in 'falling'

Fell away like a wall —Dudley Clendinen *New York Times* March 31,1985, about a publisher's declining advertising revenues

(Childhood and youth, friendship and love's first glow, have) fled like sweet dreams —Percy Bysshe Shelley

(Any thought I had for such an enterprise) fled like thunder —Richard Ford

Flown like a thought —John Keats

Fluttered away like flakes of snow —Louis Bromfield

[Ceremonial occasions] Glide swift into shadow, like sails on the seas —John Greenleaf Whittier

(He was) gone again, gone like some shadow the fire had made —Davis Grubb

Gone and out of sight like a thought —Richard Ford

Gone as a dream is gone from a dreamer waked with a shout —Lord Dunsany

Gone … as if they had evaporated —Dorothy Canfield

(That moment is) gone forever, like lightning that flashed and died —like a snowflake upon the river —like a sunbeam upon the tide —Percy Bysshe Shelley

Gone from my gaze like a beautiful dream —George Linley

Gone like a flushed toilet —Max Apple

Gone like a morning dream, or like a pile of clouds —William Wordsworth

Gone like a quick wind —Ursula Le Guin

(Our world was) gone like a scrap in the wind —Beryl Markham

Gone like a wild bird, like a blowing flame —Euripides

[Smile of a loved one] Gone like dreams that we forget —William Wordsworth

(And all the students) gone, like last week's snow —Delmore Schwartz

Gone like our change at the end of the week —Palmer Cox

(Words) gone like sparks burned up in darkness —Jayne Anne Phillips

[A funeral procession] Gone … like tears in the eyes —Karl Shapiro

Gone, like tenants that quit without warning —Oliver Wendell Holmes

Gone, like the life from a busted balloon —Palmer Cox

(I am) gone like the shadow when it declines —The Holy Bible/Psalms
The biblical "declineth" has been modernized.

Go out … just like a candle —Lewis Carroll

(The Contessina could no longer see him;) it was as though he had slipped from her vision, and the crack had closed above him forever —Elizabeth Bowen

(Maybe he wanted her to) lift up, blow away somewhere, like a kite —Margaret Atwood

Like a match struck on a stove … faded and was gone —James Agee

Like a passing thought she fled —Robert Burns
Burns' line has found its way into daily language as "vanish like a passing thought."

Like a shadow, glided out of view —William Wordsworth

Like swallows in autumn they fled, and left the house silent —John Hall Wheelock

Lost like stars beyond dark trees —Dante Gabriel Rossetti

(Her patience) melted like snow before a blowtorch —Julia O'Faolain

(Money) melting away like butter in the sun —Bertolt Brecht

Off and away like a frightened fish —Ogden Nash

Pass as if it had never existed, like a fart in a gale of wind —Richard Russo

Pass away like clouds before the wind —William Wordsworth

Passed like a ghost from view —John Greenleaf Whittier

(The wild part of her had) perished like burned grass —Ellen Glasgow

(Life was) receding … as the sea abruptly withdraws, abandoning a rock it has caressed too long —Françoise Sagan

Receding like a bad dream —Anon

(He felt the distress and suspicions of the previous night) receding like a tempest —George Santayana

[Sounds] Receding like the image of a man between two mirrors —Frank Conroy

Sank like lead into the sea —Brian Moore

Sank to the bottom as a stone —The Holy Bible/ Exodus

Scuttle away ... like moths —W. D. Snodgrass

(The cares that infest the day) shall fold their tents, like the Arabs, and as silently steal away —Henry Wadsworth Longfellow

Shrank away like an ill-treated child —W. H. Auden

Shrank like an anemone —Derek Lambert

Slip away like water —Edna St. Vincent Millay

[Thoughts] Slipped away ... like bushes on the side of a sheer precipice —Edith Wharton

Slipping silently away like a thief in a London fog —Jack Whittaker, ABC/TV, about the Goodyear blimp disappearing in the mist above the US golf open tournament in San Francisco, June 20, 1987

Slips away like a snake in a weed-tangle —Robert Penn Warren

Slips out of my life like sand —Diane Wakoski

A slow fade, like a candle or an icicle —Margaret Atwood

(The nights) snapped out of sight like a lizard's eyelid —Sylvia Plath

Suddenly disappeared with a jerk, as if somebody had given her a violent pull behind —Charles Dickens

(Her voice) suddenly disappeared, like a coin in a magic trick —Scott Spencer

Vanish ... as easily as an eel into sand —Arthur Conan Doyle

Vanish as raindrops which fall in the sea —Susan Coolidge

Vanish away like the ghost of breath —George Garrett

Vanished, ghost-like, into air —Henry Wadsworth Longfellow

Vanished like a puff of steam —H.G. Wells

A frequently used alternative is to vanish or leave "like a puff of wind."

Vanished like a sail on the sea —Oscar Hammerstein, *Pipe Dream*

(The stray cat) vanished like a swift, invisible shadow —D. H. Lawrence

[Food being served, dessert] vanished like a vision —Charlotte Brontë

Vanished like a wisp of vapor —Edith Wharton

(He had simply) vanished, like Gauguin —Lynne Sharon Schwartz

Vanished like midnight ghosts —Charles Lindberg

Lindbergh used the simile in 1927 to describe the flight of a French plane, L'Oiseau Blanc.

Vanished like some little bird that has been flushed out of the shrubbery —Mikhail Lermontov

Vanished like the last of the buffalo hunters —George Garrett

Vanished [out of his mind] like the mist before the rising sun —H. G. Wells

[The impression made upon people by a tragedy] vanishes as quickly as a delicious fruit melts in the mouth —Honoré de Balzac

Vanishes as rapidly as a road runner in a cartoon —*New Yorker,* August 26, 1985

In the "Talk of The Town" column, this referred to the speed with which a book, once finished, disappears from writer's mental picture.

(Beauty) vanishing like a long sigh —George Garrett

Vanish like a changing mood —John Hall Wheelock

Vanish like a cocktail before dinner —Anon

Vanish like a dew-drop in a rose —Gerald Massey

Vanish like a ghost before the sun —P.J. Bailey

Vanish like an echo or a dream —Johann Wolfgang von Goethe

Vanish like birds in winter —George Garrett

Vanish like lightning —Henry Taylor

Vanish like plunging stars —Don Marquis

Vanish like raindrops which fall in the sea —Anon

Vanish like smoke —Percy Bysshe Shelley

Vanish like the Witch of the North —George Garrett

Vanish like white soft crowns of dandelions in the wind —George Garrett

Vanish like writing in the sand —Anon

(My awe of Cruikback) went away like a mist in a high wind —Gerald Kersh

Went away like a summer fly —W. B. Yeats

Went gloriously away, like lightning from the sky —Edgar Allen Poe

[Sense of peace] Went out like a shooting star —Edna O'Brien

❧ DISAPPOINTMENT
See Also: DESPAIR, FACIAL EXPRESSION

Disappointed as a dieter who can't lose more than an ounce —Anon

Disappointed as a ghost without a house to haunt —Anon

Disappointed … as if he'd seen his favorite teacher drunk —Mary Gordon

Disappointing as discovering the charming man you met at a party is gay —Anon

Disappointing, like signing up for a French gourmet cooking course and learning how to make French toast —Nina Totenberg, Public Radio

Disappointment … had fallen upon him like a blow struck by some unseen hand —Sherwood Anderson

Disappointment toppled me like a wave —Susan Vreeland

Disappointment worked through me like a poison —Robertson Davies

Disillusioned … as a betrayed lover —Calder Willingham

Had a look of profound disappointment … like a child who sees a treat wafted away from him —Mary McCarthy

❧ DISAPPROVAL
See: CONTEMPT

❧ DISASTER
See: FORTUNE/MISFORTUNE

❧ DISCOMFORT
See Also: PAIN

Comfortable as a toothache —Mark Twain

[Kiss] comfortless as frozen water to a starved snake —William Shakespeare, *Troilus and Cressida*

Comfortless as salt —Sylvia Plath

Damp like a vault —Maurice Hewlett

Felt like a door-to-door salesman, pushing unwanted sets of nature encyclopedias complete with fake walnut case —Sue Grafton

Indigestible as Christmas dinner —Patricia Ferguson

I've a head like a concertina, I've a tongue like a button-stick, I've a mouth like an old potato —Rudyard Kipling

Kipling's triple simile to describe a hangover, continues as follows: "And I'm more than a little sick, but I've had my fun."

Self-conscious as a stammer —Delmore Schwartz

(Joel's fingers are cold.) The apartment is like a football game in the rain —Margaret Atwood

Uncomfortable as running a marathon in high-heeled pumps —Anon

Uncomfortable as trying to sleep standing up —Elyse Sommer

Uneasy as a dog in a vet's waiting room —Anon

An uncomfortable feeling, like finding oneself in the same cell, and for the same crime, as a man one repudiated on every ground —John Fowles

Nothing unsettles man like a bed of stinging nettles —W. S. Gilbert

♣ DISCONTENT

See Also: DEJECTION, GLOOM

Disgruntled as an under-tipped taxi driver —Anon

Dissatisfaction with himself had settled over him … as congruently as a second skin —François Camoin

Discontent follows ambition like a shadow —Anon

Discontent … had come over her like a blighting wind —George Eliot

Discontent is like ink poured into water, which fills the whole fountain full of blackness —Owen Feltham

Discontent like alum in the mouth —Wallace Stegner

His whole wounded life choked him at the throat like a death agony —Émile Zola

Looking as unhappy as an aging, wet and exhausted salesman whose luck had played out at last could possibly look —Howard Frank Mosher

Men who are unhappy, like men who sleep badly, are always proud of the fact —Bertrand Russell

Unhappiness burns like leaves —F. D. Reeve

Unhappiness inhabited me as if it were another person and it had the power to pull memories from me, as if from an open file —Scott Spencer

Unhappiness … it is like climbing up a bare wall. It is like being shut up in a cellar all your life —Vicki Baum

Unhappy as a baseball player who can't get to 3rd base —Anon

Unhappy as a character in a soap opera —Elyse Sommer

♣ DISCORD
See: AGREEMENT/DISAGREEMENT

♣ DISCOURAGEMENT
See: DEJECTION

♣ DISCRETION
See: CAUTION, TACT

♣ DISCRIMINATION
See: STYLE

♣ DISHONESTY

See Also: BELIEVABILITY, CRIME, LIES AND LIARS

All frauds, like the wall daubed with untempered mortar … always tend to the decay of what they are devised to support —Richard Whately

As honest a man as any in the cards, when the kings are out —Thomas Fuller

At length corruption, like a general flood … shall deluge all —Alexander Pope

Borrowed thoughts, like borrowed money, only show the poverty of the borrower —Marguerite Countess Blessington

Corruption is like a ball of snow … once set-a-rolling it must increase —Charles Caleb Colton

Crooked as a worm writhing on a hook —Herman Wouk

The people who are likened to worms are characters from Wouk's political novel, Inside, Outside.

(Pompous and braggadocian, he seemed to the children as flat and) false as his teeth —Ferrol Sams

Fickle and unfaithful, like false as water —William Shakespeare, *Othello*

[I pray you, do not fall in love with me] For I am falser than vows made in wine —William Shakespeare, *As You Like It*

Fraudulent as falsies —Helen Hudson

He that builds his house with other men's money is like one that gathers himself stones for the tomb of his burial —The Holy Bible/Apocrypha

The word "builds" has been modernized from "buildeth" and "gathers" from "gathereth."

It is as difficult to appropriate the thoughts of others as it is to invent —Ralph Waldo Emerson

Permit memory to paint it [a long-ago life style] falsely. Like the face of some old whore who could wish to be taken as young and innocent —George Garrett

Plays you as fair as if he'd picked your pocket —John Ray's *Proverbs*

Robbers are like rain, they fall on the just and the unjust —Josh Billings

In Billings' phonetic dialect the word "they" was "tha."

Sneaky as a rat in a hotel kitchen —William Alfred

There is something in corruption which, like a jaundiced eye, transfers the color of itself to the object it looks upon —Thomas Paine

To rob a friend even of a penny is like taking his life —Johann B. Nappaha

❧ DISILLUSIONMENT
See: DISAPPOINTMENT

❧ DISINTEGRATION
See Also: DESTRUCTION

(Shirley's childless marriage had) become unstuck like a piece of old and grubby sticking plaster —Gillian Tindall

Blown aside like thistledown —John Fowles

Fowles used this simile at one point to describe the eventual collapse of a political party and at another time to describe a mood. Some similes obviously transfer to different points of reference more easily than others.

Broke like a sea-bubble on the sand —James Montgomery

(Perhaps the hope will die stillborn,) broken up like wreckage by the tides of events —Lawrence Durrell

Come apart like wet Kleenex —Anon

(When I hit him he) comes apart like a perfect puzzle or an old flower —Philip Levine

Comes apart like meat being carved —G. K. Chesterton

(He started) coming apart like seedpod —Sharon Sheehe Stark

Cracking and fading like an old photograph —George Garrett

Crumbled like crackers into alphabet soup —Dave Anderson, *New York Times*/Sports of the Times column, November 24, 1986

This comparison referred to disintegration of once great heavyweight champion division.

Crumble like old cheese —Anon

Crumble like soda crackers —Dashiell Hammett

(Their argument) crumbles like dry rice paper —Nicholas Proffitt

(The old voice) crumpled ... like a fragile leaf —Lawrence Durrell

Crumple ... like a leaf in the fire —James Joyce

Crumple up like wet and falling roses —D. H. Lawrence

(The house was) old and decayed like the pitted trunk of a persimmon —Yasunari Kawabata

Disintegrate like a bubble at a touch —Anon

Disintegrate like a crumbling monument —Anon

(Words came to my lips and) dissipated like the wisps of children's breaths in the cold air outside —Kent Nelson

Dissolved and grew flimsy like the world after champagne —Graham Swift

[A committee] Dissolved like a summer cloud —Edith Wharton

Dissolved like spit in the wind —Wallace Stevens

Dissolve like vague promises —Elyse Sommer

(Floats on water) dissolving like a paper plate —Margaret Atwood

(The white sky) empties of its promise, like a cup —Sylvia Plath

(The shadows under the trees and bushes) evaporated like puddles after a shower —Stephen King

Evaporated like a drop of dew —Ruth Prawer Jhabvala

Evaporate … like hoar frost before the morning sun —William Somerset Maugham

Maugham's simile from The Summing Up *refers to the way changing tastes affect perceptions of an artwork's beauty.*

Fall apart and scatter like a smashed string of beads —Yaakov Churgin

Falling into decay like a layer of mulch —Jean Thompson

(Furniture) falling to pieces like dry fruitcake —William H. Gass

Goes up in smoke like so much tissue paper —Elizabeth Spencer

Go sour [as a project] like milk abandoned in the far corner of the refrigerator —Marian Sturm

Melt away like salt in water —Sholom Aleichem

Melt away like Turkish delights —Frank O'Hara

Melted away like a snail —Elizabeth Spencer

[Members of a social set] Melted away, like snow drops over a bonfire —Ayn Rand

Melted [in response to compliments] like butter on the Sahara —Tony Ardizzone

Melted like wax —The Holy Bible

(The day is) melting away like snow —Plautus

This has been used in poetry and every day language, since 200 B.C.E., and is still going strong.

Melts away like moonlight in the heaven of spreading day —Percy Bysshe Shelley

(Your mind now) moldering like a wedding-cake —Adrienne Rich

Rot and shred and peel away like old wallpaper —George Garrett

[Resolutions] Thinned away like smoke, into nothingness —Aldous Huxley

Rotted through like old shoe leather —Marge Piercy

Rotting like autumn leaves —Marguerite Yourcenar

Shredded away like leaf tobacco —Saul Bellow

(The snake slides again and again until all passed is left behind to) shrivel like a ghost without substance —Daniela Gioseffi

(The remembrance had been brought to mind so often that it was) tarnished and dull, like a trinket not worth looking at —Beryl Markham

(Her muscles came) undone like ribbons —Sharon Sheehe Stark

Wear out like a worn battery —Anon

This makes a good update for "Wears out like a run-down gramophone record."

Went to pieces like a cheap umbrella in a gale —Anon

This is updated from the original "Like a 50 cent umbrella," which today would only be possible to obtain at a rummage sale.

Will dissolve faster than an Alka-Seltzer under a waterfall —Barry Farber, WNYC radio, commenting on the endurance of communism

Wither like the flower of the field —Miguel de Cervantes

Withered like grass —The Holy Bible/Psalms

Wither like a blighted tree —Barbara Howes

Withers like the face of an aged woman —Beryl Markham

♣ DISLOYALTY
See: LOYALTY/DISLOYALTY

♣ DISORDER
See: ORDER/DISORDER

♣ DISPERSAL

Diffused charm around like an indispensable perfume —Jules Janin, about the woman who served as the role model for *The Lady With the Camellias* by Alexandre Dumas, Fils

(Consciousness) disperses itself like pollen on a spring day —Carlos Fuentes

Dispersed like a broken family —Beryl Markham

Disposed of like a branch or potato sack —Graham Swift

Here and there like teeth in an old man's mouth —Maxim Gorky

Like the chaff of the summer threshing floors; … the wind carried them away —The Holy Bible

Scatter and divide like fleecy clouds self-multiplied —William Wordsworth

Scattered as the seeds of wild grass —Beryl Markham

Scattered [audience across vacant seats in a theatre] as widely as out-fielders when the champion batter steps to the plate —O. Henry

[Shadows of doubts and weaknesses] Scattered, like a cloud in morning's breeze —John Greenleaf Whittier

(The rage that had been silent … fired and) scattered like bullets —Belva Plain

Scattered (across the map of the Land) like carelessly dropped pennies —George Garrett

Scattered, like chaff in a high wind —Donald Seaman

Scatter like confetti —Derek Lambert
> *An extension is "To scatter like confetti at a tickertape parade."*

Scattered like dusts and leaves, when the mighty blasts of October seize them —Henry Wadsworth Longfellow

Scattered like foam along the wave —George Croly

Scattered like foam on the torrent —Percy Bysshe Shelley

Scattered like mown and withered grass —Johann Wolfgang von Goethe

Scattered like rabbits to a gunshot —Lawrence Durrell

Scattered like raindrops across a window —Michael Chabon, *The Amazing Adventures of Kavalier & Clay*

(Spite, malice and jealousy) scattered like spent foam —Iris Murdoch

Scatter like a bucket of water —Erich Maria Remarque

Scatter like balls on a billiard table —Tom Shales, movie review, WNYC Morning Edition Public Radio March 20, 1987
> *In the movie Shales reviewed it was babies who were thus scattered about.*

(The sparrows) scatter like handfuls of gravel —William H. Gass

Scatter like mist before the wind —Kenzaburo Oe
> *The descriptive reference point is a feeling of contentment.*

Scatter like pigeons across grass —Anon

(His foes are) scattered like chirping sparrows —Stephen Vincent Benét

Thrown away like used paper cups —Anon

♣ DISPOSABILITY
See: TRANSIENCE

♣ DISSATISFACTION
See: DISCONTENT

♣ DISSENSION
See: AGREEMENT/DISAGREEMENT, ARGUMENT, FIGHTING

❧ DISSIMILARITY
See: DIFFERENCES

❧ DISTANCE
See: REMOTENESS

❧ DISTINCTIVENESS
See: ORIGINALITY

❧ DIVERSENESS
See Also: DIFFERENCES, PERSONAL TRAITS

(We had come up to the farm for our four summer weeks, and Maine was all before us) as various and new as the flow of the heavy tides —Barry Targan

As various as a Cook's Tour —Delmore Schwartz

As various as a duck-billed platypus —Jean Stafford

Diverse as a smorgasbord table —Anon

Diverse as weather, changeful as the wind —Robert Hillyer

(She) had as many registers as a fine old organ —Vicki Baum

He [Shakespeare] was as many-sided as clouds are many-formed —Robert G. Ingersoll

Like a Russian doll nesting ever smaller dolls inside of it, I house an infinity of selves —Daphne Merkin

Multi-faceted like a crystal chandelier —Anon

Varied as the expressions of the human face —George H. Ellwanger

With this book as an example, one might add: "And as varied as the similes to describe those expressions."

❧ DIVORCE
See: MARRIAGE

❧ DOCILITY
See: MEEKNESS

❧ DOCTORS
See Also: PROFESSIONS

As with eggs, there is no such thing as a poor doctor; doctors are either good or bad —Dr. Fuller Albright

A breast or a foot is examined [by doctors lacking in empathy] like a pack of cigarettes —Hildegarde Knef, quoted in interview with Rex Reed

Carrying his little black bag like a small sample cut from the shadow of death —Helen Hudson

This observation from Hudson's novel, Meyer Meyer, *is made by the main character about his doctor/brother-in-law.*

Commonly physicians, like beer, are best when they are old; and lawyers, like bread, when they are young and new —Thomas Fuller

A doctor knows the human body as a cabman knows the town; he is well acquainted with all the great thoroughfares and small turnings; he's intimate with all the principle edifices, but he cannot tell you what is going inside of any one of them —*Punch*, 1856

The fame of a surgeon is like the fame of an actor; it exists only as long as they live, and their talent is no longer appreciable after they have disappeared —Honoré de Balzac

Physicians are like kings —they brook no contradiction —John Webster

❧ DOGS
See: ANIMALS

❧ DOMINATION
See: POWER

❧ DOUBT
See: TRUST/MISTRUST

❧ DREAM(S)
See Also: AMBITION, HOPE, SLEEP

The arc of dreams is black and streaked with gray as dead hair is —John Logan

Dreamed of unearned riches, like Aladdin —Phyllis McGinley

The dream … hovered about her still like a pleasant, warm fog —Lynne Sharon Schwartz

A dream not interpreted is like a letter not read — *Babylonian Talmud*

Dream safely like any child who has said prayers and to whom a lullaby has been sung —George Garrett

Dreams are like a microscope through which we look at the hidden occurrences in our soul —Erich Fromm

Dreams are thoughts waiting to be thought —Jan de Hartog

Dreams descend like cranes on gilded, forgetful wings —John Ashberry

Dreams move my countenance as if it were earth being pelted by rain —Diane Wakoski

The dreams of idealists are like the sound of footsteps in a tornado —Melvin I. Cooperman, June 8,1987

Dreams pop out like old fillings in the teeth —Diane Wakoski

Dreams rising from your eyes like steam —George Bradley

Dreams withered like flowers that are blighted by frost —Ellen Glasgow

Dreamy as puberty —Karl Shapiro

Fantasy is like jam: you have to spread it on a solid slice of bread. If not, it remains a shapeless thing, like jam, out of which you can't make anything —Italo Calvino, television interview aired after his death in 1985

Kept it [private dream] locked in his heart and took it out only when he was alone, like a miser counting his gold —Margaret Millar

Like a dog, he hunts in dreams —Alfred, Lord Tennyson

Nightmares have seasons like hurricanes —Lorrie Moore

Old dreams still floated … like puddles of oil on the surface of a pail of water —Paige Mitchell

Our dreams like clouds disperse —Alfred Noyes

Toss wishes like a coin —George Garrett

You know a dream is like a river, ever changing as it flows —Garth Brooks, "The River"

♣ DRINKING

See Also: EATING AND DRINKING, FOOD AND DRINK

Alcohol is like love. The first kiss is magic, the second is intimate, the third is routine. —Raymond Chandler *The Big Sleep*

A case of beer lying at his feet like the family dog —Jonathan Valin

Drank like a camel —Robert Graves

Drank like a fire engine —Ernest William Hornung

Drink like a fish —Anon

> *There's a whole laundry list of "Drink like" and "Drunk as" similes. Those linking drinking with fish predominate with "Drunk as a lord" and "Drunk as owls" or "Boiled owls" following close on the fishes' fins. A nice twist by Mary Peterson Poole: " It's all right to drink like a fish, if you drink what a fish drinks."*

(He could) drink like a suction-hose —Thomas Burke

Drinks cognac like soda water —Isaac Bashevis Singer

Drunk as a cooter brown —Richard Ford

Drunk as an autumn wasp —Jonathan Gash

Drunk as a wheelbarrow —George Garrett

Drunk as dancing pigs —James Crumley

Drunk as puffed-up pigeons —Edward Hoagland

Drunk like wedding guests —Charles Simic

Feel the vodka melting into his bloodstream, like snow —Richard Lourie

Got as tight as a fat lady's girdle —Raymond Chandler, *Goldfish*

Half as sober as a judge —Charles Lamb

Lit up like a Christmas tree —Anon

Similes using "Lit up" with a variety of references became part of the American language around 1902. Here are some offshoots of the above: "Lit up like a cathedral," "Lit up like a church, "Lit up like Main Street," "Lit up like a skyscraper," and "Lit up like Times Square."

Pissed as a skunk —Martin Cruz Smith

Pissed as a newt —American colloquialism

This means to be very drunk.

Smell ... like a tap-room —Anton Chekov

Smells like a still —Cornell Woolrich

Some men are like musical glasses: to produce their finest tones you must keep them wet —Samuel Taylor Coleridge

Taught himself to drink as he would have taught himself Greek; like Greek it would be the gateway to a wealth of new sensations, new psychic states, new reactions in joy or misery —F. Scott Fitzgerald

(I have been) tight as a tick —Tallulah Bankhead

A hangover like a herd of elephants —Graham Masterton

(He was) so knocked out with liquor that he vomited like a whale, urinated like a dog, exposed himself like a jackass, and wallowed in his muck like a pig —St. Kitts' government newspaper *The Democrat* about leader of opposition, 1981

The stuff [liquor] was like insulin to a diabetic; he didn't need much of it at a time, but if he needed little he needed it often —Howard Nemerov

The simile describes the drinking habits of a character in Nemerov's short story "Unbelievable Characters."

Woke up with his head like a big split millstone —John Dos Passos

When drunk, his color sank to a clammy white from which it rose like a thermometer as he sobered up —Mary Ward Brown

His head still felt like a sandbag full of maggots —Sterling Hayden

Whiskey ... went through me like a rope of fire —Louise Erdrich

Whiskey ... burned his stomach like hellfire —Paige Mitchell

The spirit of the wine was rising like smoke to his head —George Garrett

The bourbon was warm in her stomach ... like a core of heat —Jayne Anne Phillips

⚜ DRIVERS/DRIVING

See: VEHICLES

⚜ DRYNESS

Arid as the sands of the Sahara —Joseph Conrad

The everyday cliché is "Dry as the Sahara."

(I'll) drain him dry as hay —William Shakespeare, *Macbeth*

Dries up like snakeskin —Kate Grenville

(Her words were) dry as the rustle of old leaves —William Beechcroft

Dry and cracking like the bindings on rare books —Diane Wakoski

(His throat was) dry as a desert —Colin Forbes

(Heart) dry as an autumn leaf —Nelson Algren

(You'll sweat until you're as) dry as an old gourd —George Garrett

Dry as ashes —Fisher Ames

Variations of this much-used cliché include "Dry as dust" as well as frame-of-reference switches such as "White as ashes."

(His sensitive palate) as dry as a bread crust —W. S. Gilbert

Dry as a spinster on a Saturday night —line from "St. Elsewhere" television drama, broadcast December 16, 1986

(I was) dry as a stick —Thomas Gray

Gray used this in combination with two other similes: "I was dry as a stick, hard as a stone, and cold as a cucumber."

(Her voice was) dry as burned paper —Susan Fromberg Schaeffer

(My heart felt as) dry as dirt —Bernard Malamud, *The Natural*, Farrar, Straus and Giroux, 1952)

(Their intellectuality is as) dry as dung that's lain on a dusty road for weeks —Louis Adamic

A shorter version seen in a poem by W. D. Snodgrass: "Parched as dung."

Dry as faded marigold —Stephen Vincent Benét

Dry as last year's crow's nest —Anon

Dry as poverty —John Ashberry

Dry as wood ash —Marge Piercy

[Feeling of teeth against lips] Dry as sandpaper —William Faulkner

(Hair) dry as spun glass —Elizabeth Spencer

(He was dry-looking, as) dry as talc —Marianne Wiggins

Dry as the white dunes under sunlight —Marge Piercy

Dry up faster than a pressed corsage —Reynolds Price

Parched like an open mouth —Charles Simic

❧ DULLNESS

See Also: BOREDOM/BORING

About as exciting as broccoli —Fred Barnes, "McLaughlin Group" television broadcast December 29, 1986

About as exciting as a ride on a stone camel —Anon

As much personality as a paper cup —Raymond Chandler about the city of Los Angeles

In his essay "The Country Behind the Hill," critic Clive James explains that this was intended as a positive simile, reflecting Chandler's fascination with the city's seediness.

Bland as a Bloody Mary without Tabasco —Anon

Bland as a martini without a twist of lemon —Anon

Bland as hominy grits —Frederick Exley

Blunt as ignorance —Samuel Rowley

(The place seemed to be as ...) dead as a Pharaoh —Raymond Chandler, *The Long Goodbye*

Dreary as an empty house —Gustave Flaubert

Dreary as an old dishrag —Anon, capsule movie review in *New York Times* television listings

Dreary as a Russian love story —William Diehl

Dry as the Congressional Record —James J. Montague

(Lies ...) dull and senseless as a stone —Elizabeth Barrett Browning

Dull as a jail cell —Ira Wood

(A day as) dull as a lead nickel —John

(A brown macramé wall hanging) dull as dirt —Patricia Henley

Dull as pig shit —Ethel Merman, about her friend Benay Venuta's Jewish society friends

Dull as brushing your teeth —Anon

Dull as ditch-water —Charles Dickens

An everyday expression modernized to "Dull as dishwater."

(When he is gone, the world will be) dull as Mars —Lorrie Moore

(The road north is ...) dull like a camel plodding through the desert —Anon

Dull ... like a cookbook written by someone who doesn't like food —Pat Conroy

An eternal sameness, like a blank wall —Robert Silverberg

Flat and insipid as a pancake —Anatole France

Anatole France loved proverbs, and so this extension of familiar wisdom.

[About an experience someone is relating] Flat as the telling at breakfast of an ecstatic dream —Stella Benson

Had the personality of a dried-out fart —Anon

His Washington [D.C.] was like going to bed with a glass of warm milk and a woman in curlers —David Auburn, *The Columnist*

Interesting as boiled potatoes —Anon

Interesting as staring at a blank wall —Anon

Interesting as watching paint dry —Dee Weber

Life as humdrum as that of a country curate —W. Somerset Maugham

Life … devoid of incident as the longest of Trollope's novels —O. Henry

Life here is as calm as a goldfish tank with one half-animate inmate: me —Julia O'Faolain

Life is as tedious as a twice-told tale —William Shakespeare, *King John*

Looked dreary, like a theater before anybody comes —Mark Twain

Looked like she had the IQ of a well-mannered houseplant —A. E. Maxwell

Mind … slept and snored like a full dog by the fire —George Garrett

Monotonous as a sailor's chantey —Raymond Chandler, *The Long Goodbye*

Monotonous like water dripping on sandstone —John MacDonald

My life is as flat as the table I write on —Gustave Flaubert

A new idea made its way into her mind with much difficulty, as if it had to traverse the meshes of a choked sieve —Stefan Zweig

Numb as a potato —Daniel Asa Rose

Obtuse as an ocelot —Gregory McDonald

Personality like a cup of yogurt —Pat Conroy

Persons without minds are like weeds that delight in good earth; they want to be amused by others, all the more because they are dull within —Honoré de Balzac

Seemed dull … as simple as a three-headed treasure-guarding troll —Anon

(The people who surrounded him) seemed like white bread, inexcusably bland —Phillip Lopate

Shadowy and uninteresting as an event in an outdated and long-unread novel —Gillian Tindall

The frame of reference for the comparison is a brief, long-ago marriage.

There are some things so dull they hypnotize like the pendulum of a clock —Karl Shapiro

Tiresome as virtue —Edith Wharton

Too dull —no stir, no storm, no life about it … like being part dead and part alive, both at the same time —Mark Twain

The condition thus described in Twain's story, Captain Stormfield's Visit to Heaven is that of running a grocery store.

Unconscious as a face of stone —H. W. Hudson

(His friends were as) uninteresting as the dead —Rumer Godden

Void of life as a block of ice —Patricia Henley

❧ DUMBNESS
See: STUPIDITY

❧ DUTY
See: RELIABILITY/UNRELIABILITY

❧ EAGERNESS
See: ENTHUSIASM

❧ EARS
See: FACIAL DETAILS

❧ EARTH
See: NATURE

❧ EASE
(I meet men in the city as) as easily as a finger stuck in water comes up wet —Marge Piercy

As easily as a hot knife cuts through butter —Ben Ames Williams

In Williams' novel Leave Her to Heaven *the simile describes the ease with which floodwaters penetrate a barrier. The simile has also cropped up in every day language to show something slipping by or through easily —as a legal decision past a judge.*

[About the availability of a woman] As hard to get as a hair cut —Raymond Chandler

(Returned to normality) as smoothly as a ski jumper landing —John Braine

Did so without effort or exertion, like a chess champion playing a routine game —Natascha Wodin

Easy as a smile —Anon

Easy as a snake crawling over a stick —Joseph Conrad

Easy as breathing in and breathing out —Louise Erdrich

Easy as climbing a fallen tree —Danish proverb

Easy as drawing a child's first tooth —Johann Wolfgang Von Goethe

Easy as falling out of a canoe —Anon

Easy as finding fault in someone else —Anon

Easy as it is for a cat to have twins —American colloquialism, attributed to New England

Easy as opening a letter —Anon

Easy as peeling the skin off a banana —Anon

Easy as pie —Anon

Easy as pointing a finger —Slogan used by Colt Patent Fire Arms Mfg. Co.

Easy as pouring a glass of water —Anon

Easy as riding down a smoothly paved road —Anon

Easy as rolling off a log —Mark Twain

Easy as running up charge account bills —Anon

Easy as scrambling an egg —Anon

Easy as shooting down a fish in a barrel —Anon

Easy as spitting —Anton T. Chekhov

Easy as stealing pennies from a blind man's can —Donald Seaman

And that's as easy as to set dogs on sheep —William Shakespeare, *Coriolanus*

Easy as turning on the TV set —Anon

Easy as turning the page in a book —Anon

Easy … like sliding into sin —Harry Prince

An easy thing to do, light and easy like falling in a dream —George Garrett

Go through … like so much dishwater —McKinlay Kantor

Stepped into his position as easily as a pair of trousers —Anon

Stepped into manhood, as one steps over a door-sill —Mark Twain

Went in … as easily as paper into a vacuum cleaner —Derek Lambert

Would happen as the turning of a light bulb on or off —John McGahern

❧ EASE, OPPOSITE MEANING
See: DIFFICULTY

❧ EATING AND DRINKING
See Also: FOOD AND DRINK, MANNERS

Ate as if there were a hidden thing inside him, a creature of all jaws with an infinite trailing ribbon of gut —T. Coraghessan Boyle

Ate like a cart-horse —H.E. Bates

Ate like a famished wolf —Louisa May Alcott

Ate like a trucker —Jonathan Kellerman

Ate silently like two starving peasants —James Crumley

Ate slowly, thoughtfully, as if fixing the taste of each spoonful in her mind —Paule Marshall

Bit off an end of it [a candy bar], like a man biting off a chaw from a plug —Peter De Vries

The bread slices collapsed like movie-set walls beneath her bite —Tom Robbins

Chewed ..., in odd little spasms, as if seeking a tooth that wouldn't hurt —Paul Horgan

Chews his granola like a Clydesdale —Ira Wood

Chomping popcorn [in a movie theatre] like their upper teeth are mad at their lower —Tonita S. Gardner

Diets, like clothes, should be tailored to you —Joan Rivers

Down poured the wine like oil on a blazing fire —Charles Dickens

Eat breakfast like a king, lunch like a prince and dinner like a pauper —Anon

Eating [voraciously] ... like a blowfly on a shit pile —Steve Heller

Eating like three men —Louis Adamic

Eating quickly and silently, like a bunch of taxi drivers eager to get back to the job —Daphne Merkin

Eating quickly and abstractedly, like a man whose habits of life have made food less an indulgence than a necessity —Elizabeth Bowen

Eat like wolves —William Shakespeare, *Henry V*

Eats like a well man, and drinks like a sick —Benjamin Franklin

Gulped the tea and felt it like sleep in her body —Frank Tuohy

He's like a camel as far as serious liquid refreshment is concerned —Iris Murdoch

Lap up the gravy just like pigs in a trough —Lewis Carroll

Mouth moving as rapidly as the treadle on Granny's sewing machine —William H. Gass

Nibble ... in quick little bites like a squirrel with a nut —George Garrett

Sip [a drink] ... as though he tasted martinis for a living —Sue Grafton

(He had) stuffed as full as an egg —Anon English ballad, "The Cork"

Swallowed it [a small sandwich] like a communion waver —T. Coraghessan Boyle

❧ ECONOMICS

Balancing the budget is a little like protecting your virtue —you just have to learn to say no —Ronald Reagan

Capital is dead labor, that, vampire-like, only lives by sucking living labor —Karl Marx

The Dow-Jones is floating up like a hot-air balloon —François Camoin

Economics is like being lost in the woods. How can you tell where you are going when you don't even know where you are? —Anon

Feeding more tax dollars to government is like feeding a stray pup. It just follows you home and sits on your doorstep asking for more —Ronald Reagan

Financial statements are like a bikini. What they reveal is interesting; what they conceal is vital —William W. Priest Jr., Managing Director BEA Associates, *Wall Street Week* television program, January 9, 1987

Forecasting economic averages is like assuring the non-swimmer that he can safely walk across the river because its average depth is only four feet —Milton Friedman

Inflation, like DC-10s, and Three Mile Islands, and Cold Wars is bad for your mental health —Ellen Goodman

It [the economy] looks more resistant to shoves and shocks than it once was. Like a clown on a roly-poly base, it swings back and forth but does not topple over —Leonard Silk, *New York Times*/Economic Scene, September 17, 1986

A little inflation is like a little pregnancy —it keeps on growing —Leo Henderson

A recession is like an unfortunate love affair. It's a lot easier to talk your way in than it is to talk your way out —Bill Vaughan, *Reader's Digest*, July, 1958

Right now being an arbitrager is kind of like being a fire hydrant at a dog show —you sure get a lot of attention —Anon arbitrager quoted in *Wall Street Journal*, 1987

The fire hydrants comparison was made in connection with the image problems resulting from arbitrage scandals.

Signs of reviving inflation are as abundant as are skeptics who read each rise in inflationary barometers as an aberration —John C. Borland, *New York Times*, September 28, 1986

The stock market climbed like the horses of Apollo —Hortense Calisher

Takeovers on a scale that would make nineteenth-century pirates look like croquet players —Harry A. Jacobs (senior director of Prudential-Bache Securities), commenting on increase in company takeovers and other economic ills, as quoted in Leonard Silk's column, *New York Times*, February 4, 1987

Tax loopholes are like parking spaces, they all seem to disappear by the time you get there —Joey Adams

To some economists, inflation is like those trick birthday candles, the ones that are impossible to blow out —Joel Popkin, *New York Times*, August 17, 1986

Turning national economic policy around is like turning the *Queen Mary* around in a bathtub —E. Gerald Corrigan, chairman of Federal Reserve Bank of New York, at Japan Society Dinner, *New York Times*, April 17, 1987

The wife economy [wherein husbands assume full economic responsibility for wives] is as obsolete as the slave economy —Elizabeth Hardwick

❧ EDUCATION

See Also: KNOWLEDGE

Alumni are like the wake of a ship; they spread out and ultimately disappear, but not until they have made a few waves —Anon

Colleges are like old-age homes; except for the fact that more people die in colleges —Bob Dylan

Education begins, like charity, at home —Susan Ferraro, *New York Times*, March 26, 1987

The charity comparison has been effectively linked with other subjects.

Education, like neurosis, begins at home —Milton R. Sapirstein

Education, like politics, is a rough affair, and every instructor has to shut his eyes and hold his tongue as though he were a priest —Henry Adams

Getting educated is like getting measles; you have to go where the measles is —Abraham Flexner

He was like an empty bucket waiting to be filled [with knowledge] —William Diehl

He who teaches a child is like one who writes on paper; but he who teaches old people is like one who writes on blotted paper —The Talmud

Human beings, like plants, can be twisted into strange shapes if their training begins early enough and is vigilantly supervised. They will accept their deformation as the natural state of affairs and even take pride in it, as Chinese women once did in their crippled feet —Milton R. Sapirstein

Sapirstein, a psychologist, used this simile to introduce a discussion of the educational impulse and its relationship to the educational process.

If it [learning] lights upon the mind that is dull and heavy, like a crude and undigested mass it makes it duller and heaver, and chokes it up —Michel De Montaigne

Learning in old age is like writing on sand; learning in youth is like engraving on stone —Solomon Ibn Gabirol

Learning is like rowing upstream: not to advance is to drop back —Chinese proverb

Learning, like money, may be of so base a coin as to be utterly void of use —William Shenstone

Learning without thought is labor lost —Confucius

Many a scholar is like a cashier: he has the key to much money, but the money is not his —Ludwig Boerne

Modern education is a contradiction. It's like a three-year-old kid with a computer in his hand who can multiply 10.6 per cent interest of $11,653, but doesn't know if a dime is larger or smaller than a nickel —Erma Bombeck

The need of a teacher to believe now and again that she fosters genius is like the writer's need to believe that he is one —Lael Wertenbaker

Rolling on like a great growing snowball through the vast field of medical knowledge —William James, writing to Dr. Henry P. Bowditch

A scholar is like a book written in a dead language: it is not everyone that can read in it —William Hazlitt

A scholar should be like a leather bottle, which admits no wind; like a deep garden bed, which retains its moisture; like a pitch-coated vessel, which preserves its wine; and like sponge, which absorbs everything —The Talmud

Soap and education are not as sudden as a massacre, but they are more deadly in the long run —Mark Twain

Students are like acorns and oaks, there's a lot more bark to the oak and a lot more nuttiness in the acorn —Anon

Study is like the heaven's glorious sun —William Shakespeare, *Love's Labour Lost*

Take it a in like blotting paper —Mavis Gallant

The teacher is like the candle which lights others in consuming itself —Giovanni Ruffini

Teachers, like actors must drug themselves, to be at their best —Delmore Schwartz

Teaching a class was in a way like making love. Sometimes he did it with great enthusiasm … sometimes he did it because it was expected of him, and he forced himself to go through the motions —Dan Wakefield

Teaching a fool is like gluing together a posherd [pottery fragment] —The Holy Bible/Apocrypha

Their learning is like bread in a besieged town; every man gets a little, but no man gets a full meal —Samuel Johnson

Johnson's simile referred to his view of Scottish education.

To study and forget is like bearing children and burying them —The Talmud

To transmit wisdom to the unworthy is like throwing pearls before swine —Moses Ibn Ezra

Your education, like … carrots, is not a manufactured article, but just a seed which has grown up largely under nature's friendly influence —William J. Long

❦ EERINESS
See: STRANGENESS

❦ EFFECT
See: CAUSE AND EFFECT

❦ EFFECTIVENESS
See: ABILITY, CAUSE AND EFFECT, SUCCESS/FAILURE, USEFULNESS/USELESSNESS

❦ EFFORTLESSNESS
See: EASE

❦ EGO
See Also: VANITY

She feeds his ego like a goose destined for pâté, —Maureen Dowd "The Great Man's Wife" *New York Times*, February 2, 2012 on presidential hopeful Newt Gingrich's third wife, Calista.

❦ ELASTICITY
See: FLEXIBILITY/INFLEXIBILITY

❧ ELATION

See: JOY

❧ ELEGANCE

See: CLOTHING, STYLE

❧ ELOQUENCE

See: PERSUASIVENESS, SPEECH MAKING

❧ ELUSIVENESS

See Also: DIFFICULTY

As elusive as a dream —Simon Mawer, *The Glass Room*

As slippery as an eel —Dutch proverb

This has seeded numerous variations such as "Slippery as an eel dipped in butter" by F. van Wyck Mason

(Love is) as slippery as greased pigskin —Delmore Schwartz

Avoided [another person] like a vampire avoids sunburn —Joseph Wambaugh

(He was) difficult as a serpent to see —D. H. Lawrence

The elusive creature being described is a fox sliding along in deep grass.

(The feeling persisted, insidious and) difficult to trace as perfume —Harvey Swados

Elusive as a collar button —Jim Murray

Murray, sports columnist for the Los Angeles Herald, *applied this simile to football player Mike Garrett.*

Elusive as a dream —William Diehl

"Fugitive as dreams" used by Tom MacIntyre in a short story, "Epithalamion," illustrates the possibility for change through word substitutions.

Elusive as a wet fish —Anon

Elusive as buried treasure —Anon

Elusive as the cure for cancer —Anon

Elusive as the cure for aging —Anon

Elusive as the source of a rumor —Anon

Elusiveness, like a thought that presents itself to consciousness and vanishes before it can be captured by words —W. Somerset Maugham

Evaded me, much like the myth of Tantalus —Marguerite Young

Evasion, like equivocation, comes generally from a cowardly or a deceiving spirit, or from both —Honoré de Balzac

Hard to hold as a flapping sail in a raging wind —Gerald Kersh

The hold to which Kersh alludes is the grip of one wrestler on another in the story entitled "Ali the Terrible Turk."

Intangible as a beautiful thought —W. Somerset Maugham

Intangible as love and fear —Andre Dubus

(A vision swarming through the mind as sudden and) irretrievable as smoke —William Styron

It [information] got away from me so easily, like the tail of a kite, when the kite's already out of your hands —Cornell Woolrich

It [trying to tie up a boxing opponent] was just like trying to hold on to a buzz-saw —Ernest Hemingway

Like fish in an aquarium, they [two girls] flashed in and out of sight —Frank Tuohy

Like sand from a clenched fist, he was slipping through her fingers —Ben Ames Williams

(She was so marvelous that, when he tried to think of her, her description) rolled away from him like a dropped coin —Mark Helprin

(She) seemed like a shadow within a shadow —D. H. Lawrence

Lawrence is describing one of the two main female characters in The Fox, *a woman the male character wants but can't seem to understand.*

She was like a rubber ball; he couldn't get a grip —Beryl Bainbridge

Slipped by like a mouse —Anton Chekov

[Something said] slipped out of me like a cork from the deep —Reynolds Price

Slipped through [guards] like a fox through a barnyard —Clive Cussler

Slippery as shadows in day's foam —Delmore Schwartz

They might as well be looking for a shoe in a swamp —Clive Cussler

❧ EMBARRASSMENT

See: SHAME, SHYNESS

❧ EMBRACE

See Also: KISSES; MEN AND WOMEN; PEO-
PLE, INTERACTION; SEXUAL INTERAC-
TION

Almost completely covered by MaButhelezi's big arms, like a blanket of flesh —Njabulo Nde-bele

Clasped each other like a pair of abandoned children —Natascha Wodin

Clinch like lovers at the final fade out —George Garrett

Curled up together like a pair of old dogs —Jean Thompson

Drawing her toward him he held her and squeezed her out like a bit of old washing —Edna O'Brien

Drew her to him, crushing her like a pale flower to his breast —Peter De Vries

Drew the child to her as if she were a springing young tree —Elizabeth Taylor

Embraced Himiko [name of a character] like a bear hugging an enemy —Kenzaburo Oe

Embraced him like a hot wet towel —William H. Hallhan

Embraced like bears —Madison Smartt Bell

Embrace like pen pals —Ira Wood

Embraces are keen like pain —Algernon Charles Swinburne

Her embrace was clumsy like a bad dancer's —John Braine

Her long thin arms came up to wind about him and inexorably, like tight thin wires, to hold him down —H. E. Bates

His arm around her felt as if she'd been born with it there —William McIlvanney

His arms are like a cradle in which she is warm and safe —Alvin Boretz, television program, 1986

Hold hands like teenagers, fingers meshed like the teeth of rusty gears —Ira Wood

Lay locked like human vines —Charles Bukowski

Let our arms clasp like Ivy —John Donne

Locked in a profound embrace … like Ahab and the whale —A.R. Guerney Jr.
Guerney's simile refers to the guests in his play
"The Perfect Party."

Marg's long tanned body entwined Fencer's like a constricting serpent —Robert Stone

Pressed herself upon me like someone pressing upon a bruise —Lawrence Durrell

She vibrated in his arms like a tuning fork —Andrew Kaplan

Snuggled up together like spoons in bed —Phyllis Naylor

They'd lie together, like a four-armed creature fearful of amputation —Julia O'Faolain

Was so huge and soft it was like embracing a cloud and sinking down —Lee Smith

❧ EMINENCE

See: FAME

❧ EMOTIONS

See Also: ANXIETY, CHEERFULNESS, DEJEC-
TION, ENVY, GLOOM, GREIF, HAPPI-
NESS, HATE, LONELINESS, LOVE, SAD-
NESS, TENSION, WEARINESS

Compulsion is a mirror in which he who looks for long will see his inner self endeavoring to commit suicide —Khalil Gibran

Emotional antagonisms that lay in us like surly dogs at the end of a chain, ready to leap up and growl at a step —Wallace Stegner

Emotional ... like a third-rate opera singer —Fred Mustard Steward

Emotions buzzed and throbbed ... like a pent-up bee —Elizabeth Bowen

Emotions got cut off ... like a broken string of beads —Susan Fromberg Schaeffer

Emotions ... swarm in my head like a hive of puzzled bees —Gertrude Atherton

(I would like my) emotions to be appropriate. This ... may be measuring them like potatoes, but it is better than slopping them about like water from a pail —E. M. Forster

Emotion akin to a physical blow —Henrietta Weigel

Fear and anger boiled up in my head like liquid air —Ross Macdonald

Feeling full of wonder and illusion —like a Columbus or a pilgrim seeing the continent of his dreams take shape in the dusk for the first time —Richard Ford

The feelings thus described are experienced as a plane comes in for a landing.

Feelings bubbled in him like water from an underground spring —Paige Mitchell

Feelings ... call, like a buzzing of flies in autumn air —Wallace Stevens

Feelings cross our flesh along nets of nerves, like a pattern of lightning flashes —Marguerite Yourcenar

Feelings here slice right through like speed skates —Jill Robinson

Robinson thus described the work of poet Amy Rothholz, building on her simile with, "Racing by with fierce, original passion." The poet's publisher extracted the simile from Robinson's review to feature in an ad for the book.

Feelings ... jumbled together like raveled wool —Frank Swinnerton

Feel mushy and wet, like a pile of leaves after they have been rained on —Daphne Merkin

Feels herself curling up like a jaundiced leaf —Alice Munro

Feel the magic building like a gathering storm —W. P. Kinsella

Felt as small and vulnerable as a calf on its first day of life —Linda West Eckhardt

Felt crazy, stupid, as though, having believed a burglar was rummaging through the house, I had found only the family cat —Kent Nelson

Felt ... inadequate, as if I were a new understudy taking on a role that had been played before, and much more effectively —Alice McDermott

Felt like a lifeline thrown out to someone —Mike Feder, *New York Times* September 7, 1986

Feder, a café storyteller, thus explained how he began his career by telling stories about his day's experiences to his housebound mother.

Felt like a man in a Rembrandt, tinged brown with sorrow and wisdom —Laurie Colwin

Felt like a man reprieved from the gallows —Wilfrid Sheed

Felt like a man who had had a tooth out that had been hurting him for a long time —Leo Tolstoy

Felt like an emotional invalid, like a balloon without the helium —T. Coraghessan Boyle

(After my husband died I) felt like one of those spiraled shells washed up on the beach ... no flesh, no life —Lynn Caine

Felt shut off like a turtle inside her skin —Laura Furman

Felt worry and joy flinging her about like a snowflake —Mary Hedin

A foul feeling, like looking over the edge of the world —Jean Rhys

Guilty and elated, as though I'd successfully committed a small theft —Christopher Isherwood

Half smiles, half tears, like rain in sun —John Greenleaf Whittier

Heart expanded like bellows —Laurie Colwin

His senses nagged at him like pampered babies —Stephen Crane

Inhibitions gave way like an earth dam collapsing in front of a winter flood —Graham Masterson

Isolation, frustration and sometimes fear run like a leitmotif through our lives —Philip Taubman, *New York Times Magazine,* September 21, 1986

It [his emotion for a woman] struck him like sickness —W. E. Bates

Love and emptiness in us are like the sea's ebb and flow —Kahil Gibran

My emotions flowered in me like a divine revelation —André Gide

My heart is like wax; it is melted in the midst of my bowels —The Holy Bible/Psalms

Old feelings gather fast upon me like vultures round their prey —Emily Brontë

Our feelings have edges and spines and prickles like cactus, or porcupines —Laurie Colwin

Colwin is likening the cactus/porcupine edges and spines to the feelings of two lovers.

Our feelings penetrate us like a poison of undetectable nature —Anais Nin

Pride and anger seemed like overblown spent clouds of thunder —John Greenleaf Whittier

Profound feelings ... swept through and racked his being like gusts of fire —George Garrett

(A feeling of) relief circles us like a spring breeze —Richard Ford

Relief courses through me like cool water —Marge Piercy

Relief had come in like a warm and welcome flood —Carlos Baker

Relieved [after things have been put right] ... like they lifted a concrete block out of my belly —John Updike

Rolled in self-pity and self-hatred like a hot sulfur spring —Marge Piercy

Self-hatred living in him like a sick dog in a cellar —Bernard Malamud

Sensations gave like snowslides in him —Larry Woiwode

Sensations ... whirling about him like snow flakes —Willa Cather

(My feelings) snapped like a glass pipette —Diane Wakoski

Stirred an emotion ... like the birth of a butterfly within a cocoon —Adela Rogers St. John

Sudden relief, like a rush of tears, came to her —Nadine Gordimer

(Their hearts were open and) sweet sensations flowed in them like honey —Ruth Prawer Jhabvala

Temperament, like liberty, is important despite how many crimes are committed in its name —Louis Kronenberger

Temper like a bed of banked coals waiting to be fired into roaring flame by a spill of brandy —Davis Grubb

They [true feelings] gathered around me like a mist, whose shape can be seen as it approaches, but not when it is on you —L. P. Hartley

Too moved to even applaud ... as if the air had been sucked out of the room —Samuel G. Freedman, *New York Times* September 7, 1986

The performer who thus moved his audience was a café storyteller.

Treats his emotions ... as vermin to be crushed in traps or poisoned with bait —Marge Piercy

Truth and jealousy, like a team of plow horses, came crashing into the fragile barn of his illusions —Louis Auchincloss

A vague uneasy stirring plagued her like some mental indigestion —Josephine Tey

A warm feeling like cocoa on a cold night —Jean Stafford

Wore his confidence like a tailored suit —Donald McCaig

Wore sorrow and anger like a worn-out coat and would not throw it away —Belva Plain

The young soldier's heart was … like fire in his chest —D. H. Lawrence

❧ EMPTINESS

See Also: ABANDONMENT, ALONENESS

(I was) as hollow and empty as the spaces between the stars —Raymond Chandler, *The Long Goodbye*

Barren as a fistful of rock —A. E. Maxwell

Barren as an iceberg of vegetation —Anon

Barren as crime —Algernon Charles Swinburne

Barren as death —John Ruskin
   William Blake voiced the same thought, using "void" instead of "barren."

Barren as routine —G.K. Chesterton

Blank and bare and still as a polar wasteland —George Garrett

Blank as a sheet —Reynolds Price

Blank as a vandalized clock —Lorrie Moore

Blank as death —Alfred, Lord Tennyson

Blank as the eyeballs of the dead —Henry Wadsworth Longfellow

Blank as the sun after the birth of night —Percy Bysshe Shelley

Clean as the sheets in a convent —Rick Elice, *Peter and the Starcatcher*
   The play's villainous Stache's declaration at finding that the treasure chest he's been after is empty.

Deserted as a park bench after a snowstorm —Anon

Desolate as a summer resort in midwinter —Richard Harding Davis

Emptied like a cup of coffee —John Ashberry

The emptiness inside was like an explosion —Eleanor Clark

Emptiness so vast it yawned like the pit of hell —George Garrett

The emptiness was intense, like the stillness in a great factory when the machinery stops running —Willa Cather

Empty-armed, empty-handed as a lone winter tree —George Garrett

Empty as a barn before harvest —Erich Maria Remarque

Empty as a broken bowl —George Garrett

Empty as a canyon —Elizabeth Spencer

Empty as a church on Monday morning —Anon

Empty as a diary without entries —Anon

Empty as a dry shell on the beach —Daphne du Maurier

Empty as an air balloon —Thomas G. Fessendon

Empty as an egg basket —Eudora Welty

Empty as an office building at night —Anon

(He was empty …) empty as an old bottle —F. Scott Fitzgerald

Empty as a person without a past, only present —Anon

(Lonely afternoons, days, evenings) empty as a rusty coffee can —Diane Wakoski

Empty as a waiting tomb —Louis Bromfield

Empty as death's head —Daniel Berrigan

(Eyes) empty as knot holes in a fence —Etheridge Knight

(The campus is as) empty as space —Babs H. Deal

Empty as the beach after a snowstorm —Anon

(The shuttle after morning rush hour is near) empty, like a littered beach after tourists have all gone home —Thomas Pynchon

Faceless as a masked bandit —Anon

Feel as dead and empty as a skeleton on a desert —Robert Traver

Feel as empty as a pop bottle in the street —Marge Piercy

A feeling of emptiness, as if I had cut an artery in my wrist and all the blood had drained out —Aharon Megged

Flat and empty as the palm of his hand —Helen Hudson

In Hudson's novel, Criminal Trespass, *the comparison's frame of reference is a flat and empty field.*

(The street below was) hollow as a bone —Peter Matthiessen

Hollow as a politician's head —Charles Johnson

Hollow as skeleton eyes —Lorrie Moore

A hollow feeling inside, big as a watermelon —Jay Parini

I'm empty … like a sand bag —Tina Howe

It's like stepping into a church in midweek: Space abounding and no one to fill it —Helen MacInnes

Look as hollow as a ghost —William Shakespeare, *The Life and Death of King John*

People, like houses, may be taken over by spirits and inhabited by ghosts when they feel they are deserted and empty —Gerald Kersh

So empty you could fire a canon and not hit anybody —Anon

Sterile as a mule —James Morrow

Sterile as a stone —Cynthia Ozick

Void as death —William Blake

The weight of his emptiness dragged like a dead dog chained around his neck —Bernard Malamud

❧ ENDURANCE
See: CONTINUITY, PERMANENCE

❧ ENEMY
See: ADVERSARY

❧ ENERGY
See Also: ACTIVENESS, BUSYNESS, ENTHUSIASM

Adrenaline bubbling in my veins like grease in a deep fryer —T. Coraghessan Boyle

Adrenaline flooded through me like water through a storm drain —Sue Grafton

Adrenalin flowing like electricity —W. P. Kinsella

Alger-like energy —Hortense Calisher

As brisk as a bee in a tar-pot —Thomas Fuller

The condensed version of this, "Brisk as a bee," can be traced back to Boswell's Life of Dr. Johnson, *where it was used to describe someone's conversational style. A variation (Also from Fuller's collection of aphorisms) is "As brisk as a body louse."*

Bracing as an Alpine breeze —Israel Zangwill

(Suddenly this Spring he's) bursting with energy, like the daffodils on the White House lawn —James Reston about Ronald Reagan *New York Times*

The collective enthusiasm works like a dose of Viagra —Francine Prose, *A Changed Man*

Electricity dripping from me like cream —Diane Wakoski

Energetic and tireless … like a shouting insect, some kind of queen aunt —J. B. Priestly

Energetic … an explosion of vitality, rather like a teapot set not to boil over but to bubble and steam —Charles Johnson

(Feeling as) energetic as a licensed jester —Clarence Major

Energy burned off him like a light —Pat Conroy

(Quick incisive) energy like quicksilver in the veins —Joan Chase

Energy … like the biblical grain of mustard-seed, will remove mountains —Hosea Ballou

Energy sings like a tea kettle —Marge Piercy

Energy ... thin and sharp like gravy —Diane Wakoski

Full of pep as an electric fan —Anon

(Little Billie was full of piss and vinegar and) full of sap as a maple tree —Robert Penn Warren

In Warren's long poem "The Ballad of Billie Potts" the maple tree comparison is followed by another simile: "And full of tricks as a lop-eared pup."

Full of vitality ... like a lighted candle —Rachel Ingalls

Had a brisk air of bristle, like a terrier bitch —Angela Carter

He's like 220 pounds worth of Duracell batteries —Mike Jameson, commenting on the untiring energy of boxer Mike Tyson, quoted in *Newsday* column by Paul Ballot, December 27, 1968

Hum with unspent power, like a machine left to run —Mary Gordon

(He is) just like a blob of mercury —Alice James writing from Europe about her brother William to her father and her brother Henry in America, 1889

Like an old volcano, which has pretty nearly used up its fire and brimstone, but is still boiling and bubbling —Oliver Wendell Holmes, Sr.

Like the grass and trees and other growing things, they were quivering and glistening with vitality —Dorothy Canfield

Refreshing, like rain at the end of a muggy day —Jay McInerney

Rings with vitality, like ax-strokes on oak —Dorothy Canfield

Sparks and twinkles like a jarred lightning bug —Sharon Sheehe Stark

The comparison refers to a lively four-year old girl in a story entitled The Johnstown Polka.

Vigorous as a run-over cat —Marge Piercy

Vitality ... like a hot flame that burnt him with an unendurable fury —W. Somerset Maugham

(She had a) vitality that warmed you like a blazing fire —W. Somerset Maugham

Warm with life as the waters of a tropic sea —Beryl Markham

We were blazing through our lives like comets through the sky —William Finn, "When the Earth Stopped Turning," *Elegies: A Song Cycle*

ENJOYMENT
See: PLEASURE

ENTHUSIASM
See Also: ENERGY, EXCITEMENT

(Parisians) applaud like pugilists —Janet Flanner

As full of spirit as the month of May —William Shakespeare, *Henry IV*

Drinking in every conceivable impression and experience like wine —George Garrett

Eager as a deb waiting for the grand march —John MacDonald

Eager as a horse player waiting for the 6th race —John MacDonald

Eager as a hostess forcing leftovers on departing guests —Ira Wood

Eager as a leashed terrier quivering to meet every challenge —Hallie Burnett

(Looked as) eager as a morning hawk —Carlos Baker

Eager as an understudy —Louis Monta Bell

Eager as a sprinter at the starting gate —Donald McCaig

Eager as bears for honey —David R. Slavitt

Eager [to buy] ... like a starving man at a banquet —Aaron Goldberg

Enthusiasm flows from X like light from a bulb —Anon

Enthusiasm is a volcano on whose top never grows the grass of hesitation —Kahil Gibran

(About as) enthusiastic as a guy going to the chair —H. C. Witwer

Enthusiastic as a sommelier rhapsodizing about wine —Amal Kumar Naj, *Wall Street Journal* November 25, 1986

Naj used the sommelier simile in an article about chili to describe the enthusiasm of a man who grows chilies as a pastime.

Fervor, whipping around ... like the flags in the stiff breeze —Sumner Locke Elliott

Follow [theatre's artistic steps] with the joy of a Mets fan checking the morning box scores —Jack Viertel, *New York Times*, June 1, 1986

Hearty as a friendly handshake —Anon

Hearty ... like a trombone thoroughly impregnated with cheerful views of life —Charles Reade

Like a racehorse in the gate; I was mad to go —Irving Feldman

Loved anatomy ... as a mother her child —Dr. David W. Cheever

The anatomy enthusiast described by Dr. Cheever is Dr. Oliver Wendell Holmes.

Stand like greyhounds in the slips straining upon the start —William Shakespeare, *Henry V*

Talked about it [business prospects] the way a man dying of thirst might talk about a cold beer —Mike Fredman

With the avidity and determination of a housewife at a Macy's white sale —T. Coraghessan Boyle

With the fervor of castaways grasping at a smudge of smoke on the horizon —Ellery Queen

Zeal without humanity is like a ship without a rudder, liable to be stranded at any moment —Owen Feltenham

Zeal without judgment is like gunpowder in the hands of a child —Ben Jonson

Zeal without knowledge is a runaway horse —W. G. Benham

Zeal without knowledge is like a fire without light —John Ray's *Proverbs*

Zeal without knowledge is like fire without a grate to contain it; like a sword without a hilt to wield it by; like a high-bred horse without a bridle to guide him —Julius Bate

Zeal without knowledge is like expedition to a man in the dark —John Newton

❧ ENTRANCES AND EXITS

See Also: BEGINNINGS AND ENDINGS, DEATH, EXITS

(A large man in white) appeared like a cuckoo out of a clock —Madison Smartt Bell

(Children don't) appear and disappear like toadstools in a lawn —Miles Gibson

Barged in ... like a Rugby forward —Frank Swinnerton

Blew in like a boisterous breeze —Cole Porter, a song from "You've Got That Thing," lyrics for 1929 musical *Fifty Million Frenchmen*

Came and went, like bees after honey —Wright Morris

Came as silent as the dew comes —Henry Wadsworth Longfellow

Came in like a swan swimming its way —Virginia Woolf

Came like swallows and like swallows went —W. B. Yeats

Came like water —Edward Fitzgerald

Comes and goes, like hearts —Elizabeth Bishop

Coming in like a kite on a string —Clive Cussler

In his novel Cyclops, Cussler used the simile to describe the entrance of a vessel.

Entered like a wind —Ruth Suckow

For added emphasis there's "Come in like a high wind" as used by Aharon Megged in his novel, Living on the Dead.

Enter ... tiptoeing like somebody trying to sneak in late to a funeral —George Garrett

Flitted in and out of the house like birds —Anne Tyler

Hopped in, light as a bird —Harvey Swados

Light upon the scene like a new-made butterfly —George Garrett

Like hoodlums come ... with neither permits nor requests —Carl Sandburg

Like Santa Claus he came and went mysteriously —Frank O'Connor

Materialize [to observe] ... like a policeman presiding over an accident —Wilfrid Sheed

Plunged into it like a rabbit into its hole —Ben Ames Williams

Popped up here and there like bubbles in a copperful of washing —Frank Swinnerton

Rolling through the front door like a drunken bear —James Crumley

Rushed into the room like a cannon-ball —Romain Gary

Rush in like a gust of wind —Anon

Slinking in like a little ailing cat —Jean Stafford

Slipped in like a cat or the wind —John J. Clayton

Strode in like a conquering prince returning to his lands —Alice Walker

Sweep in here like Zeus from Olympus, with his attendant nymphs and swains [main character and doctor] —Brian Clark

Swept vivaciously in ... like a champion ice-skater —Frank Swinnerton

Was into the living-room ... and out again with such speed that she might have been one of the mechanical weather-people in a child's snow-globe or a figure on a medieval clock, who zooms across a lower balcony as the face shows the hands on the hour —Rachel Ingalls

❧ ENTRAPMENT

See Also: ADVANCING

About as much chance of escape as a log that is being drawn slowly toward a buzz saw —Arthur Train

Captured like water in oil —John Updike

Caught in [as a war] like meat in a sandwich —Robert MacNeil, Public Television broadcast, December 1986

Caught like a forest in a blazing fire —Delmore Schwartz

(What wouldn't I give to see old Cy Lambert) caught like a monkey with his fist in the bottle —Louis Auchincloss

(The feeling came over her that she was) caught like a mouse in the trap of life —Ellen Glasgow

(I went to the war; got) clapped down like a bedbug —Clifford Odets

[Group of people] Closed in upon her, like dogs on a fox —Jean Stafford

[Four walls of room] Close in upon you like the sides of a coffin —O. Henry

[Party with many people] Engulfed him like an avalanche —Robert Silverberg

Feel like ... a shabby blackbird baked alive in a piecrust —George Garrett

Felt like a muskrat trapped in a weir —Sterling Hayden

Felt like a worm on a hook —Shelby Hearon

Gripped him like an empty belly —Cutcliffe Hyne

Held fast by circumstances as by invisible wires of steel —Ellen Glasgow

It [emotional trap] held him as with the grip of sharp murderous steel —Henry James

My heart chokes in me like a prison —Anzia Yezierska

Another example of a simile used to launch a work of fiction, in this case a short story entitled Wings.

Pinned to ... like a butterfly to a cork —F. van Wyck Mason

The butterfly image as used by Margaret Millar: "As easily trapped as a butterfly."

Struggling and captive like a newborn infant —Julia O'Faolain

Stuck with them [undesirable companions], like falling into a barrel of blackstrap molasses —Elizabeth Spencer

Thrashed about ... like a whale trying to pull free from a harpoon —William H. Hallhan

Trapped like a fish between two cats —Spanish proverb

Trapped like a peasant between two lawyers —Anon

Trapped [in traffic] like a fly in a spider's web —Donald Seaman

Felt trapped ... like a man in a cage with a sick bear and his keeper —Ross Macdonald

Trapped like a rabbit on a country road —Beryl Bainbridge

✤ ENVY

As a moth gnaws a garment, so does envy consume a man —Saint John Chrysostam

As iron is eaten by rust, so are the envious consumed by envy —Livy

Envy hit him ... like lack of oxygen —William McIlvanney

(Fools may our scorn, not envy raise, for) envy is a kind of praise —John Gay

Envy is like a fly that passes all a body's sounder parts and dwells upon the sores —George Chapman

Envy, like fire, soars upwards —Livy

Envy, like the worm, never runs but to the fairest fruit; like a cunning bloodhound, it singles out the fattest deer in the flock —Francis Beaumont

Felt a twinge of jealousy, green as a worm, wiggling deep in my center —W. P. Kinsella

Intense jealousy struck him like a missile —Mark Helprin

It [jealousy] was like a taste in his mouth —Joyce Carol Oates

Jealousy ... descended on his spirit like a choking and pestilence-laden cloud —Thomas Wolfe

Jealousy is a kind of civil war in the south, where judgment and imagination are at perpetual jars —William Penn

Jealousy is cruel as the grave —The Holy Bible/ Song of Solomon

Jealousy is like a bad toothache. It does not let a person do anything, not even sit still. It can only be walked off —Milan Kundera

Jealousy is like a polished glass held to the lips when life is in doubt; if there be breath it will catch the damp and show it —John

Jealousy that surrounds me like a too-warm room —William H. Gass

Jealousy whirled inside her like a racing motor —Milan Kundera

Stir up jealousy like a man of war —The Holy Bible/Isaiah

A wave of jealousy floats in my stomach like a cork —Ira Wood

✤ EPITAPHS
See: DEATH, PRIDE

✤ ERECTNESS
See: POSTURE

✤ ERRORS

A flaw ... would surface like an aching wisdom tooth —James Lee Burke

The defects of the mind, like those of the face, grow worse as we grow old —François Duc de La Rochefoucauld

Delusions, errors and likes are like huge, gaudy vessels, the rafters of which are rotten and worm-eaten, and those who embark in them are fated to be shipwrecked —Buddha

Errors, like straws, upon the surface flow; he who would search for pearls must dive below —John Dryden

Flaunt their folly, like a washline of dirty and patched clothes —George Garrett

Gone astray like a lost sheep —The Holy Bible/ Psalms

Great blunders are often made, like large ropes, of a multitude of fibers —Victor Hugo

Illusion forms before us like a grove —Barbara Howes

This simile is the first line and leitmotif in Howes' poem "The Triumph of Death."

(Is somehow) impure, as sacrilegious as a Coca-Cola machine in a cathedral —Tony Ardizzone

A mistake is like a mule, not always distinguishable from a horse in front, but known beyond doubt by acquaintance with its kicking qualities —*The New York Sun,* 1918

Wrong as two left shoes —Arthur Baer

❧ ETERNITY
See: CONTINUITY

❧ EVASIVENESS
See: ELUSIVENESS

❧ EVENNESS
See: STRAIGHTNESS

❧ EVIL
See Also: ACTION, CRUELTY

All sin is a kind of lying —St. Augustine

At first the evil impulse is as fragile as the thread of a spider, but eventually it becomes as tough as cart ropes —Babylonian Talmud

Bad as a rotten potato —Charlotte Brontë

Corruption is like a ball of snow, when once set a rolling, it must increase —Charles Caleb Colton

The Devil … like influenza he walks abroad —W. H. Auden

Evil actions like crushed rotten eggs, stink in the nostrils of all —John Russell Bartlett

Evil … a quality some people are born with, like a harelip —Ross Macdonald

Evil as dynamiting trout —Robert Traver

Evil enters like a needle and spreads like an oak tree —Ethiopian proverb

Evil, like parental punishment, is not intended for itself —Josepiz Albo

Evils in the journey of life are like the hills which alarm travelers on the road. Both appear great at a distance, but when we approach them we find they are far less insurmountable than we had conceived —Caleb Colton Forbes

Evils, like poisons, have their uses, and there are diseases which no other remedy can reach —Thomas Paine

An evil soul producing holy witness is like a villain with a smiling cheek —William Shakespeare, *The Merchant of Venice*

He's like a fox, grey before he's good —Thomas Fuller

Immorality in a house is like a worm in a plant —Babylonian Talmud

Immoral, like plying an alcoholic with liquor —Anon

Obscene as cancer —Wilfred Owens

Our sins, like our shadows when day is in its glory, scarce appear; toward evening, how great and monstrous they are! —Sir John Suckling

He is a man of splendid abilities, but utterly corrupt. He shines and stinks like rotten mackerel by moonlight —John Randolph

Sin is a sort of bog; the farther you go in the more swampy it gets —Maxim Gorky

Sins black as night —Robert Lowell

So awful [a crime] it was like an atrocity picture or one of Foxe's lives of the martyrs —Jonathan Valin

(You're) soft and slimy ... like an octopus. Like a quagmire —Jean-Paul Sartre

Vice is like a skunk that smells awfully rank, when stirred up by the pole of misfortune —Bartlett's *Dictionary of Americanisms*

Vice, like virtue, grows in small steps —Jean Racine

Vice repeated is like the wandering wind, blows dust in others' eyes, to spread itself —William Shakespeare, *Pericles*

Wrong as stealing from the poor box —Anon

♣ EXACTNESS
See: CORRECTNESS

♣ EXAMINATION
See: SCRUTINY

♣ EXCITEMENT
See Also: AGITATION, ENERGY, ENTHUSIASM

And then I feel a change, like a fire deep inside / Something bursting me wide open, impossible to hide / And suddenly I'm flying, flying like a bird / Like electricity, electricity / Sparks inside of me, and I'm free, I'm free —Lee Hall, lyrics from the song "Electricity" in the musical *Billy Elliot*

This is the musical's anthem number.

The blood burning in all his veins, like fire in all the branches and twigs of him —D. H. Lawrence

The blood surged through me like a sea —R. Wright Campbell

Drunk on your own high spirits, like a salesman at a convention —Dorothea Straus

Excited and happy as a bride-to-be —Gloria Norris

Excited as a cop making his first pinch —H. C. Witwer

Excited as a puppy at a picnic —Nicholas Proffitt

Excited as a starlet, on the arm of an elderly editor —Philip Roth

Excited as school children on their way to a treat —Frank Tuohy

Excited ... like a kid with his first dish of ice-cream —Louis Bromfield

Excitement caused his heart to thud all over his breast like some crazy and fateful drum —Frank Swinnerton

Excitement ... had grown to become an exhausting presence within him, like the constant company of a sleepless troop of revelers —Joseph Whitehill

Excitement rose like a hot dry wind —Marge Piercy

Exhausting and exhilarating ... it's [tracking Woody Allen's career] like mountain climbing —Vincent Canby, *New York Time*, February 9, 1986

Exhilarating like a swim in a rough ocean —Mary Gordon

Exhilarating as love —Honoré de Balzac

Exhilarating ... very much like the effects of a strong dose of caffeine —Georges Simenon

Felt exhilarated as a young man at a romantic assignation —Louis Auchincloss

(Music that) fired her blood like wine —Katherine Mansfield

(The hate excited her ... she was) fired up like a furnace in a blizzard night —Harold Adams

Flares up like a match —Sholem Aleichem

Flushed and voluble, like football fans on their way back from a match —Aharon Megged

Has about as much suspense as a loaf of bread being spread through a slicer —Scott Simon, reporting on a basketball game, *All Things Considered*, WYNC, January 31, 1987

Her excitement strummed like wire —Marge Piercy

Her excitement was deep down like a desert river under the sands —Oliver La Farge

I had felt my heart like a great snare drum beneath my lace-edged T-shirt —Claire Messud, *The Last Life*

Life at *Nightline* [Ted Koppel TV program] is like being in a popper of popcorn news —Marshal Frady, June 1987

Responding like an overheated spaniel —Clancy Sigal

Stirring as march music —Paige Mitchell

Thrilled his sleepless nerves like liquor or women on a Saturday night —John Dos Passos

Titillated … like naked flesh —Paul Theroux

Warmed by what he'd read as if it had been draughts of rum —John Cheever

❧ EXERCISE

See: MOVEMENT(S), SPORTS

❧ EXHAUSTION

See: WEARINESS

❧ EXITS

See Also: BEGINNINGS AND ENDINGS, DISAPPEARANCE, ENTRANCES AND EXITS

Bustled off … like a rolling whirlwind —Yukio Mishima

Crept away, after the fashion of a whipped dog —H. E. Bates

Fled from me like quicksilver —William Shakespeare, *Henry IV, Part II*

Fled … like damned water broken free —Z. Vance Wilson

Flits like a silky bat out of the room —Rose Tremain

Galloping out like a runaway horse —Donald Seaman

Go out like a candle, in a snuff —John Ray's *Proverbs*

A commonly used version found in a short story entitled "The Beldonald Holbein" by Henry James is to "Go out like a snuffed candle."

I'm off like a dirty shirt —John Crier speaking in the movie *Pretty in Pink*

Jumped out of that house like fleas off a dead dog —Rita Mae Brown

Leave the room as a burglar might escape from the scene of a carefully planned crime —James Stern

Like a rabbit that had been fired at, bolted from the room —John Galsworthy

Like March, having come in like a lion, he purposed to go out (of her life) like a lamb —Charlotte Brontë

Often a familiar simile gains freshness from the way it is applied, as illustrated by this example from Shirley.

Made like an arrow for the door —Christopher Isherwood

Made tracks like a jumped fawn —Thomas Zigal

Running away like sheep —Stephen Vincent Benét

Scuttled away as if he'd found a maggot in his meatball —Joseph Wambaugh

Slide away like a whisper down the wind —Richard Ford

Spook like cattle on a drive —Clinton A. Phillips, dean of faculty at Texas A & M. University, quoted on departure of some academics for better opportunities, *New York Times*, December 21, 1986

Stumping to the door … like an ancient mariner who had lost his temper —Frank Swinnerton

Took off like a big-assed bird —Army expression

Took off like a goosed duck —Harold Adams

Took off like a scalded cat —May Swenson

Turned and left, like a key in a lock —Desmond O'Grady

✿ EXPANSION
See: GROWTH

✿ EXPECTATION
See: ANTICIPATION, HOPE

✿ EXPENSIVENESS
See: COST

✿ EXPERIENCE
See: KNOWLEDGE

Experience is ... a kind of huge spider-web of the finest silken threads suspended in the chamber of consciousness, and catching every airborne particle in its tissue —Henry James

Experience is like medicine; some persons require larger doses of it than others, and do not like to take it pure, but a little disguised and better adapted to taste —Lord Acton

Experience, like a pale musician, holds a dulcimer of patience in his hand —Elizabeth Barrett Browning

Experience seems to be like the shining of a bright lantern. It suddenly makes clear in the mind what was already there, perhaps, but dim —Walter de la Mare

A new element in her experience; like a chapter in a book —Henry Van Dyke

The solitary and unshared experience dies of itself like the violations of love —Archibald MacLeish

To most men, experience is like the stern light of a ship, which illumine only the track it has passed —Samuel Taylor Coleridge

✿ EXPLOSIONS
See: BURST, SUDDENNESS

✿ EYE(S)
See Also: EYES, BRIGHT; EYEBROWS; EYE COLOR; EYE EXPRESSIONS, MISCELLANEOUS, EYELASHES; EYE MOVEMENTS

Behind the glasses his eyes looked look little bicycle wheels at dizzy speed —William Faulkner

Dull eyes set like pebbles in a puffy, unwholesome-looking face —Eric Ambler

Eye/pebble comparisons abound, with examples throughout this section.

Eye-sockets deep as those of a death's head —Thomas Hardy

Eye-sockets ... like dark caves —John Wainwright

Eyeballs like shelled hard-boiled eggs —Ivan Bunin

Eyes as big and as soft and as transparent as ripe gooseberries —Edna O'Brien

Eyes ... as cloudy as poisoned oysters —Miles Gibson

Eyes ... big and shiny, black as oil —Shirley Ann Grau

Eyes blackly circled like those of a raccoon —Lael Wertenbaker

Eyes ... carefully painted like the eyes on Egyptian frescoes —Anais Nin, *Chicago Review,* Winter/Spring, 1962

Eyes ... deep and dark like mountain nights —Mary Hedin

Eyes ... deep as a well —Walter Savage Landor

Eyes flat as glass —James Lee Burke

Eyes ... flat gold, like a lemur's —Sue Grafton

Eyes glazed and almost lightless like the little button eyes of a doll —George Garrett

Eyes ... large and gray, and baleful, like glass on fire —Norman Mailer

Eyes large as fifty-cent pieces, but pale, like dusty stones —Ludwig Bemelmans, describing William Randolph Hearst

Eyes ... large as saucers —E. N. Slocum, line from lyric of a song written in 1868 entitled "On the Beach at Cape May"

Eyes like a codfish —Frank Swinnerton

Eyes like a couple of wells —William Diehl

Eyes ... like an Arizona sunset, and they were supported on pouches as large and shapeless as badly packed duffle bags —Jimmy Sangster

Eyes like a pinwheel —Ann Beattie

Eyes ... like a spaniel's —Ouida

Eyes like a starless winter night —clear, black, bleak —A. E. Maxwell

Eyes ... like chestnuts floating on twin pools of milk —William Styron

Eyes like cold cavities in his head —Natascha Wodin

Eyes ... like crickets in daylight —Rochelle Ratner

Eyes like crosses burning on a lawn —Rochelle Ratner

Eyes like currants in a half-cooked suet pudding —Robert Graves

A simple variation of a simile from a short story by Katherine Mansfield: "little eyes, like currants."

Eyes like dark searchlights —Ross Macdonald

Eyes like dusty lapis lazuli —S.J. Perelman

Eyes like forest pools —W. Somerset Maugham

Eyes ... like forget-me-nots —Mazo de la Roche

Eyes ... like ground owls, deep in their burrows —Harold Adams

Eyes like holes burned with a cigar —William Faulkner

Eyes ... like holes were poked in a snowbank —Raymond Chandler, *The Long Goodbye*

Eyes like jelly —Hanoch Bartov

Eyes like licked stones —Virginia Woolf

Eyes like licorice gumdrops —Robert Campbell

Eyes ... like lustrous black currants —Frank Swinnerton

Eyes, like marigolds, had sheath'd their light —William Shakespeare, *Henry IV, Part II*

In Shakespeare's time "sheathed" was written as "sheath'd."

Eyes like mice peeking into my pockets —Robert Campbell

Eyes like oiled black olives —Frank Tuohy

Eyes ... like old pictures of Rachmaninoff's eyes —Henry Van Dyke

Eyes like onions —Donald Barthelme

Eyes ... like pale marble in a field of red —Linda West Eckhardt

Eyes ... like peas —T. Coraghessan Boyle

Eyes ... like pebbles at the bottom of a mountain trout pool, fixed and icy —Donald MacKenzie

Eyes like pebbles, the kind of pebbles which kids call aggies —Ludwig Bemelmans

Eyes like pebbles unwashed by the sea —Kathleen Farrell

Eyes ... like pools of oil —T. Coraghessan Boyle

Eyes ... like punctuation marks —Geoffrey Wolff

Eyes ... like rubber knobs, like they'd give to the touch —William Faulkner

Eyes like searchlights —Donald McCaig

Eyes ... like shrewd marbles —Harvey Swados

Eyes like the brown waters of a woodland stream —Henry Van Dyke

Eyes like the deep, blue boundless heaven —Percy Bysshe Shelley

(Watery gray) eyes, like the thick edges of broken skylight glass —Willa Cather

Eyes ... like those of a lobster, as if they were on stalks —William James, letter from Germany to sister Alice, January 9, 1868

Eyes ... like tiny stone wedges hammer between the lids —Ross Macdonald

Eyes like tunnels —Arthur Miller

Eyes like twin daisies in a bucket of blood —Leonard Washborn, *Inter-Ocean*, Chicago newspaper, 1880s

Eyes ... like two black seeds —Dashiell Hammett

Eyes ... like two holes burned in a blanket —Borden Deal

Eyes ... like two obeisant satellites —Cynthia Ozick

Eyes ... like two pissholes in the snow —American colloquialism

Eyes ... like violets by a river of pure water —Oscar Wilde

Eyes like washed pebbles stuck in cement (gave him a slightly aggressive look) —Donald MacKenzie

Eyes like white clay marbles —Randall Jarrell

Eyes limpid and still like pools of water —Robert Louis Stevenson

Eyes ... like glass marbles —Herman Wouk

Eye sockets ... as flat as saucers —Z. Vance Wilson

Eyes peering between folds of fat like almond kernels in half-split shells —Edith Wharton

Eyes pressed so deep in his head that they seemed ... like billiard balls sunk in their pockets —William Styron

Eyes, restless, softly brown like a monkey's —F. van Wyck Mason

Eyes ... round and shiny, like the glass bead eyes of stuffed animals —Margaret Atwood

Eyes, round as cherries —Ignazio Silone

Eyes ... round as quarters —Laurie Colwin

Eyes ... round, inane as the blue pebbles of the rain —Dame Edith Sitwell

Eyes shaped like peach pits —Bobbie Ann Mason

Eyes ... shiny and flat as mirrors —Shirley Ann Grau

Eyes ... small and dark and liquid, like drops of strong coffee —Margaret Millar

Eyes ... small and nacreous like painted ornaments —Jean Stafford

Eyes ... small and dirty like the eyes of a potato —Ross

Eyes ... small and hard and shiny like dimes —Ross Macdonald

Eyes soft as a leading lady's, round as a doe's —T. Coraghessan Boyle

Eyes, speckled and hard as pebbles at the bottom of a stream —John Yount

Eyes spoked and rimmed with black, like a mourner's rosette —Edith Pearlman
The simile is particularly appropriate as the writer is describing a character who is a widow

Eyes that looked like imitation jewels —Henry James

Eyes the size of melons —Mary Hood

Her eyes were small, so that with the mascara and the shadows painted on their lids they looked like flopping black butterflies —Eudora Welty

Her eyes looked awful [from too much liquor], as though they had been boiled —Christopher Isherwood

Her eyes lost in the fatty ridges of her face, looked like two small pieces of coal pressed into a lump of dough —William Faulkner

His eyes behind his glasses kind of all run together like broken eggs —William Faulkner

His eyes stood in his head like two poached eggs —Erich Maria Remarque

Large eyes like dark pools —Erich Maria Remarque

Little eyes like cigarette-ends —Charles Bukowski

Looked like cat's eyes do, like a big cat against the wall, watching us —William Faulkner

Mr. York's eyes bulged like doorknobs —Susan Vreeland, *Clara and Mr. Tiffany*

Our very eyes are sometimes like our judgments, blind —William Shakespeare, *Cymbeline*

Protruding eyes that looked like two fish straining to get out of a net of red threads —Flannery O'Connor

The pupils of his eyes were like disks of blue fire —Oscar Wilde

Round eyes like blue polka dots in her crimson face —Helen Hudson

Sharp stains like poor coffee under her eyes —V.S. Pritchett

She was wearing so much eyeliner that her eyes looked as if they had been drawn in ink —Jonathan Valin

Small eyes, set like a pig's in shallow orbits —Francis Brett Young

Their eyes seemed like rings from which the gems had been dropped —Dante Alighieri

Two little eyes like gimlet holes —Émile Zola

The veins in her eyeballs twisted like a map of jungle rivers —Arthur Miller

♣ EYES, BRIGHT

(Stood there ... his) black eyes burning like anthracite —Steven Vincent Benet

Burning eyes like flaming wells —Anzia Yezierska

Eyes as bright as sunlight on a stream —Christina Rossetti

Eyes blazed like molten nuggets —Robert Silverberg

Eyes like burning torches —*Arabian Nights*

Eyes like flashlights —Elizabeth Spencer

Eyes as glowing as the summer and as tender as the skies —James Whitcomb Riley

Eyes ... blazed with a sudden burst of terror, like an explosion of the heart —Robert Campbell

Eyes blazing like bonfires —Miles Gibson

Eyes bright as dance floors —Scott Spencer

Eyes bright as squirrels —John Galsworthy

Eyes bright as the lights in a valuable stone —Norman Mailer

Eyes fired up for a moment like pieces of coal. The laughter in them [eyes] was like two melting ice cubes gleaming in a dish —Alice Walker

Eyes gleam like those of a popular salesman about to hear an old, familiar joke —Hilary Masters

Eyes glittered like a wildcat's —Honoré de Balzac

Eyes glittered like razors —Jonathan Valin

Eyes ... glittering and unsteady, like a dog's when it is looking out of a car window —Frank Tuohy

(His dark) eyes glowed like brandy —Rita Mae Brown

Eyes glowed ... like fire in a cave —Nathanial Hawthorne

Eyes glowed like two tiny electric bulbs —William Faulkner

Eyes ... like black marbles lying in dust, dark and gleaming and sharp, with light —Paul Horgan

Eyes like burning torches —*Arabian Nights*

Eyes like chips of broken glass that catch the light —Joyce Carol Oates

Eyes, like cinders, all aglow —Lewis Carroll

Eyes like glow-worms —William Shakespeare, *Venus and Adonis*

Eyes like flashlights —Elizabeth Spencer

[Animal] eyes shining like wind-whipped embers on a pitch-black night —Jesse Stuart

Eyes shone brighter than the stars —Dante Alighieri

Eyes sparkled as if he'd just heard a joke or told one —Jonathan Valin

Eyes sparkled like rusty wet bolts —Abraham Rothberg

Eyes that could snap and crackle points of fire like those which sparkle from a whirling sword —Jack London

Eyes, they glow like tiger's eyes —James Baldwin

Eyes which possessed a warm, life-giving quality like the sunlight —Willa Cather

Ferocious eyes, much too shiny, like something boiling in a pot —Cynthia Ozick

Glittering eyes like rats hurrying this way and that —Louis Bromfield

Her eyes gave the impression of being lighted from within … as if she had been endowed with her own small sun —Paule Marshall

His eyes shone with certainty, like glints of shellac —Paul Theroux

The light of her eye, like a star glancing out from the blue of the sky —John Greenleaf Whittier

Lights shone in his eyes like travelers' fires seen far out on the river —Eudora Welty

Sparks burning in them [black eyes] like fire at the end of a tunnel —Paige Mitchell

✤ EYEBROWS

Black eyebrows going up like a pair of swallows —V. S. Pritchett

A brow like a thunderclap —Peter De Vries

Brows and lashes smudged like charcoal across her face —Kay Boyle

Brows like bended bows —Thomas Campion

Brows … like charcoal arches —Aharon Megged

Brows like strung bows —Ruth Prawer Jhabvala

Brows were joined above the nose like the hilt of a large dagger —Saul Bellow

Dark eyebrows like sudden brushstrokes above the deep dark eyes —Sylvia Berkman

(Raising an) eyebrow built like a wooly worm —James Crumley

Eyebrows arched like skipping ropes —Henry James

Eyebrows as big as mustaches —Jilly Cooper

Eyebrows curved like big rainbows above her eyes —J. P. Donleavy

Eyebrows drawn so closely together that they seemed like a hedge blocking her view —Carolyn Slaughter

Eyebrows lifted in pink crescents upturned like the dogwood's first leaves in spring —Eudora Welty

Eyebrows … like birds of prey —T. Coraghessan Boyle

Eyebrows like commas —John Fowles

Eyebrows like frost —James Dickey

Eyebrows like hanging gardens —Max Shulman

Eyebrows like peaked black thread —Jean Stafford

Eyebrows like unclipped hedges —Daphne Merkin

Eyebrows looking like a big iron-grey caterpillar lying along the edge of a cliff —William Faulkner

Eyebrows overhung his eyes like moustaches —John Steinbeck

Eyebrows raised, like hoods on baby-carriages —Eudora Welty

Eyebrows rising like fans —Martin Cruz Smith

Eyebrows thick and full like fur frames —Paige Mitchell

Eyebrows were thick, tough as strips of barks —Truman Capote

A great deal of brow in a face is like a great deal of horizon in a view —Victor Hugo

His brows … brindled with grey and tufted like the pelt of a beast. They looked like structural beams, raised into a position that would support the weight of his knowledge and authority —John Cheever

His eyebrows punctuate his speech like hands —Ira Wood

His eyebrows stood up furiously, like a forest of sooty straws —Cynthia Ozick, *Heir to the Glimmering World*

Knitted his brows like sharply molded steel —D. H. Lawrence

> *The text of* Women in Love, *where this appeared used the English spelling "moulded" instead of "molded" as used here.*

(When she was excited she liked to) raise first one thin eyebrow and then the other so that they almost leapt off her face like antennae —Molly Giles

Thick, black eyebrows like the wings of a swallow —Maxim Gorky

♣ EYE COLOR

See Also: BLACK, BLUE, BROWN, EYES, GRAY, GREEN

Black eyes like plum pits —Bernard Malamud

Black eyes turned shiny like the sun —Shirley Ann Grau

Blue eyes like transparent agate marbles, hard and polished and just about indestructible —Sylvia Plath

Blue eyes … round and open like two lakes —Aharon Megged

Blue eyes that sat in his lined face like a piece of sky —Erich Maria Remarque

Brown eyes like quicksand —Diane Ackerman

Eyes … black and burning as coal —Lord Byron

> *Byron's "black as coal" comparison from* Don Juan *has been much used, and with many new twists, several of which can be found here. The black as coal comparison has also been linked with many other descriptive references.*

Eyes … black as bullets and as fierce —Belva Plain

Eyes … blue and guileless as a doll's —David Brierley

Eyes … brown and irisless, like those of an old dog —William Faulkner

Eyes … deepened to the color of caramel, like sugar coming to a boil —Louise Erdrich

Eyes faded to a brittle, metallic gray, like chips of slate —James Crumley

Eyes … light, blue, like colorless water reflecting a blue sky —Jessamyn West

> *In the short story "The Calla Lily Cleaners & Dyers," from which this is taken, the simile is extended as follows: "and his face being so sun-tanned they were more like vacancies in his head than eyes."*

Eyes, like bitter chocolate —Margaret Millar

> *A more recent example of this simile appears in Ira Wood's novel* The Kitchen Man, *which is as chockfull of food imagery as a refrigerator after a weekly shopping trip.*

Eyes … like black buttons or raisins sunk in dough —Nina Bawden

Eyes … like blue cake-icing —Truman Capote

Eyes like blue-painted glass —Flannery O'Connor

Eyes like chocolate fudge still warm from the pan —Elizabeth Spencer

Eyes like the sky on a misty summer morning —Piers Anthony

Eyes … like those of a rabbit, not frightened, but utterly impenetrable —Graham Masterton

Eyes pale as the moon —Grace Paley

Eyes redder than burning coals —Gustave Flaubert

Eyes so pale they were like openings on the sky —Wright Morris

Eyes the color of water vapor —T. Coraghessan Boyle

Eyes … they didn't have much color … like, whoever was putting the color into them got a phone call in the middle and just quit —Lee Smith

Eyes … warmly blue as the glint of summer sunshine on an iceberg drifting in Southern seas —O. Henry

Grey eyes … watery like the winter sky —Frank Tuohy

Large, brown eyes like mushroom caps —Helen Hudson

In her novel Meyer Meyer, *Helen Hudson returns to this simile with another: "Her dull mushroom eyes seemed to have grown smaller, as though they had been sautéd too long."*

Light-blue eyes ... like bits of glass —Jean Rhys

Pale eyes like pools of phlegm —Richard S. Prather

Sharp blue eyes, each like a pin —Robert Browning

Small green eyes, like grapes about to burst —Mary McCarthy

Soft brown eyes, like those of a mild-tempered dog —Frank Swinnerton

Toffee-colored eyes like a spaniel's —T. H. White

Wet blue eyes, like eyes in a clear aspic —Jonathan Valin

❧ EYE EXPRESSIONS, MISCELLANEOUS

Excitement widened her eyes like periods at the end of billboard sentences —Tom Robbins

Expressionless blue eyes ... like a pair of glass marbles —Frank Swinnerton

Eyes ... alive, like blue tigers —Cynthia Ozick

Eyes ... as cold and lacking in interest as the eyes of a tortoise —Nadine Gordimer

Eyes as deep and storyless as the sea —Terry Bisson

Eyes as doleful and red-rimmed as an old hound's —Robert Traver

Eyes as hard as oysters —Raymond Chandler, *The Big Sleep*

Eyes, as hard and cold as a frozen lake —Ellen Glasgow

Eyes ... as innocent as if they had entered their sockets a half-hour ago —Ben Hecht

Eyes ... as opaque as jelly beans —Joan Hess

Eyes ... as shy as a wild stag's —Mary Lee Settle

Eyes, bland and sad as a dog's —George Garrett

Eyes ... blank, clouded with anger or grief, like the sky before a snowstorm —James Crumley

Eyes blind as woodknots —Daniel Berrigan

Eyes clear and cool as rainwater —George Garrett

Eyes clear and candid as a winter sky at dawn —Harvey Swados

Eyes clear as water —John Steinbeck

Eyes clear as window glass —Ward Just

Eyes ... cloudless as a sky in spring —George Garrett

Eyes ... cold as a crocodile's —Peter Benchley

Eyes cold as grey agate —Margaret Mitchell

Eyes cool as coins —Margaret Millar

Eyes ... dark and cold ... like water under ice —Mary Hedin

Eyes ... dark and empty, like open graves —Donald Seaman

Eyes ... dead and cold, like marbles swimming in glass —Paige Mitchell

Eyes ... expressionless as ice cubes —Clive Cussler

Eyes, fishy and staring like headlights —Harvey Swados

(When he is excited or amused ... his) eyes flare like two cigarette lighters —Bryan Miller, *New York Times* story about Yves Montand, June 24, 1987

Eyes flat and vicious like the eyes of a mean dog crouched over a bone —George Garrett

Eyes frightened as if she expected any moment the stunning blow of a fist —George Garrett

His eyes glaze over like eggs up —Ira Wood

Eyes ... grow blank as a dropped blind —Edith Wharton

Eyes ... hard as almond shells with a kernel of light —Rumer Godden

Eyes hard as buttons —Louise Erdrich

(Her inky) eyes have the look of someone who has been in prison a long time and knows they can send her back —Sharon Olds

Eyes in which intelligence and comprehension burned like two fixed stars —Edith Wharton

Eyes keen as talons —T. Coraghessan Boyle

Eyes, like a stern judge's, seemed to pierce the heart of all questions —Honoré de Balzac

Eyes like flint-stones —Donald Seaman

Eyes like glacier lakes —Donald McCaig

Eyes like marbles, hard and glazed —Borden Deal

Eyes like needles —Lord Byron

Eyes like smoking tragedies —Edna O'Brien

Eyes ... like the eyes in the statues blank and un-seeing and serene —William Faulkner

Eyes ... like the eyes of a dying man who looks everywhere for healing —James Baldwin

Eyes ... like the eyes of the dead that none has closed with love's last kiss —Johann Wolfgang Von Goethe

(Looked back at him, his black) eyes like two drill bits —Nicholas Proffitt

Eyes like two steel spikes —Flannery O'Connor

Eyes observant and curious like those of a man caught in a great catastrophe which it is his duty to record —Graham Greene

(Lying motionless on his back) eyes staring up at the ceiling like a doll's —Joseph Heller

Eyes ... steely as a bird's —Jean Garrigue

Eyes swollen with rage they look like hard-cooked eggs —T. Coraghessan Boyle

Eyes that looked as if they might warm up at the right time and in the right place —Raymond Chandler, *The Lady in the Lake*

Eyes that looked as if they were trying to see be-yond the horizon —William McIlvanney

Eyes went flat with terror, like a rabbit caught by a car's headlights —Andrew Kaplan

Eyes widened with fear, like a cat facing head-lights in the night —Z. Vance Wilson

Eyes ... wide open like a deer's —Colette

Fury flashing from her eyes like New Year's Eve sparklers —Dorothea Straus

Hard eyes ... like little metal studs (pinned into the white faces of young men) —John Updike

His eyes [Mike Wallace's] grew flat as the eyes of a movie Apache who has just taken a rifle bul-let to the stomach —Norman Mailer

The Apache comparison underscores Mailer's re-peated references to Mike Wallace as resembling a Native American.

Little eyes lit up like a cat's in a room full of yarn —Thomas Zigal

Look in his eyes like a glutted steer in a feedlot —Mary Hood

Mischief crackling like static electricity in her eyes —W. P. Kinsella

Tired, kindly eyes, like the eyes of a monkey —Elizabeth Bowen

Wide amazed eyes like an expensive china doll —George Garrett

Wide penetrating eyes, like black raisins —Rex Reed

The eyes Reed is comparing to black raisins be-long to Sophia Loren.

EYELASHES

(She was an artist of the face) drawing her long lashes out like licorice —Jay Parini

Eyelashes like the wicks of many extinguished candles —Frank Swinnerton

Eyelashes long as shish kebab —Rex Reed

The owner of the long lashes is Carol Channing

Eyelashes ... long, like flies' legs —Aharon Megged

Eyelashes stiff as bird-tails —Eudora Welty

Eyelashes ... thick and furry as tarantula legs —James Crumley

[Eyes] lash-fringed like Spanish lace —Davis Grubb

Lashes as thick and dark as raven feathers —Jonathan Kellerman

Lashes bunched together like star points —Jill Ciment

Lashes thick and black as if painted with a black tarlike material —Joyce Carol Oates

Long lashes fluttered like the feelers of a beetle on its back —Truman Capote

The lashes thus described belong to Mae West.

Thick lashes, soft as paintbrushes —Louise Erdrich

❧ EYELIDS

Eyelids drooped as though the lashes weighed intolerably —Truman Capote

Eyelids flutter like butterflies that children have impaled alive on pins —Erich Maria Remarque

Eyelids fluttering, as if assailed by gnats —Leonard Michaels

Eyelids heavy as if from too much dreaming. His dreaming lay like the edges of a deep slumber on the rim of his eyelids —Anais Nin

Eyelids … hung askew over her cloudy gray eyes [too weak to be raised or lowered], like broken blinds in the windows of a condemned house —Gerald Kersh

Eyelids like thin gray leather —Ken Kesey

Eyelids pale like a chicken's —V.S. Pritchett

Eyelids translucent as crepe —Jayne Anne Phillips

Eyelids which looked like walnut shells —Julia O'Faolain

Eyes … double-lidded like the eyes of the black bull snake —Will Weaver

Heavy eyelids … like small, brown, wrinkled eggshells —Brian Glanville

Lids … like furrows in deeply plowed soil —Anon

Lower lids as straight as ruler-edges —Dashiell Hammett

The thick red-lined lids hung over the eyeballs like blinds of which the cords are broken —Edith Wharton

❧ EYE MOVEMENTS

Blinked … as if chasing a fly away —Aharon Megged

Blinking like a frightened cat —Dan Wakefield

Blinking like a mechanical toy —Peter Benchley

Eyeballs bulged like a lizard's —Paige Mitchell

Eyes … beginning to bob like fishing corks on the sea —William Diehl

Eyes bounce like marbles —Norman Mailer

Eyes closed, almost as if he was silently praying —John Fowles

Eyes darting like astonished fish —Brian Glanville

Eyes dart like a shoplifter's —Hilma Wolitzer

Eyes dart like swallows —Marge Piercy

Eyes did a dance like two flies looking for a place to light —Robert Campbell

(He nodded his head, but his) eyes didn't move, as if they were weighted in their sockets like the eyes of a doll —Jonathan Valin

Eyes dilated like an animal's caught in a trap —V.S. Pritchett

Eyes dilate like targets on a rifle range, and each word and gesture is emphasized by a blast of cigarette smoke that makes her look like she's walking in a cumulous cloud —Rex Reed

The actress thus profiled by Reed is Bette Davis.

Eyes flashed and twinkled … like the lamps of a lighthouse —Anthony Powell

Eyes flashing like magnifying glasses —H. E. Bates

Eyes flickered like uncertain lights —Ann Rice

Eyes flicker like leaves —Marge Piercy

Eyes fluttered around the room like moths —Donald McCaig

Eyes hovered about like mosquitoes —C. J. Koch

(Yonatan's) eyes narrowed like gunslits —Amos Oz

(Schwend's hurt) eyes opened like blooming peonies —Herbert Lieberman

Eyes opened like windows —Sharon Sheehe Stark

Eyes … opened wide like a clairvoyant's —Anais Nin

Eyes roamed about like jellyfish —H. E. Bates

Eyes rolled in their sockets like loose marbles —Truman Capote

Eyes seemed to be clambering frantically, like a pair of blatant prisoners behind her heavy glasses —V.S. Pritchett

(His little) eyes snapped like two sparks. Like two sparks they glowed in the smolder of his bearded face —Katherine Mansfield

> *In this example from her short story, "Ole Underwood," Katherine Mansfield demonstrates the effectiveness of repeating a simile.*

Eyes that kept winking and twinkling at each side of his inquisitive nose, as if they were playing a perpetual game of peep-bo with that feature —Charles Dickens

Eyes … twirling around like fruit-flies —Jane Wagner

Eyes were closed like a man in violent prayer —William Styron

Furtive little eyes kept darting around in his head like rodents —Thomas Wolfe

Languidly half closes his eyes, like a cat on a sofa —Anton Chekov

Lowered her eyes like a nun beholding a statue —Honoré de Balzac

Mr. York's eyes bulged like doorknobs —Susan Vreelanc, *Clara and Mr. Tiffany*

Narrowing his eyes like someone who knows there's a mouse in the soup —Peter Meinke

Rapidly blinking eyes, as though he were caught in a constant sandstorm —Daphne Merkin

Rolled his eyes like a pair of gambler's dice —Paige Mitchell

Tightly shutting her eyes like a shot pheasant falling out of the sky —Kenzaburo Oe

Wide-spaced eyes floating like sea-slivers above his cheek bones —Julia O'Faolain

❧ FACE(S)

See Also: BLUSHES; CHEEKS; EYE(S); EYEBROWS; EYELASHES; EYELIDS; FACIAL EXPRESSIONS, MICELLANEOUS; FACIAL DETAILS; HAIR; LIPS; MOUTH; MUSTACES; PHYSICAL APPEARANCE; SKIN; WRINKLES

A beautiful face … cut as clear and sharp as a cameo —Jack London

Angular face, sharp as the face of the Knave in a deck —George Garrett

A bulky white face like that of a Mother Superior —Frank Swinnerton

The countenance is the title page which heralds the contents of the human volume, but like other title pages it sometimes puzzles, often misleads, and often says nothing to the purpose —William Matthews

A desolate, cratered face, sooty with care like an abandoned mining town —Joseph Heller

A dry energetic face which seemed to press forward with the spring of his prominent features, as though it were the weapon with which he cleared his way through the world —Edith Wharton

Face … as broad and plain as a tin pie pan —Jean Thompson

A face as creased and limited as her conversation —Hortense Calisher

Face … as creased and brown as a walnut —Marmaret Millar

Face … bunched up like a fist —Jonathan Valin

Face … changeable as an autumn sky —John O'Connor

Face … clean as a china plate —Dorothy Canfield

Face clear as a cloud —Arthur A. Cohen

Face crumpled as if it had been left out in the rain —Lael Wertenbaker

Face … doughy, like a fresh baking of bread just put out to rise —Paul J. Wellman

Face … dry and immobile, like a mummy's —Ignazio Silone

Face … has the compressed appearance, as though someone had squeezed his head in a vise —Woolcot Gibbs, about Thomas Dewey during his 1940 campaign for the Republican presidential nomination

Face … heavy as a sack —Honoré de Balzac

Face … heavy, as if little bags of sand had been painlessly sewn into various parts of it, dragging the features away from the bones —Kingsley Amis

A face in many planes, as if the carver had whittled and modeled and indented to see how far he could go —Willa Cather

(Her) face is like the Milky Way i' the sky —Sir John Suckling

Face … its beauty fortuitous like that of a Puritan woman leaning over the washtub —Walker Percy

Face lean as a hatchet —William Beechcroft

Face like a pie … out of the oven too soon —William Faulkner

A face like a 16-ounze boxing glove —Harry Prince

Face … like a badly packed suitcase —Jimmy Sangster

Face like a bad orange —Joyce Cary

Face … like a beaked bird —James Joyce

Face like a benediction —Miguel de Cervantes

Face like a butcher's block —Frank O'Connor

Face … like a fiddle and everyone who sees him must love him —Anon Irish saying

Carl Sandburg, who had a penchant for incorporating familiar similes into his work, quoted this in his poem "New Hampshire Again."

(A pale flat woman with a) face like a fillet of flounder —Helen Hudson

Face like a knotty whorl in the bark of a hoary olive tree —Amos Oz

Face … like a mail-order ax —William H. Gass

A face like a Mediterranean Lolita —Carol Ascher

Face like an anemic cat's —Colette

Face like an old purse —Mary Hedin

(A little brown monkey of a man with) a face like a nut —Ruth Rendell

Face like a peeled beet —Hanoch Bartov

Face like a picture of a knight, like one of that Round Table bunch —O. Henry

Face … like a piece of the out-of-doors come indoors: as holly-berries do —D. H. Lawrence

Face … like a pillow that has been much but badly slept on —Romain Gary

Face … like a predatory bird, beaked, grim-lipped —Wallace Stegner

Face like a raisin cookie. Eyes set wide apart and shallow —Donald McCaig

A face like a rock —Thomas Carlyle

Carlyle thus described his publisher, Frederic Henry Hedge

Face like a sack of flour —T. Coraghessan Boyle

Face like a sallow bust on a bracket in a university library —Edith Wharton

Face like a shell —Ellen Gilchrist

Face like a slab of corned beef —Oakley Hall

Face like a small pale mask —William Faulkner

Face like a sodden pie —Edgar Lee Masters

A face like a very expensive cat —Josephine Tey

Face like a very ripe peach —Christopher Isherwood

Face like lean old glove leather —Richard Ford

Face … like the cement in an old cellar, rough irregular lines lying thick and lumpy along a hard white surface —Charles Johnson

Face like the Soul's Awakening —P.G. Wodehouse

Her big powdered face was set like an egg in a cup in the frilly high-necked blouse —John Dos Passos

(He had) a face like the statue of some Victorian industrialist, heavy and firm and deeply lined, giving an impression of stern willingness —John Braine

A face like Walt Disney's idea of a grandfather —William McIlvanney

Face like warm baked clay —C. J. Koch

Face looked like a white blown-out paper bag —V.S. Pritchett

Face … massive as a piece of sculpture —Harvey Swados

Face ravaged as the dimmest memories of the past … creased and flabby, like an old bag —Kingsley Amis

Face red, swollen, like an overripe fruit —Graham Swift

Face sagged, as if its fleshy sub-structure had dried up —McKinlay Kantor

Faces bunched like fists —Irving Feldman

Faces harder than a rock —The Holy Bible/Jeremiah

Face shimmering and flat as the moon —Diane Wakoski

Face … shines in the darkness like a thin moon —Erich Maria Remarque

Face short and blunt as a cat's —M. J. Farrell

Faces like dark boxes of secrets and desires … locked safely, like old-fashioned caskets for the safe conduct of jewels on a voyage —Eudora Welty

A face like stretched leather —Helen Simonson *Major Pettigrew's Last Stand*

(Young neat unscratched boys with) faces like the bottoms of new saucers —Charles Bukowski

Face like flint —The Holy Bible/Isaiah

Face smooth and intent like a man listening to music —Ross Macdonald

Face smooth and timeless as a portrait in a darkened gallery —T. Coraghessan Boyle

Face … smooth, calculated, and precision-made, like an expensive baby doll —Ken Kesey

Face … smooth like a balmy sky where there's peace —Helga Sandburg

Face … soft and withered as an apple doll —Sue Grafton

Face so grimed with dirt it looked like a brown leather mask —John Dos Passos

Face … so old that it looked as if the flesh had been polished away —Ellen Glasgow

Face sparkles like a diamond (at mention of favorite topic, collecting) —Honoré de Balzac

Faces ruddy and wrinkled like old apples —Margaret Bhatty

Faces shimmered like they were coming out of water —Jayne Anne Phillips

Face … strong, like Greek statuary —Sue Grafton

(Their) faces were like the faces of lions —The Holy Bible/Kings

A face that looked as if it had been left out on the fire escape for over half a century —Rex Stout

A face that resembled a diseased cauliflower —Miles Gibson

A face that seemed sometimes as intimidating as a clenched fist —Frank Tuohy

Face thin as a desert saint's —Z. Vance Wilson

Face thrust forward like a hatchet —Oakley Hall

Face twitched like a snapping rubber band —James Lee Burke

(The old woman's) face was like a worn rock at which all the waves of life had smashed and beaten —Thomas Wolfe

Face was very like a crow —Lewis Carroll

Face … wizened as an old potato —Ignazio Silone

(One day his)face would collapse, like that of a beautiful woman who suddenly abandons the pretense and admits defeat —Harvey Swados

Face … wound up like a spring —Alan Sillitoe

Features … a little like a Roman emperor side-face —A. A. Milne

Features … dark and indistinct, as if they'd been rubbed with a dirty eraser —Alice McDermott

A flat face like an imprint in some thick, warm tar —Robie Macauley

Flat white face, like a pillow with eyes —Richard Connell

Front face she was shapeless like poorly impressed sealing-wax —Julia O'Faolain

Her face had filled out into two little puffs of vanity on either side of her mouth, as if she were eating or were containing a yawn —V.S. Pritchett

Her face had rounded with flesh that closed in about her eyes like a dough doll's —Will Weaver

Her face, pinched from the cold, made her look like a young girl in the Depression of the thirties —Penelope Gilliatt

Her face was like an old brown bowl —Thomas Wolfe

His countenance was like the countenance of an angel of God, very terrible —The Holy Bible/Judges

His face was as … the sun —The Holy Bible/Revelation

His face, with its thick crude lines … and large mouth, gave him the appearance of a slightly refined monkey —H. E. Bates

His unkempt face hung like a bad smell over his dirty clothes —James Crumley

Intense aquiline profile, like the prow of a boat straining forward from too close a fastening —Ruth Suckow

Looked like a miniature beside a portrait in oils —Honoré de Balzac

Old slightly wizened face, like minor characters in novels of whom one is told that "they might have been any age from 20 to 50" —Edward Marsh

A profile like a bread knife —Harvey Swados

A profile like a set of keys and a nose like a bicycle seat —Joey Adams

Profile … like the blade of a knife, cold and sharp —Honoré de Balzac

A round coarse face like a pomegranate —Frank Swinnerton

Round red face shone like freshly washed china —Katherine Mansfield

She's a charming middle aged lady with a face like a bucket of mud and if she's washed her hair since Coolidge's second term, I'll eat my spare tire, rim and all —Raymond Chandler, *Farewell, My Lovely*

A sly, pointed face with something vixen in it, the look of a child evacuee who had lost his parents and grown up too fast —Penelope Gilliatt

They had long tired faces. Their yawns, snapping and unsnapping their jaws, made them look like horses —Boris Pasternak

A thin face, pointed as a paper knife —Helen Hudson
The man thus described in Hudson's story, "The Tenant," is trying to pry information out of a troubled woman. She extended the paper knife comparison as follows: "ready to slit her open."

Weather-beaten face, like it was smoked and cured —George Garrett

Wild faces like men hopped up on dope —George Garrett

♣ FACIAL COLOR

See Also: BLUSHES, COLOR, PALLOR, RED, WHITE

A face like a raw steak —John Dos Passos

An extremely florid face, as if his blood pressure was about to pop —Peter Meinke

A bluish pallor had spread like a shadow over his face —Walter de la Mare

Carried a ruddy stain on either cheek, like a ripe apple —Robert Louis Stevenson

Cheeks and bunchy lips as red as they would have been if she had fallen into a pot of jam —Frank Swinnerton

Cheeks became pink like the delicate petals of sweet peas. —Susan Vreeland, Clara and Mr. Tiffany

Coloring as natural as a bird's egg or a leaf —Frank Tuohy

Coloring … so like the bloom of a ripe fruit, that nature in her seemed to have rivaled art —Italo Svevo

The color spread across his face like a bush fire —Mike Fredman

Face … a curious, flat color, like the inside of a raw potato —Susan Hill

A face as white and almost as smooth as a bar of soap —Scott Spencer

Face dark with furious blood, dark as a plum —Guy Vanderhaeghe

A variation by Gloria Norris: "face … turned purple as a plum."

Face … dull red, as if baked by the heat of blazing towns —Stephen French Whitman

Face glows, spotty, like there's a tiny pink bulb burning behind each cheek —Sharon Sheehe Stark

(Marley's) face … had a dismal light about it, like a bad lobster in a dark cellar —Charles Dickens

Face like a lobster —Robert Louis Stevenson

Face like a raw side of beef —Robert Campbell

Face … like a strawberry —Mary Hedin

In Hedin's short story, The Secret, the woman with the strawberry-like face had been bending over a stove.

(Passion has made his) face like pale ivory —Oscar Wilde

Face pale and lined like a map —Hugh Walpole

Face … pale as death and far more ghastly —Nathanial Hawthorne

A face … puffy and sallow, the color of old piano keys —William Boyd

In the novel, An Ice-Cream War, the author continues as follows: "as if he were just recovering from an illness or about to be seriously afflicted by one."

Face … red as a parrot's —Dame Edith Sitwell

Face … ruddy, flushed with blood, like a slaughterer's —Isaac Bashevis Singer

Face shone red as a cock's comb —Rita Mae Brown

Faces red as steak —Sharon Olds

Faces stained by the cool night like wine —Dame Edith Sitwell

Faces white like paste —Hugh Walpole

Face the color and texture of kangaroo hide —Frank Ross

Face … the color of cat's meat —James Thurber

Face turned to a dull white, like bread dough —Anon

Face went gray, like the mortar in the trough —Henry Van Dyke

Face yellow like ancient paper —Arthur A. Cohen

Great blushing face, like a Dutch cheese —Jilly Cooper

Her color had been pared away, like you pare an apple —Donald McCaig

Her color was high, as though she had been sitting near a fire —Geoffrey Wolff

Her face was … white-powdered like a marshmallow —Frank Tuohy

Her face went just as red as the side of a fire truck —Stephen King, *Carrie*

A medium dark face, like antique gold under a black light —Loren D. Estleman

Pale as a miner —Amor Towles, *Rules of Civility*

Red as a radish —Amor Towles, *Rules of Civility*

A tan like a basted turkey —David Nicholls, *One Day*

Tanned as a hound's tooth —Robert Traver

Two spots of rouge like paper discs pasted on her cheekbones —William Faulkner

Unnaturally red cheeks like varnished apples —Edith Wharton

❧ FACIAL DETAILS

A blemish on the ridge of his nose stood out like a connecting point between his eyebrows, like a town on a map —Bobbie Ann Mason

Blues under his eyes like chain links —Saul Bellow

The bones on his face stuck out like knobs under his skin —Gloria Norris

Busted blood vessels in the nose and across his cheeks look like a precinct map of the city —Robert Campbell

The dimple in her chin is like a tiny keyhole —Joan Chase

Dimples that looked as if they had been poked into her cheeks by a mischievous finger —Rex Beach

Ears as sharp as a fox —MacDonald Harris

A commonly used variation: "ears like a fox."

Ears like bat's wings —Aharon Megged

Ears like jug handles —Borden Deal

Ears like pointed spears —David Ignatow

Ears … pendulous scarlet ears that showed up like blobs of sealing wax on the pallor of his cheeks and were framed in wisps of silky white hair —Albert Camus

Ears sticking out like tabs he might be picked up and shaken by —Eudora Welty

(Large) ears … stuck out like wings —Leo Tolstoy

The features of his face were indistinct and unimpressive, as if begun in clay but never fired —Erik Larson, *In the Belly of the Beast: Love, Terror, and an American Family in Hitler's Berlin*

Freckled, as if she'd been sprinkled with nutmeg —Eudora Welty

(A mask of) freckles laid like a veil across his nose —Ben Ames Williams

Freckles like rust spots —Willa Cather

Freckles like specks of nutmeg on his cheeks —Sharon Olds

(Nose bridged with) freckles like splotches of huge summer rain on the sidewalk —William Faulkner

Freckles lingered just below the skin, like a thin wash of gold —Elizabeth Spencer

A gash as thick as a cigarette —T. Glen Coughlin

His nose was very short, just like a baby's, and he had a long blue upper lip, like a priest —Joyce Cary

A mole like a tiny cameo —Eudora Welty

(She brushed at the) mole that spotted her cheek like a tea —Truman Capote

Pale brown freckles scattered across her nose like sesame seeds —Julie Orringer, *The Invisible Bridge*

Pimples big as candy corn —Ira Wood

Pimple … shone like the sun trying to come out —Sharon Sheehe Stark

Red pimples spread across her forehead like strawberry jam —Alice McDermott

Scars ... like claw marks —Louise Erdrich

A scar ... that twained his face from forehead to chin, like a portrait sliced in half —Davis Grubb

Scratches on his face like a cat had fought him hard for every one of its lives —O. Henry

The shadows under my eyes were like a pair of leathery wings —Jean Thompson

❧ FACIAL EXPRESSIONS, BLANK

See Also: EYE EXPRESSIONS, MISCELLA-NEOUS

Anonymous, like the faces one sees in a football crowd —Robert Traver

(Her face went as) blank as a chalkboard —Jonathan Valin

(The child's expression was) blank, as if her hair was drawn back and fastened so tightly that her facial muscles couldn't function —Margaret Millar

Countenance ... like a still, dark day, equally beamless and breezeless —Charlotte Brontë

Empty look ... like an actor without a part —John le Carré

Expressionless as a smoked herring —Anon

Expressionless ... like a portrait of a great beauty by a not very great painter who had caught all the listed features, but not the living stir of loveliness —Elizabeth Taylor

Face ... cold and motionless, as of a man who is asleep —Mikhail P. Arzybashev

Face ... as blank as a target after a militia shooting-match —Mark Twain

Face ... as inanimate as a mask —Ellen Glasgow

Face as inscrutable as that of a snapping turtle —Arthur Train

A face as vacant as an untenanted house —Marcel Proust

Face, empty like that of a doll —Franz Werfel

Face had all the warmth, personality and individualism of an amoeba —Robert J. Serling

Face like a marble mask in which the lips were too rigid for speech —Edith Wharton

Face like one of those Easter Island stone carvings —Len Deighton

Face ... locked like a vault —T. Coraghessan Boyle

Face set in a fixed expression of friendly interest like a mask pulled over her skull —Frank Conroy

Face set into a stiff mask, like that of an acroterion —John Fowles

Faces that were as closed, as mysterious, and as mute as the faces of the dead who are possessed of a knowledge beyond the comprehension of the living —Joseph Conrad

Hardly ever smiling, with no cracks showing so no one could look in ... like an empty plate —Helen Hudson

Hopelessly blank, like the face of a blind man —Joseph Conrad

It [her face] was blank, as though she no longer dwelt within her own skull, as though she had gone elsewhere —Margaret Laurence

(His face was empty and impassive,) shut tight as a graveyard gate —Nicholas Proffitt

Staring blankly ahead like a man with a fever —Mark Helprin

Wooden-faced as a cigar-store Indian —Raymond Chandler, *Trouble Is My Business*
This typifies the simile that outlives the relevancy of the comparison.

❧ FACIAL EXPRESSIONS, MISCELLANEOUS

See Also: EYE EXPRESSIONS, MISCELLA-NEOUS

Always had a ready smile, so that her face with its round rosy cheeks was more like something you could eat or lick; she reminded me of nothing so much as an apple fritter —Edna O'Brien

Anger on her cheeks like rouge —Truman Capote

Anxiety and annoyance chasing each other like the hands of a clock around his wide, flat face —Helen Hudson

Blinked … like an owl surprised in daylight and annoyed at this interruption —John Galsworthy

Bright, inflamed look, as though she had just been crying or having her cheeks scrubbed by an angry nursegirl —Mary McCarthy

[Face] Cold as a cameo —Barbara Howes

His countenance was like lightning —The Holy Bible/Matthew

Expression … like a leopard who's just sighted a plump impala —Jilly Cooper

Expression like a stork that dropped a baby and broke it and is coming to explain to the parents —Mel Brooks

Face was wound up like a spring —Alan Sillitoe

Face … cold, as though warmth and tenderness were dead in her —Jean Rhys

Face … as calm as a mask —Ross Macdonald

Face … as hard as ice —Roberta Allen

Face as welcoming as an open fire —William McIlvanney

Face becoming creased and flabby, like an old bag, with the strain of making it smile and show interest and speak its permitted few words —Kingsley Amis

Face bobbing anxiously like a man bidding at an auction —Derek Lambert

Face changed a little … as if a headlight had flashed across it —Frank Tuohy

Face [of old man] crinkled into a laugh, so that it looked like a polished walnut —Lu Hsun

Face crumpled like a sheet of wadded paper —Pat M. Esslinger-Carr

Face … delicate with fear, as if it might shatter like white china —Paul Theroux

Face had clenched like a pale wax-paper mask, into a ball of hate —Louise Erdrich

Face had fallen like a waffle —Frank O'Hara

Face harmoniously fixed, as if for a camera —Elizabeth Hardwick

Face harsh and wrung and savage beneath the springing tears like sweat —William Faulkner

Face is still calm, as though she had a cast made and painted to just the look she wanted —Ken Kesey

Face laced tight as a shoe —Lorrie Moore

(When he came … her) face lighted up as if he had been sunshine —William Makepeace Thackeray

Face like a buttered scone, dripping complacency —Helen Hudson

Face lit up like a sunburst —Max Shulman

Face lit with a kind of radiant pain, as if she'd been bitten by a miracle —Sharon Sheehe Stark

(Icy anger tucked behind his) face, locked up like a store after hours —Lorrie Moore

Face looked all stiff, as if he were afraid the features would fall off —Helen Hudson

Face puckered and fierce and jowly and quizzical like a Boston bulldog —George Garrett

Face … rigid, like the face of a man in the grip of a barely controlled rage —Wallace Stegner

(Tiny's) face sagged like an old pillow propped against a headboard —Harold Adams

Faces all knotted up like burls on oaks —William Carlos Williams

Faces became red and swollen as from an interior fire which flamed out from the clear holes of their eyes —Émile Zola

Faces chipped into expressions that never change, like flint arrowheads —Ken Kesey

(The sheriff's) face seems to melt like a plate of butter left too close to the fire —George Garrett

Face shining like a great sunflower —Aharon Megged

Face shone with a bright glow ... like the terrible glow of a fire on a dark night —Leo Tolstoy

Faces ... lifted up like flowers in a kind of rapt and mournful ecstasy —Thomas Wolfe

Face squinched up like a withered apple —Robert B. Parker

Faces with the word "no" stamped like a coat of arms on them [about London landladies] —V.S. Pritchet

Face that looks as overworked as Gary Cooper trying to register an emotion —Wallace Stegner

Face twisted like a man who's accidentally swallowed a whole chili pepper —Gloria Norris

Face, vague like a shadow —Anatole France

Face ... vigilant as some small cat's —Louise Erdrich

Face was set into an expression of intense attention, like a man listening to an important broadcast which might affect his course of action in some way —John Malcolm

Face went to pieces as if by its own weight —Ross Macdonald

Fearful expression ... like the fear of an animal which has been beaten and kicked for too long —Louis Bromfield

Features ... softening like wax too close to the flame —George Garrett

Fierce and variegated countenance, appeared like war personified —Nathanial Hawthorne

A gentle, cowlike expression passed over her face like a cloud —Colette

Grimaced, like a rubber Kewpie doll being squeezed in all the wrong places —Paige Mitchell

The grin left his face and was replaced by the sort of amusement that rings like a coin slapped on a bar —Jonathan Valin

Had a face like a Requiem —Honoré de Balzac

Had an expression on his face as if he were listening for something, so that one felt one couldn't disturb him —Ruth Prawer Jhabvala

(Her eyes were still red, but she) had the happy look of a child that has outslept its grief —Edith Wharton

Had the mankind-loving look of a convert fresh from church —Harold Adams

Hard, red face like a book of rules —Anthony Carson

Has a haunted, jumpy look, as if invisible alarm clocks were going off throughout the day, to remind him of undone duties —Christopher Isherwood

Her face shut up like a suitcase —Claire Messud, *The Last Life*

His fat face opened and smiled like a distorted, gold-toothed flower —John Dickson Carr

His mangy little face lit up like a store window going on for the night —Jonathan Valin

The kid's face had as much expression as a cut of round steak and was about the same color —Raymond Chandler, *Red Wind*

Like a peddler whose wares have been turned down all day, he waited, with a look of patient expectation —Elizabeth Hardwick

Lips pursed like those of a goldfish blowing bubbles in an aquarium —Michael Korda, *Another Life*

Lips went white, like a person who has received a stunning blow without warning and who, in the first moments of shock, does not realize what has happened —Margaret Mitchell

(Every time he saw Conrad he) lit up like a fairground with hilarity and self-satisfaction —A. Alvarez

A lonely face, pulled in like rain off the wild stretches —Elizabeth Spencer

Look as startled like a hare —Joyce Cary

Looked smug … like a messenger bringing the news of a battle won —John Rechy

Looked wistful, like a kid who'd lost the magic penny —Robert Campbell

Looking as miserable as sin —Penelope Gilliatt

Looking puzzled and dismayed, like a baby who's learned to pull itself up on the sides of a crib, but hasn't figured out how to sit down again —Sue Grafton

A look of intense mirth spread over Lily's face like water released suddenly from a broken dam —Louis Bromfield

A look of surprise … as if he'd just swallowed an ice cube —T. Coraghessan Boyle

Looks perpetually surprised, but scared and insincere, like a play actor —Jayne Anne Phillips

Looks puzzled and grieved, as if he can't believe his bad luck —François Camoin

No pity or censure in her face, it was as immovable as a fact —Margaret Millar

Official faces … like death masks —Ross Macdonald

Old emotions, like old scars, savaged his face —Rita Mae Brown

One could see thoughts crossing his face like caravans of camels lurching slowly across the seemingly endless Sahara —Delmore Schwartz

Open-mouthed, like a fish —Anon

Pale astonishment in his face as if at a sudden accusation —George Eliot

Pleading look, a beg for help like a message from a powerless invaded country to the rest of the world —Lynne Sharon Schwartz

Sensuality had been eroded from his face, nibbled away, as the sea nibbles traces of meat from a shell —Julia O'Faolain

A set face, sad like a toy soldier's, wooden and clad with honor —Z. Vance Wilson

(The other diners were listening with) Shocked but rather smirking expressions, like good little boys who were going to hear the bad little boy told off —Jean Rhys

The compassionate look of a friendly dog —André Malraux

Their faces seemed unusually open, like so many windows —John Cheever

Tiredness and worry chasing one another like clouds across her face —Susan Hill

A tremor, as quick and delicate as a pulse, passed over her features … so quickly it seemed a drop of rain had simply moved like a shadow across her face —Alice McDermott

His face [as he breaks into laughter] unfolds like a peony —Erich Maria Remarque

❧ FACIAL EXPRESSIONS, SERIOUS

See Also: EYE EXPRESSIONS, MISCELLA-NEOUS

Face all clouds, like a man in need of physic —George Garrett

A face as sad and featureless as a moon by day —George Garrett

Face austere as a hermit's —Lynne Sharon Schwartz

Face … gloomy as an El Greco —John Fowles
Carlos Baker makes the El Greco comparison with "long" which expands the meaning to include mood as well as physical shape.

Face grim as flu —Reynolds Price

Face like a clenched fist —Richard Condon

A face like a stomach cramp —Loren D. Estleman

Face like a vinegar bottle —Erich Maria Remarque

Face … somber as a churchman's —Richard Ford

Face tightened up like a charley-horse —Raymond Chandler

Face was long, like a sheep's —W. Somerset Maugham

The comparison is used to describe both sadness and a long-shaped face. To emphasize the psychological there's Daphne du Maurier's "long and grave ... like a complaining sheep." To combine both meanings there's this by Margaret Atwood: "face ... long and mournful, like a sheep's, but with the large full eyes of a dog, spaniel not terrier."

Grim as an ideological bigot —Frank Swinnerton

Had the face of a man suffering the awaited death of a loved one who's terminally ill —Mario Puzo

Had the look of a boy who had just lost his puppy to the county dogcatcher —Clive Cussler

He [Calvin Coolidge] looks as if he'd been weaned on a pickle —Alice Roosevelt Longworth

His long grim face, with the mouth running across its lower hem like a slipped thread in a linen sack, was as pitted as a battlefield —Cynthia Ozick

A long sad face like a cocker spaniel —George Garrett

Looked dismayed, like a child who's been used to hearing the same story with the same happy ending, and now the ending has been changed —Margaret Millar

Looked like a man being strapped into the electric chair while his wife French-kisses the D.A. in the hallway —T. Coraghessan Boyle

Looking as if the dentist had told him he'd have to have all his teeth pulled —Ross Macdonald

Looking as pensive as a monk in a spiritual crisis —Scott Spencer

Looking like a broody hen —Margaret Kennedy

(You) look like you just swallowed a bone —Charles Johnson

Sour and gray in the face, like a man who detests the food that keeps him alive; and must yet have it —Paul Horgan

Troubled face ... like a gravel parking lot —Ken Follett

Wore a permanently pinched look, as if he had just bitten into a piece of spoiled fish that he could neither swallow or spit out —Amos Oz

Worried look, like a bird dog uncertain of the scent —Elizabeth Spencer

❧ FACIAL SHAPE

His flat face looked as if it were pressed against a window, except there was no window —Rebbecca West

Big face, broad at the bottom, narrowed upward like a Dutch cheese —Saul Bellow

An enormous flat face like an unbaked pie —J. B. Priestly

Face as huge as the bowl of the sky —George Garrett

Face as long as his arm —Henry Van Dyke

Face, as round and white and incisively marked as the face of a clock —John Updike

Face ... as round as a skillet —James Lee Burke

Face broad and oval as a meat dish —Angela Carter

Face flat as a dough pan —James Lee Burke

Face, like a large tomato, was round and very red —Kenzaburo Oe

Face long as a fence line in flat country —Linda West Eckhardt

Face long as an El Greco —Carlos Baker

Face round as a full moon —James Crumley

Face ... round as a radar dish —John Updike

Faces as long as a wet week —H. E. Bates

Face shaped like a honeydew melon —Paige Mitchell

Face shaped like a shovel —Joyce Carol Oates

Face … thin as a knife —Honoré de Balzac

A long face like a shoe —Christina Stead

A long narrow face cut like a tribal mask —Miles Gibson

A round chubby face, like a soft beachball —John Rechy

Round face like the full moon —W. Somerset Maugham

Sharp-pointed face like a cat —Honoré de Balzac

A sparkling, triangular face like a cat —Pamela Frankau

A thin face shaped like the hatchet Lizzie Borden chopped up her mama with —Davis Dresser

♣ FACTS

See Also: TRUTH

A fact is like a sack which won't stand up when it is empty —Luigi Pirandello

In his play, Six Characters in Search of an Author, *Pirandello expands upon the simile as follows: "In order that it may stand up, one has to put into it the reason and sentiment which have caused it to exist.*

Facts apart from their relationships are like labels on empty bottles —Sven Halla

Facts fled before her like frightened forest things —Oscar Wilde

Statistics are like alienists, they will testify for either side —Fiorello H. La Guardia, *Liberty Magazine,* May, 1933

Use facts … the way a carpenter uses nails —R. Wright Campbell

Use statistics as a drunken man uses lamp posts, for support rather than illumination —Andrew Lang

♣ FAILURE

See Also: COLLAPSE, DISINTEGRATION, SUCCESS/FAILURE

Our play apparently failed with a suddenness like exploding mortar. I saw the reviews.

—Martha Gellhorn, in the preface of the 1995 publication of her first and only play, *Love Goes to Press,* with fellow journalist Virginia Cowles—revived in June 2012 by the Mint Theater known for giving new life to forgotten plays.

♣ FAITH

See Also: BELIEF, RELIGION

♣ FAITHFULNESS/FAITHLESSNESS

See Also: LOYALTY/DISLOYALTY

♣ FALL

See Also: SEASONS

♣ FALLING

See Also: COLLAPSE

♣ FALSENESS

See Also: TRUENESS/FALSENESS

♣ FAME

See Also: GREATNESS

Celebrities … get consumed just as fast as new improved soaps, new clothing fashions and new ideas —Russell Baker

Celebrities used to be found in oysters, like oysters and with much the same defensive mechanisms —Barbara Walters

Celebrity is like having an extra lump of sugar in your coffee —Mikhail Baryshnikov

Fame always melts like ice cream in the dish —Delmore Schwartz

Fame grows like a tree with hidden life —Horace

Fame is a colored patch on a ragged garment —Aleksander Pushkin

Fame is like a crop of Canada thistles, very easy to sew, but hard to reap —Josh Billings

In Billings' phonetic dialect this read: "Fame is like a crop ov kanada thissels, very eazy tew sew, but hard tew reap."

Fame isn't a thing. It's a feeling. Like what you get after a pill —Joyce Cary

Fame … it's like having a string of pearls given you. It's nice, but after a while, if you think of it at all, it's only to wonder if they're real or cultured —W. Somerset Maugham

Fame, like a river, is narrowest at its source and broadest afar off —Proverb

Fame, like a wayward girl, will still be coy to those who woo her with too slavish knees —John Keats

Fame, like man, will grow white as it grows old —Abraham Cowley

Fame, like water, bears up the lighter things, and lets the weighty sink —Sir Samuel Tuke

A slight variation by Francis Bacon: "Fame is like a river, that bears (modernized from beareth) on things light and swollen, and drowns things weighty and solid."

Fame to the ambitious, is like salt water to the thirsty, the more one gets the more he wants —Emil Ebers

Glories, like glow-worms afar off, shine bright, but looked at near have neither heat nor light —John Webster

Slightly modernized from "Afar off shine bright, but look'd too near have neither heat nor light."

Glory is like a circle in the water, which never ceases to enlarge itself (till by broad spreading it disperse to nought) —William Shakespeare. *Henry VI, Part I*

Shakespeare used the Old English "ceathes."

Her life had become akin to living inside a drum with the whole world beating on the outside —Barbara Seaman

In her biography of Jacqueline Susann, Lovely Me, *this is how Seaman describes her subject's life after she becomes a famous author.*

Like grass that autumn yellows your fame will wither away —Phyllis McGinley

Like madness is the glory of this life —William Shakespeare, *Timon of Athens*

Men's fame is like their hair, which grows after they are dead, and with just as little use to them —George Villiers

Our glories float between the earth and heaven like clouds which seem pavilions of the son —Earle Bulwer-Lytton

Posterity is a switchboard to past, present and future —Karl Shapiro

The public's appetite for famous people is big as a mountain —Robert Motherwell, *New York Times,* January 22, 1986

The way to fame is like the way to heaven, through much tribulation —Lawrence Sterne

❧ FAMILIARITY

See Also: COMMONPLACE

(The donors were as) anonymous as God —Herbert Gold

(Voice) as familiar as yesterday —Wallace Stegner

Everything reliable as the newly-wed suite in the Holiday Inn —Richard Ford

The simile follows a description of the never-changing, always neat apartment of a woman's apartment in Ford's novel, The Sportswriter.

Familiar as an old mistake —Edward Arlington Robinson

Familiar as a town clock —Anon

(She became as snugly) familiar as his own armpit —Julia O'Faolain

Familiar as light or dark —Wallace Stegner

Familiar as luggage —Richard Ford

Familiar as one's own front door —Anon

Familiar as one's own face —Anon

Familiar as one's own spice shelf —Anon

Familiar as the contents of one's own broom closet —Anon

Familiar as the features of the President —Dorothea Straus

Familiar as the stars and stripes on American flag —Anon

Familiar ... as the streets of our native town —W. H. Hudson

Familiar as the voice of a favorite broadcaster —Anon

Familiar ... as things are familiar in dreams, like the dreams of falling to one who has never climbed —William Faulkner

(The agony was as) familiar ... as waking to life —Paul Theroux

Familiar as warts or some birthmark —Derek Walcott

Familiar in his mouth as household words —William Shakespeare, *Henry V*

He knows my face. He reads it like a farmer reads the sky —Marianne Hauser

Knew [her children's natures] as accurately as a bugler knows the notes of reveille —Ouida

Know him like a book —Charles F. Briggs

> *A variation that's become a popular daily is attributed to mystery writer Margaret Millar, who used it in her novel,* The Weight of the Evidence: *"I know him like I know the back of my hand."*

Know it [Boston] as an old inhabitant of a Cheshire knows his cheese —Oliver Wendell Holmes

Know ... like a rabbit knows its warren —Frank Ross

(I got men that) know (these hills) like you know your wife's geography —Ross Macdonald

(A voice as) recognizable as a train whistle —Scott Simon about sports broadcaster Harry Caray, National Public Radio, May 2,1987

Recognized (every little curve and shadow) as he would have recognized, after half a life-time, the details of a room he had played in as a child —Edith Wharton

Sounds, familiar, like the roar of trees and crack of branches —Robert Frost

Standardized as boilerplate paragraphs in a law office —Anon

Standardized, as if put together with interchangeable parts —Philip Langdon, *The Atlantic,* December, 1985

> *In an article entitled "Burger Shakes," Langdon used the simile to describe cities dotted with fast-food chains.*

The stranger is like passing water in the drain —Margaret Laurence

Stylized as the annual report message to stockholders —Anon

♣ FAMILY
See Also: PEOPLE, INTERACTION; RELATIONSHIPS

♣ FASCINATION
See Also: ATTRACTIVENESS

♣ FASHION
See Also: CLOTHING, STYLE

♣ FATE
See Also: HELPLESSNESS, LIFE

Chase destiny like a harpoonist —Edith Pearlman

Fate ... creeps like a rat —Elizabeth Bown

The Fates, like an absent-minded printer, seldom allow a single line to stand perfect and unmarred —George Santayana

Fate treats me mercilessly, like a storm treats a small boat —Anton Chekhov

Like warp and woof all destinies are woven fast —John Greenleaf Whittier

Our lives carried us in our own dimensions, like people passing on different escalators —Mary Ladd Cavell

We're like dice thrown on the plains of destiny —Rita Mae Brown

♣ FATIGUE
See: WEARINESS

FATNESS

See Also: BODY, INSULTS, PHYSICAL AP-
    PEARANCE

Blew up like a poisoned dog —Rita Mae Brown

The simile refers to a character in the novel,
Southern Discomfort, *who became fat after having a child.*

Body … encased in fat, like an insulated boiler
    —A. Alvarez

Body plump as a church rat's —Honoré de Balzac

Broad as a barn door —John Heywood's *Proverbs*

A shorter, modern version: "broad as a door."

(At the hips … she was) broad as a sofa —Saul
    Bellow

Corpulent as a fire plug —Samuel Shem Fine

Fat and sleek: a dumpling —D. H. Lawrence

Fat as a balloon —Mark Twain

Fat as a duck —John Adams

*The man Adams compared to a duck was Aaron
Burr.*

Fat as a fool —John Lyly

Fat as an owl —Miles Gibson

Fat as a pig —John Cotgrave

*This is probably the most famous and often used
"Fat as" comparison. Its earliest version "Fat as
a pork hog" appeared in to Sir Thomas Malory's
Morte d'Arthur. An offshoot, "Fat as a hen in the
forehead," has been variously attributed to the
playwrights Francis Beaumont and John Fletcher
and Jonathan Swift.*

(I shall grow) fat as a porpoise —Jonathan Swift

Fat as a whale —Geoffrey Chaucer

Fat as butter —William Shakespeare *Henry IV*

*A variation which has become an American col-
loquialism is "Fat as a butter-ball."*

Fat as plenty —Hugh Ward

The fat on her was like loose-powdered dough
    —Carson McCullers

Fat overflowed not only from her jowl to her
    neck, but from her ankles to her shoes … she
    looked like a pudding that had risen too high
    and run down the sides of the dish —Nadine
    Gordimer

(He was) fattening like a Christmas goose
    —Calder Willingham

Grew fat as a broiler —Kate Wheeler

He was fat, with a belly creased like a roll when he
    bent over —John Gunther

His stomach swells like a big cake baking
    —Carolyn Chute

I was square and looked like a refrigerator ap-
    proaching —Jean Kerr

Pudgy as a baby's hand —Jonathan Valin

Plump as an abbot —Robert Traver

Plump as a partridge —John Ray's *Proverbs*

She was round and plump as her favorite teapot
    —Peter De Vries

Stout as a stump —James Crumley

(Piglets) stout as jugs —W. D. Snodgrass

(A short man) wide as a door —Jessamyn West

A youngish plump little body, rather like a pigeon
    —Katherine Mansfield

FEAR

See Also: ANXIETY, EMOTIONS, NERVOUS-
    NESS

Afraid, as children in the dark —Dante Gabriel
    Rossetti

An air of terrifying finality, like the clap of doom
    —Herbert Lieberman

(A vague, uncatalogued) apprehension, as cold
    and disquieting as a first snowflake smudging
    the window of a warm and complacent room
    —Derek Lambert

As courage imperils life, fear protects it
    —Leonardo Da Vinci

As easily daunted as an elephant in the presence
    of a mouse —Ben Ames Williams

Brute terrors, like the scurrying of rats in a deserted attic, filled the more remote chambers of his brain —Robert Louis Stevenson

Cowardice, like alcoholism, is a lifelong condition —Susan Walton, *New York Times*, column, *New York Times*, June 4, 1987

The cowardice Walton is comparing to alcoholism is that which drives the person who always does what is expected and when.

Cowardly as the hyena —Beryl Markham

(His) cowardices ... fixed him like an invisible cement, or like a nail —Cynthia Ozick

Dreaded (her) like fire —A. S. Pushkin

The dread in his lungs lay heavy as cold mud —Peter Matthiessen

An eddy of fear swirled around her, like dust rising off the floor in some barren drafty place —Cornell Woolrich

Fear ... a little like the fear of a lover who realizes that he is falling out of love —May Sarton

Fear ... came and went like the throb of a nerve in an open tooth —James Warner Bellah

Fear ... clutching at his heart ... as if tigers were tearing him —Willa Cather

Fear ... compressed me like a vise —Aharon Appelfeld

Fear fell [on crowd] like the shadow of a cloud —John Greenleaf Whittier

Fear ... gnaws like pain —Dame Edith Sitwell

Fearing them as much ... as a nervous child with memory filled with ghost-stories fears a dark room —W. H. Hudson

Fear is like a cloak which old men huddle about their love, as if to keep it warm —William Wordsworth

Fear ... lay on me like a slab of stone —Norman Mailer

(In my body is a) fear like metal —Marilyn Hacker

The fear of failure ... blew like a Siberian wind on our unprotected backs —John le Carré

Fear oozed out (of the woods), as out of a cracked bottle —Dorothy Canfield

Fear ran through him like a sickness —Brian Moore

Fears ... fell from him like dreams from a man waking up in bed —G. K. Chesterton

Fear ... sat heavy in the center of his body like a ball of badly digested food —George Garrett

Fears came scurrying out from their hiding places like mice —Paige Mitchell

Fear ... seized all his bones like water —Hugh Walpole

Fear shot through me like a jolt of electricity —Sue Grafton

Fear spread like a common chill —Paige Mitchell

The fear [of death] ... stood silent behind them like an inflexible and cold-eyed taskmaster —Joseph Conrad

Fear stuck in his throat like a cotton hook —Charles Johnson

Fear swelled like some terrible travail —Heinrich Böll

Fear tangled his legs like a barricade —Harris Downe

Fear tastes like a rusty knife —John Cheever

Fear trills like an alarm bell you cannot shut off —John Updike

Fear worked like yeast in my thoughts, and the fermentation brought to the surface, in great gobs of scum, the images of disaster —Evelyn Waugh

Fear wrapped itself around his chest like a wide leather strap tightened by a maniac —François Camoin

Feeling as if an ice pick had been plunged into his liver —Peter Benchley

(I had) a feeling in my knees like a steering wheel with a shimmy —Rex Stout

Feel like clammy fingers were poking at my very heart —Borden Deal

Feel like a tight-rope walk high over hell —Kenneth Fearing

Feels fear, like a water bubble in his throat —Jessie Schell

Felt a chill … like swimming into a cold pocket in a lake —Tobias Wolff

Felt a driblet of fear … like a glug of water backing up the momentarily opened drain and polluting the bath with a dead spider, three lice, a rat turd, and things he couldn't stand to name or look at —Bernard Malamud

Felt like a deer stepping out before the rifle of the hunter —Piers Anthony

Felt like a nightmare that had yet to be dreamt —Stanislaw J. Lem

Felt (the beginning of) panic, like a giant hand squeezing my heart —Frank Conroy

Felt panicky, like he was in a bad dream where he did and said all the wrong things and couldn't stop —Dan Wakefield

Felt the chill of mortality … like a toddler gifted with some scraping edge of adult comprehension —Penelope Gilliatt

Felt the sick, oppressive crush of dread, like pinpoint ashes —Sylvia Berkman

A foreboding, dusky and cold like the room, crept to her side —Hugh Walpole

Frightened as Macbeth before the ghost of Banquo —Louis Veuillot

Frightened as though he had suddenly found himself at the edge of a precipice —Honoré de Balzac

Frightened … like a man who is told he has a mortal illness, yet can cure it by jumping off a fifty-foot cliff into the water. "No," he says, "I'll stay in bed. I'd rather die." —Norman Mailer

Frightening … like one of those films where ghostly hands suddenly reach in and switch off all the lights —Robert Emmet Sherwood

Fright stabbed his stomach like a sliver of glass —Arthur Miller

Full of dread and timidness as conscripts to a firing squad —Richard Ford

Gives me the creeps … like petting snakes —Raymond Chandler, *Little Sister*

Glances round him like a lamb at a convocation of wolves —T. Coraghessan Boyle

(Mildred's) heart leapt with relief like a bird in her breast —Noel Coward

A hiss of terror, like air whistling out of a punctured tire —Cornell Woolrich

Horror should rise up like a clot of blood in the throat —Dylan Thomas

[A group of children] Huddled in a corner … like so many wide-eyed, trembling mice —Gregory McDonald

I carry a scared silence with me like my smell —W. D. Snodgrass

I pretend that my right foot is like a bottle. I pour my fears down into the toes and cork the whole thing at the ankle, so none of my fears can escape into the rest of me —Dorothy B. Francis

It was as if he had entered the dark forest of a fairy tale —Erik Larson, *In the Belly of the Beast: Love, Terror, and an American Family in Hitler's Berlin*

My heart begins to pound like a thief's with the police after him —Isaac Bashevis Singer

My heart in my throat like a wad of sour grease —George Garrett

Panic, like a rabbit in front of the dogs —Peter Meinke

Panic rose as thick as honey in my throat —R. Wright Campbell

Panic shook her ... as awful as if she had been tottering on a cliff in a roaring wind —Belva Plain

Panic that was like asphyxiation —Penelope Gilliatt

Ran terror-stricken, as if death were pursuing me —Aharon Megged

Scared as a piss ant —Anon

Scared ... like a rabbit that spies a dog —Shelby Hearon

Shivered with fear like a thin dog in the cold —Stephen Vincent Benét

Take fear for granted like a drunken uncle —George Garrett

Terrifying, like a Samurai sword in motion —Robert Silverberg

Terrifying ... like fingers clamped upon your throat —Beryl Markham

Terror ebbed. Like water from a basin —Julia O'Faolain

Terror ... filled me as the sound of an explosion would fill a room —Scott Spencer

The terror inside him acted like radar —James Mitchell

Terror [of some hard to accomplish task] mocked, like some distant mountain peak —John Fowles

Terrors that brushed her like a curtain windblown against her back —Andre Dubus

(They) trail their fear behind them like a heavy shadow —Heinrich Böll

Barked like an old sergeant —Frank Swinnerton

Fierce as a comet —John Milton

Fierce as a dog with tongue lapping for action —Carl Sandburg

Fierce as a fever —Anon

Fierce as a lobster making one last lunge out of the pot —Norman Mailer

Fierce as hunger —Babette Deutsch

Fierce as vengeance —John Greenleaf Whittier

Fiery as tiger eyes —Jessamyn West

Growled ... as a dog might do at a postman —Frank Swinnerton

Savage as a bear with a sore head —Frederick Marryat

Savage as a meat-ax —American colloquialism, attributed to the Mid-South

(Hope) temptuous like a fire-cloud —Dante Gabriel Rossetti

(A fly is as) untamable as a hyena —Ralph Waldo Emerson

Wild as a monkey —Robert Silverberg

Wild as a starved cat —Elizabeth Spencer

Wild as the vultures' cry —Aeschylus

Wild as young bulls —William Shakespeare, *Henry IV, Part I.*

(Memories do not turn to dust. They live) wild as young colts —Elizabeth Spencer

(You're) wild ... just like a sea-bird —Clifford Odets

❧ FEELINGS
See: *EMOTIONS, PHYSICAL FEELINGS*

❧ FEET
See: *LEG(S)*

❧ FEROCITY
See Also: *SCREAMS*

❧ FERTILITY
See: *GROWTH*

❧ FERVOR
See: *ENTHUSIASM*

❧ FICKLENESS
See: *LOYALTY/DISLOYALTY*

❧ FICTION
See: STORIES

❧ FIGHT
See Also: FIGHTING

Clashed like stallions —Diane Ackerman

❧ FIGHTING
See Also: ARGUMENTS

Defend like a dog —Lopez Portillo

> *The former Mexican president's simile to describe how he would defend the peso gave his countrymen cause for anger and ridicule, with people sometimes barking at him in public places.*

(Self-dependent power can time) defy as rocks resist the billows and the sky —Oliver Goldsmith

Fierce strife … stirs one's old Saxon fighting blood, like the tales of "knights who fought 'gainst fearful odds" that thrilled us in our school-boy days —Jerome K. Jerome

Fight as one weary of his life —William Shakespeare, *King Henry VI, Part I*

Fight [death] … body and breath, till my life runs out like water —Stephen Vincent Benét

Fighting is like champagne. It goes to the heads of cowards as quickly as heroes —Margaret Mitchell

Fighting like a wounded puma —George F. Will

> *Wills's wounded puma simile was used to describe Richard Nixon's battle during the Watergate scandal.*

Fight like devils —William Shakespeare, *Henry V*

Fight … like lions wanting food —William Shakespeare. *King Henry VI, Part I*

Fights fierce as duels —Anon

Fought like a pagan who defends his religion —Steven Crane

Fought like one boxer and his punching bag … like mismatched twins —Erica Jong

Just when the opponents seem ready to slug each other into senselessness, they clinch and go into a clumsy waltz, like boxers in a comic film —Leonard Silk, *New York Times*, April 22, 1987

> *Silk's reference is to combatants in strained financial markets.*

Like sailors fighting with a leak we fought mortality —Emily Dickinson

A quarrel between man and wife is like cutting water with a sword —Chinese proverb

❧ FIGURE
See: BODY

❧ FINANCE
See: ECONOMICS

❧ FINGER(S)
See Also: HAND(S)

Fingernails … long as stilettos —T. Coraghessan Boyle

Fingernails that were long and curved and looked as tough as horn —Sue Grafton

Fingers are thin as ice —Marge Piercy

Fingers brown and hard as wood —Philip Levine

Fingers cool as gemstones —R. Wright Campbell

Fingers danced like midgets above a summer stream —O. Henry

Fingers fluttering … like butterflies —William Goyen

Fingers fluttering like ribbons —Sharon Sheehe Stark

Fingers … gnarled, like the roots of trees in an Arthur Rackham drawing —Antonia Fraser

Fingers … hard and inactive, like the gnarled roots of a dead tree —Frank Swinnerton

Fingers … like a bundle of broom straw, so thin and dry —Louise Erdrich

Fingers like long wax candles —Cynthia Ozick

Fingers like pliers —Donald Seaman

(The woman's) fingers rustled like branches against her face —Leigh Allison Wilson

Fingers spread apart like the talons of a predatory bird —William March

Fingers spreading out like fans —Pat Conroy

Fingers tap like a lover's fondling a girl's hard little breasts —Babette Deutsch

Fingers thick as sausages —James Crumley

Fingers tightly clenched, as if to check an involuntary gesture —Edith Wharton

Fingers … weighty as sandbags —Frank Conroy

Fingers were stiff as little darts —M. J. Farrell

Her fingers moved over his ribs gently as a harpist's —Ross Macdonald

Knuckles … like a row of little white onion [from tight grip] —Roald Dahl

(Hands crouched on the table before her, the) knuckles like miniature snow-capped mountains —Marge Piercy

Knuckles [from gripping a table very hard] shone like white stones —Mary Hedin

Long fingers arched like grapple hooks —William Carlos Williams

Long inquisitive fingers thrown out like antennae —Edith Wharton

Long thin fingers moving like knitting needles —Liam O'Flaherty

Long thin nails, like splinters —Elizabeth Spencer

My fingers fidget like ten idle brats —Wilfred Owen

Opening and closing his fingers like folding and unfolding a fan —George Garrett

Pointed his finger like a revolver —Charles Johnson

Put his fingertips together thoughtfully, like a man preparing to pray —Paul Theroux

Snapping his fingers together like a pair of scissors —Margaret Atwood

Thumb like the butt of a pistol —Sterling Hayden

❧ FIRE AND SMOKE

See Also: TOBACCO

Blaze like a box of matches —Joseph Conrad

(His house) burned like a candle —Sholem Aleichem

A cloud of black soot stood in it [the room] like a fairy-tale monster in a thick wood —Boris Pasternak

A flame as clear as a streetlight —Cynthia Ozick

The flame reared like the trunk of an animal —Steve Erickson

Flames fluttered like a school of fishes —Saul Bellow

(Suddenly the) flame shot up, leaping like a dancer in the air —Alix Kates Shulman

Oily flames curl like hair —Jean Thompson

Ribbons of flame slithered like orange serpents across the … floor —Paul Kuttner

The smoke ascended in a straight column, as though from a pagan altar —Isaac Bashevis Singer

Smoke flared through his nostrils like an old painting of a dragon —David Brierly

Smoke in the air like fog on the New Jersey flats —Carlos Baker

Smoke (from his clay pipe) lay on the air like tule fog in a marsh —Bill Pronzini

Smoke puffed from her nostril like a tiny exhaust —Ross Macdonald

Smoke rose … like a snake —Hugh Walpole

(In June when earth) smokes like slag —James Wright

Smoke … spread itself out like an infernal sort of cloud —Joseph Conrad

Smoldering embers of a fire blinked like red eyes —Ellen Glasgow

[Earth and night] Smolder like the slow, curing fire of a Javanese head-shrinker —Ted Hughes

Sparks flew against the [fireplace] screen like imprisoned birds —Margaret Millar

❧ FIRMNESS

See Also: FLEXIBILITY/INFLEXIBILITY

(Bread …) as hard as pumice —Mary Stewart

Be like a rocky headland on which the waves break incessantly, but it stands fast and the waters sink to resort —Marcus Aurelius

(Continue) firm and unmoved as a column —James Boswell

Firm as alabaster —Henry James

Firm as a monkey's tail —Creole expression

Before Jean Claude Duvalier's Haitian regime toppled in 1983, he was quoted as saying "I'm in control … firm as a monkey's tail."

[Figure] Firm as an apple —H. E. Bates

(My heart is) firm as a stone —The Holy Bible/-Jeremiah

Firm as morality —Thom Gunn

[A distant ridge] Firm as solid crystal —William Wordsworth

Firm standing like a stone wall —Bernard Bee

The term "To stonewall" comes from Bee's simile about Jackson at first battle of Bull Run.

Hard and dry as rustling corn —Dame Edith Sitwell

[A trained gangster] Hard and solid, like a shark —John Malcolm

Hard as a billiard ball —Anon

(Soil) hard as a bowling alley —E. B. White

Hard as a bulletproof vest —Russell Baker, *New York Times*, May 21, 1986

To put this in full context: "Americans like their fish, and fish roe too, fried hard as a bulletproof vest."

Hard as a heavy-duty canvas fire-hose —Sharon Olds

In the poem from which this is taken, "Six-Year-Old Boy," the fire-hose is used to describe a small boy waking up to urinate.

Hard as an egg at Easter —Michael Denham

(His body thin and stringy but) hard as armor plating —Clive Cussler

Hard as a stone pillow —Anon

Back in the Tang Dynasty chen or ceramic pillows were used during as well as after life as a means for keeping the eyes clear and preserving sight.

(The wheel of your life is … as) hard as caked clay which nothing can grow in —Amy Lowell

(Words as) hard as cannon-balls —Ralph Waldo Emerson

Hard as corkwood —Miguel de Cervantes

(Felt as) hard as dried mud —James Crumley

The descriptive frame of reference is the face of a man who's been beaten up.

(Her breasts were small but looked) hard as green apples —Anon

Hard as the knots in a whip —Yehuda Amichai

Hard as nails —Charles Dickens (*Oliver Twist*)

This now commonplace simile may well precede its appearance in Dickens' Oliver Twist. Many other writers have used it since and have modified and extended it, e.g.: "Hard and sharp as nails," attributed to S. J. Weyman; and "Hard as nails and sour as vinegar," attributed to George Beillairs.

Hardened and set like concrete —Karl Shapiro

My ass … was tight as a bull's in a thunderstorm —Lael Tucker Wertenbaker

(His jaw was) rigid as a horseshoe —Flannery O'Connor

Rigid as a starfish —Joyce Cary

Rigid as bamboo —Diane Ackerman

Rigid as iron post —Marge Piercy

(He went as) rigid as Lenin's mummy —Joseph Wambaugh

Rigid as though bound and gagged —Eudora Welty

She's hard as steel —William Shakespeare. *The Two Gentlemen of Verona*

(Heat) solid as a hickory stick —Eudora Welty

Solid as a hill —William Boyd

Stand firm as a tower, which never shakes its top, no matter what winds are blowing —Dante Alighieri

Stiff as a garden hose left out in December —Will Weaver

In Weaver's novel Red Earth, White Earth *the comparison is used to describe the physical condition of a man who's had a stroke.*

(His head) stiff as a scarab —Theodore Roethke

Stiff as a wedding night prick —Michael Connelly, *The Harry Bosh Novels*

Stiff as chessmen —Elizabeth Bowen

Stiff as icicles —Anon

Stiff as sticks —Dan Jacobson

[Bed sheet] stretched tight as a drumhead —Walker Percy

(Backside,) sturdy as baking soda biscuits —Curtis White

Taut as a sail —Barbara Howes

Taut as a tent —Karl Shapiro

(Neck tendons) taut as banjo strings —Derek Walcott

Tight as a scout's knot —Lorrie Moore

✤ FISHING
See: SPORTS

✤ FITNESS
See: HEALTH

✤ FLATNESS
See: SHAPE

✤ FLATTERY
See Also: FRIENDSHIP, WORDS OF PRAISE

As a wolf is like a dog, so is a flatterer like a friend —Thomas Fuller

Bang compliments backwards and forwards, like two asses scrubbing one another —Jonathan Swift

Bask in it [flattery] like a sunflower —Tennessee Williams

A compliment is something like a kiss through a veil —Victor Hugo

Compliments are like perfume, to be inhaled, not swallowed —Charles Clark Munn

Fawn like dogs —Percy Bysshe Shelley

Flattered me like a dog —William Shakespeare

Shakespeare's simile from King Lear *continues: "And told me I had white hairs in my beard ere the black ones were there."*

Flatterers, like cats, lick and then scratch —German proverb

Flatterers look like friends, as wolves like dogs —George Chapman

Flattering as a testimonial dinner —Anon

Flattery is like a cigarette; it is all right if you don't inhale —Adlai Stevenson

Flattery … is like a qualmish liqueur in the midst of a bottle of wine —Benjamin Disraeli

Flattery is like champagne, it soon gets into the head —William Brown

Flattery is like cologne water, to be smelt of, not swallowed —Josh Billings

Paraphrased from Billings' phonetic dialect *which reads: "Flattery is like Kolone water, tew be smelt of, not swallowed."*

Flattery is like friendship in show, but not in fruit —Socrates

Flattery is like wine, which exhilarates a man for a moment, but usually ends up going to his head and making him act foolish —Helen Rowland

(Twilight was) kind as candlelight to a bad face lift —Paige Mitchell

An overdose of praise is like ten lumps of sugar in coffee; only a very few people can swallow it —Emily Post

Praise, like gold and diamonds, owes its value only to its scarcity —Samuel Johnson

Some folks pay a compliment like they went down in their pocket for it —Kin Hubbard

Whatcha gonna do when a feller gets flirty / An' starts to talk purty / Whatcha gonna do? / S'posin' that he says / That your lips are like cherries, /Or roses, or berries —Oscar Hammerstein, "I Cain't Say No, *Oklahoma*

♣ FLAVOR

See: FOOD AND DRINK

♣ FLAWS

See: ERRORS

♣ FLEXIBILITY/INFLEXIBILITY

See Also: HABIT

Adaptable as a Norwegian wharf rat —James Mills

Adjustable as prices of goods sold in a flea market —Anon

Adjust to as your eyes adjust to darkness or sudden light —Anon

Be pliable like a reed, not rigid like a cedar —Rabbi Simeon ben Eleazar

Elastic as a criminal's conscience —Anon

Elastic as a steel spring —Anon

Flexible as a diplomat's conscience —Anon

Flexible as figures in the hands of the statistician —Israel Zangwill

Flexible as silk —Ouida

Has as much give as a tree trunk —Jimmy Breslin

Implacable an adversary as a wife suing for alimony —William Wycherly

(Softly, unhurriedly but) implacably, like a great river flowing on and on —Harvey Swados

Inflexible as a marble pillar —Anon

Inflexible as steel —Ouida

Inflexible as the rings of hell —John Cheever

Intractable as a driven ghost —Sylvia Plath

Like all weak men he laid an exaggerated stress on not changing one's mind —W. Somerset Maugham

(The adolescent personality is as) malleable as infant flesh —Barbara Lazear Acher, *New York Times*, October 23, 1986

The man who never alters his opinion is like standing water, and breeds reptiles of the mind —William Blake

Mind set like concrete —George Garrett

Pliable as wax —James Shirley

Pliant as cloth —Eugene Sue

Pliant as flesh —Linda Pastan

Rigidity yielding a little, like justice swayed by mercy, is the whole beauty of the earth —G. K. Chesterton

Set as a piece of sculpture —Charles Dickens

[She did not even pretend there would be another meeting. It was] as final as death —Laura Moriarty, *The Chaprone*

They made their hearts as an adamant stone —The Holy Bible/Apocrypha

A variation from "Hearts firm as stone" and "Cold as stone" from the Book of Job

Uncompromising as a policeman's club —Anon

Uncompromising as justice —William Lloyd Garrison

(There he was, as) unshakable as granite —Frank Swinnerton

♣ FLOWERS

See Also: NATURE

All white scented flowers, like the perfume of love in fresh sheets —Janet Flanner

Blossoms covered trees like colored powder puffs —Rita Mae Brown

Blossoms … fell to the ground like confetti —Shelby Hearon

Bluebells like grey lace —Joan Aiken

Bougainvillea … large as basketballs —William Faulkner

The bud came apart … its layers like small velvet shells —Eudora Welty

The flowers burned on their stalks like yellow tongues of flame —Dorothy Canfield

Flowers burst like bombs —Vachel Lindsay

Forsythia … sprawling like yellow amoebae —A. R. Ammons

A host of crocuses stood up like yellow trumpets —Howard Spring

Irises, rising beautiful and cool on their tall stalks, like blown glass —Margaret Atwood

The jonquils glowed like candles —Helen Hudson

Lilies bunched together in a frill of green … like faded cauliflowers —Katherine Mansfield

The little red and yellow flowers were out on the grass, like floating lamps —Virginia Woolf

Magnolia flowers … like rosettes carved in alabaster —Edith Wharton

Oleanders with their pink flowers like something spun out of sugar —George Garrett

Open blooms like ballet-skirted ladies —John Steinbeck

Orange and yellow poppies like just-lit matches sputtering in the breeze —John

Out of the earth came whole troops of flowers, like motley stars —Felix Salten

Patches of tiny wildflowers … like luminous rugs on the grass —Gina Berriault

Pink roses blooming like flesh —Bin Ramke

The plants sprang up thick as winter grass —Annette Sanford

Primroses waving gently like lazy yellow gloves —George Garrett

Roses, big as a man's fist and red as blood —Eudora Welty

Rows of white flowers … throwing shadows on the azure-colored ground like trails of shooting stars —Gustave Flaubert

Small blue flowers like points of sky —Philip Levine

The simile launches Levine's poem "The Voice."

The tiny yellow flowers danced underfoot, like jewels in the dust —Mary Stewart

The tulip-beds across the road flamed like throbbing rings of fire —Oscar Wilde

Tulips … bright as the showers —Dame Edith Sittwell

Variations of flowers are like variations in music, often beautiful as such, but almost always inferior to the theme on which they are founded —the original air —Leigh Hunt

The yellow dandelions rose up like streaks of golden light —Guy de Maupassant

♣ FOG

See Also: MIST

A churning mass of fog was welling up from the sea like a tidal wave —John Dos Passos

Fog closed in like a long sigh —George Garrett

Fog … dissolving into the sky like milk in water —Ross Macdonald

The fog … floated into the garden like gauze —Ludwig Bemelmans

Fog hung above the road like an alien intelligence —Charles Johnson

Foggy as London —Robert Traver

The fog rolled off the river like a woman rolling off a bed —Marianne Wiggins

The fog smothered sounds like an acoustical curtain —Margaret Millar

Fog that came like bitter smoke —Stephen Vincent Benét

(Pines ... wrapped with) fog that moved like bits of cloth in the wind —Shirley Ann Grau

A fog wandering like a pilgrim —Patricia Hampl

The fog was settling in and became rapidly denser. It was like wading about in dark milk soup —Erich Maria Remarque

The fog was thick and strangely white. Like wet bed sheets —Bertolt Brecht

Haze ... like a thin smoke from slowly burning money —Ross Macdonald

Night fog thick as terry cloth —Maxine Kumin

Puffs of white fog which hung there like frozen cabbage —Donald McCaig

There's a fog at the waists of the trees, like a sash —William Matthews, *A Happy Childhood*

Wreaths of white fog walked like ghosts the haunted meadows —John Greenleaf Whittier

♣ FOOD AND DRINK

See Also: EATING AND DRINKING

Appetizing as a boiled cocktail —H. L. Mencken

Blackberries big as the ball of my thumb, and dumb as eyes —Sylvia Plath

A bottle of wine brings as much pleasure as the acquisition of a kingdom, and not unlike it in kind: the senses in both cases are confused and perverted —Walter Savage Landor

The brandy went to Whit's stomach like a saber cut —John Farris

Cake ... beautiful as a palace —tall, shining and pink, outlined with balconies and battlements of white frosting —Ruth Prawer Jhabvala

Cakes ... iced like the rock of Gibraltar —Penelope Gilliatt

A chocolate [birthday] cake ... lit up like an oil refinery —Tom Robbins

Coffee ... black as the devil, hot as hell, pure as an angel, sweet as love. —Charles de Talleyrand

Talleyrand's description of good coffee once again illustrates how a simile which may sound trite by itself, will gain new momentum when appropriately combined with two or three others.

Coffee ... it tasted like swamp water —William Beechcroft

Coffee-pots breathing wisps of steam like old men talking in winter —J. G. Farrell

Coffee should be black as hell, strong as death, and sweet as love —Turkish proverb

Coffee ... tasted like a third pressing —Derek Lambert

I consider supper as a turnpike through which one pass in order to get to bed —Oliver Edwards

The inspiration for Edwards' simile was Samuel Johnson declaration that he never ate supper.

Cooking is like love. It should be entered into with abandon or not at all —Harriet Van Horn, *Vogue*, October 15, 1956

Croissants, light and warm as birds —Pat Conroy

The dining room table steamed [with hot food] like a caldron —Dan Wakefield

A fish without bones is like an artichoke without leaves, a coconut without a shell, a lobster without a carapace —Anon, from an item on an Idaho company which is trying to breed boneless fish, *New York Times* November 5, 1986

Food is a narcotic in a way, like alcohol —Edna Ferber

Good coffee is like friendship: rich and warm and strong —Slogan, Pan American Coffee Bureau, 1961

A good cook is like a sorceress who dispenses happiness —Elsa Schiaparelli

[Soup] Hot as an adulterous love —Erica Jong

This description from a poem entitled "Chinese Food," pertains to hot and sour soup. It is preceded by two other similes: "Dense as water … sour as death."

It [beer] touched his stomach like petrol on live ashes —Caryl Phillips

It [water] was heavy, tepid, and savorless and like castor oil —Vicki Baum

Lamb … hard as a wood chip … cold as Christmas —Richard Ford

Left their eggs up until the whites were glazed like plastic —Daniela Gioseffi

Lettuces like garlands of faint green roses —Cynthia Ozick

The liquid [broth] went down my throat like bones. —Maya Angelou

Margaritas flow like the Colorado River in March —Bryan Miller reviewing a Mexican restaurant, *New York Times* August 1, 1986

Martinis yellow as the rose and warm as summer rain —E. B. White

Pears … like too many women their beauty condemns them to uselessness —Bin Ramke

Pears … shapely as violins —Babette Deutsch

Rice … sticky as a snowball —Ira Wood

Roast beef, which tasted … like the uppers of an old pair of pumps —Shelby Hearon

A scrambled egg that tasted as if it had just hatched in the refrigerator —Richard S. Prather

Sherry … as thin and dry as benzene —Philip Levine

Slices the bread … into thin volumes like poetry —Sharon Sheehe Stark

Steam rose like incense from the bowl [of hot soup) —Joanna Higgins

Stick as close to that kitchen [where a gourmet cook is in residence] as the croute to a pate or the mayonnaise to an oeuf —Angela Carter

Tea … liquid and warm, like weeping —Margaret Drabble

To expand upon the comparison, The author added: "It replaced the tears."

To drink a glass of sherry when you can get a dry Martini is like taking a stagecoach when you can travel by the Orient Express —W. Somerset Maugham

Unripe oranges like dark-green golf balls —Ross Macdonald

The yolk of one of the eggs had leaked out onto the plate like a miniature pool of yellow blood —Ross Macdonald

❧ FOOLISHNESS

See Also: ABSURDITY, FUTILITY, STUPIDITY

As giddy as a drunken man —Charles Dickens, *A Christmas Carol*

This is the last of a whole string of similes uttered by a reformed Scrooge in A Christmas Carol. *"I'm as light as a feather, I am as happy as an angel, I'm as merry as a schoolboy. I am as giddy as a drunken man. A merry Christmas to everybody! A happy New Year to all the world."*

A blockhead is as ridiculous when he talks as is a goose when it flies —Lord Halifax

The words "talks" and "flies" have been modernized from the old English "talketh" and "flieth."

Comparing them [American and Oriental women] is like comparing oven broilers and banties —Bobbie Ann Mason

Felt foolishness drag like excess flesh on his face —Sharon Sheehe Stark

Foolish as to cut off the head to preserve the hair —Anon

An alternative to the cliché "As foolish as to cut off your nose to spite your face."

Foolish as to judge a horse by its harness —Anon

A fool is like other men as long as he is silent —Jacob Cats

A fool … says little, but that little said owes all its weight, like loaded dice, to lead —William Cowper

Gullible as geese —Anon

How foolish one would be to climb into the ring with love and try to trade blows with him, like a boxer —Sophocles

If all fools wore white caps, we should look like a flock of geese —English proverb

I'll not be a fool like the nightingale who is up till midnight without any ale —Dylan Thomas

Life's little suckers chirp like crickets while spending all on losing tickets —Ogden Nash

Lightheaded as a thistle —Mary Lavin

A man who commits suicide is like a man who longs for a gate to be opened and who cuts his throat before he reaches the gate —Dylan Thomas

Senseless … it's like wearing a bullet proof vest with a hole over the heart —Senator John Heinz, December, 1985, news item

Unrealistic … like someone who eats like a linebacker but yearns for the shape of a fashion model —Anon

❧ FOOTBALL

See Also: SPORTS

The ball just skittered around in the backfield like a puck on ice —Jonathan Valin

The ball peeled his head like an onion —Ken Stabler and Berry Stainback

Both players bounce up like toys —Richard Ford

My teammates were cringing in the huddle, like those scurvy hounds who live off garbage at county landfill projects —Pat Conroy

Passes faltered and tumbled like wounded ducks —James Crumley

Passes swerved like a diving duck —Y. A. Tittle, New York Giants quarterback quoted in *New York Times,* January 12, 1987

Tittle's simile dates back to 1962 when his team won the playoff game for the National Football League championship.

Pro football is like nuclear warfare. There are no winners, only survivors —Frank Gifford, *Sports Illustrated,* June 4, 1960

[Gary Anderson of the Miami Dolphins] runs like a locomotive —Craig James, Anderson's teammate, *New York Times,* September 10, 1986

Some of them [professional players] always look like brooding Pillsbury Doughboys and some of them look wizened from the start, middle-aged and beaten down, as if they'd never known what it was like to be young —Jonathan Valin

To me football is like a day off. I grew up picking cotton on my daddy's farm and nobody asked for your autograph or put your name in the paper for that —Lee Roy Jordan

Treated his players as if he had bought them at auction with a ring in their noses and was trying not to notice they smelled bad —Jim Murray about football coach Paul Brown, *Los Angeles Herald,* 1986

[Football] uniforms … heavy as mattresses —Lael Wertenbaker

When you hit that line, it gave like a sponge, and when you tackled that big long Swede, he went down like he'd been hit by lightning —Sinclair Lewis

Without a network outlet, football will disappear like cigar smoke in the wind —Harvey Meyerson, summation at NFL-USFL trial, 1986

❧ FORCEFULNESS

See: POWER

❧ FOREBODING

See: ANXIETY, FEAR

❧ FOREHEAD

See Also: FACE(S)

The artery in his forehead bulged like a snake —Richard Ford

Brow like masonry —Ted Hughes

Forehead … as wrinkled as a washboard —Harvey Swados

Forehead like a bright new moon —*Arabian Nights*

(A slim girl with) a forehead which was shiny and protuberant, like a Bartlett pear —George Ade

Forehead, with wrinkles like lines drawn all over it —Ivan Turgenev

Her forehead shines like the gleam of morning —*Arabian Nights*

A high forehead with a soft vein running indirectly down the middle like an aimless trickle of water on a windowpane —John Hersey

His brows became contorted with thick frowns, like a bull's forehead —V.S. Pritchett

His brow swells out over his face like an eroded riverbank —T. Coraghessan Boyle

His forehead bulged [with fury] as if he were horned —Jonathan Valin

His forehead rose like a gleaming dome towards the crown of his bald head —Alexander Solzhenitsyn

A pair of thin horizontal lines, like furrows in a meadow of snow, appeared on her forehead —Bill Pronzini

The skin [on a character's forehead] was wrinkled into long horizontal lines, like lines of inquiry —Dan Jacobson

❧ FORGETFULNESS
See: MEMORY, MIND

❧ FORGIVENESS

Forgiving the unrepentant is like drawing pictures in water —Japanese proverb

(God) pardons like a mother who kisses away the repentant tears of her child —Henry Ward Beecher

Forgiving without forgetting is like loving without liking —Anon

Overlooked as a favorite child's failings —Anon

(God) pardons like a mother who kisses away the repentant tears of her child —Henry Ward Beecher

❧ FORLORNNESS
See: ABANDONMENT, ALONENESS

❧ FORMALITY
See Also: ORDER/DISORDER

Formal and self-conscious as a football team in a photograph —George Garrett

Formal as a Japanese print —Ramon Delgado

Formal as an undertaker —William McIlvanney

Informal as paper napkins —Dee Weber

Ordered … like a nun's evening prayers —Charles Hanson Towne

This simile is extracted from the first stanza of Towne's poem "The Best Road of All," in which he writes about the best road being that which leads to God. The simile in full context reads: "I like … a road that is an ordered road, like a nun's evening prayers."

❧ FORTUNE/MISFORTUNE

Adversity was spreading over him like mold —Irvin S. Cobb

Bad moments, like good ones, tend to be grouped together —Edna O'Brien

Blessed as the meek who shall inherit the earth —Anon

This illustrates how a quote can be transposed into a simile.

The day of fortune is like a harvest day, we must be busy when the corn is ripe —Johann Wolfgang von Goethe

Disasters … rolling in the brain like pebbles —Denise Levertov

Fortune is as … brittle as glass —Publilius Syrus

Fortune is like glass: she breaks when she is brightest —Latin proverb

Fortune is like the market, where if you will bide your time the price will fall —German proverb

A variation by Francis Bacon begins like the above and finishes as follows: "If you can stay a little, the price will fall."

Fortunes made in no time are like shirts made in no time; it's ten to one if they hang long together —Douglas Jerrold

Fortune sits on him like a ton of shit —Irving Feldman

Fortunes made in no time are like shirts made in no time; it's ten to one if they hang long together—Douglas Jerrold

Good fortune, like ripe fruit, ought to be enjoyed while it is present —Epictetus

Good fortune seemed to be following me like a huge affectionate dog —John Braine

It's a nightmare like trying to conquer the Himalayas on roller skates or swim the English Channel lashed to a cannon —T. Coraghessan Boyle

Lord it's like a hard candy Christmas / I'm barely getting through tomorrow —Carol Hall, "Hard Candy Christmas," *The Best Little Whorehouse in Texas*

Luck is like having a rice dumpling fly into your mouth —Japanese proverb

A luckless man … the kind of man who would have gotten two complimentary tickets for the *Titanic* —William McIlvanney

The actual text in Scotch author McIlvanney's Papers of Tony Veitch reads: "The kinnaa man woulda got two complimentary tickets for the Titanic."

Luck shines in his face like good health —Anon

Misfortunes disappeared, as though swept away by a great flood of sunlight —Émile Zola

Misfortunes, like the owl, avoid the light —Charles Churchill

Misfortunes … passed over her like wild geese —Ellen Glasgow

Mishaps are like knives, that either serve us or cut us, as we grasp them by the blade or the handle —James Russell Lowell

The storms of adversity, like those of the ocean, rouse the faculties —Captain Frederick Marryatt

Sweet are the uses of adversity which, like the toad, ugly and venomous, wears yet a precious jewel in his head —William Shakespeare, *As You Like It*

Tried to conceal his misfortune as if it were a vice —Mikhail Lermontov

To wait for luck is like waiting for death —Japanese proverb

❧ FRAGILITY

See Also: WEAKNESS

As thin of substance as the air —William Shakespeare, *Romeo and Juliet*

Bones frail as a small bird's —George Garrett

Brittle as a dead tree —George Garrett

Brittle as dry wood —Miller Williams

Brittle as glass that breaks with a touch —Algernon Charles Swinburne

Brittle as straw —Ellen Glasgow

Brittle as twigs —Margaret Atwood

(Her own body seemed) fragile and empty like blown glass —Margaret Atwood

(Laughter … as) delicate and frail as new ice —Frederick Barthelme

(She was) delicate as a pig was not —Pat Conroy

Fragile and rather beautiful, like a rare kind of mosquito —Lawrence Durrell

Fragile as a bird's egg —George Garrett

Fragile as a chrysalis —John Updike

Fragile as a coquillage bouquet —Truman Capote
Capote's simile refers to Isak Dinesen.

Fragile as a cup —Reynolds Price

(Shoulder) fragile as a little bit of glass —Eudora Welty

Fragile as ancient lace or parchment —George Garrett

Fragile as a reed —Cornelia Otis Skinner

(Her conical breasts look) fragile as birds' eggs —R. V. Cassill

Fragile as snowflakes —Sharon Sheehe Stark

(She felt very weak and her plump body seemed, somehow, flat and) fragile, like a pressed leaf between the sheets —Helen Hudson

Fragile … like a spider's web —John Fowles

Fragile like her good intentions —Marguerite Yourcenar

Fragile, like the skin on scalded milk —Sharon Sheehe Stark

Frail as a blade of grass —Belva Plain

(She felt as) frail as a cobweb —Jonathan Kellerman

Frail as a fading friendship —Anon

Frail as antique earthenware —Sylvia Plath
Plath's simile describes the occupants of an old ladies' home.

Frail as April snow —Wallace Stevens

(Breasts rising) frail as blisters —Sharon Olds

Frail as flesh —Laman Blanchard

[School boys] Frail, like thin-boned fledgling birds clamoring for food —Sylvia Berkman

I feel [fragile] like a poppy; one gust of wind and everything will blow away —Carla Lane, dialogue "Solo," British sitcom, broadcast June 23, 1987
The reason the character in Lane's script feels so fragile is that she is a woman in her fifties in a relationship with a much younger man.

I felt like a moth hanging on the windowpane —Jacqueline Kennedy, *Newsweek*, January 21, 1961
The occasion being described was the first night in White House.

Insubstantial … like fake wedding cakes in a bakery window—lots of whipped cream rosettes and garlands surrounding a hollow middle —Michiko Kakutan, *New York Times*

Like a dry leaf closed into a book, he seemed frail and ready to crumble —Arthur A. Cohen

More frail than the shadows on glasses —Algernon Charles Swinburne

Promise as solid as a bundle of water —Hindu proverb

(Hair and garments) tenuous as gauze —W. D. Snodgrass

(You're so old) you're like a cup I could break in my hand —Paule Marshall

❧ FRANKNESS
See Also: CANDOR

❧ FRAUD
See Also: CRIME, DISHONESTY

❧ FRECKLES
See Also: FACIAL DETAILS

❧ FREEDOM

Abstract liberty, like other mere abstractions, is not to be found —Edmund Burke

(They just) broke free like the water —Boris Pasternak

Broke free like the sun rising out of the sea —Miller Williams

Feels freedom like oxygen everywhere around him —John Updike

Felt like a volatile gas released from a bottle —Olivia Manning

Foot-loose as a ram —Irvin S. Cobb

(I am) free as a breeze, free like a bird in the woodland wild, free like a gypsy, free like a child —Oscar Hammerstein II, from lyric for *Oklahoma*

Hammerstein used the multiple simile to paint a picture of an unattached man bemoaning the speed with which his situation can change.

Free as a fat bird —John D. MacDonald

Free as air —Alexander Pope

The simile in full context is as follows: "Love, free as air at sight of human ties, spreads his light wings, and in a moment flies."

Free as a pig in a pen —Anon, from American song, "The Lane County Bachelor"

Free, as happens in the downfall of habit when the mind, like an unguarded flame, bows and bends and seems about to blow from its holding —Virginia Woolf

Free as is the wind —Anon

A popular variation attributed to James Montgomery is "Free as the breeze."

Free as Nature first made man —John Dryden

Free as Nature is —James Thompson

Free as the grace of God and twice as plentiful —Anon

Freed, like colored kites torn loose from their strings —Rainer Maria Rilke

Freedom and responsibility are like Siamese twins, they die if they are parted —Lillian Smith

Freedom is like drink. If you take any at all, you might as well take enough to make you happy for a while —Finley Peter Dunne

Several words have been changed from Dunne's dialect: any was "nny," for was "f'r.'

Free speech is like garlic. If you are perfectly sure of yourself, you enjoy it and your friends tolerate it —Lynn White, Jr., *Look*, April 17, 1956

Free will and determinism are like a game of cards. The hand that is dealt you represents determinism. The way you play your hand represents free will —Norman Cousins

Independence, like honor, is a rocky island without a beach —Napoleon Bonaparte

Independent as a hog on ice —American colloquialism, attributed to New England

Independent as a wild horse —Anon

According to Irving Stone, author of The Passionate Journey, *this simile was used to describe the father of his fictional biography's hero, John Noble.*

A laissez-faire policy is like spoiling a child by saying he'll turn out all right in the end. He will, if he's made to —F. Scott Fitzgerald

Liberty, like charity must begin at home —James Conant

Yet another twist on the much adopted and adapted charity comparison.

Like a bird on a wire, like a drunk in a midnight choir I have tried in my way to be free —Leonard Cohen, "Bird on the Wire"

Perfect freedom is as necessary to the health and vigor of commerce, as it is to the health and vigor of citizenship —Patrick Henry

There is no such thing as an achieved liberty; like electricity, there can be no substantial storage [of liberty] and it must be generated as it is enjoyed, or the lights go out —Robert H. Jackson

Unrestricted like the rain —Mark Twain

We were free like water —Rob Thomas, "Ever the Same Again"

♣ FRESHNESS

[She looks as] clear as morning roses newly washed with dew —William Shakespeare, *The Taming of the Shrew*

Fresh as a daisy —Slogan, June Dairy Products Co.

Fresh as an unveiled statue —Henry James

Fresh as any rose —John Lydgate

The natural association between freshness and flowers has made this simile and its variants a common expression. The daisy rivals the rose as a popular comparison.

(Looking as) fresh as apple blossom among the tender leaves of late spring —Frank Swinnerton

Fresh as April grass —Karl Shapiro

Fresh [in the face] as a rain-washed rose —Reynolds Price

Fresh as a spring morning —Slogan, Little America Frozen Foods, Inc.

Fresh as hope —Susan Engberg

Fresh as paint —Francis Edward Smedley

Fresh as the dawn —Anon

An extension used as a slogan by Pacific Egg Producers: "Fresh as dewy dawn."

Fresh as the month of May —Geoffrey Chaucer

The above is modernized from, "As fresh as is the month of May."

Fresh as salt-drenched skin —Theodore Roethke

Fresh as the morning —Slogan, Campbell's corn flakes

Fresh as the morning wind that tatters the mist —Marge Piercy

Fresh as thyme or parsley —W. H. Auden

Fresh as tomorrow —James G. Hueneker

Fresh as yesterday —Shelby Hearon

In Heron's novel A Small Town, *what's fresh is a family feud.*

Fresh like frilled linen clean from a laundry —Virginia Woolf

♣ FRIENDLINESS

See: SOCIABILITY

♣ FRIENDSHIP

See Also: LOVE, SOCIABILITY

An acquaintanceship, if all goes well, can linger in the memory like an appealing chord of music, while a friendship, or even a friendship that deteriorates into an enemy ship, so to put it, is like a whole symphony, even if the music is frequently unacceptable, broken, loud and in other ways painful to hear —William Saroyan

Became like old friends, the kind who can't leave each other on deathbeds —Thomas McGuane

Comradeship … burned and flamed like dry straw on fire —Stephen Longstreet

Early friends drop out, like milk teeth —Graham Greene

Every man is like the company he won't keep —Euripides

An ironic twist on "A man is known by the company he keeps," and "Tell me the company you keep and I'll tell you who you are."

Friendship ought to be a gratuitous joy, like the joys recorded by art or life —Simone Weil

Friendship … should, like a well-stocked cellar, be … continually renewed —Samuel Johnson

A friendship that like love is warm; a love like friendship steady —Thomas Moore

Friendship with Cape was like climbing a ladder. You had to wait a while on each rung before he invited you to climb the next —Robert Campbell

Friends just can't be found / Like a bridge over troubled water / … If you need a friend / I'm sailing right behind / Like a bridge over troubled water" —Paul Simon and Art Garfunkel, from lyrics to song "Bridge Over Troubled Water"

Friends … slipping from his orbit like bees from a jaded flower —Beryl Markham

friends were like clothes: fine while they lasted but eventually they wore thin or you grew out of them —David Nicholls, *One Day*

He who helps a friend in woe is like a fur coat in the snow —Russian proverb

I keep my friends as misers do their treasure —Pietro Aretino

Aretino's simile dating back to the sixteenth century was followed by this explanation: "Because of all the things granted us by wisdom, none is greater or better than friendship."

Ill company is like a dog, who dirts those most whom he loves best —Jonathan Swift

In their friendship they were like two of a litter that can never play together without leaving traces of tooth and claw, wounding each other in the most sensitive places —Colette

It is as foolish to make experiments upon the constancy of a friend, as upon the chastity of a wife —Samuel Johnson

Life without a friend is like life without sun —Spanish proverb

Life without a friend is death with a vengeance —Thomas Fuller

Life without a friend is death without a witness —John Ray's *Proverbs*

Life without a friend is like life without sun —Spanish proverb

The light of friendship is like the light of phosphorous, seen plainest when all around is dark —Robert Crowell

Like old friends they wear well —Slogan, Meyer gloves

The loss of a friend is like that of a limb; time may heal the anguish of the wound, but the loss cannot be repaired —Robert Southey

My friendship [with Vita Sackville-West] is over. Not with a quarrel, not with a bang, but as a ripe fruit falls —Virginia Woolf, March 11, 1935 diary entry

A new friend is like new wine; you do not enjoy drinking it until it has matured —Ben Sira

A new friend is a new wine —The Holy Bible/ Apocrypha

Their association together possessed a curiously unrelenting quality, like the union of partners in a business rather than the intimacy of friends —Anthony Powell

Their friendship was like a wilted bunch of flowers that she insisted on topping up with water —David Nicholls, *One Day*

Went through our friendships like Epsom salts, draining us, no apologies, no regrets —Rosa Guy

Without a friend the world is a wilderness —John Ray's *Proverbs*

❦ FRIENDSHIP, DEFINED

Acquaintances … they're like weeds; they grow up around the real friends and choke them off —Christopher Isherwood

A broken friendship, like a broken cup, can be mended but it will never be perfect again —Anon

This can be traced to the Latin proverb "A broken friendship may be soldered but will never be sound."

A cheerful friend is like a sunny day which spreads its brightness on all around —Sir John Lubbock

Choose your friends like your books, few but choice books —James Howell

The false friend is like the shadow of a sundial —French proverb

False friends, like birds, migrate in cold weather —Anon

The feeling of friendship is like that of being comfortably filled with roastbeef; love like being enlivened with champagne —Samuel Johnson

A friendless man is like a left hand without a right —Hebrew proverb

Friends are like fiddle-strings, they must not be screwed too tight —John Ray's *Proverbs*

Friends are like melons. Shall I tell you why? To find one good, you must a hundred try —Claude Mermet

Friendship is like money, easier made than kept —Samuel Butler

Friendship is like a treasury; you cannot take from it more than you put into it —Benjamin Mandelstamm

Friendship is like two clocks keeping time —Anon

Friendship is love without his wings —Lord Byron

A friendship like a soft pillow that made her feel secure and bolstered —Mary Gordon

Friendship, like credit, is highest where it is not used —Elbert Hubbard

Friendship, like love, is destroyed by long absence, though it may be increased by short intermission —Samuel Johnson

Friendship, like love, is but a name —John Gay

Friendship, like the immortality of the soul, is too good to be believed —Ralph Waldo Emerson

The friendship of a great man is like the shadow of a bush soon gone —French proverb

A group of good friends is like the relatives you wish you'd been born with —Anon

A twist in simile form of, "You can't pick your relatives, but you can pick your friends."

A hollow friendship is like a hollow tooth —it's always best to have it out at once —*Punch*, 1862

I find friendship … like wine, raw when new, ripened with age, the true old man's milk and restorative cordial —Thomas Jefferson

An old friendship is like old wine; the longer it lasts the stronger it grows —Antonio Perez

Old friendships are like meats served up repeatedly, cold, comfortless and distasteful —William Hazlitt

Some friends are like the shadow; they follow us when our sun shines —Moses Ephraim Kuh

A variation of this attributed to Christian Nestell Bovee is, "False friends are like our shadow, keeping close to us while we walk in the sunshine, but leaving us the instant we cross into the shadow."

Some friends are like a sundial: useless when the sun sets —Judah Jeiteles

An untried friend is like an uncracked nut —Russian proverb

♣ FROWNS

See Also: FACIAL EXPRESSIONS, MICELLANEOUS; LOOKS; STARES

A dark scowl playing on his face like a spotlight —Jonathan Valin

Face was screwed up as if he had a stomach ache —Nina Bawden

Frowning like the Mask of Tragedy —Max Shulman

Frowned like a public character conscious of the interested stares of a large crowd but determined not to take notice of them —Joyce Cary

Frowning, as if at some infernal machine —Elizabeth Taylor

Frowning like a battered old bison who'd spent too many years at the zoo —Jonathan Kellerman

Frowning like a cat at a mouse hole —John Updike

The frown like serpents basking on the brow —Wallace Stevens

Glared at me like a wolf in a trap —Robert Traver

Glared slightly … like a judge intent upon some terrible evidence —Flannery O'Connor

Glares at me like a starving wolf from the forest —Bernard Malamud

Glares at us, his eyes like the barrels of a shotgun —T. Coraghessan Boyle

He was frowning, which tensed his small face up and made his deep pockmarks look like holes that went clear through his cheeks —Larry McMurtry

His lips curled away from his teeth like he was exposing so many switchblade knives —Donald McCaig

His scowl crinkled like crushed paper —F. Scott Fitzgerald

Like a ruffled old eagle on a high, bare rock, she scowled at the setting sun —Louis Auchincloss

A reddened grimace of hate and fury, like a primitive mask in a museum —Iris Murdoch

Scowl like a cap pulled over the brow —Peter De Vries

Scowl like a child about to receive an injection —Laurie Colwin

Scowl, like he'd turn a cold into cancer if you crossed him —J. W. Rider

The scowler is a doctor.

Scowled like a junkyard dog —Jay Parini

Teeth bared like the rats —Eudora Welty

❧ FRUSTRATION

See Also: DEJECTION, EMOTIONS

Feel so useless ... like a still life —Margaret Drabble

(I'm as) frustrated as a dog on a chain —Anton Chekhov

Frustrated [about career] ... as though she were peanut butter that was forced into a hypodermic syringe —Ann Jasperson

Frustration ... began to creep up his neck like a hot hand —Flannery O'Connor

Frustration lingered between her legs like an ache —Susan Lois

(The writing is becoming) more and more impossible ... I'm like a toad squashed by a paving stone, like a dog with its guts crushed out by a shit-wagon, like a clot of snot under a policeman's boot, etc. —Gustave Flaubert

(The reporters are still) running around like blind dogs in a meat house —James Reston, *New York Times*/ The Changing Guard, February 22, 1987

❧ FUN

See: PLEASURE

❧ FURNITURE AND FURNISHINGS

See Also: HOUSES, ROOMS

Armchairs angular as choir stalls —Julia O'Faolain

Bed that sagged like a hammock —John D. MacDonald

The big oriental rug glowed like a garden of exotic flowers —George Garrett

(In a mirrored room) carpeted like spring grass —William Humphrey

The carpet ... felt like fur laid over clouds —Alice McDermott

Carpeting as soft underfoot as moss —Sue Grafton

Carpets threadbare like ancient shrouds —Jaroslav Seifert

The chairs and tables looked like poor relations who had repaid their keep by a long career of grudging usefulness —Edith Wharton

Chairs that looked and felt like unbaked bread dough —Jonathan Kellerman

Chandeliers as big as locomotives —Mark Helprin

Chandeliers like crystal clouds —Gavin Lyall

Chinese lanterns ... hanging like fiery fruit —Babette Deutsch

A clock clucked like some drowsy hen on the wall —V.S. Pritchett

Colored plates, like crude carnival wheels —V.S. Pritchett

Curtain of red velvet drawn apart like lips —Beverly Farmer

Curtains billow ... as if large birds were caught in them —Charles Simic

Curtains billowed slightly like loose clothing —Bin Ramke

The curtains fluttered coyly like ladies' skirts —Margaret Millar

Curtains, flying out like flags from the opened, seaward window —Elizabeth Taylor

The curtains over the open window next to them billow suddenly like an enormous cloud —Tony Ardizzone

This simile concludes Addizzone's story, The Evening News.

Each time I'm inside [an apartment] all is precisely as it was the time before, as if riveted in place —Richard Ford

An electric night lamp that looks like a big firefly that might have come in through half-open window —Marguerite Yourcenar

The furniture around me thick as elephants —Richard Ford

Furniture like mismatched plates —Jonathan Valin

Furniture with legs like those of a very fat woman planted firmly and holding her ground —Linda West Eckhardt

A hard bench about as comfortable as a gridiron —Emily Eden

Huge chandeliers, like clusters of grapes —Helen Hudson

Lace curtains from the parlor flying like flags in the summer sky —Sharon Olds

Long gauze curtains flapping out the open window like ghosts waving —Dianne Benedict

One's chairs and tables get to be almost part of one's life, and to seem like quiet friends —Jerome K. Jerome

A polychromatic rug like some brilliant-flowered rectangular, tropical islet —O. Henry

Shadows [of flowers on window-sill] on curtains … waving like swans dipping their beaks in water —Jean Rhys

The sheets were like blankets of dry snow —Sherwood Anderson, *Winesburg, Ohio*

Some aura of grief and transient desperation clings to the curtains and the shabby upholstery like a sour breath —Herbert Lieberman

The swinging-to of a shutter was like the nervous and involuntary flicker of an eyelid —Elizabeth Bowen

The table [set for party] bloomed like a miracle of shining damask and silver spoons —Elinor Wylie

(Grandma's old long wooden dining-room) table, kept as bare and shining as an ad for spar varnish —Robert Traver

Table lamps with shades like extravagant hats —John Rechy

A threadbare carpet that looked like frayed paper —Heinrich Böll

The waxed (rectangular) table shone like a black lake —Alice McDermott

A white curtain like a wedding veil —Beverly Farmer

❧ FURITIVENESS
See: SECRECY

❧ FURY
See: ANGER

❧ FUTILITY
See Also: ABSURDITY, DIFFICULTY, IMPOSSIBILITY, USEFULNESS/USELESSNESS

Being a producer around here is like trying to direct a Broadway show full of deaf-mutes —William Diehl

Charging like Don Quixote at the windmills —George Bernard Shaw

Cleaning your house while your kids are still growing is like shoveling the walk before it stops snowing —Phyllis Diller

The twists on everyday life similes to describe ineffective actions are virtually without limit. A few examples: effective "As using a sword against cobwebs," "As trying to plug a hole with Scotch tape," "As waxing a broken car."

Confronting Assistant Secretary of Defense Richard Perle with real arms control is like confronting Dracula with a silver cross: You expect him to make loud noises and thresh about —*Wall Street Journal* editorial, March 25, 1986

Convincing her [to get an abortion]is like trying to convince her the moon's a yo-yo —Ann Beattie

Effective as redecorating a house over a corroding plumbing system —Anon

Explained to, cajoled, and bullied … but he might as well have been boxing with a feather bolster —Lael Wertenbaker

Futile as an attempt to tattoo soap bubbles —Anon

Futile as regret —Edward Arlington Robinson

Futile as to attempt to dust cobwebs off the moon —Anon

Futile as to fight an earthquake with argument —Anon

Futile … like a lacy valentine with a red heart which contains no message of love —Louis Auchincloss

Futile … like emptying a cupful of ants into a butterfly nest for safekeeping —Beryl Bainbridge

Futile [to fight unfounded suspicions] … like fighting with air, a mock battle with blank cartridges —August Strindberg

Futile like Samson pulling the roof down on the Philistine —George Garrett

Futile, like shoveling sand into the sea —Isabel Allende

Futile … like talking to a lake, a chilled lake, no reaction, not a ripple —James Kirkwood

Lending to the feckless is like pelting a stray dog with dumplings —Chinese saying

Like a spent prisoner before the moment of execution, he knew that it was too late for protest —Dorothea Straus

Maintaining classical studies in 1987 is like *Cosmopolitan* magazine obstinately advertising bustles —Dennis O'Brien, *New York Times*, February 12, 1987

O'Brien, a university president, used the comparison to support his argument that college should not be viewed as a product.

Might as well try to teach good manners to a wolf or a wild boar [as to bloody-minded soldiers who have lost whatever religion they may have had] —George Garrett

My efforts [to stir husband out of sense of doom] have been like so many waves, dashing against the Rock of Ages —Robert E. Sherwood

Sherwood wrote this simile for the character of Mary Todd Lincoln in his play Abe Lincoln In Illinois.

(About as) pointless and inglorious as steppin in front of a bus —John Osborne

Pointless as throwing birdseed on the ground while snow still falls fast —Ann Beattie

The prophesying business is like writing fugues; it is fatal to every one save the man of absolute genius —Henry Louis Mencken

Showing emotion [when with uncommunicative father] was like having a snow ball fight with a brick wall —Ann Jasperson

Speculating about it was like robbing last year's bee tree —Borden Deal

To argue with William is like arguing with Vesuvius —Delmore Schwartz

♣ FUTURE

Can see about as far ahead as a goat —Harold Adams

Doomed like a moth —Dame Edith Sitwell

A dreadful prospect, like losing your potency —Harvey Swados

The future comes like an unwelcome guest —Edmund Gosse

The future grows like a scar —Philip Levine

The future is an opaque mirror. Anyone who tries to look into it sees nothing but the dim outlines of an old and worried face —Jim Bishop, *New York Journal-American*, Oct. 15, 1959

The future is like heaven —everyone exalts it but no one wants to go there now —James Baldwin

The future was like a sunny road that wandered through a wide-flung, wooden plain —W. Somerset Maugham

The future was rushing toward her like the jaws of a trap snapping shut —A. E. Maxwell

Great promise [of a brilliant career] ... faded like his imagination —Marguerite Young

He would fly, if he could, fly in search of a future like a sycamore seed —Louis MacNeice

The years stretched before her like some vast blank page spread out to receive the record of her toil —Edith Wharton

♣ GAIETY

See Also: CHEERFULNESS

As merry as a grig —Frank Swinnerton

As merry as a mouse in malt —George Garrett

As merry as forty beggars —Proverb

As merry as notes in a tune —Dame Edith Sitwell

Merry as the day is long —William Shakespeare

> *Shakespeare used this in both* Much Ado About Nothing *and* The Life and Death of King John. *In daily conversation 'cheerful' is often substituted for 'merry.'*

Gay as the latest statistics on cancer or crime —Elyse Sommer

(Yours is) a spirit like a May-day song —Dorothy Parker

Blithe as the air is, and as free —Henry Wadsworth Longfellow

Cavorted like a mule let out to pasture —Borden Deal

Feeling like fourth of July —Stephen Vincent Benét

The gaiety of life, like the beauty and the moral worth of life, is a saving grace, which to ignore is folly, and to destroy is a crime —Agnes Repplier

Gay as a funeral procession —Anon

(As) merry as a condemned man eating his last meal —Elyse Sommer

Gay as a honey-bee humming in June —Amy Lowell

Gay as a parade —Hilda Conklin

Gay as larks —Aesop

> *The use of "gay as" and "merry as" comparisons to larks, crickets and just about any kind of humming or buzzing bird or insect abound throughout the annals of literature as well as in everyday speech.*

Heart ... lighter than a flower —Elinor Wylie

Making merry like grasshoppers —Robinson

A man without mirth is like a wagon without springs, in which one is caused disagreeably to jolt by every pebble over which it turns —Henry Ward Beecher

> *Were Beecher alive today, he might substitute "A car without shock absorbers" for "A wagon without springs"*

(Everything went as) merrily as a marriage bell —W. Somerset Maugham

A merry heart does good like a medicine —The Holy Bible/Proverbs

> *The word "doeth" has been modernized to "does," and the simile is often shortened to "A merry heart is like medicine."*

Mirth is like a flash of lightning, that breaks through a loom of clouds, and litters for a moment —Joseph Addison

♣ GAIT
See: WALKING

♣ GARDEN SCENES
See: FLOWERS, LANDSCAPES, NATURE

❧ GENEROSITY

See: KINDNESS

❧ GENIUS

See: GREATNESS

❧ GENTLENESS

See Also: KINDNESS

As gentle as an old lady singing —Raymond Chandler, *The Long Goodbye*

Gentle as a newborn colt —Rex Reed

> *In Reed's novel,* Personal Effects, *the gentle behavior is that of a man making love.*

(Looked as) gentle as a suckling dove —Arthur Train

Gently as a whisper —Slogan, door checks, Sargent & Co.

Tender as dusk —Jessamyn West

Tenderly as a mother —John Greenleaf Whittier

Tender as young love —Maxwell Anderson

They are as gentle / As zephyrs, blowing below the violet, / Not wagging his sweet head; and yet as rough —William Shakespeare, *Cymbeline*

❧ GESTURES

See: HAND MOVEMENTS

❧ GIDDINESS

See: LIGHTNESS

❧ GIFTS

See: KINDNESS

❧ GLANCE

See: LOOKS

❧ GLIMMER, GLITTER, AND GLOSS

See Also: BRIGHTNESS, LIGHTNING, SHINING

Aglow, like fruit when it colors —William Canton

All ablaze like poppies in the sun —Ouida

All glittering like May sunshine on May Leaves —Alfred, Lord Tennyson

Beams like flowers —Percy Bysshe Shelley

(Bright faces cast thousand) beams upon me, like the sun —William Shakespeare, *King Henry VIII*

Blazing like a jeweled sun —W. S. Gilbert

Blinking like a digital display —Natascha Wodin

A dull sheen, like the white of a hard-boiled egg —T. Coraghessan Boyle

(Eyes) flashed like lightning —Honoré de Balzac

Flashy as the slot machines in a gambling casino —Anon

(Evening) flickers like the midnight sun —Karl Shapiro

Gleam and glitter … like jewels in a dark velvet case —Louis Auchincloss

(His Hair) gleamed like a freshly washed blackboard —Mavis Gallant

[A car] Gleamed like a jewel in a box with an iridescent lining —Robin McCorquodale

(The Hyde Park Library, which was) gleaming like a chrome fender in the afternoon sun —Jonathan Valin

Gleaming like light on water —Beryl Markham

Gleaming like oil on water —Erica Jong

Gleaming like raw meat —James Crumley

Gleaming like water over moon-bright sand —Robert Penn Warren

Gleam like bone —Donald McCaig

Gleam like small change —Sylvia Plath

(The token woman) gleams like a gold molar in a toothless mouth —Marge Piercy

Gleams like a small coin —Philip Levine

Gleams like the cared-for brass of bank buildings —George Garrett

(The necklace) gleams, sharp as malice —Louise Erdrich

(Water) glimmered like a shower of diamonds in the broken moonlight —Joseph Sheridan Le Fanu

Glimmer ... like glow worms twinkling through the shade —Sir Walter Scott

Glimmer, sparkled like a matrix of platinum sequin laid over velvet —Richard Ford

(Eyes ...) glinted ... like crumpled tinfoil —Susan Neville

(Helmets) glinted like nail heads —Derek Walcott

[Shoulders] Glisten as silver —D.H. Lawrence

Glistened, like a globe of burnished gold —Edgar Allan Poe

Glistened like an oiled plum —Jerzy Kosinski

The descriptive frame of reference in The Painted Bird, *from which this is taken, is a snake's head.*

(The empty pavement that) glistened like a wet leather strap —Tadeusz Borowski

[A dog's coat] Glistened like black velvet —Roald Dahl

(Her neck and shoulders) glistened like liquor in a crystal bottle —Paige Mitchell

(Peas) glistened like medieval enamels —Mark Helprin

Glistened like the sun in water —Henry Wadsworth Longfellow

(The van) glistening like opal —MacDonald Harris

Glistening like satin —Ouida

Glisten like melted butter —Marilyn Hacker

[Hair] Glisten like sunshine —D. H. Lawrence

Glistens like the scaling of a snake —Mikhail Lermontov

In Lermontov's A Hero of Our Time, *the comparison refers to a river.*

(Eyes) glittered like a string of Christmas tree icicles —Donald McCaig

Glittered like bracelets —Hans Christian Andersen

Glittered like confetti —Lawrence Durrell

Glittered like steel struck with a bright light —Honoré de Balzac

Glittering like a brook —William Wordsworth

The glitter of the sea was like glass in my eyes —Steve Erickson

[Fruit wet with mist] glowed like a globe of fire —Philip Levine

Glowed like painted glass —Lincoln Kirstein

Glowed like somebody had polished her —J. B. Priestly

The narrator of Priestly's Lost Empires *is describing a showgirl in her costume.*

Glowed like the initials of an illuminated manuscript —Edmund L. Pearson

(His head) glowing like a red sun —Bernard Malamud

Glow like a sunbeam —Alfred, Lord Tennyson

Glow, like moths by light attracted and repelled —Percy Bysshe Shelley

(Water) glows ... like a crystal ball —Edward Hoagland

Glows like a drunk's nose —Hank Searls

Glows like a meteor in the distant North —William Blake

Lights glittering like Oz —Diane Ackerman

Polished like new boots —John Ciardi

Shimmered like the wing of a dragonfly —Eudora Welty

Shimmer like a vision —John Gardner

Sparkled like stars —Percy Bysshe Shelley

(Four tiny black-eyed girls ...) twinkling like Christmas trees —Hart Crane

❧ GLOOM

See Also: BEHAVIOR; DEJECTION; FACIAL EXPRESSIONS, SERIOUS; SADNESS

Bleak and uninviting as an empty hotel room —Jonathan Valin

Bleak as a winter hillside —F. van Wyck Mason

Brain which had become as inhospitable to the brighter side of life as a house without windows is to cheerful lodgers —Bertolt Brecht

Brooded over ... misfortune, like Hamlet or a character in Ibsen —Mary McCarthy

Brooding ... like a martyr —Paul Reidinger

Brooding like a woman unsatisfied —Joanne Selzer

> *The comparison as used by the author in a poem entitled "Summer Heat" refers to the atmosphere after a heavy storm. The simile in its full context beginning as follows: "The air hung heavy after the storm, brooding...."*

Brood like a ghost —Fannie Stearns Gifford

Cheerful as a turkey before Thanksgiving —Anon

> *Variants for changing seasons include: "Cheerful as a rabbit before Easter" and "Cheerful as a goose before Christmas."*

Cold and gray ... like the mortuary —Mike Fredman

Dour as a wet cat —Warren Beck

Felt heavy as Sunday —John Braine

Gloom ... dark and stagnant like a bed of straw for sick livestock —Kenzaburo Oe

Gloom, like a poisonous mist, fills the car —Ira Wood

Gloomy and melancholy, like ghosts —Mark Twain

Gloomy as a beach resort on a wet Sunday in July —Anon

> *This may be inspired by a much-used, also unattributed simile "Gloomy as a graveyard on a wet Sunday afternoon."*

[A house] Gloomy as a crypt —Michael Korda

Gloomy as a tick on Sunday —Grace Paley

Gloomy as a wet holiday —Anon

Gloomy as night —Homer

Glum as a gumboil, as sad as despair —Don Marquis

Glum as a student who's fallen hopelessly behind —John Gardner

Glum as a tongue-tied parrot —Joseph C. Lincoln

Grew clouded and closed, like the dense pallid sky —Sylvia Berkman

Ill-humor is like laziness, for it is a kind of laziness —Johann Wolfgang Von Goethe

It was the kind of day that made suicide look like a reasonable proposition —Mike Fredman

Listen to this guy, he kills me. He's like a filling station of gloom. I go away with a full tank of gloom, it lasts me all day. —Michael Chabon, *The Amazing Adventures of Kavalier & Clay*

Looked like he swallowed a lemon —William Diehl

Melancholy as a defeated politician —Herbert V. Prochnow

Melancholy as a gib (castrated) cat —William Shakespeare, *Henry IV, Part I*

Melancholy sound ... like the weeping of a solitary, deserted human heart —Guy de Maupassant

Moping around like a chicken with the dropsy —Babs H. Deal

(The men grew silent and) morose like lumps of soft coal —Richard Ford

A sense of melancholy had enveloped her like a sheath —Charles Johnson

(My grandmother had) a permanently bleak outlook ... like one of those cartoon characters with a small cloud over their heads —Susan Walton, *New York Times*, June 25, 1987

Somber and unreadable as Latin —Tony Ardizzone

Sour as port decanted too long —Truman Capote

Speak like a death's head —William Shakespeare, *Henry IV, Part II*

Sulked like a bear —Anon

We [3 motorists] drove out the lane like a funeral cortege —Ross Macdonald

♣ GLORY

See: FAME, SUCCESS/FAILURE

♣ GLUTTONY

See: GREED, EATING AND DRINKING

♣ GOD

See: FORGIVENESS, RELIGION

♣ GOLD

See: COLORS, MONEY

♣ GOLF

See Also: SPORTS

Addressed his ball as if he were stroking a cat —P. G. Wodehouse

> *Wodehouse, known for his humorous golf stories, not surprisingly coined many funny golf similes.*

The ball breasting the hill like some untamed jack-rabbit of the California prairie —P. G. Wodehouse

Before making a shot, he would inspect his enormous bag of clubs and take out one after another, slowly, as if he were playing spillikens —P. G. Wodehouse

Brooded over each shot like one whose heart is bowed down by bad news from home —P. G. Wodehouse

Drove as if he were cracking a whip —P. G. Wodehouse

Golf is like a love affair: it you don't take it seriously, it's no fun. If you do take it seriously, it breaks your heart —Arnold Daly, *Reader's Digest*, November, 1933

He stood over his ball, pawing at it with his driving-iron like a cat investigating a tortoise —P. G. Wodehouse

He whiffed that baby [the ball] so bad he torqued like a licorice twist and found his head looking straight behind him like a cockatoo —Joseph Wambaugh

I'm playing like Tarzan —and scoring like Jane —Chi Chi Rodriguez, quoted in the 1987 Masters tournament by Dick Schaap

A man ... with thirty-eight golfless years behind him ... loses all sense of proportion [when he takes up the game] ... like a fly that happens to be sitting on the wall of the dam just when the crack comes —P. G. Wodehouse

Scooped with his mashie as if he were ladling soup —P. G. Wodehouse

Stood addressing his ball [to tee off] like Lot's wife just after she had been turned into a pillar of salt —P. G. Wodehouse

That poor golf ball ... perched on the tee, as naked as a quarterback without a helmet —Dave Anderson, *New York Times*, May 11, 1987

Wielded his midiron like one killing snakes —P. G. Wodehouse

With infinite caution, like one suspecting a trap of some kind, he selected clubs from his bulging bag —P. G. Wodehouse

♣ GOOD HEALTH

See: HEALTH

♣ GOODNESS

See Also: HEART, KINDNESS

Decent men are like Daniel in the lion's den: their survival is a miracle and they do not always survive —George Bernard Shaw, *Heartbreak House*

I think your heart is the eighth wonder of the world. I think your heart is like that record-breaking tower they're building in Dubai that's going to be 2,000 feet tall and have the world's fastest elevator and look like a shining silver spiral reaching —Kate Fodor

♣ GOSSIP

[News in the computer industry] as rife with rumor as the C.I.A. or the National Security Council —Erik Sandberg-Diment, *New York Times* January 25, 1987

Collected them [rumors] as a child might collect matchbooks —W. P. Kinsella

Confirmed gossips are like connoisseurs of cheese; the stuff they relish must be stout —Holman Day

Delivered more gossip than the *National Enquirer* —Joseph Wambaugh

Far and wide the tale was told, like a snowball growing while it rolled —John Greenleaf Whittier

Fond of gossip as an old woman —Ivan Turgenev

An indiscreet man is like an unsealed letter —everybody can read it —Sebastian Shamfort

Little words of speculation drone like bees in a bottle —Beryl Markham

News as roaring in the air like a flight of bees —Truman Capote

News … would have run like a pistol shot through Faithful House [the name of publishing business around which Swinnerton's novel, *Faithful Company,* centers] —Frank Swinnerton

Rumor … it had gone like a fire in dry grass —William Faulkner

Rumors [on Iranian arms scandal's effect on Washington] are spreading like lava from a volcano —Senator Robert Byrd, CBS-TV news program, December 5, 1986

Rumors began to thicken like a terrible blizzard —Susan Fromberg Schaeffer

Rumors … flew like birds out of the unknown —Stephen Crane

Rumors swirled around his name like the waters in a riptide —Peter De Vries

Rumors that rush around … inflating as they go, like giant balloons until somebody comes along to prick them —Vita Sackville-West

Scandal, like a kite, to fly well, depends greatly on the length of the tale it has to carry —*Punch*, 1854

A secret in his [the gossip's] mouth is like a wild bird put into a cage; whose door no sooner opens, but it is out —Ben Jonson

Spits out secrets like hot custard —Thomas Fuller

Stories, like dragons, are hard to kill … If the snake does not, the tale runs still —John Greenleaf Whittier

Tale-bearers are as bad as the talemakers —Richard Brinsley Sheridan

Tell tales out of school like a child —Honoré de Balzac

They come together like the coroner's inquest, to sit upon the murdered reputations of the week —William Congreve

They [a talkative family] fly around with news in their beaks like blue jays —Susan Fromberg Schaeffer

Traded in gossip the way grown-ups play the stock market —Nora Johnson

This comparison by the teen-aged narrator in The World of Henry Orient *would be equally apt without the reference to age.*

Trumpeting it [a secret] … like an elephant in heat —William Alfred

The United States government leaks like a rusty tin can —David Brinkley, *This Week with David Brinkley,* ABC-TV, November 16, 1986

Word gets around … it's like jungle drums —George Axelrod

Word of scandal spreads like a spot of oil —Marcel Proust

♣ GOVERNMENT

See Also: LAW, POLITICS

An administration, like a machine, does not create. It carries on —Antoine de Saint-Exupéry

Any government, like any family, can for a year spend a little more than it earns. But ... continuance of that habit means the poorhouse —Franklin Delano Roosevelt

The balance of power our Founding Fathers so brilliantly contrived ... has functioned like a gyroscope to keep us from plunging irretrievably into anarchy or despotism —John R. Stockwell, *New York Times*/Op Ed, December 14, 1986

Stockwell's simile was part of the argument for open hearings on Colonel Oliver North.

Democracy is like a raft. It never goes down but, dammit, your feet are always wet —Fisher Ames

Government is like that old definition of a baby: an enormous appetite at one end and no sense of responsibility at the other —Ronald Reagan

Government ... like fire ... is a dangerous servant and a fearful master; never for a moment should it be left to irresponsible action —George Washington

Governments are like men, more or less suspicious according to their temperaments —*Punch*, 1844

Governments, like clocks, go from the motions men give them, and as governments are made and moved by men, so by them they are ruined also —William Penn

A great empire, like a great cake, is most easily diminished at the edges —Benjamin Franklin

The life of governments is like that of man. The latter has a right to kill in case of natural defense: the former have a right to wage war for their own preservation —Charles-Louis de Secondat, Baron de Montesquieu

Like a funeral or a marriage, an administration in the making creates disparate relationships and revived forgotten alliances —Maurice Edelman

Edelman put this simile into the mind of the fictional hero of his novel Disraeli Rising.

Like clowns, they [royalty] amuse the people, even with their funerals —Marie, Queen of Romania

Like knights in search of the Holy Grail, lawmakers are always looking for painless ways to raise revenues —David E. Rosenbaum, *New York Times*, March 5, 1986

A monarchy is like a man-of-war, bad shots between wind and water hurt it exceedingly; there is danger of capsizing. But democracy is a raft. You cannot easily overturn it —Joseph Cook

Monarchy is like a sleek craft, it sails along well until some bumbling captain runs it into the rocks —Fisher Ames, English Tory, former monarchist, quoted in *Money Magazine*

A nation ... is like a body contained within a circle, having a common center, in which every radius meets; and that center is formed by representation —Thomas Paine

Nations are as a drop of a bucket —The Holy Bible/Isaiah

Nations are like olives. To gentle pressure they respond with sweet oil, to hard pressure with bitter oil —Ludwig Boerne

No nation can survive if Government becomes like the man who in winter began to burn the wall boards of his house to keep warm until he had no house left —Ronald Reagan on controlling government spending, annual address to annual conference of the International Monetary Fund and World Bank September 30, 1986

States, like men, have their growth, their manhood, their decrepitude, their decay —Walter Savage Landor

States, like men, never protest their honor loudly unless they have a bad case to argue —Harold J. Laski

The superpowers often behave like two heavily armed blind men feeling their way around a room, each believing himself in mortal peril from the other whom he assumes to have perfect vision —Henry Kissinger

The entire Civil Service is like a fortress made of papers, forms and red tape —Alexander Ostrovsky

❦ GRACEFULNESS
See: AGILITY, BEAUTY

❦ GRACIOUSNESS
See: BEHAVIOR, MANNERS

❦ GRAVENESS
See: SERIOUSNESS

❦ GRAY
See Also: COLORS, GLOOM, HAIR COLOR, SKY, WEATHER

An ash-gray … like that of the first thinning of the darkness after a rain-sodden night —Dan Jacobson

(His face was) faintly gray like newsprint —John Updike

(Eyes) gray as a goose —Geoffrey Chaucer

Gray as a vault —Elizabeth Spencer

Gray as bones —Martin Cruz Smith

Gray as cement —Philip Levine

(The weather had turned as) gray as concrete —Jean Thompson

Gray as flannel —Jonathan Valin

In his novel, Life's Work, *Valin thus describes what remains of a man's hair: "bald on top, gray as flannel on the sides."*

(Eyes) gray as glass —Geoffrey Chaucer

Chaucer used the simile in The Canterbury Tales *("The Miller's Tale")* and Shakespeare used it in Gentlemen of Verona.

Gray as lava —D. H. Lawrence

(Skin) gray as lead —William Diehl

(Warships) gray as sharks —George Garrett

(Eyes) gray as storm clouds —Margaret Millar

(Max was) gray as the sky —Susan Fromberg Schaeffer

Gray like dust —Algernon Charles Swinburne

Gray [hair] like the last snows of winter —John Cheever

Gray like washed slate —John Updike

(Eyes had gone) icy gray, like winter frost —Andrew Kaplan

❦ GREATNESS
See Also: FAME, INTELLIGENCE, MIND

Early genius is like a cabbage: it doesn't head well —Bartlett's *Dictionary of Americanisms*

A fine genius, in his own country, is like gold in the mine —Ben Franklin

Genius, in one respect, is like gold—numbers of persons are constantly writing about both who have neither —Charles Caleb Colton

Genius is like a flint of many edges, but it is the edges that give the sparkle —Moritz Gottlieb Saphir

Genius, like humanity, rusts for want of use —William Hazlitt

Genius, like water, will find its level —Proverb

Genius must have talent as its complement and implement, just as, in like manner, imagination must have fancy —Samuel Taylor Coleridge

Coleridge built on this simile as follows: "in short, the higher intellectual powers can only act through a corresponding energy of the lower."

Genius without education is like silver in the mine —Benjamin Franklin

A genius without vices is like a race horse without a good jockey —Benjamin De Casseres

Great men are like mountains; we do not appreciate their magnitude while we are still close to them —Joseph Chamberlain

Great men are like meteors; they litter and are consumed to enlighten the world —Napoleon Bonaparte

Great men, like great epochs, are explosive material in whom tremendous energy has been accumulated —Friedrich Nietzsche

The simile is also quoted with the word "ages" substituted for "epochs."

Great men stand like solitary towers in the city of God —Henry Wadsworth Longfellow

Great minds are like eagles, and build their nest in some lofty solitude —Arthur Schopenhauer

It is with rivers as it is with people: the greatest are not always the most agreeable nor the best to live with —Henry Van Dyke

Men of genius are like eagles, that live on what they kill, while men of talents are like crows, that live on what has been killed for them —Josh Billings

In Billings' special phonetic dialect this read: "Men ov genius ... tha live on what tha ... while men ov ..tha live on what haz bin killed for them."

♣ GREED

See Also: EATING AND DRINKING, ENVY

(My) avarice cooled like lust in the chill grave —Ralph Waldo Emerson

Avarice is like a graveyard; it takes all that it can get and gives nothing back —Josh Billings

Avaricious ... like a pig which seeks its food in the mud, without caring where it comes from —Jean B. M. Vianney

The avaricious man is like the barren sandy ground of the desert which sucks in all the rain and dew with greediness, but yields no fruitful herbs or plants for the benefit of others —Zeno

Covetous persons are like sponges which greedily drink in water, but return very little until they are squeezed —G. S. Bowles

Greedy as a colt first loosed to pasture in the spring —Ben Ames Williams

Greedy as a vulture —Tobias Smollett

He [Donald Trump] has an appetite [for property] like a Rocky Mountain vulture —Alan Greenberg quoted in *The Wall Street Journal*, April 1, 1987

Kings, like hyenas, will always fall upon dead carcasses, although their bellies are full, and although they are conscious that in the end they will tear one another to pieces over them —Walter Savage Landor

(Love surfeits not) lust like a glutton dies —William Shakespeare, "Venus and Adonis"

Love comforteth like sunshine after rain —William Shakespeare, "Venus and Adonis"

Rapacious as a crocodile —Anon

Rapacious as a warlord —Sharon Sheehe Stark

Sucked him dry like a raw egg —Bertolt Brecht

They're [the doctors] milking you like a cow —Molière

♣ GREEN

See Also: COLORS, ENVY

Bright green like a parrot's wing —Hugh Walpole

(Eyes as) deeply green as an Amazonian jungle —Ed McBain

Green and shiny as a frog come out of the swamp —R. Wright Campbell

Green as a canker —V. S. Pritchett

Green ... as a well-watered palm —Mark Helprin

Green as jealousy —Vita Sackville-West

(Fields as) green as jellied mint —Malcolm Cowley

(Eyes) green as leeks —William Shakespeare, *A Midsummer Night's Dream*

(The trees were) green as paper money —George Garrett

Green as spring —Beryl Markham

Green as St. Patrick's Day icing —Marge Piercy

(Eyes) green as wings of horseflies —Erica Jong

Greener than envy and money —George Garrett

❧ GRIEF

See Also: SADNESS

The eye, like a shattered mirror, multiplies the images of sorrow —Edgar Allen Poe

Grief as constant as a cloud of black flies —James Crumley

Grief deep as life or thought —Alfred, Lord Tennyson

Grief floats off spreading out thin like oil —Elizabeth Bishop

Grief had flown away like a sparrow —Jean Stafford

Greif holds him like a corset —Anon

Grief is like a mine shaft, narrow and deep —Kenzaburo Oe

Grief is to man as certain as the grave —George Crabbe

Griefless as a rich man's funeral —Sidney Dobell

Grief ... like a mallard with clipped wings circles me summer and winter, settled for life in my lie's reedy lake —Denise Levertov

The simile comes from the closing lines of Levertov's poem "Visitant."

Grief rolled across the space between us like a wash of salt water —Sue Grafton

Grief sat on his chest like a dragon —Norman Garbo

Griefs ... pain me like a lingering disease —John Milton

I felt as if my chest were banded, like a barrel, with iron straps of sorrow —John Hersey

Man sheds his grief as his skin sheds rain —Ralph Waldo Emerson

Mourning had lain thick in the room, like dust —Belva Plain

The news of his death [Byron's] came down upon my heart like a mass of lead —Thomas Carlyle

Our sorrows are like thunder clouds, which seem black in the distance, but grow lighter as they approach —Jean Paul Richter

Pure and complete sorrow is as impossible as pure and complete joy —Leo Tolstoy

She had borne about with her for years like an arrow sticking in her heart the grief, the anguish —Virginia Woolf

She wore her grief like a string of pearls —Anon

Sorrow as true as bread —E. E. Cummings

Sorrow is a kind of rust of the soul, which every new idea contributes in its passage to scour away —Samuel Johnson

Sorrow like rain makes roses and mud —Austin O'Malley

Sorrows are like tall angels with star-crowns in their hair —Margery Eldredge Howell

Sorrows blurred around their edges, like a careless woman's lipstick —Jean Thompson

Sorrow was like the wind. It came in gusts —Marjorie Kinnan Rawlings

The stains of her grief became her as raindrops to the beaten rose —Edith Wharton

There are peaks of anguish in life which establish themselves as peerless, like sharp ridges above a range —Davis Grubb

Woman's grief is like a summer storm, short as it is violent —Joanna Baille

Wore his broken heart like a mourning band —Lael Tucker Wertenbaker

❧ GRIN(S)

See Also: LAUGHTER, SMILES

Face ... cut wide open by a beautiful grin ... like pumpkins with candles shining out through their strong ivory teeth —Marge Piercy

Grin at each other as if we'd just completed a double steal —W. P. Kinsella

Grinning dreamily, like a man who has just had a final fix —James Crumley

A grin like a flash of dental lightning —Don Marquis

Grin like a German Shepherd —Rick Borsten

Grin like a kid caught smoking behind the barn —W. P. Kinsella

Grin like an apple slice —Julia O'Faolain

Grin like a salesman —Richard Ford

Grin like the moon, just barely there, and like the sun, getting ready to set —Hortense Calisher

Grinned at her like a six-year-old boy caught doing something he must charm his way out of —Niven Busch

Grinned at me very engagingly, like a daddy who has just finished explaining to his little boy how the new electric train works —Harvey Swados

Grinned, filling his cheeks, as if he had food in his mouth —Paul Theroux

Grinned just like a jackass chewing briars —George Garrett

Grinned like a hungry tiger —Harvey Swados

Grinned like a pumpkin —Marge Piercy

Grinned like a shark —T. Coraghessan Boyle

Grinned like a weasel in a chicken coop —T. Coraghessan Boyle

Grinning like a cageful of monkeys —Erich Maria Remarque

Grinning like a Death's-head —Loren D. Estleman

Grinned like beans —Rita Mae Brown

Grinning like egg-sucking foxes —John D. MacDonald

A grin of recognition spread across Bunty's face like a burn —Harvey Swados

Grins like a clown with a banjo —R. H. W. Dillard

Grin ... wide as a pumpkin's —Mary Hedin

He was grinning expectantly like a salesman offering great deals on finance —David Nicholls, *One Day*

His grin was like a big wrinkle among the small ones —Robert Campbell

A lop-sided grin, like he had a lemon in his mouth —Joseph C. Lincoln

❦ GROANS AND WHISPERS

See Also: SIGHS

The continuous moaning was a simple irritant, like the clanking of a radiator pipe —Mary McCarthy

Furious whispers which sounded like the hissing of snakes roused from a summer nap in some warm garden heap —Joyce Cary

Gasped like a big fish —Brian Moore

Groaning ... like the wind in the chimney —William Faulkner

Groan like a poleaxed steer —James Thurber

Grunted ... like a goat hit with a sledgehammer —William Moseley

Grunted like a man hit with a baseball bat —James Crumley

Grunt like a water-buffalo —O. Henry

Her husky whisper, gentle as a rain breeze, was like a tender caress —Cecilia Rosas

Hissed ... like the deadliest of adders —Joseph Heller

(Nola's) husky whisper had a thrill in it like the rattle of a snake —Wallace Stegner

Like the sound of water readying to boil were the whispers of his voice —Norman Mailer

Moan and pace like captured leopards —Diane Wakoski

Moaned ... deeply, like a cello —Martin Cruz Smith

Moaned ... like some baffled prowling beast —James Joyce

Moaning like a dumbstruck giant —Scott Spencer

Moans like a bedridden grandmother —T. Coraghessan Boyle

A moan that sounded as if it had been wrenched from her chest with a steel hook —James Crumley

Wail … like wind outside a cabin window —Charles Johnson

(Felt my wrinkled heart) wheeze like a dog on a leash —Jayne Anne Phillips

Whimpering like a puppy just yanked from its mother and thrown onto the side of the road —Gloria Norris

Whimper like a well-trained pet wanting to be let out —George Garrett

A whispering moan like the rustle of wind in trees —James Stevens

Whispers dramatically, as though she were telling me a state secret —Daphne Merkin

Whisper softly as a girl's tear —Isaac Stern

Wince as if somebody had driven a red-hot spike into his head —P. G. Wodehouse

❧ GROWTH

See Also: SPREADING

Accumulate … like acorns beneath the trees of a forest —Thomas H. Huxley

Accumulate like a pile of dead leaves drifting onto the pavement of August —Barbara Pym

Accumulate like wire coat hangers in a closet —Anon

Blooming as a bride —Anon

Blooming as spring —John Dryden

Bloom like wildflowers in moss —George Garrett

[A young girl] blossomed … like a tree or a branch where every bud was breaking into flower —Rumer Godden

(Curiosity) blossomed like leprosy —Yehuda Amichai

(Life had) blossomed out like a flower in the sun —Ellen Glasgow

Blown up like a tumor —Ralph Waldo Emerson

Bred and nourished like a gardenia —Pat Conroy

Breed as quickly as cockroaches and are as difficult to stamp out —Bob Davis, in article about bugs in computer software, *Wall Street Journal,* January 28, 1987

Breed like cells under a microscope —Doris Lessing

Breeds like a rabbit —Jonathan Swift

(Ambassadors) cropped up like hay —W. S. Gilbert

(His belief … came to the surface and) expanded like some delicate flower —E. M. Forster

Expanding like the shade of a cloud on sand —Wallace Stevens

Fertile like the divine creation —Victor Hugo

(The righteous shall) flourish as a branch —The Holy Bible/Proverbs

Flourishing like a weed —Stefan Zweig

Flourish like a cabbage rose —John Ashberry

Flourish like an herb —The Holy Bible/Isaiah

Going [a criminal investigation] like a grass shack fire —Harold Adams

Grew … like a balloon being pumped full of gas —Myron Brinig

Grew like a larch —Emily Brontë

Grew like asparagus in May —W. S. Gilbert

[George Ade's popularity] Grew like Jack's beanstalk —Lee Coyle

Grew like weeds in sand —Marge Piercy

Grow and grow like a maypole —Erica Jong

Grow like a summer pumpkin —W. P. Kinsella

(His notions) grow like a tropical forest —G. K. Chesterton

Grow like savages —William Shakespeare, *Henry V*

(I watch our children) grow like stubborn weeds —George Garrett

Growth ... as fast as the light from polar regions —John Ashberry

Have grown like a bug from a bug out of the garden of Eden —Dylan Thomas

(In earth) like a man in a woman, I'll make food out of food —Daniela Gioseffi

A major advance ... it's like going from the propeller airplane to the jet —Dr. Bruce R. Baral, a dentist commenting on new cavity removal system, *New York Times,* December 31, 1986

(Disappointment) mounting higher every week, like a quick-growing hedge —Mazo de la Roche

Multiplies itself [ultimate truth about fellow men] like taxes —Ogden Nash

Multiplies like loaves and fishes —George Garrett

Multiply (thy seed) as the stars of the heaven, and as the sand which is upon the sea shore —The Holy Bible/Genesis

Multiply like fruit flies —Herbert Lieberman

Progress is like a merry-go-round. We get up on a speckled wooden horse ... we think we're travelling like the devil, but the man that doesn't care about the merry-go-rounds know that we come back where we were —Finley Peter Dunne

In Dunne's Observations by Mr. Dooley *some words were in dialect: "travellin' like the divvle."*

Proliferate, like creditors at a bankruptcy —Mike Sommer

(Plots) ripen like fruit —O. Henry

Soaring like Halley's comet —Jane Wagner

As used in Jane Wagner's stage show starring Lily Tomlin, The Search for Signs of Intelligent Life, *soaring refers to a sharp increase, as in the teenage suicide rate.*

(Poems) sprout like grain from quickened seeds —George Garrett

[Popularity] sprung up, like a grass fire —James Thurber

Stockpiled ... like grain in a grain elevator —Doug Feiden

In Feiden's novel The Ten Million Dollar Getaway, *the people doing the stockpiling are mobsters and bodies are the frame of reference for the comparison.*

Stretched out like a string released —Henri-Pierre Roché

Swelled like bullfrogs at mating time —R. V. Cassill

Cassill's bullfrogs comparison is used by a character in Hoyt's Child *to describe how policemen will fatten up their role if you let them in on your problems.*

Swelling like a balloon —Robert Silverberg

Swelling up like blowfish —Peter De Vries

Unfolding like a tree —Philip Levine

We grow like a tree from the earth —Marge Piercy

♣ GRUMBLING

See: COMPLAINTS

♣ GUILT

See Also: CONSCIENCE

Branded with his guilt as if he were tattooed —Henry Slesar

Berating himself, like an orator grading his own speech —William Diehl

Gather guilt like a young intern his symptoms, his certain evidence —Anne Sexton

Guilt is like mothers. Everyone in the world has at least one. And it's passed down like a torch to the next generation —Erma Bombeck

This has been changed to the present tense from the original which read: "I figured out long ago that guilt was like mothers. Everyone in the world had at least one. And it was passed down like a torch to the next generation."

Guilt, thick as ether, seeped into my body —Jonathan Valin

Guilt will descend on you like London Fog —Walter Allen

The heat of shame mounted through her legs and body and sounded in her ears like the sound of sand pouring —Nadine Gordimer

Looked as guilty as if he'd kicked his grandmother —Raymond Chandler, "Red Wind"

Looking behind me … as guilty as a murderer whose knife drips blood —Ann Beattie

Looks like a hound caught slipping a chop from the table —T. Coraghessan Boyle

A sense of guilt like a scent —Louis MacNeice

Shame crowding his throat like vomit —Jean Thompson

The thought of the wrong she had done … aroused in her a feeling akin to revulsion such as a drowning man might feel who had shaken off another man who clung to him in the water —Leo Tolstoy

We are all like mice: one eats the cheese and all are blamed —Solomon Ibn Vega

❧ HABIT

See Also: BEHAVIOR, FLEXIBILITY/INFLEXIBILITY

An annoying habit … like the habit of people who take nonfattening sweetness in their coffee, and order chocolate mousse —Marilyn Sharp

As the snow flakes gather, so our habits are formed —Jeremy Bentham

A bad custom is like a good cake, better broken than kept —Randle Cotgrave

The word "custom" is often interchanged with "habit."

Bad habits are like a comfortable bed; easy to get into, but hard to get out of —Rev. Watson C. Blake

The customs and fashions of men change like leaves on the bough, some of which go and others come —Dante Alighieri

(I like to) go tick-ticking along like a clock —Edith Wharton

Habit, like a crane, will bow its neck and dip its pulleyed cable, gathering me … into the daylight —Harold Monro

(All will be well, we say; it is) a habit, like the rising of the sun —Edna St. Vincent Millay

The habit (of command) was already fitting him like a tailored suit —Ken Follett

Kept on along the narrow track of habit, like a traveler; climbing a road in a fog —Edith Wharton

Set in his ways as a chunk of concrete —F. Hopkinson Smith

Set in one's way, as elderly apple trees —Allison Lurie

Shook my wild habits from me … like a worn-out cloak —O. Henry

Standard, like the salmonella in a poorly cooked chicken sandwich. —Hamilton Nolan, "Thomas Friedman Writes His Only Column Again," Gawker.com, June 25, 2012

The article took columnist Friedman to task for repetitious, boring writing practitices.

Take for granted, like running water —Anon

Used to it, like a wart —Jonathan Kellerman

Using drugs like table salt —Jimmy Breslin

We are bagged in habit like clothes back from the cleaners —Marge Piercy

Without our traditions, our lives would be as shaky as … as … as a fiddler on the roof! —Sheldon Harnick, lyrics from "Tradition" from *Fiddler on the Roof.*

❧ HAIR

See Also: HAIR COLOR; HAIR, CURLY; HAIR STYLES; HAIR TEXTURE

Bangs down over her forehead like a sheepdog's —Margaret Atwood

Bangs jitter across her forehead like magnets —Susan Minot

Bangs ... like overcooked bacon —Ann Beattie

Black hair hung like a river about her shoulders —Helga Sandburg

Braid of hair ... like a thick black snake —Ann Petry

A crest of stiff white hair, like a prophet or a cockatoo —Ellen Currie

Golden hair fountaining around her shoulders like spilled beer —Paige Mitchell

Hair as fiery as copper ivy, and eyes as blue as sky —Patricia Cornwell, *Five Scarpetta Novels*

Hair as short as a fuse —Stieg Larsson, *The Girl with the Dragon Tattoo*

Hair ... as smooth and shining as a blackbird's wing —John Braine

Hair ... auburn and abundant, like a well-nourished orangutan's coat —James Morrow

Hair ... bright and garish as brass —Margaret Millar

Hair floated around my face like wet gauze —Sue Grafton

Hair flying like a pennant —Paul Theroux

Hair foamed around her head like a dandelion cloud —Julia O'Faolain

Hair [red] ... gleaming like the sand streaked with sunset —Marguerite Young

(Gray) hair grows out of my skin like rot on an ancient tree —Anon Irish verse

Hair hanging straight as nylon cord —Alfred Gillespie

Hair ... its fine smooth loops, like slabs of snow, hung low on her cheeks —Gustave Flaubert

Hair like a field in bloom —T. Coraghessan Boyle

Hair like dry ashes —Maureen Howard

Hair like metal in the sun —Dorothy Parker

Hair ... like ripe wheat —Nelson Algren

Hair like spilled barley —T. Coraghessan Boyle

Hair ... like the rumpled wig of a clown —Hallie Burnett

Hair ... moving under her comb like a muscular skin —Gary Gildner

(Whitish) hair pointy and close as a burr or a sunflower when the seeds have been picked out of it —Saul Bellow

(The girl's black curly) hair shone like an eclipsed sun —Carol Ascher

[Blonde] Hair shone like well-polished old silver —F. van Wyck Mason

(White) hair smooth as a bird's breast —Raymond Chandler, *The Long Goodbye*

Hair spread out like feathers —Jayne Anne Phillips

Hair ... straight and sleek, and lay like black satin against her forehead —Vita Sackville-West

Hair, thick and springy like an Airedale's —Tobias Wolff, *The Garden of the North American Martyrs*

Hair ... thin and white and very short, laid over her skull like a placemat —Helen Hudson

Hair tumbled about her like a veil —Jean Stafford

Hair which resembled a horse's mane ... was like filaments of the brightest gold of Araby —Miguel de Cervantes

Hair which was long and smooth on either side of her face, like the shut wings of a raven —Mary Austin

Heavy chestnut hair hanging like a cloak about her shoulders —Marge Piercy

Heavy straight hair swinging behind like a rope —Eudora Welty

Her hair fell in bright ripples like a rush of gold from the ladle of a goldsmith —Stephen French Whitman

Her hair burned about her like a molten copper —Maurice Hewlett

In the original simile the hair was "aburned."

Her hair drooped round her pallid cheeks, like seaweed on a clam —Oliver Wendell Holmes

Her hair fell across her shoulders like a nun's veil —Sue Grafton

Her hair ... ran smooth like black water through her hands —Ross Macdonald

Her long, dark hair fell across her eyes like stray crayon marks —Joan Hess

Her long hair hung as straight as rain —Jean Stafford

Her wet hair lay flat as a second skin —Helen Hudson

His hair glittered like a skull cap of beads —Miles Gibson

His hair rose in an unruly swirl, like the topknot of some strange bird —John Yount

His hair slicks back, like a baby's or a gangster's ... shiny as a record album —Lorrie Moore

His hair stood upright like porcupine quills —Boccaccio

His thin gray hair lay on his scalp like molting feathers —John Cheever

A light fringe of hair, almost like frost —Joyce Carol Oates

A lock of black hair lay on his forehead like a leech —Jean Stafford

A man with hair like white flames —Lionel Shriver, *The Post-Birthday World*

Nearly as hairy as a dog —John Yount

Peroxide hair like rope ravelings —Paul J. Wellman

Pomaded hair slicked back like shiny Naugahyde —Paul Kuttner

The thick black hair of his chest forced its way out of the opening [of his shirt] like a jungle growth seeking sunlight —Harvey Swados

Thick shining hair, glossy as a squirt of black paint —Michael Chabon, *The Amazing Adventures of Kavalier & Clay*

A thick sprinkling of dandruff, like a fall of flour, on the shoulder of her blouse —Ruth Rendell

Thick yellow hair ... like a palm thatch —Jean Stafford

Tumbling loose dark hair like a wet mop —George Garrett

Uncombed hair hung about her face like an old dog's —H. E. Bates

Untidy hair like a lion's mane —Barbara Pym

The wild hair of his head bloomed like fallen snow —Z. Vance Wilson

Wisps of hair, like sunburst grass hanging over eyes as clear as pale grey crystals —Edith Wharton

With his tangled mane and beard, he looked like some ridiculous lion out of a bestiary —Wallace Stegner

Pale brushed heads like candles burning in the summer sunlight —John Updike

❧ HAIR, COLOR

See Also: BLACK, BROWN, GRAY, RED, WHITE

Black [hair], with only a few gray streaks like a timid motif running through it —Helen Hudson

Blond as a Zulu under the bleach —Raymond Chandler

Blond hair ... like long uncut grass but no color —Rosellen Brown

Braids, brown and shiny like a ripe hazelnut —Henry Van Dyke

A carroty mass of hair flaming round his cheeks and crown like a brush fire —T. Coraghessan Boyle

(Her long) chestnut hair was waving about like a curtain of silk —Francine du Plessix Gray

Gray hair ... like meringue —James Lee Burke

Gray hair that looks like the head of an old worn-out wet mop left out to dry and bleach in the sun —George Garrett

Gray hair, which he wore like a kind of silver beret —Robert Traver

Hair a fading mixture of black and gray, like an afternoon storm —Laura Furman

Hair … artificially streaked, as though someone had emptied a bag of feathers over her head —Lynne Sharon Schwartz

Hair, as straight and red as ironed ketchup —Tom Robbins

Redheads and their problems feature prominently in Robbins' Life with Woodpecker *and this is one of several similes about red hair.*

Hair, black and shining like mica —Jean Garrigue

Hair, black as a seal's wet fur —Jean Garrigue

Hair … bronze and silver like pear trees in full bloom —William Alfred

Hair … dark and live as snakes —George Garrett

Hair … had gray in it like streaks of milk —William Styron

Hair [red] … like a fiery wick dipped in a well of incendiary sunlight —John Farris

Hair … like Montana wheat planted in contours on a slope of hill —John Gunther

Hair looks as if it had been stained with blueberries —W. P. Kinsella

Hair, not just blonde, but radiating gold like a candle flame behind a window in winter —Stuart Dybek

Hair … streaked like old piano keys —Reynolds Price

Hair … without definable color, as though it had very early begun to rehearse for its inevitable whiteness —Doris Grumbach

Her locks were yellow as gold —Samuel Taylor Coleridge

Her long hair was naturally a light brown, but the sun had bleached tawny streaks in it, like the stripes of a very old battle flag seen through imperfect glass —R. V. Cassill

His head and his hairs were white like wool, as white as snow —The Holy Bible/Revelation

His white hair stood out from his head like the fur of a Angora rabbit —Thomas McMahon

Long yellow hair like broken egg yolks spilling down all over her head —Helen Hudson

Pale auburn with a touch of gold … like butter with paprika in it —John Gunther

Red hair … all fluffed out, like her face lived in a pink cloud —Sharon Sheehe Stark

Red hair … as glossy as plum-skins —Beverly Farmer

Red hair like a curtain that would draw down like a shade —Shirley Ann Grau

White hair … flecked all over with little rust colored dashes, like India ink put on with a fine brush —Willa Cather

White hair like a cloud —Helen Hudson

White hair made her face look like a rose in snow —L. P. Hartley

White hair shone, like mountain snow —Percy Bysshe Shelley

White-headed as a mountain —Thomas Hardy

(Her) yellow hair, like strands of gold —Anon line from early American ballad, "Locks and Bolts"

🍀 HAIR, CURLY

See Also: HAIR STYLES

A circlet of crisp curly gray hair like a laurel wreath —Marge Piercy

Curled their hair so tightly that their heads looked like bunches of black grapes —Angela Carter

(Her gold) curls hang like lazy springs —Ira Wood

Curls like those of a young hyacinth —Edgar Allen Poe

Curls of yellow hair like pine shavings —Peter De Vries

(His dark) curls were flat, plastered over his head like a wet beret —Joan Hess

Curly scented black stiff hair, like cock feathers —Janet Flanner

Hair … as tightly curled as a poodle's —Margaret Millar

A popular comparison with variations including the simplified as in "Hair … curly as a poodle" and extensions like "Hair curled like a gilded poodle's." (T. Coraghessan Boyle's Water Music*)*

Hair curled as rings of iron wire —Aharon Megged

Hair … curled like the fruit on the trees —Dame Edith Sitwell

Hair … curly as moss —Marge Piercy

Hair … curly as the wool on a ram —George Garrett

Hair that curled naturally like very young leaves —Mollie Hardwick

Hair that sprang into ringlets like gold coins —Paige Mitchell

It [hair] covered either side of her thin face in curly muffs, like a poodle's ears —Jonathan Valin

Soft gray hair curled out of his skull like smoke —Miles Gibson

Towers of hair, curled like Indian temples —Joyce Cary

❧ HAIR STYLES

Brown ringlets rising straight out of his temples like a waterfall in reverse —Cynthia Ozick, *Heir to the Glimmering World*

Close-cropped head, cut so close to the scalp that the patches of gray are like a light stain —George Garrett

Hair … almost as if ironed in place —H. E. Bates

Hair … brushed straight back —like he was wearing a hairpiece or as though a small black beaver was lying on top of his skull —Donald McCaig

Hair … cropped so short in back that he looked like a Marine in boot camp —Jonathan Valin

(Her chestnut) hair, cut short, closed about her neck like a choker —Arthur A. Cohen

Hair hanging down, straight, as if it were cut out of wood and painted —Rumer Godden

This is slightly modified from the dialect spoken by a character in Godden's story, No More Indians, *"outa" and "hangin" instead of "out of" and "hanging"*

Hair hanging … like a brush across his forehead —Ella Leffland

Hair hanging like seaweed —John Updike

Hair … hanging loose down to her shoulders, like a child's unbound for a party —Eudora Welty

Hair … lay on her forehead like a ruffled crest —James Joyce

Hair parted from the middle of her forehead like the two panels of a curtain —Saul Bellow

Hair pulled back tight as if to punish it —Marge Piercy

Hair … razor cut and blow-dried and sprayed so firmly into place that he looked like he was wearing a helmet —Robert B. Parker

Hair, so tightly braided it felt stitched on, showing her bare scalp like little seams all over her skull —Helen Hudson

Hair that grew long and thick around his face like ivy round a window —Helen Hudson

Hair … twisted like a pastry into a knot —Patricia Henley

Hair was cut close to his scalp, like freshly mowed grass —Daphne Merkin

(Her white) hair was so permanently waved and arranged that it looked like concrete —Noel Coward

Her white hair … stood high above her face like a chef's cap —Nancy Huddleston Packer

His hair … covered half his forehead like a bowl —Reynolds Price

His hair … cut short as that of a monk, seemed like a barber-college special —Thomas McGuane

His shiny brown hair was razor cut, wrapped like a scarf around his ears —Jonathan Valin

Pale fluffy hair whipped up beautifully on the top of her head like confectioner's cream —Elizabeth Bowen

Parted it [her hair] evenly, like the curtains of a neat house —Saul Bellow

Short-cropped hair hugging her head like a bangle bracelet —Arthur A. Cohen

Straight hair, cut like a little train to a point at the nape of her neck —Eudora Welty

Wore her hair away from her forehead, like a cloud which a little wind in May peels off finely —Elizabeth Barrett Browning

Wore her hair nearly to her waist, in long pastel strands like the trailing branches of a weeping willow —Harvey Swados

Wore it [hair] as though he'd had thought it indecent exposure to have allowed anyone to catch even a glimpse of his eyebrows, his ears, or the back of his neck —George Bagby

♣ HAIR TEXTURE

Dead-looking hair … as if it had been glued on —Willa Cather

Frizzy brown hair like short feathers —Marianne Hauser

A great shock of hair, like the best type of sheepskin rug —Phyllis Bottome

> The Point of Vantage *from which this is taken, leads off with a simile. Here it is in full context:* "Teobaldo Kurt Dubrik was a large stout man with a grand shock of hair, like the best type of sheepskin rug."

Hair and mustache fluffy as down —Mark Helprin

Hair as glossy as a blooded chestnut's coat —Elizabeth Spencer

Hair as sleek as a seal's fur —Sarah Bird

Hair … black and dense and glossy, like boot polish —Maeve Brennan

Hair … coarse and slightly wavy, with just a trace of oil all over it, like a well-tossed salad —Roald Dahl

Hair, frizzy like unravelled rope —D. H. Lawrence

Hair … like a coiled piece of copper —Laurie Colwin

Hair like a frizzled yellow sponge —Phyllis Bottome

Hair like blown-up gold and finer than gold —Joyce Carol Oates

Hair like dirty cotton —Loren D. Estleman

Hair like fuzz on a tennis ball —Jean Thompson

Hair like moth-eaten fur —Ellen Glasgow

Hair like Persian lambs' fur —Saul Bellow

Hair like porcupine quills —Elizabeth Tallent

Hair … like the raffia you had to soak before you could weave with it in a basket class —Saul Bellow

Hair … matted and dry, like that of a sick animal —W. P. Kinsella

Hair rich and dark, clustering thick as grapes or hyacinths —Elizabeth Spencer

Hair … rough, like a mongrel dog's —Frank Tuohy

(His curly straw) hair shone like frail golden wires on his head —James Stern

Hair smooth as a cat's —Jayne Anne Phillips

Hair … soft as milkweed silk —McKinlay Kantor

Hair … straight as a string —Dorothy Canfield

> *In her story* Married Children, *Canfield expands on this with* "She looks like a squaw."

Hair … texture like damp thread —Anthony Powell

(A mane of black) hair that was as thick as a tow rope —Sumner Locke Elliott

Hair, thick and coarse as dune grass —Marge Piercy

Hair thick and glossy like fur —Martin Cruz Smith

Hair, thick as a cushion —Helen Hudson

Hair tough as a rocking horse's —Penelope Gilliatt

(Her pale red) hair was wispy and stuck out from her head like duckling down —Tama Janowitz

Her hair, after all the combing, shone like something Marco Polo might have brought back from Far Cathay to show the peasants —William Dieter

Her locks had been so frequently and drastically brightened and curled that to caress them ... would be rather like running one's fingers through julienne potatoes —Dorothy Parker

His fine dark hair looked more like a shadow than like real hair —Katherine Mansfield

Long coarse hair, like a mop —Rosa Guy

(Black) shiny hair, hard as bristles —Ivan Turgenev

Straight shining hair like smooth straw —James Stern

Thick, bulging hair, like a bear's fur —Albert Moravia

HAND(S)

See Also: ARM(S), FINGER(S), HAND MOVEMENTS, HANDSHAKE

Big hands like the claws of a crab —Guy de Maupassant

The bones in her narrow wrists were small as chicken bones —Mary Hedin

Closed they [hands] looked like clusters of unpainted wooden balls as large as walnuts —Sherwood Anderson

A craftsman's hands ... hands quick as cats —William H. Gass

Fist like a piece of iron —Raymond Chandler

Fists ... as large as wastebaskets —Dashiell Hammett

Fists like knotty pine —George Garrett

Hand as wide as a stirrup —Richard Ford

Hand ... dry, hard and cold —rather like a chicken's foot —F. van Wyck Mason

Hand ... like a fine piece of ivory carving —Rebecca West

A hand like a aside of meat —Douglas Adams

Hand ... like a baseball catcher's glove —Frank Ross

Hand like a boxing glove —T. Coraghessan Boyle

Hand like a bundle of taut wire —Oakley Hall

Hand like a ham —Stephen Vincent Benét

Hand ... like a sharp, icy stake —Ariel Dorfman

Hand like a wood rasp —Raymond Chandler

Hand ... limp as a tassel —Frank Swinnerton

Hand, quick as a bird claw —Eudora Welty

Hands ... as soft as cotton-wool —Ivan Turgenev

Hands ... cool, muted and frail with age like the smoothness of old yellow linen —Stephen Vincent Benét

Hands ... crude and functional as if whittled out of hard wood —George Garrett

Hands folded like flower petals —Clare Boylan

Hands ... gnarled, huge and misshapen, like chunks of wood hewn from a pale tree —James Stern

Hands gnarled, twisted and earth-stained like the vigorous roots of a tree —Ellen Glasgow

Hands, horny as a laborer's —Harvey Swados

Hands hung like clusters of sausages —Louis Bromfield

Hands ... large and too thin, like empty gloves —Margaret Laurence

Hands like asbestos —Mary Hedin

Hands ... like blocks of wood and about as gentle —Leslie Thomas

Hands like bunches of bananas —Frank Swinnerton

Hands like coal shovels —Gerald Kersh

Hands ... like dangling shovels —Jonathan Gash

Hands ... like elephant's ears —Arthur Baer

Hands ... like great paws —Elizabeth Taylor

Hands like hard rubber —Helen Hudson

Hands like hunks of steak —Julia O'Faolain

Hands like lion's feet —Arthur A. Cohen

Hands ... like wings of butterflies —Hart Crane

Hands ... looked like roots in earth —Ram Dass and Paul Gorman

Hand ... soft, like worn silk —Jayne Anne Phillips

Hands ridged like topography maps —Sharon Sheehe Stark

Hands ... slender and smooth as though they had lifted nothing heavier than a knife to cut corners —Helen Hudson

Hands ... soft from the [dish] water, like old gum erasers —Jean Thompson

Hands ... steady as steel —H. E. Bates

Hands that felt ... like a scrubwoman's hands, red-knuckled and practical —Hortense Calisher

Hands that have thickened and calloused through the years so they look like tough paws —Louise Erdrich

Hands turned out flat, palms up, like a Balinese dancer —Leonard Michaels

Hands ... which projected like strings upon the finger-board of a violin, and armed with claws like those on the terminations of bats' wings —Theophile Gautier

A hand that felt as though it was reaching for you from the grave —Harvey Swados

Hand that rested like a sparrow on the table —Tony Ardizzone

Hand ... warm as a horn —Walker Percy

Hand ... wet and cold as something fished out of a pond —T. Coraghessan Boyle

Her hands were stunning like a sublime idea —Boris Pasternak

His hand felt like the tentacles of a sea anemone —Kate Grenville

His hands ... seemed large and awkward as if he was wearing invisible mittens —Stephen Crane

His wrists seemed to dangle from his cuffs as if they were sewn to the cloth —Jonathan Valin

Long hands, like pitchforks —*Arabian Nights*

An old man's hand, hooked and grimy with a couple of nailless fingers, like a hand in a horror film —Jonathan Valin

Veins [beneath skin of hands] tessellated like a blue mosaic, shining like an intricate blue design captured beneath glass —William Styron

Wrists like steel whips —H. E. Bates

❧ HAND MOVEMENTS
See Also: HANDSHAKE

Brushed at his forehead, like an insect had landed there —Donald McCaig

Clapped her hands liked someone shooing pigeons —Sharon Sheehe Stark

Clapping as loudly as if their hands were wooden slats —Louis Auchincloss

Clapping her hands like cymbals —Ann Beattie

Clasped her hands behind her back like a child embarrassed at a social function, or stuck in the middle of a recitation —Peter De Vries

Cradled his hand in his lap, like it was a ruined bird —Donald McCaig

Flapped his hand like a flag —Mary Hedin

Flashing the palms of both hands like two headlights —Ludwig Bemelmans

Folding both hands in her lap like a reprimanded schoolgirl —Ed McBain

(He flagged the car with ...) gestures like hoops —Eudora Welty

A hand, like a leaf, fell on his shoulder —Katherine Mansfield

Hands clasped like the hands of an old man round a stick —Sylvia Townsend Warner

Hands flapping like misshapen white moths —Joan Hess

Hands flew off the steering wheel like a pair of startled birds —Ed McBain

Hands fluttered like the fins of angel-fish —Frank Swinnerton

(Her delicate) hands ... flutter like birds —Phyllis McGinley

Hands gesticulating —flying through the air like two brown sparrows —Jonathan Kellerman

Hands jerked as if they were on wires —Dorothy Parker

Hands lifting out as if to smooth, like a sheet on a bed —John Updike

Hands rose and floated in the air, graceful and helpless as doves —Marge Piercy

Hands spread wide as calipers —Diane Ackerman

Hands were outspread as though he were leading an orchestra into a profound and final diminuendo —Ralph Ellison

A plain and simple variation: "Raised his hands like an orchestra conductor"

Hasty, jerky gestures like a comedian in a silent movie —George Garrett

Held up her hand like a schoolgirl asking for permission to leave the room —Harvey Swados

Held up his hand like a traffic cop signaling stop —Ross Thomas

Kept rattling the ice in her glass, rattling her beads, rattling her bracelet like an impatient pony jingling its harness —Flannery O'Connor

Long thin hand ... floated like a scarf through the air —Marge Piercy

Nervous, tentative gesture, like someone making up his mind to stroke a dog that has the reputation of biting —Francis King

Opening and closing his fingers like a neon sign flickering at night —Ariel Dorfman

Passed her hand over her eyes as if to dispel a cloud —Robert Graves

Rearranges her hair like a horse shaking away a fly —W. P. Kinsella

Rubbing his hands together as if working tobacco for a pipe —Patrick White

Spread his hands in front of him, palms up, as if he intended to read in their lines the past as well as the future —Margaret Millar

Using his hands like a sculptor to shape the words he throws out —George Garrett

Wave as regal as Henry the Eighth's —Mary Hedin

You can't do anything [practical] with your hands.... You're all gestures and waving. Cutting the air, and flapping them up and down all the time, trying to make a point, its like EMPHASISING a WORD because you DON'T know how to use them and compensating with those hands of yours.... They're like tennis rackets on the end of sticks. Like satellite dishes at the end of fishing rods —Mike Barlett, *Cock*

❧ HANDSHAKE

A grip like a trash compactor —Jonathan Valin

A grip like a weightlifter —Harvey Swados

Grip like iron —Walker Percy

A grip like pincers —Gerald Kersh

Hand gripped like bird claws —Wallace Stegner

(Your) hand grips mine like a railing on an icy night —Adrienne Rich

Hand ... pumping at mine as if he expected my fingertips to squirt milk or something —T. Coraghessan Boyle

Handshake like a bite —Leonard Michaels

Handshake like cold, cooked spaghetti —Mark Singer

Her hand was limp as a dead carp —Jay Parini

His fingers pressed my hand like pieces of wood —Aharon Megged

Shook hands ... like competitors before a match of some kind —Ross Macdonald

Shook hands like strangers —John Dos Passos

Took it (the hand) cautiously, as if he were picking up a loathsome object preparatory to dropping it in the trash basket —Evan Hunter

(She) took Jim's soft fingers and held them closely, until he felt that they had been drawn into a mangle —Frank Swinnerton

❧ HANDWRITING

Handwriting ... like driven sleet —Peter De Vries

Handwriting looks as if a swarm of ants, escaping from an ink bottle, had walked over a sheet of paper without wiping their legs —Sydney Smith

❧ HAPPINESS

See Also: CONTENTMENT, JOY, PLEASURE

All happiness is a chance encounter and at every moment presents itself to you like a beggar by the roadside —André Gide

The best advice on the art of being happy is about as easy to follow as advice to be well when one is sick —Madame Swetchine

Dry happiness is like dry bread. We eat, but we do not dine —Victor Hugo

In Les Miserables, *the hero, Jean Valjean, continues: "I wish for the superfluous, for the useless, for the extravagant, for the too much, for that which is not good for anything."*

Ecstatic as a scientist who had just discovered the key to immortality —Susan Fromberg Schaeffer

Elated as though he had stumbled on a treasure —Brian Moore

A gay, light happiness, like bubbles in wine held up against the sun —Ben Ames Williams

Glowed with happiness, like a child with expectations of a birthday party —Frank Swinnerton

The happiest women, like the happiest nations, have no history —George Eliot

Happiness as wholesome as honey on the comb —John Braine

Happiness choked my throat like an anthem. It flowed through me like a river from the beginning of the column to its end —Aharon Megged

(In the midst of happiness grows a seed of unhappiness.) Happiness consumes itself like a flame. (It cannot burn for ever) —August Strindberg

Happiness ... descended upon her heart, like a cloud of morning dew in a dell of wild-flowers —Walter de la Mare

Happiness ... filled her brain like wine —William Dean Howells

Happiness flits from branch to twig to branch like a hummingbird —Delmore Schwartz

Happiness is falling on us out of the sky ... like a blanket of snow —Jean Giraudoux

Happiness is like a sunbeam, which the least shadow intercepts —Chinese proverb

Happiness is like mana; it is to be gathered in grains, and enjoyed every day. It will not keep; it cannot be accumulated —Tryon Edwards

Happiness is like time and space; we make and measure it ourselves —George Du Maurier

Happiness, like air, is not something you can put in a bottle —Anon

Happiness like the pink and white anemones of my childhood is a flower that must not be picked —André Maurois

The happiness of the wicked passes away like a torrent —Jean Baptiste Racine

Happiness struck her like a shower of rain —Eudora Welty

Happiness … was there like light seen through moving leaves, like touching a warm stone —Sumner Locke Elliott

Happy and thoughtless as an apple on a tree —George Garrett

Happy as a bee. —Noel Coward

This is one of dozens of "happy as" similes that was a favorite Coward expression, probably re-popularized by him, as was "merry as a grig," another old simile attributed in the first edition under GAIETY to novelist Frank Swinnerton, but probably a variation of "merry as a Greek."

Happy as a butterfly in a garden full of sunshine and flowers —Louisa May Alcott

Happy as a clam —American colloquialism, attributed to New England

A variation of this found in Bartlett's Dictionary of Americanisms is "Happy as a clam at high water."

Happy as a couple of linebackers after winning a high school game —Marge Piercy

Happy as a couple of cherrystone clams —George Garrett

Happy as a dog with a bone —Anon

Happy as a lover —William Wordsworth

(I am) happy as a mother whose good baby sleeps —May Sarton

Happy as a pig in clover —American colloquialism

In the American army this gave way to "Being happy as a pig in shit."

Happy as a robin when he trills —Anon American song, "Love Letters"

Happy as a swallow —Richard Ford

Happy as a tick in a dog's ear —Jay Parini

Happy as candles that shine on a cake —Oscar Hammerstein, "A Lopsided Bus," *Pipe Dream*

Happy as trees that find a wind to sway them —Sara Teasdale

He loved happiness like I love tea —Eudora Welty

(I was) high as taxes —Loren D. Estleman

When it [happiness] comes to one, it comes as naturally as sleep —Willa Cather

I felt like an amputated leg —Raymond Chandler, *Trouble Is My Business*

I was like a river in flood … drowning in my own happiness, and buoyed up by it at the same time —Eugene Ionesco

Live together … as happily as two lobsters in a saucepan, two bugs on a muscle —Dylan Thomas

Looked like the sun at the zenith —Carlos Baker

Happy-looking as if he's just heard the foreman say "Not Guilty" —William Slavens McNutt

Looking for happiness is like clutching the shadow or chasing the wind —Japanese proverb

Looks like he is a kid holding his first puppy —John Wainwright

Moments of happiness hang like pearls on the finest silken thread, certain to be snapped, the pearls scattered away —Joan Chase

On the brink of our happiness we stop like someone on a drunk starting to weep —Galway Kinnell

The rays of happiness, like those of light, are colorless when unbroken —Henry Wadsworth Longfellow

There is nothing which has yet been contrived by man, by which so much happiness is produced as by a good tavern or inn —Samuel Johnson, March 21, 1776

The vicissitudes of life touch him [a happy man] lightly, like the wind in the aspen-tree —Anton Chekhov

Wore his new happiness like an advertisement —Nancy Huddleston Packer

❧ HARDNESS
See: FIRMNESS, TOUGHNESS

❧ HARD-HEARTEDNESS
See: CRUELTY

❧ HARDSHIP
See: FORTUNE/MISFORTUNE

❧ HARD WORK
See: AMBITION, WORK

❧ HARMLESSNESS
See Also: INNOCENCE, KINDNESS

As incapable of inflicting harm as a butterfly —Anon

Harmless and pleasant as the murmur of brook and wind —Robert Buchanan

Harmless as a Fuller Brush salesman —Raymond Chandler

Invariably topical or "brand name" similes either become obsolete or change when the name is no longer a household word. However, there's always a new name or catchword to take its place.

Harmless as a moth in a closet of Dacron —Anon

Harmless as an infant at play —William Cowper

Besides other variants meaning literally harmless ("Harmless as a baby," "Harmless as a sleeping infant"), there are also the more dramatic ones implying danger ("Harmless as an infant playing with knives/a box of pins/matches")

Harmless as a paper tiger —Chinese proverb

Harmless as doves —The Holy Bible

Attribution for the simile is often given to Christina Rosetti's Sonnet of Sonnets, which contains this line: "She spread about her beauty for a snare, harmless as doves."

Harmless as leaves —Reynolds Price

Harmless as pigeons —Robinson Jeffers

Harmless as witches that have been robbed of their terror —Ellen Glasgow

❧ HARMONY
See: AGREEMENT, COMPATIBILITY, PEACEFULNESS

❧ HARSHNESS
See Also: FIRMNESS, VOICE(S)

Austere … as an aging virgin —Paige Mitchell

Corrosive as shame —Frank Swinnerton

Harsh as the bitterness of death —Algernon Charles Swinburne

Harsh as the yelping of jackals —Gustave Flaubert

(I will be harsh as …) harsh as truth —William Lloyd Garrison

Rough as a cob and twice as corny —American colloquialism, attributed to South

Shrill and active like a flight of gulls —George Garrett

Shrill as a whistling teapot with a head full of steam —Anon

(His nerves sang a song) shriller than a dog whistle —Douglas Adams

Shrill [voice] like a blade turning on a whetstone —Clifford Irving

Spoke sternly like a ward nurse to a familiar patient —Arthur A. Cohen

Strident as mustard —Marge Piercy

Threw orders around like lashes from a cat-o'-nine-tails —Maya Angelou

❧ HASTE
See: SPEED

❧ HASTINESS

See: CARELESSNESS

❧ HATRED

Dislike ran round the table like electricity —Penelope Gilliatt

Exuded venom like a malicious old lady —Colette

The greatest hatred like the greatest virtue and the worst dogs, is silent —Jean Paul Richter

Hate … flowed like electric syrup through her veins —Marge Piercy

Hate is ptomaine, good-will is a panacea —Elbert Hubbard

Hating people is like burning down your own house to get rid of a rat —Harry Emerson Fosdick

Hatred fills my mouth like spit —Margaret Atwood

Hatred is a form of subjective involvement by which one is bound to the hated object —Lao Tzu

Hatred is like fire; it makes even light rubbish deadly —George Eliot

Hatreds, like chickens, come home to roost —Joseph Shearing

He'll (a hated individual) be getting into your beer like prussic acid; and blotting out your eyes, like a cataract and screaming in your ears like a brain tumor and boiling around your heart like melted lead and ramping through your guts like a cancer —Joyce Cary

I hate you like all-fire —Truman Capote

(Lady Charlotte would swallow back her hot feeling against Cynthia.) It [hate] was like a dark web within her, a fibrous tangle like the roots of plants in too small a pot —M. J. Farrell

My hate is like ripe fruit —Marvin Bell

The pleasure of hating, like a poisonous mineral, eats into the heart of religion and turns it to rankling spleen and bigotry —William Hazlitt

In his essay, The Pleasures of Hating, *Hazlitt continues to describe the effects on hatred: "It makes patriotism an excuse for carrying fire, pestilence and famine into other lands; it leaves to virtue nothing but the spirit of censoriousness."*

Promiscuous haters get religion as promiscuous lovers get clap —Gerald Kersh

Spite may often see as clearly as charity —Lawrence Durrell

❧ HEAD(S)

See Also: HEAD MOVEMENTS

Great head and neck rising up like a howitzer shell from out of his six-button double-breasted, after the manner of the eternal Occupation Zone commandant —Tom Wolfe

The man being profiled by Wolfe is describing Otto Preminger.

Head like a hard apple —Hugh Walpole

Head stiff and to the side like the bust of a minor Roman official —Cynthia Ozick

A head too small for the size of his face, like an underinflated balloon —Sue Grafton

Held his torso like a bit of classical rubble —Cynthia Ozick

Her head looks as if it had worn out two bodies —American colloquialism attributed to New England

Face is often substituted for head.

His skull curved like a helmet above his deep-set blue eyes —Jonathan Valin

In the novel, Life's Work, Valin *follows this with a sentence containing another simile: "His lower face fit into that helmet like a hardwood dowel driven in by a hammer."*

A sleek, round head like an umbrella's —Arthur Train

❧ HEAD MOVEMENTS

Bowed his head … as if wishing to fall at her feet —Leo Tolstoy

Craned her head back and forth like a periscope, the way people do when they are searching for a taxi at rush hour in Manhattan —Daphne Merkin

Cranes his neck like a swan —Anton Chekhov

Drew his head into his shoulders like the bellows of an accordion —Paul Olsen

Ducks his head, like a man someone has menaced and who has barely gotten out of the way —Richard Ford

Gave a shake of his head, like a dazed boxer coming to —Peter De Vries

Head, bobbing like a hollow ball —John Updike

(She was looking at her husband) head cocked like a setter bitch (as if wondering, trying to remember who she had climbed into bed with this time) —James Crumley

(The old man's) head had lowered itself into his collar like a turtle's —Flannery O'Connor

Head moving like a prison search light —T. Glen Coughlin

Heads … bent, like flowers following the sun or thrushes listening for snails —Frank Swinnerton

Head sliding forward [while dozing] like an abandoned puppet —T. Alan Broughton

(Little Nigel's) head snaps round like a weathervane in a gale —John le Carré

Head spun like a lazy susan —Jay Parini

Head thrust forward like a hungry hawk —Harold Adams

Head tilted to one side like a bib bird sitting on a branch of a tree —Harvey Swados

Head tilted to one side like a robin listening for worms —Jay McInerney

Head turning quickly from side to side, like an animal's —Eudora Welty

Head wagging like a mechanical toy —F. van Wyck

Her head dropped like a soaked tea rose —Sharon Sheehe Stark

His head droops like a sun-flower —S.J. Perelman

His head hangs limp as a sock full of sand —Ira Wood

His head moved to and fro like a foolish kitten's after a swinging tangle of wool —Vicki Baum

His head rolled about his shoulders like a balloon that wanted to break its string —James Lee Burke

His head swung like a snake's as he talked, scanning anyone who chanced to come near —Donald MacKenzie

Holds up her head like a hen drinking —Alan Ramsay's *Collection of Scots Proverbs*

Lifted his big head like a listening deer —Zane Grey

Lifted up his head like a mouse sniffing the air —Isaac Babel

Lowered her head like a slow-witted schoolgirl trying to collect her thoughts in an effort to understand the teacher's question —Franz Werfel

Lowered his head to pray, like a martyr who believed the kingdom of heaven was at hand —Z. Vance Wilson

Made the convulsive movement of his head and neck, as if his tie were too tight —Leo Tolstoy

A man with a small head is like a pin without any, very apt to get into things beyond his depth —Josh Billings

Nodded like a basking lizard —Derek Lambert

Nodded … like a leaf —William McIlvanney

Nodded smartly —like a second lieutenant's salute —Jonathan Valin

Nodding his head like a pecking bird —Beryl Markham

Nods his head like a sage old trial judge —Richard Ford

Pulls back his head, like a turtle sensing danger —Rick Borsten

Shaking her head as if to get rid of a fly —Ruth Suckow

Shaking her head impatiently … as if in a futile attempt to ease the chafing of an invisible collar —Carolyn Kizer

Shook his head like a wet retriever —Sharon Sheehe Stark

Shook his head like an overburdened professor —Martin Cruz Smith

Shook my head back and forth like a silent, solid bell —Richard S. Prather

Tossed her head with petulant violence, like a child who doesn't want her snarls combed out —John Updike

Turned her head … cocking it a little, like a pretty canary in a cage —Harvey Swados

Turning his head from side to side as though his necktie were too tight (and when he did that he usually clutched at his throat), —Ivan Turgenev

In a story entitled "Knock … Knock … Knock …" to describe a character who seemed to feel constantly cramped in the world.

Turns his head from side to side, like a turtle —Margaret Atwood

Wagged their heads like a company of cockatoos —Katherine Mansfield

Waved her head here and there like a piece of wind-worried old orange-peel —F. Scott Fitzgerald

The way he jerked his head from side to side made him seem like some sort of a little perky bird —a goldfinch, perhaps —Roald Dahl

Withdrew his head like a scared tortoise —Donald MacKenzie

♣ HEALTH

See Also: PAIN

As clean and strong and healthy as a young tree in the sun —Hugh Walpole

(Has a heart) as sound as a bell —William Shakespeare, *Much Ado about Nothing*

Drug addiction is like a light that doesn't shine —Cardinal John O'Connor, speaking at New York City ceremony to fight drug addiction, August 8, 1986

Felt like the symptoms on a medicine bottle —George Ade

(Looking) fit and taut as a fiddle —Robert Louis Stevenson

(I feel as) fit as a bull moose —Theodore Roosevelt to newspaper reporters

Fit as a fiddle —John Ray's *Proverbs*

This is the most famous of the many "Fit as" comparisons. A modernized extension by novelist Geoffrey Wolff: "Fit as an electric fiddle."

(You're looking this morning as) fit as a flea —Henry James

Gobbled pills like a famished chicken pecking up corn —Dale Kramer

[Narrator's father] Gradually sank as if he had a slow leak —Oliver Sacks

Healthy as a kayaker —Richard Ford

Healthy as a steer —Thomas Zigal

A healthy body is the guest-chamber of the soul; a sick body its prison —Francis Bacon

Hones himself down [to stay in top physical condition] sharper than a Gillette blade —Norman Keifetz

It is better to lose health like a spendthrift than to waste it like a miser —Robert Louis Stevenson

No neurotic is cured, he merely substitutes one set of neuroses for another. Like a man who stops biting his fingernails only to start scratching his head —Margaret Millar

Pent-up resentment, aggression and hostility are as bad for health as constipation —George Garrett

Radiate health and good will like a red-hot stove —Robertson Davies

Sickness fell upon me like an April cloud —Edward Marsh

So far as ailments went, Uncle Horace was like an insatiable gardener confronted by a seedsman's catalogue. He had only to get news of an untried specimen to have a go at it —Howard Spring

Sound as a bell of brass —Anon

According to Larry Gottlieb, a one-time handicapper for The New York Morning Telegraph, *this expression used to assay a thoroughbred up for sale is the most commonly used simile in racing circles, probably introduced in England in the nineteenth century.*

Sound as a nut —Mazo de la Roche

Temperature as high as a tree —Mary Lee Settle

Unhealthy as the liver of a goose intended for pate —Israel Zangwill

♣ HEART(S)

See Also: AGITATION, HEARTBEAT

Hard hearts, and cold, like weights of icy stone —Percy Bysshe Shelley

The heart errs like the head —Anatole France

The heart (especially the Jewish heart) is a fiddle: you pull the strings, and out come songs, mostly plaintive —Sholom Aleichem

The heart is like the sky, a part of heaven, but changes night and day, too, like the sky —Lord Byron

The heart is like a creeping plant, which withers unless it has something around which it can entwine —Charles James Apperley

The heart is like an instrument whose strings steal nobler music from Life's many frets —Gerald Massey

Heart like a child —Mary Hood

The heart of the wise, like a mirror, should reflect all objects, without being sullied by any —Confucius

Hearts isolated behind the bars of ribs and jumping around like monkeys —Yehuda Amichai

Hearts … mellow as well tilled soil in which good seed flourishes —Vladimir Korolenko

Hearts opening like jaws —Sharon Olds

Heart trembling a little like the door for Elijah the Prophet —Yehuda Amichai

A heart without affection is like a purse without money —Benjamin Mandelstamm

Her heart divided like two wings —Carson McCullers

Her heart sank like a wounded bird —Ellen Glasgow

His heart ached like Niagara Falls —Frank O'Hara

His heart is like a viper, hissing and spitting poison at God —Jonathan Edwards

His heart … like the sea, ever open, brave and free —F. E. Weatherly

His heart sagged in its net of veins like a rock in a sling —George Garrett

His heart swelled up in his throat like a toad —Oakley Hall

His heart was open as the day —Anon ballad, "Old Grimes"

The human heart is like a ship on a stormy sea driven about by winds blowing from all four corners of heaven —Martin Luther

The human heart is like a millstone in a mill: when you put wheat under it, it turns and grinds and bruises the wheat to flour; if you put no wheat, it still grinds on, but then 'tis itself it grinds and wears away —Martin Luther

A man's heart is like a sponge, just soaked with emotion and sentiment of which he can squeeze a little bit out for every pretty woman —Helen Rowland

A man's heart, like an automobile, is always apt to skid and ditch him just at the psychological moment when he thinks he has it under perfect control —Helen Rowland

My heart clenched like a fist —Charles Johnson

The fist comparison is also effective for describing a grim, pinched facial expression.

My heart is like an apple-tree whose boughs are bent with thick-set fruit —Christina Rossetti

The first stanza of "A Birthday," from which this is taken contains yet another heart comparison: "My heart is like a rainbow shell that paddles in a halcyon sea."

My heart is like an outbound ship that at its anchor swings —John Greenleaf Whittier

My heart is like a singing bird —Christina Rossetti

My little heart pops out, like springs —Diane Wakoski

This simile is the title of a poem which begins with yet another simile: "a little spirit in me that's wound up like a clock."

[Without my loved one] My heart's like a beet root choked with chickweed —Anon

This simile appears in a poem entitled "The Broken Hearted Gardener" found in John Ashton's 1888 compilation Modern Street Ballads.

❧ HEARTBEAT

See Also: AGITATION

Chest chiming like a cathedral gone berserk —Jonathan Gash

Feel his heart beating wildly inside his child's body, like a bird in a frail cage —Ruth Prawer Jhabvala

Heart banged like a drum —Katherine Mansfield

Heart beating like an African drum —Hugh Walpole

(Mrs. Arkin's) heart fluttered like a bird's wing —Gloria Norris

Heart jumping like a puppy —Anne Sexton

Heart noisy as a cockcrow —Walter de la Mare

Heart pulsing like a womb which has just given birth —Erica Jong

Heart … running like a hamster on a wheel —Diane Ackerman

Hearts … like muffled drums, are beating funeral marches to the grave —Henry Wadsworth Longfellow

A heart that ran up and down within the cage of ribs like a restless panther —Leonard Casper

Heart thumping like a June bug —Anne Sexton

Heart thumping like an outboard —Richard Ford

His heart … beat high and fast like the ticking of a watch under a pillow —Frank Swinnerton

His heart began to give off tremendous explosions like a rifle —Eudora Welty

His heart beating, fiercely, like a small clock —Celia Dale

His heart flapped like a mass of furled banners —Bernard Malamud

His heart fluttered like that of a small bird about to be stoned —Alice Walker

My heart leaps forward like a hungry dog —Karl Shapiro

My heart pounds away, confident as a clock —Denise Levertov

My heart pounds down on itself like an anvil —Richard Ford

My heart staggers like a drunk —George Garrett

My heart was beating intolerably like a held bird —Reynolds Price

The noise that his heart valve produced sounded like two mechanical mice making love in a spoon drawer —Tom Robbins

Heart like a bass drum in her chest —Susan Richards Shreve

[A skylark's] heart … drumming like a motor —Ted Hughes

(In his ears his) heart sounded like jungle drums —Mary Hedin

❧ HEARTINESS

See: EMOTIONS

❧ HEAT

See Also: WEATHER

The days were like hot coals —Henry Wadsworth Longfellow

A glaring, summery heat covered everything like a layer of glass —Jean Thompson

The heat came down on you like a leaden mantle, stifling you as it did so —Dominique Lapierre

[Midsummer] Heat closed in like a hand over a murder victim's mouth —Truman Capote

Heat fell on her like a blanket —Julia O'Falain

Heat gathers like fog —Angela Carter

Heat … heavy as water —Dan Jacobson

The heat … hung like a hot dust vapor —H. E. Bates

Heat lay on the pavement like a tired dog in the doorway of a house —Aharon Megged

Heat shimmered and bent the fields like the landscape was a reflection in an old mirror —Will Weaver

The heat thick as a swamp —Margaret Atwood

Heat thick as jelly —Elizabeth Enright

The heat was like a tyrant who hated his subjects —William H Hallhan

The heat was like a wasting disease —T. Coraghessan Boyle

Heat waves … rising … like fumes off kerosene —Larry McMurtry

Heat waves rose writhing like fine wavy hair —Wallace Stegner

[Sun] hot as a blast furnace —Raymond Chandler

Hot as a blister —Sir Francis C. Burnand

Hot as a draft from hell —William H. Gass

Hot as a four-alarm fire —H. C. Witwer

Heat waves rippling like lake water —Jessamyn West

Hot as a fox —Elizabeth Spencer

Hot as a jungle —T. Coraghessan Boyle

Hot as a mink in Africa —Reynolds Price

Hot as an oven —The Holy Bible

> *Writers and speakers have long repeated and enlarged upon this simile, changing the descriptive frame of reference altogether or switching from the oven to what comes out of it. Some of these old-timers include: "Hot as hell-fire" (John Dryden), "Hot as hate" (Hamlin Garland), "Hot as hammered hell/hot as hammered lightning" (American colloquialisms), and "hot as a basted turkey" (Will Carleton).*

(On some nights, New York is as) hot as Bangkok —Saul Bellow

Hot as live ash —Beryl Markham

(I am as) hot as molten lead, and as heavy too —William Shakespeare, *King Henry IV, Part I*

(I'm) hot as shit —Richard Ford

(Even the fog that day was) hot as soup —Marge Piercy

Hot as the business end of a pistol —Delmore Schwartz

Hot as the hinges of hell —Babs H. Deal

The hot days pressed people flat as irons —Susan Fromberg Schaeffer

Hot, like a furnace room —Frank Conroy

It was like being inside a radiator —David Brierley

It was more than hot: it was like being under a damp blanket in the tropics —Laurie Colwin

Scorches like nettles —Babette Deutsch

Steaming [from hot weather] like crabs in a soup pot —Margaret Laurence

(The shallow ditches were) steaming like fresh cowflap —Paul Theroux

[A hot bath] Steams like a bowl of soup —Margaret Atwood

(She was) trapped between the heat of the sun and the heat rising from the earth. It was like being struck simultaneously by gusts of fire from above and from below —Margaret Millar

Warm as a newborn child —William Alfred

Warm as summer —Walter Savage Landor

Warm as veins —Ted Hughes

(The water is) warm like my blood —Marge Piercy

(A novel that) warms like a hug —Anon book blurb, quoted in advertisement from *San Francisco Chronicle*

❧ HEAVINESS

Feel heavy … like a corpse —Penelope Gilliatt

Feel heavy like the September limbs of an apple tree —Diane Wakoski

The hand upon his shoulder weighed like a hand of lead —Oscar Wilde

Heavy and indistinct, like the consciousness of a man in a dream —Gustave Flaubert

Heavy as a lecher's kiss —Sylvia Plath

(A cold sky) heavy as a vault —Malcolm Cowley

(They are) heavy as dumplings —Henry David Thoreau

> To give added emphasis and specificity, there's "Heavy as overcooked dumplings," "Heavy as matzo balls," "Heavy as latkes," "Heavy as wontons."

Heavy as guilt —Anon

Heavy as hard luck —Philip Larkin

Heavy as ingots —Diane Ackerman

(The glass mugs were) heavy as sin —Harvey Swados

[A suitcase] heavy as some icon —Cynthia Ozick

Heavy as the weight of dreams —Henry Wadsworth Longfellow

Leaden like a bullet —Ted Hughes

❧ HELPFULNESS
See: KINDNESS

❧ HELPLESSNESS

As defenseless [without a gun] as a tethered goat in a jungle —Eric Ambler

Brutally as on a gag in her mouth, she choked on the sense of her defenselessness —Dorothy Canfield

Chucked about like a cork —Nicholas Monsarrat

Feel like a card in a deck that is being constantly shuffled —W. P. Kinsella

Feel like a rookie runner caught off base by a wily pitcher, hung up in that vast area between first and second, fluttering back and forth like a wounded bird who knows he's doomed —W. P. Kinsella

Felt as a lost sailor on a sinking ship might feel, who throws his last rope —and no saving hands to grasp it —Stella Benson

Felt [as result of being moved to another home by grandparents] as if I was being kidnapped —Elizabeth Bishop

Felt helpless, like a rape victim —Rose Tremain

Felt helpless, as if he were involved in some disgraceful fraud —Katherine Anne Porter

Felt helpless, like a dog that's been run over —Robert Lowry

Felt I was nothing but a husk blown this way and that way by the winds of misfortune —Angela Carter

Felt like a beast in a trap, whose enemy would come upon him soon —H. G. Wells

Felt like a bone between dogs —Julia O'Faolain

Felt like a man trapped in a swamp —Donald MacKenzie

Felt like a marionette, as though something outside her were jerking the strings that forced her to scream and strike —Jean Rhys

Felt like a wounded fish who faced a larger hungry fish —William Beechcroft

Felt more and more like a soldier being pitched into battle without proper orders —John Fowles

Felt ridiculous and out of control, like an engine breaking itself apart —Mark Helprin

Helpless and hopeful as a blade of grass —George Garrett

Get tossed like salad —Charles Bukowski

Helpless ... as a hooked fish swinging to land —Thomas Hardy

Helpless as a lion without teeth —F. Scott Fitzgerald

Helpless as an infant caterpillar in a nest of hungry ants —James Montgomery Flagg

Helpless as a plant without water —F. Hopkinson Smith

Helpless [against tide of emotions] as a swimmer swept away in a strong current —Margaret Kennedy

Helpless as a turtle on its back —O. Henry

Helpless as a writhing beetle on its back —Robert Traver

(I have become as) helpless as if the branch I seize and the one I stood upon both broke at the same time —Tamil

Helpless as shadows —Jean Garrigue

Helpless as the dead —W. S. Gilbert

Helpless as the owner of a sick goldfish —Kin Hubbard

Helpless ... like a man with a rumbling volcano in his pocket, trying to hold back the eruption with his naked hand —Irving Stone

Impotent yet defiant ... like a wild animal driven into a hole or fettered to a stake —Arthur Train

It almost feels out of his control now, like pattern baldness —David Nicholls, *One Day*

It was like being in an elevator cut loose at the top. Falling, falling, and not knowing when you will hit —Margaret Atwood

I was like a lamb or an ox that is brought to the slaughter —The Holy Bible/Jeremiah

Lame as a butterfly spread on a pin —Shirley Kaufman

Like elastic, stretched beyond its uttermost, his reason, will, faculties of calculation and resolve snapped to within him —John Galsworthy

Looked like sheep looking for their shepherd —W. Somerset Maugham

My will was a leaf in a gust of wind —Natascha Wodin

Powerless ... as a stone —Elizabeth Barrett Browning

Powerless as before a cataract —Simone de Beauvoir

Powerless as the wind —Percy Bysshe Shelley

The sense of being trapped ran through him like fire through dry grass —Ben Ames Williams

Sense of helplessness ... like a soft-shell crab that just shed its shell —Kenzaburo Oe

Sinking under the leaden embrace of her affection like a swimmer in a drowning clutch —Edith Wharton

The situation [of tumbling stock market prices] is like being caught in the Bermuda Triangle —Harvey P. Eisen, *New York Times*, January 1986

Tossed about like an empty can in the sea —Romain Gary

Tossed about like cattle on a train —Ignazio Silone

Tossed about like twigs in an angry water —Willa Cather

Unable to do anything ... it was like watching a big cat thrash around in a cage and being helpless to free the beast —May Sarton

Watching a friend fail … it's like a bunch of lifeguards standing and watching their friend drown —Robin Williams, "Sixty Minutes" interview, September 21, 1986

The comedian's comparison described how comedians feel when they watch one of their own fail on stage.

We're all drawn by wires like puppets, and the strongest wire pulls us in the direction in which we are meant to go —Ellen Glasgow

Without power, like a buzzing horsefly —George Garrett

Worked by strings, like a Japanese marionette —W. S. Gilbert

Wriggling helplessly, like a butterfly impaled by a pin —Louis Bromfield

❧ HESITANCY
See: UNCERTAINTY

❧ HILLS
See: MOUNTAINS

❧ HISTORY
See Also: MEMORY; PAST, THE

Americans treat history like a cookbook. Whenever they are uncertain what to do next, they turn to history and look up the proper recipe, invariably designated "the lesson of history" —Russell Baker

Carried his history with him like a tattooed sailor —Alice McDermott

History is a hill or a high point of vantage, from which alone men see the town in which they live or the age in which they are —G. K. Chesterton

Chesterton continues this simile as follows: "Without some such contrast or comparison, without some such shifting of the point of view, we should see nothing whatever of our own social surroundings. We should take them for granted, as the only possible social surroundings."

History is floated like a bond issue on the fat of banks —Marge Piercy

History is written to order like the Sunday funnies —Marge Piercy

This is one of several similes pertaining to history in Piercy's poem "For Shoshana Rihm."

History … like some lump of viscid porridge sliding slowly down a sink —Lawrence Durrell

History passes like falling rocks in the dark —Robinson Jeffers

History trails its meaning like old cobwebs caught in a cellar broom —Robert Penn Warren

(History) sifting and seeping, piddling itself away as one wastes a Sunday —William H. Gass

To the scientific eye all human history is a series of collective movements, destructions or migrations, like the massacre of flies in winter or the return of birds in spring —G. K. Chesterton

You can't escape history, or the needs and neuroses you've picked up like layers and layers of tartar on your teeth —Charles Johnson

❧ HOCKEY
See: SPORTS

❧ HOLLOWNESS
See: EMPTINESS

❧ HOME
See: FURNITURE AND FURNISHINGS, HOUSES, ROOMS

❧ HOMELESSNESS
Like a ship at sea, vainly I looked for a shore —Oscar Hammerstein, "The Man I Used to Be," *Pipe Dream*

❧ HONESTY
See Also: RELIABILITY/UNRELIABILITY

Clean as a hound's hind leg —William Beechcroft

Honest as bread —Mollie Hardwick

Honesty is a compulsion swinging a heavy sword like loving —Marge Piercy

Honesty is like an icicle; if once it melts that is the end of it —Anon

Incorruptible as a statue —Jean Garrigue

Law-abiding as a cow —G. K. Chesterton

(I'm totally legit.) Legal as a Jesuit —Jay Parini

♣ HONOR
See: REPUTATION

♣ HOPE
See Also: DREAM(S)

As renewed as a baby born to middle life —Richard Ford

As spring flowers are promised by seed-sellers in their new catalogues, you too were once full of promise —Charles Simic

Carry hope like a tallow candle —Marge Piercy

Cold hopes swarm like worms within our living clay —Percy Bysshe Shelley

Every wish is like a prayer with God —Elizabeth Barrett Browning

Full of inexpressible expectations, like a child running downstairs on Christmas morning, not knowing what wonderful things may be in the stocking —Harvey Swados

Had his hopes jerked back and forth like Pinocchio —dialogue from *Hill Street Blues*, television drama, 1987

Hope dawned in the distance like a sail —Marguerite Yourcenar

Hope is like the setting of the sun. The brightness of our life is gone —Henry Wadsworth Longfellow

(Nothing in the world is as) hopeful as knowing a woman you like is somewhere thinking about only you —Richard Ford

Hopeful, like extras at an audition —Lawrence Durrell

Hope has as many lives as a cat or a king —Henry Wadsworth Longfellow

Hope is a kind of cheat: in the minute of our disappointment we are angry; but upon the whole matter there is no pleasure without it —Lord Halifax

Hope is like the sun, which, as we journey towards it, casts the shadow of our burden behind us —Samuel Smiles

Hope is nearly as strong as despair, and greatly more pertinacious and enduring —Walter Savage Landor

Hope is to a man as a bladder to a learning swimmer; it keeps him from sinking … but yet many times it makes him venture beyond his height —Owen Feltham

Hope … it's like a fire in the wind; the slightest breeze will diminish it, but if I feed it the wind will make it blaze —Richard Maynard

Hope's as cheap as despair —H. G. Bohn's *Hand-Book of Proverbs*

Hopes like a child —Randall Jarrell

Hope springing like a Jack-in-the-box —Alice McDermott

It was as though a great eraser had swept across Stern's mind, and he was ready to start fresh again —Bruce Jay Friedman

Like our shadows, our wishes lengthen as our sun declines —Edward Young

Living on hope is like living on an 800 calorie-a-day diet —Anon
This may have its origins in a Scottish proverb: "He who lives on hope lives on a very lean diet."

Look at hopefully, like a bird with its beak open waiting for a nice juicy worm —Sara Woods

Plucked my spirits up like a hitchhiker who catches a ride when all hope was lost —Richard Ford

Through the sunset of hope like the shapes of a dream, what paradise islands of glory gleam —Percy Bysshe Shelley

Wishes, like painted landscape ... afar off they appear beautiful; but near they show their coarse and ordinary colors —Thomas Yalden

♣ HORROR

See: FEAR

♣ HOSPITALITY

Giving a party is very much like having a baby; its conception is more fun than its completion —Anon

Hospitable as Welcome Wagoners —Lisa Harris
The hospitality described in Harris' book, The World of a Hasidic Family, *is that of the Lubavitcher women in New York's Crown Heights.*

A host is like a general: it takes a mishap to reveal his genius —Horace

The service was as slow as the progress of a snail and a good-humored as Rip Van Winkle —O. Henry

♣ HOSTILITY

See: ANGER

♣ HOUSES

See Also: FURNITURE AND FURNISHINGS, ROOMS

[A modern building] All glossy undulations and shining declivities, like a razor haircut in concrete and glass —Jonathan Valin

(The place was) as conspicuously unadorned as a Presbyterian church —Jonathan Valin

(Tenement house with mean little) balconies pulled out one by one like drawers —Vladimir Nabokov

Bricks [in path to front door of house] laid close as your hairs —Sharon Olds

A building long and low like a loaf of bread —Marge Piercy

Buildings as badly painted as old whores —Larry McMurtry

Buildings, lined up like ships —Helen Hudson

Buying a new home is like raising children; there's always room for improvement —Arlene Zalesky, *Newsday*, September 27, 1986

The church has a steeple like the hat of a witch —William H. Gass

(Church) Cold, damp and smelly as a tomb —Sean O'Faolain

Cottages looking like something the three little pigs might have built —Sue Grafton

Darkened houses loomed like medieval battlements —J. W. Rider

Decrepit houses lay scattered around the landscape like abandoned machines on a battlefield —Peter Meinke

Door ... shut like an angry face —John Updike

A duplex co-op that made Lenny's [Leonard Bernstein's home] look like a fourth-floor walkup —Tom Wolfe

An estate without a forest is like a house without a chimney —Sholom Aleichem

A first home, like the person who aroused our initial awakening to sex, holds forever strong sway over our emotions —Dorothea Straus

Frame houses collapsing at their centers like underdone cakes —Jean Thompson

A glass-and-concrete air-conditioned block of a building cantilevered from the hillside like a Swiss sanatorium —Walker Percy

The great glass doors ... swished together behind him like an indrawn breath —A. Alvarez

The house is like a woman you find attractive at a distance. The closer you get, the more you wonder what you were thinking. —Jonathan Tropper, *This Is Where I Leave You*

Her house is like her chiffon cakes, all soft surfaces and pleasant colors —Bobbie Ann Mason

A home is like a reservoir equipped with a check valve: the valve permits influx but prevents outflow —E. B. White

A house like this is like some kinds of women, too expensive even —James Hilton

House narrow as a coffin —Angela Carter

Apartments ... looking like giant bricks stabbed into the ground —W. P. Kinsella

Houses, like people, have personalities, and like the personalities of people they are partly molded by all that has happened to them —Louis Bromfield

Houses that aged nicely, like a handsome woman —James Crumley

Houses, their doors and windows open, drawing in freshness, were like old drunkards or consumptives taking a cure —Saul Bellow

The house stood like a huge shell, empty and desolate —H. E. Bates

House ... trim and fresh as a birdcake and almost as small —William Faulkner

It [house] sat among ten acres of blackberry brambles, like an abandoned radio —Tom Robbins

[A ranch-style house] just too cute for words ... it looked as if it had been delivered, already equipped, from a store —Christopher Isherwood

Kept it [an old historic house] up like a museum —Ruth Prawer Jhabvala

Long rows of apartment houses stood bald and desolate, like sad old prostitutes —Erich Maria Remarque

It [a big building} looked as bleak as a barracks —Robert Silverberg

Looked as homey and inviting as the House of Usher —Sarah Bird

Houses (seen from a belfry) looked like small caskets and boxes jumbled together —Boris Pasternak

A modern building made of ... big cubes of concrete like something built by a child —Edna O'Brien

Modern buildings tend to look like call girls who came out of it intact except that their faces are a touch blank and the expression in their eyes is as lively as the tip of a filter cigarette —Norman Mailer

Paint peeled from it [an apartment house] in layers, like a bad sunburn —Paige Mitchell

A peculiar, suggestive heaviness, trapping the swooning buildings in a sweet, solid calm, as if preserving them in honey —Angela Carter

The pink stucco apartment house looked like a cake that was inhabited by hookers about to jump out of it any second —Robert Campbell

A pretty country retreat is like a pretty wife —one is always throwing away money decorating it —Washington Irving

Residences ... of brick, whitewashed and looking faintly flushed, like a pretty girl, with the pink of the brick glowing through where the whitewash had worn off —Harvey Swados

Slate roofs ... like the backs of pigeons —Don Robertson

Tents sprang up like strange plants. Campfires, like red, peculiar blossoms, dotted the night —Stephen Crane

Victorian house ... shaped like a wedding cake —Laurie Colwin

We require from buildings, as from men, two kinds of goodness: first, the doing their practical day well: then that they be graceful and pleasing in doing it —John Ruskin

❧ HOVERING
See: LINGERING

❧ HOWLS
See: SCREAMS

❧ HUMANITY
See: MANKIND

♣ HUMILITY

See: MEEKNESS, MODESTY

♣ HUMOR

See Also: CLEVERNESS, LAUGHTER

Funny as a crutch —American colloquialism

> *This typifies the ironic simile that says one thing while it means quite the opposite. A variation that takes the irony an extra step: "funny as a rubber crutch."*

Funny as a dirty joke at a funeral —William Mc-Ilvanney

Funny as your own funeral —Anon

Good jests bite like lambs, not like dogs —Thomas Fuller

Humor ... like good cheese, mellowed and ripened by age —Dorothy Canfield

Humor, like history ... repeats itself —Harold Adams

Jokes that weren't proper and which therefore went through me like an electric shock, both pleasant and intolerable —Thomas Keneally

Like clothes for the needy, they [jokes] were worn, shabby and used —Henry Van Dyke

Sarcasm should not be like a saw, but a sword; it should cut, and not mangle —Lord Francis Jeffrey

They [poorly told jokes] just lie where they fall, plop, like dropped jellyfish —Herman Wouk

True sarcasm is like a swordstick; it appears, at first sight, to be much more innocent than it really is, till, all of a sudden, there leaps something out of it —sharp and deadly and incisive, which makes you tremble and recoil —Sydney Smith

Wheezing out great lumps of irony like a cat spitting up fur —Wilfrid Sheed

♣ HUNGER

See Also: EATING AND DRINKING

Appetite ... as hot as a fire —Henry Fielding

Appetite ... as insatiable as the sun's —Wallace Stevens

Had an appetite like a chain saw —Harry Prince

Appetite like a sparrow —Jilly Cooper

Ate as heartily as a hungry pike —Howard Spring

Ate like a gang of hungry threshers —Erich Maria Remarque

Belly as empty as a wind instrument —Isaac Babel

Hunger makes beans taste like almonds —Italian proverb

Hunger stirred in him like a small animal —Carlos Baker

Hungry as a bear —John Ray's *Proverbs*

> *Of all the "hungry as" similes, the link with bears, lions and wolves is the most frequently encountered. Amongst once popular phrases which have fallen into disuse are: "hungry as a kite," "hungry as hawks," and "hungry as a hunter."*

(I came home) hungry as a hunter —Charles Lamb

Hungry as a nanny goat —Ben Hecht

> *This simple and direct comparison from a play entitled* Winkleberg *marks a departure from Hecht's bent for far-fetched similes.*

Hungry as a schoolboy —Raymond Chandler

Hungry as the grave —James Thomson

Nibbled like a minnow —Howard Spring

Passengers clustered around a food stall like ants trying to drag a crumb of cake back to their nest —Derek Lambert

Ravenous as gulls over a fishing boat —Marge Piercy

[A voracious eater] Sits down to eat as thin as a grasshopper and gets up as big as a bug in the family way —Erich Maria Remarque

So hungry, it was as if there was a hand in our stomachs, like purses, rifling through them —Susan Fromberg Schaeffer

Stomach ... as hollow as any trumpet —Henry Fielding

♣ HURRYING

See: SPEED

♣ ICICLES

See: SNOW

♣ IDEALS

See: BELIEFS

♣ IDEAS

As flowers grow in more tropical luxuriance in a hothouse, so do wild and frenzied ideas flourish in the darkness —Stefan Zweig

Every conjecture exploded like a pricked bubble —Stefan Zweig

The flow of ideas is broad, continuous, like a river —Gustave Flaubert

> *In a letter to George Sand, Flaubert refers to her easy writing style using this simile. About his own style, he said, "It's a tiny trickle."*

Get ideas like other men catch cold —Diane Ackerman

Getting an idea should be like sitting down on a pin; it should make you jump up and do something —E. L. Simpson

His fancy … ran along with him, like the sails of a small boat, from which the ballast is thrown overboard —Isak Dinesen

The idea came … like a ray of light —Vladimir G. Korolenko

The idea danced before us as a flag —Edgar Lee Masters

An idea, like a ghost … must be spoken to a little before it will explain itself —Charles Dickens

The idea remained, roaming in the dark of his mind … like a rat in the basement, too canny to be poisoned or trapped —John Gardner

Ideas are free. But while the author confines them to his study, they are like birds in a cage, which none but he can have a right to let fly; for, till he thinks proper to emancipate them, they are under his own dominion —Sir Joseph Yates

Ideas are like beards; men do not have them until they grow up —Voltaire

Ideas came with explosive immediacy, like an instant birth. Human thought is like a monstrous pendulum; it keeps swinging from one extreme to the other —Eugene Field

Ideas die, like men —Marguerite Yourcenar

Ideas good as a fat wallet —Richard Ford

Ideas, like women's clothes and rich men's illnesses, change according to fashion —Lawrence Durrell

Ideas of your own are like babies. They are all right if you can keep them quiet —Anon

Ideas should be received like guests, in a friendly way, but with the reservation that they are not to tyrannize their host —Albert Moravia

Ideas that … in the light of day, may hide but never quite go away. Like mice in old houses, one knows they're there —David R. Slavitt

Ideas winged their way swiftly like martins round the bell tower at dawn —Ivan Turgenev

The imagination is like the drunk man who lost his watch, and must get drunk again to find it. It is as intimate as speech and custom, and to trace its ways we need to reeducate our eyes —Guy Davenport

Imagination is like a lofty building reared to meet the sky —Gelett Burgess

Imagination … must be immediate and direct like the gaze that kindles it —Italo Calvino

Just like a busy bee / Each new philosophy / Can fly from tree to tree and keep me moving —Clark Gesner, "My New Philosophy," *You're a Good Man, Charlie Brown*

Lack ideas … as if someone had tied a tourniquet around the left side of his brain —Anon

Like good yeast bread, a good idea needs time to proof —Erik Sandberg-Diment, *New York Times*, August 24, 1986

(Olga's mind was sensuously slow: she) lingered over an idea like someone lingering in a hot tub —Wilfrid Sheed

Old ideas, like old clothes, put carefully away, come out again after a time almost as good as new —*Punch*, 1856

Picking up the idea by its corner like a soiled hanky —Rosellen Brown

Planted ideas ... as a gardener will plant sticks for climbing sweet pea —Lawrence Durrell

A shortsighted concept ... rather like a bankrupt saying he's invested his capital in debts —Frank Ross

The theory arrived neither full-blown, like an orphan on the doorstep, nor sharply defined, like a spike through a shoe; nor did it develop as would a photographic print, crisp images gradually emerging from a shadowy soup. Rather, it unwound like a turban, like mummy bandage —Tom Robbins

What America needs now are ideas like shafts of light —Ellen Gilchrist, National Public Radio September 22, 1986

❧ IDLENESS

See Also: SITTING

As peace is the end of war, so to be idle is the ultimate purpose of the busy —Samuel Johnson

Idle as a painted ship upon a painted ocean —Samuel Taylor Coleridge

Idle as if in hospital —Sylvia Plath

Idleness is like the nightmare; the moment you begin to stir yourself you shake it off —*Punch*, 1853

Idleness, like kisses, to be sweet must be stolen —Jerome K. Jerome

Indolent and shifting as men or tides —Kenneth Patchen

A lazy man is like a filthy stone, everyone flees from its stench —The Holy Bible/Apocrypha

Like lambs, you do nothing but suck, and wag your tails —Thomas Fuller

(I've been) lying around like an old cigarette holder —Anton Chekhov

A slacker is just like custard pie, yellow all through but without crust enough to go over the top —Don Marquis

Sloth, like rust, consumes faster than labor wears, while the used eye is always bright —H. G. Bohn's *Hand-Book of Proverbs*

❧ IGNORANCE

See Also: STUPIDITY

The fault unknown is as a thought unacted —William Shakespeare, "The Rape of Lucrece"

Ignorance is a form of incompetence —Natsume Soseki

Ignorance is like a delicate exotic fruit; touch it and the bloom is gone —Oscar Wilde

Ignorance like a fire doth burn —Bayard Taylor

Ignorant as dirt —Karl Shapiro

A man's ignorance is as much his private property, and as precious in his own eyes, as his family Bible —Oliver Wendell Holmes, Sr.

A man with little learning is like the frog who thinks its puddle a great sea —Burmese proverb

There are a great multitude of individuals who are like blind mules, anxious enough to kick, but can't tell where —Josh Billings

Here are the words as they were originally in Billing's phonetic dialect: "a grate multitude ... but kant tell whare."

❧ ILLNESS

See Also: HEALTH

Afflictions are like lightning: you cannot tell where they will strike until they have fallen —Jean-Baptiste Lacordaire

A big pulse of sickness beat in him as if it throbbed through the whole earth —D. H. Lawrence

The disease and its medicine are like two factions in a besieged town; they tear one another to pieces but both unite against their common enemy ... Nature —Lord Francis Jeffrey

Diseases ... attenuate our bodies ... shrivel them up like old apples —Robert Burton

His head seemed to be flying about like a pinwheel —Sherwood Anderson

Illness and doctors go together like priests and funerals —Armand Salacrou

Illness and medicines are invariable as costly as champagne and gaiety at a party —Janet Flanner

An illness is like a journey into a far country; it sifts all one's experience and removes it to a point so remote that it appears like a vision —Sholom Ash

Nausea lay like poison in his blood —Heinrich Böll

Our bowels were like running faucets —John Farris

Stricken as if an angel had landed on her bedpost —Gloria Norris

❧ ILL TEMPER
See: ANGER

❧ ILLUSTRIOUSNESS
See: FAME

❧ IMAGINATION
See: IDEAS

❧ IMITATION
See: SIMILARITY

❧ IMMEDIACY
See: SPEED

❧ IMMOBILITY
See Also: DEATH, LYING, POSTURE, SITTING, STANDING

(I am) comatose like a mouse in the sun —Janet Flanner
The simile was prompted by the writer's being heavily medicated.

Fixed as the garden in a wallpaper mural —Anon

Frozen like dogs waiting at night for a bitch in heat —Bertolt Brecht

Immobile as a heavily sprayed coiffure —Elyse Sommer

Immobile as despair —Yvor Winters

(Lay,) immobile, like something caught —an ungainly fish —Daphne Merkin

Immobilized like fishes caught in a net —Dominique Lapierre

Immovable, emotionless, a jade Buddha serenely contemplating some quintessential episode of a TV police show —T. Coraghessan Boyle

(The corpse still) lay like a smashed fly —G. K. Chesterton

Lay motionless, as if felled by an axe —Stefan Zweig

Lifeless as a string of dead fish —G. K. Chesterton

Motionless as a dog thrown into the street —Émile Zola

(Clouds ...) motionless as a ledge of rock —Willa Cather

Motionless as an idol and as grim —John Greenleaf Whittier

(Remained standing in the same place) motionless as if he were a prisoner —Bertolt Brecht

Motionless, in an agony of inertia, like a machine that is without power —D. H. Lawrence

Motionless, like a man in a nightmare —G. K. Chesterton

(This play has) no more action than a snake has hips —Anon

Remained rooted in place like an oak —Charles Johnson

Sat as still as a tree —Speer Morgan

Sat like a marble man —Margaret Millar

Sat ... motionless as a drowsing man —Beryl Markham

Sat there like a potted plant —Delmore Schwartz

Sat through it all like a slug —Rita Mae Brown

Sits impassive, like Rodin's *Penseur* —Frank Swinnerton

(I'd rather) sit still, like the pilot light inside the gas —Saul Bellow

Standing ... like a hydrant —Rosellen Brown

Standing there like a glee-club president in granite —Erich Maria Remarque

Standing motionless as if turned to stone —Ivan Turgenev

Standing stock still ... like George Segal plaster figures —Paul Kuttner

Standing there rigid as the Venus de Milo —T. Coraghessan Boyle

In Boyle's story, The Descent of Man, *the character voicing this simile speaks in dialect, using 'de' and 'dere' instead of "there" and "the" as used here.*

Stand motionless as a pillar of the colonial portico of a mansion in a Kentucky prohibition town —O. Henry

Stand motionless ... as though trying to make myself blend with the dark wood and become invisible —William Faulkner

Stand perfectly still, like a scarecrow —Walter de la Mare

Statue-like repose —James Aldrich

The simile from a poem entitled "A Death-Bed" reads as follows in its full context: "Her suffering ended with the day, yet lived she at its close, and breathed the long, long night away in statue-like repose."

Still as a child in its first loneliness —Theodore Roethke

Still as a cocoon on a branch —Marge Piercy

Still as a folded bat —Eudora Welty

(Became) still as a hare caught in the light of a torch —R. Wright Campbell

Still as a little hare in the hollow of a furrow —Colette

(Sitting as) still as a lizard on a stone —Mary Stewart

Still as a picture —John Greenleaf Whittier

Still as a pillar —Reynolds Price

Still as a post —Fannie Stearns Gifford

Other similes to express the same idea are to "sit still as a fence post," and "to stand like an iron post."

Still as a snapshot —Anne Sexton

Still as a turtle on a log which is stuck in the mud near some willows —Elizabeth Spencer

Still as bushes —Helen Hudson

(The air was) still as death —MacDonald Harris

(The next morning was cold and clear and) still as held breath —John Yount

(Ray lay) still as ice —Wilbur Daniel Steele

Still as if a block of ice had formed around him —William McIlvanney

Still as mummy in a case —Henry James

Still as sleeping princesses —Joyce Cary

Still as the wind's center —Theodore Roethke

Stood frozen like some sort of Mexican stone idol —Robert Silverberg

Stood still, petrified like the pillar of salt —Victor Hugo

Stood there rooted like a plant —Ellen Glasgow

They seemed [tired soldiers] as if they were of stone, without the strength to smile, or to swear —Boris Pasternak

♣ IMPARTIALITY

Feel rather like a bridge [at being caught between problems of two friends] attached neither to one side nor the other of a tumultuous river, suspended in space —May Sarton

Impartially welcoming as the host of a television show —Nadine Gordimer

Neutral as a page number —John Braine

(A voice) neutral as Switzerland —Anon

(The Yvette who assembled before me was as) objective as a police sketch —Jill Ciment

♣ IMPASSIVENESS

See: COLDNESS, REMOTENESS, RESERVE

♣ IMPATIENCE

See: RESTLESSNESS

♣ IMPERMANENCE

See: TRANSIENCE

♣ IMPOLITENESS

See: MANNERS

♣ IMPORTANCE/UNIMPORTANCE

See Also: MEMORY, NECESSITY

Brittle and meaningless as cocktail party patter —William Brammer

His influence … it is like burning a … candle at Dover to show light at Calais —Samuel Johnson

Had Johnson been an American living in America instead of an Englishman living in England, his comment on Thomas Sheridan's influence on English literature might well have illustrated with "A candle in New York to show light in Boston."

Hollow as the (ghastly) amiabilities of a college reunion —Raymond M. Weaver

I am essential to the theatre—as ants to a picnic, as the boll weevil to a cotton field —Joseph L. Mankiewicz, *All about Eve*

One of the 1950 screenplay's most memorable lines was spoken by George Sanders in the role of critic Addison de Witt.

I felt like a raisin in a gigantic fruit salad —Mark Hamill, on acting in *Star Wars*

Impact [of information] … as thin as gold —Raymond Chandler

(About as) important as a game of golf to an astronomer —Anon

Important as mathematics to an engineer —Anon

Inconsequential … like the busy work that grade school teachers devise to keep children out of mischief —Ann Petry

Insignificant as the canals of Mars —Frank Conroy

Its loss would be incalculable … like losing the *Mona Lisa* —Dr. Paul Parks, *New York Times* August 23, 1986, on the potential death of Florida's Lake Okeechobee

Meaningful as love —Kenneth Patchen

Meaningless, like publishing a book of your opinions with a vanity press —Scott Spencer

Of no more importance than a flea or a louse —Boris Pasternak

In the novel Doctor Zhivago, *a character uses this simile to compare a wife compared to workers.*

Shallow as a pie pan —Anon

[A speech] shallow as time —Thomas Carlyle

Uneventful as theory —A. R. Ammons

Worthless as withered weeds —Emily Brontë

♣ IMPOSSIBILITY

See Also: ABSURDITY, DIFFICULTY, FUTILITY, OPPORTUNITY

About as much chance as a man with a wooden leg in a forest fire —George Broadhurst

About as possible as hell freezing over —Clifford Odets

As feasible as capturing the rain in a thimble —Jonathan Kellerman

As likely as a mouse falling in love with a cat —Anon

As unlikely as a lecture by Dr. Ruth [Dr. Ruth Westheimer, sex therapist/media personality] in a fundamentalist church —Elyse Sommer

As likely as to see a hog fly —H. G. Bohn's *Hand-Book of Proverbs*

As likely to happen as hair growing on the palm of my hand —Anon

(Anything of a sexual sort seemed) as remote as landing on the moon or applying for French citizenship —Kingsley Amis

As unlikely as your car metamorphosing into a rocket ship —Elyse Sommer

Calling on [emotional] memory for so long a leap was like asking power of a machine wrecked by rust —Wilbur Daniel Steele

Getting him to join (the Federal Witness Program) was like getting the Ayatollah Khomeini to enroll in a rabbinical school —Doug Feiden

Has about as much chance as a cootie on Fifth Avenue —Maxwell Anderson/Laurence Stallings

Has about as much chance of making it into the history books as a fart in a cyclone [about a fictional President] —Peter Benchley

Have about as much chance as a woodpecker making a nest in a concrete telephone pole —Anon sports writer, about a bad baseball team

Have about as much chance as a dish-faced chimpanzee in a beauty contest —Arthur Baer

Baer's simile was part of a comment about the 1919 Willard-Dempsey fight

Impossible … like pushing a wet noodle up a hill —Anon Washington aide, *Wall Street Journal,* July 3, 1987

The aide made this comparison to illustrate the difficulty of trying to attract attention to economic issues and away from the Iran-Contra scandal.

Impossible as expecting a hook to hold soft cheese —Anon

Impossible as it would be to fire a joke from a cannon —Bartlett's *Dictionary of Americanisms*

Impossible as putting the genie back in the bottle —Peter Jennings, commenting on "World News Tonight" about trying to undo damage to Gary Hart's presidential campaign after release of story about his private life, May 7, 1987

Impossible as scratching your ear with your elbow —American colloquialism, attributable to Southwest

Impossible as setting a hen one morning and having chicken salad for lunch —George Humphrey

A comment during Humphrey's tenure as Secretary of the United States Treasury on quick economic changes

Impossible as to imagine a man without a head —Francisque Sarcey

Impossible as to pull hair from a bald man's head —Anon

Impossible as to rivet a nail in a custard pie —Anon

Impossible as to straighten a dog's tail —Anon

Impossible as trying to put on a laughter exhibition in a morgue —J. B. Priestly

Impossible as trying to blow and swallow at the same time —German proverb

Another example of usage turning a proverbial statement, "You can't blow and swallow at the same time," into a proverbial comparison.

Impossible as undressing a naked man —Anon

Another simile with proverbial origins, in this case the Greek proverb "A thousand men cannot undress a naked man."

Impossible as voting "maybe" —Maurine Neuberger

Transposed from "Many times I wished I could vote 'maybe.'"

Impossible ... like compressing the waters of a lake into a tight, hard ball —Vita Sackville-West

Impossible ... like denying a champion fighter the right to compete in the ring on the grounds that he might be hurt —Beryl Markham

Impossible ... like eating chalk or trying to suck sweetness out of paving brick, or being drowned in an ocean of dishwater, or forced to gorge oneself on boiled unseasoned spinach —Thomas Wolfe

Wolfe's writing tended towards excess. Not surprisingly, he tended to string several similes together.

Impossible ... like looking for a grain of rice in a bundle of straw —Dominique Lapierre

Impossible ... like me trying to wash the Empire State Building with a bar of soap —Don Rickles

The impossible situation described by Rickles is Eddie Fisher's marriage to Elizabeth Taylor.

Impossible ... like playing tennis with the net down —Robert B. Parker

Impossible ... like selling the cow and expecting to have the milk too —Danish proverb

Transposed from the proverbial form, "You can't expect to sell the cow and get the blood."

Impossible ... like stopping a runaway horse with your pinkie —William McIlvanney

Impossible, like trying to get blood out of a turnip —English proverb

Efforts to get new blood out of this cliché focus on changing the object out of which to try to get the blood ... anything from a stone to a corpse.

Impossible like trying to make cheesecake out of snow —Anon

Impossible like trying to write on a typewriter while riding a stagecoach —Dr. Ellington Darden

Impossible like trying to knock down the Great Wall with a nail file —Arty Shaw

Impossible [to keep a secret from my wife] like trying to sneak the dawn past the rooster —Fred Allen

Impossible to explain ... like telling a religious household you had decided God was nonsense —Harvey Swados

It [a hard-to-beat record] was like DiMaggio's consecutive game hitting streak: unapproachable —T. Coraghessan Boyle

It was like talking to a tree and expecting a reply —Clive Cussler

It was like trying to catch an eagle in a butterfly net —Wallace Turner, *New York Times*, February 4, 1987.

Turner was reporting on efforts by Washington State game wardens to capture large sea lions that had been eating game fish.

It was like trying to write a description of how to tie shoelaces in a bow for a person who has never seen shoes —W. P. Kinsella

It [changing person's mind about another] was like trying to turn a mule —H. E. Bates

It [trying to sift through events from the past] was not unlike hunting for odd-colored stones in tidal flats —Norman Mailer

(Blackmailing Laidlow would be) like trying to catch a bull with a butterfly net —William McIlvanney

No more chance than a one-legged man in a football game —Elbert Hubbard

No more possible than the development of an orchid in the middle of a crowded street —W. H. Mallock

No more chance than a motorist who passed a red light talking a policeman out of giving him a ticket —Anon

The odds were like poison —Tim O'Brien

To translate this situation to reality would be like trying to stuff a cloud in a suitcase —W. P. Kinsella

Trying to make the company [GM] competitive is like trying to teach an elephant to tap dance —Ross Perot, quoted in *Wall Street Journal* article by George Melloan, February 24, 1987

Unlikely as to see a stone statue walking —Anon

We've no more chance of surviving than an over-ripe plum has of staying on the tree —Simon Mawer, *The Glass Room*

❧ IMPROBABILITY

See Also: IMPOSSIBILITY

❧ IMPROPRIETY

See Also: PROPRIETY/IMPROPRIETY

❧ INACCURACY

See Also: ERRORS

❧ INACTIVITY

See Also: IDLENESS, IMMOBILITY

❧ INAPPROPRIATENESS

See Also: BELONGING

(I) belonged … like a pearl onion on a banana split —Raymond Chandler

Belonged … like a virgin in a brothel —William McIlvanney

Belong like a right shoe on a left foot —Elyse Sommer

Belong like a white poodle on a coal barge —Arthur Baer

Feeling like a Boston schoolteacher in Dodge City —Mary Gordon

(I) feel [out of place] like Babe Paley at a bar mitzvah in the Bronx —Sue Mengers, talent agent, quoted by Rex Reed

Felt like a gap —D. H. Lawrence

Fits in about as well as a bird-of-paradise among wrens —Leslie Bennetts, about character in Dickens' *The Mystery of Edwin Drood, New York Times,* 1985

Had about as much business teaching in college as a duck has riding a bicycle —Richard Ford

Inappropriate as a Size 20 Cinderella —Mike Sommer

Inappropriate as running shoes with a cocktail dress —Anon

It's like a thoroughbred horse pulling a milk wagon —line from movie *The Eagle Has Landed*

Looked like a greyhound puppy in a litter of collies —Michael Gilbert

A man without a place to be … that's like being alone at sea without a log to hang on —William H. Gass

Misplaced … like a dog in church —Anon

Misplaced … like a fish out of water —English phrase

Borrowed by the English from Greek, the simile has been much used and adapted since the fourteenth century.

Never fit right, like a pair of cheap shoes that sprouts a nail in the sole —Marge Piercy

(Looked as) out of place as a chicken in church —James Crumley

Out of place as matzo balls in clam chowder —Elyse Sommer

Out of place as a house boat on the high seas —Anon

Out of place as an atheist in a seminary —Anon

Out of place as a Presbyterian in Hell —Mark Twain

Out of place as some rare tropical bird —Anon

Out of place ... like an old whale stranded on the beach —George Garrett

(Harriet always seemed a little) out of things, like somebody's mother —Mary McCarthy

She was like something wrecked and cast up on the wrong shore —Elizabeth Bowen

Sticking out like a solitary violet in a bed of primroses —Tess Slesinger

❧ INCISIVENESS
See: SHARPNESS

❧ INCOMPLETENESS

Incomplete and unfinished like an apple that has begun to shrink before it has reached maturity —Louis Bromfield

Incomplete as the world on the fifth day of creation —Anon

Incomplete like a pastrami sandwich without a pickle —Ed McBain

Incomplete ... like the tree without leaves, a building without a foundation, or a shadow without the body that casts it (The knight-errand without a lady is like ...) —Miguel de Cervantes

Unfinished [sentence] like a plaster half of an ancient sculptured torso —Penelope Gilliatt

❧ INCONGRUITY
See: ABSURDITY

❧ INCORRECTNESS
See: ERRORS

❧ INCREASE
See: GROWTH

❧ INDECISION
See: CHOICES

❧ INDEPENDENCE
See: FREEDOM

❧ INDIFFERENCE
See: REMOTENESS, RESERVE

❧ INDIGNATION
See: ANGER

❧ INDISTINCTION
See: VAGUENESS

❧ INDIVIDUALITY
See: ORIGINALITY

❧ INDOLENCE
See: IDLENESS

❧ INDUSTRIOUSNESS
See: AMBITION, WORK

❧ INEFFECTIVENESS
See: FUTILITY, USEFULNESS/USELESSNESS

❧ INEVITABILITY
See: CERTAINTY

❧ INEXORABILITY
See: CERTAINTY

❧ INFATUATION
See: LOVE

❧ INFLATION
See: ECONOMICS

❧ INFLUENCE
See: POWER

❧ INFORMATION
His knowledge about the families and lives of his village friends was acquired in bits and pieces.

The information was strung like beads out of casual remarks —Helen Simonson, *Major Pettigrew's Last Stand*

Information would come slowly, like sand dropping steadily through the cinched middle of an hourglass —Michael Connelly, *The Harry Bosch Novels: The Black Echo, The Black Ice, The Concrete Blonde*

❧ INGRATITUDE

See: PARENTHOOD, SHARPNESS

❧ INHERITANCE

See: PAST, THE

❧ INJUSTICE

See: JUSTICE

❧ INNOCENCE

See Also: HARMLESSNESS

Green as apples —Sumner Locke Elliott, *Signs of Life*

Guileless as old Huck —Richard Ford

Guiltless forever, like a tree —Robert Browning

Innocence is like an umbrella: when once we've lost it we must never hope to see it back again —*Punch*

(Catherine's) innocence shone like an icon —Rita Mae Brown

Innocent and affectionate as a child —W. H. Hudson

Innocent and artless, like the growth of a flower —Isak Dinesen

Innocent as a baby —Anon

Innocent as a child unborn

> *Jonathan Swift who used the phrase in Directions to Servants is often credited as its author.*

(I was a neophyte about as) innocent as a choirboy being asked to conduct a solemn mass at the Vatican —Alistair Cooke *New York Times* interview, January 19, 1986

Innocent as a curl —Clarence Major

Innocent as a devil of two years old —Jonathan Swift

Innocent as a game —Frank Tuohy

Innocent as a new-laid egg —W. S. Gilbert

Innocent as a snowflake —Anne Sexton

(Gaze as) innocent as a teddy bear —Babs H. Deal

Innocent as a tourist's Kodak —William McIlvanney

Innocent, like a hornet that has been disarmed —Jean Stafford

(Sat there as) innocently as small boys confiding to each other the names of toy animals —Henry James

Innocuous as flowers afloat in a pond —John Updike

Perennial innocence like a chicken in a pen —William Faulkner

She was like a young tree whose branches had never been touched by the ruthless hand of man —Katherine Mansfield

❧ INQUISITIVENESS

See: CURIOSITY, QUESTIONS AND ANSWERS

❧ INSECTS

See Also: ANIMALS

Beetles and insects with legs like grass stems —Ernest Hemingway

A big black ant, shaped like a dumbbell —John Gunther

Black beetles ... crawled in all directions like animated ink —Harold Adams

Fireflies begin to rise ... exactly like the bubbles in champagne —Elizabeth Bishop

Fireflies dazzle the night like red pepper —W. P. Kinsella

Fireflies glow like planets in the moist, silent darkness —W. P. Kinsella

Fleas are, like the remainder of the universe, a divine mystery —Anatole France

A fly is as untamable as a hyena —Ralph Waldo Emerson

Insects … crooned like old women —Stephen Crane

Mosquitoes … as big as mulberries —William Styron

Moths as large and white as our hands —James Crumley

Nothing is so like a soul as a bee. It goes from flower to flower as a soul from start to star, and it gathers honey as a soul gathers light —Victor Hugo

Spiders which floated like cameos in their jars —Pat Conroy

Yellow butterflies flickered along the shade like flecks of sun —William Faulkner

♣ INSEPARABILITY

See: CLOSENESS, FRIENDSHIP, RELATION-SHIPS

♣ INSIGHT

See: WISDOM

♣ INSIGNIFICANCE

See: MEMORY, IMPORTANCE

♣ INSTINCTIVENESS

See: NATURALNESS

♣ INSULT

(It was) an affront, like a lewd remark —Scott Spencer

A day away from Tallulah (Bankhead) is like a month in the country —Howard Dietz

Has a head as big as a horse, and brains as much as an ass —Thomas Fuller

A more condensed version: "a head like a horse with the brains of an ass."

He's like a bagpipe, you never hear him till his belly is full —Thomas Fuller

He's like a man who sits on a stove and then complains that his backside is burning —W. S. Gilbert, quoted by Stephen Holden, New York Times, July 27, 1986.

While Gilbert and Sullivan's lucrative operettas provided the duo with a lavish lifestyle, Sullivan protested that he couldn't compose "fine" music because of Gilbert's light lyrics. This complaint prompted the observation by Gilbert quoted above.

He is like one of those expensive little dogs —George Bernard Shaw, *Misalliance*. Mrs. Hushabye about her daughter's fiancé

He [Napoleon] spoke like a concierge and said "armistice" for "amnesty" and "section" for "session" —Anatole France

France compared Napoleon's speech to that of a concierge to emphasize that what he said unofficially was quite different from the sayings manufactured for him by hirelings.

He thinks like Nixon, talks like Eisenhower, goofs like Goldwater —Noel Parmentel on John V. Lindsay, *Esquire*, October, 1965

His arms look like a buggy whip with fingers —Fred Allen

If he be an infidel, he is an infidel as a dog is an infidel; that is to say, he has no thought upon the subject —Samuel Johnson on Samuel Foote, October 19, 1769

I missed you like Booth missed Lincoln —Elmer Rice

This line comes from one of Rice's best known plays, Counselor at Law.

Insults are like bad coins; we cannot help their being offered to us, but we need not take them —C. H. Spurgeon

The king [Prince Albert of England] looks like a retired butcher —Oliver Wendell Holmes, Sr.

This much-quoted remark originated with a letter to Holmes' parents, June 13, 1834

Like a sewer rat that wants to scurry into a hole —Kenzaburo Oe

Like so many country people who lead a natural outdoor life, his features had hardly any definition. He gave me the impression of an underdone veal cutlet —Alexander King

Looks as if he had never been born and could not be extinguished —Harriet Martineau

She looked like a street just before they put on the asphalt —George Ade

She looked rather like a malicious Betty Grable —Truman Capote

A slight (of that kind) stimulates a man's fighting power; it is like getting a supply of fresh bile —Henrik Ibsen

Some insults come like a blow on the head the morning after, but a few are balm —Norman Mailer

They're [the Kennedy men] like dogs, they have to pee on every fire hydrant —Truman Capote

Why don't you buy some stuffing? Your bosoms look like fried eggs —Reynolds Price

Why don't you get a haircut; you look like a chrysanthemum —P. G. Wodehouse

You are like a cuckoo, you have but one song —H. G. Bohn's *Hand-Book of Proverbs*

A modern variation of this is: "He has as many good features as a cuckoo has songs."

You look as if you'd been put through a washing machine —John Dos Passos

You (Harold Ross) look like a dishonest Abe Lincoln —Alexander Woolcott

Woolcott's much quoted comparison of the New Yorker *editor Harold Ross to a dishonest Abe Lincoln is one of many quotes born around the famous Algonquin Round Table, and widely circulated in the media and books ever since.*

You look like a million dollars, green and wrinkled —Saul Bellow

You're funny as a boil on the ass —Harold Adams

Your losing one pound is like Bayonne losing one mosquito —line from the television show *The Honeymooners*

The simile was delivered by Alice (played by Audrey Meadows) to Ralph (played by Jackie Gleason).

You talk such convoluted crap you must have a tongue like a corkscrew —William McIlvanney

You've got a foot movement, kid, like a baby hippopotamus trying to side-step a jab from a humming-bird … And your knees are about as limber as a couple of Yale pass-keys (addressed to a dancer) —O. Henry

❦ INTELLIGENCE

See Also: MIND

Brain like Einstein —H.E. Bates

Compared with the short span of time they live, men of great intellect are like huge buildings standing on a small plot of ground —Arthur Schopenhauer

A country without intellectuals s like a body without a head —Ayn Rand

(I have) a head on my shoulders that's like a child's windmill, and I can't prevent its making foolish words —D. H. Lawrence

Intellect is to emotion as our clothes are to our bodies: we could not very well have civilized life without clothes, but we would be in a poor way if we had only clothes without bodies —Alfred North Whitehead

Intelligence is like money … if you don't let on how little you've got, people will treat you as though you have a lot —Anon

One good head is better than a hundred strong hands —Thomas Fuller

In Fuller's collection of aphorisms it's "better than a hundred strong heads" but common usage has made "as good as" and "like as" popular.

Smart as a whip —Anon

A simile very much in the mainstream of everyday usage.

Smart as forty crickets —American colloquialism, attributed to South

Smart ... like an idiot savant, smart enough to be dumb when he needed to —Lynne Sharon Schwartz

♣ INTENSITY

See Also: SHARPNESS, STARES

Acute as the badness of no woman out in the world thinking about you —Richard Ford

Acute like the flow of hope —Joseph Turnley

As deep into ... as a sheep is thick in wool —Anon

Burns like hate —George MacDonald

(Worries and obsessions that) come like hot rivets —Wilfrid Sheed

Deep as first love —Alfred, Lord Tennyson

Deep as earth —Madeleine L'Engle

Deep as hell —Francis Beaumont and John Fletcher

Digging in deeper and deeper, like rats in a cheese —Henry Miller

(Lonely and) furious as a hunt —George Garrett

Had a startling intensity of gaze that never wavered from its object, like that of a palmist or a seer —Mary McCarthy

(Curiosity) heating up like an iron —Susan Fromberg Schaeffer

Move through life with the intensity of one for whom each day is the last —Anon

Run deep, like old wounds —William Brammer

Sharp as a pincer —Julia O'Faolain

With the intensity of a cat following a rolling ball of yarn —Ira Berkow on Wade Boggs, Red Sox player's watching of a pitch *New York Times,* October 7, 1986

♣ INTIMACY

See: CLOSENESS, RELATIONSHIPS

♣ INTOLERANCE

Bigotry ... it's like putting your elbows on the table. You know you're not supposed to. But there's that instinct —Bonnie Currie, *New York Times,* January 24, 1986

Closed as a bigot's mind —Anon

Intolerant as a sinner newly turned saint —Anon

The mind of the bigot is like the pupil of the eye; the more light you pour upon it, the more it will contract —Oliver Wendell Holmes, Jr.

Prejudice is as a mist, which in our journey through the world often dims the brightest and obscures the best of all the good and glorious objects that meet us on our way —Anthony Ashley Cooper

Prejudices ... are like rats, and men's minds are like traps; prejudices get in easily, but it is doubtful if they ever get out —Lord Francis Jeffrey

♣ IRONY

See: HUMOR

♣ IRREGULARITY

See: REGULARITY/IRREGULARITY

♣ IRRITABLENESS/IRRITATING

See Also: ANGER, NERVOUSNESS, TENSION

Annoying as bird droppings on your windowshield —Elyse Sommer

Bitter exasperation tightened like a knot in Mr. Casper's mind —William Styron

Bristling like a panther —Victor Hugo

Cross as a sitting hen —American colloquialism, attributed to New England

Cross as nine highways —John Ray's *Proverbs*

Cross as two sticks —Sir Walter Scott

Cross ... like a beautiful face upon which some one has sat down by mistake —Victor Hugo

Disgust like powder clotted my nose —Cynthia Ozick

Disturbing as a gnat trapped and mucking about in the inner chamber of his ear —John Yount

Disturbing as decay in a carcass —Julia O'Faolain

Excitable … like a stick of dynamite just waiting for somebody to come along and light your fuse —David Huddle

Feel feisty, like a galloping colt on a Mediterranean hillside —Tony Ardizzone

In the novel from which this is taken, The Heart of the Order, *the narrator's irritability is caused by having his name shortened.*

Feeling ornery as a bunkhouse cook —Richard Ford

Felt irritably ashamed, like a middle-aged man recalling last night's party, and his unseemly capers and his pawing of the host's wife —Wallace Stegner

Gnaws like a silent poison —George Santayana

Gruff as a billy goat —Mary Hedin

Her grumpiness, her irritability, her crotchets are like static that, from time to time, give way to a clear signal, just as you often hit a pure band of music on a car radio after turning the dial through a lot of chaotic squawk —Laurie Colwin

Irritable like a hedgehog rolled up the wrong way, tormenting himself with his own prickles —Thomas Hood

The prickly hedgehog is a favorite image for describing irritability. A shorter variation of the above by Tolstoy is "bristly … like a hedgehog." Expanded versions include: "The man who rises in the morning with his feelings all bristling like the quills of a hedge-hog, simply needs to be knocked down" (Josiah Gilbert Holland), and "An irritable man is like a hedgehog rolled up the wrong way, tormenting himself with his own prickles" (Thomas Hood).

Irritated as a young stag is irritated by the velvet on his antlers —Rumer Godden

(All the mistakes of my misspent little life came down to) irritate me like so many grains of pepper —Gerald Kersh

Irritating as a coughing fit during a play —Anon

Irritating as a fly that keeps buzzing around your head —Anon

Irritating as one sock or an odd glove —Helen Hudson

Irritating, like a dish of "chulent" to an old man's gut —Stephen Longstreet

"Chulent" is a Jewish dish of meat, beans, and onions. Obviously this is the type of comparison that could easily be adapted to be more meaningful to other groups, for example: "irritating, like a dish of hot chili."

Irritating like a gun that hangs fire —Joseph Conrad

A minor nuisance, like having a tooth filled —Richard Connell

Prickly as thistles —Lawrence Durrell

Sizzle and splatter like batter in a pan —line from British television series *Bergerac*, July 1987

Snappish as a junkyard dog —Robert Campbell

Sulk, like an old man whose son had failed to make varsity —Clancy Sigal

Tempers snapping like rubber bands —Anon, WNYC, Public Radio, March 28, 1987

Troublesome as a lawsuit —Colley Cibber

♣ ISOLATION
See: ALONENESS

♣ JEALOUSY
See: ENVY

♣ JEWELRY
See Also: CLOTHING

A pear-shaped diamond, as big as your thumb —Paige Mitchell

An assortment of costly stones [of questionable taste] … very much like something Hansel and Gretel might well have plucked from the witch's house to eat —Henry Van Dyke

Bracelets seemed to grow up her arms like creeping plants —Nadine Gordimer

Bracelets … warm and heavy, alive like flesh —Elizabeth Taylor

A diamond as big as an Englishman's monocle —Lael Wertenbaker

A diamond as big as the Ritz —F. Scott Fitzgerald
This served as the title for a famous Fitzgerald story.

A diamond … as big as your fourth fingernail —Gerald Kersch

Diamond pinkie rings sputtering like neon on his manicured fingers —Jonathan Valin

Diamonds as big as grapes —Louis Adamic

Diamonds as big as potatoes —Henry James

Diamonds flashed … like drops of frozen light —Paige Mitchell

Earrings tiny as pinheads —Richard Ford

A medallion that could have anchored the *Queen Mary* —William McIlvanney

Necklace … flashed like summer lightning —Anais Nin

Pearl … shaped like the full moon, and whiter than the morning star —Oscar Wilde

(Wedding) ring … pink gold like the morning light —Anon

Rubies as big as hen's eggs, and sapphires that were like gloves with lights inside them —F. Scott Fitzgerald

Rubies like cherries, sapphires like grapes —Isak Dinesen

Rubies like headlights —Philip Levine

She was encrusted with jewels like a Maharini —MacDonald Harris

✤ JOBS
See: WORK

✤ JOKES
See: HUMOR

✤ JOURNALISM
See: PROFESSIONS, WRITERS/WRITING

✤ JOY
See Also: CONTENTMENT, HAPPINESS, PLEASURE

Agitated with delight as a waving sea —*Arabian Nights*

Exhilaration spread through his breast like some pleasurable form of heartburn —Nadine Gordimer

A joyous feeling … shot up, like the grass in spring —Ivan Turgenev

(Heart is) as full of sunshine as a hay field —Josh Billings

Bliss … as though you'd suddenly swallowed a bright piece of that late afternoon sun and it burned in your bosom, sending out a little shower of sparks into every particle —Kathine Mansfield
The simile sets the mood for one of Mansfield's best known stories, Bliss.

Ecstasy warm and rich as wine —Harvey Swados

Elated … like a lion tamer who has at last found the whip crack which will subdue the most ferocious of his big cats —John Mortimer

Enjoy life like a young porpoise —George Santayana

Gorged with joy like a pigeon too fat to fly —Marge Piercy

Great joys, like griefs, are silent —Shackerley Marmion

Gurgle like a meadowlark —W. P. Kinsella

Heart … soared like a geyser —William Peden

Her heart became as light as a bubble —Antonia White

Joy careens and smashes through them like a speeding car out of control —Irving Feldman

Joy … Felt it (joy) rumbling within him like a subterranean river —André Malraux

Joyful as carolers —David Leavitt

Joy is like the ague [malaria]; one good day between two bad ones —Danish proverb

Joy leaping within me … like a trout in a brook —George Garrett

Joy rises in me like a summer morn —Samuel Taylor Coleridge

Joys are bubble-like; what makes them bursts them too —P. J. Bailey

Joy, simple as the wildflowers —George Garrett

Joys … like angel visits, short and bright —John Norris

The angel visit comparison has been linked as effectively to goodness and fame.

Joys met by chance … flow for us fresh and strong, like new wine when it gushes from the press —André Gide

The joys we've missed in youth are like … lost umbrellas; we mustn't spend the rest of life wondering where they are —Henry James

(He is) jubilant as a flag unfurled —Dorothy Parker

Men without joy seem like corpses —Kaethe Kiwitz

My heart lifted like a wave —Norman Mailer

Our joys are about me like a net —Iris Murdoch

Rose and fell, like a floating swimmer, on easy-going great waves of voluptuous joy —Christina Stead

A strong exhilaration ran through her like the fumes of wine —Ben Ames Williams

The sun in my heart comes up like a Javanese orange —Dylan Thomas

Their joys … ran into each other like water paints mingling to form delicate new colors —Sumner Locke Elliott

Triumphant as if I'd just hurled a shutout —W. P. Kinsella

The term shutout was particularly appropriate in Kinsella's baseball novel, Shoeless Joe. *Baseball expressions do, however, work well within other contexts.*

A wonderful feeling enveloped him, as if light were being shaken about him —John Cheever

❧ JUDGMENTS
See: OPINIONS

❧ JUMPING
See Also: LEAPING, ROCKING AND ROLLING

Bouncing from foot to foot like a child in need of a potty —Joan Hess

Flapping and jumping like a kind of fire —Richard Wilbur

Hop about like mice on tiptoe —Alistair Cooke, *New York Times,* January 19, 1986

Cooke's comparison describes how a speaker's eyes move back and forth between viewer and teleprompter

Hopping about like a pea in a saucepan —Robert Graves

Hopping like a shot putter —Pat Conroy

Jogging up and down like a cheerleader —T. Coraghessan Boyle

Jumped about like sailors during a storm —O. Henry

(Mrs. Brady's mind, hopefully calculating the tip) jumped and jumped again like a taximeter —Katherine Bush

In a short story entitled The Night Club, *the character with the jumping mind is a rest room matron.*

Jumped as though he'd been shot —Katherine Mansfield

Jumped back as if he'd been struck by a snake —T. Coraghessan Boyle

Jumped like a buoy —William Goyen

Jumped like she'd seen a vampire —Dan Wakefield

Jumped like small goats —Theodore Roethke

Jumped on him like a wild wolf —Clifford Odets

Jumped out of the way like an infielder avoiding a sliding runner —Howard Frank Mosher

Jumped sideways like a startled bird —Jay Parini

Jumped up as if stung by a Tarantula —Sholom Ash

Jumped up like I was sitting on a spring —W. P. Kinsella

Jumping up and down like Jack-in-the-boxes —Barbara Pym

Jumping like a toad —Ross Macdonald

Jumping like Nijinsky —Saul Bellow

Jumping up like a squirrel from behind the log —Rudyard Kipling

Jump [with shock] like a flea on a frog's back —Walter Duranty

Jump like a flea on a frog's back —Walter Duranty

Jump like a chimp with a hot foot —Anon comment on radio show, about people doing Jane Fonda workout routines, December 10, 1986

Skipping (up the stairs) like a young ghost —Frank Swinnerton

♣ JUSTICE

Even, it [justice] is as the sun on a flat plain; uneven, it strikes like the sun on a thicket —Malay Proverb

Injustice … gathers like dust under everything —Rainer Maria Rilke

Just as a sentence meted out by a kangaroo court —Anon

Justice … inevitable as the law of cause and effect —L. P. Hartley

Justice is like a train that's nearly always late —Yevgeny Yevtushenko

Justice is like the kingdom of God; it is not without us as a fact, it is within us as a great yearning —George Eliot

Shed justice like paladins —Jonathan Valin

The tongue of the just is as choice silver —The Holy Bible/Proverbs

An unrectified case of injustice has a terrible way of lingering … like an unfinished equation —Mary McCarthy

We will not be satisfied until justice rolls down like waters and righteousness like a mighty stream —Martin Luther King Jr., speech, June 15, 1963

This is from King's famous "I Have a Dream" speech.

Your righteousness is like the mighty mountains. Thy judgments are like the great deep —The Holy Bible/Psalms

"Your" replaces the biblical "thy."

♣ KINDNESS

See Also: GENTLENESS, SWEETNESS

A heart as soft as a marshmallow —Michael Korda, *Another Life*

(You're) as good as an umbrella on a wet day —H. E. Bates

As kind as Santa Claus —Oscar Hammerstein II, from lyric for *South Pacific*

As much compassion as a toreador moving in for the final thrust —Marilyn Sharp

As occupied with worthy projects as Eleanor Roosevelt —Lisa Harris

Doing a favor for a bad man is quite as dangerous as doing an injury to a good one —Plautus

Exuding good will like a mortician's convention in a plague year —Daniel Berrigan

Gifts are as the gold which adorns the temple; grace is like the temple that sanctifies the gold —William Burkitt

Gifts are like fish hooks —Epigram c. 65 B.C.E.

Gifts are like hooks —Marcus Valerius Martialis (known in English as Martial)

As good as gold —Charles Dickens

A simile that's become a common expression. In A Christmas Carol, its most frequently quoted source, it's a response to the question "And how was Tiny Tim Today?" In The Gondoliers, W. S. Gilbert gave it a nice twist with "In the Wonder-working days of old, when hearts were twice as good as gold." In Joseph Heller's novel Good As Gold it serves as a play on the hero's name (Bruce Gold).

(He'll be) good as pie —Ring Lardner

A good heart ... a heart like a house —Irwin Shaw

The good is, like nature, an immense landscape in which man advances through centuries of exploration —José Ortega y Gassett

Good to the core like bananas —Marge Piercy

Good will ... is like gentle sunshine in early spring. It invigorates and awakens all buds —Berthold Auerbach

Great minds, like heaven, are pleased in doing good, though the ungrateful subjects of their favors are barren in return —Nicholas Rowe

A hand as liberal as the light of day —Cowper

A heart as big as a bird cage —James B. Hall

A heart as big as a mountain —Anon

A heart as warm as a desert storm —Ogden Nash

A heart like duck soup —Jean Garrigue

In his short story "The Snowfall," Garrigue elaborates on the duck soup comparison as follows: "She's the kind to want to stop a car if she hears some animal crying in the woods."

A heart like warm putty —Mary Stewart

Heart ... soft as any melon —Franklin Pierce

Heart ... was as great as the world —Ralph Waldo Emerson

In Emerson's essay "Greatness," the simile continues with "But there was no room in it to hold the memory of a wrong."

He gives up a buck as quickly as he would a tattoo —Anon

A helping word to one in trouble is often like a switch on a railroad track ... an inch between wreck and smooth-rolling prosperity —Henry Ward Beecher

He was like Florence Nightingale —Tennessee Williams, *Playboy*

Williams used the Florence Nightingale simile to describe his agent's devotion when he was ill.

(My mother) is soft as a grape —Rita Mae Brown

Kindness as large as a prairie wind —Stephen Vincent Benét

Kindness is like a baby; it grows fast —Anon

Kindness is like snow; it beautifies everything it covers —Anon caller on night-time radio talk show

Kindness, like grain, increases by sowing —H. G. Bohn's *Hand-Book of Proverbs*

A kind word is like a Spring day —Russian proverb

Made the Good Samaritan look like a cheap criminal —George Ade

Mercy among the virtues is like the moon among the stars, not so sparkling and vivid as many, but dispensing a calm radiance that hallows the whole —E H. Chapin

(My mother was as) mild as any saint —Alfred, Lord Tennyson

My bounty is as boundless as the sea —William Shakespeare, *Romeo and Juliet*

Our bounty, like a drop of water, disappears when diffused too widely —Oliver Goldsmith

The place of charity, like that of God, is everywhere —Jacques Benigne Bossuet

(She was unsparing of herself, she) poured herself out like cream (into the cups of these dull people) —Sumner Locke Elliott

The record of a generous life runs like a vine around the memory of our dead —Robert G. Ingersoll

Shone [with kindness] like the best of good deeds —Frank Swinnerton

Solicitous as St. Peter —Norman Mailer, about David Susskind

A sympathetic heart is like a spring of pure water bursting forth from the mountain side —Anon

To do a kindness to a bad man is like sowing our seed in the sea —Phocylides

Unselfish as the wind —Ken Kesey

We are never like angels till our passion dies —Thomas Dekker

"Never" is modernized from "ne'er."

♣ KISSES

See Also: INSULTS

Batted them [breast nipples] over and over with my tongue like gum —Joe Coomer

Being kissed … was something done to her, like the shampoos her mother used to give her at the kitchen sink —John Updike

He kissed her … his neck arching forward, hers backward, like a pair of swans —T. H. White

Her lips grazed mine, cool, soft, and tremulous as the wings of a moth —Robert Traver

His kiss dropped on her like a cold smooth pebble —Edith Wharton

His mouth was as soft as a flower and his breath as sweet —Ruth Prawer Jhabvala

It [kissing someone] was like putting your mouth against an automatic bank teller, where it swallows your credit card —John Updike

Kissed (the children) with an official air, as if she were conferring an honour, pinning on her kisses like orders —Rebecca West

Kisses are like confidences, one follows the other —Denis Diderot

Kisses are like grains of gold or silver found upon the ground, of no value themselves, but precious as showing that a mine is near —George Villiers

Kisses, like folks with diminutive souls, will manage to creep through the smallest of holes —J. G. Saxe

Kisses … sticky like a child's —Flannery O'Connor

Kisses strong like wine —Algernon Charles Swinburne

Kiss … felt like a drop of rain in the desert —John Updike

Kissing a person who's self-righteous and intolerant is like licking a mongoose's ass —Tom Robbins

Kissing a smoker is like licking an ashtray —Tom Robbins

Kissing her lips was like kissing warm but uncooked liver —Stephen King

Kissing her…. was like playing post office with a dead and rotting whale —Truman Capote

Kissing him would be like kissing razor blades —David Brierly

Kissing is a good deal like eating; there is not much fun when person is hungry in standing by, and seeing it done by another fellow —Josh Billings

Portions originally in the Billings phonetic dialect: "iz hungry … and see it did bi anuther fellow."

A kiss without a mustache is like an egg without salt —Spanish proverb

Moved her head and face about under the kisses as if they were small attacking waves —Doris Lessing

One more such kiss and I am ready to be roasted upon a slow fire like any chicken or duckling —Delmore Schwartz

Pecks like chicken scratchings —Mary Morris

She dug her lips into my mouth like tiger's claws —Jaroslav Seifert

She kissed me as moistly as a little girl —John Braine

She took kisses like so many coats of paint —Lawrence Durrell

A tall, willowy man, with thin lips and grave eyes and a mouth of such infinite depth, with such an inexhaustible array of recesses, that kissing him was like touring the catacombs of Notre Dame —Lionel Shriver, *The Post-Birthday World*

They kissed like two old people going to bed after the clock has been wound and the cat put out —Derek Lambert

To kiss her would be like a Becket play to a college student: She would study it, dissect it, analyze it, appraise it and inject it with the serum of significance, until at last she transformed the simple touching of four lips into a Rosetta Stone that would give meaning to her life —Peter Benchley

When she kissed him, he melted like a lump of milk chocolate —Marge Piercy

❧ KNOWLEDGE

See Also: EDUCATION, INTELLIGENCE, MIND

A body without knowledge is like a house without a foundation —Hebrew proverb

The desire for knowledge, like the thirst of riches, increases ever with the acquisition of it —Laurence Sterne

Follow knowledge, like a sinking star, beyond the utmost of human thought —Alfred, Lord Tennyson

Gleaned bits of information like a mouse hoarding pellets of bran stolen from the feed manger —Rita Mae Brown

(There are no limits to his knowledge, on small subjects as well as great;) he is like a book in breeches —Sydney Smith about Macaulay

In knowledge as in swimming he who flounders and splashes on the surface, makes more noise, and attracts more attention than the pearl-diver who quietly dives in quest of treasures to the bottom —Washington Irving

In science, as in life, learning and knowledge are distinct, and the study of things, and not of books is the source of the latter —Thomas H. Huxley

It's like swimming, once you learn it you never forget it —Miguel de Cervantes

Knowledgeable as a walking encyclopedia of universal knowledge —Louisa May Alcott

Knowledge ... is like a fire, which must first be kindled by some external agent, but which will afterwards propagate itself —Samuel Johnson

Knowledge ... like a rough diamond ... will never be worn or shine, if it is not polished —Lord Chesterfield

Knowledge, like religion, must be "experienced" in order to be known —Edwin Percy Whipple

The knowledge of man is like the waters, some descending from above, and some springing from beneath; the one informed by the light of nature, the other inspired by divine revelation —Francis Bacon

Paraphrased from Bacon's old-style: "Knowledge of man is as the waters."

Knowledge, when wisdom is too weak to guide her, is like a headstrong horse, that throws the rider —Francis Quarles

The right to know is like the right to live. It is fundamental and unconditional in its assumption that knowledge, like life, is a desirable thing —George Bernard Shaw

The struggle for knowledge has a pleasure in it like that of wrestling with a fine woman —Lord Halifax

The original simile used "hath" instead of "has."

The understanding, like the eyes, while it makes us see and perceive all things, takes no notice of itself, and it requires art and pains to set it at a distance and make it its own subject —John Locke

The fifth word is a modernization of the original, "whilst."

We deal our knowledge like a pack of cards —George Garrett

With information we can go anywhere in the world, we are like turtles, our houses always on our backs —John le Carré

In his novel A Perfect Spy, le Carré expands the simile as follows: You learn to paint, you can paint anywhere. A sculptor, a musician, a painter, they need no permits. Only their heads.

❧ LANDSCAPES

See Also: MOUNTAINS; NATURE; PONDS, RIVERS, AND STREAMS; ROAD SCENES; TREES

The corn is as high as an elephant's eye and it looks like it's climbin' clear up to the sky —Oscar Hammerstein II, from opening lyric for *Oklahoma*

The endless fields glowed like a hearth in firelight —Eudora Welty

A farm … off the road … glittering like a photo in a picture book with its twin silos pointing to heaven like two fat white fingers —Harvey Swados

Fields like squares of a chessboard and trees and houses like dolls' furniture —Hugh Walpole

The fields shone and seemed to tremble like a veil in the light —Eudora Welty

The fields were like icing sugar —Joyce Cary

The fields [in March] were white as bones and dry as meal —M. J. Farrell

Gardens, crowded with flowers of every rich and beautiful tint, sparkled … like beds of glittering jewels —Charles Dickens

Great spots of light like white wine splash over the Jardins Publiques —Katherine Mansfield

Green hummocks like ancient cannon-balls sprouting grass —Elizabeth Bishop

The land flowed like white silk … flat as a bed sheet and empty as the moon —Frank Ross

Landscape as precise and vibrant as fine writing —Sharon Sheehe Stark

The landscape boiled around her like a pan of beans —Dilys Laing

Landscape … gaunt and bleak like the face of the moon —Donald Seaman

Landscape … like a gray sink —Paul Theroux

The landscape [when it snows] lumps like flour gravy —Lisa Ress

Landscapes … like sorrows, … require some distance —Donald Justice

The landscape was bleak and bereft of color … like a painting in grisaille with its many tints of gray —Barbara Taylor Bradford

The landscape was yellowish and purple, speckled like a leopard skin —Nikos Kazantzakis

The lawn looked as expensive as a velvet carpet woven in one piece —Edith Wharton

The lawns looked artificial, like green excelsior or packing material —Saul Bellow

The lawn, spread out like an immense green towel —Ludwig Bemelmans

Light hits that field, like silk being rubbed the wrong way —John Gunther

The long slope of the park dipped like a length of green stuff with a ceiling cloth of blue and pink smoke high above —Virginia Woolf

Meadows carpeted with buttercups, like slabs of gold in the somber forest —John Fowles

Patches of earth showed through the snow, like ink spots spreading on a sheet of white blotting paper —Edith Wharton

Petals … fell on the grass like spilled paint —Laurie Colwin

Populating the field in dark humps, like elephants moving across savannah, were scores of great round straw bales —Will Weaver

Pretty cubes and loaves of new houses are strewn among the pines, like sugar lumps —Walker Percy

Smooth swelling fields, like waves —Wilbur Daniel Steele

The stony landscape … is full of craters and frozen lights like a moon —Erich Maria Remarque

Swelling smooth fields like pale breasts —Wilbur Daniel Steele

The reeds and willow bushes looked like little islands swaying in the wind —Leo Tolstoy

Vast lawns that extend like sheets of vivid green —Washington Irving

Irving's simile was inspired by English park scenery.

The view was green and rich, and breathtaking, like a photo soaked in dyes —Lorrie Moore, *Birds of America: Stories>*

The wet countryside glistened and dripped as though it had been freshly scrubbed —Robert Traver

Wet furry fields lay like the stomachs of soft animals bared to the sky —Julia O'Faolain

Wet pine growth reflects the sunlight like steel knitting needles —Walker Percy

When you drive by them [the woods] fast, the crop rows in between spin like spokes on a turning wheel —Alec Wilkinson, *New Yorker,* August 12, 1985

The whole landscape loomed absolute, as the antique world was once —Sylvia Plath

The whole [valley] was like a broad counterpane, died in rust and yellow and golden brown —Beryl Markham

♣ LANGUAGE
See Also: SPEAKING, WORD(S)

Greek is like lace; every man gets as much as he can —Samuel Johnson

It is with language as with manners: they are both established by the usage of people of fashion —Lord Chesterfield

Language, if it throws a veil over our ideas, adds a softness band refinement to them, like that which the atmosphere gives to naked objects —William Hazlitt

Language is a city, to the building of which every human being brings a stone —Ralph Waldo Emerson

Language is an art, like brewing or baking —Charles R. Darwin

Languages evolve like species. They can degenerate just as oysters and barnacles have lost their heads —F. L. Lucas

Languages, like our bodies, are in a perpetual flux, and stand in need of recruits to supply those words which are continually falling into disuse —C. C. Felton

Show them [Americans with a penchant for "fat" talk] a lean, plain word that cuts to the bones and watch them lard it with thick greasy syllables front and back until it wheezes and gasps for breath as it comes lumbering down upon some poor threadbare sentence like a sack of iron on a swayback horse —Russell Baker

♣ LAUGHTER
See Also: GAIETY, GRINS, HUMOR, SMILES

As the crackling of thorns under a pot, so is the laughter of a fool —The Holy Bible/Ecclesiastes

Basically when you laugh you have to make a fool of yourself … it's like sex —Robin Williams, interviewed on *60 Minutes TV* series, interview, September 21, 1986

Chuckles … empty and round, like bubbles —Dan Jacobson

Chuckle ... it sounded like a trapped wasp —Jonathan Gash

Chuckling like a jovial insurance salesman —James Crumley

Contralto laughter, like a violin obbligato under trills of a flute —Carlos Baker

A dry crackle like leaves crushed underfoot —Louise Erdrich

Dry laughter like the cackle of crows or the crackling of fallen leaves underfoot —Margaret Laurence

Giggled ... like a naughty child which has unintentionally succeeded in amusing the grown-ups —Christopher Isherwood

(They kissed. And) giggled like cartoon mice —Tom Robbins

Giggle, like a child watching a Hollywood adventure film —Nadine Gordimer

A good laugh is sunshine in a house —William Makepeace Thackeray

Heavy, melodious laughter, like silver coins shaking in a bag —Aharon Megged

Her braying laugh rang out like the report of a shotgun —James Thurber

Her laugh broke like a dish —Cynthia Ozick

Her laugh crackled ... like a leap of electricity —Richard Francis

Her laugh had music in it, like a climbing chord on a harp —Loren D. Estleman, *Sugartown: An Amos Walker Mystery*

Her laugh pealed out like a raven escaping into the night —Donald McCaig

Her laugh rang like the jangling of bracelets —Derek Walcott

Her laughter hung in the air like sleigh bells on a winter night —Jay Parini

Her laughter was a titanic, passionate thing that seemed to pass up like a wave from her toes to her mouth —Pat Conroy

High laugh, like a dove cry —Eudora Welty

A high laugh like a wicked witch —Carolyn Chute

His laughter thickened like a droning bell —James Wright

A hoarse, very small laugh, like a cat's cough —Frank Swinnerton

A horrifying derisive laugh, like rolling tin —Barry Hannah

Laugh ... as if a demon within him were exulting with gloating scorn —Iris Murdoch

(Louisa's) laugh begins high and descends from there like a cascade —Daphne Merkin

Laughed, a little drugged giggle, like chatter —Paul Theroux

Laughed contemptuously like a whore being offered too little money —Gary Hart

Laughed like a windup machine —John D. MacDonald

Laughed like monkeys —Richard Ford

Laughed like murmurs of the sea —W. B. Yeats

Laughed ... like the trill of a hedge-warbler —Frank Swinnerton

A laugh exploded out of me like a sneeze —Scott Spencer

Laughing, a sound like wind in the grass —T. Coraghessan Boyle

A laugh is just like sunshine —Anon rhyme
  The simile is the repeat motif running through the poem.

Laugh ... like the barking of a fox —Erich Maria Remarque

Laugh ... like a bird's carol on the sunrise breeze —John Greenleaf Whittier

Laugh like a hyena —William Shakespeare
  This simile from As You Like It *crops up in many a modern short story and novel.*

Laugh ... like a spoon tinkling against a medicine glass —Katherine Mansfield

Laugh ... like a thrush singing —Oscar Wilde

A laugh like clapboards being ripped off the side of a house —Peter De Vries

Laughs [in a film] … come out of despair, like bits of green in a graveyard —Walter Goodman about the movie *No Surrender, New York Times* August 6, 1986

Laughs like a rhinoceros —Tom Davies

The person Davies described was Samuel Johnson.

Laughs like little bells in light wind —George Garrett

Laughter … checked by small clutches of muscle, like tiny fists, at the corners of his mouth —Leonard Michaels

Laughter crackling like a schoolgirl who has not experienced enough of the world to fear it —Ira Wood

Laughter cruel as barbed wire —George Garrett

Laughter falls like rain or tears —Dame Edith Sitwell

Laughter fell like a shower of coins —George Garrett

Laughter … high and free and musical, like a happy soprano limbering up —Harvey Swados

Laughter hung smoke-like in the sudden stillness —Ralph Ellison

Laughter … keeps coming like a poison that must be ejected —Nora Johnson

Laughter leaped suddenly from her throat … then stopped, like something flung away and lost —Graham Swift

Laughter like hiccoughs —T. Coraghessan Boyle

Laughter, light and restrained like the chatter of rolling nuts —Yisrael Zarchi

Laughter lonelier than tears —Anon, *New York Times Book Review*, September 14, 1986

The laughter of a fool is like that of a horse —Welsh proverb

Laughter roared through the spectators like wind through trees —Gerald Kersh

Laughter spilled out of his prodigious frame like gravel being unloaded from a dump truck —Pat Conroy

A laugh that rippled … like the sound of a hidden brook —O. Henry

A laugh that rumbles like a freight train in the night —Michael Goodwin about sports broadcaster Steve Zabriskie, *New York Times*, October 2, 1986

A laugh that unfolds like a head of lettuce —Antler

Let out a cackle of a laugh, like the sound a hen might make if the hen were mad about something —Larry McMurtry

A little round belly that shook when he laughed like a bowl full of jelly —C. Clement Moore

Men who never laugh may have good hearts, but they are deep seated; like some springs, they have their inlet and outlet from below, and show no sparkling bubble on the brim —Josh Billings

Words originally in Billings' phonetic dialect are: "laff" for "laugh," "hav" for "have" and "sum" for "some."

A most pleasant laugh, bubbly and controlled, like fine champagne —Margaret Millar

Peal of laughter like the ringing of silvery bells —Nathanial Hawthorne

A queer stage laugh, like the cackle of a baffled villain in a melodrama —Edith Wharton

(Boutin's mouth opened from ear to ear in) a roar of laughter, like the bursting of a mortar —Honoré de Balzac

She laughed, sounding like a small barking dog —Robert Campbell

She pursed her lips each time she laughed, making laughter seem a gesture of self-control —W. P. Kinsella

A silvery laugh, like a brook running out to meet the river —Mike Fredman

A slow ripple of laughter, like a scattering of autumn leaves —Robert Traver

A snort of a chuckle like a bull-frog —Lawrence Durrell

Some … laugh just as a rat does, who has caught a steel trap, with his tail —Josh Billings

In the original phonetic dialect this was: "laff just az a rat duz, who haz caught a steel trap with his tale."

The sound [of laughter] was like the whirring of an old grandfather clock before it strikes —Frank Swinnerton

Stopped laughing as suddenly as if a string had been broken —Loren D. Estleman

A sudden fizz of laughter like soda water —George Garrett

Tittering like a small bird —Beryl Markham

Twinkled like Old King Cole —Donald McCaig

When he laughed, a satyr-like quality suffused his face —Nathaniel Benchley

When she does laugh … it's like polished crystal, like a stream in the Alps racing over a pebbly bed here below, like … like another simile —Hanoch Bartov

For anyone interested in multiple similes … here's the simile itself used to round up a medley of comparisons.

When she laughed it was as if a wren sang —Frank Swinnerton

When she was about to laugh, her tone grew higher and melodious, easing into the laugh like a singer easing from recitative to an aria —Lynne Sharon Schwartz

Wrinkles of laughter leaped into sight on his face, like small friendly insects running all over it —Romain Gary

❧ LAWS

See Also: LAWYERS

Corpuses, statutes, rights and equities are passed on like congenital disease —Johann Wolfgang Von Goethe

Exact laws, like all the other ultimates and absolutes, are as fabulous as the crock of gold at the rainbow's end —G. N. Lewis

Going to law is like skinning a new milk cow for the hide, and giving the meat to the lawyers —Josh Billings

The original in Billings' popular dialect form reads as follows: "Going tew law iz like skinning a new milch … tew the lawyers."

The Law is like apparel which alters with the time —Sir John Doddridge

Law is like pregnancy, a little of either being a dangerous thing —Robert Traver

The law often dances like an old fishwife in wooden shoes, with little grace and less dispatch —George Garrett

In Garrett's historical novel, Death of the Fox, *this simile is spoken by Sir Francis Bacon.*

Laws and institutions … like clocks … must be occasionally cleansed, and wound up, and set to true time —Henry Ward Beecher

(Written) laws are like spiders' webs; they hold the weak and delicate who might be caught in their meshes, but are torn in pieces by the rich and powerful —Anacharsis

The spiders' web comparison to the law has been much used and varied;. some examples: "Laws, like cobwebs, entangle the weak, but are broken by the strong"; "Laws are like spiders' webs, so that the great buzzing bees break through, and the little feeble flies hang fast in them" (Henry Smith); "Laws are like cobwebs, which may catch small flies, but let wasps and hornets break through" (Jonathan Swift); "Laws, like cobwebs, catch small flies, great ones break through before your eyes" (Benjamin Franklin) "Laws, like the spider's web, catch the fly and let the hawk go Free" (Spanish proverb).

Law should be like death, which spares no one —Charles de Secondat Montesquieu

Laws, like houses, lean on one another —Edmund Burke

Laws should be like clothes. They should fit the people they are meant to serve —Clarence Darrow

Laws wise as nature, and as fixed as fate —Alexander Pope

Legal as a Supreme Court decision —Anon

Legal studies ... sharpen, indeed, but like a grinding stone narrow whilst they sharpen —Samuel Taylor Coleridge

The science of legislation is like that of medicine in one respect, that it is far more easy to point out what will do harm than what will do good —Charles Caleb Colton

Suits at court are like winter nights, long and wearisome —Thomas Deloney

To try a case twice is like eating yesterday morning's oatmeal —Lloyd Paul Stryker

Violations of the law, like viruses, are present all the time. Everybody does them. Whether or not they produce a disease, or a prosecution, is a function of the body politic —Anon, quote in *New York Times*, November 28, 1986

(Law) was a system like a jigsaw puzzle, whose pieces, if you studied them long enough, all fell into place —Will Weaver

♣ LAWYERS

See Also: LAW, PROFESSIONS

A certain criminal lawyer, like a trapeze performer, is seldom more than one step from an awful fate —Paul O'Neil, *Life*, June 22, 1959

A countryman between two lawyers is like a fish between two cats —Benjamin Franklin

The glory of lawyers, like that of men of science, is more corporate than individual —Oliver Wendell Holmes, Sr., April 15, 1890

If you would wax thin and savage, like a half-fed spider, be a lawyer —Oliver Wendell Holmes

Holmes senior forsake the law for a career in medicine and literature, his son, on the other hand, loved the law and of course, distinguished himself finally becoming one of our best-known Justices of the Supreme Court.

A lawyer's face always gives warning of an ambush. Like a blockhouse. Used to conceal the artillery —Joyce Cary

A lawyer deep in his case is like a man fallen in love. Whether shaving or bathing or plain old-fashioned knaving, in bed or out, always and forever he is obsessed by his goddam case —Robert Traver

A variation of this simile from Traver's People Versus Kirk *also appears in his other famous novel,* Anatomy of a Murder.

A lawyer lacking a flock of law books is like a carpenter run out of nails —Robert Traver

A lawyer preparing for the trial of a difficult and complex case ... is like a man consulting a dictionary who winds up chasing everything but the word he needs —Robert Traver

Lawyers are just like physicians: what one says, the other contradicts —Sholom Aleichem

Lawyers, like bread, are best when they are young and new —Thomas Fuller

Lawyers on opposite sides of a case are like the two parts of shears; they cut what comes between them, but not each other —Daniel Webster

Like most corporate attorneys, he sat squarely on the fence with both ears to the ground —Anon

Years of practice had made them sensitive to every whimsy of emotion and taught them how to play upon the psychology of the jury as the careless zephyr softly draws its melody from the Aeolian harp —Arthur Train

♣ LAZINESS
See: IDLENESS

♣ LEAPING
See Also: JUMPING, ROCKING AND ROLLING

(The flashlight) leaped about like a will-o'-the-wisp —Brian Moore

Leaped from his chair as a runner leaps crouching, from the mark —Frank Swinnerton

Leaped like a fawn —Pat Conroy

Leaped like a high jumper —Frank Conroy

(Goats) leaped ... like arrows speeding from the bow —Willa Cather

Leaped like a spring released —John Updike

Leaped ... like a startled frog —Theophile Gautier

Leaped up like a little singed cat —O. Henry

Leaps like a buck in air —Caroline Finkelstein

Leaps like a flash —Maxwell Anderson and Laurence Stallings

This is a line from the Anderson/Stallings play, What Price Glory.

(The pulse in his palm) leapt like a trout in a brook —Eudora Welty

Leaping through the air like a man released from gravity —Ed Bradley about basketball star Michael Jordan, "Sixty Minutes," February 15, 1987

♣ LEARNING

See: EDUCATION

♣ LEAVES

See Also: FLOWERS, NATURE, TREES

Aspen and poplar leaves covered the road like yellow snow —Susan Engberg

The dirty leaves were hanging down from the [rain-wet] trees like dead bats —Josephine Tey

Dry leaves blew across the sidewalk like arched spiders —Joan Hess

Dry leaves chatter like a children's brigade —Diane Ackerman

A few leaves had fallen and lay like neglected toys on the grass —Carolyn Slaughter

The forest leaves moved like small rustling animals over the moss —Hayden Carruth

The last leaves of some sultry September hung stiffly, like leaves pressed between the pages of an old catechism —Nelson Algren

Leaves as light and agitated as swarms of little butterflies that hovered above the clover —Willa Cather

Leaves as limp as soiled money —George Garrett

Leaves delicately veined as a baby's hands —W. P. Kinsella

Leaves digest sun as men and women eat each other to love —Daniela Gioseffi

Leaves drooped (over white frame houses) like hands —James Reiss

Leaves fallen like wet rags —Bernard Malamud

The leaves ... fall off the branches by the hundreds, like paratroopers from their planes —David Ignatow

Leaves fell like notes from a piano —Derek Walcott

Leaves fell like rejected brown stars —John Rechy

The leaves fly up like birds —Conrad Aiken

Leaves hanging down like tongues —Jean Thompson

Leaves hissing and steaming like kettles —Philip Levine

Leaves ... hung lusterless, like drying tea-dregs —Julia O'Faolain

Leaves ... large as a lady's apron —Caroline Finkelstein

Leaves ... like a soggy blanket ... covered gutter, sidewalk, lawn, backyard, bushes and alley —Bernard Malamud

Leaves like green lace —George Garrett

Leaves like ruffled wavelets —Sylvia Berkman

Leaves like scarlet hands floated on the green slow water —Truman Capote

The leaves of the red maples glowed like fruit —Jean Thompson

The leaves paled and fell from the shedding trees like old wishes —George Garrett

Leaves peep out so fresh and green, so pure and bright, like young lives pushing shyly out into the bustling world —Jerome K. Jerome

Leaves rattled dryly together, like scales of metal —Aldous Huxley

Leaves scatter and point to every part of the sky, like famished fingers waving —Richard Wilbur

(A giant tree which bore) leaves shaped like fans —Anais Nin

The leaves sift down one by one like notes in music —May Sarton

The leaves that a few days before had been green now dropped like heat-withered cellophane —Wallace Stegner

The leaves turn and twist in the wind as if quarreling with one another —David Ignatow

The leaves were motionless on the trees, as if they were resting in the heat —Willis Johnson

Leaves, wrinkled or shiny like apples —Frank O'Hara

Some of its [a plant's] leaves had turned black and were curled up like charred Christmas ribbons —Margaret Millar

Yellow leaves like lamps of gold —John Greenleaf Whittier

The yellow leaves swam through the air as silently as fish —Jean Thompson

The young leaves were still soft and slack ... less like leaves than like petals, and drooping in the sweet forest-air like seaweeds in deep water —Isak Dinesen

♣ LEG(S)

See Also: PAIN, PHYSICAL FEELINGS

Ankles fine as an antelope's —Josephine Edgar

Ankles like door knobs —Anon

The calves of her legs were as taut and stiff as anchor chains —Mary Ellen Chase

Feet heavy as anchors —Richard Ford

Feet large as spades —Aharon Megged

Feet like canoes —Herbert Wilner

Feet ... swollen, driven through my shoes like devilled egg through a pastry bag —Ira Wood

Feet ... tripping like the feet of a restless pony —Adela Rogers St. John

(The fiddler's) feet were like the black hooves of a trotting horse that never seemed to touch the ground —Will Weaver

Her bony toes seemed as long and articulate as fingers —Thomas Williams

Her legs were shapeless ... like a fisherwoman's —H. E. Bates

His legs felt like two old rusted rain gutters —Flannery O'Connor

(She was a vast blonde girl, with) huge limbs like a piece of modern sculpture —Barbara Pym

Knees stuck out ... like two hard-boiled eggs —Anne Piper

Legs bowed like a wishbone —Ian MacMillan

Legs ... as heavy as sunken logs —Nolan Miller

Legs as shapeless and almost as thin as the lines in a child's drawing —Niven Busch

Legs as thick as newel posts —F. van Wyck Mason

Legs bent like monster springs —Richard S. Prather

Legs ... bowed, rickety, like bent pipes —George Garrett

Legs have gone mottled, like Roquefort cheese —Nadine Gordimer

Another simile to describe the effects of cellulite is "Thighs like cottage cheese."

Legs in motion like the hind parts of a dog —David Ignatow

Legs knotted and angular as whittled wood —George Garrett

Legs like a baseball bat —Delmore Schwartz

(A large man with) legs like a billiard table —Joyce Cary

Legs like an emaciated monkey's —Louis-Ferdinand Celine

Legs like redwood trees —Pat Conroy

Legs … like two pillars —Bertolt Brecht

Legs moving like the hammers of a grand piano —Paul Kuttner

Legs shaped like lion's paws —Jilly Cooper

Legs solid as tree trunks —Richard Deming

Legs … stiff as a wooden soldier's legs —William Kotzwinkle

Legs … straight as a pair of poplar trees in a storm —Ariel Dorfman

Legs were strong as old roots —Truman Capote

Legs that were too long, like a colt's —Beryl Markham

Long, thin legs like wading birds —Elizabeth Hardwick

My feet feel like balloons —Anthony Powell

(The young lady has) a pair of ankles like chianti bottles —George Jean Nathan

The pull of the tendons at his ankle like the taut ropes that control the sails of ships —Nadine Gordimer

She (a ballet dancer) has legs like a Fordham tackle —Irwin Shaw

Skinny legs, like the legs of a turkey gobbler —Ellen Glasgow

Swings his game leg like a gate, creaking on its hinges —Bette Howland

Thighs big as trees —John D. MacDonald

Thighs like a wild mare —Thomas Williams

Thighs like pillars of a temple —Peter De Vries

Thighs like twin portals —Paule Marshall

Thighs solid as poplars —Sharon Sheehe Stark

Thighs … they look like they're made of steel —Jonathan Valin

Varicose veins crawled like fat blue worms under her stockings —Ross Macdonald

Veins like big ugly worms —James Crumley

LETTER-WRITING
See: CORRESPONDENCE

LIBERTY
See: FREEDOM

LIES AND LIARS
See Also: DISHONESTY

Falsehood, like poison, will generally be rejected when administered alone; but when blended with wholesome ingredients, may be swallowed unperceived —Richard Whately

Falsehood, like the dry rot, flourishes the more in proportion as air and light are excluded —Richard Whately

A great lie is like a great fish on dry land; it may fret and fling, and make a frightful bother, but it cannot hurt you. You have only to keep still and it will die of itself —George Crabbe

(He's as) honest as the cat when the meat's out of reach —H. G. Bohn's *Hand-Book of Proverbs*

Lie as fast as a dog can lick a dish —John Ray's *Proverbs*

A lie is like a cat: you need to stop it before it gets out the door or it's really hard to catch. —Charles M.Blow "Obama For the Win," *New York Times,* June 30, 2012

Lied as often and as badly as politicians —James Crumley

Lied like a fish —John Dos Passos

Lied like an Arab —Anais Nin

Lied like a rug —Anon
In his novel private i, *Jimmy Sangster extends builds on this with "Lying like a cheap carpet."*

The lie fell as easily from his lips as a windfall apple —Donald Seaman

A lie is like a snowball; the longer it is rolled, the larger it is —Martin Luther

Lie like a trooper —American colloquialism, attributed to New England

Lie like fish —Saul Bellow

Lies are as communicative as fleas —Walter Savage Landor

Lies as fast as a dog trots —John Ray's *Proverbs*

Lies as fast as a horse can trot —Danish proverb

The comparison tends to change with use, "As fast as a dog can trot" being one of the most frequently heard variants.

Lies … buzz about the heads of some people, like flies about a horse's ears in summer —Jonathan Swift

Lies fall like flaxen thread from the skies —John Ashberry

Lies flew out of my mouth like moths —Susan Fromberg Schaeffer

Lies like a car-dealer —William McIlvanney

Lying like a book —Bertolt Brecht

Lying like an accountant at an audit —A. E. Maxwell

Lying like stink —Angus Wilson

Lying to someone is like blindfolding him: you cannot see the other's eyes to see how he sees you and so you do not know how it stands with yourself —Walker Percy

The nimble lie is like the second-hand upon a clock; we see it fly, while the hour-hand of truth seems to stand still, and yet it moves unseen, and wins at last, for the clock will not strike till it has reached the goal —Henry Wadsworth Longfellow

(Our) one white lie sits like a little ghost (here on the threshold of our enterprise) —Alfred, Lord Tennyson

The prevaricator is like an idolater —Eleazar

The telling of a falsehood is like the cut of a sabre; for though the wound may heal, the scar of it will remain —Sadi

To tell a falsehood is like the cut of a sabre; for though the wound may heal, the scar of it will remain —Sadi

When the lie was said it had the effect of leaving her breathless, as if she had just crowned a steep rise —Nadine Gordimer

❧ LIFE

See Also: AGE; LIFE DEFINED, MANKIND

(It seemed to him that) all man's life was like a tiny spurt of flame —Thomas Wolfe

And it seems to me you lived your life / Like a candle in the wind —Elton John, "Candle in the Wind"

John's tribute to the late actress Marilyn Monroe

The art of living rightly is like all arts; it must be learned and practiced with incessant care —Johann Wolfgang Von Goethe

The eventful life has dates; it swells and pauses like a plot —Paul Theroux

How ridiculous it [life] all seems … like a drop of water seen through a microscope, a single drop teeming with infusoria, or a speck of cheese full of mites invisible to the naked eye —Arthur Schopenhauer

I couldn't be content any more stuck here like a fly in molasses [the once happy New England farmer after five years as a seaman] —Eugene O'Neill, *Beyond the Horizon*

In life as in a football game, the principle to follow is: Hit the line hard —Theodore Roosevelt

I often wonder what it would be like if we could begin our lives over again … as if the life we'd already lived were just a rough draft and we could begin all over again with the final copy…. If that happened I think the thing we'd all want most would be not to repeat ourselves —Anton Chekhov, Vershinin in *The Three Sisters*

Let us play the game of life as sportsmen, pocketing our winnings with a smile, leaving our losings with a shrug —Jerome K. Jerome

Life ... empty as statistics are —Babette Deutsch

Life ... flat and stale, like an old glass of beer —Andre Dubus

Life folds like a fan with a click —Herbert Read

Life goes on forever like the gnawing of a mouse —Edna St. Vincent Millay

Life had been like a cloud rainbowed by the sun —Barbara Reid

Life imposes by brute energy, like inarticulate thunder; art catches the ear, among the far louder noises of experience, like an air artificially made by a discreet musician —Robert Louis Stevenson

A life indifferent as a star —Randall Jarrell

A life is composed of a thousand frail strands, like the rainbow tangle of telephone cables. Somehow, we make connections —Jean Thompson

Life is like a mean machine —Rob Thomas, "This Is How a Heart Breaks"

Life is like a pipe —Amy Winehouse, "Back to Black"
Many commentators believe the pipe in the lyric is a crack pipe.

Life is like riding a bicycle. To keep your balance, you must keep moving —Albert Einstein

Life is like an open book through a keyhole / If you wonder what occurs 'ere the / Lady gets her furs, have a look —Irving Berlin, "Through a Keyhole," from *As Thousands Cheer*

Life is like a sewer: what you get out of it depends on what you put into it —Tom Lehrer

Life is shapeless as a glove —Kenneth Koch

Life ... it slips through my hands like a fish —James Reiss

Life, like a child, laughs shaking its rattle of death as it runs —Rabindranath Tagore

Life, like a good story, pursues its way from beginning to end in a firm and unbroken line —W. Somerset Maugham

Life, like every other blessing, derives its value from its use alone —Samuel Johnson

Life, like war, is a series of mistakes —F. W. Robertson

Life often seems like a long shipwreck, of which the debris are friendship, glory and love —Madame de Stael

Life's bare as a bone —Virginia Wolf

Life is so like a little strip of pavement over an abyss —Virginia Woolf

Life should be embraced like a lover —Rose Tremain

Life's like an inn where travelers stay, some only breakfast and away; others to dinner stop, and are full fed; the oldest only sup and go to bed —English Epitaph
A variation of this, also found on a gravestone is "Our life is nothing but a winter's day."

Life swings like a pendulum backward and forward between pain and boredom —Arthur Schopenhauer

A life that moved in spirals turned inward like the shell of a sea-snail —Malcolm Cowley

Life was like [motion] pictures only in that it hardly every managed to be as exciting as its preview —Larry McMurtry

Like a morning dream, life becomes more and more bright, the longer we live —Jean Paul Richter

Like following life through creatures you dissect, you lose it in the moment you detect —Alexander Pope

To live is like love, all reason is against it, and all healthy instincts for it —Samuel Butler

Man's journey through life is like that of a bee through blossoms —Yugoslav proverb

A man's life, like a piece of tapestry, is made up of many strands which interwoven make a pattern; to separate a single one and look at it alone, not only destroys the whole, but gives the strand itself a false value —Judge Learned Hand

Judge Hand compared life to a piece of tapestry at the 1912 proceedings in memory of Mr. Justice Brandeis.

Men deal with life as children with their play, who first misuse, then cast their toys away —William Cowper

Moved … through her life, like a clumsy visitor in a museum —Susan Fromberg Schaeffer

Much that goes on behind Life's doors is not fixed like the pillars of a building nor preconceived like the structure of a symphony, nor calculable like the orbit of a star —Vicki Baum

My life felt like a fragile silk chemise —Marge Piercy

My life is like a stroll upon the beach, as near the ocean's edge as I can go —Henry David Thoreau

My life is like the autumn leaf that trembles in the moon's pale ray —Richard Henry Wilde

This begins the second stanza of the poem "My Life."

My life is like the summer rose that opens to the morning sky, but before the shade of evening closes is scattered on the ground to die —Richard Henry Wilde

This simile from Wilde's My Life, this one from the opening line.

My life loose as a frog's —Maxine Kumin

Our days on earth are as a shadow —The Holy Bible/Job

(I worry that) our lives are like soap operas. We can go for months and not tune in to them, then six months later we look in and the same stuff is still going on —Jane Wagner

Our lives are united like fruit in a bowl —W. H. Auden

Our lives run like fingers over sandpaper —Jaroslav Seifert

Perhaps like an ancient statue that has no arms our life, without deeds and heroes, has greater charms —Yehuda Amichai

Sometimes we do not become adults until we suffer a good whacking loss, and our lives in a sense catch up with us and wash over us like a wave and everything goes —Richard Ford

The art of life is more like the wrestler's art than the dancer's that it should stand ready and firm to meet onsets which are sudden and unexpected —Marcus Aurelius

There was a dimension missing from his life, as though trees were flat and rooflines painted on the sky —Margaret Sutherland

The vanity of human life is like a rivulet, constantly passing away, and yet constantly coming on —Alexander Pope

Viewed from the summit of reason, all life looks like a malignant disease and the world like a madhouse —Johann Wolfgang Von Goethe

Wear life like an old pair of shoes that's easy on my feet —Ben Ames Williams

When the highest stake in the game of living, life itself, may not be risked … becomes as flat, as superficial as one of those American flirtations in which it is from the first understood that nothing is to happen, contrasted with a Continental love-affair in which both partners must constantly bear in mind the serious consequences —Sigmund Freud

Would that life were like the shadow cast by a wall or a tree, but it is like the shadow of a bird in flight —Palestinian Talmud

❧ LIFE DEFINED

The course of life is like the sea; men come and go; tides rise and fall; and that is all of history —Joaquin Miller

Each person's life is like a mountain. And each person has to climb that mountain top alone —Rosamund Pilcher

Pilcher builds on the mountain simile by explaining that as a child you start in a warm and sunny valley, then you climb a somewhat steeper mountain with a wonderful view to make the end of the journey.

A human life is like a single letter in the alphabet. It can be meaningless. Or it can be part of a great meaning —essay by National Panning Committee of Jewish Theological Seminary for Rosh Hashan, September 5, 1956

Human life may be regarded as a succession of frontispieces. The way to be satisfied is never to look back —William Hazlitt

Life … a formless lump like cold tea leaves from which goodness and badness and even the last tang of bitterness have been stewed out —Gerald Kersh

The life being compared to cold tealeaves in Kersh's novel, The Angel and the Cuckoo, *is obviously deteriorating.*

Life is a big gambling game. Some are born lucky and some are born unlucky —Jack London

Life is a blister on top of a tumor, and a boil on top of that —Sholom Aleichem

Life is, after all, a kind of disaster through which we do what we can to keep each other's spirits up —Thomas Mallon, *New York Times Book Review,* October 12 1986

Life is a kind of chess, in which we have often points to gain, and competitors or adversaries to contend with, and in which there is a vast variety of good and evil events that are, in some degree, the effect of prudence or the want of it —Benjamin Franklin

Life … is a kind of stage play, where men come forth, disguised one in one array, and one in another, each playing his part —Erasmus

Life is a little like disease, with its crises and periods of quiescence, the daily improvements and setbacks —Italo Svevo

In his novel, Confessions of Zeno, *Svevo continues the simile as follows:* "But unlike other diseases life is always mortal. It admits of no cure.

It would be like trying to stop up the holes in our body, thinking them to be wounds. We should die of suffocation almost before we were cured."

Life is … a long series of challenges, like hurdles in a race —Rosamund Pilcher

Life is a long strong twisted rope made up of a number of human relationships —Mary Borden

Life is an incurable disease —Abraham Cowley

Life is a public performance on the violin, in which you must learn the instrument as you go along —E. M. Forster

Life is a train constantly crossing the border from the past to the present —Susan Fromberg Schaeffer

Life is but a day; a fragile dew-drop on its perilous way from a tree's summit —John Keats

Life … is like a beach covered with lots of pebbles, the faster we qualify ourselves to pick these pebbles the richer we will be —Evan A. Sholl

Life is like a beautiful and winding lane —George Augustus Sala

In its full context this continues as follows: "On either side bright flowers, beautiful butterflies, and tempting fruits which we scarcely pause to admire and taste, so eager are we to hasten to an opening which we imagine will be more beautiful still. But by degrees, as we advance, the tress grow bleak, the flowers and butterflies frail, the fruits disappear, and we find we have arrived to reach a desert waste."

Life is like a B-picture script. It is that corny —Kirk Douglas, *Look,* October 4, 1944

To add emphasis to his simile, Douglas added: "If I had my life story offered to me to film, I'd turn it down."

Life is like a cash register, in that every account, every thought, every deed, like every sale, is registered and recorded —Fulton J. Sheen

Life is like a cup of tea … needing love to make it sweet —Edward A. Guest

To show that the same basic simile can have different meanings, there's this line from J. M. Barrie's The Admirable Crichton: "Life, Crichton, is like a cup of tea; the more heartily we drink the sooner we reach the dregs."

Life is like a dissected map. If I could live a hundred years … I feel I could put the pieces together until they made a properly connected whole —Oliver Wendell Holmes

Life is like a fire; it begins in smoke, and ends in ashes —Arab proverb

Life is like a game of dice —Alexis

The comparison of life to the roll of the dice has been an irresistible simile throughout history. Variations include "Life is like a game of tables," the chances are not in our power but the playing is and "Life is like a game of roulette."

Life is like a game of cards —Edgar Watson Howe

Howe built on the comparison as follows: "Reliability is the ace, industry the king, politeness the queen, thrift the jack. Common sense is playing to best advantage the cards you draw." A 1978 poem by Diane Wakoski used the simile for its title and theme.

Life … is like a grapefruit … sort of orangey-yellow and dimpled on the outside, wet and squidgy in the middle —Douglas Adams

Life is like a jig saw puzzle with most of the pieces missing —Anon

Life is like a kiss that does not last long enough for a fellow to ascertain how good it is —Dow Junior

Life is like a mountain: after climbing up one side and sliding down the other, put up the sled —Josh Billings

The word "is" has been changed from the dialect form "iz."

Life is like an onion, which one peels crying —French proverb

Life is like an onion: you peel off layer after layer and then you find there is nothing in it —James G. Huneker

Life is like a school of gladiators, where men live and fight with one another —Seneca

Life is like a scrambled egg —Don Marquis

Life is like a stew, you have to stir it frequently, or all the scum rises to the top —Tom Robbins

Life is like drunkeness: the pleasure passes away, but the headache remains —Persian proverb

Life is like music, it drunkenness imposed by ear, feeling and instinct, not by rule —Samuel Butler

Life is like that, a cake-walk —Clifford Odets

Life is not a game of chess, the victory to the knowing; it is a game of cards, one's hand by skill to be made the best of —Jerome K. Jerome

Life is very much like an arms race, each side waiting for the other one to put his stick down first —Merle Shain

Life, like a dome of many-colored glass, stains the white radiance of eternity —Percy Bysshe Shelley

Human life is like the petals that fall from the rose and lie soft and withering by the side of the vase —Anon Persian poem

The life of every man is a diary in which he means to write one story, and writes another, and his humblest hour is when he compares the volume as it is with what he vowed to make it —J.M. Barrie

The life of man is like a long journey with a heavy load on the back —Japanese proverb

The race of men is like the race of leaves. As one generation flourishes another decays —Homer

Life's a library owned by an author. In it are a few books which he wrote but most of them were written for him —Harry Emerson Fosdick

Life seems to me like a Japanese picture which our imagination does not allow to end with the margin —Justice Oliver Wendell Holmes Jr.

Life's like a play: it's not the length but the excellence of the acting that matters —Seneca

A version made famous by the playwright Ben Johnson: "Our life is like a play."

Man's life is like a candle in the wind —Chinese proverb

The scenes of our life are like pictures done in rough mosaic…. There is nothing beautiful to be found in them, unless we stand some distance off —Arthur Schopenhauer

This mundane life is like a drink of salt water, which seems to quench, but actually inflames —Gaon Elijah

The way of life is like a path between two forbidding roads, one of fire and one of ice. The slightest bend in either direction is fatal (Let him walk in the middle) —Judah

Judah built on the simile with this advice: "The slightest bend in either direction is fatal. Let him walk in the middle."

A well-ordered life is like climbing a tower; the view halfway up is better than the view from the base, and it steadily becomes finer as the horizon expands —William Lyon Phelps

The whole of life of some people is a kind of partial death; a long lingering death-bed, so to speak, of stagnation and nonentity on which death is but the seal —Samuel Butler

♣ LIGHTING

See Also: BRIGHTNESS, SHINING

All lit up like warships in a foggy port —Amos Oz

Everything lit up like a disco on Saturday night —Loren D. Estleman

A glittering neon sign like wolves' eyes —Elizabeth Bowen

The gray light of the winter dawn lit the bedroom like a dreary fake impressionistic painting —Jerry Bumpus

The house [with all lights on] blazed like a stage set —T. Coraghessan Boyle

Light as a paper airplane (and as elegant) —Marge Piercy

Lighted windows [at dawn] were scattered like yellow diamonds on black velvet —Loren D. Estleman

Lighting streaked the snow. Like the urine of dogs by trees —William H. Gass

(Offices … in which) light is a kind of yellow fluid, like old shellac —Scott Turow

In his novel, Presumed Innocent, *Scott Turow uses this comparison to paint a picture of the "Dickensian" atmosphere in which the hero's fellow lawyers work.*

The light seemed to be draining away like floodwater —Kenneth Grahame

Lights glittered … like a diamond necklace round the neck of a lovely signorina —Donald Seaman

Lights … pouring over us like scalding milk —Ira Wood

The lights (of the bridge) were like strings of pearls hanging up in the air —Cornell Woolrich

The light was golden like the flesh of women —Thomas Wolfe

Like moons around Jupiter, pale moths revolved about a lone lamp —Vladimir Nabokov

(The big glass window was) lit like a stage —Frank Tuohy

(The place was) lit up like a birthday cake —Jayne Anne Phillips

Lit up like a midway —Tom Robbins

Lit up like a paper lantern —Willis Johnson

Lit up like a whorehouse on Saturday night —Loren D. Estleman

Lit up like skyscrapers or planes taking off —Marge Piercy

[A truck] Plastered with lights like a beer-joint —Carlos Baker

Streetlights cast their shadows on the wall like a sharp, white condolence —Ariel Dorfman

The streetlights shone like tiny beads on a string —David Huddle

When the lamps in the house are lighted it is like the flowering of lotus on the lake —Chinese proverb

Windows [of a building] glowing like those of a lighted cardboard house under a Christmas tree —Willa Cather

◆ LIGHTNESS

See Also: GAIETY, SOFTNESS

Airy as the holes in Swiss cheese —Anon

As giddy as a drunken man —Charles Dickens

> *This is the last of a whole string of similes uttered by a reformed Scrooge in* A Christmas Carol: *"I'm as light as a feather, I am as happy as an angel, I'm as merry as a schoolboy. I am as giddy as a drunken man. A merry Christmas to everybody! A happy New Year to all the world."*

As lightly as a cloud is blown —John Greenleaf Whittier

Flippancy, like comedy, is but a matter of visual first impressions —Joseph Conrad

(A light blue summer dress as) frothy as high tide —Jonathan Kellerman

Hands were light as moths —John MacDonald

Light as a hand among blossoms —Theodore Roethke

(Mountains ...) light and airy like balloons on a string —George Garrett

[Touch] light as a butterfly —Eleanor Farejons

> *And lighter still, there's a touch that's "light as a butterfly's kiss" from a John MacDonald novel.*

Light as a flight of tumbling birds —C. S. Lewis

Light as a fly —John Ray's *Proverbs*

Light as a leaf —Anon

> *An ancient simile which continues in use to describe lightness of heart, mind and body. "Light*

as" variants include "light as a feather," "light as wind," and "light as air." With them all, "lighter than" crops up as frequently as "light as."

Light as a milkweed puff —Richard Wilbur

[A racing jockey] Light as a monkey —Ernest Hemingway

Light as an angel —Donald McCaig

Light as a paper toy —Anon

Light as a petal falling upon stone —Theodore Roethke

(She is) light as a phantom —W. P. Kinsella

Light as a seed —Theodore Roethke

Light as breath —Robert Penn Warren

Light as cork —Henry James

Light as dandelion fluff —Mary Hedin

[Snow] Light as dust —Amy Lowell

Light as helium —Elizabeth Bishop

[Snowflakes] light as milkweed —T. Coraghessan Boyle

[Feathers on a hat] Light as mist in a breeze —Colette

Light as sea-foam, strong as the tide —Slogan for underwear, Paris-Hecker Co.

(Free and) light as the breath that clung to them like clouds —Arthur Gregor

Light as thistledown —John Yount

(We carry her indoors. She is) light as toast —Louise Erdrich

Lightly ... as a child skips rope, the way a mouse waltzes —E. B. White White on James Thurber's writing.

Lightly as a wisp of air —Harvey Swados

Weightless as an ache —Sharon Sheehe Stark

> *In Stark's novel* A Wrestling Season, *the simile is used to answer what death might be like.*

(Her body was ...) weightless as a strip of cane —Eudora Welty

Weightless as the notes rung out of bells at kindling dawn —George Garrett

♣ LIGHTNING
See: THUNDER AND LIGHTNING

♣ LIKELIHOOD
See: IMPOSSIBILITY

♣ LIKENESS
See: SIMILARITY

♣ LIMBS
See: ARM(S), LEG(S)

♣ LIMPNESS
See: SOFTNESS

♣ LINGERING

Brooded over … the way a plane caught in a fog hovers longingly over a blurred landing strip —Lynne Sharon Schwartz

The days lingered like overripe fruit —Claire Messud, *The Last Life*

(Haven't you got anything better to do than) hang around here like a prairie dog in heat? —line from the movie *Bronco Billy*

Hang around like a rent collector or a man come to fix the faucet —Harvey Swados

Hang around like sullen clouds over the sun —John Ashberry

Hanging around like a fart in a phone box —Australian colloquialism

[An idea]hang over … like a thunderstorm reluctant to break —Gavin Lyall

[The smell of circus lions] hangs like August heat —Delmore Schwartz

Hover like a moth intoxicated with light —John Galsworthy

Hover like butterflies —Lee Smith

Hover over like an ugly bird of prey —Anon

Hung around … like a herd of sheep with no sheep-dog —Ignazio Silone

(The Fraziers had refused to leave his mind; they had stayed on) imposing themselves on his consciousness and his conscience like the troubling memory of a drunken evening —Elizabeth Hardwick

Languish like a mist at noon —Herbert Read

Lingered like heat, like poppy petals, like desert sand —Kay Boyle

Lingered, like smoke after fire —Paul Kuttner

Lingering like an unloved guest —Percy Bysshe Shelley

Lingering like second thoughts —George Bradley

(Light) lingers like a lover's tongue —Bin Ramke
   This simile concludes a poem entitled "What the Weather Is Like."

Lodged like a marble in a crack —James Crumley

Loitered like a school child —Jean Stafford

(A cold notion flew into my brain and) squatted there like a buzzard, patient, in a tree —George Garrett

Stalling like a Scotchman in front of a pay toilet —Harold Adams

♣ LIPS
See Also: MOUTH

An upper lip shaped like a circumflex accent —Eric Ambler

Drew her lips into a thin wiggly line like fish bait —Sharon Sheehe Stark

Full lips like a French movie star —Ira Wood

Her lips glistened as if she'd just eaten a pound of Vaseline —Sarah Bird

Her lips looked … delicious, as though if you bit them it would be like biting into a sweetmeat, one of those candies which are filled with a pleasant warming liquid —Ben Ames Williams

His lips, like those of all men who work, were puckered up like a bag with the string drawn tight —Honoré de Balzac

His lips were tightened in a thin line, as if he had them sewn together to keep from vomiting —Robert J. Serling

His lips were too red, as if he had a hangover —Louise Erdrich

His long lips tightened, as if he sought to conquer pain —Frank Swinnerton

Lips always compressed as if to keep back a swarm of curses —George Garrett

Lips as bloodless as lips of the slain —John Greenleaf Whittier

Lips … as glossy as ripe cherries —Anton Chekov

Lips delicate as peach-toned porcelain —Jayne Anne Phillips

Lips … drawn in a tight line like the lips of a child not quite ready to take a dose of bad-tasting medicine —George Garrett

Lips … dry and faint as her tea leaves —Shirley Ann Grau

Lips full as thighs —Lyn Lifshin

Lips like a thread of scarlet —The Holy Bible/Song of Solomon

Lips like lilies —The Holy Bible/Song of Solomon

Lips … like pale velvet —Jimmy Sangster

Lips like sausages —John D. MacDonald

Lips … like the petals of a red flower —Oscar Wilde

Lips like wet cherries —Virginia Woolf

Lips moved noisily, smacking like a three-day thirst —Sharon Sheehe Stark

Lips … red as two buds —Louise Erdrich

Lips … set in exasperation, as if she had just been about to say something and found out her voice was snatched in death —Louise Erdrich

Lips … shining like rain on night streets —Jayne Anne Phillips

Lips that, like a ventriloquist's, scarcely stirred —Katherine Bush

Lips that looked as if she were permanently whistling —Mike Fredman

Lips that shine wetly, just like a Cosmo girl —George Garrett

Lips that stand out from his skin like two thick weals —Aldous Huxley

Lips tighter than any knot —Tim O'Brien

Lips trembling like elastic stretched too taut —George Garrett

A long blue upper lip, like a priest —Joyce Cary

The muscles of her chapped lips were broken and loose like the snap of an old purse —Gerald Kersh

Set her lips as though she would never speak again —Dorothy Canfield

Sharp-pointed lips stretched out like a slingshot —Bobbie Ann Mason

Thick lips … like lozenges of hard rubber —Jonathan Valin

Thin lips fitted tightly together, as though they were parts of a very well-made piece of furniture —Aldous Huxley

An upper lip that twitched softly, like a cow's in a fly-ridden summer —Penelope Gilliatt

♣ LITERATURE
See: *ART AND LITERATURE, BOOKS, WRITERS/WRITING*

♣ LIVELINESS
See: *ACTIVENESS, ENTHUSIASM, ENERGY*

♣ LOCALITIES
See: *PLACES*

♣ LOGIC
See: *SENSE*

❧ LONELINESS

See: ABANDONMENT, ALONENESS

A day without you is like a year without rain —Selena Gomez, "A Year without Rain"

And I sat by myself / Like a cobweb on a shelf —Zooey Deschanel and M. Ward, also known as She & Him, "Why Do You Let Me Stay Here?"

The immense, throbbing loneliness that was only now closing like a vise on my internal organs —Jonathan Tropper, *This Is Where I Leave You*

❧ LONGING

See: DESIRE

❧ LONG-WINDEDNESS

See: TALKATIVENESS

❧ LOOKS

See Also: FROWNS AND SCOWLS, SCRUTINY, STARES

Accusing look … as Cotton Mather might have looked at a Salem woman in the stocks —Mary Gordon

Always looked at you as if you had interrupted him in the performance of some slightly tedious but nonetheless necessary task —Louis Auchincloss

Black glance like ice —Jean Garrigue

Contemplate … with a kind of quiet premeditation, like that of a slow-witted man fondling an unaccustomed thought —Beryl Markham

Disdainful look like that of a coffee drinker sipping a cup of instant —Anon

Exchanged fidgeting looks like a pair of consternated hamsters —Sarah Bird

Exchanged wide-eyed looks that clinked in the air like fine glassware —Sharon Sheehe Stark

Eyeing me … like a starved hog watching the trough get filled —Harold Adams

Felt his eyes slide over her like a steamy wet cloak —Joseph Wambaugh

Gaze at me like chastened children sitting silent in a school —Thomas Hardy

Gazed at the pair with nudging, sympathetic smiles, like grandmothers watching babies in a play-pen —Mary McCarthy

Gaze … fixed like a snake's —Donald MacKenzie

Glance as vacant as the smoothness of the pond —David Ignatow

Glanced at one another like tigers taking measure of menacing new rival —Erich Segal

Glance … like a needle's flash —Frank Swinnerton

Glowered back like a sullen watchdog —Frank Swinnerton

Her flat dark eyes moved down Melinda like a smudge —Jessamyn West

Her gaze moved like a prison searchlight —Michael Dorris

Her gaze was like a magnet that drew towards it my will-less secret —Jean Stafford

His eyes glowed on me like a warm hand —Borden Deal

His eyes on me as hot as a bare hand —R. Wright Campbell

His eyes set on Linda's open shirtfront like a cat sighting a fat bird —Gloria Norris

His eyes slewed round to meet yours and then cannoned off again like a pool-ball —Sean Virgo

His glance came back across mine like saw teeth across a nail —Wallace Stegner

His icy-blue gaze would fall and cut you like a blade —Faith Mortimer, *The Assassins' Village*

His look was like a hand in the scruff of Bruce's neck —Wallace Stegner

Like swallows darting about a barn her deep blue eyes flickered from one to the other —F. van Wyck Mason

(Gave me) a long [forgiving] look like Christ crucified —Clare Boylan

Look at him as if he were a lamppost —Leo Tolstoy

Looked about him like the fallen archangel whose only wish was for eternal enmity —Honoré de Balzac

Looked around her at the crowd, with eyes smarting, unseeing, and tearful as if an oculist had put caustic eye-drops into them —Boris Pasternak

Looked at each other like schoolboys caught masturbating —Lawrence Durrell

Looked at each other in a flicker fast as a snake's tongue —Rosellen Brown

Looked at her like she was some kind of Italian sports car and he was ready to drive her —dialogue from "Murder She Wrote episode," television drama, broadcast March 19, 1987

The look thus described is attributed to a jealous husband.

Looked at her like a bird that has been shot —D. H. Lawrence

Looked at him as a guinea pig looks at a big dog —Frank Swinnerton

Looked at him as a sergeant in the United States Marines would look at a recruit who had just called a rifle a gun —Norman MacLean

Looked at me as if I were a mongrel that had suddenly said, "Hi" —Harold Adams

Looked at me as though I had suddenly broke out with a filthy disease —M. C. Blackman

Looked at me expectantly as a poodle —Erich Maria Remarque

Looked at me intently, as if trying to recall something —Mikhail Lermontov

Looked at me keenly, like a smart boxer stung in the first round and cagily reappraising the character of his opposition —Robert Traver

Looked at me like she was ready to carve my liver —Larry McMurtry

Looked at Whistler [character in novel] as if she'd like to crush him with her thighs or smother him with her tits —Robert Campbell

Looked at ... with an awakened air, as if she were pricking up her ears like a trooper's horse at the sound of a trumpet —Honoré de Balzac

Looked at you without really seeing you, like a TV broadcaster reading the teleprompter —Elyse Sommer

Looked him up and down like a sergeant inspecting the ranks —George Garrett

Looked knowing and quizzical, like someone smiling with a mouthful of salts —George MacDonald Fraser

Looked through us like glass —Alan Williamson

Looked towards me as towards a jury —F. Scott Fitzgerald

Looking about him as if he had a score to settle —Romain Gary

Looking at him with something cold as dislike —Rebecca West

(She was) looking at us ... like she had emptied her eyes, like she had quit using them —William Faulkner

Looking from face to face like he was judge —Jayne Anne Phillips

Looking on one another, sideways and crossways, and with lowered eyes, like guilty criminals —Anzia Yezierska

A look passed between them, like the silent exchange of two doctors who agree on a simple diagnosis without having to put it in words —Marilyn Sharp

Looks black as thunder —J.R. Planche

Looks ... like the lizard watches the fly —Leslie Silko

A look that burned like live coals on our naked bodies —Anzia Yezierska

Now there's a look in your eyes, like black holes in the sky —Pink Floyd, "Sing on You Crazy Diamond"

Playing his eyes over the other's face like the feelers of insects —Arthur A. Cohen

Regarded her with raised brows like a doctor who is considering how fully to answer a layman's question —Saul Bellow

Regarded me somberly but warily, as you might examine a particularly ferocious gorilla from the other side of a set of flimsy bars —Harvey Swados

She looked at him with that cunning which those who profess unworldliness can wield like a club of stone —Francine du Plessix Gray

She took him in as if he were frozen in a block of ice or enclosed in a cage of wires —Louise Erdrich

That look that seemed to enter him like an enormous jolt of neat whiskey —Daniel Curley

The each-for-himself look in the eyes of the people about her were like stinging slaps in the face —Anzia Yezierska

Their eyes creamed off each other like the balls on a table —Ed McBain

Their eyes rolled like marbles toward one another —Mary Hedin

Their glances crossed like blades —Stephen Crane

Triumphant look, like the fallen angel restored —D. H. Lawrence

A true-felt look ... laden with sweetness, white, mesmerizing, like the blossom that hangs from the cherry trees —Edna O'Brien

Turned to me in blank apprehension like a blind woman taken by surprise —Ross Macdonald

Uncomprehending gaze ... like an anxious monkey —Mary Stewart

Watching me as though trying to work out a puzzle —C. J. Koch

♣ LOOSENESS

(Muscle) lax as a broken shade —Diane Ackerman

(Face) lax as a wax work —Daniel Berrigan

(The gear worked) loose as a hound's shoulder —Elizabeth Spencer

Loose as a gossip's tongue —Anon

Loose as ashes —Anon

Loose as eggs in a nest —Walter Savage Landor

Loose as windblown sand —Mark Helprin

Slack as a toad —Barbara Howes

Sprawled ... lax as a drowned man —George Garrett

♣ LOUDNESS
See: NOISE

♣ LOVE
See Also: FRIENDSHIP; LOVE, DEFINED; MEN AND WOMEN

Absence in love is like waters upon fire; a little quickens, but much extinguishes it —Hannah More

All loving emotions, like plants, shoot up most rapidly in the tempestuous atmosphere of life —Jean Paul Richter

Amorous as Emma Bovary —James G. Huneker

Could love forever run like a river —Lord Byron

Falling in love is something you forget, like pain —Nina Bawden

Felt love like a lottery prize —Geoffrey Wolff

First and passionate love, it stands alone, like Adam's recollection of his fall —Lord Byron

The force of her love ... is bulky and hard to carry, like a package that keeps untying —Louise Erdrich

Going through life without love is like going through a good dinner without an appetite; everything seems flat and tasteless —Helen Rowland

Her love was like the swallow's, whose first thought is for its nest —Italo Svevo

If love were what the rose is, and I were like the leaf, our lives would grow together —Algernon Charles Swinburne

I love you as New Englanders love pie —Don Marquis

Infatuation like paralysis, is often all on one side —Helen Rowland

It [love] could, like grief, grow forgetful and weary and slowly wear away —Alice McDermott

I touch your hands / And my heart goes strong, / Like a pair of birds / That burst with song —Oscar Hammerstein, "Younger than Springtime," *South Pacific*

Just a Love Nest, cozy and warm / Like a dove —Otto Harbach, "The Love Nest," *Mary*

Knew as much about love as a pig knows about St. Valentine's Day —Harry Prince

Like a flower / Waiting to bloom / Like a light bulb / In a dark room / I'm just sitting here waiting for you / To come on home and turn me on —Norah Jones, "Turn Me On"

Like the water of a deep stream, love is always too much —Wendell Berry

This line from a poem entitled "The Country of Marriage" continues as follows: "We did not make it. Though we drink till we burst we cannot have it all, or want it all."

I begin to love, as an old man loves money, with no stomach. —William Shakespeare, *As You Like It*

Love burst out … all over our bodies, like sweat —Yehuda Amichai

Love can die of truth as friendship of a lie —Abel Bonard

Love … comes as a butterfly tipped with gold —Algernon Charles Swinburne

Love comes into your being like a tidal wave … sometimes it withdraws like a wave, till there isn't such a thing as a pool left, and every bit of your heart is as dry as seaweed beyond the wave's reach —Phyllis Bottome

Love comforts like sunshine after rain —William Shakespeare

The original simile as used in Venus and Adonis *uses "comforteth" rather than "comforts."*

Love doesn't just sit there, like a stone, it has to be made, like bread; re-made all the time, made new —Ursula K. Le Guin

Love … entered the room like a miracle —Milan Kundera

Love had seized her as unexpectedly as would sudden death —Elizabeth Taylor

(Our cook is in love.) Love hangs on the house like a mist —Phyllis McGinley

Love hung still as crystal over the bed —Louis MacNeice

Love is fierce as death —The Holy Bible/Song of Songs

Love is flower-like —Samuel Taylor Coleridge

Love is … fresh as dew when first it is new —British folk song, "The Water Is Wide"

The complete refrain includes yet another simile: "Oh, love is sweet and love is fair, fresh as the dew when first it is new, but love grows old and waxeth cold, and fades away like morning dew."

Love is like a big fat bonus that you hope kicks in after you negotiate the rest of the term sheet —Helen Simonson, *Major Pettigrew's Last Stand*

Love is like a flame / It burns you when it's hot / Love hurts —Boudleaux Bryant, from lyrics to song "Love Hurts"

Love is like the moon; when it does not increase it decreases —Joseph Alexandre Pierre Segur

Love is … lone as the sea, and deeper blue —Dorothy Parker

Love … it makes him [the lover] fluent as a tin whistle, as limber as a boy's watch chain, and as polite as a dancing master —Josh Billings

Parts transcribed from the Billing phonetic dialect: "whissel" and "perlite" as a "dansing" master.

Loveless as the multiplication table —Sylvia Plath

Love life … just about as interesting as the love life of the desert horned toad —William Saroyan

Love, like a tear, rises in the eye and falls upon the breast —Publius Syrus

Love like chicken salad or restaurant hash, must be taken on blind faith or it loses all its flavor —Helen Rowland

Love, like death, a universal leveler of mankind —William Congreve

Love, like death, changes everything —Kahil Gibran

Love, like fire, cannot subsist without constant impulse; it ceases to live from the moment it ceases to hope or to fear —La Rouchefoucauld

Love, like money, is probably best kept in the family —William Gaddis, *New York Times Book Review*, May 24, 1987

Gaddis used this simile to conclude his review of Saul Bellow's novel More Die of Heartbreak.

Love passed between them like a field of light —Ellen Gilchrist

Love … pricks like a thorn —William Shakespeare, *Romeo and Juliet*

Love … roots up the will like a leaf —Gustave Flaubert

Lovers are always in a hurry … like a racing river —Ben Ames Williams

Lovers fail like seasons —F. D. Reeve

Love's dominion, like a king's, admits of no partition —Ovid

Love sometimes is like the flower of the wild poppy: you can't carry it home —Jaroslav Seifert

Love was a treadmill, like churchgoing —Elizabeth Hardwick

Love washes on me like rain on a dead man's shoes —Ellen Gilchrist

Love without grace is like a hook without bait —Anne de Lencos

Love without respect is cold as a boa constrictor —Marge Piercy

In her poem "Witnessing a Wedding," Piercy continues as follows: "its caresses as choking."

Love without return is like a question without an answer —Anon

Making love to a woman too many times is like scratching a place that doesn't itch any more —Anon, *Playboy,* 1965

A man in love may behave like a madman but not like a dunce —François, Duc de La Rochefoucauld

Man has been substituted for gentleman to give the simile a more modern tone.

The man who is not loved hovers like a vulture over the sweetheart of others —Victor Hugo

My heart simmered with angry love like chicken soup on grandma's stove —James Atlas

My love is like foliage in the woods. Time will change it as winter changes the trees —Emily Brontë

The love described is Cathy's for Heathcliff in Wuthering Heights.

Once love is purged of vanity it is like a feeble convalescent, hardly capable of dragging itself around —Sebastien Roch Nicolas de Chamfort

Our love is like our life; there's no man blest in either till his end —Shackerley Marmion

Our love is like the misty rain that falls softly … but floods the river —African proverb

(What I want … is something organic …) potato love, natural as earth, scruffy and brown, clinging to your roots, helping you grow fit and firm —Daphne Merkin

Romance, like a ghost, eludes touching —G. W. Curtis

Romance, like alcohol, should be enjoyed but must not be allowed to become necessary —Edgar Z. Friedenberg

Romantic love is ephemeral and occasionally unavoidable ... like the viral flu —Marcia Froelke Coburn, *New York Times Book Review,* September 14, 1986

A rush of love swamped her heart ... like a tide —Vita Sackville-West

The science of love demands delicacy, perseverance, and practice, like the piano —Anatole France

The simple accident of falling in love is as beneficial as it is astonishing —Robert Louis Stevenson

(She was long married ... but she had recently) stepped out of the country of love briskly, and without a backward glance, as if she had spent too much time in its steamy jungles —John Cheever

This was a game, like bridge, in which you said things instead of playing cards. Like bridge you had to pretend you were playing for money or playing for some stakes —Ernest Hemingway

Threw herself into love like a suicide into the river —Guy de Maupassant

To love a woman who scorns you is like licking honey from a thorn —Welsh proverb

To talk of honour in the mysteries of love, is like talking of Heaven or the Deity in an operation of witchcraft, just when you are employing the devil: it makes the charm impotent —William Wycherley

Trapped in love ... like a great tortoise trapped in a heavy death-like shell —Joyce Carol Oates

It [being loved by affectionately possessive wife] was like being loved by a large moist sponge —Phyllis Bottome

Without love our life is ... unprofitable as a ship without a rudder ... like a body without a soul —Sholem Aleichem

With true loves as with ghosts: everyone speaks of them, but few have seen them —François, Duc de La Rochefoucauld

(I) wore my heart like a wet, red stain on the breast of a velvet gown —Dorothy Parker

Your love is like bad medicine —Jon Bon Jovi, Richie Sambora, and Desmond Child, from lyrics to song "Bad Medicine"

❧ LOVE, DEFINED

Falling in love is like being thrown from a horse; if you let yourself go it doesn't hurt as badly as if you try to save yourself —Edwin L. Blanchard

It's [love] very like a lizard; it wines itself around your heart and penetrates your gizzard —Anon rhyme

A love affair is like a work of art —Laurie Colwin

Love is a hole in the heart —Ben Hecht

Love is a science where great erudition and great application are needed —Anatole France

Love is like a child that longs for everything that he can come by —William Shakespeare, *Two Getlemen from Verona*

Love is like a cigar, the longer it burns the less it becomes —*Punch,* 1855

Love is ... like a coconut which is good while it's fresh, but you have to spit it out when the juice is gone, what's left tastes bitter —Bertolt Brecht

Love is like a cold. Easy to catch but hard to cure —Anon

Love is like a dizziness —James Hogg
This is the title and first line of a poem.

Love is like a dream that's too good to be true —Langston Hughes

Love is like a friendship caught on fire —Bruce Lee

Love is like a lovely rose —Christina Georgina Rossetti

Love is like a repeating decimal; the figure is the same but the value gets less and less —Anon

Love is like a wild rose-briar —Emily Brontë

Love is like butter, it goes well with bread —Yiddish proverb

Love is like electricity. It flares up for a second and is soon extinguished —Isaac Bashevis Singer

Love is like fire … wounds of fire are hard to bear; harder still are those of love —Hjalmar Hjorth Boyesen

Love is like growing pains; something we all have to experience for ourselves —Anon

Love is like heaven, a brief possession, unsearchable, hard to reconstruct with two-by-fours and building blocks —Leonard Casper

In Casper's story "Sense of Direction," the simile is in the past tense and the word "building" is spelled without the last letter.

Love is like learning to walk; we all have to go through it —Anon

Love is like linen, the more often changed, the sweeter —Phineas Fletcher

The word "changed" was written as "chang'd" in the original.

Love is like malaria. You never know when you're going to catch it —Rita Mae Brown

Love is like measles; you can get it only once, and the later in life it occurs the tougher it goes —Josh Billings

The simile in Billings' dialect: "Love iz like the meazles; we kant have it bad but onst, and the later in life we have it the tuffer it goes with us." Medical science has made this much quoted comparison obsolete, though another illness, mishap or a necessary learning experience could easily be substituted.

Love is like quicksilver in the hand … leave the fingers open and it stays in the palm; clutch it, and it darts away —Dorothy Parker

Love is like soup; it cools when the fire dies out —Anon

Love is like the devil; he whom it has in its clutches it surrounds with flames —Honoré de Balzac

Love is like the measles; we all have to go through it —Jerome K. Jerome

See the comment with Josh Billings love/measles simile above.

Love is like a well: a good thing to drink out of, but a bad thing to fall into —Anon

Love is like the wild rose-briar, friendship like the holly tree —Emily Brontë

Love is like those shabby hotels in which all the luxury is in the lobby —Paul Jean Toulet

Love is trembling happiness —Kahil Gibran

Love is very much like a tennis match … you'll never win consistently until you learn to serve well —Dan P. Herod

Love is what is called the Milky Way in Heaven, a brilliant mass formed by thousands of little stars of which each perhaps is nebulous —Stendhal

One wonders what he might have added had he known about black holes in space and their gravity so enormous it sucks up everything surrounding itself.

Love … it's like an ocean: if you're no good, if you begin a make a bad smell in it, it just spews you up somewhere to die —William Faulkner

Love, like a poker game starts with a pair; with her getting a flush, him showing a diamond and both ending up together with a full house —Anon

Love, like death, a universal leveler of mankind —William Congreve

Lovers are like drunkards; once a drunkard always a drunkard, once a lover always a lover. It is simply a matter of temperament —Guy de Maupassant

Love's like the measles, all the worse when it comes too late —Douglas Jerrod

See comment following the Josh Billings love/ measles simile above.

Love without return is like a question without an answer —Anon

Loving, like prayer, is a power as well a process. It's curative. It is creative —Zona Gale

The moods of love are like the wind —Coventry Patmore

My love is as a fever —William Shakespeare, "Sonnet #147"

Another famous author, Stendhal, also likened love to a fever, adding: "it comes and goes without the will having any part in the process."

My love is like a red red rose —John Burns

This is the first line and title of Burns' famous poem, in which the word "love" was spelled "luv."

An old man in love is like a flower in Winter —Portuguese proverb

Romance is the poetry of circumstance —Robert Louis Stevenson

True love is like seeing ghosts: we talk about it few of us have ever seen one —François, Duc de La Rochefoucauld

Some quote de La Rochefoucauld as linking the ghost comparison to perfect instead of true love.

A woman's love is like the dew. It falls as easily on the manure heap as on the rose —Donald McCaig

Young love is a flame; very pretty, often very hot and fierce, but still only light and flickering. The love of the older and disciplined heart is as coals, deep-burning, unquenchable —Henry Ward Beecher

♣ LOYALTY/DISLOYALTY

See Also: FRIENDSHIP, LOVE

Always at her side like a Great Dane —Carlos Baker

As the rolling stone gathers no moss, so the roving heart gathers no affection —Anna Jameson

Devoted and caretaking as a cat with her kittens —Katherine Anne Porter

(In the end, people's) devotion hung like rocks around your neck —Alice Munro

Endless devotion ... like a straitjacket —Lynne Sharon Schwartz

Faithful (to each other) as the Canada goose, more or less —Laurie Colwin

Fickle as spring sunlight —Carolyn Kizer

A heart true as steel —William Shakespeare

Shakespeare gave this comparison from Midsummer Night's Dream a slight twist in Romeo and Juliet: "my man's as true as steel."

Like a woman in her first love affair, he insisted on unconditional commitment —Ariel Dorfman

Loyal, like a dog —Lynne Sharon Schwartz

Loyalty ... small and hard, like buckshot lodged in her stomach —Sarah Litsey

To say that you can love one person all your life is just like saying that one candle will continue burning as long as you live —Leo Tolstoy

True to her husband as the dial to the sun —Henry Fielding

♣ LUCIDITY
See: CLARITY

♣ LUCK
See: FORTUNE/MISFORTUNE

♣ LUNACY
See: MADNESS

♣ LUSHNESS
See: ABUNDANCE

♣ LUST
See: DESIRE, SEX

❧ LYING

*See Also: BEARING, BENDING/BENT, IMMO-
BILITY, POSTURE, SITTING, SLEEP,
STANDING*

Lay … as if chloroformed —Wallace Stegner

Lay as still as a fallen doll —George Garrett

Lay in bed like a tree stump —Charles Johnson

Lay lifeless as if spellbound —Herman Melville

Lay like an aimlessly flung sack of bones —Harvey Swados

Lay on his back … rigid and ruined, like some stained window mannequin —Davis Grubb

Lay on the sofa like cast-off silk stockings —Delmore Schwartz

In his journal entry Schwartz followed this with two additional comparisons: "Like fallen buildings … like a car over turned." Had he been writing forty years later, he would have been apt to refer to pantyhose instead of silk stockings.

Lay perfectly still, as if dead with fear —D.H. Lawrence

Lay … rigid, as if she were dead —Elizabeth Taylor

Lay rigidly still, as still as if he were in his coffin —Dorothy Canfield

Lay side by side like fish —Lawrence Durrell

(Fallen and helpless, he) lay there like a pine tree that has been torn up by the roots —Ellen Glasgow

Lay there … stretched like a corpse —Hugh Walpole

Lay where she was for a few minutes like a flake of foam —Vicki Baum

(We'd) lie … like two sticks in bed —Elizabeth Spencer

The lovers like great scissors lay —Delmore Schwartz

Sprawled around … like shepherds in a frieze —Julia O'Faolain

Sprawled like a man who had been threshed —Stephen Crane

Sprawling like an exhausted dog —Mary Hedin

❧ MADNESS

As crazy as a baboon chasing shit around a tree —American colloquialism

As crazy as a loon —American colloquialism

Popular variations include "Crazy as bats" and "Crazy as a bed bug," the latter said to make its first appearance in Ernest Hemingway's For Whom the Bell Tolls.

Crazy as owl shit —Pat Conroy

As mad as a brush —Julia O'Faolain

As mad as a March hare —English phrase

Even though Lewis Carroll didn't coin the phrase as many people think, its appearance in Alice in Wonderland *probably contributed towards its common and continued usage to describe irrationality. The same is true of "Mad as a hatter" which alluded to the symptoms of madness due to chemical exposure by workers in the hat industry.*

As mad as a serpent —Carolyn See, *New York Times,* July 3, 1986

As nutty as a fruitcake —American colloquialism

In vogue since around 1935 this has seeded such twists such as "You're as nutty as a Mars bar" (Tom Robbins) and "Nuttier than a Hershey bar with almonds" (Ed McBain). Departing from the candy and cake comparison altogether, there's as "Nutty as a squirrel's nest" (Mike Sommer).

❧ MANIPULATION
See: POWER

❧ MANKIND
See Also: HELPLESSNESS, LIFE

As the clay is in the potter's hand, to fashion at his pleasure: so man is in the hand of him that made him —The Holy Bible/Apocrypha

Every man is like his affliction —André Malraux

Extraordinary men, like the stones that are formed in the highest regions of the air, fall upon the earth only to be broken and cast into the furnace —Walter Savage Landor

He [man] bolts down all events, all creeds, and beliefs, and persuasions … as an ostrich of potent digestion gobbles down bullets and gun flints —Herman Melville

Human as a kiss —Vance Thompson

Human beings are like timid punctuation marks sprinkled among the incomprehensible sentences of life —Jean Giraudoux

Humanity is like people packed in an automobile which is traveling down the highway without lights on a dark night at terrific speed and driven by a 4-year old —Lord Dunsany

It is with men as with horses; those who do the most prancing make the least progress —Baron de Stassart

Like leaves on trees, the race of man is found, now green in youth, now withering on the ground —Homer

Like the hours in the day, people come in two classes: the happy and the sad —Bin Ramke

Like the irresponsible black water bugs on summer ponds, they [people in cities] crawl and circle and hustle about idiotically, without aim or purpose —O. Henry

Man … cometh up, and is cut down, like a flower —*The Book of Common Prayer*

Man is a rope stretched between the animal and the Superman, a rope over an abyss —Friedrich Wilhelm Nietzsche

Man is as full of potentiality as he is of impotence —George Santayana

Man is like a ball tossed betwixt the wind and the billows —J.C. F. Schiller

A man is like a letter of the alphabet: to produce a word, it must combine with another —Benjamin Mandelstamm

A man is like all earth's fruit, you preserve him dry or pickled —Hayden Carruth

Man is like a musical box. An imperceptible jolt, and he plays a different tune —Ludwig Boerne

Man is like a precious stone: cut and polished by morals, adorned by wisdom —Isaac Halevi Satanov

Mankind is like the Red Sea: the staff has scarcely parted the waves asunder, before they flow together again —Johann Wolfgang von Goethe

A man like a watch is to be valued for his goings —Turkish proverb

Man's like a bird all the days of his breath, and pleasures are nets that allure him to death —Judah Al-Harizi

Man's like a candle in a candlestick made up tallow, and a little wick —John Bunyan

Men are like bricks, alike but placed high or low by chance —John Webster

Men are like ciphers: they acquire their value merely from their position —Napoleon Bonaparte

Men are like ears of corn: the emptier the head the more and the lower they stoop —Moritz Gottlieb Saphier

Men are like nuts; you can't tell what they're like till they're broken —Phyllis Bottome
This simile marks the opening of Bottome's story A Lost Leader.

Men are like plants; the goodness and flavor of the fruit proceeds from the peculiar soil and exposition in which they grow —Michel Guillaume Jean de Crevecoeur

Men are like the herbs of the field, while some are sprouting, others are withering —Babylonian Talmud

Men are like strange dogs … walk right up to them, bold as life, and they're as gentle as ducks —Owen Johnson

Men are like the stars: some generate their own light while others reflect the brilliance they receive —Jose Marti

Men are like trees … each one must put forth the leaf that is created in him —Henry Ward Beecher

Men are like weasels: weasels drag and lay up and know not for whom, and men save and hoard and know not for whom —Talmud

Men, like peaches and pears, grow sweet a little while before they begin to decay —Oliver Wendell Holmes, Sr.

Others are to us like the "characters" in fiction, eternal and incorrigible —Mary McCarthy

People are like planks of wood, soft until seasoned —St. John De Chevecoeur

People are mostly layers of violence and tenderness, wrapped like bulbs —Eudora Welty

People are somewhat like novels, we operate on beginnings, middles, and ends —Charles Johnson

In Johnson's novel, Faith and the Good Thing, *the simile includes this parenthetical comment: "Don't make too much of that simile."*

People are very much like flagstaffs. Some flagstaffs are very tall and prominent and some are small —Harry Emerson Fosdick

Fosdick's simile continued with the following observation: "But the glory of a flagstaff is not its size but the colors that it flies. A very small flagstaff flying the right colors is far more valuable than a very tall one with the wrong flag."

The race of men is like the race of leaves. As one generation flourishes another decays —Homer

Some individuals are like a brush heap, a helter-skelter, miscellaneous pile of twigs and branches —Harry Emerson Fosdick

Some men are like Einstein's theory of relativity; nobody at home understands them —Anon

Some men are like pyramids, which are very broad where they touch the ground, but grow narrow as they reach the sky —Henry Ward Beecher

Some men are like rifles with plenty of powder but no bullet … a great flow of language but no thought —Sylvanys Stall

So much of a man walks about dead … like a pianoforte with half the notes mute —D. H. Lawrence

Strong men are made by opposition; like kites they go up against the wind —Frank Harris, *Reader's Digest,* June,1936

The study of human nature is a good deal like the study of dissection, you find out a good many curious things, but it is a nasty job after all —Josh Billings

Billings wrote this in dialect which read as follows: "The studdy ov huymin natur is a gooddeal like the studdy ov dessekshun, yu finde out a good menny curis things, aut it is nasty job after awl."

To the Gods we are as flies to wanton boys —William Shakespeare, *King Lear*

We are all like vessels tossed on the bottom of the deep —Pietro Mestastasio

The simile continues: "Our passions are the winds that sweep us impetuously onward; each pleasure is a rock; the whole of life is a wide ocean."

We are like sun that rises and sheds light upon things, and then falls and leaves them in darkness again —William Goyen

We run to and fro upon the earth like frightened sheep —Robert Louis Stevenson

What a piece of work is a man! … in action, how like an angel! In apprehension, how like a god! —William Shakespeare, *Hamlet*

❧ MANNERS

See Also: BEHAVIOR, PROPRIETY/IMPROPRIETY

As chatty and polite as Rotarians —Richard Ford

Decorously polite as patients in a dentist's waiting room —Francis King

Evil manners will, like watered grass, grow up very quickly —Plautus

While bad manners might no longer be looked upon as evil, Plautus' simile in relation to how they spread remains true.

Had the manners of a disobliging steamroller ... and he was rather less particular about his dress than a scarecrow —George Bernard Shaw

His speech sounds like a spoken bread-and-butter note —W. P. Kinsella

Manners are like spices, you can't make a meal of them but they add a great deal to the meal's enjoyment —Anon

Manners are like the cipher in arithmetic; they may not be of much value in themselves, but they are capable of adding a great deal to the value of everything else —Anon

Manners ... as soft as wool —Lorenz Hart

This is part of the refrain of a song named "Moon of My Delight" written for "Chee-Chee."

Our manners, like our faces, though ever so beautiful must differ in their beauty —Lord Shaftesbury

The pleasure of courtesy is like the pleasure of good dancing —Alain

Polite as pie —F. van Wyck Mason

Politeness is like an air-cushion; there may be nothing it, but it eases our jolts wonderfully —Samuel Johnson

Rudeness (to Mrs. Dosely) was like dropping a pat of butter on to a hot plate, it slid and melted away —Elizabeth Bowen

Sedate as a judge in court —Rhys David

Sit bolt upright and smile without cease like a well-bred dinner guest —Ruth Prawer Jhabvala

To be cordial is like roughing a man's head to jolly him up, or kissing a child that doesn't want to be kissed. You are relieved when it's over —George Santayana

Ungracious as a hog —Tobias Smollett

Ungracious ... like a child who opens a birthday gift and barely glances at it before reaching to unwrap the next —Barbara Lazear Acher

An ungracious man is like a story g at the wrong time —The Holy Bible

♣ MARRIAGE

See Also: MEN AND WOMEN, RELATIONSHIPS

Adultery in a house is like a worm in poppy seeds —Babylonian Talmud

Adultery's like the common cold —if one bedfellow contracts it his companion automatically does —Robert Traver

Alimony is like buying oats for a dead horse —Arthur Baer, *New York Journal American*

Bridesmaids in their flowery frocks bloom round the bride like hollyhocks —Ogden Nash

The death of a man's wife is like cutting down an ancient oak that has long shaded the family mansion —Alphonse de Lamartine

Divorced men are like marked-down clothes; you get them after the season during which they would have made a sensation, and there is less choice, but they're easier to acquire —Judith Martin

Divorce is like a side dish that nobody remembers having ordered —Alexander King

For an artist to marry his model is as fatal as for a gourmet to marry his cook: the one gets no sittings, and the other no dinners —Oscar Wilde

For an old man to marry a young girl is like buying a new book for somebody else to read —Anon

Getting married is like a healthy man going into a sickbed —Isaac Bashevis Singer

Getting married is serious business. It's kinda formal, like funerals or playing stud poker —William Gargan to Charles Laughton in movie *They Knew What They Wanted*, 1940

He [husband of long-standing] is like an old coat, beautiful in texture, but easy and loose —Audrey Colvin, *New York Times*, July 17, 1986

A husband, like religion and medicine, must be taken with blind faith —Helen Rowland

This has been modernized from "Like unto religion."

Husbands, like governments, must never admit they are wrong —Honoré de Balzac

Husbands are like (motor) cars; all are good the first year —Channing Pollock

Husbands are like fires. They go out when unattended —Zsa Zsa Gabor

Husbands should be like Kleenex, soft, clean and disposable —Madeline Kahn, television news interview, December 1985

A husband without ability is like a house without a roof —Spanish proverbs

It [a second marriage] is the triumph of hope over experience —Samuel Johnson

It [marriage] resembles a pair of shears, so joined that they cannot be separated; often moving in opposite directions, yet always punishing any one who comes between them —Sydney Smith

It's [the permanence of marriage] like having siblings: you can't lose a brother or a sister. They're always there —Germaine Greer, *Playboy*, January, 1972

It [marriage and motherhood] was like being brainwashed, and afterward you went about numb as a slave in some private, totalitarian state —Sylvia Plath

Like suicide, divorce was something that had to be done on a thoughtless impulse, full speed ahead —R. V. Cassill

A man's wife should fit like a good, comfortable shoe —Ukrainian proverb

A man with a face that looks like someone had thrown it at him in anger nearly always marries before he is old enough to vote —Finley Peter Dunne

Many a marriage has commenced like the morning, red, and perished like a mushroom … because the married pair neglected to be as agreeable to each other after their union as they were before it —Frederika Bremer

Marriage may be compared to a cage: the birds outside frantic to get in and those inside frantic to get out —Michel de Montaigne

The simile also appeared in a play by a sixteenth century dramatist, John Webster, beginning, "Marriage is just like a summer birdcage in a garden." See the French proverb below for yet another twist in the same theme.

Marriage from love, like vinegar from wine —a sad, sour, sober beverage —Lord Byron

Marriage is a good deal like a circus: there is not as much in it as is represented in the advertising —Edgar Watson Howe

Marriage is a hand grenade with the pin out. You hold your breath waiting for the explosion —Abraham Rothberg

Marriage is like a 3-speed gearbox: affection, friendship, love —Peter Ustinov

Marriage is like a beleaguered fortress; those who are without want to get in, and those within want to get out —Quitard French proverb

Marriage is like a dull meal with the dessert at the beginning —dialogue from the movie, *Moulin Rouge*

The dialogue was spoken by Jose Ferrer as Toulouse Lautrec

Marriage is like a long trip in a tiny rowboat: if one passenger starts to rock the boat, the other has to steady it; otherwise they'll go to bottom together —Dr. David R. Reuben

Marriage is like a river. It is easier to fall in than out —Anon

Marriage is like a ship; sometimes you just have to ride out the storm —*L. A. Law*, television drama, 1987

Marriage is like buying something you've been admiring for a long time in a shop window … you may love it when you get home but it doesn't always go with everything else in the house —Jean Kerr

Marriage is like life in this … that it is a field of battle, and not a bed of roses —Robert Louis Stevenson

Marriage is like panty hose. It all depends on what you put into it —Phyllis Schlafly

Marriage is like twirling a baton, turning handsprings or eating with chopsticks; it looks so easy till you try it —Helena Rowland

Marriage like death is nothing to worry about —Don Herold

Marriages are like diets. They can be ruined by having a little dish on the side —Earl Wilson

Marriages, like houses, need constant patching —Nancy Mairs, *New York Times*, July 30, 1987

The simile was the highlighted blurb to capture reader attention. Actually it was a capsulized phrase from Mrs. Mairs' own concluding words: "Marriages, like houses, haven't got 'ever afters'. The stucco chips off and the cat fall through the screen and the bathroom runs slow. If you don't want the house falling down round your ears, you must plan to learn to weld a trowel and a hammer and a plunger."

Marriages were breaking up as fast as tires blowing in a long race —Norman Mailer

A marriage that grew like a great book, filling twenty-five years with many thousands of elaborate and subtle details —Larry McMurtry

A (seventeen-year) marriage that had been patched like an old rubber tire gone too many miles on a treadmill —Paige Mitchell

(She had decided long before that) marriage was like breathing, as soon as you noticed the process, you topped it at peril of your life —Laura Furman

A married man forms married habits and becomes dependent on marriage just as a sailor becomes dependent on the sea —George Bernard Shaw

Married so long … like Siamese twins they infect each other's feelings —Mary Hedin

Marrying a daughter to a boor is like throwing her to a lion —Babylonian Talmud

Marrying a woman for her money is very much like setting a rat-trap, and baiting it with your own finger —Josh Billings

In Billings' phonetic dialect: " … munny is vera mutch like … with yure own finger."

Matrimony, like a dip in the sea, first stimulates, then chills. But once out of the water the call of the ocean lures the bather to another plunge —Anon

Middle-aged marriages in which people seem stuck like flies caught in jelly —Norma Klein

(I am as) monogamous as the North Star —Carolyn Kizer

The sickening cords of their marriage drying everything like an invisible paste —John Updike

A successful marriage is an edifice that must be rebuilt every day —André Maurois

They [bride and groom] looked as though they belonged on top of their own enormous cake —Paul Reidinger

Wartime marriage … it's like being married on top of a volcano —H. E. Bates

Wedlock's like wine, not properly judged of till the second glass —Douglas Jerrold

What she mostly pretends, even to herself, is that her marriage was like a birthmark that turned malignant and had to be excised —Francine Prose, *A Changed Man*

Wife swapping is like a form of incest in which nobody's more guilty than anybody else —Germaine Greer, *Playboy*, January 1972

❧ MATHEMATICS AND SCIENCE

Arithmetic is where numbers fly like pigeons in and out of your head —Carl Sandburg

Every science, like a recurring decimal, has a beginning and no end —Anton Chekov

In his story "On the Way," Chekhov elaborates on this "similistic" theory as follows: "Zoology has discovered thirty-five thousand five hundred different species of insects; chemistry can count sixty-five elements; if you were to add ten zeros to the right of each of these figures, zoology and chemistry would be no nearer the end of their labors than they are now."

Science is, like virtue, its own ... great reward —Charles Kingsley

Science is love with seeing eyes —Elbert Hubbard

The study of mathematics is like climbing up a steep and craggy mountain; when once you reach the top, it fully recompenses your trouble, by opening a fine, clear and extensive prospect —Tryon Edwards

❧ MATRIMONY

See: MARRIAGE

❧ MAXIMS, PROVERBS, AND SAYINGS

Browsing through a book of proverbs ... is like taking a turn in a garden ... full of roses and fruit, where the bushes speak to you; and I come back rested, with smiles in my mind —Anatole France

Figures of speech are risky; for in art, as in arithmetic, many have no head for figures —G.K. Chesterton

Genuine proverbs are like good (kambrick) needles, short, sharp, and shiny —Josh Billings

The first word originally in Billings' phonetic dialect: "Ginowine."

His sayings are generally like women's letters; all the pith is in the postscript —William Hazzlitt

The man with the postscripts was Charles Lamb.

A man of maxims only is like a Cyclops with one eye, and that eye placed in the back of his head —Samuel Taylor Coleridge

Maxims are like lawyers who must needs see but one side of the case —Gelett Burgess

Proverbs, like the sacred books of each nation, are the sanctuary of the intuitions —Ralph Waldo Emerson

A proverb without wisdom is like a body without a foot —Moses Ibn Ezra

Rustic sayings which she [mother] threw, like flowers, into the conversation —Anatole France

A saying is like a fruit; one has first to eat it ... before one can know its taste —Sholem Ash

Sayings by wise men are like burning glasses, as they collect the diffused rays of wit and learning in authors, and make them point with warmth and quickness on the reader's imagination —Jonathan Swift

Sayings by wise men ... they are of great value, like the dust of gold, or the sparks of diamonds —John Tilletson

Similes are like songs in love: they much describe; they nothing prove —Mathew Prior

Similes dangle like baubles from me —William H. Gass

A word [that's been overused] ... lost its identity like an old coat in a second-hand shop —Anais Nin

❧ MEANINGFULNESS/ MEANINGLESSNESS

See: MEMORY, IMPORTANCE/UNIMPOR-TANCE, NECESSITY

❧ MEANNESS

See: CRUELTY

❧ MEEKNESS

See Also: MODESTY

(Quivering and) abject ... like some unfortunate dog abasing itself before its master —Jean Rhys

The quivering is being done by a young woman in the embrace of a lover, in Rhys' novel Quartet.

(Why do you sit there) apologizing to him, as if he were a fuehrer or something —Leslie A. Fieldler

Bowed to them like a tree in a storm —Edith Wharton

Complied like hostages with a gun trained on them —Louise Erdrich

Exist unthinkingly like a slave, like a working animal —Iris Murdoch

He's like a bell, that will go for everyone that pulls it —Thomas Fuller

Humble, friendly eyes looked up timidly, like the yes of a dog that is uncertain whether he is about to receive a pat or a blow —Ellen Glasgow

Like an ox, his head bent meekly, he waited for the blow of the axe which was raised over him —Leo Tolstoy

Like a victim, she waited: meek, like a sacrifice —Margaret Drabble

Looked humbly about him like a dog slipping into a strange kitchen and afraid of kicks —Honoré de Balzac

Meek as a hen —Fyodor Dostoevsky

Meek as the dew —Dylan Thomas

Meekness takes injuries like pills, not chewing, but swallowing them down —Sir Thomas Browne

A meek soul without zeal, is like a ship in a calm, that moves not as fast as it ought —John M. Mason

Obedience simulates subordination as fear of the police simulates honesty —George Bernard Shaw

Obedient as a partner in a dance —Lael Tucker Wertenbaker

Obedient as a sheep —Robert Browning

Obediently as a trained seal —Anon

The trained seal comparison has become a common cliché with many variations such as "obediently as a puppet on a string" or "obediently like a trained elephant" spotted in Aldous Huxley's After Many a Summer Dies the Swan.

Servility is like a golden pill which outwardly gives pleasure but inwardly is full of bitterness —Narun Tate

The word 'gives' has been modernized from 'giveth.'

Waiting upon her whims like a footman —O. Henry

Went meekly off ... like a repentant boy led away to reform school —Harvey Swados

Yield like a foolish mother —Emily Brontë

♣ MEETINGS

Come together as inevitably as the key to the magnet —Hugh Walpole

Converge like pulsars —Diane Ackerman

Face each other [across table] like partners at bridge —Thomas Pynchon

Like driftwood spars, which meet and pass upon the boundless ocean-plain, so on the sea of life, alas, man meets man —meets and quits again —Matthew Arnold

Like mountain streams we meet and part, each living in the other's heart —Oliver Wendell Holmes

Like two doomed ships that pass in storm we had crossed each other's way —Oscar Wilde

The simile, from The Ballad of Reading Goal *concludes as follows: "but we made no sign, we said no word, we had no word to say."*

Met [briefly] ... like a couple of trucks, side-swiping each other —Robert Emmet Sherwood

Meet like enemy generals, knocking your sabers against the table, bluffing each other —Scott Spencer

There are some meetings in life so useful, so truly wonderful, that they seem like visible interventions of Providence —Ernest Hello

♣ MELANCHOLY

See: DESPAIR

♣ MEMORY

See Also: PAST, THE

As bare of memories as a grain of sugar —Vina Delmar

As fixed in my memory ... as the flash of light that is followed by the thunder of pain when your shoulder is pulled out of its socket —Norman Mailer

Both memories give him a pleasant buzz, like a swarm of mellow bees humming between him —Francine Prose, *A Changed Man*

A breeze like the turning of a page brings back your face —John Ashberry

[Memories] came back to run through his mind like a reel of color film —Carlos Baker

(I am) clean forgotten, as a dead man out of mind —*Book of Common Prayer*

Could be forgotten as quickly and painlessly as a doubting of Jesus or a fear of death from the measles —Peter Taylor

[Memory] Drifted into my mind like a bit of weed carried in a current and caught there, floating but fixed, refusing to be carried away —Katherine Anne Porter

Eventually I thought about him [a once close friend] only once a week or so, as if he were a relative who had died years ago —Richard Burgin

Faded memories worn as a buffalo head a nickel —A. D. Winans

Felt old memories stir in him like dead leaves —Helen Hudson

Fettered to a pack of useless memories like a living person to a corpse —Ouida

Follow one after the next like cars out on the street, memories, there is just no stopping them —Tony Ardizzone

For a person blessed with a memory as full of holes as an Iran-scam scenario, life can be a continuous state of astonishment —Donal Henahan

Henahan uses this simile to introduce his comments about a revival of the musical South Pacific. *The editorial blurb writer uses a simile from the musical's lyrics "as corny as Kansas in August" to highlight to article.*

Forgotten as quickly as warm days in winter or cool days in summer —Ellen Glasgow

Forgotten like a station passed through on a train —Elizabeth Spencer

(Be) forgotten like spilt wine —Algernon Charles Swinburne

Gather memories like dry twigs, thorns and thistles —Yehuda Amichai

The ghosts of our remembrances throng around us like dead leaves whirled in the autumn wind —Jerome K. Jerome

His memory could work like the slinging of a noose to catch a wild pony —Eudora Welty

His memory lifted its skirts ... and hurried convulsively, like an old lady picking her way barefoot across a shingly beach —Noel Coward

His memory was something like his appendix —a vestigial repository —John Cheever

(He never forgets a face.) His mind is like a video camera —Ilie Nastase

If only there could be an invention that bottled up memory, like a scent —Daphne du Maurier

The image [of remembered scene] ... is like a photograph on my memory —Richard Maynard

An incident would suddenly crop up in her memory, like a piece in a jigsaw puzzle that seemed to have come from the wrong box —Mary McCarthy

It isn't a thing one forgets overnight, like losing a pencil —Mary Stewart

It was as though an endless series of hangars had been shaken ajar in the air base of his memory and from each, like a young wasp emerging from its cell, arose the memory of a plane —Ralph Ellison

I've blanked it out, like a car crash —David Nicholls, *One Day*

Like a dull actor ... I have forgot my part —William Shakespeare, *Coriolanus*

Memories are like books; a few live in our hearts through life, and the rest, like the bills we pay, are read, and then forgotten —Gerald Bendall

Memories are like stones, time and distance erode them like acid —Ugo Betti

Memories ... began to play across the surface of his mind like movies on a screen —Richard McKenna

Memories bursting in her mind like forsythia buds on the first warm day of the year —B. S. Johnson

Memories [troublesome] ... flitted like unexplained shadows across her happier thoughts —George Eliot

Memories ... floated like gossamer through her thoughts —Frank Swinnerton

Memories ... like worms eating into the flesh —William Golding

Memories lurk like dust balls at the back of drawers —Jay McInerney

Memories ... no two sets exactly the same, like fingerprints —Daphne Merkin

Memories of embarrassing things he had done and said, of mistakes he had made, buzzed and flitted in his mind like annoying little gnats —Dan Wakefield

Memories of the bad covered the good, as snow covers grass in the fall —Ann Jasperson

Memories ... no two sets exactly the same, like fingerprints —Daphne Merkin

Memories ... pierced by moments of brightness, like flashes of lightning —Yasunari Kawabata

Memories [when a lot of people one knows die] return to life as grass grows on graves —Lael Wertenbaker

Memories swept over her like a strong wind on dark waters —Carl Sandburg

Memories turned up like bills you thought you'd never have to pay —Hugh Leonard
In Leonard's play Da, *the memories are evoked as a character sorts through family memorabilia.*

Memories were like tomb paintings, thought the Major, the colors still vivid no matter how many layers of mud and sand time deposited. Scrape at them and they come up all red and blazing —Helen Simonson, *Major Pettigrew's Last Stand*

Memory ... as good as a bulldog's handshake —Loren D. Estleman In Estleman's mystery novel, *Every Brilliant Eye,* the character with the bulldog-like memory is a policeman.

Memory broke, like an old clock —Karl Shapiro

Memory can be like a dream, cause and effect non-existent —Gordon Weaver

Memory ... crawling to the surface like a fat worm after rain —Harvey Swados

The memory ... fell upon him like a weight of black water —Willa Cather

The memory [of a man] glimmered in her thoughts like a bright thread in the pattern of a tapestry —Mazo de la Roche

Memory is a rare ghost-raiser. Like a haunted house, its walls are ever echoing to unseen feet. (Through the broken casements we watched the flitting shadow of the dead, and the saddest shadows of them all are the shadows of our own dead selves) —Jerome K. Jerome

Memory is fully as chimerical as forgetfulness, deceptive as any other work of the imagination —Madison Smartt Bell

Memory is like a noisy intruder being thrown out of the concert hall … he will hang on the door and continue to disturb the concert —Theodore Reik, *Saturday Review,* January 11, 1958

Memory, is like a purse, if it's too full, it can't be shut, and everything will drop out of it —Thomas Fuller

Memory is like the moon … it has its new, its full, and its wane —Duchess of Newcastle
The word "has" modernized from "hath."

The memory is salty, like sweat, like the emissions of love-making, like the sea —Lael Wertenbaker

Memory, like a drop that, night and day, falls cold and ceaseless, wore my heart away —Thomas More

Memory, like a horrible malady, was eating his soul away —Oscar Wilde

Memory, like a juggler, tosses its colored balls into the light, and again receives them into darkness —Conrad Aiken

Memory … like an old musical box it will lie silent for long years; then a mere nothing, a jerk, a tremor, will start the spring, and from beneath its decent covering of dust it will talk to us of forgotten passion and desire —Thomas Burke

A memory like a powerful microchip —Anon

A memory like a telephone directory —William McIlvanney

A memory like a well-ordered cupboard —Anon

A memory like flypaper —Nora Johnson

Memory, like sleep, has powers which dreams obey —William Wordsworth

Memory, like women, is usually unfaithful —Spanish proverbs

Depending upon who's talking, the comparison would be as appropriate if attributed to men.

The memory of our lost friends is welcome to us like the bitter taste in wine that is very old —Michel de Montaigne

The memory of past favors is like a rainbow, bright, vivid, and beautiful, but it soon fades away —Thomas Chandler Haliburton

Memory [of something unpleasant] … pokes at him like a nightmare in the womb —T. Coraghessan Boyle

Memory returned like fire —Frank Swinnerton

Memory's like an athlete; keep it training; take it for cross-country runs —James Hilton

The [unpleasant] memory … stuck like a fishhook in her brain —Stefan Zweig

Memory transparent as a dream you strain to recall —Harryette Mullen

Memory unwound within me like a roll of film in which I played no part —Heinrich Böll

A memory, very beautiful and delicate like a flavor or a perfume —Ruth Prawer Jhabvala

Had a mind like a mainframe memory bank —William Beechcroft

The moment hung like crystal in Meredith's mind —Babs H. Deal

More than 130 years have passed since the Great Fire, but its memory lived on like a scar —Alaa Al Aswany, *Chicago*

My memory is like camphor. It evaporates with time —Dominique Lapierre

My memory kicked in; one of those wonderful little mental jolts, like a quick electric shock when a plug's gone bad —Sue Grafton

My memory's like a policeman. Never there when you want it —Ronald Harwood
This line is spoken by the main character in Harwood's play The Dresser.

Picking over the shames and humiliations … like an invalid mulling over a plate of unwanted food —Harvey Swados

Pulled up at it [gap in memory] as if his advance had been checked by a chasm in the pavement at his feet —Edith Wharton

Recollections ... collected like spit from an aging throat —Elizabeth Spencer

Recollections dropped over him like a noose —Laurie Colwin

Remembrance is a tripping stone in the path of Hope —Kahil Gibran

Remembrance ... tickles the end of his nose like the fingertips of a child —Hayden Carruth

(I have) a retentive memory, a mind like flypaper to which facts stick —Desmond Begley

Shameful memories grip me like an anchor —Delmore Schwartz

She sank from his consciousness like one of those poor people encased in concrete who are heaved over the side and plummet to the bottom of the sea —William Styron

Slipped out of her mind like a newspaper dropping from the hands of a sleepy woman —Erich Maria Remarque

Some memories are like lucky charms, talismans, one shouldn't tell about them or they'll lose their power —Iris Murdoch

Something one remembers as normal and pleasant in the past—like a very good photograph —Erik Larson, *In the Belly of the Beast: Love, Terror, and an American Family in Hitler's Berlin*

Stung by memories thick as wasps about a nest invaded —Edna St. Vincent Millay

There are many moments I cannot forget, moments like radiant flowers in all colors and hues —Jaroslav Seifert

Tries to remember like a deaf man remembering an opera he heard eleven years before —Lyn Lifshin

As unremembered as bird shadows on the grass —Henry Bellamann

Unremembered as old rain —Edna St. Vincent Millay

The world, like an accomplished hostess, pays most attention to those whom it will soonest forget —John Churton Collins

❧ MEN AND WOMEN

See Also: LOVE, MARRIAGE, SEXUAL INTERACTION

Arm in arm ... like a pair of loving turtle-doves —William Shakespeare, *King Henry VI, Part I*

Court ... as you would court a farm—for the strength of the silo and the perfection of the title —Josh Billings
  Like many Billings witticisms this one was written in phonetic dialect as follows: "as you wud court a farm—for the strength ov the sile and the parfeckshun ov the title."

Dating a grad student was like making hurried-up popcorn: lots of butter, high heat, instant noise —Will Weaver

The distance between them is like a desert, or an unswimmable body of water —Hilma Wolitzer
  In her novel In the Palomar Arms, *Wolitzer is describing an estranged husband and wife, lying far apart on a large bed.*

Felt my eyes going down across her mouth, her throat like fingers —Julio Cortázar

Finding a man is like finding a job; its easier to find one when you already have one —Paige Mitchell

Girls (on the Cripple Creek 'bout half grown) jump on a boy like a dog on a bone —American folk song, "Cripple Creek"

Handle a small woman like she's made out of steel, and a big woman like she's made out of glass —Paige Mitchell

The happiest women, like the happiest nations, have no history —George Eliot

He goes about the business of fondling you, like someone very tired at night having to put out the trash and bolt-lock the door —Lorrie Moore

He likes fat women the way a rat likes pumpkins —Rita Mae Brown

He ran through women like a child through growing hay —Louis MacNeice

A simile from a conversation overheard on a bus describes the woman as the sexual predator: "She runs through men like a fever."

He regarded women in the way that little girls regard their dolls, as toys to be dressed and undressed —Frank Swinnerton

Her responsiveness was something that fed him as wood fed the fire —Paul Horgan

He swept through her like a great ragged hawk on its journey to another prey —John le Carré

He thought she'd fall like a ripe apple —Rita Mae Brown

He was looking at me the way a butcher must size up a carcass of beef, like I was one of those drawings with the parts of the cow on it, all the choice cuts and the waste —Jonathan Valin

He would always feel for her that impersonal admiration which is inspired by anything very large, like the Empire State Building or the Grand Canyon of Arizona —P. G. Wodehouse

Holds her face in his cupped hands as carefully as a thirsty man would gather water —Hilma Wolitzer

I dropped her like a bad habit —James Crumley

It's as natural for women to pride themselves in fine clothes as 'tis for a peacock to spread his tail —John Ray's *Proverbs*

A look at fashion, both past and present, would indicate that this could well be a unisex simile.

I've never really looked at women. I find them a bit like water when you want beer. Or like a minimalist house with nothing in it, when you're someone who's really into stuff —Mike Bartlett, *Cock*

I want to steep myself in you … as if you were a South Wind —Wallace Stevens, letter to his fiancée

Just us two … like two roots joined and widening out into a flower —David Denby

Like an animal, he was aware of me at once —Robertson Davies

Like two mummies, we have been wrapped tight in love —Yehuda Amichai

Like two open cities in the midst of some vast plain their two minds lay open to each other —Katherine Mansfield

Like Ulysses tying himself to the mast to resist the song of the sirens, Jim had to brace himself to withstand the charm of Kate's voice —Henri-Pierre Roché

Making love to women is almost as old as chess —Robert Traver

A man is like a cat; chase him and he'll run … sit still and ignore him and he'll come purring at your feet —Helen Rowland

Man without woman would be as stupid a game as playing checkers alone —Josh Billings

Men like to pursue an elusive woman, like a cake of wet soap in a bathtub —even men who hate baths —Gelett Burgess

A mistress should be like a little country retreat near the town; not to dwell in constantly, but only for a night and away —William Wycherly

My blood is singing in her system, like whisky —Irwin Shaw

Paired off like the animals in the ark —Ross Macdonald

She drained me like a fevered moon —Edgar Lee Masters

She leaned easily against his shoulder … as if she had done herself up in a parcel, addressed to him, left on his doorstep from now on, his responsibility —Elizabeth Taylor

She made the blood run round in my veins like horses on a track —Ross Macdonald

Sometimes being with her is like being caught in a tornado —Alvin Boretz, television drama, 1986

Some women learn, like slaves, to study men —Charles Johnson

Take them [women] away and his (man's) existence is as flat and secure as that of a moo-cow —H. L. Mencken

(They hugged ...) their hearts shook them, like two people pounding at the same time on both sides of a very thin door —Eudora Welty

To be intimate with a foolish man is like going to bed with a razor —Ben Franklin

The trouble with being a woman is that you are supposed to enhance men; to add gaiety to their evening, like balloons, even if you feel heavy as stone —Daphne Merkin

Twenty years of romance make a woman look like a ruin; but twenty years of marriage make her something like a public building —Oscar Wilde

Two couples living together and talking openly for a week ... it was like a week in a bell jar —Joanne Kates, *New York Times*, October 2, 1986

Very gently, as to a wild animal, I reached out my hand and made her turn her head —John Fowles

A woman, I always say, should be like a good suspense movie: the more left to the imagination, the more excitement there is —Alfred Hitchcock, *Reader's Digest*, July 1963

Hitchcock topped off his simile with this bit of advice: "This should be her aim, to create suspense, to let a man discover things about her without her having to tell him."

A woman is like a salad: much depends on the dressing —Anon

There's also a saying, "clothes make the man," so this simile need not be limited to one sex.

A woman moved is like a fountain troubled, muddy, ill-seeming, thick, bereft of beauty

—William Shakespeare, *The Taming of the Shrew*

A woman's heart, like the moon, is always changing, but there is always a man in it —*Punch*

A woman's preaching is something like a dog's walking on his hinder legs. It is not done well; but you are surprised to find it done at all —Samuel Johnson

Women preachers, unlike women in other careers, are still subject to frequent discussions, which prompted a Wall Street Journal *reader to quote Johnson's simile in response to a December 24, 1986 story on this subject.*

A woman without a man is like a garden without a fence —German proverb

A woman without a man is like a wild rose which blooms fast and ... falls apart with the wind —Diane Wakoski

Women are always a touchstone ... like litmus paper or dogs before an earthquake —Iris Murdoch

Women are like flowers, a little dust or squeezing makes them the more fragrant —Josh Billings

In Billings' dialect the first part of this read as follows: "wimmin are like flowers, a little dust ov squeezing."

Women are like tricks to sleight of hand. Which to admire we should not understand —William Congreve

Women are very much like religion; we must take them on faith or go without —F. Marion Crawford

Women as compared to men are like point lace to canvas —Charles H. Hoyt

Women follow him around like flies after garbage —Paige Mitchell

Women's hearts are like old china, none the worse for a break or two —W. Somer

[Woman being addressed by a man] You've got an off-on switch like a circuit breaker —Will Weaver

❧ MERCY

See: KINDESS

❧ MERIT

See: VIRTUE

❧ MERRIMENT

See: GAIETY, JOY

❧ METHOD

See: PURPOSEFULNESS

❧ MIDDLE AGE

See: AGE

❧ MIND

See Also: ATTENTION, INSULTS, MIND DE-
FINED, THOUGHT

(You can't concentrate. You've got) a brain like a hummingbird —Jane Wagner

Brain as heavy as a grandfather clock —Diane

A brain tooled like a twenty-jewel Swiss watch —Stephen Longstreet

Emptied her mind, as if emptying a bottle —Mavis Gallant

Her mind flickered like a lizard —Elizabeth Bowen

Her mind was like a one-way thoroughfare, narrow and flat, maintained in repair —Mavis Gallant

Her mind was like a rushing stream, tumbling downhill over rocks and boulders, eddying, bouncing, shifting direction —Ward Just

Her mind was strangely empty … an empty room through which vague memories stalked like giants —Jean Rhys

His brain feels like a frail but alert invalid packed inside among a lot of deep pillows —John Updike

His brain was like a brightly-lit factory, full of flying wheels and precision —Edith Wharton

His mind [Oliver Wendell Holmes'] resembles a stiff spring, which has to be abducted violently from it, and which every instant it is left to itself flies right back —William James, letter to brother Henry from Cambridge, November 24, 1872

His mind's like the feet of a pre-civilized Chinese girl —Frank Swinnerton

The human mind should be like a good hotel — open the year round —William Lyon Phelps

It [his brain] felt like an immense dynamo running at top speed in an empty shed in the middle of the woods —Norman Mailer

Little minds, like weak liquors, are soonest soured —H. G. Bohn's *Hand-Book of Proverbs*

Mind, as clear as mountain water —Richard Wilbur

Mind … blank and enclosed as a bubble of glass —Jean Thompson

Mind flapping like a rag on a clothesline in cold wind —Saul Bellow

Mind … fluffy as a baby's crib —Louis Auchincloss

(He stood for a moment outside the room, his) mind jerking spasmodically, like a severed nerve —Storm Jameson

Mind like a bent corkscrew —Roderic Jeffries

A mind like a puddle. Things fall in and float around in it and she fishes them up later when they've gotten soggy —Jean Thompson

A mind like a sieve —Anon

A mind like a sink —Agatha Christie

Christie was thus quoted by her nephew as she spoke about Miss Marple's dark view of humankind.

Mind … like a sun-dial, it records only pleasantness —Anon

A mind like a tattered concordance —Samuel Beckett

A mind like a wedge of iron —Louise Erdrich

Mind like dead ashes —Robert Silverberg

Mind like moths —Anon

Mind … like some fertile garden —Edith Wharton

The mind, packed away like a satin wedding dress even in blue tissue, yellowing, pressing itself into permanent folds —Diane Wakoski

This simile carries through the theme and the title, also a simile: "The Mind, Like an Old Fish."

Minds fossilized like lava —Isak Dinesen

Minds [of students] so earnest and helpless that it takes them half an hour to get from one idea to its immediately adjacent next neighbor. And when they've got the next idea, they lie down on it with their whole weight and can get no farther, like a cow on a door-mat, so that you can get neither in nor out with them —William James, letter to his wife, 1896

Minds stirring like poplars in a storm —Marge Piercy

(Eleanor's) mind went whirling round like a wheel on the hub of this moment —Elizabeth Bowen

A mind wide open to absorb all it could teach him as the flowers of the date-palm to receive the fertilizing pollen —Honoré de Balzac

My brain is numb as a piece of liver —W. P. Kinsella

(I seem to have read so little of late, that) my mind is like a desert, devoid of roses and leaves —Janet Flanner

Our brains are like fruit stands; all the rubbish is in front and the good stuff is in the back —Carla Lane, dialogue from *Solo*, British television sitcom, June 23, 1987

Our unconscious is like a vast subterranean factory with intricate machinery that is never ideal, where work goes on all day and night from the time we are born until the moment of our death —Milton R. Sapirstein

Some minds are like trunks, packed tight with knowledge, no air and plenty of moths —*Life*, January 31,1918

There is no sea as restless as my mind —Derek Walcott

When you have a creative mind it sometimes backs up on you like a sewer —John Farris

❧ MIND DEFINED

As the fire-fly only shines when on the wing, so it is with the human mind; when at rest, it darkens —L. E. Landon

The brain is like the hand. It grows with using —Judge Louis D. Brandeis

The brain, like Rhenish wine, should be chilled, not iced to be at its best —A. J. Liebling

The brain of man is filled with passageways like the contours and multiple crossroads of a labyrinth. In its curved folds like the imprint of thousands of images, recordings of millions of words —Anais Nin

Brains to the sluggard are like wings to the ant, or a torch to the blind, an added load of no use or aid —Jediah Bedersi

A brilliant mind without faith is like a beautiful face without eyes —Shalom Cohen

A child's mind is like a shallow brook which ripples and dances merrily over the stony course of its education, and reflects here a flower, there a bush and yonder a fleecy cloud —Helen Keller

The conscious mind may be compared to a fountain playing in the sun and falling back into the great subterranean pool of the subconscious from which it rises —Sigmund Freud

The cultivation of the mind is a kind of food supplied for the soul of man —Cicero

The human mind is kind of like … a piñata. When it breaks open, there's a lot of surprises inside —Jane Wagner

The human mind … is like a pendulum, which the moment it has reached the limit of its swing in one direction, goes inevitably back as far as the other side and so on forever —J. R. Lowell

The human mind should be like a good hotel … open the year round —William Lyon Phelps

Many minds are like low-grade ores, there is gold in them, but it takes a vast deal of labor to get it out —John Alfred Spender

The mind is a city like London, smoky and populous —Delmore Schwartz

This simile beings a poem entitled "The Mind Is an Ancient and Famous Capital."

The mind is an iceberg … it floats with only one-seventh of its bulk above water —Sigmund Freud, quoted in his obituary, *New York Times,* September 24, 1939

The mind is like a bow, the stronger for being unbent —Ben Jonson

The mind is like a mechanical instrument that plays a great variety of tunes, but it must play them in succession —William Hazlitt

The mind is like an ocean. The surface layers of the mind function actively while the deeper levels remain silent —Maharishi Mahesh Yogi

The mind is like a sheet of white paper … the impressions it receives are oftenest, and retains the longest, are black ones —Julius Charles and August William Hare

The mind is like a slate, one thing gets rubbed out for another —Sam Slick

The mind is like the stomach. It is not how much you put into it that counts, but how much it digests —Albert Jay Nook

The mind like any other organism gradually shapes itself to what surrounds it, and resents disturbance in the form which its life has assumed —Oliver Wendell Holmes

The mind of man is like a clock that is always running down, and requires to be as constantly wound up —William Hazlitt

The mind of the people is like mud, from which arise strange and beautiful things —Walter J. Turner

Minds are like parachutes … they only function when open —Lord Thomas

Minds, like bodies, will often fall into a pimpled, ill-conditioned state from mere excess of comfort —Charles Dickens

A mind without occupation is like a cat without a ball of yarn —Samuel Willoughby Duffield

Old minds are like old horses; you must exercise them if you wish to keep them in working order —John Adams

Our minds are like crows. They pick up everything that glitters no matter how uncomfortable our nests get with all that metal in them —Thomas Merton

Our minds are like our stomachs; they are whetted by the change of their food, and variety supplies both with fresh appetite —Quintilian

The shapes which the mind assumes are like those great forms, born of undifferentiated water, which assail or replace each other on the surface of the deep; each concept collapses, eventually, to merge with its opposite, like two waves breaking against each other only to subside into the same single line of white foam —Marguerite Yourcenar

Some minds are like concrete-thoroughly mixed and permanently set —Anon

The state of a man's mind is as much a fact as the state of his digestion —Baron Charles Synge Christopher Bowen

The simile was used in reference to the legality of intent in an 1885 law case.

A weak mind is like a horoscope, which magnifies trifling things but cannot receive great ones —Lord Chesterfield

The letter to Chesterfield's son from which this was culled, addresses the question of taking a balanced view towards keeping track of expendi-

tures. *The comparison of the weak mind to a horoscope is used to underscore the author's statement that "a strong mind sees things in their true proportions."*

❧ MIRTH
See: GAIETY

❧ MISERLINESS
See: KINDESS

❧ MISERY
See: DEJECTION, GLOOM

❧ MISFORTUNE
See: FORTUNE/MISFORTUNE

❧ MIST
See Also: FOG

The hot mist ... mixed with the sun like cloudy gin —David Denby

A light morning mist like grain on film —Clive Irving

Like a blanket, the mist came down —Jilly Cooper

Mist arose on the plain and stood round about it like a guard of honor —Vladimir Korolenko

Mist draped like ragged bits of cloth over a black line of distant hills —Alice McDermott

[Thinning] Mist ... drifted away like slow smoke —Howard Spring

The mist, like love, plays upon the heart of the hills and brings out surprise of beauty —Rabindranath Tagore

The mists like flocks of trooping sheep cloudily drifted here and there —John Hall Wheelock

Mist so fine it was like cigarette smoke —Paul Theroux

Mists, whirling and winding, like snakes —Mikhail Lermontov

A mist that is like blown snow —W. B. Yeats

Mist thick as cotton batting —William Faulkner

A pure white mist crept over the water like breath upon a mirror —A. J. Cronin

A thick gray mist covered the countryside, as if to conceal the mysteries of the changes that were taking place in nature —Leo Tolstoy

❧ MISTAKES
See: ERRORS

❧ MISTRESS
See: MEN AND WOMEN

❧ MIXTURES
See: CONNECTIONS

❧ MOANS
See: GROANS AND WHISPERS

❧ MODESTY
See Also: MEEKNESS, PERSONAL TRAITS

As humbly as a guest who knows himself too late —Hart Crane

Humility is like underwear, essential but indecent if it shows —Helen Nielsen, *Reader's Digest,* March, 1959

If you really were a hero ... you made it sound routine and unglamorous, like shrugging off a ninety-yard touchdown run as "good luck and good blocking" —Dan Wakefield

I looked as if I were trying to melt into the scenery and become invisible, like a giraffe standing motionless among sunlit leaves —Christopher Isherwood

Modest as a flower —Ella Wheeler Wilcox

Modest as justice —William Shakespeare, *Pericles*

Modesty is like virtue; suspected only when it is advertised —Douglas Malloch

Modesty like a diver gathers pearls by keeping his head low —*Punch*

Modesty's at times its own reward, like virtue —Lord Byron

♣ MONARCHY

See: GOVERNMENT

♣ MONEY

See Also: COST, GREED, RICHES

Ate up money like Crackerjacks —Robert Campbell

Bargain like a gipsy, but pay like a gentleman —Hungarian proverb

The euro is like a bumblebee. This is a mystery of nature because it shouldn't fly but instead it does. —Mario Draghi

Draghi, the president of the European Central Bank, is quoted from July 2012 on his opinions about the troubled euro that this institution wanted to preserve. Mr. Draught ran with the metaphor, declaring that it flew very well for a while but has now stopped flying and graduated "to a real bee."

(There ain't a chance of putting the bee on me.... I'm) flat [broke] as a ballroom floor —H. C. Witwer

Getting money is like digging with a needle; spending it is like water soaking into sand —Proverb

Gold like the sun, which melts wax, but hardens clay, expands great souls —Antoine Rivarol

An instinct like a water diviner's where money's concerned —John Braine

Loses money the way a ... balloon loses air —Martin Cruz Smith

In Smith's novel Stallion Gate, a character is talking about nightclubs, likening a great club's money loss to a beautiful balloon's air loss.

Making money ... is, in fact, almost as easy as losing it. Almost but not quite —H. L. Mencken

A man without money is like a bird without wings; if he soars he falls to the ground and dies —Romanian proverb

He that is without money is like a bird without wings —Thomas Fuller

A man without money is like a ship without sails —Dutch proverb

Money is a bottomless sea, in which honor, conscience and truth may be drowned —Ivan Kozloff

Money is a muscle in our society like that of a leg or arm of a man with a shovel, and both muscles must have a wage —Janet Flanner

Money is in some respects like fire; it is a very excellent servant —P. T. Barnum

Money is like an arm or a leg, use it or lose it —Henry Ford, *New York Times*, November 8, 1958

Money is like an eel in the hand —Welsh proverb

Money is like a sixth sense, and you can't make use of the other five without it —W. Somerset Maugham, *New York Times Magazine*, October 18, 1958

Public money is like holy water: every one helps himself to it —Italian proverb

Money is like promises, easier made than kept —Josh Billings

In Billing's phonetic dialect: "munny ... easier maid than kept."

Money is like the reputation for ability, more easily made than kept —Samuel Butler

Money, like a boot, when it's tight, is extremely trying —*Punch*, 1864

Money is like muck, not good except it be spread —Francis Bacon

Variations include: "Money is like dung," "Riches are like muck, which stink in a heap, but spread abroad, make the earth fruitful" and "Money like manure does no good till it is spread". Two men who have been credited with barely changed versions of the above are Clint Murchison, Jr. and J. Paul Getty. Getty quoting his father's advice that, "Money is like manure. You have to spread it around or it smells" and Clint Mutchison, Jr. quoting his father's advice as "Money is like ma-

nure. If you spread it around, it does a lot of good. But if you pile it up in one place, it stinks like hell," the latter with Money is like manure. You have to spread it around or it smells."

Money, like vodka, makes a man eccentric —Anton Chekhov

Money's as cold and neutral as the universe —Hortense Calisher

Money slips from his fingers like a watermelon seed, travels without legs, and flies without wings —Bartlett's *Dictionary of Americanisms*

Money … was exactly like sex, you thought of nothing else if you didn't have it and thought of other things if you did —James Baldwin

Serious money is like cancer, it breeds itself —A. Alvarez

Spending money like a pusher —M. S. Craig

Spent her money like a spoiled empress —Marjory Stoneman Douglas

They talk about it [money] as if it were something you got pink gums from —Ogden Nash

♣ MONOTONY
See: DULLNESS, REPETITION

♣ MONTHS
See: SEASONS

♣ MOOD CHANGES
See: CHANGE

♣ MOODINESS
See: GLOOM

♣ MOON

A bright moon … like glistening silk —Amy Lowell

Curled moon … like a feather —Dante Gabriel Rossetti

Everything has in fact another side to it, like the moon —G.K. Chesterton

A full new-risen moon like a pale medallion —Hayden Carruth

The moon had lost all its brilliance and looked like a little cloud in the sky —Leo Tolstoy

A half moon sailing like a moth up the drained blue sky —Jilly Cooper

It looked like a ball of paper from the back pocket of jeans that have just come out of the washing machine, which only time and ironing would tell if it was an old shopping list or a five pound note —Douglas Adams

Bright moonlight lay against its [house] wall like a fresh coat of paint —Raymond Chandler

A little slice of moon, curved like a canoe —Helen Hudson

Like zis—ze moon, / As round as a balloon / Suspended like a bauble in ze sky —David Yazbek, "Like Zis/Like Zat," *Dirty Rotten Scoundrels*

The moon as beautiful as a great camellia —Max Beerbohm

A moonbeam … shimmers bright as a needle (in the creamy warmth of the night) —W. P. Kinsella

Moon, bright as a lemon —Tom Robbins

The moon burned like metal —Pat Conroy

The moon, but half disclosed, was cut off as by a shutter —Joyce Cary

Moon curved like a rocker —Helen Hudson

The moon floats belly up like a dead goldfish —Marge Piercy

The moon follows the sun like a French Translation of a Russian poet —Wallace Stevens

The moon hangs like a neon scythe over the countryside —W. P. Kinsella

The moon hung above the yard like a cheap earring —Isaac Babel

The moon hung like a pale lamp above the rim of the bay —William Styron

The moon is hidden by a silver cloud, fair as a halo —Christina Rossetti

The moon ... is like a cake of white soap —John Phillips

The moon leaned low against the sky like a white-faced clown lolling against a circus wall —W. Somerset Maugham

Moonlight drilling in through the window like a bit into coal —Richard Wertime

Moonlight ... dripped down like oil —Bernard Malamud

The moonlight invaded the courtyard, until it looked like a field of untrodden snow —Stefan Zweig

Moonlight so white that it looked like snow —Ruth Prawer Jhabvala

A moon like a fallen fruit reversing gravity was hoisting itself above the rooftop —Ross Macdonald

The moon like a flower in heaven's high bower, with silent delight sits and smiles on the night —William Blake

Moon like a monstrous crystal —G. K. Chesterton

The moon, like an eye turned up in a trance, filmed over and seemed to turn loose from its track and to float sightless —Eudora Welty

Moon ... like a red-faced farmer —T. E. Hulme

The complete line in the source, a poem entitled "Autumn" as follows: "I walked abroad and saw the ruddy moon lean over the hedge like a red-faced farmer."

The moon like a white rose shone —W. B. Yeats

Moon like the moving dot on sing-along lyrics —Sharon Sheehe Stark

The moon looked like the head of a golden bollard in a Venice lagoon —John Gunther

The moon, narrow and pale like a paring snipped from a snowman's toenail —Tom Robbins

The moon overhead tore through fierce cloud-wrack like a battered ship —Phyllis Bottome

Moon ... pale, full-blown as a flower —Elizabeth Spencer

Moon pitted with holes, like an old brass coin —Erich Maria Remarque

The moon rattles like a fragment of angry candy —E. E. Cummings

The moon rises like a fat white god —Diane Ackerman

The moon ... rode bonily in the sky, looking stark and abandoned like a decoration kids had put up for Halloween and forgotten to take down —William Dieter

The moon sails up out of the ocean dripping like a just washed apple —Marge Piercy

The moon shines like a lost button —Derek Walcott

The moon shone out like day —Nathanial Hawthorne

Moon slightly more than half full, like a tipped bowl —Patricia Henley

The moon stood like an arc lamp over the roofs of the houses —Erich Maria Remarque

The moon stuck like a wafer in the evening sky —Anon

The moon swelled like a plum —Philip Levine

Moon ... waning, like silver that is polished so thin that it has begun to wear away —Mary Stewart

The moon ... was like a slender shaving thrown up from a bar of gold —Joseph Conrad

The moon was like a chip of ice —Wallace Stegner

The moon was like a sickle —Edward Hoagland

The moon ... was like a slender shaving thrown up from a bar of gold —Joseph Conrad

The moon was out, cold and faraway as an owl's hoot —John Braine

The moon ... was slowly drifting into an immense, dark and transparent hole like a lake with its depth full of stars —André Malraux

A pale crescent moon shaped like a woman's earring —Katharine Haake

A pale moon, like a claw (looked down through the claw-like branches of dead trees) —Jean Rhys

Quiet moonlight lay like the smile upon a dreaming face —John Hall Wheelock

The rising moon … winding like a silver thread until it was lost in the stars —Bret Harte

Sometimes in the afternoon sky a white moon would creep up like a little cloud, without display, suggesting an actress who does not have to "come on" for a while and so goes "in front" in her ordinary clothes —Marcel Proust

The sphere hanging in the not yet darkened sky seemed like a lamp they had forgotten to turn off in the morning (a lamp that had burned all day in the room of the dead) —Milan Kundera

A stream of moonlight cut through the mist and hit the black water, like ink —Paige Mitchell

A thin moon … gray and marbled like a worn shell —Alice McDermott

A yellow moon rose like a flower blooming —Bernard Malamud

❧ MORALITY

See Also: BELIEFS, VIRTUE

As moral as any elder of the church —Rumer Godden

Morality without religion is a tree without roots —J B Shaw

Moral principles are like measles. They have to be caught —Aldous Huxley

Morals are an acquirement, like music, like a foreign language, like piety, poker, paralysis, no man is born with them —Mark Twain

The moral system of the universe is like a document written in alternate ciphers, which change from line to line —J.A. Froude

Turning the other cheek is a kind of moral jiu-jitsu —Gerald Stanley Lee

Wore her morality like long underwear —Delmore Schwartz

Schwartz followed this entry in his journal with several alternative comparisons: "Fur coat, chemise, a rope of pearls."

❧ MORTALITY

See: DEATH

❧ MOTHERHOOD

See: CHILDREN, PARENTHOOD

❧ MOTHERS-IN-LAW

See: PARENTHOOD

❧ MOTIONLESSNESS

See: IMMOBILITY

❧ MOTIVATION

See Also: AMBITION, PURPOSEFULNESS

Good intentions … like very mellow and choice fruit, they are difficult to keep —G. Simmons

(I simply) ran out of motives, as a car runs out of gas —John Barth

The true motives of our actions, like the real pipes of an organ, are usually concealed —Charles Caleb Colton

❧ MOUNTAINS

See Also: LANDSCAPES, NATURE

Cropped, long-faced hills that bristled with pine like so many unshaven cheeks —T. Coraghessan Boyle

The hills here are long and blue, like paintings —Bobbie Ann Mason

Hills like breasts —Karl Shapiro

The hillside is dotted with white plum trees like puffs of smoke —Colette

Hills … lay there like a herd of drowsing buffalo —Yitzhak Shenhar

Hills … like a young girl's breasts —William Boyd

Hills rose up like bubbles —Phyllis Bottome

Like an enormous landscape lay the mountain —Delmore Schwartz

Mountains … like crouching camels —Milton Raison

Mountains like puffs of smoke —George Garrett

The mountains rolled like whales through the phosphorous stars —Derek Walcott

The mountains rose like worn, dark-skinned fists —Carlos Fuentes

Mountains, stretching themselves like great luxurious cats in the sunshine —Hugh Walpole

Mountains … unreal like movie props —John Rechy

The mountains were jagged like a page ripped out of a book —Kate Grenville

The mountains were just visible, dusky and black, like waves of charcoal —John Fowles

The mountain tops where whitened by moonlight like crests of waves —Lee Smith

The mountain was shining like glass in colour —Paul Horgan

The scenery is funny little hills shaped like scoops of ice cream —Bobbie Ann Mason

The hills are … ribbed like the remains of antediluvian breasts stretched across the horizon —T. Coraghessan Boyle

To live in mountains is like living with someone who always talks at the top of his, or it may be her, voice —Leonard Woolf

Tree-covered folds in the mountains … lying like a gigantic crumpled velvet rug —John Fowles

❧ MOURNING
See: GRIEF

❧ MOUTH
See Also: CHEEK; CHIN; MOUTH, OPEN/SHUT

Bare his teeth like a yawning tiger —Miles Gibson

Cruel red mouth like a venomous flower —Algernon Charles Swinburne

He had his mouth all prissed up when he talked, like a man acting in a play —Iris Murdoch

Her mouth glistened like a wound —Jerry Bumpus

Her mouth hung loose like a bright ribbon —R. V. Cassill

Her mouth is wide and red as strawberry pie —Rex Reed
The mouth thus described belongs to actress Carol Channing.

Her mouth was as little suited for smiling as a frying-pan for musical purposes —Anatole France

Her peevish mouth looked like a slit cut by a knife —Stefan Zweig

His mouth ran like a thin dark crease between them [chin and nose] —Jonathan Valin

His mouth turned down like he could see death —Richard Ford

His open mouth was like a dark hole in his beard —Ross Macdonald

A loose mouth … slack with usage, like rubber bands —William Faulkner

The mouth and ear are like a bow and a fiddle; when the ear is shut the mouth is mute —Hayyim Nahman Bialik

Mouth as sweet as a ripe fig —Edith Wharton

Mouth broad as an airstrip —Loren D. Estleman

The mouth described an unsmiling straight line, as if typed with an em-dash. —Lionel Shriver, *The New Republic*

Mouth … framed in iron-gray fluffy hair, that looked like a chin-strap of cotton wool sprinkled with coal-dust —Joseph Conrad

Mouth … clamped like a spring and right as the mouth of a witch —Borden Deal

(A big, pink) mouth, curled down at one corner as if he habitually smoked a pipe —Lael Wertenbaker

A mouth drawn in like a miser's purse —Émile Zola

Mouth ... flabby like a toad's —Christopher Isherwood

A mouth like a firebucket —Raymond Chandler, *The Long Good-bye*

Mouth ... like a large wet key hole —Roald Dahl

Mouth like a fireplace —Ogden Nash

Mouth ... like a fold of skin over a skull, without the life —Paul Horgan

A mouth like an air-raid trench —Jane Wagner

Mouth like an arrowhead wound —Jean Cocteau about Colette

Mouth ... like a scarlet wound —W. Somerset Maugham

Mouth like a seam —Irvin S. Cobb

Mouth like a slit in the sidewalk —Anon

Mouth like the bottom of a parrot cage —David Niven

A mouth like the inside of a jelly doughnut —Peter De Vries

Mouth open like a funnel's —Eudora Welty

Mouth pinched inward like a fist —Joyce Carol Oates

Mouth pursed up tight like a mushroom —Roald Dahl

Mouth ... red and slightly swollen, as if somebody had been chewing on it —Ross Macdonald

Mouth ... so wide-centered and deep-cornered, so cool and so warm, so lusciously crimson, that flaring out of the pallor of her face, it was like a blood-hot signal to the senses —Inez Haynes Irwin

Mouths like donuts —F. D. Reeve

Mouths like wet velvet —Angela Carter

Mouth ... so thin that the lips seemed to hook together, like the catch of a child's purse —Frank Tuohy

Mouths pink as watermelon —May Sarton

A mouth that stretches from ear to ear when he laughs, like a mouth on a cat piggy bank —François Maspero

Mouth that looked like the prelude to a scream —Raymond Chandler, *The Big Sleep*

Mouth that was like a salmon's mouth —Roald Dahl

Mouth thin and straight, like a cut in his face —Honoré de Balzac

Mouth tight as a corset string on the preacher's wife —Harold Adams

Mouth tugged down on one side like a dead man's —John Updike

Mouth twisted like an epileptic's —Isaac Bashevis Singer

The old mouth closed like a zip —Julia O'Faolain

A quibbling mouth that would have snapped verbal errors like a lizard catching flies —Edith Wharton

A wide and expressionless mouth like the juncture of a casserole dish with its lid —Thomas McGuane

❦ MOUTH, OPEN/SHUT

Closed her mouth like a trap —Julia O'Faolain

Eyes looked like the prelude to a scream —Raymond Chandler, *The Big Sleep*

Mouth comes open like a fish for air —Robert Penn Warren

Mouth slightly open, like an idiot's —D. H. Lawrence

(Uncle Harry's) mouth dropped open, as if either in the beginning of prayer or protest —H. E. Bates

Mouth gagged open ... as if the day had stuck in his throat —William McIlvanney

Mouth hanging open like a stove lid —Charles Johnson

Mouth ... open, black and wide as an attic —Louise Erdrich

Mouth opened like a dark hole —Jerry Bumpus

Mouth opened like a folding bed —Anon

Mouth round and open like a small empty cave —William Faulkner

Mouths came open like full moons —Will Weaver

(His huge brow furrowed, his gray eyes closed down to slits, his) mouth shut like a car door being slammed —Jonathan Valin

Mouth ... slightly open, as though it froze in the middle of an unspellable word —Louise Erdrich

(Don't sit there with your) mouth sprung open like a busted letter box —William Alfred

Opened and closed her narrow lips once or twice, like some beached shellfish gasping for the tide —Edith Wharton

Opening his mouth in a kind of snarling grimace, quite without ferocity, like an old lion in a cage —Christopher Isherwood

Small mouth hung open birdlike (as she sang) —MacDonald Harris

Mouth shut abruptly, like a puppet's —Jonathan Valin

Yawned like a menagerie lion —Gelett Burgess

A yawn like an unobtrusive earthquake —G. K. Chesterton

❧ MOVEMENT(S)

See Also: ADVANCING, JUMPING, LEAPING, ROCKING AND ROLLING, RUNNING, TURNING AND TWISTING

All her movements were soft as if timed to the sleeping of children —Ada Jack Carver

Charged across ... like a cat with a kerosened ass —Harold Adams

Crawled like a worm —Denis Diderot

Creep and crawl ... stretching her fingers like a baby trying to climb the path —Eudora Welty

Creeping slowly toward him, like a lizard toward a bug —E. B. White

Crept like a man intent on crime —W. H. Auden

Crept ... like a spider on an endless thread of its own spinning —George Du Maurier

Darted about like a hummingbird —Rita Mae Brown

Darted, like a bird about the room —John Steinbeck

Darting about and banging together like bubbles in soda water —Joyce Cary

Darting off this way and that, like the wax of a burning candle —Anon

Descended the stairs like a buffalo —Joe Coomer

The director, Trip Cullman, shuffles them [the actors playing office assistants] around like scrap paper shoved into a shredding machine —Rex Reed, reviewing *Assistance* by Leslye Headland, *New York Observer*, February 29, 2012

Drifted north ... like a saddle tramp looking for a spring roundup —James Crumley

Floated like a weed —Mavis Gallant

Folded herself up like a fresh-ironed shirt —Mary Hood

Glided as though on little wheels —Jules Renard, drama critic about the actress, Sarah Bernhardt

Glide, like phantoms —John Keats

Glides to his meeting like a lover mumbling a secret, passionate message —Wallace Stevens

Go as if nine men pulled you and ten men held you —John Withal

Going back is like lifting elephants with your teeth —Paul West

Going (home) stealthily and unsteadily ... like a dissipated cat —Charles Dickens

Groped about like blind, cautious crabs —Ralph Ellison

He [a dog] dumped himself like a bag of bones —Robert Frost

He moved like a spring —Eudora Welty

He moves like a piece of darkness —Joe Coomer

His body waved like a flame in the breeze —TV obituary describing James Cagney's physical grace, 1986

I float like a butterfly, sting like a bee —Muhammad Ali

Hurried with legs stretched out ahead of me like a horse —David Ignatow

Kicking and wriggling like a retriever pup —Walter Duranty

Lethargically, like sloth on the move —Kenzaburo Oe

In the novel A Personal Matter, the lethargy described is that of a man pedaling his bike

Like a vein of gold I darted after you —Charles Simic

Like shoals of fish, they all headed one way —Elizabeth Taylor

Lowered herself [from bus] cautiously, like a climber —Elizabeth Bowen

A meandering pace that makes sweet Afton look like a white water stream —Helen Dudar reviewing Jerome Weidman's autobiography, New York Times Book Review, September 21, 1986

Moved as smoothly as light wind across water —James Crumley

Moved by as if on a treadmill —Jonathan Kellerman

Moved downhill [a street that lay on an incline] like rainwater. Like the twentieth century —Tom Robbins

Moved like a water bug, like a skipping stone, upon the glassy tense surface of his new life —John Updike

Moved like benign automata —Angela Carter

Moved passively with her head down, like a prisoner between guards —Ross Macdonald

Moved with funny little steps, like a chicken with an egg wedged up its legs —William Kotzwinkle

Move languidly ... like a hostess in her bathrobe emptying ashtrays on Sunday morning —Alice McDermott

Movement ... quick and quiet as a fish in deep water —Gerald Kersh

Move mindlessly, mechanically as a toy train through a Christmas tree town —Sharon Sheehe Stark

(Waiters) moving as deft and soft-footed as shadows —George Garrett

(Hand) moving imperceptibly like a marine plant —Marguerite Yourcenar

Moving listlessly back and forth, like a fish in an aquarium —Jill Ciment

Moving quick and light as a fairy —Dame Edith Sitwell

Moving ... slow and heavy as lead —Gerald Kersh

Moving slowly like a man recovering from surgery —David Nicholls, One Day

(The sun) moving up and down ... like a musical note —Saul Bellow

Paced around ... like a jaguar on the prowl —Jonathan Kellerman

Pace ... like impatient cats —Ira Wood

Pace like Socrates before the Court —Charles Johnson

Passed like a circus —Wallace Stevens

People moved as if groping in the dimness of the subconscious for the memory of midday warmth that lingered faintly in the skin —Kenzaburo Oe

Prowled around like a dog that has forgotten where he put his bone —Raymond Chandler

Rush sideways, like an excited crab —Jerome K. Jerome

Scampering about like frenzied ants —Brian Burland

Scamper like mice —Dame Edith Sitwell

Scuttling around it like a mouse trying to find a hole —Cornell Woolrich

Settled themselves, like chickens getting ready to roost —Christopher Isherwood

She got up and, like a vacuum cleaner with insomnia, roamed the room —Tom Robbins

Shied abruptly like a startled horse —Jack London

Shuffled about [text of a book] like a melancholy sheep in a pen —Mavis Gallant

Shuffles … around like a deck of cards —Brian Burland

Slide like lizards —Anon

Sliding like a shadow among them —R. V. Cassill

The small procession moved … slow and spaced out like a funeral —Ivo Andric

(I have seen thy waters) stealing onward, like the stream of life —Henry Wadsworth Longfellow

Step back as though I'd stepped on a snake —Dorothy Canfield

Steppin' high like a rooster in deep mud —American colloquialism

Stirred like a rustle of leaves —Maurice Edelman

> Edelman's simile is used to draw an image of whispers stirring up around the actions of the hero of his novel Disraeli Rising.

Stomped back to bed, trying to make my footsteps sound like angry exclamation marks —Dorothy Francis

Straggled on back … like tongue-dragging hounds —Thomas Zigal

Straightened up, slowly, as if she were being raised —Marguerite Duras

Swept by like a spotlight —Donald McCaig

Tore through the black-and-gold town like a pair of scissors tearing through brocade —Katherine Mansfield

Tottering … like a Chinese girl with bound feet —Jayne Anne Phillips

Travels unsteadily, as fogs do —David Ignatow

Twisted himself out like an eel —Sholem Aleichem

Twitched her shoulders like a bird shaking off water —Laura Furman

Wander like Alice —Karl Shapiro

Weave like a dreamer —John Barth

[Group of children] whirling off like autumn leaves, just as gay in their bright colors, and just as elusive —Beverly Mitchell

Wiggled like ribbons —R. V. Cassill

Wiggle [a tooth] like a loose picket in a fence —William Goyen

❧ MOVIES
See: STAGE AND SCREEN

❧ MURDER
See: CRIME

❧ MUSCLES
See Also: STRENGTH

The great muscles of his torso flickered and ran like the flank of a horse —Du Bose Heyward

Heavily defined pectoral muscles, on which the nipples stood out like pennies —Francis King

His muscles were like nylon cords —Michael Connelly, *The Harry Bosh Novels*

Muscled like a water buffalo —Gerald Kersh

Muscles [of leg] as big as a hill —Dylan Thomas

Muscles … hard and ropy like the ones on the fantastic coursing dogs in the stone friezes of ancient Persia —Beryl Markham

Muscles … hard as iron —Jack London

The muscles in his face seemed to pull together like a drawstring purse —Sue Grafton

The muscles in their arms bulge out like India rubber balls —Joanna M. Glass

Muscles in their backs rippled ... like fretted water over a stony bed —Beryl Markham

Muscles like armor plates pasted on his body —John Rechy

Muscles ... like blow-up balloons —François Camoin

In his short story, A Hunk of Burning Love, *Camoin completes the simile as follows: "Put a pipe in his mouth and he'd look like Popeye."*

Muscles like marshmallows —Carlos Baker

The muscles of his arms and back stood out beneath his fair skin like the muscles of one of Rodin's bronze men —Louis Bromfield

Muscles of his forearms ... moved in ridges and hollows from a knot above his elbow, like pistons working from a cylinder —L. P. Hartley

Muscles of strength rose like a collar from his neck —Arthur A. Cohen

Muscles ... polished like metal, pure sculpture —Vita Sackville-West

Muscles pulled like cold rubber —Tony Ardizzone

Muscles rippled like stretching cats —Stephen Vincent Benét

Muscles stretched taut as cowhide stretched over a baseball —W. P. Kinsella

Muscles that flow like a mountain stream —Ogden Nash

Muscles twitching like the flesh of a horse stung by many flies —Ralph Ellison

Remember ... the rippling of bright muscles like a sea —Dame Edith Sitwell

The ripple of muscles go along him, like a cat's back arching —Margaret Atwood

Wore faded denims through which his clumsy muscles bulged like animals in a sack —Ross Macdonald

❧ MUSIC

See Also: SINGING

As music takes up the thread that language drops, so it is where Shakespeare ends that Beethoven began —Sidney Lanier

The band wound up the tune like a train rushing into a station —Donald McCaig

The cello is like a beautiful woman who has not grown older but younger with time, more slender, more supple, more graceful —Pablo Casals

Composing is like making love to the future —Lukas Foss

Composing is like organizing a meal. The different dishes must be so arranged as to rouse the appetite and renew the pleasure with each course —Moses Ibn Ezra

A concert is like a bullfight, the moment of truth —Arthur Rubinstein

The conductor ... flapped his arms like a rooster about to crow —Katherine Mansfield

Each musician looks like mumps from blowing umpah umpah umps —Ogden Nash

Fiddles tuning up like cats in pain —Harvey Swados

Film music is like a small lamp that you place below the screen to warm it —Aaron Copeland

Good music, like land and machines, had no people in sight —Will Weaver

In Weaver's novel Red Earth, White Earth, *this simile is used to explain a character's liking for music.*

A great burst of music gushed up like a geyser —Mary Lavin

In came a fiddler, and tuned like fifty stomach aches —Charles Dickens

In music as in love, pleasure is the waste product of creation —Igor Stravinsky

It is like eating vanilla ice cream in Paradise, listening to beautiful music —Camille Lemmonnier

Musical as the holes of a flute without the flute —O. Henry

Music as loud as the roar of traffic —Marge Piercy

The music bushed from the bow [of the fiddle] like water from the rock when Moses touched it —Henry Van Dyke

The music enchanted the air ... like the south wind, like a warm night, like swelling sails beneath the stars —Erich Maria Remarque

Music is a big sublime instinct, like genius of all kinds —Ouida

Music is a sort of dream architecture which passes in filmy clouds and disappears in nothingness —Percy A. Scholes

Music is auditory intercourse without benefit of orgasm —Aldous Huxley

Music is essentially useless, as life is —George Santayana

Music is like wine ... the less people know about it, the sweeter they like it —Robertson Davies

Music is like a fickle tantalizing mistress; one is rarely happy with her, but it is sheer tormented hell ever to be long away —Robert Traver

Music is ... like mathematics, very nearly a world by itself it contains a whole gamut of experience, from sensuous elements to ultimate intellectual harmonies —George Santayana

Music is not water, but it moves like water; it is not fire, but it soars as warm as the sun —Delmore Schwartz

Music is the arithmetic of sounds as optics is the geometry of light —Claude Debussy

Music, like balm, eases grief's smarting wound —Samuel Pordage

(Drum, drum, drum, the) music like footsteps —T. Coraghessan Boyle

Music may be regarded as a thermometer that makes it possible to register the degree of sensibility of every people, according to the climate in which they live —Andre Ernest Gretry

Music throbbed like blood —T. Coraghessan Boyle

Music yearning like a god in pain —John Keats

Opera in English makes about as much sense as baseball in Italian —H. L. Mencken

The opera is like a husband with a foreign title: expensive to support, hard to understand, and therefore a supreme social challenge —Cleveland Amory

The orchestra sounds like fifty cats in agony —J. B. Priestly

Our musicians are like big canisters of gas. Light a match too close to them, and they will explode —Yevgeny Svetlanov, *New York Times*, October 20, 1986

Svetlanov, the Moscow State Symphony conductor, thus described Russian musicians in an article by Bernard Holland.

The plaintive sound of saxophones moaning softly like a man who has just missed a short putt —P. G. Wodehouse

Playing "bop" is like playing "scrabble" with all the vowels missing —Duke Ellington

Pulled music from his violin as if he were lifting silk from a dressmaker's table —Pat Conroy

Saxophones wailing like a litter of pigs —Lawrence Durrell

The string section sounded like cats in heat —Mary Hedin

(Wade and Beth could hear) the subterranean thudding of his rock music turned low, like a giant heart beating in a sub-cellar —John D. MacDonald

A symphony must be like the world, it must embrace everything —Gustav Mahler

Mahler's comment was addressed to Jean Sibelius.

To some people music is like food; to others like medicines; to others like a fan —*Arabian Nights*

Tuneless and atonal, like the improvised songs of children caught up in frantic play —Robert Silverberg

The written note is like a strait jacket, whereas music, like life itself, is constant movement, continuous spontaneity, free from restriction —Pablo Casals

♣ MUSTACHE(S)

See Also: BEARD(S), HAIR

Big mustaches that made him look like an animated mushroom —Arthur Train

A black mustache like the lowered wings of a crow —Carolyn Chute

A curled-up mustache, like two little rolls of barbed wire —Joyce Cary

A gray handlebar mustache with oiled points, like the long horns of an ox —Ira Wood

His mustache sags … like a bat —Carolyn Chute

His white mustache, of thin separate hairs like glass threads —Joyce Cary

His yellow-to-brown mustache quivered and preened over his mouth like a sparrow's wing shaking off dust —Paul Horgan

The insignificant mustache trembled like a twig in a storm —Jonathan Kellerman

A light mustache that flourished upwards as if blown that way by the breath of a constant smile —Henry James

A little black mustache like an eyebrow —George Du Maurier

Little circumflex accent mustache … like a black butterfly placed under his nose —Romain Gary

Little mustaches stiffened like a pointer's tail when he scents a bird —Arthur Train

A man without a mustache is like a woman with only one breast —M. M. Liberman

Mustache … black as India ink and big as the switch on a cow's tail —James Crumley

Mustache … black, like a charcoal smear on his upper lip —Paige Mitchell

Mustache bristled like intractable gorse —Frank Swinnerton

Mustache curling like a sultan's —Oliver Wendell Holmes, Sr.

Mustache cut short like a worn-out brush —Henry James

Mustache hanging heavy as a pelt —Carolyn Chute

Mustache like a soft black mouse —Ann Tyler

A mustache resting like a small white cloud beneath his undistinguished nose —F. Scott Fitzgerald

A mustache shadowing either side of his lip with a broad sweep, like a bird's wing —William Dean Howells

(The faded) mustaches hung like crossed pistols above his radiant smile —Eudora Welty

Mustache … thick and neat as a bristle brush —Ira Wood

Mustache … thin and straight like it was painted on —George Garrett

White mustache like a Viking's —Jo Bannister

♣ MYSTERIOUSNESS

See: STRANGENESS

♣ NAKEDNESS

See: BARENESS

♣ NAMES

See Also: MEMORY

(Alex) acquired names as other women encrust themselves with jewels —Patrick White

Fools' names like fools' faces, are often seen in public places —Thomas Fuller

Forgotten names sang through my head like forgotten scenes in dreams —Ralph Ellison

Handed [told it to her] her his name as though he were extending a card on a copper salver —Harvey Swados

His name [a politician's] has become as institutionalized as a detergent —Robert Traver

It is with you as with the seas: the most varied names are given to what is in the end only salt water —Johann Wolfgang von Goethe

Lost their names like marbles in the schoolyard —George Garrett

Making fun of your name is like making fun of your nose —Willie Morris

Names and faces eluded him like ghosts —William Diehl

Patients ... they are as patient as their name —Randall Jarrell

She called me cheri in such a way that it was a small fruit on her tongue —R. Wright Campbell

Some people have names like pitchforks, some people have names like cakes —Stephen Vincent Benét

Sounds like a name you'd see on a bracelet at Walgreen's —Richard Ford

The character who thus expresses her discontent with her name is Vicki in the novel The Sportswriter.

You carry your name forever, like a scepter alive with wings —Stephen Vincent Benét

Your name like a lozenge upon my tongue —Charles Wright

❧ NARROWNESS

See: THINNESS

❧ NATIONS

See: CHARACTERISTICS, NATIONAL; GOVERNMENTS

❧ NATURALNESS

(Her tight smile returned) as automatically as a gesundheit —Loren D. Estleman

(The doctor ... a man who listened to other people's hearts) as casually, as automatically as he blew his own nose —Helen Hudson

[His off-kilter dialogue comes to seem] as natural, and lovely, as the chirping of crickets and the sound of bird song —Charles Isherwood in a review of Will Eno's play *The Realistic Joneses*, *New York Times*, May 2, 2012

As natural a part of her life as toothpaste —Julia Whedon

As natural as a vine grows —Babette Deutsch

(She was flushed, eager, and) as natural as daylight —Frank Swinnerton

As natural ... as falling of leaves —Edith Wharton

(A faith ... as strong) as natural, as irrational as the elements —Romain Gary

As natural as NutraSweet —Anon

(Had grown up believing that overcoming handicaps was) as natural as scratching your ear —Ira Berkow, *New York Times*/Sports of the Times, September 23, 1986

Berkow's subject is Jim Plunkett, Raider quarterback.

As natural ... as the passion for air or food or drink —Stephen McKenna

As natural as the process of digestion —Walter de la Mare

He [Dr. Oliver Wendell Holmes] could no more stop it [wit flowing from him] than he could stop the blood flowing in his veins —Elizabeth Bowen

(His thoughts, his humor, his similes) rose as fast, as multitudinous, as irrepressible, as bubbles in the champagne, and nothing could prevent their coming to the surface —John T. Morse

The man whose wit is thus compared was Dr. Oliver Wendell Holmes.

Spontaneous as a child's drawing —Anon

Spontaneous as a six-course sit-down dinner —Anon

Spontaneous as the song of a bird —W. H. Hudson

Spontaneous as the time of day —*St. Elsewhere* television drama, December 16, 1986

Unconscious as an oak tree of its growth —Anon

Unconscious as the loyalty of bees to their queen —Lacfadio Hearn

Unconscious as you grow your fingernails —George Bernard Shaw

Unnatural as generosity to a miser —Elyse Sommer

Unthinkingly as a child heaping sand on its mother at the beach —Anatole Broyard, *New York Times Book Review*, January 16, 1986

❧ NATURE

See Also: FLOWERS; LEAVES; MOON; OCEAN/OCEANFRONT; PONDS, RIVERS, AND STREAMS; RAIN; SEASCAPES; SKY- SCAPES; SNOW; STARS; SUN; THUNDER AND LIGHTNING; TREES; WEATHER

Big heavy drops [of dew] … lie on the face of the earth like sweat —Shirley Ann Grau

Bushes … like heads —you could have sworn sometimes you saw them mounting and swaying in manly talk —Elizabeth Bowen

The damp stands on the long green grass as thick as morning's tears —Emily Brontë

The dawn clings to the river like a fog —Yvor Winters

Dew as thick as frost —Paul Theroux

Dew gleamed and sparkled like myriads of tiny mirrors —Dorothy Livesay

The dew is beaded like mercury on the coarsened grass —Adrienne Rich

Dew … like trembling silver leaves —Dame Edith Sitwell

Driftwood gnarled and knobby like old human bones —Charles Johnson

The earth is like the breast of a woman: useful as well as pleasing —Friedrich Nietzsche

Earth was like a jostling festival of seeds grown fat —Wallace Stevens

Flecks of ice still clung to his collar, flashing like brilliants —William H. Gass

Frost was like stiff icing sugar on all the roofs —H. E. Bates

The garden we planted and nurtured through the spring … fills out like an adolescent at summer camp —Ira Wood

The grass like a prophet's beard, thoughtful and greying —Charles Simic

The grass on the roadside moved under the evening wind, sounding like many pairs of hands rubbed softly together —H. E. Bates

Grass patches … like squares on a game board —Mary Hedin

Grass … thick as wind —David Ignatow

Hedges as solid as walls —Edith Wharton

Here a giant philodendron twined around a sapodilla tree and through the branches of a hibiscus bush like a green arm drawing two friends together —Dorothy Francis

Ice-crystals, shaped like fern-leaves —Anatole France

Light hung in the trees like cobwebs —Jay Parini

The light is in the dark river of the hot Spring evening like a dry wine in a decanter —Delmore Schwartz

Like a great poet, Nature knows how to produce the greatest effects with the most limited means —Heinrich Heine

Like a slim reed of crystal a fountain hung in the dusky air —Oscar Wilde

The moisture in the air seemed suspended like tiny pearls —Rita Mae Brown

Moss that looks and feels like felt —Brad Leit-hauser

Nature is like a beautiful woman that may be as delightfully and as truly known at a certain distance as upon a closer view —George Santayana

Santayana expanded on the simile as follows: "As to knowing her through and through, that is nonsense in both cases, and might not reward our pains."

Nature is like a revolving door: what goes out in one form comes back in another —Anon

Nature like life, she strips men of their pretensions and vanities, exposes the weakness of the weak and the folly of the fool —W. Macneile Dixon

Nature, like lives while they are being lived, is subject to laws of motion; it cannot be stopped and thereby comprehended —Margaret Sutherland

Pebbles [on the beach] lit like eggs —Jay Parini

A plant is like a self-willed man, out of whom we can obtain all which we desire, if we will only treat him his own way —Johann Wolfgang von Goethe

A rampant twining vine of wisteria ancient and knotted like muscles —Marge Piercy

Sea shells as big as melons. Others like peas —John Cheever

The [clam]shells shone like rainbows —Will Weaver

The shrubs burgeon like magic beanstalks —T. Coraghessan Boyle

The soil [being dug with spade] slices off like fudge —Sharon Sheehe Stark

Sun-baked tomatoes … hung like red balloons filled with water —Anon

The surrounding nature is soundless as if it were under water —Shohei Ooka

Thistles stood looking like prophets in the Bible in Solomon's house —Eudora Welty

Tiny, sand-sized bits of green moss hung in slanted drifts in the water like grain dust in sunlight —Will Weaver

Trees and flowers that crowded to the path's edge like children —Helen Hudson

The tufts of moss, like piles of house dust, that hang trembling on the bare winter trees —Elizabeth Hardwick

The twilight seems like a canopy —Erich Maria Remarque

Undergrowth [of a path] spotted with moonlight like a leopard's skin —Colette

The water rippled like a piece of cloth —William Faulkner

The white of the snow and sky filled my eyes like the sheet pulled over the head of a dead man —Steve Erickson

A white sky made the bare branches of the elms [in March] seem like bones —Louis Auchincloss

❧ NEARNESS

See: CLOSENESS

❧ NEATNESS

See: CLEANLINESS, ORDER/DISORDER

❧ NECESSITY

See Also: IMPORTANCE/UNIMPORTANCE

Crucial as the last game of the World Series —Anon

Essential as marrow —Curtis White

I need it like I need a hole in the head —Anon

A Yiddish simile, typical of the colorful irony that has caused so many Jewish immigrant expressions to become integrated into American English

Necessary and invisible like drafts of oxygen —Thomas Lux

Necessary as water to a healthy lawn —Anon

Necessary as a gardener to his garden —John Ray's *Proverbs*

Necessary as an anesthesiologist to an operation —Mary Morris

Necessary as applause to an actor —Anon

Necessary as a saw to a carpenter —Anon

Necessary as bytes to a computer —Anon

Necessary as Christmas to retailers —Anon

Necessary as eggs in an omelette —Anon

Necessary as gas to a car —Anon

Necessary as good lines to a play —Anon

Necessary as markings on a scale/thermometer —Anon

Necessary as paycheck to a worker —Anon

Necessary as practice to a musician —Anon

Necessary as quartz for a digital watch —Anon

Necessary as snow to a ski weekend —Anon

Necessary as sturdy shoes to a runner —Anon

Necessary as sunshine to a garden —Anon

Necessary as wages —John Braine

Necessary as workouts to an athlete —Anon

Necessary as work to a workaholic —Anon

(Men are as) necessary to her survival as water —Patricia Henley

Need as a dog needs a pocket handkerchief —Anon

"Need as" similes with opposite leanings lend themselves to endless variations.

Needed a ten minute head start like Sinatra needed singing lessons —John Lutz

Need ... like a fish needs a bicycle —Robert B. Parker

Needs as a dog needs two tails —American colloquialism, attributed to New England

The exact wording of this, as anything handed down through common usage, varies with each user. A frequent way of saying the same thing is "He don't need it any more than a dog needs two tails."

Need ... to simplify, almost like some painfully obese gourmet craving a stay at a health farm —John Fowles

Something she needs like a new navel —Richard Ford

As superfluous as a Gideon's Bible at the Ritz —F. Scott Fitzgerald

Superfluous as to light a candle to the sun —Robert South

Unnecessary like rubbish —Henia Karmel-Wolfe

❧ NECK

See Also: CHIN, CHEEKS, PHYSICAL APPEARANCE

Adam's apple bobbing like an eccentric toy —Robert Traver

Adam's apple bobbing like a fishing float —Andrew Kaplan

Adam's apple bobbing up and down like a prune seed in his throat —Calder Willingham

Adam's apple jumping up and down his throat like he got a ping-pong ball part way down and it got stuck —Carlos Baker

The Adam's apple of his thin, sinewy throat went up and down like a lift —Erich Maria Remarque

The cords in his [a man who's upset and angry] neck stick out like thumbs —Mary Hood

Her neck is like a stately tower —Thomas Lodge

Her neck rose [from folds of a shawl] like a column of slightly discolored Cararra marble —Arthur Train

His Adam's apple bulged so when he drank that it reminded Augustus of a snake with a frog stuck in its gullet —Larry McMurtry

His Adam's apple rippling up and down his skinny throat like a crazed mouse —James Crumley

His Adam's apple went up and down like an elevator —Cornell Woolrich

Limp-necked like a faded daisy —Julia O'Faolain

A long neck built like a tower —Colette

The long, pale neck rising like a beam of light from his open shirt —Helen Hudson

Neck … as a tower of ivory —The Holy Bible/ Song of Solomon

Neck as thick as a telephone pole —William Diehl

Neck like a steel truss —Jonathan Valin

Neck swiveled like a lazy susan —T. Coraghessan Boyle

Neck … wrinkled like the wattles of some big bird —Anon

The sinews of his neck … stood out like a cord of a hoist —Arthur Train

The skin of his neck, flabby and wrinkled like a turkey's cockscomb —Romain Gary

Thin neck like a goose —Jilly Cooper

Two rings of age on her neck looked like a cheap necklace —V.S. Pritchett

The veins in his thin white neck stood out like cords —Leo Tolstoy

❧ NEED
See: DESIRE

❧ NEGLECT
See: ABANDONMENT, REJECTION

❧ NEGLIGENCE
See: CARELESSNESS

❧ NERVE
See: COURAGE

❧ NERVOUSNESS
See Also: ANXIETY, TENSION, TREMBLING

All nervous and jerky like a windup toy or maybe a cockroach on its back, waving its legs and trying to turn over —George Garrett

Clucked nervously, like a mongoose —Romain Gary

Excitable … like a little rooster —Irwin Shaw

(Sat there open-mouthed) feeling the nerves of his body twitter like so many sparrows perched upon his spinal column —F. Scott Fitzgerald

Felt as if she were on the edge of a frozen pond, forced to go forward and not knowing how thick the ice was —Donald MacKenzie

Felt as if someone had taken a vegetable peeler to my nerves —T. Coraghessan Boyle

His heart smacking against his ribs like a bumblebee at a window. —Michael Chabon, *The Amazing Adventures of Kavalier & Clay*

His nerves set themselves on edge like soured teeth —H.E. Bates

His stomach felt like a volcano about to erupt —Andrew Kaplan

It's (persistent feeling of impending insanity) like my head's in a vice and all the assholes of the world are turning the goddam handle —Thomas Williams

Jumpy as a goat —James Thurber

Jumpy as a greyhound —Wallace Stegner

Jumpy as a jumping bean —Anon

Lived like an exposed nerve —Rita Mae Brown

Looked … like a nervous rabbit nibbling the smell of a gun barrel —Paul Theroux

My central nervous system has crashed as a bad hard drive —Patricia Cornwell, *Five Scarpetta Novels*

Nerves burned like open sores on a dog's neck —Hunter S. Thompson

Nerves like a bundle of firecrackers —Amy Lowell

Lowell's poem "Rosebud Wall-Paper," from which this is taken, was written in country dialogue with "of" written as "o."

Nerves like new thread —John Updike

Nerves tied in small, intricate knots, like embroidery stitching —Jean Thompson

(In rapid motion, bright) nervous as a butterfly —Marge Piercy

Nervous as a cat on a hot tin roof —Anon

In a television interview playwright Tennessee Williams stated that his father always used this phrase which became the title for one of his best-known plays and line for one of the leading characters, Margaret. Williams added that this and many other colorful phrases are attributable to Southern Blacks.

Nervous as a coyote in a pen —W. P. Kinsella

Nervous as a dog with a bone —Ben Hecht

While a dog with a bone might indeed be nervous about having another dog come along to take it away, anyone who's ever seen a dog's tail wag when finding or being given a bone, will know that "Happy as a dog with a bone" might be equally appropriate.

Nervous as a hamster —Reynolds Price

Nervous as a kitten with a duck for a foster mother —Victor Canning

Nervous as a stray dog —Amanda Hodgkinson, *22 Britannia Road*

Nervous as a whore in church —American colloquialism

Nervous as a will o'-the-wisp —F. Scott Fitzgerald

On edge, like some restless night —Yasunari Kawabata

(They felt everything, feared everything, started back at the snapping of a twig, all their) senses strained like those of nervous explorers cautiously advancing, hand on cocked trigger, into an unknown jungle —Dorothy Canfield

Shuddering and wary, like horses bewildered by lightning —Ted Hughes

Hughes' poem, "A Wind Flashes the Grass," links the comparison of the wary horses to trees suddenly silent and motionless.

White and shaken, like a dry martini —P.G. Wodehouse

Wriggle nervously like captive fish —Margaret Millar

❧ NEUTRALITY
See: IMPARTIALITY

❧ NEWNESS
See: FRESHNESS, TIMELINESS/UNTIMELINESS

❧ NEWS
See Also: GOSSIP, KNOWLEDGE

As cold waters to a faint soul, so is good news from a far country —The Holy Bible/Proverbs

Bad news travels fast like a bad shilling —line from British television program "Bless Me Father," 1986

News ... rose like a grenade across Washington —Ellen Goodman, *Newsday*, December 2, 1986

Goodman is contrasting the normalcy with which video shopping programs are working, with the scandal over arms shipments to Iran that exploded the sense of normalcy in the capital of the nation.

Share information like a basket lunch —Anon

❧ NIGHT
See Also: DARKNESS

The black night spread like glistening caviar —Diane Wakoski

The dark-blue velvet night hung like a curtain —Elizabeth Bowen

The darkness of night, like pain is dumb, the darkness of dawn, like peace, is silent —Rabindranath Tagore

Dusk was falling like blue flakes —Truman Capote

The evenings and nights were like shutters opening and closing, no more than that —Dan Jacobson

Midnight shakes the memory as a madman shakes a dead geranium —T. S. Eliot

Night, bereft of dreams, is like a deserted railway station after hours —Robert Duncan

Night brings out stars as sorrow shows us truth —P. J. Bailey

Night comes like a blackout —John Rechy

The night dives down like one great crow —Richard Wilbur

Night falls like a dropped shutter —Beryl Markham

Night falls like fire —Algernon Charles Swinburne

The night feels like a gigantic Ferris wheel turning in blackness, very slowly —Margaret Laurence

Night had fallen like a black curtain —Colin Forbes

The night is as soft as milk —Albert Camus

The night is like flower petals, the air moist as a damp cloth —W. P. Kinsella

The night is soft and silent, warm as cashmere —W. P. Kinsella

The night roars on … like an express train —Erich Maria Remarque

The nights descended on her like a benediction —Joseph Conrad

The nights stick together like pages in an old book —John Ashberry

The night stretches before me like an endless checklist —Natascha Wodin, *The Interpreter,* 1945

The night trickles on like liquid time —Natascha Wodin

The still night drifted deep like snow about me —Edna St. Vincent Millay

The summer night is like a perfection of thought —Wallace Stevens

The night, like ice, seemed to harden around her —William Dieter

🍀 NIGHTMARES
See: DREAM(S)

🍀 NOISES
See Also: IRRITABLENESS

Applause … like pebbles being rattled in a tin —Francis King

Blare, like the clearing of a monstrous throat —Richard Wilbur

(The crowd laughing and) boo-boo-booming like frogs in a barbershop quartet —Ken Kesey

Boomed like a split trombone

Boom like a military band —W. H. Auden

A branch creaked … like someone turning over in bed —Jonathan Valin

Broke into a long roar like the falling of the walls of Jericho —Katherine Anne Porter

(The house-phone …) buzzed like an angry hornet —Cornell Woolrich

Cawing like a rook —Dame Edith Sitwell

[A dog's teeth] Chattered like barbers' scissors —Frank Conroy

Clanged like fifty fire-engines —Herman Melville

Clanging [noise of truck backing out of driveway] like a half-dozen cowbells —Carolyn Chute

(Brake drums) clapped like cymbals —T. Coraghessan Boyle

Click like the snapping of a picture with an old box camera —W. P. Kinsella

A clopping sound … stung Lavinia's nerves like a box on the ears —L. P. Hartley

Creaked like a saddle when he shifted —Wallace Stegner

Creak like a rusty engine —Franz Werfel

A dissonant chord, as if somebody stepped on a cat —George Garrett

Door slam … like the crack of a bat when the opposition has hit a homerun to beat the

Mariners in the bottom of the ninth —Tom Robbins

(The phone's) dull ring ... like marbles rolling across a sheet of tin —Jean Thompson

Emitting throaty, explosive sounds like someone about to spit in someone else's face —Natascha Wodin

Fitful, hacking noise, like a dog coughing up a bone —William Styron

Footsteps echoing like gunfire in a well —T. Coraghessan Boyle

Growling away like an old mastiff with a sore throat —Charles Dickens

Growling like a fox in a trap —William Diehl

(Water) gulped and hissed like a dozen Jacuzzis —T. Coraghessan Boyle

Heels ticking on the parquet floor like the clock of a time bomb —Margaret Millar

Her steps ... made tiny, sharp pecky sounds, kind of like Mother drumming on the edge of the dinner table when Father tried to promote himself a second piece of pie —Raymond Chandler

The hinges and springs [of a door] screech like a woman with a hand over her mouth —Robert Campbell

Hissed like an adder —John D. MacDonald

(Tires) hissed like death —T. Coraghessan Boyle

(The sea) hissed like twenty thousand kettles —Joseph Conrad

Hisses and crackles like a doused campfire —Kate Wheeler

Hissing noise [as of crackling tissue paper] ... was like a nail on glass to my nerves —Cornell Woolrich

Hum, like a devout crowd on its knees —Margaret Atwood

Like a log fire the typewriter crackled —Delmore Schwartz

If Delmore Schwartz were alive and keeping a diary today instead of in 1944 when this entry was made, the crackling might be from a computer keyboard instead of a typewriter.

(A beehive as) loud as an airfield —Maxine Kumin

Loud as gunfire —Reynolds Price

Loud as the last call of God —Harold Adams

A loud cracking sound, like a frozen river breaking up in spring —Andrew Kaplan

Loud ... like a gun going off —Edith Wharton

Made a sound [in response to being kicked] like a sick cat —Loren D. Estleman

(A printer that) makes noise like a mad elephant —Edward Mendelson, reviewing computer products in *Yale Review*, 1985

Murmur like bees —Dame Edith Sitwell

(Through the audience went) a murmur, like the rustle of dead leaves —Henry Wadsworth Longfellow

The noise cracked like a whip in the still room —Margaret Mitchell

The noise Mitchell likened to the crack of a whip was made by Scarlett O'Hara when she slapped Ashley Wilkes' face in Gone with the Wind *when he rejects her declaration of love.*

Noise dwindling like a cut-back motor —Rosellen Brown

The noise level was deafening ... like some hideous unrelenting tape-loop of trains having sex —Ben Hamper in article on changes at GM, *Mother Jones*, September, 1986

Noises rise and are lost in the air like balloons —Albert Camus

Noise [of continuous lightning] that sometimes burst like metal fireworks —Marguerite Duras

(The city by day was as) noisy and busy as a pack of children —Sinclair Lewis

(She would be as) noisy as a child at a playground —Helen Hudson

Noisy as a living skeleton having a fit on a hardwood floor —Leonard Washborn, reporting on 1880s baseball game for *Inter-Ocean* newspaper

Noisy as squirrels mating on a rooftop —Elyse Sommer

Noisy as the Stock Exchange —Augustine Bire

An occasional buzz [interrupting silence], like an unheeded alarm clock —William Humphrey

Popping sounds, like hands clapped sharply together —W. P. Kinsella

[A typewriter] purrs like a seductive housecat —Tom Robbins

Rattling like a gong —Cynthia Ozick

Raucous whoop of children, spiteful and cruel like the sound of a lynch mob —Amos Oz

Resounded like a gigantic trumpet —Émile Zola

Ring like bells of glass —Elinor Wylie

Rowdy as gulls —Marge Piercy

Rumble … like a monster growl —Susan Minot

(The fiddle) screeched like a thing in pain —Elizabeth Bowen

Screeching with a noise like a buzz saw cutting through a knot —William Humphrey

Screech, like a car shifting gears on a dangerous uphill road —Yehuda Amichai

Sickening screech [of ripping metal] … like the scream of a wounded beast —Richard Moran

Slammed the door after him like a six-gun salute —Cornell Woolrich

The slamming of the door sounded like the last crack of doom —Jimmy Sangster

Sangster's comparison begins the prologue to his mystery novel Private I *with a literal and figurative bang.*

Snorted like a horse —Geoffrey Chaucer

The sound … filled the eardrums like wax —Wyatt Blassingame

Sound … it seemed to fill the vast room as breath fills a toy balloon —Frank Trippett

Sound like rhinos crashing into trees —Pauline Kael

The sounds [of the city] broke over her like a wave —Marguerite Yourcenar

Sounds came to me dully, as if people were speaking through their handkerchiefs or with their hands over their mouths —Maya Angelou

Sounds faded to a muffled warble, like a stream over pebbles —Curt Leviant

Sounds … grated and rumbled like a subway train —Norman Mailer

Sounds … hurt his ear like the thrust of a knife —Ambrose Bierce

The sound was hollow like the hammer on a coconut —Carson McCullers

The [baseball] stands sounded like gigantic drawerful of voices that had suddenly been pulled open —Bernard Malamud

Static crackled along the line, like popcorn popping —William Diehl

The steady drone of the crowds, like bees humming —Anon

A steady murmur like the crowd noises made in a movie —Frank Conroy

Tapping and ticking like nervous fingers —Sylvia Plath

A thin plaintive sound, like a starved cat —Raymond Chandler

The thud of her heart in her ears like wet dirt slapped with a spade —Reynolds Price

Ticking [of clock] … sounds like a convict rhythmically pounding a rock —W. P. Kinsella

Twitter like bats —Angela Carter

Whirring, like the buzz of a giant wasp —Eddie Cohen

A whoop woke me up … as if I'd been prodded by a cattle rod —W. P. Kinsella

❧ NOSE(S)

See Also: FACIAL DETAILS

A fabulous outsized nose attached to his face like a sheltering of stone —Pat Conroy

A flattish nose like a prizefighter —Beryl Bainbridge

His nose made two twists from bridge to end, like the wriggle of a snake —O. Henry

His nose stuck out like the first joint of a thumb —Frederick O'Brien

His nostrils heaved like a pair of blacksmith's bellows —Isaac Babel

A large nose like a trumpet —Edward Lear

Little snub nose, like a bulldog's —Colette

A long narrow nose which clung against his face as if reluctant to leave it —MacKinlay Kantor

A long nose flattened as if it had been tied down —Willa Cather

A long pink nose like a crooked beckoning finger in the middle of his face —Sue Miller

Nose … as big as an orange and the skin stretched over it was pebbled like an orange —François Camoin

Nose broad as a teacup —Carolyn Chute

Nose … crackled with tiny veins, like the nose of a hardened boozer —Gavin Lyall

A nose like a Bartlett pear —James Whitcomb Riley

A nose like a battering ram —Ross Macdonald

Nose like a bone —Ivan Bunin

A nose like a boot —Michael Gilbert

Nose like a butcher's thumb —Mary Hedin

Nose like a delicate scythe —Mary Hedin

Nose like a duck's bill —Ivan Turgenev

Nose [of a heavy drinker] like a fire ball —Erich Maria Remarque

Nose like a gherkin —Jonathan Valin

Nose like a jungle-bird's —William H. Gass

Nose like a knife blade —R. Wright Campbell

Nose like a letter opener —Jonathan Valin

Nose [Julius Caesar's] like an elephant's trunk —George Bernard Shaw

Nose like an engorged purple potato —Sarah Bird

Nose like a parrot's beak —Honoré de Balzac

Nose like a scimitar —William H. Hallhan

A nose like a spear in youth, in middle age becomes more like a shield, and in old age a little bit of a thing that looks like a button —William Saroyan

Nose like a sponge —Maxim Gorky

Nose like a turkey's ass —Robert Campbell

Nose like the beak of a bird —Anton Chekhov
> *A more specific variant by Donald MacKenzie: "Nose like a falcon's beak."*

Nose … long, like the nose in some old Italian pictures —Walter de la Mare

Nose … sharp as a pen —William Shakespeare, *The Life of King Henry V*

Nose small and laid back with about as much loft as a light iron —P. G. Wodehouse

A nose that seemed to have been bent by a tire iron —Jimmy Breslin and Dick Schaap

Nose was like a wooden peg —Truman Capote

Nose was very short, just like a baby's —Joyce Cary

Nostrils flaring like a colt's in winter —Charles Johnson

Nostrils flaring like a trotter —Joan Hess

Nostrils heaving like a stallion's —T. Coraghessan Boyle

Nostrils … shaped like the wings of a swallow —Oscar Wilde

Roman nose stuck up like the beak of a predatory bird —Carlos Baker

A straight nose, like a crusader modelled on a tomb —Antonia Fraser

This simile is culled from a novel that takes its title from a simile, Quiet as a Nun, *attributed to William Wordworth's poem "It Is a Beauteous Evening."*

An upturning nose like that of the Duchess in Alice in Wonderland —Frank Swinnerton

♣ NOSTALGIA
See: MEMORY, SENTIMENT

♣ NOURISHMENT
See: FOOD AND DRINK

♣ NOVELS
See: BOOKS

♣ NUMBNESS
See: RESERVE

♣ OATH
See: PROMISE

♣ OBEDIENCE
See: MEEKNESS

♣ OBESITY
See: FATNESS

♣ OBJECTS, MISCELLANEOUS

Beach umbrellas, bright as lollipops ... like flowers grown grossly out of proportion in a garden —Stanley Elkin

Blankets and pillows ... like loving, hugging arms —Jean Stafford

(Bernard's) camera clicks like the gnashing of a lizard's tiny teeth —R. Wright Campbell

Canes like swords —John Dickson Carr

(Dangle) a long row of credit cards like the flags on the mast of a ship —George Garrett

Opening an umbrella—like the sail of a boat snapping open in the breeze —Simon Mawer, *The Glass Room*

Pennants steam from the twin copper peaks of the roof [of the golf course clubhouse], like a castle at tournament time —Walker Percy

The phone goes off like a shrill alarm —Jay McInerney

The plow bucked and staggered like a cow with a broken back —Will Weaver

Refrigerator as big as a garden shed —François Camoin

(Sometimes I think) TVs are like dollhouses but with real, little people inside —Will Weaver
In his novel Red Earth, White Earth, *Weaver expands on this image as follows: "Close your eyes sometime, and put your ear right on the side of the T.V. It's like you're listening through a wall to the neighbors."*

Transistor radio —one of those ghetto blasters that look like assorted pie plates glued to a masonry block —Jonathan Valin

A [very small] watch ... rode her bare wrist like a rubber band around a leg of lamb —Loren D. Estleman

Umbrellas, like faces, acquire a certain sympathy with the individual who carries them —J. W. Ferrier and R.L. Stevenson

♣ OBLIVION
See: BLINDNESS, MEMORY

♣ OBSCURITY
See: VAGUENESS

♣ OBSERVATION
See: SCRUITINY

♣ OBSOLESCENCE
See: TIMELINESS/UNTIMELINESS

♣ OBSTINANCY
See: PERSISTENCE

❧ OBVIOUSNESS

See Also: CLARITY, VISIBILITY

(The magnificence of the Ambersons was) as conspicuous as a brass band at a funeral —Booth Tarkington

As conspicuous … as a butterfly among moths —George Feifer

As conspicuous as a second nose —Mike Sommer

As conspicuous as two fleas in a glass of milk, and about as welcome —Rosa Guy television review of film *Heartburn*, October 13, 1986

Blatant as a slammed door —George Garrett

Her face was as easy to read as a crooked optometrist's chart —Loren D. Estleman

[The season's coming conflicts were] hiding in plain sight, like a rifle poking out of a banker's box —John Swansburg in *Slate* about the television series *Mad Men*

It was written all over him [that he was prone to trouble] in letters like headlines —William Humphrey

Magnificence, like the size of a fortune, is always comparative —Booth Tarkington

The majority's political motives are as naked as a strip-search —Maureen Dowd, "Men in Black," *New York Times*, April 4, 2012
The title refers to the justices of the Supreme Court.

Noticeable as perfume —Wallace Stegner

(The film has a payoff that's as) obvious as a cream pie in the face —Gene Siskel

Obvious as a gesture —Stephen Crane

Obvious as an elephant's footprint —Anon

(Those two guys can't move around … without being) obvious as turds on butcher blocks —Harold Adams

Obvious, like a poster forty feet high —J. B. Priestly

(Her thoughts and her emotions had all been) outspread … like jewels —Edith Wharton

Plain as a pig on a sofa —Flannery O'Connor

(The case was as) plain as a pikestaff —Arthur Train

Plain as graffiti on a brick wall —Elyse Sommer

Plain as the nose on a man's face —Rabelais
A variation by Robert Burton: "as clear and as manifest as the nose on a man's face."

Plain as the paint on a whore's face —Stephen Longstreet

Stick out like a pregnant woman's stomach —Anon

(He was) subtle as a salvo —Jonathan Gash

There's no one so transparent as the person who thinks he's devilish deep —W. Somerset Maugham

Transparent as water in a goldfish bowl —Anon

Unobrusive as the roar of a lion —Erich Maria Remarque

❧ OCEAN/OCEANFRONT

See Also: SEASCAPES

The Alvin [a ship] … moved through the dark sea like a robot fish —Richard Moran

The beach is bare as the blue bowl of the sky —John Hall Wheelcock

The beach was splattered with people like bright rags —Nadine Gordimer

(Here in front of the summer hotel) the beach waits like an altar —Anne Sexton

A beach, white and slender like a young moon —Louis Bromfield

A breaker … roaring over the reef like a herd of crazed animals running before a forest fire —Clive Cussler

The gentle surf crested in the quick darkness with swirling phosphorous fringes of tiny animals like liquid silver —James Crumley

Long blue rollers coming in … each a neat and level line like an ironed crease —George Garrett

The ocean frowns like elephant hide —Karl Shapiro

The ocean like sleek gray stone —Robinson Jeffers

The ocean looked like a wide lavender ribbon stitched up against a pink-and-blue sky —Sue Grafton

The ocean rumbled like a train backing up —Anne Sexton

The ocean seemed to hover in the distance like a gray haze blending into the gray of the sky —Sue Grafton

The rough white crests of waves walk as if in moccasins —Diane Wakoski

The sea growled like a dog —John Mortimer

The sea has that oily sheen to it, like an empty swimming pool —William Boyd

The sea is like a human being ... always moving, always something deep in itself stirring it ... always wanting —Olive Shreiner

The sea [along the beach jetties] trembling among the stones like gelatin —Thomas McGuane

The sea whispered and hummed like a great shell held to the ear —Mary Stewart

The surf hisses like tambourines —Derek Walcott

The tide came in like ten thousand orgasms —Anne Sexton

The water ran over the sand, one wave covering another like the knitting of threads —Rachel Ingalls

Waves ... black as cypresses, clear as the water of a wishing well —Denise Levertov

Waves crashing with the sound as of breaking biscuits —Vita Sackville-West

Waves ... leaping like hounds up at the rocks —Josephine Jacobsen

Waves like small mountains rose with the shrieking wind into the black sky —James Stern

A wave like a vast castle —*Arabian Nights*

Waves, like blue animals stampeding —George Garrett

Waves like white feathers —George Garrett

The waves pulse ... like hearts —Sylvia Plath

A wave suddenly raged out like a mountain cat —Stephen Crane

Waves that rose like mountains —D. R. MacDonald

The waves were skidding in like big buildings that swayed drunkenly and then toppled over on their faces and splattered all over the hard sand —Arthur Miller

When the surf is up its roaring fills you like a shell —Marge Piercy

The whole expanse of water ... glistened like a sheet of stretched blue silk —Robie Macauley

❧ OCCUPATIONS

See: DOCTORS, LAWYERS, PROFESSIONS

❧ ODOR

See: SMELL

❧ OLD

See: AGE

❧ OPAQUENESS

See: VAGUENESS

❧ OPEN AND SHUT

Closed [a newspaper] up like a surgeon closing an incision above an inoperable truth —Elizabeth Spencer

The door is closed like the shutter of a stalled-out camera —Thomas McGuane

It [a door] came [open] easy ... like a ghost had blown it open from inside —Jay Parini

Locked up tighter than Dick's hatband —Richard Ford

Ford's simile used to describe a home business that's not open, is a variation of an American colloquialism generally linked with stinginess.

Open and shut as if cast from the shadow of a fallen angel's wing —Anon

(The elevator doors) opened suavely, like an expensive cream sliding smoothly on a flawless face —Judith Martin

(Let your mind) open like a clam when the waters slide back to feed it —Marge Piercy

Opens like a summer rose —George Garrett

(In love we) open wide as a house to a summer afternoon —Marge Piercy

(Wake up, please) open yourself like a little umbrella —Donald Justice

(Our room was closed off and) sealed, like a grave inside a pyramid —Yehuda Amichai

[Emotions] sewn up tighter than a Victorian daughter's drawers —Roderic Jeffries

Shut down (the long Minnesota winter) like the white lid of a box —F. Scott Fitzgerald

Shut firmly in like a trunk locked up when the key is lost —Eibhlin Dhubh Ni Chonnaill

[Window-blinds] shut like an eye that sleeps —H.G. Wells

Shut tight as a drum —Anon

Shut up like a rabbit trap —Noel Streatfeild

(J. B.'s face) shut with a snap like a rat-trap —Gavin Lyall

(A world had opened and) was closing … like a curtain being silently drawn —John McCahern

♣ OPENNESS
See: CANDOR

♣ OPERA
See: MUSIC

♣ OPINION
See Also: IDEAS

As men grow older, their opinions, like their diseases, grow chronic —Josh Billings

In Billings' original dialect: "Az men gro older their opinuns like thier diseazes, grow kronick."

Carried and opened this attitude like an umbrella —Delmore Schwartz

Observations … are like children's cradles … sometimes empty—sometimes full of noisy imbecility—and often lulling to sleep —Sydney Smith

Smith modestly applied this simile to his own observations.

Of three minds, like a tree in which there are three blackbirds —Wallace Stevens

Opinion gathered like a cloud and danced and then seemed to freeze —H. E. Bates

Opinion is like a pendulum and obeys the same law. If it goes past the center of gravity on one side, it must go a like distance on the other; and it is only after a certain time that it finish the true point at which it can remain at rest —Arthur Schopenhauer

Opinion polls: polls are like sleeping pills designed to lull the public into sleeping on election day. You might call them "sleeping polls" —Harry S. Truman

Opinions, like showers, are generated in high places, but they invariably descend into lower ones, and ultimately flow down to the people, as rain unto the sea —Charles Caleb Colton

Opinions, like the temperaments, fell rapidly into pre-established categories —Marguerite Yourcenar

Opinions ricocheted through the gathering like hyperactive pheromones —Susan Ferraro, *New York Times*/ Hers, February 19, 1987

Opinions stout as oak —Phyllis McGinley

Passed opinions like gas —Rita Mae Brown

Played with our ideas like jacks, pressing our fingertips against their sharp points and round protuberances, testing how many we could scoop up at once —Lynne Sharon Schwartz

Public opinion in this country runs like a shower bath. We have no temperature between hot and cold —Heywood Broun

Broun's public opinion simile is amongst the best known witticisms born at the famed Algonquin Round Table.

Sweeping judgments which are so common are meaningless ... like men who salute a whole crowd of people in the mass —Michel De Montaigne

The man who never alters his opinion is like standing water, and breeds reptiles of the mind —William Blake

The pressure of public opinion is like the pressure of the atmosphere; You can't see it—but, all the same, it is sixteen pounds to the square inch —James R. Lowell, interview with Julian Hawthorne, *New York Times*, April 2, 1922

The public buys its opinions as it buys its meat, or takes its milk, on the principle that it is cheaper to do this than to keep a cow. So it is, but the milk is more likely to be watered —Samuel Butler

Tosses off insights like the spray from a speedboat —Anon, comment about an author's work

Like many such complimentary similes, this one was later featured in an ad for the work thus praised.

To venture an opinion is like moving a piece at chess: it may be taken, but it forms the beginning of a game that is won —Johann Wolfgang von Goethe

❧ OPPORTUNENESS
See: TIMELINESS/UNTIMELINESS

❧ OPPORTUNITY
See Also: FORTUNE/MISFORTUNE, IMPOSSIBILITY

(Life was) opening up ... like an orchid in bloom —T. Coraghessan Boyle

Opportunities, like eggs, don't come but one at a time —Josh Billings

In Billings' original dialect: "Oopportunitays ... kum but one at a time."

Opportunity ... it fell like a lucky coin at his feet —George Garrett

Possibilities rising like new mountains —Richard Ford

Sometimes opportunity knocks like a loud windburst; more often it arrives like a burglar and disappears before you realize it was there —Elyse Sommer

❧ OPTIMISM
See: CHEERFULNESS

❧ ORANGE
See: COLORS

❧ ORATORY
See: SPEECHMAKING

❧ ORDER/DISORDER
See: CLEANLINESS

The big house ran like a Swiss clock —Rita Mae Brown

(The market is in absolute) chaos ... like people running out on the field after a Mets game —Howard Farber, *New York Times*, October 5, 1986

The chaos described by Farber refers to the X-rated video industry.

Chaotic as the floor of the stock exchange at the closing bell —William Diehl

(Chaos and) disorder is like a pebble in my shoe or loose hair under my shirt collar —Warren Miller

Disorder piles up like a (local California) mountain —Janet Flanner

Household ordered like a monastic establishment —Gustave Flaubert

Housekeeping, like good manners, is usually inconspicuous —Peg Bracken

Keeps house like a Dutch housekeeper —Anais Nin

The person whose neatness is likened to a Dutch housekeeper is novelist Henry Miller.

(The whole lot was) littered like a schoolroom after a paper fight —Mary Hood

Neat and bare as a GI's footlocker —George Garrett

(Withered little Filipino men, as) neat and brittle as whiskbrooms —Fletcher Knebel

Neat and dustless as a good museum —George Garrett

Neat and soft as a puff of smoke —George Garrett

Neat as a coffin —Anon

Neat as a cupcake —Laurie Colwin

(The little one-story house was as ...) neat as a fresh pinafore —Raymond Chandler

Neat as a hoop —Rosellen Brown

Neat as a morgue —Wilfrid Sheed

Neat as an employee prepared to be given a pink slip and told to clear out his desk within half an hour —Elyse Sommer

Neat as a pin —American colloquialism

This had its roots in the English expressions "Neat as a ninepence," and serves as the continuing inspiration for catchy "neat as" comparisons.

(House,) neat as a stamp collection —Marge Piercy

(He was) neat as a warm stone —Don Robertson

Neat as piecrust —Julia O'Faolain

(You are) rumpled like a sweater —Marge Piercy

Another example of a simile as an introducer, in this case of a poem entitled "Nothing More Will Happen."

Their rooms were neat as monks' cells —Babs H. Deal

(He said that) the lawn and house should be neat and pass inspection ... like a soldier's bunk and beard —Mary Morris

Untidy ... like a bird of paradise that had been out all night in the rain —Oscar Wilde

♣ ORDINARINESS
See: COMMONPLACE

♣ ORIGINALITY

As distinctive as a paper clip —Loren D. Estleman

As novel as teaching chickens to drive cars —Richard Ford

Blowing platitudes like bubbles through air —William Styron

The human mind can no more produce an original thought than a tree can produce an original fruit —Jerome K. Jerome

Individualism is rather like innocence; there must be something unconscious about it —Louis Kronenberger

A platitude like a bad postcard of the Parthenon —Karl Shapiro

Unique as the suits worn to a banker's convention —Elyse Sommer

Unlike the rest of the family as wine from water —J. B. Priestly

Unoriginal as any rabbit —Robert Frost

♣ OUTBURST
See: BURST

♣ OUT OF PLACE
See: BELONGING

♣ PAIN
See Also: HEALTH

Ached from head to foot, all zones of pain seemingly interdependent ... like a Christmas tree whose lights wired in series, must all go out if even one bulb is defective —J.D. Salinger

Ached like a bad tooth —Lawrence Durrell

The air burning my lungs like a red-hot iron or cutting into them like a sharpened razor —Albert Camus

Anguish poured out like blood from a gaping wound —Jonathan Kellerman

In Kellerman's novel When the Bough Breaks, *the anguish is being poured out by a patient to the psychologist hero.*

Bruised like a half-back in a football game —Francis W. Crowninshield

[Rash] burned like dots of acid —William Kennedy

Cut like a whiplash —Ruth Chatterton

(Walked out into) the dazzling sun that cut into his eyes like a knife —John Dos Passos

A deadly vise of pain that clamped her head like a steel helmet —Arthur A. Cohen

Exposed it [pain], like a beggar used to making a show of his sores —Julia O'Faolain

Feel like somebody stuck thumbtacks all over my head —James Lee Burke

Felt as if I'd been crushed between two runaway wardrobes —J. B. Priestly

This "similistic" comment is made by the hero of Lost Empires *after being beaten up.*

Felt as though his body were wrapped in layers of plaster cast —Kenzaburo Oe

The plaster cast comparison was used by the author to describe a character who wakes up feeling stiff and achy all over.

Felt her head was going to break open like a co-conut struck with a hammer —Marge Piercy

Felt pain like hot knives —Anon

A flash of pain darted through her, like the ripple of sheet lightning —Edith Wharton

For a second he remained in torture, as if some invisible flame were playing on him to reduce his bones and fuse him down —D.H. Lawrence

A gash ... as wide as an open grave —Jimmy Sangster

Generalized racking misery that makes him feel as if his pores are bleeding and his brain is leaking out of his ears —T. Coraghessan Boyle

A head like a sore tooth —Anon

Her stomach reacted as though she'd eaten sulfuric pancakes —Rita Mae Brown

An hour of pain is as long as a day of pleasure —English proverb

The hurt had gone through her like the split in a carcass —Julia O'Faolain

The hurt I felt ... was something like a thumb struck with a hammer —MacDonald Harris

Hurt ... like a knot passing through an artery —Donald McCaig

(My brother's laugh is small, sharp, and) hurts like gravel in your shoe —Sharon Sheehe Stark

It [the pain of failure] was like a gnawing physical disability, an ugly mark she wanted to hide —H. E. Bates

A knot of pain was set like a malignant jewel in the core of his head —Truman Capote

(Your letter was) like a bullet straight into my heart —Sholom Aleichem

My back ached as if someone were holding a welding torch against my spine, turning the flame on and off at will —W. P. Kinsella

My breast was contracted by a pain like screws clamped on my heart —Joyce Cary

My insides burned like pipes in a boiler —Governor Morris

My intestines felt as if they were playing host to a Bears-Raiders game —Penny Ward Moser, *Discover,* February, 1987

My stomach feels as if I have swallowed razor blades —W. P. Kinsella

My stomach feels like the crop of a hen —Katherine Mansfield

My whole body glows with pain as if I were being electrocuted —Iris Murdoch

Nausea coiled like a snake in her stomach —A. E. Maxwell

Pain and pleasure like light and darkness, succeed each other —Lawrence Sterne

The pain between his eyes seemed to be whirling about like a pinwheel —R. Wright Campbell

Pain comes billowing on like a full cloud of thunder —Dante Gabriel Rossetti

Painful ... like cutting the heart out of her body —Phyllis Bottome

The pain described in Bottome's short story, The Battle Field, *is that of never seeing someone again.*

The pain goes ringing through me like alarms —Delmore Schwartz

Pain ... hard as blows —John Berryman

The pain in his chest was like a tight breastplate —Graham Swift

Pain is immune to empathy ... like love —Barbara Lazear Ascher, *New York Times*, October 16, 1986

Pain is like a love affair. When it's over it's over —Elyse Sommer

Pain lifted like a fog that gives way to bright sunlight —Maurice Edelman

Pain ... like a metal bar —Graham Swift

Pain (lingering) ... like a stone pit lodged in the stomach —Anon

Pain rising as periodically as high water —William H. Gass

(The sympathy that it arouses is as) painful as charity —Mikhail Lermontov

Pains are flinging her about like an old rag, a filthy torn rag doll —Vicki Baum

The pain seemed to rock inside him like a weight that would overturn him —Graham Swift

Pains ... like streams of pulsating fire heating him to an intolerable temperature —Ambrose Bierce

Pain ... slopped through his head like water into a sand-castle —Kingsley Amis

Pains that shrieked like alarm bells —Jane Rogers

Pain tightens like a strip of hot metal across Martin's chest —Robert Silverberg

Pain ... twisting like currents in a river —Martin Amis

Pain whistled through my body like splintered glass —Ross Macdonald

Pain would advance and recede like waves on a beach —Nathaniel Benchley

People in pain are like the wandering minstrels of the Renaissance. Any occupied space becomes their court. If the story's told often enough, perhaps the demons will become manifest. Made visible and mastered through words —Barbara Lazear Ascher, *New York Times*, October 16, 1986

A persistent jabbing in her chest that tapped back and forth like an admonishing finger —Molly Giles

Pierce ... like misplaced trust —John Drury

(Though we love pleasure, we) play with pain like a tongue toying with a bad tooth —George Garrett

The pounding in his head was like ten thousand hammers —Niven Busch

Press like a blunt thumb —Lawrence Durrell

Prolonged pain is like a fire in the house, it causes you to flee and wander homeless —Barbara Lazear Ascher, *New York Times*, October 16, 1986

Shudder at the thrust of pain like a virgin at the thrust of love —George Garrett

Spine ached as if it had been twisted like a cat's tail —Bernard Malamud

Sting you like scorn —Thomas Hardy

(Irony ...) stung like squirts from a leaky hose —Geoffrey Wolff

Suffering is cheap as grass and free as the rain that falls on saint and sinner alike —George Garrett

A sweet bewildering pain, like flowers in the wind and rain —Thomas Ashe

[A broken ankle] Swelled like a soccer ball —Clive Cussler

Swollen face throbbing as if it has been pumped up with a bellows —Elena Poniatowska

Throat … like sandpaper soaked in salt —H. E. Bates

Throat … like a thicket of nettles —Arthur Train

[The lack of respect] Tormented him like a raging thirst —Marge Piercy

Woke up feeling as if someone had tied sandbags to my hair —Jonathan Valin

Writhed like a trampled snake —Oscar Wilde

(Sat on a bench) writhing like a woman in labor —Isaac Babel

Writhing … like the poor shell-fish set to boil alive —John Greenleaf Whittier

❖ PAINTINGS

See: ART AND LITERATURE

❖ PALLOR

See Also: FACIAL COLOR, GRAY, RED, WHITE

Pale as cardboard —Paige Mitchell

Pale as white wine —Sir Kenelm Digby

Blanch like conscious guilt personified —Charlotte Brontë

Bleached like the skeleton of a stranded walrus —Herman Melville

A face like paper —J. B. Priestly

Face like parchment —G. K. Chesterton

(His long, pendulous) face looked as if it had been dusted with white talc —Aharon Megged

Face … pale as a Chinese mandarin's —Nadine Gordimer

Face … pale as a dead man's —Ivan Turgenev

Face … pale as a fish —T. Coraghessan Boyle

Face, pallid and simmering like a milk pudding over a slow flame —Julia O'Faolain

He was pale as dough —Michael Chabon, *The Amazing Adventures of Kavalier & Clay*

He was pale as spaghetti, and as limp —Anon

His waxy pallor was touched along the underside of his jaw with acne, like two brush burns —John Updike

Look [pale] like Yom Kippur before sunset —Isaac Bashevis Singer

Pale as a silkfish —Diane Ackerman

Pale and dirty as a pulled root —George Garrett

Pale as a birch —Louise Erdrich

(A scar) pale as a fishgut —Davis Grubb

Pale as a ghost with pernicious anemia —Anon
   A twist on the cliché "Pale as a ghost."

Pale as a hyacinth grown in a cellar —Edith Wharton

(Looking as) pale as a magnolia blossom —Sarah Bird

Pale as a primrose —William Shakespeare, "Sonnet 30"

Pale [after donating a lot of blood] as a princess after a date with Dracula —Kenzaburo Oe

Pale as a prisoner —Carlos Baker

(Always cool and) pale as a root —Jayne Anne Phillips

Pale as a shell —James Wright

Pale as a smooth-sculptured stone —John Keats

Pale as a white rose —Nathaniel Hawthorne

Pale as bleached clay —Z. Vance Wilson

Pale as candles —Reynolds Price
   A more specific version by McKinlay Kantor is "Pale as a tallow candle."

Pale as china —Sylvia Plath

(The desert looks) pale as death —Henry Chettle

According to Stevenson's Book of Proverbs, Maxims and Famous Phrases, *Chettle was the first to use the simile in his seventeenth-century play* Hoffman. *The earliest use of the more common comparison to the complexion are variously attributed to Walter Scott's* Guy Mannering, *Thomas Hardy's* The Mayor of Casterbridge, *and Henry James'* The Madonna of the Future.

Pale as distemper —Miles Gibson

Pale as his shirt —William Shakespeare, *Hamlet*

Pale as ivory —Ouida

Pale as junket —Christina Stead

Pale as milk —William Shakespeare, *A Midsummer Night's Dream*

The similes from masters like the bard are often used "as is" or with minor additions such "Pale as cold milk" seen in Davis Grubb's novel The Golden Sickle

(Face) pale as sand —Stevie Smith

Pale as straw —William Evans

Pale as the bottom of a plate —Joseph Sheridan Le Fanu

Pale … as the mist that hangs over the river —Oscar Wilde

Pale as the soap in the dish —Jean Thompson

Pale as the tenant of a tomb —Edgar Allen Poe

Pale as waxworks —Maxine Kumin

Paler than ashes —Algernon Charles Swinburne

Paler than grass in summer —Algernon Charles Swinburne

(Thighs) pale soft as snow —Lyn Lifshin

So white she was almost transparent —Jonathan Gash

The transparent pallor of her skin was luminous like a sea-shell in green shadow of the pine-trees —Elinor Wylie

Turned white as a tablecloth —Rudyard Kipling

Wan as the Polar snows —Stephen Vincent Benét

❧ PARENTAL LOVE
See Also: PARENTHOOD

❧ PARENTHOOD

A childless person is like dead —Joshua/Talmud

The honor due to parents is like the honor due to God —The Holy Bible/Exodus

Children, grown up, now, and moved away … though they had once occupied her like a house possessing her to the fingertips —Helen Hudson

The ideal mother, like the ideal marriage, is a fiction —Milton Sabirstein

(Maybe I've got this secret kid. Chances are I have, 'cause) I probably got a sperm count like the national deficit —Jane Wagner

Love them [daughters] as sheep are loved by the shepherd —Phyllis McGinley

Marriage without children —like a garden without fruit —Phyllis Bottome

Compare this with the German proverb below about wedlock.

Mother's virtues … like a graft of a late fruit on an early apple or pear tree, do not ripen in her children until very late in the season —Oliver Wendell Holmes, Sr.

A mother-in-law and a daughter-in-law in one house are like two cats in a bag —Yiddish proverb

A mother-in-law is like the dry rot; far easier to get into a house than to get it out again —*Punch*

Not to bear children … was like a hen that did not lay eggs or a cow that was sterile or a tree that never came into blossom. (There was no point in the existence of them.) —H. E. Bates

Raising a child is like reading a very long mystery story; you have to wait for a generation to see how it turns out —Anon

Realized [after giving birth] the responsibility of launching the little creature labeled by name not of its own choosing, like launching a battleship, only instead of turrets and decks and guns she had to do with the miraculous tissue of flesh and brain —Vita Sackville-West

Sharper than a serpent's tooth it is to have a thankless child —William Shakespeare, *King Lear*

The umbilical cord stretches like a nine-hundred-and-some-mile leash —Peter De Vries

Wedlock without children [is like] a world without sun —German proverb

A woman —her heart is like an empty nest, if she has not a child —Henry Van Dyke

❧ PARTING

See: BEGINNINGS AND ENDINGS

❧ PASSION

See Also: DESIRE, LOVE, SEX

As passionate as shredded wheat —Lawrence Gilman

The echoes of passion in the emptiness of a lonely heart is like the murmurings of wind and water in the silence of the wilderness —François Rene de Chateaubriand

Genuine passion is like a mountain stream; it admits of no impediment; it cannot go backward; it must go forward —Christian Nestell Bovee

Hot as a forty-balled tomcat —Rita Mae Brown

Instant passion is like instant coffee; it's cheap and it's quick and it makes you wish you had a percolator —Carla Lane, dialogue for heroine of English television sit-com, "Solo," April 7, 1987

My passion is as mustard strong; / I sit all sober sad; / Drunk as a piper all day long, / Or like a March-hare mad —John Gay, "A New Song of Similes"

Just some of the similes Gay piled on, including even more commonly used clichés like "busy as a bee," "dead as a door-nail," "lighter than a feather," "smooth as glass," and "warm as any toast"

Our passions are in truth, like the phoenix. The old one burns away, the new one rises out of its ashes at once —Johann Wolfgang von Goethe

Our passions are like convulsion fits, which, though they make us stronger for the time, leave us the weaker ever after —Jonathan Swift

Our world passions are like so many lawyers wrangling and bawling at a bar —Owen Feltham

The comparison continues as follows: "Discretion is the lord-keeper of man that sits as judge, and moderation their contestations."

The passionate are like men standing on their heads; they see all things the wrong way —Plato

Passionate men, like fleet hounds, are apt to overrun the scent —H. G. Bohn's *Hand-Book of Proverbs*

Passion burned through her like a sunrise —Ellen Glasgow

Passion is like crime; it does not thrive on the established order —Thomas Mann

Passion is like genius: a miracle —Romain Rolland

Passionless as a clam —Gertrude Atherton

Passion … like a fire on the prairie that devours everything around it —W. Somerset Maugham

Passion … like other violent excitements … throws up not only what is best, but what is worst and smallest, in men's characters —Robert Louis Stevenson

Passions and desires, like the two twists of a rope, mutually mix one with the other, and twine inextricably round the heart —Richard E. Burton

Passions are like fire and water, good servants but bad masters —Alexander Pope

Passions are like fire, useful in a thousand ways and dangerous only in one, through their excess —François, Duc de La Rochefoucauld

Passions are like the trout in a pond: one devours the others until only one fat old trout is left —Otto Von Bismarck

A passion that had moved into his body, like a stranger —Arthur Miller

The thus passion-possessed character is Eddie in Miller's A View from the Bridge.

Passion … went over him like an ocean wave —Jean Stafford

At another point in her novel, The Mountain Lion, *Stafford used the ocean waves comparison to describe power of the smell of flowers.*

❧ PAST, THE

See Also: HISTORY, MEMORY

Events … had receded so swiftly into the near-forgotten past, like a movie seen years before and dimly remembered —Harvey Swados

The events [of the past] were astir in me, like the loosening phlegm in an attack of bronchitis, waiting to come up —L. P. Hartley

Felt himself sliding … back into a bumpy past where old humiliations still waited to confront him like hills grown taller with the dust of years —Helen Hudson

Going back is like lifting elephants with your teeth —Paul West

He [Sherwood Anderson] carried his childhood like a hurt warm bird held to his middle-aged breast —Herbert Gold

Her past years washed away like so many ridges of sand at high tide —Peter Meinke

Inheritance, like grace, is something you deserve —Hollis Summers

The inheritance being compared to grace is that of family achievement.

I think it's like childbirth, you remember the joyous part —James Lapine, looking back on the famously failed production of the musical *Merrily We Roll Along,* on the occasion of its revival as part of the 2012 Encores! Concert

It was like those years were just a ghost town she'd walked through and then decided to forget —Lee Smith

Kept coming back like a song —J. W. Rider

Like a ball of wool that kittens have got at … all the disposed-of process of my past unraveled on the floor —Louis MacNeice

The man who has not anything to boast of but his illustrious ancestors is like a potato … the only good belonging to him is under ground —Sir Thomas Overbury

Our past … clings to us like strange mystical lint —W. P. Kinsella

The past … always affected her eyes like salt water. It filled her head as if she had stayed underwater too long —Susan Fromberg Schaeffer

Past, as steep as stone, wider than water, like all land and ocean stretches —Archibald MacLeish

Past and future lie joined like a lunatic serpent —Robert Silverberg

The past … held him like a pain —Wallace Stegner

The past is a bucket of ashes —Carl Sandburg

The past is like a funeral gone by —Edmond Gosse

The past lies like an Alp upon the mind —Delmore Schwartz

Past … like a burnt book —Lynne Sharon Schwartz

The past, like an inspired rhapsodist, fills the theatre of everlasting generations with her harmony —Percy Bysshe Shelley

The past was drumming, like a train coming nearer and nearer, in her head —V.S. Pritchett

A record as long as your arm —George Garrett

The simile is the title of a short story.

Rolled up his past —Yehuda Amichai

The sense of accumulated riches of time and tradition pressed past him like a crowd moving in rank after rank, through unending centuries —G. K. Chesterton

Sometimes I want to go back to everything I had, as in a museum —Yehuda Amichai

She wears her past like other women wear perfume —Anon ambassador about Nora Astorga of Nicaragua, *New York Times Magazine,* September 28, 1986

> *True to form, the simile was pulled out of the article and used as the caption for the main illustration*

Sloughed off my past ... like a skin that shuns the light of day —Natascha Wodin

The thoughts of my past life rise like the ghosts of an unquiet dream —Percy Bysshe Shelley

Treated his past gingerly as if it were unfriendly to him —Jean Garrigue

Well it can't cut itself off from the 20th century forever. Honestly, coming here is like stepping into the middle of a Chekhov play —Athol Fugard, Elsa in *Road to Mecca*

Where she has been, she drags behind her, heavy and slurred as the speech of the deaf —Lisa Ress

Worrying about the past is like trying to make birth control pills retroactive —Joey Adams

♣ PATIENCE

Had the patience of a man who worked a step at a time through month-long laboratory experiments —Elizabeth Spencer

Mute and patient, like an old sheep waiting to be let out —Flannery O'Connor

Patience and diligence, like faith, remove mountains —William Penn

Patience is passion tamed —Lyman Abbott

Patience is so like fortitude that she seems either her sister or her daughter —Aristotle

Patient as a turtle —Mary Hedin

(I'll be as) patient as a gentle stream —William Shakespeare, *Two Gentlemen of Verona*

Patient as the matador —George Garrett

Patient, like an old man who has just dug his grave —Sharon Olds

Patiently as the spider weaves the broken web —Bulwer-Lytton

Patiently, like a weaver at his loom —Beryl Markham

Stood as patiently as a horse being groomed —John D. MacDonald

Tolerance ... like that of a grandparent for unpredictable and troublesome children —William Faulkner

Waiting patiently, in silence, as a cat does at a mouse hole —Frank Swinnerton

♣ PATRIOTISM
See: BELIEFS

♣ PAUNCHINESS
See: BODY, FATNESS, STOMACH

♣ PAUSE
See Also: CAUTION

Cease like a dropped watch —Henry James

Everybody froze with expectation like an orchestra when the conductor raises his baton —George Garrett

Faltered, chewing on his words sourly and fatuously, like an old cow —William Styron

(We) froze [at seeing an unknown, staring man] as rabbits do —Rumer Godden

Halted, suddenly trembling, like a person armed to defend himself against wild animals, but on meeting one face to face is immediately turned to stone —Jean Stafford

Hesitated like a cat testing an opening with its whiskers —William McIlvanney

Normal rules suspended. Like having a substitute teacher —Francine Prose, *A Changed Man*

A pause, barely noticeable, like a sight between one word and another —Kent Nelson

Shrieked to a trembling stop like a dog on a yanked leash —George Garrett

Slowed down gradually, like a merry-go-round after a ride —Eudora Welty

Stalled like a whale —John Malcolm Brinnin

Stopped short, like a radio cut off on a crescendo —Frank Tuohy

Stopped speaking for a moment, like a man walking who comes to a brink —John Fowles

Stopped there cold like a man raking piles of dead leaves in his yard who has turned up a severed hand —W. D. Snodgrass

Stops [suddenly] as though shot in the back —Erich Maria Remarque

Stumbled to a halt like sheep in a chute —Will Weaver

Suddenly there was a lull in my mind, like the détente after a retreating thunderstorm —L. P. Hartley

Talk died … as if the voices in the room were on tape and someone had pulled the plug —Will Weaver

(Sky and earth did one last slow turn and) wobbled to a halt like a coin coming to rest on a bar top —Loren D. Estleman

❧ PEACEFULNESS

See Also: CALMNESS

(There was) an ease of mind that was like being alone in a boat at sea —Wallace Stevens
   This is the first line of Prologues to What is Possible, *which contains a number of other similes.*

Had a certain peace, like a stone that wouldn't roll any more —Paul Horgan

Inner serenity is a lot like grace under pressure except that it's all going on inside where people might not notice and give you credit —Judith Viorst

Like a stone thrown into the smooth water of a spring, I had disturbed their peace —Mikhail Lermontov

Like the course of the heavenly bodies, harmony in national life is a resultant of the struggle between contending forces —Justice Louis D. Brandeis

A peace deep as death —Daniela Gioseffi

Peaceful as a breast —Kenneth Patchen

Peaceful as a church —Raymond Chandler

Peaceful as a leaf with its superhuman silence —Daniela Gioseffi

Peaceful as Socrates —Anon

Peaceful … like a child asleep —Phyllis Roberts

Peaceful, like being in a time machine —Lee Smith

Peaceful like New Year's —Carlos Baker

Peaceful like warm Summer nights —Amy Lowell

Peace, like a mask, hides everything —Edwin Arlington Robinson

Peace, like charity, begins at home —Franklin Delano Roosevelt

Peace, like war, can succeed only where there is a will to enforce it, and where there is available power to enforce it —Franklin D. Roosevelt, October 21, 1944 speech to Foreign Policy Association

Peacemaking is hard … hard almost as war —Daniel Berrigan
   The simile comprises the title and first line of a poem.

Peace was over her … like a mantle —Madeleine L'Engle

Peace will, like a broken limb united, grow stronger for the breaking —William Shakespeare, *King Henry IV, Part II*

[A vacation] quiet and pleasant and womblike as a slow bath in a tub of warm water —Harvey Swados

Restful as a Rembrandt background —George Ade

Rest like lizards on rocks —Etheridge Knight

(Maybe it will emerge) serene and smiling, like Daniel from the lion's den —Floyd K. Haskell, on tax reform, *New York Times*, January 17, 1986

Serene as a snowman's smile —Julie Hayden

Serene as jade buddhas —Marge Piercy

Soothing … as waves along a shore —John Gardner

Still and quiet, like a good conscience —Frank Swinnerton

Tranquility pushed their anxieties away, like a man finding a place for himself on a crowded bench —W. Somerset Maugham

Tranquilizing murmur [of a voice] like the music of a dream —Elinor Wylie

Tranquilly like the rise and fall of sand dunes —Yukio Mishima

❧ PECULIARITY
See: STRANGENESS

❧ PENETRATION
See: PERVASIVENESS

❧ PENNANTS
See: OBJECTS, MISCELLANIOUS

❧ PENSIVENESS
See: THOUGHT

❧ PEOPLE, INTERACTION
See Also: CROWDS, FRIENDSHIP, MEN AND WOMEN, RELATIONSHIPS

All her life she had looked for someone who would … settle her in the proper place like a cushion on a couch —Helen Hudson

[Different types of people] all mixed up like vegetables in soup —Flannery O'Connor

All the hurtful ugly things that happened between us got somehow wrapped around the sweetness like a hard rind around a delicate rare fruit. Like a flower garden completely surrounded with tangles of barbed wire —Harryette Mullen

(Harris) always managed to make him feel … like the character in the commercial who uses the wrong kind of deodorant soap —Andrew Kaplan

And I see the same skies through brown eyes / That you see through blue / But we're worlds apart, worlds apart / Just like the earth, just like the sun —Roger Miller, "Worlds Apart," *Big River*

Avoid them like piranhas —Richard Ford

Bitching patiently at each other like a couple married much too long —James Crumley
The people doing the bitching in Crumley's novel The Wrong Case, *are two farmers in a bar.*

Dealing with Valentine was like dealing with a king —Saul Bellow

Distance between them … like the Persian Gulf —Robert Anderson

Faced each other like scruffy bookends —Jonathan Gash

Groups gathered a moment like flies —Bin Ramke

Guided him by one elbow [to a seat], like a tugboat turning a tanker —Peter Benchley

Hoisted her up like a parcel —Henri-Pierre Roché

It was as if he could read my mind like an old tale he had by heart —George Garrett

I want to lean into her [a daughter into her mother] the way wheat leans into wind —Louise Erdrich

Lay side by side, like some old bronze Crusader and his Lady on a sarcophagus in the crypt of some ancient church —MacDonald Harris

(Take her by the lily white hand and) lead her like a pigeon —Anon

This simile is from an American dance ballad called "Weevily Heart," from the late eighteenth or early nineteenth century.

Leaned on [another person] … like a wounded man —George Garrett

Like the sun his presence shone on her —Marge Piercy

Live together like brothers and do business like strangers —Arab proverb

Loneliness sifted between us, like falling snow —Judith Rascoe

Our heart-strings were, like warp and woof in some firm fabric, woven in and out —Edna St. Vincent Millay

People, like sheep, tend to follow a leader —occasionally in the right direction —Alexander Chase

We seemed strangers [a group of three people sitting in room] waiting in a station to take a train to another city —Henry Van Dyke

People sat huddled together [on street benches] like dark grapes clustered on a stalk —W. Somerset Maugham

Read him like a label on a beer can —William H. Hallhan

[Two men who don't like each other] recoiling from one another like reversed magnets —Wyatt Blassingame

Responded to each other nervously, like a concord of music —Lawrence Durrell

Sat … like a pair of carefully-folded kid-gloves, bound up in each other —Charles Dickens

She could feel the distance between them like a patch of fog —Lynne Sharon Schwartz

She reads my silence like a page —Robert Campbell

Sitting like strangers thrown together by accident —Ross Macdonald

Something in her face spilled over me like light through a swinging door —Sue Grafton

Students, their faces like stone walls around him [a college professor] —Helen Hudson

[Many different kinds of people] swarmed around him like startled fish —Derek Lambert

Tangled together like badly cast fish lines —Katherine Anne Porter

They [a man woman with child between them] lay like two slices of wheat bread with a peanut-butter center —Will Weaver

They needed each other's assistance, like a company, who, crossing a mountain stream, are compelled to cling close together, lest the current should be too powerful for any who are not thus supported —Sir Walter Scott

They were … like two people holding on to the opposite ends of a string, each anxious to let go, or at least soon, without offending the other, yet each reluctant to drop the curling, lapsing bond between them —Hortense Calisher

Took me about like a roast [to make introductions] —Mark Helprin

This spotlights the importance of using a simile within an appropriate context. The character being taken about "like a roast" in Helprin's story, "Tamar," is the last arrival at a dinner party. If someone were being introduced in a business setting, being passed around "like a special report or a memo" might better suit the situation.

Touched him on the breast as though his finger were the fine point of a small sword —Charles Dickens

Treated him like crows treat a scarecrow: they ignored him and avoided him —William H. Hallhan

Wanted me to share her pain like an orgasm, like lovers in poems who slit their wrists together —Max Apple

Watching each other like two cats; and then, as cats do, turn away again, indifferently, as if whatever was at stake between them had somehow faded out —L. P. Hartley

(The Hendricks) were making me feel like a specimen in a jar —Jonathan Gash

We sat half-turned toward one another like the arms of a parenthesis —Cornell Woolrich

When I'm with a pistol / I sparkle like a crystal, / Yes, I shine like the morning sun. / But I lose all my luster / When with a Bronco Buster —Irving Berlin, "You Can't Get a Man with a Gun," *Annie Get Your Gun*

When I talk to him, I feel like a plant that's been watered —Marlene Dietrich on Orson Welles

You play my heart like a concertina —Harvey Fierstein

♣ PERCEPTIVENESS
See: ALERTNESS, SENSITIVENESS

♣ PERMANENCE/IMPERMANENCE
See Also: CONTINUITY

As assured of longevity as the statues on Easter Island —John W. Aldridge, *New York Times Book Review*, October 26, 1986

The work to which Aldridge ascribes the longevity of the Easter Island statues is Joseph Heller's Catch-22.

(She was) as immutable as the hills. But not quite so green —Rudyard Kipling

Bonds … as immutable as a tribal code —Anon

Changeless as heaven —John Greenleaf Whittier

Changeless as truth —William Keats

Constant as the Northern star —William Shakespeare, *Julius Caesar*

Enduring as a family feud —Anon

(A novelistic structure as harsh and) enduring as any tabby wall —John D. MacDonald

Enduring as mother love —Anon

Enduring as the Washington Monument —Anon

Enduring as the Constitution —Anon

Fixed as a habit or some darling sin —John Oldham

Fixed as a leopard's spots —Anon

Fixed as a tiger's stripes —Anon

Fixed as the cycle of life —Anon

Fixed as the days in the week —Anon

Fixed as the sun —Erasmus

(In two years he) had altered as little as the landscape —Ellen Glasgow

(My love of art seemed as) as indelible as ink —Jill Ciment

Invariable as a formula —Ellen Glasgow

Irrevocable as death —Charlotte Brontë

Lasts like iron —Oliver Wendell Holmes

Like love we seldom keep —W. H. Auden

Looking back at the years gone by like so many summer fields —Jackson Browne, "Running on Empty"

Of no more true substance than a scarecrow in a field —George Garrett

(The fine carnation of their skin is) perennial as sunlight —Herman Melville

Permanent as the bathroom fixture —Nora Johnson

In Johnson's novel The World of Henry Orient, *the frame of reference for the comparison is a woman whom the narrator of the novel likes and trusts.*

Settled … like an oil stain —Charles Johnson

Unalterable as the little paper flowers permanently visible inside the lumpy glass paperweights —Ezra Pound

Unchanging as the nation's flag —George Jean Nathan

(Ideas, though painfully acquired,) stick like nails in the best oak —Joyce Cary

(My bounded brain was as) unalterable as a ball —Jean Stafford

Binding as a wedding ring used to be —Elyse Sommer

Eternal as the sky —John Greenleaf Whittier

Eternity ... like a great ring of pure and endless light —Henry Vaughan

The simile in its full context begins as follows: "I saw eternity the other night."

[Eyes] imperishable as diamonds —Ellen du Pois Taylor

(Psychology) will live long as the pyramids —Delmore Schwartz

❧ PERPLEXITY

See: BEWILDERMENT

❧ PERSISTENCE

See Also: CLINGING, PURPOSEFULNESS

As headstrong as an allegory on the banks of the Nile —Richard Brinsley Sheridan

(Sorrow) as nagging as envy —Karl Shapiro

(The name was becoming) a teasing obsession, like a tune —Wilfrid Sheed

This crowd was sure to keep picking at the subject of Saddler like a hangnail —Lionel Shriver, *The New Republic*

Dogged as a turtle crossing a road —Marge Piercy

He followed me like a guilty conscience —Stieg Larsson, *The Girl Who Kicked the Hornet's Nest*

Hold on with a bulldog grip —Abraham Lincoln

From a telegram to General Grant, August 1864.

If there was any dirt to be dug up, she would home in on it like a cruise missile —Stieg Larsson, *The Girl with the Dragon Tattoo*

I'm like a terrier pup. Somebody tells me to do something and it gets done —Sue Grafton

Insistent as a baby's cry at feeding time —Anon

Insistent as remorse —Victor Hugo

Jabs like a prizefighter (at their feelings about each other) —Linda Barret Osborne, reviewing a novel in *New York Times*, August 31, 1986

Obstinate as a Hindu woman contemplating suttee —Frank Swinnerton

Obstinate as death —John Dryden

Persistent annoyance, like the rough place on a tooth —David R. Slavitt

Persistent as a bulldog —Oliver Wendell Holmes

Persistent as a fly on a hound's nose —Harold Adams

Persistent as a nagging backache —Anon

(Ugly and) persistent as pain —Carlos Baker

Persist ... like a terrier with a rat ... she wouldn't let go, come hell or high water —James Reeve

Prevail like the false pig in Aesop —G. K. Chesterton

Relentless as decay —Joseph Wambaugh

Relentless as a nagging tongue —Anon

Relentless as a windshield wiper —Anon

Skin ... as thick as his wallet —Jane Gross, *New York Times*, August 22, 1986

The man with the thick skin and wallet is Abraham Hirshfeld, who ran a persistent candidacy for New York State governorship, in face of many insults and putdowns.

Stick to it, like salmon swimming upstream —Anon

Stubborn and hardy as a rubber mat —Marge Piercy

(Death bugs me) as stubborn as insomnia —Anne Sexton

Tenacious as remorse —Vincente Blasco-Ibez

The thought ... unable to move [out of his head], as a jellyfish fixed on the sand —Norman Mailer

Tug at ... like a robin with a worm —T. Coraghessan Boyle

You're like a train —nothing will turn you when you get started —Joyce Cary

❧ PERSONAL TRAITS

See Also: DULLNESS

Adventurous ... like a tropical fish. His native habitat was hot water —Anon friend speaking about former C.I.A. director William J. Casey, *New York Times,* July 19, 1987

Dignified, like a clean-shaven Zeus: one who used plenty of after-shave —Kingsley Amis

Good temper, like a sunny day, sheds a brightness over everything —Washington Irving

Hears like a rabbit and strikes like an asp —William Diehl

(She would be) intent and bold and willful, like a gambler —Harold Brodkey

The author used this simile to describe a woman applying makeup.

A man or woman without personality is like a tree without leaves, or a house without pictures on the wall —Anon

Obstinacy and contradiction are like a paper kite; they are only kept up so long as you pull against them —John Casper Lavater

Quiet and smiley and polite, like a traveling salesman —George Garrett

She is like a cat, she will play with her own tail —John Ray's *Proverbs*

she was always so funny and wild … like a streak of light, or maybe a blow to the head —Helen Simonson, *Major Pettigrew's Last Stand*

Shines like a lighthouse over a dull sea of social tedium —Rita Mae Brown

Temperament … is permanent, like the color of a man's eyes and the shape of his ears —Mark Twain

A temper as explosive as a gun —Rex Beach

This is modernized from the original which read as "explosive as gun cotton."

A temper like a handsaw —Anon

✤ PERSONALITY PROFILES

An ambitious girl … that looks as though she should be kneeling before a crackling fire, stroking a pussy cat, but behind it all has nerves of iron, a will of iron, and a rigid mind cast only for the search for success —Harvey Swados

A great nose that would flare up like a swelling volcano when he was agitated, and commanding eyes like the headlights of an oncoming train, Mr. J. P. Morgan was, unshakable as a pyramid in the desert —Edward Rutherfurd, *New York*

As omnipotent and as full of faults as Jove —Wallace Stegner

As with an iceberg, only the craggy tip [of his personality] was revealed to the stranger's casual eye while the submerged seven eighths carried along an unseen, irresistible force and solidity —Irvin S. Cobb

Barely seemed human at all: more like some Chinese figurine all ivory and silk, that should suddenly have come to life, begun to dance, to quote the poets, and to laugh at everything in this ridiculous real world —George Santayana

Elegant and remote … like a statue carved in melancholy thought —Sylvia Berkman

A fascinating but sometimes uneasy presence … as if he goes around with a black cloud over his head —Daniel Philips about fellow violinist Gidoa Kremer, *New York Times,* May 10, 1987

Handsome, proud, and ingrown, "like a toe-nail" —James Baldwin

The simile is an anonymous description of Baldwin's father, quoted in his essay Notes of a Native Son.

He [Oliver Wendell Holmes] is a powerful battery, formed like a planting machine to gouge a deep self-beneficial groove through life —William James, letter to his brother Henry, July 5, 1876

He [Col. Gadhafi of Libya] is like a Bedouin in a sandstorm … He [the Bedouin] bends over until it passes and then stands up strong as ever —Abdel Halim Abu Ghazala, defense minister of Egypt, *Wall Street Journal,* September 9, 1986

He [John McEnroe] is still more like a New York cab driver, with an opinion about everything

—Peter Alfano, *New York Times*/Sports of the Times, August 6, 1986

This simile is part of Alfano's speculation about likelihood of McEnroe's becoming a "laid-back Californian."

He [waiter upon being tipped and smiled at] looked as if he had shaken hands with God —Raymond Chandler

He looked as the dead do in dreams —Mavis Gallant

He looked businesslike, efficient, crew-cut and handsome, like a Midwestern professor just after giving a lecture on Shaw or Pinero —Harvey Swados

He looked hurried, as if he were catching a train or a boat —John Cheever

He looked like a cowboy in a cigarette ad —John D. MacDonald

This simile from MacDonald's novel Free Fall in Crimson *is preceded by this description: "a lean man with a deeply grooved face, an outdoor squint."*

He [man in yellow suit, pinkish white shirt and greenish tie] looked like a friendly hound dog with light mange —Flannery O'Connor

He looked like a man secretly gnawed by a scarcely endurable pain —Margaret Mitchell

He looked like a man who had lost a penny and found a thousand pounds —Jimmy Sangster

He [Gordon Cooper, astronaut] looked like a man who played on a semi-pro football team because he wasn't big enough for the major leagues, and worked in a gas station the middle of the week —Norman Mailer

He looked like a mean mouse —Truman Capote

He looked like a piece of plot, standing there. An extra character, about to return to his mislaid car and his own life —Margaret Drabble

He looked like someone who had been long buried and then dug up again —W. Somerset Maugham

He somewhat resembled an owl, an angry, ageing bird, recently balked of a field-mouse and looking about for another small animal to devour —Anthony Powell

He was a bundle of contradictions that clashed like cymbals —Irvin S. Cobb

He was a man around whom middle-age sat like a podium —William McIlvanney

He was like a monk who'd created his own order —James Mills

Mills uses the comparison in The Underground Empire *to describe a man who is difficult to work for.*

His fifty-two years sat upon him like a finish which made youth appear crude —Edith Wharton

Horatio looked handsomely miserable, like Hamlet slipping on a piece of orange-peel —Charles Dickens

I am like a king of rainy country, wealthy but helpless, young and ripe with death —Baudelaire

I am like a martini. The gin part is New York, the vermouth, Washington, and I'm not talking about the olive —Morton B. Zuckerman at party to celebrate new Washington restaurant attended by mostly Washingtonians and some New Yorkers, quoted in *New York*, July 31, 1986

I look like a discouraged beetle battered by the rains of the Spring night —Colette

Innocent as milk and a build like a chocolate éclair —William Barry Furlon on Jack Nicklaus

It is as if he were in an incubator, breathing his own air —Mikhail Baryshnikov about Fred Astaire

Like people from Balzac, with their own individual characters and tastes —Janet Flanner

Flanner's simile is from a letter to her friend Natalia Danesi Murray about some enjoyable people with whom she spent a weekend.

Like successful nuns, they [two older single women] had a slightly married air —Elizabeth Bowen

Like the [neglected] building ... she seemed to be a victim of overuse and neglect —Margaret Millar

Like the hypochondriac who discovers a tumor under his arm with a surge of fatalistic joy, he has had his worst suspicions confirmed —T. Coraghessan Boyle

(You are a bit) like the stars; happily incomprehensible, incapable of producing anxiety —Giuseppe di Lampedusa

Looked as if she had walked straight out of the ark —Sydney Smith

Looked as wholesome, stiff and unshakable as a bowl of tapioca —Rex Reed about Robert Redford

Looked ... firm and impassable as a good privet hedge —Reynolds Price

Looked, if not like a duke, at least like an actor of the old school who specialized in dukes' parts —W. Somerset Maugham

Looked like a beautiful and highly shockable nun —David Niven about Mary Astor

> *Niven used this simile to introduce his story about the actress' sexual life, which would indeed shock a nun.*

(Dorothy Parker) looked like a bird at the mercy of every beast with teeth —Norman Mailer

Looked like a choirboy gone to seed —Pat Conroy

Looked like a man who had flown three and a half thousand miles with a hot coal in his mouth —Frank Ross

Looked like a runaway from a whiskey bottle —Rosa Guy

Looked like Lazarus risen from the dead —Mavis Gallant

> *A slight variation by Ross Macdonald: "He looked like Lazarus coming out of the tomb."*

Looked like someone whose spare time was devoted to calligraphy or stamp collecting —Jay McInerney

Looked mid to late thirties and as if she hadn't wasted any time —William McIlvanney

Looked pale, mysterious, like a lily, drowned under water —Virginia Woolf

Looked ... something like a dissipated Robinson Crusoe —Charles Dickens

Looked weak, exhausted, and helpless, like a man who has been discarded by an enemy who has no further use for him —Scott Spencer

Looking strained and intent like a woman descending voluntarily into hell —Ross Macdonald

Look like a drowned mouse —John Ray's *Proverbs*

Look like a funeral —Clifford Odets

> *Odets had a flair for pithy comparisons, like this one from* Awake and Sing.

[Tennessee Williams] looks innocent-guilty, like a choirboy who has just been caught sneaking a bullfrog into the collection plate —Rex Reed

Looks like a demented stallion sniffling out a mare in estrus —T. Coraghessan Boyle

(Now he wears black horn-rims, and having lost weight and hair,) looks like an overworked insurance agent —Richard Ford

> *In his novel,* The Sportswriter, *Ford profiles a character who has changed from looking "like a grinning tractor-trailer in a plastic helmet" in his ball-playing days, to the above description.*

Looks middle-aged and respectable like someone's favorite uncle —William Styron

A look strangely weary and solitary ... like a prospector preparing a meal in the midst of the wilderness —Christopher Isherwood

A man like an unmade bed —Angela Carter

A man of shifting contrasts, like watermarks on a desert horizon —Rex Reed

> *The man of shifting contrasts is playwright Tennessee Williams.*

Maturity, disappointment, decline of expectations had settled upon Palmer … like the wrinkles caused by smiling —Elizabeth Hardwick

A mind like a steel mousetrap and a heart like a twelve-minute egg —Jay McInerney

Proceeded through life absented-mindedly, meditatively, as if considering some complex mathematical puzzle —Anne Tyler

She looked like a woman capable of plotting a President up from his cradle —James Patterson

She looks like a flower but she's as tough as a weed —Robert Campbell

She made Narcissus look like Mother Teresa —Peter Benchley

she was always so funny and wild <3dot> like a streak of light, or maybe a blow to the head —Helen Simonson, *Major Pettigrew's Last Stand*

She was like a beautiful flower which though its petals had not yet begun to drop, was already faded and without fragrance —Leo Tolstoy

She was like a nagging itch, repellent and at the same time tempting. —Stieg Larsson, *The Girl with the Dragon Tattoo*

She [dimpled woman with conventional social responses] was like a musical box charged with popular airs —Edith Wharton

Spongy and spoiled like a child king —Wilfrid Sheed

Striped with good and evil like a giraffe —Delmore Schwartz

That man is freckled like a trout with impropriety —Marianne Moore

They looked like the people you see in ticket lines, trying to get tickets for sold-out football games —Larry McMurtry

They looked as if they had been recruited wholesale from a Jewish nightmare —Angela Carter

This girl is like a sunburn —Rob Thomas, "Smooth"

The three of them [girls sharing an apartment] … all as lovely and charming and gay as if they had been turned out by some heavenly production line —Mary Ladd Cavell

(She was radiant; she) twinkled and glittered and dazzled like a diamond —Mary Ladd Cavell

The ubiquitous cigarette in its holder makes him look brittle, like a terrible actor trapped in a "Masterpiece Theatre" production —Sharon Sheehe Stark

Was like certain vegetables; transplant them and you stop their ripening —Honoré de Balzac

While his father was often described as a force of nature, Mitt [Romney] is more like a sea of Styrofoam —Maureen Dowd, "Oedipus Rex Complex," *New York Times*, January 3, 2012

With her plump torso balanced on spiked heels, she teeters ahead faster than most people run, looking like a pheasant on amphetamines —Julie Salamon, *Wall Street Journal*, January 29, 1987

Working with Julie Andrews is like getting hit over the head with a valentine —Christopher Plummer about his *The Sound of Music* co-star

Younger than springtime, are you / Softer than starlight, are you, / Warmer than winds of June, / Are the gentle lips you gave me. / Gayer than laughter, are you, / Sweeter than music, are you —Oscar Hammerstein, "Younger than Springtime" *South Pacific*

You're like a two-piece jigsaw —David Nicholls, *One Day*

❧ PERVASIVENESS

See Also: CLINGING

As pervasive as a raging fever —Anon

(Democracy and freedom began) bouncing all over (the world) like bad checks —Ishmael Reed

Cover like a cold sweat —Anon

He's everywhere … like the mist, like some foul fog —William Diehl

He was all over him, like a cheap suit —Mark Shields

Penetrate [as through a barrier of complacency] … like the slippage of a dentist's drill through Novocain —Clare Nowell

Pervading [a woman's special magic] as a spilled perfume, irresistible and sweet —F. Scott Fitzgerald

(Egotism that seemed to) saturate them as toys are saturated with paint —O. Henry

(Allowed my thoughts to) sink in like a spoon in a pudding [in order to gain insight] —William H. Gass

❧ PHYSICAL APPEARANCE

See Also: ARM(S), ATTRACTIVENESS, BEAUTY, BODY, EYE(S), FACE(S), FAT-NESS, HAIR, HAND(S), THINNESS, UN-ATTRACTIVENESS

Anyone who looks like an unmade bed every day has no right to criticize the way anybody else looks —Anon

This letter from an anonymous reader was in response to theater critic Howard Kissell criticizing an unflattering dress actress Patti LuPone wore in a cabaret act. The simile referred to Kissel's own uncombed tresses and wrinkled clothes and was recalled on the occasion of the death of the much-liked writer on February 24, 2012

As innocent of makeup as an apple he might have polished on his sleeve —John Yount

As straight as a stick and looked as brittle —V. S. Pritchett

Awful [looking] … like an oil filter that should have been changed five thousand miles ago —Saul Bellow

Began to look like the last solitary frost-touched rose on a November bush —Honoré de Balzac

Looked like a sparrow fallen from its nest —Dominique Lapierre

Belly as bright ivory overlaid with sapphires … legs are as pillars of marble —The Holy Bible/ Song of Solomon

(He was) bowed and gnarled like an old tree —W. Somerset Maugham

Chorus-line figure, but with a face like a race-horse —Richard Ford

Dry and bony, like a handsome tree withered by blight —Louis Bromfield

Fragile-looking yet surprisingly voluptuous, she resembled a scaled-down ancient love god-dess, the gilded plastic replica sold at museum shops —T. Gertler

Gnarled as a cyprus —Mary Lee Settle

Gravity seems to hang on his lumpy body like a rumpled suit, tethering him to the ground he stands on —John Lahr, about Willy Loman as portrayed by Philip Seymour Hoffman in the 2012 revival of *Death of a Salesman*

Had a face like a barn owl. The heavy rolls of fat were covered with thick white powder and gave the appearance of a snow-covered moun-tain landscape. Her black eyes were like deep-set holes and she stared at Kern as though she might fly at him any moment with her claws —Erich Maria Remarque

An example of a colorful portrait created with a string of similes, from Remarque's novel Flotsam.

Had the aging body of a poet and the eyes of a starving panther —Ellery Queen

Had the rough, blowsy and somewhat old-fash-ioned look of a whore of the Renoir period —Thomas Wolfe

Had the threadbare appearance of a worn-out lit-igant —Sir Walter Scott

He'd been put together with care, his brown head and bullfighter's figure had an exactness, a perfection like an apple, an orange, something nature has made just right —Truman Capote

He had smooth skin and a thin moustache which made him look like the toy groom on a wed-ding cake —Andrew Kaplan

He is like a puppy with his sorrowful eyebrows and unkempt hair —Lizzie Loveridge, London critic of *Curtainup*, about the conflicted main character in Mike Bartlett's play *Cock*

He looked like a goat. He had little raisin eyes and a string beard —Flannery O'Connor

(Up till then I'd assumed that "Gross" was the man's name, but it was his description.) He looked like something that had finally come up out of its cave because it has eaten the last phosphorescent little fish in the cold pool at the bottom of the cavern. He looked like something that better keep moving because if it stood still someone would drag it out back and bury it. He looked like a big white sponge with various diseases at work on the inside. He looked like something that couldn't get you if you held a crucifix up in front of you. He looked like the big fat soft white something you might find under a tomato plant leaf on a rainy day with a chill in the air —Donald E. Westlake

A nice bit of comparative excess, something to be indulged in sparingly, which may account for the fact that Westlake's novel The Fugitive Pigeon, *contains few other similes.*

He [Marvin Hamlish] looks at certain angles, like a cheeseburger with all the ingredients oozing awkwardly out of the bun —Rex Reed

Her anxious brown eyes and full, slightly drooping cheeks gave her the look of a worried hamster —Sheila Radley

Her face and hands were as white as though she had been drowned in a barrel of vinegar —O. Henry

Her great buttocks rolled like the swell on a heavy winter sea —Miles Gibson

He was handsome, in a brooding, archaic way, like a face from early Asiatic temple sculpture —Christopher Isherwood

He was like a piece of cinnamon bark, brown and thin and curled in on himself —David Brierley

He was ruddy as a ranch hand, and dressed like one —Joyce Reiser Kornblatt

His face and body had an evil swollen look as if they had grown stout on rotten meat —Ross Macdonald

His face and head had an unfinished look, like a sculpture an artist might have left under a damp cloth until he had time to work on it again —Dorothy Francis

(The guy didn't seem to have any neck at all.) His head rested on his shoulders like a bowling ball on a shelf —Jonathan Valin

(She is tall) homely as Lincoln —Alice McDermott

A huge ruin of a woman with a face like a broken statue —Edith Wharton

In appearance she was not unlike a sea cow —Larry McMurtry

Joia whose voice had the quality of organza tearing and whose nervous system was visible through her skin, a tracery of fine blue lines like rivers on an atlas —Howard Jacobson, *The Finkler Question*

Lines around her mouth that looked like quotation marks—as if everything she said had already been said before —Lorrie Moore, *Birds of America: Stories*

A little gnarled fellow like the bleached root of a tree —Zane Grey

Look awful, all trembling and green about the gills, like a frog with shell shock —A. Alvarez

Looked and moved like an elderly gentleman with bowel problems —T. Coraghessan Boyle

[Old people] looked dry as a locust shell stuck on a pear tree —Anthony E. Stockanes

Looked like a pale specter beneath the moon —Émile Zola

Looked like a bat ... had the ears and the snout and the gray pinched mouse-face, the hunched bony shoulders that were like folded wings —Paul Theroux

Looked like a man recuperating from a coronary or just about to have one —Jonathan Kellerman

Looked like a man who has stepped on the business end of a rake and given himself a good one, whapt between the eyes —Stephen King

Looked like an animated skeleton —Jimmy Sangster

Looked like a pearl laid against black velvet —O. Henry

Looked like a seedy angel —William McIlvanney

Looking like a drooping and distracted hen —Patrick White

[Paul Newman in *The Color of Money*] looking like an only slightly worn Greek statue —Julie Salamon, *Wall Street Journal*, October 16, 1986

Look ... like a fine healthy apple —Katherine Anne Porter

Look like someone who's spent the night in a bus station —Anon

Looks as if when you touch her she'd crackle like cellophane —Harryette Mullen

Looks like a garage sale waiting for a place to happen —George V. Higgins

Looks like the side of a barn with the doors open —Ben Ames Williams

Macmillan said, and they also remember him, the prime minister of a bewhiskered old grandee, with sagging eye pouches like empty purses —Justin Cartwright, *To Heaven by Water*

Make me look like a tosser! Here I am in a skirt and heels, and I walk in with a man dressed like a dog's dinner —Lionel Shriver, *The Post-Birthday World*

Managing with his mussed fair hair and mustache to look like a shopworn model for a cigarette advertisement —Derek Lambert

A man like a scarecrow, old and storm beaten, with stiff, square, high shoulders, as if they were held up by a broomstick stuck through his sleeves —Vicki Baum

Men deteriorate without razors and clean shirts ... like potted plants that go to weed unless they are tended daily —Beryl Markham

Markham makes this observation in her autobiography West with the Night *when she lands her plane and is met by two unshaven hunters, adding this simile about one of them: (Baron Von Blixen): "Blix, looking like an unkempt bear."*

Mrs. Mitwisser, whose eyelids were so red, and whose thin nostrils trembled like a rabbit's —Cynthia Ozick, *Heir to the Glimmering World*

My doll is as dainty as a sparrow —Oscar Hammerstein, "Honey Bun," *South Pacific*

(Looks worse every time I see her, so) old and dried out, like a worn shoe —Jan Kubicki

Pink and glazed as a marzipan pig —Truman Capote about M. Soule

A pinprick of a scarlet pimple glowed like blood against the very pale skin on the side of her nose. Her freshly washed gray hair was slightly askew, and she looked ... like that demented figure in the painting of Pickett's charge at Gettysburg —Joseph Heller

Plump and sweet as a candied yam —Marge Piercy

Porgy, a man who's twisted like an old tree but transformed by Bess' love —Joe Dziemianowicz in a *Daily News* review of George and Ira Gershwin's *Porgy and Bess*

Potbellied, and bearded with extra chins like a middle-aged high school gym coach —Jonathan Valin

A profile and neck like a pharaoh's erotic dream —Loren D. Estleman

Raindrops sat on his white skin like sweat —Sue Miller

A regular old jelly ... sliding around like aspic on a hot plate —Joyce Cary

She is chipped like an old bit of china; she is frayed like a garment of last year's wearing. She is soft, crinkled like a fading rose —Amy Lowell

She [a woman of sixty] looked like a lovely little winter apple —Mary Lee Settle

She looked like a tree trunk ... her big gnarled hands seemed to protrude from her like branches —Marguerite Yourcenar

She looked, with her red-cherry cheeks and wide semicircle of smile, like something that might have briskly swung out of a weather-house predicting sunshine —Peter Kemp

She reminded him, in her limp dust-colored garments, of last year's moth shaken out of the curtains of an empty room —Edith Wharton

She was gray as a wick and as thin —Patricia Hampl

She was heavy but not unattractive, like a German grandma —Peter Meinke

She was in her mid-thirties ... faded, but still fruity —like a pear just beginning to go soft —Derek Lambert

She was like a fat little partridge with a mono-bosom —Kate Wilhelm

She [mother dancing before narrator] was like a pretty kite that floated above my head —Maya Angelou

She was tall like a lily, carried herself like a queen ... was dressed like a rose —Hugh Walpole

A short woman, shaped nearly like a funeral urn —Flannery O'Connor

Slender and tall as the great Eiffel Tower —W. H. Auden

Small, chinless and like an emasculate Eton boy —Dylan Thomas

This simile is a self-portrait

A smallish man who always looked dusty, as if he had been born and lived all his life in attics and store rooms —William Faulkner

Small, runty and rooty, she looks like a young edition of an old, gnarled tree —Laurie Colwin

Some people might think you were scrawny but I think you're like a picture drawn with a pen-cil. I like it. You haven't been coloured in, you're all wire —Mike Bartlett, *Cock*

Tall and flat like a paper doll —Elizabeth Bishop

Tan and wrinkled all over as if had been dipped and stained in walnut juice —George Garrett

There's a capacious, unused look to Gordon Brown, like an old rectory with too many rooms —Justin Cartwright, *To Heaven by Water*

They [an old couple] were brown and shriveled, and like two little walking peanuts —Carson McCullers

Thin and old-looking ... as if the frame she was strung on had collapsed and the stuffing had shifted. Like a badly stuffed toy after a month in the nursery —Josephine Tey

A thin man with a collarbone like a wire coat hanger —Penelope Gilliatt

Thin, white-whiskered ... like a consumptive Santa Claus —Dashiell Hammett

With his longish head he looked like an Egyptian king —Iris Murdoch

With his small dark eyes and jowly cheeks he looked like an intelligent bulldog —Andrew Kaplan

❧ PHYSICAL FEELINGS

See Also: HEALTH, PAIN

The cold struck him like a blow from a fist —Bernard Malamud

Deep down within her she felt as though a fish moved its tail —Sigrid Undset

This lyrical simile describes the first stirrings of life in a pregnant woman.

Disembodied feeling, like going under an anesthetic —Gavin Lyall

Feeling ... dizzy like someone who's been bound fast and is suddenly free —Cornell Woolrich

(John sat there open-mouthed) feeling the nerves of his body twitter like so many sparrows perched upon his spinal column —F. Scott Fitzgerald

(I am beginning to live a little, and) feel less like a sick oyster at low tide —Louisa May Alcott

Feel my ribs and guts flattening together like leaves in a book —Dashiell Hammett

Feels the arch of his eyebrows like drying paste on his forehead —John Updike

Felt a chill like cold water at the roots of my hair —Dorothy Canfield

Felt a pleasurable languor running through every limb as though all the blood in his body had turned to warm milk —Joseph Conrad

Felt a sudden dizziness, as though, from a mad flight through the clouds and darkness, he had dropped to safety again, and the fall had stunned him —Edith Wharton

Felt giddy, as if I had come to the bottom of a staircase and found one more step than my feet expected —Mary Gordon

Felt his body … settling down like furniture in a house at the end of a hot day —Frank Tuohy

Felt like a half-digested meal eaten in a greasy-spoon joint —Raymond Chandler

Felt like a tree that had been struck by lightning —Richard Lourie

Felt like a Whoopee cushion sat on by a fat person —Peter Benchley

Felt like I'd eaten a pound of cold buttered popcorn and washed it down with bulk saccharin —Sue Grafton

A giddy feeling in his stomach, as though he were on a swing in the middle of its downward arc —John Yount

The great cold struck him like an icy douche —Émile Zola

The ground was shifting under his feet like the trick floors at sideshows —Shirley Ann Grau

Head [of main character] clears like a hazy morning giving way to noon —T. Coraghessan Boyle

Head feels like the inside of a soggy sandwich —François Camoin

His stomach was spinning like a stunting airplane over a cow pasture —Elizabeth Spencer

Joints creak like a stiff shirt —Erich Maria Remarque

Joints … stiff as dry sticks —Gloria Norris

Legs feel stiff, as if they are all bone —Gary Gildner

Legs felt like two old rusted rain gutters —Flannery O'Connor

Leg went to sleep … it feels like a bag of nails —Thomas Williams

(Could feel all her) muscles shrinking like severed vines in the sun —William Faulkner

My belly and behind were heavy as cold iron —Maya Angelou

My face was sticky all over, like it wanted to sweat but it couldn't —Lee Smith

My throat was as dry as ginned cotton —Borden Deal

Put my head between my legs and feel the blood rush around like a heard of buffaloes trapped at the edge of a cliff —Tama Janowitz

Savoring the joy of rest as if she had twenty years' accumulation of weariness to work off —Colette

Shivering fits, like rows of cold wet needles up and down my spine —James Stern

My throat steams like a sewer —Marge Piercy

Stiff all over and felt like a sack of wet, chilly sand —Denis Johnson

The stillness soaked into her like a fine chill rain —Margaret Mitchell

Warmth ran through Bazely's body like a current of fire —Phyllis Bottome

A wonderful feeling [of pain relief after an injection] … flowed through him like some wonderful, gently warmed milk —Heinrich Böll

❧ PHYSICIANS

See: DOCTORS

❧ PICTURES

See: ART AND LITERATURE

❧ PINK

See Also: CHEEKS, COLORS, FACIAL COLOR

Pink and sweet as a magnolia —Diane Ackerman

Pink as a new baby —George Garrett

Pink as an infant's skin —Charles Wright

(Flesh-colored stockings seemed) pink as blush roses —Rebecca West

(Rosebuds) pink as girls' first lipsticks —Marge Piercy

(Belly) pink as strawberry ice cream —Marge Piercy

(Face) pink as wild roses —W. P. Kinsella

❧ PITY

See Also: KINDNESS

As fire drives out fire, so pity pity —William Shakespeare, *Julius Caesar*

Collected sympathy like a street singer catching coins in a hat —Josephine Tey

Felt a positive gush of pity … like the rising of a warm fountain —Rebecca West

Felt the dull old nagging pull of other people's trouble, like a toothache you can't leave alone —Ross Macdonald

Pity … green as grain —E. E. Cummings

Ready sympathy that can be tapped like a vat —Sharon Sheehe Stark

Wanting pity like a cat wants the mange —John Farris

Wiped the pity away like cold sweat —James Crumley

❧ PLACES

See Also: CITIES/STREETSCAPES, INSULTS

American cities are like badger holes ringed with trash —John Steinbeck

The bargain basement [of a store] where everything smelled musty and looked dull … as if a fine rain of dust fell constantly on the discounted merchandise —Joyce Reiser Kornblatt

A boarding area in an airport is a little like a waiting room in a dentist's office. Everyone tries to look unconcerned, but there's really only one thing on their minds —Jonathan Valin

Buckingham Palace … like an old prima donna facing the audience all in white —Virginia Woolf

The Capitol buildings look like a version of St. Peter's and the Vatican turned out by a modern firm —Shane Leslie

Chicago … living there is like being married to a woman with a broken nose; there may be lovelier lovelies, but never a lovely so real —Nelson Algren

(Some cities never sleep.) Cincinnati sleeps each night like it's drugged —Jonathan Valin

Cincinnati may sleep each night, yet Valin manages to infuse plenty of action into his Cincinnati-based mystery novels.

Cities, like cats, will reveal themselves at night —Rupert Brooke

The city [San Francisco] acted in wartime [WWII] like an intelligent woman under siege. She gave what she couldn't with safety withhold, and secured those things which lay in her reach —Maya Angelou

The city [New York] is like poetry; it compresses all life, all races and breeds, into a small island and adds music and the accompaniment of internal engines —E. B. White

The city spawned ugliness like a predatory insect spewing out blood-hungry larva —David Niven

Niven's simile from his autobiography, The Moon's a Balloon *could probably be applied to any high-pressure place or industry.*

[London during the day] coated with crawling life, as a blossom with blight —Jerome K. Jerome

Coming to New York from the muted mistiness of London ... is like traveling from a monochrome antique shop to a Technicolor bazaar —Kenneth Tynan

Compared to the city, the country looks like the world without its clothes on —Douglas Jerrold

Comparing the Brooklyn that I know with Manhattan is like comparing a comfortable and complacent duenna to her more brilliant and neurotic sister —Carson McCullers

Dallas, a city that treats conspicuous consumption like an art form —Peter Applebome, *New York Times,* March 6, 1986

The danger and noise make it [New York or Chicago to a country person] seem like a permanent earthquake —William James

Detroit, city of lost industrial dreams, floats around us like a mirage of some sane and glaciated life —Richard Ford

Detroit lay across the river, a mile away, like a huge pincushion stuck full of lights —Eric Linklater

Each thought, each day, each life lies here [in Moscow] as on a laboratory table —Walter Benjamin

Fifth Avenue [at Christmas] shone like an enormous blue sugarplum revolving in a tutti-frutti rain of light —Hortense Calisher

The gray cloud of Denver's smog humped over the horizon like a whale's back —James Crumley

Here, a house without a pool is like a neck with no diamond necklace; a swimming pool is like jewelry for your house —Drew Barrymore on life in Hollywood

Hollywood without Spiegel is like Tahiti without Gauguin —Billy Wilder

Wilder's simile was coined in 1986 when Aaron Spiegel died.

Ice hard as iron bands bound the streets of New York —Robert Silverberg

I'm glad to be here in Pittsburgh because I feel a sense of kinship with the Pittsburgh Pirates. Like my candidacy, they were not given much chance in the spring —John F. Kennedy, on the campaign trail

In great cities men are like a lot of stones thrown together in a bag; their jagged corners rubbed off till in the end they are smooth as marbles —W. Somerset Maugham

Ireland is something like the bottom of an aquarium, with little people in crannies like prawns —D. H. Lawrence

Italy is so tender —like cooked macaroni —yards and yards of soft tenderness, raveled round everything —D. H. Lawrence

I've seen the Leaning Tower of Pisa / it looks like somethin' up and broke —Marc Shaiman and Scott Wittman, "Seven Wonders," *Catch Me If You Can*

Japan offers as much novelty perhaps as an excursion to another planet —Isabella Bird

Leaving Los Angeles is like giving up heroin —David Puttnam

Life in Russia is like life at an English public school but with politics taking the place of sex —Isaiah Berlin

Like a resplendent chandelier, Paris in winter is made up of many parts —W. A. Poers

Like many picturesque neighborhoods, it has a chilling uniformity of character, as if the householders propped sternly in their lawn chairs or gazing out from the black space of a porch have been chosen and supplied to ornament their homes —Jonathan Valin

Living in England, provincial England, must be like being married to a stupid, but exquisitely beautiful wife —Margaret Halsey

(Looking down the wing I could see) the buildings of Manhattan, as tidy and neatly defined as an architect's model —Madison Smart Bell

Moscow ... a city landscape wanting neon and city life, as if square miles of squat building had been abandoned at the first November snows —George Feifer

Most great cities (trail their own death around with them and) sleep, like John Donne, with one foot in the coffin —Jonathan Valin

New York ... a haven as cozy as toast, cool as an icebox and safe as skyscrapers —Dylan Thomas

New York fit him [Nolan Ryan, pitcher for Astros, formerly the Mets] like a cheap suit —Paul Daugherty, *Newsday,* October 9, 1986

New York ... looked like a pagan banner planted on a Christian rampart —Douglas Reed

New York's like a disco, but without the music —Elaine Stritch

Omaha is a little like Newark, without Newark's glamour —Joan Rivers

Oaxaca sparkled like a matrix of platinum sequins laid over velvet —Richard Ford

Paris was ... all little and bright and far away like a picture seen through the wrong end of a field glass —John Dos Passos

Places as magical and removed as toy towns under glass —Robert Dunn

A public library, like a railway station, gets all kinds. They come in groups, like packaged tours —Helen Hudson

Puerto Rico ... it is a kind of lost love-child, born to the Spanish Empire and fostered by the United States —Nicholas Wollaston

The Statue of Liberty [as seen from the sky] tiny but distinct, like a Japanese doll of herself —Richard Ford

Sundays [in New York] the long asphalt looks like a dead beach —Edwin Denby

Texas air is so rich you can nourish off it like it was food —Edna Ferber

Thousands of funeral markers rise from the ground like dirty alabaster arms —Sin Ai

The scene described in Sin Ai's poem "Two Brothers" is Arlington National Cemetery.

To be raised in Philadelphia is like being born with a big nose ... you never get over it —Anon

To walk along Broadway [in New York City] is like being a ticket in a lottery, a ticket in a glass barrel, being tossed about with all the other tickets —Maeve Brennan

Transylvania without me will be like Bucharest on a Monday night —Count von Dracula, dialogue from movie *Love at First Bite*

The United Nations looked cool and pure, like its charter —Derek Lambert

Venice ... at once so stately and so materialist, like a proud ghost that has come back to remind men that he failed for a million —Rebecca West

Venice is like eating an entire box of chocolate liqueurs in one go —Truman Capote

Washington, D.C. ... at times as cold as its marble facade —Maureen Dowd, *New York Times,* March 2, 1987

Washington, D.C. ... looks as if some giant had scattered a box of child's toys at random on the ground —Captain Basil Hall

Washington, D.C. ... looks like a large straggling village reared in a drained swamp —George Combe

Writing about most American cities is like writing a life of Chester A. Arthur. It can be done, but why do it? —Clifton Fadiman

❧ PLAINNESS
See: SIMPLICITY

❧ PLANNING
See: PURPOSEFULNESS

❧ PLEASURE

See: STAGE AND SCREEN

❧ PLEASURE

See Also: GAIETY, HAPPINESS, JOY

As much fun as a newborn kitten —Mary Hood

As rewarding as a message from Billy Graham —Anon blurb about a romantic novel

A decided pleasure … as sweet as returning soldiers sometimes admit the act of killing to be —John Updike

The simile from Updike's novel, Roger's Version, *refers to the pleasure of affronting public opinion.*

Enjoyed [the difficulties of a job] … as a good fighter loves a battle —Frank Swinnerton

Fun is like life insurance, the older you get the more it costs —Abe Martin

Frank McKinney Hubbard, also known as Kin Hubbard and Abe Martin, often wrote in country dialect. In the above simile, for example, he used "git" instead of "get."

It's (talking on the telephone) as good as a warm bath and a glass of milk —Enid Nemy, quoting Hazel Duke's telephone habits in the *New York Times*, August 24, 1986

It was marvelous: like seeing a capsized boat right itself, and knowing no serious damage had been done —John Fowles

Luxuriating like a fucked-out lion —John Updike

Pleased as a well-tipped waiter —Anon

Pleased, like a young housewife going through her house and finding everything in good order —Isak Dinesen

Pleasure came like a lash —Julio Cortázar

Pleasure is frail like a dewdrop, while it laughs it dies —Sir Rabindranath Tagore

Pleasure is like a massive dose of vitamins —Anon

Pleasures are like poppies spread —Robert Burns

Pleasures are more beneficial than duties, because, like the quality of mercy, they are not strained, and they are twice blest —Robert Louis Stevenson

Pleasures are much like mushrooms. The right kind are fine, but you have to be on the lookout for the toadstools —*Boston Transcript*, May 21, 1921

Relish … like a robin-redbreast —William Shakespeare, *Two Gentlemen of Verona*

(She was as) satisfying as the morning breeze —Frank Swinnerton

Savor experience as naturally as he accepts the prismatic blessing of sunshine glancing through the glass he holds —Francis X. Clines, *New York Times*, October 19, 1986

Clines' subject is television writer John Mortimer.

Snarl at pleasure like a stoic —Lord Chesterfield

Snatches a crumb of pleasure like a dog snapping up a bone amid a host of dangers —Honoré de Balzac

❧ PLENTY

See: ABUNDANCE

❧ POETS/POETRY

See Also: WRITERS/WRITING

All good verses are like impromptus made at leisure —Joseph Joubert

Composed poetry … like a dancer working at the barre, continually exercising the power of imagining, like a muscle that demanded flexing and stretching —Arthur A. Cohen

Explaining how you write poetry … it's like going round explaining how you sleep with your wife —Phillip Larkin

He [the poet] approaches lucid ground warily, like a mariner who is determined not to scrape his bottom on anything solid. A poet's pleasure is to withhold a little of his meaning, to intensify by mystification —E.B. White

Like science, poetry must fix its thought in thing and symbol —Dilys Laing

Like a piece of ice on a hot stove the poem must ride on its own melting —Robert Frost

Like marijuana smoke are poet's verses —Jaroslav Seifert

Poems are like people ... there are not many authentic ones around —Robert Graves

The poet is like the prince of the clouds who rides the tempest ... exiled on the ground, amidst boos and insults, his giant's wings prevent his walking —Charles Baudelaire

Poetry is like light —Delmore Schwartz

Poetry is like painting; one piece takes your fancy if you stand close to it, another if you keep at some distance —Horace

Poetry ... is like spray blown by some wind from a heaving sea, or like sparks blown from a smoldering fire: a cry which the violence of circumstances wrings from some poor fellow —George Santayana

Poets ... are conductors of the senses of men, as teachers and preachers are the insulators —Karl Shapiro

The simile is taken from a prose poem entitled "As You Say (Not without Sadness), Poets Don't See, They Feel." The poem contains another simile which sheds light on the poet as one who strips away insulation: "He pulls at the seams [of insulation] like a boy whose trousers are cutting him in half."

Poets are like baseball pitchers. Both have their moments. The intervals are the tough things —Robert Frost

Publishing a volume of verse is like dropping a rose-petal down the Grand Canyon and waiting for an echo —Don Marquis, *The Sun Dial*, 1878

Rhymes you as fast as a sailor will swear —Babette Deutsch

The simile is from a poem honoring John Skelton.

They [poets] are honored and ignored like famous dead Presidents —Delmore Schwartz

To try to read a poem with the eyes of the first reader who read it is like trying to see a landscape without the atmosphere that clothes it —W. Somerset Maugham

To write a lyric is like having a fit, you can't have one when you wish you could ... and you can't help having it when it comes itself —Oliver Wendell Holmes, Sr.

Writing free verse is like playing tennis with the net down —Robert Frost

✤ POISE
See: BEARING

✤ POLITENESS
See: MANNERS

✤ POLITICS/POLITICIANS

The body politic, like the human body, begins to die from its birth, and bears in itself the causes of its destruction —Jean Jacques Rousseau

A cannibal is a good deal like a Democrat, they are forced to live off each other —Will Rogers, weekly newspaper article, April 14, 1929

The Democratic party is like a man riding backward in a railroad car; it never sees anything until it has got past it —Thomas B. Reed

The Democratic party is like a mule, without pride of ancestry or hope of posterity —Emory Storrs

The Democrats are like someone at a funeral who just found out they won the lottery —Eleanor Clift

The comparison was made during a discussion of the Iran-Contra aid scandal on The McLaughlin Group *television show, December 28, 1986.*

Elections ... are like mosquitoes, you can't very well fight 'em off without cussing 'em —Will Rogers, letter to *Los Angeles Times*, November 10, 1932

In politics as in religion, it so happens that we have less charity for those who believe the half of our creed, than for those that deny the whole —Charles Caleb Colton

In politics, as in womanizing, failure is decisive. It sheds its retrospective gloom on earlier endeavor which at the time seemed full of promise —Malcolm Muggeridge

Like American beers, presidential candidates these days are all pretty much the same —heavily watered for blandness, and too much gas —Russell Baker

A man running for public office is like a deceived husband; he is usually the last person to realize the true state of affairs —Robert Traver

A man without a vote is in this land like a man without a hand —Henry Ward Beecher

Merchandise candidates for high office like breakfast cereal ... gather votes like box tops —Adlai Stevenson

In his August 18, 1956 speech accepting the presidential nomination, Stevenson used this double simile to verbally shake his head at the idea that politics is just like product merchandising.

Ministers fall like buttered bread; usually on the good side —Ludwig Boerne

One revolution is just like one cocktail; it just gets you organized for the next —Will Rogers

Patronage personnel are like a broken gun, you can't make them work, and you can't fire them —Peter Dominick, from his monthly newsletter, August, 1966

Political elections ... are a good deal like marriages, there's no accounting for anyone's taste —Will Rogers, weekly newspaper article, May 10, 1925

Political rhetoric has become like advertising, audible wallpaper, always there but rarely noticed —George F. Will

A politician is like quick-silver; if you try to put your finger on him, you find nothing under it —Austin O'Malley

Politicians are like drunks. We're the ones who have to clean after them —Bryan Formes

Politicians are like the bones of a horse's fore shoulder —not a straight one in it —Wendell Phillips, 1864 speech

Politics are almost as exciting as war, and quite as dangerous —Sir Winston Churchill

Churchill's simile was followed by this sentence: "In war you can only be killed once, but in politics many times."

Politics are like a labyrinth, from the inner intricacies of which it is even more difficult to find the way of escape than it was to find the way into them —William E. Gladstone

Politics is like a circus wrestling match —Nikita S. Khrushchev

Politics is like a racehorse. A good jockey must know how to fall with the least possible damage —Edouard Herriot

Politics is like being a football coach. You have to be smart enough to understand the game and dumb enough to think it's important —Eugene McCarthy

Politics is like waking up in the morning. You never know whose head you will find on the pillow —Winston Churchill

Politics, like religion, hold up the torches of martyrdom to the reformers of error —Thomas Jefferson

Presidential appointments are left to us like bad debts after death —Janet Flanner

Professional politicians are like chain smokers, lighting a new campaign on the butt of the old one —Steven V. Roberts, *New York Times*, November 24, 1986

This single simile in Roberts' article was, like so many similes, lifted out of the text to be spotlighted as a boxed blurb.

The public is like a piano. You just have to know what keys to poke —John Dewey

The pursuit of politics is like chasing women: the expense is dammable, the position ridiculous, the pleasure fleeting —Robert Traver

Running for public office was not unlike suffering a heart attack; overnight one's whole way of life had abruptly to be changed —Robert Traver

So long as we read about revolutions in books, they all look very nice ... like those landscapes which, as artistic engravings on white vellum, look so pure and friendly —Heinrich Heine

(They said) the range of political thinking is round, like the face of a clock —Tony Ardizzone

A voter without a ballot is like a soldier without a bullet —Dwight D. Eisenhower, *New York Times Book Review,* October 27, 1957

Watching foreign affairs is sometimes like watching a magician; the eye is drawn to the hand performing the dramatic flourishes, leaving the other hand —the one doing the important job —unnoticed —David K. Shipler, *New York Times,* March 15, 1987

♣ PONDS, RIVERS, AND STREAMS

See Also: NATURE, SEASCAPES

The black lake was shimmering like ink —Richard Russo

Light spread across the river like an oil spill —Jay Parini

Pond ... covered with rain like sequins or crinkled up with wind like a watered silk —Joyce Cary

River ... like a sheet of polished metal —Boris Pasternak

The river in evening like a dirty window —Delmore Schwartz

The river looked like an eye which for some reason or other was growing darker and darker as happens in love at the onset of ecstasy —Bertolt Brecht

The river now all crinkled like tinfoil —Delmore Schwartz

The river raged by like a forest fire —Edward Hoagland

A river ran there as clear as the air itself, and the fish in it were like gold and silver —Hans Christian Andersen

The river ... smelled like a packing house for fish, but it looked like the melted, dark eyes of a million girls —Hortense Calisher

The river was brown and bubbly ... like cake icing —Lee Smith

The river was not gleaming, though, but lay like a huge, dark snake beside the tracks —Edward Rutherfurd, *New York*

The stream was like a silver magnet that pulled them across the prairie —Dorothy Francis

♣ POPULARITY

Favor, like disgrace, brings trouble with it —Lao Tzu

Nobody liked DeAngelo. Nobody. Not his wife, not his kids and not even the people he worked for. He was like a stain on a carpet that you couldn't get rid of or that dog that barked at all hours of the night. You want it to shut up, but you're too tired to roll out of bed, find the mutt and do him in —J. L. Stroud Jr. as Viseguy, pseudonymous winning entry of City Room's 2012 Pulp Fiction contest, for which 500 readers submitted hypothetical openings for the actual 1950s noir novel *Atlantic Avenue*

Hot as a pistol —Rex Reed

(Nothing is as ...) popular as goodness —Michel de Montaigne

She looked as if her phone had been ringing continually ever since she had reached puberty —J.D. Salinger

♣ POSSIBILITY

See: OPPORTUNITY

♣ POSTURE

See Also: BEARING, BENT, STRAIGHTNESS

Arched like a cavalry horse getting a whiff of the battlefield —Katherine Anne Porter

A back like a marine drill instructor's ... straight as a rifle shot —Loren D. Estleman

Bolt upright like drawn bayonets —Aharon Megged

Erect as a candle —Isak Dinesen

> *Dinesen used this simile in a short story, "The de Cats Family." Because it is hard to establish when a simile is the result of one writer's creative imagination, it should come as no surprise this simile also appeared in Ignazio Silone's novel* The Secret of Luca.

Erect as a cavalry officer —Francine du Plessis Gray

Erect as a Grecian pillar —Anon

Held his shoulders back as though they were braced, and he sucked in his stomach like a soldier —John Steinbeck

Her back is curved like a shell —Louise Erdrich

Her entire posture seemed to have bunched up like a fist —Robert B. Parker

He slouches in a kitchen chair, like a tire deflating —John Lahr, describing Philip Seymour Hoffman in a scene from a revival of *Death of a Salesman, New Yorker,* March 26, 2012

Her spine droops like a dying daisy —Ira Wood

Huddled up like a pale misshapen piece of pastry —Hugh Walpole

Hunched his shoulders like a fighter tensing for a blow —Harvey Swados

Hunched like a cowboy that hears a rattler —Paul Theroux

> *Theroux's simile is particularly apt to describe the photographer-heroine of the novel* Picture Palace.

Hunched, like a man made lintel-shy by too many cracks on the head through adolescence —Harold Adams

Hunched over like an old turtle —Louise Erdrich

(Sit ...) hunched up like a crow —Elizabeth Spencer

Like a schoolmistress dealing with problem pupils, sat straight-backed —Dorothea Straus

Posture ... like an emaciated old man who once had been an athlete —Kenzaburo Oe

Posture ... rigid and stylized as a pair of bookends —George Garrett

Rigid as an effigy —Gavin Lambert

(A sort of) savage stoop, like a bull lowering his horn —G. K. Chesterton

Shoulders humped like a bull's —Mary Hedin

Shoulders sagged like empty sacks —James Crumley

Shoulders ... set like those of a man carrying a banner —Hugh Walpole

Sits back, relaxed, as if she were watching an invisible TV and weeping over a soap opera —John J. Clayton

Slumped like a chimpanzee —Mary Morris

Slumped there like a bag of bones —Beryl Bainbridge

Slump ... like rags —Karl Shapiro

Slumps there like an outsized parenthesis —Marge Piercy

Standing to attention like a dead centurion at his post —John le Carré

Stands stiff as a bobby when the Queen appears —Maxine Kumin

Stands tall, straight and stern as an angel —Louise Erdrich

Stood like a dart —Brian Merriman

Stood rigid as a carving —Madison Smartt Bell

Stood stiff as a marble statue —Johann Wolfgang von Goethe

Stood up very straight like somebody in opera —Rebecca West

Stooped, as though half-crouching under an expected blow —Ben Ames Williams

Stooped like too tall visitors to an igloo —John Irving

Stooping like a decayed tree, he was so old —A. E. Coppard

Straightened like soldiers under review —Jay Parini

Tilted forward at the waist like a stick shift in third gear —Rick Borsten

Upright as the palm tree —The Holy Bible/Jeremiah Variations of this biblical simile link uprightness with a variety of other trees; for example, "upright as a pine" by Charles Cotton in his poem "Two Rural Sisters."

Upright like stalks —Aharon Megged

❧ POVERTY

See Also: ECONOMICS

Destitution, like a famished rat, begins by gnawing at the edges of garments —Stefan Zweig

Her poverty was like a huge dream-mountain on which her feet were fast rooted—aching with the ache of the size of the thing —Katherine Mansfield

(I felt as) poor as a Catholic without a sin for confession —Harry Prince

Poor as a church mouse —Anon

Like Job, mice (and rats) have long been and continue to be proverbial comparisons for poverty, dating back to the eighteenth century. The writer who is most frequently credited with originating the simile is William Makepeace Thackeray who used it in Vanity Fair.

Poor as a couple of shithouse spiders —Leslie Thomas

Poor as Job —Anon

A simile with a history dating back to the thirteenth century, and used by illustrious writers. In Henry IV *Shakespeare extended the simile to "Poor as Job ... but not so patient" while Sir Wal-*

ter Scott in The Fortunes of Nigel *made it "Proud as Lucifer, and as poor as Job." A variation that was once a popular American colloquialism is "Poor as Job's turkey."*

Poor as sin —F. Scott Fitzgerald

A poor man who oppresses the poor is like a sweeping rain which leaves no food —The Holy Bible/Proverbs

The words "oppresses" and 'leaves' have been modernized from "oppresseth" and "leaveth."

Poverty is death in another form —Latin proverb

Poverty, like wealth, entails a ritual of adaptation —Arthur A. Cohen

[Motel and Tzeitel have been married for some time now. They work very hard, and] they're as poor as squirrels in winter. But, they're so happy, they don't know how miserable they are. —Joseph Stein dialogue line for Teyve in Joseph Stein, *Fiddler on the Roof.*

Wearing squalor like a badge —Wilfrid Sheed

❧ POWER

About as influential as the p in pneumonia —Anon

Aggressive as an elbow in the side —Henry James

As omnipotent and as full of faults as Jove —Wallace Stegner

Authority shriveled as muslin in a fire —Vita Sackville-West

Authority without wisdom is like a heavy ax without an edge, fitter to bruise than to polish —Anne Bradstreet

Compelling as a gun at your head —Anon

[Choice to do something] Compelling as the sense of vocation which doctors and missionaries are supposed to experience —John Braine

(He is) consuming ... like a candle —Richard Flecknoe

Feel like a lion in a den of Daniels —W. S. Gilbert

Strong [a person's pull on others] as a riptide —Reynolds Price

Glows with power like a successful shaman —Marge Piercy

Had a ring of authority, like monarchy —Barbara Lazear Acher

Immoderate power, like other intemperance, leaves the progeny weaker and weaker, until Nature, as [if] in compassion, covers it with her mantle and is seen no more —Walter Savage Landor

Influence is like a savings account. The less you use it, the more you've got —Andrew Young

Influential as gnats —Susan Heller Anderson

It's like a Dead Sea fruit. When you achieve it, there is nothing there —Harold Macmillan, *Parade*, July 7, 1963

Like wealth and power, prestige tends to be cumulative: the more of it you have, the more you can get —C. Wright Mills

Made him fetch and carry just as if he was a great Newfoundland dog —William Makepeace Thackeray

(But her looks have) no power over me ... like a tug on a tree on a limb that has lost feeling —William Getz

Once a man of power, always a man of power. Like being a Boy Scout —Anthony Powell

(Memories ...) powerful as floods —Elizabeth Spencer

Power [in the Middle East] gravitates towards radicals like iron filings toward a magnet —Karen Elliott House

Power, like a desolating pestilence, pollutes whatever it touches —Percy Bysshe Shelley
"Whatever" replaces the old English "whate'er."

Power, like lightning, injures before its warning —Pedro Calderon de la Barca

Power, like the diamond, dazzles the beholder, and also the wearer —Caleb C. Colton

The right of commanding ... like an inheritance, it is the fruit of labors, the price of courage —Voltaire

To rule must be a calling, it seems, like surgery or sculpture —W. H. Auden

Scenting power like blood —Janet Flanner

Seemed the personification of brute strength —like a gorilla dripped in peroxide —Donald Seaman

Strode like a colossus over the [White House] staff —Dean Rusk, *New York Times*, March 1, 1987
Rusk used this image to compare Lyndon Johnson's control over the White House staff, as compared to Ronald Reagan's delegation of power.

Swept me ahead of her like a leaf —Elizabeth Bishop

There was authority in his attitude ... and its heat threatened to melt Bird [name of character] like a piece of candy —Kenzaburo Oe

They pass him on from hand to hand, like a baton in a relay race, and he ultimately becomes a puppet manipulated by others —Vladimir Solovyou and Elena Klopikova

To add a little weight to his argument he put a hand like a bunch of bananas flat on my chest —Jimmy Sangster

Tyranny, like hell, is not easily conquered —Thomas Paine

❧ POWERLESSNESS
See: HELPLESSNESS

❧ PRAISE
See: FLATTERY, WORDS OF PRAISE

❧ PRAISEWORTHINESS
See: VIRTUE

❧ PRAYER
See: RELIGION

✤ PRECARIOUSNESS
See: DANGER

✤ PRECISION
See: CORRECTNESS

✤ PREDICTABILITY
See: CERTAINTY

✤ PREJUDICE
See: INTOLERANCE

✤ PREPAREDNESS

(I was) as unprepared to meet my mother as a sinner is reluctant to meet his Maker —Maya Angelou

Got ready like a depression fighter going into the main bout at the Garden on Friday night —Norman Mailer, on preparing for television appearances

He [the district attorney] prepares his cases as if he were laying the foundations of society —Ross Macdonald

In life, as in chess, forethought wins —Charles Buxton

Like a basketball coach in a close game, he looked poised to spring —Fletcher Knebel

Poised like an acid-tipped arrow —Paige Mitchell

Prepare as though for a death —Katherine Mansfield, on travel preparations

Prepared … as healthy people are said to be prepared for death, in the sense of knowing it must come without in the least expecting that it will —Edith Wharton

Prepared for combat [in business situation], like an ambitious and hungry heavyweight boxer before a fight —Andrew M. Greeley

Prepared like a porcupine for cold weather —Anon

Stands … ready like a retriever —Erich Maria Remarque

Trained him like a race horse for academic success —Robert L. Heilbroner

The man whose educational upbringing Heilbribe likened to training a racehorse is economist John Maynard Keynes.

✤ PRESENT, THE

The present, like a note in music, is nothing but as it appertains to what is past and what is to come —Walter Savage Landor

The word "now" is like a bomb through the window —Arthur Miller

✤ PRESERVATION
See: PROTECTIVENESS

✤ PRETTINESS
See: BEAUTY

✤ PREVENTION
See: PROBLEMS AND SOLUTIONS

✤ PRICE
See: COST

✤ PRIDE

Accepts [a situation] as proudly as the mother of a Bar Mitzvah boy accepts his cracked-voice singing at the Sabbath service —Ira Wood

Beamed pride … like a mother whose son has won everything on school prize day —Louis Bromfield

Dignified and beautiful as a Beethoven Sonata —Israel Zangwill

Dignified as a state funeral —Anon

Felt as though he had feathers which had puffed up with pride —Pamela Hansford Johnson

The pride thus described in Johnson's novel The Good Husband, is caused by the admiring glances lavished upon an attractive companion.

Felt pride rising up through his chest like gas —Margaret Millar

Felt so proud, as though he head saved a life
—Mary Hood

For a man to say all the excellent things that can
be said upon one, and call that his Epitaph, is
as if a painter should make the handsomest
piece he can possibly make, and say 'twas my
picture —John Selden

Like a freshly lit lamp, expanding and bright with
triumph —Julia O'Faolain

Looking very proud like he's discovered some sort
of rare bird —Hilary Masters

My pride stung like a slapped cheek —John
Hersey

Pride is as loud a beggar as want —Benjamin
Franklin, *Poor Richard's Almanack*

Pride is to character, like the attic to the house
—the highest part, and generally the most
empty —John Gay

Pride like humility, is destroyed by one's insis-
tence that he possesses it —Kenneth P. Clark

Pride, like the magnet, constantly points to one
object, self; but unlike the magnet, it has no
attractive pole but at all points repels —Caleb
C. Colton

Pride steams off you like the stink of cancer
—William Alfred

Proud as a cock on his own dunghill —Turkish
proverb

Proud as a hen that gets a duck for a chicken
—Dion Boucciault

(Sat there …) proud as an idol —Hermann Hesse

Proud as a peacock; all strut and show —H. G.
Bohn's *Hand-Book of Proverbs*
    *Probably the best known and most used of the
    many "Proud as" similes. The original used the
    Old English "shew" instead of "show."*

Proud as a stork —John Betjeman

Proud as Satan himself (and unapproachable)
—Ivan Turgenev

(They carefully tend to their garden and show off
their vegetables like….) proud like new parents —Marian Thurm

Saw his dignity slip away like a blanket —Beryl
Markham

Show [as success or dating a beautiful woman]
off like a rose in a buttonhole —Milton R.
Sapirstein

(The curate) sounded proud, like somebody who
brushed his teeth with table salt —J. F. Powers

Swelled like a frog about to croak —Rita Mae
Brown

Swelled with pride like a turkey cock —Ben Ames
Williams

Swelling up like a robin [character proudly announcing that he knows Paul Revere]
—Stephen Vincent Benét

Wear your pride like a chevron on your sleeve
—George Garrett

❧ PROBABILITY
See: CERTAINTY

❧ PROBLEMS AND SOLUTIONS

As rust eats iron, so care eats the heart —Auguste
Ricard

Being a new employee … it's like picking up a
screenplay and starting to act your part, only
it's Act Three and you have not been in Acts
One or Two —Carol Clark quoted in *New
York Times* July 28, 1986

Burdensome as a secret —French proverb

Carry your problems with you from place to place
like a Santa Claus sack —George Garrett

Ceased to be an apparent problem … the way
crumbs swept under a rug cease to be an apparent problem —Rick Borsten

Difficulties strengthen the mind, as labor does the
body —Lucius Annaeus Seneca

(Doubt …) dug at his peace of mind like a broken fingernail —F. van Wyck Mason

(The electronics-crammed production booth is beginning to) resemble the bridge of a destroyer under air attack —Michael Cieply, writing about taping of a Bill Cosby television segment that ran into problems, *Wall Street Journal* September 26, 1986

Face a problem with all the joy of a team preparing for a game it expects to lose —Anon

Felt speaking about one's personal problems was rather like talking about one's surgery scars —a subject of consuming interest only to one's self —C. D. B. Bryan

Heading toward disaster, as certainly as a 4-year old behind the wheel of a Maserati —Vincent Canby, *New York Times*, February 28, 1986

He was like a mathematician with an abstruse problem, worrying over it, but worrying very calmly and impersonally —James Hilton

I am a man smothered with women and children, like a duck with onions —Sir Charles Napier

Napier made these comparisons when he reflected on his life in England after retiring as commander of British forces in northern India

An international crisis is like sex —as long as you keep talking about it, nothing happens —Harold Coffin

It's [being on a losing streak] like a little time box that's going to explode —John Pennywell, then a football player on Columbia University's Lions, was commenting on the team's position after a season of losses. *New York Times*, November 8, 1986

(I was) living as if I were squeezed in an iron hand —Honoré de Balzac

The whole of my life has passed like a razor —in hot water or a scrape —Sydney Smith

(My immediate) problems ... as untouchable as a raw wound —Norman Mailer

The problem stayed in the front of his mind like a sheer cliff he could not begin to climb —Ken Follett

Pry at the mouse hole of a solution like a cat with infinite patience —Bill Granger

Second-hand cares, like second-hand clothes, come easily on and off —Charles Dickens

Sign of trouble ... like seeing a cannon muzzle poke out of the woods —James Sterngold, *New York Times*, March 22, 1986

The solution rushed on him like a fire storm —T. Coraghessan Boyle

They're [troubles] piled on my head like snows on a mountain top —Bernard Malamud

They would gnaw on it for days like two puppies with a rubber bone —Charles Portis

Troubled as a plane with one wing —Anon

Trouble ... fell across her shoulders like a cloak. It was as if she had touched a single strand of a web, and felt the whole thing tremble and knew herself to be caught forever in its trembling —Ellen Gilchrist

Troublesome as a wasp in one's ears —Thomas Fuller

Troubles visited from above like tornadoes —Marge Piercy

Weaponless deterrence is like bodiless sex. It gets you nowhere —James Morrow

Women like to sit down with trouble as if it were knitting —Ellen Glasgow

Work like an antitoxin —before the complications come —Clifford Odets

❧ PROCRASTINATION
See: LINGERING

❧ PROFANITY
See: CURSES

❧ PROFESSIONS
See Also: ACTING, DOCTORS, LAWYERS, WRITERS/WRITING

Archeologists and historians ... they are like jewelers, examining every tiny aspect of each valuable thing, with exactness and care —Judith Martin

Being a screenwriter in Hollywood is like being a eunuch at an orgy. Worse, actually; at least the eunuch is allowed to watch —Albert Brooks

Being a writer in Hollywood is like going into Hitler's Eagle's Nest with a great idea for a bar mitzvah —David Mamet

Mamet's dim view of Hollywood was also reflected in his 1988 play Speed the Plow, *in which a character says, "Life in the movie business is like the beginning of a new love affair: it's full of surprises and you're constantly getting fucked."*

Business is a vocation. Philosophy is, or should be, an avocation —Elbert Hubbard

A financier is a pawnbroker with imagination —Arthur W. Pinero

(I guess) getting into nunhood is about as hard as pro football —Michael Malone

(In ordinary business, man can settle to routine. The journalist can't.) He's [the journalist] like a robin, looking in all directions at once —Frank Swinnerton

He who philosophizes is like a mirror that reflects objects that it cannot see, like a cave that returns the echo of voices that it does not hear —Kahil Gibran

Journalism, like history, is certainly not an exact science —John Gunther

The movie actor, like the sacred king of primitive tribes, is a god in captivity.... Today, many actors become like deities imprisoned in golden cells —Alexander Chase

The Notary Public like the domestic dog is found everywhere —John Cadman Roper

The philosopher is like a mountaineer who has with difficulty climbed a mountain for the sake of the surprise, and arriving at the top finds only fog; whereupon he wanders down again —W. Somerset Maugham

Philosophy is like the ocean: there are pearls in its depths, but many divers find nothing for all their exertion and perish in the attempt —Zerahiah, ha-Yevani

Police business ... it's a good deal like politics. It asks for the highest type of men, and there's nothing in it to attract the highest type of men —Raymond Chandler

Professors are just like actors. Actors got press agents that write things about them and they get so they believe it —Anon

Professors get to looking at their diplomas and get to believing what it says there —Will Rogers, radio broadcast, January 27, 1935

Psychoanalysis, like imagination, cannot be learned by rote —Theodor Reik

Psychology is like physics before Galileo's time, —not a single elementary law yet caught a glimpse of —William James, letter to James Sully, 1890

Running a liberal paper is like feeding melted butter on the end of an awl to a wild cat —Oscar Ameringer

Working journalists regularly chase wild geese. Like firemen, they answer alarms, many of them false —Richard Rovere

❧ PROFICIENCY
See: ABILITY

❧ PROFUSION
See: ABUNDANCE

❧ PROGRESS
See: GROWTH

❧ PROLIFERATION
See: SPREADING

❧ PROMISE
See Also: RELIABILITY/UNRELIABILITY

He promises like a merchant-man and pays like a man-of-war —Italian proverb

His promises are lighter than the breath that utters them —John Ray's *Proverbs*

Lovers' oaths are thin as rain —Dorothy Parker

A pledge unpaid is like thunder without rain —Abraham Hasdai

Promise as solid as a bundle of water —Hindu proverb

Modernized for non-sexist English from a woman's word is "Like a bundle of water."

Promises are like pie-crusts….Danish proverb

The promises of authors are like the vows of lovers —Samuel Johnson

When a men takes an oath, he's holding his own self in his own hands. Like water. And if he opens his fingers then —he needn't hope to find himself again —Robert Bolt

❧ PROMPTNESS

Arrived on time, and left on time, like a European train —Laurie Colwin

Punctual as a bride at a wedding —Honoré de Balzac

Punctual as a stage manager, watch in hand —Frank Swinnerton

Punctual as bills —Babette Deutsch

Punctual as death —Scott Spencer

Punctual as destiny —Edith Wharton

Punctual as lovers to the moment sworn —Edward Young

Punctually as a cuckoo in a Swiss clock —Edith Wharton

Punctually, as the tax collector —*Punch*, 1862
Paraphrased from "tax gatherer."

❧ PRONUNCIATION
See: SPEECH PATTERNS

❧ PROPRIETY/IMPROPRIETY
See Also: MANNERS

About as risqué as a bed in a hospital —George Jean Nathan

All wrong … like a priest for whom one has a great respect suddenly taking his trousers off in church —Daphne du Maurier

Decorously as an old maid on the way to get her hair dyed blue —A. E. Maxwell

Improper as thumbing your nose at the pope —Anon

Prim as Hippolytus —Stevie Smith

(Girls, at sixteen, for all our strictures, are) proper as Puritans —Phyllis McGinley

Proper like the hostesses in restaurants frequented by women shoppers —Ludwig Bemelmans

❧ PROSE
See: POETS/POETRY, WRITERS/WRITING

❧ PROSPERITY
See: RICHES, SUCCESS/FAILURE

❧ PROTECTIVENESS
See Also: WATCHFULNESS

Guard [another person] like an armed sentry —Isak Dinesen

Mothers him like an old mare —Jilly Cooper

[Trees] preserved at all costs, like Grandpa's teeth —Elizabeth Bishop

Protective [of property] as a lion in winter —Anon
This may have been inspired by James Goldman's play, The Lion in Winter.

Protectively like shepherd dogs —Harvey Swados

[Wife] Watches over my reputation like a broody hen —Luigi Pirandello

❧ PROTRUSION
See Also: BELONGING, OBVIOUSNESS, VISIBILITY

Bulges out like bubble gum before popping —Tom Robbins

Protruding like a warning finger —Beryl Markham

[A church spire] standing out conspicuously like an indicating finger —MacDonald Harris

Standing out unnaturally, like a male harpist in an all-girl orchestra —William Safire

Stand out like a blind man at a tit show —William Diehl

Stand out like a polar bear in the desert —Andrew Kaplan

Stand out like a raisin on a coconut cake —Pat Conroy

Stands out like a blackberry in a pan of milk —American colloquialism, attributed to Vermont

Stick out like a bug on a butter knife —Loren D. Estleman

Sticks out like the belly of a pregnant woman —Robert Lowell

❧ PROVERBS
See: MAXIMS, PROVERBS, AND SAYINGS

❧ PROXIMITY
See: CLOSENESS

❧ PRUDENCE
See: CAUTION

❧ PSYCHOLOGY
See: PROFESSIONS

❧ PUBLIC OPINION
See: OPINION

❧ PUBLIC, THE
See: POLITICS

❧ PURITY
See Also: VIRTUE

Incapable of taint as gold of rust —Aeschylus

Pure and white as Rainier's snows —Slogan, Mills Flour

Pure as a salamander in the flames or wool among the brambles —Miguel de Cervantes

(I'm as) pure as driven slush —Tallulah Bankhead

Pure as snow —William Shakespeare

A common formulation—pure as the driven show—wasn't found in print until around the start of the nineteenth century. However, it does stem from Shakespeare, who used snow as a simile in The Winter's Tale.

(I had grown) pure as the dawn and the dew —Algernon Charles Swinburne

Pure as the mountain air —Slogan, D. L. Clark candy

Pure as the sun —Stephen Vincent Benét

Pure in thought as angels —Samuel Rogers

She was as pure as snow and she drifted —Anon blurb for book, *New York Times Book Review* November 2, 1986

Unblemished as the cloudless sky —Anne Morrow Lindbergh

Untouched as a nun —Wallace Stegner

A variation on the same theme: "Pure as a nun" from Margaret Drabble's novel The Waterfall.

❧ PURPLE
See: COLORS

❧ PURPOSEFULNESS

Came around ... deliberately like the gun turret of a great ship —Donald McCaig

Dedicated as a Japanese artist who has found the flower he must paint all his life —William McIlvanney

Deliberate as a bee taking honey —Molly Kean

Deliberate as a dog sniffing out a buried bone —Anon

Effort as conscious and deliberate as holding his breath under water —William Peden

The simile from a short story entitled Night in Funland *refers to a character's effort to control his emotions.*

Had a plan … simple as Cain's —Alma and Paul Ellerbe

His time was organized, planned like the timetable of a battle maneuver —Arthur A. Cohen

Intent as a cannibal at breakfast —T. Coraghessan Boyle

Intent as a collector —W. H. Auden

Men, like nails, lose their usefulness when they lose their direction and begin to bend —Walter Savage Landor

Method is like packing things in a box; a good packer will get in half as much again as a bad one —Cecil

Moved like a steamroller, in a straight line, crushing everything that was in her way —Margaret Millar

My will is like a long pencil, it must be sharpened —Delmore Schwartz

(I have always envied the man who found one single role and) played it [a role or life plan], clung and grew to it like a barnacle on a ship —George Garrett

Rehearsed her sensuality like a summa-cum student —Francine du Plessix Gray

(Somewhere in the earth is a drain of) resolution filling as a fresh teapot —Daniela Gioseffi

(He had) a resolution in him like an iron bar —Wallace Stegner

Schemed like Arabs —Thomas McGuane

(Ruthless and) single-minded as birds of prey —George Garrett

Used her charm like a tennis racket —Delmore Schwartz

Will without power is like children playing at soldiers —George Canning

❧ PURSUIT

(He was) after her like a hound after a deer —Harriet Beecher Stowe

(He was) after it like a duck on a June bug —American colloquialism, attributed to the South

A twist on the duck/bug comparison is "To be after something like a pet coon into the churn."

(He was) after it like the stink after onion —American colloquialism, attributed to South

Chased him like a fox chases a turkey —Rosa Guy

Chased me … like a kid after a fire truck —Irwin Shaw

Follow after me like an old weasel tracing a rat —John M. Synge

In Synge's script for The Playboy of the Western World *'weasel' was spelled with the letter z.*

Follow each other like lemmings over the cliffs of Dover —Richard Hicks, about discount book sellers, *Publishers Weekly,* 1986

Follow every lead like a lawyer building a case —Anon

Followed her about like a little dog —William Makepeace Thackeray

Followed him like a trained sleuth —Shelby Hearo

Followed one another like insects going at dawn through the heavy grass —Eudora Welty

Follow you around like flies —Gavin Lyall

Haunted me like a passion —William Wordsworth

Held on his trail like an old hound after his last coon —James Crumley

Hounded him like bailiffs —Oakley Hall

Looked for … like a bird looking for forage in a desert —Arthur A. Cohen

Pursue as wolves pursue sheep —William Reese, a rare book dealer, quoted in *Wall Street Jour-*

nal article on how book collectors go after their finds, May 6, 1986

[A disease] pursued him like a hobgoblin —Maurice Edelman

Pursue like a dog after a bitch in heat —Anon

Pursuing him like a nemesis, like an unwanted, embarrassing relative —Donald McCaig

She tails him like the F.B.I. —Martha Gellhorn and Virginia Cowles, *Love Goes to Press* *Gellhorn and Cowles' only play revived by the Mint Theater in June 2012.*

Slivered after him like mercury —Wilfrid Sheed

Sniff out like a terrier smells a rat —Basil Blackwell

Tagging along [behind character in story], like an anthropologist tags along behind his Indian —Deborah Eisenberg

Trailing ... like a cape before a bull —Lawrence Durrell

Trotting behind like a penny dog —Rita Mae Brown

Will run him down like a greyhound catching a hare —George Garrett

Would be on my back like a bad case of sunburn —Shelby Hearon

❧ PUZZLEMENT

See: BEWILDERMENT

❧ QUESTIONS AND ANSWERS

See Also: PROBLEMS AND SOLUTIONS

Answered me as gravely as if I had asked the meaning of life —Borden Deal

Answered slow, like men who wouldn't waste anything, not even language —Carl Sandburg

Answered with the finality of a bank vault door —Dick Francis

The answer was in front of him ... like a gift-wrapped package waiting to be opened —Andrew Kaplan

Asked, like a man who didn't want to know —James Crumley

Beat back questions like a ball hitting a brick wall —Anon

A correct answer is like an affectionate kiss —Johann Wolfgang von Goethe

Curiosity ... unrolls its question mark like a new wave on the shore —John Ashberry

Deflected answers like a freight train cutting through the Mississippi Delta —Les Payne on William Rehnquist's responses to questions about his civil rights background, *Newsday,* August 3, 1986

Her questions sounded unfelt as though she were speaking from a deep well of hypnosis —Geoffrey Wolff

His answers trickled through my head, like water through a sieve —Lewis Carroll

It was like the question asked by Tennyson about the flowers in the crannied wall —Saul Bellow

One by one, neatly, like index cards out of a machine, the little questions dropped —Roald Dahl

Pursued [a question] like an inquisitor in a torture chamber who was hungry, and eager to get the signed statement before his supper —Christopher Isherwood

The question falls ... like a bird from the sky —Aharon Megged

The question hangs like music in my thoughts —W. P. Kinsella

The question immediately bursts in the sky like a shower of fireworks —Isaiah Berlin, June 1980

Question [directly] ... like a gun —Lael Tucker Wertenbaker

Questions bobbed in her mind like corks on a turbulent sea —Paige Mitchell

Questions like ordered bricks —Mary Hedin

Questions like water gushed ceaselessly —Dame Edith Sitwell

Unpleasant and unanswerable questions flopping around in his head like a bat that had mistakenly flow in through the living room window —Laurie Colwin

Was like a psychiatrist, asking questions which really were not those questions at all, but deeper ones —Elizabeth Taylor

Worried her questions like a dog does a bone —Donald MacKenzie

You start a question and it's like starting a stone. You sit quietly on the top of a hill, and away the stone goes, starting others —Robert Louis Stevenson

❧ RAIN

See Also: WEATHER

As if a mask had been peeled off, the rain ended —Tim O'Brien

Big soft drops splash on people's hands and cheeks; immense warm drops like melted stars —Katherine Mansfield

Drizzle whispered upon Joseph's umbrella like muffled applause —Rick Borsten

Droplets fired upon our windows like bullets of tin —Ira Wood

The drops like bugs stuck on the pane —F. D. Reeve

A dull rain, like a tap left running —Jean Thompson

Fall rain as fine as spray from an atomizer —Harvey Swados

Felt the rain like cold tears on his hot face —James Crumley

The good rain, like a bad preacher, does not know when to leave off —Ralph Waldo Emerson

The gray rain continued to fall, stubbornly and insensibly, like a frozen madness —Amos Oz

Hiss in the gutter [the rain] like a thousand coiled snakes —T. Coraghessan Boyle

It seemed as if the lowering clouds, heavy with water had burst, emptying upon the earth … melting it like sugar —Guy de Maupassant

It was in fact now raining, and the fat drops splattered on the window like tears —Helen Simonson, *Major Pettigrew's Last Stand*

Light rain fell around the big house and its trees like a veil —John McCahern

Light through which the slowing rain ran stitches like a sewing machine gone mad —Leslie A. Fiedler

The rain as thick as oil on the windows —Albert Camus

The rain beat down on Paris in endless steady sheets, straight down, like waterfalls —Sylvia Berkman

A nice example of a simile to introduce a story and set the mood.

Rain … beating down like a stampede, of horses —Paige Mitchell

The rain bites like a whip across a prisoner's back —Anne Morrow Lindberg

The rain came down like glass bead curtains —Joyce Cary

The rain came like an explosion in a glass factory —T. Coraghessan Boyle

The rain came sifting through the air, and settled like bloom on the fields —Mary Lavin

Another rain simile to set a fictional scene, this one for Lavin's story Brigid.

The rain came slowly and doggedly down, as if it had not even the spirit to pour —Charles Dickens

Rain comes down like the sky falling in skeins and yarny drifts —Marge Piercy

Raindrops … as warm as the tears of a child not yet consoled —Marguerite Yourcenar

Rain drops down like worms from the trees —Anne Sexton

Raindrops hitting like bullets —Joyce Carol Oates

Raindrops, plump as Malaga grapes —Paul Kuttner

Raindrops pock the surface like a plague —T. Coraghessan Boyle

Raindrops sparkled like diamonds falling through sunshine —Rita Mae Brown

Raindrops tapped at our backs like insinuating fingers —T. Coraghessan Boyle

Raindrops that whined like bullets —Kenzaburo Oe

Rained like a cow pissing on a flat rock —American colloquialism

Rain falling just past the end of his nose like a curtain —Thomas McGuane

Rain … fell like a silver veil from the dim grey sky —Mazo de la Roche

Rain … fell like iron swords out of the black sky —Paul Theroux

Rain … flowing in streaked silver patterns down the panes of the window nearby, like tears on the smooth shining face of a child —Bill Pronzini

Rain … flying down like silver needles —Frank Swinnerton

Rain glimmered like silver threads being spun from the mist —Paige Mitchell

Rain … gold as the planet system —Dame Edith Sitwell

Rain hammering at the eaves like fists —Helen Simonson, *Major Pettigrew's Last Stand*

Rain hit the roof like pennies from heaven —T. Coraghessan Boyle

Rain keeps falling like a curse —Amos Oz

Rain knocked at the windows like a smirking voyeur —T. Coraghessan Boyle

Rain … like a river falling out of the sky —Donald Seaman

Rain … like a deluge from heaven —W. Somerset Maugham

Rain, like dark-ruled lines on paper —Stephen Longstreet

The rain like pitchforks fell —Delmore Schwartz

Rain plastered the land till it was shining like hammered lead —Ted Hughes

Rain poured down like a waterfall —Jilly Cooper

Rain ran from the roof like a sea —Irving Feldman

Rain … rattling hard first on one side and then on the other like someone nailing down a case —Saul Bellow

Rains drip like the slow beat of time —Dame Edith Sitwell

Rain sheeting down like a giant waterfall —Frank Swinnerton

The rains of summer's end were very like tears, falling warm and gradually chilling where they fell —Lael Wertenbaker

Rain, so loud, like horses weeing —F. Scott Fitzgerald

Rainstorms that blacken like a headache —Amy Clampitt

The rain struck you so hard that it was like a warm gag in your mouth —Louis-Ferdinand Celine

The rain stung like whips, and from underfoot the mud oozed up over shoes and ankles like a live thing —Hugh Walpole

Rain … swept the deck in angry gusts, like a nagging woman who cannot leave a subject alone —W. Somerset Maugham

Rain thudded against the car like rotten fruit —Jean Thompson

The rain was blowing down the window glass like silk —Paul Horgan

Showers … drifting like scarves of gauze across the landscape —Jules Romains

A slanted sheet of rain swept like a scythe across Placid Cove Trailer Park —John Lutz

The scene being set with this simile is for a mystery story entitled "Ride the Lightning."

The sound of rain seemed … like the repeated attentions of a lover —John Cheever

A squall of rain driven around us in gusts like a wet veil —Erich Maria Remarque

Through the mist it was as if fine threads of rain were being teased down slowly —John McGahern

Torrents of rain streamed through the darkness, like incessant floods of tears which threatened to devour the earth and drown it in a deluge of unquenchable grief —Vladimir G. Korolenko

The [rain] water was loud as a crowd hissing —Susan Minot

When it rains, there's a wonderful lush wooden wetness in the air, and you feel as refreshed as if you were the earth itself, drinking in the water —Christopher Isherwood

The wind-blown rain was smeared like jam on the glass [of the window] —Jonathan Valin

❦ RANTING

See: ROARS

❦ RAPIDITY

See: SPEED

❦ RARITY

See Also: ORIGINALITY

Exclusive as a mail box —Raymond Chandler

He's unusual all right … like the last of the orange flamingos —Saul Bellow

A miracle as great as art —Charles Bukowski

And what is so rare as a day in June —James Russell Lowell

One of Lowell's most memorable lines!

(To think of nothing benign to memorize is as) rare as feeling no personal blemish —W. H. Auden

Rare as a man without self-pity —Stephen Vincent Benét

Rare and wonderful feeling, like the first moments of love —George Garrett

Rare as a black swan —Anon

This probably evolved from "Rare to be found as black swans," featured in Daniel Rogers' seventeenth century Matrimonial Honours.

Rare as a Cockney accent at Eton —Anon

Rare as an Emperor moth —Lawrence Durrell

Rare as a New York City subway train without graffiti —Elyse Sommer

Rare as a nine dollar bill —Anon

Rare as a politician on the stump who doesn't make promises —Anon

A partner to this simile: "Rare as a politician who lives up to his campaign promises."

Rare as a well-spent life —Anon

(A lucky man is) rare as a white crow —Juvenal

Rare as a winter swallow —Honoré de Balzac

Rare as discretion in a gossip —Anon

Rare as humility in a grizzly bear —Julian Ralph

(Movies like Paul Mayersberg's *Captive* are as) rare as peacocks' teeth —Vincent Canby, *New York Times*, April 3, 1987

Rare as rocking horse manure —Anon

Rare as snow in July —Anon

Another modern simile which can be traced to an earlier form: "like snow at Midsummer, exceeding rare"

Rare in life as black lightning on a blue sky —Fitz-Greene Halleck

(The liberal "effete snobs" that Spiro T. Agnew railed against) are as rare today as Republicans on the welfare rolls —Barbara Ehrenreich

Scarce as below par golf scores —Anon

Scarce as fat men in a long-distance marathon —Anon

Scarce as a six figure advance for a first novel by an unknown author —Elyse Sommer

(Money … was as) scarce as frogs' teeth, crabs' tails or eunuchs' whiskers —Pat Barr

Barr's colorful simile refers to the scarcity of money in Korea when the heroine of her book Curious Life For a Lady *was there during the latter part of the nineteenth century.*

Scarce as ice cream vendors on a snowy day in January —Anon

The comparative twists on this are endless; for example: "Scarce as lemonade stands in the desert," "Scarce as women in fur coats in ninety degree weather."

Scarce as low-cost, high profit ideas for an untapped market —Anon

Scarce as squirrels at a busy city street crossing —Elyse Sommer

Scarce as the buffalo that once roamed the prairie —Enid Nemy, *New York Times,* July 6, 1986

Nemy likened buffalo scarcity to newsy letters.

Scarce as the cardinal virtues —Ross Macdonald

Scarce as two dollar gourmet lunches —Anon

(One of the kindest-natured persons that I ever knew on this earth, where kind people are) as rare as black eagles or red deer —Ouida

☘ RASHNESS
See: SPEED

☘ READERS/READING
See Also: BOOKS

Deprive him [the habitual reader] of printed matter and he grows nervous, moody and restless; then, like the alcoholic bereft of brandy who will drink shellac or methylated spirit, he will make do with the advertisements of a paper five years old; he will make do with a telephone directory —W. Somerset Maugham

A person who cannot read is something like a blind man walking through a pleasant meadow, where there are flowers and fruit trees; there are many pleasant things and many wise and good things printed in books, but we cannot get them unless we read —Timothy Dwight

Reading is to the mind what exercise is to the body —Sir Richard Steele

The reading of detective stories is an addiction like tobacco or alcohol —W. H. Auden

Reading that is only whimful and desultory amounts to a kind of cultural vagrancy. It neither wets nor fortifies the mind. It merely distracts and tires it like traffic noises on an overcrowded street —John Mason Brown

Reading the same book over and over again is a mechanical exercise like the Tibetan turning of a prayer-wheel —Clifton Fadiman

Reads like some people wrestle; she gets involved —François Camoin

☘ READINESS
See: PREPAREDNESS

☘ REALIZATION
See Also: TRUTH

Awareness of failure plagued at him like a sword, twisting in his consciousness cruelly as though it had been lying in wait to murder his self-respect —Noel Coward

Began to see herself from the outside, as if she was a moving target in someone else's binoculars —Margaret Atwood

Flash of insight as pitiless as the late-autumn light —Sharon Sheehe Stark

Horror … burst upon him like an electric storm that throws a vivid light into the darkest shadow —Mazo de la Roche

It [realization] came to her slowly as a negative being developed —Elizabeth Spence

Knowledge penetrated my consciousness like a red-hot knife —Stefan Zweig

Light burst on me as if a window of my memory had been suddenly flung open on a street in the city —Joseph Conrad

Like a lover or lecher, the awareness came to her at night. Every perception rejoices in itself like a fire catching fire through itself —Delmore Schwartz

Like French women who can tell if a bottle of Cognac has been opened in the next room, Guido could tell what was happening at home as soon as he put his key in the lock —Laurie Colwin

Realization ... dawned ... like the sunrise —Donald Seaman

Realization came ... like a fist knocking the wind out of her —David Leavitt

Realization grips them like a seizure —T. Coraghessan Boyle

The realization ... made the nape of my neck feel like I'd just applied an ice pack —Sue Grafton

Saw as one sees a landscape in a flash of lightning —Virginia Woolf

Saw it like a thunderbolt —Clifford Odets

See it all like a chart unrolled —John Greenleaf Whittier

Suddenly, as if a wet sheet had been thrown over her, the truth of the matter strikes her —T. Coraghessan Boyle

The knowledge sank like a plummet —Jean Stafford

A thousand things ... suddenly added up like a column of figures in her mind —William Humphrey

(Trifles ... like a spark falling upon tinder, can) throw a flame of light into the abyss of a mind —Stefan Zweig

The truth flared in his head like a marron —Miles Gibson

The truth popped out like a jack-in-the-box —George Garrett

Trying to find it [self-knowledge] in the bosom of a Mississippi family was like trying to find some object lost in a gigantic attic, when you really didn't know what you were looking for —Elizabeth Spencer

An uncomfortable truth had come to settle like a shroud over the ... investigation —Doug Feiden

The comparison in Feiden's novel, The $10,000,000 Getaway, *pertains to the investigation of a Lufthansa airline robbery.*

Understanding fell across me like a velvet curtain —Russell Banks

❧ REALNESS/UNREALNESS

Artificial like a piece of water in a French garden —W. Somerset Maugham

Abstract and decorative as a snowstorm in a glass paperweight —George Garrett

Artificial as a false mustache —Dorothea Straus

Blurred, unreal, like a picture in the newspaper —Katherine Mansfield

Distorted as the view through the wrong end of a telescope —Anon

False as waxworks —Karl Shapiro

(Sometimes I) feel like a figment of my own imagination —Lily Tomlin

Genuine as rain —J. B. Priestly

Had a squinty close view of the truth like a jeweler studying facets and flaws, like a man at a microscope —George Garrett

He could block out reality as easily as exposing a roll of film —Jonathan Kellerman

Real and insistent as a wound in one's body —Milovan Djilas

(The pain returned) real as a toothache —John Braine

Real as hunger —Anon

Real as several grain sacks thrown on top of each other —Flannery O'Connor

Real as the passing of time —Anon

(You and I are as) real at least as the people upstairs —James Merrill

Reality met him like a swung shovel —Sharon Sheehe Stark

(The room seemed as) unreal as a stage set —William McIlvanney

Real, like a punch on the nose —Stephen Longstreet

Unreal, as ghostly as the brushing of a leaf against his face —Katherine Anne Porter

Unreal as the emptiness of the air —Leonid Andreyev

Unreal, like a poorly-played drama on the stage —Ben Ames Williams

Unreal like mid-summer sunshine remembered at Christmas —Elizabeth Bowen

❧ REAPPEARANCE

Always came back to me like a dog to his kennel —Nathan Shaham

(The day) began all over again, like a toothache, in her memory —Frank Swinnerton

(Kisses, can you) come back like ghosts —Carl Sandburg

Sandburg used this simile to open and close a poem, as well as for its title. In between are several additional similes to illustrate that love does come to an end to be put away "like a clock," "like a violin," or "like a summer day near fall time."

Double back like a fox eluding his pursuing hounds —Robert Traver

Keeps cropping up, like toadstools after a flood —Jonathan Kellerman

Like a repentant lover, I returned to that previous way of life —John Rechy

Recur like wind from a returning storm —Hallie Burnett

(Questions about her parentage) recurred like malaria —Rita Mae Brown

Recurring like a motif in music —G. K. Chesterton

(They were) returning again, like birds to their roosts —Graham Swift

Return like a bad penny —Anon

Return like a homing pigeon —Anon

Rolled like a stone back to where he'd started —Martin Cruz Smith

Turn up like an old arrest record —Marge Piercy

Turn up like a single boot after I finally threw the other away —Marge Piercy

[A deep-seated flaw] would surface like an aching wisdom tooth —James Lee Burke

❧ REASON
See: SENSE

❧ RECOLLECTION
See: MEMORY

❧ RED
See Also: BLUSHES, CHEEKS, COLORS, HAIR, LIPS, MOUTH

Red as a match tip —James Reiss

(Tongue) red as a pomegranate —Miles Gibson

Red as a radish —Anon

Red as a robin's breast —Anon

Red as a rooster's comb —Dorothy Canfield

The simile from Canfield's Sex Education describes a face turned red with embarrassment.

Red as a strong man's heart —Robert Tristram Coffin

The objects being compared are Vermont barns.

(Lips) red as a sun rising on the Atlantic and setting on the Pacific —Mary Morris

Red as a wound —Jon Silkin

[A cloak] red as blood —William Shakespeare, *Henry VI, Part II*

Similes linking the color red with blood abound throughout literature as well as everyday speech.

(Hair) red as chili powder —Saul Bellow

Red as fire —William Shakespeare, *Julius Caesar*

(Lips) red as hell —Dame Edith Sitwell

(Fingernails) red as satin ribbons —Diane Ackerman

[Leather seats of a showy car] red as spilt blood —Saul Bellow

Red like poppies —Charlotte Brontë

[Plush and] red, like the inside of a blood vessel —Simon Mawer, *The Glass Room*

Thin streaks of red, like veins in marble showed on his chalky teeth —Wright Morris

Your colour, I warrant you, is as red as any rose. —William Shakespeare, *Henry IV*

❧ REDUCTION

See: DECREASE, DISAPPEARENCE

❧ REFLECTION

See: THOUGHT

❧ REFORM

See: CHANGE

❧ REGRET

See Also: CONSCIENCE

Remorse is as the heart in which it grows —Samuel Taylor Coleridge

Coleridge's poem "Remorse" continues as follows: "If that be gentle, it drops balmy dews of true repentance; but if proud and gloomy, it is the poison tree, that pierces to the inmost."

Repentance, like the sea, is always open to the ventures —Shimoni Yalkut

Repentance, without amendment, is like continually pumping without mending the leak —Lewis W. Dilwyn

Repentance follows crime ... as changes follow time —Percy Bysshe Shelley

Regret is like a mountain-top from which we survey our dead life, a mountaintop on which we pause and ponder, and very often looking into the twilight we ask ourselves whether it would be well to send a letter or some token —George Moore

The pang of regret, sharp as a sword thrust —L. P. Hartley

Regret is like tears seeping through closed eyelids —Galway Kinnell

(When I fall) let me fall without regret like a leaf —Wendell Berry

Remorseless as an alarm clock —Anon

❧ REGULARITY/IRREGULARITY

Balance as a tail balances a kite —Anon

Balanced as the scales of justice —Anon

[A cat's purring] intermittent as a walkie-talkie —Lorrie Moore

Irregular as French verbs —Anon

Random, like love's choices —Patricia Hampl

Regular as a clock —Slogan for Serutan laxative, Healthaids, Inc.

Regular as a heartbeat —Mary Hedin

Regular as a metronome —Edward Hoagland

Regular as a motor boat —Lee Smith

A more specific variation: "regular as the chug-chug of a motor boat"

Regular as sun and tide —Wallace Stegner

Regular as the moon makes the tides —Henry James

Rhythmic as water —Amy Hempel

In Hempel's story "Beg, Sl Tog, Inc, Cont, Rep," it's the sliding knitting needles that are likened to water.

Scattered like applause during a bad set —Anon

Steadily as a shell secretes its beating leagues of monotone —Hart Crane

Symmetrical as a doily —Betsy Wade, *New York Times,* May 2, 1986

The descriptive frame of reference is a tree.

♣ REJECTION

See Also: ABANDONMENT

Cast away [anger] like spoiled milk —Marge Piercy

Discarded like outmoded customs —Elyse Sommer

Discarded (me) like yesterday's underpants —Sue Grafton

Dropped ... like a dead fish —T. Glen Coughlin

Dropped [from a list] ... like a hot rivet —Loren D. Estleman

He shook them [young women] off his back like a young stallion shaking off an unskilled rider —Russell Banks

Keep at a distance, like someone with an infectious disease —Anon

There are numerous twists on this, some referring to specific diseases (usually whatever is currently most feared) and like so many phrases that have been mainstreamed into our language, this probably owes its inspiration to Shakespeare's "barred, like one infectious."

Push her away like a clinging dog —Daphne du Maurrier

Push me aside like a kitchen chair —Philip Levine

Put (such thoughts) aside like chewed-up grape skins —Bertolt Brecht

Rejected [bad news] ... like a transplanted organ —Pat Conroy

Rejected [praise] like counterfeit money —William McIlvanney

Shoved aside like a row boat nosed away by a tanker —Mary Gordon

Shuck him off, ... hollow him from our lives like the pit from a peach —Claire Messud, *The Last Life*

Shun him like the plague —Charles Dickens

Some men, like spaniels, will only fawn the more when repulsed, but will pay little heed to a friendly caress —Abd-el-Kader

Spurn my passion like a worm —Jean Racine

Swept her aside as if she were a cobweb —Susan Kelly

They just dropped me ... like a bag of potatoes —Njabulo Ndebele

Threw aside everything ... like a contemptible burden —Heinrich Böll

[A husband caught between his wife and former girlfriend] You are talking about me like I'm a pair of shoes. —Gina Gionfriddo. *Rapture, Blister, Burn*

♣ RELATIONSHIP

See Also: MARIAGE; MEN AND WOMEN; PARENTHOOD; PEOPLE, INTERACTION

Charted his moods like a cartographer —Pat Conroy

Conroy's simile from The Great Santini *refers to the main character's understanding of and adjustment to is his father's temperament.*

Dislike shimmers between them like a heat haze —David Nicholls, *One Day*

Families are a kind of closed system; like locked trunks, they are hard to penetrate from the outside —Daphne Merkin

Families are like wine. You get the old vintage that goes right off: goes weak as colored water or old scent —Julia O'Faolain

A family, if it is large and well-connected, is like a religion —Paul Theroux

In the novel Picture Palace *from which this is taken, the author follows up the simile with the following explanation: "It serves the same purpose —to bewitch the believer with joy and offer him salvation; it consoles, it enchants, it purifies."*

Getting to know someone is like opening a safe: you have to learn the unique combination of numbers —Delmore Schwartz

Schwartz followed this entry into his journal with: "No, this is not really true."

Her life was hung upon this relationship, like the cloth of a tent that would collapse into loose folds without the central post that supported it —Tennessee Williams

Human relations just aren't fixed in their orbits like the planets —they're more like galaxies, changing all the time, exploding into light for years, then dying away —May Sarton

The idea of a step-father is like a substitute host on a talk show —Bobbie Ann Mason

In the beginning of a relationship, if you're lucky enough to find wit at the right moments, it's like getting a cab in the rain —Steve Post, WNYC/FM, December 22, 1986

(There were Ben and his father, eye to eye, as) intimate as lovers —Pat Conroy

I was there for you, like an Eye-Beam … any other beam would do —John Updike

Know each other's thoughts. Without words, as if traveling on connected bloodstreams —Mary Hedin

Know each other, crack and flaw, like two irregular stones that fit together —Adrienne Rich

Like the slowly tumbling arabesque of little cloud shapes drifting across the sand cliffs on a summer wind, neither [of two close sisters] was anything without the other —Wilbur Daniel Steele

Never got on … like a couple of dogs not liking each other's smells —Frank Swinnerton

Relationship … fragile like spindly bridges —David Leavitt, *New York Times Book Review,*1986

The relationship bumps along like a car with three tires —Ira Wood

Relationship … like two engines running at variance —D.H. Lawrence

The relationship waxed, billowed like scenery on the breeze —John Ashberry

She is eighteen years younger, a gap that incited him once but that, now he is seventy, separates them like a lake —Tom Rachman, *The Imperfectionists*

Spread herself out like a cloak for the king to walk on —Suzi Gablik, *New York Times Book Review,* 1986

This simile is used to explain the relationship between the author of My Life with Chagall *and the artist.*

The string between you wore out … like old elastic —Tess Slesinger

The sweet sorrow of loving a parent is as pure as the taste of a sourball when you are five —Norman Mailer

Their (a mother and daughter) connection had built-in tension and resiliency. Like the coiled telephone cord through which they communicated —Ellen Goodman

Their relationship had developed a gravitational pull, slow but insistent, as a planet pulls home a failing satellite —Helen Simonson, *Major Pettigrew's Last Stand*

There was room for improvement [in relationship between two men] —a sort of gap, like the Grand Canyon —J. F. Powers

Torn [between warring parents] like a plot of land they both wanted to lay claim to —Ann Jasperson

Treated her like a twenty-carat diamond —Rita Mae Brown

Understand one another like thieves at a fair —Anatole France

(After half an hour) we were as familiar with one another as if we had unbossomed our whole life histories —Erich Maria Remarque

You and Lawrence, you're like—Gibraltar —Lionel Shriver, *The Post-Birthday World*

❧ RELENTLESSNESS
See: PERSISTENCE

❧ RELIABILITY/UNRELIABILITY

See Also: FIRMNESS, STEADINESS

(I found the almond trees as) dependable as the swallows of Capistrano, announcing another spring —Wallace Stegner

As reliable as the day following the night —Dorothea Straus

[A collection of art works] as spotty as a Dalmatian and not half as beautiful —Manuela Hoelterhoff, on the new Wallace wing at the Metropolitan Museum of Art, *Wall Street Journal,* March 17, 1987

Consistent and productive as machines —Gay Gaer Luce

Dealing with Owen Roe was like walking across a bog. You never knew when the ground might give way under your feet —Julia O'Faolain

Dependable as a floating crap game —Harry Prince

Dependable as clockwork —Anon

Dependable as daylight —Beryl Markham

A duty dodged is like a debt unpaid; it is only deferred, and we must come back and settle the account at last —Joseph Fort Newton

Duty without responsibility is like pomp without power —Edward, Duke of Windsor

Fickle as a changeful dream —Sir Walter Scott

It [buying a house] was like joining a church because it committed me to spending every weekend I could get … to working on the place —George V. Higgins

(You've got) no more responsibility than a one-eyed jackrabbit —Elmer Kelton

Reliability's like a string we can only see the middle of —William McFee

(About as) reliable as a Pravda editorial —Joseph Wambaugh

Reliable as a salary —Frank R. Stockton

Reliable as crystal balls, goat innards, and prayer —Harold Adams

Reliable as he was eccentric —Mark Twain

Reliable as reading tea leaves or the bumps on one's head —Peter J. Bonacich

Responsibility rested upon him as lightly as the freckles on his nose —Alice Caldwell Hegan

Solid as tombstones —Helen Hudson

Wore, like a garment, an air of wholesome reliability —Mazo de la Roche

Would always be there … like some familiar landmark —Barbara Pym

❧ RELIEF

See: EMOTIONS

❧ RELIGION

See Also: BELIEFS

As men's prayers are a disease of the will, so are their creeds a disease of the intellect —Ralph Waldo Emerson

As religious as any man who prays daily and hangs a rabbit's foot on his windshield —Harry Prince

Beautiful women without religion are like flowers without perfume —Heinrich Heine

Catholicism's a little too much like the gold standard: a fixed weight of piety translatable into a fixed exchange rate of grace —Michael M. Thomas

The Christian is like the ripening corn; the riper he grows, the more lowly he bends his head —Thomas Guthrie

Christianity is like electricity. It cannot enter a person unless it can pass through —Bishop Richard C. Raines

The church is a sort of hospital for men's souls, and as full of quackery as the hospitals for those bodies —Henry David Thoreau

A consistently godless world is like a picture without perspective —Franz Werfel

Faith ... a stiffening process, a sort of mental starch, which ought to be applied as sparingly as possible —E. M. Forster

Faith is like love: it cannot be forced —Arthur Schopenhauer

Faith without works is like a bird without wings —J. Beaumont

Folded into his religion like a razor into its case —Anon

God's like a kid with too many toys to take care of —Sharon Sheehe Stark

People are born churchy or unchurchy, just as they are born with a tendency to arteriosclerosis, cancer or consumption —Anatole France

In religion, as in friendship, they who profess most are the least sincere —Richard Brinsley Sheridan

In religion as in politics it so happens that we have less charity for those who believe half our creed than for those who deny the whole of it —Charles Caleb Colton

Living without faith is like driving in a fog —Anon

The majority takes the creed [Calvinism] as a horse takes his collar; it slips by his ears, over his neck, he hardly knows how, but he finds himself in harness and jogs along as his fathers and forefathers before him —Oliver Wendell Holmes

A man who writes of himself without speaking of God is like one who identifies himself without giving his address —Ben Hecht

Men's anger about religion is as if two men should quarrel for a lady they neither of them care for —Marquis of Halifax

Our faith ... runs as fast as feeling to embrace —William Alfred

Our faith is too often like the mercury in the weather-glass; it gets up high in fine weather; in rough weather it sinks proportionally low —Anon

Piety, like aristocracy, has its nobility —Johann Wolfgang von Goethe

Prayed like an orphan —Wendell Berry

Prayer is a force as real as terrestrial gravity —Alexis Carrel

Priestly mannerisms clung to him like the smell of candle-wax and incense —Peter Kemp

Religion is comparable to a childhood neurosis —Sigmund Freud

Religion is like love; it plays the devil with clear thinking —Rose Macaulay

Religion is like the breath of heaven; if it goes abroad in the open air, it scatters and dissolves —Jeremy Taylor

Religion, like water, may be free, but when they pipe it to you, you've got to help pay for the piping. And the piper —Muriel Spark

Religious as a lizard on a rock —Anon

Religious sense is like an esthetic sense. You're born with it or you aren't —P. D. James, *New York Times,* October 5, 1986,

Sects and creeds of religion, are like pocket compasses, good enough to point you in the direction, but the nearer the pole you get the worse they work —Josh Billings

In Billings' phonetic dialect: "Ssekts and creeds of religion are like pocket compesses, good enuff tu point you inte the right direction, but the nearer the pole yu git."

She fought off God like an unwelcome suitor —Nancy Evans about Emily Dickenson, *First Editions*/WNYC, February 18, 1987

Some Christians are like soiled bank notes: while we acknowledge their value we wish them changed —William Lewis

Sometimes the curse of God comes like the caress of a woman's hand, and sometimes His blessing comes like a knife in the flesh —Amos Oz

The soul united to God is like a leaf united to the tree —Ignazio Silone

They treated their God like a desk clerk with whom they lodged requests and complaints —Helen Hudson

The priest who makes this "similistic" observation in Hudson's story, After Cortes, then proceeds to describe the same people's attitude towards himself: "And they behaved as though he, Father Cheney, were a mere funnel into which they poured their banal confessions no so much for penance as for pity."

Without dogma a religion is like a body without skeleton. It can't stand —James G. Huneker

✤ REMEDY

See: PROBLEMS AND SOLUTIONS

✤ REMORSE

See: REGRET

✤ REMOTENESS

See Also: RESERVE

Acting like an absentee landlord who was either unaware of or indifferent to the tenants smashing the windows or breaking up the furniture —Senator William S. Cohen commenting on President Ronald Reagan's leadership during Iran-contra affair, *New York Times*, March 1, 1987

Alienated as Camus —Richard Ford

As far apart as the sound of waves on the shore —John Updike

(Fury) as unpersonal as disease —David Denby

Behaved like a dowager queen at a funeral, acknowledging everyone's politenesses but keeping her own majestic feelings isolated —Judith Martin

Detached [from an excited crowd] as a droplet of oil —Stefan Zweig

Detached [mind from body] … like a kite whose string snaps on a windy day —Julia O'Faolain

Detached, passive, still as a golden lily in a lily-pond —Ellen Glasgow

Distant as an ocean —Reynolds Price

Distant as heart-parted lovers are —Babette Deutsch

(She was as silent and) distant as the moon —Kate Wheeler

Feeling impersonal and fragile as a piece of china waiting on a serving table —F. Scott Fitzgerald

He felt no rage, only a calm and icy distance, as if this man, who had been both a friend and an adviser, was now talking to him on a bad phone line from an ice floe in the Arctic —Helen Simonson, *Major Pettigrew's Last Stand*

He speaks to me as if I were a public monument —Queen Victoria about her prime minister, Gladstone

He was too remote, he was as uncertain for her as a rumor —Cynthia Ozick, *Foreign Bodies*

He won't listen to me—it's like talking to a lump of granite —Gita Sowerby, *Rutherford and Son*

Impassive as an apple —Laurie Colwin

Impassive as a tank —Seamus Heaney

Impersonal as a cyclone —Anon

Impersonal as the justice of God —Victor Hugo

Incurious as a stone —Robert Hass

(Until that minute she had been as) impersonal to me as a doll in a well-stocked toy department —R. V. Cassill

Indifferent as a blizzard —Anon

Remote as the moon —T. Coraghessan Boyle

Like the hermit crab, he ventured out of his shell [of reserved behavior] only on the rarest occasions —A. J. Cronin

Looked disinterested, like a Customs inspector —Julia Whedon

A look of remoteness … like cathedrals, like long gleaming conference tables, like the crackling, hissing recordings of the voices of famous men long dead —John D. MacDonald

An example to illustrate that several distinctly different similes can be effectively linked to a single reference base.

Look through 'em all like windows —Edith Wharton

Maintained a certain self-imposed distance, like high priests from different orders of the same faith —Amor Towles, *Rules of Civility*

Otherworldly like a monk —F. Scott Fitzgerald

Personal as a letter addressed to "Occupant" —Anon

(His father had always been) remote … as a figure in a pageant —Hortense Calisher

Remote as a nightmare —Walter de la Mare

[Sky scrapers] Remote as castles in a fairy tale —Bobbie Ann Mason

(Bomb shelters are as) remote as the covered wagon —Edward R. Murrow in a British broadcast from European front during World War II

Remote, unapproachable, like the expression of an animal that man has forced into sullen submission —Ellen Glasgow

Seemed like a perpetual visitor —Henry Van Dyke

(They get together and tell each other what women are like, but they never listen to find out.) Shut up in their heads like clams —Nancy Price

Stiff and remote, rather like a sleep-walker —Alice Munro

Stolid as ledgers —Julia O'Faolain

(He sat there, heavy and massive, suddenly) sunk back into himself and his drunkenness, like a lonely hill of unassailable melancholy —Erich Maria Remarque

To ask Henrietta was like asking the door knob —Sholem Aleichem

As unreachable as all the landscapes beyond the limits of my eye —John Fowles

(Face) withdrawn as a castle —Nadine Gordimer

❧ RENOWN

See: FAME

❧ REPETITION

See Also: CONTINUITY, DULLNESS

Continue unceasingly like a drip from a leaking faucet —Anon

Iteration, like friction, is likely to generate heat instead of progress —George Eliot

Kept on repeating the words like a talisman —Edith Wharton

Life as repetitive as the seasons —J. B. Priestly

Like warmed-up cabbage served at each repast the repetition kills the wretch at last —Juvenal

Monotonous … like a tap with a worn-out washer dripping … in a kitchen sink —Gerald Kersh
In Kersh's novel Repetition, *the dripping faucet image is used to describe the voice of a character.*

[Came back to that point often,] niggling at it like a tongue searching out an unfamiliar irregularity in a tooth —Simon Mawer, *The Glass Room*

Recited tirelessly as a language record —Marge Piercy
In Piercy's poem "A Cold and Married War" the narrator is reciting her sins and errors.

(Rages … which seemed to) recur in cycles, like menstruation —Ursule Molinaro

(Thought) repeated like a lesson —William H. Gass

Repeated like a rhyme —Amy Lowell

Repeats … like an advertisement in neon —Marge Piercy

Repetitive as hieroglyphs —Derek Walcott

(Disembodied and) repetitive as the sea in a shell —Elizabeth Spencer

The sweep hand (of clock) went around and around like a door-to-door salesman —Raymond Chandler

❧ REPUTATION

As for taking a good man's name from him, you might as well undertake to pull goose-quills from the wings of an angel —Dow Junior

A bad reputation in a woman allures like the signs of heat in a bitch —Aldous Huxley

Huxley's wrote Point Counter Point, *from which this is taken, long before the women's movement raised our consciousness to gender-based characterization.*

Disgraces are like cherries: one draws another —George Herbert

A good name, like good will, is got by many actions and lost by one —Lord Francis Jeffrey

A good reputation is like the cypress; once cut, it never puts forth leaf again —Francesco Guicciardini

His record's as clean as a vestal virgin's —Dialogue from a 1967 movie, *The Deadly Affair*

Honor is like a rocky island without a landing place; once we leave it we can't get it back —Nicolas Boileau

Honor is like the eye, which cannot suffer the least injury without damage; it is [like] a precious stone, the price of which is lessened by the least flaw —Jacques Benigne Boussuet

Honor, like freedom, is a luxury for those with independent incomes —John Braine

Honors trailing away behind him like the tail of a comet —Vita Sackville-West

In scandal, as in robbery, the receiver is always as bad as the thief —Lord Chesterfield

A liar's reputation ... stuck with him like a cocklebur —Carlos Baker

A person's reputation is as fragile and vulnerable as human life itself —Robert Traver

To steal it [a person's honor] is like stealing your soul —William Diehl

❧ RESENTMENT

See: ANGER

❧ RESERVE

See Also: EMOTIONS, PERSONAILTY TRAITS, REMOTENESS

Animated as a department store mannequin —Anon

Apathy dropped from her like a garment —Edna Ferber

As excited as a mortician at a cheap funeral —Raymond Chandler

As much feeling as a sphinx —Maureen Dowd, *New York Times*, 1985

(My father was) born without emotions like some people are born without little fingers —Pat Conroy

Buries her feelings as a dog buries a bone —Anon

Closed himself like a shellfish under attack —Kenzaburo Oe

Detached as a funeral director —Stanley Elkin

Detach oneself [from a situation] like a zip-out lining —Anon

(The sun is as) dispassionate as the hand of a man who greets you with his mind on other things —Beryl Markham

Drew a circle around herself, like the safe zone in a children's game where no pursuers may enter and no prisoners may leave —David Michael Kaplan

(I could) feel the armor, like a steel skin, slipping around me —William Diehl

The habit of reserve was like an iron mold —Ellen Glasgow

Keep them [emotions] tucked away, and only produce them very occasionally, like special little pots of jam, when the people whom I love come to tea —Katherine Mansfield

Like a toothpaste ... gave only a little at a time —Donald Seaman

Lived inside herself as precisely as a walnut in its shell, nothing rattling, nothing wasting —Jessamyn West

(She had withdrawn into herself and) no longer projected anything, like an actor reaching the wings, the character falling like a cape to reveal the person beneath, innocuous —Lynne Sharon Schwartz

Numb as a broomstick —William Alfred

Persons extremely reserved are like old enameled watches, which had painted covers that hindered your seeing what o'clock it was —Horace Walpole

A prudent reserve [about being open with other people] is as necessary as a seeming openness is prudent —Lord Chesterfield

Retreated into himself like a turtle —Carlos Fuentes

She was reserved … like a picture so hung that it can be seen only at a certain angle; an angle known to no one but its possessor —Edith Wharton

Shrunk into herself as though she had been touched by something coarse —Anton Chekhov

Sit inside themselves like honey in a jar and just be —Elizabeth Janeway

Spiritless as corked champagne —James G. Huneker

Taught herself to control feelings … the way an Indian fakir controls pain —Shana Alexander

❧ RESIGNATION
See: MEEKNESS

❧ RESPONSE
See: QUESTIONS AND ANSWERS, WORD(S)

❧ RESPONSIBILITY
See: RELIABILITY/UNRELIABILITY

❧ RESTLESSNESS

Always fidgeting around to go, like a horse in an antbed —Elmer Kelton

Fidgeted as though the skin on her back were as a plucked fowl's in a poulterer's shop window —Virginia Woolf

Fidgety as a child —Richard Wilbur

Fidgety, like a rabbit's nose—or a commuter —Don Marquis

Fitful as a cautery —Diane Ackerman

I'm as restless as a willow in a windstorm, I'm as jumpy as a puppet on a string —Oscar Hammerstein II, opening lines for "It Might as Well Be Spring" from *State Fair*

"It Might as Well Be Spring" is a particularly outstanding example of Hammerstein's mastery of the light-hearted simile. The lyrics also compare a nightingale without a song to a feeling of discontentment, a spider to busyness and a baby on a swing to a feeling of giddiness.

Impatience coating him like the aerosol spray —Francine Prose, *A Changed Man*

As impatient as a wedding dick —American colloquialism

(It is a night like many another with the sky now a bit) impatient for today to be over like a bored salesgirl shifting from foot to stockinged foot —John Ashberry

Pacing up and down like an animal in a cage —Elizabeth Taylor

(Walking around) restless as a big animal in the lowering weather —Elizabeth Spencer

Restless as a rolling stone —Anon

Restless as sharp desire —Arthur C. Benson

Restless as Ulysses —William Makepeace Thackeray

Restless like a man running downhill who cannot keep on his legs unless he runs on, and will inevitably fall if he stops —Arthur Schopenhauer

A restless mind, like a rolling stone, gathers nothing but dirt and mire —John Balguy

Seemed always looking for a place, like one who goes to choose a grave —Stephen Crane

(Settled on the couch) shifting and fluttering like birds in a nest —Peter Meinke

Squirming as though bitten by bugs —Bernard Malamud

Squirm like a country mule hitched beside the railroad track —American colloquialism, attributed to South

Tossed all night like a man running from himself —Paige Mitchell

Wriggling in her place, as if her chair was hot —Frank Swinnerton

❧ RESTRAINT
See: CONFINEMENT, EMOTIONS

❧ RESULTS
See: CAUSE AND EFFECT

❧ RETREAT
See: DISAPPEARANCE, EXITS

❧ RETURN
See: PAST, THE; REAPPEARENCE

❧ REVELRY
See: GAIETY

❧ REVENGE
See Also: BITTERNESS

Revenge is a kind of wild justice, which the more a man's nature runs to, the more ought law to weed it out —Francis Bacon

Revenge is like a boomerang. Although for a time it flies in the direction in which it is hurled, it takes a sudden curve, and, returning, hits your own head the heaviest blow of all —John M. Mason

Revenge is often like biting a dog because the dog bit you —Austin O'Malley

❧ REVOLUTIONS
See: POLITICS

❧ RHETORIC
See: SPEECHMAKING, WORD(S)

❧ RICHES
See Also: ABUNDANCE, FORTUNE/MISFORTUNE, MONEY, SUCCESS/FAILURE

Appearance of wealth will draw wealth to it. As honey draws hungry flies —George Garrett

Have money like sand —Louis MacNeice

His bank account swelled like a puff ball —Christina Stead

Inherited wealth is as certain death to ambition as cocaine is to morality —William K. Vanderbilt

Like our other passions, the desire for riches is more sharpened by their use than by their lack —Michel de Montaigne

A man that keeps riches but doesn't enjoy them is like an ass that carries gold and eats thistles —Thomas Fuller

"Doesn't enjoy them" has been modernized from "and enjoys them not."

More money than the telephone company's got wrong numbers —Sam Hellman

(The auction was attended by collectors with) pockets as deep as wells —Anon

Property, like liberty, thought immune under the Constitution from destruction, is not immune from regulation essential for the common good —Benjamin Cardozo

Prosperity is like a tender mother, but blind, who spoils her children —English proverb

Prosperity is like perfume, it often makes the head ache —Duchess of Newcastle

The rich are driven by wealth as beggars by the itch —W. B. Yeats

Rich as a congressman —Carson McCullers

Riches, like insects, when conceal'd they lie, wait but for wings, and in their season fly —Alexander Pope

Pope spelled the fifth word "conceal'd."

The way to wealth is as plain as the way to market. It depends chiefly on two words, industry and frugality —Benjamin Franklin

Wealth is an engine that can be used for power if you are an engineer; but to be tied to the flywheel of an engine is rather a misfortune —Elbert Hubbard

Wealth is like a viper, which is harmless if a man knows how to take hold of it; but if he does not, it will twine round his hand and bite him —Saint Clement

Wealth like rheumatism falls on the weakest parts —John Ray's *Proverbs*

Worldly riches are like nuts; many clothes are torn in getting them, many a tooth broke in cracking them, but never a belly filled with eating them —Ralph Venning

❧ RICHNESS

Rich as apricots in brandy —Robert D. McFadden

(Vellum) rich as country cream —Oliver Wendell Homes

Rich as memory —Marge Piercy

Rich as velvet brocade —Morris Philipson, describing the rich texture of language in a book, *New York Times Book Review,* April 12, 1987

❧ RIDICULE

See: INSULTS

❧ RIGHTEOUSNESS

See: JUSTICE, VIRTUE

❧ RIGHTNESS

See: CORRECTNESS, TRUENESS/FALSENESS

❧ RISING

See Also: BEARING, STANDING

Everything undulates like water weed —John Berger

Berger's simile appeared in his afterword for the published script of the movie, Nineteen-Nineteen.

Got up clumsily, cautiously, like one standing in a stalled Ferris wheel —Stanley Elkin

Lifts like a starting gate —Daniel Berrigan

Popped up … like a released spring —Elizabeth Spencer

Raising himself in his seat like a panelist answering a question from the audience —Kingsley Amis

Reared like a seal —Erich Maria Remarque

(He felt his cock) rearing up like a kite —Jilly Cooper

Rise (from sleep) like driftwood out of surf —Karl Shapiro

(Smoke that) rises like birds —D. H. Lawrence

Rising gawkily like a tame goose trying to fly —Margaret Laurence

Rising like a north wind —Lawrence Durrell

Rising like a salmon against the bullnecked river —Louis MacNeice

Rising like cakes —Thomas Lux

Rising uncomfortably, like a schoolboy in the presence of a censuring teacher —Jan Kubicki

Rose like bubbles to the surface —Ivo Andric

Rose, like royalty —Edna Ferber

Rose … slowly, like a statue coming reluctantly to life —James Crumley

Rose to go … like a business man who has wasted a valuable twenty minutes on a prospective customer —Christopher Isherwood

Rose up like a flying swan —Stevie Smith

Scrambled back out of his chair like a foot soldier ducking a grenade —Robert Lewis Taylor

Stood [up to go], like Cinderella hearing the stroke of midnight —Eric Knight

Stood up, tawny and twinkling like a mobile in a breeze —Dick Francis

Surfaced like a nugget on sinking soil —Derek Lambert

Surfaced like a trout that had spotted a dragonfly just above the water —Joan Hess

What surfaces in Hess' novel Strangled Prose, *is a character's alter ego.*

♣ RISK

See Also: DANGER

About as risky as selling the farm to buy up blocks of Xerox in the early '60s —John Stravinsky about horse syndicate investments, *Wall Street Journal*, August 15, 1986

The art of gambling is like the art of painting. You've got to know when to stop —Maurice Edelman

Betting on Martin was like betting on an aging horse that lived on sour mash whiskey —Will Weaver

(Politics with a mass of people is as) chancy and fickle as a whore's heart —Robert Traver

Chancy as trying to catch a fish in the open hand —Elizabeth Hardwick

It [the need to risk] was like statistics or gambling; you had to compute probabilities. And there was always the unforeseen, the little thing you overlooked that would catch you up in the end —Mary McCarthy

Precarious as wheat farming —Larry McMurtry

The profession McMurtry is likening to wheat farming is film making. He sticks with the image as follows: "He might raise a great crop of films … then watch them all wither in the theater."

Risky … It's like playing with a chemistry set without reading the directions —Vincent Canby, *New York Times,* January 22, 1986

The risky activity described is movie making by the inexperienced.

To remove the element of risk is like playing cards with a stacked deck —Stephen Gillers, *New York Times*, November 23, 1986

Gillers, a law professor used this simile to discuss the expose of people in the financial world who had been taking the risk out of arbitrage by dealing on specially garnered or "insider" information.

♣ RIVERS

See: PONDS, RIVERS, AND STREAMS

♣ ROAD SCENES

See Also: NOISE, VEHICLES

The cars come down them [London streets] like rats —V. S. Pritchett

Cars nestled around the place like puppies feeding off a giant tit —Dan Wakefield

Cars … run along together [on highway] like sticks on a stream —John Updike

Cars were flashing by [on highway] like toucans, bright red, hot pink and high yellow —Hortense Calisher

A dirt road that ran like string through some nearby woods —Wilfrid Sheed

The divided road looked like a striped gray snake curving across the brown landscape —A. E. Maxwell

Far off the highway … lone lights signaled like boats anchored far at sea —Louise Erdrich

Gradually the landscape on either side of the road became like an embrace —Susan Engberg

Grunting taxicabs … wallowing yellowy in the bright sun like panting porkers —Harvey Swados

The headlights of the cars in the deepening dusk were like a continuous stream of tracer-bullets aimed at anyone with temerity enough to cross their trajectory —Cornell Woolrich

The highway shimmers like a polished stove top —Mary Hedin

The interstate highway was like the ocean. It seemed to go on forever and was a similar color. Mirages of heat were shining in the distance like whitecaps —Bobbie Ann Mason

The lighted road seemed to shift like snow —Martin Cruz Smith

The motorway opened out before them like a black river, roaring —MacDonald Harris

The road, black as a ravine —Helen Hudson

The road dipped and rippled like a ribbon —Phyllis Naylor

The road lay straight as a spear —Terry Bisson

The road like a cat flattening its ears went into a straightaway —John Updike

Roads that never stopped … but looped and turned with exquisite abandon, like a ball of yarn given infinite slack —Sharon Sheehe Stark

Road that looked as smooth as a tablecloth —Wallace Stegner

The road was tree-lined, the oaks arching over the roadway from either embankment like a canopy —Jonathan Valin

The road wound like a twisted snake —Stephen Vincent Benét

Saw the train pulled like a string of black beads over the horizon —Louise Erdrich

The searchlights [of cars on the highway] coursed ahead like elongated greyhounds —Erich Maria Remarque

The sound of the traffic is as faint as the roaring of a shell —John Cheever

Steely [railway] tracks … like clean pen strokes —Dorothy Canfield

Traffic moved like flies through a sieve —Tom Robbins

ROARS

See Also: SCREAMS

Ranting like a mad prophet —Amos Oz

Roar as loud as a howitzer —Norman Mailer

(The tiger) roaring like the sea —Dame Edith Sitwell

Roar like a jetport —T. Coraghessan Boyle

Roared like a tiger —Eudora Welty

Roar [of laughter] … like a tractor backfiring —Raymond Chandler

Roar like a winter breeze —Cole Porter, from "I've Come to Wive It Wealthily in Padua" from the musical *Kiss Me Kate*, an adaptation of Shakespeare's *Taming of the Shrew*

Roars like a rhino (as she comes and comes) —Carolyn Kizer

We roar all like bears —The Holy Bible/Isaiah

A whoop like Yale making a touchdown against Princeton —Raymond Chandler

ROBBERY

See: DISHONESTY

ROCKING AND ROLLING

See Also: MOVEMENT(S), UNSTEADINESS, VIBRATION

Bobbed like a duck —F. van Wyck Mason

Bobbed like a ten-cent toy —John Updike

Like the nickel pickles and cigar, the ten-cent toy is an endangered species, but fond remembrances are likely to have comparisons like this show up for a bit longer.

Bobbing like milkweed —W. D. Snodgrass

Bobbing up and down like a barometer on an April morning —Clifford Mills

Bobbing up and down … like an apple in a bowl of toddy —Edgar Allan Poe

[Stomach from laughing hard] bounced like a cat in a sack —Gerald Kersh

Bounce … like a basketball —Raymond Chandler

Bounces like an India-rubber ball —G. K. Chesterton

(I was) bouncing around (in my seat) like a pellet of quicksilver in a nervous man's palm —Dashiell Hammett

(Testicles) bouncing ... like peas in a colander —Richard Ford

The bus rocked like a cradle —Carson McCullers

Rocking back and forth like Jews praying —Irwin Shaw

(Franklin stood) rocking from side to side like a man on the deck of a ship in an angry sea —Wilbur Daniel Steele

Roll about ... like a pea —Frank Swinnerton

Rolled down the hills like marbles —Boris Pasternak

Rolled like a stone in a riverbed —Muriel Rukeyser

Rolled like tropic storms along —Edgar Allen Poe

In Poe's poem the word "rolled" was spelled "roll'd."

Rolled off the bed like a rolling pin off a kitchen table —Rita Mae Brown

Rolled over and over like a shot rabbit —P. G. Wodehouse

[A drunk] rolling about like a ball-bearing —Mark Helprin

Rolling around like a cannon ball in a high sea —Hank Searls

[Baby in pregnant woman's body] rolling around like a basketball —Lynne Sharon Schwartz

(The words) roll on like bells —Alastair Reid

Rolls over ... like surf —Lawrence Durrell

Swayed like a bird on a twig —Arnold Bennet

(A tipsy fellow,) swaying like a wind-rocked palm —Beryl Markham

Swaying like cobras about to strike —Robert Silverberg

Sways as a wafer of light —Carl Sandburg

♣ ROMANCE

See: LOVE, MEN AND WOMEN

♣ ROOMS

See Also: FURNITURE AND FURNISHINGS, HOUSES

[An office] almost as severe as the cell of some medieval monk —J. D. McClatchy

Bathroom, mirrored like a discotheque —Diane Ackerman

Bedroom ... large as a football field and as cold —John le Carré

Black bedroom with mirrors ... looks like a wet dream from Walt Disney —Richard North Patterson

The blue and white room was ... cold and hollow as an October mist —M. J. Farrell

The cramped space of the vestibule felt like the inside of a hooded cage —Kenzaburo Oe

[Small room] done up in moist red velvet, like the interior of a womb —Angela Carter

Dusty [a windowsill] as a literal Sahara —Tom Robbins

Entry hall ... as impersonal as a hotel lounge —John Braine

Everything in the room was yellow ... it was a bit like having been swallowed by a butterfly —Pat M. Esslinger-Carr

[Wooden] floors as blonde as a movie star's hair —William Hamilton, National Public Radio, *Morning Edition*, April 15, 1987

A hall that was cool and vaulted like a cloister —Ross Macdonald

(The little den was now) hideous as a torture-chamber —Stephen Crane

It [a room] is like a monastic cell —V.S. Pritchett

It put me in mind anyhow of a monk's cell: the wall of books like mute stones set all around —Cynthia Ozick, *Heir to a Glimmering World*

The living room was spacious and divided like Gaul into three parts —John Cheever

Oak floors shone like brown glass —Rebecca West

On the ceiling the reflection of the waves of the bay outside flickered on and on like conversation —Kate Grenville

The paint [on the ceiling of the room] peeling like the surface of the moon —Jilly Cooper

(In my gray) room, bare as a barn —Randall Jarrell

Room [small and narrow] ... friendly as Death Row —Gavin Lyall

The room glows like a field of forget-me-nots in the high country —Patricia Henley

A room is like a cast-off shoe, which holds the shape of its owner's unique foot —Paul Theroux

Room ... like a cell, except that there were no bars over the one small window —Dashiell Hammett

Room like a cupboard —Katherine Mansfield

The room [at a Howard Johnson's motel] ... sat like a young bride ... wanting only to please you —Max Apple

The room was as hot as the inside of a pig's stomach —Madison Smartt Bell

The room was as quiet and empty as a chapel —Wallace Stegner

The room was filled like a pool with darkness —Josephine Jacobson

The [empty] room was like a flower plucked clean —Jean Stafford

Room ... with nothing actually matching anything else but everything living happily together, like the random sowing of flowers —Rosamund Pilcher

Study ... like the returned-letter department of a post office, with stacks of paper everywhere, bills paid and unpaid, letters answered and unanswered, tax returns, pamphlets, leaflets. If by mistake we left the door open on a windy day, we came back to find papers flapping through the air like frightened birds —Mary Lavin

Twilight came drifting into the room like a shimmering cloud of powdered glass —Natascha Wodin

Walls white like a physician's consultation room —W. D. Snodgrass

ROUNDNESS
See: SHAPE

ROWDINESS
See: NOISE

RUDENESS
See: MANNERS

RUMOR
See: GOSSIP

RUNNING
See Also: MOVEMENT(S), SPEED

Came running like a race —Lee Smith

A queer little hustling run, like a puppet jerked by wires —Ross Macdonald

Raced around ... like a migrant bird —Elizabeth Hardwick

Ran across the lawn towards us crookedly, like someone in an egg-and-spoon race —Kate Grenville

Ran after the cart like a dog after its master —Isaac Babel

Ran down the steps as if the Devil was behind her —Donald Seaman

Ran in and out ... like a squirrel —Henry Van Dyke

Ran like a blind man —Stephen Crane

Ran like a stag —Jonathan Gash

Ran like a whirlwind —Thomas Macaulay

Another simile that has outlived its source, "The Battle of Lake Regillus," as a commonly used phrase.

Run … like a blind sheep in a snowstorm —Borden Deal

(A man comes up to them with a gun, they) run like antelopes —Irwin Shaw

Run like a scalded dog —Rita Mae Brown

(Engineers and executives were) running around like ants in a burning mound —Speer Morgan

Running around in circles like crazy sheepdogs —George Garrett

Running as if on fire —Bernard Malamud

Running … like a leaf driven by the wind —Joseph Conrad

Running like a man who has jumped up in the dark and runs listening between his footfalls for the reason of his still running —Ted Hughes

[A rabbit] runs like a faucet —Marge Piercy

They [joggers] looked like an organized death march as they ran by gasping, perspiring, stumbling, their faces contorted with pain —Erma Bombeck

Trotted beside him like a frightened puppy beside an elephant —Thomas Wolfe

♣ RUTHLESSNESS

See: CRUELTY

♣ SADNESS

See Also: DEJECTION, EMOTIONS, GLOOM

As full of sorrow as the sea of sands —William Shakespeare, *Two Gentlemen of Verona*

Could feel it [the sadness] pierce him like a foreign body in his heart —Amos Oz

Crest-fallen as a dried pear —William Shakespeare, *The Merry Wives of Windsor*

Crest-fallen as a spy who had been caught by a thief —Victor Hugo

Depressing as the last day of fishing —Robert Traver

A feeling of sadness that is not akin to pain, resembles sorry only as the mist resembles rain —Henry Wordsworth Longfellow

(Scarlett) felt bereft, as though she had sold one of her children —Margaret Mitchell

The sadness which inspired the comparison was that experienced by the heroine of Gone with the Wind *when she sold her business.*

Felt melancholy grip him, like a pain in the heart —Mary McCarthy

(I felt depressed) filled to the neck with sadness like a carafe with bad wine —T. Coraghessan Boyle

His eyes, sad as a basset hound's, locked onto mine —Claire Messud, *The Last Life*

His heart throbbed like a bruise in the sigh —Norman Mailer

His heart would sink down to his bowels like lead —Thomas Wolfe

Looked and acted like a man who had just driven home from a couple of heart-rending funerals —George Ade

Melancholy as a discarded statesman —William Mountford

Melancholy as a fiddle with one string —Thomas Holcroft

My heart is within me as an ash in the fire —Algernon Charles Swinburne

My heart was as lead —Jack London

Pathetic as all final efforts —Alice McDermott

Pathetic as an autumn leaf —George Moore

(A low call) plaintive as a shepherd calling to sheep who need no strident invocation —Arthur A. Cohen

Sad as an eagle without wings, sad as a violin with only one string —Jean Rhys

Sad as night —Anon

Sad as professional mourners —F. Scott Fitzgerald

Sad as twilight —George Elliot

Saddening as a forest fire —Robert Traver

Sad like graveyards —Terry Bisson

Sad … like somebody whose pilot light got blown out a long time ago —Susan Kelly

Sadness … gnawed like a rat at his mind —Roderic Jeffries

Sadness, like that inspired by a grave strain of music —Joseph Conrad

Sadness that, over the years, had gathered in his chest like matter in a clogged drain —Joyce Reiser Kornblatt

There would come, like water washing over a sunken buoy, the little knell of sadness —Hortense Calisher

Just as similes are used to give dramatic beginnings to literary works, they can also be used to wind things up, as demonstrated by this final sentence from Calisher's novel, Point of Departure.

♣ SAFETY

See Also: DANGER, RISK

Dexter suddenly feels like he's standing on a scaffold —David Nicholls, *One Day*

Feel as safe as a lone subway rider at 2 a.m. —Anon

Feel as safe as guarded by a charm —Elizabeth Barrett Browning

Looked as dangerous as a squirrel and much less nervous —Raymond Chandler

The man who looks for security, even in the mind, is like a man who would cop off his limbs in order to have artificial ones which will give him no pain or trouble —Henry Miller

Nothing as safe as simplicity —Edith Wharton

Safe and more or less invulnerable like sulky Achilles among Trojans —George Garrett

(I thought I was) safe as a good new boat —Reynolds Price

(They think they're) safe as angels —Dashiell Hammett

Safe as a nun in a roomful of eunuchs —Donald Seaman

Safe as a tank town —W. R. Burnett

Safe as houses —Mary Gordon

Safe as in a cradle —William Wordsworth

Safe as in God's pocket —American colloquialism, attributed to New England

Safe as sunshine —Slogan, R.E. Dietz Co.

Security … tighter than the skin on a snake —William H. Hallhan

She's safe as a vault —Raymond Chandler

Squatting in safety like the yolk in an egg —Bertolt Brecht

♣ SALES
See: SUCCESS/FAILURE

♣ SARCASM
See: HUMOR

♣ SATISFACTION
See: CONTENTMENT

♣ SAYINGS
See: MAXIMS, PROVERBS, AND SAYINGS

♣ SCANDAL
See: REPUTATION, SHAME

♣ SCARCITY
See: RARITY

♣ SCARS
See: FACIAL DETAILS

♣ SCATTERING
See: DISPERSAL

♣ SCIENCE
See: MATHEMATICS AND SCIENCE

♣ SCREAMS
See Also: NOISE, ROARS

Bellowed like a locomotive —Marge Piercy

Bellowing like a wounded whale —William Diehl

Bellow, like an animal in pain —Jean Rhys

A broken shriek like a viola gone sour —T. Coraghessan Boyle

Cried out hoarsely like a bird warning the forest that a predator is on the loose —Derek Lambert

Cries … shrill, like a pig having his throat cut —W. Somerset Maugham

Gave a short roar like a lion keeping in voice —Kingsley Amis

Gave a shriek like an engine —Joyce Cary

Gave a shrill scream like a wrung hen —Hugh Walpole

He bellered like a bull calf —William A. Owens

A high-pitched wail like a cat on fire —Peter Benchley

His scream sliced the night like a hatchet —William Diehl

Howled … like a savage beast being goaded to death with knives and spears —Emily Brontë

Howling (through the streets) like an outcast dog —Erich Maria Remarque

Howl like dogs —Dante Alighieri

Howl like stabled wolves, or tigers at their prey —John Milton

A loud yell which rang through the lonely fields like the howl of an evil spirit —Charles Dickens

Screamed like a door creaking —Hugh Walpole

(Laughed and) screamed like herring gulls —Joan Aiken

Screamed like a horse in a fire —Gerald Kersh

Screamed … like an eight-legged wildcat having a fit —Harold Adams

Screamed like gulls on stormy water —Saul Bellow

Screaming at the top of her lungs like a railroad whistle —Paige Mitchell

Screaming filled the air like an icy mist —Bertolt Brecht

Screaming like a hawk making a long dive at a rabbit —W. P. Kinsella

Screaming … like a saint sent to hell by mistake —Rosellen Brown

Scream like a peacock in heat —Tennessee Williams

Scream like a village of raped virgins —Clive Cussler

In Cussler's novel Cyclops, the simile refers to protests in Washington about a space shuttle in Russian hands.

Scream like sandstorms in the desert, like the death of the universe —T. Coraghessan Boyle

Scream … like the death rattle of a slaughtered animal —Ignazio Silone

A scream of rage … like a blast from hell —Fred Mustard Steward

The scream rose like an aria —Larry McMurtry

Screams as if ice water is rippling down her back —Ira Wood

Screeched like a cage of mynas —Tony Ardizzone

Screeched like a dying pullet —Frank Ross

Screeched like a nighttime cat —Cynthia Ozick

(The women) screeching like bony parrots —H. E. Bates

She'd bellow like a rhinoceros in labor —John Osborne, Look Back in Anger

Shout as demonstrative as a lizard —George Foy

Shrieked like an old screen door —Carolyn Kizer

Shrieking … like she was at a fireman's picnic —John Dos Passos

Shriek like a knife in the heart —T. Coraghessan Boyle

A shriek like a needle-point —Elizabeth Bowen

Shriek like infuriated switch engines —Irvin S. Cobb

Shriek … louder than the loud ocean —Lord Byron

Stormed and screamed like some shrill, wet hurricane about the house —Anita Desai

Talked and shouted for hours on end like a preacher —Ignazio Silone

Yelled … as if I were being roasted alive —Natascha Wodin

Yelling and growling like savage but cowardly dogs —Lawrence Durrell

Yelping (at the captain of the waiters) like a terrier who had cornered some small defenseless animal —Ross Macdonald

Yowl like a tortured cat —Madison Smartt Bell

❧ SCRUPULOUSNESS

See: CORRECTNESS

❧ SCRUTINY

See Also: INTENSITY

Approach [society section of Sunday paper] like a lepidopterist advances on butterflies —Shana Alexander

[A maître d'] bent over (his guest list) like a conductor studying a score —Jonathan Valin

Carefully surveyed the living room and, like an auctioneer brought in for appraisal, every object it contained —Richard Russo

Examine [a face] as though it were a portrait in a public gallery —Ella Leffland

Examine like a customs inspector —Anon

Examine like a job hunter fine combs the employment ads or New York apartment hunter fine combs the real estate ads —Anon

Examine like a monkey picking fleas —Mike Sommer

Examine with care, like a horse player eyeing the "Racing Form" —Shana Alexander

Examine with care of diamond dealer examining a rare stone —Anon

Explore [feelings] … like someone trying to locate a hollow tooth —Lawrence Durrell

His scrutiny was like a well that pulled on you, making you eager to find your own face in the depths down there —Hortense Calisher

Investigate … like a burglar twirling the dial of a well-constructed safe, listening for the locks to click and reveal the combination —Mary McCarthy

Like a traveller in unfamiliar regions she began to store for future guidance the minutest natural signs —Edith Wharton

Look at as does an experienced fish at a purchased fly —Gregory Mcdonald

Looking at it [a letter] as if it were a code in need of breaking —Graham Swift

(Should be) noted with care like the names of places passed on an important journey —John McCahern

Peered around [the room] like a hungry toad —Harold Adams

Pore over … like a little-leaguer entranced by a pack of baseball cards —Jill Ciment

Pore over like possessed students of cabalist text —Joseph Weizenbaum

Weizenbaum's simile was used to describe the intensity of computer enthusiasts or hackers.

Prodding [in search of something] like a great bird rummaging for seed —Edith Wharton

Read their faces like texts and their gestures like punctuation marks —Helen Hudson

The character thus studying faces in the novel Criminal Trespass *is, not surprisingly, a librarian. The description of the gestures the librarian studies includes another simile: "the way they … yank down the volumes and riffle the contents like the Yellow Pages."*

Scrutinize as if he were a new character in a soap opera —Bobbie Ann Mason

Scrutinized … with the air of an epicure examining a fly in his vichyssoise —T. Coraghessan Boyle

Studied Barksdale's face, openly, like a man taking inventory —Paige Mitchell

Studies me like a teacher trying to decide how to discipline an unruly student —W. P. Kinsella

Study [a trip schedule] as though it were a pack of Tarot cards in some tricky configuration —Sue Grafton

Studying him like a culture —William McIlvanney

Surveyed [books] like a guard with his flashlight making the midnight rounds —Elizabeth Hardwick

Being watched like a rabbit in a laboratory —Willa Cather

Watching Bonnie is like watching a slalom champ who knows exactly when to turn, when to coast, when to switch direction —Francine Prose, *A Changed Man*

Watching people, probing like a dentist into their innermost thoughts —Ivan Turgenev

Went through everything … like detectives after fingerprints [describing antiques dealers] —Edith Wharton

Women who size you up so fast it's like they're scanning your bar code —Francine Prose, *A Changed Man*

♣ SEASCAPES

See Also: NATURE; OCEAN/OCEANFRONT; PONDS, RIVERS, AND STREAMS

The boat sails away, like a bird on the wing —Kate Greenaway

Fishing boats sleep by the docks like men beside their wives —Donald Justice

The great ships dipped low down in the water, like floating swans —Hans Christian Andersen

The lights on the canals [of Holland] like gold caterpillars —Jean Rhys

Little masted boats thick on the water, like blown leaves —Donald Justice

Sailboats moved gently in the water like large white butterflies that had dipped down to drink —Margaret Millar

The sea crinkled like foil —Derek Walcott

The sea is like a pale green fabric, stretched but not entirely smooth —Richard Maynard

The sea is sparkling like joy itself —Christopher Isherwood

The sea, like a crinkled chart, spread to the horizon —Daphne du Maurier

The sea was as smooth as a duck-pond —Rudyard Kipling

The sea [on a windless day] was like a sheet of steel —Fred Mustard Steward

The sea was quite calm, like milk-and-water —Isak Dinesen

The sea was silver, wrinkled like a snake's skin —Sir Hugh Walpole

The sea was very calm and clear like some wonderful aquarium, jade with a phosphorescent gleam; if you scooped it up it would glow in your hands —David Nicholls, *One Day*

The sea, wrinkling with light, was stretched taut like a piece of silk —Elizabeth Taylor

Smaller vessels bobbing like petals on the glass of the harbor —Francine du Plessix Gray

There was a shimmer on the sea as though a loitering breeze passed playful fingers over its surface —W. Somerset Maugham

The town seems to lean against the cliffs like a rusting ocean liner, thrown to shore by a storm —Miles Gibson

Water like glass —Joseph Conrad

The water looked flat and impervious, as if a dead membrane had been stretched over it —Cynthia Ozick

Water … pebbly-surfaced by the insistent breeze that kept sweeping like the strokes of invisible broomstraws, and mottled with gold flecks that were like floating freckles in the nine o'clock September sunshine —Cornell Woolrich

Water ... rippled like stretched grey silk in the wind —Gavin Lyall

The water that shone smoothly like a band of metal —Joseph Conrad

❧ SEASONS

August steamed in like the first slow day of creation —Shelby Hearon

The autumnal radiance fluttered like a blown shawl over the changeless structure of the landscape —Ellen Glasgow

Autumn felt as dark with life as Spring —M. J. Farrell

The autumn frosts will like upon the grass like bloom on grapes of purple-brown and gold —Elinor Wylie

In the spring ... life, like the landscape around us, seems bigger and wider and freer —a rainbow road leading to unknown ends —Jerome K. Jerome

The long gray winter settles in like a wolf feeding on a carcass —Marge Piercy

March ... comes in like a lion and goes out like a lamb —John Ray's *Proverbs*

Now that it's Spring and the blossoms fall like sighs —Louis MacNeice

October had come in like a lamb chop, breaded in golden crumbs and gently sautéd in a splash of blue oil —Tom Robbin

October morning ... sallow as a faded suntan —Jessamyn West

One of those honey-warm fall days that brought out summer habits like chilled bees —Hortense Calisher

The seasons shine like new coins —George Garrett

Sleepy winter, like the sleep of death —Elinor Wylie

The specter of winter hovering like a pale-winged bird —W. P. Kinsella

Spring, animating and affecting us all ... like a drug, a pleasant poison of annual mortal gaiety —Janet Flanner

Spring arose on the garden fair, like the Spirit of Love felt everywhere —Percy Bysshe Shelley

Spring comes like a life raft —George Starbuck

Spring sunlight flowed in the streets like good news —William H. Hallhan

Spring came that year like a triumph and like a prophecy —Thomas Wolfe

Summer ... dropping from the sky like a blanket of steam —John Rechy

Summer is like a fat beast —Wallace Stevens

Winter came down like a hammer —Lawrence Durrell

Winter [in Madison Square] ... was tamed, like a polar bear led on a leash by a beautiful lady —Willa Cather

❧ SECRECY

About as loose-lipped as a Swiss banker —Harold Adams

Another person's secret is like another person's money: you are not so careful with it as you are with your own —Edgar Watson Howe

As secret as the grave —Miguel de Cervantes

Close up like a cabbage —John Andrew Holmes

Close up like a fist —Anon

Covert as a brass band —George Wills

Fondles his secrets like a case of tools —Karl Shapiro

Furtive as a chipmunk —R. V. Cassill

Hide ... like a disgrace —George Gissing

In the mind and nature of a man a secret is an ugly thing, like a hidden physical defect —Isak Dinesen

Lydia hid her thoughts like a cat —John Prine, "Donald and Lydia"

Lurking like a pilot fish among sharks —Speer Morgan

Move ... like a rodent, furtively —John Phillips

Peered out (into the corridor) as stealthily as a mouse leaving its subterranean hole —Donald Seaman

(My face is an open secret but in my letters I) perform like a true diplomat, cunning and sly —Delmore Schwartz

Private and tight as a bank vault —Marge Piercy

Secrecy as tight as a bull's ass in fly time —Stephen Longstreet

Secret as silence —Babette Deutsch

A secret at home is like rocks under tide —D. M. Mulock

Secret operations [by a government] are like sin; unless you're good at sinning, you shouldn't do it —George Kennan, CBS/TV, March 31, 1987

Secrets are like measles: they take easy and spread easy —Bartlett's *Dictionary of Americanisms*
Now that measles is controlled by a vaccine, a virus or the common cold would probably be a more appropriate point of reference.

Secrets invisible but irritating, like sand in a shoe —Helen Simonson, *Major Pettigrew's Last Stand*

She has a mouth like a padlock —Graham Greene

Sneak away [for an acceptable, honorable activity] ... as furtively as if he were stealing to a lover's tryst —Edith Wharton

Stealthy and slow as a hidden sin —Stephen Vincent Benét

❧ SEDATENESS
See: SERIOUSNESS

❧ SELF-CONFIDENCE
See Also: PRIDE, VANITY

The acceptance of oneself ... is like falling heir to the house one was born in and has lived in all one's life but to which, until now, one did not own the title —Jean Stafford

(Sit there with) all the quiet certainty of a marauding chimp —Carla Lane, line from British television sitcom, *Solo*

As cocksure as if he had a fistful of aces —Honoré de Balzac

Confidence leaking like gas all over the room —Wilfrid Sheed

Confidence, like the soul, never returns whence it has once departed —Publius Syrus

Confident as a man dialing his own telephone number —Jack Bell

(He would be as) confident as a married man of how the evening would turn out —Alice McDermott

Confident as a master baker with a cake in the oven —Elizabeth Irvin Ross

Feel his title hang loose about him, like a giant's robe upon a dwarfish thief —William Shakespeare, *Macbeth*

Feeling power and confidence rise strongly up in her like wine filling a glass —Celia Dale

Felt like the cock of the walk —John Dos Passos

He displayed like an aura the lordly demeanor of a man who not only had dined on success throughout his lifetime but also had been born to it —Joseph Heller

I feel like a dime among pennies —Fiorello H. La Guardia, *Village Voice,* November 21, 1968
The former New York City mayor responded thus when asked how it felt to be smallest man in a group.

I'm like a cat. Throw me up in the air and I'll always land on my feet —Bette Davis, quoted in Rex Reed interview

Pitching is a rollercoaster ride through the land of confidence —Ron Darling, New York Mets pitcher, *New York Times,* August 3, 1986

(The children) roamed through the neighborhood like confident landlords —Alice McDermott

Self-confidence like an iron bar —Stephen Vincent Benét

Self-confidence surrounds him like force field —William Boyd

She was like a human duck off whose back even the most searing of words flowed liked harmless rain —H. E. Bates

A twist on the timeworn "Rolled off him/her like water off a duck's back."

Very pleased with herself … like a boa constrictor that had just enjoyed a rather large lunch —Mike Fredman

Walked the lane between the indifferently rowed cabins like he owned them, striding from shade into half-light as if he could halve the setting sun —Sherley Anne Williams

When your instinct tells you that disaster / Is approaching you faster and faster, / Then be like the bluebird and sing, / Tweet tweet, tra-la, tra-la, tra-la. —Cole Porter, lyrics from "Be Like the Bluebird," from the musical *Anything Goes*

♣ SELF-CONCIOUSNESS

See: DISCOMFORT, NATURALNESS

♣ SELFISHNESS

The force of selfishness is as inevitable and as calculable as the force of gravitation —Anon

A man is a lion in his own cause —H. G. Bohn's *Hand-Book of Proverbs*

The private life of the narcissist, like the private parts of the exhibitionist, ought not to be hung out-uninvited in the public space —Willard Gaylin

Self-Love … leaped back into her like a perpetually coiled snake —Anais Nin

Wound up in his own concerns like thread on a spool —Anon

♣ SENSATIONS

See: EMOTIONS

♣ SENSE

See Also: INTELLIGENCE

As reasonable as Latin —Anne Sexton

Beyond rationality … like stepping out into deep space, or going to the center of the world, or both at once —Susan Engberg

Common sense is as rare as genius —Ralph Waldo Emerson

Human reason is like a drunken man on horseback; set it up on one side, and it tumbles over on the other —Martin Luther

Like precious stones, his sensible remarks derive their value from their scarcity —W. S. Gilbert

Logic, like whisky, loses its beneficial effect when taken in too large quantities —Lord Dunsany

A mind all logic is like a knife all blade. It makes the hand bleed that uses it —Rabindranath Tagore

Reason in man is rather like God in the world —St. Thomas Aquinas

Reason is a bladder on which you may paddle like a child as you swim in summer waters: but, when the winds rise and the waves roughen, it slips from under you, and you sink —Walter Savage Landor

Reason is like the sun, of which the light is constant, uniform, and lasting —Samuel Johnson

Sense, like charity, begins at home —Alexander Pope

Pope's Moral Essays, can be credited with the first of many "Charity begins at home" comparisons.

Tried to size up the situation reasonably, to tote odds like a paramutual —Jonathan Valin

♣ SENSELESSNESS

See: ABSURDITY

♣ SENSITIVENESS

See Also: KINDESS

Bruise easily like a ripe pear —A.C. Greene

Ego … as delicate as tissue paper —Christopher Buckley

Exposed as if on a raft —Joseph Conrad

Felt like a shell-fish that had lost its shell —Olivia Manning

Felt like a vegetable without its skin: raw and vulnerable —Laurie Colwin

Felt myself exposed … as sharply as in a photograph —John Updike

Gentle as milk —Sylvia Berkman

Inherited sensibilities like jewels as red as rubies and blood —Janet Flanner

Interpreted the episode as sensitively as an unleashed bull would —Z. Vance Wilson

Like a toothless, clawless tiger, / Like an organ-grinder's bear, / Like a knight without his armor, / Like Samson without his hair. / My defenses are down —Irving Berlin, "My Defenses Are Down," *Annie Get Your Gun*

My sensibility begins to screech like chalk upon the blackboard scrawled —Delmore Schwartz

A person who is always having her feelings hurt is about as pleasant a companion as a pebble in a shoe —Elbert Hubbard

A non-gender specific paraphrased from the original which began with "The woman."

Sensitive as a barometer —Thomas Bailey Aldrich

Sensitive as a stick of dynamite or a hand grenade —Mike Sommer

[An alert horse, with ears turning and twitching to catch all sounds] sensitive as radar —Jilly Cooper

Sensitive as the leaves of a silver birch —Joseph Hergeshmeier

Sensitive as the money market —Thomas Hardy

(Taste buds as) sensitive as the skin on a mailman's feet —Ira Wood

Thick-skinned as a brontosaurus —Francis Goldwin, quoted on his sensitiveness to anything but imitations of his company's toy dinosaurs, quoted *Wall Street Journal,* June 15, 1987

Touchy as a second degree burn —Harry Prince

Vulnerable as one of those primitive creatures between two skins or two shells, like a lobster or a crab —David R. Slavitt

(You are) vulnerable as the first buds of the maple —Marge Piercy

With all her stubbornness and punch, she could be sliced like scrapple —Sharon Sheehe Stark

♣ SENTIMENT

Like most sentimentalists, his heart's as chilly as the Pole —Frank Swinnerton

Nostalgia … like a lover's pain in the chest —John Hersey

Nostalgic … like a letter from home —Mahalia Jackson

Jackson's frame of reference, gospel music, is particularly appropriate.

Sentimental as flowers pressed between the pages of a diary —Anon

(I've been) talking sentiment like a turtle-dove —Oliver Wendell Holmes

♣ SEPARATION

See: BEGINNINGS AND ENDINGS

♣ SERENITY

See: PEACEFULNESS

♣ SERIOUSNESS

Bearing his earnestness like an emblem —Donald MacKenzie

Every man will have his hours of seriousness; but like the hours of rest, they often are ill-chosen and unwholesome —Walter Savage Landor

Grave as a judge that's giving charge —Samuel Wesley

Grave as an old cat —Anon

Grave as an owl in a barn —George Farquhar

He was sober as a headstone. —Michael Chabon, *The Amazing Adventures of Kavalier & Clay*

Sedate as a committee-man —William McIlvanney

Serious as a doctor —Eudora Welty

Serious as an overdue mortgage —Alexander King

Serious as a pig pissin' —C. J. Koch

(This is serious, Andras, do you understand?) Serious as death —Julie Orringer, *The Invisible Bridge*

(You are so) serious, as if a glacier spoke in your ear —Frank O'Hara

Serious as if at church —Émile Zola

Serious as the Ten Commandments —W. B. Yeats

Serious like a hyacinth … which has had no sun —Virginia Woolf

Sober as a bone —Erich Maria Remarque

Sober as a coroner inspecting a corpse —Amelie Rives

Sober as a judge —Anon

> *According to Stevenson's* Book of Proverbs, Maxims and Famous Sayings, *John Arbuthnot used the simile in* John Bull *in 1712, and 22 years later, Henry Fielding used it in* Don Quixote In England. *Since then, it has come into common usage, its meaning more frequently tied to a serious manner than sobriety. In one of his* Tutt and Tutt *legal stories, Arthur Train added an interesting note of specificity with "Sober as a Kansas judge."*

Solemn as a child in shock —C. J. Koch

Solemn as a clergyman —Nina Bawden

Solemn as a lawyer at a will reading —J. B. Priestley

Solemn as a nun —R. Wright Campbell

Solemn as a soldier going to the front —Norman Mailer

Solemn as kewpie dolls —Diane Ackerman

Solemnly agreed, as though pledging allegiance to the flag —Robert Traver

Stern as a Tartar —Lorenz Hart

> *The Tartar described is Queen Elizabeth. This is also the title of this song from Hart's lyrics for "The Garried Gaieties" of 1926.*

This *Carrie* is as serious as a hostage-rescue mission —Patrick Healy, "An Outsider Gets a Nicer Date for the Prom," *New York Times*, February 5, 2012.

> *Healy is writing here about the 2012 revival of the worst-ever stage flop,* Carrie.

♣ SERMONS
See: SPEECHMAKING

♣ SERVILITY
See: MEEKNESS

♣ SEX
See Also: ATTRACTIVENESS, BODY ORGANS, BREASTS, MEN AND WOMEN, SEXUAL INTERACTION, RELATIONSHIPS

(To me they are) as asexual as money, and, like money, unless they can engender passion, they are useless to me —W. P. Kinsella

> *The frame of reference for Kinsella's double simile is the "other woman."*

Batten's [character in novel] sex had wilted like a flag in the rain —George Garrett

Celibate, like the fly in the heart of an apple —Jeremy Taylor

An erection like a steeple —Jilly Cooper

Erotic as an ape —Karl Shapiro

I felt an abrupt rush of my semen, racing through me like twin rivers —Scott Spencer

Her climax came … suddenly, like an accident —Scott Spencer

Her sex power ... hid in her eyes like a Sicilian bandit —Saul Bellow

His sex beat about like the cane of a furious blind man —Amos Oz

Horny as a tomcat —T. Coraghessan Boyle

In her passional life she was direct —like an axe falling —Lawrence Durrell

It's rather like a sneeze —Truman Capote responding to television interviewer's question as to his feelings about sex

It [a first sexual encounter] was best when it was finished ... like having a cup of really good coffee and a Havana after an indifferently cooked but urgently needed meal —John Braine

Just whispering "teenage sex" is like yelling fire in a crowded theatre —Ellen Goodman

A lack of sexuality so total that her smart clothes and too heavy-make-up made her pathetic; like an unsuccessful geisha —John Fowles

Like flowers groping toward the sun, millions of Americans are groping towards sexual nirvana —Anon

Like hatred, sex must be articulated or, like hatred, it will produce a disturbing internal malaise —George Jean Nathan

(Her husband complained she) made love like an eager, clumsy cellist —J. D. McClatchy

My sex life ... it'd make Moll Flanders look like she needed hormone therapy —Sue Miller

The only sex we were exposed to was with dreadful old whores ... like diseased orchids —Tennesse Williams, *Playboy*, April 1973

Orgasm is like a slight attack of apoplexy —Democritus

Orgasm is like the tickling feeling you get inside your nose before you sneeze —Children's sex education manual, 1972

Pornography is like peanut butter—a little goes a long way —Arthur Morowitz, *New York Times*, October 5, 1986

[Sexual] restraints fell from her like mere rags, or rather, like that dead skin which is scraped off in a steam bath —Marguerite Yourcenar

Sensual as a ripe, thick-veined scarlet fruit —John Logan

Sex becomes as routine as tying one's shoes —Deborah Phillips, *New York Times*, October 8, 1986

Sex is a subject like every other subject. Every bit as interesting as agriculture —Muriel Spark

Sex ... it's great stuff, like chocolate sundaes —Raymond Chandler

Sexless as a machine —Ellen Glasgow

Sexless as an anemic nun —Sinclair Lewis

(Some men have a) sexual disposition as vigorous, indiscriminate, and as demanding as a digestive tract —John Cheever

Sexual pleasure, like rending pain, represents the stunning triumph of the immediate —Simone de Beauvoir

She seems to regard sex as a wholesome, slightly silly indulgence, like dancing and nice dinners —Alice Munro

Sometimes I feel like a public utility —Charles Johnson

The character who makes this comparison about herself in Johnson's novel Oxherding Tale *is a woman who has had "an army" of lovers.*

There were people ... for whom love and sex came easy, without active solicitation, like a strong wind to which they had only to turn their faces —David Leavitt

Virility ... was like a gloss on him —Barbara Taylor Bradford

Wears her sex like an expensive perfume —Lawrence Durrell

(Lucille's aunt had) wrapped her own dank virginity round her like someone sharing a mackintosh —Elizabeth Bowen

☙ SEXUAL INTERACTION

See Also: INSULTS

Attacked her with a loose and greedy mouth, like a man sucking at a torn fruit —Miles Gibson

Even when they made love … it was perfunctory, as if he were listening for something else, a phone call, a footfall. He was like a man scratching himself. She was like his hand —Margaret Atwood

(She could only remember the times that he had lain with her) fleeing into her body as if it were a refuge from his daily wage of fear and frustration —Davis Grubb

Gave her whole body to me, like something without a bone —Winston Graham

Gobbled her like a ripe peach —Peter De Vries

He aroused her so excruciatingly that she wanted to lie down right now for him in the middle of the muddy road and let him plough through her like a car —Julia O'Faolain

He fell into her with the ease and velocity of a stone dropping into the sea —MacDonald Harris

He fell on me like a wave. But like a wave he washed away, leaving no sign he'd been there —Louise Erdrich

He had never before made love like this … as if he had found a twin whose body had been cast in the matching mold of his own —Amos Oz

He pulled up my clothes like a man unwrapping a parcel —Graham Swift

Her touch moving over my body like pebbles in a stream —Arthur A. Cohen

He slips into her like a thief entering a doorway —Hilma Wolitzer

He was like something washed ashore on her [after unsuccessful sexual intercourse] —Flannery O'Connor

His love making felt like having a tooth stopped by a singularly incompetent dentist —Vicki Baum

It [sexual intercourse] was as if we'd been fused together, melting into each other like amoebae but violently, like cars crashing head on —John Braine

The lovemaking wasn't exactly by the numbers, but she did order everything on the menu, like a teenage kid trying to impress his date —Jonathan Valin

Made love like monkeys —Charles Johnson

Making love with Charlie was like being taken into a big warm machine —Sue Grafton

(Harry) maneuvered her around like a load of wet wash —R. Wright Campbell

Our body warmth flowed back and forth, coursing between us like some underground hot spring —Harvey Swados

Our two bodies met like a thunderclap —Carolyn Kizer

Places her gently upon the bed like a newly pressed suit —Roger McGough

She gave herself up to me like a condemned criminal —John Hagge

She snuggled into him like a kitten at the breast of its mother —Rita Mae Brown

She stiffened on penetration and clung to him, relaxing as if unlocked with his blunt key —Paul Theroux

Spills him off her body like a pile of sand —John Updike

Their touch together was like a miniature jolt of electricity —Paul Horgan

Undressed deliberately, slowly, as if she were unwrapping a gift —Graham Swift

We crashed against one another like waves on a breakwater —Sue Grafton

We ended up in bed together, sort of, spastic and looped, doomed for failure, like two senile inventors in an upstairs room, lonely as spoons —Lorrie Moore

We flowed together again like a stream that for an instant an island had separated —Truman Capote

We half walked half stumbled towards the bed, like uncertain dancers learning a new step —Peter De Vries

❧ SEXUALITY

See: SEX

❧ SHADOW

His shadow dragging like a photographer's cloth behind him —Elizabeth Bishop

Long shadows deep as oil —Philip Levine

My shadow spilled over the grass like great leaks of ink —Henry Van Dyke

Shadows black as parts of dreams —David Denby

Shadows deep as caves —Jerry Bumpus

Shadows [of elm trees] falling all over her head and shoulder like a web —Ellen Gilchrist

Shadows lay like broad hurdles across my path —Beryl Markham

The whole shadow of Man is only as big as his hat —Elizabeth Bishop, from her poem "The Man-Moth."

❧ SHALLOWNESS

See: IMPORTANCE/UNIMPORTANCE

❧ SHAME

See Also: BLUSHES

As sheepish as a fowl —Jean de La Fontaine

Embarrassing, like showing up for a party on the wrong date and finding the host and hostess in the middle of a family squabble —Elyse Sommer

Embarrassment lay like a cloak over everyone's shoulders —Belva Plain

Embarrassment thickened in his throat like phlegm —Ross Macdonald

Embarrassing as a rich man without admirers —David Denby

Embarrassed as a nudist caught with his clothes on —Anon

He felt a drench of shame like a hot liquid over his neck and shoulders —Saul Bellow

He tasted shame like a hot fragment of metal on his tongue —Julie Orringer, *The Invisible Bridge*

In scandal, as in robbery, the receiver is always thought as bad as the thief —Earl of Chesterfield

Looked embarrassed, as if he were a spy whose cover had been blown —Robert Barnard

Red-faced ... like a puppy caught in his own piss —R. Wright Campbell

Scandal will rub out like dirt when it is dry —John Ray's *Proverbs*

Shame came over me like a blanket of steam —Mary Gordon

Shame ... it came in twenty-eight delicious flavors, like Howard Johnson's ice cream —Harvey Swados

Uncomfortable as if she had tumbled out of a warm bed into a cold room and there was no time to dress before a crowd came to view her discomfort —Henrietta Weigel

Waves of shame ran through her, like savage internal blushes —Mary McCarthy

❧ SHAPE

(Breasts) flat as paper —William Trevor

As two-dimensional as a household weather vane —Saul Bellow

Flat and pale as an empty sheet of nonerasable bond —Lyn Lifshin

(The back of his head) flat as a book —T. Coraghessan Boyle

(Suit lapels as) flat as a cardboard —Derek Lambert

Flat as a carpet —Anon

> To be more specific, there's "flat as Oriental rugs."

Flat as a fashion model's breasts —Anon

Flat as a flounder —Anon

> In his novel Death of the Fox *George Garrett* found a new application for this commonly used simile as follows: "I am panting and my body twitches and heaves. Like a man with a woman, flat as a flounder, beneath him."

[A cleft in a rock] flat as a fresco —John Farris

Flat as an empty wallet —Anon

Flat as a pancake —American colloquialism, attributed to New England

> The pancake comparison has been used to describe very flat persons and objects since the fifteenth century.

(A blue sea as) flat as a table top —Jean Stafford

Flat as a tracer bullet —Frank Conroy

Flat as a waiter's feet —Arthur Baer

Flat as melted iron —Joyce Cary

Flat as paper dolls —Elyse Sommer

Flat as the palm of one's hand —American colloquialism, attributed to New England

> A shorter version, "flat as my hand," was used by Robert Louis Stevenson.

(I lie on my single bed) flat, like a piece of toast —Margaret Atwood

(Her talk is) formless as a dream —Henry Miller

[A field of July corn] level as a mat —H. E. Bates

Long and slender like a cat's elbow —H. G. Bohn's *Hand-Book of Proverbs*

Pressed myself flat as a tick against the wood of the wall —Davis Grubb

(Pebbles …) round and white as pearls —John Cheever

Round as a ball —Alexander Hamilton

Round as a melon —Anon

Round as a pillow —William Wordsworth

(The Jewish women were as) round as the earth —Thomas Wolfe

Round as the world —Dame Edith Sitwell

(Eyes as) shapeless as a kneecap —Charles Johnson

Shapeless as fear —Beryl Markham

(The neighbors lounged on each other's steps, big and) shapeless as worn cushions —Helen Hudson

Shapeless like a slug —Heinrich Böll

(Born) a shapeless lump, like anarchy —William Drummond

They [passing lovers] are flat as shadows —Sylvia Plath

❧ SHARPNESS

See Also: PAIN, PARENTHOOD

(A whippet head) barbed like a hunting arrow —Ted Hughes

Bite … as deadly as a camel's —Wallace Stegner

Biting [language used in a book] as a chain saw —Bruce De Silva

(Her voice was) crisp as a freshly starched and ironed doily —Maya Angelou

Crisp as a handclap —Maxine Kumin

> From a poem entitled "A New England Gardener Gets Personal," the simile describes how kale comes to the salad bowl.

Crisp as frost —Babette Deutsch

Crisp as new bank notes —Charles Dickens

(A voice that) cut like a blade of ice —G. K. Chesterton

Cut like a knife —Rudyard Kipling

> Kipling's descriptive frame of reference is the wind.

[Cat's fangs] fine as a lady's needle —Ted Hughes

Incisively as an acid (a yell bit into the situation) —F. van Wyck Mason

Peppery as curry —Marge Piercy

Sharp as a bird's painted bill —Dame Edith Sitwell

Sharp as an assassin's dagger —Mike Sommer

(Face as) sharp as an ice pick —Graham Masterton

(The longing for lovely things … became as) sharp as a pang —Ellen Glasgow

Sharp as a scorpion —Dame Edith Sitwell

Sharp as a two-edged sword —The Holy Bible/ Proverbs

(The smell of smoke was) sharp as brimstone —John Gardner

(My ideas fade, yours come out) sharp as cameos —Joseph Conrad, letter to Stephen Crane

(Eyes) sharp as mica —R. Wright Campbell

(All these things fell on her) sharp as reproach —Alfred, Lord Tennyson

Sharp as the teeth of a saw —Marge Piercy

Sharp as truth —John Greenleaf Whittier

Sharp as white paint in the January sun —Wallace Stevens

Sharper than birth —Madeleine L'Engle

Sharper than ingratitude —Anon

> This may be inspired by King Lear's famous lament about a child's ingratitude being "sharper than a serpent's tooth."

Sharp like joy —Sharon Sheehe Stark

Sharp-tongued, like a sadistic dentist —Neil Gabler, a television movie commentator, thus described a colleague, Pauline Kael

A tongue like a cat o' nine tails —Ben Hecht

❧ SHINING

See Also: BRIGHTNESS, GLITTER; GLIMMER, AND GLOSS

Gleamed like dogs' eyes in a car's headlights —Frank Swinnerton

[A ballroom] polished like a skull —Lawrence Durrell

(Her face could) shine as a sack of apples —Wallace Whatley

Shine like a tear —Yocheved Bat-Miriam

[Hands] shine like old wood —Philip Levine

(A pool) shines, like a bracelet shaken in a dance —Wallace Stevens

Shines like a glowworm —Robert Penn Warren

Shines like a rhinestone in a trashcan —Nora Ephron reviewing a Jacqueline Susann novel within its context as a roman a clef

(Say to the court it glows and) shines like rotten wood —Sir Walter Raleigh

Shining and clear as white stones in a brook —George Garrett

[A table] shining like a pair of shoes —Shelby Hearon

[A room] shining like holiness —Jessamyn West

(Eyes) shining like the icing on a cake —Scott Spencer

Shone [the city in the light] as dazzling bright and pretty as money that you find in a dream of finding money —Edna St. Vincent Millay

Shone darkly, like water before a storm —Donald Seaman

Shone like a brand-new quarter —Karl Shapiro

Shone … like a cloud of lightning bugs —Eudora Welty

Shone like a meteor streaming in the wind —John Milton

Shone like patent leather —Rita Mae Brown

(The rails) shone like quicksilver —John Yount

(Her black, oiled hair) shone like a river under the moon —Colette

(Porch-slats) shone like sculpture —Alan Williamson

Sparkle like wedding cakes —Graham Swift

> In Swift's novel The Sweet-Shop Owner, the comparison is made to the effects of the sun's rays on graves.

❦ SHOCK

See Also: CAUSE AND EFFECT, SURPRISE

As dazed as a man who has just been told he hasn't long to live —Françoise Sagan

Felt amazed, as if the clouds had blown away, as if the bare bones were finally visible —Louise Erdrich

In Erdrich's novel The Beet Queen *the amazed feeling stems from a character's realization that he is homosexual.*

Felt as if I was being hit by a blast from a giant hair dryer —Dominique Lapierre

The first shock [of English society] is like a cold plunge —Robert Louis Stevenson

He happened to look at this watch, and the sight was like a douche of cold water —P.G. Wodehouse

He was white and shaken, like a dry martini —P. G. Wodehouse

(Then the familiarity of the name …) hit him like a contract cancellation —William Beechcroft

[A brutal murder] shocked me and held onto me as if I'd shaken hands with a live wire —Jonathan Valin

The shock … held everybody as in a still photo —Ray Bradbury

The shock hit me like a fist under the ribs —David Brierly

Shocking as the realization that you're not invincible —Elyse Sommer

Shocking realization … like a fist knocking the wind out of her —David Leavitt

Shock [went through room] like the twang of a bow string —Iris Murdoch

The shock numbed him out like a drug —George Garrett

(She can) shock you like a lightning bolt at high noon —Aharon Megged

(The shock and horror of the moment when he had first seen Denny's body, the disorientat-ing moonlight, had) struck him like a mental earthquake in which he no longer stood on firm ground —P. D. James, *Death Comes to Pemberly*

Stunned … as if a good boxer had just caught me with a startling left hook and a stultifying right —Norman Mailer

The sudden shock striking somewhere inside her chest like an electric bolt —William Styron

❦ SHOULDERS

See Also: BODY

Bony shoulders … like wings —Richard Ford

Protruding shoulder blades that pushed out the back of his shirt like hidden wings —Harvey Swados

Shoulder blades … almost as soft and small as a bird's wings —Penelope Gilliatt

Shoulder blades jutted like a twin hump —Harvey Swados

[Protruding] Shoulder blades … like wedges —Jay Parini

Shoulders like a buffalo —Willa Cather

Shoulders like a five-barred gate —Donald Seaman

Shoulders like a pair of walking beams —H. C. Witwer

Shoulders like a wall —Paul J. Wellman

Shoulders like the ram of a battleship —P. G. Wodehouse

Shoulders like the Parthenon —H. L. Mencken

Shoulders protruding like a Swiss chalet —Rufus Shapley

Shoulders rounded like a question mark —T. Coraghessan Boyle

Sunburned shoulders like the knobs of well-polished furniture —Nadine Gordimer

❦ SHOUTS

See: SCREAMS

❧ SHREWDNESS
See: CLEVERNESS

❧ SHRIEKS
See: SCREAMS

❧ SHUT
See: OPEN/SHUT

❧ SHYNESS
See Also: MEEKNESS, PERSONAL TRAITS

Bashful as an egg at Easter —Sir John Denham

> *This has expanded with the seasons to include "Bashful as a turkey at Thanksgiving or Christmas."*

Demure as an African violet —Maya Angelou

Demure as an old whore at a christening —Thomas Fuller

Demure as if butter wouldn't melt in his mouth —Thomas Fuller

Shy as a squirrel —George Meredith

Shy as infants —Alice McDermott

Shy as rabbits —Anon

Shy, like a hospitable country hostess anxious to give pleasure, but afraid that she has not much to offer citizens of a larger world —Phyllis Bottome

A shy man is a lonely man … between him and his fellow-men there runs an impossible barrier … a strong invisible wall —Jerome K. Jerome

❧ SICKNESS
See: ILLNESS

❧ SIDEBURNS
See: BEARD(S)

❧ SIGHS
See Also: GROANS AND WHISPERS

A collective sigh, like an escaping jet of steam —Robert Traver

Gave a deep sigh, like pain was a habit —Cornell Woolrich

Releasing a muffled sigh like a baby animal with a full belly —Kenzaburo Oe

Sighed, a rustling sound like wandering autumn leaves —Derek Lambert

Sighed like a long-suffering teacher —Ramsey Campbell

Sighed like a pair of bellows —William McIlvanney

Sighed like a poet in love —Beryl Markham

Sighed once with relief … like a low note on a bagpipe —Sue Grafton

Sighed with pain, as if a knife had twisted deep inside —Louise Erdrich

Sighing, like a bagpipe's dying breath —Patrick White

Sighing like a punctured tire —Guy Bolton

Sighing like the night wing and sobbing like the rain —Stephen Foster

> *This is a line from the song "Jeanie with the Light Brown Hair" which begins with yet another similes: "I dream of Jeanie with the light brown hair, borne like a vapor on the summer air."*

Sigh like some sweet plaintive melody —William Motherwell

A sigh of relief escaped his lips like a long-needed crap —John Lennon

Sighs as if a mountain lay on her chest —Cora Sandel

Sigh … tender and enchanting, like the wind outside a wood in the evening —Virginia Woolf

A sigh that was like a gust of sand raised and dropped suddenly by the wind —Flannery O'Connor

❧ SIGNIFICANCE
See: IMPORTANCE/UNIMPORTANCE

❦ SILENCE

See Also: SECRECY

Behaved a little like a stuffed frog with laryngitis —P. G. Wodehouse

A brief silence, like an indrawn breath —Sylvia Plath

A brittle silence stretched like iced cords through the kitchen —Anthony E. Stockanes

Dole out his words like federal grants —Shelby Hearon

Dumb as a drum with a hole in it —Charles Dickens

Dumb as a yearning brute —Martin Cruz Smith

The enfolding silence was like an echo —William Styron

Fall silently, like dew on roses —John Dryden

A great painful silence came down, as after the ringing of a church bell —Loren D. Estleman

Grew still, like a congregation in silent prayer —Edgar Lee Masters

Hears the silence … like a heart that has ceased to beat —Joyce Carol Oates

(The room was suddenly full of …) heavy silence, like a fallen cake —Raymond Chandler

Her silence bore down on him like a tombstone —Heinrich Böll

Her silence had a frequency all its own … like one of those dog whistles that make a sound only dogs can hear —a sound that cracked eggs, or something —Larry McMurtry

He tried to say something but his tongue hung in his mouth like a dried fruit on a tree —Bernard Malamud

(The crowded courtroom grew as) hushed and still as a deserted church —Robert Traver

Hushed like a holy place —Lynn Sharon Schwartz

A hush prevailed like that in an art gallery —Jean Stafford

A hush rose like a noisy fog —Bernard Malamud

I'll be like an oyster —Ivan Turgenev

The character making this statement in A Month In the Country, continues with "not another syllable."

Men fear silence as they fear solitude, because both give them a glimpse of the terror of life's nothingness —André Maurois

Moving as silently as fish under water —Ross Macdonald

Mute like a faded tapestry —Louis MacNeice

Mute as a fish —John Melton

Mute as a gargoyle —Sharon Sheehe Stark

My tongue lay like a stone in my mouth —Pat Conroy

My words, like silent raindrops fell / And echoed / In the wells of silence. —Paul Simon and Art Garfunkel, "Sounds of Silence"

Noiseless as fear in a wilderness —John Keats

Quiet as the visible murmur of their vaporizing breath —William Faulkner

Quiet and meaningless as wind in dry grass —T. S. Eliot

Quiet as a lady's fart —Harold Adams

Quiet as a lamb —William Langland

Quiet as a mouse —Anon

Quiet as an eel swimming in oil —Arthur Baer

Quiet as a nun —William Wordsworth

The English novelist Antonia Fraser borrowed Wordsworth's simile for a mystery novel about a nun.

(It was) quiet as a prayer —Mary Lee Settle

(The whole immense room … was) quiet as a sepulcher —Walter de la Mare

Quiet as a stone —John Keats

Quiet as a street at night —Rupert Brooke

Quiet as a street of tombs in a buried city —John Ruskin

Quiet as a wasp in one's nose —John Ray's *Proverbs*

Quiet as a wooden-legged man on a tin roof —Anon

This is one of many American folk similes incorporated by Carl Sandburg into his unique long poem "The People, Yes."

(The house was as) quiet as death, as the inside of a skull —John Fowles

Quiet as dust —Ken Kesey

(Her mind was) quiet, as if a needle had been lifted from a phonographic record —Ellen Gilchrist

(The town was all as) quiet as the hills —A. E. Coppard

Quiet as two tombs —Robert B. Parker

Quietly as a moth —Louis Bromfield

Quietly as smoke rising —Loren D. Estleman

Quiet ... pressed on her eardrums like a weight —Hortense Calisher

Quiet settled in the room like snow —Rumer Godden

Significant silences like fingers that point —William Bronk

The silence seemed to come drifting down like flakes of snow —Katherine Mansfield

Silence fell like a guillotine in the middle of raw, bleeding conversations —Susan Fromberg Schaeffer

The silence around them, like the silence inside a mouth, squirms with colors —James Dickey

Silence as absolute as death —Robert Penn Warren

Silence as deep as held breath —John Yount

(It was Sunday, and there was a feeling of quietness) a silence as though nature were at rest —W. Somerset Maugham

Silence beat about them like waves —Mavis Gallant

The silence between us ... it lay coiled like a sleeping cat, graceful in its way but liable to claw if stroked indelicately —Scott Spencer

Silence descending over the room like a black-winged bird —John Rechy

Silence drifting in ... settling like dust —Helen Hudson

The silence [at the other end of telephone] ... felt absolute, as if he had been trying to telephone God —William McIlvanney

Silence filled the space [of empty room] like water in a lock —Julia Whedon

Silence filled the sunlit room like gas —Harvey Swados

Silence grand as Versailles —Lorrie Moore

Silence heavy in the air like a threat —William Boyd

Silence ... hung in the air like a dead pheasant —Penelope Gilliatt

Silence is deep as eternity —Thomas Carlyle

Silence is his delight and instruction now ... as if a blessed quiet came to him like water made into music —George Garrett

Silence ... like a great hand pressed across a mouth struggling to give vent to a scream —Stephen French Whitman

Silence ... like an explosion —John Fowles

The silence like an ocean rolled, and broke against my ear —Emily Dickinson

The silence of the place was like a sleep, so full of rest it seemed —Henry Wadsworth Longfellow

Silence ... poured in between them like a drifting dune —Lawrence Durrell

The silence ran between them like a fuse —William McIlvanney

Silence, rather like somebody had died —Elizabeth Spencer

Silence ... rich and winey, like a rest in music —Zona Gale

Silence rose like a mountain —Arthur A. Cohen

Silence settled on him like a mist —Frank Ross

Silence ... so intense that it was like a third presence in the room —Antonia White

Silence so thick that he imagined he could cut a slice out of it, like a succulent melon —Ella Leffland

Silence ... steadily filling up the bare white room, like water rising in a tank —Christopher Isherwood

Silence stretched out like membrane on the point of tearing —Ross Macdonald

Silence [in tension-filled room] stretched like a wire vibrating with impulses that were never heard —Hortense Calisher

Silence that falls between them ... like deep snow —Donald Justice

Silence that fell upon her like a restraining hand —Nadine Gordimer

Silence that made his own breathing seem like the breaking of distant surf —Mark Helprin

Silence walked beside them like the ghost of a dead man —W. Somerset Maugham

The silence [in the room] was like an invasion, a possession by the great silent mountains —Gina Berriault

The silence was like a tranquilizer —Mignon F. Ballard

Silent as a burglar behind a curtain —Raymond Chandler

Silent as a cat on velvet —Reynolds Price

Silent as a country churchyard —Thomas Babington Macaulay

Silent as a ghost —Percy Bysshe Shelley

(Rooms) silent as a lantern —Daniela Gioseffi

Silent as a midnight thought —Anne Finch

Silent as a prisoner —Richard Ford

Silent as a snowflake settled on the ground —Donald Seaman

Silent as a standing pool —William Wordsworth

Silent as a stuffed sausage —Helen Hudson

Silent as a white shark —Diane Ackerman

Silent as despair —John Greenleaf Whittier

Silent as despairing love —William Blake
A modern variant: "Silent as a breaking heart."

Silent as flight —Wendell Berry

(They walk close together) silent as painted people —Julie Hayden

(An object) silent as pillows —Diane Wakoski

Silent as rain or fleece —Lawrence Durrell

[Thoughts] Silent ... as space —Lord Byron
Here is the complete simile as it appeared in Don Juan, *"There was a depth of feeling to embrace ... thoughts, boundless, deep, but silent too as space."*

Silent as the moon —John Milton
Many writers continue to link the moon with silence, with frequent twists and extensions. Some examples from contemporary literature include: "She was as silent and distant as the moon" from a short story by Kate Wheeler and "Silent as the dark side of the moon" from Water Music *by T. Coraghessan Boyle*

Silent as the pictures on the wall —Henry Wadsworth Longfellow

Silent as the rays of the sun —Slogan, Silent Glow Oil Burner Corporation

Silent as thought —Sir William Davenant

Silent as your shadow —Colley Cibber

Silent ... like an empty room —Carlos Baker

Silent like a stockpiled bomb —C. D. B. Bryan

Silently as a dream —William Cowper
"Silent as a dream" variations include "Dumb as a dream," by Algernon Charles Swinburne "Mute as any dream," by Elizabeth Barret Browning.

(Made his way through the yard as) silently as a tom-cat on the prowl —Donald Seaman

Silently as a turtle —John Hersey

Silent men, like still waters, are deep and dangerous —H. G. Bohn's *Hand-Book of Proverbs*

(The crowd was) silent ... totally, in a hush like the air in the treetops —Paul Horgan

A small silence came between us, as precise as a picture hanging on a wall —Jean Stafford

So quiet ... it felt like Sunday without church —Elizabeth Spencer

(You were) so silent it was like playing with a snowman —Martin Cruz Smith

Soundless as a gong before it's struck —Donald Justice

Soundless as any breeze —Dame Edith Sitwell

The sound of the silence was like the hum of her own nerves stretched taut —William Humphrey

Speechless as an anchorite —Lawrence Durrell

Speechless as though his tongue were paralyzed —Ouida

Stealthy silence as of a neatly executed crime —Joseph Conrad

(The house was) still as a bottomless well —Hugh Walpole

Still as a desert —Anon

Still as a mouse —Richard Flecknoe
> *An extension of this by Sir Walter Scott: "Quiet as a mouse in a hole."*

Still as a stone —The Holy Bible/Exodus

Still as mourners —Mark Strand

Still as the grave —William Shakespeare, *Othello*

Still like gulls —W. H. Auden

Stillness struck like a stopped guitar —Sharon Sheehe Stark

A sudden silence ... shook them like an inaudible explosion —Frank Tuohy

There seemed to be a lot of silence in the house, like something deep and sticky you had to wade through —Jane Rogers

There was absolute silence. It said as plainly as if silence were a language itself, "Go back." —Flannery O'Connor

Tight-lipped as a Sioux —Charles Johnson

Tongues tight as immigrants —Daniel Berrigan

Untalkative as native Vermonters —Max Lerner on commuters

Unheard like dog whistles pitched too high for human ears —George Garrett

Uses silence like a blackjack —Tim O'Brien

Vocal chords seem glued together like two uncut pages in a book —Elyse Sommer

Withdraw behind a wall of silence like children confronted with the disapproval of an authority figure —Margaret Millar

The words hung in the air like a trail of smoke. [Which Ariana blew away.] —Amy Waldman, *The Submission*

❧ SILLINESS
See: ABSURDITY, FOOLISHNESS, IMPOSSI-BILITY, STUPIDITY

❧ SIMILARITY
See Also: DISSIMILARITY

As alike as buttons on a shirt —Anon

(We're almost) as alike as eggs —William Shakespeare, *Winter's Tale*
> *Similes about things that tend to be uniform have and continue to inspire many variations ("as alike as" comparisons). The other famous author most frequently credited with this comparison is Miguel de Cervantes with "as alike ... as one egg is like another" from* Don Quixote.

As alike ... as grapes in a cluster —Edna Ferber

As alike as my finger is to my finger —William Shakespeare, *Henry V*

As alike as two drops of water —James Miller
> *This simile has become so common that no "as alike" introduction is needed, as illustrated by "just like two drops of water" used by Isaac Bashevis Singer in* The Family Moskat *to describe the resemblance between a mother and son.*

As alike as two peas in a pod —Jack London

Even in an age where more peas reach the dinner table from frozen food packages than pods, this now-commonplace expression shows no sign of diminishing use. The form shown here has supplanted older and now little used versions such as "alike as two peas to one another" and "as like each other as two peas."

As like a hand to another hand —Robert Browning

As like as like can be —William Wordsworth

As like as rain to water —William Shakespeare, *King John*

As undifferentiable … as ballots in a ballot box —Richard Ford

The simile as used by Ford in The Sportswriter describes modern parents whose lives are so lacking in mystery and difference that they are undifferentiated from their children.

[Penciled doodles] identical as tracings —Margaret Millar

[TV commentators] looked alike as bowling pins —T. Coraghessan Boyle

Looked as alike … as hair pins —Loren D. Estleman

Looked as much alike as blackbirds on a fence —John Yount

Resembled each other like waves —Gustave Flaubert

They're like as a row of pins —Rudyard Kipling

♣ SIMILES

See: MAXIMS, PROVERBS, AND SAYINGS

♣ SIMPLICITY

See Also: EASE

As devoid of any taste for luxury as a stone-deaf person of the sense of hearing —Isak Dinesen

As plain as the back of a bus —Helen Simonson, *Major Pettigrew's Last Stand*

Crude as life among farming people —Daniel Berrigan

Great men, like nature, use simple language —Vauvenargues

I am simple … just like that broken bottle. I have no secrets —John Updike

Physically as plain as a pike —Charles Johnson

[Body] plain as a cheap clothes-rack —Brian Moore

Plain as a pine door —Sumner Locke Elliott

Plain as black and white —Karl Shapiro

(Hands) plain as blank pages —Gerald A. Browne

Plain as English mutton —E. B. White

Simple as a bucket —Paul Theroux

Simple as a Hopper painting —Anon

Simple as chessboards —George Bernard Shaw

Simple as children's cradle songs —Adrienne Rich

(Words) simple as potatoes —Marge Piercy

Simple as rain —Theodore Dreiser

(Would that life were as) simple as sport —Rita Mae Brown

Simple as the golden rule —Anon

A very simple man … like a tree that has not many roots, but one tap-root that goes down deep —Willa Cather

♣ SIN

See: EVIL

♣ SINCERITY

See: CANDOR

♣ SINGING

See Also: MUSIC

As anxious about his voice as a Don Juan about his sexual equipment: a roughness was the equivalent of a dose of clap, laryngitis of impotence —Francis King

Carry a tune as well as a mouse carries an elephant —Anon

His care for his voice was like that of a parent for a sickly and therefore abnormally cherished child —Francis King

Sitting

Melody … sweetened the air like raindrops —Paul Theroux

Most of them [sopranos] sound like they live on seaweed —Sir Thomas Beecham

Sang in a drone like a far-away tractor —Mary Ward Brown

Sang without passion, like a conscientious school girl —Antonia White

Singing is as natural and common to all men as it is to speak high when they threaten in anger, or to speak low when they are dejected —William Law

Singing voice … like a bee in a bottle, a melodious slightly adenoidal whine, wavering, full of sobs and breaks, and of a pitch like a boy's before the change of voice —William Humphrey

Sing like a lark —William Makepeace Thackeray

Sings as sweetly as a nightingale —William Shakespeare

Song … old as air, and dark as doom —Mark Van Doren

Sopranos trilling loudly as if terrorized —Harvey Swados

(I tried to sing along but …) the notes themselves kept sliding away from me like water drops dancing across a hot skillet —A. E. Maxwell

A [whistled] tune … seemed to be pouring out of him as though he were a bird —James Baldwin

Tune … that climbed and plummeted like a kite in the wind —Lynne Sharon

❧ SITTING

See Also: BEARING, IMMOBILITY

Carefully lowered himself into the chair like someone entering a steaming hot bath —Andrew Kaplan

Grandly sitting like a great rock —John Ashberry

Hit his chair like a large rock —Rita Mae Brown

Hunkered down on our haunches like Indians —Stephen King

Just sits there … like a sick cat —Niven Busch

Perched [on a stool] like a night owl —Jonathan Valin

(Eight matrons) perched like pigeons around two identical card tables —Leigh Allison Wilson

Sank back [into a chair] … like a weighted diver into water —Richard Moran

The diver comparison is particularly apt within the context of Moran's novel Cold Sea Rising *which has many ocean scenes.*

Sank into a chair like stone sinking into water —Lael Wertenbaker

Sat as still as a bird sleeping on a limb —James Crumley

Sat bolt upright, like a character in a work of cheap fiction —Peter De Vries

Sat down heavily, like a farmer getting ready for Sunday dinner —Harvey Swados

Sat like a bronze figure —William Brammer

The variations on sitting, standing or being "still as a statue" are virtually limitless.

Sat like a humped stone —Flannery O'Connor

Sat like a lump of lead —Erich Maria Remarque

Sat like granite —Walter Stone

Sat like half-folded shirts, arms out of the way and knees close together —Mary Ward Brown

Sat [silently] like someone who can't remember the punch-line —William McIlvanney

Sat like some portent against the skies of the evening —E. M. Forster

Sat like wood —Leslie Thomas

Sat silent, motionless, like guests waiting to be welcomed —Helen Hudson

Sat stiff as a cockroach, waiting to spring to life —Miles Gibson

Sat stolidly, like an egg flattened on its bottom —David Ignatow

Sat there like a mountain —Eudora Welty

Sat up abruptly like a clockwork figure released by a spring —Joyce Cary

Sat up and crossed his legs like a tailor. Like a tailor with no needle —Sterling Hayden

Sat up as if she'd been shot from a cannon —Jonathan Valin

Sat up —like a soldier at reveille —Jonathan Valin

Sat up like Lazarus —Ray Bradbury

She is dumped on the seat like a barrel of ashes —Malcolm Cowley

Sitting [on the floor] like a sack —Ivan Turgenev

Sit like a frog on a chopping block —John Ray's *Proverbs*

Sit like an umbrella —Bertolt Brecht

Sit like fixed candlesticks —William Shakespeare, *Henry V*

Stood there like a mannequin —T. Coraghessan Boyle

Sit silent and still as if they were in a photograph, slightly out of focus —George Garrett

Sits like a pile of dough —Lee Smith

Sits quietly with her hands in her lap, like a pregnant woman being driven to the delivery room —Alice McDermott

Sits up high like a job applicant —Richard Ford

Sitting like somebody found at Pompeii —William McIlvanney

Sitting motionless … like a mother who affects not to notice the rude or awkward conduct of her children —Marcel Proust

(She straightened up,) sitting stiff and small, like a small mast against a storm —Elizabeth Spencer

Sitting there pop-eyed as a ventriloquist's dummy —Antonia White

You sit with your head like a carving in space —Wallace Stevens

SKEPTICISM
See: TRUST/MISTRUST

SKILLS
See: ABILITY, ACCOMPLISHMENT

SKIN
See Also: BALDNESS, COMPLEXION, FACIAL COLOR, FACIAL DETAILS, PALLOR, WRINKLES

The blue of her veins … on her breasts, under the clear white skin, like some gorgeous secret —Joe Coomer

Each summer his skin becomes like brown velvet —John Rechy

Flesh … as chill as that of a mermaid —Angela Carter

The flesh drooping like wattles beneath the jawbone —Nina Bawden

(Miss Quigg's) flesh looks as if it's been steeping in brine for years —Sharon Sheehe Stark

Flesh … luminous as though coated with milk —Cynthia Ozick

Flesh … soft and boneless as apple pulp —Margaret Millar

Flesh was as firm and clean as wood —Kay Boyle

Flesh, white as the moon —Charles Johnson

Freckles all over … like a speckled egg —Phyllis Naylor

Grained like wood (where the sweat had trickled) —Willa Cather

Hairless as a statue —Harvey Swados

Hands and forehead were deeply spotted like a seagull's egg —Frank Tuohy

Her skin cracked like skim milk —Arthur Miller

Her skin felt like plaster of Paris —Nancy Huddleston Packer

Her skin had a startlingly fine texture, like flour when you dip your hand into it —John Updike

Her skin had the bad, stretched look of the white cotton hand towels they give you in poor hotels —Maeve Brennan

Her skin was as pink as sugar icing —Georges Simenon

The simile underscores Simenon's characterization of a woman like a "bonbon."

Her skin was the color of smoked honey —R. V. Cassill

Her toadstool skin drapes her bones like cloth worn thin —William Hoffman

The simile is taken from a scene in a short story describing a dying woman.

His skin hung on his bones like an old suit much too large for him —W. Somerset Maugham

His skin is pale and looks unwholesomely tender, like the skin under a scab —Margaret Atwood

His skin was tea-colored, like a farm boy's —Ella Leffland

Like yellow parchment is his skin —Charles Hart, "Magical Lasso," *The Phantom of the Opera*

My skin hangs about me like an old lady's loose gown —William Shakespeare, *Henry IV*

Pimpled like a brand-new basketball —M. Garrett Bauman

The skin thus described in Bauman's short story "Out from Narragansett" belongs to a blowfish.

She had pale skin with the kind of texture that looked as if a pinch would crumble it —Jonathan Kellerman

Skin brown as a saddle —Linda West Eckhardt

(The waitress … has) skin dark as garden earth —Leslie Garis, *New York Times Magazine*, February 8, 1987

Skin … (slack, sallow and) draped like upholstery fabric over her short, board-like bones —Louise Erdrich

Skin felt like a series of damp veils, like the wet paper you fold over the wires when you are making papier-maché —Elizabeth Tallent

Skin felt like rawhide which hasn't been soaked —Niven Busch

Skin … flushed as if by a fresh breeze —Franz Werfel

Skin freckled like a mango leaf —Derek Walcott

Skin, freckled like a lawn full of clover —Rosellen Brown

Skin glowed like a golden peach —Lillian de la Torre

Skin … gray and rough like dirty milk —Heinrich Böll

Skin … hard and leathery … as though you could strike a kitchen match on it —Pat Conroy

Skin, hairless and white as bird droppings —Harvey Swados

Skin [when you're old and thin] hangs like trousers on a circus elephant —Penelope Gilliatt

The skin … hung from her bones like a quilt on the line —Suzanne Brown

Skin like a baby's behind —François Camoin

(One of those lovely, ageless women, with) skin like an Oil of Olay ad —Tony Ardizzone

Skin like an overwashed towel —Jean Thompson

Skin like dark flames —Margaret Atwood

Skin like flan —Scott Spencer

Skin like ice cream, like toasted-almond ice cream —T. Coraghessan Boyle

Skin like polished stone —Richard Wilbur

(He was pale, his) skin like sausage casing —Paul Theroux

Skin like shells and peaches —M. J. Farrell

Skin … like silk —*Arabian Nights*

Skin like the skin of fruit protected by shade —Paul Horgan

Skin like the under-petals of newly-opened June rosebuds —Cornell Woolrich

Skin like wax paper —Frank Tuohy

Skin like wood —Elizabeth Harris

The skin merely hung at her neck like a patient animal waiting for the rest of her to join in the decline —Max Apple

The skin of her neck was like a piece of chamois leather that had been wrung out and left to dry in brownish, uncomfortable, awkward folds —H. E. Bates

Skin pale as a snowdrop —Jaroslav Seifert

This is both the first line and title of a poem.

Skin ... pale as glossy paper —Geoffrey Wolff

Skin [around the neck] ... sagging like a turkey's —John Braine

Skin seemed as sheer as rubber, pulled over her hands like surgical gloves —Sue Grafton

Skin shines in dull gray translucence, like wax —Ira Wood

Skin shines like polished mahogany —R. Wright Campbell

Skin smelled like fresh cotton —John Updike

Skin ... smooth, as if dampened and then stretched on his skull —Wright Morris

Skin smooth as Pratesi sheets ... eyes that shimmer like Baccarat at the bottom of a Bel Air hot tub ... earrings sparkling like all the chandeliers at Lincoln Center, in Malcolm Forbes yacht and maybe even in all of Donald Trump's Tower —Stephanie Mansfield, *Washington Post*, June 21, 1986

Mansfield's string of similes sets the mood for a profile of Judith Krantz, renowned for her best sellers about glamorous people.

Skin ... soft and flabby as used elastic —Jean Rhys

Skin so unwholesomely deficient in the natural tinge, that he looked as though, if he were cut, he would bleed white —Charles Dickens

Skin ... stretched over his bones like a piece of old shining oilcloth —Dominique Lapierre

Skin stretched tight like a rubber ball —Margaret Atwood

Skin supple and moist like fine leather that had been expertly treated —Elizabeth Spencer

Skin, the color of creamed tea —W. P. Kinsella

Skin the color of ripe grapefruit —T. Coraghessan Boyle

Skin ... the texture like the pit of a peach —Stanley Elkin

Skin tight and rugged as a mountain climber's —Ward Just

The skin under the eyes was gray, as though she had stayed up every night since puberty —Ella Leffland

Skin [a baby's] was delicious to touch, fine-grained and blemishless, like silk without the worminess —John Updike

Skin was pale and drawn, her bones lay like shadows under it —William H. Gass

Skin was reddish brown like that of an over-baked apple —Jerzy Kosinski

Skin [of bald scalp] was sunburned, and ridged like dried leather —Cornell Woolrich

Skin ... weathering toward sunset like cracked glaze on porcelain —Dick Francis

The startling whiteness of her skin, lush and vulnerable, was like the petal of a gardenia —Kaatje Hurlbut

The texture of her skin was round and hard like the rind of winter fruit —Ellen Glasgow

The texture of his skin, like coffee grounds —Charles Johnson

White skin that looks like thin paper —John Cheever

❧ SKY

See Also: CLOUDS, MOON, SKY COLOR

Bleak [sky] ... as if the sun had just slipped off the edge of the world —Susan Welch

A bleak day, the sky like smudged charcoal —Erik Larson, *In the Belly of the Beast: Love, Terror, and an American Family in Hitler's Berlin*

A blue, cloudless sky spread like a field of young violets —Hugh Walpole

The cloudless sky was like an inverted bowl that hemmed it in —W. Somerset Maugham

The clouds formed like a beach and the stars were strewn among them like shells and moraine —John Cheever

A cloudy grey sky through which the sun shone opaque like an Alka Seltzer —Jilly Cooper

The evening sky, with its head dark and its scarves of color, looked like an Italian woman with an orange in her hand —Christina Stead

The expanse of the sky was like an infinite canvas on which human beings were incapable of projecting images from their human life because they would seem out of scale and absurd —Anais Nin

The gray (Seattle) sky lies around her, filmy and thick, like you could eat it —Barry Hannah

The grey, soft, muffled sky moved like the sea on a silent day —Nadine Gordimer

The horizon was like an open mouth —David Ignatow

Lifeless sky ... like the first day of creation —Edith Wharton

Light spread across the horizon like putty —T. Coraghessan Boyle

Skies like inverted cups —John Rechy

Sky ... as clear as a window —Beryl Markham

Sky as clear, as firm-looking as blue marble —David Ignatow

Sky as drab as a cast-iron skillet —Jessamyn West

Sky ... as soft as clouds of blue and white hyacinths —Ellen Glasgow

The sky bloomed like a dark rose —James Reiss

The sky covered with stars ... like dots in a child's puzzle —Helen Hudson

Sky ... flat and unreal as a glimpse of distant ocean —Sharon Sheehe Stark

The sky ... flung itself over the earth like a bolt of blue cloth —Dianne Benedict

(Over the city) the sky hangs like a giant silken tent —Erich Maria Remarque

The sky hangs like lead —Erich Maria Remarque

The sky hisses and bubbles like a cauldron —W. P. Kinsella

The sky hovering overhead like a soundless dirigible that was about to crash —Heinrich Böll

The sky hung over the valley ... like a slack white sheet —Elizabeth Bowen

The sky is darkening like a stain —W. H. Auden

The sky is like a heavy lid —Ridgely Torrence

The sky is like a human mind, with uncountable shifting pictures and caverns and heights and misty places, and lakes of blue, and big sheets of forgetting, and rainbows, illusions, thunderheads, mysteries —John Hersey

The sky is like a page from a book that hasn't been written —François Camoin

The sky is like a peach-colored sheet drawn taut at the horizon —Russell Banks

A sky like a dirty old slate —M. J. Farrell

A sky like a dustbin-lid —William McIlvanney

Sky like a forget-me-not —Joyce Cary

Sky like a great glass eye —George Garrett

Sky like an immense blue gentian —Henry Van Dyke

Sky like a pig's backside —Sylvia Plath

A sky like lead —W. H. Auden

A sky like a tinted shell —Helen Hudson

The sky looked billowy, as if you could catch the corners of it and toss the stars around as in a net —Ada Jack Carver

Sky, pale and unreal as a photographer's background screen —Katherine Mansfield

The sky seemed to be spread like a bottomless lake above them —William Styron

The sky shone like enamel —John Cheever

The sky swayed like a blue balloon on a string —Ross Macdonald

A sky that looked like water, broad, blue, its clouds rolling like great, feathery waves —Charles Johnson

The sky was full of little puffs of white clouds, like the ships we saw sailing far out to sea —Wilbur Daniel Steele

The sky [on a windy day] was like an unmade bed —Helen Hudson

The sky was like glass —James Reiss

The sky was like muslin —John Ashberry

The sky was like new-cleaned window glass full of its own shine —Joyce Cary

The sky was … like wet gray paper —Paul Horgan

The sky was overcast, monotone, as if it were made of pale gray rubber —Jean Thompson

The sky was pale and smudged like a dirty sheet —George Garrett

The sky was shining like a nickel. —Michael Chabon, *The Amazing Adventures of Kavalier & Clay*

Smoke drifted across the sky looking like a gigantic horse's mane blowing in the wind —Boris Pasternak

A starless sky as dark and thick as ink —Émile Zola

The sun bubbled in the sky, giving off clouds like puffs of steam —Helen Hudson

Up in the sky, Venus and the thinnest paring of sickle moon, like a cup and saucer, like a nose and mouth, have made the Turkish flag in the sky —Lorrie Moore, *Birds of America: Stories*

Winter skies hover over Iowa like a gray dome —W. P. Kinsella

❧ SKY COLOR

The colors hanging suspended in midair like huge, floating ostrich plumes —Paul Kuttner

The edges of the sky had a yellowish tinge like cheap paper darkening in the sunlight —Ross Macdonald

Pale blue sky like some Stuka dive-bomber —Donald Seaman

A redness in the sky, like the flame at the back of a vast baker's oven —Saul Bellow

Skies are gray as tarn —Richard Ford

Sky blue as winter milk —Joyce Cary

The sky changed through several colors and became a soft crumbled gray. It was like walking under the roof of an enormous cave where hidden fires burned low —Ross Macdonald

Sky [at dusk] … green as unripe apples —Erich Maria Remarque

The sky is gilded with red, as if intoxicated —Cora Sandel

Sky … like terra cotta —Saul Bellow

Sky so pale blue and clear as a baby's eye —Joyce Cary

Sky the color of oiled steel —T. Coraghessan Boyle

The sky was a dome of gray, stretched evenly like parachute silk at full billow —Lael Wertenbaker

The sky was as blue as the ribbon on a prize winning lamb. —Michael Chabon, *The Amazing Adventures of Kavalier & Clay*

The sky was gray as a battleship —Mike Fredman

The sky was hard blue, like bright ink —James Stern

The sky was the color of dishwater —T. Coraghessan Boyle

The sky was yellow as brass —Erich Maria Remarque

❧ SLANDER

Slanderers are like flies; they leap all over a man's good parts to light upon his sores —John Tillotson

Slander is like a hornet; if you cannot kill it dead at the first blow, better not strike at it —Josh Billings

Slander, like coal, will either dirty your hand or burn it —Russian proverb

❧ SLEEP

See Also: DREAM(S), SNORE(S)

Asleep and dreaming, like bees in cells of honey —Thomas McGuane

This simile completed McGuane's novel, The Sporting Club.

As near to sleep as a runner waiting for the starter's pistol —J. B. Priestley

As sound asleep as a coon in a hollow log —Borden Deal

Awoke … like some diver emerging from the depths of ocean —Francis King

(Paul lay in his berth) between wakefulness and sleep, like a partially anesthetized patient —John Cheever

(Mr. Samuel Pickwick) burst like another sun from his slumbers —Charles Dickens

Came out of a deep sleep slowly, like a diver pausing at each successive level —Norman Garbo

Come from sleep as if returning from a far country —Mary Hedin

The simile which begins the story, "Blue Transfer," continues as follows: "a stranger to myself, a stranger to my life."

Doze and dream like a lazy snake —George Garrett

Drowsy as an audience for a heavy speech after an even heavier dinner —Anon

Emerges from slumber like some deep-sea creature hurled floundering and gasping up into the light of day by a depth-charge —Francis King

Fell into a sleep as blank as paving-stone —Patrick White

Felt himself falling asleep like gliding down a long slide, like slipping from a float into deep water —Oakley Hall

Heavy with sleep, like faltering, lisping tongues —Boris Pasternak

I shall sleep like a top —Sir William Davenant

This simile has outlived the play from which it is taken, The Rivals, *as a colloquial expression. A somewhat different version, "slept like any top" appeared in the German children's story,* Struwelpeter, *by Heinrich Hoffman.*

I want sleep to water me like begonias —Diane Wakoski

Kept falling in and out of it [sleep] like out of a boat or a tipping hammock —Rose Tremain

Lies asleep as softly as a girl dreaming of lovers she cannot keep —F. D. Reeve

Reeve, a poet, is describing a river.

Lying awake like a worried parent —Robert Silverberg

Nodding, like a tramp on a park bench —Robert Traver

Not sleeping but dozing awake like a snake on stone —Malcolm Cowley

Sleep as smooth as banana skins —Diane Wakoski

Sleep came over my head like a gunny sack —Ross Macdonald

Sleep covered him like a breaker —Harris Downey

Sleep fell on her like a blow —Hortense Calisher

Sleeping like a lake —Theodore Roethke

Sleeping like a stone in an empty alcove of the cathedral —Clive Cussler

Sleep like a dark flood suspended in its course —Percy Bysshe Shelley

Sleep like a kitten, arrive fresh as a daisy —Slogan, Chesapeake & Ohio Railroad

Slept like a cocked pistol —Émile Zola

Slept a great deal, as if years of fatigue had overtaken him —Peter Matthiessen

Slept almost smiling, as if she had a secret —William McIlvanney

(He usually) slept like a corpse —Ring Lardner

(While the Weary Blues echoed through his head. He) slept like a rock or a man that's dead —Langston Hughes

Slept like he'd gone twelve rounds with a pro —Geoffrey Wolff

Slumber fell on their tired eyelids like the light rain of spring upon the fresh-turned earth —W. Somerset Maugham

Sunk into sleep like a stone dropped in a well —John Yount

Wake abruptly, with an alarm clock which breaks up their sleep like the blow of an ax —Milan Kundera

♣ SLIGHTNESS

See: WEAKNESS

♣ SLIMNESS

See: THINNESS

♣ SLOPPINESS

See: CARELESSNESS, ORDER/DISORDER

♣ SLOWNESS

See Also: MOVEMENT(S)

Agonizingly slow like the gradual ripening of a peach on a limb —Sue Grafton

By degrees, as lawyers go to heaven —Anon

[A locomotive] came slowly, like a bison —Saul Bellow

(An hour) crawled by like a sick cockroach —Raymond Chandler

Creeping like a snail —William Shakespeare, *As You Like It*

Dragged around … like a dog with three legs —Shelby Hearon

[An endless journey] like crossing the Sahara by pogo stick —Robert Silverberg

Gather slowly, like a storm that swirls at sea —Anon

Gradually, like a man entering a swimming pool slowly —Michael Korda

The gradual process being compared to entering a pool is a return to work.

Grew with such infinite slowness, like a stalactite —Lawrence Durrell

Happening slow motion like a baseball replay —Maxine Kumin

Have all the speed and liquidity of a slug skating across salt —Erik Sandberg-Diment, *New York Times*, January 18, 1987

Diment's comparison refers to a word-processing program.

It [the movie, *Kangaroo*] moves like a slug climbing a cornstalk —Rex Reed

It takes time … like getting your hair curled —Carlos Baker

Leisurely as the drift of continents —T. Coraghessan Boyle

Life passed him as slowly as traffic on a main artery during the evening rush hour —Anon

Moved as slow as paste —Paul Theroux

(My feet seemed deep in sand. I) moved like some heat-weary animal —Theodore Roethke

Moved slowly, like a diver with heavy boots —Graham Swift

Moved slowly through her days, like a mermaid floating in a translucent sea where all was calm, shadowy, and ambiguous —Peter Meinke

(Here and there a herd of stray cows) moves as slowly as old men on their way to the graveyard —A. D. Winans

(The government) moves like a huge blob of molasses on a two-degree slope —John D. Mac-Donald

An extension of the cliché "slow as molasses."

Moving about, slow as earthquake survivors —Brian Moore

A process about as slow and arduous as the building of the pyramids —Edith Wharton

> *The process Wharton is describing is character building.*

Pushes ahead; slow as a weight —Delmore Schwartz

Slow and silent, like old movies —Sharon Sheehe Stark

Slow as a dream —Robert Penn Warren

Slow as a hog on ice with his tail frozen —American colloquialism, attributable to Vermont

> *The way Vermonters say it: "with his tail froze."*

Slow as a tortoise —American colloquialism

> *To add emphasis there's "as old as an old tortoise."*

Slow as dough —Sharon Sheehe Stark

> *The simile is used to draw a portrait of a dull, unambitious man in a story entitled "The Horsehair."*

Slow as molasses going uphill —Jamaican expression

> *A variant of, "as slow as molasses."*

Slow as the hands of a schoolroom clock —W. D. Snodgrass

Slow as the oak's growth —John Greenleaf Whittier

Slow-blooded, like a lizard in winter —Mary Hood

Slowly, like bodies being dragged —Ross Macdonald

Slowly, like turtles cooking in the sun we rotated our heads —T. Coraghessan Boyle

Slow-moving like an old woman with a walker —Anon

Slow reluctant process [a city's morning stirrings], like the waking of a heavy sleeper —Edith Wharton

(Opened the case) with deliberate ceremonial slowness, as if breaking bread at a wedding banquet —Richard Lourie

❧ SMALLNESS

As tiny as the glint of a silver dime in a mountain of trash —Elizabeth Spencer

Big as a broom closet —Anon

> *This modern colloquialism usually applies to a small living or working space. A common variations often used with "no bigger than" is "big as a shoe box." "No bigger than" instead of "big as" is often used with either comparison.*

Big as your thumbnail —Julian Gloag

He [a very short man] with his chin up, gazing about as though searching for his missing inches —Helen Hudson

Small and undistinguishable, like far-off mountains turned into clouds —William Shakespeare, *A Midsummer Night's Dream*

Small as a breadcrumb —Anon

Small as a fly in the fair enormity of a night sky —Elizabeth Spencer

Small as a garden pea —Lawrence Durrell

Small as a snail —Babette Deutsch

> *The comparison is used to describe the subject of a poem entitled "The Mermaid."*

Small as grain of rice —Anon

Small as sesame seed —Anon

Small as snowflake —Anon

Tight as a gnats cock —English expression used by engineers to describe an extremely small space

(Paper ripped into pieces,) tiny as confetti —Ann Beattie

(Jeweled chips) tiny as grass seed —Jayne Anne Phillips

❧ SMELL

See Also: AIR, SWEAT

The air smelled like damp flannel —Jonathan Kellerman

The air smelled ... like the interior of the Bastille in 1760 —Carlos Baker

As malodorous as a badly ventilated lion house in a zoo —John Cheever

A close antiseptic odor like an empty schoolroom —George Garrett

A dark wet smell like a cave —Pat Conroy

He smelled like something that spent the winter in a cave —Sue Grafton

It [a hotel lobby] smelled like fifty million dead cigars —J. D. Salinger

A kitchen odor hung about like a bad mood —Tom MacIntyre

The lingering odor of sweat like sour wheat —Louise Erdrich

(He gave off an) odor like a neglected gym locker —Wallace Stegner

The odor of her body, like salted flowers —Bernard Malamud

The odor (of newly turned earth) steamed up around him like incense —Dorothy Canfield

The office smelled like hot coffee —Richard Ford

An old man smells old … like old clothes that need an airing —Saul Bellow

The place smells like a wrestler's armpit —Jilly Cooper

Pleasantly pungent, like the smell of one's own body —John Updike

Reek like last week's fish —Mike Sommer

The scent [from garden] rises like heat from a body —Margaret Atwood

Scent rising like incense (from the cleavage of her splendid bosom) —Jilly Cooper

The sea smelled like a sail whose billows had caught up water, salt, and a cold sun —Robert Goddard

Sexual smells, like the odor of an excellent cheese are considered foul by those who experienced them without their appetites being involved —Judith Martin

A smell [of cheap cologne] like rotten bananas in a straw basket —Jonathan Valin

[Hallway of a hotel] smelled like hot bread and clean laundry —Richard Ford

Smelled like something the cat dragged in —American colloquialism

(Mrs. Lamb) smelled like spoiled lilacs —Richard Ford

[A boy] smelled like the bottom of a calf pen where the piss settled and burned the yellow straw red and when you turned the straw over with a fork the ammonia smell made your eyes water —Will Weaver

Smell fresh as apples —John Braine

(Soft-spoken women) smelling like washed babies —Philip Levine

Smell like an open drain —Louis MacNeice

Smell like a sick skunk —Elmer Kelton

The smell of moist earth and lilacs hung in the air like wisps of the past and hints of the future —Margaret Millar

Smells like the underneath of a car —Carolyn Chute

Smells badly like things that have been too long dead —Donald McCaig

Smells fresh as melting snow —W. P. Kinsella

Smell stronger than a ton of rotten mangoes —Dr. Hunter S. Thompson

Smell (of carnations) … thick as smoke in the sun —Mary Stewart

[Honeysuckle smell] smothering, like an anesthetic —Lynne Sharon Schwartz

A stale smell like a bad embalming job —Jimmy Sangster

(The married man is grateful for) the stuffy room that smells of his wife like a bar smells of beer —David Denby

There was a foul reek of something fecund and feline, like the stench of old lion spore upon the veldt —Tama Janowitz

Wet fields reek like some long empty church —John Betjeman

♣ SMILE

See Also: BRIGHTNESS; FACIAL EXPRES-
    SION, MISCELLANEOUS; GRINS;
    LAUGHTER

Adjusted her smile like a cardboard mask —Vicki Baum

An attempt at a smile creased Willie's face like old tissue —Paige Mitchell

Beamed like a child that stops crying the moment you return his favorite toy and promise never to confiscate it again —Natascha Wodin

Beamed like a lighthouse —Clive Cussler

Beamed like an August moon —F. van Wyck Mason

Beamed like a small boy uncrating his first bicycle —Robert Traver

Beamed like the sun —Mikhail Lermontov

> The sunshine-like smile in A Hero of Our Time is in response to a nod from a young woman at a dance.

Beams like a politician —Dilys Laing

The faint, slow smile clung like an edge of light to her lips —Ellen Glasgow

Flashed her smile [and] bit it off like a thread —John Cheever

A flashing smile, like a knife gleaming briefly from concealment —Ross Macdonald

Had a smile for every occasion, like Hallmark cards —Andrew Kaplan

Her vivid smile was like a light held up to dazzle me —Edith Wharton

His smile drops from his face like a mask with a broken cord —Erich Maria Remarque

His smile lit up the world like a strobe light —Herbert Gold

His smile spread across his bearded face in crooked jerks, like a crack spreading across a dam —Rick Borsten

His smile was as stiff as a frozen fish —Raymond Chandler, The Man Who Liked Dogs

Indestructible smile cracked forever across the front of his face like the brim of a black ten-gallon hat —Joseph Heller

> The comparison is particularly apt, as it refers to a character who is a Texan.

Kept smiling, as if the corners of his mouth were strung up on invisible wires —Sylvia Plath

The lines of a smile split his jaw like a field furrow —Leigh Allison Wilson

Looked like a lizard regarding a fly —John Irving

A lovely smile, like a shining seal upon a contract —Graham Swift

On-and-off smile … like a light-switch —Eleanor Clark

Pinched-lip smile that dug deep grooves like chisel strokes in her cheeks —Anthony E. Stockanes

A pure and radiant smile suddenly shone out under her beautiful wet eyelashes, like sunshine among branches after a summer shower —Anatole France

Quick smile like somebody with a fever —George Garrett

Quick smiles that were like small coins thrown without fuss to someone who has done a service —Graham Swift

A rich, slow-spreading smile, like butter melting in a skillet over a low flame. And whenever it creeps across James Corden's face in the splendidly silly One Man, Two Guvnors, which opened on Wednesday night at the Music Box Theater, you know two things for sure: You're in for trouble, and you're already hooked —Ben Brantley, New York, April 20, 2012

She smiled like a belle —Jonathan Valin

(Smile more widely and) show his teeth like a politician visiting a high school —James Reiss

Simpering like a wolf —Dylan Thomas

A slight smile, like a knife mark in fresh dough —James Crumley

Sly, satisfied smile … like a wink, a nudge in the ribs —Ann Petry

A small puckered-up smile like an old scar —Helen Hudson

Smile as spare as the decor along Death Row —Loren D. Estleman

Smile … warm and steady as summer sun —Mary Hedin

Smile … like a crack in old plaster —Rita Mae Brown

A smile, as artificial as a last touch of makeup —Marguerite Yourcenar

Smile as cold as a polar bear's feet —Eugene O'Neill

A smile as guileless as that of a serpent —R. Wright Campbell

The smile, as it went from her face, reminded me of a flame turned off by a tap —H. E. Bates

Smile as phony as that of a trained horse —James Crumley

Smile as sharp as a blade —Ellen Glasgow

Smile broke apart like a cheap tumbler shattering —Geoffrey Wolff

A smile broke over his face like the sunrise over Monadnock —Steven Vincent Benet

Smile … cool as clean linen, friendly as beer —John Braine

Smiled as broad as a Halloween pumpkin —Charles Johnson

(Blinked and) smiled like a lizard on a rock —John D. MacDonald

Smiled like a submissive wife —Herbert Gold

Smiled like a wolf at the thought of the next meal —Mike Fredman

Smiled like a woman resigned to a fate worse than death —James Crumley

Smiled like La Gioconda —Gerald Kersh

Smiled [upon being introduced] like people who had been introduced years before and had flirted and were now hiding their acquaintance —Christina Stead

Smiled like she had just discovered a cure for the common cold —Arnold Sawislak

Smiled off and on, like a neon sign —Clancy Sigal

Smiled with all the charm and cunning of the dangerously insane —Miles Gibson

Smile, fixed like that of a ventriloquist's doll —Eric Ambler

A smile … flashed like an inspired thought across her face —O. Henry

A smile had widened her lips, spreading like oil —Hortense Calisher

Smile … it refreshes, like a shower from a watering pot —*A Broken-Hearted Gardener,* anonymous nineteenth Century verse

Smile like a cocktail gone flat —Malcolm Cowley

Smile … like a crack in an eggshell —Leslie Thomas

A smile like a cunning little flame came over his face, suddenly and involuntarily —D. H. Lawrence

Smile … like a fresh saber scar —R. V. Cassill

A smile like a large plaster ornament —Marge Piercy

Smile … like all the lights of a Christmas going on at once —George Garrett

Smile … like an invitation —Flannery O'Connor

Smile like a plastic daisy —Marge Piercy

Smile like a razor-cut before the blood comes —John Dickson Carr

Smile … like a white flower flung on an open wound —Adela Rogers St. John

A smile like Christmas morning —Harry Prince

Smile like heaven —Edith Wharton

Smile … like holiday sunshine —John le Carré

Smile … like that of the boa constrictor about to swallow the rabbit —Arthur Train

Smile ... like the crepe on a coffin —Lawrence Durrell

A smile like the first scratch on a new car —Tom Robbins

Smile ... like the smile of a chipmunk sucking on a toothpick —Don Robertson

Smile like transparent water stirred by a light breeze —Italo Svevo

(Flashes his eyes in) a smile like triumph —D. H. Lawrence

Smile of a man with a terminal headache —T. Coraghessan Boyle

A smile passed over his big face like a soundless storm —Erich Maria Remarque

A smile passed over her lined face like sunlight on a plowed field —Ross Macdonald

The smile she gave him was like a white flower flung on an open wound —Adela Rogers St. Johns

Smiles stolidly flickered like home movies —Stephen Sandy

Smiles tossed like fanciful flowers —Joan Chase

Smiles wanly ... like an actor with no conviction —Rosellen Brown

Smile sweet as cake —Lorrie Moore

A smile that came and went as quickly as a facial tick —John D. MacDonald

Smile that stretches like a rubber band —Daphne Merkin

Smile ... vacant and faint like the smile fading on an old photograph —V. S. Pritchett

A smile wide as a mousetrap —David Brierly

A smile with closed lips which was at once sorrowful and comic, very like a clown's —Storm Jameson

Smiling encouragingly but rather distantly, like friends saying good-bye in a hospital to a patient who is not expected, except by some miracle, to recover —John Mortimer

Smiling like a bailiff —Sumner Locke Elliott

Smiling like a birthday child —John Gardner

Smiling ... like a fat yellow cat —J. B. Preistly

Smiling like a winking shudder —Robert Campbell

Smiling secretly as cats do in the midst of mouse dreams —Sue Grafton

Smiling to himself like a mysterious Buddha —Margaret Landon

A soft silky smile [of mother] slipped over her [young daughter] like a new dress, making her feel beautiful —Helen Hudson

Stretching a smile across her face like a rubber band —Susan Ferraro, *New York Times*, March 12, 1987

Suddenly, like a crocus bursting out of winter earth, she [a child] looked up at Alison and smiled —John Fowles

The suggestion of an ironic smile rippled about her face like a breeze on a pond —James Crumley

(She smiled at me, and) the smile broke against my face like a cool wave —L. P. Hartley

The way you smile, with your whole face, with your eyes, it's like a certificate of trust —T. Coraghessan Boyle

When Henry smiled, showing his newly crowned front teeth, he looked like a male lead in an old silent film —Kathleen Farrell

When she smiled her eyes and mouth lighted up as if a lamp shone within —Ellen Glasgow

A wide smile, glamorous and trembly, like a movie star's —Molly Giles

❧ SMOKE
See: FIRE AND SMOKE

❧ SMOKING
See: TOBACCO

❧ SMOOTHNESS
(Her legs too are sheathed in black,) as slick and lucid as oil —Simon Mawer, *The Glass Room*

(The syllables) flow like wind on water —T. Cor-aghessan Boyle

Glib as an auctioneer —James Crumley

Go down like milk and molasses —Russell Baker

Goes down like chopped hay —John Ray's *Proverbs*

It [a drink] was about as smooth as a rusty hack-saw —Harold Adams

(Cold) polished as a marble column —Honoré de Balzac

Balzac's description deftly characterizes Gos-beck, the main character of a short novel by that name.

Sleek and pretty as a new dime —Borden Deal

(Her breasts protruded from the suds wet and) sleek as seals —Jean Thompson

Slick as a button —American colloquialism

Unlike "smooth as glass" or "smooth as al-abaster" which usually describe texture, this sim-ile generally applies to something easily done. Other widely used variation to describe a glib, shrewd person are "slick as an eel" and "slick as grease."

Slick as a cake of soap —Charles Wright

Slick as a pig —R. Wright Campbell

(Would make my life as) slick as a sonnet —Tal-lulah Bankhead

Slick as spit —James Lee Burke

Slick as a watersnake —George Garrett

[Wet streets] slick as black satin —Paige Mitchell

Slick as black marble —Donald McCaig

[An icy roof] slick as cake icing —Davis Grubb

Slick as nail polish —Rosellen Brown

Slick as snot —Jonathan Kellerman

Slick as water —Terry Bisson

(Her glasses were) slippery as icicles —Cynthia Ozick

Smooth as a carpet —John Ray's *Proverbs*

Still widely used, or as one might say: "popular and enduring as a John Ray proverb."

Smooth as a kitten's ear —Slogan, Hammond Cedar Company

Smooth as a phantom —John Betjeman

(His movement was) as smooth as a ripple of water —Raymond Chandler

Smooth as a sage —Lawrence Durrell

(Her mind, clear and as) smooth as a sea stone beaten by the waves and elements for a mil-lennium —Charles Johnson

Smooth as a suburbanized television professor —Harvey Swados

Smooth as corn syrup —Helen Hudson

(Her skin was as) smooth as glass —English bal-lad

Probably one of the most frequently "smooth as" comparisons, with "smooth" and "slick" often used interchangeably as in "The frozen lake was slick as a mirror," found in Mark Helprin's short story "Ellis Island."

Smooth as marbles —Anon

(Voice) smooth as mink oil —Linda Barnes

Smooth as monumental alabaster —William Shakespeare, *Othello*

Smooth as oil —William Shakespeare, *Henry IV, Part I*

(He is a silver imp constantly sozzled, a splendif-erous spendthrift, brittly belligerent,) smooth as olive oil —Troy Patterson, "Once More into the Clubhouse," *Slate*, about latest season of the *Mad Men* television series

(The sea was) smooth as pewter plate —Mazo de la Roche

Smooth as pine-nuts —Suzanne E. Berger

(Works as) smooth as sand running through an hour glass —William Diehl

(Glasses) smooth as sea-washed stones —Ann Beattie

(Cheeks) smooth as silk —Juvenal

Though first used to describe complexion, the simile was expanded to broader use by O. Henry when he wrote "Everything goes smooth as silk."

Smooth as skin in oil —Reynolds Price

(The fellow was) smooth as soap —Jessamyn West

(Skin) smooth as stones on the shore —Mary Morris

Smooth as the inner lips of a shell —Sharon Olds

The shell comparison is used by poet Olds to describe the reddened, sun-swollen lips of the author's daughter.

Smooth as the nose of a moth —Karl Shapiro

Smooth as the road to ruin —Anon

(He shrugged and rolled up his sleeves. Both forearms were as) unmarked as a baby's bottom —Jonathan Valin

Worn smooth and slick as a chewed bone —George Garrett

Worn smooth as a tiger's eye —Sharon Sheehe Stark

♣ SNORE(S)

See Also: SLEEP

Snored as if all the frogs of spring were inside him —Eudora Welty

(Punctuated the air with a periodic) snore like the honk of geese —Paige Mitchell

Snores go up down like a zipper —Brad Leithauser

Snores like a diesel truck —Ira Wood

(Hoffman's) snores ... like muffled lamentations —Ross Macdonald

Snores ... like stones dropped on a polished surface —T. Coraghessan Boyle

Snoring like a snare drum —John D. MacDonald

Snoring like a steamroller —Brian Burland

♣ SNOW

See Also: NATURE, WEATHER

Big flakes ... floating like parachutes in the still air —Frank Ross

Drifts [of snow] heaping themselves like scaling-ladders against the walls —O. Henry

(Those) drifts of soft snow looked like featherbeds —Scott Spencer

A dry pellety snow hitting the sidewalk like uncooked grains of rice —Marge Piercy

Falling snow ... sinking into the ground as slowly as breadcrumbs thrown to fishes sink through water —Boris Pasternak

The fine snow had melted (on his hair and his eyelashes) and sparkled now like raindrops in a sunshower —Harvey Swados

Flakes ... bob and sail like moths across the driveway —James Robison

The flakes fall like asterisks —James Reiss

Flakes of snow ... falling like feathers from the sky —Grimm Brothers

The flakes ... seemed thick as tarts —Peter De Vries

Flakes swarming around the streetlamps like soft, huge moths —George Garrett

The flakes were as large as an hour's circular tatting —O. Henry

The comparison is a vivid one, but with tatting no longer a familiar pastime, a brief explanation would be needed for any but needlework aficionados.

Flakes were like feathers —Frank Swinnerton

(The sundial was) heaped with a foot-high frosting of snow like a tall, fantastic cake —Davis Grubb

(Snow was still falling) heavy flakes like goose feathers —Jilly Cooper

A row of icicles like the crystal drops of a chandelier hung from the roof —H. E. Bates

Icicles like the teeth of fish —Saul Bellow

Icicles sparkling at the eaves like pendant blades of glass —William Styron

It [snow] fell like a great armistice, bringing all simple struggles to an end —Elizabeth Hardwick

It looks pretty in the garden [in the snow], like a living Christmas —Janet Flanner

A light fringe of snow lay like a cape on the shoulders of his overcoat and like toecaps on the toes of his galoshes —James Joyce

Lightly and whitely as wheat from the grain, thickly and quickly as thoughts through the brain, so fast and so dumb do the snowflakes come —Grace Denio Lichtfield

Like an army defeated, the snow has retreated —William Wordsworth

Long icicles, like crystal daggers —Oscar Wilde

(I looked down at the street … at the) masses of snow like dirty suds —Saul Bellow

Melted [snow], leaving the gray grass like a pallet, closely pressed —Wallace Stevens

One of those brilliant, glittery snows that ought to emit some glorious sound with each crystal falling to earth, something transcendent like a Bach cantata —Lynne Sharon Schwartz

The musical comparison is particularly appropriate to the novel, Disturbances in the Field, *in which it appeared, as its main character is a classical musician.*

The pilings of snow were like the white waves of a white sea —Truman Capote

(Her feet disperse the) powdery snow, that rises up like smoke —William Wordsworth

Snow as smooth to see as cake frosting and as light as powder —Ernest Hemingway

The snow at the roadside full of bubbles like white of egg beaten up —Joyce Cary

The snow began to spill down like quiet feathers —H. E. Bates

The snow came down last night like moths —Richard Wilbur

A simile to begin a poem entitled "First Snow in Alsace."

Snow … came in thick tufts like new wool —washed before the weaver spins it —Leslie Silko

Snow … comes down like lace —Marge Piercy

Snow … decking the fields and trees with white as for a fairy wedding —Jerome K. Jerome

Snow … driving him like a fusillade of frozen needles —T. Coraghessan Boyle

Snow fell in swift spirals, floating like gulls into the tree branches —Jean Stafford

Snowflakes dove at our window like fat moths —Donald McCaig

Snowflakes grew bigger and bigger, till at last they looked like big white chickens —Hans Christian Andersen

Snowflakes … large as white carnations —Janet Flanner

Snowflakes shone like silver —Sir Hugh Walpole

Snowflakes sifting like crumbs into the yard —Paul Theroux

The [blindingly thick] snowflakes tormented him like a swarm of silver bees —G. K. Chesterton

The snow [during a snow storm] flapped like an endless white blanket —Scott Spencer

Snow flying quick as thought —Adrienne Rich

Snow had begun to fall. It made the sidewalk a spotted hide, like leopard skin —Rosellen Brown

Snow had fallen like a fine dust —Martin Cruz Smith

The snow is now coming like dollar-sized confetti —John Wainwright

Snow … it's like inebriation because it's very pleasing when it's coming, but very unpleasant when it's going —Ogden Nash

The snow lay soft like a down pillow —Thomas Mann

Snow lies like a down mattress over the earth —Lu Hsun

Snow … lighted the streets like moonlight —Jean Stafford

Snow, like sheeps' wool only whiter —Gillian Tindall

The snow like the fuzz the morning after too much Stolichnaya —Derek Lambert

Lambert's suspense novel The Red House *is set in Russia and so the reference to a Russian drink.*

Snow poured down like salt —Helen Hudson

Snow … settling like wool on the unmown grass —H. E. Bates

Snow smooth as the sky can shed —William Wordsworth

Snow … soft as froth and easy as ashes —W. R. Rodgers

Snow sparkles like eyesight falling to earth —Wallace Stevens

Snow was falling in larger flakes, like a multitude of frozen moths —Ellen Glasgow

The snow was yellow … with orange seeping into its honey color like an aftertaste at sunset —Boris Pasternak

Snow will settle like a sheet over all live color —Frank O'Hara

❧ SOAP OPERA

See Also: STAGE AND SCREEN

❧ SOCIABILITY/UNSOCIABILITY

See Also: BEHAVIOR

Affable as a wet dog —Alfred Henry Lewis

Anti-social as death —Mary McCarthy

(About as) chummy as a pair of panthers —James Forbes

Flung himself upon Arthur like a young bear —Christopher Isherwood

Friendly as a letter from home —Slogan, wine advisory board

(He insisted on being) friendly, like a man running for sheriff —Jay Parini

Greeted me like the morning sun that had deserted the skies —Mike Fredman

The greeting I received (from Phoebe) was as damp as the weather outside —Mike Fredman

He was never alone. He wore other people like armor —William McIlvanney

(The knocking was) hostile as a kick in the balls —Harold Adams

Similes can provide attention-getting openings for a story, as this one did for Adams' mystery novel, The Fourth Widow.

Pleasant as a smile —Anon

Snarled like a raccoon (whenever she was pushed) —Miles Gibson

Unresponsive as a bag of wet laundry —David Leavitt

❧ SOCIETY

Civilization, like beauty is in the eyes of the beholder —Anon

A good civilization spreads over us freely like a tree, varying and yielding because it is alive. A bad civilization stands up and sticks out above us like an umbrella —C. K. Chesterton

A community is like a ship; every one ought to be prepared to take the helm —Henrik Ibsen

Modern society is like a Calder mobile: disturb it here and it jiggles over there, too —George F. Will

Social life is a form of do-it-yourself theater —Muriel Oxenberg Murphy, *New York Times* interview, July 23, 1976

Societies, like individuals, have their moral crises and their spiritual revolutions —Richard H. Tawney

Society is a kind of parent to its members. If it, and they, are to thrive, its values must be clear, coherent and generally acceptable —Milton R. Spirstein

Society is a masked ball, where everyone hides his real character, and reveals it in hiding —Ralph Waldo Emerson

Society is like air; very high up, it is sublimated, too low down, a perfect choke-damp —Anon

Society is like a lawn, where every roughness is smoothed, every bramble eradicated, and where the eye is delighted by the smiling verdure of a velvet surface —Washington Irving

Society is like a wave. The wave moves onward, but the water of which it is composed does not —Ralph Waldo Emerson

Society is like the air, necessary to breathe, but insufficient to live on —George Santayana

♣ SOFTNESS

Feels like walking on velvet —Slogan, Clinton Carpet Co.

Flabby as an empty sack —Luigi Pirandello

Flabby as a sponge —Guy de Maupassant

(Arm …) flabby as butter —Katherine Mansfield

Fluffy as thistledown —William Humphrey

(When I reached out to touch it, it) gave like a rubber duck —T. Coraghessan Boyle

Gentle as a pigeon's sound —Stephen Vincent Benét

(Squeezed the trigger as) gently as a bee touching down to drink from a cowslip —Donald Seaman

Gone limp as a bath towel —T. Coraghessan Boyle

Graceful as Venetian quill strokes —Clarence Major

Lank as a ghost —William Wordsworth

[A chocolate bar] limp as a slab of bacon —Margaret Atwood

Limp as calamari —Ira Wood

(Paper bags as) limp as cloth —Alice McDermott

(Arms) limp as old carrots —Anne Sexton

(The potted palms were) limp as old money —George Garrett

Looks soft as darkness folded on itself —Babette Deutsch

Soft and scented as a damask rose —Vita Sackville-West

Soft and silky as a kitten's purr —Slogan, Alfred Decker & Cohn's Society Brand Clothes

(You are) soft as a bean curd —John Hersey

(The rock was as white and) as soft as a bed —Vladimir Nabokov

Soft as a bowl of Jell-O —Anon

[A distant ridge] soft as a cloud —William Wordsworth

(Love's twilight hours) soft … as a fairy's moan —John Greenleaf Whittier

Soft as a fat woman without a girdle —Anon

(Humble love in me would look for no return) soft as a guiding star that cheers, but cannot burn —William Wordsworth

(Cheeks) soft as a hound's ear —Theodore Roethke

Soft as a kitten's ear —Slogan, for both Hews & Potter belts and Spiegel Neckwear Co. ties

Soft as a marshmallow —Anon

Used primarily to imply a kind nature. "Soft as mush" is a common variation.

(His touch was) soft as an airbrush —Molly Giles

Soft as angel hair —Susan Richards Shreve

(Snow) soft as a young girl's skin —F. D. Reeve

(Waves looked) soft as carded wool —Henry Wadsworth Longfellow

Soft as fleece —Stephen Vincent Benét

Soft as linen —Hayden Carruth

The simile, which describes a stone, continues with another: "And flows like wax." A slight twist gave Scott tissues its "Soft as old linen" slogan.

Soft as lips that laugh —Algernon Charles Swinburne

Soft as love —Hallie Burnett

(Heartbeat) soft as snow on high snow falling —Daniel Berrigan

(Her cheeks were ...) soft as suet —Raymond Chandler

Soft as the thighs of women —W. D. Snodgrass

Soft as the west-wind's sigh —W. S. Gilbert

> *This form of the west-wind comparison comes from* Ruddigore. *Using the qualitative comparison form "Softer than it" dates back to the poet Shelley.*

Soft as yesterday's ice cream —James Lee Burke

Soft as young down —William Shakespeare, *Henry IV, Part I*

Softening like pats of butter —John Updike

> *In Updike's story* Made in Heaven, *the comparison refers to the softening light in windows he describes as golden.*

(You are) soft like a shower of water —William H. Gass

Soft, like a strokable cat —Beryl Markham

Soft to the touch as a handful of yarn —Jessamyn West

[Bodies] Wobbly as custard —Alice Munro

✤ SOLIDITY
See: FIRMNESS, STEADINESS, STRENGTH

✤ SOLITUDE
See: ALONENESS

✤ SORROW
See: GRIEF

✤ SOUL

Feel my soul rolling as if it were inside an empty barrel —Yehuda Amichai

The human soul is like a bird that is born in a cage. Nothing can deprive it of its natural longings, or obliterate the mysterious remembrance of its heritage —Epes Sargent

The inner chambers of the soul are like the photographer's darkroom. Like a laboratory. One cannot stay there all the time or it becomes the solitary cell of the neurotic —Anais Nin

I thought that the soul went round like a Gladstone bag, never caring a damn for any particular station-rack or hotel cloakroom —Dylan Thomas

My soul is like a desert and the wind blows in its silent barren spaces —W. Somerset Maugham

My soul is like the oar that momently dies in a desperate stress beneath the wave, then glitters out again and sweeps the sea —Sidney Lanier

Some souls are like sponges. You cannot squeeze anything out of them except what they have sucked from you —Kahil Gibran

Soul ... as disheveled as your apartment —Jay McInerney

A soul as white as heaven —Francis Beaumont and John Fletcher

The soul dwells in the body like a spider in its web —Anon Greek Philosopher

> *A variation from the same source: "The soul resides in the body like a sailor in a ship."*

Soulless as apes. Spineless as mosquitoes or dandelions —Rick Borsten

The soul, like fire, abhors what it consumes —Derek Walcott

The soul of man is larger than the sky —Hartley Coleridge

A soul that, like an ample shield, can take in all, and verge enough for more —John Dryden

A soul through which the morning shines as through a leaf —Rainer Maria Rilke

Strong souls live like fire-hearted suns; to spend their strength in further striving action —George Eliot

The sweetest souls, like the sweetest flowers, soon canker in cities —Walter Savage Landor

Your soul was like a star, and dwelt apart —William Wordsworth

In Wordsworth's sonnet the first word was "thy."

(Even if you're racked by troubles, and sick and poor and ugly) you've got your soul to carry through life like a treasure on a platter —Alice Munro

❧ SOUNDNESS

See Also: HEALTH

❧ SOUNDS

See: NOISE

❧ SPEAKING

See Also: CONVERSATION, SPEECH PATTERNS, TALKATIVENESS

[A statement] came out flat as a sheet of onion-skin paper —Cornell Woolrich

Can speak as flashy as water runs —R. Wright Campbell

Cut short his speech, like a pang of pain —Joseph Conrad

The few sentences she uttered were like eternal judgments —Larry McMurtry

Had a habit ... of making a narrow remark which, like a plumber's snake, could work its way through the ear down the heart, halfway to my heart —Grace Paley

He [Peter O'toole] doesn't just talk, he offers his words like presents, gift-wrapped —Robert Goldberg, *Wall Street Journal,* April 21, 1987

He was gathering toward speech, like a man about to rumba, waiting to feel the beat —Leonard Michaels

His tongue [is] as a devouring fire —The Holy Bible/Isaiah

His rhetoric falls like a freight train over a bridge —David Brinkley about John L. Lewis

His talk was like a stream which runs with rapid changes from rock to roses —Winthrop Mackworth Praed

To illustrate the simile, the poem in which it appears continues with "It slipped from politics to puns; it passed from Mahomet to Moses."

If I open my mouth it's like pebbles rattling together —Albert Camus

Phrases ... looping out of her mouth like a backward spaghetti-eating process —Elizabeth Spencer

A remark thrown off like an idle dart —Sylvia Berkman

Said grimly ... like a man announcing that X-rated movies had been shown at the deacons' party —Stephen King

Said it flatly, like a tour guide reading from a Baedecker —Jonathan Valin

Sentences came ... fluently enough, even though they did sound rather like quotations from a phrase book —Christopher Isherwood

Sharpened their tongues like a serpent —The Holy Bible/Psalms

[Words] slipped out of me in a spasm of candor, like a sneeze —Paul Reidinger

Some men are like bagpipes, they can't speak till their belly's filled —Seumas MacManus

Speaking without thinking is like shooting without aiming —English proverb

Speak pleasantly ... like a stewardess in an airliner with only one wing and two engines, one of which is on fire —Douglas Adams

Spoke to them mildly as mid-May weather —Stephen Vincent Benét

Talked like birds, with a gentle malice —Dame Edith Sitwell

Talked like her eyes looked, like her eyes watching us and her voice talking to us did not belong to her. Like she was living somewhere else, waiting somewhere else —William Faulkner

Talking is like playing on the harp; there is as much in laying the hands on the strings to stop their vibrations as in twanging them to bring out the music —Oliver Wendell Holmes

Talks like his tongue is in a cramp … like he has adenoids as big as footballs … and muscles to match —John Wainwright

Tough talk … like whistling in a haunted house —John Wainwright

Voice stopped, like words written off the edge of a page —Elizabeth Spencer

❧ SPEECHLESSNESS

See: SILENCE

❧ SPEECHMAKING

An after-dinner speech is like a love letter. Ideally, you should begin by not knowing what you are going to say, and end by not knowing what you've said —Lord Jowitt

Eloquence must flow by a stream that is fed by an abundant spring —Henry St. John, Viscount Bolinbroke

A good speech is like a pencil; it has to have a point like a breathless messenger's report —James Atlas

Great eloquence, like a flame, must have fuel to feed it, motion to excite it, and brightens by burning —Tacitus

His speech was like a tangled chain; nothing impaired, but all disordered —William Shakespeare, *A Midsummer Night's Dream*

Human speech is like a cracked tin kettle, on which we hammer out tunes to make tears dance when we long to move the stars —Gustave Flaubert

Make a speech that's like a long-horned steer, with a point here and there and a lot of bull in between —Norman Mailer

Oratory, like the drama, abhors lengthiness; like the drama, it must keep doing —Edward George Bulwer-Lytton

Pompous words and long pauses which lie like a leaden pain over fever —Norman Mailer

The pompous words and pauses were heard by Mailer at the 1960 Democratic convention.

Rhetoric without logic, is like a tree with leaves and blossoms, but no root —John Selden

Sermons are like pie crusts, the shorter the better —Austin O'Malley

Speeches are like babies: easy to conceive, hard to deliver —Pat O'Malley

Speeches forgotten, like a maiden speech, which all men praise, but none remember —Winthrop Mackworth Praed

A speech is like a love affair. Any fool can start it, but to end it requires considerable skill —Lord Mancroft, *Reader's Digest,* February 1967

A speech is like an airplane engine. It may sound like hell but you've got to go on —William Thomas Piper

Piper's involvement with airplanes makes this particularly appropriate.

Speech is shallow as time —Thomas Carlyle

Speech is silver, Silence is golden —Thomas Carlyle

The speech of men is like embroidered tapestries, since, like them, it must be extended in order to display its patterns, but when it is rolled up it conceals and distorts them —Plutarch

The speech … took shape in his head as clearly and precisely as if it were an official report —Leo Tolstoy

❧ SPEECH PATTERNS

Accent … almost as authentic as that of the white-jacketed medico peddling hand cream to the TV millions —Harvey Swados

Accent … thick as porridge —W. P. Kinsella

Diction … each word distinct and unslurred, as if he were a linguistics professor moderating a panel discussion on the future of the language —T. Coraghessan Boyle

The doctor's English was perfect, pure Martha's Vineyard, he sounded like Ted Kennedy's insurance salesman —T. Coraghessan Boyle

Dragging his words along like reluctant dogs on a string —Edith Wharton

Had spoken the lines without expression, running them past, uninspired, one behind the other like passing freight cars —William Brammer

He [Edmund Wilson] spoke in a curiously strangled voice, with gaps between his sentences, as if ideas jostled and thrashed about inside him, getting in one another's way as they struggled to emerge, which made for short bursts —Isaiah Berlin, *New York Times Book Review*, April 12, 1987

His facile elocution … which had so long charmed them, was now treated like warm gruel made to put cowards to sleep —Émile Zola

His statements are often preceded by stretches of silence as painful as the space between a stutterer's syllables, as he tries to translate his images into words —Ira Wood

Inflections that rise and fall with a tidal surge equal to that of the Bay of Fundy —Richard F. Shepard about comedian Jackie Mason, *New York Times*

Intoned monotonously like a sleep-walker —MacDonald Harris

Mouthing the words and nodding to himself like an actor memorizing his lines —Donald Seaman

Repeated slowly, as if he were sounding out syllables in a book —Jonathan Valin

The rest of it [a remark] was delivered at a clipped, furious pace, like Morse code —Jonathan Valin

Said one word, carefully pursed in his mouth, spat out like a grape pip —John Fowles

The sentences were spoken like sentences from a judge summing up, bit by bit —V. S. Pritchett

Short brief staccato sentences like slaps —William Faulkner

Spaces her adjectives, like little whiplashes —John Fowles

Spacing his words as if for a particularly stupid and stubborn person —Nancy Huddleston Packer

Spat out the words like orange seeds —Dorothy Francis

Speak falteringly, like an unrehearsed actor —Anon

Speaking [in a heavy tone] … as if he were dropping words like molten lead —G. K. Chesterton

Speak like a death's head —William Shakespeare, *Henry IV, Part II*

Speak … like a telegram —Dashiell Hammett

Spitting the word from her mouth … as if it were a poisonous seed —Flannery O'Connor

Splutter and splash like a pig in a puddle —W. S. Gilbert

Spoke clearly, but in a low and hesitant voice, as if he were translating from Spanish as he went along —Norman Mailer

Spoke like a radio program —Ludwig Bemelmans

Spoke more slowly than ever before and with difficulty, like someone who fears a stammer —Dan Jacobson

Spoke slowly, with a kind of uniformity of emphasis that made his words stand out like the raised type for the blind —Edith Wharton

Spoke very slowly and deliberately, like a man reading aloud from a difficult text —Jonathan Valin

Sputtered out [words] like a wet fuse —Richard Moran

Stutter like a new-clipped crow —George Garrett

Talked flowingly like a medium —Anais Nin

Talked like she had bugs in her mouth —Madison Smartt Bell

Talked with commas, like a heavy novel —Raymond Chandler

(He had developed an unfortunate habit of) talking like a Chinese fortune cookie —John Cheever

(Tendency to) talk like a sten gun —George F. Will about Hubert Humphrey

Used the English language with dictionary precision … almost as if it were a foreign tongue he had learned perfectly —Lael Tucker Wertenbaker

Use her words cautiously, like weapons that might slip and inflict a wound —Edith Wharton

Words … dragging out like words in an anthem —G. K. Chesterton

Words, each distinct and separate, like multicolored marbles —Francis King

Words leaped out of his mouth like machine-gun bullets —Frank Conroy

Words were being mouthed like signal flags —Norman Mailer

♣ SPEED

See Also: RUNNING

(Poems have become) as instant as coffee or onion soup mix —Donald Hall

(They'll whip her back …) as quick as shit through a goose —Derek Lambert

As swift as meditation, or the thoughts of love —William Shakespeare, *Hamlet*

As swiftly as a reach of still water is crisped by the wind —Rudyard Kipling

Be not in a hurry, like the almond, first to blossom and last to ripen. Be rather like the mulberry, last to blossom and first to ripen —The Holy Bible/Apocrypha

Bills were flying through the Senate on Wednesday like great flocks of geese soaring into the turbines of a passenger jet —Gail Collins, "The Senate Overachiever," *New York Times,* March 15, 2012

The crowd was moving fast … like a big spread raveling and the separate threads disappeared down the dark streets —Flannery O'Connor

Drive [a car] like the hounds of hell —Rosamund Pilcher

Fast as a bird on the wing —Anon

Fast as a cat scurrying up a tree at the approach of a strange dog —Anon

Fast as a cook cracks eggs —Thomas Nash

Fast as a heartbeat —John D. MacDonald

Fast as a jet —Mark Helprin

Fast as a pickpocket —Anon

Fast as a propeller —Bertolt Brecht

(Scrambles into the room) fast as a spider —Robert Silverberg

Fast as greased lightning —American colloquialism

Fast as the blink of an eye —Anon

Fast-moving as the gray fox that climbs trees after squirrels —Marge Piercy

(Little and) fleet as a terrier running beside a bloodhound —Erich Maria Remarque

(To vanish) fleet as days and months and years, fleet as the generations of mankind —William Wordsworth

Flying like ice in a sleet storm —Ben Ames Williams

Fly like a donkey with pepper up its behind —Aharon Megged

Galloped through [religious mass] like a man with witches after him —Edith Wharton

Goes like a whip-lash flicked across a horse's neck —Rudyard Kipling

Going like flames —Samuel Beckett

Going like sixty —F. D. Reeve

Go like a house afire —Anon

One of many "Go like" similes that have worked their way into the American language mainstream since the late 1830s. Some other examples: "Go like a shot," "Go like hell," and "Go like mad."

Go through like a dose of salts —American colloquialism

While purgative salts are pretty much a thing of the past, the simile endures as a way to describe a very rapid pace. With the penchant for brand names, "Go through like Ex-Lax" has become a common alternative.

Go through them [reading materials] like a kid through potato chips —James Crumley

He rushed past her like a football tackle —James Thurber

(Wedding plans were) hurtling along like a train on tracks —Paul Reidinger

Insectlike swiftness —Saul Bellow

It must be done like lightning —Ben Jonson

Just a glance, like passing your eyes over the spines of books without being able to read the title … that quick —Arthur A. Cohen

(Scurried off, his) legs going like a windmill —Paige Mitchell

Like a sunbeam, swift and bright —Sir Walter Scott

Move with the speed of a Grand Prix Racer —Anon

Moving fast as a train —Anon

My days are swifter than a weaver's shuttle —The Holy Bible/Job

While this simile is not much used these days, it is the one that has seeded the many contemporary versions.

Quick and nimble; more like a bear than a squirrel —H. G. Bohn's *Hand-Book of Proverbs*

Quick as a lizard —Anthony Trollope

Quick as an attack dog —Gloria Norris

(Acted) quick as a knife —Penelope Gilliatt

(The wolf … ate her up as) quick as a slap —Anne Sexton

Quick as a striking snake —George Garrett

Quick as a weasel —Robert B. Parker

Quick as a wink —Anon

While variations such as "Quick as dust" and "Quick as scat" have faded from the American vocabulary, "Quick as a wink" endures to the point of overuse.

(Goes) quick as light —Noel Coward, lyrics for "Chase Me Charlie"

Quick as lightning —Frances Sheridan

The American variation of the simile first used by Sheridan in a play named Discovery *is "Quick as greased lightning."*

Quick as mercury —Marguerite Yourcenar

(Slipped down) quick as minnows —Marge Piercy

(Barry's eye was as) quick as sound —Frank Swinnerton

Quicker than a crab underwater —John Updike

Quicker than boiling asparagus —Caesar Augustus

According to Stevenson's Proverbs, Maxims and Famous Sayings, *Augustus used this expression whenever he wanted anything to be done fast.*

Quick on his feet as a running deer —Stephen Vincent Benét

(Lavella's brain) raced like a trapped rabbit —William Beechcroft

(Feet) rapid as the river —Henry Wadsworth Longfellow

Rash as fire —William Shakespeare, *Othello*

(Raleigh) rushed through (these hypotheses) like rosary beads —Michael Malone

(Men) rushing like they were bolt out of a cannon —Richard Ford

Rushing wildly from room to room like a flustered hen —Christopher Isherwood

Scurried like a crab —Michael Malone

She was so swift … it was like having a small cute dog with you —Isak Dinesen

Some people are too fast for their own good, like Asahel in the Book of Samuel —Saul Bellow

Sped around like intergalactic missiles —Lisa Harris

Harris's simile describes the activity of the Lubavitcher women in Crown Heights, the subject of her book The World of a Hasidic Family.

(The game) speeds along like a fast freight —W. P. Kinsella

The game speeding along is baseball, the background for The Iowa Baseball Confederacy *and other Kinsella novels.*

Speedy as steam roller —George Ade

(A wild beast) started for me (as to attack) like a streak of lightning —Rex Stout

Swift as a cloud between sea and sky —Percy Bysshe Shelley

Swift as a greyhound —Ouida

Swift as a mugger —David Leavitt

Swift as an arrow —Anon

This has been attributed to numerous sources dating back to the early seventeenth century.

Swift as a plunging knife —Rudyard Kipling

Swift as a shadow —William Shakespeare, *A Midsummer Night's Dream*

Swift as desire —Mary Pix

Swift as fear —Thomas Parnell

Swift as the eagle (flieth) —The Holy Bible/ Deuteronomy

Swift as the waters —The Holy Bible/Job

Swift as thought —William Shakespeare, *Love's Labour's Lost*

Swift as unbridled rage —Henry Abbey

Swifter than the wind —William Shakespeare, *A Midsummer Night's Dream*

Swift in motion as a ball —William Shakespeare, *Romeo and Juliet*

Swiftly as butterflies' wings —Margaret Mitchell

The girl fluttering her lashes is Scarlett O'Hara of Gone with the Wind *fame.*

Travelling fast as a wish —Elizabeth Bishop

(The race) went by like an express train —Enid Bagnold

(She dressed and) went off like a top with the whip behind it —Vicki Baum

Went past … like lightning past a hill —Jessamyn West

Went through it like a clown through a paper hoop —Temole Scott

Went through like shit through a tin horn —American colloquialism

❧ SPIRIT
See: COURAGE

❧ SPOILAGE
See: DISINTEGRATION

❧ SPONTANEITY
See: NATURALNESS

❧ SPORTS
See Also: BASEBALL, BOXING AND WRESTLING, FOOTBALL, GOLF

Batted the [tennis] ball away like an irritating gnat —Rita Mae Brown

An American winning the French bicycle race is like a Frenchman winning most valuable baseball player —Chris Wallace commenting on Greg Le Mond's winning of Tour De France race, NBC-TV, July 26, 1986

Angling may be said to be so like the mathematics that it can never be fully learnt —Izaak Walton

The [tennis] ball knifes right onto the face of the strings and stays there like a piece of cheese —Ron Carlson

Basketball is like poetry in motion —Jim Valvano, North Carolina State coach, 1987

Bathers hop across the waves agilely, aimlessly, like fleas —Malcolm Cowley

Coaching is like a monkey on a stick. You pass the same fellows on the way down as you pass on the way up —Steve Owen, New York Giants football coach

[A swimmer] floated on her back [in water] like a pink air mattress —Will Weaver

Good skiing is like good sex; it is all about instincts and movement and taking risks. Water skiing? That is even better. Water skiing is like a good orgasm. —Dr. Ruth K. Westheimer, quoted in St. Germain bio-play, *Dr. Ruth All the Way.*

Having the America's Cup yacht race in San Diego instead of Newport is like going to Mardi Gras in Pittsburg —Rhode Island Representative St. Germaine, *Wall Street Journal,* February 5, 1987

Hockey players are like mules. They have no fear of punishment and no hope of rewards —Emory Jones, general manager of the St. Louis Arena, *St. Louis Post-Dispatch,* December 26, 1963

Holds a siren yellow tennis ball up in front of her, like the torch on the Statue of Liberty, and hits it with a combination of force and grace —Daphne Merkin

If a tie is like kissing your sister, losing is like kissing your grandmother with her teeth out —George Brett, Cincinnati Royals third baseman, *Sports Illustrated,* June 23, 1986

I saw more sails biting the wind that I've ever seen before; it was like sailing through the mouth of a shark —Jean Lamuniere, September 15, 1986

Legs [bicycling] pumping like wheels —Murray Bail

Little Pat played [tennis] … like a weekly wound up machine —John Updike

Records fell like ripe apples on a windy day —E. B. White

The reel was screaming … humming like a telegraph wire in a sixty-mile gale —Arthur Train

The skaters [on the Ranger team] … perform like an electrocardiogram readout —Craig Wolff *New York Times,* September 8, 1986
Wolff's simile alluded to the team's impersonal performance.

Sports is like a war without killing —Ted Turner, baseball team owner

Swim like a cannonball —Tony Ardizzone

(I can) swim like a duck —William Shakespeare, *The Tempest*

Swimming the English Channel —it was like swimming in dishwater —Sandra Blewett, long distance swimmer, *The Evening Standard,* August 21, 1979

Tearing through the water like a seal —Rosamond Lehmann

Tennis is like a lawsuit; you can always be surprised by what happens on the other side of the court —Anon

Their arms were so high on the follow-through it looked like a mass ascension of Mount Everest —Archie Oldham
The simile, taken from a basketball story, "The Zealots of Cranston Tech," describes a team of players all shooting for baskets together.

The undulant fly line coiled out over the pond like a fleeing serpent —Robert Traver

Violent exercise is like a cold bath. You think it does you good because you feel better when you stop it —Robert Quillen

(Bicycling children) wheeled like swallows through luminous, lemon-colored air —Julia O'Faolain

Working out the [fishing] line at his feet, like a cowboy coiling a rope —Robert Traver

You will find angling to be like the virtue of humility, which has a calmness of spirit and a world of other blessings attending upon it —Izaak Walton

♣ SPREADING

See Also: GROWTH, PERVASIVENESS

(Anxiety was) as contagious as a yawn —Barbara Lazear Ascher *New York Times*, October 23, 1986

Blown up [with fever] like a tire —Elena Poniatowska

(Excuses) breaking out like pimples —Marge Piercy

Breed like guinea pigs —Raymond Chandler

Catch happiness as quickly as others catch colds —Storm Jameson

Catching like fire in dry grass —William Dean Howells

The clues must have been piling up for a while already, like unread e-mails, just a click away from being read, slapped on like an awkward coda. —Jonathan Tropper, *This Is Where I Leave You*

Contagious like the gladness of a happy child —Earle Bulwer-Lytton

Excitement swept through Jalna [the estate which is the setting for a series of de la Roche novels] like a forest fire —Mazo de la Roche

Expand like air in a pressure chamber —Penelope Gilliatt

Gather like dust on a window sill —Anon

Multiply like troubles —Marge Piercy

Passed around (German measles) like a dish of cool figs at the first rehearsal —Reynolds Price

(Houses) popping up everywhere like the heat rash. Like pimples —George Garrett

[The tendency of random thoughts to] proliferate like yeast. —Ben Dolnick, "Semicolons: A Love Story" opinion blog *New York Times*, July 2, 2012

Spread a thought … like butter on toast —Carlos Fuentes

(Feel her pleasure deepening and) spreading like a chord struck in all octaves at once, sustained, played, and then held and held till it slowly faded into its overtones —Marge Piercy

(She looked at me, recognition) spreading like a rash —Sharon Sheehe Stark

(Pain) spreading like lava —John Braine

Spreading [throughout her system] … like poison dye —Margaret Millar

In the mystery novel, The Fiend, *the author uses the simile to describe a key character's growing alertness of a dangerous situation.*

(Affection …) spread like an epidemic through the room —Jean Stafford

Spread like an unconfirmed rumor —Elyse Sommer

Spread like a quenchless fire —Percy Bysshe Shelley

Spread … like a tiny spray of ink on a piece of blotting paper —Franz Werfel

Spread like butter under a knife —Lawrence Durrell

Spread like dandelion after spring rain —Marilyn Ross about growth of directories, letter to editor, *Publishers Weekly*, June 5, 1987

(But they cling and) spread like lichen —Elizabeth Bishop

Spread like mushrooms after a fresh spring rain —Anon

Mushrooms have long lent themselves to quick growth comparisons. A variation: "Grow like toadstools."

Spread like mushrooms across an unsuspecting garden —Tom Robbins

Spread like pancake batter on a hot griddle —Elyse Sommer

Spread like the desert —Henry James

(Silence) spread ... like water that a pebble stirs —Dante Gabriel Rossetti

Spread out like a doily —Alma Stone

Spread out (the sun) like a jellyfish —John Steinbeck

(I saw the vineyards) spread out like wings —Eudora Welty

Spreads faster than panic in a plane —Donald Seaman

Spreads like a sigh —Anon

(Love that) spreads like a stain of ink in absorbent cloth —Diane Wakoski

As poet Wakoski links the spreading stain with love in her poem "My Little Heart Pops Out," so W. H. Auden uses "Ruin spreading like a stain" in Something Is Bound to Happen

Spreads like good news —Slogan for SatinWax, Economic Laboratory

Spread through like a clumsy, uninvited guest who is obese and eats too much —Lorrie Moore

The descriptive frame of reference in Moore's novel Self-Help *is cancer.*

(Enemies ... are) sprouting (around me) like tulips —Peter Benchley

♣ SPRIGHTLINESS

See: ACTIVENESS

♣ SPRING

See: SEASONS

♣ STAGE AND SCREEN

An actor is a sculpture who carves in snow —Edwin Booth

An actor is like a cigar; the more you puff him the smaller he gets —Anon

Actors are like burglars: they always change their names for business purposes —Frank Richardson

An actor's soul must be like a diamond. The more facets its got, the more shining his name —Grace Paley

The camera is a little like the surgeon's knife —Jean Renoir

Careers [in acting], like rockets, don't always take off on time. The trick is to always keep the engine running —Gary Sinise

The cinema, like the detective story, makes it possible to experience without danger all the excitement, passion, and desirousness which must be suppressed in a humanitarian ordering of society —Carl Jung

Every film is launched like a squid in an obscuring cloud of spectacular publicity —Dudley Nichols

[Danny Kaye] feels about an audience the way most men feel about a date. He woos them. He wants to make them happy —Sylvia Fine, quoted in husband Kaye's obituary, *New York Times,* March 4, 1987

Making a film is like going down a mine—once you've started, you bid a metaphorical goodbye to the daylight and the outside world for the duration —John Schlesinger

Many plays, certainly mine, are like blank checks. The actors and directors put their own signatures on them —Thornton Wilder

The movie actor, like the sacred king of primitive tribes, is a god in captivity —Alexander Chase

A movie is like a person. Either you trust it or you don't —Mike Nichols

Movie stars are like racehorses. Everybody knows their name, but they have to obey the stable boys —MacDonald Harris

A movie without sex would be like a candy bar without nuts —Earl Wilson

Not to go to the theatre is like making one's toilet without a mirror —Arthur Schopenhauer

A play is like a cigar. If it is a failure no amount of puffing will make it draw. If it is a success everyone wants a box —Henry F. Bryan

A play, like a bill, is of no value till it is accepted —Henry Fielding

Prologues like compliments are a loss of time —David Garrick

Seeing [James Earl] Jones and [Angela] Lansbury "take stage," in the blatant way they do here, is something like watching a monarch annex a neighboring province, except that the consequences are delightful rather than dire —Michael Feingold on the 2012 Broadway revival of *Gore Vidal's The Best Man, Village Voice,* April 10, 2012

Sex percolates merrily through all of the daytime soaps like grounds in a coffee pot —Carin Rubenstein, *Channels Magazine,* March 1986

Soap opera is like sex outside marriage: many have tried it, but most are ashamed of being caught —Peter Buckahm

Television is like the little girl who had a little curl. When it is good, it is very, very good, and when it is bad it is horrid —Melvin I. Cooperman, discussing quality of playwriting for stage, screen and television, *Word Warp* (electronic bulletin board for writers) May 8, 1987

The theater is a communal event, like church —Marcia Norman, quoted *New York Times Book Review* interview, May 24, 1987

Theatre is like baseball; it depends on hits and runs —Anon

You have to watch out with my plays. They're like yeast. You think they're one thing, then all of a sudden subtext gets to working —Horton Foote about his writing in Dennis Brown's *Shoptalk*

♣ STALENESS

See Also: TIMELINESS/UNTIMELINESS

As trite as the lyrics to a fifties hit —Hilma Wolitzer

Her novel In the Palomar Arms *compares the triteness of old song lyrics to what happens to the words spoken by someone once loved passionately.*

Felt about as fresh as an old piece of chewing gum —Mike Fredman

Flat and cold as the muffins of this morning's breakfast —Henry James

In James' play Pyramus and Thisbe, *this describes personality traits grown stale with overuse and familiarity.*

Flat as last night's beer —Louis Untermeyer

Stale as an old cigar —Wilfrid Sheed

Stale as yesterday's bread —Arthur A. Cohen

(But it was all unmeaningful to us, and all the proverbs seemed stiff and) stale, like dusty labels on neglected antiquities —G.K. Chesterton

Stale, like the butt of a dead cigar —Rudyard Kipling

Tired as a much-told joke —Anon

♣ STANDING

See Also: BEARING, IMMOBILITY, PERSONALITY PROFILES, POSTURE

He was standing there with his arms at his sides like a wooden soldier —Ann Beattie

(Mrs. Snow was) standing framed in the doorway like a faded vestal virgin guarding a shrine —Ross Macdonald

Standing … like a painted statue —Iris Murdoch

Stand like clockwork toys —W. S. Gilbert

Stands like the figurehead at a ship's prow —Stevie Smith

A variation on the same theme: "Stood, like a carving on the prow of a ship."

Stood around like shadows —Maya Angelou

Stood as if thunderstruck —Joseph Conrad

Stood before us, huge and dark like a colossus —Margaret Drabble

Stood like a private before his colonel —Frank Swinnerton

Stood like lead —Wallace Irwin

Stood like stocks —Dorothy Canfield

Stood stiffly as a hanged man —Leigh Allison Wilson

Stood up and stretched like a sleepy cat —Gloria Norris

❧ STARES

See Also: FROWNS, LOOKS

Dug his blue eyes into me, like nails —Jay Parini

(I've been feeling your) eyes boring into me like a pair of yellow jackets. She had a curiously intense stare, like a greedy child waiting for sweets —Beryl Bainbridge

Stared at each other quietly, like enemies —Robert Campbell

Stared at him, holding him, like the high point on a compass —Richard Ford

Stared at [a question] keenly as if it were a fly that he was waiting to swat when it came round again —V.S. Pritchett

Stared at me like blocks of wood —Donald Justice

Stared blankly at me like a dead fish —Joe Coomer

(Had no expression in his gray eyes. He) stared like a cat at an empty window —Bill Granger

Stared … with the intensity of a man having a private audience with an angel —James Morrow

Stares at me like I'm dirt he intends to one day wipe off his shoes —Robert Campbell

Stares at my idea like a crystal vase suspended in his mind's rare ether —Richard Ford

(Powell's) stare seemed to pinch her like a pair of tongs —Flannery O'Connor

(Stood there) staring at him like a stunned ox —Oakley Hall

Staring at me like unfed dogs —Dwight Garner, "The Way We Read Now," *New York Times*, March 17, 2012, about the lights on electronic reading gadgets

Staring at me with a studied air, as though measuring me —Kent Nelson

Staring into his face like a devotee before an idol —Elizabeth Spencer

Stand staring like rustics at a fair —Henry James

A way … of staring at the wall or at the window like a detective at a murder scene, depsperate for clues —Clive Barker

❧ STARS

The dipper burned like a strand of diamonds on a sable cloak —Joseph Wambaugh

The divisions between the rings [of Saturn] are furrows in which the satellites rotate … like sheepdogs running around the flocks to keep it compact —Italo Calvino

The evening star flickered like a lamp just lit —Willa Cather

In the dark vault of the sky the stars hung like muted dots of leaden silver —Heinrich Böll
This lovely simile is the first sentence of Böll's The Ration Runners.

Jupiter displays two equatorial stripes like a scarf decorated with interwoven embroideries —Italo Calvino

A lovely star … large as the full moon —Jaroslav Seifert

The Milky Way stands out so clearly that it looks as if it had been polished and rubbed over for the holidays —Anton Chekhov

A star as bright as day —Anon Christmas ballad, probably dating to Middle Ages

Starlight fell like rain —F. Scott Fitzgerald

Stars are dropping thick as stones —Sylvia Plath

(Tonight) the stars are like a crowd of faces moving round the sky —Wallace Stevens

The stars burned steadily, like the lights of far-off ships —Marjory Stoneman Douglas

The stars clung like snow crystals in the black sky —Ross Macdonald

Stars … cold, like pieces of ice —Paige Mitchell

Stars … dissolved like bubbles —Katherine Mansfield

> *The simile in full context: "In the sky some tiny stars floated for a moment and then they were gone—they were dissolved like bubbles."*

Stars gleamed and winked like searching fireflies —Robert Traver

Stars … huge, like daisies —May Sarton

Stars large as asters —Mary Stewart

Stars … like countless diamond lamps —Hans Christian Andersen

(At night,) stars rise like the bubbles of the drowned —Yehuda Amichai

The stars seemed to look down like a thousand winking eyes —William Humphrey

The stars which at midnight looked like a spillway of broken pearls, did not shine at this hour; they were holes of light, like eye squints in black masks —Paul Theroux

Twinkle, twinkle, little star how I wonder what you are, up above the world so high, like a diamond in the sky —Anne Taylor

✣ STARTING AND STOPPING

See: BEGINNINGS AND ENDINGS, PAUSE

✣ STATELINESS

See: BEARING

✣ STATISTICS

See: FACTS

✣ STEADINESS

See Also: FIRMNESS

(Believe in justice) inexorable as the decay of an isotope —Marge Piercy

Solid as earthenware —Anne Sexton

Solid as the continent —Slogan, North American Life Insurance

Stayed steady as a castle —John le Carré

(His touch is quick, sure) steady as a laser —T. Coraghessan Boyle

Steady as the moonlight —Saul Bellow

(Hands as) steady as the murder rate —Loren D. Estleman

Steady as the stare of a glass eye —Arthur Baer

Steady as the water flowing from a hydrant —James G. Hueneker

✣ STEALTH

See: SECRECY

✣ STERILITY

See: BARRENNESS, EMPTINESS

✣ STICKINESS

See: CLINGING

✣ STILLNESS

See: IMMOBILITY, PEACEFULNESS, SILENCE

✣ STINGINESS

See: THRIFT

✣ STOMACH

See Also: BODY, FATNESS, SHAPE, THINNESS

A beer gut like a beach ball —Rick Borsten

A belly like a huge alabaster bowl —Paule Marshall

Belly like a meadow —John D. MacDonald

Belly … round as a tub —Will Weaver

Belly stuck out like a full moon —Carlos Baker

(My soft) belly that hangs over my shorts like the cap of a mushroom —Ira Wood

Belly tight as a drumhead —George Garrett

Big belly all puffed out in front like he took a tube in the morning and blew it up as far as it would go —George Garrett

A big belly that hung over his pants like a melon —Gloria Norris

Carried his paunch like something stolen and badly hidden beneath his shirt —John Irving

Her belly looked like a balloon —Tony Ardizzone

Her [pregnant] belly rises, tight as a beach ball —François Camoin

Her belly split like a backside by her caesarian scar —Alice McDermott

His abdomen looked like the carapace of a lobster, all rock-hard, etched, and segmented musculature —Jonathan Valin

His gut protruded like a basketball pumped to maximum pressure per square inch —Sue Grafton

The jowls of his belly crawl and swell like the sea —Karl Shapiro

This vivid simile is the opening line of a poem entitled "The Glutton."

Stomach … hard as a cord of wood —Richard Ford

Stomach hard as a washboard —Cynthia Ozick

Stomach [of a pregnant woman] like a globe —Ruth McLaughlin

Tight potbelly like a swallowed ball —Peter Matthiessen

❧ STOP

See: PAUSE

❧ STORIES

See Also: BOOKS, WRITERS/WRITING

All circumstances in a tale answer one another like notes in music —Robert Louis Stevenson

Fiction is like a spider's web, attached ever so slightly perhaps, but still attached to life at all four corners —Virginia Woolf

A good story compels you like sexual hunger but the pace is more leisurely —Robert Hass

A good story is like a bitter pill with the sugar coating inside of it —O. Henry

A poor story is a good deal like a grist, the oftener it is told, the less there is of it —Josh Billings

In Billings' dialect this read: "The oftner it iz told, the less thare iz ov it."

Stories are like snapshots … pictures snatched out of time with clean, hard edges —James Crumley

Stories, like whiskey, must be allowed to mature in the cask —Sean O'Faolain, *Atlantic Monthly*, December 1956

Stories that meandered along like lazy streams —George Garrett

A storyteller is like a ship's captain. He takes the passengers places where they might laugh or cry, but they always feel safe —Michael Parent, storyteller, *New York Times*, May 19, 1986

A story with a moral appended is like the bill of a mosquito. It bores you, and then injects a stinging drop to irritate your conscience —O. Henry

A tale without love is like beef without mustard —Anatole France

❧ STRAIGHTNESS

See Also: POSTURE

Direct, like a guided torpedo —William Humphrey

Erect as compass in its curve —Anne Morrow Lindberg

Even as a row of West Point cadets on parade —Arthur Baer

Even as a set of false teeth —Arthur Baer

(Noses) even as buttons on a tape —Beryl Markham

Straight as a column —Louis Adamic

Straight as a gun-barrel (she carried her lengthy shadow up and down the golden sand) —Jean Stafford

(Walks) straight as a hoe —T. Coraghessan Boyle

(A woman) straight as a hunting-knife —Stephen Vincent Benét

Straight as a line —Geoffrey Chaucer

> *This is transcribed from Chaucer's old English: "streight as any lyne." An American folk variant said to originate in Maine is the much-used "straight as a ramrod."*

Straight as an arrow —Aphra Behn

> *A simile much in use, both to describe physical and moral erectness. To emphasize the latter meaning there's "straight as your sister," attributed to Jerome Barry.*

(Teeth) straight as a picket fence —Susan Fromberg Schaeffer

Straight as a plumb line —Mike Sommer

Straight as a stick and looked as brittle —V.S. Pritchett

(I felt her to be) straight as die —Colette

Straight as a fir tree —Henry Van Dyke

(The country road is wide, light grey,) straight as a ruler —Cora Sandel

Straight as the backbone of a herring —John Ray's *Proverbs*

[Lower eyelids] straight as ruler edges —Dashiell Hammett

Straight like a pine —Joseph Conrad

Straight ... like long rows of soldiers —Oscar Wilde

Straight, thin as a pencil —Miller Williams

This simile marks the opening of a poem entitled "The Writer."

(His two rifles as) upright as umbrellas —Edward Hoagland

♣ STRANGENESS

Alien and mysterious and uncanny, like sleeping out in the jungle alone —Christopher Isherwood

Eerie as a man carving his own epitaph —William McIlvanney

Miraculous as fire in the snow —Sam Shepard

Mysterious as an Agatha Christie story with the last page torn out —James Brooke

Mysterious as cells seen under a microscope —Ann Beattie

> *In Beattie's short story "Janus," the comparison refers to the bits of color in a ceramic bowl.*

Mysterious as tea leaves —Vincent Canby

Mystery emanated from her like a fire alarm —Richard Ford

Peculiar as a middle-aged man undressed —David Denby

Queer as a green kielbasa —Peter Meinke

> *A colloquialism on the same theme: "queer as a three-dollar bill."*

Queer as a jaybird —John O'Hara

The scenes and incidents had the strangeness of the transcendental, as if they were snatches torn from lives on other planets that had somehow drifted to the earth —Boris Pasternak

Strange as a wedding without a bridegroom —Anon

Strange, eerie: like something out of a fairy tale —T. Coraghessan Boyle

♣ STREETSCAPES

See: CITY/STREETSCAPES

♣ STRENGTH

See Also: BODY, COURAGE, MUSCLES, TOUGHNESS

Air of impregnability that he carried with him like a briefcase full of secrets —Derek Lambert

As indestructible as a bride's first set of biscuits —Jim Murray, about football player Mike Garrett, *Los Angeles Herald*, June 1986

Bones ... like bars of iron —The Holy Bible/Job

Built like a bouncer in a clip joint —Saul Bellow

Built like a brick shit-house —American colloquialism, popularized in U.S. Army

> *With slight alterations some of the more colorful army and country similes can be cleaned up with the original meaning still implicit. For example,*

in her novel, Love Medicine, *Louise Erdrich describes a character as "built like a brick outhouse."*

Built like a toolbox —Lee K. Abbott

A cobweb is as good as the mightiest cable when there is no strain upon it —Henry Ward Beecher

Gave off a sense of virility almost as positive as an odor —Samuel Yellen

Get the upper hand … like a strong sun —Albert Camus

Grew strong, as if doubt never touched his heart —Wallace Stevens

(Our meaning together is) hardy as an onion (and layered) —Marge Piercy

I am as strong as a bull moose —Theodore Roosevelt

I am like a forest that has once been razed; the new shoots are stronger and brisker —Victor Hugo

Looked as durable and tough as a tree growing on a stony hillside —Mazo de la Roche

Solid and strong, like a little bull —Frank Tuohy

Solid as a temple —Louis MacNeice

Strong and hard as a tree —Vicki Baum

Some other strength/tree comparisons include: "strong as an old apple tree" (Eudora Welty) and "sturdy as an oak trunk" (Ignazio Silone).

Strong as a door —Reynolds Price

Strong as a giant —Erich Maria Remarque

(A soul) strong as a mountain river —William Wordsworth

(An alibi as) strong as a twenty-foot wall —Jimmy Sangster

(And the muscles of his brawny arms are) strong as iron bands —Henry Wadsworth Longfellow

Strong as jealousy —William Blake

Strong as money —Philip Levine

What poet Levine is comparing to the strength of money is work.

Strong as the heart of a mighty Oak / With arms of steel like Hercules —Richard Adler and Jerry Ross, "Shoeless Joe from Hannibal MO," *Damn Yankees*

(Someone wakens to a life as) strong as the smell of urine —Philip Levine

Strong as the summer sun —Anon

(Had grown) strong as the sun or the sea —Algernon Charles Swinburne

(This old woman is dangerous: she is as) strong as three men —George Bernard Shaw

Strong as youth, and as uncontrolled —Henry Wadsworth Longfellow

Longfellow uses this simile to describe the ocean in his poem "The Building of the Ship."

Stronger than mahogany —Anne Sexton

Strong, like a tower —Nina Bawden

(Vemish and his wife were) strong, like rocks, not like rivers. Their strength was more in remaining than in doing —Barry Targan

(Your blunderer is as) sturdy as a rock —William Cowper

Takes brute strength like pushing a cow uphill —Anne Sexton

Using his fist the way a carpenter uses a hammer —Irwin Shaw

[Alais addressing King Henry in the play *The Lion in Winter*] You're like the rocks at Stonehenge; nothing knocks you down —James Goldman

❧ STRUGGLE

See Also: BEHAVIOR, FUTILITY, LIFE

Flailing and resisting, like a desperate moth —Claire Messud, *The Last Life*

(In his efforts with the numbing pain,) he was like a man wrestling with a creature of the air —Stephen Crane

Like the tiny coral insect, working deep under the dark waters, we strive and struggle, each for our own little ends —Jerome K. Jerome

Struggle along ... stopping and starting like a blown newspaper —J. G. Farrell

(The coalition Israeli government) struggled like two cats in a bag —Ebra Ames

Struggle like a fish —Leo Tolstoy

Struggling like a fly trapped in a glass of water —Anon

Struggling like a moth to break its chrysalis —Rumer Godden

Struggling through life like a wearied swimmer trying to touch the horizon —Israel Zangwill

❧ STUBBORNNESS

See: PERSISTENCE

❧ STUDENTS

See: EDUCATION

❧ STUPIDITY

See Also: ABSURDITY, DUULLNESS, FOOL-ISHNESS, INSULTS, MIND

Assholes are like weeds——a bitch to get rid of and when you do, another one grows back in the same place —Jonathan Kellerman

Brains like mashed potatoes —Anon

Dumb as a beetle —Anon

> The beetle has been linked to dullness and stupidity since the sixteenth century.

Dumb as a stick of wood —Anon

Dumb as pure white lead —John Updike

Had the brains of a Playboy bunny and fucked like one —Jonathan Valin

He'd be sharper than a serpent's tooth, if he wasn't as dull as ditch water —Charles Dickens

He's like the man who thinks it's raining when you pee in his eyes —Anon

His head was as empty as a politician's speech —Anon

I'm as thick as a plank —Princess Diana excusing herself from playing a game with a patient during a hospital visit

(About as) intelligent as a bundle of shawls —Henry James

Isn't very intelligent ... he's like a hound that simply follows the scent. He crumples his nose up, looking for his fleas —Henri-Pierre Roché

Like dogs, that meeting with nobody else, bit one another —John Ray's *Proverbs*

(He) looked as if he'd stood in line twice when the brains were being handed out —Christopher Hale

Look stupid as a poet in search of a simile —Thomas Holcroft

A man with a small head is like a pin without any, very apt to get into things beyond his depth —Josh Billings

(A snail's about as) smart as mud —CBS-TV news story about snails being grown for escargot lovers, November 5, 1986

(That man is) so stupid it sits on him like a halo —Emlyn Williams

(The free press in Israel has belatedly awakened to the meaning of this act, which was as) stupid as cracking the safe of your own bank —William Safire, *New York Times*, March 9, 1987

> *Safire's simile refers to Israel's recruitment of an American as a spy.*

Stupid as jugs without handles —Honoré de Balzac

Stupid as oysters —August E. F. Von Kotzbue

To serve an unintelligent man is like crying in the wilderness, massaging the body of a dead man, planting water-lilies on dry land, whispering in the ear of the deaf —Panchatantra

While he was not dumber than an ox, he was not any smarter either —James Thurber

❧ STURDINESS

See: FIRMNESS, STRENGH

❧ STYLE

See Also: CLOTHING

Dress as if having been born in a clothing store —David Ignatow

Elegance stamped on her as by a die —Henry James

Elegant as a Cole Porter lyric —Eric Pace, *New York Times,* December 1, 1986

Pace made this comparison about actor Cary Grant at the time of his death.

Elegant as a fifty-dollar whore —Raymond Chandler

Fashion is like a shadow: fly from it and it follows you; follow it and it flies from you —Anon

Had that elusive style some older women carry like blossom —Jonathan Gash

A man's style is intrinsic and private with him like his voice or his gesture, partly a matter of inheritance, partly of cultivation —Maurice Valency

Style, like the human body, is specially beautiful when the veins are not prominent and the bones cannot be counted —Tacitus

You can't get high aesthetic tastes, like trousers, ready-made —W. S. Gilbert

❧ SUBSERVIENCE

See: MEEKNESS

❧ SUBTLETY

See: TACT

❧ SUCCESS/FAILURE

See Also: BUSINESS; GROWTH; PAST, THE

Academy awards are like orgasms—only a few of us know the feeling of having had multiple ones —John Huston, who in 1948 took home the Best Director and the Best Screenplay Oscars for *The Treasure of the Sierra Madre*

The anatomy of first major success is like the young human body, a miracle only the owner can fully savor —John Fowles

As he rose like a rocket, he fell like a stick —Thomas Paine about Edmund Burke

A certain prosperity coats these people like scent or the layer of buttery light in a painting by Rubens —Jean Thompson

A conqueror, like a cannon-ball, must go on; if he rebounds, his career is over —The Duke of Wellington

(The midlist author is) dogged by his past sales record, like a utility infielder with a .228 lifetime batting average —Phillip Lopate, *New York Times Book Review,* May 24, 1987

Failed ... like an old hanging bridge —Marge Piercy

Fail like a five-year plan —Derek Lambert

Failure grabs a man like an old and shabby suit —Derek Lambert

(A great beauty) flourishing like a rose —Isak Dinesen

Flourishing like a weed in a hot-house —Susan Fromberg Schaeffer

Flourishing like trees —Hilma Wolitzer

Had risen to his great height like a man lifted to the ceiling by a sort of slow explosion —G. K. Chesterton

High office is like a pyramid; only two kinds of animals reach the summit, reptiles and eagles —Jean Le Rond d'Alembert

His life, day after day, was failing like an unreplenished stream —Percy Bysshe Shelley

Moving up hand over hand ... like a champion —Tom Wolfe

Pursued success as a knight the Holy Grail —Anon

Sailed through the world like a white yacht jubilant with flags —John Gardner

Selling like lemonade at a track meet —T. Coraghessan Boyle

Sell like hotcakes —Anon

Different industries have coined many phrases for things which sell well. This American simile, which came into usage in the middle of the nineteenth century, is probably still the most widely used. For a twist in meaning there's "selling like cold hot cakes" from The Last Good Kiss *by James Crumley.*

Sold [books by nineteenth century author Karl May] like pancakes topped by wild blueberries and heavy cream —Vincent Canby, *New York Times*, June 25, 1986

Sold like picks and pans in a gold rush —Robert Guenther on past sales successes of real estate syndicators, *Wall Street Journal*, August 6, 1986

Success is as ice cold and lonely as the north pole —Vicki Baum

Success is feminine and like a woman; if you cringe before her, she will override you —William Faulkner

Faulkner expanded on this simile still further: "So the way to treat her is to show her the back of your hand. Then maybe she will do the crawling."

Success on some men looks like a borrowed coat; it sits on you as though it had been made to order —Edith Wharton

Wanted his success acknowledged ... like the high school loser who dreams of driving to the class reunion in a custom-made sports car —Jean Thompson

Willie Loman ... He's not the finest character that ever lived. But he's a human being, and a terrible thing is happening to him. So attention must be paid. He's not to be allowed to fall in his grave like an old dog —Arthur Miller, *Death of a Salesman*

Winning an Oscar ... it's like getting thirty thousand red roses at one time —Louise Fletcher, quoted in Rex Reed interview

Wore his success like his health —George Garrett

❧ SUDDENNESS

See Also: ENTRANCES AND EXITS, SHOCK, SURPRISE

Abrupt as a sultry little thunder shower —Amy Leslie

Abruptly as string that snaps beneath the bow —Ernest William Hornung

Abruptly, like a summer rainstorm —Derek Lambert

Abrupt startling shock like the slap of a wet towel —Norman Mailer

All at once, like the wind dispersing storm clouds at a single puff —Lawrence Durrell

Appear suddenly as if out of a fold of the air —Iris Murdoch

Arbitrary as a cyclone —Anon

Burst into the room like a bullet crashing through a window —Guy de Maupassant

Didn't expect it ... like a storm on a very fine day —Ivan Turgenev

He was with them as suddenly as a gift, as if an arm had thrust in a bunch of roses or a telegram —Eudora Welty

(A reflex as) immediate as a sneeze —Leigh Allison Wilson

A common variation: "sudden as a sneeze."

Steep as a broom handle —Elizabeth Spencer

Steep as hell's half acre —George MacDonald Fraser

Stopped all of a sudden, as if he had been shot —William Makepeace Thackeray

Sudden and foolish as that almost silent fart —George Garrett

Sudden as a burst of hiccupping —Anon

This and the entries that follow typify the simile that develops new twists from conversation to conversation, writer to writer.

Sudden as a dislocated joint slipping back into place —Anon

Sudden as a massacre —Anon

Sudden as a meteor shooting across the sky —Anon

Sudden as an epileptic seizure —Anon

Sudden as a stitch in your side —Anon

Sudden as a summer shower —Anon

Sudden as a tornado swooping down on a small town —Alistair Cook, commenting on suddenness of the first World War

[Call of a jay bird] sudden as conscience —Robert Penn Warren

Sudden as the stopping of breath —Mary Lee Settle

(The end was) sudden, like a foolish play —Karl Shapiro

Suddenly, as a train comes out of a tunnel —Virginia Woolf

Suddenly, like a pair of obscene words, (there appeared on the path two boys) —Truman Capote

Sudden resolutions, like the sudden rise of the mercury in the barometer, indicate little else than the changeableness of the weather —Julius Charles Hare and Augustus William Hare

Sudden, surprising ... it is like encountering a pun in a telephone directory —Karl E. Meyer

Too sudden ... like the lightning —William Shakespeare, *Romeo and Juliet*

❧ SUMMER
See: SEASONS

❧ SUN
See Also: MOON, SKY, SUNSET

The afternoon sunlight was like gold embroidery on the grass —Paul Horgan

Autumn sunlight poured out over the rock [of Quebec] like a heavy southern wine —Willa Cather

Bars of sunlight crossed the back yard like the bars of a bright strange cell —Carson McCullers

Bits of sunlight bright as butterflies —Eudora Welty

The citronade of the pale morning sun shimmered like a multitude of violins —Angela Carter

The daylight-saving sunshine lay like custard on the oaks and mistletoe —Wallace Stegner

The fast-setting sun lighted the tops of the trees like flames of candles —Z. Vance Wilson

The heat from the scorching [California] sun hit them like a knock-out punch —Jilly Cooper

The high sun fell like balm on her body —Mary Hedin

The huge sunlight flamed like a monstrous dahlia with petals of yellow fire —Oscar Wilde

It [sunlight] licks thick as a tongue at my skin —Sharon Sheehe Stark

The last of the sun [at dusk] like a great splash of blood on the sky —George Garrett

The muffled sunlight gleamed like gold tissue through grey gauze —Edith Wharton

The new morning sun shone like a pink rose in the heavens —Kenneth Koch

A pale sun appeared over the clouds like an invalid sitting up in bed —John Mortimer

A red sun as flat and still against the sky as moonlight on pond water —Charles Johnson

The red sun was pasted on the sky like a waver —Anon

The rising sun is like a ball of blood —Robert W. Service

A scarlet sun, round and brilliant as a blooded egg yolk —Cynthia Ozick

A sharp-as-needle sun sat high over Virginia … like a heathen god sure of itself —Thomas Keneally

Sheets of incendiary sunlight flashed across the Thames, like an oil slick —Lionel Shriver, *The Post-Birthday World*

The sinking sun hung like a red balloon over the Hudson River —Belva Plain

The strong sun (of late April) pours down as though a gigantic golden basin full of light and wind were being emptied on us —Erich Maria Remarque

The sun advanced on the city and lit the topmost spines of hill, painting the olive drab slopes in crazy new colors, like the drawing of a spangled veil —William Brammer

Sun … as light and dry as old sherry —Raymond Chandler

The sun, as red as a furnace on the edge of the horizon —Émile Zola

The sun blazed like a flaming bronze mirror —Bernard Malamud

The sun breaks [over the land] like a cracked egg —T. Coraghessan Boyle

The sun breaks through the cloud like revelation —Delmore Schwartz

The sun burned feebly through the mist like a circle cut from Christmas paper —MacDonald Harris

The sun dazzled off the asphalt in fragments like breaking glass —George Garrett

The sun drew strength from them like a giant sponge —Caryl Phillips

The sun … drops on our heads like a stone —Marge Piercy

The sun, dull, like the face of an old man —Maxim Gorky

The sun fades like the spreading of a peacock's tail —John Ashbery

The sun fell thick as a blanket —Lee Smith

The sun flared in the sky, fat and red as a tangerine —T. Coraghessan Boyle
A variation by Marge Piercy: "the sun hangs like a tangerine."

The sun flashed like a torrent of warm white wine —Du Bose Heyward

The sun floats up above the horizon, like a shimmering white blimp —Margaret Atwood

The sun hangs overhead like a lantern —T. Coraghessan Boyle

The sun hits him like a slap in the face —T. Coraghessan Boyle

The sun poured in like butterscotch and stuck to all my senses —Joni Mitchell, "Chelsea Morning"

The sun … shone like a polished brass knob —Helen Hudson

The sun hung in the cloudless sky like an unblinking yellow eye —Harvey Swados

(It was a misty autumn morning,) the sun just struggling through like a great chrysanthemum —Pamela Hanssford Johnson

The sun lay like a friendly arm across her shoulder —Marjorie Kinnan Rawlings

The sun … lay on the horizon like a dissolving orange suffused with blood —John Hawkes

The sunlight dripped over the house like golden paint over an art jar —F. Scott Fitzgerald

Sunlight dropped into it (the dark foliage) like a drizzle of gold —Isak Dinesen

Sunlight fell like a shower of gold through the leaves of the chestnut trees —Silvia Tennenbaum

The sunlight hit her like a boxing glove —Jilly Cooper

The sunlight … plunged like tiny knives into my already bleary eyes —James Crumley

Sunlight splashed through the trees, the beams hazy like shafts of light filtered through stained glass —Robert J. Serling

Sunlight that was like a bright driving summer rain —Paule Marshall

Sun (is sitting atop the trees) like a big round cheddar —T. Coraghessan Boyle

The sun looks, through the mist, like a plum on the tree of heaven, or a bruise on the slope of your belly —William H. Gass

The sun lulled in the sky like a mule —Larry McMurtry

The sun overhead beat the surface of the pool like a drum —James B. Hall

The sun peeping above the trees, looked like a giant golf ball —P. G. Wodehouse

The sun … poised like a ball of fire on the very edge of the mountains —Henry Van Dyke

The sun popped over the edge of the prairie like a broad smiling face —Willa Cather

The sun poured down like fire —Isaac Bashevis Singer

Sun … reflected back to me like a shiny bedspread whose design is hundreds of wind-driven roller coasters —Richard Brautigan

The sun rested like a warm palm on the back of her neck —Francis King

The sun rolled over the horizon like the red rim of a wagon wheel —Rita Mae Brown

The sun … rose swiftly and flashed like a torch with dazzling rays —Felix Salten

The sunshine burned the pasture like fire —Rudyard Kipling

The sunshine [of a January day] cut like icicles —Edith Wharton

The sunshine made spots before your eyes … as though a thousand weddings were to be held that day —Boris Pasternak

Sunshine spread like butter over the fields —Lael Tucker Wertenbaker

Sunshine that stretched like cloth of gold all up and down Fifth Avenue —Helen Hudson

The sun shone as if there were no death —Saul Bellow

The sun shone like a million dollars —Larry McMurtry

The sun shone like Mr. Happy Face himself —Tom Robbins

The sun shone with such violence that in an illumination like a long-prolonged glare of lightning the heavens looked black and white —Eudora Welty

The sun shot upward and began to spin like a red cup on the point of a spear —Isaac Babel

Sun sizzling like a skillet in the sky —Helen Hudson

Sun slanting like a blade —Bin Ramke

The sun's rays like sheaves of wheat are gold and dry —Dame Edith Sitwell

The sun stood still like a great shining altar —Hans Christian Andersen

The sun swerves silently like a cyclist round the bend —Herbert Read

The sun throbbed like a fever —William Plomer

Sun … huge as a mountain of diamonds —Dame Edith Sitwell

The sun up in the towering sky turns like a spinning ball —Edwin Muir

The sun was high enough to sit on the roofs of buildings like a great open fire warming everything —Mark Helprin

The sun was like a burning-glass —William Plomer

This comparison from a poem entitled "In the Snake Park" refers to a lens used to focus the sun's rays to start a fire.

The sun was like a good cup of tea, strong and hot —Mike Fredman

The sun was like a hot iron on their backs —Paul Horgan

The sun was like a whip —T. Coraghessan Boyle

The sun was pouring in like maple syrup into a green bowl —Carlos Baker

The sun was shining like a congratulation —Margaret Millar

The sun was streaking the sky with strips of red and white, like a slab of bacon —Jean Thompson

[The sun] swung ... like a faded shabby orange —Sir Hugh Walpole

(While they embraced,) the sun vanished as if it had been switched off —W. P. Kinsella

The white sun twinkling like the dawn under a speckled cloud —Percy Bysshe Shelley

The yellow sun was ugly, like a raw egg on a plate —Elizabeth Bishop

❧ SUNSET

A huge sunset that drained away in the west like blood —William Styron

The sun ... drops like an angry brick at nightfall —Raymond Chandler

A sunset as thick as jam simmered in the sky —Isaac Babel

Sunset cast its colors through the leafless trees ... like panes of stained glass —Madison Smartt Bell

The (Montana) sunset lay between two mountains like a gigantic bruise from which dark arteries spread themselves over a poisoned sky —F. Scott Fitzgerald

The sunset looked like the fires of Hell were consuming it —Harry Prince

The sun was moving down slowly as if it were descending a ladder —Flannery O'Connor

The sun went down lopsided and wide as a rose on a stem —Eudora Welty

❧ SURPRISE

See Also: SHOCK, SUDDENNESS

Crops up when you least expect it, like dandruff —Robin Worthington

The news hit me like a flying hammer —Susan Vreeland, *Clara and Mr. Tiffany*

(I read the note over several times with a kind of stupid) incredulity, like an unbelieving prisoner reading the formal sentence of his own execution —Robert Traver

Started [at sound of a sudden call] like a horse at the sound of the bugle —Stefan Zweig

(She) started like a quiet, lovely insect into which someone had suddenly stabbed a pin —Elizabeth Spencer

Startling as curves in a mountain road —Lorrie Moore

(The idea was as) startling ... as if in a blank wall before her a door had opened —Dorothy Canfield Fisher

(Perception as) startling as watching a feeling cross a face on Mount Rushmore —Paige Mitchell

Startling, like a face changing in front of you, from young to old, well to ill —Wilfrid Sheed

Surprised and shocked as if she had heard an explosion and seen her own shattered legs go flying across the floor —Rachel Ingalls

Surprised as a sardine that went to sleep in the ocean and woke up in a delicatessen store —Arthur Baer

Surprised me as much as if I were a baby suddenly popped from the womb —Angela Carter

Surprise made me look like a goldfish —Rebecca West

Surprises keep us living: as when the first light surprised our infant eyes —Louis MacNeice

Surprising as a child's laugh rising higher, higher, higher —Babette Deutsch

(Sharp pain pierced his chest, as quick and) unexpected as the materialization of a hairline crack in bone —Paige Mitchell

Unexpected as aluminum siding in Buckingham palace —Anon

Unexpected as best seller status for a book of Latin quotations —Anon

Unexpected as a heart attack —Anon

Unexpected as a heat wave in February —Anon

Unexpected as gourmet food in a second rate hotel —Anon

Unexpected as snow in July —Anon

Unexpectedly wonderful treat, like blue skies and warmth in a chilly spring —Janet Flanner

You never know what somebody's got in him: like the man with germs, suddenly he's down in bed with a crisis —Clifford Odets

❧ SURVIVAL

See: IMPOSSIBILITY, SUCCESS/FAILURE

❧ SUSPENSE

See: EXCITEMENT

❧ SUSPICION

See: TRUST/MISTRUST

❧ SWEARING

See: CURSES, WORD(S)

❧ SWEAT

See Also: SMELLS

Beads of perspiration, like seed pearls —Dorothea Straus

Beads of sweat gathered on his brow like tiny blisters —William Styron

Beads of sweat … popped on his forehead like tiny, glistening prairie dogs —Joan Hess

Beads of sweat, tiny as dewdrops —Leigh Allison Wilson

(My forehead) bubbled sweat like a burning plastic bag —Ira Wood

Cold sweat burst from his pores, trickling down his back like ice water —Dorothy Canfield

A drop of it [sweat] hung like a Christmas tree ornament from the tip of his nose —Jonathan Valin

Feel the sweat like needles at my hair-roots —Randall Jarrell

Fine beads of sweat glistened [on a man's mustache] like little brilliants —Jessamyn West

Glistening with sweat like a circus seal —Ralph Ellison

I'm sweating like a prostitute in church —Susan Vreeland, *Clara and Mr. Tiffany*

Little pears of sweat had popped out like a corona around his shiny skull —Harvey Swados

Looked as if it would cost a thousand dollars to shake hands with him —Raymond Chandler

Small beads of sweat adorn his bald head like pearls on a bright dress —Erich Maria Remarque

Sweat clings like a crystal fixture to his receding brow —Mary Morris

Sweat collects in pores like ink does on fingerprints —Noel Behn

The sweat coming out on his face like somebody had squeezed it —Ernest Hemingway

Sweat crawling, like a procession of spiders and ants —George Garrett

Sweated like a coolie —Richard Wilbur

Sweated with self-consciousness and the effort to be suave, like a teen-ager dancing with a haughty girl —Derek Lambert

Sweating freely … like a squeezed sponge —Ben Ames Williams

Sweating like a swamp rat —Norman Mailer

Sweating like a very fat man in a Turkish bath —Kingsley Amis

Sweating like Judas —Samuel Beckett

Sweat like black plates under his arms —Ian Kennedy Martin

Sweat poured out … like a sprinkler —Andrew Kaplan

Sweat poured like rain —Ken Stabler, football quarterback and Berry Stainback, writer

Sweat ran down like water down a hill —American Negro ballad "John Henry"

In the original of the famous ballad "water" was spelled "watah."

The sweat ran over my back and down my arms and legs, branching, like an upside-down tree —Eudora Welty

Sweats like a mother of six, preparing lunch —Ira Wood

Sweat was pouring from his body like water coming out of a showerhead —Ann Petry

Sweat was running down behind his ears and under his collar like cold, restless worms —Margaret Millar

Under each arm of his striped shirt there was a dark semicircle like a stain of secret guilt —Margaret Millar

♣ SWEETNESS

See Also: PLEASURE, TASTE

Oh, my beautiful Rosabella, sweet like a flower … Rosabella, young like a bay —Frank Loesser, "Rosabella."

Lyric from the title character of the musical, Most Happy Fella, singing the praises of his mail order bride.

Sweet as a chaplain —Elizabeth Hardwick

"Sweet" as a comparison dates way back, probably beginning with Chaucer's "Sweet as the root of licorice" and Henry Buttes' "Sweet as a nut." Variations continue to develop, or to coin another simile, "Grow like the taste for sweet things."

Sweet as a first love affair —Isak Dinesen

(My tongue was) sweet as a fresh plum —George Garrett

Sweet as a kiss —Isak Dinesen

Sweet as a mountain lilac —Raymond Chandler

Sweet as apple cider —Eddie Cantor

This simile was immortalized by singer-vaudevillian Eddie Cantor in his musical ode to his wife Ida: "Ida … sweet as apple cidah!"

(The words) sweet as a reprieve —Delmore Schwartz

(We bit into life and life was) sweet as a ripe apple —George Garrett

Sweet as cream —Marge Piercy

Sweet as love, or the remembrance of a generous deed —William Wordsworth

Sweet as love songs —Slogan, Kerr butterscotch candy

Sweet as melancholy —Robert Burton

Sweet as new-mown hay —W. S. Gilbert

Sweet as pie —Anon

The "Sweet as pie" continues in use, both in its literal sense and to describe someone's personality.

(Kisses as) sweet as sweet mountain dew —Langston Hughes

Sweet as the hope of Paradise —F. van Wyck Mason

Sweeter than honey from a rock —Christina Rossetti

Sweeter than perfume —William Shakespeare, "Sonnet 130"

Sweet like pineapple —Marge Piercy

♣ SWIMMING
See: SPORTS

♣ SYMMETRY
See: REGULARITY/IRREGULARITY

♣ SYMPATHY
See: KINDNESS, PITY

♣ TACT
See Also: INSULTS

Diplomacy, like politics, is the art of the possible —George W. Ball

A diplomatic note is like an anonymous letter. You can call a fellow anything you want, for nobody can find out exactly whose name was signed to it —Will Rogers

Discretion like a good priest —George Garrett

Had about as much finesse as a trained elephant doing the gavotte among ninepins —Cornell Woolrich

Subtle as fanfare —William McIlvanney

Subtle as snakes —Christina Rossetti

Subtle as the London blitz —T. Coraghessan Boyle

A tactless man is like an axe on an embroidery frame —Malay proverb

❧ TALENT

See: ABILITY, ACCOMPLISHMENT

❧ TALKATIVENESS

See Also: CONVERSATION

As full of words as a hen salmon of eggs —Ben Ames Williams

Babble as one mad with wine —Algernon Charles Swinburne

Chattered like a shipload of monkeys in a storm —Anon

Chattered like squirrels —Larry McMurtry

Chattered on like a lunatic chimpanzee —Truman Capote

Chattered on like a chickadee in a feed trough —Donald McCaig

Chattering … like a flock of starlings —Jimmy Sangster

Chattering like magpies —Christina Rossetti

Chattering like one to whom speech was a new accomplishment —Calder Willingham

Chatter like a blue jay —Eleanor Clark

Chatter like a mob of sparrow —Judson Jerome

Chatter like sick flies —Algernon Charles Swinburne

Chatty as a parrot —Michael Korda, *Another Life*

Gabbled on like machines set in motion —Charlotte Brontë

Gabbling at one another like so many turkeys —Harvey Swados

Great talkers are like leaky pitchers, everything runs out of them —H. G. Bohn's *Hand-Book of Proverbs*

Had a tongue that flapped like a banner in a fair wind —George Garrett

He was like a man who'd just emerged from six months in solitary, like the sole survivor of a shipwreck, Crusoe with a captive audience: he could not shut up —T. Coraghessan Boyle

Jabbered on like a drunk old uncle —Richard Ford

Like a book in breeches … he [Macaulay] has occasional flashes of silence, that make his conversation perfectly delightful —Syndney Smith

Like a crane or a swallow, so did I chatter —The Holy Bible/Isaiah

Long-winded as a writer who gets paid by the word —Anon

Open [up, with information] like a wet envelope —Harold Adams

[Coleridge] Speaks incessantly, not thinking or imagining or remembering, but combining all these processes into one; as a rich and lazy housewife might mingle her soup and fish beef and custard into one unspeakable mass —Thomas Carlyle

Talkative persons are like barrels; the less there is in them, the more noise they make —John Gideon Mulligan

Talked and talked like a man in a high fever —Erich Maria Remarque

Talked on and on as if he was rehearsing for a speech —John Dos Passos

A tremendous talker and like a greedy eater at an ordinary dinner, keeping to himself an entire dish of which everyone present would like to have partaken —*Punch,* 1857

Went into detail … like an obstetrician describing how he got two fingers in to turn the baby's head out of breech, or, yes, like an old fisherman taking you along step by step on how to bait a hook so that the wriggler stays alive —Norman Mailer

The words came out of his throat like a cataract —Carson McCullers

Words came tumbling out of me like coins from a change dispenser —Natascha Wodin

Words flowed from him like oil from a gusher —O. Henry

Wordy like somebody with a fever —George Garrett

The world to him is a vast lecture-platform … as one long after-dinner, with himself as the principal speaker of the evening —P. G. Wodehouse

TALLNESS

I'm about as tall as a shotgun and just as noisy —Truman Capote

I towered over my parents like some big-footed freak of another species, like a cuckoo raised by sparrows —T. Coraghessan Boyle

Long and tall as a scarecrow —John Yount

Tall and gaunt as a hangman —Angela Carter

Tall as a building —Louise Erdrich

Tall as a crane —Dame Edith Sitwell

> *This simile is part of the opening and closing refrain of Dame Edith's* Aubade, *the full stanza reading: "Jane, Jane, Tall as a crane, the morning light creaks down again." In the United States, the "Tall as a crane" can be traced back to an Arkansas railroad song in which the simile is used as follows: "He was six feet seven in his stocking feet and taller than any crane."*

Tall as a stork —Angela Carter

Tall as a thunderstorm —Miles Gibson

(He was) tall as a tree in the middle of the night —Wallace Stevens

(Poppies as) tall as buildings —Arthur A. Cohen

Tall men are like houses of four stories, wherein commonly the uppermost room is worst furnished —James Howell

Tower over … like the Washington Monument —James Thurber

TASTE

A mouth on me like a Turkish wrestler's jockstrap —M. C. Beaton

As pleasingly prickly as a kitten's tongue —Slogan for Gevrey-Chamertin wine

A fastidious taste is like a squeamish appetite; the one has its origin in some disease of the mind, as the other has in some ailment of the stomach —Robert Southey

Full of rich flavor as a piece torn off an old shirt —Raymond Chandler

His mouth felt as if it had been to a party without him —Peter De Vries

His mouth was tastelessly dry, as though he had been eating dust —Joseph Conrad

My mouth [from smoking a cigarette] tasted like a cross between charred sticks and spoiled eggs —Sue Grafton

My mouth was dry and tasty as a hen-coop floor —Harold Adams

My mouth tasted like an old penny —Robert B. Parker

My tongue felt like a slice of ham in my mouth, salty and pink —Jay Parini

Palates like shoe leather —Angela Carter

(Melons … as) sweet to the tongue as gold is to the mind —Borden Deal

Tasted like a fart —Reynolds Price

Tasted like it had been fried in tar —Larry Mc-Murtry

Taste is the luxury of abeyant claims and occurs, like Wordsworth's poetry, in a kind of tranquility —Stanley Elkin

Taste like a cup of luke-warm consommé at a spinsterish tearoom —Raymond Chandler on mystery writing

(The crap still in his mouth made everything) taste like feathers —William McIlvanney

Taste like the Volga at low tide —Line from *Love at First Bite*

The character making this comparison is Count von Dracula

Tastes like cool wet sand under pearly seaside light —Slogan for Chateau Guiraud's Chateau "G" wine

Tastes like the wrath to come —Irvin Shrewsbury Cobb

Cobb used the comparison to describe the taste of corn liquor.

Tastes rather like an old attic —J. B. Priestly

Tasty as summer's first peach —Elyse Sommer

Tasty, like an angel pissing on your tongue —Anon

A commonly used simile throughout the galleys of Great Lakes steamships to describe good-tasting liquid or solid food.

♣ TEACHERS/TEACHING
See: EDUCATION

♣ TEARS
See Also: CRYING

Could feel the tears, like fire, coming up —James Baldwin

Feel the tears brimming and sloshing in me like water in a glass that is unsteady and too full —Sylvia Plath

Generally men's tears, like the droppings of certain springs, only harden and petrify what they fall on —Walter Savage Landor

He [a weeping man] was like a sponge saturated with water, and then squeezed —Leonid Andreyev

Like a summer tempest came her tears —Alfred, Lord Tennyson

This is also appears as a chapter title in Kenneth Grahame's contemporary children's classic, The Wind in the Willows.

My tears like berries fell down —W. B. Yeats

Produce tears freely like a great actor —Erich Maria Remarque

Slow as the winter snow the tears have drifted to mine eyes —Elizabeth Barrett Browning

Suspended like shimmering icicles on Maxell's cheeks were tears —Arthur A. Cohen

A teardrop hung out of each blue eye, like a fat woman leaning out of a tenement window —Tom Robbins

Teardrops come a-splashin' down his cheeks like summer rain —Edward A. Guest

A tear had slipped down to dangle like sweat at the tip of a nostril —Truman Capote

A tear ran down her cheek, turning white with powder, like a tiny ball of snow —Jonathan Valin

Tears … brightened her eyes and made them glitter like dark stars in a stormy sky —Frank Swinnerton

Tears died as laughter dies away —Dante Gabriel Rossetti

Tears fall like soft fruit juice —Rose Tremain

Tears fell like a plot —Stevie Smith

Tears fill up her eyes like a cup —Jessie Schell

Tears … flailing my face like the torn ends of shattered rope —John Updike

Tears flooded out of his eyes like the floodwater over a levee —Pat Conroy

Tears … flowed down upon him like a bower of willows —Arthur A. Cohen

Tears ... flowed like fountains —William Wordsworth

   A twist by Guy de Maupassant: "wept like a fountain."

Tears flow ... like a swollen gutter gushing through the streets —Henry Fielding

Tears gathered like small pools in the declination of his eye cups —Arthur A. Cohen

Tears glittered in her eyes, deep down, like the sinking reflection of a well —Louise Erdrich

Tears glittered like rhinestones on her lashes —Ross Macdonald

Tears, like a stream, like a ceaselessly flowing fountain, flowed and flowed —Nikolay Gogol

Tears like bits of glass formed in his eyes —Leonard Michaels

Tears like molten lead surged in her eyes —Ruth Prawer Jhabvala

Tears ... like two little brooks —Carson McCullers

Tears ... made patterns on his cheeks, like wax trickling down a candle —Julia O'Faolain

Tears on his lashes, like silver drops of dew —Ruth Prawer Jhabvala

Tears rolled down like rain —Elizabeth Spencer

Tears ... roll one from each eye, like droplets on wax fruit —Ira Wood

Tears running down like lemonade —Anne Sexton

Tears rushed forth ... like mountain mists at length dissolved in rain —Lord Byron

   This simile from Byron's famous Don Juan *has been slightly modernized and shortened. The original first line begins: "The tears rush'd forth from her o'erclouded brain, like...."*

The tears seemed to cause the features of her face to melt and soften like hot wax —George Garrett

Tears, silent as a china egg —Marge Piercy

Tears, small as sequins, glinting in her narrowed eyes —Miles Gibson

Tears steamed down her cheeks, soft and bland like the sides of a Guernsey —John Updike

Tears that slipped like melting pellets of sleet down their grieved and angered cheeks —Alice Walker

Tears that streamed ceaselessly like a veil to keep her from seeing too clearly —Paul Horgan

Tears ... they deluge my heart like the rain —Emily Brontë

Tears welled up as freely as water from a drinking fountain —Jean Stafford

Though the tears had no healing power, they took off the edge of it [pain], like cold water on a burn —Margaret Drabble

A woman's tears, like a dog's limping, are seldom real —Russian proverb

♣ TEDIUM

See: BOREDOM, DULLNESS, REPITITION

♣ TEETH

See Also: WHITE

Beautiful teeth, like china plates —Rosellen Brown

Big teeth ... like chunks of solidified milk —Frank Swinnerton

Bluhdorn's teeth seemed either too big or too many, like those of a shark. Huge and glistening white, they filled his mouth like bathroom tiles —Michael Korda, *Another Life*

Front teeth showed like those of a squirrel —George Ade

(When she opened her mouth) gaps like broken window panes could be seen in her teeth —Sholom Ash

Her front teeth overlapped each other like dealt cards —Alice McDermott

His teeth looked like a picket fence in a slum neighborhood —Stephen King

His [false] teeth moved slightly, like the keyboards of a piano —Pamela Hansford Johnson

His teeth stood out like scored corks set in a jagged row —Sterling Hayden

Lower teeth crooked, as if some giant had taken his face and squeezed them loose from his jaw —Larry McMurtry

My teeth felt like they had little sweaters on them —Anon

Sharp-worn teeth like slivers of rock —Ella Leffland

The shiny new false teeth gave him the peculiar look of someone who smiles for a living —Andrew Kaplan

Small pointed teeth, like a squirrel's —Willa Cather

Teeth all awry and at all angles like an old fence —George Garrett

Teeth, as yellow as old ivory —Frank Swinnerton

Teeth ... big and even as piano keys —Helen Hudson

Teeth ... channeled and stained like the teeth of an old horse —R. Wright Campbell

Teeth ... chattering like castanets —Maurice Edelman

Teeth clatter like ice cubes in a blender —Ira Wood

Teeth clicking like dice —T. Coraghessan Boyle

Teeth like cream —Willa Cather

Teeth like a row of alabaster Britannica —Joe Coomer

Teeth like pearls —Robert Browning

Teeth like piano keys —Elizabeth Spencer

Teeth like white mosaics shone —Herbert Read

Teeth ... tapping together like typewriter keys —Cornell Woolrich

White teeth, the kind that look like cheap dentures even when they are not —Eric Ambler

❧ TEMPER

See: ANGER

❧ TEMPERMENT

See: PERSONAL TRAITS

❧ TEMPTATION

See: ATTRACTION

❧ TENACITY

See: PERSISTANCE

❧ TENDERNESS

See: AFFECTION, GENTLENESS, KINDNESS, LOVE

❧ TENNIS

See: SPORTS

❧ TENSION

See Also: ANXIETY, NERVOUSNESS

Back ... tense as a tiger's —D. H. Lawrence

Body rigid from shoulder to belly as though he had been stricken with elephantiasis —Kenzaburo Oe

(There continued to be) a certain strain, like dangerously stretched rubber bands —Thalia Selz

Everything about him was tight and coiled as a door spring —Lorrie Moore, *Birds of America: Stories*

Feel tension rising off me like a fever —Richard Ford

Feel the tension coming out of Justin like a fever —Paige Mitchell

Felt his insides drawn together like the lips of a wound —Helen Hudson

Felt like a swimmer about to dive —Marguerite Yourcenar

His heart smacking against his ribs like a bumblebee at a window —Michael Chabon, *The Amazing Adventures of Kavalier & Clay*

His solar plexus knotted up like a sea anemone —Ursula Le Guin

In times of stress I enter into a semi-comatose state like an instinct-driven opossum —Leigh Allison Wilson

My back became like a stick —Natsume Soseki

My stomach drops as if I'm in a balky elevator —W. P. Kinsella

(Looked about as) relaxed as a safecracker —Joseph Wambaugh

Spines … stiffened like pulled twine —Louise Erdrich

Stiffen like a cat that's been hit by something —Shirley Ann Grau

(When I approach, you) stiffen like an egg white —Diane Ackerman

Stiffen like a stump —David Wagoner

Strung up like a piano wire —Elizabeth Spencer

(Body) taut like wire —Anais Nin

Tense and careful as a man handling a bomb —Dorothy Canfield

Tense and fluttering like a fish out of water —George Garrett

Tense and still like a figure in a frieze —Ross Macdonald

Tense as an animal in fear, ready to snap or go limp beneath its keeper's grasp —Louise Erdrich

(I lay) tense as a piano wire —W. P. Kinsella

Tense as a player on the bench —Maureen Howard, *New York Times Magazine*, May 25, 1986

Tense as a thoroughbred at the starting gate —Anon television features on New York marathoners, November 1, 1986

Tense as a wound spring —Joseph Heller

(Voices) tense as barks —Edward Hoagland

(People were as) tense as fiddle strings —Dorothy Canfield

Tense as if my neck were tipped back, my mouth agape, and I was preparing for the dentist's needle —W. P. Kinsella

Tense as rectitude —Norman Mailer

Tension broke like heat after a thunderstorm in a nervous burst of laughter —Lael Tucker Wertenbaker

Tension ran like a red-hot wire through the men —Marjory Stoneman Douglas

Tension stretching like taut wires across the room —Ross Macdonald

Tension … vibrates like a melancholy bell —David K. Shipler, *New York Times Book Review*, March 1, 1987

Tight as a duck —Graham Masterton

> The simile is used as part of a sex scene. In full context it reads: "With her own fingers, she slipped him inside her, and although she was as tight as a duck, she was also warm and wet and irresistible."

(His hand was) tight as a knot —Ann Beattie

Tight as a man going to the electric chair —Norman Mailer before being interviewed by Mike Wallace.

Tight as a quivering string —David Nevin

Tight as a sheet on a hospital bed —Anon

(Throats were) tight as tourniquets —Karl Shapiro

Tightly controlled … as if he was tied down to his desk by leather straps —Anon

> White House colleague speaking about Robert McFarlane during the Iran-Contra scandal, as quoted in New York Times, *March 2, 1987.*

(He always cane back from the ballfield) turned tighter than the bolts on an automobile tire —Norman Keifetz

> The simile from a novel about a baseball player The Sensation, *continues as follows:* "by that jack-handle known as 'being a pro.'"

❧ TENTATIVENESS
See: UNCERTAINTY

✣ TERROR

See: FEAR

✣ THEATER

See: STAGE AND SCREEN

✣ THEORIES

See: IDEAS

✣ THICKNESS

See Also: ABUNDANCE

Newspaper … thick as a folded bath towel —W. P. Kinsella

Richly covered … as a hen is with feathers —Anon

Thick … as a brier patch with biers —Ellen Glasgow

Thick as a mist —Percy Bysshe Shelley

Thick as autumnal leaves —John Milton

Thick as blood —Anon

> *This simile has come into fairly common usage, with many different reference points. To cite two examples from current fiction: "an aroma thick as blood," from Frank Conroy's* Stop-Time, *and "automobile traffic thick as blood" from the story "White Gardens," by Mark Helprin.*

Thick as elephant trunks —Kay Boyle

Thick as foreign coffee —Sylvia Plath

(The atmosphere of sex is) thick as the dark —John Rechy

(Exudes self-disgust) thick as the smell of a slept-in undershirt —Rosellen Brown

(Fog) thick as night —Gertrude Atherton

✣ THIGHS

See: LEG(S)

✣ THINNESS

See Also: BODY

Body … as meager as a pole —Leslie Thomas

George was slender as a willow wand and as easily bendable. —Susan Vreeland, *Clara and Mr. Tiffany.*

Lean and thin as a fallen leaf —George Garrett

Lean as a bird dying in the snow —Émile Zola

Lean as a herring —Irwin Shaw

Lean as a shadow or ghost —George Garrett

Lean as a snake —John Berryman

Lean as a whipcord —Norman Mailer

Lean as El Greco's Saint Andres —Harry Prince

Lean as the dead branch of a tree —Frank Swinnerton

Lean as Ugulino —Dylan Thomas

> *The comparison refers to Count Ugulino of Pisa, imprisoned and starved to death in Dante's Inferno.*

Leaner than wasps —Phyllis McGinley

> *McGinley's comparison referred to the stone lions at the doors of the New York Hispanic Society building.*

Looked beaky and thin, like a bird —Mavis Gallant

Looking as skinny and blue as a jailhouse tattoo —Tom Robbins

Looks as if he's been carved from a shadow —T. Coraghessan Boyle

[A red line in the sky at dawn] narrow as a needle —John D. MacDonald

Skinny as a fence post —George Garrett

Slender as a flower's stem —Arthur Sherburne Hardy

Slim and evasive as a needle's eye —Paige Mitchell

Slim as a cat —Sue Grafton

Slim as a little serpent —Anton Chekov

Slim as a mast —Geoffrey Chaucer

Slim … like a twig stripped of bark —John Updike

So skinny he looked as though, if you shook him, his bones would sound like one of those Javanese musicians who play on coconut shells —Leslie Hanscomb, *Newsday,* September 11, 1986

The thin man so described is Frank Sinatra in his early days.

So skinny he looked like he'd been pulled through a keyhole —Fred Allen

So skinny you clack like a floating crap game when you walk down the street —Russell Baker

So thin that he was like a clothed skeleton —Jean Rhys

So thin that if you touch her back you can feel the ribs, like ridges on a roll-top desk —Leslie Garis, *New York Times Magazine,* February 8, 1987

The person thus described is Joan Didion.

(She remained) thin as a baseball contract —Norman Keifetz

Thin and clear as green leaves in April —Elinor Wylie

Thin and quiet as shadows —George Garrett

Thin as a bean pole —Mikhail Bulgakov

Thin as a cobweb —Jean Garrigue

Thin as a dime —American colloquialism, attributed to New England

Thin as a file —Reynolds Price

Thin as a moonbeam —Max Apple

Thin as an empty dress —Marge Piercy

Thin as an exclamation mark —Anon

Thin as an onion shoot —Gloria Norris

Thin as a pauper's wallet —Anon

Thin as a pencil line —Mary Lee Settle

Thin as a rail —William Scarborough

[A heron] thin as a safety pin —Susan Minot

Thin as a scythe —Donald Justice

Thin as a sheet (his mother came to him) —John Berryman

Thin as a sheeted ghost —Stevie Smith

Thin as a thread —William H. Hallhan

Thin as a switch —Mark Helprin

Thin as a thermometer —Albert L. Weeks

Thin as a walking stick —Doris Grumback

(The steering wheel is) thin as a whip —John Updike

Thin as a whisper —Anon

Thin as a wire —Raymond Chandler

Thin as breath —Sharon Sheehe Stark

Thin as chop-sticks —Rumer Godden

[Partitions] thin as crackers —Tom Robbins

Thin as linguini —Anon

[Children] thin as little white haired ghosts —Carson McCullers

(The old man looked) thin as paper —Richard Ford

An extension made popular in New England is: "thin as the paper on the wall."

Thin as pared soap —Sharon Olds

In the poem in which this appears, the simile is extended to breasts as "opalescent as soap bubbles."

Thin as phantoms —Thomas Hardy

(Her face, without make-up, was an oval of white that looked as) thin as porcelain —Paul Theroux

[TV antennas] thin as skeletons —Italo Calvino

Thin as tapers —T. Coraghessan Boyle

Thin as the edge of the moon —Stephen Vincent Benét

Thin as the girl who didn't have enough to her to itch —Anon

Thin as the girl who swallowed the pit of an olive and was rushed to a maternity ward —Anon

Thin as the homeopathic soup that was made by boiling the shadow of a pigeon that had starved to death —Abraham Lincoln, October 13, 1852, speech

Thin as the line between self-confidence and conceit —Anon

Thin as the skin seaming a scar —Sylvia Plath

Thin as tissue —H. E. Bates

(Skin) thin as tracing paper —John Updike

Thin … like a skeleton —Ann Petry

The walls here are as thin as a hoofer's wallet —Raymond Chandler, *Playback*

❧ THOUGHTS

See Also: IDEAS, INTELLIGENCE

Common thoughts on common things, which time is shaking, day by day, like feathers from his wings —John Greenleaf Whittier

Each was in his own thoughts, like a sleeping-bag —William McIlvanney

Every thought is like dough; you have only to knead it well—you can make anything you like out of it —Ivan S. Turgenev

Exceptions [to theories] would crowd into her mind like a mob of unruly children —Peter Meinke

(He succeeded in starting) a familiar train of thought … like a brackish taste in his mouth —Dorothy Canfield

Great thoughts, like great deeds, need no trumpet —P. J. Bailey

Heavy on my mind, like a lump of soggy yeast dough, expanding, suffocating, blotting out all other thoughts —Mignon F. Ballard

Her thought ran like a barge along a river —Marianne Wiggins

Her thoughts ran round and round like dogs trapped behind a fence —Marge Piercy

Her thoughts rose as a veil before her vision —Charles Johnson

Her thoughts seemed to lead backwards and forwards like a shuttle weaving the moments, hours, days together in a pattern —Rumer Godden

(Booksellers were like dope-pushers to him.) He was like a junkie on thought —Saul Bellow
Bellow's simile describes an avid reader.

His thoughts like wild animals fed upon themselves —Charles Johnson

His thoughts went round and round like rats in a cage —Stephen Vincent Benét

Human thought is not a firework, every shooting off fresh forms and shapes as it burns; it is a tree growing very slowly —Jerome K. Jerome

Human thought, like God, makes the world in its own image —Adam Clayton Powell

I have thought about you until I feel like a bee —William Diehl

I will not go so far as to say that to construct a history of thought without profound study of the mathematical ideas of successive epochs is like omitting Hamlet from the play which named after him … but it is certainly analogous to cutting out the part of Ophelia —Alfred North Whitehead

Like a circle in a spiral / Like a wheel within a wheel / Never ending or beginning, / On an ever spinning wheel / As the images unwind / Like the circles that you find / In the windmills of your mind. —Noel Harrison, "The Windmills of Your Mind"

Meditative … like the chirping of a solitary little bird —Eudora Welty

Meditative, like a girl trying to decide which dress to wear to a party —O. Henry

Men's thoughts are thin and flimsy like lace; they are themselves pitiable like the lacemakers —Soren Kierkegaard

My mind paddles away like a wooden spoon in a bowl of dough —Richard Maynard

My thoughts are like sprouts, like sprouts on the branch of your brain —Edna O'Brien

My thoughts are whirled like a potters wheel
—William Shakespeare, *Henry VI, Part I*

A variation in common use: "My head is spinning like a merry-go-round."

My thoughts turn over like a patchwork quilt
—Diane Wakoski

Our thoughts are always happening ... like leaves floating down a stream or clouds crossing the sky, they just keep coming —Ram Dass and Paul Gorman

Preoccupied in following his own thought, like someone out to net a butterfly —William McIlvanney

Reasoning comes as naturally to man as flying to birds —Quintilian

Reflective as an old sextant —Richard Ford

Ripe in her thought like a fresh apple fallen from the limb —Karl Shapiro

Sudden a thought came like a full-blown rose —John Keats

Thinking is like loving and dying. Each of us must do it for himself —Josiah Royce

Thinking was like a fountain. Once it gets going at a certain pressure, well, it is almost impossible to turn it off —Walter de la Mare

Thought ascends, and buds from the brain, as the fruit from the root —Victor Hugo

A thought as neat and final as though a ticker tape had fed it into his brain and left off with a row of dots —Kaatje Hurlbut

The thought ... clanged like pipes in my mind —Scott Spencer

The thought kept beating in her like her heart —Wallace Stevens

The World as Meditation *from which this is taken, follows up the simile with this sentence:* "the two kept beating together."

The thought [of women] ... once it came it usually tended to stay for several hours, filling his noggin like a cloud of gnats —Larry McMurtry

Thoughts buzzing in his head like crazy flies —H. E. Bates

(His) thoughts drove in like a night-cloud —Stevie Smith

Thoughts ... fall from him like chantering from an abundant poet —Wallace Stevens

Thoughts flickering like heat lightning —F. van Wyck Mason

Thoughts floating like light clouds through the upper air of his mind —George Santayana

Thoughts ... flowing in unison, like a mountain-stream and a lake-stream meeting, but not yet merging, in a single river —George Santayana

Thoughts ground each other as millstone grind when there is no corn in between —Rudyard Kipling

Thoughts like fleas jump from man to man, but they don't bite everybody —Anon

The thought ... slipped through his mind like a dot of quicksilver —Stanley Ellin

(Foolish) thoughts play in her mind like firelight and shadow in a dim room —George Garrett

Thoughts ran like squirrels in the boy's head —Conrad Richter

Thoughts rising like fish to the fluid surface of his mind —Ellen Glasgow

(Lying awake with her) thoughts running round and round inside her skull like trapped mice —Josephine Tey

Thoughts spinning and tumbling like a week's wash —Julia Whedon

Thoughts that peel off and fly away at breathless speeds like the last stubborn leaves ripped form wet branches —John Ashberry

Thoughts ... tied up in knots like snakes, squeezing and suffocating them —V.S. Pritchett

Thoughts ... twisting like snakes through his brain —Alice Walker

Thoughts ... untidily stacked like dishes slanting a full sink —Lincoln Kirstein

Thoughts … vague and pale, like ghosts —Jean Rhys

Thoughts veering through her clear eyes like a flight of birds —Anon

Thoughts went on, coming and going like leaves blown in the wind —Ellen Glasgow

Thoughts wheeled like a flight of bats in her mind —Ellen Glasgow

Thoughts which moved, like the clouds, slowly, shedding dim yet vivid light —Iris Murdoch

Thoughts … whirling around on themselves, like the apocryphal snake seizing its own tail and then devouring itself —Stanley Ellin

Unusable and contradictory thoughts filled Quinn's mind with almost physical duress as though his poor head were a golf ball which, slashed open, shows its severed rubber filaments snapping and racing about in confusion —Thomas McGuane

When thought grows old and worn with usage it should, like current coin, be called in, and from the mint of genius, reissued fresh and new —Alexander Smith

♣ THREATS
See: VIOLENCE

♣ THRIFT

Act like they are bargaining with some Arab Street trader … like they are buying lemons —John Wainwright

False economy is like stopping one hole in a sieve —Samuel Johnson

Frugal as a poor farmer's wife —George Garrett

Generous as someone who would give you the sleeves out of his vest —Anon

His money comes from him like drops of blood —John Ray's *Proverbs*

Kept his wallet shut tight as an accordion —Anon

Pinches a penny like money is going out of style —George Garrett

Soliciting a miser is like fishing in the desert —Solomon Ibn Gabirol

Thrifty as a French peasant —G. K. Chesterton

Tight as a miser's wallet —Anon

Tight as a Scout knot —Geoffrey Wolff

In his novel, Providence, *Wolff expands upon the simile with: "wouldn't pay a nickel to watch an earthquake."*

Tight as a tic —Anon

Tight as Dick's headband —American colloquialism

This was coined by and is still used by Texas Rangers.

Tight as the bark to a tree —American colloquialism

This still popular simile originated in New Hampshire. A variation from Indiana, "tight as a wad," has pretty much given way to the jargon word "tightwad." The comparison was used more literally by Ulysses S. Grant when he described the pantaloons he had to wear as a West Point cadet as "being tight to my skin as the bark to a tree."

Tight as the paper on the wall —Mignon Eberhart

Watch pennies like a streetcar conductor —Irwin Shaw

♣ THROAT
See: NECK

♣ THUNDER AND LIGHTNING
See Also: NATURE, WEATHER

(There was the low boom of) distant thunder echoing like cannon —Barbara Taylor Bradford

Heard the heat thunder roll … like a hard apple rattling in the bottom of a barrel —James Lee Burke

Lightning plays over the horizon like the flicker of ideas —T. Coraghessan Boyle

Lightning and thunder spat and roared like a wounded tiger —Robert Traver

Lightning falls like silent saber blows —Erich Maria Remarque

Lightning flickers like a genie inside the bottle-shaped cloud —Walker Percy

Lightning flutters … like a wing —like a broken bird —Katherine Mansfield

Lightning … letting down thick drips of thunder like pig iron from the heart of a white-hot furnace —F. Scott Fitzgerald

Lightning snapped at the world like a whip —John Rechy

Lightning winked across the eastern sky like fitful fireflies —Fletcher Knebel

Thunder beating like tribal drums —T. Coraghessan Boyle

Thunder harried the building like a hound, brushing its crackling coat against the spandrels and mullions, snuffling all the windowpanes —Michael Chabon, *The Amazing Adventures of Kavalier & Clay*

Thunder like great stones falling —Stephen Longstreet

Thunder rolled like a cannon —Anon

Thunder rustling like water down the sky's eaves —A. R. Ammons

Thunder sounded like a far-off cracking of the earth —Martin Cruz Smith

Thunder steps down like a giant walking the earth —T. Coraghessan Boyle

A thunderstorm came rushing down … roaring like a brontosaur —Carlos Baker

❧ TIDINESS
See: ORDER/DISORDER

❧ TIGHTNESS
See: FIRMNESS, TENSION, THRIFT

❧ TIME
See Also: DAY, DEATH, LIFE

About as much time left as an ice cube in a frying pan —William Diehl

Any decent church service lasts forty-five minutes, like the sex act —Heinrich Böll

As the waves make toward the pebbled shore, so do our minutes hasten to their end —William Shakespeare, "Sonnet 60"

As the years go by me, my life keeps filling up with names like abandoned cemeteries —Yehuda Amichai

The day runs through me as water through a sieve —Samuel Butler

The days chase one another like kittens chasing their tails —H. L. Mencken

The days slipped by … like apple-parings under a knife —Stephen Vincent Benét

A decade falling like snow on top of another —Elizabeth Hardwick

Each class seemed endless to him, as if the hour were stuck to his back like his damp shirt —Helen Hudson

Each year is like a snake that swallows its tail —Robert Penn

This line is the curtain raiser for Warren's poem "Paradigm."

Every day yawned like a week —Donald Seaman

Forty-five minutes passed, like a very slow cloud —Dylan Thomas

Here [at a country inn] time swings idly as a toy balloon —Phyllis McGinley

The hours weighed like centuries on his heart —Lawrence Durrell

If time seems to pass so quickly, this is because there are no landmarks. Like the moon when it is at its heights on the horizon —Albert Camus

The hours [with nothing to do] hunted him like a pack of bloodhounds —Edith Wharton

If you let slip time, like a neglected rose it withers on the stalk with languished head —John Milton

In winter ... days were as abbreviated as a stifled sneeze —Claire Messud, *The Last Life*

It was hard to keep track of time, which had grown fat, sluggish, and lazy like an overfed cat —Lionel Shriver, *The Post-Birthday World*

The lagging hours of the day went by like windless clouds over a tender sky —Percy Bysshe Shelley

The word "over" is spelled "o'er" in the original

Leisure is like a beautiful garment that will not do for constant wear —Anon

Life goes like the river —Clifford Odets

Like a run in a stocking. It [lost time] always got worse —Anne Morrow Lindbergh

Like January weather, the years will bite and smart —Dorothy Parker

Like sand poured in a careful measure from the hand, the weeks flowed down —Paule Marshall

Like the swell of some sweet tune, morning rises into noon, May glides onward into June —Henry Wadsworth Longfellow

Looking out at the road rushing under my wheels / Looking back at the years gone by like so many summer fields —Jackson Brown, "Running on Empty"

The minutes crawl like last year's flies —Ridgely Torrence

The minutes ticked off like separate eternities —Dan Wakefield

The moment hung in time like a miner's hat on an oaken peg in a saloon abandoned ninety years ago —Loren D. Estleman

The moment shimmered like a glass of full-bodied wine —Marge Piercy

The moments [between two people] were stretching longer and longer, like so many rubber bands —Elizabeth Spencer

My days are consumed like smoke —The Holy Bible/Psalms

The passing years are like a mist sweeping up from the sea of time so that my memories acquire new aspects —W. Somerset Maugham

Saw the days of the year stretching ahead like a series of bright, white boxes, and separating one box from another was sleep, like a black shade —Sylvia Plath

She was forever saving time, like bits of string —Helen Hudson

Slowly the generations pass, like sand through heaven's blue hour-glass —Vachel Lindsay

Lindsay used this simile as a repeated refrain for his poem "Shantung."

The summer was melting away like the unfinished ice cream Sonny left on his plate —Dan Wakefield

That night and the next day swept past like the waters of a rapids —James Crumley

There is a rhythm inside a year of time, like a great mainspring that keeps it ticking from spring to summer to fall to winter —Borden Deal

Time ... a substance of some sort which existence burned up like a fire —Susan Fromberg Schaeffer

Time can be nibbled away as completely as a tray of canapé in an irresolute fat man's reach, or grandly lost in victory like the great marlin in *The Old Man and the Sea* [novel by Ernest Hemingway] —Charles Poore

Time crawled like ants —Marge Piercy

Time crouched, like a great cat, motionless but for tail's twitch —Robert Penn Warren

Time dripped like drops of blood —Yukio Mishima

Time drops sail like a ketch in a lagoon —Diane Ackerman

Time fled past us like a startled bird —James Crumley

Time flies ... like an arrow —Amy Hempel

Time goes coolly through the funnel of his fingers ... like water over stones —William H. Gass

Time has moved on like a great flock of geese —Stephen Minot

Time is a storm in which we are all lost —William Carlos Williams

Time is like an enterprising manager always bent on staging some new and surprising production, without knowing very well what it will be —George Santayana

Time is like a river made up of the events which happen, and its current is strong, no sooner does anything appear than it is swept away and another comes in its place, and will be swept away too —Marcus Aurelius

Time is like money; the less we have of it to spare the further we make it go —Henry Wheeler Shaw

Time is like some balked monster, waiting outside the valley, to pounce on the slackers who have managed to evade him longer than they should —James Hilton

Time, like a flurry of wild rain, shall drift across the darkened pane —Charles G.D. Roberts

Time like an ever-rolling stream bears all its sons away —Isaac Watts

Time, like a pulse, shake fierce through all the worlds —D. G. Rossetti

Time looked like snow dropping silently into a black room or ... like a silent film in an ancient theatre, one hundred billion faces falling like those New Year balloons, down and down into nothing —Ray Bradbury

Time moves ... like a treacle —Hortense Calisher

Time passes as on a fast day —Anon

Time pleated like a fan —Julia O'Faolain

Time pulses from the afternoon like blood from a serious wound —Hilma Wolitzer

Time roared in his ears like wind —John Barth

Time roars in my ears like a river —Derek Walcott

Time rushes past us like the snowflake on the river —Gore Vidal

Time seemed to have slowed down, dividing itself into innumerable fractions, like Zeno's space or marijuana hours —Ross Macdonald

Time ... sounded like water running in a dark cave and voices crying and dirt dropping down upon hollow box lids, and rain —Ray Bradbury

Time sticking to her like cold grease —Marge Piercy

Time swells like a wave at a wall and bursts to eternity —George Barker

Time went on like an unchanging ribbon drawn across a turbulent background —Heinrich Böll

Upon his silver hairs time like a panama hat sits at a tilt and smiles —Karl Shapiro

In his poem "Boy-Man," Shapiro expands on the simile as follows: "... And smiles. To him the world has just begun. And every city waiting to be built."

The week is dealt out like a hand —Randall Jarrell

The week passed slowly ... like a prolonged Sunday —Edith Wharton

When a man sits with a pretty girl for an hour, it seems like a minute. When he sits on a hot stove for a minute, then it's longer than any hour —Albert Einstein

When you're deeply absorbed in what you're doing, time gives itself to you like a warm and willing lover —Brendan Francis

The years are crawling over him like wee red ants —Ogden Nash

The years come close around me like a crowd of the strangers I knew once —Randall Jarrell

The years dropped from Randstalble [character in novel] like a heavy overcoat —James Morrow

The years like great black oxen tread the world, and God the herdsman goads them on behind —William Butler Yeats

The years peeled back like the skin of an onion, layer on top of layer —T. Coraghessan Boyle

The years rolled in against one another like a rush of water —Frieda Arkin

The years shall run like rabbits —W. H. Auden

The years ticked past like crabs —Randall Jarrell

Years which rushed over her like weathered leaves in a storm —Ellen Glasgow

A year that dragged like a terminal illness —Rosellen Brown

❧ TIMELESSNESS/UNTIMELINESS

See Also: STALENESS

As modern as tomorrow —Slogan, Royal Worcester Corset Co.

As out of date as the black stockings and high shoes worn by inmates of asylums that used to take up city blocks and loom large in the countryside —Eileen Simpson, *New York Times*, May 1,1987

As seasonable as snow in summer —John Ray's *Proverbs*

By the time they take place [dinner parties] the original impulse is lost … like sending a Christmas card into space and hoping an alien finds it on the right date —Maxine Chernoff

Dated as a Do-Do, but who cares —Anon capsule review, television movie listings, *New York Times*, April 1987

Dead as a failed product launch —Anon

Dead as an unsuccessful book —Henry James

Dead as Greek —Karl Shapiro

Dead as Sunday's paper on Tuesday morning —Anon

Commonly used variations include: "dead as yesterday's front page news"; and "dead as last week's ticker tape."

Extinction, like a thing of beauty is forever —Brad Leithauser, *New York Times Book Review*, June 7, 1987

Gone like the carriage-horse —Louis MacNeice

Poet MacNeice precedes the simile with this question: "What's become of the squadron of butlers, valets, grooms and second housemaids?" Clearly appropriate substitutions for the carriage-horse could give rise to as many similes beginning with "gone like" as there are obsolete customs and objects; for example: "gone … like five-cent candy and the drain board on the sink from a novel by Babs H. Deal."

Good that comes too late is as good as nothing —Thomas Fuller

It's a little like being given the captaincy of the *Titanic* after it hit the ice floe —Senator Lawton Chiles of Florida

Senator Chiles was quoted in many newspapers on the prospect of heading the Senate budget committee, after the November 1986 Democratic victory.

Like a punch line of a bad joke, the moment passed —T. Coraghessan Boyle

(Conflicts as) new as each generation —Anon, jacket copy

Because similes are so often pulled out for book jacket copy, the more a reviewer can appropriately include, the better; and so, this and the "old as literature" comparison below were both featured on one book jacket.

New as tomorrow —Slogan, Dictaphone company

(Passions and conflicts) as old as literature —Anon

No day is so dead as the day before yesterday —W. Somerset Maugham

Obsolete as books in leather bindings —Louis MacNeice

Outdated like a last year's almanac —John Greenleaf Whittier

Timing … as elegant as that of the Budapest String Quartet —Karl Shapiro

(The reference library is quite) unfrequented … like the mausoleum of a once-proud family that has died out —Robert Barnard

❧ TIREDNESS

See: WEARINESS

❧ TOBACCO

See Also: SMELLS

An acrid cigar held tightly in your teeth, you look like a banker or a psychiatrist or both —Daniela Gioseffi

Ash flow like a breaking thundercloud from his clenched cigar —Harvey Swados

Ashtray … crammed with smoked cigarettes like dead bugs —John Rechy

Blowing a cloud of coarse smoke [from a pipe], like a steam roller —Frank Swinnerton

(I lit) a cigar, a cheap twisted black thing like half a pepperoni —T. Coraghessan Boyle

Cigarette coals dotted the room like watch fires —Thomas Pynchon

Cigarettes … dangle from his lips like a second tongue —Jonathan Valin

Cigarettes tasted like hot ashes —Anthony E. Stockanes

Cigars … when lit, they exuded an overwhelming odor, like burning manure from constipated giraffes —Richard S. Prather

A dead cigar which was always in his hand, seemed to belong there, like a thumb or finger —Willa Cather

The glow in the bowl of his pipe went on and off like a firefly —Jean Stafford

A good cigar is as great a comfort to a man as a good cry is to a woman —Edgar George Bulwer-Lytton

His cheeks puffed [from smoking a cigar] like a bellows —Jay Parini

His cigar … had become a natural appendage … like a pipe stuck in the face of a snowman —Robert Traver

It [tobacco] smells like Saturday, and consequently puts me in a chronic holiday mood —Robert Benchley

It [cigarette] tasted like burning rope —Van Wyck Mason

Lit his stogy, which flared up like a burning bush —Arthur Train

My psyche felt as different without cigarettes as my body felt in moving from air to water —Norman Mailer

Removed his water-logged cigar, like a man calmly unscrewing his nose —Robert Traver

The smell of good tobacco … heavy as incense in a church —Howard Spring

Smoked like a chimney —Richard Harris Barham

The smoke of cigars and cigarettes like curtains before the lights —R. Wright Campbell

Smoking his clay pipe with the elegance of an Indian chief —André Malraux

Stubbed out the cigarette as if he were squashing a cockroach —Derek Lambert

The tip of his narrow cigarette danced like a tiny ballerina in the dark —Nelson Algren

Took another deep drag of his cigarette, letting the smoke curl up out of his mouth and around his head like ectoplasm —Margaret Millar

To smoke a cigar through a mouthpiece is the equivalent of kissing a lady through a respirator —Anon

❧ TONGUE

See Also: MOUTH, SHARPNESS

Her tongue felt like a freshly painted shingle —Edwin L .Sabin

Her tongue hung out like a yard of red hall carpet —Wilson Mizner

Her tongue [as she kissed him] was like a kitten's, soft and rough, tasting of milk —Shirley W. Schoonover

His tongue darted in and out when he talked, as if he were keeping count of the words —Shelby Hearon

(A large dog lay panting,) his tongue unrolled like a carpet —Peter Meinke

My tongue is big as a liverwurst —Marge Piercy

The tongue is like a racehorse: the less weight it carries, the faster it runs —Joseph Addison

This has been modernized from the original: "The tongue is like a race-horse, which runs the faster the lesser weight it carries."

Tongue like a pink dart —Joseph Conrad

The tongue … like a stream, could run smooth music from the roughest stone —Elizabeth Barrett Browning

Your tongue curls up in your moth like a cat lapping up cream —R. Wright Campbell

♣ TOUGHNESS

(My fate cries out, and makes each petty artery in this body) as hardy as the Nemean lion's —William Shakespeare, *Hamlet*

Babies you about as much as Perry White babies Clark Kent —Peter H. Lewis describing a tough-to-master computer program, *New York Times,* 1985

(The man is as) hard as a cash register —Dialogue, *Miami Vice* television drama, January 7, 1986

(She can be) hard as a mineral —Philip Roth

The "hard as a mineral" lady is the mother of Nathan Zuckerman, hero of several Roth novels.

Hard as flint —Larry McMurtry

Hard as my fist —Tennessee Williams

Hard as tortoise-shell —John Galsworthy

Hardboiled as a picnic egg —Edward E. Paramore

Resilient and tenacious as an ameba —Natascha Wodin

She's (Genevieve Bujold) tough as a little green apple —Rex Reed

Tough and leathery as a jockey —John Mortimer

Tough and shrill as an old bird —H. E. Bates

Tough and hard-boiled as an Easter egg —Anon

Tough as a black oak —Dee Brown

Tough as a bone —W. S. Gilbert

Tough as a fast food steak —Tim McCarver, describing baseball player Dave Parker, January 1987

Tough as a kibbutz woman —T. Coraghessan Boyle

(She was short and fat,) tough as a monkey —Rudolf Nassauer

Tough as an elephant's hide —Calder Willingham

(He was as) tough as a resistant bacterium —Patrick Suskind

Tough as a stale bagel —Anon

(Memories as) tough as a thorn —Babette Deutsch

Tough as boiled owls —Hubert H. Humphrey on his opponent for presidential election

(She's big as a damned barn and) tough as knife metal —Ken Kesey

Tough as marshmallows —Anon, *Forbes,* March 23, 1987

The simile was used as a blurb to introduce an article about the government sounding tough but not following through.

(She was a) tough lady, like a military jeep rolling from place to place on thick tires —Harvey Jacobs

(She's as) tough as old boots —Mary Bridgman

In recent years tough as "old shoe leather" has been a popular variation of this simile, which dates back to 1870.

Tough as seaweed —Linda Pastan

Tough as teak —Bryan Forbes

Tough as tire treads —Lynn Haney

> *The person being compared to tire treads is the late Edith Piaf.*

❧ TRADING

See: *ADVANTAGEOUSNESS, SUCCESS/FAILURE*

❧ TRAFFIC

See: *ROAD SCENES, VEHICLES*

❧ TRAIL

See: *PURSUIT*

❧ TRANQUILITY

See: *PEACEFULNESS*

❧ TRANSIENCE

See Also: *BREVITY, DEATH, LIFE*

About as fixed as liquid mercury —Leslie Bennetts, *New York Times*, June 8, 1986

As fleeting and elusive as our dreams —Anon

The brilliant passes like the dew at dawn —Johann Wolfgang von Goethe

> *In* Faust, *from which this is taken, Goethe continues by presenting the other side of the coin: "The true endures for ages yet unborn."*

Burnt like a faggot in a tempest —Willa Cather

Changed them like underwear —Paige Mitchell

> *In Mitchell's novel,* The Covenant, *are law clerks are what are being so changed.*

(His smile) comes and goes as quickly as snow —Robert Goldberg about film maker Alain Renais, *Wall Street Journal*, March 24, 1987

Disposable as extra income —Anon

Disposable as razor blades —Anon

Disposable as TV dinner containers —Anon

Enduring as a summer shower —Anon

Ephemeral as butterflies —Susan Heller Anderson on literary magazines, *New York Times*/Column One section, October 24,1986

Ephemeral things, like movement, are manifestations of immortality —Joanne Selzer

> *This is the closing line for the poem "Prima Ballerina."*

Flare briefly like the candles upon a cake —Donald Justice

(Embrace) fleeting as a bird's poise —Edith Wharton

Fleeting as a dream of night lost in the garish day —Aeschylus

Fleeting as a raspberry season —Line from television drama *St. Elsewhere*, broadcast December 16, 1986

Fleeting as the estate of man —Marcus Aurelius

A fleeting gratification … like alms thrown to the beggar, that keeps him alive today that his misery may be prolonged till the morrow —Lynne Sharon Schwartz

He flitted from moment to moment and topic to topic like a sparrow in a hurricane of crumbs —Edward Rutherfurd, *New York*

How fading are the joys we dote upon! Like apparitions seen and gone —John Norris

Like a rainbow—spectacular but short-lived —Anon

> *A variation: "like a shooting star—spectacular but short-lived.*

Like water thrown on the sand: it (media campaign about energy crisis) left little trace —George F. Will

Mortality weighs heavily on me like unwilling sleep —John Keats

(The moment of agitation) passed (from his gaze) like a cloud, leaving a clear blue sky —Christopher Isherwood

Passing through a certain stage, something rather like an illness —Thomas Mann

As permanent as a temporary price increase
    —Anon

Temporary as an idea in an empty head —Anon

Temporary as a wave —Anon

(Beauty is as) temporary as flowers —Anon

(His self-possession was) temporary, like a reflection in water that may be wiped out at the first swell —Saul Bellow

(His love was as) transient as the first golden streaks of dawn —Harry Prince

Transitory as childhood —Lawrence Durrell

Will last about as long as a snowball in hell —Anon

✿ TRANSPORTATION
See: VEHICLES

✿ TRAVEL

Like a chastity belt, the package tour keeps you out of mischief but a bit restive for wondering what you missed —Peg Bracken

Like film critics, the guidebooks don't always see eye to eye —Peg Bracken

Like gin or plum pudding, travel is filling —Peg Bracken

One's travel life is basically as incommunicable as his sex life is —Peg Bracken

A traveller without knowledge is a bird without wings —Sadi

Travel light, like the prayers of Jews —Yehuda Amichai

Travelling is almost like talking with men of three other centuries —René Descartes

✿ TREES
See Also: LEAVES, NATURE

Apple-trees on which the apples looked like great shining soap bubbles —Hans Christian Andersen

The bark hung in ribbons from the trunks like the flayed skins of living creatures —R. Wright Campbell

Beeches ... their beautiful bare green trunks like limbs —Elizabeth Bowen

The big pine was like greenish bronze against the October sky —Ellen Glasgow

(In the moonlight) the big trees around us looked as bare as gallows —John Braine

The birches bend like women —Caroline Finkelstein

The birches stand out ... like gay banners on white poles —Erich Maria Remarque

The birch trees wavered their stark shadows across it [snow] like supplicating arms —Leo Tolstoy

Boughs ... as rough and hornily buckled as the hands of old farmers —Margaret Laurence

[Tree] branches ... looked like the powerful contorted fingers of a gigantic hand —Sholom Ash

The branches [of a weeping willow] were thin, like the bleached bones of a skeleton —Daphne du Maurrier

Cedars ... black and pointed on the sky like a paper silhouette —William Faulkner

Chestnut trees ... their clusters of white blossoms like candelabras —Dorothea Straus

Copses of hazel and alder stood like a low, petrified forest —H. E. Bates

Cypresses rose like cathedral spires —Jilly Cooper

Elms rich like cucumbers —Joyce Cary

Evergreens as big as tents —Julia O'Faolain

Evergreens ... out of place [amid the other trees that change their foliage in Autumn] ... like poor relations at a rich man's feast —Jerome K. Jerome

Huge hardwood trees draped with clusters of Spanish moss guarded the house from the afternoon heat like overdressed sentinels —Paul Kuttner

Magnolia ... its chalices of flowers like superb classical emblems —H. E. Bates

Maples, burning like bonfires, pure yellow and pure red —Pamela Hansford Johnson

My poplars are ... like two old neighbors met to chat —Theodosia Garrison

The oaks stood silent and tired, like old, worn-out seekers after pleasure, unable to keep up in this grimy, mechanized world of ours —Anthony Powell

Palms ... like Spanish exclamation points —Sue Grafton

A pear tree glistened in bloom like a graceful drift of snow —George Garrett

The pear tree lets its petals drop like dandruff on a tabletop —W. D. Snodgrass

Pines ... moaning like the sea —John Greenleaf Whittier

Pines tossing their green manes like frightened horses —George Garrett

The pines were packed like a quiver of arrows —John Farris

The pine-trees roared like waves in their topmost branches, their stems creaked like the timber of ships —Katherine Mansfield

A poplar covered with snow looked, in the bluish mist, like a giant in a winding sheet —Anton Chekov

Poplars like dark feathers against the green and gold sunset —Sharon Sheehe Stark

The poplars stood like tall guards, attentive, at attention —Delmore Schwartz

A week after the poet entered this in his diary as a fragment, he incorporated it into a poem as follows: "The poplar stood like a rifle."

Poplars that rose above the mist were like a beach stirred by the wind —Gustave Flaubert

Red maples and orange oaks, shaped like hands —Jonathan Valin

The redwoods let sink their branches like arms that try to hold buckets filling slowly with diamonds —James Dickey

Rows of bay trees like children's green lollipops —Graham Masterton

Saw the bare branches of a tree, like fine lace, against the blackness [of the garden] —Jean Rhys

The scarlet of the maples can shake me like a cry —Bliss Carman

The shadows hung from the oak trees to the road like curtains —Eudora Welty

Tall trees like towers —Carlos Baker

A thick low-hanging [tree] branch sags like a wounded arm —John Rechy

The tops of pines moonlit, like floating Christmas trees —Frank Conroy

The tree, in full bloom, was like a huge mountain lit with candles —Alice Walker

Trees against walls, flattened like spies in old movies —Lisa Ress

The trees and the shrubbery seemed well-groomed and sociable, like pleasant people —Willa Cather

The tree sat like a party umbrella (trunk sturdy, branches gently arcing) —W. P. Kinsella

Trees bent like arches —Graham Swift

The trees cast still shadows like intricate black lace —H. G. Wells

Trees darkening like clusters of frightened wrens —Philip Levine

The trees dimmed the whiteness [of snow] like a sparse coat of hair —John Cheever

The trees drooped like old men with back problems —T. Coraghessan Boyle

Trees grew close and spread out like bouquets —Stephen Crane

The trees have a look as if they bore sad names —Wallace Stevens

Trees ... hunched against the dawn sky like shaggy dark animals, like buffalo —Alice Munro

A tree slender as life, and as tall —Kenneth Patchen

Trees ... like burnt-out torches —Oscar Wilde

Trees ... like fresh-painted green —Danny Santiago

Trees ... like prophet's fingers —Dylan Thomas

Trees like tall ships —Sharon Sheehe Stark

Trees [planted 40 years ago] ... now stately, like patriarchs whose wisdom lives in their mere physical presence, after all sight and mind have been feebled —Paul Horgan

Trees spaced out in ordered formality ... like a ballet of spinsters —W. Somerset Maugham

Trees spread like green lather —F. Scott Fitzgerald

Trees ... spread their scant shade upon the ground like fine strands of hair —Yitzhak Shenhar

The trees stood motionless and white like figures in a marble frieze —Helen Keller

(In the park) the trees stood reticent as old men —Helen Hudson

Trees ... tall and straight as the masts of ships —Donald Hall

Trees tall as mythical giants —David Ignatow

Trees ... vibrating headily like coins shaken in a dark money-box —Robert Culff

The trees were beginning to put out buds like tiny wings —Helen Hudson

The trees were plucked like iron bars —Wallace Stevens

Trees whose branches spread like hugging, possessive arms —John Rechy

Trees with branches like the groping fingers of men long dead —Loren D. Estleman

Trunks like thick skirts hanging in folds —Paul Theroux

Twigs grasped for the sky like frayed electrical wires —Z. Vance Wilson

Willow trees ... their trailing leaves hung like waterfalls in the morning air —Eudora Welty

♣ TREMBLING

See Also: ROCKING AND ROLLING, VIBRATIONS

Body quivers like a dancing animal's —Maureen Howard

Felt a tremor ... like an earthquake in a swamp —William Getz

The tremor described by the comparison is the kind that goes through a person, like a shiver.

(The handkerchief) flapped like a jib in a crosswind —T. Coraghessan Boyle

(Ali's brain) flickered and wavered like a candle flame in a draft —Gerald Kersh

(My tongue) fluttered like a dead leaf —George Garrett

Fluttered like paper in the wind —Gertrude Atherton

Fluttering around like birds in a thicket —Ariel Dorfman

Fluttering around ... like a yardful of hens —Harvey Swados

Fluttering in the wind, like a schooner in full rig —Anatole France

This referred to a feather fluttering on a hat, and while feathered hats have not been in style for many years, this simile is not limited to that descriptive reference point.

Fluttering like a white moth —O. Henry

Fluttering like pigeons —Christina Rossetti

Flutter like large butterflies —Oscar Wilde

Her hands and face shook like Jell-O —Joseph Heller

Trembling flesh and pudding make for vivid similes. Some variants: "quivering all over ... like a dish of jelly on a rickety table" (Nikolay Leskov); "The whole huge torso, the shoulders, arms and

breast and the great heaving belly, would shake and tremble like a hogshead full of jelly." (Thomas Wolfe)

His whole body was shaking and the more he tried to control it, the more violently it shook, as though the lines of communications between his brain and his muscles had been cut —Margaret Millar

(Nostrils) pulse like a heart on fire —Gertrude Atherton

Quake like mice when the cat is mentioned —Honoré de Balzac

(His whole face) quivered convulsively as if pricked by pins and needles —Luigi Pirandello

[An evening gown] quivered like a butterfly about to take wing —Dorothea Straus

Quivered like a pointer dog —Jonathan Gash

Quivered like a sob —Conrad Aiken

Quivered like forest-leaves —Dante Gabriel Rossetti

Quivering … like a wounded bird —Leo Tolstoy

Quiver like a twig in a gale —L. P. Hartley

Quiver like tuning forks —Peter De Vries

(The Saab) rattled like a trayful of china —Scott Spencer

Shaking all over like someone attached to an electric reducing belt —Cornell Woolrich

Shaking like a dog shittin' peach pits —Ken Kesey

Shaking like a drunk the morning-after —Clarence Major

Shaking like a lamb led to slaughter —Sholem Aleichem

Shaking like an ague-fit —William Faulkner

Shaking like a piece of grass —Louise Erdrich

Shaking like a treed raccoon —Harvey Swados

Shaking like a wet spaniel —T. Coraghessan Boyle

(Her breath) shaking like turning leaves —Mary Hedin

Shiver as at the sight of a bug or a repulsively dirty man in the street —Colette

Shivered, like a swimmer who has tested the water with a toe and found it exceeding chill —Stefan Zweig

Shivering like a puppy —Ross Macdonald

Shivering like a whippet on a cold day —Jilly Cooper

Shiver like a flame —George Garrett

Shiver like ostriches in a zoo —Marge Piercy

Shivers like a fish in a net —George Garrett

Shook like a harpstring —Beryl Markham

[A hand that had been beaten] shook like a loose leaf in the air —James Joyce

Shook like an autumn leaf —Dante Gabriel Rossetti

> To "shake like an aspen leaf," is a familiar variant. "I shook like a leaf … like a little leaf in a big storm," from a short story, The Actor, by Nunally Johnson exemplifies the simile extended.

(His whole body) shook like a thunder-stricken tree —Yisrael Zarchi

(His face was gray and) shook like a torn sail —Malcolm Cowley

Shook like a wet mutt [describing a dynamited building] —Tom Robbins

Shudder as if she were passing a cemetery —Elsa Schiaparelli

Shuddered all over, like a dog that recognizes the vet and smells its oncoming death —Frank Tuohy

Shuddered like a broken doll —Louise Erdrich

Shudders like an epileptic —T. Coraghessan Boyle

Shudders … like a woman gently coming —Diane Ackerman

Shuddery like a hooked fish or a stallion —W. D. Snodgrass

Silently quivering like the waters of a lake when the wind blows off-shore —Yitzhak Shenhar

Swayed like the tail of a dog attempting to be friendly —F. van Wyck Mason

Sways like a broken stalk —Elizabeth Bishop

(Her body) sways like a willow in spring wind —Robert Penn Warren

Sways like tropical seaweed —Lawrence Durrell

Trembled like an adolescent —Robert Silverberg

Trembled tensely like a released harp-string —Joseph Conrad

Tremble like an aspirin —Ogden Nash

Trembling as if something were shaking him —Ben Hecht

Trembling like a colt —Lawrence Durrell

Trembling like an invalid —Mavis Gallant

Trembling like a string —Ivan Turgenev

(Knees) trembly like water —Peggy Bennett

Tremulous as a plant in a stream —Vita Sackville-West

Twitching like a hooked fish —Gerald Kersch

Twitching like a skate [fish] in a frying pan —Lawrence Durrell

An unexpected shudder rippled over her body, like a cold wind moving across water —Madeleine L'Engle

Wobble like a skittle —Graham Swift

❧ TRITENESS
See: STALENESS

❧ TRIUMPH
See: SUCCESS/FAILURE

❧ TROUBLES
See: PROBLEMS AND SOLUTIONS

❧ TROUBLESOMENESS
See: DIFFICULTY

❧ TRUENESS/FALSENESS

Deceptive as a cat's fur —Margaret Atwood

Deceptive as a Venus flytrap —Vivian Raynor, *New York Times,* February 27, 1987
    Ms. Raynor's simile refers to the fleeting and misleading resemblance of one artist's work to another's.

Deceptive as new paint on a second-hand car —Herbert V. Prochnow

False as a lead coin —George Garrett

Falser than a weeping crocodile —John Dryden

Falser than malice in the mouth of envy —Mary Pin

Good and true as morning —Babs H. Deal

Right as rain —William Raymond
    An older, less commonly used and sarcastic variation comes from Shakespeare's Richard III: *"right as snow in harvest."*

True as life itself —Louis Bromfield

Ring as true as chapel bells on a windless morning —Anon

Ring true, like good china —Sylvia Plath

True as the dial to the sun —Barton Booth

(I found him large as life and) true as the needle to the pole —Henry James

True as the sky is blue —James Reiss

True as truth —Louis Bromfield

The true is stripped from the false like bone from meat —George Garrett

❧ TRUST/MISTRUST
See Also: UNCERTAINTY

Finding paranoia in your heart is like discovering a lump in your breast—just knowing it's there won't make it go away —Jerry Bumpus

As confiding as a doe peeping between the tree trunks —Vita Sackville-West

As suspicious of me as Hamlet was of his mother —Daphne Merkin

Carried years of suspicion strapped to her hip like a gun —Ann Jasperson

Confidence in an unfaithful man in time of trouble is like a broken tooth, and a foot out of joint —The Holy Bible/Proverbs

Confidence (in their amorous destinies) like that of birds in their wings —William Faulkner

Confidence like the soul, never returns, once it is gone —Publius Syrus

Doubt … secret and gnawing like a worm —Joseph Conrad

Doubts seemed to steam like wet flies inside his own head —Julia O'Faolain

Head … awhirl with doubts like a sky full of starlings —George Garrett

He was like a suspicion-caked old prospector —Ellery Queen

It [the thought that something was not right] was on the edge of her mind like a speck at the corner of your eye or fluff in your nostril —Julia O'Faolain

Lean on … like a man on crutches —Ross Macdonald

Mistrust swells like a prune —Marge Piercy

No more to be trusted (with news) than a cat with a saucer of milk —Christopher Isherwood

Suspicion amongst thoughts are like bats amongst birds, they ever fly by twilight —Francis Bacon

Suspicion developed like a muscle —F. Scott Fitzgerald

Suspicious … as a rat near strange bread —Patrick Kavanagh

Suspicious as a wild cat —Frank Swinnerton

Trust as I'd trust a rattlesnake —Anon

A trust, fierce and passionate, burning in her like a prayer —F. Scott Fitzgerald

Trust flourishes like a potato plant, mostly underground —Marge Piercy

As trusting to the future as a blind sky-diver —Richard Ford

Trust is like an egg and it's not like an egg. If you want to break an egg you have to do it from the outside. The only way to break up a trust is from the inside —O. Henry

Trustworthy as advice given by a cat to a mouse —Anon

A simile with clear links to an Arabic proverb: "He gives advice such as a cat gives to a mouse."

Wearing doubt like a raincoat —Carlos Baker

❧ TRUTH

See Also: CANDOR, HONESTY

All the durable truths that have come into the world within historic times have been opposed as bitterly as if they were so many waves of smallpox —H. L. Mencken

Honest as the skin between his brows —William Shakespeare, *Much Ado about Nothing*

Plain truths, like plain dishes, are commended by everybody, and everybody leaves them whole —Walter Savage Landor

Pure truth, like pure gold, has been found unfit for circulation, because men have discovered that it is far more convenient to adulterate the truth than to refine themselves —Charles Caleb Colton

Random truths are all I find stuck like burs about my mind —Phyllis McGinley

Rich honesty dwells like a miser … in a poor house; as your pearl in your foul oyster —William Shakespeare, *As You Like It*

Speaking the truth is like writing well, and only comes with practice —John Ruskin

This has been modernized from "The truth is like writing."

Truth … drag it out and beat it like a carpet —Hortense Calisher

Truth is as difficult to lay hold on as air —Walter Savage Landor

Truth is as old as God —Emily Dickinson

The truth is cold, as a giant's knee will seem cold —John Ashberry

Truth is impossible to be soiled by any outward touch as the sunbeam —John Milton

Truth … is not a thing to be thrown about loosely, like small change; it is something to be cherished and hoarded and disbursed only when absolutely necessary —H. L. Mencken

The truth is tough. It will not break, like a bubble, at a touch … you may kick it about all day, like a football, and it will be round and full at evening —Oliver Wendell Holmes, Sr.

The truth kept wandering in and out of her mind like a lost child, never pausing long enough to be identified —Margaret Millar

Truth, like a bird, is ever poised for flight at man's approach —Jean Brown

Truth, like a gentle shower, soaks through the ears and moistens the intellect —Anon

Truth, like a point or line, requires an acuteness and intention to its discovery —Joseph Glanville

Truth, like a suit of armor, stubbornly resists all attempts to penetrate it —Robert Traver

In his novel People Versus Kirk, *Traver continues the simile as follows: "While the lie, under probing, almost invariably reveals some chinks and cracks."*

Truth like a torch, the more it is shook, the more it shines —Sir William

Hamilton Modernized from the more "Tis shook, it shines."

Truth, like gold, is not less so for being newly brought out of the mine —John Locke

Truth, like light, blinds —Albert Camus

Camus prefaces his simile from The Fall *as follows: "Sometimes it is easier to see clearly into the liar than into the man who tells the truth."*

Truth, like the juice of the poppy, in small quantities, calms men; in larger, heats and irritates them, and is attended by fatal consequences in its excess —Walter Savage Landor

Truth's like a fire, and will burn through and be seen —Maxwell Anderson

A truth's prosperity is like a jest's; it lies in the ear of him that hears it —Samuel Butler

The way of truth is like a great highway. It is not hard to find —Mencius

❧ TURNING AND TWISTING

Circling like polishing rags —Diane Ackerman

(His brain) spinning around and around like a ship's propeller —Graham Masterton

Swaying like a tree in a windstorm. —Susan Vreeland

Spinning like a wind vane —William Faulkner

Spun like someone caught in a revolving door —William McIlvanney

(My whole house) spun around me like a crazy carnival ride —George Garrett

Swerving like a bird in mid-air —Lawrence Durrell

Swirling about like boiling milk —H. G. Wells

Sway like an elephant's trunk —Anon

(My senses) swivel like guns in their fixed sockets —Margaret Atwood

(We caught him red-handed and he) turned as easily as a trout in the pan —Bryan Forbes

Turned as a bucket turns in a well —Dante Gabriel Rossetti

Turning … like a chicken on a spit —Enid Bagnold

Turning like a ghost across the road —Eudora Welty

Turning like a hand in water —Philip Levine

Turns and turns like a dog making a place to lie down —Maxine Kumin

Twisted like a caterpillar —Cornell Woolrich

Twisted like a desperate fish —Peter S. Beagle

(Ryan's mouth) twisted, like a key in a lock —Julia O'Faolain

Twisting his whole body as if his bones were made of rubber —Alexander Solzhenitsyn

Went around and around like the policeman and Charlie Chaplin, both intending to fall down —Eudora Welty

Wheeled like an ambushed cat —Nelson Algren

Whipped round like a steel spring —John Fowles

Whisking about like a swallow into its nest —O. Henry

(She was always) whisking about like a clean starched napkin —H. E. Bates

Wriggle … like a snake —Mary Stewart

Writhing like a baited worm —Countee Cullen

♣ TYRANNY

See: POWER

♣ UMBRELLAS

See: OBJECTS, MISCELLANEOUS

♣ UNATTRACTIVENESS

See Also: UNDESIRABILITY

A charming middle age lady with a face like a bucket of mud —Raymond Chandler, *Farewell, My Lovely*
Chandler expanded on the simile with "if she's washed her hair since."

Disgusting, like moving cheese, like hills of ants or of flies —Ralph Waldo Emerson

(Furniture) emanating bad taste like a cold draft —Milan Kundera

Lurid as a porcelain souvenir —Derek Walcott

(It sounded) obscene, like a rarely glimpsed body part —Lorrie Moore

Plain as cement sidewalks. Plain as bread crust —Jean Thompson

Small and dry like the stump of an elm tree —Muriel Barbery, *The Elegance of the Hedgehog*

Ugly and fat as a maggot —Miles Gibson

Ugly and indestructible as the aluminum beer can —Stephen Minot

Ugly as a hairless monkey —Margaret Mitchell

Ugly as a hatful of assholes —Geoffrey Wolff

Ugly as a mud fence —American colloquialism, attributable to Southeast Southerners
Often elaborated on this as follows: "ugly as a mud fence daubed with tadpoles."

(He was like most new babies as) ugly as an artichoke —Anne Sexton

Ugly as sin —Maria Edgeworth

Ugly … like a great black spider —Rosamund Pilcher

Unappealing as a meringue with hardly any crust —Anon

As erotically stimulating as a mouthful of sardines —Miles Gibson

♣ UNAWARENESS

See: BLINDNESS

♣ UNCERTAINTY

See Also: FATE

Accidental as life —Lord Shaftesbury

I am rather like a mosquito in a nudist camp; I know what I ought to do but I don't know where to begin —Stephen Bayne
Mr. Bayne's comment was made in 1986 upon assuming a newly created job.

Indecision is like the stepchild: if he doesn't wash his hands, he is called dirty; if he does, he is wasting the water —Madagascan proverb
Modern day psychologists have adopted this as a neurosis and labeled it a "double bind."

Indecision sent me forward and back, as if I were propelled by a piston in my back —Joan Hess

Indecisive as a fellow who pulls back one leg as he moves forward with the other —Anon
Probably inspired by Arabic proverb: "He advances one leg and draws back the other."

Like children with a piece of ice ... neither able to hold it nor willing to let it go —Plutarch

Not quite sure of herself, like a new kitten in a house where they don't care much about kittens —Raymond Chandler

An obscure doubt brushed her, like a dove that wavers to a perch and is gone again without lighting —Marjorie Kinnan Rawlings

(He'd become about as) predictable as a Chinese earthquake —Joseph Wambaugh

Predictable as a Tijuana dog race —Joseph Wambaugh

Swing [uncertainly] like a hammock in the breeze —Anon

Tentative as first taste of hot soup —Anon

Tentative as a schoolgirl —Richard Ford

Uncertain as the glory of an April Day —William Shakespeare, *The Two Gentlemen of Verona*

Uncertain ... like a golf ball hit by a new golfer, continually getting close to the hole-in-one, but only getting into it by a fluke —Anon

Uncertainty ... as vertiginous as a lift descending down a bottomless shaft —Graham Masterton

Up in the air, like jugglers in a freeze-frame —John Updike

❖ UNCOMFORTABLENESS
See: DISCOMFORT

❖ UNCONCIOUSNESS
See: NATURALNESS

❖ UNDEMONSTRATIVENESS
See: COLDNESS

❖ UNDERSTANDABILITY
See: CLARITY

❖ UNDERSTANDING
See: KNOWLEDGE

❖ UNDESIRABILITY

About as inviting as Lenin's tomb —Manuela Hoelterhoff, reporting on a large wall surrounding a new museum complex in Los Angeles, *Wall Street Journal*, December 15, 1986

About as pleasant as to have an umbrella jammed down your throat, and opened there, and pulled out open, so that the broken ribs lacerate your lungs, and beaten over the head with the handle —Don Marquis

About as thrilling as swimming lessons would be to a middle-aged goldfish —H. C. Witwer

As bad as marrying the devil's daughter and living with the old folks —G.L. Apperson

As bad as offering Satan a lost soul —Emily Brontë

As desirable as meeting a former lover encountered during a honeymoon —Elyse Sommer

As much fun as a month in Gdansk —Joseph Wambaugh

(John Singer Sargent liked to make painting portraits sound) attractive as catching toads for a living —Manuela Hoeltershoff, introducing review of John Singer Sargent show at Whitney museum, *Wall Street Journal* October 15, 1986

Come like ill weather, unsent for —Brian Melbancke

(She was ...)desirable ... like a whore on a street corner —Derek Lambert

Disagreeable ... like a scent which raises fine hair on animals —John Updike

Gave him no pleasure ... it was like being invited to stretch himself out to be amputated, without an anesthetic —Storm Jameson

(Haggling about military bases) has all the joys of arm-wrestling on a sinking raft —*New York Times* editorial, March 23, 1987

Have about as much pleasure ahead of us as a pig in a butcher shop —George Garrett

Jumped at the chance like a sardine leaps for the can —John Randolph

Liked … about as much as I liked snakes or trunk murders —T. Coraghessan Boyle

Like foul weather, you come unsent for, and troublesome when you come —H. G. Bohn's *Hand-Book of Proverbs*

To love as a cat loves mustard —John Ray's *Proverbs*

Position as enviable as that of a catcher on a javelin team —George V. Higgins, on Rolland Smith's interaction with Mariette Hartley on the CBS Morning television program, *Wall Street Journal* January 19, 1987

To love as the devil loves holy water —John Ray's *Proverbs*

To love it as a dog loves a whip —John Ray's *Proverbs*

A trifle less welcome than something you would scape off the bottom of your shoe —C. W. Grafton

An unpleasant guest is as welcome as salt to a sore eye —Danish proverb

Unsatisfying as a set compliment —Heywood Broun

Unwelcome as a mouse in your shoe —Elyse Sommer

Wanted (to play baseball) like he wanted a third nostril —Max Shulman

Welcome as a guest with sneakers at a Palm Beach party —Tom Brokaw

Welcome as a mugger —Anon

Welcome as a painful and chronic disease —Elyse Sommer

Welcome as a storm —Thomas Fuller

Welcome as a tree falling across your Volkswagen —*PM-TV Magazine*

Welcome as Satan —Alfred, Lord Tennyson

Welcome as snow at harvest time —John Ray's *Proverbs*

Welcome as the season's first snowstorm —Anon

(In the rarefied upper echelons of Japanese sumo wrestling, foreigners have been about as) welcome as Visigoths were at the gates of Rome —Clyde Haberman, about wrestler from Hawaii, *New York Times*, May 28, 1987

Welcome as water in a leaking ship —John Ray's *Proverbs*

To tone down the image of disaster to common distress, there's "As welcome as water in one's shoes."

Welcomed … the way a cardiac case does chest pains —William McIlvanney

❧ UNEMPLOYMENT
See: WORK

❧ UNEXPECTEDNESS
See: SUDDENESS, SURPRISE

❧ UNFAIRNESS
See: INTOLERANCE

❧ UNFRIENDLINESS
See: SOCIABILITY

❧ UNGRACIOUSNESS
See: MANNERS

❧ UNHAPPINESS
See: DEJECTION, DISCONTENT, GLOOM

❧ UNHELPFULNESS
See: USEFULNESS/USELESSNESS

❧ UNIQUENESS
See: ORIGINALITY

❧ UNKINDNESS
See: CRUELTY

❧ UNLIKELIHOOD
See: IMPOSSIBILITY

❧ UNNATURALNESS
See: NATURALNESS

❧ UNPLEASANTNESS
See: UNDESIRABILITY

❧ UNPREDICTABILITY
See: SURPRISES, UNCERTAINTY

❧ UNPROFITABILITY
See: ADVANTAGEOUSNESS

❧ UNREALITY
See: REALNESS/UNREALNESS

❧ UNRELIABILITY
See: RELIABILITY/UNRELIABILITY

❧ UNRESPONSIVENESS
See: COLDNESS, REMOTENESS, RESERVE

❧ UNSTEADINESS
See Also: MOVEMENT(S)

Flounder around like a fish on the beach —Anon
> *A commonly used variation: "flounder around like a beached whale."*

Floundered like a waterlogged ship —James Hilton

Floundered like insects in yogurt —George F. Will, about those involved in Watergate crimes

Floundering like someone running in deep sand, blind without glasses, burdened with books —George Garrett

Flounder like a compass that's lost its needle —Anon

> *A variation: "flounder like a windup watch without a dial."*

(Was solidly built but) gave the impression of not being very stable, like a building with imperfect foundations —MacDonald Harris

Reel like a leaf that's drawn to a water-wheel —Dante Gabriel Rossetti

Stagger like a drunken man —The Holy Bible/Psalms

Staggers slightly … like a carnival clown —Hilary Masters

Staggers to his feet like a battered middleweight coming out for the fifteenth round —T. Coraghessan Boyle

Stumbled … like an old woman leaning on a cane that wasn't there —Ross Macdonald

Stumbled like fat sheep —Stephen Crane

Stumbling a little over his own feet like an adolescent not accustomed to his new growth —Margaret Millar

Tumbling … like a moth blinded by sudden brightness —Jerzy Kosinski

Unconstant as the wind; as wavering as the weathercock —William Walker

Unstable as water —The Holy Bible/Genesis

(She seemed volatile right now) unstable, like a vial of nitroglycerin —Sue Grafton

Unsteady like a pole balanced on the tip of one's finger —Arthur Schopenhauer

Wavering as the wind —John Heywood
> *Modernized from the Old English: "waueryng as the wynde."*

Wobbled like an overfed penguin —Len Deighton

(His new English) wobbles like a first bicycle —Diane Ackerman

❧ UNTIDINESS
See: ORDER/DISORDER

❧ UNTIMELINESS
See: TIMELINESS/UNTIMELINESS

❧ UNTRUSTWORTHINESS
See: TRUST/MISTRUST

❧ UNTRUTH
See: LIES AND LIARS

❧ UNWELCOMENESS
See: UNDESIRABILITY

❧ UPRIGHTNESS
See: POSTURE, STRAIGHTNESS

❧ UP-TO-DATENESS
See: TIMELINESS/UNTIMELINESS

❧ URGENCY
See: IMPORTANCE/UNIMPORTANCE

❧ USEFULNESS/USELESSNESS
See Also: FUTILITY, NECESSITY

As much use as a life preserver to a duck —Anon

Effective as a bullet —Edgar Saltus

Effective as an umbrella in a hurricane —Anon

Effective as bailing out a boat with a sieve —Anon

Effective as chicken soup. It can't hurt —Anon

Effective as dousing a fire with a Dixie cup full of water —Anon

Effective as fixing a broken leg with a Band-Aid —Anon

(Began to) feel like an old clerk on a high stool —Wilfrid Sheed

For Ian, a joke was not a single-use item but something you brought out again and again until it fell apart in your hands like a cheap umbrella —David Nicholls, *One Day*

Handy as a pocket in a shirt —Bartlett's *Dictionary of Americanisms*

Helpful as a bathing suit in a blizzard —Ed McBain

(The information was probably as) helpful as a wooden compass —William McIlvanney

Helpful as throwing a drowning man both ends of a rope —Arthur Baer

Ineffective as breaking into a bank vault and taking a bag of pennies —Anon

Ineffective like putting the steak on the fire and the skillet on top of the steak —Norman Mailer

Ineffective, like sending flies in pursuit of fly paper —Elliot Janeway, *Barron's*, January 20, 1986

(Lonely and) ineffectual as two left-handed gloves —Helen Rowland

Ineffectually as a firefly in Hell —Stephen Vincent Benét

[Medicare's health-care coverage] is like walking around in a bulletproof vest with a hole over the heart —Senator John Heinz, quoted in the *Wall Street Journal*, October 15, 1986

It's [everything valued by others] like so much fluff —Anton Chekhov

Like a bandage for a horse —Joseph Stein dialogue line for Teyve in response to the tailor's offer of help in *Fiddler on the Roof*

A lot of useless barging around, like a man with his sleeve in a thresher —Richard Ford

Making lists is like taking too many notes at school; you feel you've achieved something when you haven't —Dodie Smith

Pointless … like you'd give caviar to an elephant —William Faulkner

(Educating you would be about as) redundant as teaching a lion to like red meat —line from movie *Victor-Victoria*, spoken by Julie Andrews

Sending teacher into a classroom with no cane is like sending a boxer into the ring with one hand tied behind his back —Philip Squire

Some men are like a clock on a roof … useful only to the neighbors —Austin O'Malley

Some people are like wheelbarrows, only useful when pushed, and very easily upset —Jack Hebert

Unhelpful … like someone running round with black-currant lozenges to the victims of an earthquake —Josephine Tey

Unnecessary as another designer label —Anon

Useful as a bale of hay in a garage —Anon

Useful as a bicycle without tires —Anon

Useful as a buttonhole without buttons —Anon

Useful as a comb to a bald man —Anon

Useful as a defective parachute —Anon

Useful as an annuity —Anon

Useful as an umbrella to a fish —Anon

Useful as a pocket with a big hole in it —Anon

Useful as a sixth finger —Anon

Useful as a Swiss army knife —Anon

Useful as a thermometer or a scale without markings —Anon

Useful as a third nostril —Peter Benchley

Useful as hay fever when the pollen count is high —Mike Fredman

Useful as information trying to convey the locality and intentions of a cloud —Joseph Conrad

Useful as teats on a boar hog —American colloquialism

Useful as the marketable skill mom told you to acquire —Anon

Useless as a bell that doesn't ring —Anon

Useless as putting a Band-Aid on a gunshot wound —Anon

Useless as a broken feather —Anon

Useless as a bump on a log —Anon

> *A variation on this familiar simile from* The Last Good Kiss *by James Crumley: "stood around like a knot on a log."*

Useless as a car without gasoline —Anon

Useless as a glass eye at a keyhole —L. Monta Bell

Useless … as a half-built bridge —William H. Hallhan

Useless as an expectant lover —Ellen Glasgow

Useless as a single glove —Anon

Useless as a torn sock —Marianne Hauser

Useless as a twisted arm —Desmond O'Grady

Useless as Ronald Reagan's right ear —Joseph Wambaugh

Useless … like buying an air conditioner for a building without electricity —Anon

Useless … like the cow that gives a good pail of milk, and then kicks it over —H. G. Bohn's *Hand-Book of Proverbs*

♣ VAGUENESS

(The image) blurred … like something familiar seen beneath disturbed though clear water —William Faulkner

(The consonants) blur together like ink on a wet page —Sue Grafton

Clear as mud —Richard Harris Barham

> *This typifies the quick, humorous similes that were most often imported by New Englanders to add color to American speech.*

Obscure as a bureaucrat's memorandum —Anon

Obscure as modesty —Sidney Lanier

(Eye) opaque as a muddy pool —F. Scott Fitzgerald

Opaque as a milk-glass bowl —Linda West Eckhardt

♣ VALOR
See: COURAGE

♣ VALUE
See: IMPORTANCE/UNIMPORTANCE

♣ VANITY
See Also: PRIDE

An aura of self-love clung to him like a cloak —Robert Traver

Arrogance … was escaping from him like steam —Cornell Woolrich

Arrogant as a hummingbird with a full feeder —A. E. Maxwell

As careful about his looks as a young girl getting ready for her first dance —Carlos Fuentes

Conceit grows as natural as hair on one's head; but it is longer in coming out —Bartlett's *Dictionary of Americanisms*

Conceit like a high gloss varnish smeared over him —Rosa Guy

Conceit that plays itself in an elevated nose … that is only playing at being conceited; like children play at being kings and queens and go strutting around with feathers and trains —Jerome K. Jerome

The ego blows up like a big balloon —Delmore Schwartz

Flaunt my knowledges, like a woman will flaunt her pretty body —Borden Deal

He was like a cock who thought the sun had risen to hear him crow —George Eliot

He [a man without vanity] would be a very admirable man —a man to be put under a glass case, and shown round as a specimen a man to be stuck upon a pedestal, and copied like a school exercise [a man to be reverenced, but not a man to be loved, not a human brother whose hand we should care to grip —Jerome K. Jerome

Jerome concluded his comparison as follows: "a man to be reverenced, but not a man to be loved, not a human brother whose hand we should care to grip."

(Ed Koch) is like the rooster who takes credit for the sunrise —Jack Newfield, *Village Voice*, October 7, 1986

Looks at herself in the mirror like she was the first woman in the world —George Garrett

A man is inseparable from his congenital vanities and stupidities, as a dog is inseparable from its fleas —H. L. Mencken

A man who shows me his wealth is like the beggar who shows me his poverty; they are both looking for alms … the rich for the alms of envy, the poor man for the alms of my pity —Ben Hecht

My vanity [after hurtful remark], like a newly-felled tree, lies prone and bleeding —Carolyn Kizer

Preening himself like a courting rooster —Robert Traver

Preening like a politician after a landslide victory —Elyse Sommer

Puffed himself up like a ship in full sail —Hans Christian Andersen

Self-love is a cup without any bottom; you might pour all the great lakes into it, and never fill it up —Oliver Wendell Holmes

Sleek and smug as a full-bellied shark —T. Coraghessan Boyle

Strutting … like a pouter pigeon —Jerome K. Jerome

The pigeon thus named for its propensity for puffing out its distensible crop offers a novel variation of the more commonly used "strutting like a peacock."

Vanity is as ill at ease under indifference as tenderness is under a love which it cannot return —George Eliot

Vanity, like murder, will out —Hanna Cowley

Vanity, like sexual impulse, gives rise to needless self-reproach —Charles Horton Cooley

Cooley followed up on his simile as follows: "Why be ashamed of anything so human? What, indeed should we be without it."

Vanity may be likened to the smooth-skinned and velvet-footed mouse, nibbling about forever in expectation of a crumb —William Gilmore Simms

❧ VARIETY

See: DIVERSENESS

❧ VEHICLES

See Also: ROAD SCENES

Beechcraft Twin [airplane] … its wings flapping hectically like a fat squawking goose unable to get itself aloft —Herbert Lieberman

Brakes squawk like Donald Duck —Joyce Cary

The bus rode on the highway, like a ship upon the sea, rising and falling on hills that were like waves —Nathan Asch

Buzz of traffic … like the hum of bees working a field of newly blossomed clover —James Crumley

Car accelerated silently like a lioness which has sighted the prey —Elizabeth Spencer

A car is just like a gun. In the wrong hands it is nothing less than an instrument of death —Charles Portis

Car … ran as if lubricated with peanut butter —Peter De Vries

Cars shot by like large bees —Cynthia Ozick

Cars … their taillights like cigarette embers —Daphne Merkin

The cloud of exhaust [from the car] rose like a sail behind them —Alice McDermott

The engines [of a Mercedes] ticking like wizard-made toy millipedes —Saul Bellow

The exhaust [of the car] bloomed in the air like a bizarre, blue-white flower —William Dieter

Felt about cars the way Casanova felt about women —Mike Fredman

Guzzles gas the way computers gobble up bytes —Anon

Headlights [of the cars on a highway] flash by like a procession of candles —Stuart Dybek

Like a wasp rising from a rose, a helicopter chut-chut-chutted toward them —Will Weaver

The limousine slid to the curb and nestled there, sleek as a wet otter stretched out in the noon-day sun —Paige Mitchell

The … limousine slid up to the curb, like a great, rolling onyx —Hortense Calisher

The motor [of the car engine] sounded like a polishing drum with a dozen new agates turning inside —Will Weaver

Parked cars … stretched like a file of shiny beetles —Donald MacKenzie

Planes humming across the sky like bees —H. E. Bates

[A car] polished until light glanced off it like a knife —Jayne Anne Phillips

The power of the big tractor drew the plow through the damp earth like a potter's knife through wet clay —Will Weaver

A Rolls Royce glittering like a silver tureen —Saul Bellow

The rumbles of the big diesel engine were like ocean surf —Will Weaver

A ship … its masts jabbing the sky like upended toothpicks —Francis King

(The bus) spews out fumes black and substantial as octopus oil —W. P. Kinsella

Square black automobiles … like glossy black beetles —Robert Silverberg

Taillights [of car] gleaming like malevolent eyes —Stanley Ellin

Taillights red as smudged roses —Richard Ford

Tires humming like inflated snakes —John Hawkes

Tractors [at night] … like neon tetras drifting in the dark tank of the fields —Will Weaver

Train … wriggling like some long snake —Natsume Soseki

The windshield wipers [of the car] kicked like a weary dance team —Elizabeth Spencer

❧ VEHICLES, OPERATION OF

Drive like a nursemaid with a pramful of kids —Calder Willingham

Drove as if he were handling a hearse —Lael Wertenbaker

Drove silently, like a silent wind —Elizabeth Spencer

(Pulled out into traffic, his) engine cooking like grease on a cheap griddle —Loren D. Estleman

He [driver of a car] took the curves like a bird —Erich Maria Remarque

Keeps that engine purrin' like a whore on a hundred-dollar date —John Farris

Touchdown [of an airplane] was as smooth as arriving at the ground floor in a lift —Donald Seaman

❧ VERBOSENESS

See: TALKATIVENESS

❧ VEXATION

See: ANGER, IRRITABLENESS/IRRITATING

❧ VIBRATION

See Also: TREMBLING

Body jerking like a fish —David Mamet, dialogue from *Hill Street Blues* television show, January 13, 1987

(Light … came at him) throbbing like a drum —Mark Helprin

Jerking like a decked shark —Denis Johnson

A little ripple (went through her) like the commotion set up in a weeping willow by a puff of wind —O. Henry

Oscillate like a blancmange in an earthquake —John Wainwright

(Thoughts) rattle about … like dried seeds in a pod —Ellen Glasgow

Rattle about [a large apartment] like dried peas in a pod —Janet Hobhouse

Rattled like a dicer's cup —Davis Grubb

(The King's heart) rattled like spook chains in a horror show —Tom Robbins

Rattling like a crockery shop in an earthquake —Arthur Baer

[A cough] shook me like a coconut tree in a tornado —Dominique Lapierre

Throbbing like a heart —Marguerite Yourcenar

Throb like the heart of a coffee drinker —O. Henry

Vibrating like a dog's tail —Norman Mailer

Vibrating … like a man with a high fever —Anon

❧ VICE

See: EVIL

❧ VICTORY

See: SUCCESS/FAILURE

❧ VIGILANCE

See: ALERTNESS, WATCHFULNESS

❧ VIGOR

See: ENTHUSIASM, STRENGTH

❧ VIOLENCE

See Also: ADVANCING, BEHAVIOR

Battered to and fro as a rat is shaken by a dog —Rudyard Kipling

Came after him like an antelope —William Diehl

Came at him like a kamikaze —T. Coraghessan Boyle

Cored him like an apple —John Yount

Dealt out blows with the precision of a punch press —Natascha Wodin

Drove his fist straight in like a saber thrust —Joseph Wambaugh

Grabbed hold of me, as a cat grabs a mouse —George Garrett

Hit it [a man's chin] as if I was driving the last spike on the first transcontinental railroad —Raymond Chandler

Hit like a tank —Ken Stabler and Berry Stainback

Howling and clawing at each other like wild beasts in heat —Hunter S. Thompson

I can flatten him out like a crepe in a frying-pan —Henry Van Dyke

I could slice you down like cold meat before you could whisper, "Mercy" —Davis Grubb

In Grubb's novel The Golden Sickle, *the man making this threat is wielding a knife.*

I'll crush his ribs in like a rotten hazelnut —Emily Brontë

I'm gonna pop your eyes like busted eggs —William Kennedy

Knocked to the ground like a winged partridge —T. Coraghessan Boyle

Lunged [into the midst of a group of people] like a whirlwind on a summer's day —Flannery O'Connor

[Mobster Sam Giancana] ordered killings as easily as he ordered linguini —Kitty Kelley

The propensity for violence exists like a layer of buried molten magma underlying all human topography —Robert Ardrey

Put me in an arm lock as easily as he might twist a soft pretzel —James Crumley

Showered her blows upon him with the force and rapidity of a drummer beating his drum —Guy de Maupassant

Slapped her like a volleyball —Rochelle Ratner

Terrorism is a natural by-product of modern life. Like air pollution, family breakdown, excessively casual sexual promiscuity and exaltation of greed —Russel Baker, *New York Times*, 1986

Threw themselves at him like dogs at a bear —Mikhail Bulgakov

Violence and wrong are as a dream which rolls from steadfast truth, an unreturning stream —Percy Bysshe Shelley

Violence (was an inescapable factor of the heart) an ineradicable thing … like a bad seed —William March

Violence in a house is like a worm on vegetables —Hebrew proverb

Violence is as American as cherry pie —Eldridge Cleaver

The violence of my impulses [to harm another person] was still within me, like the sharp end of a splinter improperly removed —Scott Spencer

Violence weighed him down like a pack —Harris Downey

Violent and ruthless as a puppy —James Mills

Violent death is like a monster. The closer you get to it, the more damage you sustain —Sue Grafton

Violent death leaves an aura, like an energy field that repels the observer —Sue Grafton

Was on him like a falling tree —Jerry Bumpus

A wound like a burst fruit —Jean Stafford

⚜ VIRTUE

See Also: ACCOMPLISHMENT, MORALITY, PURITY

Admirable as the rabbit that lets the tortoise win a race —Mike Sommer

Chaste as ice —William Shakespeare, *Hamlet*

Chastity consists, like an onion, in a series of coats —Nathaniel Hawthorne

Good as a mother —Vicki Baum

Hanging on to his virtue like a thief to his loot —Paige Mitchell

Like gentle streams beneath our feet innocence and virtue meet —William Blake

Many individuals have, like uncut diamonds, shining qualities beneath a rough exterior —Juvenal Henry

Piety is like garlic. A little goes a long way —Rita Mae Brown

Rare virtues are like rare plants or animals, things that have not been able to hold their own in the world. A virtue to be serviceable must, like gold, be alloyed with some commoner but more durable metal —Samuel Butler

Rich in virtue, like an infant —Lao Tzu

True merit, like a river, the deeper it is, the less noise it makes —Halifax

Virginal as Eve before she knew Adam —Anon

Virgins are bores ... like people with overpriced houses —Thomas McGuane

Virtue and learning, like gold, have their intrinsic value; but if they are not polished, they certainly lose a great deal of their luster; and even polished brass will pass upon more people than rough gold —Lord Chesterfield

Virtue is a kind of health, beauty and good habit of the soul —Plato

A virtue is like a city set upon a hill, it cannot be hid —Robert Hichens

Virtue is like an enemy avoided —Dante Alighieri

Virtue is like a polar star, which keeps its place, and all stars turn towards it —Confucius

Virtue is like a rich stone, best plain set —Francis Bacon

Virtue is like health: the harmony of the whole man —Thomas Carlyle

Virtue is like precious odors—most fragrant when they are incensed or crushed —Francis Bacon

Virtue lies like the gold in quartz: there is not very much of it and much pain has to be spent on the extracting of it —Jerome K. Jerome

Virtue, like a strong and hardy plant, takes root in any place, if she finds there a generous nature and a spirit that shuns no labor —Plutarch

Virtues, like essences, lose their fragrance when exposed —William Shenstone

Virtuous as convict in the death house —H. L. Mencken

❧ VISIBILITY

See Also: CLARITY, OBVIOUSNESS, PROTRU-SION

Conspicuous, like giraffes —Karl Shapiro

(A trail as) faint as a wisp —Edward Hoagland

(The writing was as) faint as sparrow tracks in sand —Will Weaver

Hidden from view, like undeveloped negatives —Anon

Hide ... as a boat finds a cove until the storm passes —Mary Lee Settle

Hiding like tumors —Charles Johnson

Imperceptible as a spring breeze —Susan Richards Shreve

Imperceptible as grief —Emily Dickinson
This is both the title and the first line of a poem.

Invisible as a city sparrow —Marge Piercy

Invisible as the web in a spider's belly —Marge Piercy

Invisible, like a bad odor —Stephen Longstreet

Just out of sight like stars in the noon sky —John Farris

Lurking beneath the surface like a nest of snakes —Anon article on drugs as the X factor in National Football League violence, *New York Times*, November 30, 1986

Noticeable as a fart in a hail storm —American colloquialism

Prominent as a fried egg stain on the front of a full dress vest —Arthur Baer

Protrude like hairs from an old man's nose —F. D. Reeve

(The scene in front of him remained) unclear, like a painting so encrusted with dirt and varnish its depths refuse the investigating eye —Clive Barker

Unnoticeable as a pore —Karl Shapiro

Unobtrusive as a thief —Paul Theroux

Unseen like our shadows —Margaret Atwood

Visible ... like a goldfish in a bowl —Cornell Woolrich

❧ VIVIDNESS
See: BRIGHTNESS

❧ VOCATION
See: PROFESSIONS

❧ VOICE(S)

See Also: CRYING; GROANS AND WHISPERS; SINGING; VOICE, EFFECT OF; VOICE, HARSH; VOICE, MONOTONOUS; VOICE, MUSIC-RELATED; VOICE, SOFT

(Voice) artificial, like paper flowers or the cheapest kind of greasepaint —Heinrich Böll

Bitterness had come through into her voice, buzzing like a wasp —Ross Macdonald

A cold voice ... like a big freezer that whines slowly and precisely —Ariel Dorfman

A deep quiet voice like wrapped thunder —Loren D. Estleman

A disagreeable voice like the grating of broken glass —Aharon Megged

A frank, vaguely rural voice more or less like a used car salesman —Richard Ford

A frosty sparkle in his voice that presupposed opposition —like the feint of a boxer getting ready —Willa Cather

A grand rolling voice, like the sound of an underground train in the distance —Frank Swinnerton

Her tone clicked like pennies —Ross Macdonald

Her voice bristled like a black cat's fur —John Updike

Her voice burst from her like a bubble of blood from her mouth —Marge Piercy

Her voice was like the mirrored wind chimes in a lost lake house of long ago —John MacDonald

Her voice was rich and dark like good brandy, yet somehow lively too, like the very best champagne —George Garrett

High chirpy voice like a cricket —Marge Piercy

His voice was somehow familiar, yet ... it had a quality that made it unrecognizable, like one's own dress worn by someone else —L. P. Hartley

His voice rumbled like a bumblebee in a dry gourd —Nelson Algren

(Skinner was ready to melt with sweetness) his tone sounded like Romeo in the balcony scene —Rex Stout

In old age her voice had become thin as a bird's —Pauline Smith

His voice was as high-pitched as a bird's —Michael Korda, *Another Life*

The man with the high-pitched voice was the Hollywood agent Irving "Swifty" Lazar.

His voice stood out like thunder over rain —Erik Larson, *In the Belly of the Beast: Love, Terror, and an American Family in Hitler's Berlin*

His voice tremored defiantly, like that of a man presenting doubtful credentials at a bank —Hortense Calisher

It [her voice] sprang from her mouth like water from a spring —Guy de Maupassant

It was as clear as a radio broadcast —Amor Towles, *Rules of Civility*

It wheezed softly, like the voice of a man who had just won a pie-eating contest —Raymond Chandler, *Trouble Is My Business*

In loud enthusiastic voices like the Amens are said in country churches —Flannery O'Connor

A loud, hurrying voice, like the bell of a steamboat —Henry James

Muffled voices sobbed like foghorns —Kay Boyle

Voice(s)

A north country accent that scraped the eardrum like a dull razor —Helen Simonson, *Major Pettigrew's Last Stand*

Official-sounding, something like a radio announcer —Bobbie Ann Mason

Raised his voice like an auctioneer's —Truman Capote

Talked like she had a Jew's harp struck in her throat —Will Weaver

A terrible edge to her voice like a line of force holding back a flood —R. Wright Campbell

A thin shrill voice like the cry of an expiring mouse —Anon

Urgent tone, like a buzzer —Daphne Merkin

Voice ... like a ship lost at sea —Mike Fredman

Voice ... whining and self-pitying, like some teenage-tragedy song —Bobbie Ann Mason

Voice and lecturing style ... like a chilled aperitif: enticing you to the main course —Robert Goddard

Voice as confidential as that of a family doctor —Donald MacKenzie

Voice as freshly perked as morning coffee —Patricia Leigh Brown, *New York Times*, June 12, 1986

Voice as gravelly as a trout stream —Michael Korda, *Another Life*

Voice as intimate as the rustle of sheets —Dorothy Parker

Voice as lonely as the stars —Justin Scott

A voice as warm and tender as a wound —Julian Symons

Voice ... blunt as a blow —Ben Ames Williams

Voice ... both jarring and vulnerable: like a bloodshot eye —Tom Robbins

Voice burst up and broke like boiling water —Cynthia Ozick

Voice ... clear-pitched like an actor's —Christopher Isherwood

Voice clear as a bell, yet slithery with innuendo, it leaped like a deer, slipped like a snake —Norman Mailer

Voice ... clenched like a fist —Borden Deal

Voice ... controlled, chilly, beautiful, like a hillside spring on an August afternoon —F. van Wyck Mason

Voice ... flavored with a stout sweetness as though her words were sopped in rich, old wine —Jean Stafford

Voice ... high and clear as running water over a settled stream bed —Sherley Anne Williams

Voice ... jaggedly precise ... as if every word emitted a quick white thread of great purity, like hard silk, which she was then obliged to bite clearly off —Cynthia Ozick

A voice light and soaring, like a lark's —Joseph Conrad

A voice like a bird —Marge Piercy

Voice ... like a dull whip —Ayn Rand

Voice like a gurgling water pipe —Hugh Walpole

Voice like an iron bell —Peter Meinke

Voice like a parrot's scream —Robert Campbell

Voice ... like a wind chime rattling —Louise Erdrich

A voice like blowing down an empty straw —Helen Hudson

Voice like butter when he wanted something from you and poison if you got in the way —Victor Canning

Voice ... like gravel spread with honey —Jay McInerney

Voice like ice —Raymond Chandler

Voice ... like saw grass when the edges duel in the wind blowing over swampland —Lael Wertenbaker

[He asked weakly] his voice like that of a child being squeezed in wrestling and asking for mercy —John Updike

Voice ... like that of a helpless orphan —Ignazio Silone

Voice ... like the rolling of a funeral bell —Paule Marshall

A voice like the stuff they use to line summer clouds with —Raymond Chandler

Voice ... like the uncanny, unhuman gibber of new wine fermenting in a vat —W. Somerset Maugham

Voice ... like thin ice breaking —James Thurber

Voice ... opulent and vast like an actor's —Arthur A. Cohen

A voice queerly pitched, like a parrot's —Mary McCarthy

A voice rich as chocolate —David Tuller, *New York Times*, August 24, 1986

Voice roaring like the inside of a shell —Susan Neville

Voice ... rough-smooth, like velvet dragged over fine sandpaper —Loren D. Estleman

(Our dried voices, when we whisper together) are quiet and meaningless as wind in dry grass —T. S. Eliot

Voices [of ball field vendors], like crows cawing —W. P. Kinsella

Voices like gongs reverberate in the mind —C. S. Lewis

Voices [of children] ... like the fluttering of wings —Anon

Voices like uniforms, tinny, meaningless ... voices that they brandish like weapons —Jean Rhys

Voice ... smooth as cheesecake, sweet and proper —Patricia Henley

Voice smooth as whipping cream —Harvey Swados

Voice ... so low it sounded like a roll of thunder —Maya Angelou

(He had spoken with taut control, his) voice sounding like the steady firmness of a cello muted in the minor mode —Arthur A. Cohen

Voices ... went mad, like a chorus of frogs on a spring evening —D. H. Lawrence

A voice that boomed and echoed, like a man standing under a bridge, ankle-deep in rushing water —Paige Mitchell

Voice thin and distinct as a distant owl's call —John Updike

Voice ... very sweetly piercing, like the sight of the moon in winter —Angela Carter

A warm voice ... quivering like corn in a light summer wind —Aharon Megged

Worry remained suspended in her voice like a fly in amber —Jonathan Kellerman

❧ VOICE, EFFECT OF

Accent which tortured me as much as a fiddle with a soft G string or a clarinet reed blown through bubbles of saliva —Harvey Swados

Her low voice soothed him like honey in whiskey —Rita Mae Brown

Her voice curled around Melinda like a damp tongue —Jessamyn West

His father's voice entered Ben's ear like an icepick —Pat Conroy

His loud clear voice fell on her ears soft as snow —Margaret Millar

Loud voice that scrapes over our nerves like a brush —Erich Maria Remarque

The shrill voices stung her eardrums like sharp pebbles —Paul Kuttner

The sound of her voice drove itself into his senses like a spike —Kaatje Hurlbut

Voice ... irritating to the nerves like the pitiless clamor of the pneumatic drill —W. Somerset Maugham

Voices hitting the wall like stones —Maya Angelou

The voices were unnerving, like the dark come to life —Martin Cruz Smith

The voice (of a platoon leader) would buzz against his ear like a passing insect, undefined and rather annoying —Norman Mailer

☙ VOICE, HARSH

See Also: HARSHNESS

A hard, crushing voice like stones smashing against each other —Aharon Megged

Her voice … creaked like the hinges of a rusty iron gate —Stefan Zweig

Her voice flew around like pots and pans —Leonard Michael

Her voice sounded as brittle and sharp as a broken sliver of glass —Graham Masterton

High, irritating voice, like a razor blade —Caryl Phillips

His voice was harsh, like a great whirring mill saw —T. Coraghessan Boyle

Hoarse bass voice like an echo in an empty house —Amos Oz

A hoarse voice … like something broken —Romain Gary

A retching voice like a tin shovel scooping water off a concrete barn floor —Leonard Casper

A roughness in her voice like a grasshopper's —Virginia Woolf

[His voice] sounded like two shards of pottery being rubbed together —Norman Mailer

Their voices slash like reeds —William Meredith

A thick, husky voice that sounded as if he'd swallowed too many years of fog —Margaret Millar

A voice as hard as the blade of a shovel —Raymond Chandler

Voice … brittle as the first ice of autumn —Michael Gilbert

Voice … brittle, like overdone candy cracking on a plate —Pat M. Esslinger-Carr

Voice cracking like a trunk lid unopened for years —Patricia Henley

Voice … croaky and tense and faintly honking, as if a metal tube were involved in its production —John Updike

Voice, cruel as a new knife —George Garrett

Voice … deep, like crusted port wine —Donald Seaman

Voice flat and hard as a stove lid —James Crumley

Voice … fringed and sharp like the edge of a saw —Carson McCullers

Voice … hard as a nail on glass —William Beechcroft

Voice harsh and light as the scratching of dry leaves over the hard ground —Edna St. Vincent Millay

Voice harsh like tin and without heat like tin —William Faulkner

Voice … hoarse as a rooster —John Farris

Voice like a chair scraping across a tiled floor —Roderic Jeffries

Voice like a fingernail scraping down a dry blackboard —Reynolds Price

Voice … like a foghorn in foul weather —George Garrett

A voice like a howitzer —Thomas Carlyle about his publisher Frederic Henry Hedge

Voice … like a pointer moving sharply on a map or blackboard —Mary McCarthy

Voice, like a rusty hinge —Margaret Mitchell

Voice like a slate-pencil squeak —Paul J. Wellman

Voice like a spoon scraping a cooking pot —Annette Sanford

Voice like a tight squeak —Anon, about Marilyn Monroe by Columbia Pictures when they fired her in 1948

Voice, like barbed wire —Helen Hudson

A voice like cracking glaciers —Elinor Wylie

A voice like frosted trees in the wind —Rolaine Hochstein

A voice like hot ashes —James Agee

Voice … like sand —T. Coraghessan Boyle

Voice like scruffed gravel —Hortense Calisher

Voice like the cracked shriek of a desert wind —Phyllis Bottome

Voice … reedy like a tall-legged, tall-necked bird —Carolyn Chute

Voice … scratchily metallic as though it were being raked across miles of rusted roofing tin —Sharon Sheehe Stark

Voice … sharp as a snowflake on a sunburned nose —Rex Reed, about Tennessee Williams

Voice … sharp as porcupine quills —John Updike

Voice … sharp, splintering, like dry kindling split by an ax —Charles Johnson

Voice like pebbles in a bucket —Carlos Baker

Voice so ruined it sounded like a wood rasp —John Yount

Voice sounded like a crow with a cold —Harold Adams

Voice … sounds as if her throat is swollen shut —John Updike

Voices shrill as children's whistles —Marge Piercy

Voice that sounded like tires on a wet road —Richard Maynard

Voice … with a hardness in it like struck steel —John Yount

Voice … with an alluring crack in it, like some magisterial old woman who has smoked all her life —Lynne Sharon Schwartz

❧ VOICE, MONOTONOUS

Drone on like a dull wind at night —James Stern

Voices grind on, like machines working their way through tunnels —John Updike

Low monotonous voice like an absent-minded child haltingly reciting a lesson —Edith Wharton

No more inflection than a traffic light —John Updike

A noncommitable, no-place voice like a computer salesman, or somebody taking a poll, or an anchorman on TV —Lee Smith

Voice … low and monotonous, like a voice that had never expressed any human passions —Henry James

Voices, fixed like leeches to their solitary subject —Jean Stafford

The voice went on, like the steady pressure of a surgeon's hand on a shrieking nerve —Edith Wharton

❧ VOICE, MUSIC-RELATED

Chimed in … like a cracked bell —Angela Carter

Deep voice like a jovial bassoon —Willa Cather

His voice resonated like the bass in a barbershop quartet —Peter Meinke

Scratches in her soft voice like an old phonograph record —Wilfrid Sheed

Voice … with a monotonous beat of syllables, like the rhythm of a wide and shallow drum pounding in the heart of a jungle night —Wilbur Daniel Steele

Voice … clear and brassy, like a bugle —O. Henry

Voice … deep as a gong —Rosamund Pilcher

Voice … delicate and pleasant, like a reed pipe —Yuri Kazkov

A voice like a bassoon —Gerald Kersh

Voice like a cello solo —O. Henry

Voice like a church bell —George MacDonald Fraser

Voice like an aging church-choir soprano —Z. Vance Wilson

A voice like an old-fashioned wind instrument —Henry James

Voice like a sexual cello —Angela Carter

(Lift up thine) voice like a trumpet —The Holy Bible/Isaiah

Voice like a tuba —Charles Johnson

Voice ... like clarinets all ebony and silver —George Garrett

Voice like quiet music —Carlos Baker

Voice ... like someone relentlessly playing the kazoo during one of the more somber passages of a war requiem —Douglas Adams

Voice like the 'D' string in a cello —Henry Van Dyke

Voice like the deepest woodwind —George Garrett

Voice ... off-key, like a neglected piano —Paige Mitchell

Voice rang like a great silver bell —O. Henry

Voice roared like an organ pipe —Joyce Cary

Voices like French horns —Margaret Millar

Voice soft, like the voice of a violin —Isak Dinesen

Voice sounds like an accordion played down at the end of a dark tunnel —Charles Baxter

Voice ... thin as a flute —Ross Macdonald

Voice ... vibrant as the tones of a crystal bell —Theophile Gautier

Voice ... refined and finicky, like a tenor's in a cathedral choir —Frank Tuohy

What a little piccolo voice she had, like a living character from a Walt Disney Cartoon —Tama Janowitz

♣ VOICE, SOFT

A gentle, circling voice, as a warm hand is gentle circling the wrist —Kaatje Hurlbut

Her voice is a caress which strokes you like fingers —Jules Lemaître

Lemaître, a critic, was describing actress Sarah Bernhardt's voice.

His voice died in a frail wistful sigh, like wind through a shutter —William Styron

That beautiful voice which made everything she said sound like a caress —Virginia Woolf

Voice ... like a page of music —Pat Conroy

Voice like dark brown velvet —Josephine Tey

Voice like down feathers —William Diehl

Voice ... like liquid —Mark Helprin

Voice ... like melting honey —Jimmy Sangster

Voice like thick soup —Edith Wharton

Voices as soft and murmurous as wings —George Garrett

Voice soft and cool as a prison yard —Joseph Wambaugh

Voice soft and rich as that of a counseling angel —Henry James, letter to Thomas Sergeant Perry, November 1, 1863

Voice soft as maple syrup running into a glass container —F. Scott Fitzgerald

Voice ... soothing as running water —Dorothy Parker

When we spoke, it was softly, like TV cowboys expecting an ambush —Deborah Eisenberg

♣ VOICE, WEAK

Forced little voice, wavering like a puff of smoke —Ivan Turgenev

Her voice came soft and faint, as though another person had said the words first and she was merely passing them on —Harvey Swados

Her voice was small, as if she had to squeeze it up from the depths —Laura Furman

Little voice, that wavered like a thread of smoke —Ivan Turgenev

Voice as faint as the buzzing of a bee's wings —Kenzaburo Oe

Voice ... faded, thin away. Like a river diminishing to a stream and then to a trickle —Maya Angelou

Voice no bigger than a starling's —R. Wright Campbell

Voice ... thin as a sheet of Zig Zag —Arnold Sawislak

His voice [Tennessee Williams,] wavers unsteadily like old gray cigar smoke in a room with no ventilation, rising to a mad cackle like a wounded macaw, settling finally in a cross somewhere between Tallulah Bankhead and Everett Dirksen —Rex Reed

♣ VOTERS
See: POLITICS

♣ VULGARITY
See: TASTE

♣ VULNERABILITY
See: SENSITIVENESS

♣ WALKING

See Also: AWKWARDNESS, CAUTION, MOVEMENT(S), RUNNING

As fond of long walks as hairdressers are of fishing —Colette

As she walked she lifted her knees high, her feet far out in front of her, like a drum majorette on parade —Nancy Huddleston Packer

A curiously modest gait, like a preoccupied steer —Cynthia Ozick

A heavy man who walked as though he was still a lean one —Pat Conroy

His feet strike at the trembling earth like a bailiff pounding a door with an iron bar —Angela Carter

His stride was a sort of ambulatory Rorschach test. One could project anything one fancied into it —James Morrow

His stride was light and long, like that of a man on the moon —Mark Helprin

Light rapid steps ... like the hops of a bird —Paul Horgan

The men walked like scissors; the women trod like cats —Katherine Mansfield

My steps became extravagantly buoyant, like those of a high wire artist walking on a hidden trampoline —Robert Traver

Paced [from room to room] ... like a marathon runner cooling down —Gerald A. Browne

Paced the room like proctors at a college board examination —Scott Spencer

Picked his way as if he were walking on an iceberg —Peggy Bennett

A shambling gait like a trained bear —William Faulkner

Stalked over ... like a traffic cop —James Thurber

Step as light as summer air —John Greenleaf Whittier

Variation in common usage: "Trod as lightly as if he were walking on air."

Stiffly, like a man walking the trunk of a tree that bridges a chasm, he began to walk —Anon

Strut like a crow in a gutter —John Ray's *Proverbs*

Strut like a fighting cock —George Garrett

Struts like a bandit —Diane Ackerman

Strutting ... like an Olympic shot putter —T. Coraghessan Boyle

(I still have) a trotting bounce to my walk, like a middle-aged coyote who lopes along avoiding the cougars and hedgehogs, though still feeling quite capable of snapping up rabbits and fawns —Edward Hoagland

Unsteady but purposeful walk, as if she were on a wheel that misguided her —Eudora Welty

Up and down he went, like a sailor with a limp —Wright Morris

Walked as a man might show off a garden, stopping here and there to pluck a flower —Lawrence Durrell

Walked as if a puppet master dangled her from a set of strings —Jay Parini

Walked as if he were completely alone, like an abdicated king —Beryl Markham

Walked high on his feet, like his shoes were hurting him —Donald McCaig

Walked like a man with a pain in his gut —William H. Hallhan

Walked like two snakes —Maeve Brennan

Walked neither fast nor slow, like a man going to work at a job he didn't enjoy —Harold Adams

Walked sedately, as though he were being watched —Helen Hudson

Walked very quickly, moving his arms as he walked like a tall thin bird flapping its wings —Jean Rhys

Walk … like an invalid just liberated from the sedentary months of his sickbed —Frederick Exley

Walking sedately back and forth, like a plump abbot who has just found exquisite confirmation of his long-cherished view of Paradise —Robert Traver

Walks like a stately yacht listing disconcertingly to starboard —Frank Rich, about Robert Mitchum in television mini-series, *New York Times*, 1986

Walk slowly, like one accustomed to be alone —Karl Shapiro

Walk together, like prisoners out for exercise —W. D. Snodgrass

Wandering around like a tit in a trance —Carolyn Slaughter

When he walks, he moves like an engine —William Shakespeare, *Coriolanus*

With those long strides he looks like an antelope when he runs —Gary Thorn

❧ WAR

See Also: ARMY

The art of war is like the art of the courtesan; indeed, they might be called sisters, since both are the slaves of desperation —Pietro Aretino

The beginning of war is like the first days of peace: neither the world nor our hearts know they are there —Jane Wagner

Being a soldier [in war time] was like being on a team in a sport that drew no crowds, except for the players' own parents and friends —Dan Wakefield

Great warriors, like great earthquakes, are principally remembered for the mischief they have done —Christian Nestell Bovee

Marrying in wartime is like sowing among thorns —Ignazio Silone

Success in war, like charity in religion, covers a multitude of sins —Lord Napier

War is like an aging actress; more and more dangerous, and less and less photogenic —Robert Capa

War will disappear, like the dinosaur, when changes in world conditions have destroyed its survival value —Robert A. Millikan

Went to war with an air, as if they went to a ball —Stephen Vincent Benét

❧ WARMTH

See: COMFORT, HEAT

❧ WASTE

In delay we waste our lights in vain, like lamps by day —William Shakespeare, *Romeo and Juliet*

Wasted his wealth like spittle —Stephen Vincent Benét

Wasted more money in a day than a Boeing 747 full of proverbial welfare queens could have squandered in a century —Hodding Carter III, *Wall Street Journal*, March 30, 1986

Carter's simile referred to new defense spending policies.

Wasteful as drunkenness at undue times —Robert Browning

Wasteful as regrets —Anon

❧ WATCHFULNESS

See Also: ATTENTION, PROTECTIVENESS, SCRUTINY

Followed [by keeping eyes fixed on other person] ... like someone studying a historical figure —Lawrence Durrell

Had a way of looking around ... as if hidden cameras were photographing her —Ann Beattie

He watched her as a cat does a mouse —James Howell

Of all the comparisons linked to watchfulness, this is probably the most famous and enduring, dating back to 1624. In Robert Louis Stevenson's Kidnapped, *it appears as "We sat at table like a cat and a mouse, each stealthily observing the other."*

Hovering, like an old bird over one egg —Eudora Welty

(Each evening I) peered surreptitiously through the kitchen curtains, like a spinster keeping tab on her neighbors —W. P. Kinsella

The police hover like hawks —Gian Carlo Menotti, *The Consul*

Vigilant as cat to steal cream —William Shakespeare, *Henry V, Part I*

Watched as if from a cat's distance —Martin Cruz Smith

Watched him like musicians watching the conductor —Wilfrid Sheed

Watched ... like a warden —Anon

The warden comparison to describe watchfulness has gained considerable currency in the last decade or so. Two recent novels in which it was used are Disturbances In the Field *by Lynne Sharon Schwartz, "kept watch like a warden" and* Riders *by Jilly Cooper, "watching him like a warden."*

Watched, like Indians at a corral —Etheridge Knight

Watched me like a fish hawk —James Crumley

Watched ... tensely, like a spider lying in wait for the fly's last drop of blood —Heinrich Böll

(My mother) watches me for signs of bloom and decay, like a plant —Daphne Merkin

Watchful as a ferret —R. Wright Campbell

Watching me like a bloodhound after a convict —Shelby Hearon

Watching [someone's looks and moves] ... with an attention as intense as if an ordeal involving my life depended on them —Joseph Sheridan Le Fanu

Watch (tensely) like a cat stationed near a bird feeder —Bobbie Ann Mason

Watch ... like a dead white moon —Ross Macdonald

Watch ... like a nursemaid —Nicholas Monsarrat

Watch like one who fears robbing —William Shakespeare, *Two Gentlemen of Verona*

Watch like ravens on a tree branch —R. Wright Campbell

❧ WATER

See: OCEAN/OCEANFRONT; PONDS, RIVERS, AND STREAMS; SEASCAPES

❧ WEAKNESS

Arms felt like spaghetti —Dan Wakefield

As much strength as a seaweed —Ann Beattie

(A poor weak rag of a man with a) backbone like a piece of string —Dorothy Canfield

Boneless as poured water —George Garrett

Diminished and flat, as after radical surgery —Sylvia Plath

(The great white sails of the ships were) drooping like weary wings —Mazo de la Roche

Feeble as a babe —Ted Hughes

Feel as if I'm strung together by threads that pop and snap —Rosellen Brown

Feel diluted, like watered-down stew —Susan Minot

Felt a faintness stunning her senses as though some one had cut open the arteries of her wrists and all the blood rushed out of her body —Anzia Yezierska

Felt as if my legs had turned to warm lead —Stephen King

Forceful as a wet noodle —Anon

Forceless as a child —Aeschylus

The program has been like an elderly turtle on its back: It twitches feebly every now and then, but get nowhere —Jack D. Kirwan, *Wall Street Journal,* March 19, 1987

The turtle comparison referred to the tragedy-weakened Challenger space program.

Knees like liquid —Elizabeth Spencer

(The man sprawls … spent, empty) limp as a drowned man tossed on the sand —George Garrett

(He was) limp as laundry —W. P. Kinsella

(I must have been worked up even more than I'd thought those past weeks, for now it was all over I was) limp as a rag —Wilbur Daniel Steele

Looking like an advertisement for jelly —Mike Fredman

My legs felt as if … made of two lengths of rope —George Garrett

No more backbone than a chocolate éclair —Theodore Roosevelt

Roosevelt coined this simile about President McKinley when he was Secretary of the Navy.

She was like an overstretched bow, almost breaking —Stephen French Whitman

Softened and weakened, like a wax doll left too near the flame —George Garrett

Strength running out of him like sawdust —Vicki Baum

Was washed out like a disemboweled sack —Aharon Megged

Weak as a broken arm —Raymond Chandler

Weak as air —Ann Bradstreet

By contrast, you could say "Strong as air," especially if you've ever seen a ship in dry dock.

Weak as an nonagenarian —T. Coraghessan Boyle

(He's as) weak as a stick —Mary Lee Settle

In Settle's novel Celebration *the simile refers to emotional weakness.*

Weak as water —The Holy Bible/Ezekiel

Weak … like a cream puff with the cream squeezed out —Tom Robbins

Weak, like a moth newly broken out from its chrysalis —E. F. Benson

❧ WEALTH

See: RICHES

❧ WEARINESS

Adrenaline … seeps out of us like sawdust seeping from a stuffed toy —W. P. Kinsella

Alone in the house he felt the full weight of exhaustion settle on him like iron shackles —Helen Simonson, *Major Pettigrew's Last Stand*

An atmosphere of luxurious exhaustion, like a ripened, shedding rose —Truman Capote

Eyelids feel as if they are being held open by taxidermy needles —Jay McInerney

Fatiguing as the eternal hanging on of an uncompleted task —William James

Feel … as is if my machine has temporarily run down —Janet Flanner

Feel like a sneaker that's been through a ringer —Nicholas S. Daniloff, television interview, September 14, 1986

Daniloff's simile expressed his feelings after two weeks of Russian captivity.

Felt like an old soldier exhausted by a long retreat from battle —Kenzaburo Oe

Felt like Sisyphus taking a five-minute break, like Muhammad Ali at the end of the fourteenth round in Manila —T. Coraghessan Boyle

Felt perpetually tired, as though she were bleeding —Francis King

Felt tired as though she had spent the day on a hot beach —Mary Hedin

A flurry of fatigue swept over us like a tropical rainstorm, dropping us like sodden flies —James Crumley

Growing drowsier ... as if he had been counting a flock of pedigree Southdowns —Sylvia Townsend Warner

Had the look of an overworked nag —Sholem Aleichem

His state [from working all day] was like a flabby orange whose crushed skin is thin with pulling, and all dented in —Amy Lowell

I could lie down like a tired child, and weep away the life of care —Percy Bysshe Shelley

Looked haggard ... like a child after too much carnival —John D. MacDonald

(My time is past,) my blood is dry as my bones —Grace Paley

My fingers and back feel like I'm Quasimodo —Ray Schmidt

Schmidt's weariness was caused by a long session of entering data into his computer.

Squeezed out like an old paint-tube —Lawrence Durrell

Tired as an old coal miner —Reynolds Price

Tired as a preacher in a border town —Thomas Zigal

Tired-eyed as a diplomat —Frank Swinnerton

A wave of sleepiness knocked me over like an ocean breaker —Gloria Norris

Weariness ... like a crushing weight —Kaatje Hurlbut

(Shrugs) weary and eloquent as an ox under a yoke —George Garrett

Weary and exhausted as though I had travelled along an unending road —Stefan Zweig

Wearying as a holiday to a workaholic —Elyse Sommer

Wore me out like a fever —Sholom Aleichem

❧ WEATHER

See Also: CLOUD(S), COLDNESS, ENTRANCES AND EXITS, FOG, HEAT, MIST, RAIN, SUN, THUNDER AND LIGHTNING, WIND

The chilly drizzly June day smelled like a basement —Marge Piercy

The elements are but as qualities that change forever, like all things that have known generation —Dame Edith Sitwell

Frost made the sunny air seem like a bright keen knife —Howard Spring

Humidity ... dropped down over the city like a damp serge cloak —Carlos Baker

The humidity ... slapped me in the face like a mugger's glove —Loren D. Estleman

Rain and thaw took its [snow's] place, and now the world looks about as pleasing as a wet cat —John Wainwright

The storm crashes like god-wars —Hayden Carruth

The [hot] weather clings, like a low fever you cannot shake off —Angela Carter

Weather ... cool and gray as wash water —George Garrett

Weather in towns is like a skylark in a countinghouse—out of place and in the way —Jerome K. Jerome

The weather was like a waiter with a tray —Wallace Stevens

The whine of wind and rattle of rain and the thunder rolling terribly loud and near overhead like a thousand beer trucks roaring over the bridge —John Dos Passos

❧ WEDDINGS

See: MARRIAGE

❧ WEIGHT

See: HEAVINESS, LIGHTNESS

❧ WELCOMENESS

See: DESIRABILITY

❧ WELL-BEING

See: HEALTH

❧ WHISPERS

See: GROANS AND WHISPERS

❧ WHITE

See Also: COLORS, COMPLEXION, PALLOR

(Face) more white than sin —Dame Edith Sitwell

Pure white as china door knobs —Reynolds Price

White and bare as a winter moon —George Garrett

White and clean as driftwood —George Garrett

(A yacht) white and pretty as a birthday cake —George Garrett

White and wan, like the head and skin of a dying man —Percy Bysshe Shelley

(The desert is) white as a blind man's eye —Sylvia Plath

(He's as) white as a chicken —Honoré de Balzac

(Face) white as a bandage —Helen Hudson

White as a dog's bone —Anne Sexton

White as a foam-flower —Henry Van Dyke

(Ball) white as a leghorn egg —W. P. Kinsella

White as a lily —Anon

(In marble halls as) white as milk —Anon Old English riddle

> *Some variations to intensify the image: "white as new milk" by Dorothy Canfield Fisher and "snow white as white milk from a white cow" by Eleanor Wylie.*

White as a milk tooth —Charles Simic

(Body) white as an aspirin —Richard Ford

White as any bough that blooms in May —Geoffrey Chaucer

White as a peeled stick —Helen Hudson

(Moon) white as a sand dollar —Diane Ackerman

White as blanched almonds —Charles Cotton

(Teeth) white as detergent —Margaret Atwood

White as ermine —Dame Edith Sitwell

(Her neck and temples were) white as flour —T. Coraghessan Boyle

White as frost —G. K. Chesterton

> *An extension of this his opening line to Chesterton's poem "The Mirror of Madmen" is "white as hoarfrost."*

White as ivory —Oscar Wilde

> *An extension by a contemporary short story writer, Barry Targan: "white as polished ivory."*

White as lightning —Cynthia Ozick

> *The comparison is being used to describe the look of a woman in a nurse's uniform.*

(The air blew white in my face) white as my daughter's communion dress, white as a bridal veil —Elizabeth Spencer

(The little space between earth and sky was filled by a broken veil of drifting flakes as) white as pear blossoms —Phyllis Bottome

(Teeth) white as peeled almonds —Gerald Kersh

(Veins) white as porkfat —Sylvia Plath

White as pulverized bone —T. Coraghessan Boyle

White as rice —Reynolds Price

White as sheets and blizzards —T. Coraghessan Boyle

White as snow —The Holy Bible/Numbers

> *Similes comparing the whiteness of complexions, hair, and miscellaneous objects to snow can be found throughout literature as well as in our everyday language. Some well-known variations include: "white as new-fallen snow" by William Wordsworth, "white as dead snow" by Algernon Charles Swinburne, and "white as the snow on high hills" by Elizabeth Barrett Browning.*

(Teeth) white as sun-cured bone —Beryl Markham

(Hand) white as talcum —Mavis Gallant

(Teeth) white as the petals of a daisy —Dan Jacobson

White as the sun —Henry Chettle

White as the surf —Oscar Wilde

(Face is) white as the wall —Daphne du Maurier

(Chest ...) white as wax —Patricia Henley

(Hair) white as whipped cream —W. P. Kinsella

(Face) white like a whitewashed fence —William Faulkner

White like May-blossom —Charlotte Brontë

White like salt —Aharon Megged

White like sea foam —Joan Chase

❧ WICKEDNESS

See: EVIL

❧ WILDNESS

See: FEROCITY

❧ WIND

See Also: WEATHER

Breeze [after a very hot day] ... as torrid as the air from an oven —Ellen Glasgow

The breeze flowed down on me, passing like a light hand —Louise Erdrich

The breeze ... sent little waves curling like lazy whips along the shingle [of a house] —John Fowles

A breeze which came like a breath —Paul Horgan

A draft ... struck through his drenched clothes like ice cold needles —Cornell Woolrich

A gathering wind sent the willows tossing like a jungle of buggy whips —William Styron

High wind ... like invisible icicles —Rebecca West

Level winds as flat as ribbons —M. J. Farrell

The night wind rushed like a thief along the streets —Brian Moore

A northeaster roared down on us like a herd of drunken whales —T. Coraghessan Boyle

A northeast wind which cut like a thousand razors —Frank Swinnerton

[Wind] rustling the ... child's hair like grass —Marguerite Duras

A sandy wind blowing rough as an elephant —Truman Capote

Slight breeze came and started to stir the trees, just a little, like a whisper. It was peaceful as a lullaby —Edward Rutherfurd, *New York*

The sound of wind is like a flame —Yvor Winters

The sunless evening wind slid down the mountain like an invisible river —Dorothy Canfield

The night wind rushed like a thief along the streets —Brian Moore

There came a wind like a bugle —Emily Dickinson

This is both title and first line of a poem.

The warm spring wind fluttered against his face like an old kiss —Michael Malone

Wind ... beat like a fist against his face —Vicki Baum

The wind blew gusts of rain into his face that were much like a shower-bath —Honoré de Balzac

The wind blew him like a sail up against a lifeboat —F. Scott Fitzgerald

Wind ... blowing down from a flat black sky like painted cardboard —Marge Piercy

Wind ... driving the dry snow along with it like a mist of powdered diamonds —Henry Van Dyke

The wind drove against him like a granite cliff —Edith Wharton

Wind ... dry and faint, like the breath of some old woman —Joe Coomer

Wind ... dry and fresh as ice —Frank Ross

The wind filled his shirt like a white sail —Yitzhak Shenhar

The wind flicked about a little like the tail of a horse that's trying to decide what sort of mood it's in tonight —Douglas Adams

The wind howls like a chained beast in pain —Delmore Schwartz

The wind howls like air inside a shell —Tracy Daugherty

The wind is like a dog that runs away —Wallace Stevens

The wind is like a hand on my forehead, in caress —John Hall Wheelock

Wind like a hungry coyote's cry —Patricia Henley

Wind like a perfumed woman in heat —Clive Irving

The wind like a razor —Miles Gibson

The wind like a saw-edged knife —Paul J. Wellman

The wind [in autumn] moves like a cripple among the leaves —Wallace Stevens

The wind plunged like a hawk from the swollen clouds —Ellen Glasgow

(The gray winter) wind prowling like a hungry wolf just beyond the windows —George Garrett

The wind ran in the street like a thin dog —Katherine Mansfield

Wind ringing in their ears like well-known old songs —Hans Christian Andersen

The wind rose out of the depth below them, sounding as if it were pushing boulders uphill —Martin Cruz Smith

The wind screamed like a huge, injured thing —Scott Spencer

Wind … surges into your ear like breath coming and going —Philip Levine

The wind swept the snow aside, ever faster and thicker, as if it were trying to catch up with something —Boris Pasternak

The wind whistled … like a pack of coyotes —Paige Mitchell

A wind will … knock like a rifle-butt against the door —Wallace Stevens

The full line preceding the rifle-butt comparison in Stevens' poem "The Auroras of Autumn" reads as follows: "a wind will spread its windy grandeurs round and…."

♣ WINNING

See: SPORTS, SUCCESS/FAILURE

♣ WINTER

See: SEASONS

♣ WISDOM

See Also: EDUCATION, KNOWLEDGE

Chewing over their combined worldly wisdom like so many puppies with a shoe —Mary Ladd Cavell

The wisdom in Cavell's story "The Rotifer" is being shared by three girls sharing an apartment.

The heart of the wise, like a mirror, should reflect all objects, without being sullied —Confucius

The heart of the wise man lies quiet like limpid water —Cameroonian proverb

If a man is as wise as a serpent, he can afford to be as harmless as a dove —Josh Billings

This is an elaboration of Algernon Charles Swinburne's "harmless as a dove" which dates back to the Bible. In Billings' phonetic dialect this read: "'iz az wize az a serpent."

Insight as keen as frosty star —William Wordsworth

A learned man is a tank; a wise man is a spring —William R. Alger

String of wise jests … like gold links —Penelope Gilliatt

To learn a person's life … like learning a language, you must start with the little things, the little pictures —Susan Fromberg Schaeffer

Wisdom and virtue are like two wheels of a cart —Japanese proverb

Wisdom in a poor man is like a diamond set in lead —H. G. Bohn's *Hand-Book of Proverbs*

Wisdom is like fire: a little enlightens, much burns —Moses Ibn Ezra

Wisdom is like gold ore, mixed with stones and dust —Moses Ibn Ezra

Wisdom, like life itself, appeared to me to be comprised of continuing progress, of starting over again, of patience —Marguerite Yourcenar

Wisdom like perfume rises out of its own essence —Norman Mailer

Wisdom shook itself like a drop off a dog —Cynthia Ozick

Wise as a wisp —George Garrett

Wise as heaven —Algernon Charles Swinburne

❧ WISH

See: DESIRE

❧ WIT

See Also: CLEVERNESS, HUMOR, WISDOM

As much wit as three folks, two fools and a madman —Thomas Fuller

One wit, like a knuckle of ham in soup, gives a zest and flavor to the dish, but more than one serves only to spoil the pottage —Tobias Smollett

Sharp wits, like sharp knives, do often cut their owner's fingers —Aaron Arrowsmith

Wit and wisdom are like the seven stars, seldom seen together —Thomas Fuller

Wit is as infinite as love —Agnes Repelier

Repelier expanded upon the simile as follows: "and a deal more lasting in its qualities."

Wit ... like a quick-flashing blade —Henry James

Wit ... like champagne, not only sparkles, but is sweet —Benjamin Disraeli

Wit, like money, bears an extra value when rung down as soon as it's wanted —Douglas Jerrold

Wit must grow like fingers —John Selden

Wit ... penetrates through the coldness and awkwardness of society, gradually bringing men nearer together, and, like the combined force of wine and oil, giving every man a glad heart and a shining countenance —Sydney Smith

Wit without learning is like a tree which bears no fruit —Aristippus

Wit, without wisdom, is like a song without sense; it does not please long —Josh Billings

❧ WIVES

See: MARRIAGE

❧ WOMEN

HEART(S), MEN AND WOMEN

❧ WORD(S)

See Also: SPEAKING; WORDS, DEFINED; WORDS, EFFECT OF; WORDS OF PRAISE; WRITERS/WRITING

Applying words like bandages —William McIlvanney

[The best sentences] orient us, like stars in the sky, like landmarks on a trail —Jhumpa Lahiri, "My Life's Sentences," *New York Times*, March 17, 2012

Words should be scattered like seed; no matter how small the seed may be, if it has once found favorable ground, it unfolds its strength —Seneca

Words, like Nature, half reveal and half conceal the Soul within —Alfred, Lord Tennyson

Her words still hung in the air between us like a wisp of tobacco smoke —Evelyn Waugh

It is with words as with sunbeams, the more they are condensed, the deeper they burn —Robert Southey

Words are flowing out like / Endless rain into a paper cup —Paul McCartney, "Across the Universe"

Words, like men, grow an individuality; their character changes with years and with use —Anon

Words, like fine flowers, have their color too —Ernest Rhys

Words, like clothes, get old-fashioned, or mean and ridiculous, when they have been for some time laid aside —William Hazlitt

Words, like fashions, disappear and recur throughout English history —Virginia Graham

The word seemed to linger in the air, to throb in the air like the note of a violin —Katherine Mansfield

Her words at first seemed fitful like the talking of the trees —Dante Gabriel Rossetti

(She spoke to them slowly) dropping the words like ping pong balls —Helen Hudson

Every word hanging like the sack of cement on a murdered body at the bottom of the river —Diane Wakoski

Her words fell like rain on a waterproof umbrella; they made a noise, but they could not reach the head which they seemed destined to deluge —Frances Trolloppe

His words were smoother than oil (and yet be they swords) —*The Book of Common Prayer*

It is as easy to draw back a stone thrown from the hand, as to recall a word once spoken —Menander

Like blood from a cut vein, words flowed —James Morrow

My words slipped from me like broken weapons —Edith Wharton

An old sentence ... ran through her mind like a frightened mouse in a maze —Babs H. Deal

The rest [words meant to remain unspoken] rolled out like string from a hidden ball of twine —Lynne Sharon Schwartz

The sentence rang over and over again in his mind like a dirge —Margaret Millar

Stiff as frozen rope words poke out —Marge Piercy

They [a group at a party] flung them [words] like weapons, handled them like jewels, tossed them on air with reckless abandon as though they scattered confetti —Mary Hedin

The word hissed like steam escaping from an overloaded pressure system —Ross Macdonald

A word once spoken, like an arrow shot, can never be retracted —Anon
This simile was first used by Talmudic rabbis.

Words as meaningless and wonderful as wind chimes —Sharon Sheehe Stark

The words came out like bullets —H. E. Bates

Words came out ... tumbling like a litter of puppies from a kennel —F. van Wyck Mason

The words crumbled in his mouth like ashes —William Diehl

Words ... danced in my mind like wild ponies that moved only to my command —Hortense Calisher

Words falling softly as rose petals —Mary Hedin

Words, frothy and toneless like a chain of bursting bubbles —L. P. Hartley

Words gushing and tumbling as if a hose had been turned on —Rose Tremain

Words gush like toothpaste —Margaret Atwood

The words [just spoken] hung like smoke in the air —Doris Grumbach

Words ... like bits of cold wind —Mary Hedin

(She dealt her) words like blades —Emily Dickinson

Words like butterflies stagger from his lips —John Updike

Words, like glass, obscure when they do not aid vision —Joseph Joubet

Words ... limp and clear like a jellyfish ... hard and mean and secretive like a horned snail ... austere and comical as top hats, or smooth and lively and flattering as ribbons —Alice Munro

The narrator of Munro's story, Spelling, *is contemplating the meaning of words when while visiting an old woman.*

The word spiraled through the silence like a worm in wood —Harris Downey

The words (out) of his mouth were smoother than butter, but war was in his heart; his words were softer than oil, yet they were drawn swords —The Holy Bible/Psalms

Words ... plunked down with a click like chessmen —Yehuda Amichai

Words ... poured wetly from her red lips as from a pitcher —Lynne Sharon Schwartz

The words rang in the silence like the sound of a great cash register —Kingsley Amis

Words ran together too quickly, like rapid water —Joanna Wojewski Higgins

Words roll around in Benna's mouth [novel, *Anagrams,* by Lorrie Moore] like Life Savers on a tongue —Carol Hills, *New York Times Book Review,* November 2, 1986

Words that string and creep like insects —Conrad Aiken

Words ... tumbling out and tripping over each other like mice —Susan Fromberg Schaeffer

The words went by like flights of moths under the star-soaked sky —Adrienne Rich

Words ... white and anonymous as a snowball —Donald McCaig

(If he once ... let loose ... the) words would come like a great flood, like vomiting —George Garrett

Your words to the end, hard as a pair of new cowboy boots —A. D. Winans

❧ WORDS DEFINED

The English language is like an enormous bank account —Robert Claiborne

The great man's word is like the elephant's tusk [not to be concealed or withdrawn] —Hindu saying

Long words, like long beards, are often the badge of charlatans —F. L. Lucas

Pithy sentences are like sharp nails which force the truth upon our memories —Denis Diderot

Technical terms ... are like red, white and blue poker chips. They stand for whatever the players agree upon —John B. Kerfoot

A word fitly spoken is like apples of gold in setting of silver —The Holy Bible/Proverbs

A word is not a crystal transparent and unchanged; it is the skin of a living thought and may vary greatly in color and content according to the circumstances and the time in which it is used —Oliver Wendell Holmes

Words are like bodies, and meanings like souls —Abraham Ibn Ezra

Words are like labels, or coins, or better, like swarming bees —Anne Sexton

Words are like leaves, some wither every year —Horace

Alexander Pope's variation of this reads as follows: "and where they most abound, much fruit of sense beneath is rarely found."

Words are like money, not the worse for being common, but ... it is the stamp of custom alone that gives them circulation or value —William Hazlitt

Words are like money; there is nothing so useless, unless when in actual use —Samuel Butler

Words are, like money, a medium of exchange, and the sureness with which they can be used varies not only with the character of the coins themselves, but also with the character of the things they buy, and that of the men who tender and receive them —Allen Upward

Words are like money; and when the current value of them is generally understood, no man is cheated by them —Sir Richard Steele

Words ... a syllable which sounds like a bumble-bee breaking wind —Hortense Calisher

Words, like cavalry horses answering the bugle, group themselves automatically into familiar dreary patterns —George Orwell

Orwell's simile was used to urge against re-using any phrase once it appears in print. Anyone following his advice would use this book strictly as a guide to phrase elimination.

The words of a man's mouth are as deep waters, and the wellsprings of wisdom as a flowing brook —The Holy Bible/Proverbs

A word without thought is like a foot without sinew —Moses Ibn Ezra

❧ WORDS, EFFECT OF

Epithets, like pepper, give zest to what you write —Lewis Carroll

Carroll expanded on this simile as follows: "And if you strew them sparely, they whet the appetite: But if you lay them on too thick, you spoil the matter quite!"

Everything you say is just like scraping a wound with a knife —Iris Murdoch

Hearing a word break like a wave on the shells of my ears —John Hersey

Her words pelted me like hail —Edith Wharton

Her words showered down upon us like little glass pellets —Saul Bellow

His words dropped in Spandarian's ear like pellets of ice —Derek Lambert

Like heavy hostile fists the words pounded on Andrew's incredulous ears —F. van Wyck Mason

Listening to The Weasel [an unpleasant person] was like having a dirty hand paw through your personal belongings, leaving them in confusion; and so soiled that after the first look you were disgusted and tempted to throw them away, for they had changed —Ann Petry

The sentences ... like toy life-buoys made of paper —they carried no weight or conviction —James Stern

That terrible word caused Flora's heart to slide like frozen snow —Frank Swinnerton

The word went through Morgan's heart like a poisoned spear —Noel Coward

The word pierced her side like a sharp horn —Z. Vance Wilson

The words beat on Gerty's brain like the sound of a language which had seemed familiar at a distance but on approaching is found to be unintelligible —Edith Wharton

Words cutting like diamonds —Frank Swinnerton

Words dig at her like fingers in clay —T. Coraghessan Boyle

The words drive home like separate blows from a mallet —T. Coraghessan Boyle

The words felt like a medicine ball to the stomach —T. Glen Coughlin

Words, like daggers, enter in my ears —William Shakespeare

In Hamlet the words enter into "mine" not "my" ears. Another Shakespearean dagger image from Titus Andronicus: "These words are razors to my wounded heart."

Words ... rattle and roll like dice —George Garrett

The words shook her like a tempest —Edith Wharton

The words slid over her like water poured on stones —Ellen Gilchrist

Words that sting and creep like insects —Karl Shapiro

Words were like nails. Like little knives. —George Garrett

The words trickled through his mind like a warm and friendly brook, or a leak in a boat which filled it only slowly —MacDonald Harris

The word went home. It hit on his heart like a tennis ball in fast play —Vicki Baum

❧ WORDS OF PRAISE

For you words are like birds. They sing. They fly —Helen Hudson

The character who thus praises a friend's gift with words describes himself as someone for whom "words are worms."

(My wife … always) looks like a barrel full of stardust —Moss Hart

My doll is as dainty as a sparrow —Oscar Hammerstein II, lyrics from "Honey Bun" from musical *South Pacific*

The lyric heaps simile upon simile with "where she's narrow, she's as narrow as an arrow."

My sister, my spouse, is a secret spring —John Hall Wheelock

This is the first line and leitmotif of a poem entitled "An Old Song."

She seemed like a yellow sunrise on mountain tops —O. Henry

She shines against the backdrop of this provincial place like a jewel on a beggar's coat. She is like the moon forgotten by the pale sky of the day. She is like a butterfly over a plain of snow —Milan Kundera

When I walk with you I feel as if I had a flower in my buttonhole —William Makepeace Thackeray

When she passed it seemed like the ceasing of exquisite music —Henry Wordsworth Longfellow

When you came, you were like red wine and honey … now you are like morning bread, smooth and pleasant —Amy Lowell

When you get up, it's like the flag being raised. I want to pledge allegiance —John Updike

You're a girl like candy —Clifford Odets

You're beautiful, like a May fly —Ernest Hemingway to Mary Welsh before she became Mrs. Hemingway

You're perfect as a textbook example —Sharon Olds

Poet Olds uses the simile in a poem dedicated to her father and aptly entitled "The Ideal Father."

Your lips taste like paradise —Isaac Bashevis Singer

❧ WORK

See Also: ATTENTION, BOREDOM, DOCTORS, LAWYERS, PROFESSIONS

All the romance had been scuffed off it [playing professional baseball against small-town teams]like the gloss on a brand-new baseball after nine innings of hard use —Howard Frank Mosher

All work is as seed sown; it grows and spreads, and sows itself anew —Thomas Carlyle

The back-breaking sixteen-hour day, like a heavy hand slapping —Bernard Malamud

Being a President is like riding a tiger. A man has to keep on riding or be swallowed —Harry S. Truman

(Reagan's nostalgic wit was contributing to the feeling that he) dropped in and out of his job, like a cameo star on the love boat —Gerald Gardner

(My mom) getting paid for giving advice is like the Cookie Monster getting paid for eating cookies —Glenn Sapadin, upon hearing that his mother, Linda Sapadin, was finalist in contest to select replacement for advice columnist Ann Landers, *New York Times*/About New York, April 11, 1987

This job [being a prize fighter] needs gorgeous concentration … it's like being a priest —our work comes first —Clifford Odets

The job [dean at a university] is like being pecked to death by ducks —Dr. John Roche, lecture at Ohio State University, 1962.

Jobs are like lobster pots, harder to get out of them than into —Hugh Leonard

Labor like Hercules —William H. Gass

The only time some people work like a horse is when the boss rides them —Gabriel Heatter

Toiled like movers trying to get a refrigerator into a fifth-floor walk-up —Russell Baker

Toiling like a bee in a hive —Noel Coward, lyrics for "World Weary"

(Fifty-two Sundays a year … for three hours my mother was) unemployed in her own house. Like a queen —Philip Roth

Roth's comparison of a mother to an unemployed queen comes from his novel The Ghost Writer.

Unemployed people (actors between plays) like ghosts looking for bodies to inhabit —Gail Godwin

Work drives you like a motor —Janet Flanner

Working for Daniel is like living the last thirty minutes of *Goodfellas,* over and over again —Leslye Headland, *Assistance*

Working the rivet line [at an auto factory] is like being paid to flunk high school the rest of your life —Ben Hamper in article on changes at GM, *Mother Jones,* September 1986

Work is as much a necessity to man as eating and sleeping —Karl Wilhelm Humboldt

Work like a beaver —American colloquialism

This expression was popularized by the fur trappers who roamed the Rockies during the nineteenth century. Like many such terms it has gained much wider currency and seeded offshoots like "eager as a beaver" and "busy as a beaver."

Work like a Trojan —Anon

A popular simile dating to the Middle Ages and the depiction in the Greek classics of the Trojans as hard workers.

The work was getting to be like licking stamps eight hours a day —Loren D. Estleman

❧ WORLD

See Also: LIFE

Our world is only a practical joke of God, like a bad day —Franz Kafka

This world is like Noah's Ark in which few men but many beasts embark —Samuel Butler

Today, the world is like a cocktail party at which everybody is suffering from indigestion or some other internal ailment. People are interacting with each other, but they're mostly focused on the godawful stuff going on inside. —David Brooks, "Where Obama Shines," *New York Times,* July 20, 2012

The universe is like a safe to which there is a combination, but the combination is locked up in the safe —Peter De Vries

The world is like a beautiful book, but of little use to anyone who cannot read it —Carolo Goldon

The original simile used the word "him" instead of "anyone."

The world is like a board with holes in it, and the square men have got into the round holes, and the round into the square —Bishop George Berkeley

The world is like a cucumber, today it's in your hand, tomorrow up your arse —Arabic proverb

The world is like a drunken peasant. If you lift him into the saddle on one side, he will fall off on the other. One can't help him, no matter how one tries. —Martin Luther

The world is like a fair: people gather for a while, then part; some profit and rejoice, others lose and grieve —Bahya

The world is like a fountain-wheel: the buckets ascend full and descend empty. Who's rich today may not be so tomorrow —The Holy Bible/Exodus

The biblical passage concludes with: "who's rich today may not be so tomorrow"

The world is like a foyer leading to the world to come. —Rabbi Jacob

In the Mishna, *this continues with "Prepare yourself in the foyer, so that you may enter into the inner chamber." Another version of this reads: "The world is like an antechamber to the next. Prepare yourself here that you may be admitted to the banquet hall there."*

The world is like a great staircase, some go up and others go down —Hipponax

The world is like a house, with the sky as a ceiling, the earth spread out like a carpet, the stars arrayed like lamps, ... and man its master —Bahya

The world is like a ladder: one goes up, another goes down —Immanuel of Rome

The world is like a map of antipathies ... in which everyone picks the symbolic color of his difference —Juan Ramon Jimenez

The world is like an enormous spider web and if you touch it, however lightly, at any point, the vibration ripples to the remotest perimeter —Robert Penn Warren

The world is like an old coquette who conceals her age —Voltaire

The world is like a pump-wheel, through which the full is emptied and the empty filled —Nahman Bratzlav

The world like a cradle rises and falls on a wave of confetti and funerals —Louis MacNeice

The world waits to be made over by each man who inhabits it, and it is made over every morning like a bed —William Saroyan

A world where clichés fit like a gown by Edith Head —Tom Nolan, *New York Times Book Review,* November 9, 1986

The comparison to a Hollywood designer's gowns was most appropriate as the book being reviewed has a Hollywood background.

❧ WORRY

See: AGITATION, ANXIETY

❧ WOUND

See: PAIN

❧ WRINKLES

See Also: COMPLEXION, FOREHEAD, SKIN

All the flesh of him that showed, had creases like miniature gullies in the skin —Paul Horgan

Deep lines that looked like dark parentheses around her lips —Alice McDermott

Face as creased as his trousers —Sumner Locke Elliott

Face as lined as an Indian squaw's —John Fowles

Face creased up like a fine soft handkerchief —Lawrence Durrell

A face crisscrossed with lines like an old paper bag —Marmaret Millar

Face ... delicately wrinkled like a fine thin notepaper —Louise Erdrich

Face like a withered walnut —Edith Wharton

Face lined as soft leather —Sue Grafton

Face, lined like a much-folded map —Mollie Hardwick

Face lined like a river delta —T. Coraghessan Boyle

Face ... marked by a little cross-hatching of fine lines, as though his cheek had lain on corduroy —Harvey Swados

Face marked with gossamer lines like the craze of enamel —Samuel Yellen

Face ... savagely gouged, like the land after the passage of a fast-running rain that makes temporary rivers which plow the ground and leave sunbaked veins of rut afterward —Paul Horgan

Face so wrinkled that it was like a parchment loaded with hieroglyphics —G. K. Chesterton

Faces ... wrinkled by wind and sun like cured meat —George Garrett

Face wrinkled in deep furrows like the fissures in a red clay road after rain —Ellen Glasgow

Face ... wrinkled like the bark of the pine trees —Susan Fromberg Schaeffer

Face ... wrinkling like a bent leather glove —Harvey Swados

Grooves like gashes ran from his nostrils to his mouth-corners —Dashiell Hammett

Had a thousand wrinkles on her face, so that she looked most like an aging Barbie doll —Shelby Hearon

Her face is etched all over with fine lines, as though her skin has been caught under a butterfly net —Daphne Merkin

Her face was wrinkled like a roll-top desk —Arthur Baer

Her skin had a pattern all its own of numberless branching wrinkles and as though a whole little tree stood in the middle of her forehead —Eudora Welty

His neck all in wrinkles resembling cracks, crisscrossing one another, as though his neck were made of cork —Ivan Bunin

His skin wrinkled up like crumpled butcher paper —Jonathan Valin

Jagged lines around his eyes, lines like scars from a broken bottle —Richard Lourie

The lines deep graven in the soft skin about her eyes and mouth were like rivers in a black-and-white map —Frank Swinnerton

Lines etched by age, like frost patterns on a windowpane —Dorothea Straus

The lines on her forehead and neck were as if scored with a knife —John Braine

Pink skin scored with wrinkles like the furrows of a corn field —Carlos Fuentes

Shriveling like an overbaked potato —Ira Wood

Skin ... wrinkled like a wine-skin —W. Somerset Maugham

Skin wrinkled like an old paper bag —Margaret Millar

Skin wrinkles like paint —Derek Walcott

Stretch marks ... looked like streaky bacon held up to the light —David Niven

(On my skin) the wrinkles branch out, overlapping like hair or feathers —Margaret Atwood

Thin long lines like the lines in cracked glass or within a cake of ice —Saul Bellow

A sheaf of fine wrinkles spread [from corners of the eyes] like a fan —L. P. Hartley

Wary lines around the corners of his yes, like sparrow's claws —Derek Lambert

Wrinkled as an iguana —Richard Ford

Wrinkled as a dry plum —Anon
A much-used variation: "wrinkled as a prune."

[A newborn baby] wrinkled as a head of lettuce —Charles Johnson

Wrinkled as a walnut —Dominique Lapierre

A wrinkled, wizened face, like that of an aged monkey —William Styron

Wrinkle like an apple left uneaten too long —Anon
Simile makers are greatly drawn to comparisons between apples and wrinkled skin. Some examples from current literature: "wrinkled as a roasted apple" (Desmond O'Grady); "wrinkled like a stale apple" (Graham Greene); "wrinkled like a winter apple" (Isak Dinesen); "wrinkled like the skin of a winter-kept apple" (Wallace Stegner); "wrinkles crept into it [a woman's face] like worms" (Erich Maria Remarque).

(On my skin) the wrinkles branch out, overlapping like hair or feathers —Margaret Atwood

The wrinkles in her skin shone like a bright net —Eudora Welty

Wrinkles of delight appearing on the leathery skin like cracks in a shattered safety glass —Robert J. Serling

Wrinkles [in a forehead] ... rush together like sentinels —Irving Stone

Wrinkling like a potato —W. D. Snodgrass

❧ WRITERS/WRITING

See Also: POETS/POETRY

The act of writing itself is done in secret, like masturbation —Stephen King

Alliteration is like ivy, some of it is poison —Delmore Schwartz

As a baker bakes more bread than brown; or as a tumbler tumbles up and down; so does our author, rummaging his brain, by various methods try to entertain —Henry Fielding

An author at work is like an oyster, clam-quiet and busy —Rumer Godden

An author introduced to people who have read, or who say they have read his books, always feels like a man taken for the first time to be shown to his future wife's relations —Jerome K. Jerome

An author is like a baker; it is for him to make the sweets, and others to buy and enjoy them —Leigh Hunt

Authors are like cattle going to a fair: those of the same field can never move on without butting one another —Walter Savage Landor

Authors, like coins, grow dear as they grow old; it is the rust we value, not the gold —Alexander Pope

An author who speaks of his own books is almost as bad as a mother who talks about her own children —Benjamin Disraeli,

Being an author is like treading water in the middle of the ocean; you can never stop, you can never stop treading water —Delmore Schwartz

Being a writer in a library is rather like being a eunuch in a harem —John Braine, *New York Times*, October 7, 1961

A biographer is like a contractor who builds roads: it's terribly messy, mud everywhere, and when you get done, people travel over the road at a fast clip —Arthur Wilson

Churn out books as though his days were numbered —Michiko Kakutani, *New York Times*, February 14, 1987

In reviewing Anthony Burgess' autobiography, Little Wilson and Big God, Kakutani uses this simile to introduce her recounting the story of how Burgess began writing when he thought that his days were in fact numbered.

Clear writers, like fountains, do not seem so deep as they are —Walter Savage Landor

The simile is followed by this about the less-than-clear: "the turbid look the most profound."

Every author, however modest, keeps a most outrageous vanity chained like a madman in the padded cell of his breast —Logan Pearsall Smith

For the blocked or hesitant, the advent of the computer is like the advent of spring: the frozen river surges, the hard earth flowers —Edward Mendelson reporting on computers for writers, *Yale Review*, 1985

Getting a book published without a literary agent is like swimming dangerous waters without a shark repellent —Rae Lawrence, *New York Times Magazine* July 5, 1987

Lawrence's simile serves to introduce her experience in finding and choosing a literary agent for her first novel.

Good writing is a kind of skating which carries off the performer where he would not go —Ralph Waldo Emerson

Grammar is an art. Style is a gift. You are born with your style, just as you are born with your voice —Anatole France

The great writer finds style as the mystic finds God, in his own soul —Havelock Ellis

Hiring someone to write your autobiography is like hiring someone to take a bath for you —Mae West, quoted in *Bookviews*, February 11, 1977

I can get a kind of tension when I'm writing a short story [as compared to a novel], like I'm pulling on a rope and know where the rope is attached —Alice Munro, quoted in *New York Times Book Review,* September 14, 1986

(I enjoy the hell out of writing because) it's like an Easter egg hunt. Here's 50 pages and you say, "Oh, Christ where is it. Then on the 51st page, it'll work." —John D. Macdonald

Like thrifty French cooks, waste nothing —Leslie Garis, *New York Times Magazine,* February 8, 1987

Garis used the simile to describe Joan Didion and John Gregory Dunne's extensive note taking, all of which end up in their books.

A long preface to a short treatise is like a high hat crowning a low brow —Zevi Hirsh Somerhausen

Paraphrased for more modern English usage from: "Like a high hat crowning a low brow is a long preface to a short treatise."

Long sentences in a short composition are like large rooms in little houses —William Shenstone

Method in writing is like ceremony in living—too often used to supply the want of better things —Thomas Killigrew

Minor characters [in scripts] are rather like knights in chess: limited in movement, but handy in their capacity for quick turns, for fixing situations —John Fowles

A narrative is like a room on whose walls a number of false doors have been painted; while within the narrative, we have many apparent choices of exit, but when the author leads us to one particular door, we know it is the right one because the door opens —John Updike

Nobody can write a real drama who hasn't smelled the grease paint; it's like somebody composing who's never played an instrument —Mary McCarthy

Novels, like human beings, usually have their beginnings in the dark —Rita Mae Brown

People who write books take as much punishment as prizefighters —Norman Mailer

A pin has as much head as some authors and a great deal more point —George D. Prentice

The profession of book-writing makes horse racing seem like a solid stable business —John Steinbeck

The profession of writing is wrong, like smoking cigarettes, bad for your health, a diminisher of life expectancy —William Saroyan

Prose as smooth and burnished as well-oiled furniture —A.R. Gurney Jr., *New York Times Book Review,* 1985

Prose consists of … phrases tacked together like the sections of a prefabricated hen-house —George Orwell

Prose is like music, every word must be placed for sound, color and nuance —James G. Huneker

A sentence should read as if its author, had he held a plough instead of a pen, could have drawn a furrow deep and straight to the end —Henry David Thoreau

[George Bernard] Shaw is like a train. One just speaks the words and sits in one's place. But Shakespeare is like bathing in the sea—one swims where one wants —Vivien Leigh comparing two famous playwrights

Sitting by yourself, forcing the swirl of thoughts into a linear, systematic journey forward—it makes you smarter. It's like a pastry bag, literacy is. It presses you into one clear line —Margaret Edson quoted in a February 19, 2012, *New York Times* article by Charles McGrath in connection with revival with her Pulitzer Prize-winning play *Wit*

Sometimes writing a recipe takes me a whole day … to communicate it correctly. It's like writing a little short story —Julia Childs

To enclose him (a fictional character) as irradiantly as amber does the fly and yet the while to preserve every detail of his being has, of all tasks, ever been the dearest to me —Stefan Zweig

In his foreword to a collection of stories and novelettes, Zweig used this simile to explain that he considers his short fiction as much an accomplishment as his more "spacious" works.

Typing your own manuscript for submission is a lot like dressing to see that old lover who left you five years ago —Ira Wood

In his novel The Kitchen Man, *Wood expands the simile as follows: "Ready to walk out the door you stop one last time at the mirror, just to be sure they're going to regret what they walked out on. Well, maybe the belt is wrong, you think, throwing it on the bed, pulling out another. No, these old shoes won't do, too dowdy. After an hour, you're stripped to your socks and in tears, absolutely sure now that you are the perfect mess they said you were. And so your manuscript will be if you don't fight every urge to better every sentence."*

A well-written life is almost as rare as a well-spent one —Thomas Carlyle

Words flowed from his pen like sparkling spring water —Yoko Ono, about husband John Lennon's writing

A writer may take to long words, as young men to beards —to impress —F. L. Lucas

Writers, like teeth, are divided into incisors and grinders —Walter Bagehot

The writer's work is a little like handwriting. It comes out to be you no matter what you do —John Updike, *New York Times,* January 18, 1987

The writer who draws his material from a book is like one who borrows money only to lend it —Kahil Gibran

Writes like a comrade, the kind of friend with whom it is a pleasure to dispute —Jacques Barzun about H. W. Fowler, the author of *Modern English Usage, New York Times Book Review,* December 12, 1986

Reviewer John Gross in turn applied the simile to Barsun's book, A Word or Two before You Go.

Writing a first draft is like groping one's way into a pitch dark room, or overhearing a faint conversation, or telling a joke whose punchline you've forgotten —Ted Solotaroff

Writing for a newspaper is like running a revolutionary war; you go into battle not when you are ready but when action offers itself —Norman Mailer

Writing for him was as hard work as catching fleas —Ivan Turgenev

Writing is akin to fortunetelling … you look into someone's life, read where they have been and predict what will happen to them —Marcia Norman, quoted *New York Times Book Review,* May 24, 1987

Writing is like building a house —Ellen Gilchrist

Writing is like pulling the trigger of a gun: if you are not loaded, nothing happens —Henry Seidel Canby

Writing is like religion. Every man who feels the call must work out his own salvation —George Horace Lorimer

Writing is like serving a jail sentence —you're not free until you've done time on the rock-heap —Paul Theroux

Writing is like writing a check … it's easy to write a check if you have enough money in the bank, and writing comes more easily if you have something to say —Scholem Asch

Writing … it is rather like building a house, every separate word is another brick laid into place, cemented to its fellows, and gradually you begin to see the wall beginning to rise, and you know that the rooms inside will take their shape as you intended —Vita Sackville-West

Writing without publishing gets to be like loving someone from afar, delicious for fantasies but thin gruel for a living —Ted Solotaroff

Wrote not without puzzlements and travail; nevertheless as naturally as birds —Cynthia Ozick

You become a good writer just as you become a good joiner: by planing down your sentences —Anatole France

Your article should be like a lady's skirt: long enough to cover the essentials, and short enough to be interesting —editorial advice to freelancers, *PhotoGraphic,* January 1987

♣ YEARNING

See: DESIRE

♣ YELLOW

See Also: COLORS, HAIR

Dun-yellow color, a color like that of old lions in the zoo —Harold Brodkey

Yellow and solid as lemons —Joyce Cary

(Hair) yellow as a dandelion —Anne Sexton

(Hair) yellow as a full moon —George Garrett

Yellow as a marsh-marigold —Henry Van Dyke

Yellow as an old tooth —Howard Spring

(Dandelions) yellow as butter —Cynthia Ozick

(The field is) yellow as egg-bread dough —Randall Jarrell

(Hair) yellow as hay —Henry Wadsworth Longfellow

Yellow as mustard —Edna St. Vincent Millay

Yellow as the yolk of eggs —Marcel Proust

(Eyes) yellow like amber —Isaac Bashevis Singer

Yellow like moldy linen —Sinclair Lewis

Yellow like ripe corn —Dante Gabriel Rossetti

> *The point of reference is to the golden hair of the subject of Rossetti's famous poem "The Blessed Damozel."*

Yellow like unburnished gold —Honoré de Balzac

♣ YELLS

See: SCREAMS

♣ YOUTH

See Also: AGE

As young as truth —Dante Gabriel Rossetti

At sixty-eight, he is as pink and fat as a baby, ingenuous as a teenager —T. Coraghessan Boyle

Between eighteen and twenty, life is like an exchange where one buys stocks, not with money, but with actions —André Malraux

Childish, like believing in Beauty and the Beast —Janet Flanner

Each youth is like a child born in the night who sees the sun rise and thinks that yesterday never existed —W. Somerset Maugham

He is like one of those young-old engineers at Boeing, who at seventy wear bow ties and tinker in their workshops —Walker Percy

It is like a long hopeless homesickness ... missing those young days —Grace Paley

It would be wonderful to be young in this day and age. So many obstacles cleared from the path. Like driving right behind the snowplow. —Kate Fodor

Like the tongue that seeks the missing tooth I yearned for my extracted youth —Ogden Nash

Looked about sixteen and as defenseless as a babe at a Mafia convention —Jimmy Sangster

Midway between youth and age like a man who has missed his train: too late for the last and too early for the next —George Bernard Shaw

Seemed as perpetually youthful as movie stars —Donald Justice

She was just eighteen, rich and warm as one eagerly waiting for the play to begin —Arthur Schopenhauer

Their [young people's] impulses are keen but not deep-rooted ... like sick people's attacks of hunger —Aristotle

The young leading the young is like the blind leading the blind —Lord Chesterfield

Youth ... flashing like a star out of the twilight —Willa Cather

The simile is from an introductory poem to Cather's novel O Pioneers!

Youthful rashness skips like a hare over the meshes of good counsel —William Shakespeare

Youth is like spring, an overpraised season —delightful if it happen to be a favored one, but in practice very rarely favored and more remarkable, as a general rule, for biting east winds than genial breezes —Samuel Butler

Youth … it did not go by me like a flitting dream. Tuesdays and Wednesdays were as gay as Saturday nights —Grace Paley

Youth like summer morn … youth like summer brave —William Shakespeare, "Sonnet 73"

Shakespeare used these similes in his poem "The Passionate Pilgrim" to describe the pleasures of youth, alternating them with comparisons about age and the weather.

(My) youth passed like a sleep —Dame Edith Sitwell

♣ ZEAL
See: AMBITION, ENTHUSIASIM

AUTHOR INDEX

A

Abbey, Edward
CLOUD MOVEMENTS

Abbott, Lee K.
BODY; COMMONPLACE;
STRENGTH

Abbott, Lyman
PATIENCE

Abd-el-Kader
REJECTION

Abse, Dannie
DIFFERENCES

Ackerman, Diane
BENDING/BENT; BIRDS; BLACK;
BLOOD; BRIGHTNESS; CLARITY;
COLORS; CONNECTIONS; DESIR-
ABILITY; DESTRUCTION/DE-
STRUCTIVENESS; EYE COLOR;
FIGHT; FIRMNESS; GLIMMER,
GLITTER AND GLOSS; HAND
MOVEMENTS; HEARTBEAT;
HEAVINESS; IDEAS; LEAVES;
LOOSENESS; MEETINGS; MOON;
PALLOR; PINK; RED; RESTLESS-
NESS; ROOMS; SERIOUSNESS; SI-
LENCE; TENSION; TIME; TREM-
BLING; TURNING AND
TWISTING; UNSTEADINESS;
WALKING; WHITE

Acton, Harold
DESIRE

Acton, Lord
EXPERIENCE

Adamic, Louis
DRYNESS; EATING AND DRINK-
ING; JEWELRY; STRAIGHTNESS

Adams, Alice
BEARING

Adams, Douglas
BEARING; HANDS; HARSHNESS;
LIFE DEFINED; MOON; SPEAK-
ING; VOICE, MUSIC RELATED;
WIND

Adams, Franklin P.
CLEVERNESS

Adams, Harold
ANIMALS; BEARING; CALMNESS;
CLOTHING; CLOTHING, ITS FIT;
COLLAPSE; EXCITEMENT; EXITS;
EYES; FACIAL EXPRESSIONS,
MISCELLANEOUS; GROWTH;
HEAD MOVEMENTS; HUMOR;
INSECTS; INSULT; LINGERING;
LOOKS; MOUTH; MOVEMENT(S);
NOISES; OBVIOUSNESS; PERSIST-
ENCE; POLITICS/POLITICIANS;
RELIABILITY/UNRELIABILITY;
SCREAMS; SCRUTINY; SECRECY;
SILENCE; SMOOTHNESS; SOCIA-
BILITY/UNSOCIABILITY; TALKA-
TIVENESS; TALLNESS; VOICE,
HARSH; WALKING

Adams, Henry
EDUCATION

Adams, Joey
CLOTHING; ECONOMICS;
FACE(S); PAST, THE

Adams, John
FATNESS; MIND DEFINED

Adams, Samuel Hopkins
BLUSHES

Adams, Thomas
ARGUMENTS; BEAUTY DEFINED

Addison, Joseph
CLEVERNESS; DANCING; GAI-
ETY; TONGUE

Ade, George
COLLAPSE; FOREHEAD;
HEALTH; INSULT; KINDNESS;
PEACEFULNESS; SADNESS;
SPEED; TEETH

Adler, Felix
BELIEFS

Adler, Richard
AGILITY; CLOSENESS;
STRENGTH

Aeschylus
CHILDREN; FEROCITY; PURITY;
TRANSIENCE; WEAKNESS

Aesop
GAIETY

Agee, James
BENDING/BENT; DISAPPEAR-
ANCE; VOICE, HARSH

Ai, Sin
DESTRUCTION/DESTRUCTIVE-
NESS; PLACES

Aiken, Conrad
  LEAVES; MEMORY; TREMBLING;
  WORD(S)
Aiken, Joan
  FLOWERS; SCREAMS
Al-Harizi, Judah
  MANKIND
Alain
  MANNERS
Al Aswany, Alaa
  CITY STREETSCAPES; MEMORY;
  ORDER/DISORDER
Albo, Josepiz
  EVIL
Albright, Fuller
  DOCTORS
Alcott, Louisa May
  ATTENTION; BEARING; CAUSE
  AND EFFECT; COLDNESS; COM-
  FORT; EATING AND DRINKING;
  HAPPINESS; KNOWLEDGE;
  PHYSICAL FEELINGS
Aldiss, Brian W.
  AIR
Aldrich, James
  IMMOBILITY
Aldrich, Thomas Bailey
  BALDNESS; BENDING/BENT;
  SENSITIVENESS
Aldridge, John W.
  PERMANENCE
Aleichem, Sholem
  CROWDS; CURSES; DIFFICULTY;
  DISINTEGRATION; EXCITE-
  MENT; FIRE AND SMOKE;
  HEART(S); HOUSES; LAWYERS;
  LIFE DEFINED; LOVE; MOVE-
  MENT(S); PAIN; REMOTENESS;
  TREMBLING; WEARINESS
Alembert, Jean Le Rond d'
  SUCCESS/FAILURE
Alexander, Shana
  CLOSENESS; RESERVE;
  SCRUTINY
Alexis
  LIFE DEFINED
Alfano, Peter
  PERSONALITY PROFILES
Alfred, William
  ANGER; CHANGE; DESTRUC-
  TION/DESTRUCTIVENESS; DIS-
  HONESTY; GOSSIP; HAIR,
  COLOR; HEAT; MOUTH, OPEN
  AND SHUT; PRIDE; RELIGION;
  RESERVE

Alger, William R.
  WISDOM
Algren, Nelson
  BLOOD; DISAPPEARANCE; DRY-
  NESS; HAIR; LEAVES; PLACES;
  TOBACCO; TURNING AND
  TWISTING; VOICE(S)
Ali, Muhammad
  MOVEMENT(S)
Alighieri, Dante
  COLLAPSE; EYES; EYES, BRIGHT;
  FIRMNESS; HABIT; SCREAMS;
  VIRTUE
Allen, Fred
  IMPOSSIBILITY; INSULT; THIN-
  NESS
Allen, Roberta
  FACIAL EXPRESSIONS, MISCEL-
  LANEOUS
Allen, Walter
  GUILT
Allen, Woody
  COMEDY
Allende, Isabel
  ANGER; FUTILITY
Altringham, Lord
  COMMONPLACE
Alvarez, A.
  CERTAINTY; CLINGING; CRITI-
  CISM, DRAMATIC AND LITER-
  ARY; FACIAL EXPRESSIONS, MIS-
  CELLANEOUS; FATNESS;
  HOUSES; MONEY; PHYSICAL AP-
  PEARANCE
Ambler, Eric
  EYES; HELPLESSNESS; LIPS;
  SMILE; TEETH
Ameringer, Oscar
  PROFESSIONS
Ames, Ebra
  STRUGGLE
Ames, Fisher
  DRYNESS; GOVERNMENT
Amichai, Yehuda
  BEHAVIOR; BREASTS; DESTRUC-
  TION/DESTRUCTIVENESS; FIRM-
  NESS; GROWTH; HEART(S); LIFE;
  LOVE; MEMORY; MEN AND
  WOMEN; NOISES; OPEN AND
  SHUT; PAST, THE; SOUL; STARS;
  TIME; TRAVEL; WORD(S)
Amis, Kingsley
  BEARING; BREASTS; BREATHING;
  COLLAPSE; FACE(S); FACIAL EX-
  PRESSIONS, MISCELLANEOUS;

IMPOSSIBILITY; PAIN; PERSONAL
  TRAITS; RISING; SCREAMS;
  SWEAT; WORD(S)
Amis, Martin
  DANCING; PAIN
Ammons, A. @index theme:R., BE-
  LIEFS; FLOWERS; IMPOR-
  TANCE/UNIMPORTANCE; THUN-
  DER AND LIGHTNING
Amory, Cleveland
  MUSIC
Anarchis
  LAWS
Andersen, Hans Christian
  AGILITY; BIRDS; CLARITY;
  CLOUD MOVEMENTS; GLIM-
  MER, GLITTER AND GLOSS;
  SEASCAPES; SNOW; STARS; SUN;
  TREES; WIND
Anderson, Dave
  DISINTEGRATION; GOLF
Anderson, Maxwell
  BODY; COLDNESS; DAY; GENTLE-
  NESS; IMPOSSIBILITY; LEAPING;
  TRUTH
Anderson, Robert
  PEOPLE, INTERACTION
Anderson, Sherwood
  DESIRE; DISAPPOINTMENT; FUR-
  NITURE AND FURNISHINGS;
  HANDS; ILLNESS
Anderson, Susan Heller
  POWER; TRANSIENCE
Andreyev, Leonid
  REALNESS/UNREALNESS; TEARS
Andric, Ivo
  MOVEMENT(S); RISING
Angelou, Maya
  AIR; ATMOSPHERE; BURST; CON-
  VERSATION; FOOD AND DRINK;
  HARSHNESS; NOISES; PHYSICAL
  APPEARANCE; PHYSICAL FEEL-
  INGS; PLACES; PREPAREDNESS;
  SHARPNESS; SHYNESS; STAND-
  ING; VOICE, EFFECT OF;
  VOICE(S); VOICE, WEAK
Anouilh, Jean
  ABILITY; ALONENESS
Anthony, Piers
  EYE COLOR; FEAR
Antler
  LAUGHTER
Appelfeld, Aharon
  ATTRACTION; COURAGE; FEAR

Apperley, Charles James
HEART(S)

Apperson, G. L.
UNDESIREABILITY

Apple, Max
AGE; ATTRACTION; CHIN; CLEANLINESS; CONTENTMENT; CRITICISM, DRAMATIC AND LITERARY; DISAPPEARANCE; PEOPLE, INTERACTION; ROOMS; SKIN; THINNESS

Applebome, Peter
PLACES

Aquinas, St. Thomas
SENSE

Arcel, Ray
BOXING AND WRESTLING

Ardizzone, Tony
BREATHING; CLINGING; CLOTHING; DEJECTION; DISINTEGRATION; ERRORS; FURNITURE AND FURNISHINGS; GLOOM; HANDS; IRRITABLENESS/IRRITATING; MEMORY; MUSCLES; POLITICS/POLITICIANS; SCREAMS; SKIN; SPORTS; STOMACH

Ardrey, Robert
VIOLENCE

Aretino, Pietro
FRIENDSHIP; WAR

Aristippus
ABILITY; WIT

Aristophanes
DESTRUCTION/DESTRUCTIVENESS

Aristotle
PATIENCE; YOUTH

Arkin, Frieda
TIME

Arnold, Matthew
MEETINGS

Arrowsmith, Aaron
WIT

Arzybashev, Mikhail P.
ANGER; FACIAL EXPRESSIONS, BLANK

Asch, Nathan
VEHICLES

Asch, Sholem
BALDNESS; ILLNESS; JUMPING; MAXIMS, PROVERBS AND SAYINGS; TEETH; TREES; WRITERS/WRITING

Ascher, Barbara Lazear
DESTRUCTION/DESTRUCTIVENESS; FLEXIBILITY/INFLEXIBILITY; MANNERS; PAIN; POWER; SPREADING

Ascher, Carol
BREASTS; FACE(S); HAIR

Ashberry, John
CALMNESS; CLEANLINESS; DARKNESS; DREAM; DRYNESS; EMPTINESS; GROWTH; LIES/LIARS; LINGERING; MEMORY; NIGHT; QUESTIONS AND ANSWERS; RELATIONSHIP; RESTLESSNESS; SITTING; SKY; SUN; THOUGHTS; TRUTH

Ashe, Thomas
PAIN

Astaire, Fred
AGE

Atherton, Gertrude
EMOTIONS; PASSION; THICKNESS; TREMBLING

Atlas, James
LOVE; SPEECHMAKING

Atwood, Margaret
ADVANCING; ANIMALS; BREVITY; BRIGHTNESS; COLLAPSE; CONTINUITY; CONVERSATION; DANCING; DISAPPEARANCE; DISCOMFORT; DISINTEGRATION; EYES; FINGERS; FLOWERS; FRAGILITY; HAIR; HATRED; HEAD MOVEMENTS; HEAT; HELPLESSNESS; MUSCLES; NOISES; REALIZATION; SEXUAL INTERACTION; SHAPE; SKIN; SMELL; SOFTNESS; SUN; TRUTHNESS/FALSENESS; TURNING AND TWISTING; VISABILITY; WHITE; WORD(S); WRINKLES

Auburn, David
DULLNESS

Auchincloss, Louis
ATTENTION; BEHAVIOR; EMOTIONS; ENTRAPMENT; EXCITEMENT; FROWNS; FUTILITY; GLIMMER, GLITTER AND GLOSS; HAND MOVEMENTS; LOOKS; MIND; NATURE

Auden, W. H.
ACCOMPLISHMENT; CITIES; CROWDS; DISAPPEARANCE; EVIL; FRESHNESS; LIFE; MOVEMENT(S); NOISES; PERMANENCE; PHYSICAL APPEARANCE; POWER; PURPOSEFULNESS; RARITY; READERS/READING; SILENCE; SKY; TIME

Auerbach, Berthold
CHARACTER; KINDNESS

Augustine, St.
EVIL

Austin, Alfred
BRIGHTNESS

Austin, Mary
HAIR

Axelrod, George
GOSSIP

B

Babel, Isaac
CLOTHING; CRITICISM, DRAMATIC AND LITERARY; HEAD MOVEMENTS; HUNGER; MOON; NOSE(S); PAIN; RUNNING; SUN; SUNSET

Bach, Richard
BIRDS

Bacon, Francis
ABILITY; BEAUTY DEFINED; BEHAVIOR; DEATH; HEALTH; KNOWLEDGE; MONEY; REVENGE; TRUST/MISTRUST; VIRTUE

Baer, Arthur
DESIRABILITY; ERRORS; HANDS; IMPOSSIBILITY; INAPPROPRIATENESS; MARRIAGE; SHAPE; SILENCE; STEADINESS; STRAIGHTNESS; SURPRISE; USEFULNESS/USELESSNESS; VIBRATION; VISABILITY; WRINKLES

Baez, Joan
BLUE

Bagby, George
HAIR STYLES

Bagehot, Walter
WRITERS/WRITING

Bagnold, Enid
BURST; CROWDS; SPEED; TURNING AND TWISTING

Bahya
DAY; WORLD

Bail, Murray
SPORTS

Bailey, Nathan
  COMFORT
Bailey, P. J.
  DISAPPEARANCE; JOY; NIGHT;
  THOUGHTS
Baille, Joanna
  GREEN
Bainbridge, Beryl
  ELUSIVENESS; ENTRAPMENT;
  FUTILITY; NOSE(S);
  POLITICS/POLITICIANS; STARES
Bakeland, Brooks
  CLINGING
Baker, Carlos
  CHARACTER; EMOTIONS; EN-
  THUSIASM; FACIAL SHAPE; FIRE
  AND SMOKE; HAPPINESS;
  HUNGER; LAUGHTER; LIGHT-
  ING; LOYALTY/DISLOYALTY;
  MEMORY; MUSCLES; NECK;
  NOSE(S); PALLOR; PEACEFUL-
  NESS; PERSISTENCE; REPETI-
  TION; SILENCE; SLOWNESS;
  SMELL; STOMACH; THUNDER
  AND LIGHTNING; TREES;
  TRUST/MISTRUST; VOICE,
  HARSH; VOICE, MUSIC RELATED;
  WEATHER
Baker, Russell
  BALDNESS; BUSINESS; CER-
  TAINTY; COMPLETENESS; FAME;
  FIRMNESS; HISTORY; LAN-
  GUAGE; POLITICS/POLITICIANS;
  SMOOTHNESS; THINNESS; VIO-
  LENCE; WORK
Baldwin, James
  EYE EXPRESSIONS, MISCELLA-
  NEOUS; EYES, BRIGHT; FUTURE;
  MONEY; PERSONALITY PRO-
  FILES; SINGING; TEARS
Balguy, John
  RESTLESSNESS
Ball, George W.
  TACT
Ballard, Mignon F.
  SILENCE; THOUGHTS
Ballou, Hosea
  ENERGY
Balzac, Honoré de
  ADVANCING; APPRECIATION;
  ATTENTION; BELONGING;
  BODY; BOXING AND
  WRESTLING; CANDOR; CAU-
  TION; CONSCIENCE; COURAGE;
  CRUELTY; DISAPPEARANCE;

DOCTORS; DULLNESS; ELUSIVE-
  NESS; EXCITEMENT; EYE EX-
  PRESSIONS, MISCELLANEOUS;
  EYE MOVEMENTS; EYES,
  BRIGHT; FACE(S); FACIAL EX-
  PRESSIONS, MISCELLANEOUS;
  FACIAL SHAPE; FATNESS; FEAR;
  GLIMMER, GLITTER AND GLOSS;
  GOSSIP; LAUGHTER; LIPS;
  LOOKS; LOVE, DEFINED; MAR-
  RIAGE; MEEKNESS; MIND;
  MOUTH; NOSE(S); PERSONALITY
  PROFILES; PHYSICAL APPEAR-
  ANCE; PLEASURE; PROBLEMS
  AND SOLUTIONS; PROMPTNESS;
  RARITY; SELF CONFIDENCE;
  SMOOTHNESS; STUPIDITY;
  TREMBLING; WHITE; WIND;
  YELLOW
Bancroft, George
  BEAUTY DEFINED
Bankhead, Tallulah
  ABSURDITY; BEGINNINGS AND
  ENDINGS; DRINKING; PURITY;
  SMOOTHNESS
Banks, John
  BRIGHTNESS
Banks, Russell
  CLOTHING, ITS FIT; REALIZA-
  TION; REJECTION; SKY
Bannister, Jo
  AGILITY; MUSTACHE(S)
Barbery, Muriel
  AMBITION, UNATTRACTIVENESS
Barham, Richard Harris
  TOBACCO; VAGUENESS
Barker, Clive
  ANXIETY; STARES; VISABILITY
Barker, George
  DEATH; TIME
Barker, Paul
  DEATH
Barnard, Robert
  DAY; SHAME; TIMELINESS/UN-
  TIMELINESS
Barnes, Fred
  DULLNESS
Barnes, Linda
  CALMNESS; SMOOTHNESS
Barnum, P. T.
  MONEY
Barr, Pat
  RARITY
Barrie, J. M.
  CLINGING; LIFE DEFINED

Barron, Susan
  ANXIETY
Barrymore, Drew
  PLACES
Barth, John
  AIMLESSNESS; MOTIVATION;
  MOVEMENT(S); TIME
Barthelme, Donald
  EYES
Barthelme, Frederick
  FRAGILITY
Bartlett, John Russell
  CREDIT; EVIL
Bartlett, Mike
  HAND MOVEMENTS; MEN AND
  WOMEN; PHYSICAL APPEAR-
  ANCE
Bartov, Hanoch
  EYES; FACE(S); LAUGHTER
Baryshnikov, Mikhail
  FAME; PERSONALITY PROFILES
Barzun, Jacques
  CONVERSATION;
  WRITERS/WRITING
Bat-Miriam, Yocheved
  SHINING
Bate, Julius
  ENTHUSIASM
Bates, H. E.
  ABUNDANCE; ANGER; BOXING
  AND WRESTLING; BREASTS;
  BROWN; CONTENTMENT; CON-
  TROL; EATING AND DRINKING;
  EMBRACE; EMOTIONS; EXITS;
  EYE MOVEMENTS; FACE(S); FA-
  CIAL SHAPE; FIRMNESS; HAIR;
  HAIR STYLES; HANDS; HEAT;
  HOUSES; IMPOSSIBILITY; INTEL-
  LIGENCE; KINDNESS; LEG(S);
  MARRIAGE; MOUTH, OPEN AND
  SHUT; NATURE; NERVOUSNESS;
  OPINION; PAIN; PARENTHOOD;
  SCREAMS; SELF CONFIDENCE;
  SHAPE; SKIN; SMILE; SNOW;
  THINNESS; THOUGHTS; TOUGH-
  NESS; TREES; TURNING AND
  TWISTING; VEHICLES; WORD(S)
Bates, Lewis J.
  COLDNESS; CRUELTY
Baudelaire, Charles
  PERSONALITY PROFILES;
  POETS/POETRY
Baum, Vicki
  ANXIETY; BREATHING; CLOTH-
  ING ACCESSORIES; CROWDS;

DISCONTENT; DIVERSENESS;
FOOD AND DRINK; HEAD
MOVEMENTS; LIFE; LYING;
PAIN; PHYSICAL APPEARANCE;
SEXUAL INTERACTION; SMILE;
SPEED; STRENGTH;
SUCCESS/FAILURE; VIRTUE;
WEAKNESS; WIND; WORDS, EF-
FECT OF

Bauman, M. Garrett
SKIN

Bawden, Nina
BENDING/BENT; CLOSENESS;
CONVERSATION; EYE COLOR;
FROWNS; LOVE; SERIOUSNESS;
SKIN; STRENGTH

Baxter, Charles
VOICE, MUSIC RELATED

Bayne, Stephen
UNCERTAINTY

Beach, Rex
FACIAL DETAILS; PERSONAL
TRAITS

Beagle, Peter S.
TURNING AND TWISTING

Beaton, M. C.
TALLNESS

Beattie, Ann
ABSURDITY; ARM(S); CAUTION;
CLOTHING, ITS FIT; EYES; FU-
TILITY; GUILT; HAIR; HAND
MOVEMENTS; SMOOTHNESS;
STANDING; STRANGENESS; TEN-
SION; WATCHFULNESS; WEAK-
NESS

Beaumont, Francis
AMBITION; BLACK; ENVY

Beaumont, J.
RELIGION

Beaumont and Fletcher
CALMNESS; DESTRUCTION/DE-
STRUCTIVENESS; INTENSITY;
SOUL

Beauvoir, Simone de
HELPLESSNESS; SEX

Beck, Warren
ANIMALS; GLOOM

Beckett, Samuel
MIND; SPEED; SWEAT

Bedersi, Jediah
MIND DEFINED

Bee, Bernard
FIRMNESS

Beecham, Sir Thomas
SINGING

Beechcroft, William
ATTRACTIVENESS; BELONGING;
BODY; CERTAINTY; CONTENT-
MENT; DRYNESS; FACE(S); FOOD
AND DRINK; HELPLESSNESS;
HONESTY; MEMORY; SHOCK;
SPEED; VOICE, HARSH

Beecher, Henry Ward
BODY; CHARACTER; FORGIVE-
NESS; GAIETY; LAWS; LOVE, DE-
FINED; MANKIND;
POLITICS/POLITICIANS;
STRENGTH

Beerbohm, Max
MOON

Begley, Desmond
MEMORY

Begley, Louis
AGE

Behan, Brendan
CRITICS; CRITICISM, DRAMATIC
AND LITERARY

Behn, Aphra
BUSYNESS; STRAIGHTNESS

Behn, Noel
SWEAT

Bell, Jack
SELF CONFIDENCE

Bell, Louis Monta
ENTHUSIASM; USEFULNESS/USE-
LESSNESS

Bell, Madison Smartt
BODY; DAY; DIFFICULTY; EM-
BRACE; ENTRANCES AND EXITS;
MEMORY; PLACES;
POLITICS/POLITICIANS; ROOMS;
SCREAMS; SPEECH PATTERNS;
SUNSET

Bell, Marvin, HATRED

Bellah, James Warner
FEAR

Bellamann, Henry
MEMORY

Belloc, Hilaire
ANIMALS; BOOKS

Bellow, Saul
AGE; AIR; ANGER; ATTRACTIVE-
NESS; AWKWARDNESS; BALD-
NESS; BEARD; BEGINNINGS AND
ENDINGS; BEHAVIOR; BROWN;
CHANGE; CLOUDS; COST; DISIN-
TEGRATION; EYEBROWS; FA-
CIAL DETAILS; FACIAL SHAPE;
FATNESS; FIRE AND SMOKE;
HAIR; HAIR STYLES; HAIR, TEX-
TURE; HEAT; HOUSES; IMMOBIL-
ITY; INSULT; JUMPING; LAND-
SCAPES; LIES/LIARS; LOOKS;
MIND; MOVEMENT(S); PEOPLE,
INTERACTION; PHYSICAL AP-
PEARANCE; QUESTIONS AND
ANSWERS; RAIN; RARITY; RED;
SCREAMS; SEX; SHAME; SHAPE;
SKY COLOR; SLOWNESS; SMELL;
SNOW; SPEED; STEADINESS;
STRENGTH; SUN; THOUGHTS;
TRANSIENCE; VEHICLES;
WORDS, EFFECT OF; WRINKLES

Bemelmans, Ludwig
COMPLEXION; EYES; FOG;
HAND MOVEMENTS; LAND-
SCAPES; PROPRIETY/IMPROPRI-
ETY; SPEECH PATTERNS

Benchley, Nathaniel
LAUGHTER; PAIN

Benchley, Peter
ANXIETY; CHILDREN; EYE EX-
PRESSIONS, MISCELLANEOUS;
EYE MOVEMENTS; FEAR; IMPOS-
SIBILITY; KISSES; PEOPLE, IN-
TERACTION; PERSONALITY
PROFILES; PHYSICAL FEELINGS;
SCREAMS; SPREADING; USEFUL-
NESS/USELESSNESS

Benchley, Robert
TOBACCO

Bendall, Gerald
MEMORY

Benedict, Dianne
FURNITURE AND FURNISHINGS;
SKY

Benét, Stephen Vincent
ANIMALS; BEAUTY; BEHAVIOR;
BEWILDERMENT; BLACK;
BRIGHTNESS; CALMNESS;
CLEANLINESS; CLOTHING AC-
CESSORIES; DARKNESS; DAY; DE-
CREASE; DISPERSAL; DRYNESS;
EXITS; EYES, BRIGHT; FEAR;
FIGHTING; FOG; GAIETY;
HANDS; KINDNESS; MUSCLES;
NAMES; PALLOR; PRIDE; PURITY;
RARITY; ROAD SCENES; SE-
CRECY; SELF CONFIDENCE;
SMILE; SOFTNESS; SPEAKING;
SPEED; STRAIGHTNESS; THIN-
NESS; THOUGHTS; TIME; USE-
FULNESS/USELESSNESS; WAR;
WASTE

Benham, W. G.
ENTHUSIASM

Benjamin, Park
BEGINNINGS AND ENDINGS

Benjamin, Walter
PLACES

Bennett, Arnold
CLARITY; ROCKING AND
ROLLING

Bennett, Peggy
TREMBLING; WALKING

Bennetts, Leslie
INAPPROPRIATENESS; TRAN-
SIENCE

Benson, Arthur C.
RESTLESSNESS

Benson, E. F.
WEAKNESS

Benson, Stella
CLOUDS; DULLNESS; HELPLESS-
NESS

Bentham, Jeremy
AFFECTION; HABIT

Berger, John
RISING

Berger, Suzanne E.
SMOOTHNESS

Bergman, Ingrid
AGE

Berkeley, Bishop George
WORLD

Berkman, Sylvia
BODY; CHEERFULNESS; COLD-
NESS; CROWDS; EYEBROWS;
FEAR; FRAGILITY; GLOOM;
LEAVES; PERSONALITY PRO-
FILES; RAIN; SENSITIVENESS;
SPEAKING

Berkow, Ira
BASEBALL; CHOICES; CON-
TEMPT; INTENSITY; NATURAL-
NESS

Berlin, Irving
CHEERFULNESS; LIFE; PEOPLE
INTERACTIONS; QUESTIONS
AND ANSWERS; VULNERABILITY

Berlin, Isaiah
PLACES; SPEECH PATTERNS

Berriault, Gina
FLOWERS; SILENCE

Berrigan, Daniel
BLACK; EMPTINESS; EYE EX-
PRESSIONS, MISCELLANEOUS;
KINDNESS; LOOSENESS; PEACE-

FULNESS; RISING; SILENCE; SIM-
PLICITY; SOFTNESS

Berry, Wendell
LOVE; REGRET; RELIGION; SI-
LENCE

Berryman, John
AGE; BREATHING; PAIN; THIN-
NESS

Betjeman, John
PRIDE; SMELL; SMOOTHNESS

Betti, Ugo
MEMORY

Bhartrihari
DEATH

Bhatty, Margaret
FACE(S)

Bialik, Hayyim Nahman
MOUTH

Bible, Holy
AGE; AGREEMENT/DISAGREE-
MENT; ANGER; BARENESS;
BEAUTY DEFINED; BITTERNESS;
BLACK; BREASTS; CHEEKS; CON-
TINUITY; COURAGE; CRUELTY;
DAY; DEATH; DEATH, FINALITY
OF; DEJECTION; DESTRUC-
TION/DESTRUCTIVENESS; DIS-
APPEARANCE; DISHONESTY;
DISINTEGRATION; DISPERSAL;
EDUCATION; EMOTIONS; ENVY;
ERRORS; FACE(S); FACIAL EX-
PRESSIONS, MISCELLANEOUS;
FIRMNESS; FLEXIBILITY/INFLEX-
IBILITY; FRIENDSHIP; GAIETY;
GOVERNMENT; GROWTH;
HARMLESSNESS; HEAT; HELP-
LESSNESS; IDLENESS; JUSTICE;
LAUGHTER; LIFE; LIPS; LOVE;
MANKIND; MANNERS; NECK;
NEWS; PARENTHOOD; PHYSICAL
APPEARANCE; POSTURE;
POVERTY; ROARS; SHARPNESS;
SILENCE; SPEAKING; SPEED;
STRENGTH; TALKATIVENESS;
TIME; TRUST/MISTRUST; UN-
STEADINESS; VOICE, MUSIC-RE-
LATED; WEAKNESS; WHITE;
WORD(S); WORDS DEFINED;
WORLD

Bierce, Ambrose
BEAUTY; BELIEFS; NOISES; PAIN

Bierds, Linda
BIRDS

Billings, Josh
ADVANTAGEOUSNESS; ADVICE;
AMBITION; COLDNESS; CREDIT;
DESIRABILITY; DIFFERENCES;
DISHONESTY; FAME; FLATTERY;
GREATNESS; GREED; HEAD
MOVEMENTS; IGNORANCE; JOY;
KISSES; LAUGHTER; LAWS; LIFE
DEFINED; LOVE; LOVE, DE-
FINED; MANKIND; MARRIAGE;
MAXIMS, PROVERBS AND SAY-
INGS; MEN AND WOMEN;
MONEY; OPINION; OPPORTU-
NITY; RELIGION; SLANDER; STO-
RIES; STUPIDITY; WISDOM; WIT

Bird, Isabella
PLACES

Bird, Sarah
BALDNESS; BEARING; HAIR, TEX-
TURE; HOUSES; LIPS; LOOKS;
NOSE(S); PALLOR

Bire, Augustine
NOISES

Bishop, Elizabeth
BEHAVIOR; ENTRANCES AND
EXITS; GREEN; HELPLESSNESS;
INSECTS; LANDSCAPES; LIGHT-
NESS; PHYSICAL APPEARANCE;
POWER; PROTECTIVENESS;
SHADOW; SPEED; SPREADING;
SUN; TREMBLING

Bishop, Jim
FUTURE

Bismarck, Otto von
PASSION

Bisson, Terry
CLINGING; COLDNESS; EYE EX-
PRESSIONS, MISCELLANEOUS;
ROAD SCENES; SADNESS;
SMOOTHNESS

Blackie, John Stuart
BEAUTY

Blackman, M. C.
LOOKS

Blackwell, Basil
PURSUIT

Blake, Rev. Watson C.
HABIT

Blake, William
ABUNDANCE; CONTEMPT;
EMPTINESS; FLEXIBILITY/IN-
FLEXIBILITY; GLIMMER, GLIT-
TER AND GLOSS; MOON; OPIN-
ION; SILENCE; STRENGTH;
VIRTUE

Blanchard, Edwin L.
LOVE, DEFINED

Blanchard, Laman
FRAGILITY

Blasco Ibáñez
Vicente, PERSISTENCE

Blassingame, Wyatt
NOISES; PEOPLE, INTERACTION

Blessington, Marguerite Countess
ABILITY; DISHONESTY

Blewett, Sandra
SPORTS

Blow, Charles M.
LIES/LIARS

Boccaccio
HAIR

Boerne, Ludwig
CLEVERNESS; EDUCATION; GOVERNMENT; MANKIND; POLITICS/POLITICIANS

Boileau, Nicolas
REPETITION

Böll, Heinrich
BLUSHES; COLORS; FEAR; FURNITURE AND FURNISHINGS; ILLNESS; MEMORY; PHYSICAL FEELINGS; REJECTION; SHAPE; SILENCE; SKIN; SKY; STARS; TIME; VOICE(S); WATCHFULNESS

Bolt, Robert
PROMISE

Bolton, Guy
SIGHS

Bombeck, Erma
CLOTHING, ITS FIT; EDUCATION; GUILT; RUNNING

Bon Jovi, Jon
LOVE

Bonacich, Peter J.
RELIABILITY/UNRELIABILITY

Bonaparte, Napoleon
COURAGE; FREEDOM; GREATNESS; MANKIND

Bonard, Abel
LOVE

Booth, Barton
TRUTHNESS/FALSENESS

Booth, Edwin
STAGE AND SCREEN

Borden, Mary
LIFE DEFINED

Boretz, Alvin
ACCOMPLISHMENT; AIMLESSNESS; CHANGE; EMBRACE; MEN AND WOMEN

Borland, John C.
ECONOMICS

Borowski, Tadeusz
GLIMMER, GLITTER AND GLOSS

Borsten, Rick
BODY; GRINS; HEAD MOVEMENTS; POLITICS/POLITICIANS; PROBLEMS AND SOLUTIONS; RAIN; SMILE; SOUL; STOMACH

Bossuet, Jacques-Bénigne
KINDNESS

Boswell, James
FIRMNESS

Bottome, Phyllis
AIR; ANGER; BEAUTY; CHEEKS; DANGER; HAIR, TEXTURE; LOVE; MANKIND; MOON; MOUNTAINS; PAIN; PARENTHOOD; PHYSICAL FEELINGS; SHYNESS; VOICE, HARSH; WHITE

Boucicault, Dion
AFFECTION; PRIDE

Bourne, Randolph S.
CONVERSATION

Boussuet, Jacques Benigne
REPETITION

Bovee, Christian Nestell
PASSION; WAR

Bowen, Baron Charles Synge Christopher
MIND DEFINED

Bowen, Elizabeth
ATTENTION; DAY; DEJECTION; DESIRE; DISAPPEARANCE; EATING AND DRINKING; EMOTIONS; FATE; FIRMNESS; FURNITURE AND FURNISHINGS; HAIR STYLES; INAPPROPRIATENESS; LIGHTING; MANNERS; MIND; MOVEMENT(S); NATURALNESS; NATURE; NIGHT; NOISES; PERSONALITY PROFILES; REALNESS/UNREALNESS; SEX; SKY; TREES

Bower, Hamilton
CONSCIENCE

Bowles, G. S.
GREED

Bowles, Jane
CLINGING

Boyd, William
ATTENTION; BALDNESS; DARKNESS; FACIAL COLOR; FIRMNESS; MOUNTAINS; OCEAN/OCEANFRONTS; SELF CONFIDENCE; SILENCE

Boyesen, Hjalmar Hjorth
LOVE, DEFINED

Boylan, Clare
HANDS; LOOKS

Boyle, Kay
ARM(S); EYEBROWS; LINGERING; SKIN; THICKNESS; VOICE(S)

Boyle, Robert
CHARACTER

Boyle, T. Coraghessan
ADVANCING; AGILITY; AGITATION; AIR; ALERTNESS; ANGER; ATMOSPHERE; BASEBALL; BEARD; BEARING; BEHAVIOR; BIGNESS; BLACK; BLUE; BODY; BREASTS; BREATHING; CERTAINTY; CHEEKS; CLOTHING; CLOTHING, ITS FIT; COLDNESS; COLLAPSE; CRYING; CURSES; DANCING; DARKNESS; DAY; DEJECTION; DESTRUCTION/DESTRUCTIVENESS; EATING AND DRINKING; EMOTIONS; ENERGY; ENTHUSIASM; EYE COLOR; EYE EXPRESSIONS, MISCELLANEOUS; EYEBROWS; EYES; FACE(S); FACIAL EXPRESSIONS, BLANK; FACIAL EXPRESSIONS, MISCELLANEOUS; FACIAL EXPRESSIONS, SERIOUS; FEAR; FINGERS; FOREHEAD; FORTUNE/MISFORTUNE; FROWNS; GLIMMER, GLITTER AND GLOSS; GRINS; GROANS AND WHISPERS; GUILT; HAIR; HAIR, COLOR; HANDS; HANDSHAKE; HEAT; IMMOBILITY; IMPOSSIBILITY; JUMPING; LAUGHTER; LIGHTING; LIGHTNESS; MEMORY; MOUNTAINS; MUSIC; NATURE; NECK; NERVOUSNESS; NOISES; NOSE(S); OPPORTUNITY; PAIN; PALLOR; PERSISTENCE; PERSONALITY PROFILES; PHYSICAL APPEARANCE; PHYSICAL FEELINGS; PROBLEMS AND SOLUTIONS; PURPOSEFULNESS; RAIN; REALIZATION; REMOTE-

NESS; ROARS; SADNESS;
SCREAMS; SCRUTINY; SEX;
SHAPE; SHOULDERS; SIMILAR-
ITY; SITTING; SKIN; SKY; SKY
COLOR; SLOWNESS; SMILE;
SMOOTHNESS; SNORES; SNOW;
SOFTNESS; SPEECH PATTERNS;
STEADINESS; STRAIGHTNESS;
STRANGENESS; SUCCESS/FAIL-
URE; SUN; TACT; TALKATIVE-
NESS; TALLNESS; TEETH; THIN-
NESS; THUNDER AND
LIGHTNING; TIME; TIMELI-
NESS/UNTIMELINESS; TOBACCO;
TOUGHNESS; TREES; TREM-
BLING; UNDESIREABILITY; UN-
STEADINESS; VANITY; VIO-
LENCE; VOICE, HARSH;
WALKING; WEAKNESS; WEARI-
NESS; WHITE; WIND; WORDS,
EFFECT OF; WRINKLES; YOUTH

Bracken, Peg
    ORDER/DISORDER; TRAVEL

Bradbury, Ray
    CRYING; SHOCK; SITTING; TIME

Bradford, Barbara Taylor
    LANDSCAPES; SEX; THUNDER
    AND LIGHTNING

Bradley, Ed
    LEAPING

Bradley, George
    DREAM; LINGERING

Bradstreet, Anne
    POWER; WEAKNESS

Braine, John
    AIR; CHEERFULNESS; COMFORT;
    EASE; EMBRACE; FACE(S); FOR-
    TUNE/MISFORTUNE; GLOOM;
    HAIR; HAPPINESS; IMPARTIAL-
    ITY; KISSES; MONEY; MOON; NE-
    CESSITY; POWER; REALNESS/UN-
    REALNESS; REPETITION;
    ROOMS; SEX; SEXUAL INTERAC-
    TION; SKIN; SMELL; SMILE;
    SPREADING; TREES; WRINKLES;
    WRITERS/WRITING

Brammer, William
    BEGINNINGS AND ENDINGS;
    BIGNESS; BREASTS; IMPOR-
    TANCE/UNIMPORTANCE; INTEN-
    SITY; SITTING; SPEECH PAT-
    TERNS; SUN

Brandeis, Louis D.
    AGREEMENT/DISAGREEMENT;
    MIND DEFINED; PEACEFULNESS

Brando, Marlon
    BODY ORGANS

Brantley, Ben
    SMILES

Bratzlav, Nahman
    WORLD

Brautigan, Richard
    SUN

Brecht, Bertolt
    COLDNESS; COMPLETENESS;
    CONNECTIONS; DESIRE; DISAP-
    PEARANCE; FOG; GLOOM;
    GREED; IMMOBILITY; LEG(S);
    LIES/LIARS; LOVE, DEFINED; RE-
    JECTION; SAFETY; SCREAMS; SIT-
    TING; SPEED

Bremer, Frederika
    MARRIAGE

Brennan, Maeve
    AIR; CHOICES; CITIES; HAIR,
    TEXTURE; PLACES; SKIN; WALK-
    ING

Breslin, Jimmy
    BELIEFS; FLEXIBILITY/INFLEXI-
    BILITY; HABIT; NOSE(S)

Brett, George
    SPORTS

Bridgman, Mary
    TOUGHNESS

Brierly, David
    DIFFICULTY; EYE COLOR; FIRE
    AND SMOKE; HEAT; KISSES;
    PHYSICAL APPEARANCE;
    SHOCK; SMILE

Briggs, Charles F.
    FAMILIARITY

Brinig, Myron
    COLLAPSE; GROWTH

Brinkley, David
    GOSSIP; SPEAKING

Brinnin, John Malcolm
    CRYING; PAUSE

Britt, Stewart Henderson
    ADVERTISING

Broadhurst, George
    IMPOSSIBILITY

Brodkey, Harold
    PERSONAL TRAITS; YELLOW

Brokaw, Tom
    UNDESIREABILITY

Bromfield, Louis
    ATTRACTIVENESS; DEJECTION;
    DISAPPEARANCE; EMPTINESS;
    EXCITEMENT; EYES, BRIGHT; FA-
    CIAL EXPRESSIONS, MISCELLA-

NEOUS; HANDS; HELPLESSNESS;
HOUSES; INCOMPLETENESS;
MUSCLES; OCEAN/OCEAN-
FRONTS; PHYSICAL APPEAR-
ANCE; PRIDE; SILENCE; TRUTH-
NESS/FALSENESS

Bronk, William
    DEATH; SILENCE

Brontë, Charlotte
    BUSYNESS; CALMNESS; CAUSE
    AND EFFECT; DIFFERENCES;
    DISAPPEARANCE; EVIL; EXITS;
    FACIAL EXPRESSIONS, BLANK;
    PALLOR; PERMANENCE; RED;
    TALKATIVENESS; WHITE

Brontë, Emily
    EMOTIONS; GROWTH; IMPOR-
    TANCE/UNIMPORTANCE; LOVE;
    LOVE, DEFINED; MEEKNESS;
    NATURE; SCREAMS; TEARS; UN-
    DESIREABILITY; VIOLENCE

Brooke, James
    STRANGENESS

Brooke, Rupert
    PLACES; SILENCE

Brookes, Warren T.
    DESTRUCTION/DESTRUCTIVE-
    NESS

Brookhiser, Richard
    COMPLETENESS

Brookner, Anita
    APPRECIATION; BEAUTY

Brooks, Albert
    PROFESSIONS

Brooks, David
    WORLD

Brooks, Garth
    DREAM

Brooks, Mel
    BEHAVIOR; CRITICISM, DRA-
    MATIC AND LITERARY; FACIAL
    EXPRESSIONS, MISCELLANEOUS

Brooks, Van Wyck
    ALONENESS

Brothers, Joyce
    CREDIT

Broughton, T. Alan
    HEAD MOVEMENTS

Broun, Heywood
    ATTRACTIVENESS; BASEBALL;
    OPINION; UNDESIREABILITY

Brown, Dee
    TOUGHNESS

Brown, Jean
    TRUTH

Brown, Dr. John
CERTAINTY

Brown, John Mason
CRITICISM, DRAMATIC AND LIT-
ERARY; READERS/READING

Brown, Mary Ward
CLOTHING; DRINKING;
SINGING; SITTING

Brown, Patricia Leigh
VOICE(S)

Brown, Rita Mae
ADVANCING; ALERTNESS; AMBI-
TION; ANGER; ATTENTION;
BREASTS; BURST; BUSINESS;
CHANGE; CLINGING; CLOTH-
ING; CLOUD MOVEMENTS;
CRITICISM; DANCING; DANGER;
DEATH; DESTRUCTION/DE-
STRUCTIVENESS; EXITS; EYES,
BRIGHT; FACIAL COLOR; FACIAL
EXPRESSIONS, MISCELLANEOUS;
FATE; FATNESS; FLOWERS;
GRINS; IMMOBILITY; INNO-
CENCE; KINDNESS; KNOWL-
EDGE; LOVE, DEFINED; MEN
AND WOMEN; MOVEMENT(S);
NATURE; NERVOUSNESS; OPIN-
ION; ORDER/DISORDER; PAIN;
PASSION; PERSONAL TRAITS;
PRIDE; PURSUIT; RAIN; REAP-
PEARANCE; RELATIONSHIP;
ROCKING AND ROLLING; RUN-
NING; SEXUAL INTERACTION;
SHINING; SIMPLICITY; SITTING;
SMILE; SPORTS; SUN; VIRTUE;
VOICE, EFFECT OF; WRIT-
ERS/WRITING

Brown, Rosellen
CONVERSATION; HAIR, COLOR;
IDEAS; IMMOBILITY; LOOKS;
NOISES; ORDER/DISORDER;
SCREAMS; SKIN; SMILE;
SMOOTHNESS; SNOW; TEETH;
THICKNESS; TIME; WEAKNESS

Brown, Suzanne
SKIN

Brown, William
FLATTERY

Browne, Gerald A.
SIMPLICITY; WALKING

Browne, Jackson
PERMANENCE/IMPERMANENCE;
TIME PASSING

Browne, Sir Thomas
MEEKNESS

Browning, Elizabeth Barrett
AGE; BITTERNESS; DULLNESS;
EXPERIENCE; HAIR STYLES;
HELPLESSNESS; HOPE; SAFETY;
TEARS; TONGUE

Browning, Robert
ADVANCING; BLACK; CALM-
NESS; COST; EYE COLOR; INNO-
CENCE; MEEKNESS; SIMILARITY;
TEETH; WASTE

Broyard, Anatole
NATURALNESS

Bryan, C. D. B.
ADVANCING; PROBLEMS AND
SOLUTIONS; SILENCE

Bryan, Henry F.
STAGE AND SCREEN

Bryant, Boudleaux
LOVE

Bryant, William Cullen
DEJECTION

Buchanan, Robert
HARMLESSNESS

Buck, Pearl S.
DISAPPEARANCE

Buckley, Christopher
DIFFICULTY; SENSITIVENESS

Buckman, Peter
STAGE AND SCREEN

Buddha
ERRORS

Bukowski, Charles
ARM(S); CLOTHING, ITS FIT; EM-
BRACE; EYES; FACE(S); HELP-
LESSNESS; RARITY

Bulgakov, Mikhail
THINNESS; VIOLENCE

Bumpus, Jerry
DAY; LIGHTING; MOUTH;
MOUTH, OPEN AND SHUT;
SHADOW; TRUST/MISTRUST; VI-
OLENCE

Bunin, Ivan
BALDNESS; EYES; NOSE(S);
WRINKLES

Bunyan, John
MANKIND

Burgess, Gelett
CALMNESS; IDEAS; MAXIMS,
PROVERBS AND SAYINGS; MEN
AND WOMEN; MOUTH, OPEN
AND SHUT

Burgin, Richard
MEMORY

Burke, Edmund
BEAUTY; FREEDOM; LAWS

Burke, James Lee
ARM(S); ERRORS; EYES; FACE(S);
FACIAL SHAPE; HAIR, COLOR;
HEAD MOVEMENTS; PAIN;
REAPPEARANCE; SMOOTHNESS;
SOFTNESS; THUNDER AND
LIGHTNING

Burke, Thomas
DRINKING

Burke, William Talbot
AMBITION

Burland, Brian
MOVEMENT(S); SNORES

Burnand, Sir Francis C.
HEAT

Burnett, Hallie
ENTHUSIASM; HAIR; REAPPEAR-
ANCE; SOFTNESS

Burnett, W. R.
SAFETY

Burns, John
LOVE, DEFINED

Burns, Robert
DISAPPEARANCE; PLEASURE

Burt, Struthers
BEAUTY DEFINED

Burton, Richard E.
PASSION

Burton, Robert
CAUTION; CLINGING; CLOSE-
NESS; ILLNESS; OBVIOUSNESS;
SWEETNESS

Busch, Niven
DARKNESS; DEJECTION; GRINS;
LEG(S); PAIN; SITTING; SKIN

Bush, Katherine
JUMPING; LIPS

Butler, Samuel (novelist; 1835–1902)
ART AND LITERATURE; DEATH;
DEATH DEFINED; FRIENDSHIP,
DEFINED; LIFE; LIFE DEFINED;
MONEY; OPINION; TIME;
TRUTH; VIRTUE; WORDS DE-
FINED; YOUTH

Butler, Samuel (poet; 1612–1680)
CERTAINTY; DEATH, FINALITY
OF

Buxton, Charles
PREPAREDNESS

Byrd, Robert
GOSSIP

Byron, Lord
AGE; ANGER; ATTENTION; BEAUTY; BIGNESS; BLUE; BLUSHES; BRIGHTNESS; CLING-ING; CROWDS; CRUELTY; DARK-NESS; EYE COLOR; EYE EXPRES-SIONS, MISCELLANEOUS; FRIENDSHIP, DEFINED; HEART(S); LOVE; MARRIAGE; MODESTY; SCREAMS; SILENCE; TEARS

C

Cabanis, Dr. Pierre J. G.
AGE

Caesar Augustus, SPEED

Cain
James, BUSYNESS

Caine, Lynn
EMOTIONS

Calderóon de la Barca, Pedro
POWER

Calisher, Hortense
ADVANCING; AWKWARDNESS; CHILDREN; CHOICES; CITIES; ECONOMICS; ENERGY; FACE(S); GRINS; HANDS; MONEY; PEO-PLE, INTERACTION; PLACES; RE-MOTENESS; ROAD SCENES; SAD-NESS; SCRUTINY; SEASONS; SILENCE; SLEEP; SMILE; TIME; TRUTH; VEHICLES; VOICE, HARSH; VOICE(S); WORD(S); WORDS DEFINED

Calvino, Italo
BIRDS; DREAM; IDEAS; STARS; THINNESS

Camoin, François
CRYING; DISCONTENT; ECO-NOMICS; FACIAL EXPRESSIONS, MISCELLANEOUS; FEAR; MUS-CLES; NOSE(S); OBJECTS, MISC.; PHYSICAL FEELINGS; READ-ERS/READING; SKIN; SKY; STOM-ACH

Campbell, Joseph
AGE

Campbell, R. Wright
ARM(S); BIRDS; CALMNESS; CHIN; EXCITEMENT; FACTS; FEAR; FINGERS; GREEN; IMMO-BILITY; LOOKS; NAMES; NOSE(S); OBJECTS, MISC.; PAIN; SERIOUSNESS; SEXUAL INTER-ACTION; SHAME; SHARPNESS;

SKIN; SMILE; SMOOTHNESS; SPEAKING; TEETH; TOBACCO; TONGUE; TREES; VOICE(S); VOICE, WEAK; WATCHFULNESS

Campbell, Ramsey
SIGHS

Campbell, Robert
ANGER; BELIEFS; BODY; CALM-NESS; CHIN; CLOTHING; COM-PLEXION; CRYING; DARKNESS; EYE MOVEMENTS; EYES; EYES, BRIGHT; FACIAL COLOR; FACIAL DETAILS; FACIAL EXPRESSIONS, MISCELLANEOUS; FRIENDSHIP; GRINS; HOUSES; IRRITABLE-NESS/IRRITATING; LAUGHTER; LOOKS; MONEY; NOISES; NOSE(S); PEOPLE, INTERAC-TION; PERSONALITY PROFILES; SMILE; STARES; VOICE(S)

Campion, Nardi Reeder
DESTRUCTION/DESTRUCTIVE-NESS

Campion, Thomas
EYEBROWS

Camus, Albert
BREATHING; CITIES; FACIAL DE-TAILS; NIGHT; NOISES; PAIN; RAIN; SPEAKING; STRENGTH; TIME; TRUTH

Canby, Henry Seidel
WRITERS/WRITING

Canby, Vincent
CANDOR; CHEERFULNESS; COMPLEXITY; CRITICISM, DRA-MATIC AND LITERARY; EXCITE-MENT; PROBLEMS AND SOLU-TIONS; RARITY; RISK; STRANGENESS; SUCCESS/FAIL-URE

Canfield, Dorothy
BELIEVABILITY; BURST; CLING-ING; DISAPPEARANCE; ENERGY; FACE(S); FEAR; FLOWERS; HAIR, TEXTURE; HELPLESSNESS; HUMOR; LIPS; LYING; MOVE-MENT(S); NERVOUSNESS; PHYSI-CAL FEELINGS; RED; ROAD SCENES; SMELL; STANDING; SWEAT; TENSION; THOUGHTS; WEAKNESS; WIND

Canin, Ethan
AIR

Canning, George
PURPOSEFULNESS

Canning, Victor
NERVOUSNESS; VOICE(S)

Canton, William
GLIMMER, GLITTER AND GLOSS

Cantor, Eddie
SWEETNESS

Capa, Robert
WAR

Capote, Truman
ABSORBABILITY; ACTIVENESS; ALONENESS; BEAUTY; BROWN; CHANGE; CHEEKS; CLOTHING ACCESSORIES; CLOUDS; CON-VERSATION; CORRESPON-DENCE; EYE COLOR; EYE MOVE-MENTS; EYEBROWS; FACIAL DETAILS; FACIAL EXPRESSIONS, MISCELLANEOUS; FRAGILITY; GLOOM; GOSSIP; HATRED; HEAT; INSULT; KISSES; LEAVES; LEG(S); NIGHT; NOSE(S); PAIN; PERSON-ALITY PROFILES; PHYSICAL AP-PEARANCE; PLACES; SEX; SEX-UAL INTERACTION; SNOW; SUDDENNESS; TALKATIVENESS; TALLNESS; TEARS; VOICE(S); WEARINESS; WIND

Cardozo, Benjamin
RICHES

Carleton, Will
HEAT

Carlisle, Kitty
AGE

Carlson, Ron
SPORTS

Carlyle, Thomas
ABUNDANCE; BEAUTY; CONTI-NUITY; FACE(S); GREEN; IMPOR-TANCE/UNIMPORTANCE; SI-LENCE; SPEECHMAKING; TALKATIVENESS; VIRTUE; VOICE, HARSH; WORK; WRIT-ERS/WRITING

Carman, Bliss
ANGER; TREES

Carr, John Dickson
FACIAL EXPRESSIONS, MISCEL-LANEOUS; OBJECTS, MISC.; SMILE

Carrel, Alexis
RELIGION

Carroll, Lewis
ANGER; ATTENTION; BLACK; DISAPPEARANCE; EATING AND DRINKING; EYES, BRIGHT;

FACE(S); QUESTIONS AND AN-
SWERS; WORDS, EFFECT OF

Carruth, Hayden
  LEAVES; MANKIND; MEMORY;
  MOON; SOFTNESS; WEATHER

Carson, Anthony
  FACIAL EXPRESSIONS, MISCEL-
  LANEOUS

Carter, Angela
  BARENESS; BEAUTY; BIRDS;
  BODY; COLORS; CRYING; EN-
  ERGY; FACIAL SHAPE; FOOD
  AND DRINK; HAIR, CURLY; HEAT;
  HELPLESSNESS; HOUSES;
  MOUTH; MOVEMENT(S);
  NOISES; PERSONALITY PRO-
  FILES; ROOMS; SKIN; SUN; SUR-
  PRISE; TALLNESS; VOICE, MUSIC
  RELATED; VOICE(S); WALKING;
  WEATHER

Carter, Dyson
  AGE

Carter, Hodding, III
  WASTE

Carton, May
  ABANDONMENT

Cartwright, Justin
  APPEARANCE, BEHAVIOR

Carvell, Steven
  ADVICE

Carver, Ada Jack
  MOVEMENT(S); SKY

Carver, Raymond
  BEARING

Cary, Joyce
  BREATHING; CHIN; CLOTHING;
  CLOTHING ACCESSORIES;
  CLOUDS; COLDNESS; COLLAPSE;
  DARKNESS; FACE(S); FACIAL DE-
  TAILS; FACIAL EXPRESSIONS,
  MISCELLANEOUS; FAME; FIRM-
  NESS; FROWNS; GROANS AND
  WHISPERS; HAIR, CURLY; HA-
  TRED; IMMOBILITY; LAND-
  SCAPES; LAWYERS; LEG(S); LIPS;
  MOON; MOVEMENT(S); MUS-
  TACHE(S); NOSE(S); PAIN; PER-
  MANENCE; PERSISTENCE; PHYS-
  ICAL APPEARANCE; RAIN;
  SCREAMS; SHAPE; SITTING; SKY;
  SKY COLOR; SNOW; TREES; VE-
  HICLES; VOICE, MUSIC RE-
  LATED; YELLOW

Casals, Pablo
  MUSIC

Casper, Leonard
  HEARTBEAT; LOVE, DEFINED;
  VOICE, HARSH

Cassill, R. V.
  BLUSHES; CLOTHING; DAY;
  FRAGILITY; GROWTH; HAIR,
  COLOR; MARRIAGE; MOUTH;
  MOVEMENT(S); REMOTENESS;
  SECRECY; SKIN; SMILE

Cather, Willa
  ALONENESS; BEARING; BIRDS;
  BODY; BREATHING; CHEERFUL-
  NESS; EMOTIONS; EMPTINESS;
  EYES; EYES, BRIGHT; FACE(S);
  FACIAL DETAILS; FEAR; HAIR,
  COLOR; HAIR, TEXTURE; HAPPI-
  NESS; HELPLESSNESS; IMMOBIL-
  ITY; LEAPING; LEAVES; LIGHT-
  ING; MEMORY; NOSE(S);
  SCRUTINY; SEASONS; SHOUL-
  DERS; SIMPLICITY; SKIN; STARS;
  SUN; TEETH; TOBACCO; TRAN-
  SIENCE; TREES; VOICE, MUSIC
  RELATED; VOICE(S); YOUTH

Cats, Jacob
  FOOLISHNESS

Cavell, Mary Ladd
  FATE; PERSONALITY PROFILES;
  WISDOM

Cecil, Lord David
  PURPOSEFULNESS

Celine, Louis-Ferdinand
  LEG(S); RAIN

Centlivre, Mrs.
  BEHAVIOR

Cervantes, Miguel de
  BEAUTY DEFINED; DARKNESS;
  DISINTEGRATION; FACE(S);
  FIRMNESS; HAIR; INCOMPLETE-
  NESS; KNOWLEDGE; PURITY; SE-
  CRECY

Chabon, Michael
  DISPERSAL; GLOOM; HAIR;
  NERVOUSNESS; PALLOR; SERI-
  OUSNESS; SKY; SKY COLOR;
  TENSION; THUNDER AND
  LIGHTNING

Chamberlain, Joseph
  GREATNESS

Chamfort, Sebastien Roch Nicolas de
  LOVE

Chandler, Raymond
  ABUNDANCE; AGILITY; AGREE-
  MENT/DISAGREEMENT; ALONE-
  NESS; BALDNESS; BEAUTY; BE-

LONGING; CHIN; CLOTHING;
COLDNESS; CONSPICUOUSNESS;
DIFFICULTY; DRINKING; DULL-
NESS; EASE; EMPTINESS; EYE EX-
PRESSIONS, MISCELLANEOUS;
EYES; FACE; FACIAL EXPRES-
SIONS, BLANK; FACIAL EXPRES-
SIONS, MISCELLANEOUS; FA-
CIAL EXPRESSIONS, SERIOUS;
FEAR; GENTLENESS; GUILT;
HAIR; HAIR, COLOR; HANDS;
HAPPINESS; HARMLESSNESS;
HEAT; HUNGER; IMPOR-
TANCE/UNIMPORTANCE; INAP-
PROPRIATENESS; MOON;
MOUTH; MOUTH, OPEN AND
SHUT; MOVEMENT(S); NOISES;
ORDER/DISORDER; PEACEFUL-
NESS; PERSONALITY PROFILES;
PHYSICAL FEELINGS; PROFES-
SIONS; RARITY; REPETITION; RE-
SERVE; ROARS; ROCKING AND
ROLLING; SAFETY; SEX; SI-
LENCE; SLOWNESS; SMILES;
SMOOTHNESS; SOFTNESS;
SPEECH PATTERNS; SPREADING;
STYLE; SUN; SUNSET; SWEAT;
SWEETNESS; TALLNESS; THIN-
NESS; UNATTRACTIVENESS; UN-
CERTAINTY; VIOLENCE; VOICE,
HARSH; VOICE(S); WEAKNESS

Chapin, E. H.
  KINDNESS

Chapman, George
  ENVY; FLATTERY

Charron, Pierre
  DEJECTION

Chase, Alexander
  PEOPLE, INTERACTION; PRO-
  FESSIONS; STAGE AND SCREEN

Chase, Joan
  CHANGE; COLORS; DAY; EN-
  ERGY; FACIAL DETAILS; HAPPI-
  NESS; SMILE; WHITE

Chase, Mary Ellen
  CLINGING; LEG(S)

Chateaubriand, François René de
  PASSION

Chatterton, Ruth
  BLACK; PAIN

Chaucer, Geoffrey
  ACTIVENESS; AGILITY; BEAUTY;
  BRIGHTNESS; BROWN; FATNESS;
  FRESHNESS; GRAY; NOISES;

STRAIGHTNESS; THINNESS; WHITE

Cheever, David W.
ENTHUSIASM

Cheever, John
BASEBALL; BEGINNINGS AND ENDINGS; BODY; CAUSE AND EFFECT; CLARITY; CLINGING; CLOUDS; DESIRE; DESTRUCTION/DESTRUCTIVENESS; EXCITEMENT; EYEBROWS; FACIAL EXPRESSIONS, MISCELLANEOUS; FEAR; FLEXIBILITY/INFLEXIBILITY; GRAY; HAIR; JOY; LOVE; MEMORY; NATURE; PERSONALITY PROFILES; RAIN; ROAD SCENES; ROOMS; SEX; SHAPE; SKIN; SKY; SLEEP; SMELL; SMILE; SPEECH PATTERNS; TREES

Chekhov, Anton
ABANDONMENT; ALONENESS; BELIEVABILITY; BODY; CAUTION; CLINGING; DRINKING; EASE; ELUSIVENESS; EYE MOVEMENTS; FATE; FRUSTRATION; HAPPINESS; HEAD MOVEMENTS; IDLENESS; LIFE; LIPS; MATHEMATICS AND SCIENCE; MONEY; NOSE(S); RESERVE; STARS; THINNESS; TREES; USEFULNESS/USELESSNESS

Chernoff, Maxine
TIMELINESS/UNTIMELINESS

Chesterfield, Lord
ART AND LITERATURE; BEAUTY DEFINED; CHARACTER; KNOWLEDGE; LANGUAGE; MIND DEFINED; PLEASURE; REPETITION; RESERVE; VIRTUE; YOUTH

Chesterton, G. K.
AGILITY; ART AND LITERATURE; BELIEVABILITY; CHEERFULNESS; DIFFERENCES; DISINTEGRATION; EMPTINESS; FEAR; FLEXIBILITY/INFLEXIBILITY; GROWTH; HISTORY; HONESTY; IMMOBILITY; MAXIMS, PROVERBS AND SAYINGS; MOON; MOUTH, OPEN AND SHUT; PALLOR; PAST, THE; PERSISTENCE; POLITICS/POLITICIANS; REAPPEARANCE; ROCKING AND ROLLING; SHARPNESS; SNOW; SOCIETY; SPEECH PAT-

TERNS; STALENESS; SUCCESS/FAILURE; THRIFT; WHITE; WRINKLES

Chettle, Henry
PALLOR; WHITE

Child, Desmond
LOVE

Childs, Julia
WRITERS/WRITING

Chiles, Lawton
TIMELINESS/UNTIMELINESS

Chopin, Kate
BEWILDERMENT

Christie, Agatha
BUSINESS; MIND

Chrysostam, John
Saint, ENVY

Churchill, Charles
FORTUNE/MISFORTUNE

Churchill, Winston
CHARACTERISTICS, NATIONAL; DANGER; POLITICS/POLITICIANS

Churgin, Yaakov
DISINTEGRATION

Chute, Carolyn
ARM(S); CLOTHING; FATNESS; LAUGHTER; MUSTACHE(S); NOISES; NOSE(S); SMELL; VOICE, HARSH

Ciardi, John
ADVANTAGEOUSNESS; CERTAINTY; GLIMMER, GLITTER AND GLOSS

Cibber, Colley
IRRITABLENESS/IRRITATING; SILENCE

Cicero
BOOKS; MIND DEFINED

Cieply, Michael
PROBLEMS AND SOLUTIONS

Ciment, Jill
IMPARTIALITY; MOVEMENT(S); PERMANENCE; SCRUTINY

Claiborne, Robert
WORDS DEFINED

Clampitt, Amy
RAIN

Clark, Brian
ENTRANCES AND EXITS

Clark, Carol
PROBLEMS AND SOLUTIONS

Clark, Eleanor
ATTENTION; CONTINUITY; EMPTINESS; SMILE; TALKATIVENESS

Clark, Frank A.
CRITICISM

Clark, Kenneth P.
PRIDE

Clarke, Eleanor
ARM(S)

Clarke, John
CLEVERNESS

Clayton, John J.
ENTRANCES AND EXITS; POLITICS/POLITICIANS

Cleaver, Eldridge
VIOLENCE

Clement, Saint
RICHES

Clendinen, Dudley
DISAPPEARANCE

Clift, Eleanor
POLITICS/POLITICIANS

Clines, Francis X.
PLEASURE

Coates, Robert M.
CAUTION

Cobb, Irvin S.
ABILITY; BREVITY; BROWN; FORTUNE/MISFORTUNE; FREEDOM; MOUTH; PERSONALITY PROFILES; SCREAMS; TALLNESS

Coburn, Marcia Froelke
LOVE

Cocteau, Jean
ART AND LITERATURE; MOUTH

Coffin, Harold
ART AND LITERATURE; PROBLEMS AND SOLUTIONS

Coffin, Robert Tristram
RED

Cohen, Arthur A.
ALERTNESS; BIGNESS; BUSINESS; CHEEKS; CLINGING; COMPLETENESS; CONNECTIONS; FACIAL COLOR; FRAGILITY; HAIR STYLES; HANDS; HARSHNESS; LOOKS; MUSCLES; PAIN; POETS/POETRY; POVERTY; PURPOSEFULNESS; PURSUIT; SADNESS; SEXUAL INTERACTION; SILENCE; SPEED; STALENESS; TALLNESS; TEARS; VOICE(S)

Cohen, Eddie
NOISES

Cohen, Leonard
CLEANLINESS; FREEDOM

Cohen, Shalom
MIND DEFINED

Cohen, William S.
REMOTENESS

Coleridge, Hartley
DEATH; SOUL

Coleridge, Mary
ALONENESS

Coleridge, Samuel Taylor
ADVICE; CALMNESS; CHARAC-
TERISTICS, NATIONAL; CLARITY;
DRINKING; EXPERIENCE;
GREATNESS; HAIR, COLOR;
IDLENESS; JOY; LAWS; LOVE;
MAXIMS, PROVERBS AND SAY-
INGS; REGRET

Colette
AGITATION; BENDING/BENT;
BLUSHES; BREASTS; EYE EXPRES-
SIONS, MISCELLANEOUS;
FACE(S); FACIAL EXPRESSIONS,
MISCELLANEOUS; FRIENDSHIP;
HATRED; IMMOBILITY; LIGHT-
NESS; MOUNTAINS; NATURE;
NECK; NOSE(S); PERSONALITY
PROFILES; PHYSICAL FEELINGS;
SHINING; STRAIGHTNESS;
TREMBLING; WALKING

Colien, Arthur A.
FACE(S)

Collins, Gail
SPEED

Collins, John Churton
MEMORY

Colton, Charles Caleb
AGE; BENDING/BENT; BODY;
CRITICISM; DEATH DEFINED;
DISHONESTY; EVIL; GREATNESS;
LAWS; MOTIVATION; OPINION;
POLITICS/POLITICIANS; POWER;
PRIDE; RELIGION; TRUTH

Colvin, Audrey
MARRIAGE

Colwin, Laurie
ABILITY; BELONGING; CLOTH-
ING; DIFFICULTY; EMOTIONS;
EYES; FROWNS; HAIR, TEXTURE;
HEAT; HOUSES; IRRITABLE-
NESS/IRRITATING; LANDSCAPES;
LOVE, DEFINED; LOYALTY/DIS-
LOYALTY; MEMORY; ORDER/DIS-
ORDER; PHYSICAL APPEAR-
ANCE; PROMPTNESS;

QUESTIONS AND ANSWERS; RE-
ALIZATION; REMOTENESS; SEN-
SITIVENESS

Combe, George
PLACES

Conant, James
FREEDOM

Condon, Richard
FACIAL EXPRESSIONS, SERIOUS

Connelly, Michael
FIRMNESS; INFORMATION; MUS-
CLES

Confucius
EDUCATION; HEART(S); VIRTUE;
WISDOM

Congreve, William
ANGER; BEAUTY; GOSSIP; LOVE;
LOVE, DEFINED; MEN AND
WOMEN

Conklin, Hilda
GAIETY

Connell, Richard
FACE(S); IRRITABLENESS/IRRI-
TATING

Conrad, Joseph
ALONENESS; BITTERNESS;
BREASTS; CLINGING; CONVER-
SATION; DRYNESS; EASE; FACIAL
EXPRESSIONS, BLANK; FEAR;
FIRE AND SMOKE; IRRITABLE-
NESS/IRRITATING; LIGHTNESS;
MOON; MOUTH; NIGHT; NOISES;
PHYSICAL FEELINGS; REALIZA-
TION; RUNNING; SADNESS;
SEASCAPES; SENSITIVENESS;
SHARPNESS; SILENCE; SPEAK-
ING; STANDING; STRAIGHTNESS;
TALLNESS; TONGUE; TREM-
BLING; TRUST/MISTRUST; USE-
FULNESS/USELESSNESS;
VOICE(S)

Conroy, Frank
AGITATION; CONTENTMENT;
DISAPPEARANCE; FACIAL EX-
PRESSIONS, BLANK; FEAR; FIN-
GERS; HEAT;
IMPORTANCE/UNIMPORTANCE;
LEAPING; NOISES; SHAPE;
SPEECH PATTERNS; TREES

Conroy, Pat
ABANDONMENT; ACTIVENESS;
ARM(S); ART AND LITERATURE;
ATTRACTION; BEARING; BODY;
BREATHING; BUSYNESS; CON-
TEMPT; DULLNESS; ENERGY;

FINGERS; FOOD AND DRINK;
FOOTBALL; FRAGILITY;
GROWTH; INSECTS; JUMPING;
LAUGHTER; LEAPING; LEG(S);
MADNESS; MOON; MUSIC;
NOSE(S); PERSONALITY PRO-
FILES; PROTRUSION; REJEC-
TION; RELATIONSHIP; RESERVE;
SILENCE; SKIN; SMELL; TEARS;
VOICE, EFFECT OF; VOICE,
SOFT; WALKING

Considine, Bob
BOXING AND WRESTLING

Cook, Joseph
GOVERNMENT

Cooke, Alistair
COMMONPLACE; INNOCENCE;
JUMPING; SUDDENNESS

Cooley, Charles Horton
VANITY

Coolidge, Susan
DISAPPEARANCE

Coomer, Joe
BARENESS; DAY; KISSES; MOVE-
MENT(S); SKIN; STARES; TEETH;
WIND

Cooper, Anthony Ashley
INTOLERANCE

Cooper, Jilly
AVAILABILITY; BREASTS; COL-
LAPSE; COMPLEXION; EYE-
BROWS; FACIAL COLOR; FACIAL
EXPRESSIONS, MISCELLANEOUS;
HUNGER; LEG(S); MIST; MOON;
NECK; PROTECTIVENESS; RAIN;
RISING; ROOMS; SENSITIVE-
NESS; SEX; SKY; SMELL; SNOW;
SUN; TREES; TREMBLING

Cooperman, Melvin I.
DREAM; STAGE AND SCREEN

Coover, Robert
AGITATION

Copeland, Aaron
MUSIC

Coppard, A. E.
BEHAVIOR; POLITICS/POLITI-
CIANS; SILENCE

Cornwall, Barry
BRIGHTNESS

Cornwell, Patricia
HAIR; NERVOUSNESS

Corrigan, E. Gerald
ECONOMICS

Cortázar, Julio
CROWDS; MEN AND WOMEN; PLEASURE

Cotgrave, John
FATNESS

Cotgrave, Randle
HABIT

Cotton, Charles
WHITE

Coughlin, T. Glen
BASEBALL; BREASTS; CLINGING; FACIAL DETAILS; HEAD MOVEMENTS; REJECTION; WORDS, EFFECT OF

Cousins, Norman
FREEDOM

Coverdale, Miles
CLARITY

Coward, Noel
BEGINNINGS AND ENDINGS; CLEANLINESS; COLDNESS; FEAR; HAIR STYLES; HAPPINESS; MEMORY; REALIZATION; SPEED; WORDS, EFFECT OF; WORK

Cowles, Virginia
PURSUIT

Cowley, Abraham
FAME; LIFE DEFINED

Cowley, Hanna
VANITY

Cowley, Malcolm
DAY; GREEN; HEAVINESS; LIFE; SITTING; SLEEP; SMILE; SPORTS; TREMBLING

Cowper, William
ABUNDANCE; CONVERSATION; COURAGE; FOOLISHNESS; HARMLESSNESS; KINDNESS; LIFE; SILENCE; STRENGTH

Cox, Marcelene
CHILDREN

Cox, Palmer
BENDING/BENT; DISAPPEARANCE

Coyle, Lee
GROWTH

Crabbe, George
GREEN; LIES/LIARS

Craig, M. S.
MONEY

Crane, Hart
BRIGHTNESS; CONTINUITY; GLIMMER, GLITTER AND GLOSS; HANDS; MODESTY; REGULARITY/IRREGULARITY

Crane, Stephen
ADVANCING; BITTERNESS; COLLAPSE; CURSES; EMOTIONS; FIGHTING; GOSSIP; HANDS; HOUSES; INSECTS; LOOKS; LYING; OBVIOUSNESS; OCEAN/OCEANFRONTS; RESTLESSNESS; ROOMS; RUNNING; STRUGGLE; TREES; UNSTEADINESS

Crawford, F. Marion
MEN AND WOMEN

Crèvecoeur, Michel Guillaume Jean de
MANKIND

Crier, John
EXITS

Crockett, David
ABILITY

Croly, George
DISPERSAL

Cronin, A. J.
MIST; REMOTENESS

Cronyn, Hume
AGE

Crowell, Robert
FRIENDSHIP

Crowninshield, Francis W.
PAIN

Crumley, James
ADVANCING; AGITATION; AIMLESSNESS; AIR; ARM(S); AWKWARDNESS; BEARD; BEARING; BEWILDERMENT; BODY ORGANS; BREASTS; BREATHING; CAUSE AND EFFECT; CLOTHING, ITS FIT; COLLAPSE; CONVERSATION; CRITICISM; CROWDS; CRYING; DARKNESS; DISAPPEARANCE; DRINKING; EATING AND DRINKING; ENTRANCES AND EXITS; EYE COLOR; EYE EXPRESSIONS, MISCELLANEOUS; EYEBROWS; FACE(S); FACIAL SHAPE; FATNESS; FINGERS; FIRMNESS; FOOTBALL; GLIMMER, GLITTER AND GLOSS; GREEN; GRINS; GROANS AND WHISPERS; HEAD MOVEMENTS; HOUSES; INAPPROPRIATENESS; INSECTS; LAUGHTER; LEG(S); LIES/LIARS; LINGERING; MEN AND WOMEN; MOVEMENT(S); MUSTACHE(S); NECK; OCEAN/OCEANFRONTS;

PEOPLE, INTERACTION; PINK; PLACES; POLITICS/POLITICIANS; PURSUIT; QUESTIONS AND ANSWERS; RAIN; RISING; SITTING; SMILE; SMOOTHNESS; SPEED; STORIES; SUN; TIME; USEFULNESS/USELESSNESS; VEHICLES; VIOLENCE; VOICE, HARSH; WATCHFULNESS; WEARINESS

Culff, Robert
ALERTNESS; BEARING; DEJECTION; DESIRABILITY; TREES

Cullen, Countee
TURNING AND TWISTING

Culross, Donald
CHILDREN

cummings, e. e.
GREEN; MOON; PINK

Cuomo, Mario M.
BELIEVABILITY

Curley, Daniel
ARM MOVEMENTS; LOOKS

Currie, Bonnie
INTOLERANCE

Currie, Ellen
AVAILABILITY; HAIR

Curtis, G. W.
LOVE

Cushman, Charlotte
ART AND LITERATURE

Cussler, Clive
BODY; CHARACTERISTICS, NATIONAL; ELUSIVENESS; ENTRANCES AND EXITS; EYE EXPRESSIONS, MISCELLANEOUS; FACIAL EXPRESSIONS, SERIOUS; FIRMNESS; IMPOSSIBILITY; OCEAN/OCEANFRONTS; PAIN; SCREAMS; SLEEP; SMILE

D

Dahl, Roald
BEHAVIOR; CAUTION; CLOTHING ACCESSORIES; FINGERS; GLIMMER, GLITTER AND GLOSS; HAIR, TEXTURE; HEAD MOVEMENTS; MOUTH; QUESTIONS AND ANSWERS

Dale, Celia
HEARTBEAT; SELF CONFIDENCE

Daly, Arnold
GOLF

Dancy, John
CAUTION

Daniel, Samuel
  BEAUTY DEFINED
Daniloff, Nicholas S.
  WEARINESS
Darden, Ellington
  IMPOSSIBILITY
Darling, Ron
  SELF CONFIDENCE
Darrow, Clarence
  LAWS
Darwin, Charles R.
  LANGUAGE
Dass, Ram
  HANDS; THOUGHTS
Daugherty, Paul
  PLACES
Daugherty, Tracy
  WIND
Davenant, Sir William
  BIGNESS; SILENCE; SLEEP
Davenport, Guy
  IDEAS
David, Henry
  ACTIONS
David, Rhys
  MANNERS
Davidson, Justin
  CRITICISM; CRITICISM, DRA-
  MATIC AND LITERARY
Davies, Robertson
  DISAPPOINTMENT; HEALTH;
  MEN AND WOMEN; MUSIC
Davies, Tom
  LAUGHTER
Davis, Bette
  SELF CONFIDENCE
Davis, Bob
  GROWTH
Davis, Richard Harding
  EMPTINESS
Day, Clarence
  ANGER
Day, Edward Parsons
  AGE; BOOKS
Day, Holman
  GOSSIP
De Casseres, Benjamin
  GREATNESS
de la Mare, Walter
  BREATHING; CLEVERNESS; CON-
  VERSATION; EXPERIENCE; FA-
  CIAL COLOR; HAPPINESS;
  HEARTBEAT; IMMOBILITY; NATU-
  RALNESS; NOSE(S); REMOTE-
  NESS; SILENCE; THOUGHTS

de la Roche, Mazo
  CLOTHING; EYES; GROWTH;
  HEALTH; MEMORY; RAIN; REAL-
  IZATION; RELIABILITY/UNRELIA-
  BILITY; SMOOTHNESS; SPREAD-
  ING; STRENGTH; WEAKNESS
de la Torre, Lillian
  SKIN
De Vries, Peter
  BOOKS; BRIGHTNESS; EATING
  AND DRINKING; EMBRACE; EYE-
  BROWS; FATNESS; FROWNS;
  GOSSIP; GROWTH; HAIR, CURLY;
  HAND MOVEMENTS; HAND-
  WRITING; HEAD MOVEMENTS;
  LAUGHTER; LEG(S); MOUTH;
  PARENTHOOD; SEXUAL INTER-
  ACTION; SITTING; SNOW; TALL-
  NESS; TREMBLING; VEHICLES;
  WORLD
Deal, Babs H.
  EMPTINESS; GLOOM; HEAT; IN-
  NOCENCE; MEMORY;
  ORDER/DISORDER; TRUTH-
  NESS/FALSENESS; WORD(S)
Deal, Borden
  AGITATION; CALMNESS; CON-
  TEMPT; EYE EXPRESSIONS, MIS-
  CELLANEOUS; EYES; FACIAL DE-
  TAILS; FEAR; FUTILITY; GAIETY;
  LOOKS; MOUTH; PHYSICAL
  FEELINGS; QUESTIONS AND AN-
  SWERS; RUNNING; SLEEP;
  SMOOTHNESS; TALLNESS; TIME;
  VANITY; VOICE(S)
Debussy, Claude
  MUSIC
Defoe, Daniel
  CERTAINTY
Degas, Edgar
  ART AND LITERATURE
Deighton, Len
  FACIAL EXPRESSIONS, BLANK;
  UNSTEADINESS
Dekker, Thomas
  AGE; BLACK; CRITICISM, DRA-
  MATIC AND LITERARY; KIND-
  NESS
Delgado, Ramon
  FORMALITY
Delmar, Vina
  MEMORY
Deloney, Thomas
  LAWS

Deming, Richard
  LEG(S)
Democritus
  SEX
Demophilus
  ADVICE; CHILDREN
Denby, David
  CHOICES; CITIES; MEN AND
  WOMEN; MIST; REMOTENESS;
  SHADOW; SHAME; SMELL;
  STRANGENESS
Denby, Edwin
  PLACES
Denham, Sir John
  ACTIONS; AMBITION; SHYNESS
Denham, Michael
  BUSYNESS; FIRMNESS
Denker, Henry
  BEARING
Desai, Anita
  SCREAMS
Descartes, Rene
  BOOKS; TRAVEL
Deschanel, Zooey
  LONELINESS
DeSilva, Bruce
  ABILITY; BEAUTY; SHARPNESS
Deutsch, Babette
  AGE; AGILITY; BIRDS; BLACK;
  COLORS; CONVERSATION; DAY;
  FEROCITY; FINGERS; FOOD AND
  DRINK; FURNITURE AND FUR-
  NISHINGS; HEAT; LIFE; NAMES;
  NATURALNESS; POETS/POETRY;
  PROMPTNESS; REMOTENESS; SE-
  CRECY; SHARPNESS; SMALL-
  NESS; SOFTNESS; SURPRISE;
  TOUGHNESS
Dewey, John
  POLITICS/POLITICIANS
Dexter, Timothy
  APPRECIATION
Diana, Princess
  STUPIDITY
Diaphenia
  BEAUTY
Dickens, Charles
  ALONENESS; ANGER; ANXIETY;
  ATMOSPHERE; BEHAVIOR; BIRDS;
  CLEVERNESS; CLINGING; COL-
  LAPSE; CRYING; DESTRUC-
  TION/DESTRUCTIVENESS; DIS-
  APPEARANCE; DULLNESS;
  EATING AND DRINKING; EYE
  MOVEMENTS; FACIAL COLOR;

FIRMNESS; FLEXIBILITY/INFLEX-IBILITY; FOOLISHNESS; IDEAS; KINDNESS; LANDSCAPES; LIGHTNESS; MIND DEFINED; MOVEMENT(S); MUSIC; NOISES; PEOPLE, INTERACTION; PER-SONALITY PROFILES; PROBLEMS AND SOLUTIONS; RAIN; REJEC-TION; SCREAMS; SHARPNESS; SI-LENCE; SKIN; SLEEP; STUPIDITY

Dickey, James
ACTIONS; BRIGHTNESS; CON-NECTIONS; EYEBROWS; SI-LENCE; TREES

Dickinson, Emily
BOOKS; FIGHTING; SILENCE; TRUTH; VISABILITY; WIND; WORD(S)

Diderot, Denis
KISSES; MOVEMENT(S); WORDS DEFINED

Diehl, William
ABSURDITY; ANGER; BALDNESS; BEARING; BODY; BURST; CHIN; CHOICES; CLOTHING, ITS FIT; COLDNESS; COURAGE; CRU-ELTY; DULLNESS; EDUCATION; ELUSIVENESS; EYE MOVE-MENTS; EYES; FUTILITY; GLOOM; GRAY; GUILT; NAMES; NECK; NOISES; ORDER/DISOR-DER; PERSONAL TRAITS; PERVA-SIVENESS; PROTRUSION; REPE-TITION; RESERVE; SCREAMS; SMOOTHNESS; THOUGHTS; TIME; VIOLENCE; VOICE, SOFT; WORD(S)

Dieter, William
BEHAVIOR; DARKNESS; HAIR, TEXTURE; MOON; NIGHT; VEHI-CLES

Dietrich, Marlene
PEOPLE INTERACTIONS

Dietz, Howard
INSULT

Digby, Sir Kenelm
PALLOR

Dillard, R. H. W.
GRINS

Diller, Phyllis
FUTILITY

Dilwyn, Lewis W.
REGRET

Dimnet, Ernest
BOOKS

Dinesen, Isak
ADVANCING; AIR; ATTENTION; ATTRACTION; BEARING; BLUSHES; BODY; CALMNESS; CLINGING; IDEAS; INNOCENCE; JEWELRY; LEAVES; MIND; PLEAS-URE; PROTECTIVENESS; SEASCAPES; SECRECY; SIMPLIC-ITY; SPEED; SUCCESS/FAILURE; SUN; SWEETNESS; VOICE, MUSIC RELATED; WRINKLES

Disraeli, Benjamin
AIR; ALONENESS; BEARING; BOOKS; CRITICISM, DRAMATIC AND LITERARY; FLATTERY; WIT; WRITERS/WRITING

Dixon, W. Macneile
NATURE

Djilas, Milovan
REALNESS/UNREALNESS

Dobell, Sidney
GREEN

Doddridge, Sir John
LAWS

Dolnick, Ben
SPREADING

Dominick, Peter
POLITICS/POLITICIANS

Donleavy, Brian
BREASTS; DISAPPEARANCE

Donleavy, J. P.
CLOSENESS; EYEBROWS

Donne, John
AGE; EMBRACE

Doolittle, Hilda
AGE

Dorfman, Ariel
BLACK; DESIRABILITY; HAND MOVEMENTS; HANDS; LEG(S); LIGHTING; LOYALTY/DISLOY-ALTY; TREMBLING; VOICE(S)

Dorris, Michael
LOOKS

Dos Passos, John
ANGER; BENDING/BENT; CLOUDS; DRINKING; EXCITE-MENT; FACE(S); FACIAL COLOR; FOG; HANDSHAKE; INSULT; LIES/LIARS; PAIN; PLACES; SCREAMS; SELF CONFIDENCE; TALKATIVENESS; WEATHER

Dostoevsky, Fyodor
MEEKNESS

Douglas, Kirk
ACTING; LIFE DEFINED

Douglas, Marjory Stoneman
ABILITY; MONEY; STARS; TEN-SION

Dow, Elbridge G., Jr.
LIFE DEFINED; REPETITION

Dowd, Maureen
EGO; OBVIOUSNESS; PERSONAL-ITY PROFILES; PLACES; RESERVE

Downey, Harris
FEAR; SLEEP; VIOLENCE; WORD(S)

Doyle, Sir Arthur Conan
BURST; DISAPPEARANCE

Drabble, Margaret
BEARING; DEJECTION; FOOD AND DRINK; FRUSTRATION; MEEKNESS; PERSONALITY PRO-FILES; STANDING; TEARS

Dracula, Count von
PLACES

Draghi, Mario
MONEY

Dreiser, Theodore
SIMPLICITY

Dresser, Davis
FACIAL SHAPE

Drummond, William
SHAPE

Drury, John
PAIN

Dryden, John
BEAUTY; BUSINESS; DEATH; ER-RORS; FREEDOM; GROWTH; HEAT; PERSISTENCE; SILENCE; SOUL; TRUTHNESS/FALSENESS

du Maurier, Daphne
ABILITY; AWKWARDNESS; BOOKS; EMPTINESS; MEMORY; PROPRIETY/IMPROPRIETY; RE-JECTION; SEASCAPES; TREES; WHITE

du Maurier, George
COLLAPSE; HAPPINESS; MOVE-MENT(S); MUSTACHE(S)

Dubus, Andre
BODY; COMFORT; DECREASE; ELUSIVENESS; FEAR; LIFE

Duchess of Newcastle
MEMORY; RICHES

Dudar, Helen
BARENESS; CRITICISM, DRA-MATIC AND LITERARY; MOVE-MENT(S)

Duffield, Samuel Willoughby
MIND DEFINED

Duke of Wellington
  SUCCESS/FAILURE

Dumas, Alexandre, Pere
  AGILITY; ANGER; CALMNESS

Duncan, Robert
  NIGHT

Dunn, Robert
  PLACES

Dunne, Finley Peter
  FREEDOM; GROWTH; MAR-
  RIAGE

Dunne, James
  CHARACTERISTICS, NATIONAL

Dunsany, Lord
  DISAPPEARANCE; MANKIND;
  SENSE

Duranty, Walter
  JUMPING; MOVEMENT(S)

Duras, Marguerite
  BLACK; BODY; CHANGE; MOVE-
  MENT(S); NOISES; WIND

Durrell, Lawrence
  AGITATION; AIMLESSNESS; AIR;
  ALERTNESS; ANGER; ANTICIPA-
  TION; ANXIETY; ARM MOVE-
  MENTS; ART AND LITERATURE;
  ATTENTION; BEGINNINGS AND
  ENDINGS; BEHAVIOR; BEND-
  ING/BENT; BIRDS; BLUE;
  BREATHING; BRIGHTNESS;
  CHANGE; CHILDREN; CITIES;
  CLINGING; CLOUDS; COLLAPSE;
  CONNECTIONS; DANCING; DE-
  JECTION; DESTRUCTION/DE-
  STRUCTIVENESS; DISAPPEAR-
  ANCE; DISINTEGRATION;
  DISPERSAL; EMBRACE;
  FRAGILITY; GLIMMER, GLITTER
  AND GLOSS; HATRED; HISTORY;
  HOPE; IDEAS; IRRITABLENESS/IR-
  RITATING; KISSES; LAUGHTER;
  LOOKS; LYING; MUSIC; PAIN;
  PEOPLE, INTERACTION; PUR-
  SUIT; RARITY; RISING; ROCKING
  AND ROLLING; SCREAMS;
  SCRUTINY; SEASONS; SEX; SHIN-
  ING; SILENCE; SLOWNESS;
  SMALLNESS; SMILE; SMOOTH-
  NESS; SPREADING; SUDDEN-
  NESS; TIME; TRANSIENCE;
  TREMBLING; TURNING AND
  TWISTING; WALKING; WATCH-
  FULNESS; WEARINESS; WRIN-
  KLES

Dwight, Timothy
  READERS/READING

Dybek, Stuart
  HAIR, COLOR; VEHICLES

Dylan, Bob
  AIMLESSNESS; EDUCATION

Dziemianowicz, Joe
  PHYSICAL APPEARANCE

E

Earl of Chesterfield
  SHAME

Eban, Abba
  ADVICE

Ebb, Fred
  ALONENESS

Eberhard, Richard
  BIGNESS

Eberhart, Mignon
  THRIFT

Ebers, Emil
  FAME

Eckhardt, Linda West
  ATTRACTION; EMOTIONS; EYES;
  FACIAL SHAPE; FURNITURE AND
  FURNISHINGS; SKIN; VAGUE-
  NESS

Edelman, Maurice
  CONTROL; GOVERNMENT;
  MOVEMENT(S); PAIN; PURSUIT;
  RISK; TEETH

Eden, Emily
  FURNITURE AND FURNISHINGS

Edgar, Josephine
  LEG(S)

Edgeworth, Maria
  BIGNESS; UNATTRACTIVENESS

Edson, Margaret
  WRITING

Edward, duke of Windsor
  RELIABILITY/UNRELIABILITY

Edwards, Jonathan
  HEART(S)

Edwards, Oliver
  FOOD AND DRINK

Edwards, Tryon
  BOOKS; HAPPINESS; MATHEMAT-
  ICS AND SCIENCE

Ehrenreich, Barbara
  RARITY

Einstein, Albert
  LIFE; TIME

Eisen, Harvey P.
  HELPLESSNESS

Eisenberg, Deborah
  PURSUIT; VOICE, SOFT

Eisenhower, Dwight D.
  POLITICS/POLITICIANS

Eleazar
  LIES/LIARS

Eleazar, Rabbi Simeon ben
  FLEXIBILITY/INFLEXIBILITY

Elice, Rick
  EMPTINESS; IMPORTANCE

Elijah, Gaon
  LIFE DEFINED

Eliot, Ethel Cook
  COMPLEXION

Eliot, George
  ACTIONS; ANXIETY; BEAUTY DE-
  FINED; CAUTION; CLOTHING;
  DISCONTENT; FACIAL EXPRES-
  SIONS, MISCELLANEOUS; HAPPI-
  NESS; HATRED; JUSTICE; MEM-
  ORY; MEN AND WOMEN;
  REPETITION; SADNESS; SOUL;
  VANITY

Eliot, T. S.
  NIGHT; SILENCE; VOICE(S)

Elkin, Stanley
  OBJECTS, MISC.; RESERVE; RIS-
  ING; SKIN; TALLNESS

Ellerbe, Alma
  PURPOSEFULNESS

Ellerbe, Paul
  PURPOSEFULNESS

Ellin, Stanley
  THOUGHTS; VEHICLES

Ellington, Duke
  MUSIC

Elliott, Sumner Locke
  ANXIETY; ATTENTION; COM-
  FORT; ENTHUSIASM; HAIR, TEX-
  TURE; HAPPINESS; INNOCENCE;
  JOY; KINDNESS; SIMPLICITY;
  SMILE; WRINKLES

Ellison, Ralph
  BODY; BREATHING; HAND
  MOVEMENTS; LAUGHTER; MEM-
  ORY; MOVEMENT(S); MUSCLES;
  NAMES; SWEAT

Ellwanger, George H.
  DIVERSENESS

Elworthy, F. T.
  BENDING/BENT

Emerson, Ralph Waldo
  AGE; ART AND LITERATURE;
  BEAUTY DEFINED; BOOKS;
  CHARACTER; DEATH; DE-

CREASE; DISHONESTY; FEROC-ITY; FIRMNESS; FRIENDSHIP, DE-FINED; GREED; GREEN; GROWTH; INSECTS; KINDNESS; LANGUAGE; MAXIMS, PROVERBS AND SAYINGS; RAIN; RELIGION; SENSE; SOCIETY; UNATTRAC-TIVENESS; WRITERS/WRITING

Engberg, Susan
FRESHNESS; LEAVES; ROAD SCENES; SENSE

Enright, Elizabeth
BLUE; HEAT

Ephron, Nora
SHINING

Epictetus
FORTUNE/MISFORTUNE

Erasmus
CONSCIENCE; LIFE DEFINED; PERMANENCE

Erdrich, Louise
ANGER; ARGUMENTS; ATTRAC-TION; ATTRACTIVENESS; BEHAV-IOR; BODY; BREATHING; CLING-ING; CLOTHING; COLLAPSE; DRINKING; EASE; EYE COLOR; EYE EXPRESSIONS, MISCELLA-NEOUS; FACIAL DETAILS; FA-CIAL EXPRESSIONS, MISCELLA-NEOUS; FINGERS; GLIMMER, GLITTER AND GLOSS; HANDS; LAUGHTER; LIGHTNESS; LIPS; LOOKS; LOVE; MEEKNESS; MIND; MOUTH, OPEN AND SHUT; PALLOR; PEOPLE, INTER-ACTION; POLITICS/POLITI-CIANS; ROAD SCENES; SEXUAL INTERACTION; SHOCK; SIGHS; SKIN; SMELL; TALLNESS; TEARS; TENSION; TREMBLING; VOICE(S); WIND; WRINKLES

Erickson, Steve
FIRE AND SMOKE; GLIMMER, GLITTER AND GLOSS; NATURE

Ernst and Lindley
BUSINESS

Esslinger-Carr, Pat M.
FACIAL EXPRESSIONS, MISCEL-LANEOUS; ROOMS; VOICE, HARSH

Estleman, Loren D.
BALDNESS; BEHAVIOR; BITTER-NESS; BLACK; BLUSHES; BODY; BREASTS; CALMNESS; CLEANLI-NESS; CLOTHING ACCESSORIES;

COLLAPSE; COMMONPLACE; COMPATIBILITY; COMPLEXION; DESTRUCTION/DESTRUCTIVE-NESS; DIFFICULTY; FACIAL COLOR; FACIAL EXPRESSIONS, SERIOUS; GRINS; HAIR, TEX-TURE; HAPPINESS; LAUGHTER; LIGHTING; MEMORY; MOUTH; NAMES; NATURALNESS; NOISES; OBJECTS, MISC.; OBVIOUSNESS; ORIGINALITY; PHYSICAL AP-PEARANCE; PROTRUSION; RE-JECTION; SILENCE; SIMILARITY; SMILE; STEADINESS; TIME; TREES; VEHICLES, OPERATION OF; VOICE(S); WEATHER; WORK

Euripides
CROWDS; DISAPPEARANCE; FRIENDSHIP

Evans, Nancy
RELIGION

Evans, William
PALLOR

Exley, Frederick
BODY; DULLNESS; WALKING; WAR

F

Faber, Mark
ABILITY

Fadiman, Clifton
CRITICISM, DRAMATIC AND LIT-ERARY; PLACES; READERS/READ-ING

Fallon, Padraic
BRIGHTNESS

Farber, Barry
DISINTEGRATION

Farber, Howard
ORDER/DISORDER

Farejons, Eleanor
LIGHTNESS

Farmer, Beverly
BALDNESS; FURNITURE AND FURNISHINGS; HAIR, COLOR

Farquhar, George
CLOSENESS; CRIME; SERIOUS-NESS

Farrell, J. G.
FOOD AND DRINK; STRUGGLE

Farrell, Kathleen
EYES; SMILE

Farrell, M. J.
AGITATION; BREASTS; COLD-NESS; DAY; FACE(S); FINGERS;

HATRED; LANDSCAPES; ROOMS; SEASONS; SKIN; SKY; WIND

Farris, John
AGITATION; BEHAVIOR; BODY ORGANS; BUSYNESS; CLOUD MOVEMENTS; FOOD AND DRINK; HAIR, COLOR; ILLNESS; MIND; PINK; SHAPE; TREES; VE-HICLES, OPERATION OF; VIS-ABILITY; VOICE, HARSH

Faulkner, William
ARM(S); AWKWARDNESS; BEAR-ING; BEGINNINGS AND END-INGS; BLACK; CLARITY; CLOTH-ING, ITS FIT; CLOUDS; CROWDS; CRYING; DEATH; DEJECTION; DRYNESS; EYE COLOR; EYE EX-PRESSIONS, MISCELLANEOUS; EYEBROWS; EYES; EYES, BRIGHT; FACE(S); FACIAL COLOR; FA-CIAL DETAILS; FACIAL EXPRES-SIONS, MISCELLANEOUS; FAMIL-IARITY; FLOWERS; GOSSIP; GROANS AND WHISPERS; HOUSES; IMMOBILITY; INNO-CENCE; INSECTS; LOOKS; LOVE, DEFINED; MIST; MOUTH; MOUTH, OPEN AND SHUT; NA-TURE; PATIENCE; PHYSICAL AP-PEARANCE; PHYSICAL FEEL-INGS; SILENCE; SPEAKING; SPEECH PATTERNS; SUCCESS/FAILURE; TREES; TREMBLING; TRUST/MISTRUST; TURNING AND TWISTING; USE-FULNESS/USELESSNESS; VAGUE-NESS; VOICE, HARSH; WALKING; WHITE

Fearing, Kenneth
FEAR

Feather, William
AGE

Feder, Mike
EMOTIONS

Feiden, Doug
GROWTH; IMPOSSIBILITY; REAL-IZATION

Feifer, George
OBVIOUSNESS; PLACES

Feldman, Irving
AIR; ATTENTION; ENTHUSIASM; FACE(S); FORTUNE/MISFOR-TUNE; JOY; RAIN

Feltham, Owen
  DISCONTENT; ENTHUSIASM;
  HOPE; PASSION
Felton, C. C.
  LANGUAGE
Ferber, Edna
  ALONENESS; ARGUMENTS;
  BRIGHTNESS; DEJECTION; FOOD
  AND DRINK; PLACES; RESERVE;
  RISING; SIMILARITY
Ferguson, Patricia
  BEARING; DISCOMFORT
Ferraro, Susan
  EDUCATION; OPINION; SMILE
Ferrier, J. W.
  OBJECTS, MISC.
Ferry, James
  CHILDREN
Fessendon, Thomas G@index
theme:., EMPTINESS
Fiedler, Leslie A.
  MEEKNESS; RAIN
Field, Eugene
  IDEAS
Fielding, Henry
  CONVERSATION; HUNGER; LOY-
  ALTY/DISLOYALTY; STAGE AND
  SCREEN; TEARS; WRITERS/WRIT-
  ING
Fierstein, Harvey
  CANDOR; PEOPLE, INTERAC-
  TION
Finch, Anne
  SILENCE
Fine, Samuel Shem
  FATNESS
Fine, Sylvia
  STAGE AND SCREEN
Finkelstein, Caroline
  LEAPING; LEAVES; TREES
Finn, William
  ACTIVENESS; ENERGY
Finney, Jack
  CITIES
Fisher, Dorothy Canfield
  SURPRISE; WHITE
Fitz-Gibbon, Bernice
  ADVERTISING
Fitzgerald, Edward
  BIRTH; ENTRANCES AND EXITS
Fitzgerald, F. Scott
  AGE; BEAUTY; BELIEVABILITY;
  BOOKS; CHOICES; CLOTHING;
  DEJECTION; DESTRUCTION/DE-
  STRUCTIVENESS; DRINKING;

EMPTINESS; FREEDOM;
  FROWNS; HEAD MOVEMENTS;
  HELPLESSNESS; JEWELRY;
  LOOKS; MUSTACHE(S); NECES-
  SITY; NERVOUSNESS; OPEN AND
  SHUT; PERVASIVENESS; PHYSI-
  CAL FEELINGS; POVERTY; RAIN;
  REMOTENESS; SADNESS; STARS;
  SUN; SUNSET; THUNDER AND
  LIGHTNING; TREES; TRUST/MIS-
  TRUST; VAGUENESS; VOICE,
  SOFT; WIND
Fitzsimmons, Paul M
  AIR
Flagg, James Montgomery
  HELPLESSNESS
Flanagan, Robert
  COLORS
Flanner, Janet
  ABUNDANCE; AGREEMENT/DIS-
  AGREEMENT; BLOOD; CARE-
  LESSNESS; CLEVERNESS; CLING-
  ING; COMPATIBILITY; DESIRE;
  DESTRUCTION/DESTRUCTIVE-
  NESS; ENTHUSIASM; FLOWERS;
  HAIR, CURLY; ILLNESS; IMMO-
  BILITY; MIND; MONEY;
  ORDER/DISORDER; PERSONAL-
  ITY PROFILES; POLITICS/POLITI-
  CIANS; POWER; SEASONS; SENSI-
  TIVENESS; SNOW; SURPRISE;
  WEARINESS; WORK; YOUTH
Flaubert, Gustave
  COMMONPLACE; DEJECTION;
  DESIRE; DESTRUCTION/DE-
  STRUCTIVENESS; DULLNESS;
  EYE COLOR; FLOWERS; FRUS-
  TRATION; HAIR; HARSHNESS;
  HEAVINESS; IDEAS; LOVE;
  ORDER/DISORDER; SIMILARITY;
  SPEECHMAKING; TREES
Flecknoe, Richard
  POWER; SILENCE
Fletcher, John Gould
  ABANDONMENT; BLACK
Fletcher, Louise
  SUCCESS/FAILURE
Fletcher, Phineas
  LOVE, DEFINED
Flexner, Abraham
  EDUCATION
Fodor, Kate
  GOODNESS; YOUTH

Follett, Ken
  BELIEVABILITY; FACIAL EXPRES-
  SIONS, SERIOUS; HABIT; PROB-
  LEMS AND SOLUTIONS
Foote, Horton
  STAGE AND SCREEN
Forbes, B. C.
  ACTIONS; CRITICISM
Forbes, Bryan
  TOUGHNESS; TURNING AND
  TWISTING
Forbes, Caleb Colton
  EVIL
Forbes, Colin
  CONVERSATION; DRYNESS;
  NIGHT
Forbes, Henry Ward Beecher
  KINDNESS
Forbes, James
  SOCIABILITY/UNSOCIABILITY
Ford, Henry
  MONEY
Ford, James L.
  ATTENTION; DISAPPEARANCE
Ford, Richard
  AGILITY; AIR; ALONENESS;
  ANGER; ANXIETY; ATMOSPHERE;
  BIGNESS; BLUE; BOREDOM/BOR-
  ING; BOXING AND WRESTLING;
  COLDNESS; COMFORT; COM-
  PLEXITY; CONVERSATION; CRU-
  ELTY; DISAPPEARANCE; DRINK-
  ING; EMOTIONS; EXITS;
  FACE(S); FACIAL EXPRESSIONS,
  SERIOUS; FAMILIARITY; FEAR;
  FOOD AND DRINK; FOOTBALL;
  FOREHEAD; FURNITURE AND
  FURNISHINGS; GLIMMER, GLIT-
  TER AND GLOSS; GLOOM;
  GRINS; HANDS; HAPPINESS;
  HEAD MOVEMENTS; HEALTH;
  HEARTBEAT; HEAT; HOPE; IDEAS;
  INAPPROPRIATENESS; INNO-
  CENCE; INTENSITY; IRRITABLE-
  NESS/IRRITATING; JEWELRY;
  LAUGHTER; LEG(S); LIFE; MAN-
  NERS; MOUTH; NAMES; NECES-
  SITY; OPEN AND SHUT; OPPOR-
  TUNITY; ORIGINALITY; PEOPLE,
  INTERACTION; PERSONALITY
  PROFILES; PHYSICAL APPEAR-
  ANCE; PLACES; REMOTENESS;
  ROCKING AND ROLLING;
  SHOULDERS; SILENCE; SIMILAR-
  ITY; SKY COLOR; SMELL; SPEED;

STARES; STOMACH; STRANGE-
NESS; TALKATIVENESS; TEN-
SION; THINNESS; THOUGHTS;
TRUST/MISTRUST; UNCER-
TAINTY; USEFULNESS/USELESS-
NESS; VEHICLES; VOICE(S);
WHITE; WRINKLES

Formes, Bryan
POLITICS/POLITICIANS

Forne, Caroline
ADVANTAGEOUSNESS

Forster, E. M.
CHARACTERISTICS, NATIONAL;
EMOTIONS; GROWTH; LIFE DE-
FINED; RELIGION; SITTING

Fosdick, Harry Emerson
HATRED; LIFE DEFINED;
MANKIND

Foss, Lukas
MUSIC

Foster, Stephen
DAY; SIGHS

Fowles, John
ATMOSPHERE; CLINGING; DIS-
COMFORT; DISINTEGRATION;
EYE MOVEMENTS; EYEBROWS;
FACIAL EXPRESSIONS, BLANK;
FACIAL EXPRESSIONS, SERIOUS;
FEAR; FRAGILITY; HELPLESS-
NESS; LANDSCAPES; MEN AND
WOMEN; MOUNTAINS; NECES-
SITY; PAUSE; PLEASURE; RE-
MOTENESS; SEX; SILENCE;
SMILE; SPEECH PATTERNS; SUC-
CESS/FAILURE; TURNING AND
TWISTING; WIND; WRINKLES;
WRITERS/WRITING

Foy, George
BODY; SCREAMS

Frady, Marshal
EXCITEMENT

France, Anatole
ART AND LITERATURE; BELIEFS;
DULLNESS; FACIAL EXPRES-
SIONS, MISCELLANEOUS;
HEART(S); INSECTS; INSULT;
LOVE; LOVE, DEFINED; MAXIMS,
PROVERBS AND SAYINGS;
MOUTH; NATURE; RELATION-
SHIP; RELIGION; SMILE; STO-
RIES; TREMBLING;
WRITERS/WRITING

Francis, Brendan
TIME

Francis, Dick
QUESTIONS AND ANSWERS; RIS-
ING; SKIN

Francis, Dorothy B.
ANXIETY; ARGUMENTS; CLOUD
MOVEMENTS; FEAR; MOVE-
MENT(S); NATURE; PHYSICAL
APPEARANCE; SPEECH PAT-
TERNS

Francis, Richard
BODY; LAUGHTER

Frankau, Pamela
FACIAL SHAPE

Frankfurter, Felix
ABILITY

Franklin, Benjamin
CHEERFULNESS; COMFORT;
DEATH; EATING AND DRINKING;
GOVERNMENT; GREATNESS;
LAWS; LAWYERS; LIFE DEFINED;
MEN AND WOMEN; PRIDE;
RICHES

Franks, Lucinda
CRIME

Fraser, Antonia
FINGERS; NOSE(S)

Fraser, George MacDonald
CALMNESS; LOOKS; SUDDEN-
NESS; VOICE, MUSIC RELATED

Frayn, Michael
DEJECTION

Frederick the Great
ARMY

Fredman, Mike
ADVANCING; ARM MOVE-
MENTS; BODY; ENTHUSIASM; FA-
CIAL COLOR; GLOOM; LAUGH-
TER; LIPS; SELF CONFIDENCE;
SKY COLOR; SMILE; SOCIABIL-
ITY/UNSOCIABILITY; STALENESS;
SUN; USEFULNESS/USELESS-
NESS; VEHICLES; VOICE(S);
WEAKNESS

Freedman, Samuel G.
EMOTIONS

Freemantle, Anne
ART AND LITERATURE

Freud, Sigmund
ART AND LITERATURE; LIFE;
MIND DEFINED; RELIGION

Friedenberg, Edgar Z.
LOVE

Friedman, Bruce Jay
ANGER; HOPE

Friedman, Milton
ECONOMICS

Fromm, Erich
DREAM

Frost, Robert
CAUSE AND EFFECT; FAMILIAR-
ITY; MOVEMENT(S); ORIGINAL-
ITY; POETS/POETRY

Froude, J. A.
MORALITY

Fuentes, Carlos
DISPERSAL; MOUNTAINS; RE-
SERVE; SPREADING; VANITY;
WRINKLES

Fugard, Athol
PAST

Fuller, Roy
CLOUDS

Fuller, Thomas
ACCOMPLISHMENT; AFFEC-
TION; AGILITY; BELONGING;
BOOKS; CAUTION; DEATH; DIS-
HONESTY; DOCTORS; ENERGY;
EVIL; FLATTERY; FRIENDSHIP;
GOSSIP; IDLENESS; INSULT; IN-
TELLIGENCE; LAWYERS; MEEK-
NESS; MEMORY; MONEY; NAMES;
PROBLEMS AND SOLUTIONS;
RICHES; SHYNESS; TIMELI-
NESS/UNTIMELINESS; UNDE-
SIREABILITY; WIT

Furlon, William Barry
PERSONALITY PROFILES

Furman, Laura
EMOTIONS; HAIR, COLOR; MAR-
RIAGE; MOVEMENT(S); VOICE,
WEAK

G

Gabirol, Solomon Ibn
EDUCATION; THRIFT

Gablik, Suzi
ANGER; RELATIONSHIP

Gabor, Zsa Zsa
MARRIAGE

Gabriel, Dante
MOON

Gaddis, William
LOVE

Gale, Zona
LOVE, DEFINED; SILENCE

Gallant, Mavis
EDUCATION; GLIMMER, GLIT-
TER AND GLOSS; MIND; MOVE-
MENT(S); PERSONALITY PRO-

FILES; SILENCE; THINNESS; TREMBLING; WHITE

Galsworthy, John
CHEEKS; EXITS; EYES, BRIGHT; FACIAL EXPRESSIONS, MISCELLANEOUS; HELPLESSNESS; LINGERING; TOUGHNESS

Garbo, Norman
DARKNESS; GREEN; SLEEP

Gardner, Gerald
WORK

Gardner, John
BEAUTY; BUSYNESS; GLIMMER, GLITTER AND GLOSS; GLOOM; IDEAS; PEACEFULNESS; SHARPNESS; SMILE; SUCCESS/FAILURE

Gardner, Tonita S.
ANGER; EATING AND DRINKING

Garfunkel, Art
FRIENDSHIP, SILENCE

Gargan, William
MARRIAGE

Garis, Leslie
SKIN; THINNESS; WRITERS/WRITING

Garland, Hamlin
HEAT

Garner, Dwight
STARES

Garrett, George
ABUNDANCE; ADVANCING; AGILITY; AIR; ANGER; ANIMALS; ANTICIPATION; ARGUMENTS; ARM MOVEMENTS; ATTENTION; AWKWARDNESS; BALDNESS; BARENESS; BEARD; BEARING; BEAUTY; BEGINNINGS AND ENDINGS; BEHAVIOR; BELONGING; BIRDS; BITTERNESS; BLOOD; BLUE; BLUSHES; BODY; BREASTS; BREATHING; BROWN; CALMNESS; CARELESSNESS; CAUSE AND EFFECT; CERTAINTY; CHANGE; CHEEKS; CITIES; CLARITY; CLINGING; CLOTHING ACCESSORIES; CLOTHING, ITS FIT; CLOUDS; COLDNESS; COMPATIBILITY; COMPLEXITY; CONNECTIONS; CONTROL; COURAGE; CRUELTY; CRYING; CURSES; DESTRUCTION/DESTRUCTIVENESS; DISAPPEARANCE; DISHONESTY; DISINTEGRATION; DISPERSAL; DREAM; DRINKING; DRYNESS;

DULLNESS; EASE; EATING AND DRINKING; EMBRACE; EMOTIONS; EMPTINESS; ENTHUSIASM; ENTRANCES AND EXITS; ENTRAPMENT; ERRORS; EYE EXPRESSIONS, MISCELLANEOUS; EYES; FACE(S); FACIAL EXPRESSIONS, SERIOUS; FACIAL SHAPE; FEAR; FINGERS; FLEXIBILITY/INFLEXIBILITY; FLOWERS; FOG; FORMALITY; FRAGILITY; FURNITURE AND FURNISHINGS; FUTILITY; GAIETY; GLIMMER, GLITTER AND GLOSS; GRAY; GREEN; GRINS, GROANS, AND WHISPERS; GROWTH; HAIR; HAIR, COLOR; HAIR, CURLY; HAIR STYLES; HAND MOVEMENTS; HANDS; HAPPINESS; HARSHNESS; HEALTH; HEART(S); HEARTBEAT; HELPLESSNESS; INAPPROPRIATENESS; INTENSITY; JOY; KNOWLEDGE; LAUGHTER; LAWS; LEAVES; LEG(S); LIGHTNESS; LINGERING; LIPS; LOOKS; LOOSENESS; LYING; MOUNTAINS; MOVEMENT(S); MUSTACHE(S); NAMES; NERVOUSNESS; NOISES; OBJECTS, MISC.; OBVIOUSNESS; OCEAN/OCEANFRONTS; OPEN AND SHUT; OPPORTUNITY; ORDER/DISORDER; PAIN; PALLOR; PAST, THE; PATIENCE; PAUSE; PEOPLE, INTERACTION; PERMANENCE; PERSONAL TRAITS; PHYSICAL APPEARANCE; PINK; POSTURE; PRIDE; PROBLEMS AND SOLUTIONS; PURPOSEFULNESS; PURSUIT; RARITY; REALIZATION; REALNESS/UNREALNESS; RICHES; RUNNING; SAFETY; SEASONS; SEX; SHAPE; SHINING; SHOCK; SILENCE; SKIN; SKY; SLEEP; SMELL; SMILE; SMOOTHNESS; SNOW; SOFTNESS; SPEECH PATTERNS; SPEED; SPREADING; STOMACH; STORIES; SUCCESS/FAILURE; SUDDENNESS; SUN; SWEAT; SWEETNESS; TACT; TALKATIVENESS; TEARS; TENDERNESS; TEETH; TENSION; THINNESS; THOUGHTS; THRIFT; TREES; TREMBLING; TRUENESS/FALSENESS; TRUST/MIS-

TRUST; TURNING AND TWISTING; UNDESIREABILITY; UNSTEADINESS; VANITY; VIOLENCE; VOICE(S); VOICE, HARSH; VOICE, MUSIC RELATED; VOICE, SOFT; WALKING; WEAKNESS; WEARINESS; WEATHER; WHITE; WIND; WISDOM; WORD(S); WORDS, EFFECT OF; WRINKLES; YELLOW

Garrick, David
STAGE AND SCREEN

Garrigue, Jean
BEWILDERMENT; EYE EXPRESSIONS, MISCELLANEOUS; HAIR, COLOR; HELPLESSNESS; HONESTY; KINDNESS; LOOKS; PAST, THE; THINNESS

Garrison, Theodosia
TREES

Garrison, William Lloyd
FLEXIBILITY/INFLEXIBILITY; HARSHNESS

Gary, Romain
BURST; CLOUDS; ENTRANCES AND EXITS; FACE(S); HELPLESSNESS; LAUGHTER; LOOKS; MUSTACHE(S); NATURALNESS; NECK; NERVOUSNESS; VOICE, HARSH

Gash, Jonathan
DRINKING; HANDS; HEARTBEAT; LAUGHTER; OBVIOUSNESS; PALLOR; PEOPLE, INTERACTION; RUNNING; STYLE; TREMBLING

Gass, William H.
ADVANCING; AIR; ALONENESS; ANGER; ARM(S); BEARING; BENDING/BENT; BIRDS; BITTERNESS; COLDNESS; COLLAPSE; CONVERSATION; DARKNESS; DISINTEGRATION; DISPERSAL; EATING AND DRINKING; FACE(S); HANDS; HEAT; HISTORY; HOUSES; INAPPROPRIATENESS; LIGHTING; MAXIMS, PROVERBS AND SAYINGS; NATURE; NOSE(S); PAIN; PERVASIVENESS; REPETITION; SKIN; SOFTNESS; SUN; TIME; WORK

Gassett, Joe Ortega
KINDNESS

Gates, W. I. E.
COURAGE

Gautier, Theophile
HANDS; LEAPING; VOICE, MUSIC RELATED

Gay, John
ENVY; FRIENDSHIP, DEFINED; PASSION; PRIDE

Gaylin, Willard
SELFISHNESS

Gazzo, Michael V.
CRUELTY

Gellhorn, Martha
FAILURE; PURSUIT

Gerard, Philip
CLOTHING, ITS FIT

Gertler, T.
PHYSICAL APPEARANCE

Gesner, Clark
IDEAS

Getz, William
POWER; TREMBLING

Ghazala, Abdel Halim Abu
PERSONALITY PROFILES

Gibbs, Woolcot
FACE(S)

Gibran, Khalil
AFFECTION; AMBITION;EMOTIONS; ENTHUSIASM; LOVE; LOVE, DEFINED; MEMORY; PROFESSIONS; SOUL; WRITERS/WRITING

Gibson, Miles
BODY; BREASTS; BREATHING; CLEVERNESS; ENTRANCES AND EXITS; EYES; EYES, BRIGHT; FACE(S); FACIAL SHAPE; FATNESS; HAIR; HAIR, CURLY; MOUTH; PALLOR; PHYSICAL APPEARANCE; REALIZATION; RED; SEASCAPES; SEXUAL INTERACTION; SITTING; SMILE; SOCIABILITY/UNSOCIABILITY; TALLNESS; TEARS; UNATTRACTIVENESS; WIND

Gide, Andre
EMOTIONS; HAPPINESS; JOY

Gifford, Fannie Stearns
GLOOM; IMMOBILITY

Gifford, Frank
FOOTBALL

Gilbert, Michael
INAPPROPRIATENESS; NOSE(S); VOICE, HARSH

Gilbert, W. S.
ABUNDANCE; CLOTHING, ITS FIT; CLOUD MOVEMENTS; DAN-

GER; DEATH, FINALITY OF; DISCOMFORT; DRYNESS; GLIMMER, GLITTER AND GLOSS; GROWTH; HELPLESSNESS; INNOCENCE; INSULT; POWER; SENSE; SOFTNESS; SPEECH PATTERNS; STANDING; STYLE; SWEETNESS; TOUGHNESS

Gilchrist, Ellen
ABUNDANCE; BIRDS; BREATHING; FACE(S); IDEAS; LOVE; PROBLEMS AND SOLUTIONS; SHADOW; SILENCE; WORDS, EFFECT OF; WRITERS/WRITING

Gildner, Gary
CALMNESS; HAIR; PHYSICAL FEELINGS

Giles, Molly
BRIGHTNESS; EYEBROWS; PAIN; SMILE; SOFTNESS

Gill, Brendan
ANXIETY

Gillers, Stephen
RISK

Gillespie, Alfred
HAIR

Gilliatt, Penelope
ANIMALS; ATTENTION; BODY; CHIN; CLOTHING, ITS FIT; COLDNESS; COMPLEXION; CONTEMPT; CONVERSATION; FACE(S); FACIAL EXPRESSIONS, MISCELLANEOUS; FEAR; FOOD AND DRINK; HAIR, TEXTURE; HATRED; HEAVINESS; INCOMPLETENESS; LIPS; PHYSICAL APPEARANCE; SHOULDERS; SILENCE; SKIN; SPEED; SPREADING; WISDOM

Gilman, Lawrence
PASSION

Gionfriddo, Gina
REJECTION

Gioseffi, Daniela
CERTAINTY; COMPLETENESS; DARKNESS; DESIRE; DISINTEGRATION; FOOD AND DRINK; GROWTH; LEAVES; PEACEFULNESS; PURPOSEFULNESS; SILENCE; TOBACCO

Giraudoux, Jean
CHARACTERISTICS, NATIONAL; HAPPINESS; MANKIND

Gissing, George
SECRECY

Gladstone, William E.
POLITICS/POLITICIANS

Glanville, Brian
BODY; EYE MOVEMENTS

Glanville, Joseph
TRUTH

Glasgow, Ellen
AIR; BLUE; BREATHING; DEATH; DEJECTION; DISAPPEARANCE; DREAM; ENTRAPMENT; EYE EXPRESSIONS, MISCELLANEOUS; FACE(S); FACIAL EXPRESSIONS, BLANK; FIRE AND SMOKE; FORTUNE/MISFORTUNE; FRAGILITY; GROWTH; HAIR, TEXTURE; HANDS; HARMLESSNESS; HEART(S); HELPLESSNESS; IMMOBILITY; LEG(S); LYING; MEEKNESS; MEMORY; PASSION; PERMANENCE; PROBLEMS AND SOLUTIONS; REMOTENESS; RESERVE; SEASONS; SEX; SHARPNESS; SKIN; SKY; SMILE; SNOW; THICKNESS; THOUGHTS; TIME; TREES; USEFULNESS/USELESSNESS; VIBRATION; WIND; WRINKLES

Glass, Joanna M.
MUSCLES

Gloag, Julian
CLINGING; SMALLNESS

Goddard, Robert
SMELL; VOICE(S)

Godden, Rumer
ARGUMENTS; CRITICISM; DULLNESS; EYE EXPRESSIONS, MISCELLANEOUS; GROWTH; HAIR STYLES; IRRITABLENESS/IRRITATING; MORALITY; PAUSE; SILENCE; STRUGGLE; THINNESS; THOUGHTS; WRITERS/WRITING

Godwin, Gail
CHANGE; COMPLEXITY; WORK

Goethe, Johann Wolfgang von
BEHAVIOR; BOOKS; DIFFERENCES; DISAPPEARANCE; DISPERSAL; EASE; EYE EXPRESSIONS, MISCELLANEOUS; FORTUNE/MISFORTUNE; GLOOM; LAWS; LIFE; MANKIND; NAMES; NATURE; OPINION; PASSION; POLITICS/POLITICIANS; QUESTIONS AND ANSWERS; RELIGION; TRANSIENCE

Gogol, Nikolay V.
BLUE; CAUTION; TEARS

Gold, Herbert
ATTENTION; BODY; CHILDREN;
CONVERSATION; FAMILIARITY;
PAST, THE; SMILE

Goldberg, Aaron
ENTHUSIASM

Goldberg, Robert
SPEAKING; TRANSIENCE

Golding, William
MEMORY

Goldman, James
AMBITION; STRENGTH

Goldoni, Carlo
WORLD

Goldsmith, Oliver
ABANDONMENT; BUSYNESS;
FIGHTING; KINDNESS

Goldwin, Francis
SENSITIVENESS

Gomez, Selena
LONELINESS; YEARNING

Goodman, Ellen
ECONOMICS; NEWS; RELATION-
SHIP; SEX

Goodman, Walter
CONSCIENCE; LAUGHTER

Goodwin, Michael
LAUGHTER

Gordimer, Nadine
ATTENTION; BLUSHES; BRIGHT-
NESS; BURST; CONVERSATION;
CROWDS; EMOTIONS; EYE EX-
PRESSIONS, MISCELLANEOUS;
FATNESS; GUILT; IMPARTIALITY;
JEWELRY; JOY; LAUGHTER;
LEG(S); LIES/LIARS;
OCEAN/OCEANFRONTS; PAL-
LOR; REMOTENESS; SHOUL-
DERS; SILENCE; SKY

Gordon, Mary
BEHAVIOR; CAUSE AND EFFECT;
CERTAINTY; CLEANLINESS;
CLOTHING, ITS FIT; DESIRE; DIS-
APPOINTMENT; ENERGY; EX-
CITEMENT; FRIENDSHIP, DE-
FINED; INAPPROPRIATENESS;
LOOKS; PHYSICAL FEELINGS;
REJECTION; SAFETY; SHAME

Gore-Booth, Eva
BLACK

Gorky, Maxim
ATTENTION; CLINGING; DISPER-
SAL; EVIL; EYEBROWS; NOSE(S);
SUN

Gorman, Paul
HANDS; THOUGHTS

Gornick, Vivian
ABSORBABILITY

Gosse, Edmond
COURAGE; FUTURE; PAST, THE

Gould, Jack
ADVERTISING

Goyen, William
AGITATION; BLOOD; FINGERS;
JUMPING; MANKIND; MOVE-
MENT(S)

Gracián, Baltasar
AGE; CONTROL

Grafton, C. W.
UNDESIREABILITY

Grafton, Sue
BEARD; BODY; BREASTS;
BREATHING; CAUSE AND EF-
FECT; CLARITY; CLOUDS; CRY-
ING; DEATH, FINALITY OF; DIS-
COMFORT; EATING AND
DRINKING; ENERGY; EYES;
FACE(S); FACIAL EXPRESSIONS,
MISCELLANEOUS; FEAR; FIN-
GERS; FURNITURE AND FUR-
NISHINGS; GREEN; HAIR;
HEADS; HOUSES; MEMORY; MUS-
CLES; OCEAN/OCEANFRONTS;
PEOPLE, INTERACTION; PER-
SISTENCE; PHYSICAL FEELINGS;
REALIZATION; REJECTION;
SCRUTINY; SEXUAL INTERAC-
TION; SIGHS; SKIN; SLOWNESS;
SMELL; SMILE; STOMACH; TALL-
NESS; THINNESS; TREES; UN-
STEADINESS; VAGUENESS; VIO-
LENCE; WRINKLES

Graham, Harry
BLUSHES

Graham, Virginia
WORD(S)

Graham, Winston
SEXUAL INTERACTION

Grahame, J.
BUSINESS

Grahame, Kenneth
CRYING; LIGHTING

Granger, Bill
PROBLEMS AND SOLUTIONS;
STARES

Grant, Ulysses S.
THRIFT

Grau, Shirley Ann
EYE COLOR; EYES; FOG; HAIR,
COLOR; LIPS; NATURE; PHYSI-
CAL FEELINGS; TENSION

Graves, Robert
CROWDS; DRINKING; EYES;
HAND MOVEMENTS; JUMPING;
POETS/POETRY

Gray, Francine du Plessix
ALONENESS; BREASTS; HAIR,
COLOR; LOOKS; PURPOSEFUL-
NESS; SEASCAPES

Gray, Thomas
DRYNESS

Greeley, Andrew M.
PREPAREDNESS

Greenaway, Kate
SEASCAPES

Greenberg, Alan
GREED

Greene, A. C.
SENSITIVENESS

Greene, Barbara
CLINGING

Greene, Graham
BOOKS; EYE EXPRESSIONS, MIS-
CELLANEOUS; FRIENDSHIP; SE-
CRECY; WRINKLES

Greene, Robert
BREATHING

Greer, Germaine
BARENESS; MARRIAGE

Greer, Peter
DIFFICULTY

Gregor, Arthur
LIGHTNESS

Grenfell, Julian
AGILITY

Grenville, Kate
DRYNESS; HANDS; MOUNTAINS;
ROOMS; RUNNING

Grétry, André Ernest
MUSIC

Grey, Zane
HEAD MOVEMENTS; PHYSICAL
APPEARANCE

Grimm Brothers
SNOW

Gross, Jane
PERSISTENCE

Gross, John
CONTINUITY

Grubb, Davis
BEAUTY; BLACK; COLDNESS;
DANGER; DESTRUCTION/DE-
STRUCTIVENESS; DISAPPEAR-
ANCE; EMOTIONS; FACIAL DE-
TAILS; GREEN; LYING; PALLOR;
SEXUAL INTERACTION; SHAPE;
SMOOTHNESS; SNOW; VIBRA-
TION; VIOLENCE

Grumbach, Doris
HAIR, COLOR; THINNESS;
WORD(S)

Guenther, Robert
SUCCESS/FAILURE

Guerney, A. R., Jr.
CLOSENESS; CROWDS; EM-
BRACE

Guest, Edward A.
CHILDREN; LIFE DEFINED;
TEARS

Guicciardini, Francesco
REPETITION

Guiterman, Arthur
ATTRACTION

Gunn, Thom
FIRMNESS

Gunther, John
FATNESS; HAIR, COLOR; IN-
SECTS; LANDSCAPES; MOON;
PROFESSIONS

Gurney, A. R., Jr.
WRITERS/WRITING

Guthrie, Thomas
RELIGION

Guy, Rosa
FRIENDSHIP; HAIR, TEXTURE;
OBVIOUSNESS; PERSONALITY
PROFILES; PURSUIT; VANITY

H

Haake, Katharine
MOON

Habbington, William
BLACK

Haberman, Clyde
UNDESIREABILITY

Hacker, Marilyn
BITTERNESS; FEAR; GLIMMER,
GLITTER AND GLOSS

Hagge, John
ATTENTION; SEXUAL INTERAC-
TION

Hale, Christopher
STUPIDITY

Hale, John
DEATH

Haliburton, Thomas Chandler
BLACK; MEMORY

Halifax, Lord
FOOLISHNESS; HOPE; KNOWL-
EDGE; VIRTUE

Hall, Basil
PLACES

Hall, Carol
FORTUNE/MISFORTUNE

Hall, Donald
ALONENESS; SPEED; TREES

Hall, James B.
KINDNESS; SUN

Hall, Lee
EXCITEMENT

Hall, Oakley
COLLAPSE; FACE(S); HANDS;
HEART(S); PURSUIT; SLEEP;
STARES

Halla, Sven
FACTS

Halleck, Fitz-Greene
RARITY

Hallhan, William H.
BENDING/BENT; CLINGING; DIF-
FICULTY; EMBRACE; ENTRAP-
MENT; HEAT; NOSE(S); PEOPLE,
INTERACTION; SAFETY; SEA-
SONS; THINNESS; USEFUL-
NESS/USELESSNESS; WALKING

Halsey, Margaret
PLACES

Hamill, Mark
IMPORTANCE/UNIMPORTANCE

Hamilton, Alexander
AFFECTION; SHAPE

Hamilton, William
ROOMS

Hamilton, Sir William
TRUTH

Hammerstein, Oscar, II
AIMLESSNESS; ALONENESS;
BRIGHTNESS; CLOUD MOVE-
MENTS; COMMONPLACE; DISAP-
PEARANCE; FLATTERY; FREE-
DOM; HAPPINESS;
HOMELESSNESS; KINDNESS;
LANDSCAPES; LOVE; PERSONAL-
ITY PROFILES; PHYSICAL AP-
PEARANCE; RESTLESSNESS;
WORDS OF PRAISE

Hammett, Dashiell
BEAUTY; BLACK; BREATHING;
DISINTEGRATION; EYE EXPRES-
SIONS, MISCELLANEOUS; EYES;
HANDS; PHYSICAL APPEAR-
ANCE; PHYSICAL FEELINGS;
ROCKING AND ROLLING;
ROOMS; SAFETY; SPEECH PAT-
TERNS; STRAIGHTNESS; WRIN-
KLES

Hamper, Ben
NOISES; WORK

Hampl, Patricia
FOG; PHYSICAL APPEARANCE;
REGULARITY/IRREGULARITY

Hand, Learned
LIFE

Haney, Lynn
TOUGHNESS

Hannah, Barry
LAUGHTER; SKY

Hansberry, Lorraine
CLARITY

Hanscomb, Leslie
THINNESS

Harbach, Otto
LOVE

Hardwick, Elizabeth
ARGUMENTS; COLDNESS; COL-
LAPSE; ECONOMICS; FACIAL EX-
PRESSIONS, MISCELLANEOUS;
HAIR, CURLY; HONESTY; LEG(S);
LINGERING; LOVE; NATURE;
PERSONALITY PROFILES; RISK;
RUNNING; SCRUTINY; SNOW;
SWEETNESS; TIME

Hardwick, Mollie
WRINKLES

Hardy, Arthur Sherburne
THINNESS

Hardy, Thomas
ANXIETY; BLUE; CLARITY; EYES;
HAIR, COLOR; HELPLESSNESS;
LOOKS; PAIN; SENSITIVENESS;
THINNESS

Hare, Augustus William
MIND DEFINED; SUDDENNESS

Hare, Julius Charles
CHOICES; MIND DEFINED; SUD-
DENNESS

Harnick, Sheldon
HABIT

Harris, Elizabeth
SKIN

Harris, Frank
AMBITION; MANKIND

Harris, Lisa
HOSPITALITY; KINDNESS; SPEED

Harris, MacDonald
BODY; BREATHING; CLOTHING, ITS FIT; FACIAL DETAILS; GLIMMER, GLITTER AND GLOSS; IMMOBILITY; JEWELRY; MOUTH, OPEN AND SHUT; PAIN; PEOPLE, INTERACTION; PROTRUSION; ROAD SCENES; SEXUAL INTERACTION; SPEECH PATTERNS; STAGE AND SCREEN; SUN; UNSTEADINESS; WORDS, EFFECT OF

Harris, Richard
BALDNESS

Harrison, Barbara Grizzuiti
CRITICISM, DRAMATIC AND LITERARY

Harrison, Noel
THOUGHTS

Hart, Charles
SKIN

Hart, Gary
LAUGHTER

Hart, Lorenz
DISAPPEARANCE; MANNERS; SERIOUSNESS

Hart, Moss
ABILITY; CERTAINTY; WORDS OF PRAISE

Harte, Bret
MOON

Hartley, L. P.
CANDOR; CLOTHING ACCESSORIES; EMOTIONS; HAIR, COLOR; JUSTICE; MUSCLES; NOISES; PAST, THE; PAUSE; PEOPLE, INTERACTION; REGRET; SMILE; TREMBLING; VOICE(S); WORD(S); WRINKLES

Hartog, Jan de
ATTENTION; DREAM

Harwood, Ronald
MEMORY

Hasdai, Abraham
PROMISE

Haskell, Floyd K.
PEACEFULNESS

Hass, Robert
BIRDS; CLEANLINESS; DAY; REMOTENESS; STORIES

Hauser, Marianne
BEGINNINGS AND ENDINGS; CURSES; FAMILIARITY; HAIR, TEXTURE; USEFULNESS/USELESSNESS

Hawes, Joel
CHARACTER

Hawkes, John
DARKNESS; SUN; VEHICLES

Hawthorne, Nathaniel
CALMNESS; CLARITY; EYES, BRIGHT; FACIAL COLOR; FACIAL EXPRESSIONS, MISCELLANEOUS; LAUGHTER; MOON; PALLOR; VIRTUE

Hayden, Julie
ARM(S); PEACEFULNESS; SILENCE

Hayden, Sterling
BENDING/BENT; BODY; CHIN; DRINKING; ENTRAPMENT; FINGERS; SITTING; TEETH

Hayne, Paul Hamilton
AIMLESSNESS

Hazlitt, William
COMMONPLACE; EDUCATION; FRIENDSHIP, DEFINED; GREATNESS; HATRED; LANGUAGE; LIFE DEFINED; MAXIMS, PROVERBS AND SAYINGS; MIND DEFINED; WORD(S); WORDS DEFINED

Headland, Leslye
WORK

Healey, Patrick
SERIOUSNESS@index theme:

Heaney, Seamus
REMOTENESS

Hearn, Lacfadio
NATURALNESS

Hearon, Shelby
CLOTHING; ENTRAPMENT; FEAR; FLOWERS; FOOD AND DRINK; FRESHNESS; PURSUIT; SEASONS; SHINING; SILENCE; SLOWNESS; TONGUE; WATCHFULNESS; WRINKLES

Heart, Moss
BENDING/BENT

Heatter, Gabriel
WORK

Hebert, Jack
USEFULNESS/USELESSNESS

Hecht, Ben
ARGUMENTS; EYE EXPRESSIONS, MISCELLANEOUS; HUNGER; LOVE, DEFINED; NERVOUSNESS; RELIGION; SHARPNESS; TREMBLING; VANITY

Hedin, Mary
BEARING; CERTAINTY; EMOTIONS; EYE EXPRESSIONS, MISCELLANEOUS; EYES; FACE(S); FACIAL COLOR; FINGERS; GRINS; HAND MOVEMENTS; HANDS; HEARTBEAT; IRRITABLENESS/IRRITATING; LIGHTNESS; LOOKS; LYING; MARRIAGE; MUSIC; NATURE; NOSE(S); PATIENCE; POLITICS/POLITICIANS; QUESTIONS AND ANSWERS; REGULARITY/IRREGULARITY; RELATIONSHIP; ROAD SCENES; SLEEP; SMILE; SUN; TREMBLING; WEARINESS; WORD(S)

Hegan, Alice Caldwell
RELIABILITY/UNRELIABILITY

Heilbroner, Robert L.
PREPAREDNESS

Heine, Heinrich
ACTIONS; BOOKS; NATURE; POLITICS/POLITICIANS; RELIGION

Heine, Leonard M., Jr.
CAUTION

Heinz, John
FOOLISHNESS; USEFULNESS/USELESSNESS

Heller, Joseph
ANGER; BELONGING; BREASTS; EYE EXPRESSIONS, MISCELLANEOUS; FACE(S); GROANS AND WHISPERS; PHYSICAL APPEARANCE; SELF CONFIDENCE; SMILE; TENSION; TREMBLING

Heller, Steve
EATING AND DRINKING

Hellman, Sam
RICHES

Hello, Ernest
MEETINGS

Helprin, Mark
BLACK; BLUSHES; BREATHING; CLARITY; ELUSIVENESS; ENVY; FACIAL EXPRESSIONS, BLANK; FURNITURE AND FURNISHINGS; GLIMMER, GLITTER AND GLOSS; GREEN; HAIR, TEXTURE; HELPLESSNESS; LOOSENESS; PEOPLE,

INTERACTION; ROCKING AND
ROLLING; SILENCE; SPEED; SUN;
THINNESS; VIBRATION; VOICE,
SOFT; WALKING

Helps, Sir Arthur
BELIEFS

Hemingway, Ernest
BEARD; BIGNESS; BODY; ELU-
SIVENESS; INSECTS; LIGHTNESS;
LOVE; SNOW; SWEAT; WORDS
OF PRAISE

Hempel, Amy
BEWILDERMENT; REGULAR-
ITY/IRREGULARITY; TIME

Henahan, Donal
MEMORY

Henderson, Leo
ECONOMICS

Henley, Patricia
BREASTS; BROWN; DULLNESS;
HAIR STYLES; MOON; NECES-
SITY; ROOMS; VOICE, HARSH;
VOICE(S); WHITE; WIND

Henry, Juvenal
VIRTUE

Henry, Matthew
ANGER

Henry, O.
AIMLESSNESS; ALONENESS;
ANGER; ATMOSPHERE; BEAUTY;
BREATHING; BUSYNESS; CITIES;
CLEANLINESS; CLOTHING, ITS
FIT; CONVERSATION; DANCING;
DISPERSAL; DULLNESS; ENTRAP-
MENT; EYE COLOR; FACE(S); FA-
CIAL DETAILS; FINGERS; FURNI-
TURE AND FURNISHINGS;
GROANS AND WHISPERS;
GROWTH; HABIT; HELPLESS-
NESS; HOSPITALITY; IMMOBIL-
ITY; INSULT; JUMPING; LAUGH-
TER; LEAPING; MANKIND;
MEEKNESS; MUSIC; NOISES;
NOSE(S); PERVASIVENESS; PHYS-
ICAL APPEARANCE; SMILE;
SNOW; STORIES; TALKATIVE-
NESS; THOUGHTS; TREMBLING;
TRUST/MISTRUST; TURNING
AND TWISTING; VIBRATION;
VOICE, MUSIC RELATED;
WORDS OF PRAISE

Henry, Patrick
FREEDOM

Henson, Robert
CONTENTMENT

Hentoff, Nat
ATTRACTION

Herbert, George
ADVANTAGEOUSNESS; REPETI-
TION

Hergeshmeier, Joseph
SENSITIVENESS

Herman, Tom
CRITICISM, DRAMATIC AND LIT-
ERARY

Herod, Dan P.
LOVE, DEFINED

Herold, Don
MARRIAGE

Herrick, Robert
DAY

Herriot, Édouard
POLITICS/POLITICIANS

Hersey, John
FOREHEAD; GREEN; PRIDE; SEN-
TIMENT; SILENCE; SKY; SOFT-
NESS; WORDS, EFFECT OF

Herzog, George
ACTIONS

Hess, Joan
ADVANCING; BEARING; DEATH,
FINALITY OF; EYE EXPRESSIONS,
MISCELLANEOUS; HAIR; HAIR,
CURLY; HAND MOVEMENTS;
JUMPING; LEAVES; NOSE(S); RIS-
ING; SWEAT; UNCERTAINTY

Hesse, Hermann
PRIDE

Hewlett, Maurice
CLINGING; CRYING; DISCOM-
FORT; HAIR

Heyward, Du Bose
MUSCLES; SUN

Heywood, John
UNSTEADINESS

Heywood, Thomas
CLOTHING; COLDNESS

Hichens, Robert
VIRTUE

Hicks, Richard
PURSUIT

Higgins, George V.
COLDNESS; PHYSICAL APPEAR-
ANCE; RELIABILITY/UNRELIA-
BILITY; UNDESIREABILITY

Higgins, Joanna
FOOD AND DRINK; WORD(S)

Hill, Susan
FACIAL COLOR; FACIAL EXPRES-
SIONS, MISCELLANEOUS

Hills, Carol
WORD(S)

Hillyer, Robert
DIVERSENESS

Hilton, James
HOUSES; MEMORY; PROBLEMS
AND SOLUTIONS; TIME; UN-
STEADINESS

Hinds, Michael de Courcy
DIFFICULTY

Hipponax
WORLD

Hitchcock, Alfred
MEN AND WOMEN

Hoagland, Edward
AGILITY; ANIMALS; BOOKS;
DRINKING; GLIMMER, GLITTER
AND GLOSS; MOON; REGULAR-
ITY/IRREGULARITY; STRAIGHT-
NESS; TENSION; VISABILITY;
WALKING

Hobhouse, Janet
VIBRATION

Hochstein, Rolaine
VOICE, HARSH

Hodgkinson, Amanda
NERVOUSNESS

Hoelterhoff, Manuela
RELIABILITY/UNRELIABILITY;
UNDESIREABILITY

Hoffman, William
SKIN

Hogan, Linda
CLOTHING

Hogg, James
LOVE, DEFINED

Holcroft, Thomas
SADNESS; STUPIDITY

Holland, Josiah Gilbert
ANGER

Holm, Ken
CHARACTERISTICS, NATIONAL

Holmes, John Andrew
AGE; SECRECY

Holmes, Oliver Wendell, Jr.
AGE; BEAUTY; BURST; GOVERN-
MENT; INTOLERANCE; LIFE DE-
FINED; MIND DEFINED; WORDS
DEFINED

Holmes, Oliver Wendell, Sr.
AGE; BEHAVIOR; COLORS; CON-
VERSATION; DEATH; DISAPPEAR-
ANCE; ENERGY; FAMILIARITY;
HAIR; IGNORANCE; INSULT;
LAWYERS; LIFE DEFINED;

MANKIND; MEETINGS; MUS-
TACHE(S); PARENTHOOD; PER-
MANENCE; PERSISTENCE;
POETS/POETRY; RELIGION;
RICHNESS; SENTIMENT; SPEAK-
ING; TRUTH; VANITY

Homer
GLOOM; LIFE DEFINED;
MANKIND

Hood, Mary
BEAUTY; EYES; HEART(S); MOVE-
MENT(S); NECK; ORDER/DISOR-
DER; PLEASURE; PRIDE; SLOW-
NESS

Hood, Thomas
IRRITABLENESS/IRRITATING

Horace
ANGER; CHANGE; FAME; HOSPI-
TALITY; POETS/POETRY; WORDS
DEFINED

Horgan, Paul
AGITATION; ALERTNESS; CLAR-
ITY; CLOUDS; EATING AND
DRINKING; EYES, BRIGHT; FA-
CIAL EXPRESSIONS, SERIOUS;
MEN AND WOMEN; MOUN-
TAINS; MOUTH; MUSTACHE(S);
PEACEFULNESS; RAIN; SEXUAL
INTERACTION; SILENCE; SKIN;
SKY; SUN; TEARS; TREES; WALK-
ING; WIND; WRINKLES

Hornung, Ernest William
DRINKING; SUDDENNESS

House, Karen Elliott
POWER

Howard, Maureen
BEHAVIOR; BODY; HAIR; TEN-
SION; TREMBLING

Howard, Richard
DESTRUCTION/DESTRUCTIVE-
NESS

Howe, Edgar Watson
BELIEFS; CREDIT; LIFE DE-
FINED; MARRIAGE; SECRECY

Howe, Tina
EMPTINESS

Howell, James
FRIENDSHIP, DEFINED; TALL-
NESS; WATCHFULNESS

Howell, Margery Eldredge
GREEN

Howells, William Dean
HAPPINESS; MUSTACHE(S);
SPREADING

Howes, Barbara
ALERTNESS; CONTENTMENT;
CROWDS; DISINTEGRATION; ER-
RORS; FACIAL EXPRESSIONS,
MISCELLANEOUS; FIRMNESS;
LOOSENESS

Howland, Bette
LEG(S)

Hoyt, Charles H.
MEN AND WOMEN

Hubbard, Elbert
BUSINESS; FRIENDSHIP, DE-
FINED; HATRED; IMPOSSIBILITY;
MATHEMATICS AND SCIENCE;
PROFESSIONS; RICHES; SENSI-
TIVENESS

Hubbard, Kin
FLATTERY; HELPLESSNESS

Huddle, David
BREASTS; DARKNESS; IRRITABLE-
NESS/IRRITATING; LIGHTING

Hudson, H. W.
DULLNESS

Hudson, Helen
ACTIVENESS; AGITATION; ANI-
MALS; BALDNESS; BEHAVIOR;
BOOKS; CLOTHING; CLOTHING
ACCESSORIES; CLOUD MOVE-
MENTS; CLOUDS; DISHONESTY;
DOCTORS; EMPTINESS; EYE
COLOR; EYES; FACE(S); FACIAL
EXPRESSIONS, BLANK; FACIAL
EXPRESSIONS, MISCELLANEOUS;
FLOWERS; FRAGILITY; FURNI-
TURE AND FURNISHINGS; HAIR;
HAIR, COLOR; HAIR STYLES;
HAIR, TEXTURE; HANDS;
HOUSES; IMMOBILITY; IRRITA-
BLENESS/IRRITATING; MEMORY;
MOON; NAMES; NATURALNESS;
NATURE; NECK; NOISES; PAR-
ENTHOOD; PAST, THE; PEOPLE,
INTERACTION; PLACES; RELIA-
BILITY/UNRELIABILITY; RELI-
GION; ROAD SCENES;
SCRUTINY; SHAPE; SILENCE; SIT-
TING; SKY; SMALLNESS; SMILE;
SMOOTHNESS; SNOW; SUN;
TEETH; TENSION; TIME; TREES;
VOICE, HARSH; VOICE(S);
WALKING; WAR; WHITE;
WORD(S); WORDS OF PRAISE

Hudson, W. H.
FAMILIARITY; FEAR; INNO-
CENCE; NATURALNESS

Hueneker, James G.
FRESHNESS; STEADINESS

Hughes, Langston
LOVE, DEFINED; SLEEP; SWEET-
NESS

Hughes, Rupert
CONTENTMENT

Hughes, Ted
BEARING; BIRDS; FIRE AND
SMOKE; FOREHEAD; HEART-
BEAT; HEAT; HEAVINESS; NERV-
OUSNESS; RAIN; RUNNING;
SHARPNESS; WEAKNESS

Hughes, Thomas
BELONGING

Hugo, Victor
ACTIONS; ALONENESS; ANXI-
ETY; BENDING/BENT; BLACK;
CALMNESS; CHEERFULNESS;
CHILDREN; DEJECTION; ER-
RORS; EYEBROWS; FLATTERY;
GROWTH; HAPPINESS; IMMO-
BILITY; INSECTS; IRRITABLE-
NESS/IRRITATING; LOVE; PER-
SISTENCE; REMOTENESS;
SADNESS; STRENGTH;
THOUGHTS

Hulme, T. E.
MOON

Humboldt, Karl Wilhelm
WORK

Humphrey, George
IMPOSSIBILITY

Humphrey, Hubert H.
TOUGHNESS

Humphrey, William
AGILITY; CHIN; CLEVERNESS;
FURNITURE AND FURNISHINGS;
NOISES; OBVIOUSNESS; REAL-
IZATION; SILENCE; SINGING;
SOFTNESS; STARS; STRAIGHT-
NESS

Hundera, Milan
BELONGING

Huneker, James G.
AMBITION; CONTINUITY; LIFE
DEFINED; LOVE; RELIGION; RE-
SERVE; WRITERS/WRITING

Hunt, Leigh
AFFECTION; FLOWERS; WRIT-
ERS/WRITING

Hunter, Evan
HANDSHAKE

Hurlbut, Kaatje
  SKIN; THOUGHTS; VOICE, EF-
  FECT OF; VOICE, SOFT; WEARI-
  NESS

Hurst, Fannie
  BENDING/BENT

Huston, John
  SUCCESS/FAILURE

Huxley, Aldous
  CORRECTNESS; DEATH; DISIN-
  TEGRATION; LEAVES; LIPS;
  MORALITY; MUSIC; REPETITION

Huxley, Thomas H.
  GROWTH; KNOWLEDGE

Hyne, Cutcliffe
  ENTRAPMENT

I

Ibn Ezra, Abraham
  CORRESPONDENCE; WORDS DE-
  FINED

Ibn Ezra, Moses
  EDUCATION; MAXIMS,
  PROVERBS AND SAYINGS;
  MUSIC; WISDOM; WORDS DE-
  FINED

Ibn Vega, Solomon
  GUILT

Ibsen, Henrik
  COMFORT; INSULT; SOCIETY

Ignatow, David
  ARM(S); FACIAL DETAILS;
  LEAVES; LEG(S); LOOKS; MOVE-
  MENT(S); NATURE; SITTING;
  SKY; STYLE; TREES

Immanuel of Rome
  WORLD

Ingalls, Rachel
  BEAUTY; BITTERNESS; CLING-
  ING; ENERGY; ENTRANCES AND
  EXITS; OCEAN/OCEANFRONTS;
  SURPRISE

Ingersoll, Robert G.
  CANDOR; DIVERSENESS; KIND-
  NESS

Ionesco, Eugene
  HAPPINESS

Irving, Clifford
  HARSHNESS

Irons, Jeremy
  ACTING

Irving, Clive
  MIST; WIND

Irving, John
  POLITICS/POLITICIANS; SMILE;
  STOMACH

Irving, Washington
  CHARACTERISTICS, NATIONAL;
  HOUSES; KNOWLEDGE; LAND-
  SCAPES; PERSONAL TRAITS; SO-
  CIETY

Irwin, Inez Haynes
  BODY; MOUTH

Irwin, Robert
  CLEANLINESS

Irwin, Wallace
  AWKWARDNESS; CAUTION;
  STANDING

Isherwood, Charles
  NATURALNESS

Isherwood, Christopher
  ABSURDITY; ANGER; AWKWARD-
  NESS; BEARING; BROWN;
  CLOTHING; COMPLEXION;
  CONTENTMENT; EMOTIONS;
  EXITS; EYES; FACE(S); FACIAL
  EXPRESSIONS, MISCELLANEOUS;
  FRIENDSHIP, DEFINED; HOUSES;
  LAUGHTER; MODESTY; MOUTH;
  MOUTH, OPEN AND SHUT;
  MOVEMENT(S); PERSONALITY
  PROFILES; PHYSICAL APPEAR-
  ANCE; QUESTIONS AND AN-
  SWERS; RAIN; RISING;
  SEASCAPES; SILENCE; SOCIABIL-
  ITY/UNSOCIABILITY; SPEAKING;
  SPEED; STRANGENESS; TRAN-
  SIENCE; TRUST/MISTRUST;
  VOICE(S)

J

Jackson, Mahalia
  SENTIMENT

Jackson, Robert H.
  FREEDOM

Jacob, Rabbi
  WORLD

Jacobs, Harry A.
  ECONOMICS

Jacobs, Harvey
  TOUGHNESS

Jacobsen, Josephine
  OCEAN/OCEANFRONTS; ROOMS

Jacobson, Dan
  AIR; FIRMNESS; FOREHEAD;
  GRAY; HEAT; NIGHT; SPEECH
  PATTERNS; WHITE

Jacobson, Howard
  ANXIETY, APPEARANCE

Jacoby, Henry D.
  DIFFICULTY

James, Alice
  ENERGY

James, Craig
  FOOTBALL

James, Henry
  ABUNDANCE; ADVICE; ART AND
  LITERATURE; BELIEFS; BEWIL-
  DERMENT; CALMNESS;
  CHOICES; CLEVERNESS; CLOTH-
  ING; CRITICISM; DECREASE; EN-
  TRAPMENT; EXPERIENCE; EYE-
  BROWS; EYES; FIRMNESS;
  FRESHNESS; HEALTH; IMMOBIL-
  ITY; INNOCENCE; JEWELRY; JOY;
  LIGHTNESS; MUSTACHE(S);
  PAUSE; POWER; REGULARITY/IR-
  REGULARITY; SPREADING; STAL-
  ENESS; STARES; STUPIDITY;
  STYLE; TIMELINESS/UNTIMELI-
  NESS; TRUTHNESS/FALSENESS;
  VOICE, MONOTONOUS; VOICE,
  MUSIC RELATED; VOICE(S);
  VOICE, SOFT; WIT

James, P. D.
  ANGER; BEARING; RELIGION;
  SHOCK

James, William
  ACTIVENESS; BURST; CRITICISM,
  DRAMATIC AND LITERARY; EDU-
  CATION; EYES; MIND; PERSON-
  ALITY PROFILES; PLACES; PRO-
  FESSIONS; WEARINESS

Jameson, Anna
  LOYALTY/DISLOYALTY

Jameson, Mike
  ENERGY

Jameson, Storm
  MIND; SMILE; SPREADING; UN-
  DESIREABILITY

Janeway, Elizabeth
  RESERVE

Janeway, Elliot
  USEFULNESS/USELESSNESS

Janin, Jules
  DISPERSAL

Janowitz, Tama
  HAIR, TEXTURE; PHYSICAL
  FEELINGS; SMELL; VOICE,
  MUSIC RELATED

Jarrell, Randall
AGE; EYES; HOPE; LIFE; NAMES; ROOMS; SWEAT; TIME; YELLOW

Jasperson, Ann
FRUSTRATION; FUTILITY; MEMORY; RELATIONSHIP; TRUST/MISTRUST

Jeffers, Robinson
BREASTS; GAIETY; HARMLESSNESS; HISTORY; OCEAN/OCEANFRONTS

Jefferson, Thomas
FRIENDSHIP, DEFINED; POLITICS/POLITICIANS

Jeffrey, Lord Francis
HUMOR; ILLNESS; INTOLERANCE; REPETITION

Jeffries, Roderic
MIND; OPEN AND SHUT; SADNESS; VOICE, HARSH

Jeiteles, Judah
FRIENDSHIP, DEFINED

Jennings, Peter
IMPOSSIBILITY

Jerold, Douglas
ART AND LITERATURE

Jerome, Jerome K.
BEHAVIOR; CAUSE AND EFFECT; CONVERSATION; FIGHTING; FURNITURE AND FURNISHINGS; IDLENESS; LEAVES; LIFE; LIFE DEFINED; LOVE, DEFINED; MEMORY; MOVEMENT(S); ORIGINALITY; PLACES; SEASONS; SHYNESS; SNOW; STRUGGLE; TREES; VANITY; VIRTUE; WEATHER; WRITERS/WRITING

Jerome, Judson
TALKATIVENESS

Jerrold, Douglas
FORTUNE/MISFORTUNE; LOVE, DEFINED; MARRIAGE; PLACES; WIT

Jhabvala, Ruth Prawer
BREASTS; COLLAPSE; DISINTEGRATION; EMOTIONS; EYEBROWS; FACIAL EXPRESSIONS, MISCELLANEOUS; FOOD AND DRINK; HEARTBEAT; HOUSES; KISSES; MANNERS; MEMORY; MOON; TEARS

Jimenez, Juan Ramon
WORLD

John, Elton
LIFE

John, St.
HAIR, COLOR

Johnson, B. S.
MEMORY

Johnson, Charles
ADVANCING; AGITATION; CERTAINTY; CLARITY; CLOSENESS; EMPTINESS; ENERGY; FACE(S); FACIAL EXPRESSIONS, SERIOUS; FEAR; FINGERS; FOG; GLOOM; GROANS AND WHISPERS; HEART(S); HISTORY; IMMOBILITY; LYING; MANKIND; MEN AND WOMEN; MOUTH, OPEN AND SHUT; MOVEMENT(S); NATURE; NOSE(S); PERMANENCE; SEX; SEXUAL INTERACTION; SHAPE; SILENCE; SIMPLICITY; SKIN; SKY; SMILE; SMOOTHNESS; SUN; THOUGHTS; VISABILITY; VOICE, MUSIC RELATED; WRINKLES

Johnson, Denis
ADVANCING; BREATHING; BRIGHTNESS; PHYSICAL FEELINGS; VIBRATION

Johnson, Nora
GOSSIP; LAUGHTER; MEMORY; PERMANENCE

Johnson, Nunally
TREMBLING

Johnson, Owen
MANKIND

Johnson, Pamela Hansford
CHEERFULNESS; PRIDE; SUN; TEETH; TREES

Johnson, Samuel
BOOKS; CONTEMPT; EDUCATION; FLATTERY; FRIENDSHIP; FRIENDSHIP, DEFINED; GREEN; HAPPINESS; IMPORTANCE/UNIMPORTANCE; INSULT; KNOWLEDGE; LANGUAGE; LIFE; MANNERS; MARRIAGE; MEN AND WOMEN; PROMISE; SENSE; THRIFT

Johnson, Willis
BEARD; BODY; LEAVES; LIGHTING

Jones, Emory
SPORTS

Jones, Norah
LOVE

Jong, Erica
FIGHTING; FOOD AND DRINK; GLIMMER, GLITTER AND GLOSS; GREEN; GROWTH; HEARTBEAT

Jonson, Ben
AMBITION; CONTINUITY; COURAGE; ENTHUSIASM; GOSSIP; MIND DEFINED; SPEED

Jordan, Lee Roy
FOOTBALL

Joshua
PARENTHOOD

Joubert, Joseph
ATTENTION; CRUELTY; POETS/POETRY; WORD(S)

Jowitt, Lord
SPEECHMAKING

Joyce, James
DISINTEGRATION; FACE(S); GROANS AND WHISPERS; HAIR STYLES; SNOW; TREMBLING

Judah
LIFE DEFINED

Jung, Carl
STAGE AND SCREEN

Just, Ward
EYE EXPRESSIONS, MISCELLANEOUS; MIND; SKIN

Justice, Donald
ANIMALS; COMFORT; COMMONPLACE; LANDSCAPES; OPEN AND SHUT; SEASCAPES; SILENCE; STARES; THINNESS; TRANSIENCE; YOUTH

Juvenal
RARITY; REPETITION; SMOOTHNESS

K

Kael, Pauline
NOISES; SHARPNESS

Kafka, Franz
WORLD

Kahn, Madeline
MARRIAGE

Kakutani, Michiko
FRAGILITY; WRITERS/WRITING

Kantor, MacKinlay
EASE; FACE(S); HAIR, TEXTURE; NOSE(S)

Kaplan, Andrew
AIR; BODY; COLORS; EMBRACE; EYE EXPRESSIONS, MISCELLANEOUS; GRAY; NECK; NERVOUSNESS; NOISES; PEOPLE, INTER-

ACTION; PHYSICAL APPEAR-
ANCE; PROTRUSION; QUES-
TIONS AND ANSWERS; SITTING;
SMILE; SWEAT; TEETH

Kaplan, David Michael
BREASTS; DESTRUCTION/DE-
STRUCTIVENESS; RESERVE

Kappell, Frederick
BIGNESS

Karmel-Wolfe, Henia
NECESSITY

Kates, Joanne
CONTROL; MEN AND WOMEN

Kaufman, George
BENDING/BENT

Kaufman, Shirley
HELPLESSNESS

Kavanagh, Patrick
TRUST/MISTRUST

Kawabata, Yasunari
DISINTEGRATION; MEMORY;
NERVOUSNESS

Kaye-Smith, Sheila
ANIMALS

Kazantzakis, Nikos
LANDSCAPES

Kazkov, Yuri
VOICE, MUSIC RELATED

Kean, Molly
PURPOSEFULNESS

Keating, H. R. F.
BIGNESS

Keats, John
BEAUTY; CLARITY; DISAPPEAR-
ANCE; FAME; LIFE DEFINED;
MOVEMENT(S); MUSIC; PALLOR;
SILENCE; THOUGHTS; TRAN-
SIENCE

Keats, William
PERMANENCE

Keifetz, Norman
BASEBALL; HEALTH; TENSION;
THINNESS

Keller, Helen
BOOKS; MIND DEFINED; TREES

Kellerman, Jonathan
ARM(S); AWKWARDNESS; COL-
LAPSE; EATING AND DRINKING;
FRAGILITY; FROWNS; FURNI-
TURE AND FURNISHINGS;
HABIT; HAND MOVEMENTS; IM-
POSSIBILITY; LIGHTNESS; MOVE-
MENT(S); MUSTACHE(S); PAIN;
PHYSICAL APPEARANCE; REAL-
NESS/UNREALNESS; REAPPEAR-

ANCE; SKIN; SMELL; SMOOTH-
NESS; STUPIDITY; VOICE(S)

Kelley, Kitty
VIOLENCE

Kelly, Eleanor Mercein
BEAUTY

Kelly, Susan
REJECTION; SADNESS

Kelton, Elmer
COMPETITION;
RELIABILITY/UNRELIABILITY;
RESTLESSNESS; SMELL

Kemp, Peter
PHYSICAL APPEARANCE; RELI-
GION

Kempton, Murray
ABILITY

Keneally, Thomas
BREASTS; BURST; COLLAPSE;
HUMOR; SUN

Kennan, George
SECRECY

Kennedy, Jacqueline
FRAGILITY

Kennedy, John F.
DIFFICULTY; PLACES

Kennedy, Margaret
FACIAL EXPRESSIONS, SERIOUS;
HELPLESSNESS

Kennedy, William J.
BENDING/BENT; PAIN; VIO-
LENCE

Kennedy, William P.
BODY

Kerfoot, John B.
WORDS DEFINED

Kerr, Jean
FATNESS; MARRIAGE

Kersh, Gerald
AGE; AGITATION; BLUE; BODY;
BOXING AND WRESTLING; DAN-
GER; DARKNESS; DESTRUC-
TION/DESTRUCTIVENESS; DIS-
APPEARANCE; ELUSIVENESS;
EMPTINESS; HANDS; HAND-
SHAKE; HATRED; IRRITABLE-
NESS/IRRITATING; JEWELRY;
LAUGHTER; LIFE DEFINED; LIPS;
MOVEMENT(S); MUSCLES; REPE-
TITION; ROCKING AND
ROLLING; SCREAMS; SMILE;
TREMBLING; VOICE, MUSIC RE-
LATED; WHITE

Kesey, Ken
BIGNESS; CURSES; FACE(S); FA-
CIAL EXPRESSIONS, MISCELLA-
NEOUS; KINDNESS; NOISES; SI-
LENCE; TOUGHNESS;
TREMBLING

Khrushchev, Nikita S.
POLITICS/POLITICIANS

Kierkegaard, Soren
THOUGHTS

Killigrew, Thomas
WRITERS/WRITING

Kincaid, James
ACTIONS

King, Alexander
INSULT; MARRIAGE; SERIOUS-
NESS

King, Francis
APPLAUSE; COLLAPSE; DE-
CREASE; HAND MOVEMENTS;
MANNERS; MUSCLES; NOISES;
SINGING; SLEEP; SPEECH PAT-
TERNS; SUN; VEHICLES; WEARI-
NESS

King, Martin Luther, Jr.
JUSTICE

King, Stephen
ANGER; BREATHING; DEATH, FI-
NALITY OF; DISINTEGRATION;
FACIAL COLOR; KISSES; PHYSI-
CAL APPEARANCE; SITTING;
SPEAKING; TEETH; WEAKNESS;
WRITERS/WRITING

Kingsley, Charles
MATHEMATICS AND SCIENCE

Kinnell, Galway
AIR; HAPPINESS; REGRET

Kinsella, W. P.
AGITATION; ANXIETY; BASE-
BALL; BEHAVIOR; BLACK;
BREATHING; BRIGHTNESS;
CAUSE AND EFFECT; CHEEKS;
CLOTHING; CLOTHING, ITS FIT;
CLOUD MOVEMENTS; CLOUDS;
COLLAPSE; DEJECTION; DESIRE;
DIFFICULTY; EMOTIONS; EN-
ERGY; ENVY; GOSSIP; GRINS;
GROWTH; HAIR, COLOR; HAIR,
TEXTURE; HAND MOVEMENTS;
HELPLESSNESS; HOUSES; IMPOS-
SIBILITY; INSECTS; JOY; JUMP-
ING; LAUGHTER; LEAVES;
LIGHTNESS; MANNERS; MIND;
MOON; MUSCLES; NERVOUS-
NESS; NIGHT; NOISES; PAIN;

PAST, THE; PINK; QUESTIONS AND ANSWERS; SCREAMS; SCRUTINY; SEASONS; SEX; SKIN; SKY; SMELL; SPEECH PATTERNS; SPEED; SUN; TENSION; THICKNESS; TREES; VEHICLES; VOICE(S); WATCHFULNESS; WEAKNESS; WEARINESS; WHITE

Kipling, Rudyard
ADVANCING; AGITATION; CERTAINTY; CLEVERNESS; COLLAPSE; DEJECTION; DISCOMFORT; JUMPING; PALLOR; PERMANENCE; SEASCAPES; SHARPNESS; SIMILARITY; SPEED; STALENESS; SUN; THOUGHTS; VIOLENCE

Kirk, Eleanor
COMPATIBILITY

Kirkup, James
CHARACTERISTICS, NATIONAL

Kirkwood, James
ANGER; ATTRACTIVENESS; CRUELTY; FUTILITY

Kirstein, Lincoln
CLEANLINESS; GLIMMER, GLITTER AND GLOSS; THOUGHTS

Kirwan, Jack D.
WEAKNESS

Kissinger, Henry
GOVERNMENT

Kittman, Marvin
ACTIVENESS

Kiwitz, Kaethe
JOY

Kizer, Carolyn
HEAD MOVEMENTS; LOYALTY/DISLOYALTY; MARRIAGE; ROARS; SCREAMS; SEXUAL INTERACTION; VANITY

Klein, Norma
MARRIAGE

Klopikova, Elena
POWER

Knebel, Fletcher
ORDER/DISORDER; PREPAREDNESS; THUNDER AND LIGHTNING

Knef, Hildegarde
DOCTORS

Knight, Eric
RISING

Knight, Etheridge
EMPTINESS; PEACEFULNESS; WATCHFULNESS

Knox, William
DEATH

Knudson, Thomas J.
DIFFICULTY

Koch, C. J.
BREASTS; DEJECTION; EYE MOVEMENTS; FACE(S); LOOKS; SERIOUSNESS

Koch, Kenneth
LIFE; SUN

Koenig, Joseph
BLUSHES

Korda, Michael
ALERTNESS; CLOSENESS; ENERGY; FACIAL EXPRESSIONS, MISCELLANEOUS; KINDNESS; GLOOM; SLOWNESS; TALKATIVENESS; TEETH; VOICE

Kornblatt, Joyce Reiser
DEJECTION; PHYSICAL APPEARANCE; PLACES; SADNESS

Korolenko, Vladimir
HEART(S); IDEAS; MIST; RAIN

Kosinski, Jerzy
GLIMMER, GLITTER AND GLOSS; SKIN; UNSTEADINESS

Kotzwinkle, William
LEG(S); MOVEMENT(S)

Kozloff, Ivan
MONEY

Kramer, Dale
HEALTH

Kronenberger, Louis
EMOTIONS; ORIGINALITY

Kubicki, Jan
BREATHING; COLLAPSE; PHYSICAL APPEARANCE; RISING

Kübler-Ross, Elisabeth
DEATH DEFINED

Kuh, Moses Ephraim
FRIENDSHIP, DEFINED

Kumin, Maxine
AGILITY; FOG; LIFE; NOISES; PALLOR; POLITICS/POLITICIANS; SHARPNESS; SLOWNESS; TURNING AND TWISTING

Kundera, Milan
BREASTS; CHILDREN; DAY; ENVY; LOVE; MOON; SLEEP; UNATTRACTIVENESS; WORDS OF PRAISE

Kuttner, Paul
ANGER; ATTENTION; CLOTHING; FIRE AND SMOKE; HAIR; IMMOBILITY; LEG(S); LINGERING; RAIN; SKY COLOR; TREES; VOICE, EFFECT OF

L

La Farge, Oliver
EXCITEMENT

La Fontaine, Jean de
SHAME

La Guardia, Fiorella H.
FACTS; SELF CONFIDENCE

La Rochefoucauld, Francçois de
AGE; CRUELTY; ERRORS; LOVE; LOVE, DEFINED

Lacordaire, Jean-Baptiste
ILLNESS

Lahiri, Jhumpa
BODY; DIFFICULTY; WORDS

Lahr, John
PHYSICAL APPEARANCE; POSTURE

Laing, Dilys
LANDSCAPES; POETS/POETRY; SMILE

Lamartine, Alphonse de
MARRIAGE

Lamb, Charles
DRINKING; HUNGER

Lambert, Derek
AIR; ALONENESS; BEARING; BEWILDERMENT; BOREDOM/BORING; BREATHING; CHEEKS; COLLAPSE; DESIRABILITY; DISAPPEARANCE; DISPERSAL; EASE; FACIAL EXPRESSIONS, MISCELLANEOUS; FEAR; FOOD AND DRINK; HEAD MOVEMENTS; HUNGER; KISSES; PEOPLE, INTERACTION; PHYSICAL APPEARANCE; PLACES; RISING; SCREAMS; SHAPE; SIGHS; SNOW; SPEED; STRENGTH; SUCCESS/FAILURE; SUDDENNESS; SWEAT; TOBACCO; UNDESIREABILITY; WORDS, EFFECT OF; WRINKLES

Lambert, Gavin
POLITICS/POLITICIANS

Lampedusa, Giuseppe di
PERSONALITY PROFILES

Lamuniere, Jean
SPORTS

Landon, L. E.
MIND DEFINED

Landon, Letitia
BEAUTY

Landon, Margaret
SMILE

Landor, Walter Savage
BIGNESS; BRIGHTNESS; CLARITY; COLDNESS; COURAGE; CRU-ELTY; DAY; EYES; FOOD AND DRINK; GOVERNMENT; GREED; HEAT; HOPE; LIES/LIARS; LOOSE-NESS; MANKIND; POWER; PRES-ENT, THE; PURPOSEFULNESS; SENSE; SERIOUSNESS; SOUL; TEARS; TRUTH; WRITERS/WRIT-ING

Lane, Carla
DESTRUCTION/DESTRUCTIVE-NESS; FRAGILITY; MIND; PAS-SION; SELF CONFIDENCE

Lang, Andrew
BOOKS; FACTS

Langdon, Philip
FAMILIARITY

Langland, William
SILENCE

Lanier, Sidney
MUSIC; SOUL; VAGUENESS

Lao Tzu
CAUTION; HATRED; VIRTUE

Lapierre, Dominique
BLACK; HEAT; IMMOBILITY; IM-POSSIBILITY; MEMORY; PHYSI-CAL APPEARANCE; SHOCK; SKIN; VIBRATION; WRINKLES

Lapine, James
PAST, THE

Lardner, Ring
ATTENTION; DANCING; KIND-NESS; SLEEP

Larkin, Philip
HEAVINESS; POETS/POETRY

Larson, Erik
CHANGE; FACIAL DETAILS; FEAR; MEMORY; SKY; VOICE(S)

Larsson, Stieg
BELONGING; HAIR; PERSIST-ENCE; PERSONALITY PROFILES

Laski, Harold J.
GOVERNMENT

Laurence, Margaret
BALDNESS; FACIAL EXPRES-SIONS, BLANK; FAMILIARITY; HANDS; HEAT; LAUGHTER; NIGHT; RISING; TREES

Lavater, John Casper
PERSONAL TRAITS

Lavin, Mary
FOOLISHNESS; MUSIC; RAIN; ROOMS

Law, William
SINGING

Lawrence, D. H.
AFFECTION; AGILITY; ANIMALS; APPRECIATION; BEARING; BLOOD; BLUSHES; BREASTS; BRIGHTNESS; COLDNESS; COL-LAPSE; DESIRABILITY; DISAP-PEARANCE; DISINTEGRATION; ELUSIVENESS; EMOTIONS; EX-CITEMENT; EYEBROWS; FACE(S); FATNESS; GLIMMER, GLITTER AND GLOSS; GRAY; HAIR, TEXTURE; ILLNESS; IM-MOBILITY; INAPPROPRIATENESS; INTELLIGENCE; LOOKS; LYING; MANKIND; MOUTH, OPEN AND SHUT; PAIN; PLACES; RELATION-SHIP; RISING; SMILE; TENSION; VOICE(S)

Lawrence, Rae
WRITERS/WRITING

Le Carre, John
ARMY; ATTRACTION; BEARING; FACIAL EXPRESSIONS, BLANK; FEAR; HEAD MOVEMENTS; KNOWLEDGE; MEN AND WOMEN; POLITICS/POLITI-CIANS; ROOMS; SMILE; STEADI-NESS

Le Fanu, Joseph Sheridan
GLIMMER, GLITTER AND GLOSS; PALLOR; WATCHFULNESS

Le Gallienne, Richard
BEAUTY

Le Guin, Ursula K.
DISAPPEARANCE; LOVE; TEN-SION

Leacock, Stephen
CONVERSATION

Lean, Vincent Stuckey
BUSYNESS

Lear, Edward
NOSE(S)

Leavitt, David
JOY; REALIZATION; RELATION-SHIP; SEX; SHOCK; SOCIABIL-ITY/UNSOCIABILITY; SPEED

Lee, Bruce
LOVE, DEFINED

Lee, Gerald Stanley
MORALITY

Leffland, Ella
CLARITY; DARKNESS; HAIR STYLES; SCRUTINY; SILENCE; SKIN; TEETH

Lehmann, Rosamond
SPORTS

Lehrer, Tom
LIFE

Leitch, David
COMPATIBILITY

Leithauser, Brad
NATURE; SNORES; TIMELI-NESS/UNTIMELINESS

Lem, Stanislaw J.
FEAR

Lemaître, Jules
VOICE, SOFT

Lemmonnier, Camille
MUSIC

Lencos, Anne de
LOVE

L'Engle, Madeleine
BIGNESS; CHANGE; INTENSITY; PEACEFULNESS; SHARPNESS; TREMBLING

Lennon, John
SIGHS

Leonard, Hugh
MEMORY; WORK

Leonardo Da Vinci
FEAR

Lermontov, Mikhail
AIR; DISAPPEARANCE; FOR-TUNE/MISFORTUNE; GLIMMER, GLITTER AND GLOSS; LOOKS; MIST; PAIN; PEACEFULNESS; SMILE

Lerner, Max
CORRESPONDENCE; DANCING; SILENCE

Leskov, Nikolay
TREMBLING

Leslie, Amy
SUDDENNESS

Leslie, Shane
PLACES

Lessing, Doris
ANIMALS; GROWTH; KISSES

Levertov, Denise
FORTUNE/MISFORTUNE; GREEN; HEARTBEAT; OCEAN/OCEAN-FRONTS

Levi, Amora
BIRTH

Leviant, Curt
  NOISES

Levine, Philip
  ANGER; ARM(S); BODY;
  CHOICES; CITIES; COLDNESS;
  DEATH; DISINTEGRATION; FIN-
  GERS; FLOWERS; FOOD AND
  DRINK; FUTURE; GLIMMER,
  GLITTER AND GLOSS; GRAY;
  GROWTH; JEWELRY; LEAVES;
  MOON; REJECTION; SHADOW;
  SHINING; SMELL; STRENGTH;
  TREES; TURNING AND TWIST-
  ING; WIND

Lewes, G. H.
  CRIME

Lewis, Alfred Henry
  BEAUTY; SOCIABILITY/UNSOCIA-
  BILITY

Lewis, C. S.
  AGILITY; LIGHTNESS; VOICE(S)

Lewis, G. N.
  LAWS

Lewis, Peter H.
  TOUGHNESS

Lewis, Sinclair
  BEARD; CLEVERNESS; DEJEC-
  TION; FOOTBALL; NOISES; SEX;
  YELLOW

Lewis, William
  RELIGION

Liberman, M. M.
  MUSTACHE(S)

Lichtenberg, Georg Christoph
  BOOKS; CRITICISM, DRAMATIC
  AND LITERARY

Lieberman, Herbert
  ANGER; DISAPPEARANCE; EYE
  MOVEMENTS; FEAR; FURNI-
  TURE AND FURNISHINGS;
  GROWTH; VEHICLES

Liebling, A. J.
  MIND DEFINED

Lifshin, Lyn
  CONTINUITY; LIPS; MEMORY;
  PALLOR; SHAPE

Lincoln, Abraham
  ARGUMENTS; CHARACTER;
  DEATH DEFINED; PERSISTENCE;
  THINNESS

Lincoln, Joseph C.
  BREATHING; GLOOM; GRINS

Lindbergh, Anne Morrow
  BEGINNINGS AND ENDINGS;
  BIRDS; CONVERSATION; PURITY;
  RAIN; STRAIGHTNESS; TIME

Lindbergh, Charles
  DISAPPEARANCE

Lindsay, Vachel
  FLOWERS; TIME

Lindstrom, Pia
  ATTRACTIVENESS

Linklater, Eric
  PLACES

Linley, George
  DISAPPEARANCE

Listfield, Emily
  DESIRE

Liston, Sonny
  BOXING AND WRESTLING

Litchfield, Grace Denio
  SNOW

Litsey, Sarah
  LOYALTY/DISLOYALTY

Little, M. W.
  BEAUTY

Livesay, Dorothy
  NATURE

Livingston, David "Doc,"
  CHANGE

Livy
  ENVY

Llewellyn, Richard
  BALDNESS

Lloyd, Donald
  CONVERSATION

Locke, John
  KNOWLEDGE; TRUTH

Lodge, Thomas
  NECK

Loesser, Frank
  SWEETNESS

Logan, John
  COLORS; CONNECTIONS;
  DREAM; SEX

Lois, Susan
  BREASTS; FRUSTRATION

London, Jack
  BLOOD; CURSES; EYES, BRIGHT;
  FACE(S); LIFE DEFINED; MOVE-
  MENT(S); MUSCLES; SADNESS;
  SIMILARITY

Long, William J.
  EDUCATION

Longfellow, Henry Wadsworth
  ENTRANCES AND EXITS; GAI-
  ETY; GLIMMER, GLITTER AND
  GLOSS; GREATNESS; HAPPINESS;
  HEARTBEAT; HEAT; HEAVINESS;
  HOPE; LIES/LIARS; MOVE-
  MENT(S); NOISES; SADNESS; SI-
  LENCE; SOFTNESS; SPEED;
  STRENGTH; TIME; WORDS OF
  PRAISE; YELLOW

Longfellow, William Wadsworth
  ABUNDANCE; AGE; BREATHING;
  BROWN; CLARITY; CLOUD
  MOVEMENTS; DISAPPEARANCE;
  DISPERSAL; EMPTINESS; HOPE

Longstreet, Stephen
  ABILITY; AVAILABILITY; CHEER-
  FULNESS; CLOTHING; DANGER;
  FRIENDSHIP; IRRITABLENESS/IR-
  RITATING; MIND; OBVIOUSNESS;
  RAIN; REALNESS/UNREALNESS;
  SECRECY; THUNDER AND
  LIGHTNING; VISABILITY

Longworth, Alice Roosevelt
  FACIAL EXPRESSIONS, SERIOUS

Lopate, Phillip
  DULLNESS; SUCCESS/FAILURE

Lorimer, George Horace
  WRITERS/WRITING

Lotta, Dale
  CRITICISM

Louis IV
  DIFFICULTY

Lourie, Richard
  ALONENESS; CRITICISM, DRA-
  MATIC AND LITERARY; DRINK-
  ING; PHYSICAL FEELINGS;
  SLOWNESS; WRINKLES

Lovett, Robert
  BUSYNESS

Lowell, Amy
  BEAUTY; BEGINNINGS AND
  ENDINGS; BREASTS; COLLAPSE;
  CONTINUITY; CROWDS; FIRM-
  NESS; GAIETY; LIGHTNESS;
  MOON; NERVOUSNESS; PEACE-
  FULNESS; PHYSICAL APPEAR-
  ANCE; REPETITION; WEARI-
  NESS; WORDS OF PRAISE

Lowell, James Russell
  ALONENESS; FORTUNE/MISFOR-
  TUNE; MIND DEFINED; OPIN-
  ION; RARITY

Lowell, Robert
  EVIL; PROTRUSION

Lowry, Robert
  BEARING; HELPLESSNESS

Lu Hsün
CITIES; FACIAL EXPRESSIONS, MISCELLANEOUS; SNOW

Lubbock, Sir John
ART AND LITERATURE; FRIEND-SHIP, DEFINED

Lucas, E. V.
BLUSHES

Lucas, F. L.
LANGUAGE; WORDS DEFINED; WRITERS/WRITING

Luce, Clare Boothe
ABSURDITY; CONTROL

Luce, Gay Gaer
RELIABILITY/UNRELIABILITY

Lurie, Allison
HABIT

Luther, Martin
HEART(S); LIES/LIARS; SENSE; WORLD

Lutz, John
NECESSITY; RAIN

Lux, Thomas
BALDNESS; COMMONPLACE; NECESSITY; RISING

Lyall, Gavin
BREVITY; CLOTHING; DARK-NESS; FURNITURE AND FUR-NISHINGS; LINGERING; NOSE(S); OPEN AND SHUT; PHYSICAL FEELINGS; PURSUIT; ROOMS; SEASCAPES

Lydgate, John
BARENESS; FRESHNESS

Lyly, John
FATNESS

Lyttleton, Lord
BEAUTY DEFINED

Lytton, Edgar George Bulwer-
TOBACCO

Lytton, Edward Bulwer-
AGE; BRIGHTNESS; FAME; PA-TIENCE; SPEECHMAKING; SPREADING

M

Macauley, Robie
CLOUD MOVEMENTS; FACE(S); OCEAN/OCEANFRONTS; RELI-GION

Macauley, Thomas Babington
RUNNING; SILENCE

MacDonald, D. R.
OCEAN/OCEANFRONTS

MacDonald, George
DEJECTION; INTENSITY

MacDonald, John D.
AGITATION; ALONENESS; BALD-NESS; BEARD; BREASTS; CHOICES; CRUELTY; DULLNESS; ENTHUSIASM; FREEDOM; FUR-NITURE AND FURNISHINGS; GRINS; LAUGHTER; LEG(S); LIGHTNESS; LIPS; MUSIC; NOISES; PATIENCE; PERMA-NENCE; PERSONALITY PRO-FILES; REMOTENESS; SLOW-NESS; SMILE; SNORES; SPEED; STOMACH; THINNESS; VOICE(S); WEARINESS; WRITERS/WRITING

Macdonald, Ross
ARM(S); ATMOSPHERE; AWK-WARDNESS; BEARD; BEARING; BEHAVIOR; BODY; CHANGE; CHIN; CHOICES; CITIES; CLING-ING; CLOTHING; CLOTHING, ITS FIT; COLLAPSE; DANGER; EMO-TIONS; ENTRAPMENT; EVIL; EYES; FACE(S); FACIAL EXPRES-SIONS, MISCELLANEOUS; FA-CIAL EXPRESSIONS, SERIOUS; FAMILIARITY; FINGERS; FIRE AND SMOKE; FOG; FOOD AND DRINK; GLOOM; HAIR; HAND-SHAKE; JUMPING; LEG(S); LOOKS; MEN AND WOMEN; MOON; MOUTH; MOVEMENT(S); MUSCLES; NOSE(S); PAIN; PEO-PLE, INTERACTION; PERSONAL-ITY PROFILES; PHYSICAL AP-PEARANCE; PINK; PREPAREDNESS; RARITY; ROOMS; RUNNING; SHAME; SI-LENCE; SKY; SKY COLOR; SLEEP; SLOWNESS; SMILE; SNORES; STANDING; STARS; TEARS; TEN-SION; TIME; TREMBLING; TRUST/MISTRUST; UNSTEADI-NESS; VOICE, MUSIC RELATED; VOICE(S); WATCHFULNESS; WORD(S)

MacInnes, Helen
EMPTINESS

MacIntyre, Tom
SMELL

MacKenzie, Donald
BEHAVIOR; EYES; HEAD MOVE-MENTS; HELPLESSNESS; LOOKS; NERVOUSNESS; QUESTIONS

AND ANSWERS; SERIOUSNESS; VEHICLES; VOICE(S)

MacLean, Norman
LOOKS

MacLeish, Archibald
EXPERIENCE; PAST, THE

MacLeish, Rod
DIFFERENCES

MacManus, Seumas
SPEAKING

Macmillan, Harold
POWER

MacMillan, Ian
LEG(S)

MacNeice, Louis
ABANDONMENT; ADVERSARY; FUTURE; GUILT; LOVE; MEN AND WOMEN; PAST, THE; RICHES; RISING; SEASONS; SI-LENCE; SMELL; STRENGTH; SUR-PRISE; TIMELINESS/UNTIMELI-NESS; WORLD

MacNeil, Robert
ENTRAPMENT

Macy, John
CHANGE

Magnani, Anna
CHILDREN

Maharishi Mahesh Yogi
MIND DEFINED

Mahler, Gustav
MUSIC

Mailer, Norman
ANXIETY; BEARING; BRIGHT-NESS; COLDNESS; CONVERSA-TION; EYE MOVEMENTS; EYES; EYES, BRIGHT; FEAR; FEROCITY; GROANS AND WHISPERS; HOUSES; IMPOSSIBILITY; INSULT; JOY; KINDNESS; MARRIAGE; MEMORY; MIND; NOISES; PER-SISTENCE; PERSONALITY PRO-FILES; PREPAREDNESS; PROB-LEMS AND SOLUTIONS; RELATIONSHIP; ROARS; SAD-NESS; SERIOUSNESS; SHOCK; SPEECH PATTERNS; SPEECH-MAKING; SUDDENNESS; SWEAT; TALKATIVENESS; TENSION; THINNESS; TOBACCO; USEFUL-NESS/USELESSNESS; VIBRATION; VOICE, EFFECT OF; VOICE, HARSH; VOICE(S); WISDOM; WRITERS/WRITING

Mairs, Nancy
MARRIAGE

Major, Clarence
ENERGY; INNOCENCE; SOFT-
NESS; TREMBLING

Malamud, Bernard
ABUNDANCE; AGITATION; ANXI-
ETY; ARM MOVEMENTS; BASE-
BALL; BIRDS; BREASTS; COL-
LAPSE; DEJECTION;
DISAPPEARANCE; DRYNESS;
EMOTIONS; EMPTINESS; EYE
COLOR; FEAR; FROWNS; GLIM-
MER, GLITTER AND GLOSS;
HEARTBEAT; LEAVES; MOON;
NOISES; PAIN; PHYSICAL FEEL-
INGS; PROBLEMS AND SOLU-
TIONS; RESTLESSNESS; RUN-
NING; SILENCE; SMELL; SUN;
WORK

Malcolm, John
ABANDONMENT; FACIAL EX-
PRESSIONS, MISCELLANEOUS;
FIRMNESS

Malloch, Douglas
MODESTY

Mallock, W. H.
IMPOSSIBILITY

Mallon, Thomas
LIFE DEFINED

Malone, Michael
CLOTHING; PROFESSIONS;
SPEED; WIND

Malraux, Andre
CHEERFULNESS; FACIAL EX-
PRESSIONS, MISCELLANEOUS;
JOY; MANKIND; MOON; TO-
BACCO; YOUTH

Maltz, Albert
BEARING

Mamet, David
PROFESSIONS; VIBRATION

Mancroft, Lord
SPEECHMAKING

Mandelstamm, Benjamin
FRIENDSHIP, DEFINED;
HEART(S); MANKIND

Mankiewicz, Joseph L.
IMPORTANCE/UNIMPORTANCE

Manley, Dexter
DEJECTION

Mann, Thomas
BEAUTY DEFINED; CLOUD
MOVEMENTS; DARKNESS; PAS-
SION; SNOW; TRANSIENCE

Manning, Olivia
FREEDOM; SENSITIVENESS

Mansfield, Katherine
AGITATION; ALONENESS;
BEAUTY; CLOUDS; COURAGE;
DAY; EXCITEMENT; EYE MOVE-
MENTS; FATNESS; FLOWERS;
HAIR, TEXTURE; HAND MOVE-
MENTS; HEAD MOVEMENTS;
HEARTBEAT; INNOCENCE; JOY;
JUMPING; LANDSCAPES;
LAUGHTER; MEN AND WOMEN;
MOVEMENT(S); MUSIC; PAIN;
POVERTY; PREPAREDNESS; RAIN;
REALNESS/UNREALNESS; RE-
SERVE; ROOMS; SILENCE; SKY;
SOFTNESS; STARS; THUNDER
AND LIGHTNING; TREES; WALK-
ING; WIND; WORD(S)

Mansfield, Stephanie
SKIN

March, William
FINGERS; VIOLENCE

Marcus Aurelius
AGREEMENT/DISAGREEMENT;
ANGER; CHILDREN; DEATH DE-
FINED; FIRMNESS; LIFE; TIME;
TRANSIENCE

Marie, Queen of Romania
GOVERNMENT

Markham, Beryl
ADVANCING; ANGER; BLACK;
BOREDOM/BORING; BRIGHT-
NESS; BURST; CLARITY; CLEAN-
LINESS; COLDNESS; COURAGE;
CRUELTY; DAY; DISAPPEAR-
ANCE; DISINTEGRATION; DIS-
PERSAL; ENERGY; FEAR;
FRIENDSHIP; GLIMMER, GLIT-
TER AND GLOSS; GOSSIP;
GREEN; HEAD MOVEMENTS;
HEAT; IMMOBILITY; IMPOSSIBIL-
ITY; LANDSCAPES; LAUGHTER;
LEG(S); LOOKS; MUSCLES;
NIGHT; PATIENCE; PHYSICAL
APPEARANCE; PRIDE; PROTRU-
SION; RELIABILITY/UNRELIABIL-
ITY; RESERVE; ROCKING AND
ROLLING; SHADOW; SHAPE;
SIGHS; SKY; SOFTNESS;
STRAIGHTNESS; TREMBLING;
WALKING; WHITE

Marlowe, Christopher
ALONENESS

Marmion, Shackerley
JOY; LOVE

Marquand, John P.
DARKNESS

Marquis, Don
BLUE; DISAPPEARANCE;
GLOOM; GRINS; IDLENESS; LIFE
DEFINED; LOVE; POETS/POETRY;
RESTLESSNESS; UNDESIREABIL-
ITY

Marquis of Halifax
RELIGION

Marryat, Frederick
FEROCITY; FORTUNE/MISFOR-
TUNE

Marsh, Edward
COMPATIBILITY; FACE(S);
HEALTH

Marsh, Ngaio
COMPATIBILITY

Marshall, Paule
ANGER; ANXIETY; BEARING;
EATING AND DRINKING; EYES,
BRIGHT; FRAGILITY; LEG(S);
STOMACH; SUN; TIME; VOICE(S)

Marti, Jose
MANKIND

Martial
KINDNESS

Martin, Abe
PLEASURE

Martin, Ian Kennedy
ALONENESS; SWEAT

Martin, Judith
COLLAPSE; MARRIAGE; OPEN
AND SHUT; PROFESSIONS; RE-
MOTENESS; SMELL

Martineau, Harriet
INSULT

Marvell, Andrew
COLORS

Marx, Groucho
CORRESPONDENCE

Marx, Karl
ECONOMICS

Mascagni, Pietro
DANGER

Mason, Bobbie Ann
ATTRACTIVENESS; AWKWARD-
NESS; BEARD; BEARING;
BREASTS; COMPLEXION; EYES;
FACIAL DETAILS; FOOLISHNESS;
HOUSES; LIPS; MOUNTAINS; RE-
LATIONSHIP; REMOTENESS;

ROAD SCENES; SCRUTINY; VOICE(S); WATCHFULNESS

Mason, F. van Wyck
BARENESS; BEHAVIOR; BODY; BREATHING; CLOTHING ACCESSORIES; COLDNESS; DIFFICULTY; DISAPPEARANCE; ELUSIVENESS; ENTRAPMENT; EYES; GLOOM; HAIR; HANDS; HEAD MOVEMENTS; LEG(S); LOOKS; MANNERS; PROBLEMS AND SOLUTIONS; ROCKING AND ROLLING; SHARPNESS; SMILE; SWEETNESS; THOUGHTS; TOBACCO; TREMBLING; VOICE(S); WORD(S); WORDS, EFFECT OF

Mason, John M.
MEEKNESS; REVENGE

Maspero, François
COLORS; COMFORT; CRYING; MOUTH

Massey, Gerald
DISAPPEARANCE; HEART(S)

Masters, Edgar Lee
ABILITY; FACE(S); IDEAS; MEN AND WOMEN; SILENCE

Masters, Hilary
ANIMALS; BUSYNESS; CURSES; EYES, BRIGHT; PRIDE; UNSTEADINESS

Masterton, Graham
BEHAVIOR; BELIEFS; BENDING/BENT; DEJECTION; DRINKING; EMOTIONS; EYE COLOR; SHARPNESS; TENSION; TREES; TURNING AND TWISTING; VOICE, HARSH

Matthews, William
FACE(S); FOG

Matthiessen, Peter
BODY; EMPTINESS; FEAR; SLEEP; STOMACH

Maugham, W. Somerset
ABANDONMENT; ART AND LITERATURE; ATTENTION; BEARING; BEAUTY DEFINED; BEGINNINGS AND ENDINGS; BEHAVIOR; BODY; BREASTS; BRIGHTNESS; CLARITY; CLOUDS; COMPLEXION; CONVERSATION; CRUELTY; DAY; DEJECTION; DISINTEGRATION; DULLNESS; ELUSIVENESS; ENERGY; EYES; FACIAL EXPRESSIONS, SERIOUS; FACIAL SHAPE; FAME; FLEXIBIL-

ITY/INFLEXIBILITY; FOOD AND DRINK; FUTURE; GAIETY; HELPLESSNESS; LIFE; MEN AND WOMEN; MONEY; MOON; MOUTH; OBVIOUSNESS; PASSION; PEACEFULNESS; PEOPLE, INTERACTION; PERSONALITY PROFILES; PHYSICAL APPEARANCE; PLACES; POETS/POETRY; PROFESSIONS; RAIN; READERS/READING; REALNESS/UNREALNESS; SCREAMS; SEASCAPES; SILENCE; SKIN; SKY; SLEEP; SOUL; TIME; TIMELINESS/UNTIMELINESS; TREES; VOICE, EFFECT OF; VOICE(S); WRINKLES; YOUTH

Maupassant, Guy de
ANGER; ATTRACTIVENESS; BALDNESS; BELIEFS; COMPLEXION; CORRECTNESS; COURAGE; CRYING; FLOWERS; GLOOM; HANDS; LOVE; LOVE, DEFINED; RAIN; SOFTNESS; SUDDENNESS; VIOLENCE; VOICE(S)

Maurois, André
ART AND LITERATURE; CONVERSATION; HAPPINESS; MARRIAGE; SILENCE

Mawrer, Simon
ELUSIVENESS; IMPOSSIBILITY; OBJECTS, MISCELLANEOUS; RED; REPETITION; SMOOTHNESS

Maxwell, A. E.
AIR; ANTICIPATION; BIRDS; COLORS; DESIRE; DULLNESS; EMPTINESS; EYES; FUTURE; LIES/LIARS; PAIN; PROPRIETY/IMPROPRIETY; ROAD SCENES; SINGING; VANITY

Mayakovsky, Vladimir
CRITICISM, DRAMATIC AND LITERARY

Maynard, Richard
ANIMALS; ARM(S); BODY; DANGER; DEJECTION; HOPE; MEMORY; SEASCAPES; THOUGHTS; VOICE, HARSH

McBain, Ed
AWKWARDNESS; BEHAVIOR; BLUE; CLINGING; CONTINUITY; GREEN; HAND MOVEMENTS; INCOMPLETENESS; LOOKS; USEFULNESS/USELESSNESS

McCahern, John
OPEN AND SHUT; RAIN; SCRUTINY

McCaig, Donald
BEHAVIOR; CALMNESS; CLOSENESS; COLORS; COMFORT; EMOTIONS; ENTHUSIASM; EYE EXPRESSIONS, MISCELLANEOUS; EYE MOVEMENTS; EYES; FACE(S); FACIAL COLOR; FOG; FROWNS; GLIMMER, GLITTER AND GLOSS; HAIR STYLES; HAND MOVEMENTS; LAUGHTER; LIGHTNESS; LOVE, DEFINED; MOVEMENT(S); MUSIC; PAIN; PURPOSEFULNESS; PURSUIT; SMELL; SMOOTHNESS; SNOW; TALKATIVENESS; WALKING; WORD(S)

McCartney, Paul
WORDS

McCarthy, Eugene
CONVERSATION; POLITICS/POLITICIANS

McCarthy, Mary
ACTIVENESS; ALONENESS; ATTENTION; ATTRACTION; BEHAVIOR; BROWN; DANGER; DISAPPOINTMENT; EYE COLOR; FACIAL EXPRESSIONS, MISCELLANEOUS; GLOOM; GROANS AND WHISPERS; INAPPROPRIATENESS; INTENSITY; JUSTICE; LOOKS; MANKIND; MEMORY; RISK; SADNESS; SCRUTINY; SHAME; SOCIABILITY/UNSOCIABILITY; VOICE, HARSH; VOICE(S); WRITERS/WRITING

McCarver, Tim
TOUGHNESS

McClatchy, J. D.
ROOMS; SEX

McCorquodale, Robin
CRYING; DESIRE; GLIMMER, GLITTER AND GLOSS

McCoy, Larry
CHANGE

McCullers, Carson
CITIES; FATNESS; HEART(S); NOISES; PHYSICAL APPEARANCE; PLACES; RICHES; ROCKING AND ROLLING; SUN; TALKATIVENESS; TEARS; THINNESS; VOICE, HARSH

McDermott, Alice
ABUNDANCE; AIMLESSNESS; ALONENESS; AVAILABILITY; BEHAVIOR; BENDING/BENT; BOREDOM/BORING; COLORS; CURIOSITY; DARKNESS; EMOTIONS; FACE(S); FACIAL DETAILS; FACIAL EXPRESSIONS, MISCELLANEOUS; FURNITURE AND FURNISHINGS; HISTORY; HOPE; LOVE; MIST; MOON; MOVEMENT(S); PHYSICAL APPEARANCE; SADNESS; SELF CONFIDENCE; SHYNESS; SITTING; SOFTNESS; STOMACH; TEETH; VEHICLES; WRINKLES

Mcdonald, Gregory
DULLNESS; FEAR; SCRUTINY

McFadden, Robert D.
RICHNESS

McFee, William
BUSINESS; RELIABILITY/UNRELIABILITY

McGahern, John
CONVERSATION; EASE; RAIN

McGinley, Phyllis
BIRDS; COMMONPLACE; CONTROL; DREAM; FAME; HAND MOVEMENTS; LOVE; OPINION; PARENTHOOD; PROPRIETY/IMPROPRIETY; THINNESS; TIME; TRUTH

McGivern, William
ATTRACTION

McGough, Roger
SEXUAL INTERACTION

McGuane, Thomas
ANTICIPATION; CHEERFULNESS; COLLAPSE; DANGER; FRIENDSHIP; HAIR STYLES; MOUTH; OCEAN/OCEANFRONTS; OPEN AND SHUT; PURPOSEFULNESS; RAIN; SLEEP; THOUGHTS; VIRTUE

McGuire, Thomas
ABANDONMENT

McIlvanney, William
ARM MOVEMENTS; AVAILABILITY; BLUE; BODY; CALMNESS; CAUTION; CHEERFULNESS; CLOTHING; CONVERSATION; CRITICISM; CRUELTY; DECREASE; DIFFICULTY; EMBRACE; ENVY; EYE EXPRESSIONS, MISCELLANEOUS; FACE(S); FACIAL

EXPRESSIONS, MISCELLANEOUS; FORMALITY; FORTUNE/MISFORTUNE; HEAD MOVEMENTS; HUMOR; IMMOBILITY; IMPOSSIBILITY; INAPPROPRIATENESS; INNOCENCE; INSULT; JEWELRY; LIES/LIARS; MEMORY; MOUTH, OPEN AND SHUT; PAUSE; PERSONALITY PROFILES; PHYSICAL APPEARANCE; PURPOSEFULNESS; REALNESS/UNREALNESS; REJECTION; SCRUTINY; SERIOUSNESS; SIGHS; SILENCE; SITTING; SKY; SLEEP; SOCIABILITY/UNSOCIABILITY; STRANGENESS; TACT; TALLNESS; THOUGHTS; TURNING AND TWISTING; UNDESIREABILITY; USEFULNESS/USELESSNESS; WORD(S)

McInerney, Jay
ADVANCING; ENERGY; HEAD MOVEMENTS; MEMORY; OBJECTS, MISC.; PERSONALITY PROFILES; SOUL; VOICE(S); WEARINESS

McKenna, Richard
MEMORY

McKenna, Stephen
NATURALNESS

McKinney, Frank
AGREEMENT/DISAGREEMENT; BASEBALL

McLaughlin, Ruth
STOMACH

McMahon, Thomas
HAIR, COLOR

McMurtry, Larry
BEGINNINGS AND ENDINGS; BREATHING; CONVERSATION; DEJECTION; DESIRE; FROWNS; HEAT; HOUSES; LAUGHTER; LIFE; LOOKS; MARRIAGE; NECK; PERSONALITY PROFILES; PHYSICAL APPEARANCE; RISK; SCREAMS; SILENCE; SPEAKING; SUN; TALKATIVENESS; TALLNESS; TEETH; THOUGHTS; TOUGHNESS

McNally, Leonard
CLOSENESS

McNamara, Eugene
BODY

McNutt, William Slavens
HAPPINESS

Megged, Aharon
ADVANCING; ARM(S); BENDING/BENT; BLACK; CROWDS; DAY; EMPTINESS; EXCITEMENT; EYE COLOR; EYE MOVEMENTS; EYEBROWS; FACIAL DETAILS; FACIAL EXPRESSIONS, MISCELLANEOUS; FEAR; HAIR, CURLY; HANDSHAKE; HAPPINESS; HEAT; LAUGHTER; LEG(S); PALLOR; POLITICS/POLITICIANS; QUESTIONS AND ANSWERS; SHOCK; SPEED; VOICE, HARSH; VOICE(S); WEAKNESS; WHITE

Meinke, Peter
AIR; BIRDS; EYE MOVEMENTS; FACIAL COLOR; FEAR; HOUSES; PAST, THE; PHYSICAL APPEARANCE; RESTLESSNESS; SLOWNESS; STRANGENESS; THOUGHTS; TONGUE; VOICE, MUSIC RELATED; VOICE(S)

Meir, Golda
AGE

Meislin, Richard J.
CROWDS

Melbancke, Brian
UNDESIREABILITY

Melton, John
SILENCE

Melville, Herman
BEARING; BELIEFS; BELONGING; DESTRUCTION/DESTRUCTIVENESS; LYING; MANKIND; NOISES; PALLOR; PERMANENCE

Menander
WORD(S)

Mencius
TRUTH

Mencken, H. L.
ABSURDITY; ART AND LITERATURE; BELIEVABILITY; CANDOR; CAUTION; DEATH DEFINED; FOOD AND DRINK; FUTILITY; MEN AND WOMEN; MONEY; MUSIC; SHOULDERS; TIME; TRUTH; VANITY; VIRTUE

Mendelson, Edward
NOISES; WRITERS/WRITING

Mengers, Sue
INAPPROPRIATENESS

Menotti, Gian Carlo
WATCHFULNESS

Mercer, Johnny
CLOUDS; DAY

Meredith, George
CONTROL; SHYNESS

Meredith, William
ACTIONS; VOICE, HARSH

Merkin, Daphne
BENDING/BENT; BREASTS; CHIL-
DREN; COLDNESS; COLLAPSE;
CRITICISM, DRAMATIC AND LIT-
ERARY; DIVERSENESS; EATING
AND DRINKING; EMOTIONS;
EYE MOVEMENTS; EYEBROWS;
GROANS AND WHISPERS; HAIR
STYLES; HEAD MOVEMENTS; IM-
MOBILITY; LAUGHTER; LOVE;
MEMORY; MEN AND WOMEN;
RELATIONSHIP; SMILE; SPORTS;
TRUST/MISTRUST; VEHICLES;
VOICE(S); WATCHFULNESS;
WRINKLES

Merman, Ethel
DULLNESS

Mermet, Claude
FRIENDSHIP, DEFINED

Merrill, James
REALNESS/UNREALNESS

Merriman, Brian
POLITICS/POLITICIANS

Merton, Thomas
MIND DEFINED

Messud, Claire
CHANGE; CONVERSATION; EX-
CITEMENT; FACIAL EXPRES-
SIONS; LINGERING; REJECTION;
SADNESS; STRUGGLE; TIME
PASSING

Mestastasio, Pietro
MANKIND

Meyer, Karl E.
SUDDENNESS

Meyer, Philip K.
DIFFICULTY

Meyerson, Harvey
FOOTBALL

Michaels, Leonard
BENDING/BENT; CLOTHING, ITS
FIT; HANDS; HANDSHAKE;
LAUGHTER; SPEAKING; TEARS;
VOICE, HARSH

Michelangelo
ALONENESS

Midrash, L'Olam
ANGER

Millar, Margaret
ANIMALS; ARM(S); BALDNESS;
BEHAVIOR; BIRDS; BREATHING;

BROWN; CHANGE; CITIES;
CLINGING; CLOTHING, ITS FIT;
CONNECTIONS; DEJECTION;
DREAM; EYE COLOR; EYE EX-
PRESSIONS, MISCELLANEOUS;
EYES; FACE(S); FACIAL EXPRES-
SIONS, BLANK; FACIAL EXPRES-
SIONS, MISCELLANEOUS; FA-
CIAL EXPRESSIONS, SERIOUS;
FIRE AND SMOKE; FOG; FURNI-
TURE AND FURNISHINGS; GRAY;
HAIR; HAIR, CURLY; HAND
MOVEMENTS; HEALTH; IMMO-
BILITY; LAUGHTER; LEAVES;
NERVOUSNESS; NOISES; PER-
SONALITY PROFILES; PRIDE;
PURPOSEFULNESS; SEASCAPES;
SILENCE; SIMILARITY; SKIN;
SMELL; SPREADING; SUN;
SWEAT; TOBACCO; TREMBLING;
TRUTH; UNSTEADINESS; VOICE,
EFFECT OF; VOICE, HARSH;
VOICE, MUSIC RELATED;
WORD(S); WRINKLES

Millay, Edna St. Vincent
AGITATION; CLARITY; DISAP-
PEARANCE; HABIT; LIFE; MEM-
ORY; NIGHT; PEOPLE, INTERAC-
TION; SHINING; VOICE, HARSH;
YELLOW

Miller, Allan
ATTRACTION

Miller, Arthur
ARM(S); ATTENTION; EYES;
FEAR; OCEAN/OCEANFRONTS;
PASSION; PRESENT, THE; SKIN;
SUCCESS/FAILURE

Miller, Bryan
COLORS; EYE EXPRESSIONS,
MISCELLANEOUS; FOOD AND
DRINK

Miller, Henry
CRYING; INTENSITY; SAFETY;
SHAPE

Miller, James
SIMILARITY

Miller, Joaquin
LIFE DEFINED

Miller, Nolan
LEG(S)

Miller, Roger
DIFFERENCES; PEOPLE

Miller, Sue
BREASTS; NOSE(S); PHYSICAL
APPEARANCE; SEX

Miller, Warren
ORDER/DISORDER

Millhauser, Steven
ART AND LITERATURE

Millikan, Robert A.
WAR

Mills, C. Wright
POWER

Mills, Clifford
ROCKING AND ROLLING

Mills, James
ABILITY; ACCOMPLISHMENT;
CLOTHING; FLEXIBILITY/IN-
FLEXIBILITY; PERSONALITY
PROFILES; VIOLENCE

Milne, A. A.
FACE(S)

Milton, John
ABUNDANCE; BELIEVABILITY;
CHILDREN; DESTRUCTION/DE-
STRUCTIVENESS; FEROCITY;
GREEN; SCREAMS; SHINING; SI-
LENCE; THICKNESS; TIME;
TRUTH

Minot, Stephen
TIME; UNATTRACTIVENESS

Minot, Susan
BENDING/BENT; CHIN; CLOTH-
ING; HAIR; NOISES; RAIN; THIN-
NESS; WEAKNESS

Mishima, Yuikio
BODY; BOREDOM/BORING;
EXITS; PEACEFULNESS; TIME

Mitchell, Beverly
MOVEMENT(S)

Mitchell, Donald G.
ABANDONMENT

Mitchell, James
FEAR

Mitchell, Joni
SUN

Mitchell, Margaret
AGILITY; BEARING; BEHAVIOR;
CLINGING; EYE EXPRESSIONS,
MISCELLANEOUS; FACIAL EX-
PRESSIONS, MISCELLANEOUS;
FIGHTING; NOISES; PERSONAL-
ITY PROFILES; PHYSICAL FEEL-
INGS; SADNESS; SPEED; UNAT-
TRACTIVENESS; VOICE, HARSH

Mitchell, Paige
ANGER; ARGUMENTS; ARM(S);
BEARD; BEHAVIOR; CLOTHING;
CLOTHING, ITS FIT; CONNEC-
TIONS; COURAGE; CROWDS;

DARKNESS; DESIRE; DREAM; DRINKING; EMOTIONS; EXCITEMENT; EYE EXPRESSIONS, MISCELLANEOUS; EYE MOVEMENTS; EYEBROWS; EYES, BRIGHT; FACIAL EXPRESSIONS, MISCELLANEOUS; FACIAL SHAPE; FEAR; FLATTERY; GLIMMER, GLITTER AND GLOSS; HAIR; HAIR, CURLY; HARSHNESS; HOUSES; JEWELRY; MARRIAGE; MEN AND WOMEN; MOON; MUSTACHE(S); PALLOR; PREPAREDNESS; QUESTIONS AND ANSWERS; RAIN; RESTLESSNESS; SCREAMS; SCRUTINY; SMILE; SMOOTHNESS; SNORES; SPEED; STARS; SURPRISE; TENSION; THINNESS; TRANSIENCE; VEHICLES; VIRTUE; VOICE, MUSIC RELATED; VOICE(S); WIND

Mizner, Wilson
TONGUE

Moir, D. M.
CURSES

Molière, J. P.
CLOSENESS; GREED

Molinaro, Ursule
REPETITION

Monro, Harold
HABIT

Monsarrat, Nicholas
CRUELTY; HELPLESSNESS; WATCHFULNESS

Montague, James J.
DULLNESS

Montague, Lady Mary Wortley
CHARACTERISTICS, NATIONAL

Montaigne, Michel de
EDUCATION; MEMORY; OPINION; RICHES

Montgomery, James
DISINTEGRATION

Moor, Robert
ANGER

Moore, Brian
AGITATION; ALONENESS; BODY; CLOUD MOVEMENTS; DISAPPEARANCE; FEAR; GROANS AND WHISPERS; HAPPINESS; LEAPING; SIMPLICITY; SLOWNESS; WIND

Moore, Clement C.
LAUGHTER

Moore, George
ALERTNESS; ART AND LITERATURE; BOOKS; REGRET; SADNESS

Moore, Lorrie
APPEARANCE; ATTRACTION; CERTAINTY; DREAM; DULLNESS; EMPTINESS; FACIAL EXPRESSIONS, MISCELLANEOUS; FIRMNESS; HAIR; LANDSCAPES; MEN AND WOMEN; REGULARITY/IRREGULARITY; SEXUAL INTERACTION; SILENCE; SKY; SMILE; SPREADING; SURPRISE; TENSION; UNATTRACTIVENESS

Moore, Marianne
BASEBALL; PERSONALITY PROFILES

Moore, Thomas
CLARITY; DECREASE; FRIENDSHIP

Moran, Malcolm
DESIRABILITY

Moran, Richard
BREATHING; NOISES; OCEAN/OCEANFRONTS; SITTING; SPEECH PATTERNS

Moravia, Albert
HAIR, TEXTURE; IDEAS

More, Hannah
LOVE

More, Thomas
BELIEFS; MEMORY

Morgan, Speer
DIFFICULTY; IMMOBILITY; RUNNING; SECRECY

Moriarty, Laura
FLEXIBILITY/INFLEXIBILITY

Morris, Chuck
CRITICISM, DRAMATIC AND LITERARY

Morris, Gouverneur
PAIN

Morris, Herbert
CLOTHING, ITS FIT

Morris, Mary
KISSES; NECESSITY; ORDER/DISORDER; POLITICS/POLITICIANS; RED; SMOOTHNESS; SWEAT

Morris, William
BALDNESS

Morris, Willie
NAMES

Morris, Wright
ENTRANCES AND EXITS; EYE COLOR; RED; SKIN; WALKING

Morrow, George
BUSINESS

Morrow, James
ATTENTION; COMPLEXITY; EMPTINESS; HAIR; PROBLEMS AND SOLUTIONS; STARES; TIME; WALKING; WORD(S)

Morse, John T.
DISAPPEARANCE; NATURALNESS

Mortimer, Faith
LOOKS

Mortimer, John
AVAILABILITY; CLOTHING ACCESSORIES; JOY; OCEAN/OCEANFRONTS; SMILE; SUN; TOUGHNESS

Moseley, William
BREATHING; GROANS AND WHISPERS

Moser, Penny Ward
PAIN

Mosher, Howard Frank
BASEBALL; DISCONTENT; JUMPING; WORK

Motherwell, Robert
FAME

Motherwell, William
SIGHS

Mountford, William
SADNESS

Mourand, Paul
COMPATIBILITY

Muggeridge, Malcolm
COMPATIBILITY; POLITICS/POLITICIANS

Muir, Edwin
SUN

Mullen, Harryette
MEMORY; PEOPLE, INTERACTION; PHYSICAL APPEARANCE

Mulligan, Gideon
TALKATIVENESS

Mulock, D. M.
SECRECY

Munn, Charles Clark
FLATTERY

Munro, Alice
BOOKS; EMOTIONS; LOYALTY/DISLOYALTY; REMOTENESS; SEX; SOFTNESS; SOUL;

TREES; WORD(S); WRITERS/WRITING

Murdoch, Iris
BEAUTY; CHEERFULNESS; DISPERSAL; EATING AND DRINKING; FROWNS; JOY; LAUGHTER; MEEKNESS; MEMORY; MEN AND WOMEN; MOUTH; PAIN; PHYSICAL APPEARANCE; SHOCK; STANDING; SUDDENNESS; THOUGHTS; WORDS, EFFECT OF

Murphy, Muriel Oxenberg
SOCIETY

Murray, Jim
ELUSIVENESS; FOOTBALL; STRENGTH

Murrow, Edward R.
REMOTENESS

N

Nabokov, Vladimir
BREASTS; HOUSES; LIGHTING; SOFTNESS

Naham, Bratzlav
DESIRE

Naj, Amal Kumar
ENTHUSIASM

Najarian, Peter
DISAPPEARANCE

Napier, Sir Charles
PROBLEMS AND SOLUTIONS; WAR

Nappaha, Johann B.
DISHONESTY

Narayan, R. K.
BREASTS

Nash, Ogden
ATTRACTIVENESS; BEHAVIOR; BENDING/BENT; BODY; BURST; CALMNESS; CLEVERNESS; CLINGING; CONVERSATION; COURAGE; DISAPPEARANCE; FOOLISHNESS; GROWTH; KINDNESS; MARRIAGE; MONEY; MOUTH; MUSCLES; MUSIC; SNOW; TIME; TREMBLING; YOUTH

Nash, Thomas
SPEED

Nassauer, Rudolf
TOUGHNESS

Nastase, Ilie
MEMORY

Nathan, George Jean
ART AND LITERATURE; CHARACTERISTICS, NATIONAL; CRITICISM; LEG(S); PERMANENCE; PROPRIETY/IMPROPRIETY; SEX

Naylor, Phyllis
CLOTHING, ITS FIT; CONVERSATION; DEJECTION; EMBRACE; ROAD SCENES; SKIN

Ndebele, Njabulo
CHEEKS; EMBRACE; REJECTION

Nelson, Kent
DISINTEGRATION; EMOTIONS; PAUSE; STARES

Nemerov, Howard
DRINKING

Nemy, Enid
PLEASURE; RARITY

Neruda, Pablo
DEATH

Netanyahu, Benjamin
BEHAVIOR

Neuberger, Maurine
IMPOSSIBILITY

Neville, Susan
AIR; ARM MOVEMENTS; GLIMMER, GLITTER AND GLOSS; VOICE(S)

Nevin, David
TENSION

Newfield, Jack
VANITY

Newman, Barnett
ART AND LITERATURE

Newman, Paul
ACTING; DIFFICULTY

Newton, John
AMBITION; ENTHUSIASM

Newton, Joseph Fort
RELIABILITY/UNRELIABILITY

Ní Chonaill, Eibhlín Dubh
OPEN AND SHUT

Nicholls, David
BOREDOM; CLEVERNESS; FACIAL COLOR; FRIENDSHIP; GRINS; HELPLESSNESS; MEMORY; MOVEMENT; PERSONALITIES; RELATIONSHIPS; SAFETY; SEASCAPES; USEFULNESS

Nichols, Dudley
STAGE AND SCREEN

Nichols, Mike
STAGE AND SCREEN

Nielsen, Helen
MODESTY

Nietzsche, Friedrich
CONSCIENCE; GREATNESS; MANKIND; NATURE

Nin, Anaïs
ALONENESS; BIRTH; CAUSE AND EFFECT; CLOTHING, ITS FIT; CONVERSATION; CREDIT; EMOTIONS; EYE MOVEMENTS; EYES; JEWELRY; LEAVES; LIES/LIARS; MAXIMS, PROVERBS AND SAYINGS; MIND DEFINED; ORDER/DISORDER; SELFISHNESS; SKY; SOUL; SPEECH PATTERNS; TENSION

Niven, David
BODY; MOUTH; PERSONALITY PROFILES; PLACES; WRINKLES

Noble, Marty
BASEBALL

Nolan, Hamilton
HABIT

Nolan, Tom
WORLD

Nook, Albert Jay
MIND DEFINED

Norman, Marcia
STAGE AND SCREEN; WRITERS/WRITING

Norris, Gloria
ABANDONMENT; ANGER; BEARD; BEARING; CLEVERNESS; EXCITEMENT; FACIAL DETAILS; FACIAL EXPRESSIONS, MISCELLANEOUS; GROANS AND WHISPERS; HEARTBEAT; ILLNESS; LOOKS; PHYSICAL FEELINGS; SPEED; STANDING; STOMACH; THINNESS; WEARINESS

Norris, John
JOY; TRANSIENCE

North, Roger
CLARITY

Nowell, Clare
PERVASIVENESS

Noyes, Alfred
DREAM

Nugent, Beth
CONTROL

O

Oates, Joyce Carol
BODY; DESTRUCTION/DESTRUCTIVENESS; ENVY; EYES, BRIGHT; FACIAL SHAPE; HAIR; HAIR, TEX-

TURE; LOVE; MOUTH; RAIN; SI-
LENCE

O'Brien, Dennis
FUTILITY

O'Brien, Edna
BLUE; CLOUDS; DISAPPEAR-
ANCE; EMBRACE; EYE EXPRES-
SIONS, MISCELLANEOUS; EYES;
FACIAL EXPRESSIONS, MISCEL-
LANEOUS; FORTUNE/MISFOR-
TUNE; HOUSES; LOOKS;
THOUGHTS

O'Brien, Frederick
NOSE(S)

O'Brien, Tim
IMPOSSIBILITY; LIPS; RAIN; SI-
LENCE

O'Casey, Eileen
CONTENTMENT

O'Connor, Flannery
AGITATION; ANGER; BEARING;
BEHAVIOR; BENDING/BENT;
BLUE; BODY; BREATHING; CALM-
NESS; CANDOR; CITIES; CLOTH-
ING, ITS FIT; EYE COLOR; EYE
EXPRESSIONS, MISCELLANEOUS;
EYES; FIRMNESS; FROWNS;
FRUSTRATION; HAND MOVE-
MENTS; HEAD MOVEMENTS;
KISSES; LEG(S); OBVIOUSNESS;
PATIENCE; PEOPLE, INTERAC-
TION; PERSONALITY PROFILES;
PHYSICAL APPEARANCE; PHYSI-
CAL FEELINGS; REALNESS/UN-
REALNESS; SEXUAL INTERAC-
TION; SIGHS; SILENCE; SITTING;
SMILE; SPEECH PATTERNS;
SPEED; STARES; VIOLENCE;
VOICE(S)

O'Connor, Frank
ENTRANCES AND EXITS;
FACE(S)

O'Connor, John
FACE(S)

O'Connor, Cardinal John J.
HEALTH

O'Connor, Patrice
ANXIETY

Odets, Clifford
ATTENTION; AVAILABILITY;
BEARING; BEWILDERMENT; DE-
STRUCTION/DESTRUCTIVENESS;
ENTRAPMENT; FEROCITY; IM-
POSSIBILITY; JUMPING; LIFE DE-
FINED; PERSONALITY PROFILES;

PROBLEMS AND SOLUTIONS; RE-
ALIZATION; SURPRISE; TIME;
WORDS OF PRAISE; WORK

Oe, Kenzaburo
ANTICIPATION; BEHAVIOR;
COMPLEXION; EMBRACE; EYE
MOVEMENTS; FACIAL SHAPE;
GLOOM; GREEN; HELPLESSNESS;
INSULT; MOVEMENT(S); PAIN;
PALLOR; POLITICS/POLITICIANS;
POWER; RAIN; RESERVE;
ROOMS; SIGHS; TENSION;
VOICE, WEAK; WEARINESS

O'Faolain, Julia
ACTIVENESS; AGITATION;
ALERTNESS; ARGUMENTS; AT-
TRACTION; BEGINNINGS AND
ENDINGS; BLUSHES; CLINGING;
COLDNESS; DISAPPEARANCE;
DULLNESS; EMBRACE; ENTRAP-
MENT; EYE MOVEMENTS;
FACE(S); FACIAL EXPRESSIONS,
MISCELLANEOUS; FAMILIARITY;
FEAR; FURNITURE AND FUR-
NISHINGS; GRINS; HAIR; HANDS;
HEAT; HELPLESSNESS; HOUSES;
INTENSITY; IRRITABLENESS/IR-
RITATING; LANDSCAPES;
LEAVES; LYING; MADNESS;
MOUTH; MOUTH, OPEN AND
SHUT; NECK; ORDER/DISORDER;
PAIN; PALLOR; PRIDE; RELA-
TIONSHIP; RELIABILITY/UNRELI-
ABILITY; REMOTENESS; SEXUAL
INTERACTION; SPORTS; STO-
RIES; TEARS; TIME; TREES;
TRUST/MISTRUST; TURNING
AND TWISTING

O'Flaherty, Liam
FINGERS

O'Grady, Desmond
EXITS; USEFULNESS/USELESS-
NESS; WRINKLES

O'Hara, Frank
AIR; AMBITION; BARENESS;
CHILDREN; CITIES; CROWDS;
DEJECTION; DISINTEGRATION;
FACIAL EXPRESSIONS, MISCEL-
LANEOUS; HEART(S); LEAVES;
SERIOUSNESS; SNOW; STRANGE-
NESS

Oldham, Archie
SPORTS

Oldham, John
PERMANENCE

Olds, Sharon
EYE EXPRESSIONS, MISCELLA-
NEOUS; FACIAL COLOR; FACIAL
DETAILS; FIRMNESS; FRAGILITY;
FURNITURE AND FURNISHINGS;
HEART(S); HOUSES; SMOOTH-
NESS; THINNESS; WORDS OF
PRAISE

Olsen, Merlin
CALMNESS

Olsen, Paul
HEAD MOVEMENTS

O'Malley, Austin
CHANGE; POLITICS/POLITI-
CIANS; REVENGE; SPEECHMAK-
ING; USEFULNESS/USELESSNESS

O'Malley, Pat
SPEECHMAKING

O'Neil, Paul
LAWYERS

O'Neill, Eugene
AGILITY; LIFE; SMILE

Ono, Yoko
WRITERS/WRITING

Ooka, Shohei
NATURE

Orringer, Julie
ATTRACTIVENESS; CAUSE/EF-
FECT; FACIAL DETAILS; SERI-
OUSNESS; SHAME

Orwell, George
CRITICISM, DRAMATIC AND LIT-
ERARY; WORDS DEFINED; WRIT-
ERS/WRITING

Osborne, John
FUTILITY; SCREAMS

Osborne, Linda Barrett
PERSISTENCE

Ostrovsky, Alexander
GOVERNMENT

Otis, Amos
BASEBALL

Otway, Thomas
DESIRABILITY

Ouida
ATTRACTION; BRIGHTNESS;
EYES; FAMILIARITY; FLEXIBIL-
ITY/INFLEXIBILITY; GLIMMER,
GLITTER AND GLOSS; MEMORY;
MUSIC; PALLOR; RARITY; SI-
LENCE; SPEED

Overbury, Sir Thomas
PAST, THE

Ovid
LOVE

Owen, Steve
SPORTS

Owen, Wilfred
EVIL; FINGERS

Owens, William A.
SCREAMS

Oz, Amos
BEHAVIOR; BENDING/BENT; EYE
MOVEMENTS; FACE(S); FACIAL
EXPRESSIONS, SERIOUS; LIGHT-
ING; NOISES; RAIN; RELIGION;
ROARS; SADNESS; SEX; SEXUAL
INTERACTION; VOICE, HARSH

Ozick, Cynthia
BRIGHTNESS; BROWN; CITIES;
COMPLEXION; CRITICISM;
EMPTINESS; EYE EXPRESSIONS,
MISCELLANEOUS; EYEBROWS;
EYES; EYES, BRIGHT; FACIAL EX-
PRESSIONS, SERIOUS; FEAR; FIN-
GERS; FIRE AND SMOKE; FOOD
AND DRINK; HAIR STYLES;
HEADS; HEAVINESS; IRRITABLE-
NESS/IRRITATING; LAUGHTER;
NOISES; PHYSICAL APPEAR-
ANCE; REMOTENESS; ROOMS;
SCREAMS; SEASCAPES; SKIN;
SMOOTHNESS; STOMACH; SUN;
VEHICLES; VOICE(S); WALKING;
WHITE; WISDOM;
WRITERS/WRITING; YELLOW

P

Pace, Eric
STYLE

Packer, Nancy Huddleston
ANGER; BREATHING; HAIR
STYLES; HAPPINESS; SKIN;
SPEECH PATTERNS; WALKING

Paine, Thomas
CLOSENESS; DISHONESTY; EVIL;
GOVERNMENT; POWER; SUC-
CESS/FAILURE

Paley, Grace
COLDNESS; COLLAPSE; EYE
COLOR; GLOOM; SPEAKING;
STAGE AND SCREEN; WEARI-
NESS; YOUTH

Palladas
DEATH

Panchatantra
STUPIDITY

Paramore, Edward E.
TOUGHNESS

Parent, Michael
STORIES

Parini, Jay
BALDNESS; BLOOD; CALMNESS;
CLOTHING; EMPTINESS;
FROWNS; HANDSHAKE; HAPPI-
NESS; HEAD MOVEMENTS; HON-
ESTY; JUMPING; LAUGHTER; NA-
TURE; OPEN AND SHUT;
POLITICS/POLITICIANS; SHOUL-
DERS; SOCIABILITY/UNSOCIA-
BILITY; STARES; TALLNESS; TO-
BACCO; WALKING

Parker, Dorothy
CHARACTERISTICS, NATIONAL;
CHEERFULNESS; CORRESPON-
DENCE; GAIETY; HAIR; HAIR,
TEXTURE; HAND MOVEMENTS;
JOY; LOVE; LOVE, DEFINED;
PROMISE; TIME; VOICE(S);
VOICE, SOFT

Parker, George
COURAGE

Parker, Robert B.
ARM(S); CLOTHING; FACIAL EX-
PRESSIONS, MISCELLANEOUS;
HAIR STYLES; IMPOSSIBILITY;
NECESSITY; SILENCE; SPEED;
TALLNESS

Parks, Paul
IMPORTANCE/UNIMPORTANCE

Parmentel, Noel
INSULT

Parnell, Thomas
SPEED

Pastan, Linda
FLEXIBILITY/INFLEXIBILITY;
TOUGHNESS

Pasternak, Boris
CLOTHING, ITS FIT; CLOUD
MOVEMENTS; CLOUDS; COLD-
NESS; FACE(S); FIRE AND
SMOKE; FREEDOM; HANDS;
HOUSES; IMMOBILITY; IMPOR-
TANCE/UNIMPORTANCE;
LOOKS; ROCKING AND
ROLLING; SKY; SLEEP; SNOW;
STRANGENESS; SUN; WIND

Patchen, Kenneth
IDLENESS; IMPORTANCE/UNIM-
PORTANCE; PEACEFULNESS;
TREES

Paterson, William
BEAUTY

Patmore, Coventry
LOVE, DEFINED

Patterson, James
ARM MOVEMENTS; PERSONAL-
ITY PROFILES

Patterson, Richard North
DARKNESS; ROOMS

Patterson, Troy
SMOOTHNESS

Paulsen, Pat
ABSURDITY

Payne, Les
QUESTIONS AND ANSWERS

Pearlman, Edith
BEHAVIOR; EYES; FATE

Pearson, Edmund L.
GLIMMER, GLITTER AND GLOSS

Peden, William
JOY; PURPOSEFULNESS

Penn, William
ENVY; GOVERNMENT; PATIENCE

Penner, Jonathan
COLLAPSE

Pennywell, John
PROBLEMS AND SOLUTIONS

Percy, Walker
ACTIVENESS; ANGER; BODY OR-
GANS; CLEANLINESS; FACE(S);
FIRMNESS; HANDS; HAND-
SHAKE; HOUSES; LANDSCAPES;
LIES/LIARS; OBJECTS, MISC.;
THUNDER AND LIGHTNING;
YOUTH

Perelman, S. J.
DEATH, FINALITY OF; EYES;
HEAD MOVEMENTS

Perez, Antonio
FRIENDSHIP, DEFINED

Perot, Ross
IMPOSSIBILITY

Petronius
BLACK; COURAGE

Petry, Ann
CAUSE AND EFFECT; CLOTH-
ING, ITS FIT; HAIR; IMPOR-
TANCE/UNIMPORTANCE; SMILE;
SWEAT; THINNESS; WORDS, EF-
FECT OF

Phelps, William Lyon
LIFE DEFINED; MIND; MIND DE-
FINED

Philipson, Morris
RICHNESS

Phillips, Caryl
BENDING/BENT; FOOD AND DRINK; SUN; VOICE, HARSH

Phillips, Clinton A.
EXITS

Phillips, Daniel
PERSONALITY PROFILES

Phillips, Deborah
SEX

Phillips, H. I.
CLOSENESS

Phillips, Jayne Anne
AIR; BENDING/BENT; BODY; DISAPPEARANCE; DRINKING; FACE(S); FACIAL EXPRESSIONS, MISCELLANEOUS; GROANS AND WHISPERS; HAIR; HAIR, TEXTURE; HANDS; LIGHTING; LIPS; LOOKS; MOVEMENT(S); PALLOR; SMALLNESS; VEHICLES

Phillips, John
BLACK; MOON; SECRECY

Phillips, Wendell
POLITICS/POLITICIANS

Phocylides
KINDNESS

Picasso, Pablo
ART AND LITERATURE

Pierce, Franklin
KINDNESS

Piercy, Marge
ABUNDANCE; ADVANCING; AGE; AGILITY; ANGER; ARM MOVEMENTS; ARM(S); BENDING/BENT; BIGNESS; BIRDS; BLACK; BODY; BOREDOM/BORING; BREASTS; BRIGHTNESS; BUSYNESS; CERTAINTY; CITIES; CLINGING; COLDNESS; CORRECTNESS; CURIOSITY; DARKNESS; DAY; DEATH; DEJECTION; DESIRE; DIFFICULTY; DISINTEGRATION; DRYNESS; EASE; EMOTIONS; EMPTINESS; ENERGY; EXCITEMENT; EYE MOVEMENTS; FINGERS; FIRMNESS; FRESHNESS; GLIMMER, GLITTER AND GLOSS; GREEN; GRINS; GROWTH; HABIT; HAIR; HAIR, CURLY; HAIR STYLES; HAIR, TEXTURE; HAND MOVEMENTS; HAPPINESS; HARSHNESS; HATRED; HEAT; HISTORY; HONESTY; HOPE; HOUSES; HUNGER; IMMOBILITY; INAPPROPRIATENESS;

JOY; KINDNESS; KISSES; LIFE; LIGHTING; MIND; MOON; MUSIC; NATURE; NERVOUSNESS; NOISES; OCEAN/OCEANFRONTS; OPEN AND SHUT; ORDER/DISORDER; PAIN; PEACEFULNESS; PEOPLE, INTERACTION; PERSISTENCE; PHYSICAL APPEARANCE; PHYSICAL FEELINGS; PINK; POLITICS/POLITICIANS; POWER; PROBLEMS AND SOLUTIONS; RAIN; REAPPEARANCE; REJECTION; REPETITION; RICHNESS; RUNNING; SCREAMS; SEASONS; SECRECY; SENSITIVENESS; SHARPNESS; SIMPLICITY; SMILE; SNOW; SPEED; SPREADING; STEADINESS; STRENGTH; SUCCESS/FAILURE; SUN; SWEETNESS; TEARS; THINNESS; THOUGHTS; TIME; TONGUE; TREMBLING; TRUST/MISTRUST; VISABILITY; VOICE, HARSH; VOICE(S); WEATHER; WIND; WORD(S)

Pierson, Lewis E.
BUSINESS

Pike, James A.
CHANGE

Pilcher, Rosamund
ANTICIPATION; CLEANLINESS; CLOTHING; LIFE DEFINED; ROOMS; SPEED; UNATTRACTIVENESS; VOICE, MUSIC RELATED

Pin, Mary
TRUTHNESS/FALSENESS

Pinero, Arthur W.
PROFESSIONS

Piper, Anne
LEG(S)

Piper, William Thomas
SPEECHMAKING

Pirandello, Luigi
ABANDONMENT; AGILITY; FACTS; PROTECTIVENESS; SOFTNESS; TREMBLING

Pix, Mary
SPEED

Plain, Belva
ACCOMPLISHMENT; DISPERSAL; EMOTIONS; EYE COLOR; FEAR; FRAGILITY; GREEN; SHAME; SUN

Planche, J. R.
LOOKS

Plath, Sylvia
BIRDS; BOREDOM/BORING; CHEEKS; CLARITY; CORRECTNESS; CURIOSITY; DARKNESS; DEATH DEFINED; DECREASE; DISAPPEARANCE; DISCOMFORT; DISINTEGRATION; EYE COLOR; FLEXIBILITY/INFLEXIBILITY; FOOD AND DRINK; FRAGILITY; GLIMMER, GLITTER AND GLOSS; HEAVINESS; IDLENESS; LANDSCAPES; LOVE; MARRIAGE; NOISES; OCEAN/OCEANFRONTS; PALLOR; SHAPE; SILENCE; SKY; SMILE; STARS; TEARS; THICKNESS; THINNESS; TIME; TRUTHNESS/FALSENESS; WEAKNESS; WHITE

Plato
BODY; PASSION; VIRTUE

Plautus
DISINTEGRATION; KINDNESS; MANNERS

Plomer, William
SUN

Plummer, Christopher
PERSONALITY PROFILES

Plutarch
SPEECHMAKING; UNCERTAINTY; VIRTUE

Poe, Edgar Allan
ALONENESS; CLOUD MOVEMENTS; COLLAPSE; CONTROL; DEJECTION; DISAPPEARANCE; GLIMMER, GLITTER AND GLOSS; GREEN; HAIR, CURLY; PALLOR; ROCKING AND ROLLING

Poers, W. A.
PLACES

Pollock, Channing
MARRIAGE

Poniatowska, Elena
PAIN; SPREADING

Poole, Mary Peterson
DRINKING

Poore, Charles
TIME

Pope, Alexander
AGE; ARGUMENTS; DISHONESTY; FREEDOM; LAWS; LIFE; PASSION; RICHES; SENSE; WRITERS/WRITING

Popkin, Joel
ECONOMICS

Pordage, Samuel
MUSIC

Porter, Cole
ANGER; ENTRANCES AND
EXITS; ROARS; SELF-CONFI-
DENCE

Porter, J. Hampden
BUSYNESS

Porter, Katherine Anne
AFFECTION; ALONENESS;
BREASTS; CURSES; HELPLESS-
NESS; LOYALTY/DISLOYALTY;
MEMORY; NOISES; PEOPLE, IN-
TERACTION; PHYSICAL APPEAR-
ANCE; REALNESS/UNREALNESS

Portillo, Lopez
FIGHTING

Portis, Charles
BODY; PROBLEMS AND SOLU-
TIONS; VEHICLES

Post, Emily
FLATTERY

Post, Steve
RELATIONSHIP

Pound, Ezra
PERMANENCE

Powell, Adam Clayton
THOUGHTS

Powell, Anthony
BODY; EYE MOVEMENTS;
FRIENDSHIP; HAIR, TEXTURE;
LEG(S); PERSONALITY PRO-
FILES; POWER; TREES

Powers, J. F.
PRIDE; RELATIONSHIP

Praed, Winthrop Mackworth
SPEAKING; SPEECHMAKING

Prather, Richard S.
EYE COLOR; FOOD AND DRINK;
HEAD MOVEMENTS; LEG(S); TO-
BACCO

Prentice, Archibald
COURAGE

Prentice, George D.
WRITERS/WRITING

Price, Nancy
REMOTENESS

Price, Reynolds
BEARING; BITTERNESS; BRIGHT-
NESS; BROWN; CALMNESS;
COLDNESS; DRYNESS; ELUSIVE-
NESS; EMPTINESS; FACIAL EX-
PRESSIONS, SERIOUS;
FRAGILITY; FRESHNESS; HAIR,
COLOR; HAIR STYLES; HARM-
LESSNESS; HEARTBEAT; HEAT;
IMMOBILITY; INSULT; NERVOUS-
NESS; NOISES; PALLOR; PERSON-
ALITY PROFILES; POWER; RE-
MOTENESS; SAFETY; SILENCE;
SMOOTHNESS; SPREADING;
STRENGTH; TALLNESS; THIN-
NESS; VOICE, HARSH; WEARI-
NESS; WHITE

Priest, William W., Jr.
ECONOMICS

Priestley, J. B.
ADVANCING; BELIEFS; BODY OR-
GANS; ENERGY; FACIAL SHAPE;
GLIMMER, GLITTER AND GLOSS;
IMPOSSIBILITY; MUSIC; OBVI-
OUSNESS; ORIGINALITY; PAIN;
PALLOR; REALNESS/UNREAL-
NESS; REPETITION; SERIOUS-
NESS; SLEEP; SMILE; TALLNESS

Prince, Harry
AGITATION; ATTRACTION; AWK-
WARDNESS; BUSYNESS; CER-
TAINTY; CHEERFULNESS; COLD-
NESS; COMFORT; COMPLEXION;
COURAGE; DARKNESS; DIFFER-
ENCES; EASE; FACE(S); HUNGER;
LOVE; POVERTY; RELIABIL-
ITY/UNRELIABILITY; RELIGION;
SENSITIVENESS; SMILE; SUNSET;
THINNESS; TRANSIENCE

Prine, John
SECRECY

Prior, Matthew
MAXIMS, PROVERBS AND SAY-
INGS

Pritchett, V. S.
ATTRACTIVENESS; CORRECT-
NESS; EYE MOVEMENTS; EYE-
BROWS; EYES; FACE(S); FACIAL
EXPRESSIONS, MISCELLANEOUS;
FOREHEAD; FURNITURE AND
FURNISHINGS; GREEN; NECK;
PAST, THE; PHYSICAL APPEAR-
ANCE; ROAD SCENES; ROOMS;
SMILE; SPEECH PATTERNS;
STARES; STRAIGHTNESS;
THOUGHTS

Probst, Bethami
ATTRACTIVENESS; CRITICISM,
DRAMATIC AND LITERARY

Prochnow, Herbert V.
GLOOM; TRUTHNESS/FALSE-
NESS

Proffitt, Nicholas
ALONENESS; ARM(S); DISINTE-
GRATION; EXCITEMENT; EYE
EXPRESSIONS, MISCELLANEOUS;
FACIAL EXPRESSIONS, BLANK

Prome, Richard
BALDNESS

Pronzini, Bill
DIFFICULTY; FIRE AND SMOKE;
FOREHEAD; RAIN

Prose, Francine
ENTHUSIASM; MARRIAGE; MEM-
ORY; PAUSES; RESTLESSNESS;
SCRUTINY

Proust, Marcel
ALONENESS; BLUSHES; BOOKS;
CLOTHING; FACIAL EXPRES-
SIONS, BLANK; GOSSIP; MOON;
SITTING; YELLOW

Publilius Syrus
FORTUNE/MISFORTUNE; LOVE;
SELF CONFIDENCE; TRUST/MIS-
TRUST

Puffendorf, Baron Samuel von
DIFFICULTY

Purdy, James
COLLAPSE

Pushkin, Aleksandr
BLUE; FAME; FEAR

Puttnam, David
PLACES

Puzo, Mario
FACIAL EXPRESSIONS, SERIOUS

Pym, Barbara
BEHAVIOR; CLOTHING, ITS FIT;
GROWTH; HAIR; JUMPING;
LEG(S); RELIABILITY/UNRELIA-
BILITY

Pynchon, Thomas
EMPTINESS; MEETINGS; TO-
BACCO

Q

Quarles, Francis
DIFFERENCES; KNOWLEDGE

Queen, Ellery
ENTHUSIASM; PHYSICAL AP-
PEARANCE; TRUST/MISTRUST

Quillen, Robert
SPORTS

Quindlen, Anna
BODY

Quintilian
MIND DEFINED; THOUGHTS

R

Rabelais, François
OBVIOUSNESS

Rachman, Todd
CAUSE AND EFFECT, RELATION-
SHIPS

Racine, Jean-Baptiste
CRIME; EVIL; HAPPINESS; REJEC-
TION

Raddock, Charles
CLOTHING, ITS FIT

Radford, Dollie
BEAUTY

Radley, Sheila
COMFORT; PHYSICAL APPEAR-
ANCE

Raines, Bishop Richard C.
RELIGION

Raison, Milton
MOUNTAINS

Raleigh, Sir Walter
SHINING

Ralph, James
DIFFERENCES

Ralph, Julian
RARITY

Ramke, Bin
CLOTHING; DESTRUCTION/DE-
STRUCTIVENESS; FLOWERS;
FOOD AND DRINK; FURNITURE
AND FURNISHINGS; LINGERING;
MANKIND; PEOPLE, INTERAC-
TION; SUN

Rampolla, Cardinal Mariano
BELIEFS

Rand, Ayn
CITIES; DISINTEGRATION; IN-
TELLIGENCE; VOICE(S)

Randolph, John
EVIL; UNDESIREABILITY

Rascoe, Judith
ATTRACTION; DIFFICULTY; PEO-
PLE, INTERACTION

Ratner, Rochelle
BREATHING; EYES; VIOLENCE

Rawlings, Marjorie Kinnan
GREEN; SUN; UNCERTAINTY

Raymond, William
TRUTHNESS/FALSENESS

Raynor, Vivian
TRUTHNESS/FALSENESS

Read, Herbert
DEATH; LIFE; LINGERING; SUN;
TEETH

Read, T. Buchanan
CLINGING

Reade, Charles
ADVICE; ENTHUSIASM

Reagan, Ronald
ECONOMICS; GOVERNMENT

Rechy, John
ATTENTION; BIRDS; CHEEKS;
CLOTHING ACCESSORIES; DE-
JECTION; FACIAL EXPRESSIONS,
MISCELLANEOUS; FACIAL
SHAPE; FLOWERS; FURNITURE
AND FURNISHINGS; LEAVES;
MOUNTAINS; MUSCLES; NIGHT;
REAPPEARANCE; SEASONS; SI-
LENCE; SKIN; SKY; THICKNESS;
THUNDER AND LIGHTNING; TO-
BACCO; TREES

Reed, Douglas
PLACES

Reed, Ishmael
PERVASIVENESS

Reed, Rex
EYE MOVEMENTS; GENTLE-
NESS; MOUTH; MOVEMENT;
PERSONALITY PROFILES; PHYSI-
CAL APPEARANCE; SLOWNESS;
TOUGHNESS; VOICE, HARSH;
VOICE, WEAK

Reed, Thomas B.
POLITICS/POLITICIANS

Reese, William
PURSUIT

Reeve, F. D.
AGE; BLACK; COLDNESS; DIS-
CONTENT; LOVE; MOUTH; RAIN;
SLEEP; SOFTNESS; SPEED; VIS-
ABILITY

Reeve, James
PERSISTENCE

Reid, Alastair
AGE; ROCKING AND ROLLING

Reid, Barbara
BREATHING; DAY; LIFE

Reidinger, Paul
CLINGING; DESIRE; GLOOM;
MARRIAGE; SPEAKING; SPEED

Reik, Theodor
MEMORY; PROFESSIONS

Reiss, James
LEAVES; LIFE; RED; SKY; SMILE;
SNOW; TRUTHNESS/FALSENESS

Remarque, Erich Maria
AGE; AIR; ANGER; ANIMALS;
ARM(S); AVAILABILITY; BALD-
NESS; BEHAVIOR;
BENDING/BENT; BREASTS; BUSY-
NESS; CALMNESS; COLLAPSE;
CRUELTY; CRYING; CURIOSITY;
DARKNESS; DECREASE; DEJEC-
TION; DISPERSAL; EMPTINESS;
EYE COLOR; EYES; FACE(S); FA-
CIAL EXPRESSIONS, MISCELLA-
NEOUS; FACIAL EXPRESSIONS,
SERIOUS; FOG; GRINS; HOUSES;
HUNGER; IMMOBILITY; LAUGH-
TER; LOOKS; MEMORY; MOON;
MUSIC; NATURE; NECK; NIGHT;
NOSE(S); OBVIOUSNESS; PAUSE;
PHYSICAL APPEARANCE; PHYSI-
CAL FEELINGS; PREPAREDNESS;
RAIN; RELATIONSHIP; REMOTE-
NESS; RISING; ROAD SCENES;
SCREAMS; SERIOUSNESS; SIT-
TING; SKY; SKY COLOR; SMILE;
SPEED; STRENGTH; SUN; SWEAT;
TALKATIVENESS; TEARS; THUN-
DER AND LIGHTNING; TREES;
VEHICLES, OPERATION OF;
VOICE, EFFECT OF

Renard, Jules
MOVEMENT(S)

Rendell, Ruth
FACE(S); HAIR

Renoir, Jean
STAGE AND SCREEN

Renwick, Joyce
CLOUDS

Repplier, Agnes
GAIETY; WIT

Ress, Lisa
CHANGE; LANDSCAPES; PAST,
THE; TREES

Reston, James
CHARACTERISTICS, NATIONAL;
ENERGY; FRUSTRATION

Reuben, David R.
MARRIAGE

Rheinheimer, Kurt
COLLAPSE

Rhoden, William R.
BEHAVIOR

Rhys, Ernest
WORD(S)

Rhys, Jean
CHANGE; EMOTIONS; EYE
COLOR; FACIAL EXPRESSIONS,
MISCELLANEOUS; FURNITURE
AND FURNISHINGS; HELPLESS-
NESS; MEEKNESS; MIND; MOON;

SADNESS; SCREAMS; SEASCAPES;
SKIN; THINNESS; THOUGHTS;
TREES; VOICE(S); WALKING;
WAR

Ricard, Auguste
PROBLEMS AND SOLUTIONS

Rice, Anne
EYE MOVEMENTS

Rice, Cale Young
BREVITY

Rice, Elmer
INSULT

Rice, Grantland
ABILITY

Rich, Adrienne
AWKWARDNESS; DISINTEGRA-
TION; HANDSHAKE; NATURE;
RELATIONSHIP; SIMPLICITY;
SNOW; WORD(S)

Rich, Frank
CHANGE; CRITICISM, DRA-
MATIC AND LITERARY; WALK-
ING; WAR

Richardson, Frank
STAGE AND SCREEN

Richter, Conrad
THOUGHTS

Richter, Jean Paul
CHEERFULNESS; GREEN; HA-
TRED; LIFE; LOVE

Rickles, Don
IMPOSSIBILITY

Rider, J. W.
FROWNS; HOUSES; PAST, THE

Riedel, Michael
SEX APPEAL

Riley, James Whitcomb
CLEANLINESS; EYES, BRIGHT;
NOSE(S)

Rilke, Rainer Maria
ANTICIPATION; CHANGE; FREE-
DOM; JUSTICE; SOUL

Ríos, Alberto Alvaro
CHANGE

Rioss, J. S.
DARKNESS

Rivarol, Antoine
MONEY

Rivers, Joan
EATING AND DRINKING;
PLACES

Rives, Amélie
SERIOUSNESS

Robbins, Tom
BEHAVIOR; CRIME; DAY; EATING
AND DRINKING; EYE EXPRES-
SIONS, MISCELLANEOUS; FOOD
AND DRINK; HAIR, COLOR;
HEARTBEAT; HOUSES; IDEAS;
KISSES; LAUGHTER; LIFE DE-
FINED; LIGHTING; MOON;
MOVEMENT(S); NOISES; PRO-
TRUSION; ROAD SCENES;
ROOMS; SEASONS; SMILE;
SPREADING; SUN; TEARS; THIN-
NESS; TREMBLING; VIBRATION;
VOICE(S); WEAKNESS

Roberts, Charles G. D.
TIME

Roberts, Kenneth L.
DIFFICULTY

Roberts, Phyllis
BIRDS; PEACEFULNESS

Roberts, Steven V.
POLITICS/POLITICIANS

Robertson, Don
DAY; HOUSES; ORDER/DISOR-
DER; SMILE

Robertson, F. W.
LIFE

Robertson, William
CLEANLINESS

Robin, Leo
ABANDONMENT; AGILITY

Robinson, Edwin Arlington
BEHAVIOR; FAMILIARITY; FUTIL-
ITY; PEACEFULNESS

Robinson, Jill
EMOTIONS

Robison, James
ARM(S); SNOW

Roche, Henri-Pierre
BREATHING; GROWTH; MEN
AND WOMEN; PEOPLE, INTER-
ACTION; STUPIDITY

Roche, John
WORK

Rochefoucauld, François de la
PASSION

Rodgers, W. R.
CONTEMPT; SNOW

Rodriguez, Chi Chi
GOLF

Roethke, Theodore
CRYING; FIRMNESS; FRESHNESS;
IMMOBILITY; JUMPING; LIGHT-
NESS; SLEEP; SLOWNESS; SOFT-
NESS

Rogers, Jane
PAIN; SILENCE

Rogers, Samuel
PURITY

Rogers, Thomas
ADVICE

Rogers, Will
BELIEFS; POLITICS/POLITI-
CIANS; PROFESSIONS; TACT

Rolland, Romain
PASSION

Romains, Jules
RAIN

Rooney, Andy
CORRESPONDENCE

Roosevelt, Franklin Delano
GOVERNMENT; PEACEFULNESS

Roosevelt, Theodore
HEALTH; LIFE; STRENGTH;
WEAKNESS

Roper, John Cadman
PROFESSIONS

Rosas, Cecilia
GROANS AND WHISPERS

Rose, Daniel Asa
DESIRE; DULLNESS

Rose, Pete
BASEBALL

Rosenbaum, David E.
GOVERNMENT

Rosenquist, James
ART AND LITERATURE

Rosetti, Christina
BLUE

Ross, Elizabeth Irvin
SELF CONFIDENCE

Ross, Frank
ANGER; BREATHING; COLLAPSE;
FACIAL COLOR; FAMILIARITY;
HANDS; IDEAS; LANDSCAPES;
PERSONALITY PROFILES;
SCREAMS; SILENCE; SNOW;
WIND

Ross, Jerry
AGILITY; CLOSENESS;
STRENGTH

Ross, Marilyn
SPREADING

Rossetti, Christina
BEAUTY; BELIEFS; BREATHING;
DARKNESS; EYES, BRIGHT;
HEART(S); LOVE, DEFINED;
MOON; SWEETNESS; TACT;
TALKATIVENESS; TREMBLING

Rossetti, Dante Gabriel
AIMLESSNESS; DISAPPEARANCE;
FEAR; FEROCITY; PAIN; SPREAD-
ING; TEARS; TIME; TREMBLING;
TURNING AND TWISTING; UN-
STEADINESS; WORD(S); YEL-
LOW; YOUTH

Roth, Philip
ALERTNESS; ATTENTION; CHAR-
ACTERISTICS, NATIONAL; COR-
RESPONDENCE; EXCITEMENT;
TOUGHNESS; WORK

Rothberg, Abraham
DANCING; DEATH; EYES,
BRIGHT; MARRIAGE

Rousseau, Jean-Jacques
CHARACTER; POLITICS/POLITI-
CIANS

Rovere, Richard
PROFESSIONS

Rowe, Nicholas
KINDNESS

Rowland, Helen
FLATTERY; HEART(S); LOVE;
MARRIAGE; MEN AND WOMEN;
USEFULNESS/USELESSNESS

Rowland, Henry C.
AGE

Rowley, Samuel
DULLNESS

Royce, Josiah
THOUGHTS

Rubenstein, Carin
STAGE AND SCREEN

Rubinstein, Arthur
MUSIC

Ruffini, Giovanni
CURSES; EDUCATION

Rukeyser, Muriel
ROCKING AND ROLLING

Rule, Rebecca
BITTERNESS

Runyon, Damon
BENDING/BENT

Rusk, Dean
POWER

Ruskin, John
ADVANCING; CAUSE AND EF-
FECT; EMPTINESS; HOUSES; SI-
LENCE; TRUTH

Russell, Bertrand
DISCONTENT

Russell, John
DECREASE

Russell, Rosalind
ACTING

Russo, Richard
DISAPPEARANCE; SCRUTINY

Rutherfurd, Edward
BUSINESS; DESPERATION;
CHANGES; PERSONALITY PRO-
FILES; PONDS, RIVERS, AND
STREAMS; TRANSCIENCE;
WEATHER

Rybakof, Anatoly
BLUSHES

S

Sabin, Edwin L.
TONGUE

Sacks, Oliver
HEALTH

Sackville-West, Vita
AGILITY; AMBITION; ATTRAC-
TION; CLEANLINESS; CONTROL;
GOSSIP; GREEN; HAIR; IMPOSSI-
BILITY; LOVE; MUSCLES;
OCEAN/OCEANFRONTS; PAR-
ENTHOOD; POWER; REPETI-
TION; SOFTNESS; TREMBLING;
TRUST/MISTRUST;
WRITERS/WRITING

Sadi
CLOSENESS; LIES/LIARS; TRAVEL

Safer, Morley
AGE

Safire, William
PROTRUSION; STUPIDITY

Sagan, Françoise
DISAPPEARANCE; SHOCK

Saint-Exupery, Antoine de
CALMNESS; GOVERNMENT

Sala, George Augustus
LIFE DEFINED

Salacrou, Armand
ILLNESS

Salamon, Julie
CLOTHING; PERSONALITY PRO-
FILES; PHYSICAL APPEARANCE

Salinger, J. D.
CONTEMPT; PAIN; SMELL

Salten, Felix
FLOWERS; SUN

Saltus, Edgar
AFFECTION; USEFULNESS/USE-
LESSNESS

Sambora, Richie
LOVE

Sams, Ferrol
DISHONESTY

Sandberg-Diment, Erik
COMMONPLACE; GOSSIP; IDEAS;
SLOWNESS

Sandburg, Carl
CALMNESS; CERTAINTY; CLEAN-
LINESS; ENTRANCES AND EXITS;
FEROCITY; HAIR; MATHEMATICS
AND SCIENCE; MEMORY; PAST,
THE; QUESTIONS AND AN-
SWERS; REAPPEARANCE; ROCK-
ING AND ROLLING

Sandburg, Helga
CHEEKS; FACE(S)

Sandel, Cora
SIGHS; SKY COLOR; STRAIGHT-
NESS

Sanders, George
ACTING

Sandler, Corey
AWKWARDNESS

Sandy, Stephen
SMILE

Sandys, George
ABUNDANCE

Sanford, Annette
BREASTS; FLOWERS; VOICE,
HARSH

Sanger, David E.
DECREASE

Sangster, Jimmy
COLLAPSE; CRUELTY; EYES;
FACE(S); LIPS; NOISES; PAIN;
PERSONALITY PROFILES; PHYSI-
CAL APPEARANCE; POWER;
SMELL; STRENGTH; TALKATIVE-
NESS; VOICE, SOFT; YOUTH

Santayana, George
ART AND LITERATURE; CLING-
ING; DEATH DEFINED; DISAP-
PEARANCE; FATE; IRRITABLE-
NESS/IRRITATING; JOY;
MANKIND; MANNERS; MUSIC;
NATURE; PERSONALITY PRO-
FILES; POETS/POETRY; SOCIETY;
THOUGHTS; TIME

Santiago, Danny
BEARING; TREES

Santos,Fernanda
CROWDS

Sapadin, Glenn
WORK

Saphir, Moritz Gottlieb
GREATNESS; MANKIND

Sapirstein, Milton R.
BEAUTY; CHANGE; CHILDREN; EDUCATION; MIND; PARENT-HOOD; PRIDE; SOCIETY

Sarcey, Francisque
IMPOSSIBILITY

Sargent, Epes
SOUL

Saroyan, William
FRIENDSHIP; LOVE; NOSE(S); WORLD; WRITERS/WRITING

Sarton, May
ALONENESS; ANGER; CHANGE; CLINGING; DECREASE; FEAR; HAPPINESS; HELPLESSNESS; IM-PARTIALITY; LEAVES; MOUTH; RELATIONSHIP; STARS

Sartre, Jean-Paul
EVIL

Satanov, Isaac Halevi
MANKIND

Saul, Jamie M.
AGE

Savage, Elizabeth
BIRDS

Sawislak, Arnold
SMILE; VOICE, WEAK

Saxe, J. G.
KISSES

Scannell, Vernon
CLOTHING

Scarborough, William
THINNESS

Schaap, Dick
NOSE(S)

Schaeffer, Susan Fromberg
ALONENESS; BELONGING; BLUSHES; DAY; DRYNESS; EMO-TIONS; GOSSIP; GRAY; HAPPI-NESS; HEAT; HUNGER; INTEN-SITY; LIES/LIARS; LIFE; LIFE DEFINED; PAST, THE; SILENCE; STRAIGHTNESS; SUCCESS/FAIL-URE; TIME; WISDOM; WORD(S); WRINKLES

Schell, Jessie
FEAR; TEARS

Schiaparelli, Elsa
BELIEFS; FOOD AND DRINK; TREMBLING

Schiller, Friedrich
CALMNESS; CLINGING; MANKIND

Schlafly, Phyllis
MARRIAGE

Schlesinger, John
MOVIES

Schmidt, Ray
WEARINESS

Scholes, Percy A.
MUSIC

Schoonover, Shirley W.
CONVERSATION; TONGUE

Schopenhauer, Arthur
AGE; APPRECIATION; GREAT-NESS; INTELLIGENCE; LIFE; LIFE DEFINED; OPINION; RELIGION; RESTLESSNESS; STAGE AND SCREEN; UNSTEADINESS; YOUTH

Schulberg, Budd
CONSCIENCE

Schurz, Carl
BELIEFS

Schwartz, Delmore
ABSURDITY; AGE; AIMLESSNESS; ANXIETY; ATTENTION; CLEVER-NESS; CLOUDS; DAY; DISAPPEAR-ANCE; DISCOMFORT; DIVERSE-NESS; EDUCATION; ELUSIVENESS; ENTRAPMENT; FACIAL EXPRESSIONS, MISCEL-LANEOUS; FAME; FUTILITY; HAPPINESS; HEAT; IMMOBILITY; KISSES; LEG(S); LINGERING; LYING; MEMORY; MORALITY; MOUNTAINS; MUSIC; NATURE; NOISES; OPINION; PAIN; PAST, THE; PERMANENCE; PERSONAL-ITY PROFILES; POETS/POETRY; PURPOSEFULNESS; RAIN; REAL-IZATION; RELATIONSHIP; SE-CRECY; SENSITIVENESS; SLOW-NESS; SUN; SWEETNESS; TREES; VANITY; WIND; WRITERS/WRIT-ING

Schwartz, Lynne Sharon
ABSURDITY; ANGER; ATTRAC-TION; BEHAVIOR; COMFORT; DISAPPEARANCE; DREAM; FA-CIAL EXPRESSIONS, MISCELLA-NEOUS; FACIAL EXPRESSIONS, SERIOUS; HAIR, COLOR; INTEL-LIGENCE; LAUGHTER; LINGER-ING; LOYALTY/DISLOYALTY; OPINION; PAST, THE; PEOPLE, INTERACTION; RESERVE; ROCK-ING AND ROLLING; SILENCE; SINGING; SMELL; SNOW; TRAN-

SIENCE; VOICE, HARSH; WORD(S)

Schwartz-Borden, Gwen
CORRESPONDENCE

Scott, A. O.
CLINGING

Scott, Justin
VOICE(S)

Scott, Temole
SPEED

Scott, Sir Walter
ADVANCING; AGE; ALERTNESS; BARENESS; BUSYNESS; CLEANLI-NESS; CREDIT; DARKNESS; DEATH DEFINED; GLIMMER, GLITTER AND GLOSS; IRRITA-BLENESS/IRRITATING; PEOPLE, INTERACTION; PHYSICAL AP-PEARANCE; RELIABILITY/UNRE-LIABILITY; SPEED

Scully, Vin
BASEBALL

Seale, Jan Epton
CALMNESS

Seaman, Barbara
FAME; FINGERS

Seaman, Donald
ADVANCING; ALERTNESS; BE-WILDERMENT; BLACK; BREATH-ING; CAUTION; CHIN; CLEVER-NESS; COLDNESS; COLLAPSE; DISPERSAL; EASE; ENTRAP-MENT; EXITS; EYE EXPRESSIONS, MISCELLANEOUS; LANDSCAPES; LIES/LIARS; LIGHTING; POWER; RAIN; REALIZATION; RESERVE; RUNNING; SAFETY; SECRECY; SHINING; SHOULDERS; SILENCE; SKY COLOR; SOFTNESS; SPEECH PATTERNS; SPREADING; TIME; VEHICLES, OPERATION OF; VOICE, HARSH

Searls, Hank
AFFECTION; GLIMMER, GLIT-TER AND GLOSS; ROCKING AND ROLLING

Secondat, Charles-Louis de, Baron de Montesquieu
GOVERNMENT; LAWS

Sedgewick, Ellery
CHILDREN

Sedley, Sir Charles
CLOSENESS

See, Carolyn
MADNESS

Segal, Erich
LOOKS

Ségur, Joseph Alexandre Pierre
LOVE

Seifert, Jaroslav
FURNITURE AND FURNISHINGS; KISSES; LIFE; LOVE; MEMORY; POETS/POETRY; SKIN; STARS

Selden, John
CONSCIENCE; PRIDE; SPEECH-MAKING; WIT

Selz, Thalia
TENSION

Selzer, Joanne
GLOOM; TRANSIENCE

Selzer, Richard
AGE; DEATH; DESIRABILITY

Seneca, Lucius Annaeus (the Younger)
LIFE DEFINED; PROBLEMS AND SOLUTIONS; WORD(S)

Serling, Robert J.
FACIAL EXPRESSIONS, BLANK; LIPS; SUN; WRINKLES

Service, Robert W.
SUN

Setanti, Joaquin
CONVERSATION

Settle, Elkanah
COURAGE

Settle, Mary Lee
BEAUTY; COMFORT; EYE EXPRESSIONS, MISCELLANEOUS; HEALTH; PHYSICAL APPEARANCE; SILENCE; SUDDENNESS; THINNESS; VISABILITY; WEAKNESS

Sexton, Anne
ARM(S); BIRTH; BURST; CONVERSATION; DISAPPEARANCE; GUILT; HEARTBEAT; IMMOBILITY; INNOCENCE; OCEAN/OCEANFRONTS; PERSISTENCE; RAIN; SENSE; SOFTNESS; SPEED; STEADINESS; STRENGTH; TEARS; UNATTRACTIVENESS; WHITE; WORDS DEFINED; YELLOW

Shaftesbury, Lord
MANNERS; UNCERTAINTY

Shagan, Steve
BODY

Shaham, Nathan
REAPPEARANCE

Shaiman, Mark
PLACES

Shain, Merle
LIFE DEFINED

Shakespeare, William
ABUNDANCE; AFFECTION; AGE; AGREEMENT/DISAGREEMENT; ALONENESS; ANGER; BITTERNESS; BLACK; BOREDOM/BORING; BREVITY; CALMNESS; CERTAINTY; CLARITY; COLDNESS; CONSCIENCE; CONTEMPT; CONTINUITY; COURAGE; CROWDS; DEATH; DEATH DEFINED; DEATH, FINALITY OF; DESIRE; DESTRUCTION/DESTRUCTIVENESS; DIFFERENCES; DISCOMFORT; DISHONESTY; DRYNESS; DULLNESS; EASE; EATING AND DRINKING; EDUCATION; EMPTINESS; ENTHUSIASM; EVIL; EXITS; EYES; EYES, BRIGHT; FAME; FAMILIARITY; FATNESS; FEROCITY; FIGHTING; FIRMNESS; FLATTERY; FORTUNE/MISFORTUNE; FRAGILITY; FRESHNESS; GAIETY; GENTLENESS; GLIMMER, GLITTER AND GLOSS; GLOOM; GREED; GREEN; GROWTH; HEALTH; HEAT; IGNORANCE; KINDNESS; LAUGHTER; LOVE; LOVE, DEFINED; LOYALTY/DISLOYALTY; MANKIND; MEMORY; MEN AND WOMEN; MODESTY; NOSE(S); PALLOR; PARENTHOOD; PATIENCE; PEACEFULNESS; PERMANENCE; PINK; PLEASURE; PURITY; RED; SADNESS; SELF CONFIDENCE; SILENCE; SIMILARITY; SINGING; SITTING; SKIN; SLOWNESS; SMALLNESS; SMOOTHNESS; SOFTNESS; SPEECH PATTERNS; SPEECH-MAKING; SPEED; SPORTS; SUDDENNESS; SWEETNESS; THOUGHTS; TIME; TOUGHNESS; TRUTH; UNCERTAINTY; VIRTUE; WALKING; WAR; WASTE; WATCHFULNESS; WORDS, EFFECT OF; YOUTH

Shales, Tom
ABUNDANCE; DISPERSAL

Shamfort, Sebastian
GOSSIP

Shapiro, Karl
BRIGHTNESS; CLEANLINESS; CLEVERNESS; DISAPPEARANCE; DREAM; DULLNESS; FAME; FIRMNESS; FRESHNESS; GLIMMER, GLITTER AND GLOSS; HEARTBEAT; IGNORANCE; MEMORY; MOUNTAINS; MOVEMENT(S); OCEAN/OCEANFRONTS; ORIGINALITY; PERSISTENCE; POETS/POETRY; POLITICS/POLITICIANS; REALNESS/UNREALNESS; RISING; SECRECY; SEX; SHINING; SIMPLICITY; SMOOTHNESS; STOMACH; SUDDENNESS; TENSION; THOUGHTS; TIME; TIMELINESS/UNTIMELINESS; VISABILITY; WALKING; WAR; WORDS, EFFECT OF; WRINKLES

Shapley, Rufus
SHOULDERS

Sharp, Marilyn
HABIT; KINDNESS; LOOKS

Shaw, Artie
IMPOSSIBILITY

Shaw, George Bernard
ART AND LITERATURE; BEHAVIOR; CHARACTERISTICS, NATIONAL; DANGER; DEATH; FUTILITY; GOODNESS; INSULTS; KNOWLEDGE; MANNERS; MARRIAGE; MEEKNESS; NATURALNESS; NOSE(S); SIMPLICITY; STRENGTH; WRITERS/WRITING; YOUTH

Shaw, Henry Wheeler
TIME

Shaw, Irwin
AGILITY; ATTRACTIVENESS; BOXING AND WRESTLING; BREASTS; BUSYNESS; KINDNESS; LEG(S); MEN AND WOMEN; NERVOUSNESS; PURSUIT; ROCKING AND ROLLING; RUNNING; STRENGTH; THINNESS; THRIFT

Shaw, J. B.
MORALITY

Shearing, Joseph
HATRED

Shedd, William Greenough Thayer
BELIEFS

Sheed, Wilfrid
AGREEMENT/DISAGREEMENT; ALERTNESS; AWKWARDNESS;

BELIEFS; COLLAPSE; EMOTIONS; ENTRANCES AND EXITS; HUMOR; IDEAS; INTENSITY; ORDER/DISORDER; PERSISTENCE; PERSONALITY PROFILES; POVERTY; PURSUIT; ROAD SCENES; SELF CONFIDENCE; STALENESS; SURPRISE; USEFULNESS/USELESSNESS; VOICE, MUSIC RELATED; WATCHFULNESS

Sheen, Fulton J.
LIFE DEFINED

Sheiner, Robin
CLEVERNESS

Shelley, Percy Bysshe
BEAUTY; BLACK; BLUE; BRIGHTNESS; CALMNESS; CHANGE; CLINGING; COLDNESS; COLLAPSE; COURAGE; DEATH; DESTRUCTION/DESTRUCTIVENESS; DISAPPEARANCE; DISINTEGRATION; DISPERSAL; EMPTINESS; EYES; FLATTERY; GLIMMER, GLITTER AND GLOSS; HAIR, COLOR; HEART(S); HELPLESSNESS; HOPE; LIFE DEFINED; LINGERING; PAST, THE; POWER; REGRET; SEASONS; SILENCE; SLEEP; SPEED; SPREADING; SUCCESS/FAILURE; SUN; THICKNESS; TIME; VIOLENCE; WEARINESS; WHITE

Shenhar, Yitzhak
MOUNTAINS; TREES; TREMBLING; WIND

Shenstone, William
EDUCATION; VIRTUE; WRITERS/WRITING

Shepard, Richard E.
BREVITY; SPEECH PATTERNS

Shepard, Sam
STRANGENESS

Sheridan, Frances
SPEED

Sheridan, Richard Brinsley
AGREEMENT/DISAGREEMENT; GOSSIP; PERSISTENCE; RELIGION

Sherwood, Robert Emmet
FEAR; FUTILITY; MEETINGS

Shields, Mark
PERVASIVENESS

Shipler, David K.
TENSION

Shirley, James
ABUNDANCE; FLEXIBILITY/INFLEXIBILITY

Sholl, Evan A.
LIFE DEFINED

Shreiner, Olive
OCEAN/OCEANFRONTS

Shreve, Susan Richards
ABANDONMENT; CITIES; DANCING; HEARTBEAT; SOFTNESS; VISABILITY

Shriver, Lionel
APPEARANCE; DESPERATION; DIFFICULTY; HAIR; KISSES; MOUTH; PERSISTENCE; RELATIONSHIPS; SUNLIGHT; TIME

Shulman, Alix Kates
FIRE AND SMOKE

Shulman, David
CONTENTMENT

Shulman, Max
BEARD; CHARACTERISTICS, NATIONAL; EYEBROWS; FACIAL EXPRESSIONS, MISCELLANEOUS; FROWNS; UNDESIREABILITY

Sidney, Sir Philip
BLACK

Sigal, Clancy
CALMNESS; EXCITEMENT; IRRITABLENESS/IRRITATING; SMILE

Signoret, Simone
ACTING

Silk, Leonard
ECONOMICS; FIGHTING

Silkin, Jon
RED

Silko, Leslie
LOOKS; SNOW

Sillery, C. D.
DEATH

Sillitoe, Alan
FACE(S); FACIAL EXPRESSIONS, MISCELLANEOUS

Silone, Ignazio
BEARING; DEJECTION; EYES; FACE(S); HELPLESSNESS; LINGERING; RELIGION; SCREAMS; VOICE(S); WAR

Silverberg, Robert
BODY; DULLNESS; ENTRAPMENT; EYES, BRIGHT; FEAR; FEROCITY; GROWTH; HOUSES; IMMOBILITY; MIND; MUSIC; PAIN; PAST, THE; PLACES; ROCKING AND ROLLING; SLEEP; SLOW-

NESS; SPEED; TREMBLING; VEHICLES

Simenon, Georges
EXCITEMENT; SKIN

Simic, Charles
BEAUTY; BEHAVIOR; BIRDS; BLOOD; DRINKING; DRYNESS; FURNITURE AND FURNISHINGS; HOPE; MOVEMENT(S); NATURE; WHITE

Simmons, Charles
CORRECTNESS

Simmons, G.
AMBITION; MOTIVATION

Simms, William Gilmore
VANITY

Simon, Kate
BRIGHTNESS

Simon, Neil
CONVERSATION

Simon, Paul
FRIENDSHIP, SILENCE

Simon, Scott
EXCITEMENT; FAMILIARITY

Simonson, Helen
WEARINESS; FACE; INFORMATION; LOVE; MEMORIES; PERSONAL TRAITS; PLAINNESS; RAIN; RELATIONSHIPS; REMOTENESS; SECRECY; VOICE(S)

Simpson, E. L.
IDEAS

Simpson, Eileen
TIMELINESS/UNTIMELINESS

Singer, Isaac Bashevis
ABUNDANCE; BEGINNINGS AND ENDINGS; BLACK; DRINKING; FACIAL COLOR; FEAR; FIRE AND SMOKE; LOVE, DEFINED; MARRIAGE; MOUTH; PALLOR; SUN; WORDS OF PRAISE; YELLOW

Singer, Mark
HANDSHAKE

Sinise, Gary
ACTING

Sira, Ben
FRIENDSHIP

Siskel, Gene
OBVIOUSNESS

Sitwell, Dame Edith
BIGNESS; BLACK; BLUE; BRIGHTNESS; CALMNESS; COLORS; DANCING; DISAPPEARANCE; EYES; FACIAL COLOR; FEAR; FIRMNESS; FLOWERS; FUTURE;

GAIETY; HAIR, CURLY; LAUGH-
TER; MOVEMENT(S); MUSCLES;
NATURE; NOISES; QUESTIONS
AND ANSWERS; RAIN; RED;
ROARS; SHAPE; SHARPNESS; SI-
LENCE; SPEAKING; SUN; TALL-
NESS; WEATHER; WHITE;
YOUTH

Skinner, B. F.
AGE

Skinner, Cornelia Otis
FRAGILITY

Slaughter, Carolyn
ABANDONMENT; CHEERFUL-
NESS; EYEBROWS; LEAVES;
WALKING; WAR

Slavitt, David R.
CONVERSATION; ENTHUSIASM;
IDEAS; PERSISTENCE; SENSI-
TIVENESS

Slesar, Henry
GUILT

Slesinger, Tess
ALONENESS; BREATHING; INAP-
PROPRIATENESS; RELATIONSHIP

Slick, Sam
MIND DEFINED

Slocum, E. N.
EYES

Smedley, Francis Edward
COST; FRESHNESS

Smiles, Samuel
CHILDREN; CREDIT; HOPE

Smith, Alexander
THOUGHTS

Smith, Dodie
USEFULNESS/USELESSNESS

Smith, F. Hopkinson
HABIT; HELPLESSNESS

Smith, Henry
LAWS

Smith, John
CLEANLINESS

Smith, Lee
AIR; AVAILABILITY; BLUE; CER-
TAINTY; CLOUDS; DAY; EM-
BRACE; EYE COLOR; LINGER-
ING; MOUNTAINS; PAST, THE;
PEACEFULNESS; PHYSICAL
FEELINGS; REGULARITY/IRREG-
ULARITY; RUNNING; SITTING;
SUN; VOICE, MONOTONOUS

Smith, Lillian
FREEDOM

Smith, Logan Pearsall
WRITERS/WRITING

Smith, Martin Cruz
ARM MOVEMENTS; AWKWARD-
NESS; DRINKING; EYEBROWS;
GRAY; GROANS AND WHISPERS;
HAIR, TEXTURE; HEAD MOVE-
MENTS; MONEY; REAPPEAR-
ANCE; ROAD SCENES; SILENCE;
SNOW; THUNDER AND LIGHT-
NING; VOICE, EFFECT OF;
WATCHFULNESS; WIND

Smith, Pauline
VOICE(S)

Smith, Stevie
ART AND LITERATURE; PALLOR;
PROPRIETY/IMPROPRIETY; RIS-
ING; STANDING; TEARS; THIN-
NESS; THOUGHTS

Smith, Sydney
BELIEFS; CORRESPONDENCE;
HANDWRITING; HUMOR;
KNOWLEDGE; MARRIAGE;
OPINION; PERSONALITY PRO-
FILES; PROBLEMS AND SOLU-
TIONS; TALKATIVENESS; WIT

Smollett, Tobias
GREED; MANNERS; WIT

Snodgrass, W. D.
ABUNDANCE; ANGER; BELIEV-
ABILITY; BLACK; BREATHING;
CONTROL; DARKNESS; DISAP-
PEARANCE; FATNESS; FEAR;
FRAGILITY; PAUSE; ROCKING
AND ROLLING; ROOMS; SLOW-
NESS; SOFTNESS; TREES; TREM-
BLING; WALKING; WAR; WRIN-
KLES

Socrates
FLATTERY

Solotaroff, Ted
WRITERS/WRITING

Solovyou, Vladimir
POWER

Solzhenitsyn, Alexander
CLOUDS; FOREHEAD; TURNING
AND TWISTING

Somerhausen, Zevi Hirsch
WRITERS/WRITING

Sommer, Elyse
ABUNDANCE; ACTIVENESS; AD-
VERSARY; ANXIETY; ATTRAC-
TION; BELIEVABILITY; BLACK;
BREVITY; BRIGHTNESS; CAN-
DOR; CHARACTERISTICS, NA-

TIONAL; CHEERFULNESS;
CLINGING; COMFORT; COM-
MONPLACE; COMPATIBILITY;
COMPETITION; COMPLETE-
NESS; COST; CRUELTY; CURIOS-
ITY; DECREASE; DIFFICULTY;
DISAPPEARANCE; DISCOMFORT;
DISCONTENT; DISINTEGRA-
TION; GAIETY; IMMOBILITY; IM-
POSSIBILITY; INAPPROPRIATE-
NESS;
IRRITABLENESS/IRRITATING;
LOOKS; NATURALNESS; NOISES;
OBVIOUSNESS; OPPORTUNITY;
ORDER/DISORDER; ORIGINAL-
ITY; PAIN; PERMANENCE; RAR-
ITY; REJECTION; SHAME; SHAPE;
SHOCK; SILENCE; SPREADING;
TALLNESS; UNDESIREABILITY;
VANITY; WEARINESS

Sommer, Mike
ABSURDITY; ANXIETY; AVAIL-
ABILITY; CAUTION; COLLAPSE;
COMPETITION; COMPLEXITY;
COURAGE; DECREASE;
GROWTH; INAPPROPRIATENESS;
OBVIOUSNESS; SCRUTINY; SEN-
SITIVENESS; SHARPNESS; SMELL;
STRAIGHTNESS; VIRTUE

Sondheim, Stephen
COLORS

Sophocles
FOOLISHNESS

Soseki, Natsume
IGNORANCE; TENSION; VEHI-
CLES

Soutar, Bill
CRITICISM

South, Robert
ABSURDITY; NECESSITY

Southern, Terry
CLINGING

Southey, Robert
BENDING/BENT; CURSES;
FRIENDSHIP; TALLNESS;
WORD(S)

Sowerby, Gita
REMOTENESS

Spalding, John Lancaster
BELIEFS

Spark, Muriel
AGE; RELIGION; SEX

Spencer, Elizabeth
ABUNDANCE; BLUE; CONVERSA-
TION; CRITICISM; CRYING;

DEATH; DIFFICULTY; DISINTE-GRATION; DRYNESS; EMPTINESS; ENTRAPMENT; EYE COLOR; EYES, BRIGHT; FACIAL DETAILS; FACIAL EXPRESSIONS, MISCEL-LANEOUS; FACIAL EXPRES-SIONS, SERIOUS; FEROCITY; FIN-GERS; GRAY; HAIR, TEXTURE; HEAT; IMMOBILITY; LOOSENESS; LYING; MEMORY; MOON; OPEN AND SHUT; PATIENCE; PHYSICAL FEELINGS; POLITICS/POLITI-CIANS; POWER; REALIZATION; REPETITION; RESTLESSNESS; RISING; SILENCE; SITTING; SKIN; SMALLNESS; SPEAKING; STARES; SUDDENNESS; SUR-PRISE; TEARS; TEETH; TENSION; TIME; VEHICLES; VEHICLES, OP-ERATION OF; WEAKNESS; WHITE

Spencer, Herbert
CERTAINTY

Spencer, Scott
ABSURDITY; ACCOMPLISHMENT; AGITATION; BEGINNINGS AND ENDINGS; CLOTHING, ITS FIT; DIFFICULTY; DISAPPEARANCE; DISCONTENT; EYES, BRIGHT; FA-CIAL COLOR; FACIAL EXPRES-SIONS, SERIOUS; FEAR; GROANS AND WHISPERS; IMPOR-TANCE/UNIMPORTANCE; IN-SULT; LAUGHTER; MEETINGS; PERSONALITY PROFILES; PROMPTNESS; SEX; SHINING; SI-LENCE; SKIN; SNOW; THOUGHTS; TREMBLING; VIO-LENCE; WALKING; WIND

Spender, John Alfred
MIND DEFINED

Spofford, Harriet Prescott
BEAUTY DEFINED

Spring, Howard
FLOWERS; HEALTH; HUNGER; MIST; TOBACCO; WEATHER; YELLOW

Spurgeon, C. H.
INSULT

Squire, Philip
USEFULNESS/USELESSNESS

St. John, Adela Rogers
EMOTIONS; LEG(S); SMILE

St. John, Henry
CHARACTERISTICS, NATIONAL; SPEECHMAKING

Stabler, Ken
FOOTBALL; SWEAT; VIOLENCE

Staël, Madame de
LIFE

Stafford, Jean
AGILITY; AIR; ANGER; ATTEN-TION; BEWILDERMENT; CLAR-ITY; CONTINUITY; CONVERSA-TION; DAY; DIVERSENESS; EMOTIONS; ENTRANCES AND EXITS; ENTRAPMENT; EYE-BROWS; EYES; GREEN; HAIR; IN-NOCENCE; LINGERING; LOOKS; OBJECTS, MISC.; PASSION; PAUSE; PERMANENCE; REALIZA-TION; ROOMS; SELF CONFI-DENCE; SHAPE; SILENCE; SNOW; SPREADING; STRAIGHTNESS; TEARS; TOBACCO; VIOLENCE; VOICE, MONOTONOUS; VOICE(S)

Stainback, Berry
FOOTBALL; SWEAT; VIOLENCE

Stall, Sylvanys
MANKIND

Stallings, Laurence
BODY; IMPOSSIBILITY; LEAPING

Stanton, Theodore
BOOKS

Starbuck, George
SEASONS

Stargell, Willie
BASEBALL

Stark, Sharon Sheehe
ACTIVENESS; AGE; AGITATION; AIR; ARM(S); ATTENTION; BARE-NESS; BENDING/BENT; BODY; BURST; CALMNESS; CERTAINTY; CLARITY; CLEVERNESS; COL-LAPSE; COLORS; COMFORT; CONTINUITY; CROWDS; DAY; DEATH; DISINTEGRATION; EN-ERGY; EYE MOVEMENTS; FACIAL COLOR; FACIAL DETAILS; FA-CIAL EXPRESSIONS, MISCELLA-NEOUS; FINGERS; FOOD AND DRINK; FOOLISHNESS; FRAGILITY; GREED; HAIR, COLOR; HAND MOVEMENTS; HANDS; HEAD MOVEMENTS; LANDSCAPES; LEG(S); LIGHT-NESS; LIPS; LOOKS; MOON;

MOVEMENT(S); NATURE; PAIN; PERSONALITY PROFILES; PINK; REALIZATION; REALNESS/UNRE-ALNESS; RELIGION; ROAD SCENES; SENSITIVENESS; SHARPNESS; SILENCE; SKIN; SKY; SLOWNESS; SMOOTHNESS; SPREADING; SUN; THINNESS; TREES; VOICE, HARSH; WORD(S)

Stassart, Baron de
MANKIND

Stead, Christina
BOOKS; DEJECTION; FACIAL SHAPE; JOY; PALLOR; RICHES; SKY; SMILE

Steele, Sir Richard
READERS/READING; WORDS DE-FINED

Steele, Wilbur Daniel
ARM(S); BROWN; IMMOBILITY; IMPOSSIBILITY; LANDSCAPES; RELATIONSHIP; ROCKING AND ROLLING; SKY; VOICE, MUSIC RELATED; WEAKNESS

Steffens, Lincoln
ART AND LITERATURE

Stegner, Wallace
ACTIVENESS; ADVANCING; ALERTNESS; ANGER; BRIGHT-NESS; CLEANLINESS; DAY; DIS-CONTENT; EMOTIONS; FACE(S); FACIAL EXPRESSIONS, MISCEL-LANEOUS; FAMILIARITY; GROANS AND WHISPERS; HAIR; HANDSHAKE; HEAT; IRRITABLE-NESS/IRRITATING; LEAVES; LOOKS; LYING; MOON; NERV-OUSNESS; NOISES; OBVIOUS-NESS; PAST, THE; PERSONALITY PROFILES; POWER; PURITY; PUR-POSEFULNESS; REGULARITY/IR-REGULARITY; RELIABILITY/UN-RELIABILITY; ROAD SCENES; ROOMS; SHARPNESS; SMELL; SUN; WRINKLES

Stein, Joseph
POVERTY; USEFULNESS/USE-LESSNESS

Steinbeck, John
AGITATION; EYE EXPRESSIONS, MISCELLANEOUS; EYEBROWS; FLOWERS; MOVEMENT(S); PLACES; SPREADING; WRIT-ERS/WRITING

Stendhal, LOVE, DEFINED

Stern, Isaac
GROANS AND WHISPERS

Stern, James
EXITS; HAIR, TEXTURE; HANDS; OCEAN/OCEANFRONTS; PHYSICAL FEELINGS; SKY COLOR; VOICE, MONOTONOUS; WORDS, EFFECT OF

Stern, Steve
CHEEKS

Sterne, Laurence
BITTERNESS; FAME; KNOWLEDGE; PAIN

Sterngold, James
PROBLEMS AND SOLUTIONS

Stevens, James
GROANS AND WHISPERS; STRENGTH

Stevens, Wallace
ACTIVENESS; BARENESS; CLOUDS; COLDNESS; DAY; DISINTEGRATION; EMOTIONS; FRAGILITY; FROWNS; GROWTH; HUNGER; MEN AND WOMEN; MOON; MOVEMENT(S); NATURE; NIGHT; OPINION; PEACEFULNESS; SEASONS; SHARPNESS; SHINING; SITTING; SNOW; STARS; TALLNESS; THOUGHTS; TREES; WEATHER; WIND

Stevenson, Adlai
FLATTERY; POLITICS/POLITICIANS

Stevenson, Robert Louis
ACTIVENESS; CHOICES; CITIES; CONVERSATION; CRUELTY; DESTRUCTION/DESTRUCTIVENESS; EYES; FACIAL COLOR; FEAR; HEALTH; LIFE; LOVE; LOVE, DEFINED; MANKIND; MARRIAGE; OBJECTS, MISC.; PASSION; PLEASURE; QUESTIONS AND ANSWERS; SHOCK; STORIES

Stewart, Fred Mustard
EMOTIONS; SCREAMS; SEASCAPES

Stewart, Mary
FIRMNESS; FLOWERS; IMMOBILITY; KINDNESS; LOOKS; MEMORY; MOON; OCEAN/OCEANFRONTS; SMELL; STARS; TURNING AND TWISTING

Stockanes, Anthony E.
BUSINESS; CLOUDS; PHYSICAL APPEARANCE; SILENCE; SMILE; TOBACCO

Stockton, Frank R.
RELIABILITY/UNRELIABILITY

Stockwell, John R.
GOVERNMENT

Stone, Alma
SPREADING

Stone, Irving
ABANDONMENT; AGITATION; ALONENESS; HELPLESSNESS; WRINKLES

Stone, Robert
EMBRACE

Stone, Walter
SITTING

Storrs, Emily
POLITICS/POLITICIANS

Stoughton, John
BOOKS

Stout, Rex
ANGER; FACE(S); FEAR; SPEED; VOICE(S)

Stowe, Harriet Beecher
CRUELTY; PURSUIT

Strand, Mark
SILENCE

Straus, Dorothea
AWKWARDNESS; BEARD; CHOICES; CITIES; CONTINUITY; EXCITEMENT; FAMILIARITY; FUTILITY; HOUSES; POLITICS/POLITICIANS; REALNESS/UNREALNESS; RELIABILITY/UNREALITY; SWEAT; TREES; TREMBLING; WRINKLES

Stravinsky, Igor
MUSIC

Stravinsky, John
RISK

Streatfeild, Noel
OPEN AND SHUT

Strindberg, August
ANTICIPATION; FUTILITY; HAPPINESS

Stritch, Elaine

Stroud, J. L.
POPULARITY
PLACES

Stryker, Lloyd Paul
LAWS

Stuart, Jesse
EYES, BRIGHT

Sturm, Marian
DISINTEGRATION

Styron, William
AGITATION; BLACK; ELUSIVENESS; EYE MOVEMENTS; EYES; HAIR, COLOR; HANDS; INSECTS; IRRITABLENESS/IRRITATING; MEMORY; MOON; NOISES; ORIGINALITY; PAUSE; PERSONALITY PROFILES; SHOCK; SILENCE; SKY; SNOW; SUNSET; SWEAT; VOICE, SOFT; WIND; WRINKLES

Suckling, Sir John
EVIL; FACE(S)

Suckow, Ruth
ENTRANCES AND EXITS; FACE(S); HEAD MOVEMENTS

Sue, Eugène
FLEXIBILITY/INFLEXIBILITY

Summers, Hollis
CONTENTMENT; PAST, THE

Süskind, Patrick
CLARITY; CONTENTMENT; TOUGHNESS

Sutherland, Margaret
ADVANTAGEOUSNESS; AVAILABILITY; CLOUDS; CONTENTMENT; LIFE; NATURE

Svetlanov, Yevgeny
MUSIC

Svevo, Italo
FACIAL COLOR; LIFE DEFINED; LOVE; SMILE

Swados, Harvey
ACTIONS; ALONENESS; ANTICIPATION; ARM MOVEMENTS; ATTENTION; BEARD; BEARING; BLOOD; BLUSHES; CERTAINTY; CHIN; CLOTHING; CLOTHING, ITS FIT; CONNECTIONS; CONVERSATION; DESIRE; ELUSIVENESS; ENTRANCES AND EXITS; EYE EXPRESSIONS, MISCELLANEOUS; EYES; FACE(S); FLEXIBILITY/INFLEXIBILITY; FOREHEAD; FUTURE; GRINS; HAIR; HAIR STYLES; HAND MOVEMENTS; HANDS; HANDSHAKE; HEAD MOVEMENTS; HEAVINESS; HOPE; HOUSES; IMPOSSIBILITY; JOY; LANDSCAPES; LAUGHTER; LIGHTNESS; LINGERING; LOOKS; LYING; MEEKNESS; MEMORY; MUSIC; NAMES; PAST, THE; PEACEFULNESS; PERSON-

ALITY PROFILES;
POLITICS/POLITICIANS; PRO-
TECTIVENESS; RAIN; ROAD
SCENES; SEXUAL INTERACTION;
SHAME; SHOULDERS; SILENCE;
SINGING; SITTING; SKIN;
SMOOTHNESS; SNOW; SPEECH
PATTERNS; SUN; SWEAT; TALKA-
TIVENESS; TOBACCO; TREM-
BLING; VOICE, EFFECT OF;
VOICE(S); VOICE, WEAK; WRIN-
KLES

Swansburg, John
OBVIOUSNESS

Swartz, Joshua
BOOKS

Swenson, May
EXITS

Swerdlow, Joel
BEHAVIOR

Swetchine, Madame
HAPPINESS

Swift, Graham
ARGUMENTS; BEARING; CLOTH-
ING ACCESSORIES; DISINTEGRA-
TION; DISPERSAL; FACE(S);
LAUGHTER; PAIN; REAPPEAR-
ANCE; SCRUTINY; SEXUAL IN-
TERACTION; SHINING; SLOW-
NESS; SMILE; TREES;
TREMBLING

Swift, Jonathan
ABANDONMENT; AGE; ANGER;
BARENESS; BEAUTY DEFINED;
BEGINNINGS AND ENDINGS;
BOOKS; CLEVERNESS; CLOTH-
ING, ITS FIT; CONTINUITY; FAT-
NESS; FLATTERY; FRIENDSHIP;
GROWTH; INNOCENCE; LAWS;
LIES/LIARS; MAXIMS, PROVERBS
AND SAYINGS; PASSION

Swinburne, Algernon Charles
ACTIVENESS; AGE; BARENESS;
BEAUTY; BENDING/BENT; BIT-
TERNESS; BLACK; BRIGHTNESS;
CLARITY; COLDNESS; CONNEC-
TIONS; COURAGE; CRUELTY;
EMBRACE; EMPTINESS;
FRAGILITY; GRAY; HARSHNESS;
KISSES; LOVE; MEMORY;
MOUTH; NIGHT; PALLOR; PU-
RITY; SADNESS; SOFTNESS;
STRENGTH; TALKATIVENESS;
WISDOM

Swinnerton, Frank
ADVANCING; ALERTNESS;
ANGER; ANXIETY; ATTRACTIVE-
NESS; BEARD; BEARING; BOOKS;
BREATHING; CALMNESS; CAU-
TION; CLARITY; CLINGING;
COMFORT; COMPLEXION; CON-
NECTIONS; CRUELTY; CURIOS-
ITY; DARKNESS; DAY; EMO-
TIONS; ENTRANCES AND EXITS;
EXCITEMENT; EXITS; EYE
COLOR; EYE EXPRESSIONS, MIS-
CELLANEOUS; EYES; FACE(S);
FACIAL COLOR; FACIAL EXPRES-
SIONS, SERIOUS; FEROCITY; FIN-
GERS; FLEXIBILITY/INFLEXIBIL-
ITY; FRESHNESS; GAIETY;
GOSSIP; HAND MOVEMENTS;
HANDS; HANDSHAKE; HAPPI-
NESS; HARSHNESS; HEAD MOVE-
MENTS; HEARTBEAT; IMMOBIL-
ITY; JUMPING; KINDNESS;
LAUGHTER; LEAPING; LIPS;
LOOKS; MEMORY; MEN AND
WOMEN; MIND; MUSTACHE(S);
NAMES; NATURALNESS;
NOSE(S); PATIENCE; PEACEFUL-
NESS; PERSISTENCE; PLEASURE;
PROMPTNESS; RAIN; REAPPEAR-
ANCE; RELATIONSHIP; REST-
LESSNESS; ROCKING AND
ROLLING; SENTIMENT; SHIN-
ING; SNOW; SPEED; STANDING;
TEARS; TEETH; THINNESS; TO-
BACCO; TRUST/MISTRUST;
VOICE(S); WEARINESS; WIND;
WORDS, EFFECT OF; WRINKLES

Symons, Julian
VOICE(S)

Synge, John M.
PURSUIT

T

Tabley, Lord de
CLARITY

Tacitus
SPEECHMAKING; STYLE

Tagore, Rabindranath
LIFE; MIST; NIGHT; PLEASURE;
SENSE

Tallent, Elizabeth
HAIR, TEXTURE; SKIN

Talleyrand, Alexandre de
CHARACTER

Talleyrand, Charles de
FOOD AND DRINK

Tamil
HELPLESSNESS

Targan, Barry
BELONGING; DIVERSENESS;
STRENGTH; WHITE

Tarkington, Booth
DISAPPEARANCE; OBVIOUSNESS

Tate, Narun
MEEKNESS

Taubman, Philip
EMOTIONS

Tawney, Richard H@index theme:.,
SOCIETY

Taylor, Anne
STARS

Taylor, Bayard
ALONENESS; IGNORANCE

Taylor, Elizabeth
CALMNESS; CLOTHING ACCES-
SORIES; DANGER; EMBRACE; FA-
CIAL EXPRESSIONS, BLANK;
FROWNS; FURNITURE AND FUR-
NISHINGS; HANDS; JEWELRY;
LOVE; LYING; MEN AND
WOMEN; MOVEMENT(S); QUES-
TIONS AND ANSWERS; REST-
LESSNESS; SEASCAPES

Taylor, Ellen du Pois
BLACK; PERMANENCE

Taylor, Fred
DANGER

Taylor, Henry
DISAPPEARANCE

Taylor, Jeremy
RELIGION; SEX

Taylor, Pat Ellis
AGITATION

Taylor, Peter
MEMORY

Taylor, Robert Lewis
RISING

Teasdale, Sara
BELIEFS; HAPPINESS

Temple, Sir William
ABILITY; BOOKS

Tennenbaum, Silvia
SUN

Tennyson, Alfred, Lord
AMBITION; ARGUMENTS;
BEAUTY DEFINED; BRIGHTNESS;
BURST; CLARITY; DESIRABILITY;
DREAM; EMPTINESS; GLIMMER,
GLITTER AND GLOSS; GREEN;

INTENSITY; KINDNESS; KNOWL-
EDGE; LIES/LIARS; SHARPNESS;
TEARS; UNDESIREABILITY;
WORD(S)

Tey, Josephine
BEARING; BODY; EMOTIONS;
FACE(S); LEAVES; PHYSICAL AP-
PEARANCE; PINK; THOUGHTS;
USEFULNESS/USELESSNESS;
VOICE, SOFT

Thackeray, William Makepeace
BLACK; FACIAL EXPRESSIONS,
MISCELLANEOUS; LAUGHTER;
POVERTY; POWER; PURSUIT;
RESTLESSNESS; SINGING; SUD-
DENNESS; WAR; WORDS OF
PRAISE

Theroux, Paul
ABILITY; ANIMALS; BEARING;
BIRDS; CLOUDS; EXCITEMENT;
EYES, BRIGHT; FACIAL EXPRES-
SIONS, MISCELLANEOUS; FAMIL-
IARITY; FINGERS; GRINS; HAIR;
HEAT; LANDSCAPES; LAUGHTER;
LIFE; MIST; NATURE; NERVOUS-
NESS; PHYSICAL APPEARANCE;
POLITICS/POLITICIANS; RAIN;
RELATIONSHIP; ROOMS; SEXUAL
INTERACTION; SIMPLICITY;
SINGING; SKIN; SLOWNESS;
SNOW; STARS; THINNESS; TREES;
VISABILITY; WRITERS/WRITING

Thomas, Dylan
ABILITY; BELIEFS; BREASTS;
CHOICES; CLOUDS; CORRE-
SPONDENCE; DEJECTION; FEAR;
FOOLISHNESS; GROWTH; HAPPI-
NESS; JOY; MEEKNESS; MUS-
CLES; PHYSICAL APPEARANCE;
PLACES; SMILE; SOUL; THIN-
NESS; TREES

Thomas, Leslie
ARM(S); HANDS; POVERTY; SIT-
TING; SMILE; THINNESS

Thomas, Lord
MIND DEFINED

Thomas, Michael M.
RELIGION

Thomas, Rob
FREEDOM; LIFE; PERSONALITY
PROFILES

Thomas, Ross
ATTENTION; HAND MOVE-
MENTS

Thompson, H. W.
BLACK; BUSYNESS; COMMON-
PLACE

Thompson, Hunter S.
NERVOUSNESS; SMELL; VIO-
LENCE

Thompson, James
FREEDOM

Thompson, Jean
ACTIVENESS; BALDNESS;
CHEEKS; CLOUDS; DISINTEGRA-
TION; EMBRACE; FACE(S); FA-
CIAL DETAILS; FIRE AND
SMOKE; GRAY; GREEN; GUILT;
HAIR, TEXTURE; HANDS; HEAT;
HOUSES; LEAVES; LIFE; MIND;
NERVOUSNESS; NOISES; PALLOR;
RAIN; SKIN; SKY; SMOOTHNESS;
SUCCESS/FAILURE; SUN; UNAT-
TRACTIVENESS

Thompson, Richard
ATTRACTION

Thompson, Vance
MANKIND

Thomson, James
CRUELTY; HUNGER

Thoreau, Henry David
AGE; BELIEVABILITY; HEAVI-
NESS; LIFE; RELIGION; WRIT-
ERS/WRITING

Thorn, Gary
WALKING

Thurber, James
ATTRACTION; CONTENTMENT;
FACIAL COLOR; GROANS AND
WHISPERS; GROWTH; LAUGH-
TER; NERVOUSNESS; SPEED;
STUPIDITY; TALLNESS; VOICE(S);
WALKING

Thurm, Marian
PRIDE

Tillotson, John
CANDOR; MAXIMS, PROVERBS
AND SAYINGS; SLANDER

Tindall, Gillian
DISINTEGRATION; DULLNESS;
SNOW

Tittle, Y. A.
FOOTBALL

Tolstoy, Leo
ANXIETY; COLDNESS; COL-
LAPSE; CRITICISM, DRAMATIC
AND LITERARY; EMOTIONS; FA-
CIAL DETAILS; FACIAL EXPRES-
SIONS, MISCELLANEOUS;

GREEN; GUILT; HEAD MOVE-
MENTS; LANDSCAPES; LOOKS;
LOYALTY/DISLOYALTY; MEEK-
NESS; MIST; MOON; NECK; PER-
SONALITY PROFILES; SPEECH-
MAKING; STRUGGLE; TREES;
TREMBLING

Tomlin, Lily
REALNESS/UNREALNESS

Tomlinson, Gerald
BREATHING

Toohey, John Peter
BURST

Toole, John Kennedy
CITIES

Torrence, Ridgely
SKY; TIME

Totenberg, Nina
DISAPPOINTMENT

Toulet, Paul Jean
LOVE, DEFINED

Towles, Amor
ACTIONS; CLEANLINESS; FA-
CIAL COLOR; REMOTENESS;
VOICE

Towne, Charles Hanson
FORMALITY

Townsend, Sylvia
COLDNESS

Train, Arthur
CHIN; CONSCIENCE; CRIME;
ENTRAPMENT; FACIAL EXPRES-
SIONS, BLANK; GENTLENESS;
HEADS; HELPLESSNESS;
LAWYERS; MUSTACHE(S); NECK;
OBVIOUSNESS; PAIN; SMILE;
SPORTS; TOBACCO

Traver, Robert
BARENESS; BEARING; BEHAVIOR;
BEWILDERMENT; CLINGING;
CLOUDS; CONTROL; COST;
EMPTINESS; EVIL; EYE EXPRES-
SIONS, MISCELLANEOUS; FA-
CIAL COLOR; FACIAL EXPRES-
SIONS, BLANK; FATNESS; FOG;
FROWNS; FURNITURE AND FUR-
NISHINGS; HAIR, COLOR; HELP-
LESSNESS; KISSES; LANDSCAPES;
LAUGHTER; LAWS; LAWYERS;
LOOKS; MARRIAGE; MEN AND
WOMEN; MUSIC; NAMES; NECK;
POLITICS/POLITICIANS; REAP-
PEARANCE; REPETITION; RISK;
SADNESS; SERIOUSNESS; SIGHS;
SILENCE; SLEEP; SMILE; SPORTS;

STARS; SURPRISE; THUNDER
AND LIGHTNING; TOBACCO;
TRUTH; VANITY; WALKING; WAR

Tremain, Rose
AGE; AIR; BLACK; BREASTS;
DARKNESS; EXITS; HELPLESS-
NESS; LIFE; SLEEP; TEARS;
WORD(S)

Trevor, William
BEAUTY; SHAPE

Trippett, Frank
NOISES

Trollope, Anthony
SPEED

Trollope, Frances
WORD(S)

Tropper, Jonathan
ADAPTABILITY; CANDOR;
HOUSES; LONELINESS; SPREAD-
ING

Truman, Harry S.
OPINION; WORK

Tuckwell, Barry
DIFFICULTY

Tuke, Sir Samuel
FAME

Tuller, David
VOICE(S)

Tuohy, Frank
EATING AND DRINKING; ELU-
SIVENESS; EXCITEMENT; EYE
COLOR; EYES; EYES, BRIGHT;
FACE(S); FACIAL COLOR; FA-
CIAL EXPRESSIONS, MISCELLA-
NEOUS; HAIR, TEXTURE; INNO-
CENCE; LIGHTING; MOUTH;
PAUSE; PHYSICAL FEELINGS; SI-
LENCE; SKIN; STRENGTH;
TREMBLING; VOICE, MUSIC RE-
LATED

Turgenev, Ivan
COMFORT; DEATH DEFINED;
FOREHEAD; GOSSIP; HAIR, TEX-
TURE; HANDS; HEAD MOVE-
MENTS; IDEAS; IMMOBILITY;
JOY; NOSE(S); PALLOR; PRIDE;
SCRUTINY; SILENCE; SITTING;
SUDDENNESS; THOUGHTS;
TREMBLING; VOICE, WEAK;
WRITERS/WRITING

Turner, Ted
SPORTS

Turner, Wallace
IMPOSSIBILITY

Turner, Walter J.
MIND DEFINED

Turnley, Joseph
INTENSITY

Turow, Scott
LIGHTING

Twain, Mark
ALONENESS; CALMNESS;
CROWDS; DARKNESS; DESIR-
ABILITY; DISCOMFORT; DULL-
NESS; EASE; EDUCATION; FA-
CIAL EXPRESSIONS, BLANK;
FATNESS; FREEDOM; GLOOM;
INAPPROPRIATENESS; MORAL-
ITY; PERSONAL TRAITS; RELIA-
BILITY/UNRELIABILITY

Tyler, Anne
BITTERNESS; CITIES; COMPLEX-
ION; ENTRANCES AND EXITS;
MUSTACHE(S); PERSONALITY
PROFILES

Tyler, W. T.
BEARD

Tynan, Kenneth
PLACES

U

Undset, Sigrid
PHYSICAL FEELINGS

Untermeyer, Louis
STALENESS

Updike, John
ADVANCING; AIR; ARM(S); ART
AND LITERATURE; ATTENTION;
ATTRACTIVENESS; BEARING; BE-
LONGING; BRIGHTNESS; CALM-
NESS; CAUSE AND EFFECT; CAU-
TION; CITIES; CLINGING;
COLLAPSE; CRYING; DANCING;
DEATH; EMOTIONS; ENTRAP-
MENT; FACIAL SHAPE; FEAR;
FRAGILITY; FREEDOM; FROWNS;
GRAY; HAIR; HAIR STYLES; HAND
MOVEMENTS; HEAD MOVE-
MENTS; HOUSES; INNOCENCE;
KISSES; LEAPING; MARRIAGE;
MIND; MOUTH; MOVEMENT(S);
NERVOUSNESS; PALLOR; PHYSI-
CAL FEELINGS; PLEASURE; RE-
LATIONSHIP; REMOTENESS;
ROAD SCENES; ROCKING AND
ROLLING; SENSITIVENESS; SEX-
UAL INTERACTION; SIMPLICITY;
SKIN; SMELL; SOFTNESS; SPEED;
SPORTS; STUPIDITY; TEARS;

THINNESS; UNDESIREABILITY;
VOICE, HARSH; VOICE, MONOT-
ONOUS; VOICE(S); WORD(S);
WORDS OF PRAISE; WRIT-
ERS/WRITING

Upward, Allen
WORDS DEFINED

Ustinov, Peter
MARRIAGE

V

Valency, Maurice
STYLE

Valin, Jonathan
ABSURDITY; ANGER; ARM(S);
BEARING; BELONGING; BLOOD;
BODY; BREASTS; CANDOR;
CAUSE AND EFFECT; CITIES;
COLLAPSE; COMMONPLACE;
CONSCIENCE; CONVERSATION;
CRUELTY; DRINKING; EVIL; EYE
COLOR; EYE MOVEMENTS; EYES;
EYES, BRIGHT; FACE(S); FACIAL
EXPRESSIONS, BLANK; FACIAL
EXPRESSIONS, MISCELLANEOUS;
FATNESS; FOOTBALL; FORE-
HEAD; FROWNS; FURNITURE
AND FURNISHINGS; GLIMMER,
GLITTER AND GLOSS; GLOOM;
GRAY; GUILT; HAIR, CURLY; HAIR
STYLES; HANDS; HANDSHAKE;
HEAD MOVEMENTS; HEADS;
HOUSES; JEWELRY; JUSTICE;
LEG(S); LIPS; MEN AND
WOMEN; MOUTH; MOUTH,
OPEN AND SHUT; NECK;
NOISES; NOSE(S); OBJECTS,
MISC.; PAIN; PHYSICAL APPEAR-
ANCE; PLACES; RAIN; ROAD
SCENES; SCRUTINY; SENSE; SEX-
UAL INTERACTION; SHOCK; SIT-
TING; SMELL; SMILE; SMOOTH-
NESS; SPEAKING; SPEECH
PATTERNS; STOMACH; STUPID-
ITY; SWEAT; TEARS; TOBACCO;
TREES; WRINKLES

Valois, Marguerite de
ATTRACTION

Valvano, Jim
SPORTS

Van Doren, Mark
SINGING

Van Dyke, Henry
BELONGING; BLACK; COMPLEX-
ION; EXPERIENCE; EYES; FACIAL

COLOR; FACIAL SHAPE; GREAT-
NESS; HAIR, COLOR; HUMOR;
JEWELRY; MUSIC; PARENT-
HOOD; PEOPLE, INTERACTION;
REMOTENESS; RUNNING;
SHADOW; SKY; STRAIGHTNESS;
SUN; VIOLENCE; VOICE, MUSIC
RELATED; WHITE; WIND; YEL-
LOW

Van Horn, Harriet
FOOD AND DRINK

Van Vechten, Carl
ACTIVENESS

Vanderbilt, William K.
RICHES

Vanderhaeghe, Guy
ABANDONMENT; BIRDS; FACIAL
COLOR

Vaughan, Bill
ECONOMICS

Vaughan, Henry
PERMANENCE

Vaughan, M. E.
AGE

**Vauvenargues, Marquis de Luc de
Clapiers**
ADVICE; SIMPLICITY

Vecsey, George
BASEBALL

Venning, Ralph
RICHES

Veuillot, Louis
FEAR

Vianney, Jean B. M.
GREED

Victoria, Queen
REMOTENESS

Vidal, Gore
ABUNDANCE; AMBITION; STAGE
AND SCREEN; TIME

Viertel, Jack
ENTHUSIASM

Villiers, George
FAME; KISSES

Vincent, Steven
ATTENTION

Vinez, Robert
DIFFICULTY

Viorst, Judith
PEACEFULNESS

Virgo, Sean
LOOKS

Voltaire
AIMLESSNESS; BOOKS; CALM-
NESS; CERTAINTY; CLOUDS;
IDEAS; POWER; WORLD

Von Kotzbue, August E. F.
STUPIDITY

Vreeland, Susan
ANXIETY; CALMNESS; DIFFI-
CULTY; DISAPPOINTMENT; EYE
MOVEMENTS; EYES; FACIAL
COLOR; SURPRISE; SWEAT;
THINNESS; TURNING AND
TWISTING

W

Wade, Betsy
REGULARITY/IRREGULARITY

Wagner, Jane
ABILITY; BREATHING; EYE
MOVEMENTS; GROWTH; LIFE;
MIND; MIND DEFINED; MOUTH;
PARENTHOOD; WAR

Wagoner, David
TENSION

Wainwright, John
ABSURDITY; BENDING/BENT;
DULLNESS; EYES; HAPPINESS;
SNOW; SPEAKING; THRIFT; VI-
BRATION; WEATHER

Wakefield, Dan
ART AND LITERATURE; ATTRAC-
TION; BOREDOM/BORING;
CALMNESS; CLOTHING; CLOTH-
ING, ITS FIT; EDUCATION; EYE
MOVEMENTS; FEAR; FOOD AND
DRINK; JUMPING; MEMORY;
MODESTY; ROAD SCENES; WAR;
WEAKNESS

Wakeman, Frederic
BRIGHTNESS

Wakoski, Diane
AFFECTION; AGILITY; ALONE-
NESS; ANGER; DEJECTION; DIF-
FICULTY; DISAPPEARANCE;
DREAM; DRYNESS; EMOTIONS;
EMPTINESS; ENERGY; FACE(S);
GROANS AND WHISPERS;
HEART(S); HEAVINESS; MEN
AND WOMEN; MIND; NIGHT;
OCEAN/OCEANFRONTS; SI-
LENCE; SLEEP; SPREADING;
THOUGHTS; WORD(S)

Walcott, Derek
AGITATION; CAUTION; CITIES;
FAMILIARITY; FIRMNESS; GLIM-
MER, GLITTER AND GLOSS;
LAUGHTER; LEAVES; MIND;
MOON; MOUNTAINS;
OCEAN/OCEANFRONTS; REPETI-
TION; SEASCAPES; SKIN; SOUL;
TIME; UNATTRACTIVENESS;
WRINKLES

Waldman, Amy
SILENCE

Walker, Alice
BODY ORGANS; CLEVERNESS;
ENTRANCES AND EXITS; EYES,
BRIGHT; HEARTBEAT; TEARS;
THOUGHTS; TREES

Walker, William
UNSTEADINESS

Wallace, Chris
SPORTS

Walling, R. A. J.
CALMNESS

Walpole, Hugh
BEGINNINGS AND ENDINGS; BE-
HAVIOR; BIRDS; BRIGHTNESS;
CLOUD MOVEMENTS; CLOUDS;
COMMONPLACE; COST; FACIAL
COLOR; FEAR; FIRE AND
SMOKE; GREEN; HEADS;
HEALTH; HEARTBEAT; LAND-
SCAPES; LYING; MEETINGS;
MOUNTAINS; PHYSICAL AP-
PEARANCE; POLITICS/POLITI-
CIANS; RAIN; RESERVE;
SCREAMS; SEASCAPES; SILENCE;
SKY; SNOW; SUN; VOICE(S)

Walters, Barbara
FAME

Walton, Izaak
SPORTS

Walton, Susan
FEAR; GLOOM

Walworth, Clarence
BOOKS

Wambaugh, Joseph
AGE; AGITATION; ATTENTION;
BODY; BUSYNESS; CANDOR;
CLARITY; COLLAPSE; COMPLEX-
ITY; ELUSIVENESS; EXITS; FIRM-
NESS; GOLF; GOSSIP; LOOKS;
PERSISTENCE; RELIABILITY/UN-
RELIABILITY; STARS; TENSION;
UNCERTAINTY; UNDESIREABIL-
ITY; USEFULNESS/USELESSNESS;
VIOLENCE; VOICE, SOFT

Ward, Edward
BARENESS

Ward, Hugh
　FATNESS

Ward, M.
　LONELINESS

Wardle, Jane
　ART AND LITERATURE

Warner, Charles Dudley
　CONVERSATION

Warner, Sylvia Townsend
　HAND MOVEMENTS; WEARI-
　NESS

Warren, Robert Penn
　AIMLESSNESS; BEAUTY; BROWN;
　CLEVERNESS; CORRECTNESS;
　DISAPPEARANCE; ENERGY;
　GLIMMER, GLITTER AND GLOSS;
　HISTORY; LIGHTNESS; MOUTH,
　OPEN AND SHUT; SHINING; SI-
　LENCE; SLOWNESS; SUDDEN-
　NESS; TIME; TREMBLING;
　WORLD

Washburn, Leonard
　EYES; NOISES

Washington, George
　CERTAINTY; CLARITY; GOVERN-
　MENT

Watts, Alan
　DIFFICULTY

Watts, Isaac
　ACTIVENESS; TIME

Waugh, Evelyn
　ANXIETY; BOREDOM/BORING;
　FEAR; WORD(S)

Weatherly, F. E.
　HEART(S)

Weaver, Gordon
　MEMORY

Weaver, Raymond M.
　IMPORTANCE/UNIMPORTANCE

Weaver, Will
　AIR; ARM(S); BREASTS; CLING-
　ING; FACE(S); FIRMNESS; HEAT;
　LANDSCAPES; LAWS; LEG(S);
　MEN AND WOMEN; MOUTH,
　OPEN AND SHUT; MUSIC; NA-
　TURE; OBJECTS, MISC.; PAUSE;
　PEOPLE, INTERACTION; RISK;
　SMELL; SPORTS; STOMACH; VE-
　HICLES; VISABILITY; VOICE(S)

Weber, Dee
　DULLNESS; FORMALITY

Webster, Daniel
　LAWYERS

Webster, John
　BITTERNESS; DOCTORS; FAME;
　MANKIND

Weeks, Albert L.
　THINNESS

Weigel, Henrietta
　EMOTIONS; SHAME

Weil, Simone
　FRIENDSHIP

Weisbrod, Rosine
　AIR

Weizenbaum, Joseph
　SCRUTINY

Welch, Susan
　SKY

Wellman, Paul J.
　FACE(S); HAIR; SHOULDERS;
　VOICE, HARSH; WIND

Wells, H. G.
　CONNECTIONS; DIFFICULTY;
　DISAPPEARANCE; HELPLESS-
　NESS; OPEN AND SHUT; TREES;
　TURNING AND TWISTING

Welty, Eudora
　ABANDONMENT; ACTIVENESS;
　ANIMALS; CALMNESS; CAU-
　TION; CHEEKS; CLOUDS; COL-
　LAPSE; COLORS; COMPLEXITY;
　CONTENTMENT; DANGER;
　DARKNESS; DIFFERENCES;
　EMPTINESS; EYEBROWS; EYES;
　EYES, BRIGHT; FACE(S); FACIAL
　DETAILS; FIRMNESS; FLOWERS;
　FRAGILITY; FROWNS; GLIMMER,
　GLITTER AND GLOSS; HAIR;
　HAIR STYLES; HAND MOVE-
　MENTS; HANDS; HAPPINESS;
　HEAD MOVEMENTS; HEART-
　BEAT; IMMOBILITY; LAND-
　SCAPES; LAUGHTER; LEAPING;
　LIGHTNESS; MANKIND; MEM-
　ORY; MEN AND WOMEN; MOON;
　MOUTH; MOVEMENT(S); MUS-
　TACHE(S); NATURE; PAUSE; PUR-
　SUIT; ROARS; SERIOUSNESS;
　SHINING; SITTING; SNORES;
　SPREADING; SUDDENNESS; SUN;
　SUNSET; SWEAT; THOUGHTS;
　TREES; TURNING AND TWIST-
　ING; WALKING; WATCHFUL-
　NESS; WRINKLES

Werfel, Franz
　ACTIONS; BEHAVIOR; FACIAL
　EXPRESSIONS, BLANK; HEAD
　MOVEMENTS; NOISES; RELI-
　GION; SKIN; SPREADING

Wertenbaker, Lael
　AGITATION; ANXIETY; ARGU-
　MENTS; BEARING; BEHAVIOR;
　BLUSHES; DESIRE; EDUCATION;
　EYES; FACE(S); FIRMNESS;
　FOOTBALL; FUTILITY; GREEN;
　JEWELRY; MEEKNESS; MEMORY;
　MOUTH; QUESTIONS AND AN-
　SWERS; RAIN; SITTING; SKY
　COLOR; SPEECH PATTERNS;
　SUN; TENSION; VEHICLES, OP-
　ERATION OF; VOICE(S)

Wertime, Richard
　MOON

Wesley, Samuel
　SERIOUSNESS

West, Jessamyn
　CONVERSATION; DAY; EYE
　COLOR; FATNESS; FEROCITY;
　GENTLENESS; HEAT; LOOKS; RE-
　SERVE; SEASONS; SHINING; SKY;
　SMOOTHNESS; SOFTNESS;
　SPEED; SWEAT; VOICE, EFFECT
　OF

West, Kanye
　CRUELTY

West, Mae
　WRITERS/WRITING

West, Paul
　MOVEMENT(S); PAST, THE

West, Rebecca
　ART AND LITERATURE; BLACK;
　COLDNESS; CRUELTY; FACIAL
　SHAPE; HANDS; KISSES; LOOKS;
　PINK; PLACES; POLITICS/POLITI-
　CIANS; ROOMS; SURPRISE; WIND

Westcott, Edward Noyes
　CLINGING

Westheimer, Ruth K.
　SPORTS

Westlake, Donald E.
　BEAUTY; PHYSICAL APPEAR-
　ANCE

Weyman, Stanley
　ANGER

Wharton, Edith
　ABANDONMENT; AGE; ARGU-
　MENTS; ART AND LITERATURE;
　ATTRACTION; BEARING; BEHAV-
　IOR; BELIEFS; BREATHING;
　CALMNESS; CHANGE; CHARAC-
　TER; CHEEKS; COLLAPSE; CON-
　NECTIONS; CONTROL; CORRE-

SPONDENCE; CROWDS; CRYING; DECREASE; DEJECTION; DISAPPEARANCE; DISINTEGRATION; DULLNESS; EYE EXPRESSIONS, MISCELLANEOUS; EYES; FACE(S); FACIAL COLOR; FACIAL EXPRESSIONS, BLANK; FACIAL EXPRESSIONS, MISCELLANEOUS; FAMILIARITY; FINGERS; FLOWERS; FURNITURE AND FURNISHINGS; FUTURE; GREEN; HABIT; HAIR; HELPLESSNESS; KISSES; LANDSCAPES; LAUGHTER; MEEKNESS; MEMORY; MIND; MOUTH; MOUTH, OPEN AND SHUT; NAMES; NATURALNESS; NATURE; NOISES; OBVIOUSNESS; PAIN; PALLOR; PERSONALITY PROFILES; PHYSICAL APPEARANCE; PHYSICAL FEELINGS; PREPAREDNESS; PROMPTNESS; REMOTENESS; REPETITION; RESERVE; SAFETY; SCRUTINY; SECRECY; SKY; SLOWNESS; SMILE; SPEECH PATTERNS; SPEED; SUCCESS/FAILURE; SUN; TIME; TRANSIENCE; VOICE, MONOTONOUS; VOICE, SOFT; WIND; WORD(S); WORDS, EFFECT OF; WRINKLES

Whately, Richard
DISHONESTY; LIES/LIARS; SHINING

Whedon, Julia
CONTINUITY; NAMES; NATURALNESS; REMOTENESS; SILENCE; THOUGHTS

Wheeler, Kate
FATNESS; NOISES; REMOTENESS

Wheelock, John Hall
ARGUMENTS; CLOUD MOVEMENTS; CLOUDS; COLLAPSE; CONTINUITY; DECREASE; DISAPPEARANCE; MIST; MOON; OCEAN/OCEANFRONTS; WIND; WORDS OF PRAISE

Whipple, Edwin Percy
KNOWLEDGE

White, Antonia
BEHAVIOR; JOY; SILENCE; SINGING; SITTING

White, Curtis
FIRMNESS; NECESSITY

White, E. B.
BREVITY; FIRMNESS; FOOD AND DRINK; HOUSES; LIGHTNESS; MOVEMENT(S); PLACES; POETS/POETRY; SIMPLICITY; SPORTS

White, Lynn, Jr.
FREEDOM

White, Patrick
BALDNESS; CHEEKS; CLINGING; CLOTHING, ITS FIT; HAND MOVEMENTS; NAMES; PHYSICAL APPEARANCE; SIGHS; SLEEP

White, T. H.
CLARITY; EYE COLOR; KISSES

Whitehead, Alfred North
INTELLIGENCE; THOUGHTS

Whitehill, Joseph
EXCITEMENT

Whitman, Stephen French
FACIAL COLOR; HAIR; SILENCE; WEAKNESS

Whitman, Walt
ALERTNESS

Whittaker, Jack
DISAPPEARANCE

Whittier, John Greenleaf
BEAUTY; BENDING/BENT; BLUE; CALMNESS; DEJECTION; DISAPPEARANCE; DISPERSAL; EMOTIONS; EYES, BRIGHT; FATE; FEAR; FEROCITY; FOG; GENTLENESS; GOSSIP; HEART(S); IMMOBILITY; LAUGHTER; LEAVES; LIGHTNESS; LIPS; PAIN; PERMANENCE; REALIZATION; SHARPNESS; SILENCE; SLOWNESS; SOFTNESS; THOUGHTS; TIMELINESS/UNTIMELINESS; TREES; WALKING

Wiggins, Marianne
DRYNESS; FOG; THOUGHTS

Wilbur, Richard
AIMLESSNESS; AWKWARDNESS; BIRDS; CALMNESS; DARKNESS; JUMPING; LEAVES; LIGHTNESS; MIND; NIGHT; NOISES; RESTLESSNESS; SKIN; SNOW; SWEAT

Wilcox, Ella Wheeler
MODESTY

Wilde, Oscar
ACTIONS; AGITATION; BEAUTY; BLACK; BLUSHES; BODY; CITIES; CONVERSATION; CRITICISM, DRAMATIC AND LITERARY; CRYING; EYES; FACIAL COLOR; FACTS; FLOWERS; HEAVINESS; IGNORANCE; JEWELRY; LAUGHTER; LIPS; MARRIAGE; MEETINGS; MEMORY; MEN AND WOMEN; NATURE; NOSE(S); ORDER/DISORDER; PAIN; PALLOR; SNOW; STRAIGHTNESS; SUN; TREES; TREMBLING; WHITE

Wilde, Percival
BALDNESS

Wilde, Richard Henry
LIFE

Wilder, Billy
PLACES

Wilder, Thornton
STAGE AND SCREEN

Wilhelm, Derek
PHYSICAL APPEARANCE

Wilhelm, Kate
PHYSICAL APPEARANCE

Wilkinson, Alec
LANDSCAPES

Will, George F.
ANGER; BASEBALL; CRITICISM, DRAMATIC AND LITERARY; DESTRUCTION/DESTRUCTIVENESS; FIGHTING; POLITICS/POLITICIANS; SECRECY; SOCIETY; SPEECH PATTERNS; TRANSIENCE; UNSTEADINESS

Williams, Ben Ames
AGITATION; CERTAINTY; CLEANLINESS; CRITICISM, DRAMATIC AND LITERARY; DEJECTION; EASE; ELUSIVENESS; ENTRANCES AND EXITS; FACIAL DETAILS; FEAR; GREED; HAPPINESS; HELPLESSNESS; JOY; LIFE; LIPS; LOVE; PHYSICAL APPEARANCE; POLITICS/POLITICIANS; PRIDE; REALNESS/UNREALNESS; SPEED; SWEAT; TALKATIVENESS; VOICE(S)

Williams, Emlyn
STUPIDITY

Williams, Joe
CALMNESS

Williams, Joy
ACTIVENESS

Williams, Miller
BENDING/BENT; DISAPPEARANCE; FRAGILITY; FREEDOM; STRAIGHTNESS

Williams, Robin
HELPLESSNESS; LAUGHTER

Williams, Sherley Anne
SELF CONFIDENCE; VOICE(S)

Williams, Tennessee
ALONENESS; BEAUTY; CLEANLI-NESS; DARKNESS; FLATTERY; KINDNESS; RELATIONSHIP; SCREAMS; SEX; TOUGHNESS

Williams, Thomas
CURSES; LEG(S); NERVOUSNESS; PHYSICAL FEELINGS

Williams, William Carlos
FACIAL EXPRESSIONS, MISCEL-LANEOUS; FINGERS; TIME

Williamson, Alan
LOOKS; SHINING

Williamson, Joy
CLARITY

Willingham, Calder
ADVANCING; ALERTNESS; ANXI-ETY; BREASTS; DISAPPOINT-MENT; FATNESS; NECK; TALKA-TIVENESS; TOUGHNESS; VEHICLES, OPERATION OF

Willis, N. P.
AMBITION

Wilner, Herbert
LEG(S)

Wilson, Angus
LIES/LIARS

Wilson, Arthur
WRITERS/WRITING

Wilson, C. P.
BRIGHTNESS

Wilson, Earl
MARRIAGE; MOVIES

Wilson, Leigh Allison
AGITATION; ARM MOVEMENTS; BEARING; BEHAVIOR; BLACK; FINGERS; SITTING; SMILE; STANDING; SUDDENNESS; SWEAT; TENSION

Wilson, Louis D.
CAUSE AND EFFECT

Wilson, Thomas
ATTENTION

Wilson, Woodrow
CHARACTERISTICS, NATIONAL

Wilson, Z. Vance
BREATHING; CHEEKS; COL-LAPSE; CRYING; EXITS; EYE EX-PRESSIONS, MISCELLANEOUS; EYES; FACE(S); FACIAL EXPRES-SIONS, MISCELLANEOUS; HAIR;

HEAD MOVEMENTS; PALLOR; SENSITIVENESS; SUN; TREES; VOICE, MUSIC RELATED; WORDS, EFFECT OF

Winans, A. D.
BARENESS; CRYING; MEMORY; SLOWNESS; WORD(S)

Winehouse, Amy
LIFE

Winerip, Michael
DIFFICULTY

Winter, William
CARELESSNESS

Winters, Yvor
COLDNESS; IMMOBILITY; NA-TURE; WIND

Withal, John
MOVEMENT(S)

Witwer, H. C.
BLUSHES; ENTHUSIASM; EX-CITEMENT; HEAT; MONEY; SHOULDERS; UNDESIREABILITY

Wodehouse, P. G.
ADVERSARY; AGITATION; DANC-ING; DEJECTION; FACE(S); GOLF; GROANS AND WHISPERS; INSULT; MEN AND WOMEN; MUSIC; NERVOUSNESS; NOSE(S); ROCKING AND ROLLING; SHOULDERS; SILENCE; SUN; TALKATIVENESS

Wodin, Natascha
AGILITY; ATMOSPHERE; CLAR-ITY; CONVERSATION; DANGER; DARKNESS; DEJECTION; EASE; EMBRACE; EYES; GLIMMER, GLITTER AND GLOSS; HELPLESS-NESS; NIGHT; NOISES; PAST, THE; ROOMS; SCREAMS; SMILE; TALKATIVENESS; TOUGHNESS; VIOLENCE

Woiwode, Larry
EMOTIONS

Wolcott, John
CONSCIENCE

Wolfe, Thomas
AGE; AGILITY; BODY; CER-TAINTY; COMPLEXION; DEJEC-TION; DISAPPEARANCE; ENVY; EYE MOVEMENTS; FACE(S); FA-CIAL EXPRESSIONS, MISCELLA-NEOUS; HEADS; HOUSES; IMPOS-SIBILITY; LIFE; LIGHTING; PHYSICAL APPEARANCE; RUN-NING; SADNESS; SEASONS;

SHAPE; SUCCESS/FAILURE; TREMBLING

Wolff, Craig
BASEBALL; SPORTS

Wolff, Geoffrey
CALMNESS; CONVERSATION; EYES; FACIAL COLOR; LOVE; PAIN; QUESTIONS AND AN-SWERS; SKIN; SMILE; THRIFT; UNATTRACTIVENESS

Wolff, Tobias
FEAR; HAIR

Wolitzer, Hilma
EYE MOVEMENTS; MEN AND WOMEN; SEXUAL INTERAC-TION; STALENESS; SUCCESS/FAILURE; TIME

Wollaston, Nicholas
PLACES

Wondersford, O. S.
BEAUTY

Wood, Ira
AGITATION; ANGER; BODY; BREASTS; DIFFICULTY; DULL-NESS; EATING AND DRINKING; EMBRACE; ENTHUSIASM; ENVY; EYE EXPRESSIONS, MISCELLA-NEOUS; EYEBROWS; FACIAL DE-TAILS; FOOD AND DRINK; GLOOM; HAIR, CURLY; HEAD MOVEMENTS; LAUGHTER; LEG(S); LIGHTING; LIPS; MOVE-MENT(S); MUSTACHE(S); NA-TURE; PRIDE; RAIN; RELATION-SHIP; SCREAMS; SENSITIVENESS; SKIN; SNORES; SOFTNESS; SPEECH PATTERNS; STOMACH; SWEAT; TEARS; TEETH; WRIN-KLES; WRITERS/WRITING

Woods, Sara
HOPE

Woolcott, Alexander
ARGUMENTS; CERTAINTY; IN-SULT

Woolf, Geoffrey
SLEEP

Woolf, Leonard
MOUNTAINS

Woolf, Virginia
BEHAVIOR; BRIGHTNESS; CLING-ING; CLOTHING; CRUELTY; EN-TRANCES AND EXITS; EYES; FLOWERS; FREEDOM; FRESH-NESS; FRIENDSHIP; GREEN; LANDSCAPES; LIFE; LIPS; PER-

SONALITY PROFILES; PLACES; REALIZATION; RESTLESSNESS; SERIOUSNESS; SIGHS; STORIES; SUDDENNESS; VOICE, HARSH; VOICE, SOFT

Woolrich, Cornell
AIMLESSNESS; ALERTNESS; ARM(S); BREATHING; CLOSE-NESS; COLLAPSE; CRIME; DANC-ING; DESTRUCTION/DESTRUC-TIVENESS; DRINKING; ELUSIVENESS; FEAR; LIGHTING; MOVEMENT(S); NECK; NOISES; PEOPLE, INTERACTION; PHYSI-CAL FEELINGS; ROAD SCENES; SEASCAPES; SIGHS; SKIN; SPEAK-ING; TACT; TEETH; TREMBLING; TURNING AND TWISTING; VAN-ITY; VISABILITY; WIND

Wordsworth, William
AIR; ALONENESS; BARENESS; BEAUTY; CALMNESS; CHEER-FULNESS; CONTINUITY; COURAGE; DISAPPEARANCE; DISPERSAL; FEAR; FIRMNESS; GLIMMER, GLITTER AND GLOSS; HAPPINESS; PURSUIT; SAFETY; SHAPE; SILENCE; SIMILARITY; SNOW; SOFTNESS; SOUL; SPEED; STRENGTH; SWEETNESS; TEARS; WISDOM

Worthington, Robin
SURPRISE

Wouk, Herman
ABUNDANCE; CARELESSNESS; DISHONESTY; EYES; HUMOR

Wright, Charles
BENDING/BENT; DECREASE; NAMES; PINK; SMOOTHNESS

Wright, James
CRUELTY; FIRE AND SMOKE; LAUGHTER; PALLOR

Wycherley, William
CONTROL; FLEXIBILITY/INFLEX-IBILITY; LOVE; MEN AND WOMEN

Wylie, Elinor
ARM(S); BLUSHES; DIFFICULTY; DISAPPEARANCE; FURNITURE AND FURNISHINGS; GAIETY; NOISES; PALLOR; PEACEFUL-NESS; SEASONS; THINNESS; VOICE, HARSH; WHITE

Y

Yaari, Yehuda
CLOUD MOVEMENTS

Yalden, Thomas
HOPE

Yalkut, Shimoni
REGRET

Yankowitz, Susan
BREASTS

Yannis, Alex
DESTRUCTION/DESTRUCTIVE-NESS

Yates, Sir Joseph
IDEAS

Yazbek, David
MOON

Yeats, W. B.
BLACK; CLEVERNESS; COM-PLEXION; CONVERSATION; DAY; DISAPPEARANCE; ENTRANCES AND EXITS; LAUGHTER; MIST; MOON; RICHES; SERIOUSNESS; TEARS; TIME

Yellen, Samuel
CHARACTERISTICS, NATIONAL; STRENGTH; WRINKLES

Yevtushenko, Yevgeny
JUSTICE

Yezierska, Anzia
BEHAVIOR; CALMNESS; ENTRAP-MENT; EYES, BRIGHT; LOOKS; WEAKNESS

Yngve, Rolf
BIRDS

Young, Andrew
POWER

Young, Edward
HOPE; PROMPTNESS

Young, Francis Brett
EYES

Young, Marguerite
ACTIVENESS; BREASTS; ELU-SIVENESS; FUTURE; HAIR

Yount, John
AGE; ATTRACTION; CAUTION; CHIN; EYES; HAIR; IMMOBILITY; IRRITABLENESS/IRRITATING; LIGHTNESS; PHYSICAL APPEAR-ANCE; PHYSICAL FEELINGS; SHINING; SILENCE; SIMILARITY; SLEEP; TALLNESS; VIOLENCE; VOICE, HARSH

Yourcenar, Marguerite
BEHAVIOR; BIRTH; CLEVERNESS; CLINGING; CRITICISM; DISINTE-

GRATION; EMOTIONS; FRAGILITY; FURNITURE AND FURNISHINGS; HOPE; IDEAS; MIND DEFINED; MOVEMENT(S); NOISES; OPINION; PHYSICAL AP-PEARANCE; RAIN; SEX; SMILE; SPEED; TENSION; VIBRATION; WISDOM

Z

Zalesky, Arlene
HOUSES

Zangwill, Israel
ALONENESS; BLUE; CAUTION; CONTENTMENT; ENERGY; FLEX-IBILITY/INFLEXIBILITY; HEALTH; PRIDE; STRUGGLE

Zarchi, Yisrael
BELONGING; LAUGHTER; TREM-BLING

Zeno
GREED

Zerahia, Ha Yevani
PROFESSIONS

Zigal, Thomas
BUSYNESS; CONTEMPT; EXITS; HEALTH; MOVEMENT(S); WEARINESS

Zola, Émile
ABILITY; ANGER; BIRDS; CITIES; COMFORT; DISCONTENT; EYES; FACIAL EXPRESSIONS, MISCEL-LANEOUS; FORTUNE/MISFOR-TUNE; IMMOBILITY; MOUTH; NOISES; PHYSICAL APPEAR-ANCE; PHYSICAL FEELINGS; SE-RIOUSNESS; SKY; SLEEP; SPEECH PATTERNS; SUN; THINNESS

Zuckerman, Morton B.
PERSONALITY PROFILES

Zweig, Stefan
ALONENESS; ARM(S); BLACK; BLUSHES; CALMNESS; DAY; DE-CREASE; DIFFICULTY; DULL-NESS; GROWTH; IDEAS; IMMO-BILITY; MEMORY; MOON; MOUTH; POVERTY; REALIZA-TION; REMOTENESS; SURPRISE; TREMBLING; VOICE, HARSH; WEARINESS; WRITERS/WRITING